MW01194132

PSALMS, VOLUME 2

THE NIV
APPLICATION
COMMENTARY

From biblical text . . . to contemporary life

ZONDERVAN ACADEMIC

Psalms, Volume 2
Copyright © 2018 by W. Dennis Tucker Jr. and Jamie A. Grant

ISBN 978-0-310-52855-5 (ebook)

Requests for information should be addressed to:
Zondervan, 3900 Sparks Dr. SE, Grand Rapids, Michigan 49546

Library of Congress Cataloging-in-Publication Data

Names: Tucker, W. Dennis, Jr., author. | Grant, Jamie A., author. | Wilson, Gerald Henry. Psalms. Volume 1.
Title: Psalms. Volume 2 / W. Dennis Tucker Jr. and Jamie A. Grant.
Other titles: NIV application commentary.
Description: Grand Rapids, Michigan : Zondervan, [2018] | Series: The NIV application commentary series | This volume completes the commentary on the Psalms for the NIV series. Volume 1 of the Psalms was written by Gerald Wilson, published in 2002. | Includes bibliographical references.
Identifiers: LCCN 2018038920 | ISBN 9780310206705 (hardcover)
Subjects: LCSH: Bible. Psalms--Criticism, interpretation, etc.
Classification: LCC BS1430.52 .T83 2018 | DDC 223/.206--dc23 LC record available at https://lccn.loc.gov/2018038920

Printed in the United States of America

22 23 24 25 26 27 28 29 30 31 /TRM/ 21 20 19 18 17 16 15 14 13 12 11 10 9 8 7 6 5 4

THE NIV APPLICATION COMMENTARY

From biblical text . . . to contemporary life

W. DENNIS TUCKER JR. & JAMIE A. GRANT

ZONDERVAN
ACADEMIC

Contents

7
Series Introduction

11
General Editor's Preface

13
Authors' Preface and Acknowledgments

15
Abbreviations

19
Introduction

39
Outline

43
Select Bibliography

57
Text and Commentary

Psalms 73–106, Jamie A. Grant

Psalms 107–150, W. Dennis Tucker Jr.

1046
Scripture Index

1063
Subject Index

1068
Author Index

The NIV Application Commentary Series

When complete, the NIV Application Commentary
will include the following volumes:

Old Testament Volumes

Genesis, John H. Walton
Exodus, Peter Enns
Leviticus/Numbers, Richard E. Averbeck
Deuteronomy, Daniel I. Block
Joshua, Robert Hubbard
Judges/Ruth, K. Lawson Younger
1–2 Samuel, Bill T. Arnold
1–2 Kings, Michael S. Moore
1–2 Chronicles, Andrew E. Hill
Ezra/Nehemiah, Thomas Petter and
　　Donna Petter
Job, Dennis R. Magary
Psalms, Volume 1, Gerald H. Wilson
Psalms, Volume 2, W. Dennis Tucker Jr.
　　and Jamie A. Grant
Proverbs, Paul Koptak
Ecclesiastes/Song of Songs, Iain Provan
Isaiah, John N. Oswalt
Jeremiah/Lamentations, J. Andrew
　　Dearman
Ezekiel, Iain Duguid
Daniel, Tremper Longman III
Hosea/Amos/Micah, Gary V. Smith
Jonah/Nahum/Habakkuk/Zephaniah,
　　David M. Howard Jr.
Joel/Obadiah/Malachi, David W. Baker
Haggai/Zechariah, Mark J. Boda

New Testament Volumes

Matthew, Michael J. Wilkins
Mark, David E. Garland
Luke, Darrell L. Bock
John, Gary M. Burge
Acts, Ajith Fernando
Romans, Douglas J. Moo
1 Corinthians, Craig Blomberg
2 Corinthians, Scott Hafemann
Galatians, Scot McKnight
Ephesians, Klyne Snodgrass
Philippians, Frank Thielman
Colossians/Philemon, David E. Garland
1–2 Thessalonians, Michael W. Holmes
1–2 Timothy, Titus, Walter L. Liefeld
Hebrews, George H. Guthrie
James, David P. Nystrom
1 Peter, Scot McKnight
2 Peter/Jude, Douglas J. Moo
Letters of John, Gary M. Burge
Revelation, Craig S. Keener

NIV Application Commentary
Series Introduction

THE NIV APPLICATION COMMENTARY SERIES is unique. Most commentaries help us make the journey from our world back to the world of the Bible. They enable us to cross the barriers of time, culture, language, and geography that separate us from the biblical world. Yet they only offer a one-way ticket to the past and assume that we can somehow make the return journey on our own. Once they have explained the *original meaning* of a book or passage, these commentaries give us little or no help in exploring its *contemporary significance*. The information they offer is valuable, but the job is only half done.

Recently, a few commentaries have included some contemporary application as *one* of their goals. Yet that application is often sketchy or moralistic, and some volumes sound more like printed sermons than commentaries.

The primary goal of the NIV Application Commentary Series is to help you with the difficult but vital task of bringing an ancient message into a modern context. The series not only focuses on application as a finished product but also helps you think through the *process* of moving from the original meaning of a passage to its contemporary significance. These are commentaries, not popular expositions. They are works of reference, not devotional literature.

The format of the series is designed to achieve the goals of the series. Each passage is treated in three sections: *Original Meaning, Bridging Contexts,* and *Contemporary Significance.*

THIS SECTION HELPS YOU UNDERSTAND the meaning of the biblical text in its original context. All of the elements of traditional exegesis—in concise form—are discussed here. These include the historical, literary, and cultural context of the passage. The authors discuss matters related to grammar and syntax and the meaning of biblical words.[1] They also seek to explore the main ideas of the passage and how the biblical author develops those ideas.

---

1. Please note that in general, when the authors discuss words in the original biblical languages, the series uses a general rather than a scholarly method of transliteration.

After reading this section, you will understand the problems, questions, and concerns of the *original audience* and how the biblical author addressed those issues. This understanding is foundational to any legitimate application of the text today.

THIS SECTION BUILDS A BRIDGE between the world of the Bible and the world of today, between the original context and the contemporary context, by focusing on both the timely and timeless aspects of the text.

God's Word is *timely*. The authors of Scripture spoke to specific situations, problems, and questions. The author of Joshua encouraged the faith of his original readers by narrating the destruction of Jericho, a seemingly impregnable city, at the hands of an angry warrior God (Josh 6). Paul warned the Galatians about the consequences of circumcision and the dangers of trying to be justified by law (Gal 5:2–5). The author of Hebrews tried to convince his readers that Christ is superior to Moses, the Aaronic priests, and the Old Testament sacrifices. John urged his readers to "test the spirits" of those who taught a form of incipient Gnosticism (1 John 4:1–6). In each of these cases, the timely nature of Scripture enables us to hear God's Word in situations that were *concrete* rather than abstract.

Yet the timely nature of Scripture also creates problems. Our situations, difficulties, and questions are not always directly related to those faced by the people in the Bible. Therefore, God's word to them does not always seem relevant to us. For example, when was the last time someone urged you to be circumcised, claiming that it was a necessary part of justification? How many people today care whether Christ is superior to the Aaronic priests? And how can a "test" designed to expose incipient Gnosticism be of any value in a modern culture?

Fortunately, Scripture is not only timely but *timeless*. Just as God spoke to the original audience, so he still speaks to us through the pages of Scripture. Because we share a common humanity with the people of the Bible, we discover a *universal dimension* in the problems they faced and the solutions God gave them. The timeless nature of Scripture enables it to speak with power in every time and in every culture.

Those who fail to recognize that Scripture is both timely and timeless run into a host of problems. For example, those who are intimidated by timely books such as Hebrews, Galatians, or Deuteronomy might avoid reading them because they seem meaningless today. At the other extreme, those who are convinced of the timeless nature of Scripture but who fail to discern its timely element may "wax eloquent" about the Melchizedekian priesthood to a sleeping congregation or worse still try to apply the holy wars of the Old Testament in a physical way to God's enemies today.

The purpose of this section, therefore, is to help you discern what is timeless in the timely pages of the Bible—and what is not. For example, how do the holy wars of the Old Testament relate to the spiritual warfare of the New? If Paul's primary concern is not circumcision (as he tells us in Gal 5:6), what *is* he concerned about? If discussions about the Aaronic priesthood or Melchizedek seem irrelevant today, what is of abiding value in these passages? If people try to "test the spirits" today with a test designed for a specific first-century heresy, what other biblical test might be more appropriate?

Yet this section does not merely uncover that which is timeless in a passage but also helps you to see *how* it is uncovered. The authors of the commentaries seek to take what is implicit in the text and make it explicit, to take a process that normally is intuitive and explain it in a logical, orderly fashion. How do we know that circumcision is not Paul's primary concern? What clues in the text or its context help us realize that Paul's real concern is at a deeper level?

Of course, those passages in which the historical distance between us and the original readers is greatest require a longer treatment. Conversely, those passages in which the historical distance is smaller or seemingly nonexistent require less attention.

One final clarification. Because this section prepares the way for discussing the contemporary significance of the passage, there is not always a sharp distinction or a clear break between this section and the one that follows. Yet when both sections are read together, you should have a strong sense of moving from the world of the Bible to the world of today.

 THIS SECTION ALLOWS the biblical message to speak with as much power today as it did when it was first written. How can you apply what you learned about Jerusalem, Ephesus, or Corinth to our present-day needs in Chicago, Los Angeles, or London? How can you take a message originally spoken in Greek, Hebrew, and Aramaic and communicate it clearly in our own language? How can you take the eternal truths originally spoken in a different time and culture and apply them to the similar-yet-different needs of our culture?

In order to achieve these goals, this section gives you help in several key areas.

(1) It helps you identify contemporary situations, problems, or questions that are truly comparable to those faced by the original audience. Because contemporary situations are seldom identical to those faced by the original audience, you must seek situations that are analogous if your applications are to be relevant.

(2) This section explores a variety of contexts in which the passage might be applied today. You will look at personal applications, but you will also be encouraged to think beyond private concerns to the society and culture at large.

(3) This section will alert you to any problems or difficulties you might encounter in seeking to apply the passage. And if there are several legitimate ways to apply a passage (areas in which Christians disagree), the author will bring these to your attention and help you think through the issues involved.

In seeking to achieve these goals, the contributors to this series attempt to avoid two extremes. They avoid making such specific applications that the commentary might quickly become dated. They also avoid discussing the significance of the passage in such a general way that it fails to engage contemporary life and culture.

Above all, contributors to this series have made a diligent effort not to sound moralistic or preachy. The NIV Application Commentary Series does not seek to provide ready-made sermon materials but rather tools, ideas, and insights that will help you communicate God's Word with power. If we help you to achieve that goal, then we have fulfilled the purpose for this series.

—The Editors

General Editor's Preface

IT MAY BE THAT THE BOOK OF PSALMS IS THE most complete revelation in all of Christendom. What do I mean when I say a "complete revelation?" I mean that properly read, the 150 psalms touch every aspect of what it means to be fully human, created in the image of God. This commentary by Dennis Tucker and Jamie Grant shows that the Psalter tells the story of God working in the world and with humanity. Yet the psalms tell the story using one of our primary means of art: song. And, yes, there is a moral to each of the 150 mini-stories in David, Solomon, and others' compositions, sometimes more than one. When you put the wisdom, art, and ethics of the psalms together it feels like one can almost reach out and touch God as our head, heart, and hands fade away in a wave of blissful relationship.

It may be that my sense of the completeness of the book of Psalms has a lot to do with my past experiences. The earliest thing I remember about Psalms is trying to memorize Psalm 23, "the LORD is my shepherd, I lack nothing" (v. 1). I was not a great memorizer, but since I was the pastor's son, after all, I was expected to show the way. I liked Psalm 23 very much, but I didn't like the pressure of having to recite it from memory. I'm pretty sure my understanding of who God is, his sovereignty and glory, comes primarily from psalms like 41, "Praise be to the LORD, the God of Israel, from everlasting to everlasting" (v. 13) and Psalm 72, "Praise be to the LORD God, the God of Israel, who alone does marvelous deeds" (v. 18). The musicality of the psalms surely was enhanced by my wife Frances' beautiful piano renditions of psalm-based hymns from the *Little Flock* hymnbook, a reminder of her youth. And I will never forget the unique chanting-style of the psalms by the brothers at St. John's Abbey in Collegeville, Minnesota, where we spent a year in sabbatical study.

The book of Psalms is complete in another way. It is both revelation—God's words to us—and meditation—our words to God. Perhaps it was for this reason Martin Luther called the Psalter "The Little Bible," a distillation of the Torah's 613 commands down to the handful the psalmist emphasizes. There is a reason why the psalms are read every day in liturgies around the world. They are like public prayer conversations with God set to music. They can be read privately or corporately, but never without a two-way engagement with the author of our being.

When the psalms were written, their function was what Sigmund Mowinckel called "cultic," referring to their use in worship as either praise or lament or thanksgiving. The wholeness and simplicity of that function in Old Testament times has been shattered and dispersed today. We talk about the psalms' usefulness—what is of advantage to us. And we talk about the psychological, the sociological, and the philosophical (probably even the evolutionary) functions of the psalms. They are valuable, yes. They have "economic" worth to each of us, and to us as communities, they spread across the disciplines of life. Yet there must be more to it than that.

In the midst of this complexification of the psalms' utility, something has been lost, something we might call the wholeness of the worship of God. And this is precisely what the Psalter can restore to us. When we read the psalms, God's promises come alive. When we sing the psalms our hearts are filled with joy. God speaks through the psalms to our everyday burdens and cares. All of this is enhanced by learning more about the text we have before us. We read, then, this commentary with one eye on learning all we can, but with our other eye on being embraced by the wholeness of God's amazing love.

—Terry C. Muck

Authors' Preface and Acknowledgments

To write a commentary on a biblical book is a humbling task indeed. It asks the interpreter both to receive and give—to receive the heritage that comes with these texts and to give a faithful rendering of them for the current generation. In pouring over these psalms and the related secondary material, we have been reminded of a long heritage of able scholars and faithful followers who have also poured over these texts. They have studied faithfully, thought deeply, and written carefully. Names such as Augustine, Gregory of Nyssa, John Calvin, Martin Luther, and Hermann Gunkel, to mention but a very few, represent the breadth of this heritage, as do the many other names that appear in the footnotes of this commentary. They have cast a long shadow, and we are all the beneficiaries of their diligent work. Beyond the luminaries we know, however, we are also well aware of the countless number who remain nameless but who, through the ages, sought to read, teach, and preach these texts faithfully. And while in many cases we do not have the benefit of their writings, we remain well aware that they too cast a long shadow—one in which we all stand as well. What unites them all, however, is the primacy they gave to the study of the text. Because they were careful readers, they provided faithful renderings of it.

It is our prayer that those who use this commentary will receive with gratitude the heritage that comes with these texts and that they too will be humbled by the thought of stepping into this broad stream of faithful interpreters. But even more, it is our hope that users of this commentary, like those before them, will give primacy to the study of the text—that they too will study faithfully and think deeply and, in so doing, give a faithful rendering of the biblical book that Luther termed "the Little Bible."

There are a number of people who have played a critical role in seeing this project to completion. Chief among them are Terry Muck, the general editor for the NIV Application Commentary series, and Tremper Longman, consulting editor for the series. Both men patiently awaited the completion of our work and provided guidance where needed. In addition to these scholars, Katya Covrett, executive acquisitions editor at Zondervan, and Nancy Erickson, senior editor at Zondervan, have been helpful interlocutors and wise guides. We would also like to thank the colleagues at our two institutions: the George W. Truett Theological

Seminary at Baylor University and Highland Theological College UHI. These colleagues have offered encouragement at every turn in this project. Finally, we thank our families, who have graciously and generously allowed us the time necessary to complete this work. Like the psalmist, we count ourselves blessed because of them (cf. Ps 127).

Gerald H. Wilson wrote *Psalms, Volume 1* in the NIV Application Commentary series, and he was slated to write the second volume.[1] Tragically, however, Gerald died far too young and well before his work on this commentary had commenced. Like those commentators mentioned above, Gerald Wilson cast a long shadow. Few people produce scholarship that actually shapes a discipline for a generation, but with the publication of *The Editing of the Hebrew Psalter* in 1985, Wilson did just that.[2] The influence of his research and the paradigm shift he initiated cannot be adequately measured or fully appreciated. In 2010, some 25 years after the release of his 1985 monograph, a group of psalms scholars convened to consider the lasting impact of Gerald Wilson on the larger guild, and on psalms scholarship in particular.[3] Within that volume most contributors noted that, while scholarly investigation on the Psalter continues to pursue new avenues of research, the work of Gerald H. Wilson remains a formative influence on the discipline. His influence is keenly felt throughout the pages of this commentary.

Finally, we would like to dedicate this commentary to our students— past, present, and future—at the George W. Truett Theological Seminary at Baylor University and Highland Theological College UHI. These students are faithful servants of the church who lean fully into the unfolding of God's reign in the world.

—W. Dennis Tucker Jr. and Jamie A. Grant

---

1. Gerald H. Wilson, *Psalms, Volume 1*, NIVAC (Grand Rapids: Zondervan, 2002).
2. Gerald H. Wilson, *The Editing of the Hebrew Psalter*, SBLDS 76 (Chico, CA: Scholars Press, 1985).
3. Nancy L. deClaissé-Walford, ed., *The Shape and Shaping of the book of Psalms: The Current State of Scholarship*, AIL 20 (Atlanta: SBL Press, 2014).

Abbreviations

AB	Anchor Bible
ABD	*Anchor Bible Dictionary.* Edited by David Noel Freedman. 6 vols. New York: Doubleday, 1992
ABS	Archaeology and Biblical Studies
AcBib	Academia Biblica
AIL	Ancient Israel and Its Literature
AOAT	Alter Orient und Altes Testament
AOTC	Abingdon Old Testament Commentaries
AOTS	Augsburg Old Testament Studies
ATANT	Abhandlungen zur Theologie des Alten und Neuen Testaments
BBB	Bonner biblische Beiträger
BBR	*Bulletin of Biblical Research*
BCOTWP	Baker Commentary on the Old Testament Wisdom and Psalms
BDB	Brown, Francis, S. R. Driver, and Charles A. Briggs. *A Hebrew and English Lexicon of the Old Testament*
BETL	Bibliotheca Ephemeridum Theologicarum Lovaniensium
BHS	*Biblia Hebraica Stuttgartensia.* Edited by Karl Elliger and Wilhelm Rudolph. Stuttgart: Deutsche Bibelgesellschaft, 1983
Bib	*Biblica*
BN	*Biblische Notizen*
BTB	*Biblical Theology Bulletin*
BZ	*Biblische Zeitschrift*
BZAW	Beihefte zur Zeitschrift für die alttestamentliche Wissenschaft
CBQ	*Catholic Biblical Quarterly*
CBQMS	Catholic Biblical Quarterly Monograph Series
CC	Continental Commentaries
ConBOT	Coniectanea Biblica: Old Testament Series
COS	*The Context of Scripture.* Edited by William W. Hallo. 3 vols. Leiden: Brill, 1997–2002
CThM	Calwer Theologische Monographien
ESV	English Standard Version

Abbreviations

ETL	*Ephemerides Theologicae Lovanienses*
EvT	*Evangelische Theologie*
FAT	Forschungen zum Alten Testament
FBBS	Facet Books, Biblical Series
FOTL	Forms of the Old Testament Literature
FRLANT	Forschungen zur Religion und Literatur des Alten und Neuen Testaments
GKC	*Gesenius' Hebrew Grammar.* Edited by Emil Kautzsch. Translated by Arther E. Cowley. 2nd ed. Oxford: Clarendon, 1910
HALOT	*The Hebrew and Aramaic Lexicon of the Old Testament.* Ludwig Koehler, Walter Baumgartner, and Johann J. Stamm. Translated and edited under the supervision of Mervyn E. J. Richardson. 4 vols. Ledien: Brill, 1994–1999
HAR	*Hebrew Annual Review*
HAT	Handbuch zum Alten Testament
HBS	Herder Biblische Studien
HBT	*Horizons in Biblical Theology*
HKAT	Handkommentar zum Alten Testament
HThKAT	Herders Theologischer Kommentar zum Alten Testament
HUCA	*Hebrew Union College Annual*
ICC	International Critical Commentary
Int	*Interpretation*
IVP	InterVarsity Press
JAOS	*Journal of the American Oriental Society*
JBL	*Journal of Biblical Literature*
JBTh	*Jahrbuch für Biblische Theologie*
JETS	*Journal of the Evangelical Theological Society*
JNSL	*Journal of Northwest Semitic Languages*
JSOT	*Journal for the Study of the Old Testament*
JSOTSup	Journal for the Study of the Old Testament Supplement Series
JSS	*Journal of Semitic Studies*
JTS	*Journal of Theological Studies*
KUB	*Keilschrifturkunden aus Boghazköi.* Berlin: Akademie, 1921–
LHBOTS	The Library of Hebrew Bible/Old Testament Studies
LXX	Septuagint
MLBS	Mercer Library of Biblical Studies
MT	Masoretic Text
NASB	New American Standard Bible

NCBC	New Century Bible Commentary
NET	New English Translation
NETS	*A New English Translation of the Septuagint.* Edited by Albert Pietersma and Benjamin G. Wright. New York: Oxford University Press, 2007.
NIB	*The New Interpreter's Bible.* Edited by Leander Keck. 12 vols. Nashville: Abingdon, 1994–2004.
NIBCOT	New International Biblical Commentary on the Old Testament
NICOT	New International Commentary on the Old Testament
NIDOTTE	*New International Dictionary of Old Testament Theology and Exegesis.* Edited by Willem A. VanGemeren. 5 vols. Grand Rapids: Zondervan, 1997
NIV	New International Version
NIVAC	NIV Application Commentary
NKJV	New King James Version
NRSV	New Revised Standard Version
NSBT	New Studies in Biblical Theology
OBO	Orbis Biblicus et Orientalis
OBT	Overtures to Biblical Theology
OTE	*Old Testament Essays*
OTG	Old Testament Guides
OTL	Old Testament Library
OTS	Old Testament Studies
OTWSA/OTSSA	Die Ou-Testamentiese Werkgemeenskap in SuidAfrika/ The Old Testament Society of South Africa
PRSt	*Perspectives in Religious Studies*
RB	*Revue biblique*
RevExp	*Review and Expositor*
SBB	Stuttgarter biblische Beiträge
SBET	*Scottish Bulletin of Evangelical Theology*
SBLAB	Society of Biblical Literature–Academia Biblica
SBLABS	Society of Biblical Literature Archaeology and Biblical Studies
SBLDS	Society of Biblical Literature Dissertation Series
SBS	Stuttgarter Bibelstudien
SJOT	*Scandanavian Journal of the Old Testament*
SJT	*Scottish Journal of Theology*
THOTC	Two Horizons Old Testament Commentary
ThSt	Theologische Studiën
TOTC	Tyndale Old Testament Commentaries

Abbreviations

TS	*Theological Studies*
ThWAT	*Theologisches Wörterbuch zum Alten Testament.* Edited by G. Johannes Botterweck and Helmer Ringgren. Stuttgart: Kohlhammer, 1970–
VT	*Vetus Testamentum*
VTSup	Supplements to Vetus Testamentum
WBC	Word Biblical Commentary
WMANT	Wissenschaftliche Monographien zum Alten und Neuen Testament
WTJ	*Westminster Theological Journal*
WW	*Word and World*
ZAW	*Zeitschrift für die alttestamentliche Wissenschaft*
ZTK	*Zeitschrift für Theologie und Kirche*

Introduction

To appreciate both the literary and poetic sophistication of the psalms, as well as their theological depth, requires that the contemporary interpreter have some familiarity with the various features of Hebrew poetry on display in the Psalter. A number of these features were explained in *Psalms, Volume 1*.[1] In addition to explaining the Psalter's title and its implications for interpretation of the book, *Psalms, Volume 1* also introduced the dominant forms or genres found in the Psalter, with particular attention given to praise, lament, and thanksgiving psalms. Understanding the content, literary features, and theology associated with each type of psalm proves helpful in the interpretive process. Moreover, because the psalms are in fact poetry, interpreters will benefit from a general understanding of the poetic conventions present in each psalm. Parallelism, for example, is often mentioned as the most distinctive characteristic of Hebrew poetry. Because parallelism is omnipresent in the Psalter, interpreters should understand how Hebrew parallelism works and to what end. Other noted features in Hebrew poetry include merism, chiasm, word pairs, and even acrostically structured psalms. *Psalms, Volume 1* provides a thorough introduction to these matters in "The Art of Hebrew Poetry," and the reader here is encouraged to review the introduction in that volume prior to studying the psalms under consideration in the present volume.[2]

Two topics were not addressed in the first volume: the shape of the Psalter and the theology of the Psalter. Gerald Wilson indicated that these subjects would be covered in the second volume once the entirety of the Psalter had been carefully studied. These two topics, therefore, comprise the balance of the introduction in *Psalms, Volume 2*.

The Shape of the Psalter

Attention to the shape and shaping of the Psalter is a fairly recent development in the study of the book of Psalms. For much of the twentieth century, the methodological approaches formulated by Hermann Gunkel and Sigmund Mowinckel dominated the analysis of psalms.[3] The work

---

1. Gerald H. Wilson, *Psalms, Volume 1*, NIVAC (Grand Rapids: Zondervan, 2002).
2. Ibid., 35–57.
3. Hermann Gunkel, *The Psalms: A Form Critical Introduction*, FBBS 19, trans. Thomas M.

of these scholars cast a long and formative shadow across the discipline.[4] Gunkel identified various genres or "forms" of psalms found in the Psalter, along with the features that are characteristic of each form (e.g., lament, thanksgiving, praise). Gunkel suggested that these forms, and their common literary features, had a particular *Sitz im Leben*, a particular "setting in life." In asserting this, however, he did not claim that he could establish the precise historical context that prompted the writing of each psalm (as earlier scholarship had attempted to do), but instead that each form of psalm (e.g., lament) likely emerged from a common context that can be generally established. For example, a lament psalm was likely written when a psalmist or group of worshipers was in need of deliverance from an enemy, illness, oppression, or even individual and communal sin.

Mowinckel, a student of Gunkel, pressed the insights of his teacher further by arguing that each psalm was used in temple worship and that appropriate interpretation necessitated the analysis of individual psalms to determine their "cultic function." This view naturally led to Mowinckel's conclusion concerning the very purpose of the Psalter: "the Psalter was transmitted as the songbook of the second temple, and was unquestionably used as such."[5] As a result of form-critical analysis, the emphasis remained on the study of individual psalms. Any discussion of the Psalter as a whole, much less its shape, was purely secondary.

In 1979 Brevard Childs released his *Introduction to the Old Testament as Scripture* and, in many ways, opened new avenues for the examination of Scripture writ large, including the Psalter.[6] Childs argued that the "final form" of biblical books should be of primary consideration. Integral to his new proposal was the belief that the final form of these texts had been intentionally shaped by later editors or redactors. Attention to the "shape" of the biblical book, Childs argued, could yield insights that are central to the interpretive task of individual texts and of the book as a whole. For example, in his *Introduction* Childs posed the simple but insightful question: "Why is Psalm 1 the first psalm in the Psalter?"[7] In making such a query, Childs makes two assumptions: first, that Psalm 1 was placed in its current

---

Horner (Philadelphia: Fortress, 1967); Sigmund Mowinckel, *The Psalms in Israel's Worship*, 2 vols., trans. D. R. Ap-Thomas (Nashville: Abingdon, 1962).

4. In *Psalms, Volume 1*, 59–64, Gerald H. Wilson outlines in greater detail the monumental contributions of Gunkel and Mowinckel.

5. Quoted in Herman Gunkel, *An Introduction to the Psalms*, MLBS, trans. James D. Nogalski (Macon, GA: Mercer University Press, 1998), 340.

6. Brevard Childs, *Introduction to the Old Testament as Scripture* (Philadelphia: Fortress, 1979).

7. Ibid., 512.

location intentionally, and second, that its placement has interpretive implications for understanding the Psalter as a whole.

The work started by Childs on the shape of the Psalter was more fully explored in the work of his student, Gerald H. Wilson, in his groundbreaking study *The Editing of the Hebrew Psalter*.[8] Wilson explored collections of Sumerian hymns and identified indicators of editorial activity within those collections. Wilson observed that some collections included the name of the scribe who had gathered the collection, while other collections included a similar first line (an "incipit"), which likely explained their organizational structure. Other Sumerian collections appear to share a common theme, and that commonality bound the collection together. When Wilson turned to the book of Psalms, he noted evidence of "major editorially significant structures in the arrangement of the canonical Hebrew Psalter."[9] Some of these indicators had been noted previously (i.e., the five-book structure of the Psalter), but they took on new and added meaning in the light of the shift in psalms study. In the pages that follow, a brief review of the indicators of structure in the Psalter will appear, followed by a summary of Books 1–5 in the Psalter.

Preliminary Observations Concerning the Shape of the Psalter

COLLECTIONS. Although the Psalter is often considered a collection of 150 separate psalms, closer inspection, especially of the headings or superscriptions, suggests otherwise. Embedded within the larger Psalter are a number of smaller collections that appear to be grouped in various ways.

The presence of personal names in the superscription appears to be the feature that unites some collections:[10]

The Davidic Collection	Psalms 3–41, 51–72, 108–10, 138–45
The Korahite Collection	Psalms 42–49, 84–85, 87–88
The Asaphite Collection	Psalms 50, 73–83

---

8. Gerald H. Wilson, *The Editing of the Hebrew Psalter*, SBLDS 76 (Chico, CA: Scholars Press, 1985). For an assessment of Wilson's work and its influence on the discipline after more than two decades, see the collection of essays in Nancy deClaissé-Walford, ed., *The Shape and Shaping of the Book of Psalms: The Current State of Scholarship*, AIL 20 (Atlanta: SBL Press, 2014).

9. Gerald H. Wilson, "The Structure of the Psalter," in *Interpreting the Psalms: Issues and Approaches*, eds. David Firth and Philip S. Johnston (Downers Grove, IL: InterVarsity, 2005), 229–46.

10. Other personal names appear in the Psalter as well, but with far less frequency: Heman (Ps 88); Solomon (Pss 72; 127); Moses (Ps 90); and Ethan (Ps 89).

In the NIVAC *Psalms, Volume 1,* Wilson considers the meaning of personal names in the superscripts. Traditionally these names have been associated with authorship, but as Wilson rightly notes, the issue remains a matter of considerable debate. The Hebrew preposition *le* is attached to each personal name, but because the preposition can mean "of," "by," "for," "to," "concerning," or "about," the precise meaning of the designation remains unsettled. Rather than making a claim of authorship, these designations (i.e., *leDavid*) may well refer to a style of composition, or it may refer to whom the psalm is dedicated, or even who might be responsible for reading the psalm in temple worship (i.e., Korahites).[11] In the present line of discussion, the primary point is not to debate the question of authorship but instead simply to acknowledge the presence of collections in the Psalter based upon common name designations in the superscriptions.

Other collections appear throughout the Psalter but are grouped thematically. For example, Psalms 93 and 95–99 appear together in Book 4 of the Psalter (see below) and comprise a collection of "Enthronement Psalms," as is evident by their common reference to Yahweh as the Divine King. Psalms 42–83 comprise a collection termed the "Elohistic Psalter." In this collection of psalms, the name *'elohim* ("God") is preferred over *Yahweh* ("the LORD") throughout the collection, even though *Yahweh* is the preferred designation throughout the remainder of the Psalter. Whether these psalms originally included the name *'elohim* or the name *Yahweh* was replaced with *'elohim* remains a matter of debate. Either way, these psalms function as a collection within the final form of the Psalter.[12] A third collection can be found in Psalms 120–34, a collection united by the common designation in their superscription, "A Song of Ascents." Prior to their present location in the Hebrew Psalter, these psalms may have existed separately as a small collection used by pilgrims as they made their way to Jerusalem for festivals. Two other collections appear to be grouped by their opening line, "Hallelujah" (Pss 111–18; 146–50). Similar to the incipits identified by Wilson in the Sumerian hymns, these opening calls to "praise the LORD" serve to bind these psalms together. Whether these opening incipits were original to the psalm or added in the process of collection by

---

11. Wilson, *Psalms, Volume 1,* 78–79.

12. J. Clinton McCann Jr., "The Book of Psalms," in *The New Interpreter's Bible,* vol. 4, ed. Leander Keck (Nashville: Abingdon, 1996), 658, contends that *'elohim* was original to the psalms in this collection. For an alternative view, see Joel S. Burnett, "A Plea for David and Zion: the Elohistic Psalter as Psalm Collection for the Temple's Restoration," in *Diachronic and Synchronic: Reading the Psalms in Real Time. Proceedings of the Baylor Symposium on the Book of Psalms,* ed. Joel S. Burnett, W. H. Bellinger Jr., and W. Dennis Tucker Jr., LHBOTS 488 (New York: T&T Clark, 2007), 96–113.

the editor remains a matter of some debate. Either way, the incipits suggest that these psalms are meant to be understood as a collection. While generations of scholars have recognized the presence of collections within the Psalter, their role within the editorial shaping of the Psalter and its "final form" has become a matter of inquiry only within the last three decades.

Five-book Structure. At some point, perhaps late in its compositional history, the Hebrew Psalter was divided into five "books": Psalms 1–41; 42–72; 73–89; 90–106; and 107–50. Evidence for this five-book structure in the Hebrew Psalter can be found at the conclusion of each of the first four books. Following the last psalm in each book, the editors inserted a doxology.

> Praise be to the LORD, the God of Israel,
>> from everlasting to everlasting,
>>> Amen and Amen. (Ps 41:13)

> Praise be to the LORD God, the God of Israel,
>> who alone does marvelous deeds.
> Praise be to his glorious name forever;
>> may the whole earth be filled with his glory.
>>> Amen and Amen. (Ps 72:18–19)

> Praise be to the LORD forever!
>> Amen and Amen. (Ps 89:52)

> Praise be to the LORD, the God of Israel,
>> from everlasting to everlasting.
> Let all the people say, "Amen!"
> Praise the LORD. (Ps 106:48)

That the word "amen" occurs in each of the four doxologies but nowhere else in the Psalter suggests editorial intentionality in shaping the conclusion to each book. Gerald Wilson observed additional markers in the first three books that indicate a shift from one book to the next. He notes that in the movement from Psalm 41 to 42, 72 to 73, and 89 to 90 there are shifts both in the genre of the psalm and the name mentioned in the superscription, thus once more suggesting the presence of editorial intentionality in the Psalter. The fifth book, comprised of Psalms 107–50, does not conclude with a similar doxology but instead is followed by a lengthy doxological conclusion to the Psalter (Pss 146–50) that calls on all people to praise God.

The recognition of a "five-book" arrangement to the Psalter is not a recent development in scholarship but extends far back in history.

The Midrash Tehillim explains that, "As Moses gave five books of laws to Israel, so David gave five books of Psalms to Israel."[13] While the analogy between the Torah of Moses and the psalms of David provides an interesting explanation for the five-fold structure of the Psalter, contemporary scholarship has provided alternative explanations for its current structure (as suggested below).

The Editorial Purpose of the Psalter

To speak of the editorial purpose of the Psalter does not suggest that there is a rationale for the location of *each and every* psalm within the Psalter, but it does suggest that selected psalms do appear at strategic locations and that, through careful analysis, those psalms might provide clues for understanding the Psalter as a whole.[14] Like any good book, the Psalter has an introduction and a conclusion, along with intervening material. To determine the editorial purpose of the Psalter requires that one give careful attention to the psalms that appear at these strategic locations in the Psalter.

The Introduction: Psalms 1–2. Although they are two separate psalms, Psalms 1 and 2 function together to introduce two overarching themes for the Psalter. The opening psalm reflects the wisdom tradition and presents the reader with two fundamentally different options for life. Though the psalm opens with reference to the "happy" or "blessed" person, the identity of that individual is established based on a comparison with the "wicked," "sinners," and "mockers." Unlike these people, the righteous individual delights in the "law of the Lord." And unlike the wicked, whose path will perish (v. 6), the righteous who meditate on the law will prosper

---

13. William G. Braude, *The Midrash on Psalms* (New Haven, CT: Yale University Press, 1954), 1:5.

14. Largely under the influence of Frank-Lothar Hossfeld and Erich Zenger, German scholarship has also focused on matters related to the editorial purpose of the Psalter. The scholars' methodological assumptions are clearly on display in their two commentaries: *Psalms 2*, Hermeneia (Minneapolis: Fortress, 2005), and *Psalms 3*, Hermeneia (Minneapolis: Fortress, 2011). Hossfeld and Zenger, along with much of the German work on the Psalter, reflects a more decidedly diachronic approach to the text. While they focus on the final form, they are particularly interested in the historical processes that were at work in reaching that final form. North American scholarship, as a rule, has been more synchronic in orientation—less concerned with *how* the final form reached its current state than in what the final form means. See, for example, McCann, "The Book of Psalms," and Nancy deClaissé-Walford, Rolf A. Jacobson, Beth LaNeel Tanner, *The Book of Psalms*, NICOT (Grand Rapids: Eerdmans, 2014).

in their path and the Lord will watch over their way (vv. 3, 6). Thus Psalm 1 exhorts readers to a type of torah-piety rooted in the law of the Lord.

The second psalm likely reflects a coronation ceremony during the pre-exilic period, yet its position at the beginning of the Psalter raises questions as to its function in the corpus. The royal psalms (and particularly Ps 2) appear to have been reinterpreted by subsequent generations, especially following the exile.[15] Although human kingship is mentioned in Psalm 2:6–9, the psalm builds to an acknowledgment of Yahweh as the ruler over the kings of all the earth (v. 10). Thus, as Childs has observed and others after him have confirmed, the location of Psalm 2 appears to emphasize "the kingship of God as a major theme of the whole Psalter."[16] So together Psalms 1 and 2 call the reader to heed the instruction of Yahweh and acknowledge that, despite circumstances which appear to the contrary, the LORD reigns.

Books 1–3: Psalms 2–89. In his analysis of the Psalter, Wilson observed two distinct "blocks" of psalms, Psalms 2–89 and Psalms 90–145.[17] The superscriptions proved invaluable in discerning the organizational and compositional strategy for grouping together Psalms 2–89. Strikingly, in this portion of the Psalter, eighty-six of the eighty-eight psalms have a superscription, while of Psalms 90–145 less than half have some form of superscription.

In Books 1–3 the superscriptions are dominated by author designations and genre information (e.g., "a psalm," "a maskil"), and all but one of the thirteen "historical" superscriptions connected with the life of David (e.g., Ps 51) can be found in this collection.[18] In fact, David is mentioned in fifty-eight of the eighty-eight psalms, with two large Davidic collections dominating the first two books (Pss 3–41 and 51–72). David figures prominently in the organizational strategy of the first two books (Pss 2–72). In addition, Korahite and Asaphite collections are only found in this portion of the Psalter, thus reinforcing the importance of author designations as an organizational principle in Psalms 2–89.

In addition to the superscriptions, the lament genre plays a formative role in Psalms 2–89 by appearing with far more regularity than any other genre of psalm. Within Book 1, 24 of the 41 psalms are laments; in Book 2,

---

15. Scott A. Starbuck, *Court Oracles in the Psalms: The So-Called Royal Psalms in their Ancient Near Eastern Context*, SBLDS 172 (Atlanta: SBL Press, 1999), 205–12.

16. Childs, *Introduction to the Old Testament as Scripture*, 516.

17. Wilson argued that Ps 1 was added quite late as an introduction to the Psalms corpus, and Pss 146–50 as a conclusion.

18. The only other historical superscription is in Ps 142.

20 of the 31 psalms are laments; and in Book 3, 8 of 17 are laments. Nearly two-thirds of this initial collection (Pss 2–89), therefore, is comprised of laments. The dominance of lament contributes to the theological trajectory of the collection as a whole.

What proves most striking about Books 1–3, however, is the placement of royal psalms at the "seams" of the books. Psalm 2 opens the collection with a reference to Israel's kingship as something divinely sanctioned. Psalm 72, the final psalm in Book 2, references Solomon in the superscription, thus suggesting that the divinely sanctioned office of king continues with Solomon.[19] Strikingly, however, Book 3 contains a large number of communal laments, with two psalms in particular referencing the destruction of Jerusalem (Pss 74 and 79). These references suggest that the entirety of the collection was influenced by the events associated with the exile. Psalm 89 concludes Book 3 (and the larger collection of Pss 2–89) with a lament over what appears to be Yahweh's apparent rejection of the Davidic covenant—or, as Wilson has summarized,

> Psalm 2 describes the inauguration of the Davidic dynasty in words reminiscent of 1 Samuel 7:1–17. At the end of the combined prayers of David, Ps 72 (attributed 'to/for' Solomon) articulates the hope for successive Davidic monarchs to 'endure forever . . . as long as the sun' (72:17). This happy hope of eternal blessing comes crashing down at the end of the third book. There Ps 89, after beginning with the exalted expectations grounded in the inviolable word of God himself, turns swiftly to agonized confusion over the destruction of kingdom and monarch in exile.[20]

With their temple destroyed (Pss 74; 79) and the throne of David tossed into the dirt (Ps 89:44), the people wonder how they will endure the insults and taunts of the enemy nations (89:50–51). How will Israel endure the humiliation of exile and, worse yet, the dismantling of the nation's theological worldview? Israel's response to these questions follows in Books 4 and 5.

Books 4–5: Psalms 90–145. As suggested above, Books 1–3 were grouped according to author and genre designations in the superscriptions, but in Pss 90–145 superscriptions occur far fewer times: only sixteen of these fifty-six psalms contain a superscription, thus suggesting that a

---

19. Pharaohs and other ancient Near Eastern kings frequently uttered prayers to their respective deities asking for divine blessing and prosperity for their sons/successors. Brevard Childs contended that Ps 72 should be understood as a prayer for Solomon offered up by David (Childs, *Introduction to the Old Testament*, 516).

20. Wilson, "The Structure of the Psalter," 234.

different editorial technique was employed in assembling the latter third of the Psalter. Wilson argued that two words functioned as organizing principles in this section: *halleluyah*, "praise the LORD," and, *hodu*, "give thanks." That one of the two terms appears in nearly every psalm in Book 5 provides a strong hymn-like quality to the final third of the Psalter. In addition to the terms' sheer repetition, Wilson noted that they assume a particular role in the organizational structure of the collection: *halleluyah* appears in psalms that conclude a section, and *hodu* signals the start of a new collection. For example, Psalms 104–106 end with *halleluyah*, followed by a new section that begins in Ps 107 with the presence of *hodu* in the opening line. Psalm 117 concludes with *halleluyah* and so suggests the close of that section, while Psalm 118 begins with *hodu* and so indicates the start of the next section. Similarly, Psalm 135 concludes the section with *halleluyah*, and the appearance of *hodu* in Psalm 136 signals the start of a new collection.

While Wilson's observations concerning *haleluyah* and *hodu* are instructive, they do not explain in full the structure of Book 5.[21] What complicates the structure of Books 4 and 5 further are the various collections that comprise the latter third of the Psalter. In addition to the Enthronement Psalms in Book 4 (Pss 93 and 95–99), there are several collections in Book 5, including the Psalms of Ascent, two David collections (Pss 108–10; 138–45), and the massive acrostic psalm, Psalm 119. The way in which these collections intersect with the organizing terms suggested by Wilson (*halleluyah* and *hodu*) has yielded a number of proposals but little agreement.[22] Despite the challenges associated with assessing the editorial structure of Books 4 and 5, the two books do provide a theological response to the crisis of exile articulated in the first three books. The Psalter shifts from lament (Books 1–3) to praise and thanksgiving (Books 4–5).

Following the lament in Psalm 89, Book 4 opens with a psalm of Moses, the only psalm in the Psalter that includes Moses in the superscription.

---

21. Erich Zenger also signals a cautionary note regarding Wilson's claim. See Zenger, "The Composition and Theology of the Fifth book of Psalms, Psalms 107–145," *JSOT* 80 (1998): 77–102.

22. See Zenger, "The Composition and Theology of the Fifth book of Psalms"; Klaus Koch, "Der Psalter und seine Redaktionsgeschichte," in *Neue Wege der Psalmenforschung*, HBS 1, ed. Klaus Seybold and Erich Zenger (Freiburg: Herder, 1994), 243–77; Richard Kratz, "Die Tora Davids: Psalm 1 und die doxologische Fünfteilung des Psalters," *ZTK* 89 (1996): 1–34. Among the more recent assessments of the structure of Book 5, see Frank-Lothar Hossfeld and Erich Zenger, *Psalms 3*, Hermeneia (Minneapolis: Fortress, 2011), 1–7, and Michael K. Snearly, *The Return of the King: Messianic Expectation in Book V of the Psalter*, LHBOTS 624 (London: Bloomsbury T&T Clark, 2016).

Some have referred to Book 4 as a "Moses book" because of the considerable attention given to Moses, as well as the exodus and wilderness traditions.[23] The mention of Moses returns the reader to a time in Israel's history when the nation was led by only one king, Yahweh. This theme is reinforced with the appearance of the Enthronement Psalms in the middle of this collection. Of the seventeen psalms in this collection, six are Enthronement Psalms (Pss 93; 95–99) celebrating the kingship of Yahweh. (On the implications of this collection, see below.) The final two psalms in Book 4 (Pss 105–6) provide a recitation of Israel's history with a decidedly theological assessment of the covenantal relationship between Yahweh and Israel. Psalm 105 celebrates Israel's deliverance out of Egypt by focusing entirely on God's faithfulness to his people and the covenant that binds them together. Like Psalm 105, Psalm 106 provides a historical recital, but this recitation moves in a markedly different direction. The psalmist recounts key episodes in Israel's historical narrative, beginning with Israel's deliverance out of Egypt and culminating with their arrival in the land, yet the psalmist does more than simply track Israel's travel. Book 4 closes by giving considerable attention to the obstinate and rebellious spirit of God's people as they made their way to the promised land. God had been faithful (Ps 105), his people had not (Ps 106).

Although Book 3 closes with a lament over the fallen Davidic monarchy, Book 4 offers a daring word of hope declaring that Yahweh remains Israel's true king, thus ensuring that hope remains. The historical recitals at the end of Book 4 provide both a word of instruction and a word of caution. Israel is reminded of God's utter faithfulness to his people (Ps 105) and at the same time that their history is one of rebellion and waywardness (Ps 106). Israel's hope rests with the Divine King, who remains faithful; in turn, they must resist the ways of their ancestors and choose to respond to the Divine King in faithfulness.

Following the recounting of Israel's faithlessness in Psalm 106, the psalm closes with a petition for Yahweh to gather his dispersed people from among the nations—a request that ties Psalm 106 with the first psalm in the fifth book of the Psalter (Pss 107–50). Psalm 107 opens by referencing "those he redeemed from the hand of the foe" and those he "gathered from the lands" (vv. 2–3). The psalmist calls on this "gathered people" to

---

23. Note that beyond the superscription in Ps 90, Moses is also mentioned in Pss 99:6; 103:7; 105:26; 106:16, 23, 32; he is only mentioned in the Psalter one time outside Book 4 (Ps 77:20). On Book 4 as a "Moses book," see Marvin E. Tate, *Psalms 51–100*, WBC 20 (Waco, TX: Word, 1990), xxvi. See also the comments in Wilson, *The Editing of the Hebrew Psalter*, 217–19.

celebrate the steadfast love (*hesed*) of God. Such an opening statement might lead one to believe that the crisis is over and the world has been fully righted because of the steadfast love of the Divine King. Yet Psalm 107 portends a more ominous claim. In a wisdom admonition, the psalmist concludes the song by declaring, "Let the one who is wise heed these things and ponder the loving deeds of the LORD" (v. 43). The community would do well to remember the saving work of Yahweh because the world remains a place fraught with dangers and threats, as reflected in Psalms 107–45. The nations still stand in opposition (Pss 108–10). God's people remain in need of deliverance, similar to those he once delivered from Egypt (Pss 113–18). Those who give faithful attention to God's law find themselves "scorned and persecuted" even as they wait for God's reign to be unfurled fully.[24] The Psalms of Ascents (Pss 120–34) recall regularly the threats posed by hostile forces and the need for the people of Israel to lift their eyes to God for deliverance (Ps 121). Even in the final Davidic collection (Pss 138–45), the psalmist acknowledges the need for God to rise up and put down the threats posed by the foreign powers (Ps 144). The book concludes with a lengthy acrostic poem that celebrates the kingship of Yahweh (Ps 145).

Books 4 and 5 declare that from beginning to end that God reigns. Although the kingship of God was picked up in earlier portions of the Psalter (cf. Pss 2, 46, and 48), the latter portion of the Psalter makes this confession "amid circumstances that seem to deny and belie it."[25]

The Conclusion to the Psalter: Psalms 146–50. The final five psalms in the Psalter provide an emphatic conclusion to the entire work. Overall, these psalms offer a sustained call to "praise the LORD." Each of the five psalms contains an *inclusio* that opens and closes with the expression *halleluyah*, "praise the LORD." This sustained call to praise God reaches a crescendo in Psalm 150. The entirety of the psalm is an extended call to worship the God who reigns. (See the comments on Ps 150.) The opening and closing lines in the final psalm contain the phrase *halleluyah*, "Praise the LORD," and in the intervening verses (vv. 1b–5b) the verb *halal*, "to praise," appears in every half-line in the psalm. Thus, while the earlier psalms (particularly Pss 3–89) were filled with lament, most notably lamenting the loss of kingship in Psalm 89, the final run of psalms suggests that lament does not have the final word in the lives of those who rely on the steadfast love of God—praise does. The final verse issues the invitation to acknowledge this confession: "Let everything that has breath praise the LORD" (Ps 150:6).

---

24. McCann, "The Book of Psalms," 663.
25. Ibid.

Theological Themes in the Book of Psalms

BECAUSE THE BOOK OF PSALMS is such a complex book, any attempt to construct *a* theology of Psalms will invariably fall short. Individual psalms, collections of psalms, and the Psalter itself were composed, collected, and edited by various individuals across a considerable period of time. Further, each psalm and certain collections of psalms (e.g., the Psalms of Ascents, Pss 120–34) appear to have been created to address particular theological, social, and existential concerns. For the most part, the "setting in life" (*Sitz im Leben*) of individual psalms has been lost to history, but their theological claims remain firmly embedded within the texts themselves. Despite the complexity of the Psalter and its lengthy compositional history, the book of Psalms demonstrates a remarkable consistency in its theological confession concerning God, humanity, and the interaction between the two.

In the opening chapter of his *Institutes of the Christian Religion*, John Calvin declares that it is impossible to speak meaningfully about God without also speaking meaningfully about humanity, and similarly it is impossible to speak meaningfully about humanity without speaking about God. He writes, "Nearly all the wisdom we possess, that is to say, true and sound wisdom, consists of two parts: the knowledge of God and of ourselves."[26] In many ways the Psalter does just that; it makes manifold theological claims concerning both God and humanity. In short, the Psalter is at once both theological and anthropological, about God and about humanity.

The pairing of Psalms 1 and 2 as the introduction to the Psalter suggests that perhaps these twin emphases were indeed intended to be the interpretative lenses through which to read the entire book. William Brown suggests that the first psalm serves "as the Psalter's hermeneutical entry point."[27] The psalm gives attention to the torah of Yahweh and the covenantal life of the "blessed" person. Moreover, this psalm presses the reader to a particular way of living before God and in some sense prefigures the call for "unobstructed reverence to God," a call that appears repeatedly throughout the remainder of the Psalter.[28] In lament and in praise,

---

26. John Calvin, *Institutes of the Christian Religion* I.1.1, ed. J. T. McNeil; trans. F. L. Battles (Philadelphia: Westminster, 1960), 35. See the larger discussion concerning Calvin's reading of the Psalter in Herman J. Selderhuis, *Calvin's Theology of the Psalms* (Grand Rapids: Baker Academic, 2007), 21–43.

27. William P. Brown, *Seeing the Psalms: A Theology of Metaphor* (Louisville: Westminster John Knox, 2002), 55.

28. Ibid., 78.

in petition and in thanksgiving, the psalmist calls the people of God to a life of faithful worship and obedient living.

While Psalm 1 illumines the reader on the proper stance of humans before God (Ps 1:1–3), Psalm 2 provides a stunning reminder of God's stance before the world. Although Psalm 2 was originally a royal psalm and likely part of a coronation ceremony for a human king, in its present location in the Psalter its primary function is to introduce "the pervasive proclamation of God's reign," a declaration that appears repeatedly in the Psalter.[29] This proclamation of the reign of God is set alongside the announcement that there are nations who conspire and peoples who "plot in vain" against God and his people. While the reign of God is certain in the book of Psalms, its unfolding remains plagued by the "enemies" that seek to confound the work of God in the world. Despite their presence in the world, the psalmists confess that these enemies (and nations) are not a formidable threat because they are as weak as the idols they serve (Ps 115:8). In contrast, the people of God confess that Yahweh "is the great God, the great King above all gods" (Ps 95:3).

Many of the subsequent affirmations about the work and activity of Yahweh are predicated on the assumption that Yahweh reigns as king. Given the breadth of the Psalter, an exhaustive assessment of its theology is not possible here. For those interested in further work on the theology of the Psalter, the works of Brown, Kraus, and McCann have proven to be reliable guides in that investigation.[30] In the brief treatment below, the themes of "Yahweh as King" and "Humans in the World" will be considered before concluding with a brief assessment concerning the two-fold function of the Psalter.

Yahweh as King. Although the book of Psalms employs a number of metaphors, the image of Yahweh as king has been identified as the "root metaphor." Tryggve N. D. Mettinger suggests that a root metaphor "feeds a whole family of extended metaphors; it comprises the genetic code of a broad complex of ideas."[31] As suggested above, the kingship of Yahweh is referenced first in Psalm 2 but finds its most forceful articulation in Book 4 of the Psalter (Pss 90–106). Embedded within this collection are a number of psalms designated as Yahweh *malak* psalms, so named because they contain two Hebrew words, which can be translated "the LORD Reigns."[32]

---

29. McCann Jr., "The Book of Psalms," 665.

30. Brown, *Seeing the Psalms*; Hans-Joachim Kraus, *Theology of the Psalms*, trans. Keith Crim (Minneapolis: Fortress, 1992); J. Clinton McCann Jr., *A Theological Introduction to the Book of Psalms* (Nashville: Abingdon, 1993).

31. Tryggve N. D. Mettinger, *In Search of God* (Philadelphia: Fortress, 1987), 92–93.

32. McCann Jr., *A Theological Introduction to the Book of Psalms*, 41–50.

In addition to the declaration of the reign of God, these psalms also depict Yahweh as a king, as one "robed in majesty" (Ps 93:1), as one who executes justice and equity in the world (Pss 96:10; 99:4). Beyond the collection found in Book 4, other psalms (e.g., Ps 145) make explicit reference to Yahweh as a king (*melek*), thus reinforcing the Psalter's proclamation concerning the kingship of God. Whether explicitly announced (Ps 97:1) or more subtly claimed (Ps 82), the reign of Yahweh stands as the central theological claim of the Psalter.

Yahweh as Creator. In attempting to portray the rule of God, the psalmists often refer to God's power as creator. Several psalms (Pss 29, 93, and 104) invoke ancient Near Eastern images of a cosmic combat with primeval chaos. For the psalmist, these images of a primeval battle support the claim that Yahweh reigns and, further, that the reigning King has the capacity to create order out of chaos anew. Other texts affirm Israel's confession that Yahweh is indeed the maker of heaven and earth (e.g., Pss 95:6; 121:2); he is the one enthroned in the heavens and is continuing his faithful work in governing all of creation (Pss 147:8–9; 148:8). As the Creator King, Yahweh rules the cosmos, his created kingdom, thus ensuring the people of Israel that their past, present, and future are not open to the whims of fate or the malevolence of foreign powers but, instead, are guided by the one who has called all things into being and thus can be trusted to continue sustaining his people. The image of God as creator celebrates what God has done and the power associated with such acts, but even more this image celebrates and anticipates what God may yet do through his continued creative work in the world as the Divine King.

Yahweh as Refuge. Following the work of Jerome Creach, William Brown has argued that the metaphor of "refuge" (*mahseh*) is critical to the theology of the Psalter.[33] Psalm 2 concludes with the declaration, "blessed are all who take refuge in him [Yahweh]." Much of the Psalter proves to be a theological reflection on that confession. Yet the complexity of the confession "Yahweh is a refuge" requires further explication and necessitates another set of metaphors to make the meaning clearer. To capture the larger sense of refuge, the psalmists refer to Yahweh as a "rock" or "cleft," a place of protection when life is under threat (Ps 62:6–7). Still other psalms draw from military imagery in declaring Yahweh as refuge. He is a "shield" and "fortress" (cf. Ps 144:1–2) for those enduring the hostile actions of others. In the well-known Psalm 46, the psalmist refers to the roaring of the chaotic waters and the uproar of the nations, yet the psalm opens

---

33. Brown, *Seeing the Psalms*, 15–30; Jerome F. D. Creach, *Yahweh as Refuge and the Editing of the Hebrew Psalter*, JSOTSup 217 (Sheffield: Sheffield Academic, 1996).

with the confession that "God is our refuge and strength" and then twice that Yahweh is a fortress of protection for his people (vv. 7, 11). In other psalms, the psalmists refer to being in the shadow of Yahweh's wings (e.g., Pss 17:8; 36:7). Although this metaphor emerges from the constellation of images associated with animals, particularly those from the ornithological world, the metaphor of wings is connected with a notion of refuge meant to connote the protective and nurturing capacity of God.

Although the descriptions of Yahweh as refuge draw from a broad array of images, they are rooted in the confession that God is king.[34] Only the king has sufficient power and authority to provide this kind of protection.

The City of the Great King. The city of Jerusalem, Zion, is the city of the Great King. This declaration may appear at odds with the earlier confession concerning Yahweh as the Creator King. As noted above, the psalmists often refer to God as one enthroned in the heavens, the Divine King who stands over all. In other places, however, an earthly counterpart to Yahweh's heavenly throne is mentioned—the city of Jerusalem. In referring to heavenly and earthly thrones, the psalmists confess through metaphorical language both the transcendence and immanence of God. To be the Divine King, Yahweh must rule over all. He must sit over the cosmos as both Creator and Sustainer. But for Israel to be the beneficiaries of that rule, he must be accessible and present to his people.

A number of psalms confess that Zion functions as the place where God has chosen to make his presence known to his people (e.g., Pss 46, 48, 84, and 87). Yet such confessions are not meant to confine or limit God; instead, they serve as reminders of the significance of God's presence among his people. Because of the nearness of God and his felt presence in Zion, people made pilgrimages to Zion, as evident in the Psalms of Ascents (Pss 120–34). Yet even those pilgrimage psalms held in tension the nearness of God in Zion with the power of the God enthroned in the heavens (cf. Pss 123:1; 124:8).

Because Yahweh was present in the city of Zion, the people trusted in the power of God to protect them. In Psalm 48:3 God is said to be in the citadels of the city, thus causing the kings of the nations to flee in terror at the sight of him and leading Israel to confess, "In the city of the LORD Almighty, in the city of our God: God makes her secure forever" (Ps 48:8). Because the Divine King is enthroned in Zion, the people enjoy not only the felt presence of God but, even more, the protection afforded them by the presence of the Divine King.

---

34. Creach, *Yahweh as Refuge*, 51–52.

Humans in the World

THE PSALTER OPENS WITH THE DECLARATION *'ashre ha-'ish,* "blessed is the one." While the Psalter is rooted in the confession that Yahweh reigns, the collection also gives considerable attention to what it means to be human in the world. Athanasius, in his *Letter to Marcellinus,* explained, "For I think that in the words of this book all human life is covered, with all its states and thoughts and that nothing further can be found in man."[35] Or, as Thomas Merton put it, "This is the secret of the Psalms. Our identity is hidden in them. In them we find ourselves and God. In these fragments, He has revealed not only himself to us, but ourselves to him."[36] Thus to read the psalms is indeed to worship the living God, but it is also to reflect theologically on what it means to be human.

The Way of Human Life. Psalm 1 concludes with the reminder that "the LORD watches over the way of the righteous." William Brown has rightly noted that the metaphor of the pathway plays an important role in the theology of the Psalter, particularly as it pertains to the theological anthropology found in and across this collection of texts.[37] Psalm 1 is properly labeled a torah psalm, not simply because of its reference to torah in verse 2 but, more generally, because of its didactic intention. The psalm calls the people of God to meditate on the torah and then to walk in the ways of the righteous. As a collection of prayers and liturgies, the Psalter has a morally formative function; these words call people to a particular way of life.

Similar to Psalm 1, the *sui generis* Psalm 119 unites the metaphor of the "way" with that of the torah of Yahweh. The opening verse reads, "Blessed are those whose ways [*derek*] are blameless, who walk according to the law [*torah*] of the LORD." The remaining 175 verses in Psalm 119 guide the praying person into the way of life that is consonant with and reflective of God's torah.[38] Although most psalms do not mention the torah explicitly, they do model human life as it is meant to be lived amid the darkness of lament and the glory of praise.

The instructive nature of psalms is quite evident in the entrance liturgies found in Psalms 15 and 24. Both psalms point to a particular way

---

35. Athanasius, "The Letter of St. Athanasius to Marcellinus on the Interpretation of the Psalms," in *On the Incarnation: The Treatise "De incarnatione Verbi Dei"* (Crestwood, NY: St. Vladimir's Seminary, 1996), 97–119; see p. 116.

36. Thomas Merton, *The Sign of Jonas* (New York: Image Books, 1956), 248.

37. Although the Hebrew term *derek* ("way") appears in Ps 1:6, other terms appear throughout the Psalter as synonyms, all referring to a "path" or "way."

38. On the role of Ps 119 as a morally formative text, see Brown, *Seeing the Psalter,* 31–34.

of life for the faithful by responding to the questions, "Who may dwell in your sacred tent?" (Ps 15:1) and "Who may ascend the mountain of the LORD?" (Ps 24:3). Early Jewish interpreters understood the role these psalms played in shaping the "way" of the reader. In the Babylonian Talmud (Mek. 23b–24a), a discussion ensues concerning the 613 commandments of the Torah, but amid this discussion the text explains that Psalms 15 and 24 actually contain a truncated version of the entirety of the Torah. The text reads:

> R. Simlai when preaching said, "David came and reduced them to eleven [principles], as it is written. A Psalm of David. Lord who shall sojourn in Thy tabernacle? Who shall dwell in Thy Holy Mountain? [i] He that walketh uprightly and [ii] worketh righteousness and [iii] speaketh truth in his heart; that [hath no slander upon his tongue, [v] nor doeth evil to his fellow, [vi] nor taketh up reproach against his neighbor, [vii] in whose eyes a vile person is despised, but [viii] he honoureth them that fear the Lord, [ix] He sweareth to his own hurt and changeth not, [x] he putteth not out his own money on interest, [xi] nor taketh a bribe against the innocent. He that doeth these things shall never be moved.[39]

Thus as R. Simlai observed, the psalms function as instructional guides meant to point people to a faithful life that is lived consistently in the ways of God.

Human Life Amid Hostile Forces. The Psalter not only calls people to a particular way of life, the book also acknowledges the realities that accompany life. Repeatedly throughout the Psalter, the psalmist alludes to the threats and taunts of enemies that endanger human life. In the psalms of the individual, those who offer such threats are identified by various terms: "enemies" (Pss 3:7; 6:10; 7:5; 41:5); "foes" (Pss 3:1; 13:4; 23:5); "evildoers" (Pss 26:5; 27:2); and "the wicked" (Pss 3:7; 12:7; 26:5). In addition to excessive hubris (Pss 10:6; 14:1), the enemies appear to have turned their attention on the psalmist, whom they persecute in both word and deed. The psalmist invokes three metaphors in an attempt to capture the seriousness of the threat to human life: (1) the enemies are frequently compared to a hostile army that attacks a helpless people (Pss 27:3; 55:18); (2) the enemies of the individual are compared to hunters stalking their prey (Pss 9:15; 35:7–8); and (3) the enemies are compared to wild beasts that attack unsuspecting

---

39. Quoted in John Barton, "Sin in the Psalms," *Studies in Christian Ethics* 28 (2015): 49–58; see p. 55.

victims (Pss 22:12–13; 27:2).[40] In other psalms, particularly communal laments and royal psalms, the enemy refers to those nations hostile to Israel and Judah. Frequently they mock God's people even as they mock God by asking, "Where is their God?" (Ps 115:2). In such contexts, the community implores Yahweh to act not only to redeem his people but also and more critically to restore "the glory of [his] name" (Ps 79:9).

The presence of enemies and hostile forces prompts the people of God to lament and cry out. In crying out to God about their present plight, the people are making a fundamental confession, namely, that the world remains in discord, far from the creational design of the Divine King. Although life under duress was never the design of Yahweh, the world remains awash in disruption and chaos nevertheless. Yet as Claus Westermann notes, "the point of the lament is not a self-depiction of suffering or self-pity, but to bring the end of suffering. The lament is an appeal to the one who can end suffering."[41] The psalmist declares that "the LORD watches over all who love him, but the all the wicked he will destroy" (Ps 145:20). Thus, the frequent references to the enemy validate the brokenness of human experience while also reinforcing Israel's confession that Yahweh and Yahweh alone remains the only hope for a world absent of hostility and filled with *shalom*.

God's Word to Humanity, Humanity's Word to God

TO CONSIDER THE RICH TEXTURE of the theological claims in the Psalter, we must learn to read the Psalter in all of its fullness. As suggested above, the psalms guide us in thinking about God, but they also guide us in thinking about our own human condition. In other words, the psalms function theologically in two different directions: they speak of God and they also speak of us. In addition to the bifurcated theological vision across the book of Psalms, the Psalter also functions at two different levels. These texts are both God's word to humanity and humanity's word to God. Like all texts in Scripture, we are meant to pour over them, learn from them, and preach from them. We are called to listen to them and be shaped by them. But unlike the rest of Scripture, the words of the Psalter have the capacity to become our words to God, whether in corporate worship or in private devotion. They are our words when our hearts are filled with thanksgiving

---

40. Hans-Joachim Kraus, *The Theology of the Psalms*, trans. Keith Crim (Minneapolis: Augsburg, 1992), 130–31.

41. Quoted in Bernd Janowski, *Arguing with God: A Theological Anthropology of the Psalms*, trans. Armin Siedlecki (Louisville: Westminster John Knox, 2009), 45.

---

and bursting forth in praise. And they are our words when our hearts are devoid of words because of the circumstances of life.

At one church, I was asked to lead a series of Sunday morning conversations on the book of Psalms. During the session on lament, I was waxing on about the formal features of lament psalms and the theological claims inherent in such raw texts. I then mentioned, somewhat off-handedly, "the psalms of lament become our words when we have no words left to utter." I continued on in my presentation but slowly became aware of the mother sitting next to me who was gently wiping tears from her face. Class members had long since stopped listening to me, as their attention had rightly turned to her. I paused. And then I asked if she had any comments. She reminded us about her autistic daughter, who was down in the children's wing with the rest of our children. She explained that when her daughter was younger, she would go to the preschool room, like the rest of us who were parents, to pick up her child. And when all the children would run and jump into the arms of their parents and embrace them, her daughter stood in place, barely aware of her mother's presence. She said, "I never received a hug from her; I never heard her utter the words 'I love you, Mommy.'" The mother explained that after one painful Sunday, she remembered saying to herself, "I can no longer worship a God that would allow this to happen to a child, to my child." She went home, gathered all her Bibles, placed them in a closet, and vowed never to return to church.

A year later, she said she was cleaning around the house and came across a Bible. As providence would have it, she opened this Bible to a familiar lament psalm and began to read, "My God, my God, why have you forsaken me? Why are you so far from saving me, so far from my cries of anguish?" With tears in her eyes she said, "That was what I had wanted to say to God for so long, but I did not have the words." *Those* words became *her* words. She joined the great cloud of witnesses throughout history who, through liturgy, worship, and private devotion, have prayed these psalms as prayers to the living God.

To read the Psalter theologically necessitates both listening and speaking. This commentary gives considerable attention to the former by inviting us to listen to the claims being made about God, humanity, and the interaction between the two. But the call to listen must always be balanced by the call to speak, to make these texts our words to God. In listening *and* in speaking, we are sure to be transformed by the living God, to whom these words bear witness and to whom they are directed.

—*W. Dennis Tucker Jr.*

I. Book 3 (Psalms 73–89)

A. Psalms 73–83: Crisis for the Community (Asaph Psalms)
  1. Psalm 73   The Wicked Prosper
  2. Psalm 74   A Communal Prayer for Help
  3. Psalm 75   Thanksgiving for the Coming Judgment of God
  4. Psalm 76   God's Divine Rule from Zion
  5. Psalm 77   An Individual Prayer for God's Aid
  6. Psalm 78   A Recollection of God's Work in History
  7. Psalm 79   A Communal Prayer in Light of National Disaster
  8. Psalm 80   A Communal Plea for God's Faithfulness
  9. Psalm 81   A Call for Covenant Renewal
  10. Psalm 82   God's Commitment to Justice
  11. Psalm 83   A Plea for Deliverance from National Enemies

B. Psalms 84–89: A Focus on Zion
  1. Psalm 84   Longing to Return to Zion
  2. Psalm 85   A Plea for God to Restore His People
  3. Psalm 86   A Plea for God to Act on Behalf of the Psalmist
  4. Psalm 87   A Celebration of Zion
  5. Psalm 88   Anguish over God's Apparent Abandonment
  6. Psalm 89   Anguish over the Loss of the Davidic Monarchy

II. Book 4 (Psalms 90–106)

A. Psalms 90–92: Introduction to Book 4
  1. Psalm 90   A Communal Plea for Deliverance from God's Wrath
  2. Psalm 91   Acknowledgment of God as Refuge
  3. Psalm 92   Declaration of God's Just Rule over the World

B. Psalms 93–99: The Enthronement Psalms
  1. Psalm 93   God's Kingship over the World
  2. Psalm 94   The Divine Judge of the World
  3. Psalm 95   The Divine King in History
  4. Psalm 96   The Coming Judgment of the Divine King
  5. Psalm 97   The Appearance of the Divine King
  6. Psalm 98   The Celebration of the Divine King
  7. Psalm 99   The Divine King Rules from Zion

    C. Psalms 100–106: Responses to the Kingship of God
       1. Psalm 100   Invitation for All Creation to Praise God
       2. Psalm 101   A Prayer to Walk in God's Ways
       3. Psalm 102   A Prayer for Healing and Restoration
       4. Psalm 103   A Celebration of the Goodness of God
       5. Psalm 104   A Celebration of the Creative Power of God
       6. Psalm 105   The Faith*fulness* of God to His People
       7. Psalm 106   The Faith*lessness* of God's People

III. Book 5 (Psalms 107–150)
    A. Psalm 107: The Return from Exile
    B. Psalms 108–110: A Davidic Collection
       1. Psalm 108   Communal Prayer for Deliverance from the Enemies
       2. Psalm 109   Prayer for Divine Judgment Against the Enemies
       3. Psalm 110   Assurance of God's Divine Rule in the World
    C. Psalms 111–112: Calls to Praise God
       1. Psalm 111   In Praise of God's Wonderful Acts
       2. Psalm 112   A Description of the Righteous Life
    D. Psalms 113–118: The Egyptian Hallel
       1. Psalm 113   God's Concern for the Needy
       2. Psalm 114   Israel's Deliverance out of Egypt
       3. Psalm 115   A Celebration of the Sovereignty of God
       4. Psalm 116   Thanksgiving for Deliverance from Death
       5. Psalm 117   A Call for All Nations to Praise God
       6. Psalm 118   Thanksgiving for Deliverance from the Nations
    E. Psalms 119: A Meditation on the Torah's Centrality for All of Life
    F. Psalms 120–134: The Songs of Ascent
       1. Psalm 120   A Prayer for Deliverance in a Warring World
       2. Psalm 121   A Song of Confidence in God's Protective Care
       3. Psalm 122   A Celebration of Zion
       4. Psalm 123   A Communal Prayer for Deliverance from Enemies
       5. Psalm 124   A Communal Thanksgiving for Deliverance
       6. Psalm 125   A Communal Prayer for Deliverance from Enemies
       7. Psalm 126   A Community Petition for Divine Aid
       8. Psalm 127   A Reflection on Home and Family
       9. Psalm 128   A Meditation on the Blessings of God
      10. Psalm 129   A Community Prayer Against National Enemies
      11. Psalm 130   A Plea for Personal Deliverance
      12. Psalm 131   A Confession of Trust in God

13. Psalm 132   A Celebration of Zion and the Davidic Dynasty
14. Psalm 133   A Celebration of the Unity of God's People
15. Psalm 134   A Concluding Blessing upon the Pilgrims
G. Psalms 135–36: An Appendix to the Songs of Ascent
   1. Psalm 135   In Praise of God's Work in History
   2. Psalm 136   In Praise of God's Steadfast Love in History
H. Psalm 137: An Imprecation against the Enemies of Israel
I. Psalms 138–45: A Final Davidic Collection
   1. Psalm 138   Thanksgiving for God's Steadfast Love
   2. Psalm 139   A Reflection on the Presence of God
   3. Psalm 140   A Prayer against the Enemies
   4. Psalm 141   A Prayer to Resist the Ways of the Wicked
   5. Psalm 142   A Prayer for Deliverance from Persecution
   6. Psalm 143   A Prayer for Deliverance from the Enemies
   7. Psalm 144   A Royal Prayer for Divine Help from Foreign
                   Powers
   8. Psalm 145   A Hymn Praising the Divine King
   9. Psalms 146–50: The Final Hallel
   10. Psalm 146   A Hymn Praising the Divine King
   11. Psalm 147   A Hymn Praising God for his Governance of
                   the World
   12. Psalm 148   An Invitation for All of Creation to Praise God
   13. Psalm 149   A Hymn in Praise of God's Rule
   14. Psalm 150   A Culminating Hymn of Praise

Select Bibliography

Psalms Commentaries

Allen, Leslie C. *Psalms 101–150, Revised Edition.* WBC 21. Nashville: Nelson, 2002.

———. *Psalms 101–150.* WBC. Waco, TX: Word Books, 2002.

Alter, Robert. *The Book of Psalms: A Translation with Commentary.* W. W. Norton: New York/London, 2007.

Anderson, A. A. *The Book of Psalms, Volume I, Psalms 1–72.* NCB. Grand Rapids: Eerdmans, 1972.

———. *The Book of Psalms, Volume II, Psalms 73–150.* NCB. Grand Rapids: Eerdmans, 1972.

Brueggemann, Walter. *The Message of the Psalms: A Theological Commentary.* Minneapolis: Fortress, 1984.

Brueggemann, William and William H. Bellinger Jr. *Psalms.* NCBC. New York: Cambridge University Press, 2014.

Broyles, Craig. *Psalms.* NIBCOT. Carlisle: Paternoster, 1999.

Briggs, Charles Augustus and E. G. Briggs. *The Book of Psalms.* ICC. Edinburgh: T&T Clark, 1906.

Clifford, Richard. *Psalms 73–150.* AOTC. Nashville: Abingdon, 2003.

Dahood, Mitchell. *Psalms III: 101–150.* AB 17A. New York: Doubleday, 1970.

Davidson, Robert. *The Vitality of Worship: A Commentary on the Book of Psalms.* Grand Rapids: Eerdmans, 1998.

deClaissé-Walford, Nancy, Rolf A. Jacobson, and Beth LaNeel Tanner. *The Book of Psalms.* NICOT. Grand Rapids: Eerdmans, 2014.

Eaton, John. *The Psalms: A Historical and Spiritual Commentary with an Introduction and New Translation.* London: T&T Clark International, 2003.

Gerstenberger, Erhard S. *Psalms, Part 2; and Lamentations.* FOTL XV. Grand Rapids: Eerdmans, 2001.

Gillingham, Sue. *Psalms through the Centuries: Volume One.* Blackwell Bible Commentaries. Oxford: Blackwell, 2008.

Goldingay, John. *Psalms: Volume 1, Psalms 1–41.* BCOTWP 1. Grand Rapids: Baker, 2006.

———. *Psalms: Volume 2, Psalms 42–89.* BCOTWP 2. Grand Rapids: Baker, 2007.

———. *Psalms: Volume 3, Psalms 90–150.* BCOTWP 3. Grand Rapids: Baker, 2008.

Grogan, Geoffrey W. *Psalms*. THOTC. Grand Rapids: Eerdmans, 2008.

Hossfeld, Frank-Lothar, and Erich Zenger. *Psalms 2: A Commentary on Psalms 51–100*. Translated by Linda M. Maloney. Hermeneia. Minneapolis: Fortress, 2005.

———. *Psalms 3: A Commentary on Psalms 101–150*. Translated by Linda M. Maloney. Hermeneia. Minneapolis: Fortress, 2011.

Kidner, Derek. *Psalms 1–72*. TOTC. Leicester: Inter-Varsity Press, 1973.

———. *Psalms 73–150*. TOTC. Leicester: Inter-Varsity Press, 1973.

Kirkpatrick, A. F. *The Book of Psalms*. Cambridge: Cambridge University Press, 1910.

Kraus, Hans-Joachim. *Psalms 1–59: A Commentary*. CC. Translated by Hilton C. Oswald. Minneapolis: Augsburg, 1988.

———. *Psalms 60–150: A Commentary*. CC. Translated by Hilton C. Oswald. Minneapolis: Augsburg, 1989.

Longman, Tremper. *Psalms: An Introduction and Commentary*. TOTC. Leicester: Inter-Varsity Press, 2014.

Mays, James L. *Psalms*. Interpretation. Louisville: John Knox, 1994.

McCann, J. Clinton. "The Book of Psalms." In *1 & 2 Maccabees; Introduction to Hebrew Poetry; Job; Psalms*. NIB IV. Nashville: Abingdon, 1996.

Oesterley, W. O. E. *The Psalms: Translated with Text-Critical and Exegetical Notes*. London: SPCK, 1959.

Okorocha, Cyril. "Psalms." In *African Bible Commentary: A One-Volume Commentary*. Edited by Tokunboh Adeyemo. Grand Rapids: Zondervan, 2006.

Schaefer, Konrad. *Psalms*. Edited by David W. Cotter. Berit Olam. Collegeville, MN: Liturgical Press, 2001.

Seybold, Klaus. *Die Psalmen*. HAT 1/15. Tübingen: Mohr Siebeck, 1996.

Tate, Marvin E. *Psalms 51–100*. WBC 20. Waco, TX: Word Books, 1990.

Terrien, Samuel. *The Psalms: Strophic Structure and Theological Commentary*. Eerdmans Critical Commentary. Grand Rapids: Eerdmans, 2003.

Weiser, Artur. *The Psalms: A Commentary*. OTL. Translated by H. Hartwell. Philadelphia: Westminster, 1962.

Wesselschmidt, Quentin F., ed. *Psalms 51–150*. Ancient Christian Commentary VIII. Downers Grove, IL: InterVarsity, 2007.

Wilson, Gerald. *Psalms—Volume 1*. NIVAC. Grand Rapids: Zondervan, 2002.

Other Studies

Attridge, Harold W. "The Psalms in Hebrews." Pages 197–212 in *The Psalms in the New Testament*. Edited by S. Moyise and M. J. J. Menken. London: T&T Clark International, 2004.

Ballhorn, Egbert. *Zum Telos des Psalters: Der Textzusammenhang des Vierten und Fünften Psalmenbuches*. Bonner biblische Beiträge 138 (Berlin: Philo, 2004).

Bar-Efrat, Shimon. "Love of Zion: A Literary Interpretation of Psalm 137." Pages 3–11 in *Tehillah le-Moshe*. Edited by Moshe Greenberg, et al. Winona Lake, IN: Eisenbrauns, 1997.

Barth, Christoph. *Die Errettung vom Tode in den individuellen Klage—und Dankliedern des Alten Testaments*. Zollikon: Evangelischer, 1947.

Bautch, Richard J. *Developments in Genre between Post-Exilic Penitential Psalms and the Psalms of Communal Lament*. SBLAB 7. Atlanta: SBL Press, 2003.

Bechtel, Lyn M. "Shame as a Sanction of Social Control in Biblical Israel: Judicial, Political, and Social Shaming," *JSOT* 49 (1991): 47–76.

Becking, Bob. "Does Exile Equal Suffering: A Fresh Look at Psalm 137." Pages 181–202 in *Exile and Suffering: A Selection of Papers Read at the 50th Anniversary Meeting of the Old Testament Society of South Africa OTWSA/OTSSA, Pretoria August 2007*. Edited by B. Becking and D. Human. Leiden: Brill, 2009.

Bellinger, Jr., William H. "Poetry and Theology: Psalm 133." Pages 3–14 in *The Psalter as: Poetry, Theology and Genre*. Edited by W. Dennis Tucker, Jr. and William H. Bellinger, Jr. Waco, TX: Baylor University Press, 2017.

Beyerlin, Walter. *Im Lichte der Traditionen: Psalm LXVII und CXV. Ein Entwicklungszusammengang*. VTSup 45. Leiden: Brill, 1992.

_____. *We are Like Dreamers: Studies in Psalm 126*. Edinburgh: T&T Clark, 1982.

_____. *Werden und Wesen des 107. Psalms*. BZAW 153. Berlin: de Gruyter, 1979.

_____. *Wider die Hybris des Geistes: Studien zum 131. Psalm*. SBS 108. Stuttgart: Katholisches Bibelwerk, 1982.

Birkeland, Harris. *The Evildoer in the Book of Psalms*. Oslo: Jacob Dybwad, 1955.

Botha, Phil J. "Psalm 108 and the Quest for Closure," *OTE* 23 (2010): 574–96.

_____. "Social Values and the Interpretation of Psalm 123." *OTE* 14 (2001): 189–98.

_____. "'Wealth and Riches are in His House' (Ps 112:3): Acrostic Wisdom Psalms and the Development of Anti-materialism." Pages 105–28 in *The Shape and Shaping of the Book of Psalms: The Current State of Scholarship*. Edited by Nancy L. deClaissé-Walford. Atlanta: SBL Press, 2014.

Booij, Th. "Psalm CX: 'Rule in the Midst of Your Foes.'" *VT* 41 (1991): 396–407.

_____."Psalm CXXXIX: Text, Syntax, Meaning." *VT* LV.1 (2005): 1–19.

Brown, William P. "A Royal Performance: Critical Notes on Psalm 110:3 aγ-b," *JBL* 117 (1998): 93–110.

_____. *Seeing the Psalms: A Theology of Metaphor*. Louisville: WJKP, 2002.

Broyles, Craig C. *The Conflict of Faith and Experience in the Psalms: A Form-Critical and Theological Study*. JSOTSup 52. Sheffield: JSOT Press, 1989.

Brueggemann, Walter. *Abiding Astonishment: Psalms, Modernity, and the Making of History*. Literary Currents in Biblical Interpretation. Louisville: Westminster John Knox, 1991.

———. "Bounded by Obedience and Praise." *JSOT* 50 (1991): 63–92.

———. *The Land: Place as Gift, Promise and Challenge in Biblical Faith*. Overtures to Biblical Theology. Philadelphia: Fortress, 1978.

———. *Spirituality of the Psalms*. Minneapolis: Fortress, 2002.

Brueggemann, Walter, and Patrick D. Miller. "Psalm 73 as a Canonical Marker." *JSOT* 72 (1996): 45–56.

Bullock, C. Hassell. *Encountering the Book of Psalms: A Literary and Theological Introduction*. Grand Rapids: Baker Academic, 2001.

Butler, Trent C. "Piety in the Psalms." *RevExp* 81 (1984): 385–94.

Buysch, Christoph. *Der letzte Davidpsalter: Interpretation, Komposition, und Funktion der Psalmengruppe Ps 138–145*. SBB 63. Stuttgart: Katholisches Bibelwerk, 2009.

Ceresko, Anthony. "Psalm 149: Poetry, Themes (Exodus and Conquest) and Social Function." *Bib* 67 (1986): 177–94.

Cheung, Simon Chi-Chung. *Wisdom Intoned: A Reappraisal of the Genre "Wisdom Psalms."* LHB/OTS 613. London: Bloomsbury, 2015.

Clifford, Richard J. "The Function of Idol Passages in Deutero-Isaiah," *CBQ* 42 (1980): 450–64.

———. "The Hebrew Scriptures and the Theology of Creation." *TS* 46.3 (1985): 507–23.

———. "Style and Purpose in Psalm 105." *Bib* 60.3 (1979): 420–27.

Cornelius, Izak. "The Visual Representation of the World in the Ancient Near East and the Hebrew Bible." *JNSL* 20.2 (1994).

Creach, Jerome F. D. *The Destiny of the Righteous in the Psalms*. St. Louis: Chalice, 2008.

———. *Yahweh as Refuge and the Editing of the Hebrew Psalter*. JSOTSup 217. Sheffield: Sheffield Academic, 1996.

Croft, Steven J. L. *The Identity of the Individual in the Psalms*. JSOTSup 14. Sheffield: JSOT Press, 1987.

Crow, Loren D. *The Songs of Ascents [Psalms 120–134]: Their Place in Israelite History and Religion*. SBLDS 148. Atlanta: Scholars Press, 1996.

Currid, John D. *Ancient Egypt and the Old Testament*. Grand Rapids: Baker Books, 1997.

Daly-Denton, Margaret. "The Psalms in John's Gospel." Pages 119–37 in *The Psalms in the New Testament*. Edited by S. Moyise and M. J. J. Menken. London: T&T Clark International, 2004.

Davis, Ellen F. "Expository Article: Psalm 98." *Int* 46.1 (1992): 171–75.

Dobbs-Allsopp, F.W. *On Biblical Poetry*. Oxford: Oxford University Press, 2015.

Doyle, Brian. "Metaphora Interrupta: Psalm 133." *ETL* 77 (2001): 5–22.

Eaton, John H. *Kingship and the Psalms.* The Biblical Seminar 3. Sheffield: JSOT Press, 1980.

———. "Proposals in Psalms XCIX and CXIX." *VT* 18.4 (1968): 555–58.

Ego, Beate. "'Der Herr blickt herab von der Höhe seines Heiligtums:' Zur Vorstellung von Gottes himmlischen Thronen in exilisch-nachexilischer Zeit." *ZAW* 110 (1998): 556–69.

Eidevall, Göran. *Prophecy and Propaganda: Images of Enemies in the Book of Isaiah.* ConBOT 46.Winona Lake, IN: Eisenbrauns, 2009.

Emerton, J. A. "The Text of Psalm LXXVII 11." *VT* XLIV.2 (1994): 183–94.

Firth, David G. *Surrendering Retribution in the Psalms: Responses to Violence in the Individual Complaints.* Paternoster Biblical Monographs. Milton Keynes: Paternoster, 2005.

Fleming, Daniel. "House/City: An Unrecognized Parallel Word Pair." *JBL* 105 (1986): 689–93.

Fokkelman, J. P. *Major Poems of the Hebrew Bible: At the Interface of Prosody and Structural Analysis, Volume II: 85 Psalms and Job 4–14.* Studia Semitica Neerlandica. Leiden: Brill, 2000.

Freedman, David N. "The Structure of Psalm 137." Pages 187–205 in *Near Eastern Studies in Honor of W. F. Albright.* Edited by H. Goedicke. Baltimore: Johns Hopkins, 1971.

Gerstenberger, Erhard S. "Singing a New Song: On Old Testament and Latin American Psalmody." *WW* V.2 (1985): 155–67.

Gillingham, Susan E. "The Exodus Tradition and Israelite Psalmody." *SJT* 52.1 (1999): 19–46.

Goulder, Michael D. *The Psalms of the Return: Book V, Psalms 107–150.* JSOTSup 258. Sheffield: Sheffield Academic, 1998.

Gosling, F. A. "Were the Ephraimites to Blame?" *VT* 49.4 (1999): 505–13.

Grant, Jamie A. "Creation and Kingship: Environment and Witness in the Yahweh *Mālāk* Psalms." Pages 92–106 in *As Long as Earth Endures: The Bible Creation and the Environment.* Edited by Jonathan Moo and Robin Routledge. Leicester: Apollos, 2014.

———. "Determining the Indeterminate: Issues in Interpreting the Psalms." *Southeastern Theological Review* 1.1 (Winter 2010): 3–14.

———. "Editorial Criticism." Pages 149–56 in *IVP Dictionary of the Old Testament: Wisdom, Poetry & Writings.* Edited by Tremper Longman III and Peter Enns. Downers Grove: IVP, 2008.

———. "The Hermeneutics of Humanity: Reflections on the Human Origin of the Laments." Pages 182–202 in *A God of Faithfulness: Essays in Honour of J. Gordon McConville on His 60th Birthday.* Edited by Jamie A. Grant, Alison Lo, and Gordon J. Wenham. LHBOTS 538. London: T&T Clark, 2011.

————. "Psalms 73 and 89: The Crisis of Faith." Pages 61–86 in *Praying by the Book: Reading the Psalms*. Edited by C. G. Bartholomew and A. West. Carlisle: Paternoster, 2001.

————. "Singing the Cover Versions: Psalms, Reinterpretation and Biblical Theology in Acts 1–4." *SBET* 25.1 (Spring 2007): 27–49.

————. *The King as Exemplar: The Function of Deuteronomy's Kingship Law in the Shaping of the Book of Psalms*. AB 17. Atlanta/ Leiden: SBL/ Brill, 2004.

————. "'When the Friendship of God Was Upon My Tent': Covenant as Essential Background to Lament in the Wisdom Literature." Pages 323–39 in *Covenant in the Persian Period: From Genesis to Chronicles*. Edited by Richard I. Bautch and Gary N. Knoppers. Winona Lake, IN: Eisenbrauns, 2015.

————. "'Why Bother with the Vulnerable?': The Wisdom of Social Care." Pages 51–67 in *Transforming the World? The Gospel and Social Responsibility*. Edited by Jamie A. Grant and Dewi A. Hughes. Leicester: Apollos, 2009.

Grant, Jamie A., and Dewi A. Hughes, eds. *Transforming the World? The Gospel and Social Responsibility*. Leicester: Apollos, 2009.

Gunkel, Hermann. *An Introduction to the Psalms: The Genres of the Religious Lyric of Israel*. MLBS. Translated by James Nogalski. Macon, GA: Mercer University Press, 1998.

Hauge, Martin R. *Between Sheol and Temple: Motif Structure and Function in the I-Psalms*. JSOTSup 178. Sheffield: Sheffield Academic, 1995.

Heibert, Theodore. "Theophany in the OT." Pages 505–11 in *Anchor Bible Dictionary, Volume 6:Si-Z*. Edited by David N. Freedman. New Haven: Yale University Press, 1992.

Heim, Knut M. "The (God-)Forsaken King of Psalm 89: A Historical and Intertextual Enquiry." Pages 296–322 in *King and Messiah in Israel and the Ancient Near East: Proceedings of the Oxford Old Testament Seminar*. Edited by J. Day. JSOTSup 270. Sheffield: Sheffield Academic, 1998.

Hess, Richard S. *Israelite Religions: An Archaeological and Biblical Survey*. Leicester: Apollos, 2007.

Holman, Jan. "The Semiotic Analysis of Psalm CXXXIII (LXX)." *OtSt* 26 (1990): 84–100.

Holst, Søren. "Psalmists in Cramped and Open Spaces: A Cognitive Perspective on the Theology of the Psalms." *SJOT* 28 (2014): 266–79.

Howard, David M. Jr. "Psalm 94 Among the Kingship-of-Yhwh Psalms." *CBQ* 61.4 (O 1999): 667–85.

Human, Dirk J. "Be'rit in Psalm 74." *Skrif en Kirk* 16.1 (1995): 57–66.

————. "Ethical Perspectives from the *Sîrê Hamaʿalôt* Psalm 127." Pages 523–36 in *The Composition of the Psalter*. Edited by Erich Zenger. BETL 238. Leuven: Peeters, 2010.

_____. "Psalm 136: A Liturgy with Reference to Creation and History." Pages 73–88 in *Psalms and Liturgy*. Edited by Dirk. J. Human and C. J. A. Vos. JSOTSup 410. London: T&T Clark, 2004.

Hunter, Alastair. *Psalms*. Old Testament Readings. London: Routledge, 1999.

Jacobson, Rolf A. "'The Faithfulness of the Lord Endures Forever': The Theological Witness of the Psalter." Pages 111–37 in *Soundings in the Theology of Psalms: Perspectives and Methods in Contemporary Scholarship*. Edited by Rolf A. Jacobson. Minneapolis, MN: Fortress, 2011.

Janowski, Bernd. *Arguing with God: A Theological Anthropology of the Psalms*. Translated by Armin Siedlecki. Louisville: Westminster John Knox, 2013.

_____. "Dankbarkeit: Ein anthropologischer Grundbegriff im Spiegel der toda-Psalmen." Pages 91–136 in *Ritual und Poesie: Formen und Orte religiöser Dichtung im Alten Orient, im Judentum und im Christentum*. Edited by Erich Zenger. HBS 36. Freiburg: Herder, 2003.

_____. "Dem Löwen gleich, gierig nach Raub. Zum Feindbild in den Psalmen." *EvT* 55 (1995): 155–73.

_____. *Die Welt als Schöpfung*. Beiträge zur Theologie des Alten Testament 4. Neukirchen-Vluyn: Neukirchener Verlag, 2008.

Jarick, John. "The Four Corners of Psalm 107." *CBQ* (1997): 270–87.

Jensen, Joseph E. "Psalm 75: Its Poetic Context and Structure." *CBQ* 63.3 (2001): 416–29.

Jeremias, Jörg. "Ps 100 als Auslegung von Ps 93–100." *Skrif en kerk* 19 (1998): 605–15.

Johnston, Philip. *Shades of Sheol: Death and Afterlife in the Old Testament*. Downers Grove, IL: InterVarsity, 2002.

Kee, Min Suc. "The Heavenly Council and its Type-scene." *JSOT* 31.3 (2007): 259–73.

Keel, Othmar. *The Symbolism of the Biblical World: Ancient Near Eastern Iconography and the Book of Psalms*. Translated by T. J. Hallett. Winona Lake, IN: Eisenbrauns, 1997.

Keesmaat, Sylvia C. "The Psalms in Romans and Galatians." Pages 139–61 in *The Psalms in the New Testament*. Edited by S. Moyise and M. J. J. Menken. London: T&T Clark International, 2004.

Keet, Cuthbert C. *A Study of the Psalms of Ascent: A Critical and Exegetical Commentary upon Psalms CXX to CXXXIV*. London: Mitre, 1969.

Kellerman, Ulrich. "Psalm 137." *ZAW* 90 (1978): 43–58.

Kimelman, Reuven. "Psalm 145: Theme, Structure, and Impact." *JBL* 133 (1994): 37–58.

Kitz, Anne Marie. "Effective Simile and Effective Act: Psalm 109, Numbers 5, and *KUB* 26." *CBQ* 69 (2007): 440–56.

Kline, Meredith G. *The Structure of Biblical Authority.* 2nd ed. Eugene, OR: Wipf and Stock, 1989.

Klingbeil, Martin. "Metaphors that Travel and (almost) Vanish: Mapping Diachronic Changes in the Intertextual Usage of the Heavenly Warrior Metaphor in Psalms 18 and 144." Pages 115–35 in *Metaphors in the Psalms.* Edited by Pierre van Hecke and Antje Labahn. BETL 231. Leuven: Peeters, 2010.

Knowles, Melody. *Centrality Practiced: Jerusalem in the Religious Practice of Yehud and the Diaspora in the Persian Period.* ABS 16. Atlanta: SBL Press, 2006.

Koch, Klaus. "Sühne und Sündenvergebung um die Wende von der exilischen zur nachexilischen Zeit." *EvT* 26 (1966): 217–339.

Körting, Corinna. *Zion in den Psalmen.* FAT 48. Tübingen: Mohr Siebeck, 2006.

Krašovec, Jože. "Merism—Polar Expression in the Hebrew Bible." *Bib* 64 (1983): 231–39.

Krawelitzski, Judith. "God the Almighty? Observations in the Psalms." *VT* 64 (2014): 434–44.

_____. *Theology of the Psalms.* CC. Translated by Keith Crim. Minneapolis: Fortress, 1992.

Kselman, John S. "Janus Parallelism in Psalm 75:2." *JBL* 121.3 (2002): 531–32.

Labahn, Michael. "The Psalms in Q." Pages 47–60 in *The Psalms in the New Testament.* Edited by S. Moyise and M. J. J. Menken. London: T&T Clark International, 2004.

Ladd, George E. *A Theology of the New Testament.* Rev. ed. Edited by Donald A. Hagner. Grand Rapids: Eerdmans, 1993.

Launderville, Dale. *Piety and Politics: The Dynamics of Royal Authority in Homeric Greece, Biblical Israel, and Old Babylonian Mesopotamia.* Grand Rapids: Eerdmans, 2003.

Lee, Archie C. C. "Genesis I and the Plagues Tradition in Psalm CV." *VT* XL.3 (1990): 257–63.

Leuenberger, Martin. *Konzeptionen des Königtums Gottes im Psalter: Untersuchungen zu Komposition und Redaktion der theokratischen Bücher IV–V im Psalter.* ATANT 83. Zürich: Theologischer Verlag Zürich, 2004.

Levenson, Jon. "The Sources of Torah: Psalm 119 and the Modes of Revelation in Second Temple Judaism." Pages 559–74 in *Ancient Israelite Religion.* Edited by Patrick D. Miller Jr., Paul D. Hanson, and S. Dean McBride. Philadelphia: Fortress, 1987.

Levin, Christoph. "The Poor in the Old Testament: Some Observations." Pages 281–300 in *Re-reading the Scriptures: Essays on the Literary History of the Old Testament.* Tübingen: Mohr Siebeck, 2013.

Liess, Kathrin. "Von der Gottesferne zur Gottesnähe: Zur Todes-und Lebensmetaphorik in den Psalmen." Pages 167–96 in *Metaphors in the Psalms*. Edited by P. van Hecke and A. Labahn. BETL 231. Leuven: Peeters, 2010.

_____. *Der Weg des Lebens: Psalm 16 und das Lebens-und Todensverständnis der Individualpsalmen*. FAT 2/5. Tübingen: Mohr Siebeck, 2004.

Limburg, James. "Psalm 121: A Psalm for Sojourners." *Word and Way* 5 (1985): 180–87.

Longman, Tremper. "The Messiah: Explorations in the Law and Writings." Pages 13–34 in *The Messiah in the Old and New Testaments*. Edited by Stanley E. Porter. Grand Rapids: Eerdmans, 2007.

———. "Psalm 98: A Divine Warrior Victory Song." *JETS* 27.3 (1984): 267–74.

Longman, Tremper, and Daniel G. Reid. *God is a Warrior*. Grand Rapids: Zondervan, 1995.

López, Félix García. "Le Roi d'Israel: Dt 17,14–20." Pages 277–97 in *Das Deuteronomium: Entstehung, Gestalt und Botschaft*. Edited by N. Lohfink. Leuven: Leuven University Press, 1985.

Macleod, Donald. "Faith beyond the Forms of Faith: An Exposition of Psalm 73." *Int* 12.4 (1958): 418–21.

Malchoz, Christian. "Psalm 136: Exegetische Beobachtungen mit methodogischen Seitenblicken." Pages 177–86 in *Mincha. Festgabe für Rolf Rendtorff zum 75. Geburtstag*. Edited by E. Blum. Neukirchen-Vluyn: Neukirchener, 2000.

Martilla, Marko. *Collective Reinterpretation in the Psalms*. FAT 2/13. Tübingen: Mohr Siebeck, 2006.

Mathys, Hans-Peter. *Dichter und Beter: Theologen aus spätalttestamentlicher Zeit*. OBO 132. Göttingen: Vandenhoeck & Ruprecht, 1994.

Mays, James L. *The Lord Reigns*. Louisville: Westminster John Knox, 1994.

———. "Psalm 73: A Microcosm of Old Testament Theology." Pages 247–58 in *The Listening Heart: Essays in Wisdom and the Psalms in Honor of Roland E. Murphy, O.Carm*. Edited by K. G. Hoglun, E. F. Huwiler, J. T. Glass, and R. W. Lee. JSOTSup 58. Sheffield: JSOT Press, 1987.

———. *A Theological Introduction to the Books of Psalms: The Psalms as Torah*. Nashville: Abingdon, 1993.

McConville, J. Gordon. *Deuteronomy*. AOTC. Leicester: Apollos, 2002.

McKelvey, Michael G. *Moses, David and the High Kingship of Yahweh: A Canonical Study of Book IV of the Psalter*. Gorgias Dissertations Biblical Studies 55. Piscataway, NJ: Gorgias Press, 2010.

Mejía, Jorge. "Some Observations on Psalm 107." *BTB* 5 (1975): 56–66.

Menken, Martin J. J. "The Psalms in Matthew's Gospel." Pages 61–82 in *The Psalms in the New Testament*. Edited by S. Moyise and M. J. J. Menken. London: T&T Clark International, 2004.

Mettinger, Tryggve N. D. *In Search of God: The Meaning and Message of the Everlasting Names*. Minneapolis: Fortress, 1988.

Middleton, J. Richard. "Created in the Image of a Violent God? The Ethical Problem of the Conquest of Chaos in Biblical Creation Texts." *Int* 58.4 (2004): 341–55.

Miller, Patrick D. "Gift of God: Deuteronomic Theology of the Land." *Int* 23.4 (1969): 451–65.

———. *Interpreting the Psalms*. Philadelphia: Fortress Press, 1986.

———. "The Poetry of Creation: Psalm 104." Pages 178–92 in *The Way of the Lord*. FAT 29. Tübingen: Mohr Siebeck, 2004.

———. *The Religion of Ancient Israel*. Library of Ancient Israel. London: SPCK, 2000.

———. *They Cried to the Lord: The Form and Theology of Biblical Prayer*. Minneapolis, MN: Fortress, 1994.

Mitchell, David C. *The Message of the Psalter: An Eschatological Programme in the Book of Psalms*. JSOTSup 252. Sheffield: Sheffield Academic Press, 1997.

Sigmund Mowinckel, *The Psalms in Israel's Worship. Vol 1*. Translated by D. R. Ap-Thomas. Oxford: Basil Blackwell, 1962.

Moyise, Steve. "The Psalms in the Book of Revelation." Pages 231–46 in *The Psalms in the New Testament*. Edited by S. Moyise and M. J. J. Menken. London: T&T Clark International, 2004.

Murphy, Roland E. *Wisdom Literature: Job, Proverbs, Ruth, Canticles, Ecclesiastes and Esther*. FOTL XIII. Grand Rapids: Eerdmans, 1981.

Murphy, Todd J. *Pocket Dictionary for the Study of Biblical Hebrew*. Downers Grove, IL: InterVarsity, 2003.

Nasuti, Harry P. "God at Work in the World: A Theology of Divine-Human Encounter in the Psalms." Pages 27–48 in *Soundings in the Theology of the Psalms: Perspectives in Contemporary Scholarship*. Edited by Rolf A. Jacobson. Minneapolis: Fortress, 2011.

———. "'Who is Like the Lord our God?' Relating Theology and Ethics in Psalm 113." Pages 27–45 in *The Psalter as Witness: Poetry, Theology, Genre*. Edited by W. Dennis Tucker Jr. and W. H. Bellinger. Waco, TX: Baylor University Press, 2017.

Nelson, Richard D. "Psalm 114," *Int* 63 (2009): 172–74.

Niehaus, Jeffrey J. *God at Sinai: Covenant and Theophany in the Bible and Ancient Near East*. Studies in Old Testament Biblical Theology. Grand Rapids: Zondervan, 1995.

O'Dowd, Ryan. *The Wisdom of Torah: Epistemology in Deuteronomy and the Wisdom Literature*. FRLANT 225. Göttingen: Vandenhoeck & Ruprecht, 2009.

Ollenburger, Ben C. *Zion the City of the Great King: A Theological Symbol of the Jerusalem Cult*. JSOTSup 41. Sheffield: JSOT Press, 1987.

Peels, H. G. L. *Shadow Sides: God in the Old Testament*. Translated by Hetty Lalleman. Carlisle: Paternoster, 2003.

Perdue, Leo. *The Sword and the Stylus: An Introduction to Wisdom in the Age of Empires*. Grand Rapids: Eerdmans, 2008.

Phillips, Elaine A. "Speaking Truthfully: Job's Friends and Job." *BBR* 18.1 (2008): 31–43.

Prinsloo, Willem S. "Psalm 149: Praise Yahweh with Tambourine and Two-edged Sword." *ZAW* 109 (1997): 395–407.

Prothero, Rowland E. *The Psalms in Human Life*. London: Nelson, 1903.

Rasmussen, Michael D. *Conceptualizing Distress in the Psalms: A Form-Critical and Cognitive Semantic Study of the צרר^1 Word Group*. Gorgias Biblical Studies 66. Piscataway, NJ: Gorgias Press, 2018.

Reynolds, Carol Bechtel. "Psalm 125." *Int* 48 (1994): 272–75.

Reynolds, Kent Aaron. *Torah as Teacher: The Exemplary Torah Student in Psalm 119*. Leiden: Brill, 2010.

Richter, Sandra L. *The Deuteronomistic History and the Name Theology: leshakken shemo sham in the Bible and the Ancient Near East*. BZAW 318. Berlin: de Gruyter, 2002.

Riede, Peter. *Im Netz des Jägers: Studien zur Feindmetaphorik der Individualpsalmen*, WMANT 85. Neukirchen-Vluyn: Neukirchener Verlag, 2000.

Roberts, J. J. M. "God's Imperial Reign According to the Psalter." *HBT* 23 (2001): 211–21.

_____. "Of Signs, Prophets, and Time Limits: A Note on Psalm 74:9." *CBQ* 39 (1977): 474–81.

Rooker, M. F. "Theophany." Pages 859–64 in *Dictionary of the Old Testament: Pentateuch*. Edited by T. Desmond Alexander and David W. Baker. London: Inter-Varsity Press, 2003.

Schaeffer, Francis A. *The Church Before the Watching World: A Practical Ecclesiology*. Downer's Grove: IVP, 1971.

Scaioloa, Donatella. "The End of the Psalter." Pages 701–10 in *The Composition of the Book of Psalms*. Edited by Erich Zenger. BETL 238. Leuven: Peeters, 2010.

Schmid, Konrad. "Himmelsgott, Weltgott, und Schöpfer: 'Gott' und der 'Himmel' in der Literatur der Zeit des Zweiten Tempels." Pages 111–48 in *Der Himmel*. Edited by D. Sattler and S. Vollenweider. Neukirchen-Vluyn: Neukirchener Verlag, 2006.

_____. *The Old Testament: A Literary History*. Translated by Linda Maloney. Minneapolis: Fortress, 2012.

Schniedewind, William M. "'Are We His People or Not?' Biblical Interpretation During Crisis." *Bib* 77 (1995): 540–50.

Scoralick, Ruth. "'Hallelujah für einen gewalttätigen Gott?': Zur Theologie von Psalm 135 und 136." *BZ* 46 (2002): 253–72.

_____. "Psalm 111—Bauplan und Gedankengang." *Bib* 78 (1997): 190–205.

Smick, Elmer B. "Mythopoetic Language in the Psalms." *WTJ* 44 (1982): 88–98.

Snyman, Fanie. "Reading Ps 117 against an Exilic Context." *VT* 61 (2011): 109–18.

Soll, William M. *Psalm 119: Matrix, Form and Setting*. CBQMS 23. Washington, DC: Catholic University of America Press, 1991.

Tournay, Raymond J. "Psaumes 57, 60 et 108. Analyse et Interprétation." *RB* 96 (1989): 5–26.

Tsevat, Matitiahu. "God and the Gods in Assembly: An Interpretation of Psalm 82." *HUCA* 40–41 (1970): 123–37.

Tucker Jr., W. Dennis. *Constructing and Deconstructing Power in Psalms 107–150*. Ancient Israelite Literature 19. Atlanta: SBL Press, 2014.

_____. "Is Shame a Matter of Patronage in the Communal Laments?" *JSOT* 31 (2007): 465–80.

_____. "A Polysemiotic Approach to the Poor in the Psalms." *PRSt* 31 (2004): 425–39.

_____. "Revisiting the Plagues in Psalm CV." *VT* LV.3 (2005): 401–11.

_____. "The Role of the Foe in Book 5: Reflections on the Final Composition of the Psalter." Pages 179–92 in *The Shape and Shaping of the book of Psalms*. Edited by Nancy L. deClaissé-Walford. Ancient Israelite Literature 20. Atlanta: SBL Press, 2014.

van der Meer, William. "Psalm 110." Pages 207–34 in *The Structural Analysis of Biblical and Canaanite Poetry*. Edited by W. van der Meer and J. C. de Moor. JSOTSup 74. Sheffield: Sheffield Academic, 1988.

van der Merwe, Christo H. J., Jackie A. Naudé, and Jan H. Kroze. *A Biblical Hebrew Reference Grammar*. Biblical Languages: Hebrew 3. London: T&T Clark, 2002.

Van Rensburg, J. F. J. "History as Poetry: A Study of Psalm 136." Pages 80–90 in *Exodus 1–15: Text and Context*. Edited by J. J. Burden, P. J. Botha, and H. F. van Rooy. OTWSA/OTSSA 29. Pretoria: V & R Printing, 1987.

von Waldow, H. E. "Israel and Her Land: Some Theological Considerations." Pages 493–508 in *A Light Unto My Path: Old Testament Studies in Honor of Jacob M. Myers*. Edited by H. N. Bream, R. D. Heim, and C. A. Moore. Philadelphia: Temple University Press, 1974.

Walker, Christopher and Michael Dick. *The Induction of the Cult Image in Ancient Mesopotamia*. Helsinki: Neo-Assyrian Text Corpus Project, 2001.

Wallace, Howard Neil .*Words to God, Word from God: The Psalms in the Prayer and Preaching of the Church*. Burlington, VT: Ashgate, 2005.

Waltke, Bruce K. and Michael O'Connor. *An Introduction to Biblical Hebrew Syntax*. Winona Lake, IN: Eisenbrauns, 1990.

Walsh, Jerome T. *Ahab: The Construction of a King*. Interfaces. Collegeville, MN: Liturgical Press, 2006.

_____. *The Mighty from Their Thrones: Power in the Biblical Tradition*, OBT (Philadelphia: Fortress, 1987.

Walton, John H. *Ancient Israelite Literature in its Cultural Context*. Grand Rapids: Zondervan, 1989.

_____. *Ancient Near Eastern Thought and the Old Testament: Introducing the Conceptual World of the Hebrew Bible*. Leicester: Apollos, 2007.

Watson, Wilfred G. E. "The Hidden Simile in Psalm 133." *Bib* 60 (1979): 108–09.

_____. "Reversed Rootplay in Ps 145." *Bib* 62 (1981): 101–02.

Weber, Beat. *Werkbuch Psalmen II: Die Psalm 73 Bis 150*. Stuttgart: Kohlhammer, 2003.

Westbrook, Raymond. *"Vitae Necisque Potestas."* *Historia: Zeitschrift Für Alte Geschichte* 48.2 (1999): 203–23.

Westermann, Claus. *The Living Psalms*. Translated by J. R. Porter. Grand Rapids: Eerdmans, 1989.

_____. *Praise and Lament in the Psalms*. Translated by Keith Crim. Atlanta: John Knox, 1961.

_____. *The Praise of God in the Psalms*. Richmond, VA: Knox, 1965.

Weippert, Manfred H. E. *Jahwe und die anderen Götter*. FAT 18. Tübingen: Mohr Siebeck, 1997.

Whitekettle, Richard. "Bugs, Bunny, or Boar? Identifying the Zîz Animals of Psalms 50 and 80." *CBQ* 67.2 (2005): 250–63.

Whybray, R. Norman. "The Wisdom Psalms." Pages 152–60 in *Wisdom in Ancient Israel: Essays in Honour of J. A. Emerton*. Edited by J. Day, R. P. Gordon, and H. G. M. Williamson. Cambridge: Cambridge University Press, 1995.

Williams III, H. H. Drake. "The Psalms in 1 and 2 Corinthians." Pages 163–80 in *The Psalms in the New Testament*. Edited by Steve Moyise and Maarten J. J. Menken. London: Continuum, 2004.

Wilson, Gerald H. *The Editing of the Hebrew Psalter*. SBLDS 76. Chico, CA: Scholars Press, 1985.

———. "Evidence of Editorial Divisions in the Hebrew Psalter." *VT* XXXIV.3 (1984): 337–52.

————. "The Shape of the Book of Psalms." *Int* 46.2 (April 1992): 129–41.

————. "Shaping the Psalter: A Consideration of Editorial Linkage in the Book of Psalms." Pages 72–82 in *The Shape and Shaping of the Psalms.* Edited by J. Clinton McCann. JSOTSup 159. Sheffield: JSOT Press, 1993.

————. "The Structure of the Psalter." Pages 229–46 in *Interpreting the Psalms: Issues and Approaches.* Edited by P. S. Johnston and D. G. Firth. Leicester: Apollos, 2005.

————. "The Use of Royal Psalms at the 'Seams' of the Hebrew Psalter." *JSOT* 35 (1986): 85–94.

Wolff, Hans Walter. *Anthropology of the Old Testament.* Translated by Margaret Kohl. Philadelphia: Fortress, 1974.

Wright, N. T. *The Case for the Psalms: Why They Are Essential.* San Francisco: HarperCollins, 2013.

Zenger, Erich. *A God of Vengeance? Understanding the Psalms of Divine Wrath.* Louisville: WJKP, 1996.

————. "Psalmenexegese und Psalterexegese." Pages 17–65 in *The Composition of the Book of Psalms.* Edited by Erich Zenger. BETL 238. Leuven: Peeters, 2010.

————. "Torafrömmigkeit. Beobachtungen zum poetischen und theologischen Profil von Psalm 119." Pages 380–96 in *Freiheit und Recht. Für Frank Crüsemann zum 65. Geburtstag.* Edited by Christof Hardmeier, Rainer Kessler, and Andreas Ruwe. Gütersloh: Kaiser, 2003.

Zevit, Ziony. "Psalms at the Poetic Precipice." *HAR* 19 (1987): 351–66.

Zimmerli, Walther. "Zwillingspsalmen." Pages 105–13 in Wort, Lied und Gottesspruch, II: Beiträge zu Psalmen und Propheten. Edited by Joseph Schreiner. Würzburg: Echter, 1972.

Psalm 73

A psalm of Asaph.

Surely God is good to Israel,
    to those who are pure in heart.
² But as for me, my feet had almost slipped;
    I had nearly lost my foothold.
³ For I envied the arrogant
    when I saw the prosperity of the wicked.
⁴ They have no struggles;
    their bodies are healthy and strong.
⁵ They are free from common human burdens;
    they are not plagued by human ills.
⁶ Therefore pride is their necklace;
    they clothe themselves with violence.
⁷ From their callous hearts comes iniquity;
    their evil imaginations have no limits.
⁸ They scoff, and speak with malice;
    with arrogance they threaten oppression.
⁹ Their mouths lay claim to heaven,
    and their tongues take possession of the earth.
¹⁰ Therefore their people turn to them
    and drink up waters in abundance.
¹¹ They say, "How would God know?
    Does the Most High know anything?"
¹² This is what the wicked are like—
    always free of care, they go on amassing wealth.
¹³ Surely in vain I have kept my heart pure
    and have washed my hands in innocence.
¹⁴ All day long I have been afflicted,
    and every morning brings new punishments.
¹⁵ If I had spoken out like that,
    I would have betrayed your children.
¹⁶ When I tried to understand all this,
    it troubled me deeply
¹⁷ till I entered the sanctuary of God;
    then I understood their final destiny.
¹⁸ Surely you place them on slippery ground;

you cast them down to ruin.
[19] How suddenly are they destroyed,
　　completely swept away by terrors!
[20] They are like a dream when one awakes;
　　when you arise, Lord,
　　you will despise them as fantasies.
[21] When my heart was grieved
　　and my spirit embittered,
[22] I was senseless and ignorant;
　　I was a brute beast before you.
[23] Yet I am always with you;
　　you hold me by my right hand.
[24] You guide me with your counsel,
　　and afterward you will take me into glory.
[25] Whom have I in heaven but you?
　　And earth has nothing I desire besides you.
[26] My flesh and my heart may fail,
　　but God is the strength of my heart
　　and my portion forever.
[27] Those who are far from you will perish;
　　you destroy all who are unfaithful to you.
[28] But as for me, it is good to be near God.
　　I have made the Sovereign LORD my refuge;
　　I will tell of all your deeds.

PSALM 73 IS BOTH UNUSUAL and significant. It is unusual because it gives us a perspective on lament that we do not normally witness in the book of Psalms. It is significant because of its placement within the Psalter. Several commentators have pointed out that, theologically if not arithmetically, Psalm 73 is the centerpiece of the Psalter,[1] and the importance of its position within the canonical collection of psalms should not be underestimated. In some ways Psalm 73 marks an important transition within the Psalms. It is the first psalm of Book 3, and this third collection of psalms indicates changes that are about to occur.

---

1. J. Clinton McCann, "Psalm 73: A Microcosm of Old Testament Theology," in *The Listening Heart: Essays in Wisdom and the Psalms in Honor of Roland E. Murphy, O.Carm.*, JSOTSup 58, ed. K. G. Hoglund et al. (Sheffield: JSOT Press, 1987), 247–58; Walter Brueggemann and Patrick D. Miller, "Psalm 73 as a Canonical Marker," *JSOT* 72 (1996): 45–56.

First, we see a movement away from the figure of David, who dominates so much of Books 1–2, and second, we see an intensity of lament in Book 3. Each of these factors plays its role in the movement that we witness in the Psalter from lament to praise.[2] Walter Brueggemann argues that this transition from lament to praise takes the reader through a process of orientation, disorientation, and reorientation. Psalms of orientation are poems that declare faith in God and certainty of his justice (e.g., the torah psalms, such as Ps 1, or the creation psalms, such as Ps 8). Psalms of disorientation are those poems that express the doubts, fears, and uncertainties of the psalmist with regard to God's justice in the world around him (e.g., the complaints of the individual, such as Ps 13, or community laments, such as Ps 74, or the imprecations, such as Ps 137). Psalms of reorientation are the poems in which the writer has expressed his doubt, come to a new understanding of God, and thus been enabled to praise him all the more fully (e.g., the personal thanksgiving songs that declare God's deliverance, such as Ps 40).[3] Book 3 of the Psalter is marked by a preponderance of psalms of disorientation, and the voice of Book 3 sets the scene for the transition to praise that follows in Books 4–5. This process of orientation, disorientation, and reorientation occurs on a macro level within the book of Psalms but is also reflected on a micro level in Psalm 73 itself. In this way Psalm 73 sheds light on the journey the individual undertakes in reading the whole of the Psalter. A closer study of Psalm 73 illustrates the way in which the Psalter as a whole encourages us toward a more mature spirituality.

The Heading (73:0)

PSALM 73 IS SIMPLY DESCRIBED as a "Psalm of Asaph." The designation *mizmor* ("a psalm") is the most common title for the compositions of the Psalter and probably refers to a poem or song to be accompanied with music (as indicated by the verbal root *zmr*). Asaph was known as a liturgical leader appointed by David to orchestrate public worship in the temple (1 Chr 16:4–7). But since most of the psalms ascribed to Asaph in Book 3 of the Psalter (Pss 73–89) are based on the events of the exile, it is unlikely that this specific Asaph is in view in these psalm headings. It seems possible that—just as all succeeding kings in the line of David are known as sons of David—all those appointed to lead God's people in temple worship may have been seen in the line of Asaph. So, the Asaph designation may simply refer to a temple or formal worship setting.[4]

---

2. Walter Brueggemann, "Bounded by Obedience and Praise," *JSOT* 50 (1991): 63–92.

3. See also Walter Brueggemann, *Spirituality of the Psalms* (Minneapolis: Fortress, 2002).

4. See Gerald H. Wilson, *Psalms, Volume 1*, NIVAC (Grand Rapids: Zondervan, 2002),

Orientation (73:1)

MANY PSALMS, EVEN PSALMS OF LAMENT, begin with a focal statement of faith that celebrates the nature of God. As we shall see below, Asaph's psalm is a poem of brutal honesty in which he does not hold back from expressing his complaint against Yahweh, his God. However, even in doing so there are certain things the poet wants the reader to remember. Here we see one of them: *"Surely God is good to Israel."* The Hebrew word for "good" (*tov*) marks an important theme in Psalm 73 because it both begins and ends the poem. In verse 1 Asaph reminds the reader that "surely God is good," and in verse 28 he states that "it is good to be near God." This common Hebrew poetic technique is known as an *inclusio*—basically a bracketing function that draws the reader's attention to the key theme of the poem or text. So somehow, unlikely as it may seem as we read through parts of Psalm 73, we should remember that this poem is ultimately about a God who is good.[5] Even when confronted with the injustices of life and the judgment of God, the reader is encouraged to remember that this God is a *good* God.

Initially, Asaph's opening statement sounds like many of the faith statements that introduce complaint poems—the declaration is that God is good regardless of present circumstances. But there is, perhaps, a certain poignancy to the opening words of Psalm 73: *"Surely God is good to Israel."* The small Hebrew particle that begins the poem (*'ak*) is more significant than its stature suggests. The inclusion of the word "surely" seems to reflect the doubts of the psalmist's heart that later become apparent in the psalm itself. The experiences he faces on a day-to-day basis have caused him to doubt the goodness of God, and something of that tension comes out in the emphatic and, at the same time, dubious expression, *surely* God is good to Israel. This expression is what Asaph knows cognitively and also what he hopes for experientially. It is an expression of both his theological conviction and his hope for the future despite the doubt caused by his present experience.[6]

This opening verse is what we could describe as a statement of *orientation.* It is a statement of faith that all Old Testament believers would, as a matter of course, accept as true. It is a statement that reflects the faith

---

127–28; Frank Lothar Hossfeld and Erich Zenger, *Psalms 2*, Hermeneia, trans. Linda M. Maloney (Minneapolis: Fortress, 2005), 237.

5. Konrad Schaefer, *Psalms*, Berit Olam (Collegeville, MN: Liturgical Press, 2001), 177.

6. Zenger comments that this word "surely" "emphasizes that the confessional statement it introduces is meant to convey the drama of a passionate struggle *and* its outcome" (Hossfeld and Zenger, *Psalms 2*, 226).

community's creedal position. God is good to his people, in particular to those who genuinely walk in his ways. The opening statement of verse 1 reflects the theology of Psalm 1. The worldview of Psalm 1 and Psalm 73:1 is remarkably simple. To walk in the ways of God is a lifestyle that reaps his blessing. Explicitly in Psalm 1, and by implication in Psalm 73:1, the flip side of that coin is clear. Those who reject God and his ways rob themselves of his blessing and place themselves under his punishment. Such is the statement of faith implied in 73:1. God is good to those who are pure in heart, who walk in his ways. It is a statement of orientation. This declaration would have been one of the many foundational (liturgical) statements of the worshiping community through which the people "articulate the joy, delight, goodness, coherence, and reliability of God, God's creation, and God's governing law."[7] Orientation statements express what we believe about God and about life with him.

Disorientation (73:2–17)

THE REALITY OF OUR EXPERIENCE of life with God in the world, however, often conflicts with our expectation of how that life should look. The statements of faith that we hold lead us, rightly or wrongly, to formulate certain expectations with regard to the life that we live. Disorientation occurs when our experience of life does not match up to our faith-based expectations. So went Asaph's experience in the next section of Psalm 73.

But as for me. Asaph moves quickly from his statement of orientation in verse 1 to a description of his personal crisis of faith in verses 2–17. His disorientation occurs in his observation of life round about him. These observations make uncomfortable viewing for the poet because the reality of life in the world around him does not appear to match the theology of his statements of faith. Asaph's is a very personal crisis, but it is one to which many believers today, as throughout the centuries, can relate. Why do the wicked prosper when God's people seem to struggle so much?[8] Verse 2 describes how close Asaph came to losing his way in life because of his doubts. The "way" imagery of the Psalter is a common means of referring to questions of lifestyle. It seems that Asaph is telling us that his doubts almost led him to reject his life of faith (see also vv. 13–14).[9]

---

7. Brueggemann, *Spirituality of the Psalms*, 8.

8. The Psalms are kept deliberately vague in terms of their background and setting so that they may be adopted in the broadest range of settings by the widest number of people as their own prayers regarding the specifics of their own lives. See Patrick D. Miller, *Interpreting the Psalms* (Philadelphia: Fortress, 1986), 18–28; Wilson, *Psalms, Volume 1*, 23–31.

9. Schaefer, *Psalms*, 179.

For I envied the arrogant. With the benefit of hindsight, Asaph sees that the root of his problem was based on his own attitude and perspective at least as much as it was grounded in the reality of his situation. A major part of the problem was the way he *perceived* things. That is not to say that this problem had no grounding in reality, but Asaph clearly comes to realize that his own attitude toward that reality exacerbated the issue at hand. "The psalmist now begins a confession of foolishness which almost led to a fatal fall from God."[10]

When I saw the prosperity of the wicked. The statement that Asaph makes here is really something of a theological hand grenade. Some of the power of this verse is lost in translation, for what the poet actually says is that he envied the arrogant when he saw the *shalom* of the wicked! Imagine the reaction of the first hearers of this psalm. "The *shalom* of the wicked . . . Asaph, are you mad? The wicked do not have . . . *cannot have* . . . *shalom!*" The idea of *shalom* in the Old Testament is associated with the powerful, holistic blessing of God for his people. Surely only the "righteous" can have *shalom*, not the wicked. In terms of Psalm 1, only those blessed people who delight in the torah of Yahweh can expect to receive his *shalom*, for the wicked have set themselves on a way that is perishing. So how can Asaph possibly say that the root of his problem lay in the "peace" and "welfare" that was broadly thought to be a privilege dependent on nearness to God?[11] Yet this was exactly how it appeared to Asaph. It was not he, as one numbered among the righteous, who was experiencing the *shalom* of Yahweh; rather, it was those who rejected God and oppressed the weak in society who experienced the welfare that Asaph could only long for. How is a believer to resolve such a conundrum?

They have no struggles. . . . they are not plagued by human ills. Asaph's problem of perspective results in a somewhat idealized view of the reality of those who rejected Yahweh. Asaph's external perspective on the wicked presents them as trouble free, well fed, and somehow immune to the trials of life that are common to everyone else. It would be interesting to know whether those people whom Asaph observed from a distance would describe their lives in the same way. It strikes me that we are to read these verses as an indication of Asaph's state of mind rather than as a sober presentation of the reality of life for the godless oppressor. In verse 4 Asaph describes the wicked as being "fat" (NIV: "healthy and strong").

---

10. John H. Eaton, *The Psalms: A Historical and Spiritual Commentary with an Introduction and New Translation* (London: T&T Clark International, 2003), 266. See also A. A. Anderson, *The Book of Psalms, Volume II, Psalms 73–150,* NCB (London: Marshall, Morgan & Scott, 1972), 530.

11. Craig C. Broyles, *Psalms,* NIBCOT (Carlisle: Paternoster, 1999), 299.

In ancient Near Eastern agrarian society, being fat was generally seen as a sign of wealth, so the poet is indicating that the people he envied were among the prosperous of his society. This description of the wicked, then, may also indicate that Asaph's perspective is not entirely to be trusted in his assessment of their reality because, from a human perspective, it has always been easy to envy those who have more than we do.[12]

Therefore pride is their necklace. . . . their evil imaginations have no limits. Not only do the wicked (a term we will discuss later in the Bridging Contexts section) reject Yahweh and yet prosper, but they are also marked by the classic signs of arrogant godlessness. "Pride" adorns them as a necklace. Pride is a characteristic roundly condemned in Scripture (e.g., 2 Sam 22:26–28; Prov 6:16–19; 16:18 et al.), yet one thing worse than simply *being* proud is being blatant about that pride. Along with the arrogance of the wicked come violence and willingness to oppress others in order to get what they want. The strange idiom in verse 7a (literally in the Hebrew, "Their eye goes out [bulges] with fat") is genuinely difficult to translate. It may simply refer to the extent of their wealth and greed so that even their eyes bulge with fat, but this explanation does not make much sense of the second part of the parallelism. It may well be that the "fatted eye" is a reflection of their "fatted hearts." Just as their lack of moderation and care for the needs of others leads to their bodies becoming fat (v. 4), so the metaphor of their eyes being fat points to the same self-centered perspective on life as a whole. The way in which they see things—all their thoughts and plans—reflects the same selfish attitude, hence the NIV's "From their callous hearts comes iniquity."[13] And this is certainly the tone of verse 7b, where the psalmist speaks of the evil imaginations of their minds as running riot. "They are evil to the core; their hearts spill over with evil (v. 7)."[14]

They scoff, and speak with malice. . . . "Does the Most High know anything?" Asaph uses a series of height metaphors in order to emphasize the extent of the arrogance of the people he envied, the people whose prosperity precipitated such a deep crisis of faith for him. Scoffing, threatening oppression, and mocking God are all indicative of the type of arrogance that is roundly condemned in the Bible as detestable in God's eyes (Prov 6:16–19). What is more, despite all these characteristics that should have led to societal condemnation and alienation, Asaph sees that the wicked have become *popular* in his day (v. 10). This development indicates that others besides Asaph have found the lifestyle of this group

---

12. Anderson, *Psalms*, 531.
13. Hossfeld and Zenger, *Psalms 2*, 228.
14. Schaefer, *Psalms*, 178.

of individuals attractive, regardless of their dubious morality and their outright rejection of Yahweh.

Not only do these people oppress others when they can get away with it, but they are also open in their mocking rejection of God. Interestingly, it is not that they do not believe in God, for their words indicate that they do. Perhaps even more alarming than the rejection of atheism, however, is the trivialization of God by those who are focused entirely on self.[15] As far as they are concerned, there may well be a God, but he is irrelevant in their lives, hence their shameless pride and unconcealed oppression of others. They are not afraid because they have not experienced God as judge . . . yet![16] We will see that this caveat is important in the resolution of Asaph's crisis of faith.

There is a sense in which Asaph's frank description of these people makes his envy of them all the more surprising. These people are not just the "ordinary" wicked who simply refuse to walk in the ways of the Lord: rather, they are the "oppressive" wicked who exploit the weak and mock the Creator in doing so. Asaph's presentation of the wicked is far from appealing, so what was it about them that so drew his envy?

Always free of care, they go on amassing wealth. So it is that we get to the heart of Asaph's problem of perspective. The poet's envy is rooted in the observation of an easy, *wealthy* life. The life of the wicked seemed to be untroubled with the burdens that normal people experienced and, despite their obvious rejection of God and the oppression of the weak, the rich just seemed to get richer. The essence of the matter from Asaph's perspective seems to be that *wealth, however it is gained, makes life easier*—an attitude often echoed in our own day! Ultimately, Asaph comes to the realization that his conclusion was not true in his day, just as it remains untrue in ours. As we shall see in a moment, Asaph's envy was based on an illusion. Real life for those who reject God is never actually as attractive as their lifestyle may seem to indicate.[17] This was Asaph's eventual realization as his concept

---

15. Zenger describes this view as "practical atheism," that is, "an attitude to life and a worldview that not only rejects God as giver and protector of a world order, but proclaims God's factual and even principled lack of interest in the world and human action" (Hossfeld and Zenger, *Psalms* 2, 228).

16. There is a question as to the translation of verse 9a inasmuch as the preposition can be translated in a couple of ways. The Hebrew could be read (with the NIV and others) as indicating a claim upon heaven, which makes sense in light of the parallel clause. But the same preposition could be read as speaking out against heaven, which also makes sense in view of verse 11. (See Hossfeld and Zenger, *Psalms* 2, 221, 228).

17. "What a man envies is not usually the best, but the second best. . . . He was not coveting the best, but something far inferior. He was jealous of success that is measured

of wealth is transformed. For the time being, however, the observation of an easy life, wealth, and power[18] proved all too seductive for Asaph, thus causing him to experience the genuine crisis of faith he recounts in these verses of his complaint.

Surely in vain have I kept my heart pure. The poet's confusion at the unmerited prosperity of those who reject God's ways is further compounded by his own experience of hardship. With a lovely sense of artistry the psalmist picks up on the language of verse 5 in verses 14 and 16. He tells us that the wicked are not "burdened" (*'amal*) like other men, nor are they "plagued" (*naga'*) by human ills (v. 5). Asaph complains that his own experience has been just the opposite. He has been "afflicted" (*naga'*) *all day long* (v. 14), and when he came to consider his own experience in the light of his observations of the world round about him, the whole equation was "burdensome" (*'amal;* NIV "oppressive") to him (v. 16).[19] The irony of this symmetry is unmistakable. The worldview in verse 1 indicates a world in which the wicked could reasonably expect to be those who are "burdened" and "plagued." But when Asaph thinks about the reality of his life in the light of events witnessed around him, he realizes that the reverse is the case. *They* prosper and *he* is plagued![20]

Note the second "surely" here. It echoes the element of doubt implied in Asaph's statement of faith in verse 1. Reading this verse back into the opening statement of Psalm 73, we see the scenario that has led to Asaph's doubting the goodness of God. He *believes* that God is good (v. 1), but he *knows* that he is suffering (vv. 13–14). Herein lies the crisis of faith and experience—Asaph believes one thing, but his experience tells another. A third "surely" is yet to come in verse 18, where we begin to see a resolution.

Asaph's confusion over his observation of the prospering of the wicked was further exacerbated by his own experience of suffering—it was like rubbing salt into his theological wounds. So, in his inner being, he came to the conclusion that his quest for a godly lifestyle was "vain" or "empty" (v. 13). Asaph's analysis of his own experience in the light of his observation

---

in terms of all one can grab with moral impunity and not in terms of real meaning and values" (Donald Macleod, "Faith Beyond the Forms of Faith: An Exposition of Psalm 73," *Int* 12.4 [1958]: 421).

18. The Hebrew word translated "wealth" (*hayil*) here in verse 12 can also be translated as "power." So it is possible that Asaph envied their influence and status (vv. 10–11) as much as their wealth, though his lament seems to indicate that he sees these things as going hand in hand.

19. Schaefer, *Psalms*, 178.

20. We will consider the language of "them and us" in the Bridging Contexts and Contemporary Significance sections below.

of reality in the world around him caused him to question the very value of his faith—was it all worth the cost?

If I had spoken out like that. This stanza (vv. 15–17) marks a turning point in Ps 73. It is at this point that, in tone, the poem pivots from lament to praise and declaration of faith. Clearly, Asaph comes to the realization that there was something skewed in his perspectives. Looking back on the way in which he had been thinking, he confesses that to declare these thoughts publicly would have, in some sense, been a betrayal of the community of faith (v. 15). It is interesting to notice the preserving effect of the worshiping community. In the previous verses (vv. 13–14) we are given insight into Asaph's inner turmoil, which has caused him to doubt the value of his life with God. Asaph is willing to question God in his heart but somehow is unwilling to express this doubt among his people. Craig Broyles comments, "It is surprising that what restrains the speaker is not his loyalty to God but his loyalty to [God's] children."[21] It is difficult to define precisely what happens in these verses; however, it appears that Asaph's presence among God's people begins the poet's dawning realization that his perspectives are awry.[22]

It troubled me deeply. The importance of community is accentuated by the confession that individual contemplation, in this case, has failed to provide any sort of resolution for Asaph (v. 16). There is something quite emotive about Asaph's plaintive plea in this verse. He has genuinely struggled to understand why the observed reality of life around about him does not conform to the expectations derived from his theological belief system. He has genuinely sought resolution, but the tension between his observations, on the one hand, and his allegiance to both God and community of faith, on the other, means that his reflections have been burdensome to him.[23] Until . . .

Till I entered the sanctuary of God. Clearly, it is in meeting with God in his sanctuary that Asaph's internal torment finds release.[24] Verse 17 is the pivot around which the whole psalm rotates. It is the turning point that transforms Asaph's perspective and changes the tone of the poem. It is important to note, however, that the transformation occurs not in Asaph's circumstances; rather, it occurs in his *perception* of the circumstances. As far

---

21. Broyles, *Psalms*, 300.

22. "What prevents the psalmist from defection is the sense of obligation to the community" (Schaefer, *Psalms*, 179).

23. Hans-Joachim Kraus, *Psalms 60–150: A Commentary*, trans. Hilton C. Oswald (Minneapolis: Augsburg, 1989), 88–89.

24. "In other words, the psalmist's experience of the presence of God recalibrated his perspective" (Tremper Longman, *Psalms: An Introduction and Commentary*, TOTC [Leicester: Inter-Varsity Press, 2014], 276).

as we are aware, the reality that led to Asaph's crisis of faith remains the same, but verse 17 points to the utter transformation of Asaph's *appreciation* of the events that surround him. Asaph's crisis resulted from his limited, temporal perspective on the events of the world around him. In meeting with God he begins to see things from a more eternal, divine perspective. The essence of the solution that eases Asaph's inner turmoil is really quite simple—the wicked may prosper now, but ultimately they will not. This realization restores harmony to Asaph's worldview. The tension between observed reality and his theological belief system is resolved. Until now it seemed that the wicked stood on solid ground, whereas Asaph's feet were slipping (v. 2), but in meeting with God the psalmist comes to the realization that he stands on ground that is firm, whereas the apparent stability of the wicked is illusory.

What happened in the sanctuary? There is no specific indication of precisely what Asaph experienced in the "sanctuary of God" to lead to such a radical transformation of attitude. This lack has led to much debate about whether verse 17 refers to a physical visit to the temple in Jerusalem or to a metaphorical experience of God on Asaph's part.[25] There are good arguments to be made either way, and, clearly, both the physical and metaphorical interpretations of verse 17 point to a spiritual reality that goes beyond mere outward experience of formalized religion.[26] So the essence remains the same: whether literally in the temple or metaphorically wherever the psalmist happened to be, Asaph met with God, and his understanding of the reality of his life and the world round about him was radically transformed by that encounter.

We can only speculate as to whether it was the public reading of the Torah or the entrance rituals that would point to the holiness of God and the exclusion of the wicked—or the experience of singing together with the massed ranks of the believers, or perhaps simply Asaph's consciously placing himself in the presence of God in prayer. One way or the other, the psalmist came to see things from God's perspective and in this way came to the realization that his complaint reflected an attitude that was entirely wrong (vv. 21–22).

---

25. For fuller discussion see Hossfeld and Zenger, *Psalms 2*, 230–32.

26. Broyles, for example, points out the lexical and conceptual similarities between Ps 73 and a number of the psalms that are associated with entrance into the temple and that thus may indicate a background in the experience of God in the worship of the temple (Broyles, *Psalms*, 301). Zenger, however, argues on the basis of the strongly metaphorical language throughout the rest of Ps 73 (amongst other things) that this should be understood as a metaphorical "meeting with God in the sanctuary" (Hossfeld and Zenger, *Psalms 2*, 231–32).

This transformation of thought leads Asaph to a spiritual, intellectual, and experiential reorientation that brings new depths of maturity to his understanding of who God is and what he, Asaph, has in relationship with the God of the covenant.

Reorientation (73:18–28)

SURELY YOU PLACE THEM ON SLIPPERY GROUND. The eternal angle on his temporal circumstance totally transforms Asaph's perception of those wealthy individuals who had rejected a godly lifestyle. Before his encounter with God, these people seemed to "have it all going for them" as far as Asaph was concerned. "Always free of care, they go on amassing wealth" (v. 12). They were to him people to be envied. Yet here in verses 18–20 we witness Asaph's dawning realization that, despite their present wealth, societal significance, boasting arrogance, and easy lifestyle, those who reject the ways of Yahweh are as insubstantial as the dust of the street. In the ideology of Psalm 1, which describes the wicked as "chaff" (the lightweight dust and residue that is blown away by the wind as part of the process of winnowing grain), Asaph ultimately sees that those who reject God amount to little more than passing images on the landscape of history. There is a sense of the prophetic about Asaph's pronouncement in verses 18–20.[27] The direct intervention of God breaks in to Asaph's logical deliberations and provides a resolution by means of revelation. It is significant that the solution Asaph sought was to be found in meeting with God and not in contemplation alone.[28]

Interestingly, we see the echo of the word "surely" from verses 1 and 13 here again in verse 18. Whereas we read an element of doubt and pleading hope into the "surely" cry of verse 1, as well as the definiteness of his own suffering in verse 13, this particle takes on a greater element of certainty and hope after Asaph's meeting with God. Now he sees that the hoped-for goodness of God is in fact a present reality that will be borne out in ultimate judgment. The psalmist's encounter with the Creator has filled him with a trust and assurance that was lacking when he tried to find a resolution to his problem by himself. This "surely" stands in marked contrast to the doubts of verse 13. A different temporal perspective on the issue of God's justice in this world fills Asaph with a renewed confidence—doubt has given way to hope.[29]

I was a brute beast before you. Asaph's encounter with Yahweh leads him to the reassessment of his previous state of mind. He sees that which

---

27. Kraus, *Psalms II*, 89.
28. See Contemporary Significance below.
29. Broyles, *Psalms*, 301–2.

strikes the neutral observer as odd. His presentation of the wicked in verses 2–12 is far from pleasant. Apart from their wealth, why would anyone envy such people? So it is that, after his transformation of mind, Asaph comes to the realization that his previous perspective was entirely skewed. "I was senseless and ignorant; I was a brute beast before you" (v. 22). The words of the Hebrew text are perhaps even stronger: Asaph speaks about his heart as being embittered and his kidneys (the Hebrew metaphor that speaks of the seat of human emotions) as being pierced. He describes himself as "brutishly stupid" and "without knowledge" before Yahweh. It was this ignorance of God's mystery and his inability to bring to mind the fact that God is simply bigger than our human understanding that led, in this case, to Asaph's over-emphasis on temporal reality as opposed to eternal reality. The moment of divine theophany, however, set those perspectives right, and now, looking back, the poet easily sees just how wrong he had gotten things.[30]

Yet I am always with you. As we have seen above, the root of Asaph's envy of the wicked seems to have been based primarily in the wealth that they possessed. (There is little or nothing else that is attractive in Asaph's description of them otherwise.) Here we see a beautiful transition between Asaph's previous state of mind and his present spiritual and mental well-being. Asaph's brutally frank description of his previously warped perspectives begins with the words, "But as for me" (v. 22, author's translation). In the following verse, the same words (translated "yet" in the NIV) open Asaph's celebration of the riches he comes to realize are his in relationship with Yahweh. "But as for me, I am always with you." The repetition of this emphatic phrase draws attention to the total transformation of attitude that Asaph has undergone.

The change from the expected subject and object in this sentence also makes the reader stop and think. We are quite used to the many statements of Scripture in which *God* declares his presence with and commitment to his people. But here it is *Asaph* who speaks of his constant presence with the Almighty. The poet declares that *he* is always with God. There is a surprise factor at work here that makes us stop and think about the divine-human relationship. Asaph's declaration reminds us of the reality of the covenantal relationship as "real" relationship. It is not a one-way street, where God does all the "relating" and we do all the "receiving"; rather, this relationship is analogous to all our human interactions, in which friendship and depth of contact requires effort on both sides. Asaph also realizes that he was with God—and God was with him—even throughout the darkness

---

30. Eaton, *Psalms,* 267.

---

and confusion of his crisis of faith. He was and is *always* with God, and the Creator had been near and was helping him even in his dark days of doubt.[31] His meeting with God awakens the poet to a profound awareness of the immense gift of divine presence.

This short phrase is telling in its magnitude. Asaph had been jealous of the wealthy wicked because of their apparent ease of life and their significance in society. But if there is a God who created all things and all people, a God of love, one who desires relationship with his creations, can there possibly be any greater blessing than to know and love that God? Asaph comes to the realization that nothing can possibly compare to the true wealth of knowing God and being loved by him.

You hold me by my right hand. Asaph's new awareness that he is always with God is further strengthened by the knowledge that it is Yahweh who tenaciously maintains relationship even through the darkness of human doubt.[32] The image of a hand held is a metaphor that speaks powerfully not only of presence but also of care. This God who is always present with Asaph is also the God who actively protects his people, just as a parent holds the hand of his child while crossing the street or when her small child walks on a wall.[33] The image of being held by God's right hand is particularly poignant in the light of verse 2, in which Asaph describes how close he was to stumbling and falling. Why is it that he only *almost* slipped? He realizes now that it is because Yahweh had held him by his right hand.

You guide me with your counsel. The imagery here is that of the royal court, where the king, faced with all the challenges of government, seeks counsel from his royal advisors. It is a picture that will be familiar to all those who grew up reading Shakespeare, in whose plays the tension is often to be found in the very issue of whose advice the king will follow. But Asaph turns the imagery on its head by celebrating advice *from* the King rather than *for* the king. Not only is God near, not only does God protect, but Asaph has also come to see that God guides by his direct intervention—guidance that is life and attitude transforming. The imagery of a deity's taking someone by the hand and guiding him was commonly applied to kings in the ancient Near East, but here Asaph—as an "ordinary" believer—celebrates these same privileges.[34] Yahweh takes *him* (and by implication every believer) by the hand and guides him by his divine counsel.

---

31. James L. Mays, *Psalms*, Interpretation (Louisville: John Knox, 1994), 243.
32. Broyles, *Psalms*, 302.
33. "God's hand-clasp expresses both his choice and support (often of king or Israel, cf. 18:35; 63:8; 80:17; 39:10; Isa 41:10; 45:1)" (Eaton, *Psalms*, 267).
34. Hossfeld and Zenger, *Psalms 2*, 233–34; Kraus, *Psalms II*, 90.

And afterward you will take me into glory. This final privilege of the four power-packed statements of verses 23–24 has evoked much discussion in the scholarly literature. It is often pointed out that the ancient Hebrews probably did not have a developed sense of the afterlife, so this statement must refer to something physical in the "here and now." Some scholars suggest that this statement actually refers to the poet's final entry into the presence of God in the temple, his transformation (v. 17) having occurred during the entrance rituals.[35] Other interpreters suggest that the statement is simply a reference to the period after Asaph's crisis of faith has passed, rather than one to life after death.[36] But reading this statement as a reference to the psalmist's eternal security in relationship with Yahweh makes a great deal of sense in contrast to the fleeting and temporal nature of the wicked.[37] The Hebrew word for "afterward" (*ahar*) is from the same root as the word used to describe the "final destiny" of the wicked in verse 17 (*aharit*). There is little doubt that the reference in verse 17 is to the final judgment of those who reject the ways of Yahweh, so it makes sense to read the adverbial form here in verse 23 as a reference to the "final destiny" of the psalmist.[38] Certainly this idea implies future security for God's people in all that they face in life and, even if the poet did have such ideas in mind at the time of writing, there can be little doubt that in its reception over the years this text has come to be seen as a reference to eternal security beyond death.[39]

Whom have I in heaven but you? Asaph's realization that, in terms of ultimate reality, he is the one who is truly rich, not the arrogant wicked, continues in the following verses (vv. 25–27). He begins with a rhetorical question in verse 25a that implies an answer to the question of verse 25b. Just as there is no one else in heaven who can hear and answer Asaph's prayers, so the earth holds nothing of remotely comparable value to friendship with God. Those people whose lifestyle precipitated Asaph's crisis of faith may have *things*, but things are nothing compared to an eternity of community with the Creator God! Asaph has come to remember where

---

35. Broyles, *Psalms*, 302.

36. Schaefer, *Psalms*, 180.

37. Mays, *Psalms*, 243.

38. Andrew E. Hill, "אַחֲרִית," *NIDOTTE* 1:361–2. Longman comments, "Contrary to the opinion of many scholars, it seems likely that the psalmist himself harboured an eternal hope, and by the time of the New Testament, readers would (and did) read this language as indicating eternal life" (Longman, *Psalms*, 277).

39. For further discussion see Hossfeld and Zenger, *Psalms 2*, 234–35; J. Clinton McCann, *A Theological Introduction to the Books of Psalms: The Psalms as Torah* (Nashville: Abingdon, 1993), 144–45.

both security and meaning are truly to be found, and neither is to be found in possessions. There can be no greater treasure than covenantal relationship with the God who is near and involved in the lives of human beings.

God is the strength of my heart and my portion forever. Continuing this theme of true wealth and reward, Asaph expresses his final understanding that, whatever he may gain in life, it is nothing compared to the reward that is to be found in life with God. He points out the passing nature of physical life (v. 26a) and contrasts that with the sure certainty of an unchanging deity who is in himself a reward for his people. The "strength" of my heart (NIV) is, more literally, the "rock" of my heart—an image that speaks of lasting certainty and stability (Ps 18:1–2), a stability Asaph was lacking when he took his eyes off his God (Ps 73:2). The idea of a "portion" in the Old Testament is associated with reward (Num 18:10; Deut 10:9; Josh 14:4–5), and Asaph now declares that his reward is not to be found in the trivial things such as possessions or money.[40] His reward is knowing God and walking in his ways.

Final Summary (73:27–28)

THOSE WHO ARE FAR FROM YOU WILL PERISH. Asaph's final realization is that in reality there was no divergence between his theology and his observation concerning the world around him. What lay at the heart of Asaph's crisis of faith was really a question of chronology. The poet's expectation was that God would work out his justice in the temporal realm (and sometimes he does).[41] But Asaph came to accept that Yahweh, in the mystery of his sovereignty, sometimes stays his hand and does not intervene in our present reality; therefore, Asaph's final conclusion is expressed both negatively and positively. With regard to the wicked, they may prosper today and tomorrow or even for a generation, but ultimately they will not. Those who are "unfaithful" to God (lit., "who prostitute themselves from God") are on a road to ruin whether they realize it or not. God's justice will not be denied. Sometimes it is realized by his intervention into current events of humankind; always it will become clear at the final judgment. Ultimately, the wicked do not prosper.[42]

But as for me, it is good to be near God. The spatial imagery continues in the final verses. Those who are *far* from God perish (v. 27), but for the psalmist it is "good to be *near* God" (emphasis added). Asaph's

---

40. Hossfeld and Zenger, *Psalms 2*, 235–36; William P. Brown, *Seeing the Psalms: A Theology of Metaphor* (Louisville: Westminster John Knox, 2002), 202–4.

41. See the discussion of Ps 109 below.

42. Mays, *Psalms*, 243.

---

summary openly confesses that the theology of Psalm 1 is entirely correct. Fellowship with God and a lifestyle based on his ways is a blessing in and of itself. Whereas the declaration of God's goodness in verse 1 seems wracked with doubt as we read the succeeding verses, now Asaph simply rests and rejoices in the goodness of God. Come what may, in this life or the next, it is *good* to be near God. As the Creator God himself, Yahweh has become a refuge for the psalmist. The term "refuge" is particularly signif- icant throughout the Psalter as both a declaration of affiliation to Yahweh and also a description of the security that the community of faith finds in him.[43] Having come to this realization, Asaph is now able to proclaim openly the good works of God on his behalf. This open proclamation stands in marked contrast to Asaph's earlier reluctance to speak out of fear that he would betray God's people (v. 15). Now he knows that true reward is to be found in close relationship with God, and about this relationship he *will* speak because both the covenant community and those whom he once envied need to hear the ultimate truth that Asaph has discovered.

 **OF THE RIGHTEOUS AND THE WICKED.** The big issue for modern readers of Psalm 73 seems to be the identity of "the wicked" in this poem. During a recent home-group Bible study when we were discussing this psalm, my friends were fairly unequivocal in their condemnation of the group of people described in the psalm and found it difficult to understand why any believer would be envious of such individ- uals. Another aspect of the psalm that goes hand in hand with this issue is the "them and us" nature of the language adopted by Asaph. There seems little empathy for those whom Asaph initially envies. Some interpreters even read a note of adulation or boasting in Asaph's final summary, which speaks of the ultimate destruction of those who reject the Lord. How are we to understand the language of "the righteous and the wicked" in this psalm and throughout the Psalter?

In our contemporary Christian understanding of these terms, we tend to think about "the righteous" as the very, very good,[44] whereas "the wicked" are the very, very bad. Few Christians would number themselves among

---

43. Jerome F. D. Creach, *Yahweh as Refuge and the Editing of the Hebrew Psalter*, JSOTSup 217 (Sheffield: Sheffield Academic, 1996).

44. The Hebrew word for "the righteous" (*tsaddiqim*) is not actually used in Ps 73; however, in his marked contrast between himself and "the wicked," Asaph is conceptually framing his discussion in those terms that are commonly found in the Psalter.

the former and, equally, few would see their neighbors as being numbered among the latter. For us, generally speaking, our contemporary use of these terms points to extremes that are beyond the normal human experience of the majority. This manner, however, is not the way in which the psalmist uses these ideas. Basically, "the wicked" (*resha'im*) are all those who walk in a way that is contrary to the way of the Lord. We see this meaning most clearly in the book of Psalms itself and in the Old Testament's wisdom literature. For example, Psalm 1:6 contrasts the "way of the righteous" with the "way of the wicked." These "ways" are alternative lifestyles. The former indicates a person's affiliation with Yahweh, whereas the latter indicates a person's rejection of that lifestyle ordained as pleasing to God. So, essentially, the language of "the righteous and the wicked" at its most basic level speaks about an individual's allegiance to God or rejection of him. The assumption is that the affiliation of "the righteous" will be evidenced in obedience to and proper worship of Yahweh. But the flip side of that coin is that the psalmists fully expect that the rejection of Yahweh by "the wicked" will ultimately be made plain in their patterns of behavior.

This understanding, therefore, provides the background for the somewhat stark "them and us" language of Psalm 73. Asaph voices the equation in very black and white terms because that is exactly how he views life: each individual is either with God or against him—there is no middle ground. In reading this text we should probably assume that some of those individuals whom Asaph envied would be present at the public reading of this psalm, as they were likely members of the visible covenant community. So, far from being indifferent to their attitude or rejoicing in their fate, Asaph's poem is a clarion call for change. He has met with God and has gained an appreciation of the ultimate outworking of the choices we all make here and now. His poem, therefore, is an affirmation for those who trust in God but struggle with the apparent prosperity of those who reject him and the impunity with which they persecute others. But Psalm 73 is also a wake-up call to "the wicked." They believe in a God who *exists* (v. 11), but they do not believe in a God who *judges*, in a God who *intervenes*. In this way Asaph's poem, in and of itself, is the very act of proclamation that he promises (v. 28). It is both affirmation for those who love the Lord but also warning for those who reject him. That their path is far from firm and their ultimate end far from happy is why Asaph speaks with such frank (some would say simplistic) language—he does not want any to be unaware of their "final destiny" (v. 17).

Psalm 73 in the New Testament. Surprisingly for such a significant psalm, Psalm 73 is not cited anywhere in the New Testament either by direct quotation or allusion. But the theological equation presented by

Asaph is readily observable in Jesus' teachings, especially in the Sermon on the Mount. Lifestyle as a choice between two ways—one affiliating with God and one rejecting God—lies at the heart of much of Christ's teaching in the Gospels (e.g., Matt 7:13–27). Equally, Asaph's warning that wealth and riches are illusory when it comes to ultimate meaning in life is echoed clearly in Jesus' words about laying up treasure in heaven (Matt 6:19–34). As to the warning that the wicked find themselves on slippery ground and the strong distinction between the righteous and the wicked, these ideas are also made even more explicit in the New Testament's teaching on final judgment (e.g., Matt 13:24–30, 36–50 et al.). Finally, Asaph's great celebration of the privileges inherent to being a believer is echoed forcefully in Paul's great statement of eternal security in Romans 8:28–39.

HONESTY IN PRAYER. There are many aspects of Psalm 73 that are of great significance in our contemporary setting; however, perhaps the most significant avenue of application is also the one we find most difficult. Asaph is brutally honest in his poem, and his honesty is of a type we find difficult to replicate in our own life with God. There is an interesting dynamic at work in Psalm 73. Asaph refuses to voice his complaint against God before the community of faith, but we are probably meant to assume that Asaph did voice his complaint *to God* (though the text does not say so explicitly).[45] Indeed, it could be argued that Asaph's honest expression of the way in which he viewed life around him *was essential* to his reorientation. Asaph ultimately came to a more mature, fuller understanding of the true identity of his God and a better understanding of the riches he possessed in relationship with God. But the question we must ask is whether he would have come to this transformation of perspective had he not been honest in his prayer before Yahweh.

In this psalm (as in all the laments), we are confronted with the implication that we *must* be absolutely honest with God in prayer. The psalmists were never reluctant to give voice to their grief and sense of covenantal disappointment. From their perspective it often seemed that God had let them down, that he had not kept his part of the covenantal deal, and in their prayers they openly voiced their doubts to Yahweh. Neither the Old Testament songwriters nor the community of faith in general were

---

45. The anguished confession of verse 22 ("I was a brute beast before you") seems to me to imply that Asaph did actually voice his complaint to Yahweh.

reluctant to speak honestly to God of their distress, even when they viewed God as the source of their distress.[46]

We are not very comfortable with such openness and honesty in our contemporary Christian spirituality. It strikes us as impolite and inappropriate to speak to God in these ways, yet so much of the Bible is made up of laments of this type.[47] Why was it appropriate then but seems inappropriate to us now? What is more, Jesus chose laments to voice his own feelings before his Father (e.g., Ps 22:1 in Mark 15:34; Ps 69:5 in John 15:25). Why was it appropriate for Jesus to speak and pray using this language, yet we are so uncomfortable with it? In the contemporary church in the Western world, there is an unwritten pressure placed upon Christians that assumes that we are always "Fine!" In fact, if we are not "fine" there must be something seriously wrong with our faith. This is not the attitude of the Bible! The Scriptures meet with us in all our humanity—good and bad, strong and weak, soaring with faith and wracked with doubt. In the Bible we find language that is appropriate to our every situation, and laments, like Asaph's, are appropriate to those days when we ourselves are filled with doubts and uncertainties. It is important that we, today, make these prayers our own when they reflect our heart and mind and view of life.

Such honest spirituality may be new and uncomfortable for us, but two things we should bear in mind: (1) Asaph's change of perspective would not have occurred without his *honest* meeting with God—voicing his complaint was part of his reorientation; (2) Why would we ever offer to God prayer that amounts to no more than a polite lie? The sovereign God sees our hearts and knows our moods and precisely how we see things. If we are disappointed or angry with God, he is fully aware of that fact, and there is no point in offering a politely dishonest prayer when it is only in the honest expression of our real mood and mindset that he can begin to heal, correct, restore, and reorient.

Seeing other people as God sees them. Another difficulty in contemporary society is the challenge to view our friends and neighbors from a godly perspective rather than from a worldly perspective. It is very easy to look round about us and see people who seem perfectly happy—people with a nice family, a good job/house/car, earning more money than we do, with no visible problems or tensions or turmoil. Very often those people

---

46. Wilson, *Psalms, Volume 1*, 139–48.

47. There are more psalms of lament in the Psalter than there are psalms of any other individual type. Also we find laments in large chunks of the books of Jeremiah and Isaiah, not to mention the whole of the book of Lamentations. There is much lament in the Old Testament; it cannot simply be ignored.

---

around us who do not know Christ seem to have life sorted out and do not really appear to lack anything. So it is that today we can often fall into the same trap as Asaph did. We too can envy the wicked. But even if we do not envy the wicked in and of themselves, we can subconsciously assume that these folks have no needs. By the standards and priorities of the world, often they may not.

Christians today, however, need to remind themselves of Asaph's sanctuary experience with God: "Then I understood their final destiny." It is important to see our family, friends, and neighbors who are without Christ not from a worldly perspective of success and happiness but from the eternal perspective of a God who one day will judge. We must never forget Asaph's lesson that those who are without the gospel stand on slippery ground. Success from a human perspective and worldly wealth are meaningless at the point of a person's death. Ultimately, only one thing really matters—relationship with God through Christ! Those of us who believe must look beyond the physical wealth of others and remember their spiritual poverty, which can only be met through the declaration of all God's deeds in Christ (Ps 73:28; cf. Rom 10:14–17).

Remember the richness of all that we have in Christ. Just as we can see others from the wrong perspective, so also we can misperceive ourselves. Certainly in contemporary Western Europe it would be fair to say that the tide of society flows against Christianity. In a world that is becoming more and more radically secularized, it is very easy for Christians to lapse into the type of mentality that thinks, "Woe is me! Life is hard! Everyone is against us!" But we must never forget that the reality of life in Christ is so very different from such pessimistic navel gazing. We have been given blessing after blessing, good gift after good gift, promise after promise, and encouragement after encouragement in and through the work of the Lord Jesus Christ![48] We must never forget the riches we have as the people of God—friendship with the Creator; eternal security guaranteed; meaning and purpose in life; kinship with a family that transcends every barrier of race and nationality; the promise of divine protection, guidance, provision, and help; and so much more besides. Just as Asaph came to realize that it is not worldly wealth which brings true richness, so we too must remember the great wealth we have as children of the Father through the sacrifice of the Son as we are strengthened through the Spirit.

Crisis and community. It is significant that the community of faith had a substantial influence in Asaph's refusal to turn completely away

---

48. John 1:16; 10:10; Jas 1:17.

from his life of faith. Crises of faith are best dealt with not alone but in the community of believers. Living only with our own thoughts, doubts, and fears in isolation from other believers will only worsen the tensions we face. We find help in community—others who have already experienced these things and who, therefore, can offer meaningful advice and prayers. Christian fellowship is essential to any healthy life of faith, but all the more so in days when we struggle in our own relationship with God (Heb 10:19–25).

Resolution in relationship. Psalm 73 addresses another question that is often a major problem for people contemplating the life of faith in the light of the suffering visible in this world. Time and time again, the question of theodicy has proven to be a stumbling block for philosophers and theologians alike. It is the type of question concerning which human beings, with all our limitations, can never attain an entirely satisfactory answer. Throughout the generations, some of the greatest minds in Christianity have sought to explain in terms of abstract logic the tension between the justice of God and the sufferings of this world. It appears to me that Asaph's autobiographical story in Psalm 73 tells us that the solution to such problems can never be found in the realm of contemplation and logic alone; rather, Asaph's story points to *resolution in relationship*. It was in meeting with God that Asaph's crisis was resolved. His perspectives were transformed through the renewal of right relationship rather than through the logical deliberation that proved so burdensome to him (v. 16). Quite simply, the limitations of human logic are such that things only begin to make sense when we seek right relationship with the Creator rather than making complete logical understanding a prerequisite for entering into relationship with God.

Psalm 74

A maskil of Asaph.

¹ O God, why have you rejected us forever?
  Why does your anger smolder against the sheep of your
    pasture?
² Remember the nation you purchased long ago,
  the people of your inheritance, whom you redeemed—
  Mount Zion, where you dwelt.
³ Turn your steps toward these everlasting ruins,
  all this destruction the enemy has brought on the sanctuary.
⁴ Your foes roared in the place where you met with us;
  they set up their standards as signs.
⁵ They behaved like men wielding axes
  to cut through a thicket of trees.
⁶ They smashed all the carved paneling
  with their axes and hatchets.
⁷ They burned your sanctuary to the ground;
  they defiled the dwelling place of your Name.
⁸ They said in their hearts, "We will crush them completely!"
  They burned every place where God was worshiped in
    the land.
⁹ We are given no signs from God;
  no prophets are left,
  and none of us knows how long this will be.
¹⁰ How long will the enemy mock you, God?
  Will the foe revile your name forever?
¹¹ Why do you hold back your hand, your right hand?
  Take it from the folds of your garment and destroy them!
¹² But God is my King from long ago;
  he brings salvation on the earth.
¹³ It was you who split open the sea by your power;
  you broke the heads of the monster in the waters.
¹⁴ It was you who crushed the heads of Leviathan
  and gave it as food to the creatures of the desert.
¹⁵ It was you who opened up springs and streams;
  you dried up the ever-flowing rivers.
¹⁶ The day is yours, and yours also the night;

you established the sun and moon.
¹⁷ It was you who set all the boundaries of the earth;
    you made both summer and winter.
¹⁸ Remember how the enemy has mocked you, LORD,
    how foolish people have reviled your name.
¹⁹ Do not hand over the life of your dove to wild beasts;
    do not forget the lives of your afflicted people forever.
²⁰ Have regard for your covenant,
    because haunts of violence fill the dark places of the land.
²¹ Do not let the oppressed retreat in disgrace;
    may the poor and needy praise your name.
²² Rise up, O God, and defend your cause;
    remember how fools mock you all day long.
²³ Do not ignore the clamor of your adversaries,
    the uproar of your enemies, which rises continually.

PSALM 74 IS A TRADITIONAL LAMENT (complaint) voiced by the Old Testament community of faith. It is a response to the loss of the temple as their central place of worship as well as a response to the hiddenness of God's plans for their future amidst their present sufferings. The destruction of Jerusalem in 586 BCE and the exile of Judah that followed engendered great trauma both in political *and* religious terms. The Old Testament covenant community had lost the three great signs of their religious identity: the land, the Davidic king, and the temple—the visible evidences of the salvation God had worked for them in the past, his rule in the present, and his presence among his people. The removal of these external confirmations of Yahweh's active allegiance to his people caused a communal crisis of faith much akin to the individual crisis of faith faced by Asaph in Psalm 73.[1] How are God's people to cope with such a public failure and the doubts that result from it?

---

1. The apparent setting of this psalm as a response to the exile illustrates the uncertainty with which we must view the "authorial" designations of the Psalms. Psalm 74 is described as a *maskil* (probably a musical or liturgical term) *of Asaph*. The original Asaph was appointed by David as worship leader within the temple (1 Chr 6:39; 16:5); however, this psalm seems to find its setting in the destruction of Jerusalem and the temple some four hundred years later. Just as the psalms that bear a Davidic superscription can refer to any of the "sons of David" (i.e., any of the kings of David's line), so it appears that the designation "of Asaph" (*le'asaph*) probably applies to any of the temple worship leaders who followed Asaph. A *maskil* seems to refer to some sort of wisdom or teaching psalm. The Septuagint

The "Why" Question (74:1–3)

AMONG THE MOST POWERFUL CRIES of the Old Testament laments are the often-repeated questions "why?" (*lamah*) and "how long?" (*ad mah*). That both of these questions appear in Psalm 74 (see vv. 1, 9–11) reflects the darkness, insecurity, doubt, and uncertainty God's people felt during the period of the exile. That which was most important to them, both in terms of national identity and the practice of their faith, had been removed and destroyed. At that time it genuinely seemed that Yahweh had turned his back on his people, and the communal psalms of lament found in Book 3 of the Psalter indicate that reciting such psalms—the people together offering their honest prayers of complaint—was a means of coping with this incomprehensible disaster (see also Pss 78, 80, 83, and, perhaps most powerfully, 89). They asked the hard questions because they knew that ignoring them would never lead to a resolution of their present tragic situation.

O God, why have you rejected us forever? Note once again the forceful directness of the psalmist. This tone is a familiar one throughout the book of Psalms but one that is often alien to us. The poet refused to accept that the current circumstances of the people of God could be attributed to the vagaries of international politics in that day. It may well have been the Babylonian armies who ransacked the temple, but the psalmist was well aware that ultimately God was in control. To ask "why have you rejected us *forever*" could indicate the doubts that arose among the people of God with the lengthy passage of time in exile. Seventy years is a long time by anyone's standards, but it appears that the Judeans in Babylon only became aware of Jeremiah's prophecy regarding the length of the exile toward the end of their period in captivity (Dan 9:1–2). There are also indications from the prophetic texts around the time of the exile that the people feared the seventy years had passed, yet they remained in captivity (Zech 1:12).[2] So the psalmist's prayer may reflect his (and the people's) fears over the passage of time without any change in their circumstances. But the question may also be a reference to the totality of destruction that confronted the people in the fall of Jerusalem. Although the word

---

(an ancient Greek translation of the Old Testament) refers to the thirteen psalms with the designation *maskil* as psalms "of understanding," presumably because the word *maskil* seems to be derived from the Hebrew verb *sakal*, meaning "to be prudent or to have insight" (see *HALOT* 2:1328). Although a couple of these psalms refer to imparting wisdom (32:8; 78:1), none of them really fits the classic mould of a wisdom psalm, so again the true meaning of the word is hidden to us. See Derek Kidner, *Psalms 1–72*, TOTC (Leicester: Inter-Varsity Press, 1973), 38.

2. J. J. M. Roberts, "Of Signs, Prophets, and Time Limits: A Note on Psalm 74:9," *CBQ* 39.4 (1977): 474–81.

netsah (translated "forever" in the NIV) normally refers to duration and the passage of time, it can also refer to extent; hence, Eaton translates this verse, "Why, O God, have you so utterly rejected us?"[3] Either way, this opening verse reflects the desolate feeling of abandonment experienced by the exiled people.

Why does your anger smolder against the sheep of your pasture? The pain of God's rejection of his people is accentuated by their recollection of their own identity as a flock under the care of Yahweh. The metaphor of the shepherd speaks of provision, protection, and guidance (cf. Ps 80:1). By stark contrast, however, the people presently experience rejection (Ps 74:1a) and divine anger. In the ancient Near East, one of the main responsibilities of the shepherd would be to protect the flock from its natural enemies (e.g., wolves, bears, lions). It was patently obvious to the psalmist that in this particular area of shepherding responsibility, Yahweh had chosen not to meet the duty of care expected by his "flock." At the same time, the poet knew that their plight was not the result of divine inability. It was God's active punishment that had led them into exile rather than the relative power of the Babylonian armies. The imagery of God's anger "smoldering" paints a picture that speaks both of the destructive power God used in rebuking his people and also of the hiddenness of God's way (see Ps 80:4).[4] The cry of Psalm 74:1 is an emotive expression of confusion and despair. The people see a hopeless future and find it difficult to come to terms with their God's continued anger with them.

Remember the nation you purchased long ago. As is so often the way in the Psalms, despair leads to prayer. The plaintive cry "why?" turns to appeal that this same God should "remember" and return (vv. 2–3). The language of verse 2 is reminiscent of the events of the exodus from Egypt. The exodus is often described in terms of Yahweh's "remembering" his covenant and his people and, based on that remembrance, working purposefully for their liberation from captivity (e.g., see Exod 2:24; 6:5). In fact, God's "remembering" his people becomes something of a shorthand for his powerful answering of prayer in the Old Testament (e.g., 1 Sam 1:11–20). So the psalmist's call to "remember" is actually an appeal that God would hear and respond to the prayers that follow in Psalm 74. The reminder that they are also his people from "long ago" is designed to call to mind the long track record between Yahweh and his people. The implication is that there are responsibilities that accompany such long-standing ties.[5]

---

3. Eaton, *Psalms*, 268.
4. Hossfeld and Zenger, *Psalms 2*, 244.
5. Broyles, *Psalms*, 306.

The association with the liberating work of the exodus is accentuated by the way the psalmist describes the covenant community. He refers to them as a people who were "purchased long ago" and as a people whom "you redeemed." The combination of "purchased" (*qanita*) and "redeemed" (*ga'alta*) resonates with the language of the Song of Moses (Exod 15:13, 16, 17), a poem that celebrates the salvific work of Yahweh in bringing his people out of captivity. It is not accidental that the psalmist chooses this terminology to remind God of his relationship with his people. Yahweh has brought Israel out of foreign captivity with great signs of his power once before, and the psalmist's call to remember is a prayer that he will do so again. What is more, Psalm 74:2 actually refers to *"your congregation* [*'adateka*] that you purchased of old" (author's translation.) In the release of the exodus, Yahweh did not just create for himself a people but actually formed a *worshiping community*. The prayer of the psalmist is grounded in the fact that they are now a worshiping community robbed of their place of worship. The poet's additional plea that God should remember "Mount Zion, where you dwelt," as well as remembering his people, is a request that Yahweh would resolve this tension for his worshiping community who can no longer worship as ordained because of the circumstances of the exile.

Turn your steps towards these everlasting ruins. This unusual phrase seems to be an invitation to the absent God to return to his former dwelling in order to inspect the ruins. Of course, the irony of verses 1–3 is that Yahweh's anger burns against his flock and not against his/their enemy! The *enemies* of Judah have become the *instruments* of Yahweh in the outworking of his purposes for his people. This concept would be almost beyond comprehension for the psalmist and God's community. The temple was so associated with the name and presence of Yahweh that the thought of his withdrawal from it and the subsequent destruction of the temple were almost beyond belief for the Old Testament people of God.[6] But the poet is all too aware that God has not only *allowed* these events to occur but was also *proactive* in bringing them about. We should not imagine that the psalmist was unaware of the causes of the Babylonian exile. Much as in the book of Lamentations, the fact that the exile resulted from the people's constant failure to respond to God's correction is assumed in Ps 74 rather than explicitly discussed. The point of the psalmist's prayer is not to debate the appropriateness of God's punishment. It is rather to plead for mercy in the face of continued suffering and confusion. The language of "purchase" and "redemption" is associated with God's grace in the exodus.

---

6. See the discussion of Pss 46 and 48 in Wilson, *Psalms, Volume 1*.

These words conjure up memories of God's past liberation of his people based solely in his covenant love. So, Psalm 74 is a plea for the renewal of this unmerited grace rather than a deliberation over the equities or inequities of the events that resulted in the exile.

Destruction and Doubt (74:4–9)

YOUR FOES ROARED IN THE PLACE WHERE YOU MET WITH US. Here we see another aspect of lament that is somewhat strange to us. Essentially, the psalmist is declaring to Yahweh things that he already knows. The psalmist makes this presentation as though God were unaware of the events that had occurred! He is telling God about all the unbelievably horrible things that happened in the temple because, surely, if God were aware of them he would do something to rectify the situation. Of course, the poet does not really believe that the Creator is unaware, but from his perspective he cannot comprehend why God allowed these things to happen, and his recapitulation of these destructive acts is designed to stir into action the God who previously met with his people in that now desolate temple. From the perspective of the psalmist and the community of faith, it is as though Yahweh were unaware of the true significance of the events that had taken place and needed to be awakened to their significance through prayer.[7]

This stanza points to the great offence perpetrated by Judah's enemies in their assault on the temple. They roared like animals in a place designed for worship; they set up their military standards in the temple (most likely, emblems that proclaimed their victory over God's people and the victory of their god over Yahweh);[8] they destroyed all the wooden paneling in the temple like woodsmen chopping down a forest; and, ultimately, they burned the edifice to the ground. The visible symbol of God's presence on earth had been destroyed . . . yet he had done nothing in response! The psalmist's account of this destruction reflects his amazement. There is a real sense in which even the retelling of these events would have been absolutely staggering for the poet and the people. According to the Zion theology of the Psalter, *the very stability of the world order* is founded on the immovability of Yahweh's temple in Jerusalem.[9] Yet the sanctuary, the symbol of an immanent God, has been removed, and the people are faced with nothing but silence in response.[10]

---

7. Eaton, *Psalms*, 270.
8. Marvin E. Tate, *Psalms 51–100*, WBC 20 (Waco, TX: Word, 1990), 248–49.
9. See Pss 46 and 48. See also the discussion in Hossfeld and Zenger, *Psalms 2*, 245.
10. There is, of course, a question over what is meant by the phrase in verse 8b, "They

We are given no signs from God. This statement could be another reference to the exodus, thus completing the psalmist's description of the people's present calamity. God's liberating work on behalf of his people by freeing them from slavery in Egypt was accompanied by his "miraculous signs" (*otot* [Exod 10:1–2]), and now the exiled community of faith awaits liberation from Babylon, yet no miraculous signs are worked in *their* behalf. "Why so?" is the psalmist's confused plea.[11] The lack of "signs," however, may also refer to the silence of God in response to the fall of Jerusalem. The same word is also used of prophetic oracles in the Old Testament (e.g., see Isa 38:7; Jer 44:29), and it is possible that the poet completes his lament by saying, "We have suffered so much, yet you remain silent!" There are no prophetic signs providing hope for the future. What is more, there are no prophets left declaring the will of God, and the people have no idea for how long this state of affairs will continue (v.9).[12] "The people's isolation reaches critical proportions. Even communication with God, which was accomplished by means of the prophetic oracles, has been severed (v. 9; see Lam 2:9, 'her prophets obtain no vision from the Lord'). The complaint reflects God's silence."[13] The suffering of a worshiping people who cannot worship is compounded by their belief in an immanent God who refuses to speak to them.

How Long? (74:10–11)

How long will the enemy mock you, God? Since no one in the congregation of God's people knows the duration of their suffering, the psalmist is forced to fire this question at God. Again, his complaint is voiced as though Yahweh were unaware of all that was going on in those days. In asking "How long?" the psalmist is also saying, "Do you not realize that you are being mocked by nations that worship other gods?" There is an obvious

---

burned every place where God was worshiped in the land." The difficulty of this idea is that the temple in Jerusalem was the only legitimate site of worship in the time prior to the exile, so what other sites is the psalmist referring to? There is a wide variety of theories regarding what the psalmist had in mind in this reference, but probably the most convincing argument is that, while the Jerusalem temple was the only official place of festal worship and sacrifice, there were other sites throughout Judah where God's people met for prayer and non-sacrificial worship. It is possible that, following Josiah's reforms, some of the "high places," which had formerly been sites of idolatrous worship, became places where local congregations would meet to pray and worship without practicing those religious activities that were the sole preserve of Temple worship. See 1 Macc 3:46 for a reference to such a place of prayer at Mizpah; also Tate, *Psalms 51–100*, 249–50.

11. Hossfeld and Zenger, *Psalms 2*, 245–47.
12. Roberts, "Of Signs, Prophets, and Time Limits."
13. Schaefer, *Psalms*, 182.

pathos in the prayer of verses 10–11 inasmuch as the psalmist is aware of the true nature of Yahweh, the Creator and Sustainer of the whole universe (vv. 12–17), yet daily he must hear the mocking voice of the Babylonians who would treat Yahweh as a weak and insignificant provincial deity. The poet offers his prayer because he knows that Yahweh is powerful to respond. He is jealous for God's name—yet God himself does not seem to be so. The psalmist's confusion is palpable, and it is made worse by the open-ended chronology of this situation. For how much longer must they wait?

Why do you hold back your hand, your right hand? Yahweh's inactivity is a complete mystery to the poet. The writer is fully aware that God is capable of acting. He knows that the Creator is more than powerful enough to free them from captivity in exile and is able to hush the mocking of their captors by his powerful right hand. Knowing that Yahweh is capable of acting makes his inactivity all the more inexplicable from the psalmist's perspective. The image of Yahweh as hiding his hand in the folds of his garment is the exact opposite of his activity in the exodus (Exod 15:6). His right hand "shattered the enemy" to free the people from Egyptian bondage, but now God refuses to stretch out his hand to end their Babylonian captivity. This creedal awareness of what God had done in the formation of his worshiping community rubs salt into the wounds of their present experience. If God did harder things in the past on behalf of a previous generation, why will he not act now in behalf of this present generation? It is a question that is genuinely burdensome to the psalmist, hence the angst of his psalm of lament. Surely Yahweh should prove his true character and powerful being to these insolent enemies, should he not?[14]

The Power of the Creator God (74:12–21)

BUT GOD IS MY KING FROM LONG AGO. A remarkable confession of faith, given the psalmist's present circumstances, follows the lament of verses 1–11. We are privy to the psalmist's reminding himself and the community of the ultimate truth about their God, regardless of the indications to the contrary in their current experience. Whatever anyone else may say,

---

14. Broyles, *Psalms*, 307. The call to "destroy them" at the end of verse 11 is a difficult phrase to translate. It may well indicate the psalmist's call to put an end to the mocking of Judah's enemies; however, the command bears no object, so it is unclear whether the psalmist is referring specifically to the enemies or to the situation in which they find themselves. The Hebrew command (*kalleh*) may mean "destroy," but a more frequent definition of this verb is "to end or complete something." It is therefore possible to translate verse 11 as, "Why do you hold back your hand, your right hand? Take it from the folds of your garment—end it!" (that is, to take it as an appeal for Yahweh to end the people's plight in exile). See Tate, *Psalms 51–100*, 240, 243.

Yahweh has been and remains king over his people. In these verses we see movement from lament to a hymnic profession of faith that emphasizes the awesome power of God in a series of statements addressed directly to him. The psalmist speaks publicly to God about what he is like as a reminder to all those who would listen. First, he reminds himself of Yahweh's sovereign rule throughout many generations. Yahweh has been king from "long ago" and, mysterious though they may be, the people's present circumstances cannot change the reality of Yahweh's identity as king. "The God to whom the prayer is made is identified and evoked in the confession (v. 12) and its hymnic exposition (vv. 13–17)."[15] Second, the people are reminded of the associated benefits of having Yahweh as their king. He is, after all, the one who "brings salvation on the earth" (v. 12b). More literally, the Hebrew describes God as "the worker of salvations in the midst of the earth." The way in which the phrase is formed (using a participle to describe God, the "doer" or "worker") shows that this characteristic is something foundational to Yahweh's identity, and the fact that he works "salvations" (plural) points to a God who is not reluctant to intervene—in fact, he does so frequently for the benefit of his people and humankind in general. There is something profoundly important about these recollections. The psalmist speaks of Yahweh's intrinsic character, which cannot change even if the community's present circumstances are difficult to understand.

It was you who split open the sea by your power. In verses 13–17 the psalmist speaks about the awesome power of God as creator. The creation of the universe is undoubtedly the most awesome display of power imaginable, far outweighing any of the destructive displays of power that humankind has been able to muster. The creative authority of God remains an unchangeable fact throughout all human history. Although God may be staying his hand at present, the poet knows that he prays to the God who made everything—therefore, he knows that he prays to a God of unbelievable power and authority. To make this point forcefully and visually, the psalmist adopts the language of other ancient Near Eastern cosmogonies (creation mythologies). The nations that surrounded Israel all had their own accounts of the creation of the universe, and most of these myths describe creation in terms of a conflict between the gods. Many of these cosmogonies saw the creation of the earth and humankind as some sort of by-product of a cosmic battle between the high god of their religion and the forces of chaos. In these mythologies, the forces of chaos were most commonly represented by some sort of personification of the

---

15. Mays, *Psalms*, 224.

sea, and it is this imagery that the psalmist draws upon to make his point about the awesome power of the God to whom he prays.[16]

So the graphic presentation of Yahweh as the one who broke open "the heads of the monster in the waters," "crushed the heads of Leviathan," and displays his control over the sea, springs, streams, and flowing rivers (vv. 13–16) is designed to illustrate his power over chaos. Both the sea monsters and the waters themselves would have been understood as forces of chaos by the original hearers of this psalm. So Psalm 74 presents Israel's God as victorious in the struggle with chaos (*Chaoskampf*), as defeating—metaphorically speaking—all the chaotic powers that stood against him. It was not that the psalmist actually believed this was the process by which God created the universe, but he uses this well-known imagery as a means of illustrating the greatness of God's creative power and, at the same time, his control over disorder. Quite simply, the psalmist points the reader's attention to the fact that God is the Creator who has more power than we can ever imagine. The NIV captures well the poet's emphatic use of the pronoun "you" (seven times) in verses 13–17. "It was you who" accomplished all these amazing feats in creating the universe and overcoming chaos. This prayer to God is a proclamation of the ultimate nature of his power, probably as a reminder both to the psalmist himself and to the exiled people of God.[17] The worshiping community in exile must listen to an ideology that presents Yahweh as a weak and defeated god from a remote and insignificant province. "Not true!" declares the psalmist—"This is the God who created the world, who controls the seas and the seasons, who fixed the boundaries of the earth and set the sun and the moon in place!" This prayer declares God to be all-powerful and reminds his people that, whatever the reason for Yahweh's apparent inactivity at this time, their experience in the exile is not caused by a lack of divine power.

---

16. Although there are several ancient Near Eastern mythologies that adopt broadly similar imagery, it is most likely that the poet has the creation myths of Canaan in mind in verses 12–17. Found in the ancient cuneiform tablets discovered at Ras Shamra, the Canaanite (Ugaritic) mythology presents Baal as defeating the primordial enemy known as Yam (also known as "Prince Sea" or "Judge River") in a battle that results in the creation of the world. The other enemies with which Baal contends are quite similar to some of the figures that appear in verses 12–17 (e.g., the great, multiheaded sea beast Leviathan, alongside other dragons and sea serpents). For an interesting discussion of the implications of these cosmogonies, see J. Richard Middleton, "Created in the Image of a Violent God? The Ethical Problem of the Conquest of Chaos in Biblical Creation Texts," *Int* 58.4 (2004): 341–55; also Longman, *Psalms*, 280–81.

17. Samuel Terrien, *The Psalms: Strophic Structure and Theological Commentary*, Eerdmans Critical Commentary (Grand Rapids: Eerdmans, 2003), 542–43.

This creational proclamation is important as it reminds the hearers that the God to whom they pray is a potent God capable of overcoming chaos. Yahweh has proven himself powerful in the exodus and, before that, in creation. In reminding God of his past activity, the people hope to draw his favor upon their present chaotic reality.[18]

Remember and Rise Up! (74:18–23)

REMEMBER HOW THE ENEMY HAS MOCKED YOU, LORD. Based on the preceding confession of faith in the power of the Creator God, the psalmist goes on to pray with great confidence using direct commands to provoke God to activity not just on behalf of his maligned people but also in defense of his own character. Again we are reminded that the problem over which the poet laments is as much religious as it is political or experiential. Along with the community of God's people, he laments not just because they are in exile in Babylon but also because Yahweh's name is mocked by people who know no better. Yes, there is a human cost to the exile that grieves the poet, but he is also saddened by the way God is dishonored as a result of the present situation.[19]

There is a real intensity about the language of remembering and forgetting in these final verses of Psalm 74. Yahweh is encouraged to remember the mocking of his name by Judah's enemies (vv. 18, 22), to remember his covenant (v. 20),[20] and not to forget his afflicted people forever (v. 19).[21] Seven imperatives, positive and negative, dominate the final verses of the psalm: "remember," "do not hand over," "do not forget," "have regard for" (or, more literally, "look to"), "rise up," "defend your cause" (or "bring your charges"), and "do not ignore." The urgency of the psalmist's prayer comes from his desire that Yahweh not forget his people and his promise (vv. 2, 19, 20).[22]

---

18. Richard J. Clifford, "The Hebrew Scriptures and the Theology of Creation," *TS* 46 (1985): 507–23.

19. Schaefer, *Psalms*, 184.

20. Dirk Human makes a compelling case that the covenant referred to here in verse 20 is specifically the Davidic covenant and that this plea is a call for the restoration of the Davidic king (see Human, *"Berit* in Psalm 74," *Skrif en Kirk* 16.1 [1995]: 57–66).

21. The description of God's people as his "dove" in verse 19a is probably an allusion to the divine covenant with Noah, which granted life to humankind (Gen 9:8–17), thus serving as a further reminder of God's promise to his people. This interpretation makes sense of the echoing parallelism in verse 19b, which petitions Yahweh not to forget his afflicted ones. He has promised life, and the psalmist is keen to remind Yahweh of that promise. The imagery also speaks of the fragile nature of Judah in exile (or even in the postexilic period)—they are like a dove at risk of being savaged by wild beasts. See Hossfeld and Zenger, *Psalms 2*, 250.

22. Mays, *Psalms*, 246.

The underlying attitude in this prayer is that the people have suffered enough and for long enough. The poet's urgent petition reminds Yahweh first of his unimaginable power and second of the plight of the people to whom he is bound by covenant. The psalmist is saying, "Enough!" From his perspective, God's people have suffered enough and God's name has suffered too much. As with Psalm 73, the psalmist refuses to couch his prayers in "polite" terminology. He says how he sees things, and he knows that it is pointless to pray to God out of any other attitude. He prays, therefore, with the confidence and directness that we find difficult to emulate.[23]

Psalm 74 concludes with a rousing battle cry—"Rise up, O God!" (v. 22). The command to "rise up" is an exhortation to action directed toward Yahweh as Judge. His name, character, and power have been besmirched in the event of the exile, and the psalmist prays that God would now arise and "defend your cause" (v. 22). The loss of the temple in Jerusalem was not just a socio-political phenomenon resulting from the vagaries of Near Eastern politics at that time. It was a challenge to the very nature of Yahweh and, therefore, to the faith of his people. "The petitions show that the congregation does not yield its faith to experience but instead shapes its bitter experience by faith into poignant urgent prayer."[24] Psalmist and people know their God: their prayer in Psalm 74 is that God will reveal himself once again to be in visible reality the one they know him to be by creed and faith.

TEMPLE AND HOLY SPACE. One of the challenges in reading Psalm 74 is determining how we should respond to the temple theology and the ideas of "holy space" that we see in such psalms. Jerusalem was seen as the "city of God" (Ps 46:4), and the most holy place within the temple was, in a sense, seen as the place where God's presence dwelt on earth (1 Kgs 8:22–66). Of course, the Israelites were fully aware that God could not be contained by any building (1 Kgs 8:27); however, they also believed that there was a special sense in which God did make himself present in the temple (2 Chr 7:1). So it is completely understandable that the fall of Jerusalem and the destruction of the temple were cataclysmic events for the psalmist and the Old Testament community of faith. For the proper worship of God, pilgrimage festivals had

---

23. "Like other psalms with 'of Asaph' in the caption (Psalms 50, 73–83), Psalm 74 is vigorous and blunt" (Schaefer, *Psalms*, 184).

24. Mays, *Psalms*, 246.

been ordained, and they had to be held in the central sanctuary (Deut 16); sacrifices for the forgiveness of sin could only take place in the temple (2 Chr 2:1–6); and it was a place where God's people could meet with him in a special sense (Ps 48).

The concept of holy space has been entirely transformed by the coming of Christ. The New Testament describes the recontextualization of the concept of the temple by Jesus and the New Testament writers. The Old Testament concepts of temple and holy space were inextricably linked with a physical site in Jerusalem. Going to an actual place was an essential part of the Old Testament worship schema, but Jesus transformed ideas of the divine presence on earth through the incarnation. In Christ, God literally comes to dwell on earth with humanity. He is present in the midst of his people in a way that was previously unimaginable. Since the coming of Christ to dwell among humanity, the notion of temple has been transformed. Now, rather than referring to a physical place to which believers must make a pilgrimage, the concept of temple has been spiritualized.

The idea of temple has two connotations in the Christian era. First, Jesus likens himself (his own body) to the temple in John 2:19–22. In doing so, he is pointing to the ultimate act of sacrifice that he was about to accomplish on the cross, thus vitiating the need for the sacrificial work of the temple. Speaking of these verses Gary Burge comments, "Jesus is predicting his death and resurrection, which will create a new covenant with God and make the services of the Jerusalem temple obsolete."[25] Jesus goes even further in his conversation with the Samaritan woman in John 4. Part of the discussion centers on this question of locus—that is, where does true worship take place? The Samaritans believed that Mount Gerizim, at the foot of which Abraham had first built an altar to the Lord upon entry into the land (Gen 12:7), was a holy site where people could meet with God in a special way (John 4:19–20). Jesus makes it clear that the Samaritans were wrong in their belief (v. 22), but he goes on to make a fascinating comment that transforms the whole question of holy space. Verses 21–24 read:

> "Woman," Jesus replied, "believe me, a time is coming when you will worship the Father neither on this mountain nor in Jerusalem. . . . a time is coming and has now come when the true worshipers will worship the Father in the Spirit and truth, for they are the kind of worshipers the Father seeks. God is spirit, and his worshipers must worship in the Spirit and in truth."

---

25. Gary M. Burge, *John*, NIVAC (Grand Rapids: Zondervan, 2000), 97.

So the Messiah points to a time after his death when the need for a specific holy place is removed and to the fact that those who truly worship God will worship him in a spiritual manner. These words would have been shocking for both the Jewish and Samaritan communities of faith! In the coming of Christ, the very nature of religious practice is revolutionized. God, at that time, had quite literally come to dwell on earth, so a special place for a meeting with him becomes redundant. Since that time, God dwells spiritually on the earth with his people through his Holy Spirit, so the concept of sanctuary or holy space is magnified to encompass the whole earth, at least wherever his people are present. The need for sacrifice is removed in Christ, and the need for a place of intermediary representation is also removed by his association with humanity and his constant intercession in our behalf (Heb 4:14–16; 7:23–28).

Second, Paul makes it clear that the "dwelling place" of God on earth is now to be found in his church. Even in the Old Testament period everyone acknowledged that God could not be contained within one geographic space—he is always present everywhere. The same is true in the Christian era. In one sense God is present absolutely everywhere, but the place where he dwells in a special sense is now in the midst of his people wherever they gather. First Corinthians 3:16–17 describes the church universal, and by implication particular congregations of God's people, as the new temple, where it is possible to meet with God in a heightened sense. "Just as Jewish and pagan temples were believed to be the dwelling place of God (or the gods), so also the Christian fellowship is the special place of the Spirit's presence."[26]

We see in the Christian era, therefore, the transformation of the idea of temple and holy space. Aspects of this Old Testament theology are consummated in Christ, and other aspects are expanded by the spiritualizing work of Christ. That believers can meet with God anywhere and worship him fully was true under the old covenant (1 Kgs 8:27–30), but it is all the more true because of the completed sacrificial work of Jesus.[27] Also, the

---

26. Craig Blomberg, *1 Corinthians*, NIVAC (Grand Rapids: Zondervan, 1994), 75.

27. Note that the people did not have to be present in the temple to pray and be heard. Solomon's suggestion was that the people could turn to Jerusalem to pray as a mark of respect for this place of God's special dwelling, but the Old Testament community of faith could also meet with God anywhere. Through the intermediary work of Christ, our ability to meet with God is, in some sense, heightened—not least by the removal of the sacrificial system. So it is not that the removal of the temple affords the believer in the Christian era something that the Old Testament believer did not have, but our access to the presence of God is made easier through the representation of a Son who knows what it is like to be human.

place where God's presence dwells "especially" on the earth is in the midst of his people. In a very real sense, wherever people gather to worship God, he is present, and the opportunity to meet with him intensifies.[28]

Alternative worldviews. It is interesting to note that the psalmist adopts the terminology of a worldview that is not his own in order to make a particular theological point. Verses 13–14 speak of Yahweh in terms of Canaanite creation mythologies by describing him as the High God who overcomes the forces of chaos personified by the sea and sea monsters. Why is it that the poet chooses to adopt the concepts and language of a religious worldview that the covenant community would hold to be false? Is the psalmist actually saying that God did, in fact, create the world in this way? Psalm 74 does not run counter to the creation narratives of Genesis 1–2; rather, it adopts language and imagery that would have been common currency to the readers of the day in order to make a particular theological point that was relevant to the psalmist's purpose in writing the poem. The Old Testament community of faith felt under such pressure from the "chaos" of current events that they wanted to remind themselves (and God) in their liturgy that he is the one who overcame all "chaos" in the act of creation and, therefore, is the one who is able to overcome all chaos in their present circumstance.[29]

There are some overlaps with the imagery of the ancient Near Eastern cosmogonies in the Genesis 1–2 creation accounts—so many, in fact, that some scholars have considered these connections to be examples of *Chaoskampf* in the Old Testament creation account. Having said so, it is now generally acknowledged that the Old Testament's connections with "chaos ideologies" regarding the formation of the universe are much more understated than the ancient Near Eastern equivalents. We do see that initially the created order was *tohu wabohu* ("formless and empty") and "darkness was over the surface of the deep" (Gen 1:2). This picture does present the idea of God's overcoming the unformed chaos by his command, but it is far removed from the rebellious forces of chaos personified as sea gods or sea monsters in the creation myths of Israel's neighbors. Equally, Genesis 1:21 points to God's creation of the "great creatures of the sea"—again, imagery that bears some similarity to the alternative creation accounts—but, as before, the similarities are fairly superficial. The sea monsters do not compete with God in some sort of cosmic battle; rather, they are created

---

28. For a fuller treatment of the important theme of the temple in biblical theology, see Greg K. Beale, *The Temple and the Church's Mission: A Biblical Theology of the Dwelling Place of God*, NSBT (Leicester: Apollos, 2004).

29. Clifford, "Theology of Creation," 512.

by him and therefore entirely under his control. In fact, these similarities of language and imagery, but differences of content and ideology, illustrate the fact that the Genesis 1–2 creation account probably serves as a polemic against the alternative cosmogonies of the ancient world. The imagery of the Old Testament's creation narrative cannot really be described as *Chaoskampf* because there is no obvious sign of struggle (*Kampf*). In the mind of the Old Testament writers, there was no conflict in creation because there is no power comparable to that of Yahweh's creative word.[30]

The psalmist adopts a similar approach in Psalm 74. He makes use of imagery that would be familiar to his hearers in order to make a particular point without implying that the alternative creation account has any authoritative status or factual accuracy. The sea monsters and dragons would be understood by his readers as shorthand for forces of chaos. The Hebrews in exile (and even in the postexilic period) would see their own lives as being shrouded in such chaos. The image of the Creator God who overcomes chaos, therefore, is one that would speak powerfully to them. Liturgically, these verses would be an encouragement to the exilic community. In prayer, these words serve as a reminder to God of his foundational character, thus voicing the expectation of the people that he will work in accordance with his nature.[31]

Psalm 74 in the New Testament. While we find no direct citations from or allusions to Psalm 74, clearly the whole concept of the temple as holy space is one that undergoes quite a transformation in the New Testament (see the above discussion, pp. 90–93).

SEEING THE WORLD THEOLOGICALLY. We saw in our study of Psalm 73 that the way in which we view and respond to life is often shaped by our perspectives on it. The poet who wrote Psalm 74 had a relentlessly *theological* perspective on life.[32] Together with the author of the book of Lamentations, the psalmist looks beyond the outward circumstances of life to see God's hand at work in the events that he and his fellows were experiencing. It would have been very easy for

---

30. Gordon J. Wenham, *Genesis 1–15*, WBC (Waco, TX: Word, 1987), 36–40.

31. The apostle Paul did similarly in some of his own writing and speaking. To make a particular point to a particular audience, he sometimes adopted the language of local writers or thinkers when illustrating something about God or the gospel (e.g., see Acts 27:22–24, esp. v. 28).

32. Mays, *Psalms*, 244–45.

the psalmist to focus on the destructive power of the armies of Babylon or the political weakness of Judah in his day, but instead he realizes that the events experienced in the exile had a theological root rather than a geopolitical one.

Jesus himself serves as an example of this type of thinking. In John 19:10–11 Pilate thinks that he has authority and control in his confrontation with Jesus, but even in the most trying of circumstances the Messiah sees things from the perspective of theological reality rather than political reality. "You would have no power over me if it were not given to you from above" (v. 11a). Jesus was fully aware of the spiritual reality at work behind the current, traumatic events of his own life. He saw beyond the physical and consciously viewed things theologically.

Do we do the same in our own day and reality? As we read the newspapers and watch 24-hour news channels, do we look beyond the tangible scheme of things and ask how God is at work in the events of our time and our nations? It may be hard for us to discern just how God's hand is at work in the (often traumatic) events of our own experience, so—as with Psalm 74—this practice is one best worked out communally in our congregations of faith. Challenging as it may be, however, we should practice such discernment. We should ask God to reveal to us how and where he is at work in our own situations and, also, ask what role he would have us play as his people in this generation.

Remembering the character of God. Another important line of application to be drawn from Psalm 74 is the psalmist's insistent belief that the God to whom he prays works in human history. The poet points to the great works of God in the creation of the universe and reminds himself that his prayer is directed to this Creator God who has worked in the creation of human history and who still works in human history today. We must ask ourselves whether or not our prayers actually reflect the fact that we pray to the one who made everything we see around us. Our intercession is directed to a God of incomparable power, so our prayers should be marked by faith of a similar magnitude. I fear that often our prayers do not reflect the fact that "our God is a great, big God."[33] Rather, it seems to me that, were a stranger who had no idea about Christianity to listen to our prayers, he would think that we actually believe in a God of limited power—a God who is able to provide "journeying mercies" and "bless" all sorts of people and events, certainly, but perhaps not the Creator of all things who is able radically to transform the world in which we live. The author of Psalm 74

---

33. "Great Big God," by Jo Hemming & Nigel Hemming © 2001 Vineyard Songs (UK/Eire).

clearly believed in such a God, and his prayer echoed his belief. Our prayer should echo our belief in the God who "crushed the heads of Leviathan" and who "established the sun and moon."

God's anger and today's church. We should not think that God's anger against his covenant people is something that is limited to the Old Testament and the people of the wilderness experience or the exile. The story of the exile in Babylon makes it clear that he will use the means necessary to enable us to walk well with him. Sometimes our stubbornness and unwillingness to submit will mean that God will use measures that are difficult or unpleasant for us in order to help and enable us to receive the blessing that results from walking in his ways. We should not deceive ourselves into believing that God no longer works in this way today! Peter makes it clear that the Christian church is every bit as liable to God's corrective redirection as was Israel in the Old Testament. First Peter 4:17 makes it plain that sometimes judgment begins with the family of God, so the church today needs to be aware of the multitude of means God uses to bring about his will and our obedience to his purposes in the world.

Psalm 75

*For the director of music. To the tune of "Do Not
Destroy." A psalm of Asaph. A song.*

¹ We praise you, God,
    we praise you, for your Name is near;
    people tell of your wonderful deeds.
² You say, "I choose the appointed time;
    it is I who judge with equity.
³ When the earth and all its people quake,
    it is I who hold its pillars firm.
⁴ To the arrogant I say, 'Boast no more,'
    and to the wicked, 'Do not lift up your horns.
⁵ Do not lift your horns against heaven;
    do not speak so defiantly.'"
⁶ No one from the east or the west
    or from the desert can exalt themselves.
⁷ It is God who judges:
    He brings one down, he exalts another.
⁸ In the hand of the LORD is a cup
    full of foaming wine mixed with spices;
he pours it out, and all the wicked of the earth
    drink it down to its very dregs.
⁹ As for me, I will declare this forever;
    I will sing praise to the God of Jacob,
¹⁰ who says, "I will cut off the horns of all the wicked,
    but the horns of the righteous will be lifted up."

FROM A CANONICAL PERSPECTIVE Psalm 75 is a response to the doubts and questions of Psalm 74, in which we read about the crises and tensions that were caused for God's people by the exile in Babylon. The problems raised by the psalmist and the congregation in Psalm 74 are partly based on the suffering they faced as a result of the political and social turmoil of exile, but the heart of their problem is fundamentally religious. The temple has been destroyed, therefore they cannot worship as ordained in the Old Testament Scriptures. What is more,

Yahweh's name is mocked by the nation's captors. The Babylonians believed that the military victory they had won over Judah and Jerusalem proved that their gods were stronger than Yahweh, so God's people were forced to listen to his name being derided (74:10–11, 18, 22) even though they knew him to be the Creator of all things (vv. 13–17) and King over all the universe (v. 12). Lack of divine response to this unbearable situation lay at the root of the lament of Psalm 74. The psalmist could not understand why God would allow his name to be mocked and remain inactive when he could easily prove his sovereignty and power. Psalm 75 speaks in response to the doubts of Psalm 74. This poem assures the congregation both that God is Judge (Ps 75:7) and that God *will* judge (vv. 2, 4, 7–8, 10), but that he will do so *in his own time*, when he deems it to be right. So, effectively, Psalm 75 responds to Psalm 74 with assurance of judgment to come— God's name will not be mocked forever![1]

The Heading (75:0)

THE HEADING HERE IS A MORE COMPLICATED ONE. It contains the designation *lamenatseah*, meaning "To the director" or "For the director." The root verb from which the office of director is derived (*ntsh*) means "to direct" or "to supervise."[2] With the passage of time it became unclear precisely what this "director" did, but the term implies an instruction or dedication to one who had responsibility for the leading of temple worship, be that oversight of the music or the singing.[3] "Do not destroy" probably refers to a known tune. The remaining phrases of the heading identify the psalm as a continuing part of the Asaphite collection begun with Psalm 73 and describe the composition as a "song," one of the standard descriptions of a psalm.

Giving Thanks for a God Who Is Near (75:1)

THE GREAT MYSTERY OF PSALM 74 was the inactivity of God in the face of the suffering of his people. The Old Testament community of faith was in exile, Yahweh's name was mocked, sacrificial worship was made impossible by the destruction of the temple, and in the face of all this calamity God seemed distant! How can such realities be reconciled? Well, the editors of the book of Psalms resolve this tension by placing Psalm 75 as a response

---

1. See Joseph E. Jensen, "Psalm 75: Its Poetic Context and Structure," *CBQ* 63.3 (2001): 418–19.

2. See its use in Ezra 3:8–9 for those who supervised the rebuilding of the temple and 1 Chr 15:21, where it is used in the context of musical direction within the temple.

3. See Tate, *Psalms 51–100*, 4–5, for further discussion of the possible meanings of this office.

---

to the turmoil of Psalm 74. The "distant God" who seems to have rejected his people (Ps 74:1) is now celebrated as the God whose "Name is near" (Ps 75:1). In a marked contrast of tone compared with Psalm 74, the psalmist here leads the people in celebration of the nearness of God and his "wonderful deeds."[4]

It is interesting that the psalmist gives thanks to God for the nearness of his "Name." Effectively, the name of God is an extension of God himself. It refers to the very essence or being of God, so in a sense the psalmist is simply celebrating the nearness of God. But on another level, the fact that the God of the exodus chose to reveal himself to this newly formed worshiping community by using a personal name (Exod 3:13–15) was a radical act of self-revelation that indicated a degree of intimacy between the deity and his people that was uncommon in the ancient Near East.[5] What is more, God chose to place his name in the temple as a sign of his dwelling there (Deut 12:4–14; 1 Kgs 8:15–21). So, it is particularly poignant that the psalmist chooses to celebrate the nearness of God's "Name" following a lament over the loss of the temple. These verses serve as a reminder to the reader that God is near even when circumstances seem to indicate otherwise. The temple may be gone, but its absence cannot separate God's people from his presence, so the psalmist calls on the community of faith to give thanks (Rom 8:31–39).[6] As well as remembering God's nearness as a reason for thanksgiving, the poet also reminds readers of how men speak of the "wonderful deeds" of God.[7] These "wonderful deeds" (*nipla'ot*) that

---

4. Unusually, the verb for "we give thanks" (*hodinu*) takes a Hebrew perfect form in Ps 75:1. Some commentators suggest that this verb should be rendered in the narrative past ("we have given thanks"; e.g., see Hossfeld and Zenger, *Psalms 2*, 252–53). But it seems more likely that the call to give thanks in verse 1 is the present basis upon which the assertion in verses 9–10 is built, namely, the assertion that the psalmist will declare God's judgment and sing his praise in the future. Hence the contemporary English translations, as we see with the NIV, translate verse 1 with a temporally neutral present tense.

5. For further discussion of the divine name in the Psalms see Wilson, *Psalms, Volume 1*, 200.

6. As well as responding to the crisis of Ps 74, it seems likely that Ps 75:1 deliberately echoes the conclusion of Ps 73, where the poet declares on an individual level that it is "good to be near God" (v. 28). Here the entire community gives thanks for the nearness of God. See Hossfeld and Zenger, *Psalms 2*, 255.

7. There is no explicit subject in the Hebrew text, which reads, "we give thanks because your name is near; *they* tell of your wonderous works." Most of the modern English versions add either "men" or "people" to make explicit what is probably implied in the Hebrew text. The ESV chooses to make this clause read, "We recount your wondrous deeds"; however, the verb form in the Hebrew is clearly a third-person plural rather than a first-person plural, so it is probably better to supply an explicit subject ("men/people") than to assume that the author intends us to see "we" as the continued subject. Kselman

people recount are normally associated with Yahweh's work in creation and salvation. So, the psalmist reminds God's people that he is near and that he is the God who has worked in the creation of the universe and intervened to bring salvation into the historical reality of his people in the past. They therefore have reason to give thanks, because he is able to work with such power in their present reality.[8]

Divine Proclamation (75:2–5)

IN THE POEMS OF THE ASAPH COLLECTION, it is quite common for the psalmist to introduce a divine oracle (Pss 50; 81; 82), as here in Psalm 75:2–3. It is actually quite difficult to delimit the extent of divine speech within this poem for at least two reasons: ancient Hebrew did not make use of punctuation marks (so there are no quotation marks to make things easy for us), and the divine oracles contained within the poems lack introductory announcements that a message from God follows. We are therefore left to decide on the extent of the divine proclamations the psalmist records simply based on the flow and sense of the text. To make the extent of God's speech within the poem clear for the contemporary reader, the NIV (with some justification) adds the words "You say" at the beginning of verse 2 and places quotation marks around verses 2–5.[9] When we come to discuss verse 10, we will see just how difficult it is to know for certain when the psalmist is speaking for himself, as it were, and when he is relating God's speech to us.

You say, "I choose the appointed time; it is I who judge with equity." This divine declaration seems to be a very direct response to the

---

makes an interesting argument for the existence of a Janus parallelism in this verse, where the Hebrew word for "your Name" (*shemka*) could be read as the subject of the first clause and also repointed as "your heavens" (*shameka*), thus giving the object of the second clause (John S. Kselman, "Janus Parallelism in Psalm 75:2," *JBL* 121.3 [2002]: 531–32). Doing so would give a reading of the text as "we give thanks . . . for near is your name [*shemka*]/ your heavens [*shameka*] recount your wondrous deeds"—an ingenious reading of the text and one that in many ways makes good sense of the theology of the passage. The extent to which Janus parallelism was actually practised in the Hebrew poetic texts, however, remains unclear, and there is no indication that the passage has ever been read with this *double entendre* in mind in either the Jewish or the Christian history of interpreting Ps 75.

8. Eaton, *Psalms*, 273.

9. Some contemporary translations follow the example of the NIV by including the introductory formula "You say," as well as making use of quotation marks (e.g., NET). Others, however, use only quotation marks (e.g., ESV, NASB), whereas still others follow the pattern of the Hebrew text by including neither (e.g., NRSV). It seems most likely that these verses do indicate divine speech which the psalmist relates to the reader, so it is important to distinguish this speech clearly for the modern reader.

doubts and lament of Psalm 74. The writer of the preceding psalm challenges God to, "Rise up . . . and defend your cause" (v. 22), and here, in the very next psalm, God responds with words of assurance not only that he *will* judge but also that he will judge in *his* time. The lament of Psalm 74 is born out of the people's inability to listen to any more mocking of their God. From their perspective this mocking had gone on quite long enough, and it was time for Yahweh to respond. But words of assurance come through the divine oracle of Psalm 75:2–5. Not only will God judge (v. 2), but it is God who holds the earth and keeps it secure (v. 3)—he will deal with the arrogant and the mocker in the day that he appoints for judgment (vv. 4–5).

Here there is a subtle play on words between Psalms 74 and 75. The Hebrew word *mo'ed* can refer to either God's "appointed place" or God's "appointed time." In Psalm 74:4 we read, "Your foes roared in the place [*mo'ed*] where you met with us," whereas in Psalm 75:2 we read, "I choose the appointed time [*mo'ed*]." The appointed *place* may have been desecrated, but the appointed *time* for judgment is entirely within God's control. From the perspective of God's people in Psalm 74, they felt that they could take no more—things seemed out of control and they wanted God to act now! Psalm 75 responds with the assurance that God is in control and that he will act when the time is right in his eyes.

When the earth and all its people quake. Verse 3 contains a promise that judgment is Yahweh's and will come at the time that suits his purposes. Justice and vindication for the righteous, although not apparent in the present, will come (cf. Hab 2:1–4). In verse 4, this assurance is linked to the steadiness of the earth itself: Yahweh who created and sustains the world and all that is in it can be depended upon to establish justice upon it in good time. Yahweh is the basis both of the world's stability and of the moral order. If either is challenged, chaos may erupt, but Yahweh's steadying hand will be there to restore order.[10]

From Psalm 74, we see that the delay in God's intervention appeared to challenge the very order of things in the minds of his people. As far as they were concerned, the failure of God to act struck at the very foundations of their worldview and their understanding of the way in which the universe works. In Psalm 75:3 God speaks in response to their fears. He "holds its pillars firm," no matter how—from our perspective—the earth may seem to be shaking.

To the arrogant I say, "Boast no more." God's control over all things extends every bit as much to rebellious humanity as it does to the natural

---

10. Tate, *Psalms 51–100*, 258–59.

order. This part of the divine oracle (vv. 4–5) reminds the people hearing this psalm that Yahweh does work in human history. His judgment is not only eschatological, but when he sees fit, he also intervenes in the reality of daily lives in the here and now to rebuke those who reject his moral standards, so curtailing their arrogant rebellion. These verses begin a motif of "raising up and bringing down" that runs throughout the remainder of the psalm. God speaks emphatically to the boastful by telling them "Do not boast," and he instructs the wicked not to "lift your horns." The imagery here speaks of self-exaltation, and the divine oracle speaks in rebuke against all those who would exalt self. The metaphor of "lifting a horn" is an ancient image that speaks about taking delight in one's own power. Generally speaking, the horn refers to strength and power, so here the divine rebuke is addressed to those who glory in the power they hold over others. It is a rebuke that works on two levels. First, it speaks to the arrogant military forces of Babylon who mock Yahweh and his people because of their capture of Jerusalem and the temple. The prophecy of Habakkuk picks up on very similar imagery by addressing the armies of Babylon with a warning of divine judgment (Hab 1:5–11; 3:1–13). Second, however, the same vocabulary is often applied to all those who would exalt their own status and power by exploiting others within Israel (see Pss 5:5; 73:3, both of which use the same word we see in Psalm 75:4 to describe the arrogant). So, God's divine oracle gives comfort to people in their present circumstances by reminding them that judgment will come on all those who reject Yahweh; but it also serves as a reminder of the attitude that they themselves should display in their dealings with one another—an attitude of humility and dependence on God rather than self.[11]

The Exalting and Humbling God (75:6–8)

THE PSALMIST'S ACCOUNT of the divine oracle is followed by his own poetic discussion of the same subject matter. In the preceding verses God speaks of himself as Judge and as the one who brings down the boastful who arrogantly take delight in their own power. In these verses the psalmist himself, in turn, portrays God first as the exalting and humbling God (vv. 6–7) and then as Judge (v. 8).

No one . . . can exalt themselves. Verse 6 draws attention to the sole source of success and failure in life. Using imagery employed elsewhere in the Old Testament, the psalmist points out that exaltation does not come from the east, the west or, by implication, the south (i.e., "the

---

11. Mays, *Psalms*, 249.

desert").[12] Interestingly, reference to "the north" is omitted from this verse. While it may be appealing both to Scotsmen and Yankees to think of "the North" as the only source of exaltation, that is not what the author implies! "The north" (*tsaphon*) was also associated with Mount Zaphon, which was thought to be the site of a special mountain sanctuary of God (see Ps 48:2; Isa 14:13).[13] The implication, therefore, is that exaltation comes from God alone, which is exactly the point the psalmist goes on to make in Psalm 75:7.

It is God who judges. The poet makes absolutely explicit the point that he has been emphasizing throughout this psalm—God alone is Judge, and he *will* judge. It is God who "brings one down" and "exalts another" (v. 7). He is the ultimate source of all human success and failure. If a group of people is on the ascendancy, it is because God has so ordained. Equally, if another people group is in dire straits, this situation, too, is part of God's plan. It is not difficult to see how directly these words communicated to a people in exile. The (temporary) triumph of the Babylonians and the (equally temporary) demise of the Judahites under their power are both under the hand of God. For the time being and in accordance with his purposes, he has exalted the Babylonians and brought down his own people. This turn of events is all under his control. The exilic and postexilic prophets made it clear that Judah's present experience was the result of divine judgment as a corrective for sin (e.g., see Ezek 39:23). Equally, however, the time was soon coming when Yahweh would judge the Babylonians and provide release for his own people. In response to their lament of Psalm 74, the poet reminds God's people that *every aspect* of the current experience is *entirely* under Yahweh's control.

In the hand of the LORD is a cup full of foaming wine. Once again, the overlap of imagery with Psalm 74 shows how this poem serves as a response to the preceding psalm of lament. Here the image of the divine hand's pouring out God's judgment on the wicked, as though he were pouring out a cup full of foaming wine, responds directly to the psalmist's anguished question in 74:11 as to why Yahweh holds back his powerful hand from judgment. The image of God's cup of judgment was a common one among the prophets.

---

12. Hebrew often uses geographic features to refer to the points of the compass; therefore, reference to "the sea" in Hebrew (i.e., the Mediterranean Sea) is often meant to indicate "the west" in general. Equally, reference to "the river" (i.e., the Euphrates) frequently symbolizes "the east." In the same way, "the desert," meaning the Sinai desert to the south of Israel, is often used to refer to "the south," as seems to be the case here in Ps 75:6.

13. Cleon L. Rogers, Jr., "צָפוֹן," *NIDOTTE* 3:834–6.

The psalm uses a metaphor that was a favorite of the seventh-and sixth-century prophets to personalize and dramatize judgment. God has a cup whose content is his decreed destiny for those under judgment, and he will pour a draught from it for all the wicked of the earth to drink (Jer 25:15; 49:12; Ezek 23:32–34; Isa 51:17; Hab 2:15–16). When that will happen is a matter of God's choice, but the divine saying in verse two makes it very clear that God will set an appointed time in his judgment.[14]

So Psalm 75 responds to the community's prayer in Psalm 74. The psalmist assures the community of faith that, although Yahweh may have stayed his hand at the present time, the righteous judgment they call for will arrive, but it will arrive in God's time, not theirs.

Praise and Justice (75:9–10)

THE PSALM CLOSES WITH A DOUBLE declaration in which both statements are made in the first-person singular. The first statement (v. 9) is the psalmist's determined declaration that he will both declare God's authority and judgment forever and, as a result, "sing praise to the God of Jacob," while the final declaration of judgment is another divine oracle (v. 10).[15]

I will sing praise to the God of Jacob. The modern reader often finds the juxtaposition of praise and judgment to be incongruous. There was, however, no tension in the mind of the psalmist. He was fully aware that the world in which he lived was not as it should be—events happened that were abhorrent to God and contrary to his created order. The removal from the face of the earth of the counter-creational injustice, persecution, exploitation, and violence perpetrated by the wicked was a prospect that inspired praise in the heart of the poet. He was therefore willing to declare the coming judgment of God to all who would listen (v. 9), and the anticipated results of this judgment gave him reason to praise.[16]

The horns of the righteous will be lifted up. It is interesting to note that the final verse of Psalm 75 refers to "the wicked" in the plural (*resha'im*) but to "the righteous" in the singular (*tsaddiq*). Singular nouns may often serve a representative function in Hebrew, so we should not put too much store in the singularity of "the righteous one" in verse 10. But we should

---

14. Mays, *Psalms,* 249.

15. Broyles, *Psalms,* 311; Tate, *Psalms 51–100,* 259; Hossfeld and Zenger, *Psalms 2,* 257.

16. For further consideration of the importance of divine justice, see Erich Zenger's excellent work on the psalms of imprecation (Erich Zenger, *A God of Vengeance? Understanding the Psalms of Divine Wrath* [Louisville: Westminster John Knox, 1996]).

at least be aware of the possibility that this word in the closing divine oracle may refer to the Lord's Anointed, who was often described in the Old Testament and the intertestamental literature as Yahweh's *tsaddiq*, his "Righteous One."[17] It does seem that, especially during the exile and in the period after it, a sense of messianic expectation grew strong among God's people. The expectation was that a future king would come who would work out the purposes of God in righteousness. Psalm 75:10—where the divine oracle states that Yahweh will cut off the power of the wicked but lift up the horn (i.e., power) of the righteous, or the Righteous One—may be a reference to this type of messianic expectation.[18]

READING THE PSALMS IN CANONICAL CONTEXT. One of the key features of Psalm 75 is its positioning within Book 3 of the Psalter. Reading through the book of Psalms in order gives the clear impression that psalms are deliberately placed alongside each other in order to influence our interpretation of the individual poems. For example, it is more than fortuitous that Psalm 23:1 ("The LORD is my Shepherd, I lack nothing") immediately follows the anguished plea of Psalm 22:1 ("My God, my God, why have you forsaken me?"). The editors who compiled the Psalter deliberately placed psalms alongside one another so that the voice of each psalm would speak to its neighbors. In this way, we see a clear response to the doubts of Psalm 74 here in Psalm 75 and, indeed, the conversation that begins between these two psalms continues on into Psalm 76, as we shall see below.[19] The community pours out its lament over the inactivity of God in Psalm 74, but the divine oracle of Psalm 75 provides assurance that God will work, though he will accomplish his work in his time. Just as we read any other passage of Scripture in its context within the book in which it appears, so we should be careful to do the same with the psalms in their context within the Psalter.[20]

---

17. Tremper Longman, "The Messiah: Explorations in the Law and Writings," in *The Messiah in the Old and New Testaments*, ed. Stanley E. Porter (Grand Rapids: Eerdmans, 2007), 13–34.

18. Eaton, *Psalms*, 273. Reading Ps 75 from a contextual perspective, if we assume that the covenant referred to in Ps 74:20 is Yahweh's covenant with David, then it makes the interpretation of Ps 75:10 as a reference to a coming Davidic king all the more likely. See Human, "*Berit* in Psalm 74."

19. Jensen, "Psalm 75."

20. The question of canonical interpretation is discussed more fully in the section The Shape of the Psalter at the beginning of this commentary. The work of Gerald Wilson,

Culture-bound metaphor. Another question that arises from Psalm 75 is, "How are we to understand metaphors that are meaningless to us?" Essentially, a metaphor is a pictorial means of expressing an idea or concept by way of comparison with something else. For example, Robbie Burns compares the abstract concept of love to "a red, red rose":

> O my love's like a red, red rose,
>   That's newly sprung in June;
> O my love's like the melody,
>   That's sweetly played in tune.[21]

The comparison of his love with both the rose and the melody is meant to conjure up images in the mind of the reader—these are images of beauty, warmth, pleasure, harmony, and so on. The pictorial image of the metaphor shapes our understanding of the way Burns viewed his love for this anonymous woman.

Metaphors in the Psalms function in the same way. The pictorial value of the metaphor describes the idea that the poet seeks to explain. For example, in Psalm 1 the blessed person who delights in the instruction of Yahweh is described as being like "a tree planted by streams of water" (v. 3). Obviously, in the dry climate of the Near East, a tree planted by a water source will stand out in terms of growth, strength, fruitfulness, and stability when compared to other trees. The metaphor tells us that this kind of thriving is what we are to expect for the believer who delights in God and his word.

Most metaphors communicate well because the imagery is fairly universal and can be observed throughout the world. Burns's metaphor of the rose communicates well in every country and culture that knows the sight and scent of the rose in bloom, as does the image of "the tree planted by streams of water." In Psalm 75, however, we read about "the horn" (vv. 4–5, 10), an image that does not communicate so universally today, at least in

---

who wrote the preceding *Psalms, Volume 1*, has been key in understanding the importance of interpreting the Psalms contextually. His article "The Shape of the Book of Psalms," *Int* 46.2 (April 1992): 129–41, is a particularly helpful introduction to the canonical interpretation of the Psalter, as is one of his later articles published not long before his untimely death ("The Structure of the Psalter," in *Interpreting the Psalms: Issues and Approaches*, eds. P. S. Johnston and D. G. Firth [Leicester: Apollos, 2005], 229–46). See also Jamie A. Grant, "Editorial Criticism," in *IVP Dictionary of the Old Testament: Wisdom, Poetry & Writings*, ed. Tremper Longman III and Peter Enns (Downers Grove, IL: InterVarsity, 2008), 149–56.

21. Robert Burns, "A Red, Red Rose," written in 1794. http://www.robertburns.org/works/444.shtml.

Western cultures.[22] The meaning or inference of such images is lost to us—they were once clear in their meaning to a particular community, but the understanding of them has been lost with the passage of time. The "horn" is one such image.

It seems that the image of the horn in Hebrew poetry had a multivalent meaning. Sometimes it appears to symbolize strength (e.g., see Ps 18:2). This usage of the horn metaphor is probably derived from the physical hardness of the horn and the strength and power of horn-bearing animals, such as the wild ox.[23] In some instances the horn metaphor symbolizes ideas of status or dignity, though this symbolism may too have overtones of power (e.g., Ps 112:9).[24] In other instances the horn may also represent Yahweh's appointed strong one, normally a reference to the king (e.g., Ps 132:17).[25] But the imagery of Psalm 75 relates specifically to lifting and cutting off horns (vv. 5, 10). These activities symbolize, respectively, triumph and defeat.[26] Hannah, for example, rejoices with the words, "in the LORD my horn is lifted high" (1 Sam 2:1), so symbolizing her transition from humiliation to restoration and blessing. Effectively, she has triumphed because of the Lord's grace in answering her prayer.

Psalm 75 warns against exulting in the victories won according to human perspectives, because ultimately these victories are short-lived and ephemeral. God can and will intervene to right the balance toward the standards of his justice. He will "cut off the horns of all the wicked," thus showing every alleged victory won contrary to his standards ultimately to be illusory. On the other hand, those who walk in his ways may appear downtrodden now, but their ultimate restoration is never far away (v. 10). Learning from dead metaphors takes a bit of research. When we come across imagery in the Psalms that we do not understand, it helps to look to commentaries and Bible dictionaries to grasp the meaning of such symbols for their original readers and hearers.

Psalm 75 and Hannah's prayer. Another point of interest with regard to Psalm 75 is its similarity to Hannah's prayer in 1 Samuel 2:1–10. Hannah's prayer reflects many of the themes that we find in Psalm 75—for example, the image of the horn's being lifted high (1 Sam 2:1), the arrogance and

---

22. It may well be that this imagery is still commonly understood in cultures where bulls, elephants, and rhinos are more commonly seen than they are in the industrialized world.

23. Eaton, *Psalms*, 105.

24. Leslie C. Allen, *Psalms 101–150*, WBC 21, rev. ed. (Waco, TX: Word, 2002), 94.

25. Broyles, *Psalms*, 473.

26. Michael L. Brown, "קֶרֶן," *NIDOTTE* 3:990–2.

boasting of enemies (v. 3), the humbling of those who are apparently victorious and the uplifting of those who are apparently defeated (v. 4), Yahweh as the one who exalts and humbles (v. 7), and God as providing stability to the world (v. 8). The close of Hannah's prayer, where she prays for God's strengthening of the king, his anointed one, may further strengthen the suggested reading of Psalm 75:10, which sees "the righteous" as a reference more specifically to the "righteous one." It is very difficult to ascertain the precise relationship between Psalm 75 and Hannah's prayer. Is one borrowing from the other, or do both simply reflect a common theology and perspective? Due to the lack of concrete historical settings in the Psalms, it is very difficult to answer such questions with any degree of certainty.[27] But it is certainly worth noting that Hannah's words are very similar—an example for us all to follow. It is good to take the words of the psalms and make them our own prayers in the wide variety of settings in which the prayers of the psalmist reflect our own hearts and minds.

Psalm 75 in the New Testament. The imagery of the wine of Yahweh's judgment being poured out on the wicked finds an echo in Revelation 14:10. It is important to remember that judgment is not an issue limited entirely to the Old Testament. This misunderstanding is frequently repeated in contemporary Christian circles. But both Jesus in the Gospels (e.g., Matt 11:20–24) and the apostle John in Revelation (e.g., 14:6–13) make it absolutely clear that ultimately God will bring his judgment on humanity. Often this idea is one we would prefer not to think about, but the Scriptures make it absolutely plain that judgment will be a historical reality which every created human being must face. Ignoring that fact does no one any good. The judgment passages give us comfort that the blatant injustices of this world will not go unpunished, and they should also serve as a spur to take the gospel to those who have not yet responded to God's good gift in Christ. Comfort, with regard to the judgment imagery of Psalm 75, is found in the fact that, ultimately, it is Jesus who drank the cup of God's punishment on behalf of all those who turn to him for refuge. In Matthew 26:39 and 42 (see also Mark 14:36 and Luke 22:42), we see Jesus praying to his Father that this "cup" be taken from him. Jesus' prayer is a reference to the punishment for sin that he would receive on the cross. He is referring to the "cup full of foaming wine" in the hand of the Lord (Ps 75:8), the cup of judgment. Ultimately, God the Son drank the cup of the Father's righteous judgment so that we ourselves would not have to drink that wine.[28]

---

27. Miller, *Interpreting*, 18–28.
28. Longman, *Psalms*, 284.

PERSPECTIVE, PATIENCE, AND PRAYER. Psalm 75, as an answer to Psalm 74, is a reminder that very often things are not what they seem. This theme is one that is repeated in *The Voyage of the Dawn Treader,* one of C. S. Lewis' Narnia Chronicles books. During the heroes' lengthy sea voyage, they visit various islands in their quest for the seven lost lords of Narnia, and on each of the islands appearances prove to be deceptive. For example, on the "Duffers' Island" they come across a group of creatures that live in terror of a fearful and powerful wizard, who has "cast a spell" on these poor creatures to make them invisible. Described from the Duffers' perspective, the wizard sounds like a fearsome villain, except that he actually turns out to be a faithful servant of Aslan, Narnia's Christ-figure, who works for their good despite their failure to realize so. We too can be like the Duffers and fail to recognize when God is doing something for our good.

The problem of perspective in prayer is one that every Christian has to endure. Just like the people of God in Psalm 74, we often wonder why God stays his hand when we pray for his intervention (v. 11). Yet Psalm 75 corrects that perspective with the reminder that God's hand is still active in human history (v. 8). Often the way in which we see our reality is very different from God's perspective of intending to bless us for our *eternal good,* though not necessarily for our *present ease.* What does this difference mean for us in terms of our own prayer life? It means that we must be a people who are: (1) Honest in prayer. As mentioned in our study of Psalm 73, it is essential that we discuss our life openly and honestly with God. Even if our perspectives are wrong, there is no point in denying the reality of our human view. If our perspective is wrong, the starting point of its correction is honesty before God. (2) Patient in prayer. If God does not answer our prayers or does not answer them in the way we expect, we must be patient in prayer. Psalm 75 reminds us that God's timing and ours very often do not coincide. Psalm 74 is the prayer of a people who felt it was high time that God worked in judgment against those who mocked him (vv. 10–11, 22–23). In response, Psalm 75 reminds them that Yahweh will judge in the time that *he* knows to be right (v. 2). Our perspective on God's timing can be just as mistaken as our perspective on our reality, so our prayer should also be marked by patience. (3) Open to change. Psalms 74 and 75 show us that we can be wrong in our perspective on reality and wrong in our appreciation of God's timing, so we should always be a people who are open to change at God's leading as we pray. As with Asaph in Psalm 73, where our perspective is skewed, God will change it when we are open and honest as we draw near to meet with him.

Psalm 76

For the director of music. With stringed instruments. A psalm of Asaph. A song.

¹ God is renowned in Judah;
  in Israel his name is great.
² His tent is in Salem,
  his dwelling place in Zion.
³ There he broke the flashing arrows,
  the shields and the swords, the weapons of war.
⁴ You are radiant with light,
  more majestic than mountains rich with game.
⁵ The valiant lie plundered,
  they sleep their last sleep;
not one of the warriors
  can lift his hands.
⁶ At your rebuke, God of Jacob,
  both horse and chariot lie still.
⁷ It is you alone who are to be feared.
  Who can stand before you when you are angry?
⁸ From heaven you pronounced judgment,
  and the land feared and was quiet—
⁹ when you, God, rose up to judge,
  to save all the afflicted of the land.
¹⁰ Surely your wrath against mankind brings you praise,
  and the survivors of your wrath are restrained.
¹¹ Make vows to the LORD your God and fulfill them;
  let all the neighboring lands
  bring gifts to the One to be feared.
¹² He breaks the spirit of rulers;
  he is feared by the kings of the earth.

Original Meaning

PSALM 76 CONTINUES the discussion begun in Psalm 74 concerning the crisis of exile and the fall of Jerusalem.[1] Psalm 74 laments the desecration of the temple when the armies of Babylon

---

1. Jensen, "Psalm 75," 418–22.

captured Zion. It asks why God stayed his hand and queries why he does not respond to those who continue to mock his name. Psalm 75 picks up on this discussion and argues that God's hand will stretch out in judgment (v. 8), but in his time and not according to anyone else's agenda (v. 2). Psalm 76 continues the response to the lament over the loss of the temple by pointing out that God still dwells in Jerusalem and that he is still mighty in battle regardless of the appearances of the present circumstance. In Psalm 76 the voice of faith sings out clearly, thus pointing the reader of this poem to a reality that far outweighs circumstances.

God Who Is Known in Zion (76:1–3)

THE FIRST THREE VERSES OF PSALM 76 make three statements of faith that set the tone for the song as a whole. First, the psalmist reminds his readers that God is not distant; rather, he has revealed himself to his people (v. 1). Second, regardless of the geographic location of the exiled people, God himself still dwells in Zion (v. 2)! That reality remains undiminished by the people's plight. And third, Israel's God is presented as the one who ends wars—the one who is always able to quell the warmongering of men (v. 3).

God is renowned in Judah. In different ways, Psalms 73 and 74 reflect on questions of the hiddenness of God. Individually in Psalm 73 and corporately in Psalm 74, the poets question the hiddenness of God in the midst of their distress. These reflections center on the thorny issue of what Luther describes as the *deus absconditus*—the hidden God. Psalm 76 continues the response begun in the preceding psalm by reminding the readers that their God, in fact, is not the *deus absconditus*, he is rather the *deus revelatus*—the God who reveals. Yahweh is known to his people, and this revelation of his awesome character remains an established fact regardless of all variations in the present circumstances of those who meditate on this psalm. The passive verb that in the NIV is translated "renowned" (*noda'*) can also be translated "has revealed himself." God has revealed his true character to his people. So, continuing the response to the lament of Psalm 74, the psalmist reminds God's people that those who draw conclusions from historical events alone are inclined to arrive at the wrong conclusion (as in Ps 74:10, 22). Israel's God may appear to have been defeated when Jerusalem fell to the armies of Babylon, but the Creator God *has spoken* of his true nature, and this word of revelation remains untainted by the appearances of historical events. Here in Psalm 76, therefore, the psalmist says, "in Israel his name is great" (v. 1b). For the community of faith, for those who believe in divine revelation despite temporal appearances, Yahweh is still the Great One! His revealed character points to one who remains in complete control regardless of what others may think. God's people are to base their knowledge of him on his spoken word rather than on their apprehension of their current experience.

His tent is in Salem, his dwelling place in Zion. The psalmist's response to the exile and to the lament of Psalm 74 continues in his bold assertion that Yahweh still dwells in Jerusalem on Mount Zion! It is the people who have been displaced, not Yahweh. The temple may have been destroyed, but the spiritual reality of God's chosen place of dwelling continues regardless. Just as Psalm 76:1 points to the revealed character of God that remains unchanged, so verse 2 proclaims that Yahweh's chosen place of "dwelling" on earth remains unchanged. The people have been taken into exile as part of his plan to bring about their repentance (Ps 75), but Yahweh has not been exiled. His greatness remains unchanged, and his choice of dwelling place remains unchanged.

There he broke the flashing arrows. God's greatness is unaffected by historical events; God's dwelling place remains unchanged despite the exile of his people; and third, the community of faith is reminded that their God is the one who brings an end to all wars, the implication being that God has nothing to fear from the axes and destruction of the armies of Psalm 74:4–8. The mention that he has previously brought wars to an end in Jerusalem (Ps 76:3) is probably a reference to the siege of Jerusalem by Sennacherib, king of Assyria, during the reign of Hezekiah around 701 BCE (see 2 Kgs 18–19). The point the psalmist makes to the exiled people of God in response to Psalm 74's lament is that Yahweh has previously turned powerful armies away from the gates of Jerusalem, and, had he wished to do so, he could have done the same in their case. Their circumstances have not come about through weakness or inability on God's part—he shatters the weapons of war! Their present reality is part of his design for their restoration.

The Warrior God (76:4–6)

YOU ARE RADIANT WITH LIGHT. The psalmist continues the theme of God's power in the next stanza of Psalm 76. The imagery of God's being "radiant with light" (v. 4a) speaks of God's great and unquestionable majesty.[2] The picture is of a deity who burns more brightly than the dawning sun. His power is incomparable—even the inherent majesty of the mountains pales in comparison to it. Why they are mountains "rich with game" is something of a mystery, but the description may well refer to the known ancient Near Eastern image that often presented the divine Judge as a lion. The words

---

2. Terrien, *Psalms*, 550.

used for "tent" and "dwelling place" in verse 2 can also refer to the lairs of wild animals,[3] and the language of "breaking" (or perhaps more properly, "shattering") the weapons of war (v. 3) is also commonly applied to the effect of a lion's attack.[4] So the reference to God as being "more majestic than mountains rich with game" may continue this leonine language. Mountains are inherently majestic, and the fact that they are filled with prey for the lion provides a link with the first stanza. But Israel's God is by nature more glorious than the hills and stronger than the lion.

Not one of the warriors can lift his hands. The "hand" theme continues to run through these linked psalms. In the lament of Psalm 74, the people ask why God holds back his "hand" (v. 11). Psalm 75 responds with the voice of assurance that God will act in his time and that he holds the cup of judgment in his "hand" (vv. 2, 8). Psalm 76 inverts this imagery to emphasize the reality of the Creator's awesome power. In Psalm 74 it is the armies of Babylon that are active and powerful, and the people lament Yahweh's inactivity. In Psalm 76 the God who ends wars leaves rebellious armies devastated and powerless—to the extent that "not one of the warriors can lift his hands" (v. 5). Literally, the Hebrew says that they cannot "find" their hands. Far from being powerless, as was the fear of Psalm 74, God's "rebuke" (or "battle cry") is enough to leave those who would seek to prevent his will and purpose incapacitated with fear (v. 6). God's word alone is capable of this effect without his even stirring his "hand" to activity.

Awesome God (76:7–10)

You alone . . . are to be feared. The psalmist's direct speech to God continues in the next stanza with another emphatic use of "you" (v. 7). There is probably something of a play on words in the Hebrew of this verse. The Hebrew word for "radiant with light" (*naor* [v. 4]) and the word for "to be feared" (*nora*) are very similar in appearance and sound, and both are linked to the pronoun "you." These wordplays probably indicate the transition of stanzas and the beginning of a new theme.[5] God is feared as Warrior in verses 4–6 and now he is to be feared as Judge. The Hebrew poetry is perhaps a little more emphatic than the translation found in the NIV and may be rendered, "You are to be feared, YOU!" The words of the psalmist explode with emphasis. The idea of a sovereign's "being feared" in the ancient world was used in much the same way we would use the word

---

3. Eaton, *Psalms*, 275.
4. Hossfeld and Zenger, *Psalms 2*, 265.
5. Schaefer, *Psalms*, 186–87.

"awesome."[6] The imagery of verse 7 tells the reader that any individual who might enter the real presence of God would simply be struck down by the inherently awesome reality of his being, especially were he to be seen when angry. The assurance for the reader is plain. The awesome power of God the Judge is unquestionable, even if at any given moment in time it is shrouded from the eyes of his people.[7]

From heaven you pronounced judgment. The NIV's translation misses the symmetry of the parallelism in verse 8.[8] The first line of the parallelism declares the divine pronouncement of judgment "from heaven." The second part of the parallelism shows the response of absolute silence "on earth." The Hebrew word translated as "the land" (*'erets*) in verse 8 can mean either "the land" or "the earth" as a whole. With the divine pronouncement coming from *heaven*, a parallel reading seems to suggest that it was not the *land* that feared and was silent; rather, the *whole earth* feared and was silent before Yahweh's declaration of judgment.[9] Once again, the imagery speaks of the earth's humble and awestruck response to the majestic power of the living God. Whenever God speaks his decree from heaven, the earthly response is not to debate its merits; rather, the earth is hushed to silence by the inherent power and wisdom of the divine word and waits in silence for the outworking of divine justice.

When you, God, rose up to judge. Again, the psalmist's reminder probably refers to Yahweh's miraculous relief of the Assyrian crisis during the reign of Hezekiah. The people were in a situation that was beyond all human hope. There was nothing they could do to save themselves from the massed armies of the Assyrians, who were famed for their brutality and mercilessness in war. As far as Jerusalem was concerned, the siege was set, and nothing but suffering and death awaited them. This outcome would have been their reality had it not been for the fact that the God who made Jerusalem his dwelling place rose up to judge (2 Kgs 19:35–36). This historical reminder would, of course, be poignant for a people responding to the crisis of exile. In their relatively recent past, God had risen in power to save them from military oppression—the reminder for a lamenting people is that, in working out his justice, their God is capable of saving his people again.

---

6. John Goldingay, *Psalms: Volume 2, Psalms 42–89*, BCOTWP 2 (Grand Rapids: Baker Academic, 2007), 454.

7. Mays, *Psalms*, 250.

8. See the discussion of parallelism in volume 1 of this commentary (Wilson, *Psalms, Volume 1*, 35–57).

9. "The world as a whole thus looks on with awe as Yhwh's decision about the destiny of Israel's attackers is announced" (Goldingay, *Psalms 2*, 454).

While the statement of Psalm 76:9 may well refer to the concrete histor-ical setting of the Assyrian crisis of 701 BCE, we must never forget that the poetry of the Psalter has become generalized so that the lessons learned from concrete historical events can be reapplied to a wide variety of settings.[10] So in reminding the reader of what God did in 701 BCE outside the gates of Jerusalem, the psalmist is also making a general point applicable in all times and all places. Just as God *judged* in power, so the reader should be aware that God *judges* in power. A general principle is derived from a specific event.

To save all the afflicted of the land. It is interesting to note the objective of God's miraculous intervention in the events of humankind. God's judgment "aims at putting an end to violence and the misery from which 'all the poor of the earth' suffer."[11] The working of God's justice is never capricious or nasty. The aim is always to bring peace and restore righteousness on the earth. In the context of the Assyrian crisis, "the afflicted of the land" would refer to the many thousands of innocents who would suffer as a result of the siege of the city. But once again, this principle also can be generalized to describe the way in which Yahweh works as a matter of course. His *spoken judgment* reflects his declared will and purpose for the right ordering of the earth in which we live. His *active judgment* serves these ends. In accordance with his nature, God works to end violence, bring wholeness, and restore the oppressed.

Surely your wrath against mankind brings you praise. Psalm 76:10 is a difficult verse to translate, but the NIV's footnote probably gives the better rendering of the Hebrew ("Surely the wrath of mankind brings you praise, /and with the remainder of wrath you arm yourself."). At this point the verse seems to be talking about human wrath rather than God's, and it gives a different perspective on the machinations of men. In the light of the preceding verses the psalmist is indicating that, ultimately, the anger-filled rebellion of humankind serves God's purposes by giving scope for the full display of his sovereign power. When God does so, those who rebel against Yahweh are ultimately compelled to confess his greatness.

[God's wrath] is also, however, the expression of a militant readiness to bring to reality his universal royal rule, especially against the nations and individuals who oppose it. To that extent divine wrath is not aimed at destruction, but at changing, indeed transforming, the "enemies of God."[12]

---

10. Miller, *Interpreting*, 18–28.
11. Hossfeld and Zenger, *Psalms 2*, 270.
12. Ibid.

God's righteous judgment, forcefully worked out in historical reality, is a sign that points even those who reject him to the greatness and reality of his being. "No-one can resist God when he appears as Warrior to judge his enemies."[13]

The second line of this parallelism refers to God's girding or binding "the survivors of your wrath" to himself. Once again, the Hebrew here is quite difficult to translate; therefore, it is difficult to arrive at the intended meaning of this text with absolute certainty. As with the preceding line of this parallelism, however, it seems that the translation offered in the footnotes of the NIV is probably closer to the truth. "And with the remainder of wrath you arm yourself" is probably a reference to the work of transformation that occurs when Yahweh's enemies are confronted with his glory in Zion. This feature occurs commonly within the psalms celebrating Zion: the expectation that those who rebel against God and his people will somehow be transformed by a dawning realization of his unquestionable presence and power when faced with his glory in Jerusalem (e.g., see Pss 46:8–10; 48:4–7; 72:8–11; also Isa 60; 66:18–24). The powerful implication of this verse is that ultimately the angry rebellion of humankind brings glory to God and will also result in the radical metamorphosis of some to allegiance to Yahweh. Eaton comments that "mankind is won from rebellion to worship God in thanksgiving. Verse 10b then follows with the thought that God girds on the saved people as a garment in closeness to him (cf. Jer 13)."[14] The point of this verse seems to be that not only does God save his own people by bringing human rebellion to an end but in doing so he also brings about the transformation of those very people who rebel against him.

Responding to the Awesome God (76:11–12)

THE CLOSING TWO VERSES OF PSALM 76 address the question of response to such a God. The first three stanzas of the psalm speak about God as Warrior and Judge, the one who ends all wars and rebellion. This final stanza sets out to answer the question of how we respond to such a God.

Make vows to the LORD your God and fulfill them. The fourth stanza is marked by a change from direct speech to God to direct speech to the reader. The reminder is a poignant one: Given that the God who rules

---

13. Longman, *Psalms*, 285.

14. Eaton, *Psalms*, 276. See also Hossfeld and Zenger, who note that "divine wrath is not aimed at destruction, but at changing, indeed transforming, the 'enemies of God.' It is one of the essentials of the Zion theology that the 'enemy nations' subject themselves to the royal rule of the God of Zion and praise his name . . . and it becomes a crucial theme of exilic and postexilic hopes for salvation" (Hossfeld and Zenger, *Psalms 2*, 270).

the universe is this leonine Warrior Judge, be careful how you respond to him! As creatures we have an obligation toward our Creator. The psalmist warns us that we should be diligent in responding properly to the Warrior God. It is interesting to consider who is addressed in this command. Most naturally, of course, the phrase "the LORD your God" seems to indicate that Israel is in the psalmist's mind when he commands fealty to God.[15] The universal implications of verse 10 should not be ignored, however. If the psalmist envisions a remnant from the rebellious nations as ultimately coming to offer allegiance to God, then the extent of this command in the following verse surely must encompass that remnant as well as Israel. In fact, such a command makes sense with an expanded worshiping community in mind. The divine name, Yahweh, appears for the first time in verse 11 as a reminder to Israel and as instruction to the nations that there is only one true God and that he alone is worthy of our gifts of tribute.[16] The more universal aspect of this command is accentuated in verse 11b, where it is the people of neighboring lands who bring their tribute to God, thus acknowledging that he (i.e., not their own gods) is the one to be feared.

He is feared by the kings of the earth. Psalm 76:12 provides an interesting counterpart to verse 1. The first verse of the poem acknowledges that God's revealed character is known in Judah and that his name is great in Israel. But here at the close of the psalm, "the kings of the earth" fear Yahweh. Continuing the eschatological Zion theology of the psalm, verse 12 foresees the day when all the rulers of the earth will acknowledge the undisputed greatness of Israel's God. As is so often the way in the Old Testament, the particular expands to the universal. Israel's acknowledgment of God's greatness serves a purpose; namely, that one day all the nations of the earth will see and acknowledge God's greatness.

THE WARRIOR GOD. An image with which we are relatively unfamiliar in contemporary Christianity is the picture of God as the Warrior-Judge—a picture we see in Ps 76 and in other parts of the Old Testament.[17] How does this square with the presentation of God as loving Father in the New Testament? We should be careful not to misrepresent God in one way or the other; rather, we should view his

---

15. Goldingay, *Psalms 2*, 455.

16. Hossfeld and Zenger, *Psalms 2*, 270–71.

17. For an excellent discussion of this presentation of God in Scripture, see Tremper Longman and Daniel G. Reid, *God is a Warrior* (Carlisle: Paternoster, 1995).

full character as it is represented in both of the Testaments. It has become a popular caricature that the God of the Old Testament is angry, judging, and war-like, whereas the God of the New Testament is peace-loving, gentle, and full of grace. Psalm 76, along with many passages of the Scriptures (in both the Old and New Testaments), testifies to the fact that both images of God faithfully reflect aspects of his character and being. The fact of the matter is that God is both Judge and Father—he is presented as such in the Old Testament, and his nature remains so in the New Testament.

A god who does not or cannot judge is not much of a god. Equally, a god who judges capriciously and out of spite is not to be trusted. In Psalm 76, however, the poet paints a picture of Israel's God as the one who acts decisively in power when needed (vv. 3–10) but also as the God who meets with his people and dwells with them (vv. 1–2). He is the one who brings peace (vv. 3, 8) and justice to the afflicted (v. 9) and who expands his community of blessing to all who acknowledge him, regardless of their starting point (v. 10).

Why would we worship a god who did not care for the weak and oppressed? Why would we follow a god who was impotent to bring about his right purposes? If we are often appalled by the events we see around us, how much more is God horrified by these injustices? What sort of god would he be were he unable or unwilling to rectify wrongs? In a world that is often full of wickedness and oppression of the worst kind, the God who has revealed himself in the Scriptures sometimes breaks into our historical experience in warrior-like power in order to bring an end to abuse. Psalm 76 shows God as being lion-like in power, capable of bringing all violence to an abrupt end. The psalm, however, also shows that his aim in every display of power is the restoration of justice and right order to the earth. Why would we worship any other kind of god?

Psalm 76 in the New Testament. There are no direct citations from Ps 76 in the New Testament; however, the book of Revelation throws up a number of interesting images that bear striking similarity to the language and theology of this poem. Perhaps the most striking of these allusions is John's reference to Jesus as the "Lion of the tribe of Judah" (Rev 5:5). Just as Yahweh is presented as a lion-like Warrior-Judge, so the elders standing before God's throne in heaven proclaim Jesus to be the lion of Judah who has triumphed and who holds the eternal destiny of humankind in his hands. The surprise factor, of course, is that when John looks to see this triumphant lion he actually sees a sacrificed lamb standing in the center of the throne (Rev 5:6). Once again, the New Testament uses Old Testament imagery to equate Jesus with Israel's God. Just as Yahweh is the leonine victor of Psalm 76, so Jesus is also "the Lion of the tribe of Judah"—victorious in power even though that power was ultimately expressed in self-sacrifice. The book of Revelation also, however, points to the day when the Lion's power will be displayed in judgment (Rev 6).

The other interesting connection between Psalm 76 and the close of the New Testament is the question of the incorporation of the nations into the worshiping community of Israel. If we follow the NIV footnote to verse 10, we see that human rebellion ultimately serves God's purposes and results in the inclusion of a remnant of these "rebels" into the community of those who worship God. What is more, the psalmist repeatedly draws our attention to his presentation of God as the awesome, majestic King who is feared by the whole of the created order (vv. 4, 7–8, 11–12). It is interesting to compare Psalm 76's presentation of Yahweh dwelling in Jerusalem in might and power with John's presentation of the New Jerusalem in Revelation 21–22. Psalm 76:11–12 presents the princes and leaders of the nations as making offerings of allegiance to Yahweh because of his indisputable power. The psalm closes with the words, "he is feared by the kings of the earth," and we see an interesting parallel in the imagery of the New Jerusalem as a temple-city—"The nations will walk by its light, and the kings of the earth will bring their splendor into it" (Rev 21:24). Psalm 76 alludes to a day when Yahweh's unquestionable authority leads the world's powerbrokers to offer their allegiance to him. Revelation 21–22 points to the fulfillment of this imagery in the aftermath of the outworking of God's final judgment on humanity.

IMPORTANCE OF REMEMBERING. One of the key lessons from Psalm 76 is the importance of remembering God's works in the past as we consider the challenges we face in the present. As we have charted the connections between Psalms 74–76, it has become apparent that Psalm 76 speaks in response to the crisis of the Babylonian exile. One element of the psalmist's response to Israel's present plight is to direct the people's attention to God's remarkable work of salvation in the past. Previously, God had miraculously relieved a siege of Jerusalem when the Assyrians attacked (2 Kgs 18–19), and the point of the psalmist's reminder is quite simple: God had saved Jerusalem from an impossibly powerful military attack once before, and he is perfectly capable of doing so again; therefore, the fact that he stayed his hand in the present must be part of his purposes for his people. The reminder of God's work in the past was designed to have an impact on the worshiping community's perception of their present circumstances. The practice of remembering is a repeated theme in the Psalter and is one of the central ideas of Psalm 77, so we will consider the importance of remembrance in the life of faith as part of our discussion of the next psalm.

Christus Victor. "Christians using this psalm will think of Christus Victor, whose defeat of the powers of sin and death deepens hope in the sovereign God."[18] Psalm 76's imagery of God as a lion-like Warrior defeating the enemies of his people has been a picture of great encouragement for many generations of faith. It remains so for us today. As James Mays suggests in the above quotation, the absolute victory of God grants us great assurance as people who still struggle with the effects of sin in our lives. It is important for us to realize that our continuing struggle with sin is waged not from a position of human weakness but from a position of divine power. The apostle Paul writes in Colossians 2:13–15:

> When you were dead in your sins and in the uncircumcision of your flesh, God made you alive with Christ. He forgave us all our sins, having canceled the charge of our legal indebtedness, which stood against us and condemned us; he has taken it away, nailing it to the cross. And having disarmed the powers and authorities, he made a public spectacle of them, triumphing over them by the cross.

Just as God's victory over the Assyrians demonstrated his undeniably great power over all of the created order, so Christ's victory over the powers of sin and Satan provides us with an unshakable salvation. Yes, we still struggle with sin, but our struggle is from the position of ultimate victory rather than from a position of weakness and defeat. Jesus made a public spectacle of all the powers of evil that would keep us from coming to God—he triumphed over them by the cross. All such powers have been totally vanquished, and Christians today must remember that truth in our quest for holiness. The God who provides salvation for the oppressed (Ps 76:9) has provided just such a release for all those who find faith in Christ. Day by day it is important to remind ourselves that our struggle with temptation and sin is one in which victory has already been secured. In many ways, this victory over temptation comes down to a question of attitude. Often, due to our repeated failures, we feel weak in our struggle with temptation. Psalm 76 reminds us that the God whom we follow is the Warrior-Judge—the Lion springing forth from his lair—who destroys his people's enemies and provides release from oppression. Daily we must remind ourselves of this truth and turn to this God in expectant prayer. Such acts of remembrance shape the way in which we face the ongoing struggle with sin in our lives.

---

18. Mays, *Psalms*, 251.

Psalm 77

For the director of music. For Jeduthun. Of Asaph. A psalm.

¹ I cried out to God for help;
  I cried out to God to hear me.
² When I was in distress, I sought the Lord;
  at night I stretched out untiring hands,
  and I would not be comforted.
³ I remembered you, God, and I groaned;
  I meditated, and my spirit grew faint.
⁴ You kept my eyes from closing;
  I was too troubled to speak.
⁵ I thought about the former days,
  the years of long ago;
⁶ I remembered my songs in the night.
  My heart meditated and my spirit asked:
⁷ "Will the Lord reject forever?
  Will he never show his favor again?
⁸ Has his unfailing love vanished forever?
  Has his promise failed for all time?
⁹ Has God forgotten to be merciful?
  Has he in anger withheld his compassion?"
¹⁰ Then I thought, "To this I will appeal:
  the years when the Most High stretched out his right hand.
¹¹ I will remember the deeds of the LORD;
  yes, I will remember your miracles of long ago.
¹² I will consider all your works
  and meditate on all your mighty deeds."
¹³ Your ways, God, are holy.
  What god is as great as our God?
¹⁴ You are the God who performs miracles;
  you display your power among the peoples.
¹⁵ With your mighty arm you redeemed your people,
  the descendants of Jacob and Joseph.
¹⁶ The waters saw you, God,
  the waters saw you and writhed;
  the very depths were convulsed.
¹⁷ The clouds poured down water,

the heavens resounded with thunder;
your arrows flashed back and forth.
¹⁸ Your thunder was heard in the whirlwind,
your lightning lit up the world;
the earth trembled and quaked.
¹⁹ Your path led through the sea,
your way through the mighty waters,
though your footprints were not seen.
²⁰ You led your people like a flock
by the hand of Moses and Aaron.

PSALM 77 IS A POWERFUL reminder of the importance of remembrance and remembering in the life of faith. It is a psalm marked by the transition in the heart of the poet from lament and lostness to hope and praise. That transformation of attitude results from the psalmist's conscious decision to focus his attention on the saving works of God in the past. It is this act of remembering that is key to the heart of Psalm 77's message.

The Heading (77:0)

THE SUPERSCRIPTION OF PSALM 77 indicates that it belongs to the collection of Asaph psalms begun with Psalm 73. "Jeduthun" in the title probably refers to one of the other temple music leaders who was a contemporary of Asaph (1 Chr 16:41–42). The preposition 'al (NIV: "For Jeduthun") should probably be read as "according to the style of."[1] The psalm is described as a *mizmor*, the most common designation for the poems of the Psalter, appearing in the titles of some fifty-seven psalms. The term *mizmor* seems simply to mean "a composition."[2]

The Call of Lament (77:1–2)

I CRIED OUT TO GOD FOR HELP. Psalm 77 begins with a description of the appeal to God by the pray-er in his time of distress. In many ways these verses seem typical of the tone of lament that we see in many psalms in Books 1–3. The key difference in comparison with other laments, however, is that in Psalm 77, verses 1–9 refer to the poet's lament in terms

---

1. See Wilson, *Psalms, Volume 1*, 78–81.
2. John Goldingay, *Psalms: Volume 1, Psalms 1–41*, BCOTWP (Grand Rapids: Baker Academic, 2006), 592; Wilson, *Psalms Volume 1*, 127.

of a past narrative. Typically, lament is addressed directly to God in the second person, and the address is very much based on the poet's present experience. Here, however, the psalmist relates his past experience to the reader.[3] He speaks of days of distress (v. 2) when he called out to the Lord in prayer, yet these prayers remained unanswered.[4] The intensity of these prayers is seen in the language used—the language of crying out, being in distress, seeking the Lord, stretching out untiring hands, and refusal to be comforted. These were not the light prayers that we so often offer without any real expectation that God will answer. The psalmist is telling us about deep prayers of the heart. He is relating an account of a protracted time when he grappled with God in prayer.[5] The Hebrew text makes it clear that this pleading to the Lord is vocal—these prayers are cried out audibly. That the poet does so constitutes another sign of the intensity of his plea for divine intervention.

When I was in distress, I sought the Lord. Clearly, the psalmist did the right thing! His trouble was real. The Hebrew word translated "distress" (*tsarah*) in verse 2 conjures up the image of "straits" or "narrows." It is a tight spot, a time when the psalmist feels hemmed in and unable to breathe. But the poet responds rightly to his undefined calamity. Rather than panicking, he seeks the Lord, and he does so day and night. The refusal to be comforted indicates the full extent of his suffering and the greatness of his need for God's help (see Jer 31:15).[6] The fact that the psalmist's soul "would not be comforted" is not meant to reflect intransigence on his part. It is rather an indication that his prayer remains unanswered and, therefore, his grief continues.[7] The poet's attitude in these verses also reflects his awareness of his complete dependence on God. We do not know what challenges he faced, but we see clearly that he was aware that resolution could only be found by the hand of God. Such an attitude of complete dependence on Yahweh is considered meritorious in the Old Testament (Ps 62:7).

Painful Reflection (77:3–6)

I REMEMBERED YOU, GOD, AND I GROANED. In these verses we witness the dissonance between the suppliant's memories of God and his present

---

3. Mays, *Psalms*, 251.
4. Broyles, *Psalms*, 315.
5. Eaton, *Psalms*, 278.
6. Hossfeld and Zenger, *Psalms 2*, 277.
7. "[T]his sentence signifies that the psalm singer is ill-disposed toward all superficial comforting. Psalm 77 lets us discern a seriousness and a depth of enquiry after God that amazes us again and again" (Kraus, *Psalms II*, 115).

experience of unanswered prayer. His memory of past grace made his present suffering all the more difficult to bear. Looking back, he points the reader's attention to a time when not even his reflection on God brought comfort—even his own meditation on God was somehow burdensome. As Craig Broyles comments, "These lonely musings yield pain and longing, leaving the speaker sleepless, speechless and lost in nostalgia."[8]

You kept my eyes from closing. This is the only statement in verses 1–9 that addresses God directly, and these words show us that the psalmist views God as the source of his insomnia. The opening verses of Psalm 77 highlight the dedication and commitment of the poet in prayer, but his reflection and meditation bring him no peace. Sleep would have been a release; verse 4a, however, paints a picture of a God who refused the psalmist sleep, thus forcing him to maintain his vigil of reflection. This very visual image speaks of God as having "seized" (*'ahazta*) the eyelids of the speaker, of keeping his eyes open and refusing to grant him sleep.[9] Despite his wakefulness, the psalmist finds himself unable to speak (v. 4b). Is he intimidated by God's absence and his forceful action in denying him rest? Or is it that he does not want to voice his abject and hopeless meditations? We do not know, but clearly even prayer has become difficult for the poet.[10]

I remembered my songs in the night. Psalm 77:5–6 points to the speaker's reflection on years gone by. The poet realizes that his experiences with God in the past have been different from his present experience and that this contrast is worthy of further consideration. The act of "remembering his songs in the night" indicates that the psalmist consciously contrasts his present experience of exile with times that were much more favorable. It is possible that the songs which the speaker remembered in the night were songs of praise to Yahweh.[11] If so, it is likely that this remembrance of past praise was influential in the transformation that is so clear in Psalm 77. James Mays notes that the praise psalms served an important creedal function in Israel's public worship:

---

8. Broyles, *Psalms*, 316.

9. Goldingay's argument that Yahweh is, in fact, holding the speaker's eyes closed rather than open seems counter-intuitive in the context of the psalm. He suggests that the reason for the poet's failure to find satisfaction in his meditation is that God has refused to reveal himself; hence, the psalmist's eyes are held tight shut (Goldingay, *Psalms 2*, 464). But the image of God as grappling with the speaker, just as the speaker grapples with God, seems to make more sense of the metaphor here. The poet attributes his insomnia to divine activity, thus giving him yet another reason to lament (see Tate, *Psalms 51–100*, 274; Kraus, *Psalms II*, 115; and others).

10. Mays, *Psalms*, 251.

11. Goldingay, *Psalms 2*, 465.

[P]salmic praise is *confessional*. Praise as doxology declares *that* God is. Praise as confession says *who* God is. The hymns of the Psalter were Israel's confession of faith. In them the people of God said— and say—who it is they trust and obey. In the history of worship, we have come to associate the confession of faith with the literary form of the creed, but in the biblical world the congregations' declaration of whom they served took the form of praise.[12]

It is, therefore, not surprising that the remembrance of past hymns of praise sparks a train of thought that leads to transformation. In reciting hymns of praise to himself, the poet is reminded of the true nature of the God who is praised; hence, "my heart meditated and my spirit asked" (v. 6b). The words of the songs begin a process of contemplation that is much more fruitful than the lonely meditations of the preceding verses.

Powerful Rhetorical Questions (77:7–9)

"**WILL THE LORD REJECT FOREVER?**" In speaking of the rhetorical questions that Yahweh fires at Job in response to his complaint, John Eaton writes, "Questions are the most arresting form of address and here bring home the full the weight of the theme."[13] Precisely the same effect is at work here in Psalm 77:7–9, except that it is the psalmist's self-interrogation that brings home the full weight of realization. Singing psalms of praise, with all their creedal statements about the faithfulness of Yahweh and the fact that his steadfast love endures forever, triggers a train of thought that is inescapable for the speaker in this psalm. "Will the Lord reject forever? Will he never show his favor again? Has his unfailing love vanished forever? Has God forgotten to be merciful?"

The rhetorical questions speak for themselves and lead the psalmist to a conclusion grounded in faith that belies the difficulties of his present circumstances. The whole point of "unfailing love" is that it is *unfailing*![14] God's promise never fails, and, even at the time of Israel's great rebellion in worshiping the golden calf, Yahweh reveals himself to be slow to anger and abounding in steadfast love (Exod 34:6–7). The psalmist is asking questions to which he already knows the answer. The songs he sang in the night reminded him of what he already knew—the faithfulness of God

---

12. James L. Mays, *The Lord Reigns* (Louisville: Westminster John Knox, 1994), 65.

13. John H. Eaton, *Job*, OTG (Sheffield: Sheffield Academic, 1996), 26.

14. It is, of course, possible that these questions are accusatory (Longman, *Psalms*, 287); however, a transformation clearly occurs in the following stanza, and it seems that this rhetorical reflection paves the way for that change of heart and mind.

never fails. The pray-er focuses on attributes of God that are inextricably linked with his good character—his favor (*ratsab*), his covenantal love (*hesed*), his promise (*'omer*), his grace (*hinnen*), and his mercy (*raham*). These key terms are intimately linked with God's unchanging faithfulness toward his people based on the binding promise between him and them. These attributes are non-negotiables of Yahweh's character. He can no more deny these characteristics of his being and his sworn means of relationship with his people than deny his own existence. This self-interrogation reminds the speaker of what he knows about his God and, once again, this reminder brings remarkable transformation.

Appeal to the Past (77:10–15)

THEN I THOUGHT, "TO THIS I WILL APPEAL: THE YEARS WHEN THE MOST HIGH STRETCHED OUT HIS RIGHT HAND." Psalm 77:10 serves as the pivot around which this poem revolves. The psalmist's questions reveal to him the course of action he must take. He realizes that, if his God is truly gracious and merciful, then his appeal must be directed to God and based on the reminder of Yahweh's own works in the past.

There is much debate about the translation of this verse. Several translations follow an alternative rendering of this statement along the lines of the NRSV, namely, "And I say, 'It is my grief that the right hand of the Most High has changed.'" From a purely linguistic perspective, both translation options are valid and, indeed, many of the commentators translate verse 10 along the lines of the NRSV.[15] But consideration of how we translate

---

15. See, for example, Goldingay, *Psalms 2*, 476; Mays, *Psalms*, 252. See also the discussion of an alternative translation of this verse in J. A. Emerton, "The Text of Psalm LXXVII 11," *VT* XLIV.2 (1994): 183–94. Acknowledging that it is more likely that verse 10 should be read positively rather than negatively, Emerton suggests that a slight emendation of the original Hebrew text would leave our reading along the lines of, "And I said, 'That is my hope; the years of the right hand of the Most High.'" While this rendering is certainly possible and makes good sense of the transition from lament to confidence in the psalm, it is always difficult with any degree of certainty to establish changes that may have occurred in the text. The problem revolves around the translation of the Hebrew verb *halah* and the linked term *shanot*. *Halah* can carry two major meanings: either "to be grieved or sickened" by something or "to entreat the favour of someone" ("חלה," *HALOT* 1:316). *Shanot* can either be a plural noun meaning "years" (as in v. 5) or an infinitive form of the verb *shanah*, meaning "to change." What is more, when *halah* is used to refer to an appeal or entreaty, it is normally followed by the preposition *pene*, meaning "before" or "in the presence of" someone. This preposition, however, does not appear in verse 10. The complexity of these various options gives rise to genuine difficulty in arriving at a definitive translation for this verse, as is reflected in the different approaches of the commentators. But on balance and despite difficulties with the translation, the NIV's rendering is probably the right one. As Broyles

this verse must take its cue from the context and natural flow of the poem itself. The rhetorical questions that precede this statement (vv. 7–9) all imply the answer that God will not reject his people forever and that he will be faithful to his promise. Equally, the verses that follow speak of the poet's remembrance of the saving works of Yahweh in the past and his goodness toward his own people (vv. 11–15). It is striking that the most logical translation of verse 10 is not as a lament over the fact that God's dealings with his people have changed but rather as a pivotal statement of reorientation for the psalmist. The speaker's present experience is difficult, but he consciously decides to make his appeal to God based on divine faithfulness in the past and the unchangeable nature of his character. Eaton is correct when he writes,

> This pivotal verse has been rendered in widely differing ways, the Hebrew being ambiguous. . . . However, the preceding occurrence of the 'pause' [Hebrew *selah*], and also the force of 'And/But I say', make it more probable that this verse introduces the hymnic section, countering the preceding questions. As in the Asaph Psalm 74, the ancient work of God is to be recounted as plea for its renewal.[16]

The poet's decision to appeal to "the years when the Most High stretched out his right hand" suggests he has found a new focus for his prayer that had somehow fallen by the wayside in his previous intercession. He focuses his mind on the saving works of God in the past. The right hand of God is a metaphor that points to his power and ability to deliver his people from any threat, as perhaps most clearly seen in the saving works of God in the exodus. Exodus 15:6 celebrates the work of Yahweh's right hand in delivering his people from the impossible situation at the Red Sea. The massed ranks of the Egyptian army on one side, the impassible waters of the sea on the other—how could people possibly be delivered from this threat? "Your right hand, LORD, was majestic in power. Your right hand, LORD, shattered the enemy" rings the Song of Moses after God has worked out a remarkable salvation for them. What is more, the speaker acknowledges that the people of God have experienced such works of deliverance throughout many generations in the past. The experience of deliverance has been their norm for many years, and, despite the present difficulty, Israel's God has not changed. So the poet decides to refocus

---

comments, "In view of the striking change that takes place in the psalm's appeal at this point, the latter rendering [i.e., "To this I will appeal: the years when the Most High stretched out his right hand"] is more appropriate for this transitional verse" (*Psalms*, 318).

16. Eaton, *Psalms*, 278.

his prayers through a new prism—the conscious remembrance of the faithfulness and powerful works of God in the past.

I will remember the deeds of the Lord. This re-centering of the psalmist's intercession is echoed in verses 11–12. Note the language that is used here: "I will remember," "I will remember," "I will meditate," and "I will consider." These acts are conscious on the part of the speaker. He makes a decision to view his current experience in the light of God's deeds in the past. And what are the objects of this remembrance? Yahweh's miracles, his works, his mighty deeds. The psalmist realizes that remembering what the Lord has done in the past makes it easier to face the challenges of the present. God, of course, is never bound by his previous activity—his interaction with his people, however, reveals his changeless character, which therefore legitimately shapes the expectations of his people.

Your ways, God, are holy. What god is so great as our God? It seems reasonable to ask what has changed in the heart of the poet between his burdensome remembrance of God in verse 3 and the release-providing remembrance of God's deeds in verses 10–15. The same activities are indicated both in the initial lament and in the hymn of praise and hope that follows (i.e., remembering and meditating). How can they produce such different effects? While it is impossible to enter into the inner thought processes of the psalmist, there does seem to be a transformation in the *type of remembrance* practiced in each section of the psalm. Could it be that verses 1–5 smack just a little bit of self-pitying nostalgia? These verses paint an image of the psalmist as alone with his thoughts, possibly reminiscing about former and better days in an unproductive way. Verses 10–15, however, reveal a dynamic wherein remembrance leads not to nostalgia but to prayer. Having reminded himself of the works of the Lord (vv. 10–12), the speaker goes on to remind *God* of his saving works in the past. At this point in the psalmist's experience the act of remembering becomes a spur to pray. Remembering has unleashed a new confidence that is reflected in the *activity* of the psalmist as opposed to his *passivity* in the earlier lament. Clearly, calling to mind the activities of God in behalf of his people has given the poet new confidence by reminding him that his God is worthy of trust because he has proved himself countless times in the past. No other god can compare with the God who has delivered his people time and time again. Such a God can be trusted even when circumstances would indicate otherwise—hence the psalmist's transformation of attitude.

> The speaker now not only remembers God in his own heart and spirit (vv. 3, 6, i.e., privately); he reminds God of the saving precedent that he established himself by his own acts. When left to ourselves,

memories can lead to nostalgia and despair, but when presented to God they can become a powerful appeal for renewal.[17]

In reminding himself and God of God's miraculously powerful saving works in the past, the psalmist discovers new hope.

Remembering Past Victory (77:16–20)

THE WATERS SAW YOU AND WRITHED. The psalmist moves from generic celebration of God's salvific work in the past to specific commemoration of the ultimate example of divine salvation in the Old Testament, namely, the exodus from Egypt. Even more particularly, the poet commemorates what is arguably the most miraculous of all the miracles worked by Yahweh to secure the release of his people from slavery, namely, the parting of the Red Sea (Exod 14). The author personifies the sea as a combatant in a struggle with Yahweh—a combatant who is utterly defeated in the divine work of salvation. Neither the armies on one side of Israel nor the sea on the other constitute any sort of risk or danger for God's people, for he is the Warrior God working on their behalf. The waters were entirely vanquished at the coming of the Lord—his appearance established his power and the salvation of his people.

The imagery of verses 17–18 is typical of psalmic accounts of theophany (cf. Ps 18:7–15). Clouds, thunder, lightning, and the quaking of the earth typically mark the physical manifestation of God on earth in the Old Testament (e.g., see Exod 20:18–21; Deut 5:22–27). The psalmist is clearly implying that Yahweh was really present with his people in the outworking of the miraculous act of salvation that was the parting of the Red Sea (Exod 15:6–12). Perhaps the most interesting aspect of the divine theophany at the Red Sea in the presentation of Psalm 77 is that Yahweh, although present, went unseen.

Your path led through the sea, your way through the mighty waters, though your footprints were not seen. Of course, there are challenges in following an invisible God. His power was made manifest in the parting of the sea, but the people had to follow with the water piled up on both sides. The psalmist implies that God's presence and power are always without question, yet his purposes and ways are sometimes hidden to his people. It is easy to see how this lesson would be deeply meaningful to Israel in the exilic or postexilic period. Yahweh is still the God of miraculous salvation even though his purposes are opaque for his

---

17. Broyles, *Psalms*, 316.

people at this time. "Even in the most magnificent of God's revelations, he remains profoundly hidden. His acts must be recognized by faith."[18]

The Good Shepherd (77:20)

THE FINAL VERSE OF PSALM 77 speaks through the emotive imagery of care implied by the shepherd-flock metaphor. Once again, we find language that echoes the Song of Moses, which celebrates Yahweh's leadership and guidance of his people. Interestingly, there the term translated "your holy dwelling" (*naveh* [Exod 15:13]) is often used to refer to a place for pasturing sheep.[19] Moses acknowledges Yahweh's shepherding of his people through many dangers to a place of divine provision and protection. The same imagery is in play here in Psalm 77:20. The image of God as Shepherd in the ancient Near East speaks of both divine kingship and of divine care. Just as the flock is obliged to follow the shepherd, so also the shepherd is expected to look after the sheep. Following on from verse 19 it seems significant that Yahweh led the people by the hand of Moses and Aaron. Seen through the eyes of faith, it was God who led the way through the raging waters of the Red Sea; however, visibly speaking it was Moses and Aaron who guided the people through the waters onto dry land. As is most often the case in the Scriptures, God worked through human agents in the exodus, yet the release of the Israelites was *God's* work. The divine activity underlying the political exchange between Pharaoh and Moses is seen through faith. The question of whether our focus falls on the work of agents or the activity of the Prime Mover is entirely dependent upon the attitude of the observer. This abrupt ending to the psalm leaves the reader with that challenge. Will we look beyond the external appearance of present circumstances and seek out the divine purpose in the events we face? God led the way through the raging waters of the Red Sea, yet his footsteps were invisible. In terms of appearances, Moses and Aaron led the flock. The psalmist finishes with a clear reminder to the people that appearances can be deceptive. The turmoil of exile can make it appear that God is not in control. Conscious acts of remembrance, however, remind us of the true nature of God, the unfailing character of his love, the greatness of his salvation, and the hiddenness of his ways. Psalm 77:20 is a reminder to view life through the eyes of faith and in the knowledge of God. "The psalm invites us as readers to ponder the mystery of the 'unknown tracks' of God in the midst of our distress. Has his loyal-love (v 9) failed? Can we

---

18. Broyles, *Psalms*, 317.
19. Goldingay, *Psalms 2*, 472.

still trust his promises? Verses 12–21 give us the basis for an affirmative answer, but the decision is ours."[20]

THE SHEPHERD-KING IN THE PSALTER. The image of God as Shepherd and Israel as his flock is one we will return to when we examine the "LORD reigns" psalms (Pss 93–100), but this rich theme is worthy of mention here because of its significance to the overall theology of Psalm 77. When we chart the flow of this poem, we see the movement from the psalmist's doubt-filled lament to a confident trust based on his remembrance of Yahweh's past saving deeds. A significant part of this transition is rooted in the final climactic statement of Psalm 77. The speaker remembers that Yahweh is a Shepherd who guides his people by the agency of servants, who are also meant to shepherd the people. Clearly, the shepherd metaphor speaks of protection and care, for these duties comprise the herdsman's primary responsibility toward his flock— protecting them from the dangers of thieves and wild animals and leading them to places where they will find pasture and water. In the context of the ancient world, however, the shepherd metaphor also speaks about rule and authority, with marked royal connotations. We see an example of this meaning in Ezekiel 34, where the kings of Israel are criticized by the prophet because of their failures with regard to their role as shepherds. They failed to provide leadership and care for Israel (Ezek 34:1–10) to such an extent that Yahweh himself had to intervene in order to gather his wandered flock, protect them, and provide for them (Ezek 34:11–16);[21] hence the rich significance of Psalm 23's declaration of the Lord as the psalmist's Shepherd. But the reminder of the rod and staff that comfort (v. 4) is also a reminder of the kingship and rule of God. The images of the rod and the staff are more commonly associated with the scepter of the king. They are symbols of rule as much as they are signs of protection.[22] The significance of this royal symbolism here at the close of Psalm 77 is vital to the transformation experienced by the psalmist. The act of remembering the salvific deeds of God worked on behalf of his people in the past (vv. 10–12) reminds the psalmist of the true nature and identity of his God (vv. 12–20). This remembrance of God's identity culminates in the confession of his leadership as Shepherd-King (v. 20). Essentially, the

---

20. Tate, *Psalms 51–100*, 276.
21. McCann, *Theological Introduction*, 129.
22. Wilson, *Psalms, Volume 1*, 435.

speaker remembers that God rules. Sometimes his purposes are difficult for us to understand (the unseen footprints of v. 19), but his sovereign governance over all things is beyond question. Sometimes there may be a gap between our knowledge of God's providential rule on our behalf and the experience of it on a daily basis. Herein lies the root of the psalmist's problem in verses 1–9—there was a gap between his awareness of divine power and protection and his experience of it. But the confessional value of singing psalms of praise in the night redirected the psalmist from his focus on the subjectivity of present difficulties to his remembrance of the objective and unchangeable truth of Yahweh's powerful care for his people as the Shepherd-King whose sovereignty is absolute.

The exodus in the Psalter. Another interesting aspect of Psalm 77 is the psalmist's recourse to the exodus from Egypt as the greatest expression of God's salvific work on behalf of his people. This theme becomes even more explicit in the following poems—Psalms 78, 80, and 81—and perhaps comes to the fore most fully in Book 4 of the Psalter. Given that Book 3 (Pss 73–89) is dominated by the language, imagery, and anguish of the exile, it is perhaps not surprising that the exodus is foregrounded in the "story" of this section of the book of Psalms. The exodus represents the clearest example of God's powerful, redemptive work to bring release to his oppressed people. It is easy to see how these psalms provide comfort for people in need of release from foreign power and oppression.

> In the postexilic period, the use of the two other pairs of "Exodus Psalms" [including Pss 77 and 78] is admittedly less subversive, for the context concerns the raising up of a people brought low by the exile; in this sense there is a greater continuity between the essence of the Exodus tradition (God's protection of the oppressed) and its later interpretation.[23]

The reminder of God's power expressed in the exodus gives hope to people requiring release from oppression in their present reality. Just as Moses said to Israel when they were faced with the Red Sea on one side and the terrors of the Egyptian army on the other, "Do not be afraid. Stand firm and you will see the deliverance the LORD will bring you today" (Exod 14:13), so also remembrance of that salvation gives hope to people without strength in every generation.[24]

---

23. Susan E. Gillingham, "The Exodus Tradition and Israelite Psalmody," *SJT* 52.1 (1999): 45.

24. C. Hassell Bullock, *Encountering the Book of Psalms: A Literary and Theological Introduction* (Grand Rapids: Baker Academic, 2001), 106–107.

Psalm 77 in the New Testament. There are no direct citations or allusions from Psalm 77 in the New Testament. Some of the imagery of this poem, however, represents themes that are richly apparent throughout the whole Bible. In particular, and in a manner somewhat akin to that in Psalm 74, Jesus' authority over the waves echoes Yahweh's dominance of the seas in Psalm 77:16–19 (e.g., see Matt 8:23–27). Yahweh's unseen footprints leading through the sea (Ps 77:19) may be more specifically echoed in Jesus' walking on the water (Matt 14:22–36). Here again Christ shows his absolute mastery over the waves and demonstrates that his way cannot be limited by meaningless obstacles such as "mighty waters." The absolute sovereignty of Yahweh in Psalm 77 is reflected in the absolute sovereignty of Christ over the seas in the Gospels. Similarly, Romans 11:33 may well echo Psalm 77:19—"his paths beyond tracing out." Paul's doxology in Romans reflects upon the inscrutability of God's ways, as do the poet's words in Psalm 77.

 THE IMPORTANCE OF REMEMBERING. As mentioned briefly in our consideration of Psalm 76, we see once again the importance of remembering the works of God in the past if we are to have a right perspective on our present reality. We do not know the specifics of the speaker's difficulties in Psalm 77, but clearly his days and nights have been dark and his distress has been great. Even meditating on God has not helped him find comfort in his problem (v. 3). There is a difference, however, between nostalgia and remembrance. The poet's transition from distress to confidence is triggered by remembrance of "the years when the Most High stretched out his right hand" (v. 10). This pivotal verse marks the movement from what was, perhaps, general and aimless reflection to a purposeful bringing to mind of the ways in which God has saved and helped his people in the past.

Altars are of great significance in the Old Testament. Whenever God made a promise to his people, an altar was built as a physical act of remembrance of that promise (e.g., Abram in Gen 12:7)—an altar that served as a physical reminder of the promise made by God. As time passed and circumstances changed, the recipient of the promise could return to the altar as a reminder of the certainty of the divine word even when present circumstances indicated a different reality. Altars were also raised in order to commemorate God's mighty works of help or salvation on behalf of the community of faith (e.g., after the crossing of the Jordan in Josh 4). Building an altar serves as an act of remembrance that reminds the people of God's care, power, and help (Josh 4:19–24). Time and time again the Old Testament makes clear the importance of remembering for the spiritual health of God's people. Observing the Passover is an act of remembrance that speaks to the people of God's power and salvation (Exod 13). Phylacteries tied to hands and heads or doorposts and gates were meant to remind the people of the importance of holistic love for God (Deut 6:8). Tassels on cloaks served as reminders of the importance of keeping God's laws (Num 15:38–41). The Old Testament is full of indications that remembering the character, works, and faithfulness of God is essential for healthy spirituality and a proper perspective on the life we live.

The book of Deuteronomy is designed to be an expression of the covenantal relationship between God and his people for their new situation as those who were soon to dwell in a land of their own. The people are about to experience a change of status from being a nomadic people entirely dependent on God as they wandered through the desert to being a landed people who are able to plant and grow crops, raise up vineyards, and dig wells for themselves. The danger that accompanies their new situation is, of course, that the people turn their hearts from an attitude of dependence on God to an attitude of self-sufficiency (Deut 8). So it is that Deuteronomy is absolutely full of exhortations to remember God and his gracious works.[25] The text of this Old Testament book makes it absolutely plain that right relationship with God requires a good spiritual memory, and the same is absolutely true for the Christian community of faith in our generation. Just as the Passover was a reminder of God's saving work for the covenant community in the pre-Christian era, so also the Lord's Supper is a commemoration of Christ's saving work on behalf of the Christian community of faith (Luke 22:18–19). Taking the bread and wine reminds us of Jesus' body and blood, which were willingly given and spilt so that all who believe in him can enjoy renewed and eternal relationship with God. "Taking communion" is an act of remembrance. In celebrating this sacrament, we are reminded of all that we have in Christ (forgiveness, cleansing, restored standing in the eyes of the Father, etc.), and we are also reminded of the great cost at which this change of status was bought for us. If we are to *go on* in our walk with God, we must remember what has *gone before* in our walk with him. New days and new circumstances will present new challenges, but it is only forgetfulness with regard to God's faithfulness in the past that will place us in a position of fear as we face

---

25. See, for example, Deut 4:10; 5:15; 7:18; 8:2, 18; 9:7, 27; 11:2; 15:15; 16:3, 12; 24:9, 18, 22; 25:17; 32:7, and the corresponding exhortations not to forget in 4:9, 23; 6:12; 8:11; 25:19.

uncertainties in the future. The memories of yesterday in the conscious bringing to mind of God's past activity on our behalf, on the other hand, brings confidence for tomorrow.

Psalm 77 also speaks of the important role that song can play in remembering God and maintaining the right perspective in difficult days. Verse 6 indicates that remembering songs in the night moved the psalmist's thought processes in a much more positive direction. These songs reminded him that the Lord does not reject forever and that his love his unfailing (vv. 7–9). It is, of course, quite possible that the poet is referring to the Psalms themselves, and in singing these songs he is reminded of the true character of God that remains unchanged and unchangeable. As suggested above, it is quite possible that the speaker reverted to singing the songs of praise that played something of a creedal role in the worship life of Israel. It is interesting to note that the psalmist reverts to songs of praise even at a time when his heart would be disinclined to praise. These praises spoke about the true nature of God, and there is a lesson here for contemporary readers of Psalms as well. The Psalter makes it absolutely plain that there are times when it is appropriate to express honest complaint against God, but Psalm 77 reminds us that sometimes our problems lie in forgetfulness with regard to God's faithfulness in the past. In singing praises to God, sometimes we will discover newfound confidence based on these songs' professions of faith. Songs of praise, ancient hymns, Christmas carols, and the like all celebrate the goodness of God toward his people and the works he has done on their behalf. Reminding ourselves of these truths can result in a dramatic change of perspective, from hopelessness to confidence, as we think deeply and powerfully about God's faithfulness to his people in the past.

If we are to go on in the faith, our spirituality must be marked by remembrance of the past as much as it is marked by vision for the future. The trials and difficulties of today remain real, but our view of them is transformed by the practice of remembrance. The insurmountable becomes doable as we remember the God who in the past has worked miracles to help his people. It is important to remember.

Psalm 78

A maskil of Asaph.

¹ My people, hear my teaching;
    listen to the words of my mouth.
² I will open my mouth with a parable;
    I will utter hidden things, things from of old—
³ things we have heard and known,
    things our ancestors have told us.
⁴ We will not hide them from their descendants;
    we will tell the next generation
the praiseworthy deeds of the LORD,
    his power, and the wonders he has done.
⁵ He decreed statutes for Jacob
    and established the law in Israel,
which he commanded our ancestors
    to teach their children,
⁶ so the next generation would know them,
    even the children yet to be born,
    and they in turn would tell their children.
⁷ Then they would put their trust in God
    and would not forget his deeds
    but would keep his commands.
⁸ They would not be like their ancestors—
    a stubborn and rebellious generation,
whose hearts were not loyal to God,
    whose spirits were not faithful to him.
⁹ The men of Ephraim, though armed with bows,
    turned back on the day of battle;
¹⁰ they did not keep God's covenant
    and refused to live by his law.
¹¹ They forgot what he had done,
    the wonders he had shown them.
¹² He did miracles in the sight of their ancestors
    in the land of Egypt, in the region of Zoan.
¹³ He divided the sea and led them through;
    he made the water stand up like a wall.
¹⁴ He guided them with the cloud by day

and with light from the fire all night.
¹⁵ He split the rocks in the wilderness
    and gave them water as abundant as the seas;
¹⁶ he brought streams out of a rocky crag
    and made water flow down like rivers.
¹⁷ But they continued to sin against him,
    rebelling in the wilderness against the Most High.
¹⁸ They willfully put God to the test
    by demanding the food they craved.
¹⁹ They spoke against God;
    they said, "Can God really
    spread a table in the wilderness?
²⁰ True, he struck the rock,
    and water gushed out,
    streams flowed abundantly,
but can he also give us bread?
    Can he supply meat for his people?"
²¹ When the LORD heard them, he was furious;
    his fire broke out against Jacob,
    and his wrath rose against Israel,
²² for they did not believe in God
    or trust in his deliverance.
²³ Yet he gave a command to the skies above
    and opened the doors of the heavens;
²⁴ he rained down manna for the people to eat,
    he gave them the grain of heaven.
²⁵ Human beings ate the bread of angels;
    he sent them all the food they could eat.
²⁶ He let loose the east wind from the heavens
    and by his power made the south wind blow.
²⁷ He rained meat down on them like dust,
    birds like sand on the seashore.
²⁸ He made them come down inside their camp,
    all around their tents.
²⁹ They ate till they were gorged—
    he had given them what they craved.
³⁰ But before they turned from what they craved,
    even while the food was still in their mouths,
³¹ God's anger rose against them;
    he put to death the sturdiest among them,
    cutting down the young men of Israel.

³² In spite of all this, they kept on sinning;
  in spite of his wonders, they did not believe.
³³ So he ended their days in futility
  and their years in terror.
³⁴ Whenever God slew them, they would seek him;
  they eagerly turned to him again.
³⁵ They remembered that God was their Rock,
  that God Most High was their Redeemer.
³⁶ But then they would flatter him with their mouths,
  lying to him with their tongues;
³⁷ their hearts were not loyal to him,
  they were not faithful to his covenant.
³⁸ Yet he was merciful;
  he forgave their iniquities
  and did not destroy them.
Time after time he restrained his anger
  and did not stir up his full wrath.
³⁹ He remembered that they were but flesh,
  a passing breeze that does not return.
⁴⁰ How often they rebelled against him in the wilderness
  and grieved him in the wasteland!
⁴¹ Again and again they put God to the test;
  they vexed the Holy One of Israel.
⁴² They did not remember his power—
  the day he redeemed them from the oppressor,
⁴³ the day he displayed his signs in Egypt,
  his wonders in the region of Zoan.
⁴⁴ He turned their river into blood;
  they could not drink from their streams.
⁴⁵ He sent swarms of flies that devoured them,
  and frogs that devastated them.
⁴⁶ He gave their crops to the grasshopper,
  their produce to the locust.
⁴⁷ He destroyed their vines with hail
  and their sycamore-figs with sleet.
⁴⁸ He gave over their cattle to the hail,
  their livestock to bolts of lightning.
⁴⁹ He unleashed against them his hot anger,
  his wrath, indignation and hostility—
  a band of destroying angels.
⁵⁰ He prepared a path for his anger;

he did not spare them from death
but gave them over to the plague.
⁵¹ He struck down all the firstborn of Egypt,
the firstfruits of manhood in the tents of Ham.
⁵² But he brought his people out like a flock;
he led them like sheep through the wilderness.
⁵³ He guided them safely, so they were unafraid;
but the sea engulfed their enemies.
⁵⁴ And so he brought them to the border of his holy land,
to the hill country his right hand had taken.
⁵⁵ He drove out nations before them
and allotted their lands to them as an inheritance;
he settled the tribes of Israel in their homes.
⁵⁶ But they put God to the test
and rebelled against the Most High;
they did not keep his statutes.
⁵⁷ Like their ancestors they were disloyal and faithless,
as unreliable as a faulty bow.
⁵⁸ They angered him with their high places;
they aroused his jealousy with their idols.
⁵⁹ When God heard them, he was furious;
he rejected Israel completely.
⁶⁰ He abandoned the tabernacle of Shiloh,
the tent he had set up among humans.
⁶¹ He sent the ark of his might into captivity,
his splendor into the hands of the enemy.
⁶² He gave his people over to the sword;
he was furious with his inheritance.
⁶³ Fire consumed their young men,
and their young women had no wedding songs;
⁶⁴ their priests were put to the sword,
and their widows could not weep.
⁶⁵ Then the Lord awoke as from sleep,
as a warrior wakes from the stupor of wine.
⁶⁶ He beat back his enemies;
he put them to everlasting shame.
⁶⁷ Then he rejected the tents of Joseph,
he did not choose the tribe of Ephraim;
⁶⁸ but he chose the tribe of Judah,
Mount Zion, which he loved.
⁶⁹ He built his sanctuary like the heights,

like the earth that he established forever.
⁷⁰ He chose David his servant
and took him from the sheep pens;
⁷¹ from tending the sheep he brought him
to be the shepherd of his people Jacob,
of Israel his inheritance.
⁷² And David shepherded them with integrity of heart;
with skillful hands he led them.

THIS HISTORICAL PSALM represents a challenge to every generation of the community of faith by calling on them to remember the failures of past generations as a reminder and warning that they should not fall prey to the mistakes of their forefathers. It is a lengthy psalm (the longest in the Psalter apart from Ps 119), and a number of ancient commentators seem to find its length and tone wearisome.[1] Unlikely as it may seem to us, however, this psalm is framed in the context of public worship, or at least in the context of some sort of public performance ("My people, hear my teaching" [v. 1]). Psalm 78 focuses on the failures of God's people to live in accordance with his teaching—despite the fact that they had seen his great power and love at work in the plagues that secured their release from captivity in Egypt and resulted in the formation of Israel as a nation. Although the psalm covers the whole swathe of Israel's history from the exodus through to David's reign, there is a sense in which the reader is drawn rhetorically to read the psalm from the perspective of the wilderness generation (vv. 12–43) and the people living in the time of the Judges (vv. 56–64). The *reading* locus centers on those generations of God's people who failed in their call to be faithful to him. The *teaching* locus of the psalm is that the current generation of God's people should not make the same mistake (v. 8). The connection between Psalm 78 and the preceding poems of Book 3 is found in the theme of remembrance. As with Psalms 76 and 77, it is in remembering the past (whether positive or negative examples from it) that the reader finds direction for the present.

The Heading (78:0)

AS WE HAVE SEEN PREVIOUSLY (in the heading of Ps 74), Psalm 78 is also described as a *maskil* of Asaph. While it is impossible to determine for

---

1. Goldingay, *Psalms* 2, 479. Jerome, for example, describes the psalm as "endless," and Cassiodorus remarks that its length induces "weariness."

certain what is implied by this Hebrew term, it does appear to have wisdom or contemplative overtones. The Hebrew verb *sakal* (from which the noun *maskil* is derived) generally means "to understand" or "to have insight."[2] The *maskil*, therefore, is often thought of as referring to a didactic or meditative poem.[3] Clearly, not all the psalms that take the heading *maskil* can be described as wisdom psalms. But the strongly didactic flavor of Psalm 78 combined with the first two verses, which are couched in wisdom terminology, means that we have fairly good reason to assume this poem is in fact the product of Israel's ancient wisdom schools.[4]

Learning from History (78:1–8)

MY PEOPLE, HEAR MY TEACHING. The opening words of Psalm 78 are replete with the language of Old Testament wisdom literature. The public call to "hear my teaching" (lit., "give ear to my instruction [*torati*]" [v. 1]) would normally be associated either with the office of prophet (e.g., see Isa 28:23) or wisdom teacher (Job 33:1). But the "parable" and the "hidden things" (more literally, "proverb" [*mashal*] and "riddle" [*hidot*], Ps 78:2) are the domain of the wisdom teacher.[5] Psalm 78:1–2 present the reader with a context for understanding what is to follow: "Heads up! This is important instruction. Watch out for the lessons to be learned from this poem." Such was the purpose of the wisdom teacher—to instruct God's people in the way of life and fear of the Lord. This interpretive call applies just as much to readers of our generation. We too are forewarned that teaching follows the psalmist's call, so we should be prepared to see and heed concrete lessons from this poem.

Things we have heard and known, things our ancestors have told us. The psalmist continues his instructional theme by discussing the transmission of teaching from one generation to the next (vv. 3–4). He will teach "hidden things, things from of old" to the present generation of God's people (v. 2). These weighty matters are not new teachings; rather,

---

2. "שָׂכַל," *HALOT* 2:1329.

3. Herbert Wolf, "*maskil*" *TWOT* 2:877–88.

4. R. Norman Whybray, "The Wisdom Psalms," in *Wisdom in Ancient Israel: Essays in Honour of J. A. Emerton*, ed. J. Day, R. P. Gordon, and H. G. M. Williamson (Cambridge: Cambridge University Press, 1995), 158.

5. It is difficult to assess whether there is an idea of "hiddenness" implied by the psalmist's use of the word "riddle." Often the word is used in wisdom literature to speak of hidden truths that require wisdom in order to discern their meaning. But in the context of Ps 78:2, it seems more likely that the speaker is simply referring to "mysteries" or "deep truths" that are to be derived from the history of Israel's dealings with God. See Eaton, *Psalms*, 283.

this is wisdom that had been taught by the preceding generation of God's people. The teacher's exhortation is that the current generation should not fail in its responsibility to teach these selfsame lessons to the succeeding generation (v. 4).

This emphasis on the importance of the transmission of God's teaching from one generation to the next is reminiscent of the instruction of Deuteronomy. The centerpiece of Old Testament faith is known as the Shema—"Hear, O Israel: The LORD our God, the LORD is one. Love the LORD your God with all your heart and with all your soul and with all your strength" (Deut 6:4–5). This call to singularity of worship and whole-hearted devotion to the living God is immediately followed by instruction concerning the transmission of this foundational teaching from one generation to the next (vv. 6–9). Clearly, it is never enough for any particular generation to be so focused on their own piety that they should fail in their responsibility to instruct the generations that follow. In the theology of Deuteronomy, practice and instruction are inseparable. As each generation learns what it means to have the commandments of the Lord on their own hearts in their own context (v. 6), so too, simultaneously, they bear the obligation to teach these commandments to the succeeding generation (v. 7; see also 4:9).

This tone is very much that of Psalm 78:1–8. The speaker has learned important lessons from faithful people of a previous generation, and he declares his determination that these lessons should not die out with the present community of faith—rather, they *must* be taught to the coming generation. There is a note of determination in the imperfect verbs of v. 4: "We will *not* hide them from their descendants; we *will* tell the next generation the praiseworthy deeds of the LORD" (emphasis added). The intent of the author is quite clear: neither the present nor the coming generation of faith should forget these important lessons from Israel's history. "It is vital that the present generation plays its role as a link between the past generation and the next generation. Without this, the chain of learning will be broken."[6]

The praiseworthy deeds of the LORD, his power, and the wonders he has done. We should take careful note of the object of this instruction from generation to generation. The ancestors of the faith told the psalmist about "the praiseworthy deeds of the LORD, his power and the wonders he has done." This statement is programmatic for what follows throughout the rest of the psalm. The hearer and reader of the psalm should focus

---

6. Goldingay, *Psalms* 2, 485.

their attention on Yahweh's awesome, salvific deeds in the history of his dealings with his people, *and*, by implication, they should think about the proper response to such a God in their generation.

Focus on "praiseworthy deeds" grounds this reminder within the paradigmatic celebration of divine salvation that is Exodus 15 (see comments on Ps 77:16–20). The Song of Moses also delights in God's "praiseworthy deeds" (Exod 15:11, rendered "awesome in glory" in the NIV but translated more literally, "awesome in praiseworthy deeds"[7]). Over and above this delighting, the psalmist encourages remembrance of Yahweh's "power" (possibly implying "powerful acts" in the context of the verse[8]) and "the wonders he has done."[9] The primary focus of the memory must be on the amazing faithfulness of God directed toward his people in the past. He has worked powerfully in human history for the benefit of his children—let them not forget that fact. We will see later that there is a secondary focus of memory (the inappropriate response of previous generations to God's awesome saving power), but the primary reminder occurs here in Psalm 78:4. The God of the covenant, Yahweh, has performed praiseworthy, powerful, and wondrous acts in order to help his people—no generation of the believing community should ever be allowed to forget them. As Craig Broyles notes, if God's people are to trust him as they ought, "A living memory of God and his acts is the crucial factor."[10]

He decreed statutes for Jacob and established the law in Israel. Remembrance of God is not an illusive task based entirely on an oral tradition. Clearly, the psalmist's opening exhortation is that this generation should remember for themselves who God is and pass that message of hope on to their children. Often in the ancient Near East the remembrance and transmission of foundational teaching was based on the memorizing of stories verbatim by a professional class of teachers or storytellers. Normally, this elite endeavor was specialized; but Israel's task is made easier by the gift of revelation. By decreeing *written* statutes and establishing a written law for his people, God has made cross-generational education much easier. His people have been entrusted with a written pool of teaching by which they can know him and make him known to others. The psalmist's point is, again, very similar to the message we read in Deuteronomy. Foreseeing the

---

7. This rendering is reflected in some of the other modern English translations of this passage. See, for example, the ESV, NASB, and NET translations of Exod 15:11.

8. Hossfeld and Zenger, *Psalms 2*, 295.

9. These two terms ("power" [*'ezuz*] and "wonders" [*nipla'ot*]) continue the link between Pss 77 and 78 (see Ps 77:11, 14).

10. Broyles, *Psalms*, 320.

written form of the sermons and laws currently being delivered by Moses, Yahweh declares to his people in Deuteronomy 30:11–14,

> Now what I am commanding you today is not too difficult for you or beyond your reach. It is not up in heaven, so that you have to ask, "Who will ascend into heaven to get it and proclaim it to us so we may obey it?" Nor is it beyond the sea, so that you have to ask, "Who will cross the sea to get it and proclaim it to us so we may obey it?" No, the word is very near you; it is in your mouth and in your heart so you may obey it.

The point of written revelation is that knowing God becomes easier. People are not dependent on hearsay accounts or epic tasks to discover the truth—decreed statutes and established law bring God closer to the people. Such is the purpose of written revelation from God: it brings God closer than we could otherwise imagine (Deut 4:7–8).

So the next generation would know them. Deuteronomy is equally clear that as we receive God's revelation, we also assume the responsibility to teach its message to the coming generations (Deut 4:9; 6:7, 19–25). The psalmist stresses the importance of continuing instruction about living lives of remembrance and devotion to God from one generation to the next. "Continuity is underscored by the repetitions, ancestors (vv. 3, 5, 8), children (vv. 4, 6), generations (vv. 4, 6, 8), 'tell' (vv. 3, 4, 6), 'know' or 'teach' (vv. 3, 5, 6)."[11] It is not enough just to respond to our own knowledge of God. Each generation must both respond to *and teach* true knowledge of God.

Then they would put their trust in God. The purpose of learning from God's word is clear—that each generation would know and love God (Ps 78:7). Equally, the purpose of passing on God's revelation is not for children simply to acquire head knowledge or learn only about Israel's history. Teaching God's saving miracles and his revealed word serves a specific purpose, namely, that the next generation should meet with God and respond to him. Transmission of Israel's foundational knowledge of God is not an academic task. It is, rather, a formative endeavor designed to shape the next generation into a community of believers who fear and respond to the Lord. Trusting, remembering, and keeping are the active images of a healthy community of faith. Every community of God's people must respond to God for themselves[12] by remembering his works in behalf of his people and being shaped by his word.

---

11. Schaefer, *Psalms*, 191.
12. The overtones of the Hebrew idiom used in verse 7a imply the placing of one's

They would not be like their ancestors. The purpose of the present generation's teaching task is expressed both positively (v. 7) and negatively (v. 8). As well as cultivating trust and torah-obedience, the aim of this act of education is also that those who follow should avoid the failings of those who have gone before. Not being loyal in heart or faithful in spirit stands in contrast to the practice of trusting, remembering, and keeping in the previous verse and describes the lack of proper, holistic response to the goodness of God. The NIV misses something of the nuance of the original text by translating the verb as a stative rather than the Hebrew's causative. The translation should really read, "a stubborn and rebellious generation that *did not establish* its heart." It is not the case that the hearts of the desert generation *just happened* not to be loyal, whereas the hearts of other generations *just happened* to be faithful. The psalmist clearly implies that the responsibility for making their hearts firm or loyal lay firmly with each particular group of God's people. It was their responsibility to establish their hearts—to make their hearts loyal to God—but they singularly failed to do so; therefore, they strayed. "[T]he psalm assumes that *we do* the firming of our heart. The result of the people's failure to do so was that their spirit was not true to God. This is the tendency the psalm will illustrate."[13]

So, the first section of Psalm 78 is an exhortation addressed to the current generation of God's people to learn lessons of faith and devotion from Israel's history and to pass these truths on to succeeding generations of the covenant community.

Failures of Faith and Miracles Galore (78:9–16)

THE ESSENCE OF THE EXHORTATION in verses 1–8 is that God's people should learn to trust him based on the great works of salvation he has accomplished for them in the past. Verse 8 speaks of previous generations who have failed to learn this lesson, and verses 9–11 go on to give a historical illustration of such failure.

The men of Ephraim, though armed with bows, turned back on the day of battle. The Old Testament and later Jewish traditions relate a number of battle-related incidents in which the tribe of Ephraim does not

---

confidence (*kesel*) in God. The psalmist does not use the normal Hebrew word for trusting God (*batah*); rather, the question of the locus of our *kesel* is one that applies to our whole world and life view. For example, Eliphaz challenges Job that his "confidence" (*kesel*) should be in his piety, and he parallels this with "blamelessness" (Job 4:6). In a similar manner, Psalm 78:7 parallels confidence in God with remembrance and obedience. The same word is also used negatively to imply folly or stupidity when one places one's trust in the wrong source of confidence (Ps 85:8, Eccl 7:25).

13. Goldingay, *Psalms* 2, 487. Emphasis added.

cover itself with glory. It is therefore difficult to establish with any degree of confidence which particular event the psalmist has in mind in making his statement.[14] What is more, it is not entirely clear what links the military failure mentioned in verse 9 with the failure of covenantal devotion in verses 10–11. The Hebrew phrase translated "though armed with bows" is unclear, but the meaning of the verse seems to imply that Ephraim failed despite being well equipped for the task that they faced.[15]

They did not keep God's covenant. Verses 10–11 give clear reasons for Ephraim's failure. Whichever events the psalmist had in mind, there is no doubt about the cause of Ephraim's defeat. The poet describes their downfall as having a threefold root: failure to keep God's covenant with them, refusal to walk in the ways of God's law, and forgetfulness regarding God's miraculous works in the past. This assessment of Ephraim's failure provides the paradigm of judgment the poet uses in this psalm as a warning for the present generation. Failure to remember the works of God in behalf of his people is associated with failure to keep the covenant and rejection of the law. This thought continues the theme of remembrance emphasized so clearly in Psalm 77. Not remembering is like not obeying—clearly a serious matter in the mind of the poet.

The dominant tribe of Ephraim simply *forgot*, which had serious consequences.

---

14. F. A. Gosling, "Were the Ephraimites to Blame?" *VT* 49.4 (1999): 505–6. Various scholars have associated this verse with the failure of the tribe of Ephraim to occupy their allotted land properly (Judg 1). Some suggest that the loss of the ark of the covenant when the tabernacle was at Shiloh (Ephraimite tribal territory) is the incident referred to here (1 Sam 4–6). Others argue that this verse refers to the account of Ephraim's alleged cowardice in 1 Chr 7:20–24. It has also been suggested that the references to Ephraim here may be applied to those tribes that sided with Saul and were defeated by the Philistines at Mount Gilboa during the period when Saul was preoccupied with the pursuit of David (1 Sam 31). Also from the biblical tradition, it has been suggested that this verse may be speaking of the fall of Samaria under the Assyrian attack, when the Northern Kingdom was permanently destroyed (2 Kgs 17; cf. Hos 10:14, which also uses the phrase "the day of battle"). The Targum points to a Jewish tradition that tells of the tribe of Ephraim's rebelling against Egypt three years prior to the exodus and retreating in the face of military defeat. A later Jewish tradition, based on 1 Chr 7, also refers to Ephraim's breaking away from Egypt prior to the main exodus but being defeated in battle by the men of Gath. So it is difficult to know which of these incidents, if any, the psalmist had in mind. It may well be that in the mind of psalmist and his hearers these biblical and extrabiblical accounts combined to associate Ephraim with such failure. But of these options, it seems most likely that the loss of the ark of the covenant in 1 Sam 4–6 provides the backdrop, for the psalmist returns to this narrative later in the psalm (Ps 78:56–66).

15. That the failures of Ephraim reappear later in the psalm (v. 67) sheds additional light on the meaning of this verse.

If wisdom is the fruit of the collective memory so as to avoid repeating past mistakes, forgetfulness dooms one to repeat past errors. Analogously, forgetfulness of God's benefits is tantamount to their nullification, while remembering them reactivates God's wonders for the present and stimulates the people's faith and faithfulness.[16]

He did miracles in the sight of their ancestors in the land of Egypt. Moving on from the failures of the tribe of Ephraim, the psalmist reminds his hearers of the arch-paradigm of divine salvation, namely, the exodus from Egypt. Effectively, in Psalm 78:12–16 the psalmist is outlining the miraculous past deeds that Yahweh worked in behalf of his people—deeds that should have been remembered by the men of Ephraim. Interestingly, the Hebrew word translated "miracles" in the NIV (v. 12) is actually a singular noun ("miracle").[17] The implication seems to be that the exodus functions as *the* paradigmatic miracle of salvation to be remembered by all generations of God's people. But that overarching miracle consists of many miraculous parts. Israel's release from the control of the ancient world's greatest superpower was clearly an event beyond all comprehension apart from the intervention of God. What is more, Yahweh actually performed many miracles in securing their release and nationhood (Exod 13–17). So the psalmist draws attention to the parting of the Red Sea (Ps 78:13), the pillars of cloud and fire that led Israel through the desert, and the astonishing provision of water from a rock in the middle of the desert. Just as the exodus itself defies natural explanation, so also do each of these scenarios. Israel's release from Egypt was impossible, crossing the Red Sea was impossible, surviving the trials of the desert was impossible—yet all of these things happened. The point the psalmist makes is clear: such events should never be forgotten, and such a God should never be forgotten!

Miracles, Rebellion, and Retribution (78:17–31)

BUT THEY CONTINUED TO SIN AGAINST HIM. Forgetfulness is a cross-generational phenomenon. Its effects go far beyond the people involved at first instance, as is reflected in the psalmist's use of "they" in verse 17. Who are the "they" in question? At first it seems that the most likely candidates are the men of Ephraim, as they are the obvious subject in verse 9; but the acts described in verses 17–31 show that the psalmist actually has in mind the equally forgetful "ancestors" mentioned in verse 12. It is interesting to note this progression through the generations. The exodus generation

---

16. Schaefer, *Psalms*, 192.
17. Kraus, *Psalms II*, 127.

was unfaithful, and they set the tone for the generations to follow. As their forgetfulness led to covenantal unfaithfulness, so also they set the example that was followed by the "men of Ephraim" (v. 9). The psalmist's desire is to keep the present generation of believers from falling into the same trap.

They willfully put God to the test. The language used here draws us back to the rebellion of Israel's wilderness wanderings (Exod 16; Num 11). The NIV rightly brings out the "willfulness" of the people's testing. These challenges were not the natural ones posed by the barrier of the Red Sea and the people's need for water in the wilderness. This testing of God was based on *desire*, not *need*. Yahweh had without fail stepped up to the plate for Israel when they were faced with a situation of need—miracles to secure their release from Egypt, parting the waters of the sea, providing water in the desert. The testing here in Psalm 78 is of a different ilk. First, it calls either God's character or his competence into question (vv. 19–20). "Testing" is the theme word of the book of Numbers—it is the primary characteristic of the wilderness generation (Num 14:20–25). They constantly tested Yahweh, and by doing so they cast doubt on both *his love* for them (Exod 14:11) and, as in this case, *his ability* to help them (Ps 78:19–20). Either way, there is an implied accusation in their testing of God. Their challenge represents that lack of covenantal faithfulness echoed in the actions of the "men of Ephraim" (v. 10). Moreover, their craving leads them to a skewed perspective on the reality of their experience. Numbers 11:4–5 reflects the amazing perverseness of their rebellion against God: "The rabble with them began to crave other food, and again the Israelites started wailing and said, 'If only we had meat to eat! We remember the fish we ate in Egypt at no cost—also the cucumbers, melons, leeks, onions and garlic.'"

The perverse nature of their response to the miracles of Yahweh in the desert shows that lapses of memory work in two ways: forgetting the goodness of God and forgetting the true nature of life without God. Slavery, brutality, and genocide in Egypt are forgotten in the remembering of cucumbers, onions, and garlic! Here we see another example of how remembrance is not a question of intellectual capacity but, instead, a question of obedience and right relationship with God. (We will return to this matter under Contemporary Significance.)

They spoke against God. The psalmist's assessment of the thoughts of Israel in the desert informs us of the tone with which the words of Psalm 78:19–20 were spoken. These expressions were not genuine questions seeking an answer. They were accusations leveled *against* God. Their failing is as much in the way they spoke as it is in the words they uttered (see Exod 16:2–3; 17:7). Their skeptical interrogation belittles the miracles they had seen. The implication is, "Well, anyone can bring water from a rock, but setting a table of meat in the desert . . . now that would be a true miracle!" Their doubt denies the logic of the miracles they had witnessed. Surely the God who brings water from stone can also provide bread and meat, yet the people were consumed with doubt rather than the confidence their previous experience should have engendered (Exod 16).[18]

When the LORD heard them, he was furious. The harm of forgetfulness is illustrated by God's response in Psalm 78:21–22. The people's grumbling attitude damaged the covenantal relationship and had to be addressed. God never hesitated to perform miracles when his people were in need, but his anger was aroused by their illogical lack of faith, which denied the people's own experience with Yahweh. They questioned his goodness and competence, but they had no just cause for doing so; therefore, God was angry. Their forgetfulness was not passive carelessness—it was an act of disbelief and lack of trust (v. 22). Effectively, their failure to remember God's good provision amounted to an act of rebellion.[19]

Yet . . . he gave them the grain of heaven. Despite the rebellion of the people, Yahweh continued to prove his good character and unquestionable competence by providing the very things they had so skeptically demanded. Verses 23–25 first draw attention to the provision of manna from heaven. The exodus generation did not believe it was possible to "spread a table in the wilderness," yet that is exactly what God did for them. They needed a staple food, and God provided it for them. The irony of the poet's historical presentation lies in the very ease with which God met this requirement. Verses 19–20 imply that providing food in the desert was a task beyond even Yahweh's ability, yet these verses present the accomplishment of this miracle by no more than the command of the Lord. In imagery reminiscent of the creation narratives of Genesis 1–2, God speaks and his purpose becomes reality. He simply *commands* bread from heaven, and this bread appears. The psalmist reemphasizes the astounding nature of this miracle. Just as familiarity with the manna

---

18. The psalmist changes the chronology of Israel's complaints and grumbling in the desert. According to Exod 16–17, the people first complained with regard to food (Exod 16) and then with regard to water (Exod 17), but the poet reverses this order in his presentation of their forefathers' failings. Of course, the point of the psalm is not to discuss historical chronology but is rather to bring to life the failures of the exodus generation as a negative example, one to be avoided. It seems that the psalmist makes this point by conflating the "grumbling" accounts from Exod 16–17 and Num 11.

19. The statement that "fire broke out against Jacob" is probably another intertextual association with Num 11, thus showing again that the poet is synthesizing the rebellion/grumbling stories of the Torah.

eventually resulted in the people's contempt (Num 11:4–6), so also familiarity with the account of the miracle can breed an apathetic response
from subsequent generations of God's people. Every one of the poet's
hearers knew about the provision of manna, and familiarity with any
miracle story removes something of its sense of awe and power. By way of
this vivid poetic presentation, the poet seeks to renew the "wow factor"
in his contemporaries' response to this miracle. Literally the Hebrew says,
"Men ate the bread of heroes!" Sometimes heroes (*'abirim*) refers to mighty
warrior types (Ps 76:5; Lam 1:15); but the image can also refer to God
himself (Gen 49:24; Ps 132:2, 5), and here it seems to refer to heavenly
beings.[20] The vividness of the imagery is designed to reinvigorate the
present generation's response to a familiar account and toward the Author
of the miracle it records: "Can you imagine?" the poet says to his hearers—
"They ate the bread of angels!"

He rained meat down on them like dust. Verses 26–29 then retell
the miraculous provision of meat in the flocks of quail that landed in the
Israelite camp (Exod 16). There are interesting repetitions in the poetic
retelling of the provision of both the manna and the birds. Both the
manna and the meat "rained down" upon them (Ps 78:24, 27); both events
clearly have their origin "in the heavens" (vv. 23–24, 26); and in both
cases God provided more than the people could actually eat (vv. 25, 29).
These themes highlight the divine origin of the miraculous events—they
were not happenstance—and the themes also emphasize the expansive
generosity of God. The idea of bread and meat as "raining down" suggests
massive volume as well as heavenly source. The imagery is of provision that
is gracious and generous rather than reluctant and miserly.

He had given them what they craved. The imagery seems idyllic despite the previous rebellion of the people (vv. 17–21). Once again,
the psalmist picks up on the language of exodus in describing the people's experience of plenty thanks to the provision of God (Exod 16:8;
Num 11:4), but these references to the desert stories also ring warning
bells in the ears of the psalmist's listeners. His language is the language of
Exodus and Numbers, but when these words are found in the Pentateuch
their association is with judgment and God's punishment. The intertextual
references of Psalm 78:29 serve as a warning that not all is as idyllic as it

---

20. The angelic nature of the heroes in this verse is seen most clearly in the Septuagint's
translation of *'abirim* as "angels" (as with the Syriac version of the Psalter and the Targum).
Psalm 103:20 also uses a synonym of *'abirim* to describe angels. So it seems likely the
psalmist is saying that the people ate the bread that was reserved for heavenly beings alone.
See Tate, *Psalms 51–100*, 282; Goldingay, *Psalms 2*, 495.

seems. The words used in this verse remind the people of God's wrath and punishment toward the wilderness generation, and this bridging verse leads the psalmist into a more explicit discussion of that very theme.

God's anger rose against them. Yahweh had provided for them the very things they craved, but his provision should not be seen as a tacit acceptance of the people's rebellious behavior and distrust of God (vv. 17–21). God's miraculous provision of the things the people craved proved his capability despite their doubts. The fact that God condescends to meet the people's grumbling demands, however, does not mean that their wayward attitude has been forgotten. There was a real sense in which religious practice in the ancient Near East revolved around attempts to manipulate one's god. Whether it be by offering sacrifices that did not really cost the individual all that much, or by making promises one had no intention of keeping, the purpose was to make the god work in the manipulator's behalf even by way of trickery or deception. Could it be that this attitude was that of the exodus generation? Having just come out of Egypt, where there was a slew of gods and a marketplace of religious practices, it is just possible that this rebellious and forgetful people thought they had managed to manipulate Yahweh into providing the very thing they desired. But verses 30–31 make it quite clear that Israel's God is not to be toyed with! As C. S. Lewis writes in *The Lion, the Witch and the Wardrobe*, "Aslan is not a tame lion," and clearly Yahweh is not a tame god.[21] There is a sense in which the trickery of the people is met by a "trick" from God—before they had even turned away from their food, God's punishment struck.[22]

The Stubbornness of Rebellion (78:32–39)

IN SPITE OF ALL THIS, THEY KEPT ON SINNING. Throughout the Bible, God's punishment is presented as a means of securing repentance (e.g., see Deut 29:22–29; cf. 30:1–10). God sent plagues or storms or enemies, all under his control, in order to prompt his people to repent and change when they were being rebellious. Despite divine judgment, however, this generation *continued* in rebellion against Yahweh (Ps 78:32).[23] The people would not learn their lesson—they still refused to believe. Constantly, the Scriptures

---

21. C. S. Lewis, *The Lion, the Witch and the Wardrobe* in *The Complete Chronicles of Narnia* (London: HarperCollins, 2000), 132.

22. Anderson comments, "God gave the rebels the object of their desire, and he punished them by answering their own prayers" (*Psalms*, 569).

23. "[T]his evidence of dramatic retribution does not convert them, for 'they were sinning still' (v. 32)" (Terrien, *Psalms*, 567).

make a connection between failure to believe God or his word and way-ward behavior.[24] The people's failure to relate rightly to Yahweh inevitably led to wrong behavior and empty lives (v. 33). The irony, of course, is that this generation is the one freed from Egyptian slavery. What an amazing opportunity to enjoy and delight in their release, yet their faithless rebel-lion led them to futility, not freedom.[25]

Their hearts were not loyal to him. Verses 34–35 present a picture similar to the one we find in the book of Judges. God's repeated rebuke would bring a "repentance" that was far from genuine (v. 36). The people would, in a sense, say the right things (v. 35)[26] and, in a sense, do the right things (v. 34).[27] But their words and deeds were only superficial and did not reflect a true change of heart (v. 37).

The psalmist contends that the old truism is, in fact, true: namely, "the heart of the problem is the problem of the heart." That previous gen-eration, which is being used as a warning to the present generation of God's people, put up only a *facade* of repentance, and it remained on a superficial level. They were not "loyal" in heart (lit., "their hearts were not firm toward him") and "they were not faithful to his covenant." The whole point of a covenant, like a modern contract, is that it puts under obligation both parties to the agreement. The poet paints a picture of a community who desired all the benefits of covenant without being will-ing to accept its obligations. They saw God's miraculous provision, yet they did not believe (v. 32). They received God's rebuke—designed to bring real transformation—yet they would not change (vv. 34, 37). Still it appears that the people thought of God as a plaything in their own hands—one to be manipulated at their own will. It is evident from the psalmist's presentation of Israel's exodus generation that genuine devotion to Yahweh was far from them. Their response to God was more functional than it was real, and this kind of response is always a danger in the practice of religion. (See Contemporary Significance for further discussion.)

---

24. Broyles, *Psalms*, 232.

25. Interestingly, in verse 33 the poet uses the word *hebel* to describe the futility of rebellious lives. This word *hebel* is the same one we find in the thematic verse of Ecclesiastes: "Meaningless! Meaningless!" says the teacher—"Utterly meaningless! Everything is meaningless" (Eccl 1:2).

26. This language is found often in the psalms and normally reflects a right attitude toward God (see Pss 18:1–2; 19:14). Clearly, however, there was something wrong with the exodus generation's appropriation of these ideas.

27. Equally, the activities of "seeking," "eagerly turning to," and "remembering" God are all practices that are commended in the Psalms (Pss 22:27; 34:10; 77:11 et al.), yet Ps 78:37 calls the genuineness of these actions into question.

Yet he was merciful. Remarkably, Yahweh did not respond to his people in kind. His character remains unchanged despite his people's failings (v. 38). Who God is fundamentally is an absolute that does not change in response to the weakness of his followers. The fabled old man trying to save a scorpion from drowning shows this kind of unchangeability—and notes the same characteristic in the scorpion. Each time the man reaches out to rescue the venomous insect, it stings his hand. A passerby mocks the futility of this exercise, but the old man replies, "What the scorpion is by nature, does not change who I am by nature." It is interesting that, before continuing with the narrative of Psalm 78, the poet interjects an emphatic statement of God's true identity (literally, *"But he* is merciful").[28] The people's attitude of heart led to negative behaviors, but the good character of God shapes his activity for the benefit of his people.

He forgave their iniquities. Verse 38 is an unusual verse in the Old Testament because it speaks of God's atoning for his people's sin (*yikapper*, translated "forgave" in the NIV). It is unusual for God to be the one who performs atoning activity; normally in the Old Testament this work is that of the priest. Here, however, Yahweh himself takes on the role of the one who does what is necessary to deal with his people's sinfulness. "God's compassion expresses itself in taking the initiative to solve the problem caused by the people's waywardness."[29]

Time after time he restrained his anger. Once again echoing the desert experience of the exodus generation, God's compassionate character manifests itself in merciful action toward the ill-deserving people. At the point of Israel's iconic failure in the incident of the golden calf (Exod 32–34), God reveals his true nature to Moses (Exod 34:6–7):

> And he passed in front of Moses, proclaiming, "The LORD, the LORD, the compassionate and gracious God, slow to anger, abounding in love and faithfulness, maintaining love to thousands, and forgiving wickedness, rebellion and sin. Yet he does not leave the guilty unpunished; he punishes the children and their children for the sin of the fathers to the third and fourth generation."

God's compassion and slowness to anger are evidenced in the history of Israel on the countless occasions in which the nation's behavior merited divine rebuke, yet Yahweh, true to his character, stayed his hand.

He remembered that they were but flesh. Whereas Israel's remembering God in Psalm 78:35 lacked sincerity, we see here that God *remembers*

---

28. Hossfeld and Zenger, *Psalms* 2, 297.
29. Goldingay, *Psalms* 2, 500.

his people's human frailty, and this remembrance leads him to compassion. Even though the exodus generation failed to keep their covenantal obligations, Yahweh remained true to his side of the bargain. Remembering their weakness, he showed mercy that was true to his character and promise. Yet the following verses show that ultimately, and even taking into account his fundamentally compassionate nature, God cannot allow himself to be mocked by the flagrant rebellion of his people.

Rebellion Despite Release (78:40–55)

THE SECTION OF THE PSALM covering verses 40–55 addresses the people's continued rebellion despite the fact that they were witnesses to the miracles of the exodus from Egypt.

How often they rebelled against him in the wilderness. Verses 40–41 draw attention to the repeated failures of the exodus generation while they were in the desert. Their rebellion was not just a one-off or even an occasional matter. Time and again, this newborn nation rebelled against their Father and Redeemer.

They did not remember his power. Once again, the root of Israel's rejection of God is found in their failure to *remember*. Literally, the psalmist laments the people's failure to "remember his hand," a metaphor that occurs frequently in the Old Testament to refer to Yahweh's powerful, saving activity in behalf of his people in the exodus from Egypt (Exod 13:3, 14–17; Deut 6:21; 7:8 et al.). The main point of Psalm 78:42–51 is simple: Remembering the redemptive miracles of the exodus that secured the people's release from torture and slavery should have been enough to maintain their fidelity to Yahweh. They did not remember, and they were not faithful.[30]

But he brought his people out like a flock. Israel's rebellion is made all the more difficult to comprehend because they were forgetful not only of God's miraculous salvific power but also of his shepherding care for

---

30. There is much debate in some commentaries about why we do not have a full account of the plagues in Ps 78 (where only seven of the ten plagues are mentioned). Some question whether this psalm refers to an older traditional account of the plagues (see the discussions in Hossfeld and Zenger, *Psalms 2*, 297–98; Eaton, *Psalms*, 284). We must remember, however, that Ps 78 gives a *poetic* account of Israel's historical failures and that the poet is at liberty to use as much or as little of the historical narrative as he sees fit in order to make his point. As we have seen above, the psalmist also blends the Exod 16 and Num 11 accounts of Israel's failure in the desert to make his own specific point about the importance of remembering God and learning from the failings of ancestors. As a poet, he is not a slave to known narratives but, instead, is at liberty to make use of them in the manner that best suits his poetic and didactic purpose.

them (vv. 52–55). The miracles they had witnessed in the plagues that secured their release demonstrated the awesome power and remarkable ability of Yahweh. His provision and care for them in the desert demonstrated his fatherly heart and loving care for his chosen people. God's manifest power should have made Israel fearful of forgetting. His loving care should have inspired an affection that kept Israel from forgetting.[31] To the amazement of the psalmist, neither one proved to be the case.

He guided them safely. The miracles of God's provision and care are no less amazing than the spectacularly destructive plagues that broke the might of a superpower in order to secure Israel's freedom from slavery. The imagery in this section (vv. 40–55) speaks of God's multifaceted intervention in behalf of his people. The underlying image is of the God of promise who is at work in the temporal realm to do whatever is necessary to benefit his people. Sometimes this work is a display of power *against* those who oppose his children (vv. 42–51, 55). Sometimes his power miraculously *opens pathways* for his people (vv. 52–54). Sometimes his power *provides* for the needs of his flock (vv. 25–29). Whatever the specific expression of God's power may be, the psalmist reminds his readers that his multivalent activity serves the purpose of blessing his people.

He settled the tribes of Israel in their homes. Ultimately, the divine activity of these verses serves the aim of providing a home and place of rest for God's people. To deliver them from being a landless, downtrodden, exploited people, Yahweh works to give Israel a home, with all the implications of rest that accompany that image (e.g., "settled" implies dwelling in safety[32]). This prominent biblical theme finds many echoes in the Psalter (see the discussion of Ps 84). Yahweh's purpose was to provide rest for his people—a rich image illustrating the aim of following God in obedience, the aim of discipleship. The psalmist presents Yahweh as the absolute owner of Canaan whose right to dispose of the land as he pleases is beyond question (Ps 78:54–55); therefore, he can give it to whomever he pleases. This theme picks up on the Pentateuchal teaching that the nations living in the promised land lost it because of their failure to adhere to God's standards (Gen 15:13–16) and on the warnings that the same will happen to Israel should they fail to follow God's ways (Deut 8). The rest that was

---

31. Eaton comments, "The plagues had to reach their climax before the liberation was conceded. . . . Then the shepherd got his flock on the move and led them through desert and water; the warmth of the shepherding image (common in the Asaph psalms—vv. 70–2; 74:1; 77:20; 80:1) contrasts with the preceding account of Israel's rebelliousness" (Eaton, *Psalms*, 284–85).

32. See Goldingay, *Psalms 2*, 507.

God's aim for Israel could only come as a result of covenantal faithfulness and commitment. Would Israel finally learn this lesson as they transitioned from being a nomadic, desert people to being a nation with a land?

Failure and Withdrawal (78:56–64)

BUT THEY PUT GOD TO THE TEST. There is an almost inevitable sense of disappointment as the poet again recounts the failings of previous generations. This time the focus switches from the exodus generation to Israel throughout the period of the Judges until the reign of David. This generation of God's people is different—generations, in fact, are implied—but they did not learn from the historical events of those who experienced the exodus from Egypt yet forgot the God who had saved them. The settled people repeated the mistakes of their ancestors in *testing* God and *rebelling* against him (Ps 78:56; cf. vv. 18, 41), as is made explicit in verse 57, where the poet compares the failures of the generations in the land with those of their forefathers. Interestingly, Hosea 7:16 also describes Ephraim (named in Ps 78:67) as a "faulty bow." Possibly picking up on this Hosea tradition, the poet in Psalm 78:57 plays on his earlier description of Ephraim, who in verse 9 is said to have turned away despite their being "armed with bows." Their bows were useless then, and the poet makes the point that the current generation is equally deceptive. A bow gives the appearance of strength and threat, but a faulty bow is absolutely useless. "Israel is compared to a bow from which an arrow suddenly shoots off in the wrong direction."[33] There is no point in such a weapon. Equally, Israel gives the appearance of covenantal relationship with Yahweh, but the reality is drastically different. Their spiritual aim is skewed, as evidenced by their idolatry in the high places (v. 58).

They angered him with their high places. While *forgetting* was the order of the day for the exodus generation (vv. 11, 42), the people in the land resorted to idolatry (v. 58). In itself, this turning is arguably a type of forgetfulness—forgetfulness of the true God, who is able to work miracles, in favor of gods of wood and stone that can do nothing.[34] But it is forgetfulness exacerbated by adultery. The idea of *arousing God's*

---

33. Kraus, *Psalms II*, 129.

34. Sometimes the Hebrew word for high places (*bamot*) can refer to local sanctuaries, and idols (*pesilim*) can refer to manmade images that were actually meant to be a physical representation of Yahweh. So this verse may refer to aberrant types of Yahweh worship (see Goldingay, *Psalms 2*, 508). But the jealousy of Yahweh (v. 58) is often associated with the worship of false or foreign gods (see Exod 34:14; Deut 6:14–15 et al.), as seems to be the more natural reading of the text here.

jealousy is an image similar to that of a betrayed spouse. The covenantal relationship between God and his people is commonly held in parallel with the marriage relationship in the Old Testament (e.g., see Hos 1–3; Jer 31:32). Israel's idolatry gave rise to God's justifiable jealousy just as a betrayed spouse has a right to be jealous, but without that jealousy's leading into sin.

He rejected Israel completely. Psalm 78:59–64 highlights the full extent of Israel's unfaithfulness by recounting the severity of Yahweh's response to it. The people repeatedly turned to useless idols rather than to God. So when God hears their prayers to lifeless statues—with the ironic implication that *Yahweh alone* hears these prayers—he becomes very angry. (This anger echoes God's response to the selfish and arrogant prayers of the exodus generation in v. 21.) His anger led to rejection of his people—a rejection manifested in the removal of the caring intervention witnessed by Israel in Egypt and the desert and celebrated by the psalmist in verses 42–55. All the things he did for the benefit of his people in bringing them out of Egypt, leading them through the desert, and bringing them into the land, he now refuses to do for them in an attempt to cause them to repent.

He abandoned the tabernacle of Shiloh. Psalm 78:60 reflects on the conundrum that lies at the heart of much of the biblical narrative, namely, How can an absolutely holy God dwell in the midst of a sinful people? The overarching story of the Bible makes it clear that God never rejects his people entirely; however, from time to time the excessive sinfulness of God's people is met by the removal of his presence for a period of time. This was the people's experience at Shiloh (1 Sam 4–6).[35] Israel's behavior in the land was much the same as her behavior in the desert following the people's release from Egypt, and the psalmist points out that the rejection of Yahweh in the land led to even worse consequences for such behavior. Yahweh had threatened to destroy Israel in response to their idolatry over the golden calf (Exod 32:9–10). Though he relented in response to Moses's prayer, a further threat remained, namely, that God would not go with Israel because of his anger against them (Exod 33:1–3). Once again, however, Moses's relentless prayer appears to cause God to relent, and in the end he did not remove his presence from his people (vv. 12–17). But such

---

35. There is some debate about whether these verses refer to the experiences of Israel during the time of Eli or whether the verses are actually a reference to the fall of the Northern Kingdom of Israel in 722 BCE. While there are definitely some lexical similarities between the psalmist's presentation and the language of exile (Hossfeld and Zenger, *Psalms 2*, 298–99), the poet seems quite deliberately to echo the narrative of 1 Sam 4–6 in this section of the psalm (see also Tate, *Psalms 51–100*, 293–94; Broyles, *Psalms*, 325).

was the rebellion of the people in the land (seen throughout the book of Judges) and the corruption among the priesthood (1 Sam 2:12–36) that Yahweh took the step of rejecting Shiloh as the place of his dwelling—despite the fact that his tabernacle and the ark of the covenant were there. The external symbols of divine presence were not sufficient to retain the reality of presence because the sinfulness of the people and priesthood had forced the holy God to remove his presence. The dichotomy of a righteous God who desires relationship with an unrighteous people is a tension that ultimately only finds release in the cross (see Bridging Contexts).

While God's withdrawal from his people was not permanent, the consequences were stark. The ark of the covenant was taken into captivity by the Philistines (Ps 78:61; cf. 1 Sam 4:1–11), Israel suffered a great military defeat and loss of life (Ps 78:62–63;1 Sam 4:10–11), and the priestly line of Eli fell to the sword as a result of their godlessness (Ps 78:64;1 Sam 4:11, 19–22). The psalmist is keen to remind the people that the exodus generation was not the only one marked by unfaithfulness toward God and that the consequences of spiritual forgetfulness are stark.

Forgiveness and Renewal (78:65–72)

THEN THE LORD AWOKE AS FROM SLEEP. To mark the sudden change in circumstances that Israel experienced, the psalmist adopts two extremely uncommon metaphors to describe God—the sleeping god and the drunken warrior. The point of these metaphors, of course, is not to imply that God was either sleeping or drunk, but whatever the cause, he seems to have been inattentive. The imagery used here communicates the suddenness of Yahweh's transition from anger and inactivity to dynamic action in behalf of his people. From their perspective, it is as though God has awoken from a bad-tempered, drunken sleep and finally struck out at their enemies. Of course, the psalmist is well aware that Yahweh's inactivity did not result from sleepy inattention (hence the use of the simile "like"), but he uses word pictures to express the sudden change of Yahweh's disposition.

He beat back his enemies. The image of the drunken warrior awaking from his stupor is not entirely accidental. Once Yahweh's attention is refocused on Israel's plight, the people witness again the raw power of the Warrior God who freed his people from Egypt with a mighty hand (Ps 78:42–51). This same God rose up again in power in behalf of his people when they were persecuted in the land of promise, just as he had when Abraham's children were exiled outside the land of promise. As the following verses indicate, the Lord's striking back against his enemies seems to be a reference to the military success and political emancipation won by David as God's chosen instrument (2 Sam 5, 8).

He chose the tribe of Judah, Mount Zion, which he loved. The remarkable surprise of these verses is compounded by the very fact that no reason is given for the sudden change of heart that surprised the people so much. The psalmist does not draw attention to any act of national repentance. He does not point to a change of heart on the part of God's wayward people. The images of the sleeping god and the drunken warrior (Ps 78:65) further compound the sense of sudden change from inactivity to action that results in the release of his people. So why this sudden change of heart? Quite simply, the poet makes it plain that divine intervention is based on divine choice. Yahweh chose Judah and Zion and David. No rationale is given for his choice to intervene, but the psalmist is aware that the roots of God's election are to be found in divine love. Broyles is helpful here:

> Yahweh acts unilaterally—for no prior reason he acts graciously. Although Israel's repentance amounted to lying to him, yet he was merciful (vv. 34–39). Now **the LORD** acts suddenly and the abruptness is underscored by two graphic similes (sleep and intoxication) one would normally think inappropriate for God (v. 65). He chooses **Judah, Mount Zion**, and **David**. No reasons are given for these choices. Nothing is said that they possess the qualities that **Ephraim** lacked, such as remembering God's saving acts, believing God, or keeping his covenant. Focus is given to God's free choice.[36]

God's forgiveness and his decision ultimately not to withdraw his presence from his people are based on his gracious, sovereign will—based on his love. *Why* he chooses to be merciful will always be beyond our understanding. *That* he chooses to be merciful should always bring great hope to weak and wayward people.

He built his sanctuary like the heights. The symmetry with the previous stanza further emphasizes the sovereignty of God in his dealings with his people. Just as he rejected Shiloh as the place where his presence symbolically dwelt (v. 60), so he chooses Zion as the place of his presence. These choices are God's choices. He will not allow himself to be manipulated by the selfish whims of his people—be they the desire for food on the part of the exodus generation (vv. 17–20) or Israel's attempt to use the ark of the covenant as a talisman in their conflict with the Philistines (vv. 60–64)—but he will show his grace in his time and in accordance with his will. Interestingly, the psalmist associates the Jerusalem temple not with

---

36. Broyles, *Psalms*, 325. Emphasis original.

Solomon, its builder, but with David, the originator of the idea (2 Sam 7).
Perhaps the poet does so because of Solomon's ultimate association with
the type of idolatry he critiques (Ps 78:58), or perhaps the psalmist simply
wants to draw attention to the one who serves as the paradigm for godly
rule in Israel despite all his failings.

Like the earth that he established forever. The description of the
Jerusalem temple bears all the hallmarks of Old Testament eschatological expectation. Drawing a comparison between the establishment of
God's sanctuary on Mount Zion and the foundation of the earth shows
the centrality and significance of the worship of the one true God. "God
'loves' Zion (cf. 47:4; 87:2) and there himself built the temple, high as the
heavenly heights and deep as the foundations of the earth; it has thus a
cosmic significance, center of the divine rule on earth."[37] This psalm is
part of a collection that was probably gathered in response to the exile of
Judah (see comments on Ps 74). At this time Judah was a bit-part player on
the political stage of the ancient Near East, yet the author of this poem is
aware that a universal and eternal significance remains in God's dwelling
place on earth. Zion is presented as stable, like the earth, even though the
previous psalms in this collection have lamented the temple's destruction.
Somehow, the poet was aware that the choice of Zion and the choice of
David would have profound ramifications far beyond the borders of Israel
and the time in which he lived, even though often it did not appear that
way throughout history.

He chose David his servant and took him from the sheep pens.
This lengthy psalm ends with the poignant image of David as the shepherd-
king. He is chosen by God, and the pastoral imagery of caring for sheep is
transposed to caring for God's people on a national scale. The presentation
of David is idealized. He is described as the shepherd who looked after
God's people with "integrity of heart" and who led God's people with
"skillful hands" (Ps 78:72). From the reader's knowledge of David based on
the Old Testament historical books, however, it would be fair to say that
this idealistic image of David is only partially true. We are not meant to
assume that the psalmist was unaware of David's failings, rather—as with
his description of the temple as still having cosmic significance even after
its destruction in the fall of Jerusalem—we see here the author's hope in a
coming king from the line of David who would truly represent the best of
everything the historical David offered. The concluding voice of Psalm 78
speaks clearly of a future hope. God's people may well be rife with failure

---

37. Eaton, *Psalms*, 285.

and sin, but God's grace, based on his love, is still alive and well. The temple may have been destroyed, but it is as stable as the foundations of the earth itself. And at the time in which this collection was added to the Psalter, there was no Davidic king reigning in Jerusalem, yet the psalmist is fully aware that Yahweh's promise to David still holds true. For a poem that is dominated by warnings concerning the unfaithfulness of the covenant community, Psalm 78 concludes with a voice of hope. This hope, however, is not based on any confidence in the inherent ability of God's people to keep his law. It is rather based on the sure knowledge of the God who loves his people and is still full of grace and forgiveness. The psalmist's hope is founded on the remembrance of a God who keeps his promises.

DARK PAST. Psalm 78, like its neighbors, emphasizes the importance of learning from the past. On a human level, our natural desire is to learn from the high points of human history. In some ways it is easier for us to look to the examples of our heroes and to seek to emulate them. We tend to try to brush embarrassing events under the carpet. We do not speak about those relatives who have brought shame upon the family or those activities we would rather forget. But the twice-repeated focus of Psalm 78 is on the failings of past generations of God's people, and it is clear that we must learn from the errors of those who have gone before us as much as from the examples of those who have lived well. It is significant that the poet chooses to focus on two separate generations of Hebrews who failed to remember their God. As we see above, the psalmist first focuses on the rebellion of the exodus generation (vv. 12–55), but he also draws our attention to the repetition of this type of unfaithfulness during the reign of the latter judges (vv. 56–64). So not only does the psalmist point out the failings of a past generation—he also considers the failure of a separate generation *to learn* from the failings of their forefathers.

It is a clear biblical maxim that God expects his people to learn from his past dealings with their ancestors. And just as we are expected to follow the examples of those who honor God (Heb 11), so also we are meant to learn from the failings of both Israel and the church. Both the Bible and church history are full of good examples to be emulated, and also examples of the types of behavior we should avoid at all cost. Psalm 78 makes it clear that learning from negative examples is just as important as celebrating that which is positive. The early verses of the poem (vv. 1–8) set the tone for the historical account that follows. It is all about teaching and learning. The failure of God's people to remember God's character and works will always be disastrous for them. Failure to learn from the mistakes of those who have gone before us condemns us to repeat those mistakes. The introductory verses of this historical account set the tone for the life of faith of each successive generation of the Christian community. Each new generation of the church should go beyond those who have gone before them. Today's generation bears the responsibility to teach tomorrow's generation, and tomorrow's generation, in learning from our experiences, should be equipped to go farther than we have done in our experience of God. Each generation has the responsibility both to learn from the past and to teach for the future. In this way, God's people should grow and mature as the generations pass. The process of discipleship is not exclusive to the New Testament—we see the same ideas at work here in Psalm 78.

Future hope. Focusing on the inadequacies of those who have gone before us should not, however, lead us to an attitude of negativity. Given the extensive consideration of the ways in which Israel had failed God, the concluding verses of Psalm 78 (vv. 65–72) seem unduly positive. How is it that the psalmist is able to celebrate the stability of Mount Zion and the temple in Jerusalem when the neighboring psalms of this book of the Psalter (e.g., Ps 74) lament the demise and destruction of these symbols of God's permanent presence? How is it that the psalmist is able to celebrate the leadership of David so fulsomely (Ps 78:70–72) when the hearers of this psalm would be fully aware of David's moral failings and also of the fact that, in the postexilic period, there was no Davidic king on the throne? Of course, it could be the case that this poem was written before the fall of Jerusalem and the removal of the Davidic line from power. But even if that be the case, Psalm 78 is found in its place in the Psalter amidst a collection that is in many ways dominated by the fall of Jerusalem. Why would the editors who collected these psalms include such a poem here? Jerusalem has fallen. The temple is destroyed. No son of David sits on the throne. How is it, then, that the psalmist is able to conclude on such a positive note of future hope?

Verses 65–72 are fully focused on the character of God and his gracious, sovereign power. Ultimately, the psalmist celebrates the fact that relationship with God is not dependent on the ability of God's people to keep the covenant. Were that the case, each and every successive generation would experience the withdrawal of God's presence from their midst. The final voice of Psalm 78 celebrates a God who is gracious simply because he is who he is . . . and not because of anything in us. So there is always hope for the future of God's people, for his character remains unchanged and his promise cannot be broken.

These truths are the basis for the eschatological hope we see in the Old Testament. Despite all the failings of past generations, the psalmist sees that Yahweh still loved his people and chose Judah as the place of his dwelling and David as his own vicegerent. As far as we can tell from the psalmist's presentation, Yahweh did these things not because of any inherent worth in either Judah or David but simply out of love and his sovereign willingness to do so. Even in the postexilic period, therefore, when Judah had been marginalized and the temple destroyed, the people of the covenant were able to look upon both Zion and David with hope. The temple may have been destroyed and the throne of David may have lain empty, but Yahweh had been faithful to his promise in the past, and the psalmist knew that he would be faithful again in the future. So throughout many of the psalms we see this continuing tone of hope when Zion and David are mentioned. Somehow, these concepts that were so richly symbolic in the past would become significant again.

Psalm 78 in the New Testament. It is possible that Psalm 78 is quoted in the Gospel of John. When the Pharisees question Jesus' ability to work miracles in John 6:31, the statement they make is probably drawn from Psalm 78:24.[38] Effectively, the Pharisees point out that Yahweh gave Israel "bread from heaven," and their implied critique of Jesus is, "What can you do that compares with such an amazing miracle?" Jesus points them to the greater miracle he will work in behalf of God's people. Rather than *giving* his people bread that feeds them in the moment but eventually allows their hunger to return, God—in his son Jesus—has *become* for his people the Bread of Life from heaven so that they may never hunger again (John 6:32–41). What miracle could be greater than the provision of manna in the desert? Jesus, the God-Man, *gives himself* so that all who participate in him and his sacrifice will find eternal life in fellowship with God— something that the exodus generation could only dream of. "Bread from heaven" takes on a whole new meaning in the sacrificial work of Christ—a new meaning that we celebrate every time we take the Lord's Supper in an act of remembrance of the type encouraged in Psalm 78.

A holy God and the question of presence. One of the other classic Old Testament questions that Psalm 78 brings to the fore poses the problem of how an absolutely holy God can dwell in the midst of a people who are anything but holy. This tension begins in Genesis 3 with the first sin of humankind and is expressed in different ways throughout the pages of the Old Testament. Adam and Eve were distanced from the presence of God by

---

38. Margaret Daly-Denton, "The Psalms in John's Gospel," in *The Psalms in the New Testament*, ed. S. Moyise and M. J. J. Menken (London: T&T Clark, 2004), 133–34.

being removed from the garden. Cain is forced to wander farther away from the garden following his act of fratricide. We see the same problem throughout the many generations of Israel's relationship with God as it is recorded in the Old Testament. How can a God who tolerates no sin maintain relationship with a sinful people? How can God dwell among humankind?

This thorny issue is one that reaches resolution only in the incarnation of Christ. In John 1:14 we read, "The Word became flesh and made his dwelling among us. We have seen his glory, the glory of the one and only Son, who came from the Father, full of grace and truth." The tension of the holy God's dwelling in the midst of the unholy is resolved when God himself takes on human form. First, in the physical incarnation of Jesus for the thirty-three years of his life on earth, God literally lived in the midst of sinful humanity. So on one level that tension is resolved in the incorporation of perfect humanity and divinity in the same living being— Jesus of Nazareth. Second, of course, the incarnation was not an end in itself—rather, it was the means by which Jesus the Messiah could secure salvation and restoration of relationship with God for all who believe in him. In taking human form and paying the price for human sin, Jesus offers everyone who has come to faith in him the possibility of complete cleansing and therefore restoration of relationship with the God who is pure. The need for holy places and priests to act as intermediaries and sacrifices to take away sin has been removed entirely through the work of Christ. Cleansing is secured in his perfect act of sacrifice, so the problem of presence is removed. Sin still distances one from God, but the cleansing made available through the sacrifice of Jesus enables us to "walk in the light, as he is in the light" (1 John 1:5–2:2).

PROPER PERSPECTIVE ON THE COST OF DISCIPLE-SHIP. Psalm 78:18 reminds us of an example not to be followed—the willful rebellion of the children of Israel in the desert. The psalmist picks up on the imagery of Exodus 16 and Numbers 11 to remind his generation not to follow this example of stubborn rejection. The great irony that we see in the behavior of the wilderness generation is how they idealized their previous life. With miraculous displays of awesome power, Yahweh had just brought people out of Egypt and was in the process of leading them through the desert to a new and promised land of bounty. God had freed them from slave labor, from ethnic oppression, and from the tyranny of a genocidal dictator. Yet in these desert months, how did Israel come to think about their time in Egypt? Numbers 11:4–6 tells us:

The rabble with them began to crave other food, and again the Israelites started wailing and said, "If only we had meat to eat! We remember the fish we ate in Egypt at no cost—also the cucumbers, melons, leeks, onions and garlic. But now we have lost our appetite; we never see anything but this manna!"

Thoughts of violence and suffering have made way for reminiscences about cucumbers, melons, and garlic. Since God had only provided them with miracle bread to eat in the desert, the people had become upset! They wanted meat to go along with this bread that had been so amazingly provided. In their discontent, Israel's perspective had become totally skewed. They failed to see the miracle of the provision of manna in a place where there would be no food for them otherwise. They failed to remember the extremes of suffering they faced while in Egypt. For the people at that time, and for reasons that are difficult for us to discern from our historical perspective, the perceived cost and sacrifice of following Yahweh had become too great. They longed to return to the life they had before.

Christians living in the twenty-first century should not be too quick to shake our heads at the fickleness of the exodus generation, for we often fall prey to exactly the same tendencies. For a generation in which Christianity is becoming increasingly marginalized in the Western world, it is easy to look at the license and permissiveness of the world in which we live and to say, "It's too hard to be a Christian! I want to go back to the life I had before!"

We can all face this tendency on the journey that is the Christian life of faith. Sometimes the cost of being different just seems too high. Sometimes we feel that God is asking too much of us. Sometimes we just get tired of fighting with the world, the flesh, and the devil. It is at these times that we start to idealize a "normal" life—a life without the costs of faith. Just as the exodus generation lost their grip on the reality of what life was like before they started to walk with Yahweh, so we too can glamorize or idealize our past lives, thus making them seem to be a better option than they ever really were.

On days such as these, we need to follow the advice of the author of Psalm 78 by remembering the true nature of the God we worship. As we think about the God of grace and all that he has done for us in his Son, our perspectives are transformed. As we meditate on the true character of God, as we consider the self-sacrifice of Christ, as we recall the indwelling presence of God the Holy Spirit in our hearts, our perspectives on life now and life before are transformed. On days such as these, we too need to "put [our] trust in God, . . . not forget his deeds, . . . [and] keep his commands" (v. 7).

Functionality and reality. In Psalm 78:32–39 it becomes apparent that the people believe they can manipulate God. Somehow they think they can get what they want out of God without actually upholding their responsibilities within the covenantal relationship. They would remember that "God was their Rock" and "Redeemer" and "flatter him with their mouths" (vv. 35–36), but "their hearts were not loyal to him, they were not faithful to his covenant" (v. 37). In any form of organized religion, it is always a danger for worship to become all about the worshiper rather than the object of worship, and we are not immune from this danger within the Christian church. Given our fundamentally selfish human nature, it is very easy for worship to become more about what we can get out of God than it is about what we offer to him. Our prayers become shopping lists, and we demand that God fulfill his obligations toward us. It is often easy to forget that God is . . . *God!* He is all-powerful and more than slightly terrifying. (Notice how human beings become terrified when confronted by any sort of manifestation of the real presence of God [e.g., Isa 6:5; Mark 9:5–6 et al.]).

The challenge, once again, is to think properly as we worship God. Psalm 78 makes it clear that remembrance is the key to right relationship with him. As we worship, we must always remember that God is the one who is *worthy* of praise. We must remember all that he has done for us. We must be aware of human frailty and the offense we often cause. We must also ponder his great character, his awe-inspiring love, and the immeasurable grace God shows to us day by day. It is in remembering who God is and who we are that we are protected from falling into a relationship with God that is purely functional (what we can get out of God) rather than a relationship that rejoices in the reality of loving God and being loved by him.

Psalm 79

A psalm of Asaph.

¹ O God, the nations have invaded your inheritance;
    they have defiled your holy temple,
    they have reduced Jerusalem to rubble.
² They have left the dead bodies of your servants
    as food for the birds of the sky,
    the flesh of your own people for the animals of the wild.
³ They have poured out blood like water
    all around Jerusalem,
    and there is no one to bury the dead.
⁴ We are objects of contempt to our neighbors,
    of scorn and derision to those around us.
⁵ How long, LORD? Will you be angry forever?
    How long will your jealousy burn like fire?
⁶ Pour out your wrath on the nations
    that do not acknowledge you,
on the kingdoms
    that do not call on your name;
⁷ for they have devoured Jacob
    and devastated his homeland.
⁸ Do not hold against us the sins of past generations;
    may your mercy come quickly to meet us,
    for we are in desperate need.
⁹ Help us, God our Savior,
    for the glory of your name;
deliver us and forgive our sins
    for your name's sake.
¹⁰ Why should the nations say,
    "Where is their God?"
Before our eyes, make known among the nations
    that you avenge the outpoured blood of your servants.
¹¹ May the groans of the prisoners come before you;
    with your strong arm preserve those condemned to die.
¹² Pay back into the laps of our neighbors seven times
    the contempt they have hurled at you, Lord.
¹³ Then we your people, the sheep of your pasture,

will praise you forever;
from generation to generation
we will proclaim your praise.

PSALM 79 CONTINUES the tone of lament over the loss of Jerusalem and the temple that we have seen throughout Book 3 so far.[1] Although the setting is familiar, the tone of this psalm is much more forceful than the tone we see in its neighbors. Psalm 79 gives us a much more powerful insight into the human cost of the exile, as the poem dwells on both the physical and spiritual torment caused by God's apparent rejection of his people (vv. 1–6). So, Psalm 79 brings us more of the same, yet also confronts us more intensely with the pain God's people experienced in the Babylonian exile.

The Heading (79:0)

PSALM 79 BEGINS with the most basic of superscriptions—"A psalm of Asaph." A *mizmor* is one of the most common designations for the poems of the Psalter. The phrase is derived from the Hebrew verbal root *zmr*, probably indicating a song accompanied by music.[2] But it is the continuing association of this poem with the psalms of Asaph that is the telling factor in this superscription. We have observed the tone of lament that accompanies the psalms of Asaph in Book 3, and the continuation of this grouping inclines us to expect more of the same.

Reminding God of the Cost (79:1–4)

O GOD, THE NATIONS HAVE INVADED YOUR INHERITANCE. The opening verses of Psalm 79 are perhaps surprising for modern readers. This psalm

---

1. There is some debate about whether the original setting for this poem is to be found in the fall of Jerusalem and the exile. Psalm 79 is certainly a powerful lament of God's people in a time of great distress, and, given the placement of this psalm alongside others that deal with the crisis of exile, it seems most likely that the original setting to this poem is to be found in the suffering of the siege and fall of Jerusalem and the destruction of the temple. (For further discussion, see Hossfeld and Zenger, *Psalms 2*, 304–5.) Some scholars suggest that although this psalm is undoubtedly based on the events of the exile, it should be seen as the prayer not of those taken into Babylonian captivity but of the broken and captive people still living in Jerusalem (Goldingay, *Psalms 2*, 527–28). While it is difficult to be so specific, there are definitely merits to this argument.

2. See Eaton, *Psalms*, 68, and the first volume of this commentary (Wilson, *Psalms, Volume 1*, 127 n. 1).

begins by *reminding God* of the events that his people have faced in the fall of Jerusalem and the exile. First the poet reminds Yahweh that it is *his* inheritance which has been invaded and *his* temple that has been defiled—and by the *goyim*, the nations! The people of Israel were Yahweh's inheritance and the land of Israel was designed to be their inheritance. We see this dynamic throughout the Old Testament. Moses' prayer in Deuteronomy that Yahweh would spare the people describes Israel as God's "inheritance" (Deut 9:26–29), and the same book describes the land of Israel as the people's inheritance (4:37–38). Both land and people have been invaded and defiled by the rampant Babylonian armies. The following verses make it clear that it is not only the land but also the people who have been defiled in the fall of Jerusalem. "The nations" are those who "do not acknowledge [lit., *know*] you . . . that do not call on your name" (Ps 79:6). This powerfully terse imprecation makes the stakes absolutely clear from the very beginning: God's chosen people have been defiled, God's chosen land has been captured, the place that God chose as the symbol of his special presence has been destroyed, and all these calamities have been perpetrated by nations who worship other gods! Clearly, the psalmist does not believe in flowery introductions. He gets straight to the point, and the point is that Yahweh's people and place have been violated by pagan nations who worship false gods.

They have left the bodies of your servants as food for the birds of the sky. The psalmist goes on to elucidate the human costs of the defilement that has taken place. Many of the psalms emphasize the cost of the exile in terms of infrastructure—the temple destroyed, the city in ruins (e.g., Ps 74:4–7)—but here the psalmist reminds God of the human cost of Jerusalem's capitulation. His "servants" have not only been killed, but their bodies have also been left to rot in the open air. Surely this complaint is of a survivor. Insult has been added to injury. Not only has Jerusalem fallen, not only have the armies of Israel been defeated, but also the survivors have not been allowed to bury their dead. The psalmist and his compatriots are forced to look upon the bodies of friends and family, of men and women and children who have fallen within the city walls. Burial brings closure, and God's people have been denied that closure.[3] The pain is all the more stark because the psalmist knows that these corpses are those of Yahweh's "servants" left for the birds of the air, and it is the "flesh of your own

---

3. Eaton, *Psalms*, 288. Kraus comments, "It was considered a special misfortune and a terrible outrage when a human being was not buried (cf. Deut 28:26; 2 Sam 21:10; Jer 7:33). The poet gives prominence to these two recollections, the desecration of the sanctuary and the violation of corpses; all other events fade into the background" (Kraus, *Psalms II*, 135).

people" that is torn apart by the wild animals of the earth. These people are God's people. Good people. Not only have servants and saints been killed by the godless, but God's people who remain have actually been forced to look upon this tragedy without being able to do anything about it, thus increasing the sense of grievance that goes along with the sense of loss. Their treatment is an insult, and the psalmist reminds God that, by implication, any insult to the servants casts a shadow on their Master.

They have poured out blood like water all around Jerusalem. The intensity of human suffering caused by the fall of Jerusalem is further illustrated in Psalm 79:3, where the psalmist uses the language of sacrifice to describe the extent of the people's misery. For the Old Testament community of faith, the idea of pouring out blood (*shapak damam*) is one that would be readily associated with the act of sacrifice (see Lev 4). In Jerusalem during any one of the annual festivals, the temple would be stained by the blood of animals poured out in sacrifice to Yahweh. There seems to be a poignant irony in the psalmist's choice of words here: blood has been poured out all around Jerusalem, but it is the blood of Yahweh's people rather than the blood of sacrifices to Yahweh. The temple has been defiled (Ps 78:1), so there is no scope for the pouring out of blood in sacrifice, but blood *is* still being poured out—the blood of God's people. And, once again, the pain of being unable to bury the dead vexes the psalmist.

We are objects of contempt to our neighbors. In verse 4 the poet continues his lament over the shame experienced by God's people. There is shame in the fact that Judah has been invaded, shame in the desecration of the temple, shame in the fall of the city of Jerusalem, shame in the bodies lying around the city unburied. In this verse the psalmist makes that sense of shame explicit. Neighboring nations mock the Judahites because of the fall of their capital and the defilement of their place of worship (vv. 10, 12). In the ancient world, the conquering of one nation by another was seen as proof that the victorious nation's god was more powerful than the deity of the defeated people. So, we can only imagine the verbal torment that accompanied the physical pain of loss in the months and years following Jerusalem's fall. The human cost of the exile is poignantly laid bare in these opening verses of Psalm 79—it is the pain of loss, but it is also the pain of shame.

Lament: The Cry of Despair and Hope (79:5–8)

HOW LONG, LORD? WILL YOU BE ANGRY FOREVER? The question "How long, LORD?" is a common one in the lament psalms of the Psalter (Pss 6:3; 13:1; 89:46 et al.). These two Hebrew words (*'ad mah*) reflect the great pain of present experience. The following verses make it abundantly clear that the poet is aware of the causes of Israel's present suffering (Ps 79:8–9), but the fact that it results from the people's own sinfulness does nothing to ease the pain of their present suffering. The psalmist knows that Yahweh has the right to be angry with his people, yet their present suffering is so great that the poet feels compelled to voice the longing of the community that his wrath would pass in order for the tension and difficulty of the people's present circumstances to ease. God has every right to be angry with the inhabitants of Jerusalem, yet the psalmist is forthright in his questioning. Yes, God has the right to punish his people for their faithlessness, but should that punishment go on forever? Just as there is an explicit reminder to God in verses 1–4, so we see an implied reminder in the psalmist's questions. In asking "How long?" and "Will you be angry forever?" the psalmist is reminding God of his underlying character—a character that is merciful and disinclined to continue punishment beyond what is necessary to meet the intended ends.

How long will your jealousy burn like fire? This question shows that the poet knows the root cause of Yahweh's activity in punishing his people. God is jealous because the people of Jerusalem refused to trust in him and, instead, turned to false gods. In the Old Testament the covenantal relationship between God and Israel is often likened to the relationship between a husband and wife (e.g., see Hos 1–3), so the worship of other gods echoes the act of adultery (Deut 31:16–18). "God's 'jealous wrath' (v. 5) is his zeal for Israel's exclusive relation to him and is the term used for God's response to Israel's commerce with other gods (Exod 20:5; 34:14; Deut 5:9; 32:16, 19; Josh 24:19: Ps 78:58)."[4] God's anger burns against his people because of their apostasy, but the rhetorical questions of Psalm 79:5 mark the psalmist's plea that God's anger be removed from his people and redirected toward the nations.[5]

Pour out your wrath on the nations that do not acknowledge you. The psalmist's prayer is not just that God's anger will be removed from his people but also that the punishment they have experienced would be diverted to those nations that have destroyed and mocked Israel in the events of the exile. "Let divine wrath, at first aroused by the covenanted

---

4. Mays, *Psalms*, 261.

5. "There is a sense in which the first question [of Ps 79:5] is seeking information, though it also implies what sort of reply it looks for. The second and third will look like requests for information, but they are nothing of the sort. They look for denial. At the same time they are also scarcely disguised petitions, appropriate for beginning the petition section. They implicitly urge, 'Do not be angry forever—in fact, stop now; your passion must not burn like fire'" (Goldingay, *Psalms 2*, 523).

community, be now oriented against the *goyim* [nations] for their unspeakable crimes. The *goyim* perpetrated these crimes because they did not know Yahweh. Perhaps the meaning should be that they refused to know."[6] It is clear in the poet's mind that the people of Judah deserved their punishment, but this reversal in Psalm 79:6–7 urges Yahweh to respond to the gross criminality of the nations during the fall of Jerusalem, hence the explicit reminders of verses 1–4. In the mind of the psalmist, the fact that the nations still go unpunished for the barbarism that accompanied Jerusalem's seizure serves as an indication that Yahweh's activity is not yet complete. Yes, God's people deserved punishment for their spiritual adultery, and there can be no denying that the horrible brutality perpetrated against the citizens of Jerusalem must also draw down God's anger. There is no doubt in the psalmist's mind about the ultimate nature of divine justice—the people of Jerusalem deserved their punishment, but so too do the nations who were the temporal instruments of that punishment. So the psalmist cries out that the punishment of the covenant community has run its course—they have suffered enough. Now it is time for Yahweh to exact justice upon the nations who brutalized, then mocked his people. These nations "poured out [*shapak*] blood like water all around Jerusalem" (v. 3), and now it is time for Yahweh to "pour out [again the verb *shapak*] your wrath" in punishment upon the peoples who have refused to acknowledge him and doubt his very existence (v. 10).

The rationale for this reversal of punishment is their very destruction of Jerusalem and devastation of God's people. The irony is that God's people brought this punishment on themselves, yet the nations who inflicted the punishment on Jerusalem cannot be held guiltless for the brutality of their own actions. The armies of Babylon "devoured Jacob" and "devastated his homeland" (v. 7). They dared to mistreat the chosen people of God and to wreak havoc on the very land that Yahweh had chosen as a place of rest for his people. Although these events were all somehow part of God's plan for his covenant community, the psalmist knows that the brutal injustice of these activities against his people and the promised land will not go unpunished.

May your mercy come quickly to meet us. The psalmist has no other grounds for appeal than to call on the mercy of God's character. He is aware of the sins both of his forefathers (v. 8) and of his own generation (v. 9).[7] The psalmist knows that he cannot base his plea to God in the

---

6. Terrien, *Psalms*, 573.

7. As such Ps 79 echoes strongly the themes of Ps 78, which also addresses the problem of failing to heed lessons that should have been learned from the failures of a previous generation.

righteousness of his people. Their forefathers were not faithful, so the exile occurred; but the people in exile are no more true to God's commands than their forefathers were, so no plea can be made on the grounds that the present generation has changed. The psalmist's only basis for hope as he prays is that God will be true to *his* nature because he is merciful. The psalmist's prayer is based on his knowledge of God's character and practice. There is no other sure basis for confidence in prayer. The people have not suddenly changed. The poet's confidence is based on his knowledge that neither has God suddenly changed!

The psalmist asks for forgiveness of sins (v. 8a) and the swift expression of God's mercy (v. 8b), and he puts these requests in context by stressing the great need in which the people find themselves (v. 8c). The psalmist's hope is based on his knowledge of Yahweh as the God of the exodus. There is a sense in which Exodus 34:6–7 is foundational to the Old Testament's presentation of the fundamental character of God:

> And he passed in front of Moses, proclaiming, "The LORD, the LORD, the compassionate and gracious God, slow to anger, abounding in love and faithfulness, maintaining love to thousands, and forgiving wickedness, rebellion and sin. Yet he does not leave the guilty unpunished; he punishes the children and their children for the sin of the fathers to the third and fourth generation."

These verses are widely quoted in one form or another throughout the Old Testament.[8] There is a sense in which this exodus revelation of God's character—which is his response to the sinfulness of Israel in the golden calf incident—becomes something of a confessional statement for the people of God. Based on her experience of God throughout many generations since the exodus, Israel has come to know God as merciful in character. This understanding of Yahweh's basic nature shapes the psalmist's prayer. He has no plea to make based on his own worth or in the merit of this generation of God's people—his only hope is to thrust their present

---

8. Fretheim points to direct quotations of these verses in Num 14:18; Neh 9:17; Ps 103:8, 17; Jer 32:18–19; Nah 1:3 and also to strong allusions to these verses (although not exact quotations) in Deut 5:9–10; 1 Kgs 3:6; Lam 3:32. No other description of God is cited this frequently throughout the Old Testament. Fretheim goes on to comment, "It is important to note that this statement has a certain abstract, even propositional character. It cuts across the Old Testament as a statement of basic Israelite convictions regarding its God. It thus constitutes a kind of 'canon' of the kind of God Israel's God is, in the light of which God's ongoing involvement in its history is to be interpreted" (Terence E. Fretheim, *Exodus: A Commentary for Teaching and Preaching*, Interpretation [Louisville: Westminster John Knox, 1991], 302).

situation into the hands of the God he knows to be gracious, compassionate, and merciful. The people's need is great. The response of Psalm 79 encourages the reader toward an attitude of absolutely dependent prayer.

A Prayer for Mercy, a Prayer for Justice (79:9–13)

HELP US, GOD OUR SAVIOR. The remaining verses of Psalm 79 expand the prayer voiced in verse 8. In praying for God's help, the psalmist uses the address "God our Savior." While in contemporary Christianity we tend to think of the idea of God as Savior in spiritual terms, the Old Testament community viewed the saving nature of God in terms of divine activity in their behalf. Salvation is a much more physical and practical concept in the Psalter. So, the call for God's help is actually a call for his practical intervention into the grim circumstances of the people in exile in Babylon. Once again, the rationale for this prayer is based on God's nature, not in humankind. The psalmist prays for Yahweh's help "for the glory of your name"; similarly, he asks for forgiveness "for your name's sake." Verse 10 highlights the fact that God's name is mocked among the nations because of the present downtrodden circumstances of Israel. So, the psalmist grounds his prayer in the desire to see Yahweh's name glorified among the nations once again. The mocking question "Where is their God?" implies that Yahweh is not a god at all or, at the very least, that he is not a god to be reckoned with. The true nature of the all-powerful Creator of the universe and all of humankind is called into question because of the moral and religious failure of Israel that resulted in the rebuke of exile. In his prayer, the psalmist basically says, "Enough is enough!" The character of Yahweh has been besmirched among the nations, and they continue to mock the one true God. The psalmist therefore bases his prayer in the desire to see God's name glorified among the nations once again. And his prayer implies that the best way to restore Yahweh's standing among the nations is through the restoration of Israel and the bringing of God's just punishment on those nations who have mocked his character.

Make known among the nations that you avenge the outpoured blood of your servants. There is no doubt in the psalmist's mind that Yahweh cannot tolerate injustice. Despite all the ambiguity surrounding the causes of the exile, the poet knows there can be no doubt with regard to God's view of the events lamented in verses 1–4. Yes, in one sense, the people of Judah and Jerusalem "deserved" the rebuke of exile because they had betrayed their God and failed to heed the warnings of his messengers. God had warned them that the result of such behavior would be exile (Deut 28:64–68). But the fact that exile was part of the divine economy to bring his people to repentance does not change God's view of brutality and injustice. Why God allows such traumatic national and international events will always be a mystery to us, but there should be no doubt with regard to God's perspective on such matters. He hates injustice and will always avenge the blood of innocents (e.g., see Num 35:19, 21; Deut 19:12; Ps 9: 12). Once again, the psalmist sees the public act of divine retaliation as part of the defense of God's true might and character among the nations. Deuteronomy 32:43 calls on the nations to rejoice with Israel, for should other peoples exploit them, Yahweh will avenge the blood of his servants. Here the psalmist calls on God to make good his promise so that his name will no longer be mocked by those who worship gods of wood and stone. "The jeering quotation from the foreign nations . . . held up to Yahweh at the beginning of this section (v. 10) makes unmistakably clear that this conflict between Israel and the nations is not simply about the survival of Israel (cf. the second section vv. 5–9), but about Yahweh's own, specific divinity."[9]

May the groans of the prisoners come before you. The psalmist's prayer in verse 11 picks up on exodus imagery by calling on God to intervene in behalf of his people. The book of Exodus reminds the exilic generation that Yahweh heard the groaning of his people once before and remembered his covenant (Exod 2:23–26, which uses a synonym for groaning). He heard their groaning and responded by displaying the strength of his arm (15:16). So, effectively, the psalmist is calling on Yahweh to respond in behalf of the generation in exile in the same way that he did for the exodus generation. Once before he displayed his power to the nations by bringing freedom and release to his people. The prayer of the author of Psalm 79 is that God will do the same thing again. The people feel as though they are under a sentence of death (v. 11c), and only God can save them now.

Pay back into the laps of our neighbors seven times the contempt they have hurled at you, Lord. Imprecation is a concept that is alien to contemporary Christianity. It is often seen as being vindictive and vengeful—the antithesis of the gospel ethics taught by Jesus (Matt 5:43–48) and Paul (Rom 12:18–21). Here the poet prays that those who have mocked God's people as a result of the fall of Jerusalem would experience such derision, but in a manifestly more powerful way.[10] We will consider the theology and practice of imprecation more fully in the Bridging Contexts section, but suffice it to say here that the poet refuses to encourage

---

9. Hossfeld and Zenger, *Psalms 2*, 306–7.

10. This imprecation is probably addressed against those neighboring nations who encouraged the attacking Babylonian armies and continued to deride the Judahites after the fall of the city rather than against the Babylonian superpower itself (see Goldingay, *Psalms 2*, 528).

the people to take any sort of revenge themselves. Of course, this refusal may simply be an expression of the people's weakened and oppressed state—they have no capability of taking action against their mockers; yet I suspect that there is a more profound reason behind the psalmist's prayer. He calls for a severe response from God, but he entrusts that rebuke to God. The poet prays for what he sees to be an appropriate punishment but, in the very act of prayer, subjects his own will and wisdom to the one who answers prayer.

It is interesting to note precisely what it is that draws the psalmist's request for divine retribution. His prayer is not directed at the armies that laid waste to Jerusalem in such brutal fashion (Ps 79:1–4); rather, it is addressed at the mockers of verse 10. He has already prayed concerning the injustices of the invading armies (vv. 6–7), but he wants to make sure that the mockery that has called the very nature of God into question does not go without response. God has been slandered among the nations. They have claimed their own gods (worthless idols) to be more powerful than Yahweh. From the psalmist's perspective, such falsehood must be publicly rectified so that the nations realize that Yahweh is the true God above all gods.

Then we . . . will praise you forever. Much of Psalm 79 is simply a prayer in which the psalmist reminds God of things he already (clearly) knows. Yahweh is fully aware of the brutalities suffered by his people when Jerusalem was captured, yet the psalmist reminds him of these pains (vv. 1–4). Equally, God is fully aware of the mockery that his name was subjected to following the capture of his people, yet the psalmist reminds him of these events as well (vv. 10, 12). For today's readers this dynamic is strange, yet it is one that we see often in the Psalms. The poets of the Psalter often remind God of events that have occurred and of his promises to his people.[11] Once again, at the very end of Psalm 79, the poet reminds God of something God knows, namely, that they are his people and are under his care. The psalmist states this reminder in a promise of praise. When God responds to the prayers of his people and "sets things right," then the people's public voice shall change from the lament of the present song to a voice of continuous praise.

This assurance, however, comes with a reminder that is implicit throughout the whole of Psalm 79. The people singing this psalm of lament are "*your* people, the sheep of *your* pasture" (v. 13, emphasis added; cf. Ps 100:3). In the same way, it was "*your* inheritance" that was invaded and "*your* holy temple" that was defiled (Ps 79:1, emphasis added). The slain of Jerusalem

---

11. See Contemporary Significance for further discussion of this strange yet powerful dynamic in prayer.

are described as "your servants" and "your own people" (v. 2). Equally, the punishment that Jerusalem had experienced was a result of "your jealousy" (v. 5), and the flip-side of this coin is that it is "for your name's sake" (v. 9) and by "your strong arm" (v. 11) that the psalmist believes the people will be saved. This prayer is all about God and his relationship with his people. Such is the voice of lament. Although subtle, the poet voices the expectations of the people. They are "the sheep of" Yahweh's pasture—under his protection and care—and this reality gives rise to expectations on their part. Their covenantal expectations are voiced in the prayer of Psalm 79.[12] The people have sinned and received God's rebuke for it. Their lament is grounded in their view of their own circumstances, and they believe they have suffered enough and have learned their lesson—hence their reminder to God that they are his people; hence their prayer for release from their present suffering; and hence their appeal that God will restore the honor of his own name and prove himself once again to be Lord over all the nations.[13] Then his people will praise his name from generation to generation. Their prayer is for permanent restoration and that renewed community will be marked by continual, grateful praise.

TWO ELEMENTS OF THE PRAYER that is Psalm 79 make contemporary Christians profoundly uncomfortable—imprecation and lament. First, we are uncomfortable with the idea of asking God to do nasty things to other people (vv. 6, 12). This type of prayer is known as imprecation, and psalms that include such elements are described as imprecatory psalms—psalms that ask the Lord to take vengeance on one group of people or another. Second, we are uncomfortable with the lament aspects of many of the psalms. How is it that the psalmist dares to tell God his people have suffered enough? How dare he insist, as he clearly does,

---

12. For discussion on the spiritual dynamics of prayers of lament see Jamie A. Grant, "Psalms 73 and 89: The Crisis of Faith," in *Praying by the Book: Reading the Psalms*, ed. C. G. Bartholomew and A. West (Carlisle: Paternoster, 2001), 73–79.

13. "[T]he nations mock Israel, a people who dwell in exile, and they mock their God, Yahweh, who is apparently unable to deliver Israel from the hands of the Babylonians. The psalmist's climactic assertion in 79,13 then is a response to the two explanations of Israel's situation: 1) as the nations would claim, Yahweh is not God; or 2) Israel is not his people. . . . The psalmist challenges Yahweh to restore his own name and to deliver his servants, and thereby Prove that Yahweh is God and that Israel is indeed his people and the sheep of his pasture" (William M. Schniedewind, "'Are We His People or Not?' Biblical Interpretation During Crisis," *Bib* 77 [1995]: 546).

"We have suffered enough! We get the point! It's time to show mercy!" There is an undercurrent of complaint in this poem, and our contemporary brand of Christian spirituality just doesn't like that way of approaching God. So how to deal with these two issues?

Imprecation. Imprecatory psalms need to be seen for what they are: prayers! Their identity is significant to the whole dynamic. David Firth wrote a book about the imprecatory psalms and titled it *Surrendering Retribution in the Psalms*.[14] This surrendering is precisely what occurs in the imprecatory psalms. Rather than encouraging God's people themselves to seek vengeance against the Babylonians or the mocking nations, the psalmist encourages the people of God to offer these offenses over to him in prayer. What is more, the psalmist seeks only that retribution from God which is appropriate to the wrongs meted out against God's people. Neighboring nations such as Edom mocked the Judahites when Jerusalem fell in 586 BCE, so the psalmist prays that the reproach that they hurled at Yahweh should be revisited on them sevenfold. Obviously, there is an element of intensification here, but the prayer is that reproach will be met with reproach, not that reproach should be met with annihilation from the face of the earth. So, the psalmist prays that God will meet mocking with mocking, and he leaves the act of retribution in God's hands rather than taking it into his own hands. The imprecatory psalms are characterized by these two key features: giving over the act of retribution into the hands of God, who will respond to the prayers of his people precisely in the manner that he sees fit; and seeking no more than an appropriate response from God, not a vindictive one. (The psalms of imprecation are not vindictive.) Such prayers break cycles of violence because prayer is the substitute for a violent response to violence.[15]

Even with this awareness that prayer is better than responding violently and that vindictiveness is not "allowed" in the imprecatory psalms, I suspect that many readers would still consider these requests for God's vengeance to be less than Christian. Before rejecting these canonical songs out of hand, however, we should consider some complementary questions. Just how should the Christian community respond to the injustices of this world—by being nice? Surely it is a more appropriate response to bring this question to God in prayer. German Old Testament scholar Erich Zenger asks the same question in his book *A God of Vengeance?*[16] and makes several

---

14. David G. Firth, *Surrendering Retribution in the Psalms: Responses to Violence in the Individual Complaints*, Paternoster Biblical Monographs (Milton Keynes: Paternoster, 2005).

15. Ibid., 139–44.

16. Zenger reminds us that, "Without jumping into the conversation too quickly,

compelling arguments that the imprecatory psalms should be part of our communal spirituality in the church today. Among other observations, Zenger points out that imprecatory prayers treat social injustice and exploitation seriously. All too often Christians simply wring their hands in the face of oppression, as though we were powerless to do anything to stop it. But such injustice is an offense against God's created order and therefore deserves to be laid before him in prayer. Imprecation does just that by saying, "Your world was never meant to be like this! Do something to set things right!" So imprecation treats injustice seriously as an offense against God's plan for life on earth. Second, imprecation challenges our ambivalence toward injustice. Such prayers shape the way we think as much as anything else. In bringing injustice to God in prayer, we are forced to consider the daily reality of the world in which we live in the light of his design and plan for life on earth. Christians tend to be overly spiritual, yet we live in the real world. Responding to violent injustice in prayer forces us to focus on the world we live in rather than overfocusing on our future hope. Third, as Firth also points out above, imprecation leaves the right response in the hands of God. He knows what is best, so offering prayer to the one who is able to do all things is the best response to violence and injustice. There is no place for selfish vindictiveness in our prayers, for God will not tolerate such an attitude, which in prayer would also constitute a denial of the divine plan for life on earth. The whole point of imprecation is that we must let that prayer be an honest assessment of reality in the light of God's design. In giving these matters over to God, we acknowledge that he alone truly knows what course of action is appropriate to the circumstances. "Imprecations affirm God by surrendering the last word to God. They give to God not only their lament about their desperate situation, but also the right to judge the originators of that situation. They leave everything in God's hands, even feelings of hatred and aggression."[17]

Lament. We are equally ill at ease with the undisguised honesty of the psalmist's complaint in Psalm 79. In part we have addressed this issue already in our discussion of Psalm 73. Today's Christian spirituality often discourages us from *reminding God* in the way the psalmist does here (e.g., see Ps 79:1–4). In our churches we would not often say something like, "How long, LORD? Will you be angry forever?" (v. 5). Basically, the poet

---

without shoving them aside in know-it-all fashion, without expressing judgment out of a sense of Christian superiority, we need to try to understand these texts in their historical context, their linguistic shape, and their theological passion. That is the first task" (Zenger, *A God of Vengeance?* 25).

17. Ibid., 15.

points out injustices that have as yet gone unpunished and declares that God's people have already suffered enough! Would we have the confidence to pray together in such a way as we bring our daily reality before God in prayer? We should. Just as individual prayer to God must be absolutely honest, so must be our prayer in community. It is in offering these prayers that we begin to see matters more clearly from God's perspective. Also, such prayer reminds us of the character and activity of God. The Bible tells us what our God is like by nature and how he acts in this world. In making his complaint to God, implicitly the psalmist becomes convinced that the violent brutality suffered by the Jerusalemites will one day be avenged because such behavior is an offense against God (vv. 1–4). The psalmist is reminded of the true nature of God's character—he is a God of mercy (v. 8). And, ultimately, he becomes convinced that one day God's people will see his response and then in turn will respond to him by offering songs, not of complaint but of endless praise (v. 13). Honest prayer to God in community shapes the way we think of God and the way we view the reality of our present experience. Such prayer may sound forceful and, in some sense, inappropriate, but if as communities of God's people we cannot be honest with God in prayer, our experience of life with him is poorer as a result. (See Contemporary Significance for more thoughts on this matter.)

Psalm 79 in the New Testament. "How long, LORD?" There are echoes of Psalm 79 in the words of the persecuted church in Revelation 6:10. In John's apocalyptic vision, the martyred people of God call out to him seeking justice for the persecution the church had suffered on earth. Like the clear message of the poet's voice in Psalm 79, there is no doubt regarding the divine perspective on their suffering. The martyred believers know that the injustices that led to their death merit God's response. The issue is not whether God will respond. The only question is, When will God respond? As with the experience of the Old Testament community in Psalm 79, those who have died for their faith and now stand before God's throne are told that they will have to wait a little longer for their vindication. Justice will be done, but it will be done in God's time, not ours.

WHY PRAY IF GOD ALREADY KNOWS? One of the interesting dynamics of Psalm 79 is this whole idea of reminding God of things that have happened. This reminding may seem strange to us, since we know that God already sees and knows everything. So why does the psalmist remind God of things that have happened? It would probably be legitimate to expand that question somewhat to address an issue that many Christians ask from time to time: Why pray when God already knows what is happening and what we need? Probably every Christian has experienced thoughts along these lines—if God knows everything and sees everything, if God is a caring Father and knows what we need, why should we bring these things to him in prayer? Does he not see, or is he unwilling to respond to our needs?

Therein lies the error of our thinking. So much of our practice of prayer is based on an attitude of functionality. We pray to get things done. We pray to accomplish something. The end of our prayer is to meet the needs of others (or, all too often, of ourselves). Prayer is the way to "get things done." We have much to learn from Psalm 79 in terms of our attitude in prayer. Imagine coming home from a day at work in which you and three of your colleagues had just been fired. You decide not to say anything to your spouse because, after all, there is nothing that he or she can do about it. That same day you wreck the car but, again, do not talk to your family about what has happened. Later that week you are mugged at knifepoint, but once more you decide to keep the incident to yourself. The point, of course, is obvious: we talk about things with the people we love!

At the end of each and every day, wives and husbands talk with each other about their experiences at work or their day with the kids or what has been happening in the neighborhood. Each and every day, friends chat about everything and nothing, siblings catch up on what has been going on in their lives (good or bad), and parents endeavor to extract a fuller response than "Fine" to the question, "How was school?" Why is it so? The truth of the matter is that people who love each other talk with each other about their lives.

Did the psalmist believe that God had been asleep when Jerusalem fell and the temple was destroyed? No. Did he think that perhaps it had slipped God's mind? No. Did he perhaps believe that God was not really very interested in the plight of his people? No. So why remind God of these events? People who love each other talk with each other about the things that are important to them. It is what we do. Prayer is about more than "getting things done"—it is about relationship with a Father who loves us and whom we love. So we talk about all the stuff in our lives—the big things and the little things. We talk about things as we see them, and we let God shape us to see things from his perspective. We pray as an expression of love, not as a means to an end. That is why we pray even though God already knows.[18]

---

18. Douglas F. Kelly, *If God Already Knows, Why Pray?* (Fearn: Christian Focus, 2005).

Psalm 80

For the director of music. To the tune of "The Lilies of the Covenant." Of Asaph. A psalm.

¹ Hear us, Shepherd of Israel,
   you who lead Joseph like a flock.
You who sit enthroned between the cherubim,
   shine forth ² before Ephraim, Benjamin and Manasseh.
Awaken your might;
   come and save us.
³ Restore us, O God;
   make your face shine on us,
   that we may be saved.
⁴ How long, LORD God Almighty,
   will your anger smolder
   against the prayers of your people?
⁵ You have fed them with the bread of tears;
   you have made them drink tears by the bowlful.
⁶ You have made us an object of derision to our neighbors,
   and our enemies mock us.
⁷ Restore us, God Almighty;
   make your face shine on us,
   that we may be saved.
⁸ You transplanted a vine from Egypt;
   you drove out the nations and planted it.
⁹ You cleared the ground for it,
   and it took root and filled the land.
¹⁰ The mountains were covered with its shade,
   the mighty cedars with its branches.
¹¹ Its branches reached as far as the Sea,
   its shoots as far as the River.
¹² Why have you broken down its walls
   so that all who pass by pick its grapes?
¹³ Boars from the forest ravage it,
   and insects from the fields feed on it.
¹⁴ Return to us, God Almighty!
   Look down from heaven and see!
Watch over this vine,

¹⁵ the root your right hand has planted,
the son you have raised up for yourself.
¹⁶ Your vine is cut down, it is burned with fire;
at your rebuke your people perish.
¹⁷ Let your hand rest on the man at your right hand,
the son of man you have raised up for yourself.
¹⁸ Then we will not turn away from you;
revive us, and we will call on your name.
¹⁹ Restore us, LORD God Almighty;
make your face shine on us,
that we may be saved.

 PSALM 80 CONTINUES the call for restoration that we see in Psalm 79. In the previous psalm, this call concludes with the promise that the restored people of God will be marked by continuous praise: "Then we your people, the sheep of your pasture, will praise you forever; from generation to generation we will proclaim your praise" (v. 13). Psalm 80 picks up on this pastoral imagery in its opening verse, "Hear us, Shepherd of Israel, you who lead Joseph like a flock" (v. 1), and echoes its neighbor's call for restoration.

The Heading (80:0)

THE HEADING OF PSALM 80 IS COMPLICATED. Following the frequently occurring designation *lamenatseah* ("To/for the director"),[1] we come across what is probably the name of a tune (*'el-shoshannim*, "According to Lilies") and what is probably best seen as another, uncommon designation for a type of psalm, namely, an *'edut*. The difficulty lies in knowing how to translate this phrase as a whole. Very often in the psalms' headings, each phrase should be treated as an individual instruction or designation. For example, "To the director [of music]. According to [the name of a tune]. Of Asaph. A psalm." We see this type of heading frequently in the Psalter (e.g., Ps 75:0). So, the most natural way of translating *'edut* would be to treat it as the description of a type of psalm, thus giving the word its normal meaning, "statute."[2] The difficulty in the case of the heading for Psalm 80 is that the psalm would then have two designations. It would be described as both a "statute" (*'edut*)

---

1. See the discussion of this designation under Ps 75:0.
2. *'Edut* is frequently used as a synonym for the *torah* of Yahweh, another word for God's teaching and instruction (see Pss 19:7; 119:14 et al.).

and a "psalm" (*mizmor*). So the translators of the NIV decided the term *'edut* should be read as part of the psalm's tune designation: "According to 'The Lilies of the Covenant'" (since *'edut* can be used as a synonym of the idea of covenant). Such a reading is certainly possible, but *'edut* may also be read as a stand-alone term describing this poem as both a "statute" and a "song" (see the ESV, NRSV, and several commentators). It is difficult to come to any definitive conclusion on the matter, since both readings are credible. Neither interpretation particularly colors our understanding of the poem as a whole.[3]

Calling on the Shepherd God (80:1–2)

HEAR US, SHEPHERD OF ISRAEL. Psalm 80 begins where Psalm 79 ends, that is, with a focus on God as Shepherd of his people. Psalm 79:13 concludes with the assurance of lasting praise from God's people—who describe themselves using the language of the flock—once they experience God's restoration. Of course, this description implies care—the flock comes under the protection and provision of the shepherd. He protects from attack, leads to good pastures, ensures they have water, and so on. The flock comes under the shepherd's care, but the imagery of the ancient Near East also implies that the flock will follow the shepherd. So, there is a dual responsibility implied through the shepherd-flock imagery: care from the shepherd and obedience from the flock. The shepherd figure is often used as a metaphor for the king in the ancient world. We see this metaphor in the literature of many of Israel's neighbors; it is also a common image in the Old Testament (e.g., see 2 Sam 5:2; 7:7 regarding David's leadership, and 1 Kgs 22:17; Ezek 34 regarding the failings of human kingship). The idea of God as the Shepherd-King is a poignant and graphic image in the Psalter as well, as is illustrated most famously in Psalm 23.[4]

Psalm 80 renews the call for restoration by the Shepherd-King. The plea for renewal in Psalm 79 seems to come from the perspective of Judah and Jerusalem,[5] and Psalm 80 echoes this appeal but from the perspective of the northern tribes of Israel. (Note the specific references to Joseph, Ephraim, and Manasseh, all often used as shorthand references to Israel during the period of the divided kingdom.)[6] Not only is the content similar

---

3. For discussion of the almost identical superscription to Ps 60 see Tate, *Psalms 51–100,* 100–101.

4. For other examples of the shepherd-flock imagery in the book of Psalms see Wilson, *Psalms Volume 1,* 431–32; Pss 28:9; 77:20; 78:71; 95:7; etc.

5. See the comments on Ps 79:1–4.

6. The explicit inclusion of Benjamin (part of the southern kingdom of Judah) probably indicates that, although we have a northern perspective on the events of exile, the author still views the twelve tribes of Israel as a single kingdom in God's eyes. We encounter this

to that in Psalm 79, but also the tone is equally forceful. Literally, Psalm 80:1 says, "O Shepherd of Israel, give ear!" Effectively, the psalmist and people call on God to *pay attention* to their cry for help. "The need for this plea suggests that the people believe that God is inattentive (see v. 4)."[7] This call is accentuated by the fact that the opening verses of Psalm 80 go on to make four more similar pleas for divine activity: "awaken your might . . . come and save us . . . restore us . . . make your face shine on us" (vv. 1–3). Clearly, the psalm reflects the people's attitude that God has distanced himself from them and is not responding to their prayers. Interestingly, their response to this terrible, existential conundrum *is to pray!* As in Psalm 79, the poet is reminding God of his covenantal responsibilities. He is, by covenantal promise, the one who both shepherds and leads Israel.[8] The address to God is actually a reminder of the functions he has promised to fulfill—the protection of a shepherd and the guidance of his flock to safe places. The covenantal community does not see this type of divine activity, and they call out for it with great confidence because they know that such relationship has been promised to them.

Awaken your might; come and save us. The imagery of "shepherding Israel" and "leading Joseph like a flock" and Yahweh's "sitting enthroned between the cherubim" is strongly associated with the exodus from Egypt. Just as we have seen in both Psalm 78 and Psalm 79, the experience of exodus was particularly significant to the exiled community of God's people. Exodus was something they knew of theologically but was also something they longed *to experience in reality.*[9] The exodus narrative was in every way

---

theological notion—disregarding the geopolitical reality—from time to time throughout the history of the divided kingdom (e.g., see Isa 5:7; 11:11–16; Hos 1). The Septuagint's addition to the heading of the phrase "Concerning the Assyrians" may further support the northern locus of this poem. All this evidence taken together may well indicate that this psalm was originally written in Israel as a response to the Assyrian exile of 721 BCE but, with the passage of time, was included within the Psalter as part of the psalmic response to the Babylonian exile of 587 BCE that we see in Book 3. Certainly Ps 80 seems to continue the theme of exile begun in Ps 74 and is closely linked with the language and imagery of Pss 78 and 79.

7. J. Clinton McCann, "The book of Psalms," in *1 & 2 Maccabees; Introduction to Hebrew Poetry; Job; Psalms, NIB*, vol. 4 (Nashville: Abingdon, 1996), 999.

8. Both the noun "Shepherd" and the phrase "you who lead" are verbal participles in the Hebrew text. So the text could equally well be translated, "You who shepherd Israel, give ear; You who lead Joseph like a flock." The problem is that the exiled people have little or no sense of God as the one who shepherds and leads. See Goldingay, *Psalms 2*, 534.

9. We see the language of shepherding and leading Israel in the desert in Exod 13:18; 15:22 and in the idea of the pillar of fire and cloud. This shepherding of the exodus community is celebrated in Deut 8 and echoed, as we saw above, in Ps 78:52–55.

foundational to their theological reckoning; their present prayer is that what they know will be reflected in the reality of what they experience. They longed for the God of the exodus from Egypt to lead them out from their foreign captivity, whether that was in Assyria or in Babylon.

The exodus imagery is also replete with military imagery that becomes all the more explicit in the following verses. Of course, God displayed miraculous power in the plagues to secure the release of his people.[10] The psalmist's plea seeks a fresh expression of Yahweh's mighty works in the exodus. Hence he prays for God to "awaken your might"—an appeal for activity; to "come"—an appeal for God's approach, since the people feel that he has withdrawn from them in their plight; and to "save us"—a call for direct divine intervention to resolve their situation. This prayer asks God to respond in power to secure the release of his people.

The Refrain (80:3, 7, 19)

RESTORE US, O GOD. The three parts of Psalm 80 are divided by a repeated chorus in verses 3, 7, and 19. Although the nomenclature used to address God differs slightly, the essential content of these verses is the same: an (ambiguous) call for restoration followed by an appeal for blessing toward the specific end of deliverance for the people. Unpacking this repeated refrain slightly, we note that the prayer—"Restore us, O God/ God Almighty/ LORD God Almighty"—can be read in two ways. Most obviously, on one level the refrain is simply a plea for the restoration of the fortunes of God's people, a plea that they would be released from their present suffering and restored to the more favorable circumstances they enjoyed before. This is probably the way in which the plea for restoration is best understood,[11] but perhaps there is a deliberate ambiguity in the language used in this appeal for restoration.

The Hebrew imperative for "restore us" (*hashiybenu*) is the causative form of the verb *shub*, which is frequently used to describe repentance in the Old Testament. So the causative command form could equally well be read, "Cause us to repent, O God." Whether or not this reading is the intent of the psalmist's prayer, the ambiguity may simply reflect the inseparability of relationship with God from the restoration of their circumstances.

---

10. For example, the imagery of God as "enthroned between the cherubim" is an obvious reference to the ark of the covenant, which preceded the people into battle as they were led by God in the desert (Num 10:33) and entered the land (Josh 3). So the imagery of Ps 80:1c speaks of the Warrior God as leading his people in victory (see Broyles, *Psalms*, 330–31).

11. Goldingay, *Psalms 2*, 536.

This group of psalms dealing with Israel's exilic plight shows awareness that the people brought their present traumatic circumstances on themselves by rejecting God's ways. We see an example of this awareness in Psalm 78's repeated warnings not to echo the sinful behavior of the exodus generation and in Psalm 79:8–9's plea for deliverance from the effects of a previous generation's sins as well as from the present generation's sin. So, the immediate canonical context within Book 3 of the Psalter shows clear awareness that the exile and the people's present suffering resulted from their sinful rejection of God. The prayer in the refrain of Psalm 80, therefore, is particularly poignant: "Restore us" and/or "cause us to repent." The two realities are inseparably intertwined because there can be no restoration of circumstances without restoration of relationship with Yahweh.[12] For Zenger, the ambiguous call for restoration was clearly an appeal for a literal change of circumstance, but "it was at the same time a question of the restoration of the original relationship to God in which Israel had experienced a proximity of salvation that was summarized in the metaphor of the 'shining countenance.'"[13]

Make your face shine on us. Here the psalmist's call is for Yahweh's blessing to rest on his people once again. In an echo of the richly emotive Aaronic blessing of Numbers 6:22–27, the poet pleads for the experience of God's full blessing to replace the experience of pain and loss that has become their daily norm.[14] The psalmist seeks God's *shalom* to replace exile's sorrow.

O God . . . , God Almighty . . . , LORD God Almighty. While the repeated refrain is essentially the same in verses 3, 7 and 19, it is worth noting the changes in the way in which God is addressed. The prayer for restoration is first addressed to "God," then to "God Almighty," and finally to "Yahweh God Almighty." The movement in Hebrew is from *'elohim* to *'elohim tsebaot* to *Yahweh 'elohim tsebaot*—"O God," is followed by "O God of Hosts/Armies," which concludes with the covenantal name for God, Yahweh, and the description "God of Hosts/Armies." The progression is telling. The psalmist prays to *God* for blessing in verse 3. He reminds

---

12. See Broyles, *Psalms*, 331; McCann, "Psalms," 999.

13. Hossfeld and Zenger, *Psalms 2*, 314.

14. "The LORD said to Moses, 'Tell Aaron and his sons, "This is how you are to bless the Israelites. Say to them: 'The LORD bless you and keep you; the LORD make his face shine on you and be gracious to you; the LORD turn his face toward you and give you peace.' So they will put my name on the Israelites, and I will bless them'" (Num 6:22–27). Similar imagery is found in written prayers to other gods and goddesses in the ancient Near East, and the tone of all these texts implies that "the turning and bestowing of a shining face results in the bestowal of mercy" (Roy Gane, *Leviticus, Numbers*, NIVAC [Grand Rapids: Zondervan, 2004], 541).

the people in his prayer that this God is the commander of armies—the heavenly hosts at his disposal in verse 7 ("God Almighty" in the NIV). And verse 19 concludes that this God who commands armies is *their* God, the God who has made a covenantal promise to deal well with his people ("LORD God Almighty"). So, the prayer is offered to God, to a strong God, and finally, to a strong God who is bound to his people.

Calling on the Warrior God (80:4–6)

LORD GOD ALMIGHTY. After praying for restoration in the refrain, the poet addresses God in a telling manner. "LORD God Almighty" literally reads as "O Yahweh, God of Hosts [or armies]" in the Hebrew. This address is significant when compared to the prayer that follows.

How long . . . will your anger smolder? Verses 4b–6 offer the sufferings of the people to God in prayer, just as we have seen in so many of the psalms in this section of Book 3 of the Psalter. But in these verses the poet makes plain the cause of their plight. The events they suffer are not accidents of international politics. The psalmist's prayer is directed toward the almighty, all-powerful God *who is the cause* of their present suffering! *His* anger smolders against the prayers of his people (v. 4). *He* fed his people with the bread of tears (v. 5). *He* caused the enemies of his people to mock them (v. 6).

The psalmist knows that their present suffering has not arisen out of accident or circumstance. Nor, indeed, has their suffering resulted from divine inactivity. It is not the case that God has simply turned his back for a second. From the poet's perspective, Yahweh the God of Armies has turned his might against his people to bring them to their present circumstance! The shepherd imagery of verses 1–2 is transformed into the warrior imagery that is common in the book of Psalms (e.g., Pss 24:10; 46:7, 11; 48:8 et al.). The twist in the tale we see in these verses is that the Warrior God is fighting *against* his people rather than for them. For this reason—and for this reason alone—are the people experiencing their present humiliation. "The wrath of God (v. 4) has brought on the distress of the people of God. It has been active a long time already. All petitions were in vain."[15] There seems to be an implied acceptance that God was right to act in this way—against the temporal good of his people and for their ultimate good—but the prayers of the refrain make it clear the poet believes that the people have now suffered enough. Each prayer for restoration in verses 3, 7, and 19 is a call for Yahweh, the God of Armies, to start fighting again *for* Israel rather than against them.

---

15. Kraus, *Psalms 60–150*, 142.

The Parable of the Vine (80:8–18)

YOU TRANSPLANTED A VINE FROM EGYPT. Psalm 80:8–18 recounts the exodus story using the vine as an extended metaphor for God's people, Israel. Once again we see that the exodus story is an important one for God's people in exile. The undercurrent we have already seen in Psalms 77, 78, and 79 is that if Yahweh freed his people from bondage in Egypt, then he can free his people from Assyrian or Babylonian bondage as well.

You drove out the nations and planted it. The language of Psalm 80:8–11 echoes the Warrior-God language in verses 4–6. Just as Yahweh is the ultimate cause of the people's present distress, so Yahweh's hand was behind Israel's preexilic success, as we see in the psalmist's use of "you" throughout this section. "*You* transplanted . . . *you* drove out . . . and planted . . . *you* cleared the ground" (emphasis added). The exodus and conquest of Canaan was God's work. He was the one who made all these things possible. Israel's establishment in the land in the days before the exile (vv. 10–11) was all due to the efforts of the Warrior God in behalf of his flock. These verses also show the great care taken by Yahweh to ensure that this vine takes root and bears fruit—bringing, planting, clearing the ground. Equally, verses 10–11 recall the halcyon days of Israel's history when the nation was a major player on the stage of the ancient Near East.[16] The image of Israel as vine is common throughout the Old Testament (Isa 5:1–7; Ezek 17:1–10; Hos 10 et al.). But it is a metaphor that becomes synonymous with the failure of Israel and Judah to keep the covenant. The Song of the Vineyard in Isaiah 5:1–7 is the perfect illustration of this association. In these verses (as in Ps 80), Yahweh does everything possible to ensure that the vine is protected and properly tended, yet it yields only bad fruit; therefore, God threatens to break down its protecting wall. So the metaphor of the vine is one that speaks of the establishment of Israel in the land, but it is also one that reminds the people of their own covenantal failures, which led to their removal from the land.

Why have you broken down its walls? The recollection of the people's previous, positive circumstances in the land leads the praying psalmist back to lament over their current fallen state and to intercession for the restoration of the people to the land. Cultivated vines would often be enclosed within a walled courtyard to keep out scavenging animals that would uproot the vine.[17] The psalmist turns again to the poignant (almost

---

16. The reference to "the Sea" (i.e., the Mediterranean) and "the River" is designed to recall the full extent of the united kingdom of Israel in the days of David and Solomon (see Tate, *Psalms 51–100*, 315).

17. Kraus, *Psalms 60–150*, 142.

desperate) question, "Why?" As readers, we can almost feel the confusion and tension of the psalmist's question, "Why did God allow these protecting walls to be broken down and the vine to be uprooted?" The confusion results from the contrast between the care taken to transplant the vine in the land, on the one hand, and the subsequent removal of all protection on the other hand. The memory of the past experience of blessing (the exodus) makes their current experience of distress (exile) all the more unpalatable. Along with this confusion, however, there is probably also an element of tension in the poet's questioning lament. He himself adopts the metaphor of the vine to illustrate the establishing of Israel in the land. Surely the psalmist was aware of the metaphor's baggage. Surely he was aware of the prophetic critique of Israel as the vine planted by Yahweh's hand. Surely he himself realized that the fate of the vine resulted from the fruit borne by the people. There is tension in the question "Why?" because—at least in part—the psalmist *knows* why the exile happened. The imagery he chose to illustrate his lament suggests the answer to his own question.

Boars from the forest ravage it. Psalm 80:12–13 returns to the effects of the removal of divine protection—passersby pick the fruits of the vine, boars ravage it, and field creatures feed on it.[18] This poetic imagery points to the spoiling of Israel by foreign nations. Whether this imagery refers to the exile of Israel in the north or of Judah in the south (or to both), the psalmist laments the removal of the people from the land. The psalmist again sees Yahweh's hand in these events. God broke down the wall, and the uprooting of the vine from the land is a result of that intentional removal of protection. So it is that the psalmist sees that his only recourse is prayer. If God is the prime mover in bringing the exile about, then he alone is capable of bringing restoration.

Return to us, God Almighty! Again, the Hebrew here literally reads, "Return to us, O God of Armies" (see comment on vv. 4, 7). If the exile resulted from the removal of Yahweh's protection, then restoration could only result from the renewal of that security which comes from God's presence. This plea is that the Warrior God return to fight on the side of his people. Presence and protection go hand in hand in the Old Testament. It is assumed that if Yahweh is present in a place, then that place is under his

---

18. There is much debate concerning what type of animal the *ziz* of verse 13b actually is. While it is probably impossible to say with any specificity, Richard Whitekettle makes a good argument for seeing the *ziz* as a "small herbivorous terrestrial animal" (Richard Whitekettle, "Bugs, Bunny, or Boar? Identifying the Zîz Animals of Psalms 50 and 80," *CBQ* 67.2 [2005]: 264).

protection (see Pss 46 and 48); therefore, the removal of protection implies to the psalmist that God has removed *himself* from the midst of his people. So it is that he prays forcefully for God's return in power to dwell among his covenant community. In the psalmist's mind, this return will inevitably bring national restoration.

The poet's "why?" has been replaced by an appeal for God to relent. The psalmist knows why the people are in exile, but his prayer makes it clear that—from his perspective—the people have suffered enough. We see this pattern of prayerful questioning transition to a cry for mercy elsewhere in the Old Testament. "Following Israel's apostasy, Moses twice asks 'Why?' before requesting that God 'turn' (Exod 34:12). Thus the renewed request in Psalm 80:14 implies that the answer to the question in verse 12 is that God is punishing Israel for its sin."[19] The psalmist knows why the people are in exile—because they rejected Yahweh. But he prays for God to "return" because he knows that restoration is not to be found in logical debate with God but rather in appealing to his mercy. The people may well deserve their distress, but only by God's hand will they ever be restored from that humiliation. So, the only recourse left to both poet and people is to pray!

Look down from heaven and see! The second appeal in Psalm 80:14b is a prayer for a renewed exodus. About the exodus from Egypt we are told that "God looked on the Israelites and was concerned about them" (Exod 2:25). So the psalmist challenges God to "look down from heaven and see." Implied in this appeal is a challenge to God that he be moved toward mercy by what he sees. If Yahweh was moved to mercy by the conditions of his people in Egypt, then surely the conditions of his people in exile will have the same effect. Again, the poet's appeal implies that the people believe God has removed himself from among them. He needs to visit them again in order to see their sad state of being—surely then he will act out of mercy for their benefit. "The great middle section closes with the plea addressed to Yahweh that he would return (from hiddenness) and mercifully look down from heaven."[20]

Watch over this vine. The psalmist returns to the vineyard imagery by praying that God would once again "tend to" or "attend to" his vine.[21] As Goldingay points out, however, there is edginess to this final appeal in verse 14, since,

---

19. McCann, "Psalms," 1000.

20. Kraus, *Psalms 60–150*, 143.

21. The Hebrew verb *paqad* most commonly refers to God's "visiting" someone or "seeing to" something (see "פקד," *HALOT* 2:955–8).

When Yahweh attends to something (*paqad*), this often implies pun-ishing wrongdoing (again cf. 59:4 [5]). "I will attend to the altars of Bethel," Yahweh said through Amos (Amos 3:14). But Yahweh also attends in order to bless, deliver or restore (e.g., Pss 8:4 [5]; 65:9 [10]; 106:4). The supplicants look Yahweh boldly in the face and urge that kind of attention.[22]

There is a real sense in which the psalmist prays, "Do what must be done—whatever that might be—to bring the restoration of your people, your vine!"[23]

The root your right hand has planted. The psalmist goes on to remind God of the strength and intimacy of relationship with his own people. They are not some easily forgotten, passing tribe that Yahweh stumbled upon at some point. This vine was planted by him, with all the implications of care discussed in the comments on verses 8–9. God planted the vine. He cleared the rocks from the ground. He did the weeding. He made sure the vine was fed and watered. God himself has put a great deal of care into the development of his people. "Right hand" implies strength and effort of activity. Yahweh has worked hard for his people to grow. And now the poet changes the imagery from raising the vine to raising a son just to make the point of his prayer absolutely clear. It is not simply a question of the *effort* that God has put into Israel's growth—it is a question of the *relationship* that binds them regardless of past efforts. Israel is God's son! Surely Yahweh cannot turn his back on his own kin! Thus pressure is brought to bear in the plea to God. "Return to your people. Look and see their plight for yourself. Do whatever needs to be done for restoration to occur. Remember the efforts you put into this relationship in the past! Remember the ties that bind you to Israel!" the psalmist prays. His prayer is forceful and indicative of the way in which God's people are still able to speak to him today. Such powerful prayer indicates the reality of covenantal relationship.

Your vine is cut down. The psalmist's implied willingness to endure God's scrutiny (v. 14c), however uncomfortable doing so might be, is explained in verse 16. The vine is being destroyed, and anything must

---

22. Goldingay, *Psalms* 2, 541.

23. Terrien comments, "Ardently, the poet petitions the vintner to 'visit' this vine-yard—namely, to take care of it and to nurse it back to health. The primary sense of the verb 'to visit' is negative, 'to encounter in order to punish.' Perhaps this meaning still haunts the background of the psalmist's mind, and the ambivalence is partly preserved, but the notion that dominates is positive: 'to visit in order to heal and to bring back to life'" (Terrien, *Psalms*, 579–80).

be better than what they currently endure. The verbs used indicate the violence of the situation: "cut down," "burned with fire," "perish." Again, the psalm is clear about the origins of this violence. It may be perpetrated upon the people by foreign armies, but they are the proximate rather than the ultimate cause. "At *your* rebuke *your* people perish" (v. 16, emphasis added). So it is that the psalmist (and the people?) are willing to experience God's corrective scrutiny—they would rather endure fire that purifies than fire that simply destroys. Things could not possibly be worse. It is time to seek God's mercy even if, first, they must face God's rebuke for past sinful behavior.

Let your hand rest on the man at your right hand. The references to "the man at your right hand" and "the son of man [or, possibly, Adam]" in verse 17 are enigmatic but probably refer to Israel as God's son. Given the context of the psalm as a whole and the more immediate context of the extended vine/vineyard imagery, it is most likely that this verse seeks for God's blessing to fall on Israel once again. It is possible that this language (as elsewhere in the Psalms) refers to the king of Israel and is a plea for the restoration of the line of David.[24] The same vocabulary, however, is used in verse 15 to refer to the people of God, and in that light the most natural reading seems to be seeing this language as referring to Israel.[25] When God's hand rests upon ordinary human beings, they are enabled to do extraordinary things (Pss 17:7; 18:35; 20:6 et al.). God's resting his hand on his people is his sign of presence, help, salvation, and protection (see Ezra 8:31), and this situation is precisely what the psalmist sought for the people.

Then we will not turn away from you. Here the vicious cycle is explained in full! Israel suffers in exile because of their sin. The people seek the help of the one who brought this punishment upon them because he alone can provide resolution to their crisis. They call even for his scrutiny as part of their restoration because they know that *apart from his presence with them they can never please him!* It is only when God's hand rests on his people that they are enabled to remain true to him. The psalmist makes no grand declaration of future obedience on the part of Israel. He simply prays for God's hand of blessing to rest on the people, for it is only by way of Yahweh's merciful help that they will ever be able to live in the manner that pleases him. Only with divine mercy and help can the people remain true. Equally, only with that same divine mercy and help can Israel live aright— "Revive us, and we will call on your name." Calling on God's name was a complex concept in Israel's worldview. It meant worship. It meant witness.

---

24. Broyles, *Psalms*, 331.
25. See McCann, "Psalms," 1000.

It meant lifestyle. Yahweh was the source of life for the ancient Israelites, so to call on his name was to seek his engagement with every aspect of the individual's being and the community's life.[26] But in order to worship and witness and live properly in God's eyes, the psalmist first acknowledges that the people need his restoration. Apart from the reviving work of God, a right lifestyle and a right attitude of worship remain far removed from his people. It is only by his mercy that we are strengthened by God and enabled to live life in a manner that pleases him.

The psalm closes with the final rendering of the refrain, which seeks the blessing and practical help of Yahweh, the God of Armies.

THE VINE. Psalm 80's extended metaphor describing Israel as a vine would have communicated powerfully to the psalm's original hearers. It is an image replete with meanings and associations. The idea of Israel as a vineyard planted by God is a prominent image to describe God's care for the people and their own waywardness in response. It is a recurring picture in the prophetic literature. As mentioned above, Isaiah 5:1–7 is typical of the prophetic vine imagery. This passage focuses on the great care and provision that Yahweh had lavished on his people—yet the vine produced bad fruit. In the context of Isaiah's opening chapter, the "bad fruit" probably refers to empty, formulaic worship and lack of social justice within Israel. The people were not behaving in a manner concomitant with the care that Yahweh had taken over them. He took care to provide and protect, but the people did not do the same within their own ranks. So Yahweh decided to remove his protection as a wake-up call to his people, who had become calloused to his challenge to change their patterns of behavior.

This imagery is particularly powerful because it illustrates the reality of God's unwillingness to bring hardship on his people. He has put in all the effort of nurturing their growth. It is well known even today how difficult is it to cultivate grapes for use in the wine industry. How much more so was this difficulty the case in the ancient world. The idea of God as vine grower was designed to illustrate the great care he takes over the growth of his people. He provides them with everything they need to grow and to produce good grapes. The implications are clear. If God's people do not follow God's ways, he cannot be blamed for their rejection

---

26. Hossfeld and Zenger, *Psalms 2*, 316–17.

of his standards, for he has done everything possible to make faithfulness a reality. But sometimes God removes his protection as a means of prodding his people to realize their error and return to him (Isa 5:5–6). He did so via the exile, and the exiles' circumstances led to the lament of Psalm 80.

From the psalmist's use of the vine image, it seems that at least the poet—and probably some of God's people in exile—had come to the realization that their exilic suffering was a heart cry from God to return to him—hence the prayer for God's restoration and his renewed help in the people's quest for faithfulness (v. 18). This forceful prayer indicates that the people had, at last, learned the lesson of the vineyard and were now turning back to God. Ironically, the starting point of that process was, of course, to be found in the one who had previously removed his protection from his people. They realized that if Yahweh had removed the protecting wall (Isa 5:5; Ps 80:12), then he alone could restore it. So the psalmist leads the people in *lament* over their suffering and in *prayer* for renewal. There was (and is) nowhere else to begin.

The son of man. As explained above, I understand "son of man" in Psalm 80:17 as a reference to the nation of Israel in its original context. This view seems to make the most sense in the flow of the vine "narrative" that we read in verses 12–18. But several commentators point out that the "son of man" language is often used in the Psalms and other books of the Old Testament to refer to the Davidic king.[27] While I do not believe the poet intended this meaning in the original setting of the psalm, clearly the concept of the "son of man" takes on royal (and, later, messianic) overtones with the passage of time, and ultimately the reference to the "son of man" in verse 17 came to be read in this manner. The Greek translation of Psalm 80 sees this verse as referring to a future kingly figure. The translators ensure this eschatological focus by translating "son" in verse 15b as "son of man" as well.[28] So the whole section (vv. 14–18) takes on a much more messianic overtone—through the restoration of the "son of man" the people will be enabled to remain faithful. The Aramaic Targum of the Psalms goes even further by rendering verse 15b as "the King Messiah . . . who you made strong for yourself." With these amendments of verse 15b it becomes much more natural to see the "son of man" in verse 17 as a reference to a renewed

---

27. See, for example, Eaton, *Psalms*, 291; Broyles, *Psalms*, 331. Tate takes a mediating route by pointing out "the confluence of kingship and nation in the ancient Near Eastern thought; the king embodies the nation and his fortunes are those of his people, and vice versa" (Tate, *Psalms 51–100*, 315).

28. There is no indication that the original Hebrew texts ever used "son of man" in verse 15b. The appearance of the phrase in the LXX was a later addition.

Davidic king who will be responsible for the restoration of the people's fortunes. Arguably, Daniel also seems to use the "son of man" language with messianic overtones (Dan 7:13–14), so it is not surprising that Jesus frequently adopts vine imagery both in his teaching (Matt 20:1–16; 21:33–41 et al.) and with reference to his own identity and ministry (John 15).

Psalm 80 in the New Testament. While Psalm 80 is not quoted directly, as mentioned above, the vine imagery of the poem is echoed frequently in the New Testament and there functions on two levels. First, the imagery is used as warning to the people of Jesus' day not to behave like Israel, the vine of the Old Testament (e.g., Mark 12:1–12). Jesus uses the parable of the vineyard as a warning to the religious leaders of his day that they are in danger of missing God's rebuke, voiced first by the prophets and now by God's Son, and therefore are in danger of missing out on the reward promised to God's people. This use of the imagery is very similar to how the vineyard metaphor functions in the Old Testament. Second, however, in John 15 Jesus frames his own life and ministry in terms of the vine metaphor. In the Farewell Discourse of John 13–17, where Jesus teaches his disciples prior to his passion and crucifixion, he describes himself as the "new vine," a description that is pregnant with meaning. In the Old Testament, the vine was the community of God's people and therefore the "son of God." Here Jesus describes himself as the "true vine," that is the true Son of God. As we see elsewhere in the Gospels (e.g., Matt 1–4), Jesus as the Son of God is compared to Israel as the son of God. The Gospel writers go on to present Jesus as the true or faithful "Son," whereas Israel failed in their sonship. Here Jesus is the "true" vine, the Son who did not fail in his relationship with the Father. By inference, therefore, all those who remain *in* the true vine will continue in right relationship with Yahweh, the Father. The imagery of sonship and relationship with God continues. But John 15 makes it plain that the only way to find true and fruitful relationship with God is through ingrafting into the "true vine." In other words, fruitful relationship with God can only be maintained through continuing right relationship with the Son.

SEEKING GOD IN ALL CIRCUMSTANCES. One of the practical lessons we can learn from Psalm 80 is the importance of seeking God when life is difficult—even when we believe him to be the cause of our present reality! The psalmist and community believed in a God who is strongly sovereign; therefore, they had to accept that God was at work even in the painful circumstances of the exile. If we assume

Psalm 80 had a northern setting, the Assyrian armies may well have been the immediate cause of the people's present pain. But the psalmist was well aware that armies only wield power when allowed to by Yahweh, the God of Armies. For the psalmist there was no getting around the fact that God's control over all things meant that his hand was, in some sense, active in bringing about their distress. In the modern world, we tend to philosophize over questions of God and suffering. The psalmist believed in a God who was in complete control and who had allowed the exile to happen.

This perspective, however, leads to an important example for our own spirituality. The psalmist was clearly frustrated with apparent divine inactivity (v. 4), yet he continued to believe in a strong God who was in control of all things. The psalmist was also frustrated by God's apparent lack of concern with the difficulties faced by the people (v. 14), yet he continued to believe that God was the Shepherd of Israel. The lesson for us to learn is that God remains unchanged by the circumstances we face. Not unmoved, but unchanged. God's sovereign power was not changed by the fall of either Israel or Judah. Equally, God had not become indifferent to his people when they suffered the pains and indignities of exile. The psalmist knew this truth, so he prayed. He prayed honestly, and he kept praying even though he believed God to be responsible for their loss and distress.

In times of difficulty it is often easy to focus on the circumstances we face and forget about the God we worship. We can get so caught up in the difficulties of our daily reality that we forget about the one who orders every aspect of that reality. In trying situations, it is easy to fall into an attitude of complaint and dissatisfaction. The psalms we are reading make it clear that it is good to be honest before God. Psalm 80 echoes that principle absolutely, but it also stresses the importance of remembering who God really is even if we find it difficult to recognize aspects of his character. God is in control . . . even when life seems chaotic to us. God does love us . . . even when he seems distant and removed. The important lesson to learn is that we must continue to pray to God based on who and what we know him to be. Our prayers should be shaped according to our knowledge of God, not according to our perception of God by present experience. In Psalm 80, the psalmist's exemplary response was to keep praying even though he thought everything was God's fault.

Attitude of dependence. Psalm 80 and the vine imagery also speak to us about the importance of complete dependence on God. Today's world celebrates independence: the self-made man, the rags to riches story, "God helps those who help themselves," and so on. Our twenty-first-century society does not see dependence as a virtue. For many of us dependence is, rather, a blight: welfare, people sponging off of society/the government/ parents, and so on. Yet the poet in Psalm 80 is fully aware of his complete dependence on God. There is a sense in which an attitude of dependence is counterintuitive in the world in which we live. Clearly, there is also something quite contradictory in the psalmist's prayer in Psalm 80. He knows God to be the ultimate cause of his distress, yet his response is to pray to God! Why so?

The prayer of Psalm 80 is addressed to "Yahweh, the God of Armies/ Hosts." The prayer for restoration we see in verses 3, 7, 14, and 19 implies awareness that it was not by human means that Israel had enjoyed well-being in the past, and neither would future restoration come about by human effort. The prayer for God's face to shine upon his people again shows the poet's realization that temporal blessing comes from God—it is only in prayer, therefore, that national renewal will follow. Equally, verse 18 shows the poet's solemn realization that only with God's help will the people be able to be faithful to him. The psalmist makes no grand declaration of some newfound, innate ability of the people to remain loyal to God. He knows that only when God's hand of blessing is upon his people will they be able to remain true to him. Equally, Jesus' description of himself as the "true vine" in John 15 encourages a healthy attitude of dependence: "Apart from me you can do nothing" (v. 5). It is by remaining in him and relying on him that we are enabled to be fruitful. An attitude of dependence is realistic and drives us to prayer—dependence *has* to be a good thing.

Psalm 81

For the director of music. According to gittith. *Of Asaph.*

¹ Sing for joy to God our strength;
    shout aloud to the God of Jacob!
² Begin the music, strike the timbrel,
    play the melodious harp and lyre.
³ Sound the ram's horn at the New Moon,
    and when the moon is full, on the day of our festival;
⁴ this is a decree for Israel,
    an ordinance of the God of Jacob.
⁵ When God went out against Egypt,
    he established it as a statute for Joseph.

I heard an unknown voice say:
⁶ "I removed the burden from their shoulders;
    their hands were set free from the basket.
⁷ In your distress you called and I rescued you,
    I answered you out of a thundercloud;
    I tested you at the waters of Meribah.
⁸ Hear me, my people, and I will warn you—
    if you would only listen to me, Israel!
⁹ You shall have no foreign god among you;
    you shall not worship any god other than me.
¹⁰ I am the LORD your God,
    who brought you up out of Egypt.

Open wide your mouth and I will fill it.
¹¹ "But my people would not listen to me;
    Israel would not submit to me.
¹² So I gave them over to their stubborn hearts
    to follow their own devices.
¹³ "If my people would only listen to me,
    if Israel would only follow my ways,
¹⁴ how quickly I would subdue their enemies
    and turn my hand against their foes!
¹⁵ Those who hate the LORD would cringe before him,
    and their punishment would last forever.
¹⁶ But you would be fed with the finest of wheat;
    with honey from the rock I would satisfy you."

 PSALM 81 IS A COMBINATION of hymn and pro-
phetic oracle—it combines celebration with
declaration.[1] The psalm also gives the reader a
different insight into the plight of Israel's exile,
which is the major focus of Book 3. As we have seen in our discussion of
the preceding psalms, the pains, humiliations, and causes of the exile have
been the central focus of the poems from Psalm 74 onward. Psalm 81 also
examines this traumatic event in Israel's history, but the prophetic oracle
in verses 6–16 gives God's take on these events. The prophet declares to
the people how God sees the tragedy of exile and, clearly, the exile is every
bit as much a tragedy to God as it is to the people, but for very different
reasons! The effect of Psalm 81 is stark in the context of the Asaph laments
of Book 3. We have heard many prayers from a human perspective. Now
we hear God's declaration in response.

The Heading (81:0)

THE TITLE OF PSALM 81 CONTAINS an instruction to the director (see comments on Ps 75:1) that the psalm should be performed according to the
gittith—another one of the mysterious names we find in the superscriptions
of the psalms. (For *gittith*, see also Pss 8:0; 84:0.) There are three main theories regarding the *gittith*: (1) the designation refers to a type of instrument
originating in Gath; (2) the word names a tune; or (3) it associates the
psalm with the "winepress" (Hebrew *gat*), and therefore probably with the
harvest festival. It is difficult to draw any definitive conclusion regarding
the meaning of *gittith*, but since the nearby Psalm 84 also seems to have a
festival context, the third option may be the most likely.[2]

The Call to Worship (81:1–5b)

SING FOR JOY TO GOD OUR STRENGTH. The opening verses of Psalm 81 are a
real surprise for the reader of the Psalter. Since Psalm 74, we have been lost

---

1. Psalm 81 is often described as one of "the trio of so-called festival psalms" (Hossfeld
and Zenger, *Psalms 2*, 320). Along with Pss 50 and 95, these three psalms combine the call
to praise in a festival context with a declaration of divine speech in the first person. In
the case of each of these songs, some scholars posit the bringing together of two separate
compositions at a later date. Of course, this possibility exists, but as Tate points out the
association of markedly different types of material in a single psalm is hardly surprising or
uncommon (Tate, *Psalms 51–100*, 322). That these three psalms are unusual in their form
makes them particularly evocative, as they focus on the divine rather than the human
perspective.

2. See Tate, *Psalms 51–100*, 318.

in lament over the exile of God's people and the desecration of the temple. Psalm 80 ends with a desperate plea for restoration, and then its neighbor begins with this powerful imperative toward praise! The language of praise, of course, is not alien to the Psalms and becomes increasingly prevalent in Books 4 and 5. But this call to voluble praise is out of step with the tone of the poems of Book 3 up to this point.

Note the compelling nature of the commands that we read in these opening verses: "sing for joy . . . shout aloud . . . begin [or better, *raise*] the music . . . strike the timbrel . . . play the melodious harp . . . sound the ram's horn." As we see in many of the Psalter's calls to praise God, there is something almost vociferous about the psalmic expectation regarding our worship of God (e.g., see Pss 47:1; 66:1; 149; 150 et al.).[3] Psalmic worship is not a tepid affair—rather, it is whole-hearted and full of gusto.

There is something of a conundrum in terms of the locus of interpretation in this psalm. Verses 1–3 indicate a festival setting. The command to "sound the ram's horn at the New Moon, and when the moon is full, on the day of our festival" (v. 3) points to an original setting in one of the great pilgrimage festivals of the Old Testament.[4] Most likely Psalm 81 is to be associated with the Feast of Tabernacles, which commemorated God's protection of the Israelites during the years of their wilderness wandering (Lev 23:33–43; Num 29:12–40).[5] So on the one hand the opening verses of Psalm 81 point to Israel's festival celebrations—which imply that God's people are in the land and worshiping in the temple.[6] On the other hand, however, the canonical context (i.e., reading Ps 81 in the light of its neighbors) suggests a poem addressed to the exilic community.[7] The effect of

---

3. "The celebration begins with gusto with five invitations to worship (sing aloud, shout for joy, raise a song, sound, blow), and five musical ways to celebrate (choral and instrumental)" (Schaefer, *Psalms*, 199).

4. See Deut 16:1–17 for a description of the three Old Testament pilgrimage festivals, and see Lev 23:23–25 and Num 29:1 for descriptions of the blasting of "trumpets" in the celebration of festivals. This trumpet blasting is probably what the psalmist has in mind when he calls for the ram's horn to be sounded on the feast day.

5. Note the instruction to hold a holy assembly on the fifteenth day of the seventh month, that is, on the occurrence of the full moon (Ps 81:3).

6. This implication would mean that the opening verses of Ps 81 could be rooted in the preexilic period, if we assume that the psalm is the result of the combination of two preexisting poems, one early and one late. But the opening verses could also come from the Second Temple period, when Israel was restored to the land of promise. The poem's locus in that case would allow for the combination of both festal worship and reflection on the exile.

7. As J. Clinton McCann writes, "Following two communal complaints and placed in the midst of Book III, which recalls the crisis of exile, . . . Psalm 81 serves both as an

the prophetic oracle in verses 6–16 also places this psalm in the setting of the community of God's people in exile. And if we are meant to read this psalm as a call to Israel in exile, there is something forcefully defiant about this requirement to praise. There was no temple for the people to journey to, yet they are to remember Yahweh, the Provider, just as though they were celebrating the Feast of Tabernacles in Jerusalem. It is almost as if the psalmist says, "Regardless of our present distress, we *will* praise Yahweh!" These opening verses call them to an act of vocal and musical praise in defiance of their lamentable situation. Why so?

At least part of the rationale for this praise is found in verse 1a—sing for joy to *God our strength*. The praise command is a reminder that God remains unchanged even in the people's experience of distress. He is still *their* God ("the God of Jacob" [v. 1b]), and he is still their *strength*, regardless of how it might appear. Verses 5c–16 explain the reality of God's sovereign power in much greater detail, but the opening verse immediately clarifies the object of the people's worship. They are to sing for joy to their God, who is still their strength![8]

Begin the music, strike the timbrel. The poet calls the community to offer fulsome praise to God. The emphasis on praise with loud song (v. 1) and melodious instruments (v. 2) points to heartfelt worship of Yahweh. This call is not to stifled praise out of a sense of obligation. The poet demands a strong level of engagement in the act of public worship. "Sing for joy . . . shout aloud . . . strike the timbrel . . . play the melodious harp . . . sound the ram's horn!" The encouragement is toward an act of worship in which the people are fully engaged. The Hebrew commands are also all in the plural—the whole community is to be involved in this public proclamation of Yahweh's worth.[9]

Sound the ram's horn at the New Moon. Verse 3 poses a few challenges for the reader. Normally the ram's horn (Hebrew *shophar*) is associated with entry into battle (Josh 6; Judg 7), but it is also associated

---

explanation for the people's suffering (vv. 11–12) and as a hopeful, encouraging word if Israel will but listen and respond (vv. 8–10, 13–16). Beyond its possible original festal setting and its literary setting, Psalm 81 can function as a call to commitment at all times and in all places" (McCann, "Psalms," 1003).

8. The references to "Jacob" in verse 1 and again in verse 4, and also to "Joseph" (Hebrew *Yehosheph*) in verse 5, may well point to this poem's origin in the northern kingdom of Israel, just as we saw with Ps 80. See Terrien, *Psalms*, 585.

9. By way of example, it appears that the timbrel was normally played by women in worship as a rhythm instrument (possibly with accompanying dancing [see Ps 150:4]). So the explicit mention of this instrument implies the involvement of the the the whole community in worship. See Goldingay, *Psalms 2*, 548.

with the giving of the law at Sinai (Exod 19–20). (This latter point is interesting because the prophetic oracle in Psalm 81:6–16 focuses on the first commandment.) But it appears that the command to sound the ram's horn is probably akin to the blowing of trumpets at the three great pilgrimage festivals. This act was not part of the worship itself, but it did call the people together to give their praise and offerings to Yahweh (see Lev 23:24; Num 10:10). The references to the new moon and full moon probably point, more specifically, to the Feast of Tabernacles (see Lev 23:23–34), as these celebrations encompassed both the beginning and middle of the seventh month.[10] This command is an interesting one if we are meant to read Psalm 81 through the eyes of the people of God in exile. The psalmist calls on the people to celebrate God's provision for the exodus generation in the desert, for such was the focus of the Feast of Tabernacles. The symbolism is poignant. The people in the desert after their exodus from Egypt have been released from bondage, whereas the generation of Hebrews in exile do not yet share that experience. The call is to celebrate something that they hope for intensely. They also long for the experience of God's provision on the way to the promised land. So there is a real sense in which the psalmist's call to worship is a call to exercise faith in the face of difficult circumstances.

This is a decree for Israel. Psalm 81:4–5b reminds the people that remembrance of the Feast of Tabernacles is commanded by Yahweh. It is an act of worship that has been ordained by God. Of course, under normal circumstances, the celebration of this feast would occur in the temple following the pilgrimage of the people. But the loss of the temple and the inability to journey there do not change the importance of the act of remembrance. Just because the feast cannot be celebrated "properly" does not mean that its root lesson should be forgotten. God's provision for his people, which was triggered when they left Egypt ("when God went out against Egypt" [v. 5a]) must always be remembered, even amid circumstances in which that care is less than obvious to the community of faith.

It may seem strange to Christians today that worship can be commanded. We think of public worship as being an act of free expression, so *commanding* worship brings the genuineness of the activity into question. The command to celebrate the pilgrimage festivals, however, redresses our natural human tendencies toward forgetfulness and taking things for granted. The miracle of the exodus should never be forgotten (thus the

---

10. Broyles, *Psalms*, 333.

celebration of Passover), nor should the provision of God in the harvest (thus the Feast of Weeks). Equally, the miraculous provision in the desert must be remembered (thus the Feast of Tabernacles). The danger is always that such regular celebrations become no more than routine, but the fact that they can become empty ceremony does not diminish the appropriateness of regular reminders. The psalms of Book 3 of the Psalter underline the importance of remembrance, and Psalm 81 is no different.[11] If we are to think rightly about God, we must remember who he is and what he has done. This memory serves to shift our focus from the temporality of our experiences to the unchangeability of our God.

The Prophetic Oracle: Part 1 (81:5c–10)

I HEARD AN UNKNOWN VOICE SAY. There is an issue over the extent of the divine oracle from 81:5c onward. The NIV reads these as the words of the psalmist, introducing the oracle of God that follows in verses 6-16. This is possible, of course; however, the first person singular proclamation in verse 5c could also be read as part of the voice of Yahweh, which speaks through to the end of the psalm. Quite literally, the Hebrew reads, "I heard a speech [or 'voice' or 'language'] I did not know." The change in the person speaking is marked in the Hebrew, and the first-person singular who speaks through the rest of the poem is clearly Yahweh. So what options are open to us? The NIV reads this statement as a prologue to Yahweh's pronouncement made through the poet-prophet: "I heard an unknown voice: 'I removed the burden from your shoulders'" (81:5c–6a). So, effectively, the prophet who declares what is Yahweh's revelation to the people in verses 6–16 precedes his proclamation with an expression of special revelatory experience, Yahweh's voice being the previously "unknown voice." This interpretation is certainly possible, but it requires two voices both speaking as "I": the poet-prophet and Yahweh.[12] Another option of a similar nature is proposed by Goldingay, who suggests the translation, "I listened to lips I had not acknowledged." Goldingay sees the "I" to be the entire community of Israel who are now listening to the voice of Yahweh, whereas they had previously

---

11. See the interesting discussion of the putative office of the *mazkir* in David C. Mitchell, *The Message of the Psalter: An Eschatological Programme in the book of Psalms*, JSOTSup 252 (Sheffield: Sheffield Academic, 1997), 94. Based on these psalms in Book 3, Mitchell suggests the possibility that Israel's public worship included an official role for one who brought to mind the remembrance of Yahweh's character and past activity. Whatever the case historically, remembering dominates the message of this part of the Psalter.

12. Eaton (*Psalms*, 294), Hossfeld (*Psalms 2*, 319–21), and Tate (*Psalms 51–100*, 317–20) all follow this option, as do several modern versions of the English Bible (NRSV, NET, NASB, and ESV).

refused to acknowledge him and his verdict on their exilic experience.[13] The "I" of 81:5c is a collective in this view. However, this still requires two speakers who identify as "I."

It may be, however, that we should read the whole of the prophetic oracle as the words of Yahweh—in other words, as God who is speaking in the first-person singular from verse 5c to the end of the psalm. Were we to read the verse in this manner, *Yahweh* now listens to a voice that previously he had not acknowledged. This understanding makes sense in the context of Book 3, where the preceding poems desperately seek answers to the questions, "Why the exile?" and "How long will this suffering last?" These very questions are posed in the immediately preceding poem (see Ps 80:12 for the "Why?" question and Ps 80:4 for the "How long?" question). Canonically speaking, until this point the psalms of Book 3 imply that these questions regarding God's rationale for the exile and the length of its duration remain unanswered. So in that sense, the people's voice remains unrecognised. Here in Psalm 81, we hear Yahweh's response to these questions. Finally, Yahweh hears the speech of his people that previously he had not acknowledged. So, I would suggest that verse 5c begins Yahweh's response to the people's interrogation regarding the exile. Previously, as part of their punishment, God did not listen or respond. Now, in this prophetic oracle, he both listens and responds.[14]

I removed the burden from their shoulders. Verses 6–7 once again recall God's liberating work in the exodus from Egypt. Yahweh, here speaking through the prophet-poet, reminds the people of his redemptive activity in the past. He "removed the burden from their shoulders; their hands were set free from the basket"—these observations probably refer to the Hebrews' forced carrying labors when they were slaves in Egypt.[15]

In your distress you called and I rescued you. As well as reminding Israel of his powerful work in securing their release, God also reminds them of the fact that he did hear and answer the prayers of his enslaved people. At that time, the Hebrews called out to God and he rescued them from the suffering they faced (v. 7a). But the prophet reminds the people that even in the day of the exodus there was a degree of inscrutability in Yahweh's response to their prayers. Verse 7b points to Yahweh's response as "out of a thundercloud" and as followed by the testing of the people's faith. The Old

---

13. Goldingay, *Psalms 2*, 551.

14. Reading the psalm in this way brings out an interesting parallel in verse 13. Now Yahweh is listening to the people, and simultaneously he longs for them to listen to him (v. 13).

15. Eaton, *Psalms*, 294.

Testament's thundercloud imagery often points to the mystery and sovereignty of God's activity. He acts as he sees fit, even if that activity is shrouded in mystery to human participants in these events. For example, in the book of Job, God "spoke to" (though in Hebrew a synonym for the word used in Ps 81:7) from the midst of the storm (Job 38:1), and, as part of his interrogation of Job, Yahweh asks, "Do you have an arm like God's, and can your voice thunder like his?" (40:9). The thunder imagery tends to stress God's sovereign might and power, as we also see in the association of thunder with the divine theophanies in which Yahweh reveals himself as the Warrior God (e.g., Pss 18:13; 29:3; 77:18; et al.).[16] So the subtle emphasis of Psalm 81:7b is that, while the Warrior God did indeed answer the prayers of the exodus generation, he did so in his time and as he saw fit. He was sovereign then, and the implication for the exilic community is that he will answer once again as and when he sees fit.

I tested you at the waters of Meribah. There is an element of ironic surprise in verse 7c because Meribah (along with Massah) is known in the tradition of the Old Testament as the place where *Israel* "tested" God (see Exod 17:2, 7). The psalmist here, however, presents Yahweh's take on the same scenario as *God's* testing Israel's faith and trust in his sovereign power, even though the exodus tradition sees it the other way around. It may be that here the poet conflates the water tests of Exodus 15:22–27 and 17:1–7, for in 15:25 the same scenario is described as a test of the people set by Yahweh.[17] But whatever referent the poet has in mind, the issue is whether the people will trust Yahweh—and Yahweh alone—as becomes clearer in the following verses (Ps 81:8–10).[18]

If you would only listen to me, Israel. Again we return to the "listening" theme begun in verse 5c and continued in verses 11 and 13. This time, however, it is *God* who laments over *Israel's* failure to listen! Throughout the psalms of Book 3 we have seen several instances where Israel complains about Yahweh's inattentiveness to their prayers (e.g., Pss 77:1–2; 80:1–2), but here verse 8 turns the tables. Inattentiveness is Israel's problem, not Yahweh's. The people did not listen to God's warnings and failed to obey his command, so they are confronted with the reality of exile; yet the question is *still* open as to whether or not they are listening now (verses 13–16).[19]

---

16. Tate, *Psalms 51–100*, 323.

17. See Goldingay, *Psalms 2*, 552.

18. Note similar themes developed in Pss 78:9–22; 95:7–9. In the psalmic tradition, these stories from the wilderness experience of Israel become synonymous with the failure truly to trust God, and they serve as warnings to every generation of God's people.

19. Schaefer, *Psalms*, 199–200.

Verse 8 is a heartfelt appeal from God voiced through the prophet-poet. The audience would instantly associate the call, "Hear . . . , my people," with the Shema of Deuteronomy 6:4–5 ("Hear, O Israel: The LORD our God, the LORD is one. Love the LORD your God with all your heart and with all your soul and with all your strength").

In many ways the Shema formed the heart of the Old Testament community's religious focus. It was a summary statement regarding both the identity of Israel's God and what worship of him means. Though often seen as a statement of abstract monotheism, the Shema is rather a call to monolatry—singular love for and worship of Yahweh.[20] So the call for God's people to "hear" was a poignant one that reminded the listeners/readers of the importance of singular love for and devotion to Yahweh.

You shall have no foreign god among you. Verses 9–10 make explicit what is implied in the preceding verse. The reminder of the Shema draws the reader to thoughts of devotion to Yahweh alone, and that singular devotion becomes the express focus of verses 9–10. These verses, of course, echo the first of the Ten Commandments (Exod 20:1–3). The absolute prohibition of the worship of alien gods (Exod 20:3; cf. Ps 81:9) is tied to the very identity of Yahweh (Exod 20:2; cf. Ps 81:10a). He alone is their covenantal God, and he alone brought them out of slavery in Egypt; therefore, he alone is worthy of their worship and devotion. Psalm 81:10a shows clearly that Israel's duty of allegiance to Yahweh is based on two grounds: first, relationship (he alone is *their* God), and second, obligation (he alone freed them from slavery in Egypt). So, in terms of God's response to the prayers of his people in Book 3 of the Psalms, Yahweh finally speaks, and he laments their failure to listen. He reminds them that it was their failure to keep covenant with him which led to the exile experience they currently endure.

> The first commandment is the true meaning of the Exodus. Any commerce with other gods meant that Israel had not listened to the God who listened to their cry of distress. The concluding self-presentation of God says it all: "I am the LORD your God, who brought you up out of the land of Egypt." That was God's word at Sinai; that is the word which introduces and founds the ten words of the covenant of Israel. With that word the confrontation between God and people at Sinai is reenacted (Exod 20:1–3).[21]

---

20. See Nathan MacDonald, *Deuteronomy and the Meaning of 'Monotheism,'* FAT (Tübingen: Mohr Siebeck, 2003).

21. Mays, *Psalms*, 267.

So these words in Psalm 81 remind the readers of their covenantal obligations under the Ten Commandments—obligations that they had singularly
failed to keep in the generations prior to exile.

Open wide your mouth and I will fill it. This enigmatic statement
following the reprise of the first commandment is probably a reference
to God's natural desire to give good things to his people of promise. He
has cut a covenant with them, and part of that promise is his duty of care
for his people. It was that care that took them out of Egypt and that care
that fed and watered the people miraculously in the desert. This sentence
probably reflects the promise in verse 16 to feed Israel with the "finest
of wheat" and "with honey from the rock." This command continues the
idea of trust in Yahweh alone that we see in the preceding references to
Meribah and to having no foreign gods. The point is that Yahweh is more
than able (and willing) to provide abundantly for his people, if only they
will put their trust solely in him. He provided generously in the exodus
and will provide generously again for his people . . . if only they will listen
and trust.

The Prophetic Oracle: Part 2 (81:11–16)

THE SAME THEMES OF LISTENING, trust, and obedience are developed again
in the second part of the prophetic oracle.

But my people would not listen to me. The people's failure to keep
the terms of the covenant made at Sinai is key for the reply of Psalm 81
to the questions of Psalm 80. In Psalm 80 the psalmist asks God "Why?"
and "How long?" with regard to the exile. The second part of Yahweh's
soliloquy in Psalm 81:11–16 answers both questions. First, the answer to
the "Why?" question of Psalm 80:12 comes in Psalm 81:11–12. The exile
occurred because Israel would not listen! Nor would they submit to God.
The point of these verses is that, in the Sinai covenant and its restatement
in Deuteronomy (cf. Ps 81:8–10), God told his people how they should
live, but they refused to listen and obey. He had laid out a plan for life in
community based on the two tablets of the law. Israel was called to live in
right relationship with Yahweh and right relationship with one another, but
the prophets make it clear that they did neither one. They refused to listen
to God's original plan, they refused to listen to the rebuke and redirection
of the prophets, and they refused to change their behavior. These refusals
give the reason why the exile happened. Exile was the ultimate tool in
God's hand to lead his people back to repentance (cf. Deut 28:64–68).

**So I gave them over to their stubborn hearts to follow their own
devices.** Literally, the Hebrew text of Psalm 81:12 says, "So I sent them
off in their stubbornness of heart, so they could follow their own counsel."

The point made is that the people would not bend, so God allowed them to experience the consequences of their own worldview. They prioritized their own wisdom over God's and ended up bearing the consequences of that decision.[22] Their refusal to worship Yahweh alone ultimately led to their forced worship of gods of wood and stone in exile. So Yahweh, through Psalm 81's prophetic voice, answers the "Why?" question: the exile occurred because Israel would not listen.

If my people would only listen to me. The prophet-poet's answer to the "How long?" question follows in verse 13. How long will the exile last? Well, if the people would finally *listen*, they would then see just how quickly Yahweh responds to their change of heart! In this verse there is an element of appeal in the words of the Lord. It is as though God is simply *longing* for his people *finally* to hear what he has been saying to them all along, and, as soon as they do so, they will witness the outpouring of his grace, restoration, and liberation, as did the exodus generation so many years earlier. Once again, the importance of listening properly is paramount in terms of the dynamic that must come into play before the people will be released from exile. "The essence of Israel's identity as God's people is found in the ability to listen. For not listening Israel was punished (v. 12). If only she would again listen, God would rescue and provide for her."[23]

How quickly would I subdue their enemies. Restoration is focused on two factors in the closing verses of Psalm 81. The first factor is political renewal in the defeat of Israel's enemies. Reading this poem as original to the exilic setting would point to liberation from Israel's present captivity. Reading the psalm from a postexilic perspective would mean that it points to a renewal of Israel's disappointing fortunes following the community's return to Jerusalem and the rebuilding of the temple and city. Once again the Warrior God would fight on Israel's side (cf. Ps 80), and the enemies of his people would feel the fullness of his power (Ps 81:15)—the same power that was poured out on Egypt, one of the world's great superpowers at the time of the exodus.

But you would be fed with the finest of wheat. The second focus of the restoration that would follow the people's active repentance is voiced in terms of provision. Just as Israel experienced God's power in the exodus, so also they experienced his great provision in the desert wanderings. Equally, here in Psalm 81 power is promised for the defeat of enemies and provision is promised as a sign of God's rich blessing. Not just any old food will be given—rather, the people will be fed with the choicest

---

22. Ibid.
23. Schaefer, *Psalms*, 200.

grain. The divine source of this splendid provision is implied in the idea of "honey from the rock." Honey is inevitably associated with the good produce promised in the land of Canaan, and the combination of honey from the rock with choice grain is probably to be associated with Deuteronomy 32:13–14. God's desire is to bless his restored people in the same way that he blessed them in the beginning. This imagery speaks of God's abundant blessing on his children if they will but listen and follow his ways rather than rebelling and following their own (Ps 81:13).

There is an intriguing open-endedness about the close of Psalm 81. "If only my people would listen, then they would know my blessing." The question is left hanging, "Will they listen and respond appropriately?" The openness of the conclusion makes it a vital question addressed to every generation of God's people. Will we listen to God, or will we follow our own wisdom?

PSALM 81 IN THE CONTEXT OF BOOK 3. Psalm 81 plays an important role in the flow of thought we can see in Book 3 of the Psalms. This third book is dominated by laments over the exile of Israel. Some seem to have a northern origin in the Israel of the divided monarchy (Pss 80; 81); others are rooted very clearly in the fall of the Jerusalem temple (e.g., Pss 74, 76, and 79); yet others seem to combine Israelite and Judahite traditions (e.g., Ps 78). But Psalm 81 is significant because it is the first psalm to provide God's perspective on the crisis of exile. Up to this point we hear the voice of human lament over the suffering faced by the people. Those in exile want to know why this suffering has been allowed to happen, and they want to know how long their suffering will last. The voice we hear up to this point in Book 3 is very human. But now, in Psalm 81, God speaks! This change makes the psalm significant as a response to the community laments that dominate the flow from Psalm 74 onward.

As we have seen above, Psalm 81 is closely linked with Psalm 80 in terms of its response to the "Why?" and "How long?" questions of the exile. God's answers are quite simple. Why? Because the people rejected their covenantal obligations and worshiped more than just Yahweh. How long? Until the people learn to listen to God and follow his ways again. So, Psalm 81 provides the reader with a very different perspective on Israel's reality. As we will see below, however, Psalm 81 is also closely linked with Psalm 82, in which God speaks once again as a corrective to the attitudes that prevailed in Israel—attitudes that ultimately led to the exile. Here in

Psalm 81 it is Israel's syncretism that is condemned—their refusal to worship Yahweh alone—and also their unwillingness to listen to God and keep the covenant. As this "narrative" develops, another area of national failure that resulted in the punishment of exile is condemned in Psalm 82, namely, Israel's failure to maintain social justice within their society.

We see both strands in the texts of the prophets. The refusal to love God, to listen to him, and to follow his ways were key factors that resulted in the exile (e.g., see Jer 7). Equally, however, the social injustices that dominated Israelite and Judahite society contributed to the divine condemnation that led to both kingdoms' removal from the land (e.g., see Isa 1). So, Psalm 81 fills an important role as a response to the complaints of Book 3 (especially the complaints in Pss 79 and 80). Psalm 81 also begins the divine response to the complaints of the people that continues in Psalm 82.

Psalm 81 in the New Testament. Psalm 81 is not cited directly in the New Testament, but the key theme of listening to God occurs frequently in the Gospels. Central to God's response to the people's complaint over the crisis of exile is the expectation that they should listen and hear the message that he has been trying to teach them through their circumstances. Of course, the implication from Psalm 81 is not that the people of the community simply hear his message physically but that they hear, absorb, and respond to the rebuke constituted by their exile. We see similar language and ideas in Jesus' warnings to his hearers in the Gospels. A frequently recurring refrain on Jesus' lips is the challenge, "Whoever has ears, let them hear" (Matt 11:15; 13:9; 13:43). Christ's challenge is that the people should truly listen and respond to this new message of the kingdom. It was not enough to hear—they had really to listen to what he was saying and respond accordingly. Similarly, the letters to the churches in the book of Revelation issue the same warning to listen (Rev 2:7, 11, 17, 29; 3:6, 13, 22). The churches in Asia Minor are supposed to listen properly to God's word to them (whether it be challenge or encouragement) and respond accordingly. Clearly, this theme of listening and responding to God continues as an important one in the New Testament.

PRAISE GOD WELL. We will return to this line of application when we discuss psalms later in the Psalter (esp. Pss 146–50), but here it is worth pointing out the importance of praising God properly. Psalm 81:1–3 encourages us to holistic and wholehearted praise of God. Our praise should involve joyful shouting and loud declaration of God's goodness and love. It should also be musically uplifting. The imagery speaks of praise that is both fully engaged and engaging. Sometimes while standing in church on a Sunday morning, it seems to me that most people would rather still be in bed, and this attitude is reflected in the way God's praise is sung there! Is it too much to ask that we should go to bed a little earlier on Saturday night in order to be in a better frame of mind to praise God properly on Sunday morning?

The opening verses of this psalm emphasize the importance of hearty praise of God. It is also possible that they stress the importance of praise even in difficult circumstances. If we read Psalm 81 as a response to the community laments of Psalms 79 and 80 in particular, then the call to praise is quite surprising. In Psalm 80, both psalmist and people wonder how long the exile will continue and why it has occurred in the first place. They get their answer in Psalm 81:6–16, but the opening call to praise seems incongruous in the light of their present suffering. So it may well be that the psalmist encourages the people to praise God even when they are not experiencing the type of situation in which they might naturally want to do so—hence the reminder that the festal remembrance of God in praise is a command to be obeyed (vv. 4–5), even if it is not an act we feel naturally drawn to because of present circumstances of hardship. Why so? The prophetic declaration that follows the call to praise God reminds the hearer of God's true nature and practice. Psalms of praise were, for the Hebrews, also creedal declarations of God's character and activity.[24] In praise we are reminded of who God is and how God works, so our praises can be important in shaping our perspective on our life and present experience.

I recently encountered this principle in reality in my home church in Scotland. For some weeks, as a church family we had been praying for a newborn baby who was desperately ill from the moment of birth. For some six weeks, we prayed with a great deal of intensity for healing for this baby girl and for strength for her family. But this beautiful little baby girl died at the age of six weeks, and there was an almost tangible sense of disappointment in the church. At the evening service of the Sunday following her death, the worship leader spoke very honestly of his disappointment and anger with God. He told the congregation how he had almost resented

---

24. "Second, psalmic praise is *confessional*. Praise as doxology declares *that* God is. Praise as confession says *who* God is. The hymns of the Psalter were Israel's confession of faith. In them the people of God said—and say—who it is they trust and obey. In the history of worship, we have come to associate the confession of faith with the literary form of the creed, but in the biblical world the congregations' declaration of whom they served took the form of praise" (Mays, *The Lord Reigns*, 65).

the fact of having to prepare a service of worship after just hearing the tragic news. Nevertheless, we proceeded to praise God in song regardless of our common feeling of disappointment verging on anger. The ensuing time of worship in song—focused on the character of God—was both precious and, in some way, healing. Praise had brought hope and restored our vision of a caring, sovereign God who holds all things in his hands and knows better than we do. Community praise is important, and it is important that it is done well.

Listening to God. All Christians will readily acknowledge that it is important to pray. Unfortunately, we often think of prayer as an act of speech rather than conversation. What is more, in our twenty-first-century culture we do not, generally speaking, feel comfortable with silence. Our lives tend to be full of constant noise and bustle from TVs, iPods, elevator music, traffic noise, and the like. This predisposition toward "noise and movement" can affect our spirituality as well. Being still and quiet do not come naturally to us any longer. Yet Psalm 81 is clear that we need to listen to God. We must hear what he says and allow that to influence our lives. So it is vitally important for the spiritual health of the contemporary church that we relearn disciplines of silence and meditation.

Rather than just praying and reading the Scriptures (both of which activities can become very task orientated—we speak, God hears; we read, then we go), it is important that we also take time to listen in our personal times of devotion. How might we do so? By *taking time* with God. Rather than reading quickly as a task, we should read slowly and prayerfully while asking the Holy Spirit to shape our hearts and minds and wills through his word. Equally, in prayer it is important that we take time just *to be* in the presence of God, to sit in an attitude of prayerful stillness. In prayer we must take time to listen as well as to speak. Otherwise, we—like the Israelites—can miss God's word of rebuke or redirection, encouragement and blessing. Christians today need to redevelop the discipline of spiritual listening.[25]

---

25. There are many helpful books on the spiritual disciplines in general, including stillness and listening. Dallas Willard's *The Divine Conspiracy: Rediscovering our Hidden Life with God* (San Francisco: Harper, 1998) and Richard Foster's *Celebration of Discipline: The Path to Spiritual Growth* (London: Hodder, 1998) are particularly good starting points for considering how to develop our walk with God.

Psalm 82

A psalm of Asaph.

¹ God presides in the great assembly;
　he renders judgment among the "gods":
² "How long will you defend the unjust
　and show partiality to the wicked?
³ Defend the weak and the fatherless;
　uphold the cause of the poor and the oppressed.
⁴ Rescue the weak and the needy;
　deliver them from the hand of the wicked.
⁵ "The 'gods' know nothing, they understand nothing.
　They walk about in darkness;
　all the foundations of the earth are shaken.
⁶ "I said, 'You are "gods";
　you are all sons of the Most High.'
⁷ But you will die like mere mortals;
　you will fall like every other ruler."
⁸ Rise up, O God, judge the earth,
　for all the nations are your inheritance.

JOHN DOMINIC CROSSAN refers to Psalm 82 as "the single most important text in the entire Christian Bible."[1] A surprising claim indeed! How many of us would choose this relatively unknown psalm as the single most important text of the Bible? Yet Crossan's overstatement makes an important point, because Psalm 82 provides the reader with a remarkable insight into God's standards and priorities. It shows us just how much social justice matters to the God of Christian Scripture. With Crossan, it has to be said that the lessons we learn from Psalm 82 are of remarkable importance and should not be passed over lightly by today's church.

Psalm 82 continues the voice of God begun in Psalm 81. Apart from the opening and closing verses, it is God who declares his judgment over all

---

1. John Dominic Crossan, *The Birth of Christianity: Discovering what Happened in the Years after the Execution of Jesus* (San Francisco: Harper, 1998), 575.

other gods for their lack of justice and discernment. This voice is unusual in the book of Psalms (and Book 3), which is dominated by the prayers and perspectives of God's people. Essentially, Ps 82 is a reminder to the people of God of his absolute sovereignty.

The Heading (82:0)

PSALM 82 IS SIMPLY DESCRIBED as a "Psalm of Asaph." The designation *mizmor* ("a psalm") is the most common title for the compositions of the Psalter and probably refers to a poem or song to be accompanied with music (see comments on Ps 73:0).

God and the Assembly of "the Gods" (82:1)

GOD PRESIDES IN THE GREAT ASSEMBLY. The context and setting of Psalm 82 is fairly alien to the mindset of contemporary Christians. The NIV translates this verse as referring to the "great assembly." Sometimes the Hebrew words *'el* and *'elohim* can be translated as meaning "great" or "mighty,"[2] but the more "normal" rendering would be to see these words as referring to "God" or "the gods." So, God's presiding in the *'edat-'el* (v. 1) is probably better understood as God's standing with authority over the "assembly of God" or "divine assembly."

What difference is borne out by these varying translation options? Basically, the choices that we make concerning the translation of the opening verse of Psalm 82 affect whether we read the poem as a rebuke of the corrupt leaders (either of Israel or the nations) or as addressed against the gods of the nations. In translating verse 1 as a reference to the "great assembly" and by placing in quotation marks the reference to the "gods" in the second part of this verse, the NIV's translators make it clear that they see this as a figurative reference to leaders rather than a literal address to the gods. But if we see verse 1a as speaking about the "divine assembly" and verse 1b as addressing the "gods," then this psalm takes on much more spiritual and cosmic overtones.

For a variety of reasons, I believe the latter translation option to make better sense of Psalm 82. First, Psalm 82 continues the response to the laments voiced by God's people in the community complaints of Psalm 74 and the following psalms, and particularly the prayers of Psalms 79–83, which seem to form a contextual unit. One of the questions asked in these preceding psalms is, "Why should the nations be allowed to mock Israel's God?" (see Pss 74:10, 18, 22; 79:4, 10, 12; 80:6 et al.). In securing military

---

2. See, for example, the reference in Ps 80:10 to the "mighty cedars," which could be translated as the "cedars of God."

victory over Israel and Judah, the surrounding nations believed their gods to be more powerful than Yahweh. They therefore exalted their gods and mocked the God of Israel as a direct result of the exile. From a contextual reading of these psalms, Psalm 81 begins Yahweh's response to the people by answering the "Why?" and "How long?" questions of the exilic people. Here in Psalm 82 God responds (again by prophetic utterance), but this time he addresses the issue of spiritual rule and reality that is brought up in Psalms 79 and 80. The divine response in Psalm 82 reminds the community that Yahweh still rules absolutely despite their moral and military failures.

There are also linguistic reasons for seeing Psalm 82 as having in mind the gods and the heavenly realms. Reference to the "sons of the Most High" (v. 6) is often seen as an indication that human rulers are in view.[3] But even this concept is frequently used in the Old Testament and Psalter with reference to heavenly beings (e.g., see Job 1:6; 2:1; Ps 29:1). The references in Job point to the "sons of God" (i.e., heavenly beings) as taking part in a "heavenly assembly," a scenario much like the one we read of here in Ps 82:1. Equally, the Psalms frequently refer to God as being praised or being incomparable "among the gods" (Pss 86:8; 95:3; 96:4; 97:9). So, although the concept of a heavenly council over which God rules may be an alien one to the modern mindset, this would not be so among the original hearers and early readers of this psalm.[4]

In Psalm 82:1, therefore, the psalmist provides the setting for the proclamation of Yahweh that follows in verses 2–6. The voice of the poet is heard again in the closing prayer of verse 8, where the poet seeks God's arousal. The psalmist paints a picture (akin to the imagery in Job 1–2) in which Yahweh stands in authority over the heavenly assembly. He has called a meeting, and all the heavenly beings, the gods, are obliged to attend in order to hear his authoritative judgment against them.[5] John Eaton comments on this verse:

> "God" (originally probably "Yahweh") is presiding at the divine assembly (*'edat 'el*), thought of as the solemn event where affairs of the world are reviewed and decisions of destiny made. It is a

---

3. Kings, both in Israel and throughout the ancient Near East, were often referred to "sons of God" or "sons of the gods" (see John H. Walton, *Ancient Near Eastern Thought and the Old Testament: Introducing the Conceptual World of the Hebrew Bible* [Leicester: Apollos, 2007], 278–86).

4. For further discussion see Broyles, *Psalms*, 335–36; Min Suc Kee, "The Heavenly Council and Its Type-Scene," *JSOT* 31.3 (2007): 259–73.

5. For discussion of the divine assembly in the worldviews of the ancient world, see Walton, *ANE Thought*, 92–97.

question whether to translate in v. 1a "stands" (Tate) or . . . "pre-sides" (see Dahood); for the former, nearer the usual sense of the verb, the point would be that the enthroned God now stands to announce his verdict, while the latter rendering has him seated in majesty throughout before the standing servants. These underlings are indeed "holy ones / gods," but the psalm will vividly illustrate the limits of their power (cf. 29:1; 95:3; 96:4). In v. 1b the verb "he judges . . ." probably refers to the conclusion of his judging, the verdict which will now follow.[6]

Gods of Injustice (82:2–4)

HOW LONG WILL YOU DEFEND THE UNJUST? In the Old Testament we often encounter the question, "Who is a God like you?" (e.g., see Exod 15:11; Pss 35:10; 71:19; 89:8; Mic 7:18 et al.). We tend to read this question as entirely rhetorical; however, for the writers of these verses their question would be genuinely comparative. They lived in a world where there were hundreds, even thousands of gods, and each one made its own claims. Some would claim to offer fertility of crops or children, others control over the storm, and still others would grant power over enemies.[7] The genuinely comparative nature of this question comes to the fore in the verses of this prophetic oracle in which Israel's God—the true High God—pronounces judgment on the other gods in the heavenly assembly. Their activity is assessed by Yahweh and found to be corrupt and to fall short of the High God's standards, as highlighted in Psalm 82:2 by Yahweh's interrogation of the gods for their unjust activity. "How long will you defend the unjust and show partiality to the wicked?" Yahweh expects the gods to adhere to his standards in their activity. Since they have failed to do so, they receive his rebuke. In this metaphor of the heavenly assembly, it is as though Yahweh—the High King—has delegated power to the gods to rule over portions of the earth (see the NIV's footnote on Deut 32:8) but expects them to do so in accordance with his own absolute standards. Since the gods have failed Yahweh's expectation of them, he calls them to task. The High God's verdict is that they have defended the unjust and showed preferential treatment to the wicked. Such behavior is diametrically opposed to the "divine order of law that is meant to be defended and carried out by the gods within the territories assigned to them on behalf of the nations that are subject to their jurisdiction."[8]

---

6. Eaton, *Psalms*, 297.
7. Walton, *ANE Thought*, 87–112.
8. Hossfeld and Zenger, *Psalms 2*, 333.

The "How long?" question takes a different slant in Psalm 82. In Psalms 79 and 80 we see this question directed at God concerning the duration of his people's suffering, and in Psalm 81 Yahweh answers that question. In Psalm 82, however, it is Israel's God who takes up the question and asks it of the gods of the nations. In this instance, we can see that the question is entirely rhetorical because it leads into command. Yahweh does not sit powerless and wondering when the minor gods might stop their bad behavior. He sits in authority and commands obedience (vv. 3–4). In this instance the "How long?" question lays bare the basic character inadequacies of the gods—they do not maintain societal justice in line with the character of God. "In this psalm, the provision of delivering justice is made the decisive criterion for the authenticity of deity! It is not one of the features, it is the sole issue."[9]

Defend the weak and the fatherless. There then follows a fourfold command from God addressed at the gods. Clearly, from the perspective of the psalmist, these "deities" are entirely under the authority of Yahweh and subject to his control. The focus of the divine order is singular. These gods do not maintain social justice as they ought. Gods were thought to be territorial in the ancient world, their rule thought to extend to the limits of "their" kingdom. So, the rule of Re, the high god of Egypt, was thought to extend throughout the Egyptian kingdom. Since the time that Israel had been taken into exile, they had witnessed firsthand the social order of the nations, and according to the psalmist the society of the kingdoms "ruled" by the gods was found seriously wanting. These spiritual "rulers" do not secure justice for the poor and weak of the nations under their supposed aegis.

> The conception is that the government of the earth's nations has been delegated to [the divine beings] as ministers of the supreme King, the Lord. As generally in the Near East, the acid test of good government is held to be the care of the vulnerable and afflicted, such as widows, orphans, the poor and migrants (cf. 72.f.).[10]

The gods have been found wanting. These commands in Psalm 82:3–4 do not imply a recommissioning of the gods to their task of stewardship; rather, the commands remind the gods of their failure to do what was required by Yahweh. The pronouncement of judgment follows in verse 5.

---

9. Mays, *Psalms*, 270.
10. Eaton, *Psalms*, 297.

Judgment in the Divine Assembly (82:5)

THE "GODS" KNOW NOTHING, THEY UNDERSTAND NOTHING. Yahweh's voice continues with a public declaration of his ultimate verdict concerning the gods. He no longer speaks to them ("you" plural [vv. 2–4]) but speaks about them to the listening community of his people ("they" [v. 5]). The emptiness that the gods have to offer is described in terms of their lack of knowledge. Inherent to the concept of deity is the fact that a divine being *knows* more than a human being. A "god" should be more knowledgeable of those things that are of vital importance than a human being is, yet Yahweh's verdict on these deities is that they are profoundly lacking in their knowledge of ultimate reality. They have not shown the wisdom that could be expected of them in the natural scheme of things. "[T]hey have not 'known' or 'recognized' the context of justice or injustice, or their own personal share in the situation, or the consequences of their behavior."[11] Yahweh's judgment does not just address the fact that they failed to behave as they should have done—even more damning is the fact that these so-called deities did not even realize that social justice is the hallmark of a good society. The injustice of their activity is compounded by their ignorance of the effects of their praxis.

They walk about in darkness. The imagery of verse 5b is sardonic. Gods are supposed to have greater insight than humans, but the psalmic presentation is of deities who cannot see in the dark. This is chaos imagery that underlines the inadequacy of their activity. The prophets draw a link between justice and light (e.g., see Isa 51:4), whereas injustice brings nothing but darkness (Isa 59:9–10). The justice and righteousness of Yahweh bring order—light by which the people can live. Injustice and the rejection of God's ways bring chaos—darkness in which both gods and people stumble.[12]

All the foundations of the earth are shaken. Herein lies the essence of Crossan's claim mentioned above, namely, the notion of the foundations of the earth as being shaken speaks to the fundamental significance of the gods' injustice. Their behavior counters the very fabric of the divinely created order. According to the biblical writers, when Yahweh created the universe he instilled in it certain innate processes that are basic to the proper running of creation. Justice is one of these creation ordinances (e.g., see Pss 89:14; 97:2; Prov 8:20). It is foundational to Yahweh's rule over the earth, and the universe only works properly when God's justice is

---

11. Hossfeld and Zenger, *Psalms* 2, 334.
12. Ibid.

maintained. So it is that the gods' rejection of justice strikes at the very fabric of the created order (Ps 85:5b). That there are nations in which justice is not honored rocks the very core of the world. "Criminality and social irresponsibility upset the stability and goodness of creation. The earth will shake and quake in revulsion to human unfairness."[13]

The Mortality of the "Gods" (82:6–7)

I SAID, "YOU ARE 'GODS.'" Yahweh's judgment now returns to addressing the gods directly. Israel's God has declared to the covenant community the inadequacies of the divine beings (v. 5). Now he once again addresses the gods directly with the pronouncement of judgment. He reminds them that they owe their status to the High God in the first place. By his ordinance alone have they attained their rank. The gods are reminded that whatever authority they command is apportioned to them—it is not theirs by right. Their status as "sons of the Most High" is conferred on them, much as authority was conferred on the king in Israel as the "son" of Yahweh (Ps 2).

But you will die like mere mortals. Yahweh declares his judgment on the inadequacies of the rule of these divine beings. They are no more gods than the rulers of the earth (Ps 82:7) and can face death like anyone else because they too are subject to God's decree. He conferred status on them and can remove that status just as quickly. In much the same way as immortality was removed from Adam and Eve following their sin in the garden (Gen 3:4–5; cf. 22–24), so the failure of the gods results in the declaration of their mortality.[14] Rejection of Yahweh's standards leads to death—"gods" are subject to the same rules as humans.

The Psalmist's Appeal (82:8)

RISE UP, O GOD, JUDGE THE EARTH. The psalmist closes with a prayer that echoes his declaration in the opening verse. In verse 1, the psalmist presents the God of Israel as presiding over the heavenly assembly, as judging in the midst of the gods. This spiritual reality the psalmist knows to be unchanging—Yahweh rules over all of the gods of the nations. The poet's concluding prayer calls on Yahweh to make that spiritual reality

---

13. Terrien, *Psalms*, 590.

14. Interestingly, the Hebrew of Ps 82:7a is singular rather than the plural of the NIV's translation, so it actually reads, "Surely, like a man [*'adam*] you will die." The *Midrash on the Psalms* and at least one early commentator have read this verse as comparing the fall of these "gods" to the fall of Adam in the garden. Sin inexorably leads to death, and it may be that the removal of Adam's immortality as result of his sin is echoed in this declaration of lost immorality for the gods. See Goldingay, *Psalms 2*, 567.

visible truth once again. From the spiritual perspective of the psalmist, the absolute rule of Israel's God over the nations is undisputed. From the perspective of the nations, however, Israel's exilic circumstances point to a different reality. As far as the peoples of the ancient Near East were concerned, a nation defeated means a god defeated. So, Israel and Judah's defeat means that Yahweh is *seen* among the nations as being weaker than the gods of the Assyrians and Babylonians. The psalmist prays to Yahweh to address that misperception by judging these gods, by proving himself sovereign over them. The prayer is the logical conclusion that follows from the neutralizing of the gods by Yahweh's judgment on them (vv. 6–7). They have failed to secure justice, so let Yahweh now arise to do what the gods have not done. "[Yahweh] is the supreme ruler and judge who alone can bring justice to the oppressed peoples of the world. Verse 8 calls for a 'realignment of world order' . . . with Yahweh himself assuming the duties of the neutralized gods."[15]

For all the nations are your inheritance. The gods of Israel's neighbors would all be imperialistic. They were based in the land where their temple was located, but, like kings, they sought to expand their sphere of influence through military advancement.[16] Yahweh has no need for military expansion because he rules over all the nations—they belong to him as his inheritance to apportion as he wishes. Herein we see the theological backbone of Psalm 82. Gods may quarrel and strive after power, but Yahweh simply rules. As part of that rule, he may apportion authority to lesser divine beings for the purpose of fulfilling his will, but should they fail to do so they, too, will come under Yahweh's judgment just like the rest of the created order, for the whole universe is his.

Psalm 82:8 is reminiscent of the language and theology of Deuteronomy 32, particularly if we take into account the variant reading of Deuteronomy 32:8 mentioned above. The NIV reads: "When the Most High gave the nations their inheritance, when he divided all mankind, he set up boundaries for the peoples according to the number of the *sons of Israel*. For the LORD's portion is his people, Jacob his allotted inheritance" (Deut 32:8–9). But both the Dead Sea Scrolls and the Septuagint, as well as several of the contemporary English translations (e.g., see ESV, NRSV, NET), translate the phrase highlighted "sons of Israel" as the "sons of God." This seems to be the more likely original reading, and Matitiahu Tsevat explains the idea behind these verses:

---

15. Tate, *Psalms 51–100*, 339.
16. Walton, *ANE Thought*, 103.

In the distant past, Yahweh, the Most High, divided mankind into nations, whose number He determined by the number of the sons of "God/El," i.e., the minor gods; each of these gods received a nation as his portion. . . . Only one nation was not given over to these gods—Israel; that people Yahweh retained for himself.[17]

Psalm 82 declares Yahweh's judgment on the failure of the gods to fulfill the purposes of their Sovereign. The psalmist cries out in prayer to Yahweh, therefore, that he reassume control over *all nations* as his inheritance, not just Israel. The gods failed to rule justly, so the psalmist calls for Yahweh to reappropriate that which he had delegated in the past. Yahweh is the one true and just King—only he can secure justice for the poor, needy, marginalized, and neglected in any and every society.

ISRAEL'S GOD AND THE GODS. There is a profound question of ontology when we come to Psalm 82, namely, just what did the Israelites believe about the gods of the nations? In particular, were they real or were they not? There seems to be something of a contradiction between the language of Psalm 82 and other references to the gods in the psalms. Perhaps the starkest contrast would be to read this psalm in the light of Psalm 96:5, which reads: "For all the gods of the nations are idols, but the LORD made the heavens." The psalmist there clearly sees the gods as empty and untrue, so how is it that the poet who penned Psalm 82 appears to place greater credence in the existence of the gods? There are at least three ways to read passages such as Psalm 82.

1. *Polemic:* Often scholars treat the language of the divine assembly as an example of polemic in the literature of the Old Testament. Clearly, the religious history of the Old Testament points to Israel's belief in Yahweh as the one true God, so the concept of an assembly of gods seems incongruous. Many readers, therefore, view Psalm 82 as an example of Israelite borrowing from the religious beliefs of the nations and twisting their known ideologies to make a particular point about Yahweh. Many of the nations around Israel—and certainly the Babylonians, who had taken Israel into captivity—believed in a pantheon or assembly of gods. In such an assembly of gods there would be a high god (often called *'el*) who ruled over the parliament of deities. It may well be the case that

---

17. Matitiahu Tsevat, "God and the Gods in Assembly: An Interpretation of Psalm 82," *HUCA* 40–41 (1970): 133.

the psalmist is simply borrowing these familiar concepts and figuratively adapting them to point out the absolute, sovereign rule of Yahweh over all things—including the divine assembly. If we read Psalm 82 as a polemic, we do not have to form a conclusion about what the Israelites believed regarding the gods; rather, we are simply saying that polemic makes use of a linguistic and conceptual tradition that is alien to the orthodox religious beliefs of the people in order to emphasize some aspect of their theology. So, if Psalm 82 is polemic, it is not actually addressing the existence or nonexistence of gods, and it merely adopts a common currency in order to say something profound about Yahweh, namely, that if there were a divine assembly, Yahweh would be the absolute Ruler over it.[18]

2. *Progression in Israel's religious awareness:* Some scholars believe that compositions such as Psalm 82 reflect the complex religious history that ultimately resulted in the developed monotheism we now see in the Old Testament. The idea is that in the early days of Israel's community life, the people were polytheists like all the other people groups of the ancient world. Gradually, with the passage of time, Israel developed a more complex and holistic theological belief system which resulted in the realization that God is singular rather than many. So, some see Psalm 82 as a relic of the ancient, naïve, premonotheistic beliefs adhered to by Israel before belief in Yahweh as the one, real God became the dominant theological view.[19]

3. *Monotheism not excluding other gods:* In more recent years there has been increasing and fruitful discussion of just what the monotheism of Israel actually meant. From a modern perspective we assume that the existence of only one God precludes the existence of any other gods. But it is far from clear that the Israelites held *precisely* this view in their day. In particular, when we examine the book of Deuteronomy more closely, we see that Israel's belief in the oneness of God did not necessarily preclude their belief in the possible existence of other gods. If we look at passages such as Deuteronomy 4 and 32:8–9 (mentioned above), we see that the monotheism of this book is really a call to singularity of devotion, worship, love, and affiliation rather than an ontological claim that only Yahweh exists.[20] In fact, these texts seem to imply a belief in the "reality" of the

---

18. For further discussion of Israel's use of ancient Near Eastern mythological concepts in the psalms see Elmer B. Smick, "Mythopoetic Language in the Psalms," *WTJ* 44 (1982): 88–98.

19. W. O. E. Oesterley, *The Psalms: Translated with Text-Critical and Exegetical Notes* (London: SPCK, 1959), 375.

20. See the helpful and careful discussion in MacDonald, *Deuteronomy and the Meaning of 'Monotheism.'*

existence of other gods. So, it could be argued that the call to monotheism in the Old Testament is actually a call to monolatry (that Yahweh alone is to be worshiped) rather than a statement of abstract ontology (that only Yahweh exists). With this being the case, Psalm 82 would fit well within Israel's conceptual understanding of monotheism. As far as the psalmist is concerned, other gods *may* exist in reality, but, if they do exist, they too are under the judgment of the God of Israel just like *every* other created being.[21]

What conclusions can we draw from these deliberations? It is highly unlikely that Psalm 82 remains as some relic of a previously polytheistic worldview in Israel. On another level, the poem clearly fills a polemic function. The belief systems of the nations are critiqued in Psalm 82's presentation of Yahweh as the one who rules in the divine assembly, who delegated authority to the gods, and who ultimately finds them wanting and, therefore, judges them. The Babylonians may have believed that the capture of Jerusalem proved Marduk more powerful than Yahweh, but the psalmist paints a picture of a spiritual reality that goes far beyond geopolitical events. So, polemic is definitely in play in Psalm 82. But we should also bear in mind the possibility that Israel's understanding of the singularity of Yahweh and the people's responsibility to worship him alone did not necessarily preclude (in their understanding) the existence of other gods. In fact, if we do ascribe some degree of literality to the psalmist's understanding of the imagery in Psalm 82, the poem becomes all the more vivid and its lessons all the more pointed. (See Contemporary Significance for further discussion.)[22]

---

21. This ambivalent view of the gods seems to continue in the New Testament, where, on the one hand, Paul's view is described as being that "gods made by human hands are no gods at all" (Acts 19:26), yet on the other hand, we see Paul discussing the spiritual powers and realities that lie behind idols in 1 Cor 10:19–20. Indeed, in 1 Cor 8 Paul seems to be deliberately ambivalent about the ontological existence of gods. In verse 4 he writes, "'We know that an idol is nothing at all in the world' and 'that there is no God but one'"; yet in verses 5–6 he goes on to say, "For even if there are so-called gods, whether in heaven or on earth (as indeed there are many 'gods' and many 'lords'), yet for us there is but one God, the Father, from whom all things came and for whom we live; and there is but one Lord, Jesus Christ, through whom all things came and through whom we live." It is difficult to know precisely what Paul is saying in these thoughts, but at the very least he seems to be ambiguous about whether or not other "gods" exist. He is absolutely clear about the fact that there is only one God worthy of worship—the Creator—but ambivalent about whether other heavenly entities may or may not exist.

22. Hess points out that the heavenly assembly language features elsewhere in the Old Testament to refer simply to an assembly of heavenly beings: "As with Baal and others, this establishment of kingship entails first rulership over the divine assembly, which in the myths is made up of gods. In the accounts of Yahweh, it is made up of angelic beings

Psalm 82 in Book 3 of the Psalter. We see a flow of question and response in the psalms of this mini-collection. The compositions from Psalms 79–83 seem to be particularly closely related through the repetition of words and themes and the asking and answering of questions.[23] Psalms 79 and 80 ask the questions "Why?" and "How long?" and Psalms 81 and 82 provide the answers to those questions. In Psalm 81 Yahweh reminds the people that they face the crisis of exile because they refused to listen. Psalm 82 continues the voice of Yahweh and responds to both questions asked in the laments of the earlier psalms. Why does Israel face the exile? Like the "gods" of the nations, God's people also failed to execute justice for the poor and needy, so they too had to face divine judgment. They had refused to listen to the prophetic critique of their society and had to face the consequences. So, Psalm 82 confirms the message of Psalm 81: God's people had not listened to the challenge to maintain godly justice in their society. But Psalm 82 also answers the "How long?" question of Psalm 80:4. God's people are reminded that all the gods of the nations are subject to the absolute, sovereign rule of Yahweh. Israel's God is the undisputed Ruler over every god and therefore over every nation! So, Psalm 82 reminds the community of faith that their exile does not continue because of the strength of nations; rather, it continues according to the will of the God who rules. Exile will end when *his* purpose is fulfilled.

Psalm 82 in the New Testament. Psalm 82:6 is quoted by Jesus in John 10:34–38 when he is challenged by the Pharisees about his claim to be one with God the Father. Jesus uses the unusual message of this verse to make the point that his claim to divinity—unmistakable, as seen by the reaction of the religious leaders of the day—is not unprecedented within the Scriptures of the Old Testament. Jesus uses the Scriptures to make the very point the psalm itself makes: namely, that true divinity is marked by the characteristics of God. He goes on to point out that the deeds he has done, the miracles he has worked, and the way he has lived in the midst of the people all evidence the true nature of his deity because they are in keeping with the character of God himself. In Psalm 82 the gods come under Yahweh's judgment because they fail to reflect the priorities and

---

(1 Kgs 22; Job 2; Ps 82; Isa 6) who act in accordance with Yahweh's will. Unlike the mythologies there is no disagreement in the divine assembly of Israel's God. All obey God alone. More than any other text, Psalm 82 demonstrates the absolute dominion of Yahweh over all the assembly, so that he can and does depose the ones given authority to rule over various nations of the world" (Richard S. Hess, *Israelite Religions: An Archaeological and Biblical Survey* [Leicester: Apollos, 2007], 163).

23. Hossfeld and Zenger, *Psalms 2*, 336.

expectations of the High God. The point Jesus makes in John 10 is that his actions precisely mirror the priorities and expectations of Yahweh. He truly is the one and only "son of the Most High" who is faithful to the purposes of his Father.

HOW DO WE JUDGE OUR SOCIETY? While there are undoubtedly complexities in Psalm 82 with regard to its perspective on the existence or nonexistence of other gods, there is absolutely no doubt about the main teaching thrust of the psalm: Yahweh expects nations and societies to be run justly, and if they do not enact justice, they will receive his punishment. The failure of the "gods" to maintain justice for the poor is the sole criterion for the declaration of their mortality. They failed to do that which was expected by Yahweh, and judgment was the consequence. The singularity of God's assessment should function as a stark warning for all of us as we assess our own societies from the divine perspective. As Crossan says, "Psalm 82 tells us how we are to be judged by God but also how God wants to be judged by us. Everything else that God says or does in the Bible should be judged by that job description."[24] Social justice is properly basic to the nature of the God of the Bible.

We tend to allow other factors to shape our assessment of the world in which we live. Fiscal wealth, economic and political stability, comfort for the majority of people, low crime rates, good housing or public services, or "quality of life" and plenty of entertainment—these are the features constantly used in surveys to discover the best places in the world to live. Psalm 82 is a stark warning to the church today, particularly to the church in the comfortable, developed world. There is only one standard by which our societies are assessed by God—how we care for the weak, the poor, the marginalized, the voiceless, and the disenfranchised. God judges our societies today, and Psalm 82 gives us the standard by which he views the "success" or "failure" of our communities. Whether we have cable or multiplex cinemas is not high on God's list of priorities, but how we care for the single mother or the troubled teenager is.

So, the challenge for the church today revolves around our influence within our societies. Are we a constant, nagging, prophetic voice that calls out, "Remember the poor!"—or have we been shaped by the standards of our world to such an extent that we are simply happy being comfortable?

---

24. Crossan, *The Birth of Christianity,* 575–76.

What are we doing with the money our congregations collect? We are often quick to build new buildings or invest in the fabric of our structures, but what are *we* doing for the poor? We should not expect the needy to come to us—for too long churches have been disengaged from the needs of the poor; rather, we should seek every opportunity to minister practically and spiritually to all those who have less than we do.

The message of Psalm 82 is unmistakable: Defend the cause of the weak and fatherless; maintain the rights of the poor and oppressed. Rescue the weak and needy; deliver them from the hand of the wicked. How are we, as congregations of God's people, going to be proactive in delivering social justice to the weak, fatherless, poor, oppressed, and needy of our day? We have no right to delegate this task to the state, for this singular standard is the one by which God will judge us as his representatives on the earth.

Justice in the human realm was a concern of all Near Eastern religions, but in Psalm 82 the *cosmic* realm also depends upon justice in the social order. Indeed the very foundations of cosmic order are shaken in the presence of injustice. The cosmos, the universe, the divine world, depends upon the maintenance of justice in the human community—not only in Israel's midst but in all communities. When justice is not maintained, then the very foundations of the earth are shaken, the world threatens to fall apart into chaos once more. That is how much justice matters. It is not just one of the virtues. It is not even a high ethical demand. Justice is the issue on which the very claims of deity are settled. Justice, just rule, is that central activity by which God is God. Without it the very universe cannot survive.[25]

---

25. Miller, *Interpreting*, 124.

Psalm 83

A song. A psalm of Asaph.

¹ O God, do not remain silent;
  do not turn a deaf ear,
  do not stand aloof, O God.
² See how your enemies growl,
  how your foes rear their heads.
³ With cunning they conspire against your people;
  they plot against those you cherish.
⁴ "Come," they say, "let us destroy them as a nation,
  so that Israel's name is remembered no more."
⁵ With one mind they plot together;
  they form an alliance against you—
⁶ the tents of Edom and the Ishmaelites,
  of Moab and the Hagrites,
⁷ Byblos, Ammon and Amalek,
  Philistia, with the people of Tyre.
⁸ Even Assyria has joined them
  to reinforce Lot's descendants.
⁹ Do to them as you did to Midian,
  as you did to Sisera and Jabin at the river Kishon,
¹⁰ who perished at Endor
  and became like dung on the ground.
¹¹ Make their nobles like Oreb and Zeeb,
  all their princes like Zebah and Zalmunna,
¹² who said, "Let us take possession
  of the pasturelands of God."
¹³ Make them like tumbleweed, my God,
  like chaff before the wind.
¹⁴ As fire consumes the forest
  or a flame sets the mountains ablaze,
¹⁵ so pursue them with your tempest
  and terrify them with your storm.
¹⁶ Cover their faces with shame, LORD,
  so that they will seek your name.
¹⁷ May they ever be ashamed and dismayed;
  may they perish in disgrace.

¹⁸ Let them know that you, whose name is the LORD—
that you alone are the Most High over all the earth.

PSALM 83 CONCLUDES the mini-collection of poems focused on the exile, its causes, and how long it will last. Psalms 79–83 all revolve around the great national crisis of exile. The removal of the people from the land of promise, from the "holy city" of Jerusalem, and from the symbol of God's presence among his people, the temple, struck at the very core of Israel's religious identity. This challenge was real and lasting for Israel's understanding of her relationship with Yahweh and her place in God's purposes for the world, so it is not surprising to see the issue of exile dealt with so prominently in the prayers of the Psalter. Psalms 79 and 80 are laments that question why God allowed the exile to happen in the first place and how long it will last. In Psalms 81 and 82 Yahweh speaks to his people in response. First, he reminds them that they are in exile because of their failure to listen to his warnings. Second, he points out his absolute control over the nations (and their gods). Psalm 83, once again, returns to the prayers of the people, with the psalmist's call for divine justice to be worked out in human history.

The Heading (83:0)

THE TWO MOST COMMON DESCRIPTIONS of psalms combine here: "A song. A psalm of Asaph." These two Hebrew designations (*shir* and *mizmor*) are frequently found together in the headings to the psalms and, broadly speaking, seem to function as synonyms, with both terms implying a composition to be sung with musical accompaniment.[1] Psalm 83 concludes the Asaph collection that dominates Book 3.

The Nations Conspire (83:1–8)

PSALM 83 DIVIDES INTO TWO PARTS. In verses 1–8 the psalmist reminds God of the nations that have joined together to conspire against the nation of Israel and against Yahweh, their God. Verses 9–18 then voice the psalmist's prayer that God will work powerfully against these conspirators to reestablish his reputation as Lord over all the earth.

---

1. It is possible that at one point *shir* referred to a composition primarily to be sung, whereas *mizmor* described a song with musical accompaniment. But with the passage of time this distinction seems to have lapsed, and in time the two terms began to function synonymously (see "מִזְמוֹר," *HALOT* 1:566).

O God, do not remain silent. The opening verse of Psalm 83 follows intriguingly from the final verse of Psalm 82. Psalm 82:8 ends with the call for Yahweh to rise up and judge the earth, for all the nations belong to him. The poet knows that Israel's God rules absolutely over the nations (see 83:1–7), but he ends the Psalm 82 with a call for Yahweh to pronounce his judgment over the whole earth. Psalm 83:1 then picks up on this theme with a threefold prayer that God will not be silent! The implication is that the poet calls for God's silence over the exile to end as he pronounces judgment on the nations, their rulers, and their gods.

The three verbs used (*damah, harash,* and *shaqat*) all seem to be synonyms implying voicelessness rather than inactivity. The prayer is for Yahweh finally to speak. The implication is that, though the people may by faith have come to accept the fact that God does still rule over the nations, their desire is for his sovereignty to *be proclaimed* to those nations that still mock the Creator and King of the universe. Psalm 82:8 encourages Yahweh to "rise up," which is a frequent call to activity. The activity desired in Psalm 83:1 is one of *speech*. According to the psalmist, it is time for God to declare his verdict over the nations and, by doing so, to address their mockery (cf. Ps 79:10). The brute fact of God's silence during the experience of exile added to Israel's dismay.[2] As far as the people are concerned, it is time for God to break silence and to speak in judgment over the injustices of the nations.

The psalmist/speaker stands as the representative of the people in this psalm. He prays publicly, thus exercising the only—and the most powerful—weapon at the disposal of the community of faith in the midst of their turmoil. In the Hebrew text this opening verse is bracketed by the two most common words for God (*'elohim* and *'el*), thus focusing on the sole locus of hope for Israel in exile.[3] God alone can bring release. God alone can pronounce judgment. So the people, through the psalmist, pray. "God seems indifferent to the danger of His people: their enemies are mustering unrebuked: but He has only to speak the word, and their schemes will be utterly frustrated."[4]

See how your enemies growl. The psalmist moves from intercession (Ps 83:1) to lament (vv. 2–8). He begins by praying for Yahweh to speak in judgment and then lays out the reason why that pronouncement should

---

2. See Hossfeld and Zenger, *Psalms* 2, 341: "This silence of God is unbearable to those praying the psalm, not least because the enemies speak and act all the more loudly, as the two causal clauses in vv. 3–5 and 6–9 deplore."

3. Schaefer, *Psalms*, 203.

4. A. F. Kirkpatrick, *The Book of Psalms* (Cambridge: Cambridge University Press, 1910), 500.

come, namely, because the nations are in rebellion against God and his design for the world. The silence of God stands in marked contrast to the very vocal nature of the nations' rebellion. They "growl" (better "rage," as the Hebrew is stronger than the NIV's translation here), they "conspire" and "plot" and "say." In the poetry of the psalm, the speaker paints a picture of a loud mass of rebellious people in contrast to a God who, to date, remains silent. The imagery is powerful and conveys the urgency of the intercession in verse 1.[5] The use of pronouns is also significant in verse 2. The psalmist makes it clear that these enemies—who are described elsewhere in this collection as Israel's enemies (Pss 80:6; 81:14) are actually *Yahweh's* enemies as well. They hate not only Israel as a state but also Yahweh as their God. In the mind of the poet, standing against God's people is standing against God's will and purpose and, therefore, against God himself (Ps 83:3–5). So, in the lament, which provides the rationale for the prayer of verse 1, the speaker makes it plain that the peoples deserve judgment not just for the injustices of the exile but also for their rebellion against God.[6]

"Come," they say, "let us destroy them as a nation." Psalm 83:4 displays the extent of the opposition Israel has faced. It is not just a minor political conflict—the aim of the enemies listed in this psalm is to wipe Israel out.[7] Psalm 83:4b is particularly poignant. Memory was a significant concept in the ancient world, and for a nation to be forgotten entirely would be the darkest of fates.[8] We see the same tendency in our own day. Politicians are forever thinking about their "legacy," and we all want to be remembered after we are gone. The significance of the conspiracy in Psalm 83 is the way in which it runs counter to God's plan for the world. As we read the unfolding story of God's design to restore his relationship with sinful humanity, we see quite clearly that Abraham and his descendants have a role to play within that plan. From Genesis 12 onward we read about the Creator's choice of a particular individual, his family, and the

---

5. Broyles, *Psalms*, 339.

6. McCann, "Psalms," 1009–10.

7. Of course, there may be an element of poetic hyperbole in the psalmist's presentation of the risk that Israel faces. But Haman and Hitler serve as warnings not to pass over a literal interpretation of this verse too quickly.

8. Walton, *ANE Thought*, 313. Jeremiah 11:19, Ezek 21:32, and Zech 13:2 all speak about someone's being remembered no more. In the first of these passages, this nonremembrance is precisely what Jeremiah's opponents wish for him. The second passage, significantly for Ps 83, is Yahweh's pronounced judgment on the kingdom of Ammon, one of the nations listed in Ps 83:7. In the text from the book of Zechariah, it is the false gods and idols that will be remembered no more in the "day of the Lord."

nation born out of his family. In choosing that particular individual, Yahweh always maintained the intent of working out his plan to bless the whole of the created order through him (Gen 12:1–3). So, the narrative of the Bible, unfolding from the fall of humankind in Genesis 3 onward, displays God's design to restore right relationship with sinful humanity. Clearly, Israel has their role to play within that design. Through Israel God sought to display his true nature to the nations, and Israel, as a society driven by his revealed word, was meant to attract the nations to turn back to Yahweh (e.g., Deut 4).[9] Even though they singularly failed in this task, Israel remained a part of God's purpose for the outworking of his salvation on the earth. So, the nations' plan to wipe out the memory of Israel from the earth was also an act of rebellion against Yahweh and his purposes for the world.

They form an alliance against you. The Hebrew of Psalm 83:5b is powerfully telling. Literally, the Hebrew text of this verse says, "Against you, they cut a covenant." The notion of covenant governed the relationship between Yahweh and his people, Israel. God's relationship with his people is structured and ordered by the covenants he makes with them.[10] Covenant is the means by which God makes his expectations clear regarding how his people behave, live, act, think, speak, worship, and so on. Covenant is also the means by which the Creator lets his people know what they can expect *from him* as a result of their allegiance to God. Covenant is a solemn and serious agreement of association. As well as working on a divine-human level, covenants could also be made between human parties to an agreement. They could either function between individuals, much like a modern-day contract, or between nation states, much like a treaty. It is the latter that the psalmist refers to here. The idea of "cutting" a covenant seen here in the Hebrew text is linked with the ceremonies that accompanied the making of a covenant. Often these ceremonies would involve the bloody sacrifice of animals as a graphic warning that failure to keep the covenant would lead to the same end result. Genesis 15 gives us a biblical example of just such a covenant-making ceremony. The point is that entering into a covenant is a serious and solemn matter. The psalmist is making it clear that we are not simply talking about a difference of

---

9. For example, see Christopher J. H. Wright, *Deuteronomy*, NIBCOT (Peabody, Mass./ Carlisle: Hendrickson/Paternoster, 1996), 45–60, and Christopher J. H. Wright, *The Mission of God: Unlocking the Bible's Grand Narrative* (Leicester: Apollos, 2006), 357–96, for further discussion of Israel's witness to the nations.

10. For example, see the covenants with Noah in Gen 9; Abraham in Gen 15 and 17; Moses and Israel at Sinai in Exod 19–24; David in 2 Sam 7; and Jeremiah's discussion of the "new covenant" in Jer 31.

opinion regarding foreign policy here. The nations listed in Psalm 83:6–8 are clearly and purposefully intent on conscious rebellion against Yahweh through the annihilation of his people, God's instrument for working out his purposes on the earth at that time.

The tents of Edom and the Ishmaelites. Ten neighboring nations are listed in verses 6–8 as those who have entered into covenant against Israel. This list is probably not intended to mark a particular historical incident in which all these nations combined to attack Israel; rather, the recorded nations have all opposed Israel at some point in the past, and the psalmist is calling to mind their aggression. That geographically these nations surround Israel emphasizes the people's great need of divine intervention (vv. 9–18).[11]

The special mention of Assyria in verse 8 is interesting. If Psalm 83 is part of a mini-collection focused on the challenge of exile, it would be more logical to see Babylon as the great and dominant threat rather than Assyria. There are a number of possible explanations for the psalm's focus on Assyria. First, and perhaps most likely, this psalm could originally have been of northern, Israelite origin (note also the lack of specific reference to Jerusalem). This explanation would make sense of seeing Assyria as the greatest threat, as it was the great military power on Israel's doorstep during the years of the divided kingdom. Nonetheless, an original setting in the experience of Israel would not prevent the editors who gathered the psalms together as a book from seeing Psalm 83 as a composition appropriate to this discussion of the problem of exile. Although the original setting may have been in the context of Israel's experience, the indeterminacy of the psalms means that they can readily be read and adopted in different circumstances. So, it is entirely possible that a psalm originating in the north, where Assyria was the oppressor, would be adopted as the prayer of a Judean audience when they faced similar circumstances. Other suggestions include the possibility that Assyria may have been chosen as a foil to establish the sovereign ability of Yahweh because, despite their great power and military success, they failed in their attempt to capture Jerusalem.[12] So the use of Assyria as the superpower behind the other nations reminds the people of God's ability to deliver them even from the

---

11. Eaton, *Psalms*, 300. Hossfeld and Zenger point out that the list of nations in these verses may well echo the typical ancient Near Eastern pattern of a "tableau of nations" that oppose a particular country. Basically, this roster is a formal list of opposing nations and is often represented in the iconography of Egyptian royal tombs (see Hossfeld and Zenger, *Psalms* 2, 342–43).

12. Hossfeld and Zenger, *Psalms* 2, 343.

mightiest of oppressors. A third alternative may be that Assyria functions as a kind of code referring to Persia, the superpower of the day in the early postexilic period (fifth century BCE). The Persian kingdom of this period encompassed the territory of Assyria, and Ezra 6:22 uses the phrase "king of Assyria" to refer to Darius, king of Persia.[13] Whatever the rationale behind the use of Assyria as the archenemy in Psalm 83:8, these verses emphasize the extent of opposition faced by Israel over the years. This climactic verse of the psalmist's lament leads into the prayer that follows.

Intercession Seeking Intervention (83:9–18)

DO TO THEM AS YOU DID TO MIDIAN. In counterpoint to the list of opposing nations in the lament part of Psalm 83, the poet then moves on in the ensuing intercession to list some of the great victories of God in behalf of his people. From the attacks of Edom, Moab, Assyria, etc., the psalmist refocuses on Israel's great victories over Midian, Sisera, and Jabin. The essence of the psalmist's heartfelt plea is that Yahweh would deal with their present oppressors as effectively as he has done in behalf of his people in the past. It seems that in verses 9–12 the psalmist is focusing particularly on the victories of God during the time of the judges.[14] Sisera and Jabin were defeated by Deborah and Barak, with Sisera meeting a particularly gruesome demise involving a woman and the business end of a tent peg (Judg 4:17–24). The poet's reference to Oreb, Zeeb, Zebah, and Zalmunna continues the judges theme by bringing to mind another great Israelite victory over the Midianite military. These four Midianite noblemen died in Gideon's campaign against this people's oppression of Israel (Judg 6–8).[15]

There are two key features of these campaigns that suit the psalmist's purposes in writing Psalm 83. First, in Judges 4–8 Israel was helpless before the might of Midian, and the emphasis of these stories is upon the people's absolute reliance on Yahweh for deliverance. Such reliance is a key thrust of the Gideon narrative in particular, in which Yahweh whittles away the

---

13. Goldingay, *Psalms 2*, 579.

14. Reference to Midian could also bring to mind one of Israel's earliest military victories under the leadership of Yahweh. Numbers 31 describes the victory of the newly formed Israel over Midian on the Hebrews' way out of Egypt. But the association of Midian with Sisera and Jabin in Ps 83:9 indicates that the psalmist probably has Gideon's victory over the Midianites in mind (Judg 6–8).

15. The reference to their becoming "like dung on the ground" (Ps 83:10) is simply a description of the completeness of the victory over the Midianites. No one was left to bury the bodies, so they were left to rot into the soil. Hossfeld and Zenger point out the irony that "those who wanted to take possession of God's pastures (cf. v. 13) remain in those very pastures—but as fertilizer!" (Hossfeld and Zenger, *Psalms 2*, 344).

numbers of Gideon's army to prove that it is the Warrior God who brings victory rather than the skill of Israel's generals or armies. Israel stood no chance against Midian in the days of Gideon, yet God brought them victory. So, the psalmist calls to mind this triumph in his present prayer for deliverance—God's people in exile stood no chance against their enemies, yet, just as in the days of the Judges, he is still capable of bringing release. Second, the Judges narrative is poignant because in those days Yahweh won his people's release from oppression *despite* their sin and rebellion. One of the dominant motifs of the book of Judges is the repeated cycle of Israel's rebellion against God, resulting in their oppression from a neighboring state as a means of divine rebuke, followed by their prayer for release from this punishment, and issuing in Yahweh's intervention in behalf of his people by sending a deliverer who leads the people to freedom from military oppression. Key to this repeating narrative throughout Judges 2–16 is the grace of God in hearing the prayers of his people despite their rebellion against him.[16] Understandably, this nuance of the Judges story is significant in forming the prayer of Psalm 83. The mini-collection of Psalms 79–83 makes it plain that God's people had brought the crisis of the exile on themselves through their sinful refusal to listen (Ps 81) and through their own failure to maintain justice in the land (Ps 82). Yet God had brought release to a sinful people in times past, and the psalmist prays that he will do so once again for the present generation.

Who said, "Let us take possession of the pasturelands of God." The attitude of the nations currently oppressing the psalmist and the praying congregation is aligned with the arrogant rebellion of those defeated by God in the past (Ps 83:4; cf. v. 12). The Midianites had arrogantly assumed that their might allowed them to take whatever they wanted. But these tracts were the "pasturelands of God," not just of Israel. Thus, their arrogant pride truly led to their fall when their plotting took them up against the Warrior God of Israel. The intercession of verses 9–12 invokes the same treatment of the arrogant military oppressors of the psalmist's day. They plot against Yahweh when they plot against his people, and the poet seeks the same end for these modern enemies as was experienced by ancient enemies in the time of the judges. "Yhwh gave Israel spectacular victory on these occasions. These verses take these acts of God as a pattern for their prayer, seeking Yhwh to act in the same way again."[17]

Make them like tumbleweed, my God. Psalm 83:13–15 expands this prayer for divine deliverance from military persecution. The victory

16. K. Lawson Younger, *Judges, Ruth*, NIVAC (Grand Rapids: Zondervan, 2002), 34–43.
17. Goldingay, *Psalms 2*, 580.

requested in verses 9–12 is spelled out in these subsequent verses. The poet demands that these forces, which seem so substantial, become inconsequential before the power of Yahweh. Just as the awesome might of Midian is transformed into fertilizer for the ground, so the psalmist prays that the solid power of their present oppressors becomes as slight as "tumbleweed" or "chaff." This imagery echoes the theology of Psalm 1, where the wicked are described as being "like chaff" (v. 4, though this verse uses a different word for "chaff "from that used in Ps 83:13). Psalm 1 speaks of the stability, strength, and fruitfulness of those who love the Lord and delight in his revealed word. This stability is contrasted with the ethereal nature of those who reject God's ways. Those who reject Yahweh are like chaff—passing, insubstantial, here today and gone tomorrow. As an act of faith, the psalmist sees beyond the reality of his present experience to view the possibilities that exist when God answers prayer (see Contemporary Significance). Just as Gideon came to see what God was capable of despite the "objective" military might of the Midianites (Judg 6–8), so the speaker and the people praying with him see beyond the reality of their present experience. The Babylonians were strong enough to take the people of Judah and Jerusalem into captivity. In that sense, they were a substantial threat. Yet the psalmist knows that before God they may be as lightweight as chaff.

As fire consumes the forest . . . so pursue them with your tempest. The prayer for restoration builds to a crescendo. The pray-er moves from the prayer that the enemies of God's people will become "tumbleweed" and "chaff" to asking that they will be consumed by "fire" and "flame." So the prayer is that the oppressors' great strength will be removed from them and that they will be engulfed by the consuming power of God's judgment. Then the psalmist calls for the unleashing of all God's furious power on those who would spoil his purposes. The imagery of "tempest" and "storm" speaks of the revelation of God's power in theophany. When God makes his presence tangibly real on the earth, his appearance is accompanied by powerful storm manifestations (Exod 19; Deut 5; Ps 18). The poet prays that the people's (and Yahweh's) enemies will be terrified before this manifestation of God's raw power, just as Israel was terrified at Mount Sinai (Exod 20:18–21). This petition becomes significant as the prayer develops because the speaker does not pray that God will visit on Israel's enemies the same end that these enemies sought for Israel (Ps 83:4). The prayer is that God will relentlessly pursue his enemies until they are absolutely convinced of his absolute power.[18]

---

18. "The words 'terrify' (v. 15) and 'dismayed' (v. 17) translate the same Hebrew root (בהל *bahal*) that is used to assert God's sovereignty over enemies of God and the people (Exod 15:15 . . . , Ps 2:5; 48:5)" (McCann, "Psalms," 1010).

Cover their faces with shame, LORD, so that they will seek your name. In some ways we naturally balk at the violent overtones of the prayer in Psalm 83:9–15, yet the end purpose of the prayer is quite remarkable. The psalmist lived in a violent world, and people of Israel were faced with the threats of that merciless reality (v. 4). But the psalmist's prayer is not that Yahweh will mete out punishment in line with the intent of the rebellious nations. Instead he prays that the Warrior God of Israel will absolutely establish his power over the nations *so that they would seek him!* In many ways this request is uncanny. The pray-er asks God to confound his enemies with his power so that ultimately they may know that he is the one, true God and seek relationship with him. This desired result makes Psalm 83 quite remarkable among the psalms that seek God's intervention. The psalmist effectively prays that Yahweh would make the enemies who had conspired to eradicate the covenant community part of that selfsame family of God's people! So, the psalmist views the military victories of the past as essential to establishing the true nature of Yahweh as God over all the nations. His prayer for divine intervention is not vengeful but salvific in intent. His desire is for the nations who reject God and conspire against him to acknowledge his lordship and join with the community who worship him. He prays that those separated from God will find a truth that surprises them.

May they ever be ashamed and dismayed. The means by which the psalmist sees this transformation occurring is also interesting. In Psalm 83:16–17 we see a threefold emphasis on the imagery of shame ("shame," "ashamed," "disgrace"). Why so? As far as the Bible is concerned, any act of rebellion against God finds its root cause in human pride.[19] Before the nations listed in verses 6–8 can truly see the error of their ways and seek the name of Yahweh (v. 16), they must first be humbled by God. The prayer is poignant because it reflects the experience of Israel and Judah in exile. Their own arrogant refusal to hear God and to bow to his will led to their humiliation in the loss of their capital, their land, their king, and their temple. God's people first had to be humbled in order to seek him again. Having apparently learned this lesson, the psalmist prays that the peoples of the alliance of rebellious nations will also be humbled in order that they may seek and find the truth and blessing of life with God.

---

19. For example, see Lev 26, especially verses 18–20, and Isa 13:11. Psalm 10 is also telling in the context of Ps 83:16–17. For example, Ps 10:4 says, "In his pride the wicked man does not seek him; in all his thoughts there is no room for God." The psalm frames the rejection of God and the mockery of others in terms of human pride and arrogance. Only divine rebuke can change such an attitude of arrogant rejection (vv. 12–18).

Let them know that you . . . are the Most High over all the earth.
In an echo of Psalm 82, the psalmist prays that, through the act of divine
humiliation, the nations will realize that Yahweh alone is the one who rules
over the whole of creation. The temporary military success of the nations
inclined them to believe that their gods ruled, but the poet prays that
God will work to show them the reality of the situation: Yahweh alone is
the High King over the entire world. He is sovereign over the rhythms of
the world in which we live, and human beings only find their true role in
created order when they accept his kingship and their part in his purposes.
The psalmist prays that the people of the nations will come to know Yahweh as the Most High. In doing so they will find the blessing, meaning,
and purpose that comes from complying with his design for this planet.

THE NATIONS IN THE PSALMS. Normally in the
psalms, as in much of the Old Testament, the
nations are presented as being the enemies of
Israel and in rebellion against God. Psalm 2
is the prime example of the general attitude we find in the Psalter. The
enemies conspire against God (vv. 1–3), and they come under his judgment
(vv. 10–12). As we have seen in the psalms of Book 3, often the psalmist
laments because of the military victory of the nations and the mockery
they direct against Yahweh because of these geopolitical events (e.g., see
the discussion of Pss 74 and 79). But on occasion in the book of Psalms,
the discussion of the nations takes on missional intensity. Psalm 83 is one
of these poems, and this theme returns in Book 4 with the discussion of
the reign of Yahweh in Psalms 93–100.

As modern readers, we often balk at the militaristic overtones we
encounter from time to time in the Old Testament. It is easy for us to take
a patronizing view of these ancient texts and to reject them as brutal, simplistic, and sectarian. But such an attitude would simply display our own
lack of awareness of the realities of the ancient world from which the psalms
were penned. Military expansionism reflected the supremacy of the gods
of the nations that happened to be in ascendency, so often the psalmists'
prayers reflect no more that the desire for Yahweh to be seen for who he is in
reality—sovereign over all the earth. In the language of the world in which
the poets lived, renewal and restoration of God's people out from under
control of their oppressors was the only means by which the true nature of
God as Creator and Controller of the universe could be established.

What is more, Psalm 83 shows us that the attitudes toward the nations
reflected in the psalms were not necessarily vindictive. Often the prayers

regarding the nations simply seek divine redress for undeniable injustices perpetrated on their people. The psalmists were becoming aware that the exile, with all of its accompanying suffering, was part of God's plan to bring his people to repentance and right relationship with him. But injustice was still injustice. Brutality was still brutality. War crimes were just that—crimes. The only appropriate response to such national tragedy was to bring the whole situation before God in prayer. The poets knew that the exile was part of Yahweh's plan to bring his people to repentance, but their exile did not mean that he was blind or indifferent to the horrors perpetrated on them by the armies of the nations. Such behavior was still wrong in the eyes of God, so the psalmists were under no doubt that offering prayers seeking divine justice for such offenses was an entirely appropriate response to the actions of the nations. Furthermore, Psalm 83 shows us that in the book of Psalms, the prayers seeking divine retribution were not necessarily as simplistic as we sometimes believe.

Psalm 83 prays for military victory over the nations who had conspired against Israel and Yahweh. But battle honors were not the ultimate aim of the psalmist's prayer. Much as the exile served as a means to an end with regard to the spiritual restoration of Israel, so the psalmist prays that military triumph over the nations, of the type witnessed during the time of the judges (see comments on vv. 9–12 above), *would serve as a witness drawing these nations into the worshiping community of God's people.* It is difficult to overemphasize the significance of the prayer in verses 16–18. The speaker prays publicly that these very nations who had conspired to eradicate the nation of Israel should experience Yahweh's rebuke so that they too could become a part of the family of God's people! Psalm 83:17 shows us that the psalmist still sought God's justice if the nations refused to learn the lessons that would come from Yahweh's activity in Israel's behalf (just as the Midianites failed to learn that lesson in Judg 4–8), but the ultimate goal of this prayer is that those who hate God's people would become a part of them. Psalm 83 is a prayer that the nations would see the true God and respond to him. It is fundamentally missional in nature. We should not oversimplify the psalmic view of the nations to one of simple hostility. Clearly, there were those in Israel who realized that their divine election did not mean divine rejection of all other nations. Israel's function as light and witness to the nations (e.g., Deut 4:14) had not been entirely forgotten, even in the crisis of the exile.

Psalm 83 in the New Testament. While there are no direct quotations from Psalm 83 in the New Testament, the psalmist's attitude toward the nations is remarkably consistent with the teaching of Jesus and the apostolic writers regarding how we should treat enemies. For example, the prayer of verses 16–18 is remarkably consistent with Jesus' challenging teaching in Matthew 5:4–48. Setting aside the norms of bygone eras, Jesus challenges those hearing the Sermon on the Mount, "pray for those who persecute you" (Matt 5:44).[20] This challenge is precisely what the psalmist takes up in Psalm 83. Having highlighted the extent of the opposition to God's people (vv. 2–8), the poet then goes on to pray that the opponents would become part of the worshiping community of God's people. It is often claimed that the New Testament displays a higher ethic than the Old Testament does. Equally, we encounter frequent assertions that the psalms vilify other nations and that these poems are marked by a characteristic hatred of those outside the covenant community. But here in Psalm 83, we see the kernel of Christ's teaching regarding the right attitude toward enemies. We also see that the psalmic view of the nations is more nuanced than is often realized.

PRAYING FOR THE PERSECUTED CHURCH. In terms of application to the contemporary world in which we live, Psalm 83 models for us the attitude we should share in prayer for our brothers and sisters in Christ who are persecuted for their faith. The psalmist is unwilling to see injustice persist, yet his prayer is couched in terms of seeking repentance and change in the hearts of those who persecute God's people.

In the (still fairly) comfortable Western church, we often forget the realities of Christians who daily face persecution and even martyrdom simply because they call Jesus their Lord. Many believers in many countries throughout North Africa, the Middle East, and East Asia daily face the threat of serious maltreatment or death at the hand of those who conspire against God and his people. Fellow Christians have their property confiscated, their businesses ruined, and their educational opportunities removed—they are beaten, tortured, humiliated, and all too frequently killed by those who worship other gods or insist that there is no God. How should we respond to such outrages against the created order that God has instilled in this world? Psalm 83 models for us the type of prayer we ourselves should adopt in behalf of those who face persecution for their faith.

---

20. The essential teaching of Ps 83 regarding enemies and opponents is also consonant with the teaching of Paul on this matter. If we compare Ps 83:16–18 with Rom 12:14–21, we see a remarkable correspondence between the psalmist's community prayer and the teaching of Paul.

First, we should pray! Praying is precisely what the poet does. He does not just shake his head silently or rage impotently against the injustices of life among the nations—he does the right thing by adopting the most efficacious course of action available to any believer in any situation. All too often we pray when all else fails. The fact that we have not quickly turned to prayer is frequently the reason why all else has failed! It may be true to say that prayer was the only recourse open to the exiled psalmist. He had no human power upon which he could call to remedy the people's situation. But the theology of Psalm 83 clearly demonstrates the pray-er's realization that intercession is always the *best* course of action regardless of circumstances. It is not accidental that the psalmist calls on God to act as he did in the time of the judges. There were many victories the poet could have called to mind as examples; he chose to focus attention, however, on these particular incidents in which the power of God rather than human military expertise is the primary point of the text. Psalm 83 reminds us that prayer is the best course of action we can ever take and should, therefore, be the first course of action we do undertake. In this light, it is important that we remember to pray regularly and in an informed manner for Christians in the suffering church, for therein lies the power to effect real change.

Second, we must be honest in prayer. There is no point in brushing over the brutality of oppression some Christians face. We need to investigate the reality of their daily lives and bring these facts before God in prayer. Organizations such as Christian Solidarity Worldwide and Release International provide detailed and timely information about the events that affect churches and individuals worldwide. With access to email and the internet, we have every means open to us to find out about the situations that our Christian family encounter on a daily basis. Yes, of course God knows these things, but acknowledgment of that fact did not stop the psalmist from describing his reality to God in prayer (vv. 2–8). We too must lay out present realities before our Father, who hears our prayers through his Son (Rom 8:31–3).

Third, our prayers should focus on repentance and justice. The poet's first focus of intercession is that the enemy nations might discover the truth about God and (by implication) join the community of his people in worship (Ps 83:16–18). But injustice and violence are offensive to God as much as they cause harm to individuals, and such situations cannot be allowed to continue unchecked. The psalmist's desire is that the nations will repent and know that God is the Most High and, therefore, the only being worthy of worship. There is no doubt from the poet's prayer, however, that the persecution perpetrated by the enemies should stop (vv. 13–18). So also in our prayers for the persecuted church, we should focus on repentance and justice. We should pray that, in the providence of God, he will intervene to bring a realization of error and repentance to those who persecute. God has done so many times in the past—in the experience of the apostle Paul through to military and police figures of the present day. But should repentance not occur for whatever reason, our prayers should also invoke God's justice into the situation—prayers beseeching the all-sovereign God to punish wrong and wrongdoers who rebel against his standards and purposes. Some Christians balk at such forceful prayer—and, of course, we should be careful when we pray such things for ourselves. Christians, however, should be advocates and intercessors seeking God's kingdom to come on this earth. Injustice and evil should be named for what they are, and our prayers should reflect the revulsion the Creator feels when his laws and his people are violated. That repentance and justice should be the focus of our prayers is also part of the message of Psalm 83.

> Imprecations affirm God by surrendering the last word to God. They give to God not only their lament about their desperate situation, but also the right to judge the originators of that situation. They leave everything in God's hands, even feelings of hatred and aggression.[21]

---

21. Zenger, *A God of Vengeance?* 15. Zenger's book is an excellent study of the forceful prayers of imprecation (the type of prayer against enemies and persecutors we see in Ps 83) and the concept of divine justice in the world in which we live.

Psalm 84

For the director of music. According to gittith.
Of the Sons of Korah. A psalm.

¹ How lovely is your dwelling place,
    Lᴏʀᴅ Almighty!
² My soul yearns, even faints,
    for the courts of the Lᴏʀᴅ;
my heart and my flesh cry out
    for the living God.
³ Even the sparrow has found a home,
    and the swallow a nest for herself,
where she may have her young—
    a place near your altar,
Lᴏʀᴅ Almighty, my King and my God.
⁴ Blessed are those who dwell in your house;
    they are ever praising you.
⁵ Blessed are those whose strength is in you,
    whose hearts are set on pilgrimage.
⁶ As they pass through the Valley of Baka,
    they make it a place of springs;
    the autumn rains also cover it with pools.
⁷ They go from strength to strength,
    till each appears before God in Zion.
⁸ Hear my prayer, Lᴏʀᴅ God Almighty;
    listen to me, God of Jacob.
⁹ Look on our shield, O God;
    look with favor on your anointed one.
¹⁰ Better is one day in your courts
    than a thousand elsewhere;
I would rather be a doorkeeper in the house of my God
    than dwell in the tents of the wicked.
¹¹ For the Lᴏʀᴅ God is a sun and shield;
    the Lᴏʀᴅ bestows favor and honor;
no good thing does he withhold
    from those whose walk is blameless.
¹² Lᴏʀᴅ Almighty,
    blessed is the one who trusts in you.

 PSALM 84 BEGINS a new collection of psalms within Book 3 and sets a very different tone from the compositions that come before it. The tone shifts from lament to worship—from the loss of exile to the joy of being in God's presence. Psalm 84 is a Zion psalm, a psalm of pilgrimage that focuses on the people's pilgrimage to the temple in Jerusalem to celebrate one of the great festivals (probably the Feast of Tabernacles[1]). Although this psalm finds its roots in the literal, physical pilgrimages of the period before Judah's exile, the imagery of the day soon became spiritualized and associated with the life of faith. Thus, the significance of Psalm 84 continued after the destruction of the temple as a psalm celebrating the privileges of life with God.

The Heading (84:0)

SEE THE COMMENTS ON PSALM 81:0 regarding the heading. Psalm 84, however, is a psalm of the Sons of Korah rather than an Asaph composition. The Sons of Korah are associated with worship in the temple during the Solomonic period. Korah himself was one of the musicians appointed to lead the people's worship at this temple in Jerusalem (1 Chr 6:16–47), and the literal "Sons of Korah" were appointed as gatekeepers of the tent of meeting before the building of the temple (1 Chr 9:17–22). So Korah and his sons are associated with the public worship of Yahweh in the central sanctuary. Second Chronicles 20:19 also describes the Korahites as one of the singing groups that led public worship in the temple during the reign of Jehoshaphat. It is this thoroughgoing association with corporate praise and the temple that probably led to the attribution of psalms to the "Sons of Korah." For the purpose of our reading of the book of Psalms, the heading indicates a change of subgroup within Book 3. We have moved from the Asaphite collection, dominated by lament (Pss 73–83), to a Korahite collection that is more mixed in tone, including both praises and laments and both corporate and individual psalms (Pss 84–88, apart from Ps 86). Effectively, from the perspective of the editorial shape of Book 3, we move on to a different discussion in Psalms 84 and following. The laments over the loss of the temple and Jerusalem have been answered in Yahweh's responses in Psalms 82 and 83, so the conversation moves on to consider other matters, namely, worship and what it means to walk with Yahweh.

---

1. Reference to the "early rain" or "autumn rains" in verse 6 points to a setting in the Festival of Booths (see Deut 16:13–16).

Dwelling with the Lord (84:1–4)

HOW LOVELY IS YOUR DWELLING PLACE, LORD ALMIGHTY. Psalm 84 begins with a eulogy to the beauty and benefits of dwelling in the presence of God. "Lovely" here is slightly misleading inasmuch as the root word points to the dwelling place of God as being "well loved" (*yadid*) rather than simply having aesthetic beauty. The latter may also be implied in the description of the divine sanctuary, but the root word and the context point more naturally to the psalmist's *response* to the presence of God—he loves to be where God is, so the dwelling place of God is a *beloved* place in that sense. For the pilgrim people there may be an element of amazement at the beauty of the temple complex when it comes into view for the first time,[2] but these opening verses speak more to the immense desire the psalmist voices (on behalf of the people) to be in the presence of God.[3]

There is an interesting juxtaposition of language in this opening verse of Psalm 84. The tone is very gentle and contemplative. It is focused on the delights of dwelling in the presence of God, yet the psalmist addresses his exclamation to the "LORD Almighty" ("Yahweh of Hosts [or 'Armies']"; see comments on Ps 80:4, 7, 14, 19). The contrast of foci is surprising, but the point seems quite clear. The God who is King dwells with his people. The Warrior God is also the God who meets with his people. It is a remarkable conjunction of imagery—the people love to dwell in the presence of the God of Armies. He may well be terrifying to all enemies, but those under his protection are *attracted* to his presence. There is an element of surprise in this opening verse, but its meaning is clarified by the parallel closing verse of Psalm 84. Those who dwell in the presence of the Lord of Hosts come under his blessing (v. 12)—that God is knowable and capable is the point of the surprising language of verse 1. Basically, the God whose presence the people love is also strong to hear and to answer prayers (v. 8) because he is the strong and sovereign King.

My soul yearns, even faints, for the courts of the LORD. This delight in God's presence is expressed in terms of longing and desire. The language of the "soul" and "heart" and "flesh" is used to express the completeness of this desire. *Every* aspect of the psalmist's being deeply yearns for the presence of the Lord, the Warrior God of Israel. There is nothing

---

2. Eaton, *Psalms*, 303.

3. Hossfeld and Zenger describe the one praying this psalm as being moved by the "'inner' quality of the Temple area." They go on to say, "This closeness to . . . God . . . is something that the one praying also desires to experience. His or her thinking, desiring and feeling, literally everything in him or her . . . revolves, full of longing, around this place of God's special presence" (Hossfeld and Zenger, *Psalms 2*, 355).

superficial about this longing—it is physical, spiritual, and emotional. It is positively all-consuming.

Even the sparrow has found a home. That the sparrow and swallow find their dwelling places in the temple courts furthers the psalmist's expression of desire. The comparison here is the common Jewish association of the lesser to the greater. If the birds of the air can make their homes at the temple, how much more so should God's people be able to do so? The reference to the sparrows and swallows is a reminder of something of the greatness of the Solomonic temple. It was a vast structure with outer and inner courts surrounded by walls and buildings of substantial stature. Birds would easily be able to make nests for themselves within the temple complex, and the pilgrim people would have witnessed their flight to and from their nests. So, the comparison is one that would come readily to mind: if swallow and sparrow can make their home there, how much more should the people of God be able to do so?

A place near your altar, LORD Almighty, my King and my God. There is some debate in the commentaries regarding why birds would congregate near the place of the altar. It is, after all, a busy, smoky place where animals are sacrificed. For that reason, it seems to be an unlikely place for birds to find shelter.[4] Focusing on this detail misses the point, however, inasmuch as the poet is not really thinking about birds—he is expressing his own desire! And once again, proximity is the focus of the poet's desire. *His* longing is to be close to God, and the temple with its altar is the means by which this closeness can happen. The poet's concern is not precision regarding where birds are found in the temple complex; rather, he uses birds as a literary device to express his own desire—to be near the place of sacrifice. The significance of the altar is, of course, its role in the restoration of relationship between God and his people. It is at the foot of the altar that sacrifices were made. Blood was sprinkled on that altar for the forgiveness of sins (Lev 1–9). So, the psalmist's longing is to dwell, like the birds, close to the altar, where forgiveness of sins may readily be sought and received.

We should note also the seeming dissonance of terminology used to describe the psalmist's God in Psalm 84:3. Clearly, the psalmist's desire is for presence with God, yet the language he uses to describe his God is the language of authority, not intimacy—"LORD Almighty, my King and my God." But the terminology of verse 3 actually implies a strong degree of intimacy that goes beyond the distance of the titles Lord, King, and God.

---

4. See Charles Augustus Briggs and E. G. Briggs, *The Book of Psalms*, ICC (Edinburgh: T&T Clark, 1906), 226–27.

"LORD Almighty," as it is translated in the NIV, literally means "Yahweh of Armies." This imagery points to the great power of God in that he commands hosts of heavenly warriors, but this same God is *Yahweh*—a personal God who reveals himself to his people using a personal name. The comments from Terrence Fretheim are helpful:

> Moreover, in God's giving of God's name (e.g. Exod 6:2–3), God thereby identifies himself as a personal, individual, distinctive member of the community of those who have names. In fact, naming entails a certain kind of relationship. Giving the name opens up the possibility for, indeed admits a desire for, a certain intimacy in relationship. A relationship without a name inevitably means some distance. Naming the name makes for a certain closeness of relationship, enabling truer encounter and communication. God and people can now meet and address one another, and at a level that makes for intimacy and depth.[5]

What is more, the powerful images of "King" and "God" are personalized by the psalmist's confident declaration that he is talking about *his* King and God. The use of the personal pronoun "my" adds intimacy to the idea of approach before such an all-powerful being. This being is not just any king or God, but the poet's King and God. "The titles, **my king and my God** (i.e., my personal guardian Deity), bring together the corporate and individual roles that Yahweh fulfills for the people."[6] So, despite the titles that may at first glance seem to distance God, the language of this verse really points toward intimacy of relationship with God for every singer of this psalm.

Blessed are those who dwell in your house. This statement summarizes the overall message of the opening verses. The pilgrim on his way to Jerusalem is excited by the possibility of being "physically" present before his God in the temple. We tend to take a spiritualized view of the idea of blessedness, but in reality the psalmist is simply pointing out that those who meet with God in his temple are *happy.* Hebrew uses two different words for the idea of blessing: *baruk,* which seems to have the more typically religious connotations of blessing, and *'ashre,* which presents an image of happiness flowing from the experience of God's goodness.[7]

---

5. Terrence E. Fretheim, "The Color of God: Israel's God-Talk and Life Experience," *WW* 6.3 (1986): 263.

6. Broyles, *Psalms,* 342.

7. Hans-Joachim Kraus, *Psalms 1–59: A Commentary,* trans. Hilton C. Oswald (Minneapolis: Augsburg, 1988), 115. See also Wilson, *Psalms, Volume 1,* 93–94.

The pilgrim poet's thoughts are absorbed with the simple joy that there is to be found in relationship with God—happy are those who dwell in his presence. In the psalm's original, historical context there is probably an element of delight in the protection provided by God's house because Zion was seen as impregnable (Pss 46; 48), but the real joy is to be found in the ability to praise God continuously (Ps 84:4b).

The Blessings of the Way (84:5–7)

PSALM 84:1–4 ANTICIPATES ARRIVAL in Jerusalem and the delights of worshiping God in the temple, but verses 5–7 address the joys and challenges of the pilgrims' journey to Jerusalem.

Blessed are those whose strength is in you. Again, the Hebrew points to the root of true and lasting happiness in this statement. Happy are those whose strength is in God! Plain and simple. To use a modern idiom, "It's not rocket science!" True and deep human happiness can never be found apart from right relationship with God the Creator. The image in verse 5a implies the need of God's help for the way—the pilgrim people need to seek and find strength in their God. In its original context this implication would refer to the challenges and difficulties associated with pilgrimage to Jerusalem over long distances, challenging terrain, and all the other dangers implicit in journeying in the ancient world. But as the psalm has passed through the generations of God's people and the concept of pilgrimage has become spiritualized, this verse has come to be seen as a truth for all who walk the paths of a life of faith. Just as the original pilgrims needed God's help to reach Jerusalem, so also do today's spiritual pilgrims need God's strength if we are to go on in discipleship.[8]

Interestingly, this verse clearly implies God's presence with and protection of his people even while they are away from Jerusalem and the temple. So although the poet speaks longingly of his desire to enjoy God's *special presence* in Jerusalem, he is fully aware that God's blessing and protection are with his people wherever they may be. This awareness really reflects the Old Testament's theology of temple. From its beginning it was seen as a physical manifestation of God's presence on earth, but with complete awareness that no building could conceivably contain the fullness of God, who is present everywhere (see 1 Kgs 8; 2 Chr 6). So, we see the juxtaposition of the psalmist's longing to be in the temple (possibly associated especially with the cleansing found at the altar [Ps 84:3]) and his awareness that God's blessing and strengthening are to be found anywhere at all.[9]

8. Mays, *Psalms*, 275.
9. Goldingay, *Psalms 2*, 592.

Whose hearts are set on pilgrimage. The Hebrew for verse 5b is somewhat elusive. Literally it reads, "Happy are those whose strength is in you, the highways are in their heart." This ambiguous image has prompted much debate and many different translations over the years. Of course, although the language is opaque, the concept is not difficult: "Happy are those who find strength in God, who are committed to a life of pilgrimage toward him" is what the psalmist seems to be saying to us. Whether that commitment is evidenced by literal pilgrimage to Zion, as in the days of the psalmist, or spiritually by an attitude of devotion to God and willingness to change as part of the process of discipleship, does not really matter. The psalmist points us to the lifestyle of "the way"—a life of pilgrimage toward God. It is with such an attitude of heart that we experience the blessing and strengthening of God.[10]

As they pass through the Valley of Baka. Presumably, verse 6a refers to an actual valley that was part of the pilgrimage route to Jerusalem, but it is unclear which valley is in mind. The Hebrew *baka'* seems to refer to "balsam trees,"[11] but this referent remains obscure, for these kinds of trees are seldom mentioned in the Old Testament (2 Sam 5:23; 1 Chr 14:13–16; NIV renders "poplar trees"), and there is no indication that they were characteristically associated with a particular valley or area.[12] Because the similar, more common Hebrew word *bakah* means "weeping" or "tears,"[13] this phrase in verse 6a is sometimes translated "the Valley of Tears" (see the LXX and NLT).[14] If we are meant to understand this place as "the Valley of Tears," then clearly, for some reason, it implies that the journey is not altogether easy and without its trials. The fact that there is blessing in gathering to worship in Jerusalem and that there is true happiness to be found in the pilgrimage to Zion does not mean that pilgrims are immune to all trouble. Whatever the cause, the imagery of verse 6 points to a hostile environment and difficult circumstances.

---

10. Hossfeld and Zenger, *Psalms 2*, 355.

11. "בָּכָא," *HALOT* 1:129.

12. Hossfeld and Zenger imply that the significance of the name Baka is that it refers to a shrub which only grows in arid places (Hossfeld and Zenger, *Psalms 2*, 355).

13. Although they are not from the same word root, these two words are pronounced the same way. For *bakah*, see "בָּכָה," *HALOT* 1:129.

14. The commentators suggest various reasons why this may be a place of weeping. Goldingay suggests that this location was on the route where raiders would attack parties of pilgrims (*Psalms 2*, 593), and others say simply that the tears reflect the difficulty of a dry and barren place, a particularly difficult part of the way to Zion (e.g., see Eaton, *Psalms*, 303). It is impossible to establish the location or reason—if, indeed, weeping is implied in the name—why this place would cause such despair.

They make it a place of springs. The second part of this verse may be taken to affirm the opinion of those commentators who see "the Valley of Tears" as simply a dry and barren place and, therefore, a hostile environment for pilgrims to get through. The point is that the very presence of the pilgrims *en route* to Jerusalem transforms this challenging landscape into a more amenable place of streams and pools. In other words, the psalmist's implication lies in the fact that those with a pilgrim's heart are where they are—no matter how dry and barren that place is, their presence changes its landscape. The imagery for the succeeding generations who did not participate in the pilgrimage to Jerusalem remains poignant: God's strengthening enables God's people to make a positive impact on the difficult environment in which they live—wherever and whenever that environment may be.

They go from strength to strength, till each appears before God in Zion. Returning to the strength imagery of verse 5, the psalmist suggests two thoughts: (1) the vitality of God's empowering, and (2) the completion of the pilgrimage. Although a different word for "strength" is used here in verse 7 (*hayil*, as opposed to *'oz* in v. 5), the two words are functional synonyms that both denote strength or power. The implication is that the pilgrims who have set their heart on the worship of Yahweh do not journey as others do, for they are equipped with divine strength. This gift enables them to complete the pilgrimage where others may have given up along the way. For the many generations for whom the pilgrimage had become spiritual rather than literal, this verse provides the same encouragement. God strengthens his people so that they can finish well. As the apostle Paul wrote to the Philippians, "being confident of this, that he who began a good work in you will carry it on to completion until the day of Christ Jesus" (Phil 1:6).

The Psalmist's Prayer (84:8–9)

THE NEXT SECTION OF THE PSALM moves from celebration of the delights of God's presence to a prayer for protection in behalf of the king. These verses are perhaps a surprising interlude in the flow of the psalm, but we should remember that the king was intrinsic to temple worship in the days before the exile of Judah.

Hear my prayer, LORD God Almighty. The prayer for the king is marked by great sincerity and earnestness. The psalmist beseeches God—again, presented as the Lord of Armies—to hear his prayer. The serious tone of the prayer indicates that the psalmist is fully aware of the importance of the king's role as the sponsor of temple worship.

Look on our shield, O God. Verse 9 indicates the role of the king as vicegerent and, in some sense, representative of Yahweh on earth.

The description of the king as a "shield" echoes the psalmist's later description of God as a "sun and shield" (v. 11), indicating that the king bears responsibility to fulfill the purposes of God on earth. Ultimately, of course, the poet sees Yahweh as both light for and protector of the people, but the prayer indicates that the Davidic king—as representative of Yahweh's order on earth—also plays his role in protecting the people and securing access for worship in the temple.[15] In the period after the exile, this prayer would probably be offered in behalf of the high priest, who was the senior figure with regard to worship in the Second Temple.

The Locus of Hope (84:10–12)

THE POEM CONCLUDES WITH THE PSALMIST'S declaration that it is better to be in the presence of God than anywhere else.

Better is one day in your courts. The poet's longing for the special presence of God in the temple is fully reflected in this statement of priorities. One day in the "real" presence of God in the Jerusalem temple is better than a thousand days spent anywhere else. This statement shows the real heart of the pilgrim worshiper whose normal daily existence is far from the temple, and it indicates just how precious these times of festal worship were to the genuine believer. The hyperbole of the "one" to "one thousand" comparison is designed to challenge the readers to consider just what is of ultimate importance in their lives. That one day with God is better than a thousand without him becomes another metaphor for lifestyle choices for all those readers living in the period after the great pilgrimage festivals ceased to exist. All who recite this psalm are challenged to think about where their priorities lie.

I would rather be a doorkeeper in the house of my God. The reference to the doorkeeper in verse 10b is probably not meant to refer to the Levitical office of doorkeeper (1 Chr 26). This task was one which only the Levitical priests could fulfill, not one that could be taken up by the vast majority of pilgrims on their way to Jerusalem. It is more likely that the reference to being a doorkeeper in the house of Yahweh speaks about the long queues of worshipers waiting to enter the temple compound

---

15. The books of 1 and 2 Chronicles clearly present David as the sponsor of temple worship (e.g., see 1 Chr 22–29). Although it was in fact his son Solomon who built the temple, David was the progenitor of the idea, gathered resources for the building of the structure, and also made plans for the conduct of worship within the temple. In this way David served as an example to all future kings of Judah. They too were responsible for securing the place of temple worship in the life of the community, and this responsibility would include protection for the people as they traveled to Jerusalem and provision for the proper functioning of the temple as a place of worship. See Eaton, *Psalms*, 303–4.

to make sacrifices for their sins. Again, the poet is saying that it is better to be here, waiting to enter the place of sacrifice as an act of devotion to God, than to be among those who refuse to devote themselves to Yahweh. Kraus sees this statement as saying, "I would rather lie at the border of the sacred area as a pilgrim who desires to enter and is waiting than to be far from God and to live in the [tents of the wicked]."[16]

The psalmist does not specify where or what the "tents of the wicked" might be. Some people see this phrase as a reference to the gentile nations, but such specificity is unmerited.[17] The "tents of the wicked" simply refers to the community of people who refuse to worship Yahweh and seek his presence. It may well be that the reference to the "tents" of the wicked is a critique of those who reject pilgrimage. The wicked are those who refuse to participate in the journey of pilgrimage toward God—they prefer to remain in their tents. Whether or not this view is correct, the "tents of the wicked" clearly stand in opposition to the "house of my God," and the psalmist knows without a doubt where he would rather be.

For the LORD God is a sun and shield. Verse 11 crystallizes the hope that is evident throughout the psalm. In the whole poem we note a tone of confidence despite even difficult circumstances, and it is here we come to see just why the poet is so sure that ultimately all will be well. Verse 11 gives three good reasons for confidence that also act as a spur to all those who recite this psalm. First, Yahweh is a sun and shield for the pilgrim people of God. The two images, of course, speak of light and protection. Nowhere else in the Old Testament is Yahweh referred to as a "sun," so the reference in this verse results in some debate among commentators regarding the translation of this phrase.[18] Nevertheless, images that speak of God as being or giving light are not uncommon in the Psalter (e.g., Pss 27:1; 36:9; 43:3 et al.)[19] and, in the context of the pilgrimage theme, make abundant sense. Particularly in the ancient world, where roads (such as they were) were rough and artificial sources of light were not practicable for journeying, the idea of God's being sun to his people is a particularly evocative image. He gives the light that pilgrims need to make the journey to Jerusalem and, for the postexilic generations who have sung this psalm,

---

16. Kraus, *Psalms 60–150*, 170. Longman comments that the psalmist "would rather be on the outer edges of the temple (as a *doorkeeper*) than live in a tent belonging to the wicked" (Longman, *Psalms*, 311).

17. See Artur Weiser, *The Psalms: A Commentary*, OTL, trans. H. Hartwell (Philadelphia: Westminster, 1962), 569.

18. For example, see Tate, *Psalms 51–100*, 361.

19. Psalm 43:3 also associates the themes of God's light and worship in the temple.

he provides the light (i.e., wisdom) they need to live life. The image of God as shield is a common one in the book of Psalms (Pss 3:3; 5:12;[20] 7:10; 18:1 et al.) and communicates the reassuring message that God watches over and protects his people in all circumstances.

The LORD bestows favor and honor. Second, we see that God is not begrudging in his care for his people. He freely grants both grace and glory to all those who walk in his ways and seek to worship him properly. These two Hebrew words (*hen* and *kabod*) both speak to the blessing of God. *Hen* is the grace or favor of God, and *kabod* ("glory") means that this honor is poured out visibly on the recipient for all to see.

No good thing does he withhold. Third, the psalmist summarizes the blessings of the Lord in the fact that his generosity is without compass or measure. It is this all-encompassing blessing that gives the psalmist and the pilgrim people of God great confidence that their pilgrimage is not in vain. Yahweh, their God, generously gives them everything they need to be able to walk in his ways. For the original festal community, this declaration implied God's protection and provision during the journey to Jerusalem. For postexilic communities of faith, these assurances are spiritualized, thus providing confidence that God will be an ever-present help throughout the pilgrimage that is a life of discipleship. Mays sums up this verse beautifully:

> The Lord is the living God, a title that means "lively," as the giver of life, rather than "alive," as opposite of dead. God is sun, the source of life, and shield, the protection of life (v. 11). God gives grace and glory; the good in life comes from the Lord. He is, says the psalm, "my king and my God," a double title that means something like "the sovereign power of the universe and the center of my personal life, the one who makes all things cohere for the life I have to live." To draw near to such a God is the *summum bonum*. Pilgrimage to God's place is a profound symbol of the centering and direction of all life.[21]

From those whose walk is blameless. The three images of God's rich blessing serve as reminders to the people of God that encourage them to continue in the way of pilgrimage. These blessings are open to all whose walk is blameless (v. 11). In the contemporary world, the notion of blamelessness is one that we associate with innocence or perfection; however, the

---

20. Psalm 5:12 describes God's favor as surrounding his people like a shield. There is a similar association of imagery in Ps 84:11.

21. Mays, *Psalms*, 274–75.

Hebrew word *tamim* implies wholeness or integrity.[22] "Those whose walk is blameless" is not referring to those whose walk is perfect but, instead, to all those individuals who seek honestly to walk in the ways of the Lord. So, the blessings of verse 11 are available to all those who are committed to live a lifestyle ("walk") that genuinely seeks to please God.

Blessed is the one who trusts in you. Psalm 84 closes with another beatitude (cf. vv. 4–5). Echoing the sentiments of the previous blessing statements, verse 12 points to the source of true happiness as being found in an attitude of dependence on the Lord of Hosts ("LORD Almighty" in the NIV). Just as those who dwell in the house of the Lord find happiness (v. 4), as do all those who find the strength in God (v. 5), so also, according to the psalmist's closing reminder, does the truly blessed person who trusts in Yahweh, the God who commands armies. The final two verses of Ps 84 provide readers of every generation with a powerful motivation for prayer. First, we see in verse 11 the goodness of God and his generosity toward his people. Then, in verse 12 we are reminded that this good and generous God is also "Yahweh *tseba'ot*"—the Lord of Hosts, the God of Armies. Because he is the God who reigns, not only is he inclined to do good toward people, but he is also capable of ordering all circumstances for their benefit! Surely trust in him brings great blessing.

PRESENCE, SACRIFICE, AND FORGIVENESS. In some ways Psalm 84 is one of these passages of the Old Testament that subtly reveals to the Christian reader just how full and freeing is the redemption secured for the believer in Christ Jesus. Imagine the deep longing of the pilgrim believer who knows that in sacrificing on the altar in Jerusalem he receives forgiveness yet is also fully aware that, soon after leaving the temple sanctuary, he will require forgiveness and restoration again. That first flash of anger, that first ill-considered choice of words, thoughts that dishonor God—all these matters and a thousand beside place the pilgrim worshiper in need of redemption again. The believer is left needing the comfort of knowing that his sins are forgiven and that he is right with God again—hence the *deep* desire expressed by the pilgrim poet in verses 1–4 for God's presence and for nearness to the altar, for it is at the altar that oneness with God is attained. I do not mean to imply that the Old Testament believer had no experience of forgiveness apart from

---

22. "תָּמִים," *HALOT* 2:1748–50.

---

sacrifice in the temple. There is substantial evidence in the Psalter itself that the Old Testament believer could and did experience the forgiveness of sins even apart from sacrifice in the temple (e.g., see Pss 50:15; 51:16–17 et al.). But inescapably, the Old Testament system of belief accentuates the cleansing of sins resulting from sacrifice, and this cleansing becomes irrevocably associated with the central sanctuary. So, it is easy to understand the poet's longing for the experience of forgiveness secured before the "real" presence of God in the temple.

The book of Hebrews emphasizes the rich fullness of forgiveness that is won for the believer through the work of Jesus on the cross. Hebrews speaks of Jesus as being a high priest in the line of Melchizedek, the priest-king who met with Abraham in Gen 14. The writer of this letter draws our attention to the fact that Jesus is a better high priest, a better sacrifice, and the guarantor of access before the throne of grace (Heb 7–10). The price for sin is paid once for all through the great sacrificial work of Jesus on the cross (Heb 9:23–28; 10:11–14); therefore, the significance of holy space is transformed for believers in the Christian era. We do not have to go to a special place to meet with God. Our longing for the presence of God is met by way of the sacrifice of Christ. We now have access into the very throne room of God's presence because of the all-encompassing work of Jesus on the cross. So yes, we may share the same longing to meet with God as is expressed in Psalm 84, but our pilgrimage is not a physical one to Jerusalem; rather, a spiritual one in a Godward direction: "by one sacrifice he has made perfect forever those who are being made holy" (Heb 10:14). That one sacrifice has transformed our spiritual reality. We are made right with God and therefore can delight in immediate access into his presence. But, at the same time, we are still people who are "being made holy"—this transformation is our pilgrimage.

Psalm 84 in the New Testament. No direct citations from Psalm 84 are found in the New Testament, but the poem's central theme is radically transformed through the ministry of Christ Jesus. The major threads running through this psalm are the ideas of pilgrimage and presence—access into the real presence of God. Both of these ideas are radically transformed in the New Testament. Not only is the concept of sacrifice and access completely fulfilled through the work of Jesus, but so too is the idea of pilgrimage.[23] Being a pilgrim in the Christian era does not involve long journeys on foot to a particular holy place. From the time of Christ onward, for the community of faith pilgrimage has become basically

---

23. Longman, *Psalms*, 312.

equivalent to discipleship. Pilgrimage now is all about lifestyle choices. It is about choosing "the Way" (Acts 9:2; 19:9, 23 et al.). Both of these ideas, presence and pilgrimage, are completely renewed through the work Jesus has done on behalf of humanity.

IMPORTANCE OF FELLOWSHIP AND COMMUNITY WORSHIP. One message is absolutely clear in Psalm 84: public worship is vital to the spiritual experience of every believer! The delight of the psalmist in gathering together with the people of God is absolutely unmistakable. He desires to experience the presence of God amid the community of the saints. Clearly, he delights in the place of worship and celebrates pilgrimage together with the massed ranks of other believers. As far as the poet is concerned, the whole package of gathering with others to praise God and meet with him is a source of great joy and happiness (vv. 4–5).

Somehow, fellowship and public worship seem to have become optional in contemporary Christianity. The faith of the individual believer is elevated to such an extent that attending church to worship with other Christians has come to be seen as an act that is, at best, a chore and, at worst, completely unnecessary. The attitude of the psalmist explodes that myth with shouts of joy and great celebration as a massive community of the people of God gathers together for the sole purpose of meeting with him and praising his name! From the days of Abraham onward, to be a believer means to be in community, and we neglect that community at our own peril because worship in togetherness has always been part of biblical faith. Just as any pilgrim would be in great danger on the journey to Jerusalem were he or she to make that trip in isolation, so believers who separate themselves from fellowship place themselves in great danger with regard to their spiritual pilgrimage.

There is great happiness to be found in coming together with other believers to worship God (v. 4). There is great strength to be derived for the journey of discipleship by making the pilgrimage in community (vv. 5–7). Why then would people neglect meeting together with the family of believers? Such fellowship is a source of great joy and a reservoir of strength to keep going in the Christian faith, so let us "not give up meeting together, as some are in the habit of doing, but encouraging one another— and all the more as you see the Day approaching" (Heb 10:25).

Holy space. Clearly, in Christ and through his sacrifice we enjoy real and immediate access to the presence of God wherever we are. The New

Testament makes it plain that the Jerusalem temple is replaced in spiritual form by the body of Christ, that is, the universal church. Collectively, the family of believers is that point of access between God and the surrounding world. There is a real sense in which the church is designed to fulfill the idea of holy space that we see in Psalm 84 (Eph 2:11–22).

The psalmist longed to meet with God in the temple. The holy space of the temple precinct provided a forum in which business could be done with Yahweh—praises were sung, prayers voiced, sacrifices offered up, and sins forgiven. The holy space where all those things happened was the temple itself. As a physical site, it fulfilled an intermediary function as the place where people could meet with God and experience the reality of relationship with him. Today, the church of Christ fulfils that same intermediary function. We are not "space" in the same sense that the temple was a physical place, but the church is meant to provide the same sort of forum in which people can come to do business with God—where they too can praise and pray and hear the good news that sins can be forgiven and peace with God secured. The real question that every local community of faith has to answer is, do we genuinely provide an arena for the people around us to meet with God?

Another aspect of the question of holy space concerns the relationship between physical place and spiritual experience. Undoubtedly, there is no *need* for holy places in the life of the Christian. We do not need to make pilgrimage to specific holy places, be they particular meccas in our own country or elsewhere in the world. We are not obliged to visit the biggest churches or the most beautiful cathedrals. There is no sense that any particular place is more "holy" than another in the Christian economy. As in the Old Testament, God is everywhere, and because we can meet with God everywhere, every single place on this earth may be or become holy ground. Nevertheless, the fact that there is no *need* for holy places in our Christian reality does not mean we cannot benefit from the beauty or stillness or peace of particular places that can enhance our spiritual experience of God.

Many a climber describes the summit of a hill or mountain as a spiritual place. There is just something special about standing high enough to see all the beauty of creation displayed before you. Often mountaintops seem like sacred places, so in the ancient world shrines tended to be built on the tops of mountains. There is, therefore, a sense in which place can heighten our experience of God. Equally, many of us have probably sat in one of the great cathedrals of the world and understood why it was built as a meeting place with God. The length of the nave draws us forward to meet with God at the communion table and pulpit, and the height of the transept directs our attention upward to consider the Maker of heaven and earth. Perhaps there is a space in your house where you just find it easier to meditate, where, in some increased sense, you "feel" the presence of God. Or maybe there is a particular walk or view that inspires you to worship.

It may well be true that there is no *need* for particular holy places in the Christian faith, but we should be aware that physical space can influence our spiritual awareness. So, we should make the most of our environment and enjoy those places that heighten our awareness of God's presence with us.[24]

---

24. See William Dyrness's *Visual Faith: Art, Theology and Worship in Dialogue* (Grand Rapids: Baker Academic, 2001) for helpful discussion of the relationship between the aesthetics of architecture and the experience of worship.

Psalm 85

For the director of music. Of the Sons of Korah. A psalm.

¹ You, LORD, showed favor to your land;
   you restored the fortunes of Jacob.
² You forgave the iniquity of your people
   and covered all their sins.
³ You set aside all your wrath
   and turned from your fierce anger.
⁴ Restore us again, God our Savior,
   and put away your displeasure toward us.
⁵ Will you be angry with us forever?
   Will you prolong your anger through all generations?
⁶ Will you not revive us again,
   that your people may rejoice in you?
⁷ Show us your unfailing love, LORD,
   and grant us your salvation.
⁸ I will listen to what God the LORD says;
   he promises peace to his people, his faithful servants—
   but let them not turn to folly.
⁹ Surely his salvation is near those who fear him,
   that his glory may dwell in our land.
¹⁰ Love and faithfulness meet together;
   righteousness and peace kiss each other.
¹¹ Faithfulness springs forth from the earth,
   and righteousness looks down from heaven.
¹² The LORD will indeed give what is good,
   and our land will yield its harvest.
¹³ Righteousness goes before him
   and prepares the way for his steps.

PSALM 85 IS ONE OF THE GREAT prayers of human piety in the Psalter. This song delights in the freeing and forgiving grace that flows from God to his people yet, at the same time, is fully aware of the day-by-day tensions of the life of faith. Psalm 85 gives the reader a beautiful insight into the reality of a heart that longs to walk with

God. Along with Psalm 80, this psalm has been particularly important to the church in my own country, Scotland, during times of revival or spiritual renewal. Often these two psalms have provided a focal voice for the prayers of God's people during these periods of increased spiritual awareness. It is perhaps not surprising that each of these poems contains a strong awareness of sin and the need for forgiveness as well as the realization that such forgiveness and restoration is only to be found in the free grace of God.

The Heading (85:0)

PSALM 85 IS THE SECOND SONG of the Korahite collection in the Psalter's Book 3. For discussion of the dedication to the "director of music," see the comments on Psalm 77:0.

Rich Forgiveness (85:1–3)

THE OPENING VERSES OF PSALM 85 are among the richest found even among the great wealth of literary masterpieces in the Psalter. The poet celebrates the completeness of Yahweh's forgiveness of his people in terms that rival anything we read in the New Testament.

You, LORD, showed favor to your land. As we so often see in the psalms, this composition begins with a focal thought that is developed throughout the rest of the poem. In some ways, the description we find in verse 1 immediately highlights for us the theme of the psalm as a whole. The God of the psalmist is a God who shows favor. The God of Psalm 85 is the God who restores his people. The language used in this verse is strong and emotive, and our English translations do not quite do justice to the tone of this verse. The Hebrew verb *ratsah* perhaps more closely reflects "delight" rather than simply "showing favor." John Goldingay comments, "Here, as in 44:3[4], it denotes an unexplained if not inexplicable delight that Yahweh feels. . . . It is the pleasure and the liking that issue in practical favoring, and acting in a loving way. It is the attitude of a father to his son (Prov 3:12)."[1] The object of this divine affection is the land itself— Yahweh's own. But the second line of verse 1 makes it clear that God's pride is not much rooted in the geography of Palestine; rather, it is rooted in the land's being an appropriate home for his people.

You restored the fortunes of Jacob. Given the context within which Psalm 85 falls, it seems likely that this reference to restoration calls to mind Israel's return to the land following their release from the Babylonian exile.

---

1. Goldingay, *Psalms 2*, 606.

In fact, the phrase "you restored the fortunes of Jacob" can alternatively be read as "you turned [or 'returned'] the captivity of Jacob."[2] Verse 1 points to the Lord's great delight in his people and the fact that they are able to return to the land promised to them as their home. The psalmist is fully aware that this restoration is not really a question of the political and military machinations of the Near East in his day. The following verses of the psalmist's prayer show that the restoration of the people to the land is rooted in one thing alone: God's gracious forgiveness of his people's sin. Yes, Yahweh has restored his people to the land, but this political restoration is actually rooted in an underlying *spiritual* restoration that has been worked by Yahweh himself in behalf of his people.

You forgave the iniquity of your people. While the translation of this sentence is perfectly accurate, the limits of the English language mean that we miss out on a very rich metaphor contained in the Hebrew of verse 2. The language of the forgiveness of sins in Hebrew is rooted in the idea of God's "lifting off" or "carrying away" the sins of his people (*nasa'ta 'awon 'ammeka*). The concept behind this language understands sin to be a burden that weighs down the people of God. Through the forgiveness of their sins, God reaches down and lifts that weight from their shoulders. It is in the removal of the burden of sin and guilt that Israel has found restoration.

And covered all their sins. The image of the removal of sin and guilt is complemented by the idea of God's "covering" their moral failings. We should not think of all this activity as being akin to the contemporary notion of a "cover-up." It does not refer to concealment in that sense. The image of covering here adds to the above idea of the removal of sin. In the divine act of covering sins, God decides to bring them to mind no more. At this point in the poem the psalmist does not indicate the instrument of this covering, but verse 7 and Proverbs 10:12 (which uses the same type of language) lead the reader to the conclusion that Yahweh has covered over the sins of his people with his steadfast love. The verb that is used for "covered" (*kissitah*) is elsewhere used to describe the effects of a flood on the land (Ps 104:6; Exod 15:5, 10 et al.), and the imagery of Psalm 85:2b symbolizes God's covering over the sins of his people with his great love just as the waters of a flood cover the land. So, verse 2 conjures up an image of the completeness of Yahweh's forgiveness—the burden of sin and guilt has been removed, and God no longer sees those wrongs because he has covered them over with his love. This imagery of grace in the heart of the Old Testament is indeed very rich.

---

2. Broyles, *Psalms*, 344.

You set aside all your wrath. The concept of forgiveness, however, often takes a twofold manifestation in the Bible. First, as we see in verse 2, God proactively removes the burden of sin and guilt from his people. Second, as we see here in verse 3, in forgiving the sins of his people God also sets aside his righteous anger. As a result of their sin and rebellion, Yahweh has every right to be angry with his people, and for a period of time that anger was manifested in the judgment of the exile. But in his prayer the psalmist celebrates the totality of God's forgiving restoration, for he has not only removed the burden of guilt, but he has also chosen to abrogate his anger. The forgiveness celebrated by the psalmist in prayer is the complete package—both the sinful acts themselves and God's righteous response of anger are completely removed, and therefore the people are completely restored.[3]

The Conundrum (85:4–7)

RESTORE US AGAIN, GOD OUR SAVIOR. There is a strong element of surprise in the second stanza of Psalm 85. It seems absolutely contradictory that the psalmist should move from his prayerful celebration of God's all-encompassing forgiveness in verses 1–3, where he delights in restoration of Yahweh, to this heartfelt plea that God would once again restore his people. Restoration is received yet still required. How so? The movement seems to be a bit backward. As with Psalm 126, logically speaking it appears that the second stanza should precede the first. The normal flow in psalms of this type seems to be that restoration is first sought and then celebrated once it is received. But the psalmist is not driven by logic in his prayer but by experience. He is fully aware that the experience of forgiveness does not remove *the need* for forgiveness. The people have been forgiven and restored, but they are still in constant need of forgiveness and restoration. The sins that led to Israel's removal from the land and exile in Babylon have been publicly forgiven, thus resulting in the rebirth of the nation in the land. But a change of address does not automatically mean a change of heart. The psalmist is aware of the continuing sinfulness of the people and of the displeasure (lit., "vexation" [*ka'as*]) this sinfulness brings to the Lord (v. 4b).

Obviously, there is an inherent tension in this situation, but the psalmist is able to pray because he knows the true nature of the God whom he

---

3. The language of verses 1–3 is reminiscent of the language used in Exod 32–34, which speaks of God's merciful decision not to destroy his people completely following the golden calf incident. Just as Yahweh turned from his "fierce anger" (Exod 32:11–14) in the formation of his people, so here in Ps 85 we see Yahweh turning from his righteous anger in the restoration of his people (see Hossfeld and Zenger, *Psalms 2*, 364).

worships—he is the "God of salvation" (NIV: "God our Savior"); therefore, the psalmist is emboldened to pray. There is an element of bare-faced gall about his prayer. One would think that after such public and gracious grace in the restoration of Israel to the land the poet would be almost embarrassed to seek forgiveness yet again. But he is confident to pray because he knows that salvation is something properly basic to the character of God.

Will you be angry with us forever? If we do posit a setting for this psalm in the return to Jerusalem and the restoration of the people to the land, then the questions of verses 5–6 become particularly poignant. The poet asks, "Will you be angry forever? Will you prolong your anger through all generations?" But these questions are rhetorical, for in the return from exile the psalmist has *witnessed* the fact that Yahweh does not prolong his anger through all generations. The psalmist asks questions to which he already knows the answers. Asking questions to which we already know the answers can seem pointless, but effectively this contemplative interrogation serves as a reminder to readers and hearers alike. They have witnessed God's salvation in the return from exile, therefore, though they sin, they can still have confidence that they will experience generous renewal again.

Will you not revive us again, that your people may rejoice in you? Again, the question is rhetorical. The poet is confident that, just as the anger of God will not linger unnecessarily, so he will also bring life to the people again. The idea of revival in verse 6a speaks to God's breathing spiritual and moral life into the community of faith. In contemporary Christianity we tend to think of revival in terms of mass conversions and the growth of the church, but this prayer simply asks God to breathe spiritual life back into his people.[4] Such spiritual renewal results in a people who are grateful in heart and rejoice in their relationship with God (cf. Ps 80:18). Only in right relationship with God can human beings truly delight in their humanity.

Show us your unfailing love, LORD, and grant us your salvation. The passion of the psalmist's plea is found in the awareness that forgiveness, salvation, and spiritual renewal are only to be found in the unmerited love of God (his *hesed*). The prayer of Psalm 85:4–7 is rooted in the people's experience of seventy years of exile. God alone can restore and renew. He alone can hear and forgive. That there is nothing the people can do

---

4. The prayer that the Lord would "revive" the people again is rooted in the Hebrew verb *hayah*, meaning "to live" or "to bring to life." So effectively the psalmist prays that God will restore the people to spiritual life.

to earn or merit the reviving work of God constitutes the reason for the psalmist's offering this the impassioned appeal—prayer alone can bring about the end the psalmist seeks. The poet is fully aware that forgiveness is found entirely in the grace of God and that grace can only be sought in prayer. Salvation in Old Testament terms is God's intervention into the historical reality of his people (see the discussion of Ps 74:12), and the clear desire voiced in this prayer is that God's intervention will bring about spiritual renewal in the hearts of his people. Physical restoration to the land and the city is not enough; the poet's desire is that true, spiritual transformation would accompany the outward restoration of the return from exile. Such renewal can result only from God's unfailing love and is rooted in his intervention to carry out a work of transformation in the hearts of his people.

Psalm 85:1–3 celebrates the completeness of forgiveness that results from God's gracious favor, and verses 4–7 deal with the inherent conundrum of the life of faith. The people have been forgiven, but they are also constantly in need of forgiveness. They have been restored, but they are constantly in need of restoration. Such is the dichotomy of life with God for every generation of God's people. We are forgiven, but in our weakness we constantly need forgiveness. We are restored to right relationship with God, yet we still constantly require restoration. Is it possible to find some sort of resolution to this tension?

God Speaks Peace (85:8–9)

I WILL LISTEN TO WHAT GOD THE LORD SAYS. The tension voiced in Psalm 85 is one with which surely every believer has grappled in the life of faith. But the author of the psalm also points the reader to the sole solution to this experiential dichotomy—the promise of God. The solution for poet and reader alike is the same: listening to what God has to say to us. Our listening to God is an act of the will. We can choose to focus on the tension we face and the inadequacies we experience—or we can actually listen to the declaration of God himself with regard to his people. The poet declares his willingness to listen and, in doing so, finds the solution to his conundrum of faith.

He promises peace to his people, his faithful servants. The problem of being forgiven yet still needing forgiveness has a twofold solution that is both theological and experiential. The psalmist starts with theology in verse 8b—God *speaks* peace to his people. The NIV translates this part of verse 8 as "he promises peace to his people," but the Hebrew is much more prosaic, yet at the same time profound. The Hebrew text says simply, "He speaks [*yedabber*] peace [*shalom*] to his people." It is the ordinary word for speaking that is used, but of course the concept is far from ordinary, for speech is the means by which God accomplishes that which he accomplishes. In Gen 1–2 God speaks the whole of the created order into being. God speaks each new day into being (Ps 50:1). The speech of God is a creative act. It brings things into being. It transforms reality. The voice of God *creates* a new reality—from nothing, God's speech brings order and beauty beyond imagination.

It is this same creative speech that declares a new *spiritual* reality into being for the people of God. Peace between God and his people is disrupted by sin, but God himself—by his spoken word—recreates that peace and wholeness of relationship. If Yahweh speaks *shalom*, then *shalom* is precisely what results. This theological reality resolves the tension of Psalm 85. God has unilaterally declared peace with his people, and in that declaration harmony is restored. So goes the theological reality from the perspective of God—by his gracious, recreative word, the Creator has declared his people forgiven and, therefore, at peace with him. This state is a declared, unchangeable fact for all his "faithful servants," that is, for all those who seek to be faithful to him.[5]

But let them not turn to folly. The psalmist is aware, however, that our cognizance of our own moral failings can skew our theological understanding. We may "know" the theological reality of God's declaration, but we do not *feel* that reality because our waywardness and sin lead us to believe that harmony with God has been irrevocably broken. Often the experiential, because it is so immediate, outweighs our appreciation of theological truth. So the psalmist points to a practical solution to the conundrum of faith that should accompany the theological truth of the divine declaration of peace. If our sinfulness means that we no longer appreciate the truth of restored relationship with God, then we should turn away from these practices that mar our understanding of spiritual reality. It is because of sin that God's people find it difficult to accept his acceptance. So the psalmist urges his readers to turn away from such patterns of behavior, thus removing the tension between theological knowledge and the doubts that spring from the experiential. Most of the English versions adopt a fairly polite translation of the Hebrew word *kislah* ("folly" or "foolish ways"), but the original is more blunt. "Stupidity" is perhaps a better understanding of the term.[6] And "stupid" is how the poet

---

5. Interestingly, Terrien sees this three-line, first-person interjection in verse 9 as being central to the message of the psalm, set apart from the two-line verses that surround it (*Psalms*, 605–6).

6. "כִּסְלָה," BDB 493.

wants the hearers of the psalm to view their sinful behavior. He is not talking about "alternative lifestyles"; turning away from God's paths is, quite simply, stupid—and to be avoided at all costs.[7]

The solution is rooted, first, in God's declaration of peace with his people. His spoken word changes their spiritual reality. By his gracious love, God has established harmony between himself and his people. But to be able to appreciate that harmony fully, without being wracked with doubt, God's people should also turn away from all behaviors that lead them to doubt God's love and acceptance.

Surely his salvation is near those who fear him. The psalmist comes to the realization that salvation is to be found only in the grace of God. His people will never merit his help or deliverance. Yet that salvation is near to those who fear him (v. 9a). This realization is profound because the tension of Psalm 85 can only ever be resolved in the unilateral action of God himself, for his people will never be able to merit his goodness. Yet those who "fear him" do receive his help. This truth is significant because fearing God is an attitude of heart and a determination of will rather than an absolute standard of moral goodness. What does it mean to fear God? Deuteronomy 10:12–13 indicates that fearing God is all about walking in his ways, loving him, serving him, and keeping his word.[8] Those who fear God are not necessarily perfect, but they genuinely desire to please the God whom they worship and to devote their lives to him. The psalmist sees that the tension of forgiveness for an unfaithful people is never going to be resolved in the will and purpose and righteousness of those individuals. It is, rather, to be resolved by accepting the full and free grace of the God

---

7. Goldingay comments, "they had better make sure that they do not turn away from Yhwh into the kind of stupidity that reckons they can make their own decisions and safeguard their own future (see 49:10, 13 [11, 14])" (*Psalms 2*, 611).

8. In his discussion of Prov 1:7, Raymond Van Leeuwen helpfully outlines the concept of the "fear of the Lord": "The great phrase 'the fear of the LORD' grounds human knowledge and wisdom (cf. 9:10) in humble service of Yahweh. . . . Without the God of Israel, the best human wisdom becomes folly, because God alone holds the world and all outcomes in God's hands (2 Sam 16:15–17:23; 1 Cor 1:18–31, with its OT quotations). Although this phrase has its origin in the experience of God's numinous majesty (as at Sinai, Deut 4:9–10), *it eventually has come to express the total claim of God upon humans and the total life-response of humans to God*" ("The book of Proverbs: Introduction, Commentary and Reflections," in *The New Interpreter's Bible*, vol. 5, ed. Leander Keck et al. [Nashville: Abingdon, 1997], 33). Basically, the idea of the "fear of the LORD" finds its origins in the people's experience of the raw power and majesty of God at Sinai, but with the passage of time the idea has come to represent a lifestyle that is fully devoted to Yahweh. The psalmist realizes that this is enough and that, although not perfect, those who genuinely love and seek to serve God receive his help even though they do not deserve it.

who forgives and by genuinely seeking to walk in his ways day by day. This God dwells with his people (v. 9b). He is present despite their weakness, and he will help those who genuinely seek relationship with him.[9]

Covenantal Tensions Resolved (85:10–13)

THE DILEMMA OF FAITH AND EXPERIENCE is summed up in the final verses of Psalm 85, where the psalmist turns his attention to the tension God's people have always felt in their covenantal relationship with God. Any covenantal relationship, just like any contract, brings benefits to both parties but also places responsibilities on them. Israel always took great delight in the covenantal promises and the blessings they brought. We see many of them in the psalms themselves—for example, protection (Pss 46 and 48), forgiveness (Pss 51 and 103), presence (Pss 23 and 91), and so on. But Israel also faced the tension of keeping the covenantal responsibilities placed upon them. Book 3 of Psalms is replete with poems dealing with the problem of the exile—a problem brought about by Israel's failure to keep their covenantal responsibilities (e.g., Pss 74, 75, 76, 78 et al.). God's people had failed to keep up their end of the covenantal bargain, so to speak, so Yahweh had, in a sense, been forced to use the punishment of exile as a means of reawakening his people's awareness of their covenantal responsibilities. Having discussed the tension of being individuals who are both forgiven and in need of forgiveness in Psalm 85:1–9, the poet applies the same principles to his consideration of the covenantal relationship. God's people long for the blessings of the covenant yet constantly fail to keep the covenant—how can this tension be resolved? Once again, the psalmist realizes that covenantal relationship can only be maintained through the grace of God.

Love and faithfulness meet together; righteousness and peace kiss each other. This language is very much that of covenant and, at heart, highlights the tension God's people felt in being a covenant people. The chiastic structure of this verse highlights both the blessings and responsibilities of covenant. At the center of the chiasm are the responsibilities of faithfulness (*'emet*) and righteousness (*tsedek*)—terms that every Hebrew would associate with covenantal responsibility. Bracketing the central idea of covenant obligation are the terms that speak of the privileges or blessings of covenant—steadfast love (*hesed*) and peace (*shalom*). These blessings are the upsides of being in relationship with God. He pours out his devoted love on his people, and he brings wholeness and satisfaction to their lives.

---

9. McCann, "Psalms," 1017.

Love	Faithfulness
Righteousness	Peace

The harmony of covenant was to be found in the meeting of God's love with the faithfulness of his people, and the righteousness of Israel would be met with the kiss of God's *shalom*.[10] The problem for God's people in the covenantal relationship has always been their inability to be faithful or righteous. Through all generations, communities of faith have rejoiced in the benefits of being in covenantal relationship with God but struggled to keep their responsibilities under the covenant. Much like the conundrum of being a people who have received forgiveness yet who are in need of forgiveness, the concept of covenant brings with it great tension: we long for the blessings of covenant but know that we are too weak to keep our side of the promise. God promises steadfast love and wholeness for his people who enter into covenant with him, but the expectation of covenantal relationship is that they, in turn, will maintain faithfulness and righteousness. The tension arises in the inability of God's people to do just that. In the context of Book 3 of the Psalter, the psalmists devote a great deal of attention to meditating upon Israel's covenantal failure. That both faithfulness and righteousness were far from them explain why they experience the rebuke of exile. How then can there be hope that the covenantal relationship will be any different this time?

Faithfulness springs forth from the earth, and righteousness looks down from heaven. Once again the psalmist realizes that the only resolution to this tension is to be found in God's gracious and unilateral work in behalf of his people. Both psalmist and people long for Yahweh's steadfast love and peace, yet they know they are far from being faithful or righteous. Are the blessings of the covenant therefore lost to them? With a beautiful sense of the poetic, the psalmist points the readers again to a God of grace and unmerited love, a God who does for them what they could not do for themselves. The people were supposed to be faithful and righteous if they were to receive God's strong love and holistic blessing, but such loyalty eluded them. So Yahweh, the Creator God of heaven and earth, provides these standards for them by his own will! Faithfulness bubbles up from the earth, and righteousness looks down from heaven. What the people lack in order to make the covenantal relationship work flows from the created order. In poetic terms, Psalm 85:11 tells the singers of the psalm that God will

---

10. "Verse 11 continues to personify faithfulness and righteousness, but this time in combination with a word pair (*heaven* and *earth*) to indicate that these qualities permeated the entire cosmos" (Longman, *Psalms*, 314).

provide what is needed to make the covenantal relationship a living, ongoing reality. That God will do so is always true in the covenantal relationships of Scripture. While normally obligations are placed on all human parties to a covenant with God (as in his covenants with Adam, Noah, and Abraham, for example), still it was always only by God's gracious forgiveness and provision that these relationships were able to continue. The psalmist has come to realize that the solution to the tension of covenant is never going to be discovered in the strength, will, or ability of God's people. The covenant between God and humanity can only ever work because of the grace of God.

The LORD will indeed give what is good. Verse 12 echoes the opening verse of the psalm. Just as the poet celebrated the goodness of God in the past in the introduction to his poem, so he also trusts in the goodness of God for the future. Verse 1 calls to mind Yahweh's favor toward the land and his restoration of the people. Verse 12 looks to the future—the psalmist states his trust that God will prove himself to be "good" to his people again and that this favor will be evidenced in practical terms in future harvests yielded by the land. The stigma of sin, failure, and exile is passed. God has restored his people, and with that restoration his blessing is renewed on the land itself.

Righteousness goes before him. The final metaphor of Psalm 85 is somewhat enigmatic—righteousness goes before Yahweh and prepares a way for his steps (v. 13). It is not entirely clear what the psalmist has in mind here. It could be judgment imagery that reminds people of God's absolute moral standards and, in doing so, warns them of future judgment should Israel turn from him again. The phrase could also be an exhortation to remind the people that they are to be instruments of Yahweh's purpose on earth— walking in righteousness, they themselves prepare a way for him to inhabit the land. Either way, the psalm ends with a reminder of the righteousness of God, his *tsedek* (cf. vv. 10–11). Such is the psalmist's emphasis on God's grace via the forgiveness of sin and maintenance of the covenantal relationship that he wants to remind the singers of the psalms that such grace is not an excuse for license. Those who genuinely fear God (v. 9) will strive after his righteousness as his ambassadors on earth (cf. Rom 5:20–6:2).

GOD'S FIERCE ANGER. It is difficult for Christians who do not often delve into the Old Testament to understand how God—whom we see as Father, Savior, and Comforter—can also be a God of wrath and fierce anger (Ps 85:3). This idea seems alien to a "New Testament" understanding of God. How are we to understand this notion of God's fierce anger?

God's fierce anger is a proper response to our covenantal failure, as is perhaps best illustrated by considering one of the covenantal ceremonies we find in the Bible itself. Genesis 15 is one of these Old Testament passages that seems strange and alien to modern readers. In this passage, God enters into a covenant with Abram. He promises to the old man an heir of his own flesh and blood, something that seemed impossible to Abram. So, to establish the certainty of this promise, God enters into a covenant with him. The ceremony itself seems strange to us but was common enough in the ancient Near East. Abram was to take a heifer, a goat, and a ram, as well as a dove and a young pigeon (Gen 15:9), split the larger animals in two, and lay out the halves (along with the birds) to create a path, albeit a bloody and fairly gruesome one.

Normally, the covenant would be entered into by both parties to the contract via the walking of each one through the path of sacrificed animals.[11] The symbolism of this solemn act communicated a vow: "Should I fail to keep my side of the covenant, may I be treated as harshly as these animals." This ceremony illustrates just how seriously a covenant should be viewed.

It is in this context of covenant that we should understand God's fierce anger. Covenantal relationship is a serious thing. Failing to keep the covenant has serious consequences. Should either party to the promise fail to uphold his or her side of the deal, the offended party has the right to be angry and to execute justice. Israel failed (as have God's people in every generation) to meet their covenantal promises. They bound themselves to keep God's law and singularly failed to do so. God had faithfully and patiently kept his side of the covenantal deal, but his people not only failed to keep but also openly rejected their covenantal responsibilities. They were meant to love God and follow in his ways, but they rejected his law and chased after other gods.

So it was that, eventually, God vented his justifiable anger against Israel and Judah through their respective exiles. Covenant is a serious matter, and breaking covenant has serious consequences. It is in this context that the psalmist speaks about God's "wrath" and "fierce anger" in Psalm 85. Thankfully, he only raises the matter to speak about the grace of God in choosing not to act upon the righteous anger he felt.

---

11. The interesting thing about Gen 15, however, is that Abram did not walk through this path—it was a unilateral covenant on God's part. He was solemnly binding himself to grant Abram's desire for a son despite his and Sarai's advanced years.

Two significant themes run through Psalm 85, and to one degree or another Christians struggle with each of these ideas. The psalm celebrates the grace of God and our dependence on that grace, but underpinning that meditation is the idea of God's anger. God's grace means that he turns away from anger and maintains relationship with a sinful people. There are many people in today's church who struggle with each of these concepts—God's unmerited grace and his righteous anger. By way of application it is important that we allow each of these themes to speak to the way we think about God, ourselves, and the world in which he has placed us.

Embracing God's grace. There is something immensely human about our struggle to accept God's free grace. We find it difficult to accept that there is nothing—absolutely nothing—that we bring to the table to merit God's love and acceptance. We long to be good enough. We desire a quantifiable righteousness that means we are just good enough to be considered worthy of relationship with God. But Psalm 85 is clear that forgiveness is not found in our ability to obey. It is based solely in God's gracious decision simply to forgive (vv. 2–3). The covenantal relationship works because God chooses to see us as faithful even when we are not (vv. 10–11).

Christians struggle with grace on two levels. First, it is hard to accept our unworthiness, and we can tend to think of ourselves as better than we really are. Second, we can struggle to accept that God still loves us and that his grace is sufficient to forgive all our sins.

1. Conditionality: Human beings are used to conditionality. Our love for one another is often predicated on what we receive from the object of that love. We love because we are loved back. We serve others because (or so that?) they, in turn, help us. But we feel that we must always do something to merit the love, service, or acceptance of others. This conditionality often affects our relationship with God. Although we would never actually voice such ideas, we can feel that God loves us because of all that we do for him. We serve in church (whether that be preaching or setting out the chairs); we are kind to others (though we expect them to be kind back); we take care to read the Bible and pray (most of the time). And in some sense we feel that we deserve God's love because, after all, we try our best to love and serve him. We do not like to be beholden . . . but that is exactly what we are! God loves us not because of what we do for him—he loves us just because he has chosen to do so. It is important for us to realize that we are completely dependent on God's grace, for one day our self-righteousness will fail us. One day we will fail to do the things that we feel make us acceptable, and the world will come crashing down around us. The psalmist makes it clear that God's desire for relationship with and forgiveness of us are unmerited. It is important for us to remember this truth if we are to have any sense of security in our life with God and if we are to view ourselves with the humility we ought to have.

2. *Accepting forgiveness:* The second reason for our need to think properly about God's grace is that if we do not do so, we will become crippled by guilt and useless to God. In various churches, I frequently encounter Christians who find it hard to believe that God can *still* love them and forgive them *again* for the sins they have committed. Some struggle because of the number of times they sin—and that they commit the same sins over and over again. Others cannot accept God's grace because of the perceived seriousness of the sins they commit. But Psalm 85, as a clear precursor of what we see in the New Testament, points readers to the fullness of God's forgiveness. Verses 2–3 make it clear that all sin (and its associated guilt) is thoroughly removed from us. God lifts the burden of sin from us, he covers it over so that he sees it no more, and he chooses to turn away from rightful anger. His grace is absolutely full. His forgiveness is totally complete. As far as the psalmist is concerned, this truth is an absolute and unquestionable fact—our responsibility is simply to accept that fact.

If we are to make Psalm 85 real in our lives, we must embrace the grace of God fully in our hearts and minds. Only then we will see and understand our relationship with him properly.

Embracing God's anger. As contemporary Christians we tend to struggle with the idea of an angry God. This is not the way we see God; rather, we view him as Father and Friend. We often encounter statements that relegate this idea of a God of wrath to the pages of the Old Testament alone, as though God underwent a personality transplant at the point of the incarnation. We certainly do not like to think of God as being angry, because the image is not comfortable for us. Yet in Psalm 85 the anger of God is the important background theme against which the main theme of God's rich grace is played out. Is it right for modern Christians to marginalize the idea of God's wrath? In doing so, do we run risks?

The wrath of God is inescapable in the Scriptures and certainly cannot be limited to the Old Testament. Frequently, God's anger is described as burning against sin, injustice, and oppression (e.g., Exod 32:11; Ps 7:6, 11 et al.). The Bible often talks about the sinful activities of human beings as "provoking" God to anger (for example, see the historian's presentation of the kings of Israel who turned their backs on God in 1 Kgs 15:30; 16:13, 26, 33 et al.). Jesus' anger at the hypocrisy and callousness of the religious rulers of his day is unmistakable, the cleansing of the temple in John 2 being just one of many examples of the wrath of God displayed during the period of the Messiah's earthly incarnation. And the concept of God's righteous anger does not disappear in the Christian era. Both Paul and John are clear that God's anger has not ceased because of the work of Jesus (e.g., see Rom 1:18; 3:5; Col 3:6; Rev 16). So, we cannot easily rid ourselves of an angry God, but how are we to understand these passages and others like them?

Clearly, God's anger is linked with human sin and rebellion, as we see in Psalm 85. God's righteous anger at the persistent sin of Judah and Jerusalem led to the exile, yet God turned from that wrath and restored the people to their home (vv. 1, 3). But the people still sinned, so the poet prays for God's grace in once again turning from his anger (vv. 4–5).

This link between anger and sin is important for believers of every generation to remember. God's anger against sin remains real and true today. It has not changed. God has not "chilled out" over the passing generations so these things simply do not matter anymore. Failure to grapple with the concept of an angry God will lead the current generation of believers into a state of complacency, one in which we are not filled with horror at sin as we should be. God's anger should be reflected in our own response to sinful behavior both in ourselves and in the world in which we live. If we have no concept of God's anger, then we will grow to tolerate sin in our own hearts and become indifferent to injustice in the world. We embrace the angry God because his anger is our guide—his anger shapes our perspectives of life.[12]

Ultimately, a God who cannot be angry is toothless and stands for nothing. Perhaps that is why contemporary Christians are uncomfortable with the wrath of God—we are actually quite happy with a God who does not place awkward demands or expectations on his people. Yet the Bible is clear that, at some point in the future, God's anger will be worked out in human reality.

It is clear from how God revealed himself to Moses that God controls his anger and does not express his wrath in ways that he might. Exodus

---

12. In his discussion of the imprecatory psalms, Erich Zenger points out that the church today often fails to reflect God's disgust at the sins of the world in which we live (see *A God of Vengeance?*). There are many injustices perpetrated every day (rape, exploitation, destruction of the environment, and countless other acts) that should fill us with horror and righteous anger. If we do not respond in this way, then we are out of step with God the Creator. We should not seek to do away with the idea of an angry God in the church. We should allow that anger to shape our prophetic voice in the world of today.

34:6–7 powerfully portrays God as compassionate in nature, as keeping his anger in check. Yet that anger still teaches us. God's wrath must be allowed to shape the life of believers in our (and every) generation. Otherwise we will never have the absolute abhorrence of sin (both personal and societal) that we should have. So, it is not the place of the church to marginalize the wrath of God. Yes, we rejoice in God's grace, as did the psalmist, but we also embrace God's anger as a flawless guide that shapes our view of our hearts and of the world in which we live.

Psalm 86

A prayer of David.

¹ Hear me, LORD, and answer me,
   for I am poor and needy.
² Guard my life, for I am faithful to you;
   save your servant who trusts in you.
You are my God; ³have mercy on me, Lord,
   for I call to you all day long.
⁴ Bring joy to your servant, Lord,
   for I put my trust in you.
⁵ You, Lord, are forgiving and good,
   abounding in love to all who call to you.
⁶ Hear my prayer, LORD;
   listen to my cry for mercy.
⁷ When I am in distress, I call to you,
   because you answer me.
⁸ Among the gods there is none like you, Lord;
   no deeds can compare with yours.
⁹ All the nations you have made
   will come and worship before you, Lord;
   they will bring glory to your name.
¹⁰ For you are great and do marvelous deeds;
   you alone are God.
¹¹ Teach me your way, LORD,
   that I may rely on your faithfulness;
give me an undivided heart,
   that I may fear your name.
¹² I will praise you, Lord my God, with all my heart;
   I will glorify your name forever.
¹³ For great is your love toward me;
   you have delivered me from the depths,
   from the realm of the dead.
¹⁴ Arrogant foes are attacking me, O God;
   ruthless people are trying to kill me—
   they have no regard for you.
¹⁵ But you, Lord, are a compassionate and gracious God,
   slow to anger, abounding in love and faithfulness.

¹⁶ Turn to me and have mercy on me;
    show your strength in behalf of your servant;
save me, because I serve you
    just as my mother did.
¹⁷ Give me a sign of your goodness,
    that my enemies may see it and be put to shame,
    for you, LORD, have helped me and comforted me.

PSALM 86 IS A SURPRISING POEM in the flow of Book 3 of the Psalter. In the midst of groups of psalms by Asaph and the Sons of Korah, we come across a Davidic psalm that is reminiscent of the individual prayers of Books 1 and 2. This psalm is a passionate plea that God will hear the poet's prayer by responding to his need and, in doing so, publicly vindicate him before his opponents, who seem to be the source of his undefined problem. It is a prayer grounded in the sure knowledge of God's grace toward his people—a knowledge that trusts in the goodness of God despite the difficulty of the circumstances faced.

The Heading (86:0)

IT IS SOMETHING OF A SURPRISE to come across the name of David in Book 3. This collection in the Psalter (Pss 73–89) is dominated by the cultic groupings of Asaph and the Korahites, so the appearance of a Davidic subscription seems somewhat out of place. But the Davidic title is appropriate in two ways. First, the lament is similar to the tone of the anonymous "I" laments of Books 1 and 2, in which Davidic psalms predominate. Second, the missional tone of the nations' joining the worshiping community in Zion fits well with the kingship and Zion psalms, which also take Davidic superscriptions.

Psalm 86 seems to fill a transitional role within the flow of poems. It continues the tone of intercession and meeting with God (as encountered in Pss 84 and 85); it affirms the superiority of Israel's God over the gods of the nations (as do Pss 82 and 83); it laments over enmity and oppression (Pss 74–76); and it seeks the wisdom of God (as does Ps 73). Not only does Psalm 86 fit in with what has gone before—it also points toward what follows in Book 3. Psalm 87 again points to the sovereignty of God over the nations. Psalm 88—very bleakly—returns to the complaint of the individual. Psalm 89 picks up on each of these voices by first celebrating God's rule over the nations before lamenting the apparent removal of his blessing from his people. So, it appears that those who compiled this collection of psalms saw this Davidic poem as fitting well within the ongoing "discussion" of Book 3. The description of this psalm as a prayer (*tephillah*) indicates for us the tone of the poem and the attitude in which we should read it—this poem is best read prayerfully.

The Poet's Intercession (86:1–7)

HEAR ME, LORD, AND ANSWER ME. The psalm's tone of prayer is poignantly voiced by the opening words of the poem. Literally, the psalmist calls in anthropomorphic terms to his God: "Turn your ear, O Yahweh, and hear me!" The opening line of Psalm 86 gives insight into the psalmist's heart. Above all else at this time, the poet needs God to hear his prayer—to hear and respond. This experience is common to many of the psalms and to many who have adopted the psalms as their own prayers throughout the many generations since they were penned.

For I am poor and needy. The reason for this sense of prayerful urgency becomes immediately obvious. The poet is desperate for his prayers to be heard because he is in a desperate situation. "Poor and needy" should be understood in their Old Testament senses. "Poor" (*'ani*), for example, does not refer to the psalmist's financial status, as we would normally read the word today. Such poverty really refers to weakness and affliction.[1] "Needy" (*'ebyon*), again, is not necessarily a reference to financial lack but, in this context, seems to point to oppression.[2] So the psalmist's burning desire for his prayer to be heard is rooted in his circumstances of affliction and oppression. He is under severe pressure, apparently inflicted upon him from outside, and he desperately needs God's help in order to have any hope for the future.

Guard my life, for I am faithful to you. The NIV captures well the essence of the psalmist's motivational justification as to why God should hear his prayer. "Guard my life" seems to emphasize the deep urgency of the poet's circumstances—he feels that his life is literally endangered. So the poet prays for divine protection because he is "faithful" (*hasid*). Modern Christian readers have a tendency to read forensic New Testament understandings into Old Testament texts such as the psalms—therefore we balk at the type of self claims we find here in verse 2. But the poet is not claiming perfection in his walk with God; rather, he is reminding God of his honest devotion. The psalmist reminds God of this devotion as a rationale for his prayers to be heard, and this tactic continues into the second line of verse 2. Here the psalmist reminds God of both the relationship

---

1. "עָנִי," *HALOT* 1:856.
2. "אֶבְיוֹן," *HALOT* 1:5.

they share ("your servant . . . You are my God") and the fact that he relies on God for his sufficiency.[3] As one who is devoted to Yahweh, he does not rely on the loci of strength that are common in this world—wealth, power, or influence—nor does he rely on his own strengths, gifts, and abilities; rather, he has placed his trust in the Lord and therefore is entirely dependent on God's response to his prayers. Such trust is the very essence of devotion to God, and the psalmist, being faced with such extremes, is compelled to remind God both of the reality of their relationship and the totality of his (the psalmist's) dependence.

Have mercy on me, Lord, for I call to you all day long. The complete dependence that lies at the heart of verse 2 is echoed in the prayer of the following verse. In the face of great trouble, the psalmist calls out to God for mercy (*hanan*, sometimes translated as "grace" or "favor"[4]) because prayer is his only source of hope. The poet is entirely aware that he has no hope for the future if God does not come to his aid. His is an attitude of complete dependence. Again, for contemporary Christian readers, this strategy seems incredibly "high risk." But from the psalmic perspective such dependence is a sign of true devotion to God, a mark of a real and deep spirituality.

Bring joy to your servant. The essence of the psalmist's daily prayer is that God would change his circumstances. Presently, the poet is "poor and needy" (v. 1); he wants God to restore some joy to his life. The overtones of the opening verses of Psalm 86 imply that for a period of time the poet has been in a situation of great personal suffering, whatever its source. This adversity has robbed him of all the joy and happiness in his life, so he prays for a restoration of joy to his inner being, literally, "Bring joy to *the soul of* your servant." The image conjured up by this plea is of one who has been worn down by the hardship and oppression he has faced—his longing, quite simply, is to feel joy and happiness once more. This sentiment is echoed in the second line of verse 4, where the psalmist offers his "trust," literally, his "soul" (his inner being, his whole life) to his Lord as a sign of ongoing devotion.[5] Almost in desperation, the psalmist is renewing

---

3. "The petition is supported by various considerations: humility that acknowledges poverty and hopelessness . . . ; the bond that God himself has made, so that the psalmist is his 'servant' (vv. 2b, 4a, 16) and steadfast covenant-partner (*hasid* v. 2a)" (Eaton, *Psalms*, 309).

4. Robert Alter translates this line, "Grant grace to me, Master" (Robert Alter, *The Book of Psalms: A Translation with Commentary* [W. W. Norton: New York/London, 2007], 303).

5. Alter sees this phrase as an idiom referring to intercessory prayer in general but comments, "'My being,' *nafshi*, also has the sense of 'my very self,' 'my life breath'" (ibid.).

his absolute dedication to Yahweh in the hope that this commitment will ensure God's hearing of his prayer and returning of some joy to his life.

You, LORD, are forgiving and good, abounding in love to all who call to you. Some are troubled by this statement of faith in the midst of the psalmist's continued appeal to God for mercy. Rather than being an inappropriately positioned indication of the psalmist's transformation of heart and mind, verse 5 is a further motivation clause presented by the psalmist as part of his overall rationale to explain why the Lord should hear his prayer. The poet is reminding God of God's very nature! To the modern mind this approach seems illogical, yet it is very much part of the prayer life of ancient Israel and is a common feature in the psalms. In prayer, the psalmist's words to God remind God of the essence of his nature, and in the process of speaking thus to God, the poet reminds himself that he prays to a God who is not reluctant to respond but who is by nature "forgiving," "good," and "abounding in love to all who call" on him. This act of "stating the obvious" shapes *the psalmist*, regardless of the pessimism of his present reality. The poet is calling on the solid truths of the nature of God that his people had celebrated for generations. His forebears in the faith had found God to be such a Master, and the author of Psalm 86 pleads that the God of his devotion will prove himself to be of that nature in his case as well. Broyles notes, "Moreover, the assuring hymnic praise of verse 5 is not an ad hoc attempt to pacify the fears of a worshipper, but is a famous confession tested through generations of believers (Exod 34:6; Num 14:18; Neh 9:17; Jonah 4:2; Joel 2:13; Pss 103:8; 145:8)."[6] The poet finds strength in the knowledge of God shared by this community throughout many generations. The psalmist moves beyond the facts of who he is (Ps 86:1–2) and what he does (vv. 3–4) as motivations for God to hear his prayer. The ultimate reason why God will hear and respond is not to be found in the character or the works of the speaker-psalmist (though these elements are also significant to the prayer); God will hear because of who *he* is rather than because of who the supplicant is or what the supplicant does.[7]

When I am in distress I call to you, because you answer me. Following on from his renewed appeal that God would hear his prayer in verse 6 (cf. v. 1), the author concludes this introductory section with a recapitulation of both his distress and his hope. In the Psalter, "When I am

---

6. Broyles, *Psalms*, 347–48.

7. Goldingay points out that here alone in the Old Testament "'forgiving' is an adjective, *sallah*, suggesting that Yhwh is not merely one who does forgive but one who is forgiving by nature" (*Psalms 2*, 622–23).

in distress," literally, "the day of my distress" (*tsar*), is a relatively common idiom that implies constraint, trouble, and pressure from which the petitioner needs to be delivered by a powerful external hand. A recent doctoral study describes this concept of distress as indicating a type of suffering that is oppressively painful, salient, and ever present, and a trouble from which the supplicant is powerless to deliver himself.[8] Verse 7 reflects the conundrum of faith that many believers have faced over the years: God does not seem to be answering their prayers, yet they know that their only hope is found in the expectation that God will answer their prayers. Such is the very essence of lament in the Psalms. Israel's ancient poets cry out in complaint that Yahweh does not hear their prayers. Yet *they do cry out*, for they believe it is only in prayer to Yahweh that they will ever find release. There is a real sense in which the declaration of verse 7 becomes a statement of faithful determination to cling to Yahweh regardless of present circumstances. The psalmist knows that Yahweh hears the prayers of his people even though his present reality seems to deny that fact. The prayer of verses 1–7 is, in itself, a declaration of faith in the face of contrary circumstances.

The Incomparability of God and the Inclusion of the Nations (86:8–10)

FOLLOWING ON FROM THE OPENING INTERCESSION (vv. 1–7), the psalmist turns to praise of God based on the incomparable greatness that sets him apart from all the gods of the nations. In a remarkable statement of faith, the author goes on to predict a day in which all the surrounding nations will come to realize that the God of Israel is better in his nature and action than the gods whom they presently worship. The "pagan" gentile nations will therefore join Israel's worshiping community of faith.

Among the gods there is none like you. Once again, the poet picks up on the language of the book of Exodus in declaring Yahweh's incomparable greatness (cf. v. 5). In adopting the language of the Song of the Sea (Exod 15:11), the psalm draws our attention to Yahweh's great might in providing deliverance for his people. When they were powerless to save themselves, God provided miraculous salvation. It is perhaps unsurprising that the psalmist adopts such imagery in the time of his present distress. In dire need of saving from his own distressful circumstances, the poet needs to remind himself and his readers that theirs is the God of miraculous deliverance—there is none like him.

---

8. Michael D. Rasmussen, *Conceptualizing Distress in the Psalms: A Form-Critical and Cognitive Semantic Study of the* צרר¹ *Word Group*, Gorgias Biblical Studies 66 (Piscataway, NJ: Gorgias Press, 2018).

All the nations you have made will come and worship before you.
The logical conclusion of the incomparability of Yahweh when compared
to the gods of the nations is that, ultimately, the nations themselves will
come to realize that Yahweh is far greater than the gods they worship.
This realization is the very essence of the meaning of the English word
"worship." Worship is acknowledging the great worth of the object of one's
praise. Although the same is not implied in the Hebrew verb used in verse
9, clearly the poet's argument in verses 8–10 implies the objective worthi-
ness of Yahweh to receive honor. Echoing the prophets, the declaration in
verse 9 is one of the great missionary statements of the Psalter. The author
envisions a day in which the pagan nations surrounding Israel will join with
the community of faith in worshiping Yahweh, who created all humankind.
Broyles comments, "We should not quickly assume this refers merely to
a future reality at the end of time, because other psalms describe foreign
nations offering tribute to Yahweh at the pre-exilic temple (see Ps 47, esp.
v. 9 and Ps 68 esp. vv. 18, 29; cf. 66:4)."[9] Whether this event is meant to
be seen as a future eschatological happening or an ever-increasing reality
within the history of Israel is something of a moot point—the psalm does
not say. But the clear expectation is that one day, whether in the near or
distant future, the worshiping community of God's people would extend
far beyond ethnic Israel and incorporate those nations of people who did
not yet acknowledge Yahweh as God. There is a sense of inescapable logic
about the psalmist's vision of the future: Yahweh is so great in his character
and deeds that everyone who stops to consider the reality of his being will
surely come to realize that he alone is the true God (Ps 86:8, 10).

A Prayer of Devotion in Times of Trouble (86:11–17)

THE CONCLUDING SECTIONS OF THIS PSALM INCLUDE A PRAYER OF devotion to
Yahweh (vv. 11–13) and a renewed, desperate plea for divine intervention
in the psalmist's distress (vv. 14–17). The latter section very much echoes
the tone and language of the initial supplication in verses 1–7.

Teach me your way, LORD, that I may rely on your faithfulness.
Interestingly, following on from the psalmist's declaration of devotion to
Yahweh (vv. 2–3), the poet now prays for God's help that he might continue
to live a life of commitment to Yahweh. The first aspect of this prayer for
devotion is cognitive (v. 11a): the poet prays that God will "teach" him so
he is able to live in a way that pleases his Lord. (The Hebrew idiom "I will
walk in your truth" reflects a desire to live a life that is consistent with

---

9. Broyles, *Psalms*, 348.

divine revelation in the torah.) This prayer indicates the speaker's desire to continue in a godly lifestyle even in the face of all of the difficulties and opposition he faces in his daily reality. It is a declaration of trust and determination as well as a prayer for strengthening in this task.[10]

Give me an undivided heart, that I may fear your name. The second element of this prayer of devotion to Yahweh centers more on the idea of holistic, heartfelt devotion to God (v. 11b). The idea behind the "undivided heart" is actually a prayer that God would "unite" or "concentrate" the heart of the intercessor.[11] It is a plea for a singularity of devotion on the psalmist's part. Perhaps implied in this prayer is just a hint that the poet's commitment to Yahweh had been affected by the difficulty of his daily circumstances. It seems likely that the temptation to put his trust in sources of strength other than his God would have been a strong one. But the psalmist was aware that, "if Yahweh is the only real God, as Yahweh's deeds indicate, then the suppliant's heart cannot be divided. . . . Yahweh's singleness needs to be matched by an undivided commitment of the person."[12] Therein lies the objective of the prayer in verse 11.[13]

I will praise you, Lord my God, with all my heart. This singularity of devotion is repeated in the poet's commitment to holistic praise of Yahweh and the desire to bring glory to him (v. 12). The declaration of praise "with all my heart" echoes the Shema's call to whole-life, singular devotion to Yahweh (Deut 6:4–5). Once again, the psalmist is making a confident declaration that his commitment to God remains unshaken even by torturously difficult circumstances and that he will continue to live such a lifestyle if God hears and answers his prayer for an undivided heart (Ps 86:11b). "This petition seeks for Yahweh's influence not only in the worshipper's actions but also in his inner attitudes: **give me an undivided heart**, that is, a single heart to will one thing. As a result, he can promise, **I will praise you . . . with all my heart**. The psalm thus seeks a single heart to worship the one God (v. 10)."[14]

For great is your love toward me; you have delivered me from the depths, from the realm of the dead. Verse 13 gives a clear reason for the exemplary devotion witnessed in the preceding verses. The poet has experienced the great love of God and his deliverance in the past, and because of those experiences he is able to continue in faith that God will hear his

---

10. Goldingay, *Psalms 2*, 625.
11. "לֵב," *HALOT* 1:513–15.
12. Goldingay, *Psalms 2*, 625.
13. For discussion of the fear of the Lord see the comments on Ps 85:9.
14. Broyles, *Psalms*, 348.

prayers despite all the counter-indications in his present experience. The fact that Yahweh has previously delivered the psalmist "from the realm of the dead" (lit., "lowest Sheol" or "nethermost Sheol"[15]) indicates that he has previously faced such serious distress that he was in real fear of death. But the God who loves him had rescued him once before gives the supplicant confidence that God will do so again in his present circumstances.

Arrogant foes are attacking me, O God. Verses 14 and 17 give some insight into the background of the poet's current difficulties. He faces persecution from those who oppose him and reject God (v. 14). Readers are given no more insight into the circumstances of this opposition, but clearly the speaker feels himself to be in real and immediate danger from a "ruthless" (lit., "violent"[16]) enemy. That clearly the stakes are high further emphasizes the depth of devotion seen in the preceding verses of this song. This arrogant band of ruthless men who seek the poet's life are also described as "those who have no regard for you" (lit., "they do not set you in their sight"). This attitude characterizes the foolish, wealthy wicked (Ps 73:11) and the arrogant men of power who oppress the weak (Ps 10:4). The theology of the Psalms is quite clear: such people are setting themselves up for a fall. They may prosper in the present day, but ultimately they will not. As Erich Zenger puts it, "Their 'faith in God' has no ethical consequences."[17] The poet is confident that God will hear his prayer because clearly such enemies have also made themselves enemies of God.

But you, Lord, are a compassionate and gracious God. The poet is aware that he need not fear the character of his enemies because he knows the character of God. His enemies may be violent persecutors determined to attack him, but his God is "compassionate and gracious . . . abounding in love and faithfulness" (Ps 86:15). As in the opening stanza, the intercession is marked also by reflection on the character of God (cf. v. 5). The speaker gains confidence in his prayer from meditation on the true character of God. We should also note that the psalmist's prayer in verse 11a is reflected in the nature of God described here in verse 15. Note that in verse 11 the psalmist asks God to enable him to walk in his "truth" (Hebrew *'emet*), and here in verse 15 Yahweh is described as abounding in love and "faithfulness" (again, Hebrew *'emet*).[18] The psalmist asks that

---

15. Alter, *Psalms*, 304.

16. "עָרִיץ," *HALOT* 1:884.

17. Hossfeld and Zenger, *Psalms 2*, 375.

18. The NIV translates 86:11 as "Teach me your way, LORD, that I may rely on your faithfulness." While this shows well the correspondence between verses 11 and 15, I would

his life might reflect the very character of God—even in the face of trial and hardship.[19]

Show your strength in behalf of your servant. The closing intercession continues to reflect the tone and language of the opening prayer (vv. 1–7). Having asked God to "hear" him in verse 1, the poet again pleads that God would "turn" to him and "have mercy" (v. 16; cf. "mercy" in v. 3). These motional verbs indicate the pray-er's feeling that God has distanced or removed himself from him, and he pleads for God's return. Again, the speaker reminds God that he is God's servant—they share relationship, and that relationship is characterized by devoted service to God on the part of the poet. So, the poet intercedes that Yahweh would grant him strength. It is unclear whether this plea for strength is simply a request for God to provide refuge and protection (cf. v. 5) or is a more categorical prayer that God would not only give the psalmist strength to endure in the face of trouble but also go further by enabling the one who is oppressed to triumph over his oppressors. In the context of the psalm as a whole, the latter idea seems the more likely. The fact that the poet is not only Yahweh's servant but that he is also "the son of your maidservant" further emphasizes the sense of obligation that falls upon Yahweh.[20] Not only is the poet himself devoted in his service to God, but he also comes from a line of forbears who shared that devotion. Should not God, therefore, be all the more inclined to hear and answer his prayer?

Give me a sign of your goodness, that my enemies may see it and be put to shame. The second section of intercession concludes with the request for a sign—a sign of God's goodness toward the psalmist. A public display of God's blessing would constitute an act of vindication before his persecutors. "It is some expression of the master's commitment that will put in their place the people who are against the suppliant, showing them to be wrong and exposing them to themselves and to the community

---

read the request in 11b as the psalmist seeking divine help to walk in Yahweh's truth. See also Alter, *Psalms*, 304.

19. The Hebrew word *'emet* can mean either *truth* or *faithfulness*. Particularly in poetic texts, it can sometimes be difficult to ascertain which concept is implied. In fact, the TNIV translates verse 11, "Teach me your way, LORD, that I may rely on your faithfulness." Such a translation better reflects the echo that exists between the objective of the prayer in verse 11a and the description of God's character in verse 15. Equally, however, it would be possible to translate both verses using the language of *truth* (e.g., see the NKJV and Edward Cook's English translation of the Psalms Targum).

20. The NIV translates 86:16c as "save me, because I serve you just as my mother did." However, this line is probably better translated as "save the son of your maidservant" (cf. ESV and Hossfeld and Zenger, *Psalms 2*, 375.)

as a whole."[21] The psalmist believes in a God who intervenes, not in the redundant God of his persecutors (v. 14). The God who is known to the poet is a God who actively provides *help* and *comfort* to his people (v. 17c). Ultimately, the source of this psalmist's great confidence lies in his belief in a God who is real, a God who is near, and a God who is active in behalf of his people. So, the psalmist is able to pray with confidence even when present circumstances present a challenge to that confidence.

Facing a horde of terrible foes, the psalmist lifts up his soul to God and continues long in prayer. His plea is grounded in relationship which binds him to the Lord, a bond where he, the servant, is in himself poor and needy, but his faithful and compassionate Lord is the sole God, able to do marvels.[22]

ATHEISM IN THE ANCIENT WORLD. Psalm 86 gives an interesting insight into the idea of godlessness in the ancient Near East. Atheism—at least as we know it in the modern, Western world—did not really exist in the ancient world, as far as we can tell. There would have been few people in Israel who would point-blank deny the existence of God. Equally, among Israel's neighbors in the ancient Near East, there would have been few who denied the existence of the gods. Psalm 86:14 illustrates the reality of the "atheism" of biblical times. The psalmist's persecutors had "no regard," and this idiom gives us insight into the reality of "atheism" in that era. More literally, the Hebrew text of this phrase can be translated "and they did not place you before their sight" (*welo' samuka lenegdam*). This statement really reflects the essence of godlessness from the psalmic perspective. The real question is not one of ontology (whether or not God exists); rather, it is a question of ethics (whether belief in God affects human behavior). The men who were persecuting the psalmist may well have believed in the existence of God, but that cognitive realization made no impact on the daily reality of their behavior, hence the above quotation from Erich Zenger: "Their 'faith in God' has no ethical consequences."[23] From the perspective of the Psalms, belief in the existence of a deity that does not bring profound consequences in the lifestyle of the believer is of no value whatsoever. Qualitatively, it is atheism.

---

21. Goldingay, *Psalms 2*, 629.
22. Eaton, *Psalms*, 310.
23. Hossfeld and Zenger, *Psalms 2*, 375.

God and the gods. For discussion of the psalmists' perspective on Israel's God and the gods of the nations (v. 8), see the comments on Psalm 82, Bridging Contexts.

Psalm 86 in the New Testament. While there are no direct citations from Psalm 86 in the New Testament, there is a strong parallel between the vision of the nations drawing near to worship God in verses 9–10 and the declaration found in Revelation 15:3–4.[24] In the context of each passage we find reference to the Song of Moses from Exodus 15; reference to the mighty, revelatory acts of God; discussion of the absolute uniqueness of God; and the confident declaration that the nations will worship God, thus bringing glory to his name. Both Psalm 86:9 (*kol-goyim*) and Revelation 15:4 (*panta ta ethnē*) emphasize the ultimate gathering together of *all* nations to worship God. This eschatological image is shared by both the Old and New Testaments—one day people from every nation of the earth will gather to worship God. This expectation is fulfilled in part today, but we will not see ultimate fulfillment before the return of Christ. The voice of both Testaments points to a day when the full, international community of faith will gather together to glorify God and declare his great worth—it will be a celebration to remember.

PRACTICAL ATHEISM. Contemporary society has seen a very vocal reawakening of public atheism in recent years. With the increasing popularity of the works of Richard Dawkins and others, atheism has once again become a focal point of public debate. But Psalm 86 reflects a concern that is far more pressing than presuppositional atheism. The poet's concern is more focused on those who have "no regard" (v. 14). As indicated in the discussion above (Bridging Contexts), this disregard is not ontological atheism—not a denial of the existence of God. It is practical atheism. Those who oppressed the poet simply did not believe that the existence of God had any relevance for the way they lived their lives. As far as they were concerned, God may well be real, but so what? Theirs was a practical atheism—a belief that the existence of God had no bearing on who they were as people or how they lived their lives day by day.

Ironically, such practical atheism is a reality in the church today. Many are vocal in terms of their public declaration of belief in God but fail to

---

24. Steve Moyise, "The Psalms in the Book of Revelation," in *The Psalms in the New Testament*, ed. S. Moyise and M. J. J. Menken (London: T&T Clark, 2004), 235–36; Longman, *Psalms*, 317.

work out in their daily lives the practical implications of belief. Such practical atheism has two common manifestations. First, it is manifested in a lack of holy living; second, it is seen in a lack of practical concern for others. In terms of holy living, the people of God should be markedly different from the world around us. We should be characterized by a family likeness to God our Father (Lev 19:2; 1 Pet 1:15–16), a likeness that sets us apart from the common standards of the world in which we live (1 Pet 1:17). All too often the church is influenced by the world rather than being salt and light in a world that has strayed from the standards of Scripture. This failure is a result of our practical atheism—our failure to realize that our belief in God affects every area of our daily life and practice. Real belief in God influences the way we complete our tax returns and the way we view copyright laws when we are downloading music to our iPods. Real belief in God influences what we watch on TV and where we surf the Net. Real belief in God has an impact in all areas of our life—our family, work, free time, how we use our gifts, and how we spend our money. If we truly believe in God through his Son, that faith must affect every area of our behavior every day. Real belief means that our lives are characterized by the desire to bring glory to God in every area of our being (Ps 86:9–12).

The second common manifestation of practical atheism is a lack of care and concern for others who are in need. This was James's concern in his epistle, as expressed in James 2:17–19:

> In the same way, faith by itself, if it is not accompanied by action, is dead. But someone will say, "You have faith; I have deeds." Show me your faith without deeds, and I will show you my faith by my deeds. You believe that there is one God. Good! Even the demons believe that—and shudder.

James was warning his hearers that faith without the implications of faith is empty. Real belief will mean that we care for the poor and needy. We provide for the hungry and clothe those who are cold. All too often the church has treated such practical manifestations of care as somehow subsidiary to evangelism and mission. The biblical reality, however, is that mission and social care always go hand in hand.[25] The challenge of Psalm 86 for the community of faith today is that we should never be guilty of lapsing into practical atheism. Of course, we would never deny *the existence* of God, but we should be careful that our lives do not lapse into reflecting the practical atheism that is the poet's concern here in Psalm 86.

---

25. For fuller discussion of this matter, see Jamie A. Grant and Dewi A. Hughes, eds., *Transforming the World? The Gospel and Social Responsibility* (Leicester: Apollos, 2009).

The essence of mission. Psalm 86:8–10 reflects the heart of what mission is all about. Many in the church today have concerns about the practice of mission. An awareness of the cultural imperialism that characterized some of (but by no means all!) the missional activity of previous centuries has made many Christians sensitive with regard to cross-cultural mission activity today. We want to be sure to avoid social elitism and the imposition of our own cultural norms in spreading the good news of Christ. The missional vision of Psalm 86 shows how to avoid cultural imperialism in the practice of outreach. "Among the gods there is none like you, Lord; no deeds can compare with yours. All the nations you have made will come and worship before you, Lord; they will bring glory to your name. For you are great and do marvelous deeds; you alone are God" (vv. 8–10).

Mission is simply talking about God. True mission is entirely God focused. Biblical outreach is all about the presentation of the character and works of God. It is to talk about a God who is great and whose works are incomparably wonderful. As mentioned above, a large part of mission is about our care for others, but it also involves speaking to others about the reality of who God is and asking them to compare the God of the Scriptures with the ultimate realities that shape and form their life (i.e., their own religion or worldview). Missional activity that is biblically based speaks about the reality of a God of love and forgiveness who has done wonderful things for humanity. In his love he has sent his Son to restore alienated humanity to himself. His deeds are full of love and grace and restoration. This message-bearing is the very essence of mission: simply to talk about the incomparably great God and to manifest his character and deeds in our lives.

Psalm 87

Of the Sons of Korah. A psalm. A song.

¹ He has founded his city on the holy mountain.
² The LORD loves the gates of Zion
 more than all the other dwellings of Jacob.
³ Glorious things are said of you,
 city of God:
⁴ "I will record Rahab and Babylon
 among those who acknowledge me—
Philistia too, and Tyre, along with Cush—
 and will say, 'This one was born in Zion.'"
⁵ Indeed, of Zion it will be said,
 "This one and that one were born in her,
 and the Most High himself will establish her."
⁶ The LORD will write in the register of the peoples:
 "This one was born in Zion."
⁷ As they make music they will sing,
 "All my fountains are in you."

PSALM 87 IS AN INTERESTING (if linguistically awkward) little psalm that picks up on the imagery of Psalm 86:9 and the inclusion of the nations into the worshiping community of God's people. It is a Zion psalm along with Psalms 46, 48, 76, 84, and 122. The celebration of the centrality and importance of Zion is neither exclusive nor jingoistic, however; rather, it is inclusive and expansive. Zion is the place of privilege in Yahweh's eyes, but the psalmist invites people of all nations to be reborn as citizens of Zion under the blessing of her King.

The Heading (87:0)

WE RETURN TO THE KORAHITE psalms that, along with the Asaph grouping, characterize the bulk of Book 3, thus suggesting an origin for the Korahite collection in Israel's public worship during the Second Temple period. Otherwise, the poem is described using the common designations of "Psalm" and "Song." As discussed elsewhere, these titles probably indicate compositions that are intended to be sung as part of the community's public worship.[1] The position of Psalm 87 in Book 3 is interesting. The poem seems to arise naturally out of the eschatological, international, and missionary vision of Psalm 86:8–10. Psalm 87 consolidates this vision with the imagery of adoption. The nations normally thought of as being Israel's enemies are described as having been born in Zion, thus including them in the community of faith. This development is truly fascinating in terms of the Psalms' theological representation of the nations.

The Centrality of Zion (87:1–3)

SOME OF THE ORIGINAL HEBREW and some of the sentence structures are quite awkward in this psalm, thus making it difficult to translate. But the opening verses refer to the divine possession of Zion as the place of his delight.

He has founded his city on the holy mountain. The opening stanza is one of the awkward verses in this composition. It is unusually brief, being only a single line, and its content is slightly oblique. Literally, the Hebrew reads, "His foundation is among the holy hills."[2] Although the designation of Zion as being among the holy *hills* (plural) is slightly unusual (cf. Ps 133:3, which also uses the plural), the essential meaning of Psalm 87:1 is clear: Zion is founded by God as a place of special holiness, as becomes explicit in the following verse. Yahweh has made it so. Zion's significance is not an accident of geography or the result of David's geo-political machinations (2 Sam 5). The city's greatness is derived from the fact that it is founded by God. It is, as far as the psalmist is concerned, the special place of God's choice and therefore unique among the cities of the earth. The plurality of the *holy hills* is probably not a reference to Zion as part of a mountain range but likely implies the uniqueness of Zion among the other mountain sanctuaries of the ancient Near East that were claimed to be major seats of worship (cf. Ps 48:1–3).[3] Jerusalem is unique because it is the sanctuary founded by Yahweh. Its origin is what gives it unique importance.

The LORD loves the gates of Zion more than all the dwellings of Jacob. The implication of Psalm 87:2 is that Zion bears unique significance even within Israel as a whole. There is a sense in which the whole of the promised land is holy and, therefore, significant. But this significance is especially true of Jerusalem, for it is where the temple represents the particular dwelling place of God on earth. The "gates of Zion" can serve as an idiom for the city as a whole or, more specifically, for the people within

---

1. See Wilson, *Psalms Volume 1*, 78–81.

2. Alter, *Psalms*, 306; Eaton, *Psalms*, 311.

3. For example, Mount Zaphon was connected with the worship of Baal; Mts. Mašu and Simmiria were sites of worship in Mesopotamia. See Walton, *ANE Thought*, 96, 173–75.

the city (see Ps 78:68; Isa 14:31–32). "For Zion, that also personifies all his worshippers, the Lord has the utmost love and devotion."[4] Normally, gates are to be thought of as significant for their defensive purpose—they can be locked to keep out every threat. Often in the Old Testament it is the nations who were kept at bay by the gates of Zion (see Lam 2:9 regarding the effects of the fall of the gates). The irony of Psalm 87 is that the gates of Zion, so loved by Yahweh, are wide open and welcome the nations into the heart of the city!

Glorious things are said of you, city of God. The singer—probably a temple prophet—concludes this introductory celebration of Zion's exalted status by addressing the personified city itself. Great things are spoken of Jerusalem, and the implication is that this positive testimony is the result of Jerusalem's being the "city of God." Zion's importance is not the result of political or military greatness or of size or influence. Jerusalem is important because it lies at the very heart of God's plan for the earth. It is founded by him and is the object of his love; thus it is the recipient of the "glorious things" that are about to be spoken in the prophetic oracle of verses 4–7.

The Rebirth of the Nations in Zion (87:4–7)

THE FOLLOWING VERSES CONSTITUTE the "glorious things" that are spoken of Zion in a prophetic oracle. The oracle begins with God's proclamation regarding Zion and is interspersed with linking statements from the prophetic speaker.

I will record Rahab and Babylon among those who acknowledge me. Remarkably, God's proclamation of Zion's greatness begins with the inclusion of Israel's archenemies among those who acknowledge (lit., "know," with all the relational overtones of the Hebrew verb *yada'*) him. Rahab—the chaos monster of the sea who opposes Yahweh—is frequently used as a metaphor for Egypt (see Ps 89:10; Isa 30:7).[5] God now numbers the two great superpowers that held his people in exile (Egypt prior to the exodus and Babylon following the fall of Jerusalem) as *part* of his community. There are two ways to read the phrase "among those who acknowledge me." The Hebrew preposition *le* can mean "among" (as with the NIV and other translations) but is more commonly translated "to." So, the declaration of Psalm 87:4 can be the public proclamation that Egypt and Babylon are now numbered among God's people. Alternatively, the verse could be read as a declaration to Israel about these two nations,

---

4. Eaton, *Psalms,* 312.
5. See the NIV footnote to 87:4.

namely, that Israel should view them also as Yahweh's nations.[6] Whichever way we read the preposition, the meaning is clear: Israel's enemies are included in the family of God's people!

The idea of Yahweh's "recording" of Egypt and Babylon as belonging among his peoples is also an interesting and unusual image and receives fuller discussion in the comments on verse 6 below.

The inclusion of Philistia, Tyre, and Cush along with Egypt and Babylon in the list of God's peoples gives us further insight into the extent of the inclusiveness of the divine kingdom. Philistia and Tyre are near neighbors to Israel (to the south and north, respectively), whereas Cush (modern-day Sudan/Ethiopia) represents the farthest reaches of the known world. The implication seems to be that this eschatological image of the nations as being gathered into the worshiping community of God's people applies not only to Israel's great enemies but also to all nations both near and far.

This one was born in Zion. The concluding statement of verse 4 clearly implies that a sense of belonging is extended to nations outside Israel. By accident of birth their origin may lay elsewhere. But all those who respond to the call to join Israel in the worship of Yahweh will be viewed as though they were born in Jerusalem and thus bear all the rights and privileges of any member of the covenant community.[7]

This one and that one were born in her. The Hebrew of verse 5 is awkward. More literally, the Hebrew reads, "A man and a man are born in her," in echo of the statements in verses 4 and 6: "This one was born in her." (The NIV makes the object explicit by naming Zion in these verses.) As mentioned above, the statements imply that some sort of honorary citizenship of Jerusalem—and by extension, Israel—is proffered to all those who acknowledge the kingship of God (cf. Ps 86:8–11). Robert Alter comments, "The wording is certainly cryptic but it might convey a universalist message about Jerusalem. Though as a biographical fact every person is born in his or her native place in the surrounding region, all who come up to Zion to acclaim God's kingship there are considered to be born in Zion."[8]

And the Most High himself will establish her. As with Psalm 87:1, the significance of the temple city, Jerusalem, is neither ethnic nor political—it is derived from divine choice. Yahweh is the great God and King, and he both founded and continues to establish Zion (v. 5). The strength

---

6. Goldingay, *Psalms 2*, 636.

7. This international call to worship comes into sharp focus in the Yahweh *malak* psalms (Pss 93–100). For further discussion see the commentary on Ps 96 in particular.

8. Alter, *Psalms*, 307.

and significance of Zion is based on Yahweh's choice of the city as the epicenter for the outworking of his purposes for humanity. Obviously, from the perspective of biblical theology, this choice comes to make much more sense in the light of the New Testament. Throughout many centuries of Israel's existence there would be a strong degree of dissonance whenever the Zion psalms were read, for the elevated view of the city presented in Psalms 46, 48, 87, and others did not match the historical reality of Jerusalem's role within the world order. Yet Jerusalem was the city chosen by Yahweh, and poems such as Psalm 87 were constant reminders to God's people that the city was still central to his purposes, regardless of how things appeared on the broader world stage.[9]

The Lord will write in the register of the peoples. Further elaborating the imagery of verse 4a is this unusual image of Yahweh as clerk or record keeper. God himself enters these nations in his list of citizens! Again, the idea of a "register of the peoples" is unusual but is probably to be associated with the lists of those who belonged to the tribes of Israel. The nations of peoples written in the register were, therefore, entitled to enter the tabernacle/temple to worship God (e.g., see Num 1–3; Exod 32:32; Ezek 13:9). Psalm 87:6 makes it quite clear that this record is a written one; that it is so emphasizes the legally binding nature of this invitation to a new citizenship. Just as someone who changes his or her citizenship today receives a certificate or a new passport, so also Yahweh's register constitutes a legal document affirming that these nations are included within the worshiping community.[10]

"All my fountains are in you." In verse 7 we again see Hebrew that is quite difficult to translate. First, it is not clear whether the verse refers to people who are "singing and dancing" or "singing and making music," so both options are reflected in the modern English translations. Second, it is not absolutely clear how the second line of verse 7 relates to the first line. Whether we are to understand the people as singing and dancing or singing and making music makes little difference in the end—the image is clearly that the people are celebrating their newfound citizenship and the privileges that go with it. The imagery pictures the masses of people now added to the ranks of Israel's numbers as joining in exuberant celebration of their inclusion in the family of God. The relationship between the two lines of verse 7 is perhaps slightly less obvious, but the second line of the verse is probably meant to be read as a statement of celebration voicing the people's song (as with the NIV and other translations). The "you" of the

---

9. We discuss this matter more fully in the Bridging Contexts section below.
10. Hossfeld and Zenger, *Psalms 2*, 383.

statement "All my fountains are in you" clearly refers to Zion, and the imagery of one's fountains or wellsprings as being in the city probably refers to Jerusalem as being the source of life or the heartbeat of the nations. In the arid landscape of the ancient Near East (today's Middle East), the source of water was the source of life, so the nations celebrate the new life they have found inside the city by way of their new citizenship.

Psalm 87 provides readers with this rich image of the nations' being reborn into the family of Yahweh so that they may become full-fledged members of the worshiping community of faith. It is a rich eschatological image that would be very different from the reality of Jerusalem's historical experience. Yahweh's city was often subjected to hardship at the hands of the nations listed in this psalm, but the psalmist points to a future reality—ordained and brought into being by Yahweh himself—in which these countries will ultimately become part of God's people.

ZION IN THE HISTORY OF INTERPRETATION. Psalm 87 is another example of a Zion psalm, as are Psalms 46, 48, and 84 (discussed above). Each of these songs holds Jerusalem in high regard—to an extent, in fact, that is almost mythical in tone. They each celebrate Zion's exalted status. Some point to her military impenetrability as a fortress or refuge. Most celebrate the worship of Yahweh practiced in the temple city. But one thing is common to most of the Zion psalms, namely, that the city of God is central to Yahweh's plans for and governance of the whole earth. In the case of Psalm 87, Zion's significance is painted in terms of love and inclusion. The gates of the city—that is, its inhabitants (v. 2)—are loved by God. The city is the focus of his affection and blessing more than any other place, even other places in Israel. But that love is inclusive rather than exclusive. So many of the tabernacle/temple rituals outlined in Leviticus and elsewhere are actually about exclusion. Such is the amazing holiness of Yahweh that only through cleansing sacrifice could one approach the presence of God. All sorts of issues, both moral (sin of any type) and practical (e.g., the eating of shellfish [Deut 14:10]), excluded one from entering the holy presence of God Almighty. But the tone of Psalm 87 is quite the opposite—it is all about inclusion. It is about the people who were normally excluded from worship becoming part of the worshiping family of God. As so often in the Psalter, Zion is central to that act of inclusion. It is there that the nations receive their adoption as citizens of a new kingdom. The peoples are declared *to have been born there* (vv. 4, 6). Zion is the necessary and unique place of that rebirth and new citizenship.

It is entirely understandable that the early church began to read the significance of Zion in terms of the events that occurred in the city through the life and ministry, death and resurrection of Jesus of Nazareth. It was in Zion that Jesus overturned the money lenders' tables in the temple. It was in the courts of the same complex of buildings that he taught the people, debated with the Pharisees and teachers of the law, walked and talked with the disciples, people watched and used the events he saw as teaching illustrations. It was to Jerusalem that Jesus led his disciples with great purpose and determination, even though he knew that the great city would also be the place of his death. It was outside the city walls that he was nailed to a tree and killed—and outside the walls of Jerusalem that the grave could not hold him. It was in that selfsame city that the church of Christ was born and began to grow. So, it is not surprising that Christians of the early centuries would view the significance of the Zion psalms in terms of the Christ event.

But clearly the Zion psalms meant something to the people of God throughout the generations before the coming of Christ. Where did that meaning lie when the reality of Jerusalem's history fell far short of the exalted status celebrated in these poems?

To understand the meaning of the Zion psalms for the original readers of the Psalter, we must consider these poems in the light of their history of appropriation. Some of the poems celebrating Zion probably date from the time of Kings David and Solomon, when Israel was a relatively major player on the stage of the ancient Near East, and these psalms would have borne some similarity to the transnational, political reality of the day. Jerusalem was the capital of the Davidic nation, and that nation was not to be trifled with. So, the significance of Zion would be read in the light the political and military realities of the day. But even for a reader in the days of David and Solomon there would still have been an element of dissonance—Jerusalem was great . . . but the nations were not flocking there by the thousands, nor was it the seat of rule over all the countries of the earth, as implied in Psalm 2. So even for readers of the Zion psalms during the height of Jerusalem's significance, there would have been a degree of surprise at the highly effusive language used to describe the significance of the city.

This surprise would reach the realms of disbelief in the historical period that followed the death of Solomon and the division of Israel. For believers singing the Zion psalms at that time, the theology and imagery of these poems would have stood in marked contrast to the geopolitical reality of the day. Effectively, Judah was a bit-part player on the world stage and entirely dominated by superpowers to the south (Egypt) and north

(Assyria, then Babylon). The songs that celebrate the impregnability of Zion would have sounded hollow in the light of the military dominance of Israel's and Judah's near neighbors. How then would believers in the days after the death of Solomon but before the exile read psalms such as Psalm 87? It seems clear that they would have read these psalms with an attitude of future expectation. The Zion psalms did not resonate with the Hebrews' current experience, so the people would have read them in the belief that Zion's significance would rise again at some point in the future.

This proleptic rereading would become all the more common in the years following the fall of Jerusalem at the hands of the Babylonians. Ideas regarding the impregnability of the city and Yahweh's rule over the whole world from Jerusalem bore no similarity to Zion's historical and political reality; therefore, the community of faith would have read these psalms with a forward-looking attitude of mind. The Zion psalms bore little resemblance to the Hebrews' present reality, so they came to be read with a sense of future expectation.[11] Thus it is not surprising that early Christian readers of these poems read them as descriptive of the life and events surrounding Jesus of Nazareth played out in the city of Jerusalem. While the Zion psalms may not originally have been "about Jesus," all the psalms lend themselves to reinterpretation by each succeeding generation, and, even at the height of Zion's fame, Psalm 87 would probably have been read by Old Testament believers as referring to future climactic events through which Yahweh would transform the world.[12] Certainly in later years Psalm 87—which is probably postexilic in origin—would have been read with a sense of looking forward to future events. For Christian readers looking back, we see that the rebirth of the nations worked out in Zion became possible and real through the climactic events of the cross of Jesus Christ.

Psalm 87 in the New Testament. There are no direct citations from or allusions to Psalm 87 in the New Testament. But the image of the nations' finding new citizenship and entering the family of God through climactic events in Zion obviously echoes strongly with the passion narratives in the Gospels and with the events of Pentecost (and all that followed) in the book of Acts. Truly, Jerusalem lay at the heart of all the historical events that led to the rebirth of the nations as the people of God through Christ Jesus and to the spread of the good news of Yahweh's salvation throughout the earth.

---

11. Susan E. Gillingham, *Psalms Through the Centuries: Volume One*, Blackwell Bible Commentaries (Oxford: Blackwell, 2008), 5.

12. On the reinterpretation of the psalms, see Jamie A. Grant, "Singing the Cover Versions: Psalms, Reinterpretation and Biblical Theology in Acts 1–4," *SBET* 25.1 (2007): 27–49.

INCLUSION. One of the great challenges of Psalm 87 for its original hearers would have been the image of Israel's enemies somehow being reborn as the people of God. Egypt and Babylon were synonymous with Israel's two great enslavements and all the horrors and brutality that went with them.[13] It would have been no easy thing for those who had returned from exile to consider accepting Babylonians as worshiping brothers in Zion, especially since Jerusalem was the site of so much suffering at the hands of the Babylonians. The challenge of *inclusion* would have been real and difficult. The thought of including in worship in the second temple those who had destroyed the first temple (Ps 74), killed the Hebrews' forefathers (Ps 79), and brutally murdered their ancestors' children (Ps 137) would have been far from appealing. The image of future inclusion would not have been an easy one to accept.

The Christian church today faces a similar challenge on two levels. First, persecution is still real for Christians in many parts of the world, and while we certainly pray for justice, we must also pray for transformation of hearts and incorporation into the body of Christ's people. Those who do not experience the reality of persecution cannot really imagine how difficult this act must be—but it is part of the challenge of Ps 87. We must pray that our enemies and oppressors (on whatever level they might be) come to know God and become part of the community of faith—our very own communities of faith. The history of the church is littered with examples of persecutors-turned-evangelists—from the apostle Paul right down to the present day. So, while we do pray for peace, justice, and the cessation of violence against our brothers and sisters in Christ, we should also pray that the enemies of God's people become members of his worshiping family.

There is, however, a second and perhaps more prevalent challenge of inclusion that faces the church today, namely, the challenge of including in our church families those who are very different from us. In an increasingly secularized, postmodern world, the general standards of people in the world around us will inevitably differ greatly from the standards we would profess and adhere to based on Scripture. So, we face an ever-increasing challenge in terms of incorporation, but the onus is on those of us in the church to make newcomers and seekers feel welcomed and loved despite the differences that may exist between us. It is of particular importance that we do not place unrealistic expectations on those who have yet to

---

13. See the discussion of Pss 74 and 79 above and of Ps 137 below.

accept Christ. The church has often been guilty of placing prerequisites on people who desire to find out more about Jesus but who have not yet come to faith in him. We expect people coming into the church to speak and behave as we do. This expectation, however, is often a barrier to inclusion within the community of faith.

People who are not yet followers of Christ but who desire to find out more about him may well use language that we find unpalatable, or may be living with a partner, or may do recreational drugs, or engage in a whole host of behaviors we find objectionable. Often an important part of one's journey *to* faith is the acceptance and friendship of those who are in the Christian community *of* faith. Very often friendship and hospitality make the love of Christ become real in the heart of a seeker. So, it is of vital importance that our Christian communities are welcoming and inclusive even toward those whose ethical standards—at this point in their journey—are very different from our own. Our first responsibility is to include. Then, as people come to know and love the Lord Jesus Christ, they will become increasingly aware of his standards as they are discipled in the way of Lord. But we should never make the standards a prerequisite for inclusion. Instead, our local communities of faith should be shaped by the offer friendship and hospitality to all those seeking to know more about the message of the gospel.

Psalm 88

A song. A psalm of the Sons of Korah. For the director of music. According to mahalath leannoth. *A maskil of Heman the Ezrahite.*

[1] LORD, you are the God who saves me;
  day and night I cry out to you.
[2] May my prayer come before you;
  turn your ear to my cry.
[3] I am overwhelmed with troubles
  and my life draws near to death.
[4] I am counted among those who go down to the pit;
  I am like one without strength.
[5] I am set apart with the dead,
  like the slain who lie in the grave,
whom you remember no more,
  who are cut off from your care.
[6] You have put me in the lowest pit,
  in the darkest depths.
[7] Your wrath lies heavily on me;
  you have overwhelmed me with all your waves.
[8] You have taken from me my closest friends
  and have made me repulsive to them.
I am confined and cannot escape;
  [9] my eyes are dim with grief.
I call to you, LORD, every day;
  I spread out my hands to you.
[10] Do you show your wonders to the dead?
  Do their spirits rise up and praise you?
[11] Is your love declared in the grave,
  your faithfulness in Destruction?
[12] Are your wonders known in the place of darkness,
  or your righteous deeds in the land of oblivion?
[13] But I cry to you for help, LORD;
  in the morning my prayer comes before you.
[14] Why, LORD, do you reject me
  and hide your face from me?
[15] From my youth I have suffered and been close to death;
  I have borne your terrors and am in despair.

¹⁶ Your wrath has swept over me;
    your terrors have destroyed me.
¹⁷ All day long they surround me like a flood;
    they have completely engulfed me.
¹⁸ You have taken from me friend and neighbor—
    darkness is my closest friend.

PSALM 88 IS UNIQUE IN ITS BLEAKNESS. Though there are other psalms that clearly present the author as being in a dark place in his relationship with his Creator, Psalm 88 is unmatched in its tone of darkness and despair. Accordingly, it is very easy for us to brush over this poem, fail to grapple with it, and think it to be nothing more than the bitter ramblings of a disappointed soul. It is very easy to marginalize Psalm 88. It is convenient and comfortable for us contemporary readers to limit its applicability to our own lives. But Psalm 88 is every bit as canonical as Psalm 23, and we do a great disservice to this poet when we distance ourselves from his words and experiences. For almost every believer who has sought honestly to walk with God in this good but fallen world, Psalm 88 has come to express the reality of our experience at some point in our own personal history. So, not only do we do a great disservice to the psalmist when we marginalize Psalm 88, but we also do a great disservice to ourselves when we exclude this avenue of expression from our vocabulary of prayer.

The Heading (88:0)

THE POEM IS DESCRIBED IN THREE WAYS—as a song (*shir*), a psalm (*mizmor*), and a *maskil*, or "meditation." While it is not unexpected to see Psalm 88 described as a *maskil* (with the contemplative, wisdom overtones of that term), it is certainly more of a surprise that this composition is described as a song and a psalm, for both terms are associated with public worship and community voice.[1] It is relatively easy to see Psalm 88 as a meditative poem, albeit a fairly bleak meditation, but it is altogether more difficult for us to grasp the use of these words in public worship. Yet the heading also ascribes a tune to accompany these words. The fact that we find it difficult to place Psalm 88 within the realm of public worship, however, is more a reflection on us and our attitudes than it is an implied criticism of the original use of this psalm.

---

1. Wilson, *Psalms, Volume 1*, 127.

The Prayer of Desperation (88:1–5)

LORD, YOU ARE THE GOD WHO SAVES ME. Given what follows, the opening statement of Psalm 88 is both surprising and enlightening. The tone of the remainder of the poem is full of darkness and despair—it is unmatched in the Psalter in terms of its sheer bleakness. Yet the psalmist begins by addressing Yahweh as "the God who saves me." It is unclear whether the poet bases this invocation on his past experience ("God who saves *me*") or theoretical knowledge (vv. 10–12), but he certainly knows something of the character of God, and his present experience does not match his understanding of what God's character should be like. He knows that the God he calls on is a God who saves his people. Yet being saved by God is not the poet's present personal experience. The despair of this meditation stems from the strong dissonance between the poet's expectation of God and his experience of the reality of life with him.[2]

Undoubtedly there is something telling about the address of verse 1. Whether or not a tone of irony is meant to be read into this description, the fact that the psalmist continues to address his God is probably meant to indicate that his one avenue of hope in the face of hopelessness is still to be found only in God. The element of irony present in every lament is seen clearly in Psalm 88. The poet lambastes God for failing to hear and respond to his prayers . . . yet he continues to pray to God. This seeming illogic illustrates the incongruity of lament, and it is particularly vivid in this psalm. The poet sees himself as being ignored and afflicted by God, but he continues to pray in the hope that Yahweh will once again prove himself to be the God of *his* salvation. Herein lies the essence of lament: though seemingly rejected by God, the petitioner will not cease to pray honestly.

Day and night I cry out to you. Verse 1b shows the poet's consistency of intercession. But this poetic merism also shows the consistency of the speaker's suffering, and it implies the passage of time without response to his prayer. Daily he prays, and daily he sees no change in his condition—no response to his prayer. Yet he turns to God in prayer once again in the following verse in the hope that, despite his experience, the Sovereign will this time turn his ear to the poet's cry. Until now, it appears that God has not been listening, but the poet prays again in the hope that time this he might be heard.

I am overwhelmed with troubles. Verses 3–5 give us insight into the depths of the psalmist's despair. His soul is "full of trouble" (v. 3).

---

2. Hence the title of Craig Broyles' book on the lament psalms, *The Conflict of Faith and Experience in the Psalms: A Form-Critical and Theological Study*, JSOTSup 52 (Sheffield: JSOT Press, 1989).

The Hebrew term is the same as the word used to describe one whose stomach is full after a good meal. The speaker's life is sated with troubles—he is full to bursting with torments of various types (indicated by the Hebrew's use of the plural).

And my life draws near to death. These verses continue with the description of the poet's proximity to death. We have no insight into the causes of his anguish and suffering, but whatever they are they leave him close to death.

I am set apart with the dead. Verse 5 summarizes the full extent of the psalmist's pain and suffering. He is so close to death as to be indistinguishable from the dead.[3] The psalmist's great fear is voiced in verse 5c and 5d. He fears he has been forgotten by God and is no longer subject to God's care. "Remembering" is an immensely significant concept in the Old Testament. God's people are to remember his character and works,[4] but they also rely entirely on the fact that God will remember them in their time of need.[5] In the darkness of the poet's lengthy suffering he fears that Yahweh, in fact, remembers him no more and that, in God's forgetting of him, he has been cut off from the divine hand (v. 5d) of care and protection. So deep is his pain and so lengthy its extent that the poet believes God has forgotten him—a spiritual dynamic that adds to the torment of his present physical suffering.

Note the language of these verses: "my life draws near to death" (Sheol, the place of the dead; see Bridging Contexts for further discussion), "counted among those who go down to the pit," "set apart with the dead," "like the slain who lie in the grave." Whatever the source of the psalmist's pain and suffering, it leaves him at death's door—such is the extent of his suffering. The clear picture of these opening verses is that the speaker's suffering is genuinely very great. These verses are meant to draw us into the speaker's reality, and we are meant to, in a very real and genuine sense, "feel his pain." Since we struggle with the accusatory tone of Psalm 88,

---

3. The Hebrew here literally reads "set free among the dead." This idea, however, does not imply a desirable situation—it rather gives the image of the psalmist as clinging to life by his fingertips and trying desperately not to be cut loose from life to enter the realm of the dead.

4. This duty is one of the key themes of the book of Deuteronomy (e.g., see Deut 8–9 and the constant calls to remembrance in this passage). For further discussion of this important idea, see Ryan O'Dowd, *The Wisdom of Torah: Epistemology in Deuteronomy and the Wisdom Literature*, FRLANT 225 (Göttingen: Vandenhoeck & Ruprecht, 2009), 49–52.

5. For example, see the role of divine remembrance in the account of the exodus (e.g., Exod 2:24; 6:5).

our subliminal response to it is to castigate the psalmist as deluded or rebellious, thus marginalizing his message rather than truly grappling with its truth. In much the same way as the prologue to the book of Job (Job 1–2), these opening verses of Psalm 88 are designed to draw us in to the psalmist's plight. We should accept the genuineness of his suffering, and we should be aware of its full extent. The poet has suffered *greatly*. This suffering has brought him close to death. Throughout it all, from his honest perspective, God has been silent. This situation is the picture painted in verses 1–5, and we as readers are meant to empathize with the poet in his plight.

The Source of Suffering (Psalm 88:6–9)

YOU HAVE PUT ME IN THE LOWEST PIT, IN THE DARKEST DEPTHS. Clearly, the hardest part of the poet's suffering comes from his awareness of its source. Take note of the pronouns used throughout this section of the psalm: "*you* put me in the lowest pit"; "*your* wrath lies heavily on me"; "*you* have overwhelmed me"; "*you* have taken from me my closest friends" (emphasis added). While there is clearly an objective cause to the psalmist's suffering, the pain he feels is accentuated by his awareness of God's role in his present experience. Yahweh, the covenantal God in whom he believes, is sovereign and able to do all things, so the poet's present suffering is exacerbated by divine inactivity in response to his prayer (vv. 9, 13–14). But the issue is not simply a matter of the mystery of divine inactivity, for from the psalmist's perspective God is actually *proactive* in causing his suffering. Naturally, we balk against such readings. There is something in us that automatically suggests the poet must have gotten it wrong. As we will discuss in the Contemporary Significance section, however, such a knee-jerk reaction is not necessary. Our response as readers should be to associate with the speaker, to empathize with him rather than to deny the legitimacy of his conclusions. Any such rejection of the poet's perspective on his current providence aligns us with Job's friends, who were quick to deny the legitimacy of his conclusions. They were condemned for their unwillingness to sympathize and, as readers of the Bible, we do not want to put ourselves in the same position.

God's providence has been dark for the writer of the psalm. This providence seems to include depression (v. 6), punishment (p. 7), and isolation from his friends (v. 8). It is no wonder that the poet's "eyes are dim with grief" (v. 9). He is worn out from crying because his suffering has been compounded by the belief that it finds its source in the God he worships. Who are we to say that he is wrong?

Unanswered Prayer and Rhetorical Questions (88:9b–12)

I CALL TO YOU, LORD, EVERY DAY. Herein we find the very essence of lament. The psalmist is suffering. He believes that the God to whom he prays is in some way responsible for the suffering, yet he continues to pray to this selfsame God. This seemingly paradoxical activity emblematizes the natural tension of lament. The poet lays out his complaint because he believes that God has not been faithful. But his only source of hope is the faithfulness of God. So it is that the poet, having just declared God to be the source of all his pain and suffering, expresses his continued commitment to prayer. The irony is obvious, but it is clear that the psalmist desires to maintain relationship with his God despite experiencing what that might mean (see Contemporary Significance for further discussion).

Do you show your wonders to the dead? There then follows a series of six rhetorical questions that are probably designed to serve as reminders both to the psalmist himself and also to Yahweh, the God to whom his prayers are addressed (v. 9). Each of the questions has an implied negative answer: "Do you show your wonders to the dead? Do their spirits rise up and praise you? Is your love declared in the grave, your faithfulness in Destruction?" The implied answer to these and the other questions in these verses is "No."[6] This rhetorical device gives courage to the poet himself as he is reminded that God is faithful to the living, not the dead. So, if God is going to show his wonders, he will do it while the poet is still alive. If God is going to declare his love for the suffering speaker, he will do it while the appellant is still alive. These "reminders to self" serve as an encouragement to the one who prays. These rhetorical questions constitute self-instruction as the psalmist reminds himself of the true nature of God and how he works among his people. "Ultimately, God is faithful and he will *surely* show his faithfulness while I am still alive." This self-assuring statement conveys the net effect of the psalmist's rhetorical interrogation in these verses.

But there is another effect of this questioning, namely, a reminder to Yahweh of his true character. The thought that God may need to be reminded of his good character comes as something of a surprise to modern readers, but the notion would not necessarily have surprised readers in

---

6. Actually, it is probably not that straightforward. In reality, the poet probably believed that Yahweh *is absolutely capable* of working for his benefit even in Sheol, the place of the dead. But it was generally accepted that Yahweh did not do such works in Sheol; therefore, if God still wanted to receive the psalmist's praise (v. 10b), then he must act for the poet's benefit while the poet is still alive, for the dead cannot "rise up and praise" God. For fuller discussion see Goldingay, *Psalms 2*, 653–55.

the ancient Near Eastern world, in which the gods would be reminded of their obligations by those who prayed to them.[7] The psalmist, of course, did not doubt that God knew his own character, but these rhetorical questions served as motivating reminders encouraging Yahweh to hear the psalmist's prayer.

> An additional element of the appeal is the rhetorical questions that argue that "the dead do not praise Yahweh" (vv. 10–12; see further on Ps 30). Here the psalm points to Yahweh's praiseworthy attributes and deeds—his wonders, his love, his faithfulness, his righteous deeds—and asks, If you permit your worshipers to die, who then will you save and who will extol your kindness?[8]

Or, as Longman puts it, "The series of questions in verses 10–12 almost taunt God to provoke him to action."[9]

Darkness is my Closest Friend (88:13–18)

WHY, LORD, DO YOU REJECT ME AND HIDE YOUR FACE FROM ME? Given the rhetorical questions that precede this final outpouring of the speaker's pain and anguish, his words in these verses are all the more poignant. "Do their spirits rise up and praise you? Is your love declared in the grave . . . ?" The implied answer to these questions is "No." So the accusation of these concluding verses is all the more bitter. It is the living who praise God, so why will Yahweh not hear the prayer of the psalmist and respond to it? As Broyles asks above, "If you permit your worshipers to die, who then will you save and who will extol your kindness?" The poet is one of those whose desire is to praise God, and all he needs in order to do so is to live. Why is it, then, that he is "set apart with the dead"? Why is it that the God whom he worships "rejects" him and "hides his face from" him?

There is no mistaking the bitter disappointment in the psalmist's final plea. His prayer is constant (v. 13), yet it remains unheard (v. 14a), and God has removed himself from the speaker (v. 14b). Clearly, the poet is abundantly aware that his suffering has lasted a long time, and this awareness is made all the more difficult as he considers the root of his affliction (vv. 15b–16). His suffering has been great, and somehow he sees that suffering as being rooted in the will and purpose of God for his life. The anguish in this final stanza is unmistakable. Quite simply, his circumstances

---

7. Walton, *ANE Thought*, 87–112.
8. Broyles, *Psalms*, 354.
9. Longman, *Psalms*, 320.

have taken him to a point that is beyond his ability to bear. The psalmist feels like he is drowning (v. 17), and despair has taken over.

Darkness is my closest friend. The final verse of Psalm 88 speaks of the climactic suffering the psalmist has experienced. On top of everything else, over and above all of the suffering he has encountered, his pain is compounded by the loss of friendship—again, he believes, at the hand of his God. "You have taken from me my closest friends." That the Hebrew in this verse is awkward leads to a certain ambiguity in the various English translations. It is likely that verse 18 actually speaks of the threefold removal of friendship and simply closes with the desperate summary exclamation, "utter darkness!"[10] But whether or not the NIV's rendering of the final line is the most accurate translation, it gets to the heart of the psalmist's complaint. Truly, all that is left to Heman (see the superscription) is darkness. All hope, all light, all friendship, fellowship, and companionship have been removed from him. Truly the darkness has become his closest friend. The poet is left with nothing but darkness, and in his poem he is unwilling to betray the reality of his experience by trying—artificially and dishonestly—to mitigate his message by concluding with a voice of hope that he does not feel. So, Psalm 88 closes with the cry of dereliction—*utter darkness!*

SHEOL AND THE WORSHIP OF GOD. One of the themes we see throughout the Psalter is the idea that the dead do not, indeed cannot, praise and worship God. We see this notion discussed in Psalm 88:4–6 and 10–12, and it is an issue encountered throughout the Psalter (e.g., see Pss 6:5; 30:9; 115:17). In order to understand the mentality of the psalmist, it is important to grasp how readers of the Old Testament thought about the afterlife. Modern Christians, reading with the benefit of the New Testament, have a much more rounded and complete view of life with God following our natural life on earth. The concepts of a resurrected body, eternal life, heaven, and the new earth all come into much clearer focus following the death and resurrection of Jesus. The Old Testament authors and readers did not have the benefit of this more fully orbed perspective on life after death, so the concept of the afterlife was

---

10. Literally, the Hebrew text of verse 18 reads, "You have removed from me loved one and neighbor, my friends—utter darkness." See Geoffrey W. Grogan, *Psalms*, THOTC (Grand Rapids: Eerdmans, 2008), 155.

a fairly shadowy and ill-defined one in the period during which Psalm 88 was written.

In terms of an understanding of the world and the created order, Israel shared with her neighbors a tripartite view of the cosmos. The universe was made up of three spheres: heaven, the place where God (or, for Israel's neighbors, the gods) lived; the earth, obviously the abode of humanity; and Sheol (or the underworld), the dwelling place of the dead. Sheol was a dark and shadowy, twilight-type of netherworld. No one really knew what happened there, but certainly it was a place to which you did not want to go if you could possibly avoid it.[11]

From the perspective of the Psalms, however, there is an interesting connection of ideas regarding the place of the dead and the concept of worship. Expressed positively, in the religious experience of the Hebrews there was a strong sense in which being alive meant praising God (e.g., see Ps 150:6). The theology throughout the Psalter conveys a very profound sense that the life of faith implies a life of praise. If one is truly alive in God, then, to one degree or another, that person's life must be marked by praise. "In the Psalter praise is the nerve center of the spiritual life. Even lament moves in the direction of praise. The Psalms themselves . . . inform the reader from time to time how central praise is in the faith of Israel, and thus in the Christian faith."[12]

The flip side of this coin, which we see discussed here in Psalm 88, is that descent into the place of the dead removes the very possibility of praise. "Do their spirits rise up and praise you?" the psalmist asks (v. 10). Just as life is intrinsically linked to praise, so death is a "praiseless" reality. Both conclusions are associated with the issue of relationship with God. Whoever lives a life of faith in God will find that praise is never far from his or her lips. The place of the dead, however, was seen as removing the believer from the very presence of God, so praise is not offered.[13]

While our concept of life after death may be more developed in the Christian era than in the ancient Near Eastern world, there are probably still lessons we can learn from the Hebrew attitude toward praise, life, and death. First, do we associate our Christian walk with praise in the same inseparable manner that Old Testament believers did? The dominant trend in our materialistic society is toward an attitude of perpetual

---

11. Walton, *ANE Thought*, 320–21.

12. Bullock, *Encountering the Psalms*, 132. None of this theology, of course, denies the legitimacy of lament in the spiritual experience of God's people. But the book of Psalms is quite clear as to the central significance of praise in the life of faith.

13. Walton, *ANE Thought*, 321.

dissatisfaction. We may have a house and a car and a job, but the ethos of contemporary, Western secularism means that we often end up desiring a bigger house, a nicer car, and a better job—with higher pay. Christians are also affected by this attitude of permanent dissatisfaction. The psalms make it clear that our attitude should be quite the opposite—life with God should be marked by praise and thankfulness. The apostle Paul describes this attitude in terms of contentment (Phil 4:10–19)—here is a lesson we need to learn and relearn. Second, we are given cause to ponder the link between death and a praiseless attitude. For the poets of the Psalter, to be alive in relationship with God meant to praise. If our spiritual lives have become devoid of an attitude of grateful praise, we need to ask whether some sort of spiritual death has separated us from God like Sheol did in the mind of the psalmist. If we do not find reason for praise, are we really alive in Christ?

LAMENT AND SPEAKING TO GOD. Very often, Christian readers are uncomfortable with the tone of Psalm 88. There is an almost natural reaction to marginalize the psalmist's voice as an extreme one within the Psalter. But we can learn lessons from the lament of Job and apply them to the poet's situation. At points throughout the book of Job, its central character berates God for causing his suffering and becoming his enemy (e.g., Job 29:2–5; 30:19–23 et al.). The concluding speeches by Yahweh show us that Job was in fact wrong in many of his conclusions about God, yet in the end Job is elevated to the role of intercessor. Job got things wrong, yet he was the one accepted by God. Why so?

Job is commended by Yahweh *because he spoke to him throughout his whole experience.* While the friends deliberated over philosophical questions regarding justice, creation, chaos, and the nature of God, Job grappled with God himself while interacting also with the friends. It appears that one implication of Yahweh's commendation of Job is to be found in the *relational* aspect of his lament. The man from Uz did not understand what was happening. He resented God for what he perceived to be God's role in his experience of suffering, yet he continued to pray—he continued to address God directly. Although Job was mistaken in some of what he said against God, and although he was extremely forceful in voicing his erroneous complaint against God, Yahweh commends him for praying rather than condemning him for his prayer. *The essential element of the spirituality of lament as exemplified by Job is found in the express desire to maintain relationship despite the present circumstances.* Elaine Phillips is helpful here:

God declared unequivocally (two times) that speaking correctly meant speaking *to* him, and in the process properly representing both Job's situation and God himself. Job did so; the friends did not, suggesting that, in addition to their limited view of the situation, *they completely lacked the relationship that infused Job's every utterance.*[14]

Furthermore, Phillips adds:

On the other side, God's endorsement of Job's words silences those who say that we ought not to articulate those difficult truths about the apparently gratuitous evil infesting our fallen world. That had been implicitly the position of the friends who were unnerved by the force of his protest. It is evident that God welcomes the exercise of moral judgment that was the focus of Job's verbal quest. *What Job said represented reality although it was an incomplete picture, as is that of any human observer.* Job's expressed anguish and his refusal to back down were what prompted the unparalleled revelation of God in the whirlwind, and what God said at that point was only that Job spoke in ignorance (38.2).[15]

Surely this analysis has a significant impact on our thinking when we return to the contextless Psalm 88. It expresses none of the great statements of faith that we frequently come across in the other psalms of lament, yet the very act of offering a prayer in a time of great despair and disillusionment with God is, in itself, arguably the greatest act of faith. So, Job's example points to the importance of relationship regardless of knowledge. *When it comes to the spirituality of prayer in general and lament in particular, engaging directly with God is more important than being right.*

Such a realization affects how we view the prayer of Psalm 88. Our knee-jerk reaction to the bleakness of this poem is to question whether or not the speaker is correct. The lesson learned from Job's lament is that this question is entirely irrelevant. In certain matters Job is declared wrong, yet still Job is commended because he has *done* rightly in wrestling directly with God rather than withdrawing from relationship. Job accuses, he cajoles, he complains, he charges God with wrong while declaring his own innocence, he accuses God of breach of covenant . . . yet "he has spoken in a right manner to me," declares Yahweh after his miraculous self-revelation from the whirlwind.[16] What conclusions, then, can we draw

---

14. Elaine A. Phillips, "Speaking Truthfully: Job's Friends and Job," *BBR* 18.1 (2008): 41. Emphasis added.
15. Ibid., 42. Emphasis added.
16. Ibid., 39.

regarding Psalm 88? It does not matter if the speaker is right or wrong. With regard to the spirituality of lament, such a question is an error of categories. Right or wrong must play second fiddle to human observation and experience. If bleakly is how the poet experiences his reality, then his lament is "right." Honest expression of relationship—even if it amounts to accusation and even if that accusation is "factually" inaccurate—is more important than saying nothing out of a desire to be sure that one has the facts correct.

> From the darkness and the questions believers flee to God, who reveals himself as the faithful One who will not abandon the work of his hands. They keep talking about "my God," even with a lump in their throat, so to speak. Even in the darkest psalm, Psalm 88, the author calls the Lord "the God who saves me," though he is overwhelmed by distress.[17]

We should not be quick to condemn or sideline Psalm 88 because of its acerbic tone of lament, for one day our experience may echo his, and we may find within ourselves the desire to pray these words as our own. As it was for the poet and so is for us, the important thing is to keep praying even when the most that our hearts can muster is complaint and accusation.[18]

---

17. H. G. L. Peels, *Shadow Sides: God in the Old Testament*, trans. Hetty Lalleman (Carlisle: Paternoster, 2003), 36–37.

18. For fuller discussion of Ps 88 and the spirituality of lament, see Jamie A. Grant, "The Hermeneutics of Humanity: Reflections on the Human Origin of the Laments," in *A God of Faithfulness: Essays in Honour of J. Gordon McConville on His 60th Birthday*, LHBOTS 538, ed. Jamie A. Grant, Alison Lo, and Gordon J. Wenham (London: T&T Clark, 2011), 182–202.

Psalm 89

A maskil of Ethan the Ezrahite.

¹ I will sing of the LORD's great love forever;
    with my mouth I will make your faithfulness known
    through all generations.
² I will declare that your love stands firm forever,
    that you have established your faithfulness in heaven itself.
³ You said, "I have made a covenant with my chosen one,
    I have sworn to David my servant,
⁴ 'I will establish your line forever
    and make your throne firm through all generations.'"
⁵ The heavens praise your wonders, LORD,
    your faithfulness too, in the assembly of the holy ones.
⁶ For who in the skies above can compare with the LORD?
    Who is like the LORD among the heavenly beings?
⁷ In the council of the holy ones God is greatly feared;
    he is more awesome than all who surround him.
⁸ Who is like you, LORD God Almighty?
    You, LORD, are mighty, and your faithfulness surrounds you.
⁹ You rule over the surging sea;
    when its waves mount up, you still them.
¹⁰ You crushed Rahab like one of the slain;
    with your strong arm you scattered your enemies.
¹¹ The heavens are yours, and yours also the earth;
    you founded the world and all that is in it.
¹² You created the north and the south;
    Tabor and Hermon sing for joy at your name.
¹³ Your arm is endowed with power;
    your hand is strong, your right hand exalted.
¹⁴ Righteousness and justice are the foundation of your throne;
    love and faithfulness go before you.
¹⁵ Blessed are those who have learned to acclaim you,
    who walk in the light of your presence, LORD.
¹⁶ They rejoice in your name all day long;
    they celebrate your righteousness.
¹⁷ For you are their glory and strength,
    and by your favor you exalt our horn.

¹⁸ Indeed, our shield belongs to the LORD,
  our king to the Holy One of Israel.
¹⁹ Once you spoke in a vision,
  to your faithful people you said:
"I have bestowed strength on a warrior;
  I have raised up a young man from among the people.
²⁰ I have found David my servant;
  with my sacred oil I have anointed him.
²¹ My hand will sustain him;
  surely my arm will strengthen him.
²² The enemy will not get the better of him;
  the wicked will not oppress him.
²³ I will crush his foes before him
  and strike down his adversaries.
²⁴ My faithful love will be with him,
  and through my name his horn will be exalted.
²⁵ I will set his hand over the sea,
  his right hand over the rivers.
²⁶ He will call out to me, 'You are my Father,
  my God, the Rock my Savior.'
²⁷ And I will appoint him to be my firstborn,
  the most exalted of the kings of the earth.
²⁸ I will maintain my love to him forever,
  and my covenant with him will never fail.
²⁹ I will establish his line forever,
  his throne as long as the heavens endure.
³⁰ "If his sons forsake my law
  and do not follow my statutes,
³¹ if they violate my decrees
  and fail to keep my commands,
³² I will punish their sin with the rod,
  their iniquity with flogging;
³³ but I will not take my love from him,
  nor will I ever betray my faithfulness.
³⁴ I will not violate my covenant
  or alter what my lips have uttered.
³⁵ Once for all, I have sworn by my holiness—
  and I will not lie to David—
³⁶ that his line will continue forever
  and his throne endure before me like the sun;
³⁷ it will be established forever like the moon,

the faithful witness in the sky."
³⁸ But you have rejected, you have spurned,
you have been very angry with your anointed one.
³⁹ You have renounced the covenant with your servant
and have defiled his crown in the dust.
⁴⁰ You have broken through all his walls
and reduced his strongholds to ruins.
⁴¹ All who pass by have plundered him;
he has become the scorn of his neighbors.
⁴² You have exalted the right hand of his foes;
you have made all his enemies rejoice.
⁴³ Indeed, you have turned back the edge of his sword
and have not supported him in battle.
⁴⁴ You have put an end to his splendor
and cast his throne to the ground.
⁴⁵ You have cut short the days of his youth;
you have covered him with a mantle of shame.
⁴⁶ How long, LORD? Will you hide yourself forever?
How long will your wrath burn like fire?
⁴⁷ Remember how fleeting is my life.
For what futility you have created all humanity!
⁴⁸ Who can live and not see death,
or who can escape the power of the grave?
⁴⁹ Lord, where is your former great love,
which in your faithfulness you swore to David?
⁵⁰ Remember, Lord, how your servant has been mocked,
how I bear in my heart the taunts of all the nations,
⁵¹ the taunts with which your enemies, LORD, have mocked,
with which they have mocked every step of your anointed one.
⁵² Praise be to the LORD forever!
Amen and Amen.

 IN MANY WAYS PSALM 89 is one of the most poignant poems in the whole of the Scriptures, and it is also one of the most significant in the Psalter. Psalm 89 closes Book 3 with a lament that both echoes and exceeds the others in this collection that is so dominated by the theme of exile. Other psalms of Book 3 lament the fall of Jerusalem (Ps 76) or the loss of the temple (Ps 74), but Psalm 89 focuses on the demise of the line of Davidic kings. In the psyche of the Old Testament

community of faith, certain symbols of the covenantal relationship with God became key: the city of Jerusalem and its impregnability; the temple as the dwelling place of God on earth; and the royal line of David, chosen by Yahweh to rule on this earth as his vicegerent. The psalms of Book 3 (Pss 73–89) have already voiced the people's anguish over the destruction of the temple and the fall of the city, but it is the issue of the apparent failure of God's covenantal promise to David that stands as the climax to this collection. Psalm 89 is also a psalm of three parts. The first section of the psalm (vv. 1–18) celebrates the covenantal faithfulness of God to his people, whereas the second part of the poem (vv. 19–37) reviews the covenant between Israel's God and Israel's king. The third part (vv. 38–51) consists in a fairly dark lament over the demise of the Davidic king.[1] Psalm 89 is significant in all sorts of ways, and we will unpack some of its great symbolism in the discussion that follows.

The Heading (89:0)

PSALM 89 IS DESCRIBED AS A *MASKIL* of Ethan the Ezrahite. The description *maskil* gives a wisdom-based, contemplative overtone to the composition. It is a song—and a subject matter—that requires meditation. It is a poem that asks hard questions without providing easy answers; therefore, the reader is obliged to pay careful attention to the deliberations that follow. This psalm is one of only two psalms written by an Ezrahite. Psalm 89 is associated with Ethan the Ezrahite, and the preceding psalm with Heman the Ezrahite.[2] It is not coincidental that these neighboring psalms are powerfully significant because of their content of forceful lament. Psalm 88 is the darkest of the individual laments that we find in the Psalter, whereas Psalm 89 is one of the most challenging community laments in the book of Psalms. The juxtaposition of these psalms illustrates that both the individual and the community feel compelled to voice their complaints against God—a pattern we also find at the beginning of Book 3, where Asaph's individual lament in Psalm 73 is followed by the people's cry of despair over the destruction of the temple in Psalm 74. Each of the laments that begin Book 3 find an answer. Asaph discovers the answer to

---

1. Anderson, *Psalms*, 630–31.
2. Both Ethan and Heman are described as "wise men" in 1 Kgs 4:31, and it is probably for this reason that their names are adopted for the headings of these two *maskils*. Of course, it is unlikely that it was the Ethan mentioned in 1 Kgs 4 who wrote Ps 89, for the psalm seems to respond to the collapse of the Davidic line in the Babylonian exile, events that occurred some 400 years after that Ethan would have died. But as with many of the "psalms of David," Ethan is an appropriate figurehead for a contemplation of this type.

his complaint when he meets with God in the temple (see the discussion of Ps 73 above). The answer for the despairing people of Psalm 74 follows in the succeeding Psalm 75, where God assures them that his judgment will happen when the time is right and his justice will be worked out once and for all. So, the opening laments of Book 3 are met with answers, but what about Psalm 89? Is there an answer to follow the people's complaint about the loss of the Davidic line? Perhaps, but that answer is not to be found in Book 3 itself, so we will have to return to this question in our consideration of Psalm 90.

The God of Covenant (89:1–4)

I WILL SING OF THE LORD'S GREAT LOVE FOREVER. Psalm 89 begins with a voice of personal praise and covenantal confidence. The Hebrew text draws attention to the object of the sentence: "Of Yahweh's great love [*hesed*] I will sing forever!" The immediate focus of the psalm is on the covenantal love of Yahweh and his faithfulness to his people. The psalmist begins with a confident outpouring of praise to God because of his devoted love and faithfulness to the community of faith. The poet's confidence is so great that he is determined to make this declaration of divine faithfulness to each succeeding generation (v. 1b). The irony, of course, is that this very point comes into question in the latter stages of Psalm 89 (v. 49), but we will return to this tension when we come to that section of the psalm. The opening voice of this poem is one of confident praise—God is a God of steadfast love and faithfulness. Surely he will never fail his people!

You said, "I have made a covenant with my chosen one." The root of this great and confident celebration is to be found in the promise of God to David (vv. 3–4). Yahweh himself had spoken his decree that a king in the line of David would rule throughout all the ages, and this promise filled the poet with a great sense of assurance. The thing to remember here is that this promise was not just an indication of privilege for a particular family; it was the guarantee of God's ordaining authority over the whole earth. God had promised peace for Israel through the governance of David and his line (2 Sam 7:8–11). This promise came to be read as the assurance of Yahweh's rule over the whole earth mediated through his appointed line of kings from David's line. This type of ideology is seen clearly in the Psalter in some of the royal psalms, such as Psalms 2, 18, 72, and 110. So, from the poet's perspective, Yahweh's invisible rule over the whole of the earth and humankind was, in a sense, "incarnated" through the line of the sons of David. Their political rule was the visible symbol of Yahweh's absolute governance over the whole earth. Herein lies the root of the poet's confident joy: God's king reigns in Jerusalem as the visible confirmation of the fact that God is in control over all of the events of humanity, including the events of his own life and those of the nation to which he belongs.[3]

The Created Order Declares Yahweh's Praise (89:5–18)

THE HEAVENS PRAISE YOUR WONDERS, LORD. The next major section of Psalm 89 focuses on Yahweh's great and awesome rule over the whole of the created order. Israel's God is sovereign in the heavens (vv. 6–7), over the seas (vv. 9–10), and over the whole earth (v. 11). As far as the poet is concerned, there can be absolutely no doubt about God's majestic rule over the whole of the created order.

Your faithfulness too, in the assembly of the holy ones. Once again, the focus of attention is drawn to one particular characteristic of God's being, namely, his faithfulness (v. 5b). The psalmist is absolutely confident of the fact that God will be 100 percent true to the promises he makes. For the author, this faithfulness is an absolutely non-negotiable characteristic of Yahweh's identity and, just as the heavens praise God for all of his wondrous works (e.g., creation itself), so they also celebrate his steadfastness in the divine assembly. It is interesting that the psalmist comes back to this particular feature of Yahweh's being time and time again in Psalm 89 (e.g., vv. 1, 2, 5, 8, 14 et al.). His focus on God's faithfulness in the early part of this psalm stands as a fascinating counterpoint to his troubled lament in the latter stages of this composition (vv. 38–51).[4]

For who in the skies above can compare with the LORD? Verses 5–8 take the reader into the realm of the metaphorical "heavenly council." As in Psalm 82, the psalmist asks questions that modern readers take to be rhetorical: "For who in the skies above can compare with the LORD? Who is like the LORD among the heavenly beings?" But for the original readers of Psalm 89, these questions would have been genuine calls to make comparisons. The imagery, common throughout the psalms, is of a notional parliament of gods in the heavens where it must be universally

---

3. Bill Arnold comments, "The interrelated themes of the Davidic covenant include the long-awaited rest in the land, peace and security, political stability provided by an eternal dynasty, and the construction of a permanent temple for Yahweh's great name. Moreover, by embedding this text in the historical narrative of 2 Samuel, and especially coming immediately after the turning of Jebus into Zion the city of David (5:1–6:23), the Davidic covenant interrelates with even more of Israel's broad themes: the resplendent Zion and the security of Jerusalem, the Ark of the covenant with the *mysterium tremendum*, the sovereignty of Yahweh in holy war, and many other important theological themes" (Bill T. Arnold, *1 & 2 Samuel*, NIVAC [Grand Rapids: Zondervan, 2003], 489).

4. We will talk more about this tension in the Contemporary Significance section below.

acknowledged that Israel's God, Yahweh, is the only true God over all creation. None can compare to his greatness and awesome power (v. 7); neither are any of these "competing" gods comparable in terms of character (v. 8). The implication of verse 8 is that Yahweh can be trusted implicitly ("your faithfulness surrounds you"), whereas the other gods of the ancient world are capricious and changeable. Again, this implication is key to the prayer of lament that supplements these opening verses of praise.[5]

You rule over the surging sea. Verses 9–10 speak to God's control over all the powers of chaos in the created order. The seas and waters in the ancient world were viewed as the most uncontrollable of all of the forces of the natural order. In other ancient Near Eastern creation accounts, the earth is often presented as coming into being as a byproduct of a cosmic conflict between the high god (sometimes called *'el*) and the forces of chaos personified as a sea god or goddess.[6] The language of "sea . . . waves" (and so on) became shorthand for all that is powerful, terrifying, chaotic, and fear-inducing in creation.[7] Once again, however, the psalmist knows that his God is more powerful even than the most chaotic force imaginable. So God is faithful to his promises, and God is powerful over chaos. The poet is painting a picture that speaks to his concluding plea.

The heavens are yours, and yours also the earth. The tripartite imagery in these verses is completed in verses 11–13, where the poet also declares Yahweh's sovereign power (symbolized by the language of his "arm," "hand," and "right hand") over the whole earth, as well as the heavens and the sea. God's sovereign rule is asserted through the language of possession. Just as the heavens belong to Yahweh (vv. 5–8), so the earth is his also. As Owner he is also Ruler, implies the psalmist.[8] These verses also point to the universality of Yahweh's rule over the earth. North, south, Tabor, and Herman may indicate the four points of the compass[9] but could equally refer to the sites of pagan shrines, thus implying "the subordination of their deities to God."[10] The language of "founding" or "establishing" the

---

5. For a fuller discussion of the idea of the heavenly assembly in the Psalms see the discussion of Ps 82 above.

6. Walton, *ANE Thought*, 184–88.

7. See the language of Psalm 69 as an example of the use of water imagery to present the overwhelming chaos that life can sometimes bring. See Gerald Wilson's helpful discussion of this psalm in the first work in this series (Wilson, *Psalms, Volume 1*, 947–62). See also the discussion of Psalms 77 and 93 in this present volume for a fuller discussion of the ramifications of sea and water imagery in the psalms.

8. Goldingay, *Psalms 2*, 673.

9. Ibid., see 673 n. 32.

10. Schaefer, *Psalms*, 220.

earth (v. 11) speaks once again about Yahweh's control over the whole of creation but also about his faithfulness. An established earth is a place of peace and security—such is the world order that God has created, and this order is another sign of his faithfulness to his people.

Your arm is endowed with power. This section closes with a confident statement regarding Yahweh's absolute power over everything in his creation. The metaphors of "arm," "hand," and "right hand" do not simply speak about God's power in the abstract. Instead, these metaphors commonly refer to God's ability to work out his purposes in the historical reality of his people.[11] The convictions of the poet are univocal: as Creator, Yahweh is capable of doing all things in behalf of his people.

Righteousness and justice are the foundation of your throne. Just as God's might and rule are unquestionable, so also is his character. Verse 14 uses the language of covenant, the concept that is so central to this poem. "Righteousness" (*tsedeq*), "justice" (*mishpat*), "love" (*hesed*), and "faithfulness" (*'emet*) are all key components of the covenantal relationship between Yahweh and his people and, more significantly in terms of this psalm, key components of the relationship between Yahweh and David. As the symbol of Yahweh's authority, his throne is characterized by righteousness and justice—precisely what was expected of the kings in David's line (Ps 72:2). As is Yahweh's rule, so should be the rule of his chosen leaders. Could there be an underlying critique of the human rule by David's line here? The poet tells the reader clearly what characterizes Yahweh's throne. In doing so it is quite possible that he also presents an implied criticism of the human kingship that was meant to echo Yahweh's ruling style.

Love and faithfulness go before you. Again, the poet calls to mind the character of God's being. He is a God of steadfast love and faithfulness (an echo of the opening verse of the psalm). Given the lament over the loss of the Davidic king that follows in verses 39–51, it is perhaps not surprising that the psalmist needs to keep reminding himself and his hearers of the basics of Yahweh's character. Fundamentally, he is a God of love and faithfulness regardless of how things may appear at any given point in human history. So inherent are these features to Yahweh's being that they are personified here as royal pages preceding his coming and announcing his true nature. Israel's God cannot be separated from love and faithfulness. The psalmist knows that he must remind himself and his hearers of this fact.

Blessed are those who have learned to acclaim you. The truth of God's character and covenantal faithfulness (vv. 1–4, 14) and the truth of

---

11. For example, see the use of "hand" imagery to describe Yahweh's liberation of Israel from slavery in Egypt (Exod 3:19–20; 6:1; 15:6 et al.).

his sovereign rule over all creation (vv. 5–13) can lead to only one proper response from any created person: worship (vv. 15–16). The beatitude "blessed" (*'ashre*) implies a lifestyle of true happiness (see comments on Ps 84:4). It is as we respond to God's character and works by worshiping him that human beings find the essence of happiness in their lives. In learning to acclaim God, men and women find fulfillment (see further discussion under Contemporary Significance).

For you are their glory and strength. Again, rooted in the idea of covenant, the psalmist celebrates the exalted status enjoyed by Israel as a result of their relationship with Yahweh. More literally this line reads, "For you are the grandeur of their strength,"[12] and the implication is that Israel delights in strength and status beyond what is natural to them precisely because of Yahweh's association with them. The following reference to the lifting up of Israel's horn emphasizes this point. The "horn" is the symbol of strength and power, and whatever strength Israel has is in accordance with Yahweh's favor.

Indeed, our shield belongs to the LORD, our king to the Holy One of Israel. The second line of Psalm 89:18 elucidates the first. Just as the nation belongs to Yahweh, so does its king. The kings of Israel had no might or grandeur in their own right—they were vicegerents of Yahweh's ultimate kingship. In that sense, the king's primary duty was always to Yahweh and secondarily to the people. Just as ownership of the earth implies sovereignty over it (v. 11), so in verse 18 does God's ownership of the Davidic line imply his sovereignty over the human kings of Israel. The idea of vicegerency is seen also in verse 18a's description of the king. He is Israel's "shield," yet the people know who their ultimate shield is (Ps 84:11). Just as Yahweh is a shield and refuge for the people, so should the king be. The human office of kingship in Israel is meant to reflect the activities of Yahweh in his rule over Israel (see comments on Ps 89:14 above). A criticism of the kings of Israel may be implied here: Have the kings of Israel forgotten their owner and the obligation they bear to reflect his character and activity in their ruling over the people?

Calling to Mind the Covenant with David (89:19–37)

PSALM 89:19–37 RECALLS IN POETIC FORM the covenant made between God and David as king of Israel (see 2 Sam 7; 1 Chr 17). In the development of the covenants in the Old Testament, the promise to David brings a new chapter to the people of God. It reflects a new reality for Israel as a settled

---

12. Alter, *Psalms*, 313.

nation-state resident in the land. New structures have come into place for the governance of the people under God's hand, and part of that divinely instituted reorganization involves the intermediation of a king between the people and their God. The inception of that arrangement is recounted in these verses in stylized form. The essence of Yahweh's promise to David is repeated as a reminder to God himself and to the psalm's hearers. From the psalmist's perspective, the very fact that God has made a promise must be worth something.

Once you spoke in a vision, to your faithful people you said. Psalm 89:19a stands alone as an introductory formula to the account of the Davidic covenant that follows. The idea of Yahweh's speaking in a vision is probably meant to be deliberately reminiscent of 2 Samuel 7, according to which God spoke to David via a vision given to the prophet Nathan. The idea of Yahweh's speaking is always a profound one in the Old Testament, where there is the absolute expectation that what God speaks will be done. So, this introductory formula highlights the sense of expectation inherent to Israel's understanding of the Davidic covenant.

I have bestowed strength on a warrior. The first stanza of this account of the Davidic covenant focuses on David as a warrior. The psalmic representation of the covenantal promise focuses on the fact that David, as king of Israel, would neither be defeated by those who would attack the nation (vv. 22–23) or thwarted by those nations that he would attack (v. 25).[13] Given the lament that follows, it is perhaps not surprising that Psalm 89's presentation of the covenant centers on David as a warrior. According to the psalm, David is chosen to lead the people to military security under God's hand. Of course, this picture is not a full and complete representation of the covenant as it is recorded in 2 Samuel 7, but this ensured security is a key feature of Yahweh's contract with the kings of Israel. Due to God's promise to David, the nation of Israel was meant to be secure; therefore, if this psalm is a response to the fall of Jerusalem and the loss of the Davidic line (as is likely), it is hardly surprising that the psalmist focuses on the promise of national stability.

Through my name his horn will be exalted. Here in Psalm 89:24b we see a reflection of the promise to the people in the promise to the king (see v. 17). Yahweh provides strength for the people beyond their status, and he does just the same for their king. This provision reflects the closely interwoven structures of the covenantal relationship between God, people, and human ruler. God promises blessing to the people through the king.

---

13. Alter describes Ps 89:25 as "an image of imperial dominion" (*Psalms*, 314).

As the king is blessed, so the people are blessed. When the king is faithful, the people walk in faithfulness. As God's rule is righteous and just, so the king's governance must be, and in this way the people are blessed. Yahweh's covenant with the king has the people in mind—it does not just privilege David and his family apart from a larger goal. The purpose of the covenant is the blessing of the people and the blessing of the nations through the people (see the discussion of Ps 87).

He will call out to me, "You are my Father, my God, the Rock my Savior." This verse further develops the privileged position of the Davidic king in the divine economy. The imperfect verb (*qara'*) is probably better translated transitively, that is, without the indirect object "to me." This omission gives a slightly more nuanced reading, "He will call me [saying], 'You are my Father, my God, the Rock of my salvation.'"[14] This address shows the privilege of direct, forthright, and honest relationship between David and his God.[15] Contemporary readers may be uncomfortable with the idea of summoning God, but as Goldingay points out, "To summon Yahweh to our help is not a peremptory act if it is the summons that Yahweh invites."[16] This reference to David's God-given ability to call out to Yahweh shows the depth of covenantal relationship. The Old Testament notion of covenant is neither formal nor theoretical—it bears real depth and makes a real difference in the life of the covenantal participant.

I will appoint him to be my firstborn. The second aspect of the promise to David is that of a continuous line of successors to perpetuate the monarchic dynasty (vv. 27–29). There is a sense in which the divine promise assures David of the steadfast love of God, and that love for David extends beyond him to his heirs in perpetuity (v. 28). Along with security, the covenantal promise of 2 Samuel 7 guarantees a royal line forever. But both issues are questioned in the lament that follows.

If his sons forsake my law. Following this discussion of security for the nation and a line for David is a caveat (vv. 30–37): What happens if David's heirs do not love Yahweh in the manner that he did? Clearly, covenantal election can never be an excuse for license. This truth applied to Israel (Deut 28) and also to the Davidic dynasty (Ps 89:32). God will not be mocked by the kings who follow in David's footsteps, and we know from the historical books of the Old Testament that many of those kings did, in a wholesale and reprehensible manner, fully reject the love of the Lord. Yet it is interesting to note that, of the eight verses which discuss

---

14. Ibid.
15. Goldingay, *Psalms 2*, 679.
16. Ibid.

this question of wayward heirs to the promise, only a single verse (v. 32) actually deals with punishment as a response. The rest of this strophe focuses on the promise of God's continuing love for David, expressed by way of God's continuing grace toward his ancestral line (vv. 33–37). This divine grace continues because the issue at stake is not the obedience of the Davidic kings. The issue at stake is, instead, the faithfulness of God to his promise. Observe the language used in these verses:

> But I will not take my love from him,
>> nor will I ever betray my faithfulness.
> I will not violate my covenant
>> or alter what my lips have uttered.
> Once for all, I have sworn by my holiness—
>> and I will not lie to David. (Ps 89:33–35)

These verses show clearly the passion and seriousness with which the Creator God enters into covenantal relationship with his servant David. God's covenant is based on his sovereign choice. Once it is made, the ramifications of that promise are more far reaching than finite human minds can ever fathom. God's faithfulness to the promise he made to David could not be thwarted even by the unfaithfulness of David's heirs. Yahweh's love for David, the psalmist tells us, far outweighed the subsequent kings' lack of love for Yahweh. Yet here a tension arises: If God is absolutely faithful to his promise, then why has the Davidic line ceased to exist, as the psalmist acknowledges it has? In these verses the psalmist has praised the unquestionable faithfulness of Yahweh. He now goes on to question that very faithfulness in his prayer of lament (vv. 38–51).

The Faithfulness of God Questioned (89:38–51)

BUT YOU HAVE REJECTED, YOU HAVE SPURNED. The change in tone could not be more marked. Having just recounted the unchangeable promise of God, the psalmist pours out his heartfelt complaint in prayer to God. As readers, we need to feel the passion of the poet's prayer born out of the confusion that comes from a present reality that does not match his beliefs. The sure promise of God was for a continuous line of kings descended from David:

> [T]hat his line will continue forever
>> and his throne will endure before me like the sun;
> it will be established forever like the moon,
>> the faithful witness in the sky. (Ps 89:36–37)

The psalmist believed this promise, but he now faces a historical reality that contradicts his beliefs. In that confusion he cries out in verses 38–39:

But you have rejected, you have spurned,
you have been very angry with your anointed one.
You have renounced the covenant with your servant
and have defiled his crown in the dust.

We should read these verses with the same tone of shocked surprise that was undoubtedly voiced by the poet. "But *you have* rejected, *you have* spurned" (emphasis added). The inconceivable has happened, and the author is rocked to his very core. Lament is described by Craig Broyles as being "the conflict of faith and experience," and this conflict is precisely the experience voiced in verses 38–51.[17]

You have broken through all his walls. The promise of security (v. 22) has been dashed by the humiliation of military defeat (vv. 40–41). The promise of divine strength (v. 21) seems to have been transferred to his enemies (v. 42). The promise of an eternal line of descendants (vv. 27–29) has been brought to a crushing end in real time (vv. 44–45). The once exalted status of the anointed one (*mashiah*) of Yahweh (v. 20) has been rejected and cast down to the very dust of the earth (vv. 39, 44–45). How is the poet, how are the people, to make sense of all these disasters? The firm belief in the faithfulness of Yahweh on the one hand (vv. 1–37) has collided horribly with their present experience on the other (vv. 39–51). The psalmist's prayer tries to make sense of the ensuing theological train wreck.

How long, LORD? The very essence of lament is found in these words that we see repeated so often throughout the Psalms.[18] The exclamation "How long?" seeks an end to the conflict of faith and experience. The psalmist is looking for reconciliation between his theology and the present circumstances that do not match his beliefs. Geoffrey Grogan comments:

The psalm's whole burden is concentrated into a cry of bewildered agony. "How long?" is often asked in the Psalms (see esp. 13:1). Life is short, but God's promises are long-lasting. How is it then that this covenant promise has apparently failed? The shame of defeat and the king's exile have involved others, the psalmist included, and he concludes with the word translated "anointed one," a poignant reminder of the Davidic covenant. Where, though, is the promise undergirding it now?[19]

---

17. Broyles, *Conflict of Faith and Experience*, 35–53.
18. This prayer is found in Pss 6:3; 13:1; 35:17; 74:10; 79:5; 80:4; 82:2; 90:13; 94:3; 119:84. There are many similar variants on this prayer.
19. Grogan, *Psalms*, 157.

So goes the thrust of the remainder of Psalm 89. It all boils down to the essential question in verse 49: "Lord, where is your former great love, which in your faithfulness you swore to David?" The poet simply cannot comprehend how the God of faithfulness whom he worships could possibly have turned his back on the promises made to his servant David. Yes, the poet was fully aware that kings could and would be rebuked if they rejected Yahweh (v. 32). But such rebuke was never going to affect the perpetuity of the kingly line (vv. 33, 36). Yet here the psalmist stands contemplating the broken city walls of Jerusalem, a defiled temple, and an empty throne. It is clear that the psalmist cannot make sense of this incongruity, and the only conceivable response is to offer this brutally honest prayer. He calls on Yahweh to remember (vv. 47, 50)—to remember the brevity of human experience and to remember the king. There is a real sense in which the psalmist pours out all the angst that results from his human fallibility and lack of comprehension. There is no way for him to reconcile his understanding of God's nature with his historical experience. With that lack of understanding comes prayer, for he believes that it is only in relationship with Yahweh that he can make sense of all the theological incongruities of life.[20]

The Final Doxology (89:52)

P**RAISE BE TO THE** L**ORD** **FOREVER!** A**MEN AND** A**MEN.** So, the core content of the psalm finishes with the words "your anointed one." Clearly, the poet is calling on Yahweh to remember the covenant with David and to restore the monarchy to Jerusalem. But what is the effect of this concluding doxology in verse 52?

Most scholars accept that the doxologies found at the end of each of the books of the Psalter (Pss 41:13; 72:19–20; 89:52; 106:48; 146–50) function as editorial signs that indicate the conclusion of each of the books of the book of Psalms.[21] It is not absolutely clear why the editors who put the Psalter together as a collection wanted to divide the overall canonical book into smaller books, but it is broadly accepted that they used these doxologies to indicate the close of one book and, by implication, the beginning of the next. So, there is a sense in which Psalm 89:52 applies to the whole of Book 3 of the Psalms, thus concluding the collection that is Psalms 73–89.

But it is equally inescapable that this verse is added to the end of Psalm 89 as a part of the poem itself, so verse 52 has an influence on this psalm as

---

20. Grant, "Hermeneutics of Humanity."

21. Gerald H. Wilson, "Evidence of Editorial Divisions in the Hebrew Psalter," *VT* XXXIV.3 (1984): 337–52.

well as concluding the book as a whole. The editors must have been aware of what they were doing in adding this voice of praise at the end of the lament in verses 38–51. Knut Heim argues that the postscript anticipates divine intervention along the lines of the prayer offered. He sees verse 52 as a statement of faith that the psalmist's prayer has been heard and will be answered.[22] John Goldingay, on the other hand, sees a more nuanced effect of this verse upon the psalm as a whole. He argues that the coda "reminds us of the daring profession of faith that the Psalter as a whole makes."[23] There is no resolution implied in verse 52. It does not change or deny the paradox voiced in the lament; rather, as with every lament, this verse simply acknowledges the dichotomy. The psalmist cannot understand how God is being faithful to his promise, and he says as much. But he realizes that resolution—whatever form it may take—is only to be found in a relationship of faith in Yahweh, so he declares that blessing of praise on Yahweh forever.

Psalm 89 and Book 3 close with an expression of Yahweh's inestimable worth despite the psalmist's continued confusion over a historical reality that conflicts with his beliefs. The doxology reminds the reader that God is worthy even when his people are conflicted in their experience of him.

 **POSITION OF PSALM 89 IN THE PSALTER.** It is broadly acknowledged that Psalm 89 lies at a significant juncture within the book of Psalms and contributes to the overall flow of the book's "narrative." Gerald Wilson was influential in formulating this theory, and his ideas have since attained broad acceptance among scholars of the Psalter.[24] Wilson argued that royal psalms have been placed at significant junctures throughout the book of Psalms, and that the placement of these psalms tells a "narrative" of the rise and fall of the Davidic monarchy.[25] According to Wilson, Psalm 2 gets the ball rolling with a celebration of kingship in this Enthronement Psalm. Although Psalm 2 does not bear an "of David" superscription, the poem is similar in tone and content to the Davidic royal psalms of Books 1–3. The next major juncture in the

22. Knut M. Heim, "The (God-)Forsaken King of Psalm 89: A Historical and Intertextual Enquiry," in *King and Messiah in Israel and the Ancient Near East: Proceedings of the Oxford Old Testament Seminar*, JSOTSup 270, ed. J. Day (Sheffield: Sheffield Academic, 1998), 304–5.

23. Goldingay, *Psalms 2*, 694.

24. Gerald H. Wilson, *The Editing of the Hebrew Psalter*, SBLDS 76 (Chico, CA: Scholars Press, 1985), 199–228; Wilson, "Shape."

25. Gerald H. Wilson, "The Use of Royal Psalms at the 'Seams' of the Hebrew Psalter," *JSOT* 35 (1986): 85–94.

Psalter actually comes at the seam of Books 2 and 3 where we find the only postscript in the Psalms (Ps 72:20). According to Wilson, this postscript suggests the end of "the prayers of David son of Jesse" and groups Books 1 and 2 together (Pss 2–72).

So, the psalmic narrative moves from inception in Psalm 2 to continuation in Psalm 72. It is possible that Psalm 72 is meant to be read as David's prayer *for Solomon* as the royal line promised by Yahweh is continued through his descendants. If this view is correct, then David prays for his son's reign to be marked by the same righteousness and justice that characterizes Yahweh's rule (Ps 72:1–2; cf. Ps 89:14). Psalm 72 creates an expectation of the kind of kingship that should typify the rule of David's progeny; societal justice (vv. 1–4, 12–14) and worship of Yahweh (vv. 18–20) should characterize the rule of David's son. Book 3 of the Psalter, however, makes it clear that God's people and God's rulers all too often did not follow in his ways and so bore the consequences of their actions. As reflected in the covenantal blessings and curses of Deuteronomy 28, Israel was warned that if they consistently rejected Yahweh and his ways they would inevitably face punishment, and the punishment would culminate in exile. Exile is, in many ways, the subject matter of Book 3 of the Psalter as it focuses on the loss of the city of Jerusalem (Ps 74), the temple (Ps 76), and ultimately the king (as we have seen here in our study of Ps 89).

So, Wilson argues, Books 1–3 of the Psalter chart the rise and fall of the Davidic line of kings—inauguration in Psalm 2 and continuation in Psalm 72 are finally countered by the demise of the monarchy in Psalm 89. The hope and promise that arose out of Yahweh's covenant with David have been spoiled by his sons' rejection of a lifestyle that should have been characterized by adherence to the instruction of Yahweh as an example for the people (Deut 17:14–20).[26] The promise to David was meant to bring hope to the people, but the constant rejection of justice and righteousness by Judah's kings robbed both ruler and nation of the security promised by God and left them open to his punishment. So, the psalms at the seams of Books 1–3 present the story of the failure of human kingship. Book 4 brings a renewed focus on the kingship of *Yahweh*, but the Davidic king is not lost from the voice of the Psalter. The figure of David will return in Book 4, but the presentation of human kingship will be quite different from what we have read here in Psalm 89 and in Books 1–3 in general.

Changing symbols. As well as being significant because of its importance within the canonical Psalter, Psalm 89 represents a culmination in

---

26. Jamie A. Grant, *The King as Exemplar: The Function of Deuteronomy's Kingship Law in the Shaping of the book of Psalms*, AB 17 (Atlanta/Leiden: SBL Press/Brill, 2004).

terms of the reconsideration of Israel's major symbols of national identity. Book 3 has already focused on the loss of the city of Jerusalem (Ps 74) and the temple (Ps 76) before contemplating the significance of the demise of the Davidic monarchy here in Psalm 89. Jerusalem (Zion), temple, and king were all significant symbols of Yahweh's various promises to Israel—assurances of his protection, presence, and governance. But in Psalm 89 the psalmist has to confront the reality of the loss of the monarchy, just as other poets confront the fall of Jerusalem and the destruction of the temple. In each case, the people probably believed in a permanent promise that these special symbols would continue forever, and in the postexilic period they attempted to make sense of their removal. In order to understand how they could do so, we have to take the long view of God's plan for the salvation of humankind.

The original call and election of Abraham, the father of Israel, in Genesis 12:1–3 presents that choice as part of God's plan to bless *all* the nations. That call—though clearly privileging Abraham and his descendants—was always intended to bring good to the whole of humankind, even those who were not directly part of Abraham's line. This emphasis is repeated in the election of Israel and their call to be a "kingdom of priests and a holy nation" (Exod 19:5–6). Once again, Israel is Yahweh's "treasured possession" (*segullah*), but their purpose is to be intermediaries (priests) between Yahweh and the other nations. This representative function is repeated prior to Israel's entry into the land (Deut 4:1–14): Israel is meant to be a light to the nations to bring to them as well the blessing promised to Abraham. So, Israel is special in God's eyes, but that unique place in his economy was always maintained with a particular end in mind, namely, the incorporation of the nations into God's plan of blessing.[27]

We see throughout the Old Testament a constant struggle, first within the united kingdom of Israel and later within the southern kingdom of Judah, regarding the effects of election. Many within the ranks of ethnic Israel came to see their election as a simple end in itself, an end that set them apart from the nations in an absolute sense. The net effect of this way of thinking was a type of ethnic elitism whereby the people believed that the covenantal relationship with Yahweh made them qualitatively better than other nations. The external signs of the covenant with Yahweh—Zion, temple, and Davidic king—therefore became symbols of Israel's ethnic superiority rather than evidences of God's blessing for the purpose of being a blessing. The prophets often struggled with these skewed

---

27. For a fuller discussion of divine election and the nations see Christopher Wright's excellent *The Mission of God*, 189–264.

attitudes toward Jerusalem, the temple, and the Davidic king (e.g., see Jer 6–7). The signs of the covenant had become a talisman that many in Israel believed would protect them regardless of their actions and real relationship with Yahweh. The signs had replaced the essence of loving and obedient relationship with God.

So it was that God came to remove the external trappings of the covenant by means of the fall of Jerusalem and the exile. Having warned his people repeatedly that exile would be the tool in his hands to bring them back into right relationship with him, Yahweh finally allowed Jerusalem to fall to the Babylonians in 586 BCE. As we have seen from our study of the psalms of Book 3 of the Psalter, this event had a climactic impact on the people of God. The signs of city, sanctuary, and monarchy emblematized the promises God had made to his people, and their loss caused many to question the faithfulness of God, just as we have seen here in Psalm 89.

But it is important to remember that these symbols were merely signs of a far greater reality present in the relationship between God and his people. Jerusalem symbolized security for Israel, but the people were secure under God's hand even given the events of the exile. The temple symbolized God's presence, but he was just as much present with his people in exile in Babylon as he ever was in the temple during the morning and evening sacrifices. The Davidic king symbolized God's control and governance over the nations, yet God controlled the armies of Nebuchadnezzar, king of Babylon, and Cyrus, king of Persia, regardless of whether or not a Davidide reigned on the throne in Jerusalem.

In forgetting the broader plan of bringing blessing to the nations and focusing on the trappings of election, Israel found the loss of these symbols almost unbearable. For God, however, the essence of covenantal *relationship* was more important. The removal of the symbols in no way changed his love for his people with all the practical ramifications that love brings. So, the loss of the Davidic king was tragic for the psalmist and caused him to question the very faithfulness of God. But God was looking to the essence of his promise: his rule over the earth administered through his servant, who is his son and anointed one (Ps 2). For the psalmist, that "son" had to be the Davidic king, but even throughout the reign of David and his line Yahweh was looking toward another Son, who was his Servant and Anointed One and through whom he would visibly establish his rule over all the earth. A greater spiritual reality lay behind the symbol.

So it is that the very physical symbols of the Old Testament are transformed into a greater spiritual reality in the New Testament. Israel as the elect is transformed into a multinational, multiethnic, multicultural church that still seeks to be a blessing to all the nations. The physicality of Jerusalem and the temple as the place of God's presence is expanded in the new covenant to fill the whole earth (Rev 21–22). And the role of the Davidic king as the instrument of God's purpose on the earth is radically transfigured by great David's greater Son. As we see in Isaiah 55, God always had in mind a far greater reality for the line of David than his people at that time ever suspected.[28] His promise to David encompassed a type of rule and governance beyond the wildest imagination of the author of Psalm 89. A "Son" of David continued on the throne throughout the exile, just as he had ruled before David's birth. That this reality was, of course, far beyond the understanding of the author of Psalm 89 explains why he offered his lament to God. But in all these things—in the loss of important symbols and even in the suffering of his people—God was at work to fulfill a greater plan of blessing for Israel and for the nations. It would be several hundred years before that plan became visible to the people of God (Acts 1–4), hence the confusion of the psalmist. But that hope is exactly why the psalmist kept praying even in his confusion. He prayed to Yahweh because he knew that his God was faithful, even though he did not understand how. Symbols were being transformed, but the removal of the symbols paved the way for a far greater spiritual reality to be worked out in and through Jesus the Christ, "the son of David . . . the son of God" (Luke 3:31, 38).

Psalm 89 in the New Testament. The strongest resonances of Psalm 89 in the New Testament come in the book of Revelation. In Revelation 1:5 Jesus is described as "the faithful witness, the firstborn from the dead, and the ruler of the kings of the earth." This description resonates strongly with the words of the psalmist depicting David in Psalm 89:27 and the covenant in verse 37. The sun and moon serve as faithful witnesses to the covenant with David in Psalm 89; now Jesus shines out as the "faithful witness." He is the "firstborn," just as David was the firstborn of the line of Davidic kings. And Jesus is also the "ruler of the kings of the earth" in the same manner that David was granted that dominance by God for the outworking of his purposes on earth. John uses the language of Psalm 89 to make his point that Jesus is the promised Son of David, the one who brings a greater reality to the psalmic idea of the king as the instrument of God's governance on earth. But the fact that Jesus is the "firstborn from the dead" reminds the reader that the exalted status of Jesus the Messiah came at great personal cost—exaltation and suffering are closely linked, thus drawing us back to the parallels between Psalm 89 and the suffering servant in Isaiah 55. Revelation 1:5 presents Jesus as the true King who

---

28. Knut Heim draws out interesting parallels between the text of Ps 89 and the role of the servant in Isa 55 ("Psalm 89," 306–14).

fulfilled the Davidic role in a manner that neither David nor his sons were ever able to do.[29]

WORSHIPING EVEN WHEN WE DO NOT FEEL LIKE IT. Several times throughout our consideration of the psalms in Book 3 (Pss 73–89), we have discussed the importance of practicing lament. Honest prayer is important to God, and well-intentioned, polite lies are pointless when we pray to the God who sees our hearts. But the apparently contradictory parts of Psalm 89 teach us an equally important spiritual lesson.

Over the years, scholars have struggled to hold together the tension that arises from the very different nature of the two sections of Psalm 89. The hymn of praise (vv. 1–37) is so very confident regarding the faithfulness of God that the vigor of the lament (vv. 38–51) catches the reader by surprise. Some interpreters have suggested that these were actually two (or possibly even three) completely different psalms that have been combined by a later editor as a poetic account of the origin, development, and demise of the monarchy.[30] But this approach seems unnecessary as an explanation of the tensions found in Psalm 89, for these tensions are inherent to the life of faith.

The psalmist knew absolutely what he *believed* regarding the promises of God and the role of the Davidic king. He also knew what he had *seen* happen to the Davidic line. The tension was inescapable for all followers of Yahweh in the exilic and postexilic period, and the only possible response was one of prayerful honesty. "Here is what I believe about you and your promise, Lord, and here is what I see," the poet prays. That the tension is unresolved but the prayer is still offered teaches us an important lesson in terms of our perspectives in praise, prayer, and worship.

God, quite simply, is bigger than we are! So we pray honestly and openly in accordance with the way we see things, but we pray also with the awareness that God is eternal and all-knowing, so what we think we know may be entirely wrong! Given the tone of the lament in verses 38–51, it seems reasonable to assume that the psalmist did not feel much like worshiping God, yet he chose to recite all that he knew about the faithfulness

---

29. For further discussion see Moyise, "Psalms in Revelation," 236–38, and Heim, "Psalm 89," 316–21. Sylvia Keesmaat also suggests that there are resonances of Ps 89's lament in Paul's presentation of Jesus as the Suffering Servant in Galatians. See Sylvia Keesmaat, "The Psalms in Romans and Galatians," in *The Psalms in the New Testament*, ed. S. Moyise and M. J. J. Menken (London: T&T Clark, 2004), 159–60.
30. Oesterley, *Psalms*, 396.

of God and his covenantal promise to David. This knowledge did not keep him from voicing his complaint, but neither did he allow his experience to become so overarching that he rejected his theology of God. There is a subtle indication in Psalm 89 that the poet has experienced God's faithfulness in the past, so he has decided to declare that faithfulness despite his present confusion (vv. 1–2).

Herein lies an important lesson for us as contemporary believers—a lesson that is affirmed in Psalm 89 itself. Verses 15–17 give the basis for this idea of worshiping through our questions:

> Blessed are those who have learned to acclaim you,
> who walk in the light of your presence, LORD.
> They rejoice in your name all day long;
> they celebrate your righteousness.
> For you are their glory and strength,
> and by your favor you exalt our horn.

As mentioned above, the idea of "blessedness" here reflects the experience of true and deep human happiness. The poet reminds the reader that this happiness can only be found in the habitual practice of worship. As created human beings we only find our true meaning in the worship of the Creator. If God is good and made us in his image, then something deep within us yearns to worship him.

Often our experiences in life will leave us feeling disinclined to worship, but Psalm 89:15 paints the picture of "learning to acclaim God" (literally from the Hebrew, "who know the horn's blast"). The image is one of participating in the public worship of Yahweh, thus answering the call to worship that, in the psalmist's day, was made by the blowing of a horn.[31] It is as we learn the worship of God that we are equipped to deal with the complexities and incongruities of life. In worship we are shaped and equipped to find our strength in God, even when we do not really understand what God is doing. This lesson is an important one for all of us to learn if we are to "walk in the light of his presence" and to find "our glory and strength" in God. Worship shapes who we are and how we see the world. Joining with the community of faith to offer praise to and to consider the character of our God and Savior equips us to face those experiences of life that leave us flummoxed. So, with the psalmist, we must remember that it is important to worship even when we do not really feel like it.

---

31. Tremper Longman, "רוע," *NIDOTTE* 3:1083.

Psalm 90

A prayer of Moses the man of God.

¹ Lord, you have been our dwelling place
   throughout all generations.
² Before the mountains were born
   or you brought forth the whole world,
   from everlasting to everlasting you are God.
³ You turn people back to dust,
   saying, "Return to dust, you mortals."
⁴ A thousand years in your sight
   are like a day that has just gone by,
   or like a watch in the night.
⁵ Yet you sweep people away in the sleep of death—
   they are like the new grass of the morning:
⁶ In the morning it springs up new,
   but by evening it is dry and withered.
⁷ We are consumed by your anger
   and terrified by your indignation.
⁸ You have set our iniquities before you,
   our secret sins in the light of your presence.
⁹ All our days pass away under your wrath;
   we finish our years with a moan.
¹⁰ Our days may come to seventy years,
   or eighty, if our strength endures;
yet the best of them are but trouble and sorrow,
   for they quickly pass, and we fly away.
¹¹ If only we knew the power of your anger!
   Your wrath is as great as the fear that is your due.
¹² Teach us to number our days,
   that we may gain a heart of wisdom.
¹³ Relent, LORD! How long will it be?
   Have compassion on your servants.
¹⁴ Satisfy us in the morning with your unfailing love,
   that we may sing for joy and be glad all our days.
¹⁵ Make us glad for as many days as you have afflicted us,
   for as many years as we have seen trouble.
¹⁶ May your deeds be shown to your servants,

your splendor to their children.
¹⁷ May the favor of the Lord our God rest on us;
establish the work of our hands for us—
yes, establish the work of our hands.

PSALM 90 IS SIGNIFICANT for two reasons. First, it is the only psalm in the Psalter associated with Moses in its title. Second, Psalm 90 functions as the immediate response to the huge national crisis outlined in Book 3 and, especially, Psalm 89. Book 3 (Pss 73–89) is dominated by the imagery of exile with the associated theological crises that event brought to the people. In the canonical book of Psalms, it is Psalm 90 and Book 4 (Pss 90–106) that respond to the crises of faith voiced in the previous collection. The response found in Psalm 90 sets the broad tone for much of what follows in this next collection of seventeen psalms. The decision of the editors to place a "prayer of Moses" as the response to the crisis caused by the fall of the Davidic monarchy in Psalm 89 is profound and significant. Effectively, those who gathered this collection of psalms invite the readers to look back to a time before there ever were any human kings leading Israel, to look back to the time of the birth of the nation when Moses was Israel's leader without being Israel's king. In allowing Psalm 90 to respond to Psalm 89, the editors seem to be saying: "Do not worry too much about the loss of the monarchy because Yahweh is still the true King! He was King in the time of Moses *before* David had ever been born, and he is still King now *after* the loss of the line of David. Take a long view of things and remember that Yahweh *always* reigns, regardless of the events of our human history!" The essence of Psalm 90's message is: Yahweh is King and he is our Refuge.

The Title (90:0)

A PRAYER OF MOSES THE MAN OF GOD. The simplicity of the title belies its profundity. This prayer is the only psalm associated with Moses, and that association will automatically trigger certain thoughts in the mind of the audience. It seems reasonable to assume that Book 4 was gathered together and added to Psalms 1–89 at some point during the exilic or early postexilic period. Book 3, as we have seen, is dominated by the crisis of exile, and Book 4 provides a poetic response to that historical and theological turmoil. In choosing a prayer associated with Moses as the first psalm of this collection, the editors draw their readers' attention to a time way back before the exile, before the monarchy, before even the entry into the land—a time when Yahweh in his power brought his people out from exile and defeated a superpower in doing so. If Book 4 was gathered during the exile (when the people were held in exile by the superpower of their day), it is very easy to see why this psalm was chosen to initiate this collection.

The fact that this is *"a prayer* of Moses" (emphasis added) would also be significant for the original readers of this collection because Moses's prayers were deemed to be efficacious. For example, the Lord heard Moses's plea for the people following their idolatry during the golden calf incident and appears to have turned from his original intent to destroy Israel as a result of their unfaithfulness (see Exod 32–34, esp. 33:11). Of course, there are many imponderables when it comes to the will of God and the course of human history, but in Israel's religious understanding Moses became known as a pray-er—as one whose prayers were heard and answered by God (see Ps 99:6). This reminder of God's responding to the prayers of his people would also be a significant encouragement to the exilic community because it no doubt appeared to them that their prayers recorded in Book 3 are going unanswered. The reminder that Yahweh showed mercy—even to an unfaithful people—by hearing and answering their prayers would give the community confidence that perhaps even *their* own prayers might be answered by God.

There is a third important reminder in this superscription, namely, that Moses was "a man of God." This description would be poignant for the exilic community for a couple of reasons. First, it would remind them of what their own, much-lamented kings were not. And second, it would remind the people of what they must be. Book 3 of the Psalms decries the unfairness of the exile from the perspective of the psalmists, but Book 4 begins with a reminder of the priorities that should characterize the community of faith. Their first and most important call, following Moses's example, is to be "men and women of God." It is not a complicated calling, but it is one to which they must aspire.

Psalm 90:0 is a brief and simple title, but it is profound nonetheless. It reminds the people of Yahweh's absolute rule regardless of the question of monarchy. It encourages them to think about answered prayers. And it reminds them of their calling to walk in the ways of their God.

Sovereign throughout History (90:1–6)

LORD, YOU HAVE BEEN OUR DWELLING PLACE THROUGHOUT ALL GENERATIONS. The tone for Book 4 is set with a metaphor that has provided comfort for God's people throughout the ages (Ps 90:1). The Creator God is presented as having been a place of rest and comfort for his people regardless of their circumstances throughout all generations. Jerome Creach comments,

"This statement of confidence reminds that Yahweh was a source of security and protection before Israel had a human king."[1] The juxtaposition of Psalm 90 as a response to the crisis of kingship lamented in Psalm 89 points to a deeper historical understanding that goes far beyond the most recent experience of God's people. Kingship may have been the visible sign of Yahweh's governance over the whole earth (see the discussion of Ps 89), but that is all it was—a visible sign. The loss of the human king did not change the *reality* of Yahweh's kingship in any way, shape, or form. Yahweh reigned over the whole earth before there was a David or a Davidic king, and he continues to reign following the demise of David's line. He is still—and is always—the "dwelling place" of his people. McCann points out that he is, "really, the only dwelling place that counts."[2] Jerusalem may have been seen as an impenetrable and secure place for the people—hence its loss hit them very hard (Ps 74)—but the ultimate expression of secure dwelling for Israel was never in a city but always, spiritually, in their God. Terrien writes that this idea of a dwelling place "transcends the idea of temple, sanctuary or refuge" and is "the symbol of spirituality for God's people (Pss 71:3; 91:3)."[3] The neighboring composition further elucidates the concept of Yahweh as a "dwelling place" or "refuge" in Psalm 91:9b, where the same word (*ma'on*) is used. Clearly, what is being encouraged in this verse is that the Israelites should consciously find spiritual refuge and strength in Yahweh because this practice has implications for living life in real terms.[4] And therein lies the very point of Psalm 90:1: Yahweh has always been a refuge for his people—before there was a king in Jerusalem, and now after the king has gone.

From everlasting to everlasting you are God. The essence of the people's security is found in the eternal and unchangeable nature of God (v. 2). Before the world came into being God was *'el*, the great and high Creator God and Sovereign over all he had made. This focus on the eternal nature of God contrasts strongly with the discussion of the brevity of *human* life in verses 3–6. The reminder is that the events of human history, although significant for each generation in turn, are but a moment from God's perspective and are all under his control as Creator and the one who ordains life and death.

---

1. Creach, *Yahweh as Refuge*, 94.
2. McCann, "Psalms," 1041.
3. Terrien, *Psalms*, 643.
4. McCann comments, "The relationship between Psalms 90 and 91 is established by the occurrence of the relatively rare word 'dwelling place' (*ma'on*) in Psalm 90:1 and 91:9" (McCann, "The book of Psalms," 1047).

You turn people back to dust. God's eternity gives him absolute authority over the days of humankind. The reference to returning men to dust (v. 3) appears to have a double meaning in this verse. A more literal translation of verse 3 would be, "You return men to dust, and you say, 'Return, sons of men.'" The words "to dust" in the NIV's translation of verse 3b are not actually in the original Hebrew, but they might be implied from the preceding line of the parallelism. This ambiguity means that the verse could, on the one hand, be a reference to a divine act of humbling and an ensuing call to repentance. That is, God causes humans to humble themselves—in the Old Testament, one of the frequently occurring con-notations of "dust" (*dakka'* here rather than the more common *'aphar*). After humbling the people by placing them in the dust, in verse 3b he calls his people "to return" (*shub*), which is a term often used metaphorically to symbolize repentance. So, effectively, one reading would be to see verse 3 as an act of divine subjugation followed by a call to repentance.[5] The alternative is to assume (with the NIV) that verse 3 implies the continua-tion of the indirect object ("to dust") from the first line of the verse into the second. This reading, therefore, adopts the second major connotation of "dust" in the Old Testament, namely, that all humanity is created out of dust (Gen 2:7) and that all human beings return to dust after their death (Gen 3:19). Both translations are feasible options, but given the content of the following verses that speak of the transitory nature of humanity, the latter translation seems the more likely.[6] This tone of the brevity of human life is continued in verses 3–6, where human beings are compared to the Palestinian grass: fresh and green in the cool of the morning but dry, parched, and lifeless by the evening. The message of these verses is clear: human life is brief, and then it is gone.

These opening verses contrast the eternal power of God (vv. 1–2) with the brevity of life under the divine ordinance that all human beings shall "return to dust" (v. 3; cf. Gen 3:19). The point the psalmist seems to be making is that security can only be found in the lasting strength and stability of God, whereas all people (including kings?) are marked by the frailty and temporality of the human condition. God is in control because he is the eternal Creator God.

Divine Rebuke and the Human Experience (90:7–11)

WE ARE CONSUMED BY YOUR ANGER. Attention shifts from God's eternity in the first stanza to God's anger in the second. The combination of "anger"

---

5. Alter, *Psalms*, 318.
6. See Kirkpatrick, *Psalms*, 549; and Eaton, *Psalms*, 323.

(*'aph*) and "indignation" (*hemah*) is reminiscent of the warnings in Deuteronomy about what will happen to the people if they fail to keep the covenant once they have entered the land. (Deut 29:21, 28 combine these two words.) This combination of synonyms for God's wrath is particularly poignant because the pairing of these words is associated with the warning of exile as the ultimate punishment in response to the people's continued unfaithfulness (see Deut 28–29). So, the description of God's wrath as anger that terrifies and consumes is not to be seen as capricious. These words reflect God's righteous response to the persistent rebellion of his people.[7]

You have set our iniquities before you. Psalm 90:8 gives the clear reason for the divine anger mentioned in the previous verse—human sin has provoked a response from God. The combination of the vocabulary of sin ("iniquities" and "secret sins") with the language of presence ("before you" and "in the light of your presence") exposes the real problem: How can an absolutely holy God cohabit with a sinful people? God's anger is provoked by the continuous sins—both known and unknown—of his people. As Eaton points out, "The present distress of the worshippers is now laid before God. It seems to be a protracted period of hardship; they interpret it as sent by God in anger at their sins, which he is not covering or forgiving, but keeping exposed to his judgment."[8] Psalm 85:1–3 makes it clear that forgiveness is found in Yahweh, but Psalm 90:7–8 lays out the turmoil of God's people when they do not experience that forgiveness. God's holiness provokes an angry response to sin, and verse 8 shows the people's complete dependence on the grace of God if they are to maintain relationship with him.

All our days pass away under your wrath. Experiencing God's anger simply adds to the frustration of living a brief and troubled life (vv. 9–11). Knowing that the possibility of a life well lived (e.g., see comments on Ps 89:15) is removed by God's angry response to human sin further embitters the psalmist in his view of life. A short life could be a good one if lived in happy communion with God, but a life under divine wrath is bitter and frustrating. It is both short and full of difficulty and grief (Ps 90:10), thus culminating in a groan of frustration upon death (v. 9).[9]

---

7. As Schaeffer writes, "Chronic guilt sparks the divine wrath, thus making time even more of a cause of mortals fretting" (Schaefer, *Psalms*, 227).

8. Eaton, *Psalms*, 323.

9. Verse 9b might also be translated, "We finish our years like a sigh," thus once more reflecting on the brevity of life rather than its difficulty. But the NIV's translation of *hegeh* as "moan" seems preferable because the root verb *hagah* ("to mutter, murmur, plot") always seems to have a vocal overtone.

Your wrath is as great as the fear that is your due. The psalmist cuts to the quick at the culmination of his reflection on the frustrations of life in the light of divine wrath (v. 11). Although this pithy statement is quite awkward to translate, the basic meaning seems clear enough: God's righteous anger should always provoke a response of faithfulness in his people. There are two ways to read verse 11b: "with good reason people are afraid of You because the manifestations of your anger are indeed awesome,"[10] or alternatively, "whoever truly understands the burning intensity of God's wrath will respond in faithful obedience to the measure of that anger."[11] "Fear of God" is a catchphrase borrowed from Israel's wisdom literature that signifies a holistic response to God's call to follow him (see discussion of Ps 85:9). The poet is saying that anyone who understands the full extent of God's righteous anger will respond with a sincere desire to walk in his ways by rejecting sin and striving after his holiness. This use of wisdom language in Psalm 90:11 sparks the transition from meditation to supplication.

The Prayer of the Finite (90:12–17)

As is so often the case with the psalms, there is a degree of uncertainty about the structure of Psalm 90.[12] But from verse 12 to the end of the psalm, each verse contains a direct plea of one sort or another (e.g., "teach," "relent," "have compassion," "satisfy"), thus making it more likely that verses 12–17 are meant to be read as a unit reflecting the poet's concluding prayer based on his preceding meditation.[13]

Teach us to number our days. Psalm 90:11 resonates with the language of the Old Testament wisdom literature in its call to respond to God's wrath by exercising the fear of the Lord. This wisdom overtone continues in verse 12 with the prayer that God would "teach" his people. And the focus of the prayer for instruction really reflects the totality of Psalm 90.[14] "Teach us to number our days, that we may gain a heart of wisdom" reflects the central theme of this psalm, namely, awareness of our human finitude and weakness and the importance of responding properly to that realization. The first object of the poet's supplication is that the

---

10. Alter, *Psalms*, 319.

11. Kirkpatrick, *Psalms*, 552.

12. The NIV breaks the stanza after verse 12, whereas the ESV, for example, ends the preceding stanza at verse 11.

13. These petitions take either the command form in Hebrew (e.g., "teach" [*limnot*], "relent" [*shubah*]) or a jussive form (e.g., "may the favor of the Lord our God rest on us" [*wihi no'am 'adonay 'elohenu 'alenu*]), but both forms of expression clearly represent the psalmist's petition to Yahweh.

14. Alter, *Psalms*, 319.

people of God should return to right relationship with him—the sort of relationship indicated in verse 1, where God is the sure dwelling place of his people. Verse 12b employs language of the harvest—the psalmist prays that God would teach the people awareness of their limits in order that they might "gain" (*nabi'*) a heart of wisdom.[15] Simply put, we reap a heart of godly wisdom when we approach life with prayerful awareness of our weakness and complete dependence on God.

Relent, LORD! How long will it be? The ensuing petitions follow the typical pattern of laments in the psalms, but the language used is quite different from the laments of Book 3. Those are replete with the language of complaint and a sense of the injustice. In Psalm 90:12–17, however, the poet's prayer seeks the *mercy* of God. His intercession is not based on what the people felt to be their right as a result of the promise of God; rather, he seeks the grace and mercy of God, as clearly seen in the language of the poet's requests ("relent," "have compassion," "may the favor of the Lord our God rest on us"). Combined with the language of sin, repentance, and divine wrath in the previous stanza (vv. 7–11), this change of tone in the lament of Psalm 90 is quite profound. Whereas the laments of Book 3 were focused on the profound injustice and divine abandonment felt by the people, the lament of Psalm 90 centers on the mercy of God in response to the sin of the people. The supplication of verses 12–17 is not grounded in demands based on the covenantal promises; it seeks a gracious response from God *despite* the people's sin. There is an implied awareness in Psalm 90 that the events of the exile took place as a result of Judah's sin and rejection of God. The appeal against injustice is replaced by an appeal for grace in the face of their iniquity.

Interestingly, in verse 13 we encounter the first use of the divine name, Yahweh, in Psalm 90. Until this point in the psalm, God is referred to as "Lord" or "Master" (*'adonay*) and as "God" (*'el* and *'elohim*), but here the psalmist prays to God using his covenantal name, "Yahweh," which takes the reader back into the narrative of Exodus 32–34 and the prayer of Moses (see comments on Ps 90:0 above). It is in this passage, describing the great sin of Israel in rejecting God and worshiping an idol, that Yahweh reveals his true nature in Exodus 34:6–7:

> And he passed in front of Moses, proclaiming, "The LORD, the LORD, the compassionate and gracious God, slow to anger, abounding in love and faithfulness, maintaining love to thousands, and forgiving wickedness, rebellion and sin. Yet he does not leave the guilty

---

15. Eaton, *Psalms*, 323–24.

unpunished; he punishes the children and their children for the sin of the fathers to the third and fourth generation."

So, when the poet turns from meditation to prayer he adopts the divine name, Yahweh, in remembrance of this act of self-revelation at the time of Israel's rebellion during the exodus. The resonance with Exodus 34:6–7 is twofold in its effect. It reminds the psalmist's hearers that Yahweh is, by nature, a God of grace, love, and forgiveness even when confronted by the sins of his people. But it also reminds the people that God, by nature, will punish sin. These two aspects of the divine nature must be held in tension, and the "Mosaic" nature of Psalm 90 reminds those who recite this poem that both characteristics are real in their present experience. Judah has sinned, and their present experience is the natural consequence of that behavior; but Yahweh is also a God of grace, so they can hope for and seek forgiveness despite their rebellion.

Make us glad for as many days as you have afflicted us. The focal point of the prayer in the final stanza of Psalm 90 is the return to joy. The underlying realization played out by the poet in Psalm 90 is that joy is only to be found in renewed relationship with God. The prayer for the renewal of joy is a prayer for the renewal of right relationship with Yahweh, Israel's God.

May the favor of the Lord our God rest on us. The psalm is permeated by an awareness of human frailty and rebellion, on the one hand, and divine wrath on the other. The concluding prayer of verse 17 presents the inescapable resolution to this tension: it is only by the undeserving grace of God that any relationship with the holy God can be maintained. The final supplication requests God's "favor" (*no'am*, his mercy or compassion) to be upon his people, for without that favor there is no hope of restoration to right relationship, and without right relationship there is no hope at all.

Establish the work of our hands. The prayer for grace in verse 17 is echoed in the repeated prayer that God would establish the work of the people's hands. God's grace is always evidenced in the concrete historical experiences of his people, and it is this expression of grace that the psalmist seeks. Israel frequently "punched above her weight" because of the intervention of Yahweh in her historical reality to protect and prosper his people. So, the prayer for favor is extrapolated in the prayer that God will establish the work of his people. "This is how the reality of human life appears when seen from the other side, that is, the Godward side: it is God's grace alone which gives purpose to life and durability to the work of man."[16]

---

16. Weiser, *Psalms*, 603.

THE PROBLEM OF SIN AND HUMAN SIGNIFICANCE. There is a conundrum that is voiced repeatedly throughout the Old Testament: How can a holy God dwell with a rebellious people? Psalm 90 gives us a clear presentation of the problem and the solution, as seen in the component parts of the poem: (1) God is infinite, whereas human beings are finite (vv. 1–6); (2) God is angered by the sins of his people, and that anger should inspire us to change our behavior (vv. 7–11); (3) it is only by the unwarranted favor of the covenantal God that we can experience fellowship with him and live lives that leave a godly mark on the world we live in (vv. 12–17). The solution to this problem is to be found only in God himself. Without his grace and favor there is no hope of living rightly before him and no way of making a lasting impact on the world around us.

Of course, the essential solution to the holiness and presence conundrum finds its ultimate resolution in the person and work of Jesus the Messiah. How, ultimately, could a holy God dwell with an unholy people? By becoming one of them and *literally* dwelling in their midst (John 1:14). Not only does Jesus deal with the problem of human sin definitively (Heb 9:26), but he also provides the solution to any sense of brevity and futility with regard to human life (John 10:10). In the work of Christ, our sins are taken away, thus enabling rich relationship with God. What is more, Jesus brings significance to the lives we live and to the work we seek to accomplish. Though it is probably not original to the text of Mark's Gospel, there is a lovely image at the end of Mark 16, where it is said that "the Lord worked with them" (Mark 16:20).

There is a profound sense in which the key issues of Psalm 90 are resolved in Christ, yet this resolution is not wholly accomplished. It is true that we find the forgiveness of sins, a holiness that is not our own, and eternal life through Jesus and his sacrifice, so why is it that Christians still struggle with feelings of unworthiness, finitude, and lack of purpose? The conundrum we face as Christians is similar to the one faced by the community of faith in the exilic and postexilic periods. The root of Israel's problem was that they had lost sight of their Refuge—they had forgotten that God was their "dwelling place" (Ps 90:1). The same can be true for every Christian. If we forget the work that Christ has accomplished for us, then we soon fall into the trap of worrying about life, health, purpose, and the sins we have committed. In Psalm 90 the poet encourages the people to turn again to God in his mercy because only then is relationship restored. The same is true for believers today. It is by maintaining relationship through the grace of God the Father, worked out in his Son and sealed by his Spirit, that we find a solution to the problems of our own sin and the significance of our lives. Created in the image of God and adopted as children of the King, it is by walking close to God and receiving his grace that we find significance in life regardless of its brevity and difficulty. The challenge for Israel was to allow God to be their "dwelling place" in their own hearts, and that challenge remains the same for believers today. It is only a healthy sense of dependence that brings wholeness to human life.

Prayer and the God who relents. The Hebrew word *shub* is of some significance in Psalm 90. This word, in its most literal sense, means "to turn" or "to return" (as is seen in v. 3, for example), but in the Old Testament it often functions in a metaphorical sense. We have already discussed the use of this word to signify human repentance (see the discussion of Ps 85 above), but we also see another important metaphorical use of *shub* in this composition. This same verb *shub* is used in verse 13 in the poet's intercession that God would "relent" from his punishment of the people and allow them to experience joy once again. In the poet's intercession, this choice of verb—along with many other features of this psalm—resonates with the book of Exodus, and in particular the whole issue of God's response to the golden calf incident (Exod 32–34). In Exodus we read that God is prepared to destroy the whole nation of Israel and begin a new line of his choice through Moses and his sons (Exod 32:9–10), but Moses intercedes for the people and God relents from his anger (vv. 11–14). In verse 12 of that passage Moses uses the same language that is used in Psalm 90:13 when he calls on Yahweh to "turn from your fierce anger; relent and do not bring disaster on your people." And, quite remarkably, we read in Exodus 32:14 that Yahweh heard Moses's prayer, relented (using a different word but with the same sense), and did not bring catastrophe on the people. In the same way, the psalmist has the courage to ask God to relent from his punishment and have mercy on his people.

It is a mind-blowing concept to think that the almighty God might, at the behest of one of his servants, relent from a course of action he has decided to undertake. Yet this divine response is what happened for Moses, and the author/speaker of Psalm 90 clearly also believes that it could happen again in response to the prayers of the people. Of course, we can talk about the permissive and prescriptive will of God, or we can debate the causality of an all-knowing God's undertaking to do something while knowing full well that someone would pray and he would respond to that prayer. But such philosophical discussion of predestination and the will of God somewhat misses the point. With regard to Psalm 90, the debate should not be a philosophical one, for the lesson here is clear and simple: the psalmist believes that prayer changes the very heart of God!

Now, I am aware that the words "God" and "change" in the same sentence will set alarm bells ringing in the hearts of many a theologian, but again, let us not run the risk of missing the point in Psalm 90. The psalmist's prayer does not affect God's ontology, but it does affect the reality of the poet's experience! This prayer is bold, but it is clearly one that the psalmist believes will be answered. Just as Moses the lawgiver interceded for the people and God heard, so the "Moses" of Psalm 90—the man of prayer and the man of God—fully believes that God will change the course of action he seems to have ordained at this time. The whole point is that we pray in our suffering *because* we pray to a God who relents and changes the course of human history. The psalmist's bold prayer in verses 12–17 provides the reader with a model to follow: we pray boldly because we pray to a God who, because of his grace and mercy, changes our experience.

Psalm 90 in the New Testament. There are no specific citations of Psalm 90 in the New Testament, but the philosophical themes are dealt with throughout its books. The seriousness of sin and the wrath of God are seen clearly in the suffering of Jesus in the passion narratives of the Gospels. As the apostle Peter puts it:

> Since you call on a Father who judges each person's work impartially, live out your time as foreigners here in reverent fear. For you know that it was not with perishable things such as silver or gold that you were redeemed from the empty way of life handed down to you from your ancestors, but with the precious blood of Christ, a lamb without blemish or defect. (1 Pet 1:17–19)

The problem of sin and relationship with God was dealt with conclusively in Christ Jesus, as is the issue of insignificant lives ("redeemed from the empty way of life"). Psalm 90 may not be quoted directly, but its topics of discussion certainly find their equivalents in the New Testament.

 **BRIEF LIVES.** Late on a Sunday evening BBC Radio 5 Live used to run a fascinating weekly broadcast entitled "Brief Lives." Basically, it was an obituary program looking at the lives of famous or significant people who had died during the preceding week. The title of the show was a deliberate play on words. The show itself lasted only for half an hour, so each obituary was only six or seven minutes long, but in presenting these potted summaries of people's lives there was always the sense that, regardless of how long the featured individuals had lived, their lives had been all too brief.

One of the messages of Psalm 90 is to be aware of the brevity of life (vv. 7–12). Verse 10 reads:

> Our days may come to seventy years,
>   or eighty, if our strength endures;
> yet the best of them are but trouble and sorrow,
>   for they quickly pass, and we fly away.

When we are young, the span of seventy or eighty years seems like an eternity, but as time passes we soon realize that it is not. Having entered my late forties at the time of writing these thoughts, I have become deeply aware of the things I have not yet done in my lifetime, and a sense of pressing urgency begins to creep in as I consider my life ahead. Seventy does not seem so very far away, yet there is still so much to be accomplished in life! Such thoughts would never have crossed my mind at the age of eighteen, but now, as my kids gradually leave behind their teenage years, I myself have become all too aware of the reality of "brief lives." This realization comes on us all at some point in life, and Ps 90 gives us guidance as we are confronted by the brevity of human life.

First, it is important to come to the realization arrived at by the psalmist in the second stanza of the poem. Our lives are brief and frail, and without that realization we will never adopt the right attitude of dependence on God that should characterize our every day! As human beings we are weak and sinful (vv. 7–9). It is only God who can deal with our sins (vv. 13–15), and it is he who decides exactly how long each life is going to last (v. 3). The truth of the matter is that none of us can demand our next breath, and each and every breath is a gift from God. The sooner we realize this fact, the fuller our lives will be. We often rebel against our status of "creature," yet as creatures we only find the fullness of meaning in relation to the Creator. So, a healthy awareness of our own dependence on God is the only way to view our lives properly.

Second, Psalm 90 gives us some good advice as to how we can live these brief lives well. Verses 12 and 17 are particularly significant for this purpose. Verse 12 is the first request of the psalmist's supplication: "Teach us to number our days, that we may gain a heart of wisdom." A right sense of awareness is important: "teach us to number our days." There are not so many of these days, so it is vital that we value each one of them and attribute a right sense of perspective to the daily lives we live. When we do consider the brevity of seventy years, perhaps watching that show or movie on TV is not really as important as we might think. Not that I am advocating rampant activism and drivenness, but "numbering our days" will mean that we have a sense of the important and of that which has eternal value. "Numbering our days" means that we will have a clear sense of priorities in the way we live. But the aim of "numbering our days" is to "gain a heart of wisdom." A heart of wisdom is one that is attuned to God and his will and purpose, one that seeks to live life according to the rhythms of his created order. Wisdom theology is a creational theology.[17] It is all about "how to negotiate life successfully in God's good but fallen world."[18] A heart of wisdom seeks God's pattern for life: worship, work, rest, family, good food, stunning views—all these things should play their part in a life well lived. The aim is to seek God's will and purpose for our lives day by day and to live each day in this vibrant relationship with him as our "dwelling place" (v. 1).

Third, the psalmist's closing supplication in verse 17 helps us deal with the brevity of life as well: "Establish the work of our hands for us—yes, establish the work of our hands." We all seek a sense of meaning, purpose, and significance in what we do. Whether we are homemakers or world-stage statesmen, teachers or Wall Street traders, farmers or civil servants, we all want there to be some lasting significance from our labor. Ultimately this desire is a spiritual reality. We tend to think of the aim of work as paying the bills, but God has made us for something more than that. The psalmist's closing prayer is born out of the realization that any work whose value is going to be lasting must be a work of the eternal God, who sees beyond our present generation. So our life and labor should be prayerful, for only then can we have a permanent impact on the world around us. Only by God himself, through the indwelling of his Son (John 15:5) and the work of his Spirit (1 Cor 12:11), are we able to build a spiritual legacy that goes beyond anything the world around us values. The psalmist's prayer echoes the advice of Proverbs 16:3: "Commit to the LORD whatever you do, and he will establish your plans." Only this sense of prayerful devotion to God and his purposes will lead us through lives that are brief but resonant with meaning.

17. Roland E. Murphy, *Wisdom Literature: Job, Proverbs, Ruth, Canticles, Ecclesiastes and Esther,* FOTL XIII (Grand Rapids: Eerdmans, 1981), 5.

18. Craig G. Bartholomew, *Reading Proverbs with Integrity* (Cambridge: Grove Books, 2001), 8.

Psalm 91

[1] Whoever dwells in the shelter of the Most High
will rest in the shadow of the Almighty.
[2] I will say of the LORD, "He is my refuge and my fortress,
my God, in whom I trust."
[3] Surely he will save you
from the fowler's snare
and from the deadly pestilence.
[4] He will cover you with his feathers,
and under his wings you will find refuge;
his faithfulness will be your shield and rampart.
[5] You will not fear the terror of night,
nor the arrow that flies by day,
[6] nor the pestilence that stalks in the darkness,
nor the plague that destroys at midday.
[7] A thousand may fall at your side,
ten thousand at your right hand,
but it will not come near you.
[8] You will only observe with your eyes
and see the punishment of the wicked.
[9] If you say, "The LORD is my refuge,"
and you make the Most High your dwelling,
[10] no harm will overtake you,
no disaster will come near your tent.
[11] For he will command his angels concerning you
to guard you in all your ways;
[12] they will lift you up in their hands,
so that you will not strike your foot against a stone.
[13] You will tread on the lion and the cobra;
you will trample the great lion and the serpent.
[14] "Because he loves me," says the LORD, "I will rescue him;
I will protect him, for he acknowledges my name.
[15] He will call on me, and I will answer him;
I will be with him in trouble,
I will deliver him and honor him.
[16] With long life I will satisfy him
and show him my salvation."

 WITHIN THE FLOW of Book 4 of the Psalter, Psalm 91 seems to function as a response to Psalm 90. The preceding poem focuses on the brevity and difficulty of life, whereas Psalm 91 draws the reader's attention to God's protection of his people even in the face of great adversity. One psalm does not contradict the other; they merely reflect the realities that are part of life and the life of faith. On the one hand, it is important to be aware of the fleeting and frequently challenging nature of human existence (see comments on Ps 90), but on the other hand, the believer should remember that God's real presence makes a difference in life, especially when we face trial and challenge. There are various lexical and conceptual links between Psalms 90 and 91 that confirm this association between the two compositions, and the voice of Psalm 91 that speaks of personal security drawn from relationship with God must be heard alongside Psalm 90's warning that life is brief and can be full of trouble.

Two voices are heard in Psalm 91: first the poet narrates the protection of Yahweh (vv. 1–13), including a personal declaration of his own determination to trust in God (vv. 1–2), and then Yahweh speaks words of assurance in response to the poet's trust in him (vv. 14–16).[1]

A Determined Declaration of Faith (91:1–2)

WHOEVER DWELLS IN THE SHELTER OF THE MOST HIGH. Psalm 91 begins with a very strong echo of Psalm 90. The preceding composition began with the poignant reminder that God had been a "dwelling place" for the people throughout all generations. This call to remember God's protection of his people from the time of Moses onward was in itself a response to the great crisis of Psalm 89 (see comments on Ps 90 above). Essentially, Psalm 90 served as a challenge to the hearer through encouragement to find true strength in and through relationship with Yahweh alone, regardless of how things looked on the world or local stage. The basic point being made in Psalm 90 is that God's people should look away from the apparent crisis of their present political situation and see the *ultimate* security that is theirs

---

1. See Hossfeld and Zenger, *Psalms 2*, 427–28, though Robert Alter suggests that the speaker in verse 2 is actually a third voice (*Psalms*, 321). This latter suggestion seems unlikely, since verses 3–13 seem to comprise a voice of assurance directed to the individual who makes the declaration of trust in Yahweh in verses 1–2, thus drawing these verses together as a unit (see Schaefer, *Psalms*, 227).

because of their covenantal relationship with the Creator God. Psalm 91 continues that line of thought by painting a very vivid and graphic picture of the individual who chooses to trust in Yahweh above all else.

"Dwells" (*yashab*), "shelter" (*seter*), "rest" (*lin*), and "shadow" (*tsel*) in Psalm 91:1 echo the idea of God as a "dwelling place" seen in Psalm 90:1. Psalm 90 encourages its hearers consciously to find their rest and security in God, and Psalm 91:1–2 responds with a determined declaration to do just that. As so often in the psalms, Psalm 91 begins with a simple statement of faith in the opening verse, and this statement constitutes the primary or guiding thought that summarizes the basic content of the poem. Choosing to dwell in the shelter of God Most High leads to a position of rest under his protective care. Strictly speaking, the verb that is used in verse 1b for "rest" (*lin*) conveys the idea of staying or sojourning in a particular place, thus leading some scholars to suggest that Psalm 91 is a psalm of vigil or asylum in the temple. But as Terrien suggests, Psalm 91 reflects on "the consciousness of psychological security, not a geographical construction of public worship."[2] The ideas of dwelling and resting seen in this verse do, however, indicate a degree of permanence in the attitude displayed. The psalmist is encouraging the people to be consciously and constantly aware of God's protecting presence.[3] God is described as the "Most High" (*'elyon*) and the "Almighty" (*shadday*) in this verse, and both terms reflect Yahweh's absolute authority and power, thus giving the reader reason to trust him.

I will say of the LORD, "He is my refuge and my fortress." The effect of the abstract endorsement in verse 1 is doubled in verse 2 by the psalmist's resolute declaration of his own personal determination to find protection in Yahweh. The descriptions of Yahweh as "refuge" and "fortress" give a military overtone to the protection he provides. The peoples of the ancient Near East lived under constant threat of military invasions by neighboring powers that were frequently brutal in their tactics, so the overtone of verse 2a is that Yahweh is able to protect his people from the very worst of their fears.[4] But God's shelter is guaranteed in the face of

---

2. Terrien, *Psalms*, 649.

3. Such is the extent of the poem's emphasis on divine protection that one scholar has suggested Ps 91 should be classified as an "amulet psalm," the idea's being that a reader struck by doubt would repeatedly recite this psalm to obtain a sense of God's real presence and protection (cited in Alter, *Psalms*, 321). Of course, however, people from many cultures in the ancient Near East would actually trust in amulets or charms to protect them from harm, whereas the purpose of Ps 91 is to encourage trust in Yahweh, not in trinkets or gods of wood and stone (Broyles, *Psalms*, 362–63).

4. John Goldingay, *Psalms: Volume 3, Psalms 90–150*, BCOTWP (Grand Rapids: Baker Academic, 2008), 42.

a wide variety of dangers (e.g., hunting, plague, and wild animals), thus broadening the potential areas of appropriation so that an individual could find encouragement from this poem regardless of the specific type of threat being faced.[5]

My God, in whom I trust. Verse 2b gets to the very core of the psalmist's purpose. His desire in writing this poem is to engender trust among the people of God—to generate a deeply rooted and determined desire to find their ultimate security in relationship with Yahweh rather than in any external source of security. This response seems to address the great sense of loss that is apparent in Book 3 with regard to the removal of all the external signs of covenantal promise (Jerusalem, temple, and Davidic king). The clear point of Psalm 91 is that trust must have the right object. Zion, with its temple and king, was the external, visible sign of Yahweh's presence on earth, but the removal of the sign does not equate with the removal of the reality. The signs of the covenant were never intended to be objects of trust in and of themselves—they all served to point people to the deeper reality that was to be found in relationship with Yahweh himself. So, the declaration of verse 2b is a clear statement of proper focus. It is not enough that the people have trust, for faith is not an abstract entity. It is the object of their trust that is important: God himself, and nothing less.

Divine Protection in the Face of Trial (91:3–13)

FOLLOWING THE OPENING FOCAL STATEMENT of faith, the next two stanzas (vv. 3–8 and 9–13) outline in vivid detail the protection God provides for his people.[6]

Surely he will save you. Herein lies the overriding thought of verses 3–13—surely Yahweh, the God of the covenant, will rescue his people regardless of the danger that threatens them. The "he" of the sentence is emphatic. Again, the poet is being explicit about the correct *object* of one's trust. He then goes on in verses 3–8 to paint a picture of a world full of a wide variety of dangers. The imagery speaks of "the fowler's snare" and "deadly pestilence," which suggest threat from the devious plotting of other people or from endemic disease. Either way, Yahweh ensconces his people under the protection of his wings (v. 4)—the imagery of a mother bird's protecting her young from attack.

---

5. Broyles, *Psalms*, 361.
6. Each stanza begins with the Hebrew preposition *ki* ("for") and contains a description of the individual's faith combined with the promise of divine protection and the believer's security (Hossfeld and Zenger, *Psalms 2*, 428; Broyles, *Psalms*, 361).

You will not fear the terror of night. Verses 5–6 elaborate the variety of dangers that can target the believer: the unnamed terrors of night or the arrows of military attack (v. 5) or the invisible danger of rampant and deadly illness (v. 6) that cuts a swath through the people (vv. 7–8). The point of this graphic imagery, of course, is that the life of the believer need not be spent in fear and worry. Although the future may well contain untold dangers, the believer's trust is in the God who is Most High and Almighty. He is in control of every experience, so the individual who trusts in him need not live a life marked by fear of the future.

You will only observe with your eyes. Each of the two stanzas in this section of Ps 91 ends with a description of the believer's status in the thick of surrounding turmoil. Verse 8a describes the one who trusts in Yahweh as an *observer* of the effects of tragedy on the world. Such is the extent of God's protection of his people that the petitioner merely looks on as the events of divine judgment are worked out around him. The reason for this removal from the tragedies taking place seems to be explained in verse 8b. "And see the punishment of the wicked" seems to imply that the tragic events affecting so many people (v. 7) are all under God's control because they are his interventions into the history of humankind. Because the person of faith has taken Yahweh's side—and by implication lives in accordance with his ways rather than rejecting them—he is protected from God's hand of punishment on those who refuse to live in line with their Creator's sense of justice. As Zenger points out, we get an insight into the implied scenario in these verses: "The petitioner feels himself alone, persecuted, physically and mentally threatened in the midst of an environment experienced as hostile and criminal—and in this very environment he seeks strength and confidence in and with his God."[7]

If . . . you make the Most High your dwelling. The second stanza in this section of Psalm 91 reprises the themes of the first with an even more elevated expression of divine protection. Although this verse is quite difficult to translate,[8] its point is clear: God must be a dwelling place for his people, a refuge and place of security even in dark and troubled times. This act is a spiritual one—the adoption of an attitude of mind and heart that

---

7. Hossfeld and Zenger, *Psalms* 2, 431.

8. There is some discussion as to whether the text should be read as "my refuge" (v. 9a) or "your refuge," which, arguably, makes the sentence read more smoothly (see NRSV). Either way, the Hebrew is awkward, and some imagination has to be exercised to make sense of the sentence whichever option one chooses. It is possible that the psalmist is using the terms "Most High," "Yahweh," and "my refuge" as synonyms, as is suggested in the NIV (Goldingay, *Psalms* 3, 46).

transcends all present circumstances. Schaefer points out that although this imagery may find its roots in the asylum afforded by the temple, verse 9 points to a spiritual reality that transcends the physical protection offered by the temple courts. "The image enlarges the horizon beyond time and space. Anyone who trusts in God has the right to asylum. Thus, any person within the faith community may be addressed. The sanctuary is transcended (v. 9); 'the Lord' and 'the Most High' is our refuge and support."[9]

No harm will overtake you. Verse 10 goes beyond the suggested specifics of the previous stanza. Rather than implying that God protects his people from one type of harm or another, the poet states that no harm will befall the one who trusts in Yahweh, nor will it even approach that person's home—a remarkably all-encompassing assurance.

For he will command his angels concerning you. The spirituality of the idea of refuge in God comes to the fore in the promise of angelic protection, and these verses are probably making a deliberate association with God's protection of his people during the exodus from Egypt (Exod 23:20–23; 33:2). Of course, if Psalm 91 was written, or at least recited, during the period of the exile, these words would have been particularly poignant and seen as a promise of God's protection on the long journey home to Jerusalem ("your ways," "strike your foot against a stone").[10] But the concept of pilgrimage and journey had become largely spiritualized by the time the book of Psalms was finalized, so these promises were likely to be read as the assurance of divine help for the community of faith as they sought to live out Yahweh's purposes on earth, even in an environment that had become hostile to his will and purpose. With this spiritualized concept of pilgrimage in mind, "your ways" came to be seen as a reference to lifestyle, and "striking feet against stones" would be seen as a metaphor for the obstacles one faces in daily life.

You will tread on the lion and the cobra. Just as verse 8 closed out the first stanza of this section with a statement of the petitioner's status as observer, so also verse 13 concludes with the image of the believer as victor. The reference to "lion," "cobra," "great lion," and "serpent" may, of course, simply refer to the types of natural danger that pilgrims would face on their way to Jerusalem. But references to wild animals in the Psalter frequently have metaphorical overtones—the serpent in particular often symbolizes the forces of chaos that threaten the created order (e.g., see the

---

9. Schaefer, *Psalms*, 229.

10. Broyles suggests an early origin to this psalm and points out that this language would be appropriate to the community pilgrimages to celebrate the great feasts in Jerusalem (Broyles, *Psalms*, 362).

discussion of Ps 74:14 above). "The lions and serpents in verse 13 may be a symbolic representation of *all* actual and potential enemies and dangers."[11] Whether literal or symbolic, verse 13 presents the believer as triumphant over these troubles. The language of "treading" and "trampling" frequently symbolizes military victory, thus granting the one who takes refuge in Yahweh a particular status: he comes to represent "the one who fights against chaos."[12] So throughout verses 3–13 there is a transformation of the believer from one who is constantly buffeted by the dangers and misfortunes of life to one who triumphs over these selfsame challenges, thus bringing order out of chaos.

Yahweh's Assurance of Protection (91:13–16)

THE FINAL STANZA OF PSALM 91 affirms the statements of faith made in the preceding verses by introducing an oracle spoken by God that confirms the grand claims of the preceding verses. Gerstenberger describes these verses as "the most spectacular final part of Psalm 91,"[13] and there is indeed something quite astonishing in hearing these words of remarkable assurance from "God's lips."

"Because he loves me . . . I will rescue him." The NIV adds the words "says the LORD" in order to make the change of speaker absolutely clear. But we have already seen different voices within the psalm, and none of them are explicitly marked (vv. 2, 9). It becomes immediately apparent who the speaker is, given the language of these verses (e.g., "acknowledges my name," "call on me," "with long life I will satisfy him"), so perhaps this addition is not really necessary. The "rhetorical" transformation is remarkable because it moves the poem from making statements of faith *about* God and his protection to statements *from* God about his protection. This shift brings a whole new level of certainty to the reader's experience of Psalm 91. It is one thing to be encouraged by the poet to believe these things; it is quite another experience to hear this promised protection in the form of a prophetic word "directly" from God. Concepts of faith and assurance blur as the Most High comes down to offer a level of assurance that goes beyond anything the psalmist could engender even with his fine words and images.

I will be with him in trouble. Here we find the very essence of the concept of divine protection: God is with his people even in their distress (v. 15b). The accusation of so many of the psalms of lament found in Book 3

---

11. Anderson, *Psalms*, 659.

12. Hossfeld and Zenger, *Psalms 2*, 431.

13. Erhard S. Gerstenberger, *Psalms, Part 2; and Lamentations*, FOTL XV (Grand Rapids: Eerdmans, 2001), 166.

of the Psalter (Pss 73–89) is that their God was absent. Where was he . . . when the city fell . . . when the temple was violated . . . when the people were dying? The assurance that rings out from the divine oracle of Psalm 91:14–16 speaks precisely to this issue because it speaks of a covenantal God who is *never* absent from those who take refuge in him, and especially not in their times of greatest distress. He does hear and answer prayers (v. 15a). He does protect and rescue all those who *know* (NIV *acknowledge*) him (v. 14). He does save and honor all those who love him (v. 15c). And perhaps most poignantly of all, Psalm 91 closes with a voice of assurance that responds to the great uncertainty of Psalm 90. Did not Psalm 90 remind the pray-er that life is short and full of difficulty (v. 10)? Surely it is, yet Psalm 91 closes with the promise of God that he will *satisfy* his people "with long life" and help them as they live it out. This final imagery speaks of a life that is full and rich, of one that experiences God's practical help throughout its entire length (the implication of "salvation" language in the Psalter).

PSALM 91 IN THE NEW TESTAMENT. One of the fascinating aspects of Psalm 91 is, of course, that it becomes the subject of a theological debate between Jesus and the devil in the Gospels. Both Matthew and Luke include a detailed account of Satan's attempts to derail Jesus' ministry before it really gets going (Matt 4:1–11; Luke 4:1–13). Satan can never be accused of being slow on the uptake, so—having been rebuked by Jesus, using Scripture—the devil attempts to deflect Jesus from the purposes of his Father by quoting Scripture, and it is Psalm 91:11–12 that he chooses for this purpose. Though the order of the verbal exchange is different in each of the Gospel accounts, the conversation surrounding Psalm 91 is essentially the same. Luke 4:9–12 describes this fascinating scenario in this way:

> The devil led [Jesus] to Jerusalem and had him stand on the highest point of the temple. "If you are the Son of God," he said, "throw yourself down from here. For it is written:
>
> > 'He will command his angels concerning you
> >   to guard you carefully;
> > they will lift you up in their hands,
> >   so that you will not strike your foot against a stone.'"
>
> Jesus answered, "It is said: 'Do not put the Lord your God to the test.'"

One of the interesting things about this exchange is that, on one level, the devil's use of Psalm 91 seems quite appropriate. Clearly, the basic message of this poem is that God protects his people from harm, and superficially this protection seems to be the object of his challenge to Jesus. But Jesus' rebuttal of Satan's argument shows clearly that Christ views the devil's use of Scripture as a perversion of the real intent of Psalm 91. Jesus responds by quoting from Deuteronomy 6:16. The broad context of this passage revolves around the challenge to love God above all else, and the particular expression of devotion to him should be displayed in trusting him even when circumstances do not look good.[14] Interestingly, the following verses of Deuteronomy 6 focus on the importance of obedience to God's command and leading as an expression of the people's love for him. And this obligation of obedience seems to be the essence of Satan's deliberate misinterpretation of Psalm 91.

It is interesting that in both Matthew's Gospel and in Luke's account of the same story, the devil's citation of verses 11–12 is incomplete. Matthew 4:6 omits the entire phrase "to guard you in all your ways," and in Luke 4:10 the phrase becomes "to guard you carefully." In both versions of the temptation account, the devil omits the phrase "in all your ways." This omission is telling because in this phrase we encounter the essence of the promise of Psalm 91. As discussed above, the idea of "your ways" reflects the normality of everyday life and lifestyle. The wisdom language of "the way," though possibly originating in a pilgrimage setting as far as Psalm 91 is concerned, is in later biblical Hebrew thought often used as shorthand for the way in which one lives one's life. This usage nuances the all-encompassing promises of Psalm 91 since the assurance, therefore, seems to refer to divine presence and protection as we go about the business of living for God in our everyday routine.

Satan seeks evidence of God's presence and protection in the spectacular. The underlying suggestion is that evidence *is required* in order to prove God's presence and protection. Effectively, the devil attempts to sow seeds of doubt in the mind of God's Son. Jesus' response is telling because the context of the verse he quotes (Deut 6:16) recognizes that the claims of the nations regarding their gods may sow seeds of doubt in the mind of Israel. Whereas Israel failed and ran after the benefits promised by these foreign gods, Jesus stood strong because he trusted in the promise and character of his Father, thus requiring no spectacular affirmation of a reality he knew to exist.[15]

---

14. Wright, *Deuteronomy*, 102–3.
15. Félix García López, "Le Roi d'Israel: Dt 17,14–20," in *Das Deuteronomium: Entstehung, Gestalt und Botschaft*, ed. N. Lohfink (Leuven: Leuven University Press, 1985), 332.

Effectively, Jesus believed the promise of Psalm 91 without requiring proof of its veracity. Accepting the devil's challenge would imply that Jesus doubted his Father was really present and involved in the undertaking he was about to begin. Knowing his Father as he did, Jesus required no external verification of the reality of God's presence and help:

> It is not the content of the devil's address that is wrong, but his aim is to "tempt God," and this is not in accordance with the nature of the Son of God. Reading the context of Psalm 91 we find that the pious one who is searching for God's protection (91:2, 9a) is the one who will be protected; protection is connected with piety and faith. Piety, faith and obedience . . . are evoked by quoting Deuteronomy 6. By refusing the aim of the devil, Jesus is characterized as the true Son of God who is obedient.[16]

The aim of Psalm 91 is to encourage all God's people to employ a quiet and simple trust in him, regardless of how threatening our circumstances may feel. Psalm 91 is not the poetic meditation of a spiritual kamikaze; it is the call to trust in God's presence and help even when everything around us screams that he is not real and not involved. Psalm 91 helps the believer to remember that God is both near to us and intimately engaged with our reality.

WHEN BAD THINGS HAPPEN TO GOOD PEOPLE. The amazing claims of Psalm 91 are a challenge for any Christian believer who looks around his or her church congregation. At least these claims are a challenge for any *honest* observer of the life of faith. How can we reconcile the great promises of protection with the difficulties believers face in the reality of daily life? In the days that I write these lines, ten fieldworkers from an aid agency with a Christian ethos have been killed in Afghanistan—Psalm 91 seems to have been patently untrue in

---

16. Michael Labahn, "The Psalms in Q," in *The Psalms in the New Testament*, ed. S. Moyise and M. J. J. Menken (London: T&T Clark, 2004), 52. Chris Wright comments in a similarly helpful manner: "The suggestion that [Jesus] should 'prove' God's protective commitment to him by jumping off the temple in Jerusalem when he still had ringing in his ears the voice of his Father God, with its combination of recognition, approval, and commissioning, was rightly resisted as utterly out of line with the command of Deuteronomy 6:16. Where Israel, God's first-born son (Exod 4:22), had so often distrusted and disobeyed, in spite of spectacular demonstrations of God's benevolence, the Son of God would trust and obey" (Wright, *Deuteronomy*, 102–3).

their experience. What of the suffering church in North Korea? What do believers tortured for their faith make of the promise that "no harm will overtake you" (v. 10)? And we all know fine Christian women and men of faith who labor under great suffering from illness or loss or a thousand different challenges in their daily reality. What can Psalm 91 mean in the light of the heart-rending human tragedies that people of faith from every background and culture face every day?

Such has been the challenge in reconciling the words of Psalm 91 with the reality of Christian experience that it has led some to question the continuing validity of the Old Testament for the Christian faith.[17] Broyles is quick, and probably correct, to point out that the extent of the divine promise in verses 14–16 is more circumspect than the claims made by the poet in verses 1–13.[18] Yet this observation does not ease the tension, for there is no sense in which the divine pronouncement corrects or denies the content of the preceding stanzas. Anyone reading Psalm 91 as a whole will naturally read it as an assurance of God's protection and—far from minimizing the effect of this assurance—the effect of the prophetic oracle in verses 14–16 strengthens that prescription. So how can we reconcile Psalm 91 with the reality of our experience? Does the composition simply consist in poetic hyperbole?

Clearly a degree of hyperbole is implied in the language of this poem, but that implication, in and of itself, is not sufficient to provide a resolution to the tension we face in reconciling the theological content of Psalm 91 and the frequent bitterness of Christians' human experience. In order to understand the core theological message of Psalm 91, we need to ground ourselves in the rhetoric of the poem. Picking up on the imagery of Psalm 90, the poet's desire is to engender in the hearer an attitude of conscious refuge in God—an attitude of rest in God in the face of a turbulent present. The fact that the present experience of the reader/hearer of the psalm may be turbulent is clearly seen in the language and expectations of Psalm 90 but is also present in the multiplicity of threats that are outlined in Psalm 91 itself. Psalm 91's promise ultimately is that God will be present, not that life will be easy. Yet the promise of deliverance and salvation is still there in verses 15–16, and clearly this experience is not universal for God's people.

It is possible, and perhaps even necessary, to spiritualize the promise of absolute protection so that it becomes entirely about the ultimate salvation

---

17. See the discussion in Hossfeld and Zenger, *Psalms 2*, 433. Yet, as Erich Zenger points out, the voice of Ps 91 is echoed in summary in Rom 8:28–31.

18. Broyles, *Psalms*, 362–63.

that is the reality for all believers in Christ. Yet it is not clear that Old Testament believers had such a strong sense of certainty regarding life after death. The Old Testament points to a confidence in God's ultimate justice, but the whole question of "life after death" was shady and uncertain before the coming of Christ and his resurrection. So how then can we reconcile Psalm 91 with Christians' experience of hardship?

The answer to this difficult question is rooted in one of the many mysteries of the interface between spiritual reality and human life. It is perhaps best illustrated by the words of Hananiah, Mishael, and Azariah—or, as they are better known, Shadrach, Meshach, and Abednego. In Daniel 3 (vv. 16–18), when these three men are confronted with the palpable human reality of being thrown into a furnace, they responded to the dictator, Nebuchadnezzar, in this manner:

> Shadrach, Meshach and Abednego replied to him, "King Nebuchadnezzar, we do not need to defend ourselves before you in this matter. If we are thrown into the blazing furnace, the God we serve is able to deliver us from it, and he will deliver us from Your Majesty's hand. But even if he does not, we want you to know, Your Majesty, that we will not serve your gods or worship the image of gold you have set up."

God's intervention into the affairs of humanity is invariably shrouded in mystery.[19] The response of Daniel's friends reflects an understanding that echoes the aim of Psalm 91. God saves. He does intervene in the reality of human affairs to help his people, but when and how he does so is entirely his choice and subject to his sovereign purpose. Effectively, Psalm 91 declares with Shadrach, Meshach, and Abednego, "he is able to deliver us" (Dan 3:17; cf. Ps 91:3); but correct interpretation of this poem also acknowledges that sometimes, in accordance with God's understanding, which is higher than ours, he chooses not to do so. Psalm 91, however, is clear that in every ultimate sense God saves his people. At times he evidences this salvation in human history.[20] Sometimes he does not. But either way his people can be at rest and take refuge in him because they need not fear even the most difficult of human experiences (v. 5).

Faith that attempts. On the one hand, Psalm 91 sparks questions about the interface of our theology and our experience. But on the other hand,

---

19. In all likelihood, God's presence and protection is often at work in our lives behind the scenes, even when we are entirely unaware of his providential help.

20. So it would be wrong to view Ps 91 purely in terms of a spiritual guarantee, for the poem points to a God who impinges upon human reality.

the intent of the psalmist who penned it was to instill great confidence into the hearts of all those who take up the words of this psalm as their own. Rowland Prothero describes the effect that singing Psalm 91 had in the life of Theodore de Beza, one of the second generation of Reformation leaders who faced great persecution in France:

> In 1548, when he, for the first time, attended the service of the Reformed Assembly, the congregation was singing Ps xci, "Whoso dwelleth under the defence of the Most High shall abide under the shadow of the Almighty." He never forgot the effect of the words. They supported him in all the difficulties of his subsequent life; they conquered his fears, and gave him the courage to meet every danger.[21]

The effect that Psalm 91 had on Beza was precisely the type of effect that it should have on us. The great promises of Psalm 91 should give us great courage to step out in faith and attempt things for the kingdom of God. It is a poem that we should allow to permeate our beings, so that it gives us strength to witness with great courage and to speak with a prophetic voice even in a hostile world. William Carey, who is often described as the father of modern missions, once said: "Expect great things from God and attempt great things for God."[22] Psalm 91 gives us every confidence to do the former and great courage to do the latter.[23]

---

21. Rowland E. Prothero, *The Psalms in Human Life* (London: Nelson, 1903), 173.
22. See Timothy C. Tennant, "William Carey as Missiologist: An Assessment," in *Expect Great Things, Attempt Great Things: William Carey and Adoniram Judson, Missionary Pioneers*, eds. A. Yeh and C. Chun (Eugene, OR: Wipf & Stock, 2013), 16–20.
23. López, "Le Roi d'Israel," 331.

Psalm 92

A psalm. A song. For the Sabbath day.

¹ It is good to praise the LORD
  and make music to your name, O Most High,
² proclaiming your love in the morning
  and your faithfulness at night,
³ to the music of the ten-stringed lyre
  and the melody of the harp.
⁴ For you make me glad by your deeds, LORD;
  I sing for joy at what your hands have done.
⁵ How great are your works, LORD,
  how profound your thoughts!
⁶ Senseless people do not know,
  fools do not understand,
⁷ that though the wicked spring up like grass
  and all evildoers flourish,
  they will be destroyed forever.
⁸ But you, LORD, are forever exalted.
⁹ For surely your enemies, LORD,
  surely your enemies will perish;
  all evildoers will be scattered.
¹⁰ You have exalted my horn like that of a wild ox;
  fine oils have been poured on me.
¹¹ My eyes have seen the defeat of my adversaries;
  my ears have heard the rout of my wicked foes.
¹² The righteous will flourish like a palm tree,
  they will grow like a cedar of Lebanon;
¹³ planted in the house of the LORD,
  they will flourish in the courts of our God.
¹⁴ They will still bear fruit in old age,
  they will stay fresh and green,
¹⁵ proclaiming, "The LORD is upright;
  he is my Rock, and there is no wickedness in him."

Original Meaning

PSALM 92 SHOULD BE READ in parallel with Psalm 73, for it looks at the same sort of circumstances but from a slightly different perspective. Psalm 73 is dominated by its opening voice of lament, whereas Psalm 92 has all the characteristics of a hymn of praise. Yet these two poems arrive at the same conclusion: the righteous win out in the end, regardless of how it appears at any given moment in time. Of course, each psalm represents the psalmist's particular journey to this conclusion, and each poem is the legitimate expression of the poet's relationship with Yahweh at the time of writing. In Psalm 73, deep crisis leads to a position of faith by way of vocal lament. In Psalm 92, the psalmist approaches the same question from a position of faith at the outset. These different perspectives probably represent the differing ways believers come at the question of the prosperity of the wicked at various times and stages of life: sometimes it appears that the wicked are winning out all too easily in society (Ps 73), whereas on other occasions we have faith to "see" that the wicked will not win out in the end (Ps 92). So, either one of these psalms may voice our perspective depending on where we are at spiritually.

The Title (92:0)

PSALM 92 IS DESCRIBED AS A PSALM "for the Sabbath day," but there is no obvious link with the Sabbath in terms of the poem's content. The title may simply reflect the composition's use during Sabbath services at some point in its history. Psalm 92 is the only psalm with a Sabbath-related title—a surprising fact when one considers the Psalter's association with Israel's worship. Some commentators suggest that Psalm 92's link with the Sabbath points to a sort of eternal, eschatological rest rather than to the Sabbath day.[1] Given the poem's overtones of final judgment and the blessing of the righteous in the presence of Yahweh, this suggestion is quite possibly the case.[2]

The Joy of Praise (92:1–3)

IT IS GOOD TO PRAISE THE LORD. Psalm 92 begins with a fundamental statement of deep satisfaction: "It is good to praise/give thanks to the LORD!" There is a simplicity to the summary statement that begins the psalm. While he is aware of the complexities of life (as is evidenced by all the discussion of the prosperity of the wicked that follows), the poet begins with a bare statement of fact: it is a good thing to praise the living God! This goodness has been his experience of worship, and the joyful simplicity of that practice of praise shapes the opening thoughts of this poem.

---

1. Hossfeld and Zenger, *Psalms* 2, 437; Schaefer, *Psalms*, 230.

2. Zenger points to an early Jewish tradition in the Mishnah that reads Ps 92 eschatologically: "The commentary in *m. Tamid* 7.4: 'A psalm, a song for the future that is coming, for the day that is altogether a Sabbath of rest for eternal life.'" See Hossfeld and Zenger, *Psalms* 2, 437 n. 5.

And make music to your name, O Most High. The psalmist's delight in praise is vocal, musical, and noisy! This praise is not quiet or understated—it is vibrant, colorful, and exuberant. So, his praise of the Lord is combined with "making music,"[3] "proclamation," and more music on the "ten-stringed lyre" and the "harp."[4]

Proclaiming your love in the morning. Verse 2 provides the rationale for the poet's assessment of praise as good. It is good to praise Yahweh because of Yahweh's good character. Morning and night (a merism that implies "at all times"), God is steadfast in his love and faithfulness. For this reason it is good to praise God, because he is truly a God who is worthy to receive praise. In the ancient Near East it was common to praise gods for fear that they might turn nasty at any moment. Praise was offered because the gods could be capricious, and if their egos were not massaged they could turn against the people.[5] But it is good to praise Israel's God because he himself is good.

Works, Thoughts and Judgment (92:4–8)

YOU MAKE ME GLAD BY YOUR DEEDS, LORD. The second stanza gives a more detailed rationale for the psalmist's great willingness to praise. Just as it is good to praise God because of his character (v. 2), so also the works of the Lord give the psalmist reason to delight in worship. In the Old Testament, the idea of the Lord's deeds or actions is associated with either (1) the mighty works of God (creation, the exodus, etc.) or (2) God's saving work in the life of an individual. Given the personal declaration of praise in these verses, it is likely the latter that is in mind here. The positive experience of divine intervention has led the poet to this position of happiness. God has worked in his behalf, and he finds great gladness in this realization.

I sing for joy at what your hands have done. This recognition of God's presence and personal help fills the speaker with a level of determination regardless of circumstances. The verb here may be read as either habitual or future action, that is, the poet generally *sings* for joy because of the works of God's hands or he *will sing* for joy in the future because of

---

3. The verb used here is *zamar*, from which is derived the Hebrew term for a "psalm" (*mizmor*). It is not absolutely clear whether this word refers to making music or singing praise, but either way something vibrant and noisy is in mind (see *HALOT* 2:273).

4. Again, it is not clear precisely which instruments are in view in verse 3, but there is a strong sense of musicality behind the psalmist's declaration of praise. Zenger comments, "The types of lyre mentioned in v. 4 project the picture of a great orchestra, with v. 4b even indicating different performance techniques" (Hossfeld and Zenger, *Psalms* 2, 437).

5. Walton, *ANE Thought*, 105–12.

his awareness of God's help.[6] Both options are grammatically possible, but, given the future focus of the following verses, verse 4b may well be read as a defiant declaration of a stable, future hope regardless of the prospect of difficult circumstances to come.

How great are your works, LORD, how profound your thoughts! Not only are the Lord's works a great encouragement, so are his thoughts. The reference to the thoughts of Yahweh seems to apply specifically to the verses that follow, that is, to the divine perspective on reality that goes beyond the human perspective. Echoing the discussion found in Psalm 73, the poet ponders the difficult issue of the justice of God and the prosperity of the unjust. Some see the apparent well-being of the blatantly wicked oppressor as proof of a godless human reality. Psalm 92, however, summarizes the essence of the issue in a straightforward manner: God's thoughts are higher than a human's thoughts, and anyone who fails to realize this truth is nothing other than a fool (vv. 5–6).

Though the wicked spring up like grass . . . they will be destroyed forever. The author of Psalm 92 has none of the angst that is displayed in Psalm 73's consideration of the same issue. No crisis of faith is implied in Psalm 92. The poet sees a spiritual reality that goes beyond the observable circumstances of the world around about him and has every confidence that God's justice will be established unequivocally and for all time (v. 7). John Eaton comments, "The 'works' that give rise to the praise are now indicated a little more fully. They concern the judgment of the evildoers— judgment hidden, mysterious, sometimes apparently long delayed, but yet sure and inevitable."[7] The NIV's rendering of this verse does not quite reflect the full force of the psalmist's statement, which seems to imply a causal relationship between the prosperity of the wicked and their punishment to follow. The Hebrew text of verse 7 is perhaps better translated, "When the wicked spring up like grass and all the evil-doers flourish it is so that they might be destroyed forever."[8] This difference may seem relatively slight from a linguistic perspective, but the net effect is to present a strong image of Yahweh as just Judge. More than that, so embedded is Yahweh's justice in his created order that it must inevitably come to the fore when injustice is perpetrated within that creation. The psalmist seems to suggest that the only possible purpose of the prosperity of the wicked is

---

6. See Goldingay, *Psalms 3*, 55.

7. Eaton, *Psalms*, 330.

8. Broyles, *Psalms*, 365. Broyles points out that the Hebrew text "lacks the concessive **though**."

to establish once again the indisputable righteousness and the all-powerful judgment of Yahweh as King of the universe.

The imagery associated with time in this verse is also interesting. The wicked "spring up like grass," an image that refers to the sudden flourishing of grasses and plant life after rains or heavy morning dew in the Middle East. But just as the sudden appearance of such grass is surprising, so equally the brevity of its existence is stark, as it is burned up by the strong, daytime, Palestinian sun.[9] The poet's point is unmistakable. In this imperfect world in which we live, those who reject God's ways may indeed prosper, but they will do so only for a moment, whereas their punishment is long lasting.

But you, LORD, are exalted forever. Whatever exaltation oppressors may enjoy in this world, it is brief and ultimately empty. The Creator King, however, will always be praised (vv. 1–3) because of his justice (v. 7), because of his intervention into the real lives of human beings (vv. 4–5), and because of his good character (v. 2). In every generation there arise those who exalt themselves and demand the praise of their peers because of their great power or influence. But history teaches us that such tyrants, tycoons, and superstars are little more than blips on the radar of time. The eternal Creator, on the other hand, is praised forever because he is forever good and he is forever King.

The Fall of the Lord's Enemies (92:9–11)

FOR SURELY YOUR ENEMIES, LORD . . . WILL PERISH. Psalm 92 evidences the poet's certainty of what the author of Psalm 73 comes to see only eventually. In Psalm 92 the poet is confident of the demise of the wicked and sure of their ultimate fate—things the author of Psalm 73 came to see only after an encounter with God in the place of worship (Ps 73:17). The unnamed author of Psalm 92 takes the long view on present circumstances and, based on his knowledge of God's character, is confident that those who are unjust can never prosper in any ultimate sense under the rule and economy of a just God. The idea of the perishing of the wicked seems to be deliberately ambiguous. It may refer to the expectation that those who wield the sword will perish by the sword (as is so often evidenced in the machinations of kingship and succession in the books of Kings and Chronicles; e.g., see the fate of Zimri in 1 Kgs 16). But as seen in the previous stanza, Psalm 92 displays an absolute certainty that the wicked will *inescapably* face judgment at some point under the divine economy

---

9. Goldingay, *Psalms 3*, 57.

(cf. v. 7). The evildoers who appear to flourish (v. 7) will certainly meet their just deserts at some point in the future.[10]

You have exalted my horn like that of a wild ox. Just as the passing nature of injustice is emphasized in this strophe, so also the blessing and stability of the righteous comes to the fore as the concomitant effect of divine intervention in the events of this world. This idea becomes the focal point of the following strophe (vv. 12–15), but a foretaste of this theme is voiced in contrast to the ultimate demise of those who oppose Yahweh (v. 10; cf. vv. 9, 11). The metaphor of the horn in Old Testament poetic language can have several referents: strength (Ps 18:2), the strong one (often a reference to the king; e.g., Ps 89:17), or dignity/honor (Ps 112:9). Here the metaphor seems to apply to God-given strength that enables the psalmist to face up to the challenges of those who are hostile to God and his followers. The "wild ox" (*re'em*) is probably a reference to the auroch, a now-extinct wild bull common in the Syrian mountain region.[11] In the ancient Near East the bull was often used to symbolize power and military victory (cf. Deut 33:17).

Fine oils have been poured on me. There is quite a contrast between the imagery of strength and victory in the bull (v. 10a) and the imagery of tranquil celebration in the pouring of oils (v. 10b). It is possible that the imagery in verse 10b is meant as a royal reference and that the anointing of the king is what the poet has in mind here.[12] But the verb employed is probably *balal* (to moisten)[13] rather than *mashah*, which is more typically used when the anointing of individuals to offices is in mind. The use of *balal* suggests an act of hospitality and refreshment—the pouring of oils on an honored guest.[14] So the imagery combines to describe the strength and restoration of the believer at the hand of Yahweh. He intervenes in a hostile world to provide strength and to refresh his once-wearied people.[15]

---

10. The idea of *scattering* (v. 9) is often associated with judgment imagery in the Psalter (e.g., see Ps 1:4–5). The idea of scattering seems to correspond to notions of power and permanence. The wicked often abuse the power they hold and seem unshakable in their positions of social control. But from God's perspective they are but chaff—lightweight, ephemeral, and passing—scattered by the slightest of winds.

11. Eaton, *Psalms*, 330.

12. Ibid.

13. There is a degree of complexity involved in reconstructing the verb here (see Th. Booij, "Psalm CXXXIX: Text, Syntax, Meaning," *VT* LV.1 [2005]: 1–19), and if the root verb is *balal*, then the form is slightly awkward but not impossible (see Eaton, *Psalms*, 330).

14. Schaefer, *Psalms*, 231.

15. Goldingay, *Psalms 3*, 57.

My eyes have seen the defeat of my adversaries. Verse 11 is awkward inasmuch as there is no explicit mention of either the "defeat" or the "rout" noted in the NIV's translation of this verse. Literally, the Hebrew reads, "My eye has seen my adversaries, those wicked ones rising up against me, my ears have heard." There is no explicit notice of what it is that the poet has seen and heard regarding his enemies. This lack leads to a variety of approaches and translations among the commentators, but it is probably best to infer that what the psalmist "saw" was the defeat of his enemies and what he "heard" were the sounds associated with that defeat. Schaefer comments, "Just as the wicked thrive, their tragic and sudden end has been determined, and this is in sharp contrast to the righteous destined for God's loving regard. The poet is an ear and eyewitness to this fact (v. 11)."[16] Whatever was involved in the seeing and hearing by the poet, it is linked to the judgment brought about by God (v. 9). Interestingly, Yahweh's enemies (v. 9) have become the psalmist's enemies in verse 11. But we should probably not read too much into this development. Perhaps it simply implies that all enemies of Yahweh are necessarily enemies of those who side with Yahweh. Or perhaps verse 11 is a specific word of testimony that affirms the general principle—the poet has seen God's judgment worked out in his own historical reality.

The Righteous Flourish (92:12–15)

THE RIGHTEOUS WILL FLOURISH LIKE A PALM TREE . . . LIKE A CEDAR OF LEBANON. The contrasting imagery in the closing verses of Psalm 92 points to the growth, fruitfulness, and permanence of the people of God when they live life in his presence. Those rejecting Yahweh are like grass—they flourish quickly but soon wither (v. 7). The righteous, however, are like the palm tree and the cedar—both grow slowly but live long (v. 12). These arboreal similes communicate images of perpetual growth and fruitfulness. Zenger points out that the cedars of Lebanon, "even at the age of three thousand years, can still produce seed-bearing cones."[17] Picking up on the tree imagery of Psalm 1:3, the poet again draws the reader's attention to the notion that human stability and personal growth are dependent on right relationship with the Creator.[18]

Planted in the house of the LORD, they will flourish. Continuing the same theme, the poet makes a strong association between the temple and the fruitful life. This association stems from the idea of the temple's being a

---

16. Schaefer, *Psalms*, 231.

17. Hossfeld and Zenger, *Psalms 2*, 440.

18. "The righteous are like a stately and fertile tree, while the wicked are like short-lived grass" (Longman, *Psalms*, 334).

type of edenic, garden sanctuary—the locus of great fruitfulness (note the imagery associated with the temple in 1 Kgs 6).[19] But with the passage of time the physical temple comes to be read also as a metaphorical image of divine presence. In remaining close to Yahweh the believer lives life under his blessing, protection, and providential care, thus allowing her to experience the fullness of human existence that springs only from communion with God.

They will still bear fruit in old age. Like the cedars of Lebanon, fruitfulness should never diminish with age. The type of fellowship with God implied in these verses leads to a lifestyle that remains constantly fertile. The believer is continually growing and bearing fruit—she never reaches a stage in which continued growth becomes optional.

Proclaiming, "The LORD is upright; he is my Rock, and there is no wickedness in him." The concluding voice of Psalm 92 is a voice of praise and assurance. Echoing the confidence of the opening verses (vv. 1–3), the poet declares Yahweh to be both morally dependable ("upright," "there is no wickedness in him") and his source of strength ("my Rock"). Verse 15 seems to be a deliberate echo of Moses's song in Deuteronomy 32:4. The focus of both passages is on the ultimate and inescapable justice of God. This thought brings great hope to the poet because he knows that ultimately the wicked, who appear to prosper in the here and now, will not succeed. But equally, Yahweh's justice is the guarantee of his support for those who desire to walk in his right paths. God's reign is celebrated in Psalm 92. He is described as the "Most High" at the beginning of the psalm (v. 1). In the middle (v. 8) he is "forever exalted" (i.e., "on high forever"— another reign image). And finally, here at the end, he is the Rock "who renders unshakable both the cosmos and every individual righteous person."[20] God rules undeniably, and in this truth his followers find sure hope.

LINKS BETWEEN PSALMS 90–92. It seems that Psalms 90–92 form a mini-collection within Book 4 of the Psalter, linked around the figure of Moses. Psalm 90 is the only composition in the Psalter to carry a specific heading associating it with Moses. Psalm 91 uses the language of Deuteronomy to describe the psalmist's devotion to God (Ps 91:14; cf. Deut 7:7; 10:15, where the same language is used to describe God's love for Israel) and Yahweh's protection of his people under his wings (Ps 91:4; cf. Deut 32:11). Deuteronomy, of course, is dominated

---

19. Hossfeld and Zenger, *Psalms 2*, 440–41.
20. Ibid., 442.

by the presence and voice of Moses. Psalm 92, as we have seen above, is a "Song of the Sabbath," and the Sabbath is associated with the giving of the law, which was mediated by Moses (Exod 20; Deut 5). So, this mini-collection of poems harks back to the days of Moses.[21] Why so?

The inclusion of a Mosaic collection at the start of Book 4 seems to have resulted from a deliberate decision by the Psalter's editors in response to the crisis of Davidic kingship, the theme that ends Book 3. Psalm 89 concludes Book 3 (Pss 73–89) with a voice that cries out in despair over the loss of the Davidic line, and this final voice echoes the desperation of the people expressed earlier in Book 3 over the loss of the temple and the fall of Jerusalem (see comments on Pss 74 and 76 above). So, from the perspective of the Psalter as a whole, Book 3 is dominated by a voice of lament and concludes with a strong expression of loss and discomfit concerning the demise of the Davidic line in the events of the exile. The basic tenor of the preceding collection is a voice that asks, "How are we to survive without the temple, without Zion, and without a king in the line of David to rule us?"

Psalms 90–92 respond to that voice of loss by pointing the readers of the Psalter to a time when there was no temple, when Jerusalem was still a "pagan" town, and when the concept of kingship barely registered in the psyche of God's people, yet everything was fine! The editors respond to the multiple crises of the exile, as presented in Book 3, by redirecting the reader's thoughts to the period of Moses's leadership of an embryonic Israel. When Moses was in charge, the concepts of temple, holy city, and human king were (broadly speaking) meaningless—*yet God still ruled and was still able to bless his people!* So, this collection of poems encourages readers to look beyond their despair, caused by the losses they had experienced, to a spiritual and historical reality in which God's rule was undeniable despite the nonexistence of the physical trappings of that rule. The point seems quite clear: Yahweh reigned over Israel before there was a temple or a Zion or a David, so can he not still govern the affairs of his people now that these things no longer exist?

Pointing to Moses in Psalms 90–92 directs the readers to think of realities that predate their own existence and experience of God. Had the people come to focus their attention on the physical signs over and above the spiritual reality? Perhaps they had. So, the editors remind the people of a time when the reality of God's rule was undeniable even though the

---

21. Michael G. McKelvey, *Moses, David and the High Kingship of Yahweh: A Canonical Study of Book IV of the Psalter*, Gorgias Dissertations Biblical Studies 55 (Piscataway, NJ: Gorgias, 2010), 281–96.

signs were not present. Equally, however, there is movement within this collection as it transitions from petition (Ps 90) to promise (Ps 91) and, finally, to thanksgiving (Ps 92).

Psalm 90 begins as a lament over the susceptibility of humans to death and an expression of fear of an unpredictable divine wrath, culminating in the petition that Yahweh, in his steadfast love (*hesed*), might counter this wrath. This petition in Psalm 90 is answered in Psalm 91 with a twofold assent or promise. That this assent is not an empty word, but is fulfilled in the one who trusts in it, is then attested by the hymnic account of rescue in Psalm 92; in the process, individual formulations in Psalm 92 acquire additional dimensions of meaning in light of Psalms 90–91.[22]

In particular, there appears to be a thematic unity based on the idea of dwelling in the presence of God. The Mosaic Psalm 90 begins with the celebration of God as the "dwelling place" of generations of believers. Psalm 91 points to the protection afforded to those who take refuge in Yahweh— those who make the Most High their dwelling (v. 9). And, picking up on this same theme, Psalm 92 paints a picture of growth and fruitfulness for those who are "planted in the house of the LORD" (v. 13). The message of Psalms 90–92 is one that speaks of a faithful God who is a Rock and Refuge for his people. The rhetorical challenge of this collection of poems encourages the readers to place their trust in this God and to do so actively, with a real sense of hope and assurance. "Moses" speaks in Psalms 90–92 with a voice of certainty: "Place your trust in God because he *is* in control!"

Psalm 92 in the New Testament. There are no direct citations of Psalm 92 in the New Testament; however, "the song of God's servant Moses and of the Lamb" in Revelation 15:3–4 celebrates both the works of the Lord (cf. Ps 92:4) and the great justice of God (cf. Ps 92:15). Similarly, Revelation 16:5–7 focuses on the absolute justice of God in the exercise of judgment. In the book of Revelation there are, of course, strong echoes of the idea of eschatological justice found in Psalm 92. John's Apocalypse also points to the ultimate justice of God despite the present injustices perpetrated by the wicked. Again, in the New Testament we see a scenario in which the oppressor may seem to hold the upper hand at various points of historical reality, but we also see that God's undeniable justice will come to the fore in his time.

The idea of taking rest in Christ also echoes the overall theme of this Sabbath song. The famous verses of Matthew 11:28–29 point to Jesus as the Messiah who brings the Sabbath experience to his people. It is in

---

22. Hossfeld and Zenger, *Psalms 2*, 442.

relationship with him that his people find this peace, just as those who dwell in the house of Yahweh experience an edenic fruitfulness and idyll. Equally, Matthew 12:1–14 echoes this type of Sabbath experience as depicted in Psalm 92. The Sabbath is not about legalism and rule but about fullness and wholeness in relationship with God.

FLEETING TYRANNY. For those of us in the Western world, tyranny is something that we normally experience from afar. Twenty-four hour news channels and the speed of the Internet give us almost instant access to eyewitness accounts of events happening thousands of miles and several time zones away. We are often faced with the unpleasant reality of seeing tyrants and dictators rise to authority at great cost to those dwelling in the lands where those rulers wield power. Such realities are all the more difficult for the many thousands of people who do not watch it from afar but experience it as their daily norm. It is one thing to hear and read about the killing fields of Cambodia or even to watch the news stories—it was quite another thing to experience the persecutions of Pol Pot.[23] You can fill in the blanks today and every day. In the 1930s and 1940s it was Hitler in Germany. In the 1940s and 1950s it was Stalin in Russia. In the 1960s, Papa Doc Duvalier and the Tonton Macoutes ruled Haiti with an iron fist. In the 1970s, it was Idi Amin in Uganda and Pol Pot in Cambodia who wreaked havoc on their own peoples. In the late 1980s, the old communist dictatorships of Central and Eastern Europe began to crumble, but that did not prevent Slobodan Milošević from rising to power in Serbia and propagating his hateful ideology of ethnic cleansing in the Balkans in the early 1990s. The early years of the twenty-first century have been no better, and selective "regime change" by Western governments left countless other dictators in destructive power over their people—Kim Jong-un in North Korea, Bashar al-Assad in Syria, not to mention the Castros in Cuba or Lukashenko in Belarus or the apparently indeterminate power of ruling royal families throughout the Middle East. How is the person of faith to view such brutal regimes?

The answer as found in Psalm 92 is surprisingly simple on one level, yet incredibly challenging on another. The simple side of the problem of dictators is that, though they rule now with severe prejudice, justice

---

23. See Don Cormack, *Killing Fields, Living Fields: Faith in Cambodia* (Fearn, UK: Christian Focus, 2009), for a moving account of those who experienced Pol Pot's persecution yet refused to turn their backs on the God they loved.

and judgment are certain in God's economy. They may inflict untold pain today and tomorrow or for some years to come, but ultimately their absolute demise and judgment at the hand of a righteous God is certain (vv. 6–8). Herein lies the "simple" side of seeing things from the divine perspective—all those who practice injustice shall face the judgment of a just God (vv. 9, 15). The more difficult side of this equation is "When?" Why should God's judgment be "ultimate" and not "now"? Why are dictators left to reign for so long? Here is the imponderable question—but one that has to be asked. It is the "How long?" question of so many of the psalms of lament. The answer may not always satisfy us, but it is only right to ask the question. Injustice is always something that the church should lament, but it laments with a degree of hope because we rest in the sure knowledge that justice will be worked out—if not in our present experience, in God's good time (see comments on Ps 75 above).

So, the message that Psalm 92 gives the reader is a perspective unattainable by "fools" (v. 6). God is forever exalted, whereas the wicked are forever destroyed (vv. 7–8).

Rejoicing in judgment? This perspective gives rise to a second question of practical application: Is it ever right to rejoice in judgment (and the associated suffering) of anyone, even the wicked? Clearly, the tone of thanksgiving in Ps 92 includes (or at least implies) giving thanks for judgment poured out on others. Can doing so ever be morally "right"? Does it not deny the New Testament's teaching that we should "love [our] enemies and pray for those who persecute [us]" (Matt 5:44)? Superficially, this tone of thanksgiving at judgment may seem to be so very Old Testament, yet we are told that it is this same Jesus who "*will* judge the living and the dead" (2 Tim 4:1, emphasis added). Equally, Paul encourages *us* not to take vengeance for wrongs inflicted on us (Rom 12:18–21), yet he does so in the awareness that *God* will take such revenge. Is there a contradiction here?

As Christians longing to show compassion that reflects the grace we have received, we must never forget the innate sense of justice that God has instilled in his created order. Is it wrong to celebrate the demise of oppressive governments? Surely not, for the Bible makes it clear that Yahweh himself is the advocate pleading the case of the oppressed poor (Prov 22:22–23), and we should never ignore the advocacy of the Lord. In fact, Christians should be agents for change and advocates for the voiceless. While accepting that God will judge in accordance with his perfect timing, we should strive to make use of every means of influence we have to support those who suffer under cruel and vindictive rule. Every human being is imbued with inherent worth as one created in the image of God;

therefore, Christians should be constantly active in defending the rights of the defenseless and speaking up for the voiceless.

So, is it wrong to give thanks for judgment worked out in history or eternity? No, because injustice should always grieve us, and the practice of justice should cause us to rejoice. C. Hassell Bullock comments: "Psalms give us a realistic view of the world. That is, they will not permit us to ignore the violence and evil of the world we live in."[24] Thanksgiving for divine judgment echoes of the indignation we should feel when injustice reigns on the earth. We pray "Thy kingdom come; Thy will be done, on earth as it is in heaven," and we rejoice when that kingdom does come little by little, more and more fully in our day.

---

24. Bullock, *Encountering the Psalms*, 246.

Psalm 93

¹ The LORD reigns, he is robed in majesty;
  the LORD is robed in majesty and armed with strength;
  indeed, the world is established, firm and secure.
² Your throne was established long ago;
  you are from all eternity.
³ The seas have lifted up, LORD,
  the seas have lifted up their voice;
  the seas have lifted up their pounding waves.
⁴ Mightier than the thunder of the great waters,
  mightier than the breakers of the sea—
  the LORD on high is mighty.
⁵ Your statutes, LORD, stand firm;
  holiness adorns your house
  for endless days.

PSALM 93 IS A BRIEF POEM of great power that begins a group of psalms celebrating the high kingship of Yahweh. Although this poem is one of the shorter psalms in the Psalter, it is a composition packed with very visual imagery that testifies to the great power of the Creator God. This metaphoric presentation speaks clearly of the rule, power, and absolute authority of God, thus beginning a theme that resonates throughout Pss 93–100.[1] The "high kingship" of Yahweh is succinctly encapsulated in the phrase "the LORD reigns," which runs through this mini-collection like the motif melody of a Broadway musical (Pss 93:1; 96:10; 97:1; 99:1). The author and editors of Book 4 of the Psalter want to remind readers that God is in control regardless of how their circumstances may appear. The second aspect of the imagery of Psalm 93 is a "fashion" image. It may be true that "the devil wears Prada," but Psalm 93 highlights those characteristics of God's being so fundamental to his nature that it is as though he were *clothed* in them (vv. 1, 5). These attributes are his majestic power and holiness. The introductory statement of Yahweh's rule ("The LORD reigns") is followed by two lines focusing on

---

1. We will examine the connections within this collection as we progress through these psalms.

the "appearance" of God (v. 1b–c) that in turn are followed by two lines centering on the establishment of the earth based on the establishment of God's throne (vv. 1d–2). Next comes a couplet of verses comparing God's power with the awesome strength of the sea (vv. 3–4). The psalm closes with a reminder of certain characteristics basic to God's being (v. 5). Essentially, "[t]his psalm gives those who sing it a way to imagine the kingship of God and to understand its meaning."[2]

Yahweh Reigns (93:1a)

THE LORD REIGNS. Although Psalm 93 bears no official heading or a title, the opening words of the composition are probably meant to be seen as a thematic statement for this psalm and the collection that follows.[3] This opening declaration, therefore, functions effectively as a title not only for Psalm 93 but also for Psalms 94–100. While there is much debate about how to translate this phrase (and we will return to this question below), these two Hebrew words comprise a powerful focus statement for all readers of the Psalms. *Yahweh malak*, "Yahweh reigns!" This simple proclamation makes a declaration that would have spoken powerfully to the original readers of Psalm 93, just as it speaks powerfully to modern readers. *Yahweh rules!* These words summarize the key theme of Book 4, and Book 4 is key to our understanding of the whole Psalter.[4] As James Mays puts it, "The declaration *Yahweh malak* involves a vision of reality that is the theological center of the Psalter."[5] The author of this psalm and the editors who gathered the individual poems into a book had a clear aim, namely, to influence the way God's people viewed their present reality. The aim was one of worldview formation—to shape the way the covenant community viewed their own historical circumstances and present reality.[6] The formative message was as simple as it was powerful:*"No matter how chaotic things may appear, Yahweh is in control! He reigns!"*

There has been much discussion as to how the phrase *Yahweh malak* should be translated. For many years scholars, following Mowinckel,

---

2. Mays, *Psalms*, 300.

3. Hossfeld and Zenger, *Psalms 2*, 353.

4. Gerald Wilson describes Book 4 as the "editorial center" of the Psalter (Wilson, *Editing*, 215). It refocuses the reader's attention away from the crises of human history onto the eternal reign of God. Book 4 presents that divine control as an unchanging reality regardless of the way in which our human circumstances may appear to God's people at any given point in time.

5. Mays, *The Lord Reigns*, 22.

6. See the discussion of Ps 90 for further information on the historical circumstances that probably influenced the composition of Book 4.

suggested that the most appropriate translation was "Yahweh has become king." Their argument was twofold. First, the type of verb used to define God's rule may point to a specific act rather than a general fact. Second, some scholars associated this psalm with the hypothetical autumn festival, which, it was argued, celebrated annually the enthronement of Yahweh.[7] While this translation is grammatically possible given the type of verb used, there is certainly nothing in the verb itself to give preference to this rendering. Also, there is no strong reason to translate the verb in the past tense ("*has become* king"). Should one decide to translate the verb *malak* with reference to the office of king rather than the activity of ruling, then the most natural translation would be simply, "the LORD *is* King." Conceptually, such a translation is not far removed from the preferred option, "the LORD reigns." But perhaps the best argument for translating the words *Yahweh malak* as "the LORD reigns" is found in the literary context of verse 1. This psalm, and the succeeding compositions, focus on the activity of God's rule and reign—as Creator, Judge, and King—throughout all the created order, at all times, and forever! This collection of psalms does not focus on a particular act of divine enthronement but rather concentrates the minds of its readers on the ongoing and universal rule of Yahweh. From a literary perspective, the NIV's translation, "the LORD reigns," better represents the tone and content of this psalm and its neighbors than does the alternative suggestion.

The "Clothing" of the Lord (93:1b–c)

HE IS ROBED IN MAJESTY . . . AND ARMED WITH STRENGTH. This powerful affirmation of God's rule is followed by two lines that present what we might call "a divine fashion statement"! The psalmist describes certain characteristics so intrinsic to God's very being that it is as though he were clothed in them—"he is robed in majesty; the LORD is robed in majesty and armed with strength." There are actually three "clothing" verbs used in these statements: the repeated idea that Yahweh is "clothed" in majesty,

---

7. For fuller discussion of Mowinckel's theory, see Wilson, *Psalms, Volume 1*, 62–64. As Wilson shows, there are substantial weaknesses in Mowinckel's argument that the psalms were closely related to this purported annual fesitival. Primarily, it seems unlikely that such a prominent festival could escape mention entirely in the rest of the Old Testament! Surely such a significant and annually occurring event would at least be mentioned elsewhere in the Old Testament, if not described in great detail (as are some of the annual festivals, such as Passover in Deut 16:1–17). Second, the argument that all 150 psalms of the Psalter are somehow related to this festival fails to take account of the great diversity of material found in the book of Psalms. To posit a festal background for all the psalms leads to forced and unnatural interpretations of many of the texts.

and the verb translated "armed," which carries the connotation of "girding" or "putting on."[8] The notion would have been immediately obvious to the original readers of the psalm. The attire of any king in the ancient world would clearly set him apart from all others by indicating his high office. In a parallel manner, Yahweh is characterized by such evident glory and power that there is no mistaking his high office within the created order. As Anderson comments, "the ancient kings were often distinguished by their magnificent robes . . . but Yahweh is clothed in majesty and might. . . . [T]he description of Yahweh's robes is really a metaphorical account of his nature."[9]

Of course, the psalmist could have chosen to celebrate any of God's inherent characteristics in the way that he does here. It is equally true to say that Yahweh is clothed in holiness, justice, love, and mercy. So why does the poet choose to present God as being clothed in "majesty" and "strength"? The two words used (*ge'ut* and *'oz*) are linked via the concept of power. Psalm 89:9 speaks of God's rule over the "surging [*ge'ut*] sea." The sea is effectively described as being "majestic" in its natural power, and in both verses the poets present Yahweh as ruling over the sea despite all its natural majesty and strength. The term translated "strength" (*'oz*) is often applied not only to the power inherent to Yahweh's being (e.g., Ps 65:6) but also to the salvific power he makes available to his people (e.g., Exod 15:2; Ps 21:1). Yahweh creates all things in his *strength* (Ps 65). Moses rejoices in the *strength* made available to him by Yahweh in Exodus 15, as does the king in Psalm 21. This connection between God's inherent power and its accessibility for his people is surely significant to the application of this psalm, as we shall see below.

The purpose of the psalmist's choice of divine characteristics is clear. His desire is to present God as "the war hero on a cosmic scale, Yahweh is girded with strength, as a fighter constantly awaiting combat."[10] The didactic purpose of this presentation is straightforward—Yahweh is the heavenly Warrior King![11] There is none like him in terms of his intrinsic power, might, and rule! The visual image presented reminds the singers of this psalm that the God whom they worship rules over heaven and earth absolutely, and their present circumstances have no bearing on that absolute fact. If, as we should probably suppose, the original recipients of

---

8. "אות," *HALOT* 1:28.

9. Anderson, *Psalms*, 667.

10. Terrien, *Psalms*, 659. Hossfeld adds that this presentation "confirms the impression that YHWH is enthroned in the garments of the divine warrior" (*Psalms 2*, 448).

11. Longman, *Psalms*, 334–35.

the psalm are living in the postexilic period of national crisis—without a Davidic king, the external symbol of Yahweh's rule on earth—then this image would indeed speak powerfully to them. The symbol of God's rule on earth may be gone, but God's rule remains undiminished because it is inherent to his very being. He is still the Warrior King fighting in behalf of his people and ruling over all the earth.

Establishment and Security (93:1d–2)

THE WORLD IS ESTABLISHED, FIRM AND SECURE . . . . YOUR THRONE WAS ESTABLISHED LONG AGO. The next two parallelisms point to the profound consequences of God's reign for all humanity. The opening verses proudly proclaim Yahweh's rule over all creation, and these lines point out the significant consequences of that heavenly rule. The key term here is the Hebrew verb *kun*—"established." Why can the cosmos not be moved? Because Yahweh's "throne was established long ago" (v. 2a). The two facts are inextricably linked. The stability of the created realm is based on the stability of God's rule. In one sense the former only exists because of the latter, and without the stability of God's rule there is no hope of stability within the natural order. This fact is brought home once again by reference to God's essential nature: "you are from all eternity" (v. 2b). The eternal, unchangeable nature of God's being is what brings lasting stability to the universe—it remains because Yahweh rules, just as he always has done.

There is a sense in which God has always been King because of his very nature and being. But that kingship becomes a "visible" reality in the creation of the universe. It is in that act of creation that he "becomes" King over creation. Hence the establishment of God's throne and the stability of the universe are inseparable realities.

When the psalm says that the world is established and cannot be shaken, it means that the stability and the continuity of the human home is [sic] secure against unstable chaos, from which it was created by God. The two are coordinate because in the way the psalm thinks about reality, the establishment of the world was the deed by which the Lord gained kingship, and his kingship is a guarantee of the stability of the ordered inhabitable world.[12]

The meaning of the imagery is clear: God rules over all the created order, and the whole universe owes its continued existence to the reign of God.

---

12. Mays, *Psalms*, 301.

Yahweh: Mightier than the Seas (93:3–4)

THE SEAS HAVE LIFTED UP, LORD. These two powerfully poetic verses paint a picture of Yahweh, exalted on high, mightier than the amazing force of the seas. Again, the meaning of the metaphor is clear: the sea is a mighty power, but Yahweh is *more* powerful! The discussion of the seas in these verses was probably meant to be ambiguous for the original readers. First, as contemporary readers readily understand, the sea represents a natural force of great power that is much to be feared. The devastation caused by the tsunami that struck the Asian subcontinent on Boxing Day 2004 is only one of many instances that illustrate the terrible power of the sea. In the ancient world also, readers were only too well aware of the raw power of the seas. In fact, their awareness was probably greater because of the comparatively insubstantial nature of their boats and also because relatively few people in those days could swim. Second, the "waters" of the Old Testament sometimes symbolized the opposition of the nations against Israel. Just as the waters of the sea seek to break the boundaries of the land and pour over it, so the nations are sometimes pictured as wild waters seeking to pour over Israel's national boundaries (see Isa 8:7;17:12).[13] Third, the "waters" could be a metaphoric reference to the creation traditions of Israel's neighbors. All the nations of the ancient world had their own cosmogonies—traditions regarding how the world began. Although each national account differs in detail, often the core ideas were quite similar. Normally in these stories the creation of the earth is the byproduct of a conflict among the gods, and one of the parties to that conflict (the bad guy or girl) is represented by the sea as the ultimate force of chaos. In the Babylonian tradition, the high god, Marduk, is victorious in battle with the goddess, Tiamat, who rules over the primordial deep. Marduk then creates the heavens and the earth from her body. Similarly, in the Canaanite tradition we read of a great celestial conflict between Baal, the storm god, and Yam, the god of the sea.[14] In these traditions we see a conflict between the

---

13. See Anderson, *Psalms*, 668; Kirkpatrick, *Psalms*, 564–65.

14. It is far from clear whether the Baal Cycle, which recounts Baal's mythical victory over Yam, is in fact a cosmogony. It does not make an *explicit* link between Baal's battle with the sea god and the creation of the heavens and the earth—largely because the following text is broken. But many scholars assume that a creation ideology is implied because the story depicts the type of struggle with the forces of chaos that is commonly associated with other ancient Near Eastern creation myths. (For fuller discussion see Thorkild Jacobsen, "The Battle between Marduk and Tiamat," *JAOS* 88 [1968]: 104–8.) We can say with a fairly strong degree of certainty that there was in the ancient world a connection between creation mythologies and overcoming the chaotic power of the seas. So it seems reasonable that Ps 93 picks up on that common currency and twists it to meet the ends of

high god and the forces of chaos that ultimately results in the formation of the universe. These stories are known as *Chaoskampf* myths. They recount the struggle with chaos, which must be defeated for order (creation) to appear, and these forces of chaos are typically represented by the sea.[15] So the sea imagery of Psalm 93 could be "a culturally relevant way of saying that Yahweh, not Baal, is king over all cosmic forces."[16]

Each of these three readings is possible, given that the psalms seldom make concrete reference to the specific background of their writings—in that sense they are without context.[17] So the ambiguity of the seas in Psalm 93 is probably deliberate. The seas of verses 3–4 could refer more literally to the naturally destructive power of the sea or, more metaphorically, either to the surrounding nations that oppose Israel or to the mythical forces of chaos that are constant threats to the order of creation. Whichever the specific referent, the psalmist makes use of this imagery to emphasize his point further—*Yahweh is greater than the seas!* Whatever power the sea imagery might represent, Israel's God is *more* powerful!

Lifted up. In the Old Testament the idea of *lifting up*, found in verses 3–4, is commonly associated with rebellion (see Ps 75). The seas are pictured as being in rebellion against Yahweh, but their rebellion is futile because he made everything and rules over all things. "These would-be kings rose up to do battle, proud waters that reared and dashed with thunderous voices. But the outcome proved that it was to Yahweh, high above them, that true majesty belonged."[18]

The LORD on high is mighty. The threefold *lifting up* of verse 3 is met by a threefold *mightier than* in the next verse! The seas lift themselves up, with their voice and their waves in rebellion. In beautiful poetic symmetry, Yahweh is presented in verse 4 as being mightier than the "thunder of the great waters" (the "voice" of v. 3), mightier than the "breakers" (the "pounding waves" of v. 3), and then, simply stated, Yahweh is declared to be both "on high" and "mighty" (therefore, mightier than the "sea" of v. 3).

---

the psalmist's own theological purposes. For further discussion see Walton, *ANE Thought*, 179–99.

15. There are probably overtones of this type in the presentation of the sea in the book of Revelation. The *sea* is presented as the home of the rebellious beast (Rev 13:1), and the *waters* are a tool of the serpent (Rev 12:15). The "great prostitute Babylon"—the symbol of human rebellion against God—*sits on many waters* (Rev 17:1, 15). In Revelation the seas and waters represent chaos and the rejection of God's design.

16. Anderson, *Psalms*, 668.

17. Jamie A. Grant, "Determining the Indeterminate: Issues in Interpreting the Psalms," *Southeastern Theological Review* 1.1 (Winter 2010): 3–14.

18. Eaton, *Psalms*, 332.

Both of these words (*bamarom* and *'adir*) portray images of rule. Height reflected rule in the ancient world, and though the seas may have rebelled, their rebellion is futile, for Yahweh is the truly *Mighty* One.

Stability and Decoration (93:5)

THE FINAL IMAGE OF PSALM 93 adds a slightly surprising note to the images of rule that have dominated the poem to this point. Verse 5 focuses attention on the stability of God's word and the holiness of his dwelling. In the psalmist's mind, there is no doubt as to God's power. Equally, *his character* is beyond question.

Your statutes, LORD, stand firm. Echoing the establishment of the earth based on the establishment of God's throne (vv. 1d–2), the statutes of Yahweh are presented as *standing firm.* Although a different verb is used (*'aman* here, as opposed to *kun*) the idea is the same, and in the mind of the poet the establishment of the created order and moral order are inseparable. God's revelation is 100 percent dependable because he is who he is. Just as the earth is secure because of God's inherent rule, so also God's word is sure because of his intrinsic character. He governs the world because of his authority as Creator and Sovereign. He also orders the reality of his people through his word. Just as there is a divine rule that holds together the universe, so too there is a divine rule for life within that universe. Both "rules" are unshakable because of Yahweh's nature and intrinsic authority. The sea must obey the High King . . . so too must his people!

> In our view of the world, there is no direct continuity between creation and society. What we call natural laws and moral laws seem quite different things. But, in the view of the psalmist, the commandments that order human life are the decrees of the sovereign of the universe. The ordering of the world and the ordering of society are expressions of one and the same rule.[19]

The word "statutes" represents the Hebrew word *'edut,* which in earlier periods has traditionally been translated "testimonies." But the NIV's translation ("statutes") adds some of the force implied by the original Hebrew. *'Edut* are not just general observations that we can accept or ignore as we please. In courtrooms worldwide, jurors accept or reject the testimony of witnesses as they choose. The *'edut* of the Old Testament is, however, used basically to refer to God's revealed instruction. Sometimes the word refers to the tablets of the Ten Commandments (Exod 31:18; 32:15), and in the Psalter this word

---

19. Mays, *Psalms,* 301.

tends to represent the torah in general (Ps 19:7; 78:5).[20] So the psalmist is reminding his readers that the entirety of the revelation they read—the psalms and the whole canon—is completely trustworthy as a guide for life. The implication is clear: Yahweh rules as sovereign over everything, so his word can be trusted and must be obeyed as a pattern for life.

Holiness adorns your house. The final thought of Psalm 93 brings us back to the clothing imagery of verse 1. Just as majesty and strength are Yahweh's robes, so also "holiness" is the decoration of his dwelling place. Holiness as a concept dominates the presentation of the real presence of God throughout the Old Testament. The fall of humanity in Eden caused separation from a *holy* God. Yahweh's presence is always marked by holiness. Adam and Eve had to leave Eden because sin meant that they could no longer dwell in his real presence (Gen 3). Moses had to remove his sandals in the real presence of God at the burning bush because it was *holy* ground (Exod 3). The presence of God in the *most holy* place in the tabernacle had to be shrouded from a sinful people (Exod 26:30–37), and so on. God's presence is always a holy presence. So, it is no surprise that God's house is decorated in holiness just as he himself is robed in majesty and strength. The "house" referred to here could be Yahweh's heavenly dwelling, but it may also refer to the restored temple in the postexilic period. Wherever Yahweh dwells, holiness adorns that place, and this circumstance is true throughout all eternity ("for endless days").

The psalmist ends with this thought for good reason. He celebrates the absolute power of Yahweh throughout Psalm 93. But absolute power is also a fearful thing, since it is abundantly open to abuse. The psalmist tells the reader that she need not fear, for God's absolute power is matched only by his perfection of character! "Holiness is not defined but it clearly determines the fundamental character of God as King! Awe is based on veracity, and the sanctity of the shrine is due not to its geographic location but to the rectitude of God and his worshippers."[21] The holiness of God means that his power can ever only be used in accordance with the right standards that are natural to his being. His power always corresponds with his goodness and righteousness.

His rule is ultimately without challenge. His words are entirely trustworthy. His character is matchlessly perfect. Power in this context breeds a willing respect and submission from all who "see" this reality—not a submission drawn from absolute terror before a capricious god but a willing submission to the God who is all-powerful *and* all-good. Psalm 93 is,

---

20. Wilson, *Psalms, Volume 1*, 367.
21. Terrien, *Psalms*, 660.

indeed, an act of imagining. "Imagine God," the psalmist says, "Perfect in power, ruling over all things regardless of appearances. He speaks in a way that we can trust and is characterized always by sublime moral perfection." Such a picture surely breeds celebration . . . especially when the reader comes to realize that this God is *his* or *her* God!

THE SECURITY OF SOVEREIGNTY. While some of the imagery of Psalm 93 might not be immediately obvious to the modern reader, the message of the poem remains timely for believers in this generation. We may not be familiar with the idea of kings regaled in finery that declares their high office. (Apart from very formal state occasions, the constitutional monarchs of today are disappointingly "normal" in their appearance!) Nor do we think of powers of chaos, symbolized by the sea, as striving on a daily basis to overcome the natural order. These images are rooted in the thought world of the psalm's original hearers. The metaphors are appropriate to the original readers, but the point made by the psalmist is applicable in all generations of believers: *God is in control regardless of how it may appear.*

The turmoil experienced by the original hearers of Psalm 93 may not be the turmoil of the twenty-first century, but the specific circumstances are not the point. The universal and eternal reign of God is the point the psalmist makes. The author does not need to specify the source of the apparent chaos because the details do not matter. The covenantal God is sovereign and in control, whatever the particular challenge may be.

This is the message of the whole of Scripture. Yahweh rules in and over all things. From the creation accounts of Genesis 1–2 onward we read of a God whose mere speaking makes everything jump to attention. He *declares* light and matter into being because he is King over all such things. We see that rule in the ordering of the events of human history for the fulfillment of his purposes. Yahweh promises Abraham a line of descendants, which will become a nation, which in turn will be a blessing to all the families of the earth (Gen 12:1–3). The rest of the Bible, in one sense, is the story of how Yahweh orders all the events of human history toward the specific end of fulfilling that promise. He is in control when challenges confront the promise (e.g., the barrenness of Sarah, Rebekah, and Rachel). He is in control when the stupidity of his chosen instruments puts the promise at risk (e.g., Abraham's passing Sarah off as his sister, Jacob's stealing a blessing, and Israel's constantly worshiping other gods). He is in control even when the main players on the stage of human history openly oppose the ends of that promise (e.g., Pharaoh's attempts to destroy the line of Israel and to oppress God's people, and Herod's attempts to kill Israel's true King while he was still a child). Yahweh is in control of all the events of human history; he orders them to fulfill that promise made to Abraham and his declared purpose of bringing blessing to all the families of the earth.

The voice of the Bible is universally the same: Yahweh is always in control, regardless of how it may appear from our human perspective. He reigns! This message is plain and simple and without qualification of any kind. So speaks Psalm 93, and in so doing it joins in the consistent chorus of the rest of Scripture.

As well as being an unmistakable theme throughout the Bible as a whole, the reign of Yahweh is perhaps the single most significant theme found in the Psalter. The Yahweh *malak* psalms (Pss 93–100) repeat the same idea with a variety of specific foci. The royal psalms (e.g., Pss 2, 20–21, 72, and 110) all celebrate Yahweh's universal rule over all the earth through his king. The Zion psalms (e.g., Pss 46 and 48) proclaim God's kingship over all the earth as a result of his presence on the earth. The many cries and prayers of the anonymous psalmists that God would hear their prayers and respond (e.g., Ps 22) only make sense when such pleas are offered to One *who is able to change and order their circumstances.* The message of Psalm 93 is consistent with the dominant voice of the Psalter—*Yahweh reigns.* This fact is unchangeable. The point of poems such as Psalm 93 is to *remind* God's people of that absolute fact.

The security of Scripture. The dominant imagery of Psalm 93 is based on metaphors pointing to God's rule. But the psalmist also reminds the people that Yahweh is not simply a God of raw power. He is also a God who has revealed himself to his people—one whose character we know through his word, and that character is good! So, the psalmist points to reliability in two ways. First, readers can trust in God because he rules over everything imaginable. Second, we can also trust in his word because it *stands firm*—it is fully dependable and absolutely trustworthy for life. The same term is used to describe the divine revelation in Psalm 19:7, "The statutes ['edut] of the LORD are *trustworthy*, making wise the simple" (emphasis added). The psalmist there implies that we can rely completely upon God's word as a rule for life. The "simple" of this verse are not people of weak mind or mental incapacity; rather, this word refers to the youth who lacks the wisdom to live well—wisdom that comes from experience.[22] God's teaching in his word equips those willing to learn by enabling them to make right choices in life. Just as God orders the universe, so his revealed

---

22. "פֶּתִי," *HALOT* 1:989.

word provides a secure path through life. That path is designed to reflect the character of God himself, a character marked by holiness.

The two dominant images found in Psalm 93—security based on God's sovereignty and security based on God's word—serve as reminders for the readers of this psalm throughout all generations. They encourage trust in *God's control* in the (often) chaotic events of life. They encourage trust in *the Scriptures* as an accurate guide for life in all its complexity. Much goes on in the world that is beyond our comprehension, but we can still trust that God is in control. But belief that "in all things God works for the good of those who love him" (Rom 8:28) does not in itself equip us to live life well in the midst of such confusion. So the author reminds us that we can also trust in *God's word* as a reliable guide by which to live. The people of God know how they should live, regardless of the vicissitudes of life around them. Following in the ways of his instruction offers a security that remedies life's complexities, a sure path through the quagmires of human folly that often surround us. Psalm 93 speaks of this double security for the community of God's people.

Psalm 93 in the New Testament. While there are no direct citations of Psalm 93 in the New Testament, the psalm resonates with the New Testament in at least a couple of ways. First, of course, Jesus' calming of the storm (Matt 8:23–27; Luke 8:22–25) is an action that reflects his true nature. Yahweh alone is mightier than the seas, and the obedience of the wind and the waves in response to Jesus' rebuke testifies to his divine nature. Second, we noted above the similarities between the sea imagery in Psalm 93 and the book of Revelation.[23] The final word regarding the sea in Revelation, however, also points to the complete sovereignty of God. John's vision tells us, "Then I saw 'a new heaven and a new earth,' for the first heaven and the first earth had passed away, *and there was no longer any sea*" (Rev 21:1, emphasis added). God's ultimate victory over chaos is finally established in the complete removal of chaos in the new created order.

BELIEVING IN A STRONG GOD. Anyone who has seen the film *The Perfect Storm* will have been struck by the iconic image that served as the film's poster. A small fishing trawler looks as though it is about to be swamped by a massive wave. The New England fishing boat is not large but is sturdy, with a strong, sea-going motor. It is

---

23. See note 15 above.

trying to make its way back to port through the storm of the century. The crewmembers are making progress back to their home base when all of a sudden they are confronted by a massive, freak wave that towers high above the boat. Left with no other choice, they try to ride out the wave. The boat climbs higher and higher toward the crest of the giant wave and . . . it is here that the poster image pictures. Will they make it? Can they do it? They have gone so far—can they survive this greatest of challenges? I will not spoil the film for those who have not seen it!

The advertising picture from *The Perfect Storm* reflects the reality of what many people feel on a day-to-day basis. Many live life with the feeling that they are just about to be swamped. The wave—like the seas in Psalm 93—may represent any one of many things—debt, sickness, unemployment, family troubles, bereavement, a bullying boss, a failing marriage. For Christians in some parts of the world, that "wave" may be persecution. Just as the seas are undefined in Psalm 93, so too may there be many different types of challenge that seem as though they are about to take us under in today's world. The ambiguity is deliberate. The psalmist does not wish to limit applicability to a certain sphere of reality because he wants the reader to remember the absolute sovereignty and control of God over *every* circumstance. The particular definition of the rebellious sea is in one sense irrelevant because there is absolutely nothing within the created order that represents a real challenge to the power of the Creator God!

We may feel out of our depth or that life is beyond our control. The wave is about to engulf us. The reality is that we *are* often out of our depth, and many things in life *are* entirely beyond our control. That is why the psalmist reminds us not only of the power of God but also of his character. "Holiness adorns [his] house." He is in control, *and* he will always do what is right! Yahweh's good character directs the exercise of his power. We may not see the grand plan or design, but God always leads us toward the end of developing the family likeness (Rom 8:29). He is holy, and his desire is for his people to reflect that holiness. The wave may be huge, but the question we should ask is not, "Why is this massive wave in my face?"—rather, we should ask, "How can this wave make me more like Christ?" "Both the one who makes people holy and those who are made holy are of the same family. So Jesus is not ashamed to call them brothers and sisters" (Heb 2:11).

Inevitably a storm seems like chaos to us. The trials of life represent our own personal *Chaoskampf*. But the imagery of God's might and power in Psalm 93 reminds us to view things from a different perspective—the divine perspective. Verse 3 presents the seas and waves as *lifting up* in rebellion. They attempt to rise up. They attempt to flex their muscles and exercise their power. But there is irony in the psalmist's response to this saber rattling, of which we read in verse 4. The seas raise themselves up, but Yahweh simply *is* on high. The rebellious forces of chaos are intimidating to us, but they are small and insignificant to God. He is above them all. From the divine perspective there is no *Kampf* in the *Chaoskampf*. There is no struggle. There is no breach in the order he has ordained. From the divine perspective there is only order. The truth of the matter is that our God, the God of the covenant, is mightier than the greatest difficulties of our lives.

This reminder is not a passive act. The *strength* ('oz) of Yahweh in which he is robed (v. 1) is a strength that he makes available to his people. "The LORD is *my* strength ['oz] and my defense; he has become my salvation. He is my God, and I will praise him, my father's God, and I will exalt him" (Exod 15:2). God's strength and God's rule are never simply abstract facts—they make a difference to God's people.

> "A cry means something only in a created universe. If there is no creator, what is the good of calling attention to yourself?" . . . Psalm 13 is a cry at the center of which is a plea: "Notice me! Answer me!" (v. 3). The plea is addressed to the LORD, the creator of heaven and earth and of Israel. The psalm is language in which the desperate loneliness of human life is offered to God, who is its ultimate source and only final help. It is a prayer in which mortals in anxiety and anguish speak of themselves to God and in doing so speak *about* God to those of us who read the prayer as scripture.[24]

The psalmists pray in their psalms because they believe that there is one who hears their prayers and that he is powerful to change their reality in response to those prayers. The God of whom we are reminded in Psalm 93 is not just any god—he is *our* God. His rule is not an abstract fact but a present reality that affects the life of the reader and is accessed through offering prayers of the type the psalmists offer. This God makes his strength available to his people by responding to their prayers.

The people of Israel living in the postexilic period had to remind themselves of a greater reality. The Davidic king was gone. Jerusalem had been devastated. The temple was rebuilt, but it was just not the same as Solomon's temple. Israel was a puppet state under the control of a succession of foreign powers, some of whom exercised their power with much brutality. *God's people needed to be reminded that the* LORD *on high is mighty!* As James Mays points out above, Psalm 93 is an act of imagination. Refocusing on the powerful, sovereign rule of *our* God has given and gives believers throughout all generations courage to face an uncertain world.

---

24. Mays, *The Lord Reigns*, 55.

Psalm 94

¹ The LORD is a God who avenges.
O God who avenges, shine forth.
² Rise up, Judge of the earth;
pay back to the proud what they deserve.
³ How long, LORD, will the wicked,
how long will the wicked be jubilant?
⁴ They pour out arrogant words;
all the evildoers are full of boasting.
⁵ They crush your people, LORD;
they oppress your inheritance.
⁶ They slay the widow and the foreigner;
they murder the fatherless.
⁷ They say, "The LORD does not see;
the God of Jacob takes no notice."
⁸ Take notice, you senseless ones among the people;
you fools, when will you become wise?
⁹ Does he who fashioned the ear not hear?
Does he who formed the eye not see?
¹⁰ Does he who disciplines nations not punish?
Does he who teaches mankind lack knowledge?
¹¹ The LORD knows all human plans;
he knows that they are futile.
¹² Blessed is the one you discipline, LORD,
the one you teach from your law;
¹³ you grant them relief from days of trouble,
till a pit is dug for the wicked.
¹⁴ For the LORD will not reject his people;
he will never forsake his inheritance.
¹⁵ Judgment will again be founded on righteousness,
and all the upright in heart will follow it.
¹⁶ Who will rise up for me against the wicked?
Who will take a stand for me against evildoers?
¹⁷ Unless the LORD had given me help,
I would soon have dwelt in the silence of death.
¹⁸ When I said, "My foot is slipping,"
your unfailing love, LORD, supported me.

¹⁹ When anxiety was great within me,
     your consolation brought me joy.
²⁰ Can a corrupt throne be allied with you—
     a throne that brings on misery by its decrees?
²¹ The wicked band together against the righteous
     and condemn the innocent to death.
²² But the LORD has become my fortress,
     and my God the rock in whom I take refuge.
²³ He will repay them for their sins
     and destroy them for their wickedness;
     the LORD our God will destroy them.

PSALM 94 IS A LINKING PSALM. First, it continues the theme of Yahweh's kingship from
Psalm 93. Although Psalm 94 does not contain
the emblematic words *Yahweh malak* that we
find in Psalm 93 and other psalms of this collection (e.g., Pss 96:10; 97:1;
99:1), this poem certainly continues the theme of Yahweh's unquestionable rule over all creation. This particular composition emphasizes
Yahweh's ultimate authority as Judge over all humanity and in this way
echoes the theme of God's rule in Psalm 93. Second, Psalm 94 functions
as what might be described as a "binding" psalm. For anyone reading
the psalms in order, it will be immediately obvious that Psalm 94 in
many ways echoes the themes of Psalm 92—the injustice and apparent
prosperity of the wicked and the ultimate judgment of God as Creator.
So, Gerald Wilson suggests that Psalm 94 *binds* together these two
mini-collections of psalms,[1] his point being that, though the groupings
are separated from each other in their immediate context, there is still a
general commonality of theme throughout the psalms of Book 4, with
its broad focus on the absolute rule of God regardless of external signs
and circumstances.

The focus on Yahweh as the high Judge comes to the fore from the
outset of Psalm 94 as it emphasizes God's vengeance on the wicked in
response to their oppression of the weak.

---

1. Gerald H. Wilson, "Shaping the Psalter: A Consideration of Editorial Linkage in the
book of Psalms," in *The Shape and Shaping of the Psalms*, JSOTSup 159, ed. J. Clinton McCann
(Sheffield: JSOT Press, 1993), 76. See also McKelvey, *Moses, David and the High Kingship of
Yahweh*, 84–86.

How Long Will the Wicked Be Jubilant (94:1–3)

THE LORD IS A GOD WHO AVENGES . . . . [S]HINE FORTH. The initial supplication of the psalmist could not be clearer. He calls on Yahweh—whom he names "the God who avenges" (in Hebrew a plural, "God of vengeances")—to "shine forth." This opening plea is clearly a call for God's justice to be worked out in the face of present oppression (see vv. 4–7 below). The idea of shining forth is probably a reference to divine appearance and, clearly, the psalmist is calling on God to manifest himself in power with the aim of restoring justice. Robert Alter comments:

> *God of vengeance.* This boldly aggressive characterisation of God, *'el neqamot,* which occurs only here, is fudged by the modern translations that render it in mitigating language as "God of retribution." As in many psalms of supplication, to which this poem is roughly allied, the speaker is filled with rage at the dominance of injustice in the world and exhorts God to manifest a spectacular appearance ("shine forth") in order to exact vengeance against the perpetrators of evil.[2]

Rise up, Judge of the earth. Verse 2, however, immediately goes on to clarify this stark and unusual characterization of God as the "God who avenges." The psalmist's plea is not based on some sort of understanding of God as a wrathful vigilante; rather, his appeal is to the ultimate Judge of humanity to work out justice within his present historical setting.[3] Throughout this poem the psalmist focuses discussion on the wicked and their ultimate fate, and he uses a variety of terminology to describe these individuals. Here they are described as "the proud," which is a term with universally negative connotations in the Old Testament. Naturally, this term refers to an attitude of heart and mind, but the Hebrew mindset assumes that pride goes beyond questions of attitude to particular patterns of behavior. Normally in the Hebrew Bible, "the proud" are those who by means of their wealth and power see God as an unnecessary abstraction who has absolutely no relevance in their lives (Prov 16:5; Isa 2:11–12). Equally, "the proud" are often characterized as perpetrators of social injustice (e.g., see Prov 16:19), and it is a concept that is frequently associated with blatant wickedness (Job 40:11–12). The poet here calls on God to bring just recompense to this situation. He does not ask for vindictive

---

2. Alter, *Psalms,* 331.

3. "Although there is a clear call for vengeance in the opening verse, we must not presume it is a personal, emotional reaction. The next verse and the whole psalm make clear that it is characterized by just judgment (O Judge of the earth), that is, repayment for wrongs committed (vv. 2, 23)" (Broyles, *Psalms,* 371).

retribution, merely an equitable response to the harm that these proud individuals have caused.

How long, LORD, will the wicked be jubilant? Characterized by that typical question of lament—"How long, O Lord?"—the poet's interrogation of God implies that the social inequity caused by the behavior of the proud has been going on for some time. The implication of the "How long?" question is that, from the psalmist's perspective, this inequity has already been going on for far too long and that it is now high time for God to intervene by bringing some sort of resolution to this injustice. The description of the proud as "jubilant" ('*alaz*) points to a scenario in which those who oppress the weak not only perpetrate their injustices but actually delight in doing so. This description paints a picture of flagrant disregard for any concept of social justice. Not only do the wicked oppress (Ps 94:4–7), but they also publicly elevate themselves as they do so. As Goldingay points out, this act of jubilation or exulting is entirely appropriate in the right setting, but the idea of the wicked and exulting "do not go together." He concludes, "As in v. 1, then, the closing verb brings the line to a forceful close: in this case, a scandalous one."[4] Verse 3 shows just how serious the present state of affairs is for the psalmist and the people. Those who perpetrate injustice should, at least, be so obviously out of step with the norms and expectations of society that they are forced to be secretive about their behavior. This verse points to a reality in which not only do the powerful get away with unacceptable behaviors, but also their dominance is such that they need not even fear public opinion.

They crush your people, LORD (94:4–7)

THEY POUR OUT ARROGANT WORDS. Continuing the emphasis from verse 3, the poet voices his indignation at the open arrogance of those who do evil in society. They trumpet those activities of which they should be ashamed. Their pride is vocal as well as behavioral. Such flagrant self-glorification of their own power and ability to oppress rubs salt into the wounds of the community already scarred by the activities of their oppressors.

They crush your people. . . . They slay the widow and the foreigner. The poet's plea for justice is accentuated by the relational language of verse 5. In seeking Yahweh's intervention, the psalmist points out that it is *Yahweh's* people and inheritance who are crushed and oppressed by the behavior of those who practice evil. The rhetoric of this verse clearly implies that the unspecified oppressors whose actions have provoked this

---

4. Goldingay, *Psalms 3*, 77.

prayer are laying some sort of claim of entitlement over the people who belong only to God. The oppressors' practices imply a possessive claim of authority over God's people. So, verse 5 reminds God of his ownership of the community of faith and points out the affront implied by these patterns of behavior. This is not simply a matter of social injustice—it is a power grab by those who would set themselves up as gods among their peers.

In practical terms, these behaviors manifested themselves primarily in the oppression of the weak and marginalized in society. Verse 6 highlights the ruthlessness of the wicked with regard to the widow, alien, and orphan—three categories of Israel's society who were particularly vulnerable but who also come under the peculiar protection of Yahweh.[5] Again there is particularly strong rhetoric in the psalmist's plea in this verse. He is aware that oppression of the people in these specific categories reflects a practice that would be especially abhorrent to Yahweh, therefore making it more likely that he will hear and respond to the poet's supplication. There is some discussion in the commentaries about whether the verbs used in verse 6 should be read figuratively or literally. (In other words, did the oppressors mentioned in Ps 94 actually kill the weak in society, or is this characterization a hyperbolic reference to other, less drastic oppressive practices?).[6] Of course, it is not beyond the bounds of possibility that the poet is using hyperbole here; however, the Old Testament's concern for people in these three categories (widow, orphan, and alien) is based on an awareness that they are the people most open to oppression of all sorts, *including* the very worst.

They say, "The Lord does not see." The oppression of the wicked is matched only by their godless arrogance. Not only do they reject God's rules concerning the protection of the weak in society, but they are blatant in their declaration that they are able to do so because God, in their opinion, either does not see or is not paying attention. The attitude of the oppressors in Psalm 94 is very similar to the voice of the wicked in Psalm 73:11—they assume their wickedness will go unpunished because God *does not* intervene. But the poet points out their folly in the following stanza.

---

5. "They do great harm to those for whom God has a special concern, namely the widows and orphans and those who are strangers in the land. God makes it clear that rulers (and ordinary believers) have a duty to help people who live in poverty and have special needs (see Exod 22:21–24; Deut 26:12; 27:19; Isa 1:17; Jer 7:5–7; 22:3; Zech 7:8–10; Mal 3:5)" (Cyril Okorocha, "Psalms," in *African Bible Commentary: A One-Volume Commentary*, ed. Tokunboh Adeyemo [Grand Rapids: Zondervan, 2006], 701).

6. See Oesterley, *Psalms*, 417–18; Anderson, *Psalms*, 672.

The truth is not as it appears to the wicked fools because the reality of the matter is not that God does not intervene in the events of humanity—he simply *has not* intervened *yet!*

The Folly of Disdain (94:8–11)

DOES HE WHO FASHIONED THE EAR NOT HEAR? Verse 8 rebukes the arrogant for their blind stupidity that is voiced in verse 7. They claim that God does not see, and if he does see he's not really interested in the events of humanity. "Folly!" replies the psalmist. "How stupid can you possibly be?" Their error is a theological one—they simply have no idea what God is really like. So, the poet asks a series of rhetorical questions: Does the Maker of the ear not hear? Does the Maker of the eye not see? How about the God who punishes nations—will he not intervene in the matters of individuals? Does the God who brings light to humanity lack understanding? The implied answers are a profound warning to those who would take advantage of the weak in any society. Effectively, the poet addresses the oppressors and says, "God hears the prayers of your victims! He sees each and every one of your actions! He controls the destiny of nations! Do you really think he cannot deal with you? You have no knowledge apart from him, and you think you can pull the wool over his eyes? Fools! Folly!" We can almost hear the tone of mocking laughter on the psalmist's lips.

The LORD knows all human plans . . . they are futile. The foolish wicked of verses 4–7 show their great disdain for God in the words of verse 7, but the true reality is that God has nothing but disdain for them! The thoughts of man are *hebel* (NIV "futile"). This term is resonant with connotations in Israel's wisdom circles, for it is the frequent refrain of the speaker in Ecclesiastes that "everything is *meaningless*" (*hebel* [Eccl 1:2]). In the same way, in arrogant rebellion against God, the thoughts of humans are futile, meaningless, empty, and vain. The evildoers who are so "full of boasting" (v. 4) are really just full of wind. From the divine perspective they are but pathetic specks of dust. For all their pomp and arrogance, they and their bragging boastfulness are all simply meaningless in the divine economy.

> Verse 11 should be heard in relation to v. 7. It is not an abstract affirmation of God's omniscience, but an affirmation that the arrogantly stated intentions of the wicked will come to nothing (see Ps 39:11). God will deal with humanity's evil "thoughts" (see Gen 6:5). In short, God is sovereign.[7]

---

7. McCann, "Psalms," 1058.

The Blessing of Discipline (94:12–15)

BLESSED IS THE ONE YOU DISCIPLINE, LORD. Contemporary Western society does not readily associate the ideas of "discipline" and "blessing." The poet does so because he sees a reality that reaches beyond the priorities and perspectives of the world around him. While the same word (*yasar*) is used here as is used in verse 10, the implied meaning is quite different. God's discipline can mean "discipline" (v. 10), but it can also mean "teaching," and this ambiguity is probably deliberate on the part of the psalmist. On one level, discipline serves as an implied warning to the wicked regarding the potential of God's punishment to come. On another level, however, both verse 10 and verse 12 make the link between discipline and teaching. The implication of this association is probably intended to point out that there is a lesson that can still be learned *before* God brings his punishment on the arrogant oppressors. They reject Yahweh's ways, but verse 12 declares that true happiness (NIV "blessed" [*'ashre*]; cf. Ps 1:1) is to be found in *walking in God's paths,* not rejecting them!

The one you teach from your law. This makes explicit the link between divine instruction and blessing/happiness. A truly full and fulfilled life is to be found in the revelation of Yahweh—his law or, perhaps better here, instruction is the avenue via which humanity finds true happiness in life. Rejection of his instruction may have seemed like the better option to the oppressors because of their dominant self-interest. Exploiting the poor may have been a means of arriving at some short-term financial gain, but the psalmist is clear that this strategy is not the means of long-term happiness in life. Such blessing only comes through a lifestyle grounded in the teaching of Yahweh.

You grant them relief from days of trouble, till a pit is dug for the wicked. Psalm 94 is clear, however, that we are not just talking about better or worse lifestyle choices. Yes, it is better to be disciplined by God and to walk according to his torah, but we are not ultimately talking about two valid lifestyle choices, one of which is preferable over the other. The "way of the Lord" (cf. Ps 1:6) is a lifestyle that falls under divine protection—even when the righteous believer is surrounded by the machinations of the wicked. But the "way of the wicked" (again Ps 1:6) is a path that will ultimately lead to judgment, and this tone is what we find in Psalm 94:13b. Yahweh will protect the believer through all the days of domination by oppressors ("from days of trouble" [Hebrew *mime ra'*, lit., "from evil days"]) until God's judgment is worked out on them ("a pit is dug"). The irony, of course, is that the digging of a pit is frequently a metaphor for the perfidious ambushes the wicked set to attack others (e.g., see Ps 35:7–8), but here, as often in the psalms, the evil intentions of the schemer become his own downfall (cf. Pss 7:15; 9:15;

57:6). The implication of Psalm 94:13b seems to be that the pit is dug for the oppressor by God himself as an act of judgment—he protects the righteous until his judgment is worked out on the wicked.

For the LORD will not reject his people; he will never forsake his inheritance. The psalmist calls to mind the language of the exodus and the election of Israel (Deut 31:6–8; Lev 26:40–45) to remind the people of the ultimate and unquestionable faithfulness of God. There may come "evil days" that God's people must go through, but they never experience those days apart from the presence of God—herein lies the poet's reminder.

Judgment will again be founded on righteousness. The promise of presence is accompanied by the assurance of the ultimate restoration of justice. The winds of society and culture may presently blow contrary to God's standards, but verse 15 points to a change in the wind's direction. One day God's standards will be restored. This somewhat elusive idea (the Hebrew being slightly awkward) may point either to societal reform in the here and now or to ultimate judgment to come on a more eschatological level. The mood of Psalm 94 seems to reflect on both possibilities—God's judgment will come ultimately, but don't be surprised if you see it sooner than anticipated.

God's Comfort in Difficult Days (94:16–19)

WHO WILL RISE UP FOR ME AGAINST THE WICKED? This rhetorical question comes as something of a surprise and reflects the speaker's hope in Yahweh despite the difficulties experienced in his present reality. The voice of lament here is typical of the classical dynamic of such prayers: God may not have acted to date, but the poet is aware that the only possibility of finding a solution will be from the hand of Yahweh himself. The psalmist develops this thought by way of testimony (vv. 17–19). He considers the psychological comfort and practical support he has received from Yahweh in the past, and they serve as consolation and encouragement regarding the difficulties presently faced. Clearly the psalmist's view is that Yahweh will respond by arising and standing up against the evildoers, but the question also makes a rhetorical challenge to hearers and readers of the psalm, namely, the challenge that they claim the courage of their convictions by taking a stand against social wrongs.[8]

Unless the LORD had given me help. The overarching thought of these words of testimony in verses 17–19 is the idea that all would have been lost long ago were it not for the help of Yahweh. There is a real sense that the psalmist has been here before—and to such an extent that he had

---

8. Broyles, *Psalms*, 372.

been close to death (v. 17b). But the fact that his God saved him while *in extremis* in times past gives him courage and strength to face the present challenges outlined in the poem and to stand up for the vindication of the marginalized.[9] The voice of testimony in these verses is didactic. It does not just reminisce; rather, it remembers so as to shape the reader's perception of the difficulties presently faced. Testimony teaches us and transforms our perspectives.

An End to Oppression (94:20–23)

CAN A CORRUPT THRONE BE ALLIED WITH YOU—A THRONE THAT BRINGS ON MISERY BY ITS DECREES? Just as there was a surprise factor in the preceding rhetorical question (see v. 16 above), so also there is something somewhat unexpected in the question of verse 20. Until this point in the psalm there seems to be no association between Yahweh and the oppressors mentioned throughout the poem. Indeed, we have been led to believe that they are arrogant in their dismissal of Yahweh and his standards (vv. 4, 7). So why does the poet pose this particular question: "Can a corrupt throne be allied with you?" It seems clear that the ones referred to in this verse are the oppressors described for us throughout the psalm, so it lacks any obvious association of them with Yahweh. Why then include this rhetorical question about corrupt rule and allegiance to Yahweh at this point in the psalm? The "corrupt throne" (literally, "throne of destruction") of verse 20 probably refers to a judicial seat of office, for it is an office that issues *decrees* which bring on misery (v. 20b).[10] The irony here, of course, is that despite the vocal rejection of God in verses 4 and 7, the corrupt judges in question, simply by dint of being judicial office holders, would be seen as somehow representing Yahweh in the land. So, the very office of these oppressors, in a formal and official sense, associates them with Yahweh, but the speaker makes it plain that such formal associations are meaningless in the eyes of Yahweh. It is one's behavior that draws a person near to or distances from the Creator God—offices and titles are meaningless. Yahweh will have nothing to do with these officials who bring oppression, and their official status will in no way protect them from judgment.

The wicked band together against the righteous and condemn the innocent to death. This verse names the worst kind of societal oppression and abuse of office. The officials conspire to work against the justice of the Lord, presumably for personal gain and self-interest. This statement shows

---

9. "Just as God has defended, rescued and comforted the poet, so may the divine judge vindicate the oppressed righteous" (Schaefer, *Psalms*, 234).

10. Hossfeld and Zenger, *Psalms 2*, 455.

the extent to which these corrupt judges are prepared to go—even as far as judicial murder (as implied in v. 6).

But the LORD has become my fortress. Regardless of the conspiracies of the powerful and influential, the psalmist acknowledges a security that goes far beyond the reach of those who hold temporal office. Yahweh himself is the psalmist's fortress and refuge—his support and protection against all attacks. The speaker has the courage to stand up for justice because he knows that his protection goes far beyond the reach of the conspirators despite their influential positions in society.[11]

He will repay them for their sins and destroy them for their wickedness; the LORD our God will destroy them. The poet is absolutely certain of the ultimacy of divine judgment, hence the repetition of the destruction imagery in verse 23. For the psalmist the ultimate equation is simple: corrupt officials may prosper now, but their final judgment is certain unless they change their patterns of behavior. There is an interesting association in the use of "the LORD our God" in the final statement of the psalm. Effectively, the speaker is making his stand alongside the poor and voiceless of society—he is absolutely with them in their struggle and certain of their vindication.[12]

THE PLACE OF PSALM 94 IN THE YAHWEH *MALAK* PSALMS. One of the interesting aspects of the interpretation of Psalm 94 is that it does not immediately resonate with the language of the other psalms of the Yahweh *malak* collection (Pss 93–99, or 93–100 if we include Ps 100 as a doxology to this collection, as we probably should), so questions arise about its place in the collection. As discussed above in our consideration of Psalm 93, the overarching tone of Psalms 93–100 is summarized in the repeated statement "the LORD reigns" (Pss 93:1; 96:10; 97:1; 99:1). Not all the psalms contain these exact words, but they all, at the very least, include connected imagery that points to the absolute sovereignty of Yahweh over all creation. Psalm 94, however, is somewhat different in its tone (see Original Meaning above). The poem is a song that considers the oppression of the vulnerable in society and points to their ultimate

---

11. "The Rock is not to be understood as the omphalos or center of the earth, standing in the most sacred room of the Zion sanctuary, but it must be taken as the stony shield that the hills offer warriors and, metaphorically, the defender who brings to justice his moral balance and integrity" (Terrien, *Psalms*, 666).

12. Hossfeld and Zenger, *Psalms 2*, 455.

vindication at the hand of Yahweh their Protector. Another interesting point that feeds into this discussion is the apparent similarity between Psalms 92 and 94, both of which deal with the final fate of the wicked. On a superficial level it might seem that Psalm 94 has been misplaced and that it does not really belong among the Yahweh *malak* psalms. David Howard summarizes the differences in this way:

> Psalm 94 stands amidst the kingship-of-Yahweh psalms surrounding it as something of an anomaly, however. For one thing, it is much longer than most of the surrounding psalms. More significantly, it sounds a more discordant note than most of the psalms in an otherwise praise-oriented section. Furthermore, it is a complex poetic composition composed of an individual lament (vv. 1–7), a wisdom interlude (vv. 8–15), and a community lament (vv. 16–23), whereas most of the surrounding psalms are much simpler in form and are more thoroughly unified. Finally, few of the great kingship-of-Yahweh motifs are found in this psalm; it does not belong to this form-critical genre in any scholar's estimation. What, then, is Psalm 94 doing in its present position? What function does it perform?[13]

While the structure, tone, and form of expression of Psalm 94 are quite different from those of the other psalms in the collection, as Howard suggests, the presentation of Yahweh is clearly in line with the views expressed in these other psalms. The ultimate presentation of God in Psalm 94 insists that Yahweh is the righteous Judge who will deliver a final verdict on all corrupt authorities—a message that resonates strongly with presentations of God in Psalms 96, 98, and 99. The imagery of God as Judge and Avenger combines nicely with the metaphors of kingship that are prevalent in the collection's remaining psalms, in which Yahweh is pictured as great God, great King, mighty King, Most High, Maker, Creator, etc. Psalm 94 is different from the other poems of this grouping in that it is not the same type of didactic praise poem. The other psalms represent vibrant, objective contemplations of the nature of Yahweh, whereas Psalm 94 is focused on earthly realities of social injustice and abuse of office. Nonetheless, Psalm 94 still paints a very similar picture of Yahweh to the one we find throughout the collection. He is the ultimate Sovereign in every aspect of life and being. In most ancient Near Eastern cultures the king was normally the ultimate arbiter of justice. While each nation would have some sort of judiciary functioning at a lower level, the ultimate right of appeal for justice would

---

13. David M. Howard Jr., "Psalm 94 Among the Kingship-of-Yhwh Psalms," *CBQ* 61.4 (1999): 667–68.

be to the king. In the ancient world, therefore, the judicial imagery is also rule imagery, so the representation of Yahweh in Psalm 94 is not at odds with the rest of the collection despite its differences from the other poems.

Psalm 94 in New Testament. Psalm 94:11 is cited in 1 Corinthians 3:20. Paul's basic thought echoes the basic idea of Psalm 94, namely, that even that the highest heights of human wisdom are inevitably limited when compared to the wisdom of God. In 1 Corinthians 3 Paul applies this principle to human approaches regarding the strengths and weaknesses of particular leaders. And Paul's corrective to the Corinthian church points out that old traditional human categories of assessing and valuing leadership are meaningless when applied to spiritual leadership because ultimately every true spiritual accomplishment is the work of God and not a human work. So such debates based on personality affiliations are really meaningless from a kingdom perspective.[14]

There also seems to be an echo of Psalm 94:14 in Romans 11:1–2. Verse 14 of Psalm 94 states that "the LORD will not reject his people," and Paul echoes this thought in Romans 11:1. Though Israel has not yet responded to the gospel of Christ as they ought, their slowness to do so does not mean that the "original" people of God have been abandoned by him. Paul firmly believes there will come a time when the Jewish people do turn to the good news of Jesus the Messiah and therefore also that Yahweh has not given up on ethnic Israel.[15]

Considering the themes of Psalm 94 more broadly, the New Testament appears rife with imagery that speaks of God as Judge over all creation. This theme is, of course, a frequent one in the book of Revelation (e.g., see Rev 6 and 20), but this imagery is also found throughout the literature of the New Testament (e.g., Heb 12:23–24; Jas 4:11–12; 1 Pet 4:5–6 et al.).[16]

CHRISTIANS AND POLITICS. The closing verses of Psalm 94 provide the reader with a salient warning about our primary responsibility to our Creator to live in accordance with his created order. Inevitably, this warning will make the community of faith cautious about the affiliations we make with those who wield power, regardless

---

14. For fuller discussion see H. H. Drake Williams III, "The Psalms in 1 and 2 Corinthians," in *The Psalms in the New Testament*, ed. Steve Moyise and Maarten J. J. Menken (London: Continuum, 2004), 164–67.

15. Keesmaat, "Psalms in Romans and Galatians," 153–54.

16. Longman, *Psalms*, 338.

of their political hue. Verse 20 asks, "Can a corrupt throne be allied to you—a throne that brings misery by its decrees?" This question is rhetorical, the obvious answer being "No," and is designed to make the people of God think critically about all political allegiances. Social governance that brings misery by its decrees is something that runs counter to the creative ordinances regarding the sanctity of life and the fundamental dignity of every human being created in the image of God. So, while it is entirely appropriate for Christians to be fully involved and engaged in the political realm, it is important for all believers to maintain a critical distance from any and all policies that contradict God's purposes for humanity and this world. To that end, together with the poet the contemporary church must never lose its prophetic voice. So, although it is important for Christians to be engaged in the political realm because otherwise we cede all influence to those who do not follow the ways of the Lord, our involvement should always allow scope to take a step back and say, "No, this decree brings on misery, and it would be wrong to implement such a policy." Psalm 94 is clear about the faith community's responsibility to care for those who are socially marginalized (vv. 4–7). This responsibility must always be the priority of the people of God because it is the priority of our God, who is Judge (vv. 8–11, 15).

Association with the oppressed. The concluding verse of Psalm 94 points to the poet's willingness to side with the oppressed against the oppressor (vv. 16–23). The speaker believes that God will act to protect the vulnerable (vv. 16–17), but he is also clearly willing to take his own stand against injustice. There are parts of the world where Christians are oppressed and persecuted simply because of their love for and devotion to Jesus. In these instances the call to protect the oppressed is real, vivid, and personal. But for the majority of the church in the Western world, we are seldom subject to oppression and marginalization of this type. Indeed, this more protected position seems to be the psalmist's position as well. It is not the psalmist who is being oppressed, but he stands with the oppressed because he knows that social injustice is abhorrent in God's eyes. He expresses willingness to stand up for what is right simply because it is right and not because it brings some benefit to himself. I feel that the church in Europe and North America often finds itself in this position. We may feel somewhat sidelined by increasingly marked trends toward secularism in our culture, but the worst excesses of what might be called oppression in our society are seldom directed toward the Christian community. Surely it is the task of the church, however, to root out oppression of any type and to speak up for the voiceless in our communities, whoever they may be.

As I write these words I am sitting in a friend's home in King William's Town, South Africa, where I have been teaching in a theological college that seeks to serve the Xhosa community of the Eastern Cape. The college is called Dumisani Theological College, and one of its buildings previously belonged to the Biko family. It was in the garden of that building that the black political activist Steve Biko met with Donald Woods, a white journalist who had become convinced that the wrongs of the apartheid system must be opposed. I certainly do not want to oversimplify a complex social and political equation, but we can see echoes of Psalm 94 in this scenario. Donald Woods, and many other white anti-apartheid campaigners both within and outside the church, associated themselves with an oppressed community even though they themselves were not the objects of that oppression. The psalmist makes this call clearly in Ps 94 and provides an example for the Christian church in every locality. Who are the voiceless, marginalized, oppressed of our area, and how can we stand with them to fight for a justice that is pleasing to God our Creator? My fear is that local churches are often so disengaged from the world around them that we are even unaware of injustices that exist not far from our own doorstep. Psalm 94, however, encourages us proactively to seek out those who are in need and to make a stand on their behalf. This is an awkward calling but one that sees the full value of all people created in the divine image. It is also a ministry that foreshadows the ultimate work of God. Our task is to associate actively with the voiceless and to declare his justice in our societies before he comes to avenge and judge the earth (vv. 1–3).

Power of shared testimony. Verses 17–19 give a great example of the power and encouragement of shared testimony. The poet relates his experience of God's protection and deliverance in the past knowing that this testimony will be an encouragement to the readers of the poem as they face their own challenges and difficulties. The Lord had helped the psalmist when he faced death (v. 17), and this testimony strengthens readers to take their stand against social injustice in their own society (v. 16), even though doing so involves risk on their part. So, the reader hears the challenge to stand up for the oppressed and thinks, "Yes, this is risky but it is the right thing to do. Yahweh saved the psalmist in his day of need; surely he will help me in mine!" Testimony of God's intervention in our lives encourages others to take risks in the service of his kingdom.

I often find that Christians are reluctant to share testimonies of God's intervention and help because we fear that we will be seen as "hyperspiritual" or seeking to draw attention to ourselves. We are happy enough to speak about everything else *apart* from the work that God has done and is doing in our lives—weather, sports, news, politics, but not anything that might be described as "testimony." In so doing we rob ourselves of a rich source of spiritual exhortation and affirmation. Grounding biblical truth in the framework of real daily human experience communicates powerfully. It's not just about the exodus or the resurrection or other biblical narratives. God is at work today in the lives of his people, and we need to share with one another that living, daily narrative of his deliverance and empowering as an encouragement to take risks in seeking to fulfill God's purposes on earth. The author of the letter to the Hebrews writes, "And let us consider how we may *spur one another on* toward love and good deeds, not giving up meeting together, as some are in the habit of doing, but *encouraging one another*—and all the more as you see the Day approaching" (Heb 10:24–25, emphasis added). We do these things as we share openly with one another about God's work in our lives, so it is important that God's people are never shy to do so.

Psalm 95

¹ Come, let us sing for joy to the LORD;
  let us shout aloud to the Rock of our salvation.
² Let us come before him with thanksgiving
  and extol him with music and song.
³ For the LORD is the great God,
  the great King above all gods.
⁴ In his hand are the depths of the earth,
  and the mountain peaks belong to him.
⁵ The sea is his, for he made it,
  and his hands formed the dry land.
⁶ Come, let us bow down in worship,
  let us kneel before the LORD our Maker;
⁷ for he is our God
  and we are the people of his pasture,
  the flock under his care.
Today, if only you would hear his voice,
⁸ "Do not harden your hearts as you did at Meribah,
  as you did that day at Massah in the wilderness,
⁹ where your ancestors tested me;
  they tried me, though they had seen what I did.
¹⁰ For forty years I was angry with that generation;
  I said, 'They are a people whose hearts go astray,
  and they have not known my ways.'
¹¹ So I declared on oath in my anger,
  'They shall never enter my rest.'"

PSALM 95 CONTINUES the Yahweh *malak* psalms with a powerful reminder of past failure as a spur toward present devotion to God. The poet reminds the current community of God's people of the failures of the exodus generation in the desert and, by doing so, encourages them not to fall into the same trap. The right communal attitude toward Yahweh as Creator and God of the covenant is one of responsive worship as opposed to an attitude of reluctance and resistance. This psalm serves as a vivid challenge and reminder to every generation of God's people to learn from the mistakes of the past.

Psalm 95 divides into three stanzas made up of verses 1–5, 6–7c, and 7d–11. The first two stanzas begin with a public exhortation for the community of faith to "Come" in order to worship their God.[1]

Come and Worship the Creator God (95:1–5)

COME, LET US SING FOR JOY TO THE LORD. Psalm 95 begins with an exhortation to very vocal praise of Yahweh. The exhortation to draw near is plural, thus addressing the whole community of God's people, and the verbs call for noisy worship.[2] Our English renderings ("sing," "shout aloud," and "extol") are perhaps somewhat weak compared to the Hebrew, which uses the same verb in verses 1b and 2b. The emphasis of the Hebrew is very much on the "shouting aloud" in praise to Yahweh. This language is often associated with Old Testament festival worship, for which the people came together to declare publicly and vocally their praise of God.[3]

The Rock of our salvation. The description of God as the "Rock of our salvation" resonates both with Psalm 18 and Deuteronomy 32,[4] but this description of God is also found in laments such as Psalms 88 and 89. As discussed above,[5] remembering God as the "Rock of our salvation" points to a God who is actively involved in our daily realities and difficulties. The *rock* imagery refers to God as fortress or protective crag, and the idea of *salvation* in the Old Testament is not a spiritualized concept of belief and its effects—rather, it is the understanding that this God, who is our protective rock, intervenes to help his people in the here and now. As Schaefer points out, the idea of a God who *is* "our salvation" resonates with exodus imagery, and, of all the events of Israel's history, perhaps it is the exodus that points most powerfully to God's practical and physical intervention in behalf of his people.[6]

For the LORD is the great God. The ensuing verses (Ps 95:3–5) provide the rationale that lies behind the call to worship. Why should the people worship Yahweh as opposed to any other God? Because he is the "great God" and "great King" (v. 3). This greatness is evidenced by his ultimate power, expressed in his creation of the universe (vv. 4–5). He alone made the earth in all its amazing mystery and thereby has proven himself

---

1. Two different commands are used in verses 1 and 6 (*leku* and *bo'u* respectively), but each verb serves as an invitation to the community to come together in approach to God in worship.
2. Goldingay, *Psalms 3*, 90.
3. Hossfeld and Zenger, *Psalms 2*, 460.
4. See Ps 18:2, 31, 46; Deut 32:4, 15, 18 et al.
5. See the discussion of Ps 74:12 above.
6. See Exod 14:13; 15:2; Schaefer, *Psalms*, 362.

to be the "great God" and "great King." These verses include two merisms that show the full extent of God's creative power. The "depths of the earth" and the "mountain peaks" both belong to God as Creator, and the "sea" and "dry land" were both formed by him.[7] Of course, there is symbolism attached to the terminology chosen by the psalmist: the "depths of the earth" would often be associated with the underworld, which was seen as the domain of shadowy powers, and the "mountain peaks" were thought to be the dwelling places of the gods. But the poet asserts, quite simply, that these extremes belong to him as Maker, and in turn his ownership of them implies his absolute power in every realm.[8] Equally, Yahweh made the sea and dry land, and as Progenitor he is also Ruler.[9]

Come and Worship the God of the Covenant (95:6–7c)

COME, LET US BOW DOWN IN WORSHIP. The worship imagery of the second stanza moves from the vocalizing of worship (vv. 1–2) to deference and obedience in worship (v. 6). As a community, the worshipers celebrate their God loudly because he is Creator, but they also bow before him because he is King. The language used in these verses (especially in v. 7) is the language of covenant, and the position adopted in worship ("bow down") is the appropriate response as one approaches the greatest Suzerain (see Bridging Contexts). He is the high King and, as such, is entirely worthy of deference and respect.

For he is our God and we are the people of his pasture. Verse 7 echoes the covenantal formulas seen throughout the Old Testament but particularly in Deuteronomy (e.g., Deut 26:17–19) and the Deuteronomic literature (e.g., Jer 23:1–4). The phrase "he is our God" is often associated with strong declarations of loyalty to Yahweh, Israel's God, over and above all other gods (e.g., see Josh 24:16–18). This association makes sense in the international and pluralistic context in which we find Ps 95. "The Lord reigns" psalms of this collection (Pss 93–100) are voiced in the literary presence of the watching world. They call all the nations to worship (see comments on Ps 96) and declare Israel's God to be sovereign over all nations and superior to all gods. So, this declaration that Yahweh is both Maker (Ps 95:6)

---

7. The language used to describe the "depths of the earth" in Hebrew seems to imply the "unfathomable depths" of the created order. These are areas that cannot be properly plumbed or searched out by human beings, yet they are held in God's hand (see "מֶחְקָר," *HALOT* 1:413–14 and "יְבַּשֶׁת," *HALOT* 1:384–5; Goldingay, *Psalms 3*, 92).

8. Weiser, *Psalms*, 626.

9. "Yahweh's dominion over nature rests upon the fact that he created it, and that he is its undisputed Lord" (Anderson, *Psalms*, 678).

---

and Owner (v. 7) of his people is also a proclamation of his supremacy over everything else that claims any sense of rule, divinity, or power. This God— the indisputably sovereign God of the universe—is Israel's God. He alone, and no other. So, there is a strong sense of communal identification with the absolute Ruler of the universe, but this identification works two ways, for Israel is also Yahweh's possession, his flock. Israel declares its affiliation with Yahweh, and Yahweh claims Israel is his people in a special sense of belonging. The need to experience a sense of identity and belonging is something of fundamental importance to human experience, and Psalm 95 speaks profoundly about that basic need (see Contemporary Significance).

Learning from Past Mistakes (95:7d–11)

THE FINAL STANZA IN PSALM 95 focuses on the mistakes of the present community's forebears in the faith by encouraging the present generation—and every succeeding generation, for that matter—to avoid the waywardness of the exodus generation. This stanza sees a marked change in tone and genre from the preceding verses. We move from praise to a prophetic rebuke that reflects the voice of God to the current generation of the faith community.

Today, if only you would hear his voice.[10] Once again we see similarities with Deuteronomy in the psalmist's call to obey (e.g., see Deut 5:1; 11:13; 15:5; 28:1 et al.). The translation "if only you would hear his voice" does not, perhaps, fully reflect the force of the language used in the Hebrew text. The issue is not about whether God's voice is audible to his people—it is rather that the worshiping community should be careful to *listen* to his voice when they hear it. The combination of God's "voice" (*qol*) and the verb "to hear or listen" (*shama'*) has a particular nuance, especially when used in a Deuteronomic context: the verb takes on an implication of *obedience* rather than the simple physicality of hearing or listening.[11] The implied undercurrent is that the hearers of the psalm should listen to *and obey* the voice of the Lord in contradistinction to the behavior of their forefathers of the exodus generation. The "if" of this line is not really meant to indicate the possibility of doubt about whether or not the people will hear God's voice; rather, it expresses an appeal to the current generation to be different from their founding fathers by actually obeying God's voice![12]

---

10. There is an apparent mistake in the versification here. This phrase has been traditionally included as the conclusion to verse 7, but it reads much more naturally as the introduction to the ensuing lines of verse 8 (Alter, *Psalms*, 337).

11. Equally, for the desert generation the problem was not that they failed to hear God's voice or that his direction was unclear to them. It was, rather, that they failed to listen and obey.

12. With some justification, Hossfeld translates this line as: "Oh, that today you would hearken to his voice!" (Hossfeld and Zenger, *Psalms 2*, 458).

Do not harden your hearts. Meribah and Massah are place names redolent with images of faithlessness, hardheartedness, and rebellion. Referring to the exodus generation's unwillingness to trust God in the desert (Exod 17:1–7) despite the miraculous deliverances they had witnessed in their release from captivity and the miraculous provision of food and drink (Ps 95:9), Massah and Meribah became names synonymous with the wrong attitude toward God. The opening praise of Psalm 95 (vv. 1–7c) encourages the right attitude toward God—one of worship, trust, and obedience—and this second section (vv. 7d–11) illustrates the type of attitude and behavior to avoid at all costs.

For forty years I was angry with that generation. In verses 6–7c the call to worship with a right attitude emphasizes the intimacy of relationship that exists between Yahweh and his people. But verse 9 points out that this very intimacy of relationship can be impaired by the people's failure to bow the knee to God. Yahweh's plan was to bless and provide for his people, but their constant attitude of careless rebellion, on some level, spoiled the covenantal relationship between God and Israel. That relationship was not irreparably ruined—covenantal relationship is still offered to the generation of the psalmist; but the exodus generation's enjoyment of the covenantal relationship with their Creator and Redeemer was spoiled by their consistent refusal to listen and trust ("I was angry with that generation").

They have not known my ways. Several instances of rebellion associated with the desert generation are recounted for us in the Pentateuch. First, there is the incident at Massah and Meribah, where the people rebelled because they were thirsty (Exod 17). Second, there is the rebellion following the report of the spies who entered the promised land (Num 14). Third, there is the rebellion in Numbers 20, once again over lack of water in the desert. And fourth, in Numbers 21 we see a similar rebellion over food and water and the hardship of the desert wanderings. Actually, the Pentateuch records many more instances of Israel's rebellion, but in each of these cases the people end up questioning Yahweh's character by questioning his intent and purpose for his people. In Exodus 17:3 and Numbers 14:3, 20:4, and 21:5, the people all ask whether Yahweh had brought them out of Egypt with the intent of letting them die in the desert. This is the attitude reflected in Psalm 95:9, where through the psalmist God says, "They have not known my ways." Basically, the first generation after the exodus never fully accepted the goodness of God's character despite all the evidences he gave them of its goodness. And in many ways this disbelief was the most repugnant aspect of their rebellion. Despite being given every evidence of God's care and keeping, that generation continued

405

to question the fundamental goodness of his nature. Their example is given as a stark warning to the psalmist's generation to remember that God loves his people and that he is in control regardless of the appearance of present circumstances. Yahweh is their Maker and King, and the people can trust in him.

They shall never enter my rest. According to the psalmist this is the very reason that the people failed to enter the promised land.[13] It was because the desert generation explicitly and continually denied God's good character that they were excluded from entry into the land as a place of rest.

The conclusion of Psalm 95 is purposefully open-ended. Much like the book of Jonah and, as we have seen, Psalm 78, Psalm 95 lacks a clear conclusion. The poem simply ends by voicing the effect of the forefathers' rebellion: they robbed themselves of the promised rest. The open nature of the psalm's conclusion is quite deliberate. It invites readers to draw their own conclusion, to supply their own ending. The abrupt ending to the psalm effectively challenges the hearer to decide for herself: "Will I harden my heart, or will I bow down in worship?"

 **COVENANT IN THE OLD TESTAMENT.** Psalm 95 revolves around the important theological concepts of covenant and covenantal faithfulness. The language used is the language of covenant in the Old Testament, and the challenge presented by the psalmist to the people is the challenge of being faithful to the covenant. The essence of covenant is relational. It is about God's relationship with his people and about their response to him. As Patrick Miller illustrates:

> The close relationship between deity and tribe . . . expressed itself in covenantal forms, at the heart of which was the binding together of the people in a sociopolitical relationship with the deity that recognized the involvement of Yahweh in the guiding and protecting of the people and that obligated them to maintain allegiance to him.[14]

The heart of covenant is the divine promise of presence, protection, and blessing. The people's response to that promise is one of fealty—obedience to the ways of God. This promissory relationship, while fundamentally

---

13. This understanding is indicated by the consequential use of *'asher* in verse 11 (lit., "So that I swore an oath"; see "אֲשֶׁר," *HALOT* 1:98–99).

14. Patrick D. Miller, *The Religion of Ancient Israel*, Library of Ancient Israel (London: SPCK, 2000), 4.

religious and worship-based at heart, follows social and political patterns that were well known in the ancient Near East. Miller again comments:

> In its simplest form . . . that covenantal bond rested in the reciprocal claim and promise of Yahweh, "You are my people," and of Israel, "You are my God" (Hos. 2:25[23]). In its more complex form, the covenant bond has been compared to the international political treaties of the first and second millennium that spelled out the way in which a great king (in this case, Yahweh) has dealt beneficially with a vassal (in this case, Israel), set forth stipulations that such benevolence places upon the vassal, and built in provisions for sanctions, witnesses safekeeping of the treaty document, and its regular reading by the vassal.[15]

Basically, the covenantal forms that we see in the Bible, especially as represented in the book of Deuteronomy, seem to reflect the patterns of the suzerain-vassal treaties of the ancient Near East.[16] The implications of this known background for the biblical concept of covenant are quite profound. Clearly, a suzerain-vassal treaty encompasses more than just religious practice, and so it is in terms of the biblical concept of covenant. While Psalm 95 clearly encompasses the legitimate religious expression of covenant—worshiping Yahweh and him alone—the implications of Yahweh's being both "great King" (v. 3) and "Maker" (v. 6) point to a type of allegiance that goes beyond our worship practice. Ancient Near Eastern covenants would stipulate in great detail acceptable behavior on the part of the vassal. In the same way, covenantal allegiance to God affected not only Israel's worship practice but also the political, social, familial, trade, and other practices of the nation.

The type of covenant implied in Psalm 95 is based on worship but goes far beyond it, as is evidenced by the Deuteronomic language used in the composition. The failures of the exodus generation highlighted in verses 7d–11 stress the fact that true covenantal loyalty will influence every area of life and practice. As the ultimate suzerain, God lays a holistic claim over every aspect of the people's lives. They are to follow his ways (v. 10) in every aspect of their life and practice. The covenantal relationship affects every aspect of society and if in practice it does not do so, then serious questions are to be asked about whether the people are truly being faithful to the covenant.

---

15. Miller, *Religion*, 5.

16. For much more detailed background discussion, see Moshe Weinfeld, *Deuteronomy and the Deuteronomic School* (Oxford: Clarendon, 1972); Meredith G. Kline, *The Structure of Biblical Authority*, 2nd ed. (Eugene, OR: Wipf and Stock, 1989).

Psalm 95 in the New Testament. Psalm 95 is used powerfully in Heb 3:1–4:13 as part of the author's rhetorical challenge to the first generation of Christians to remain faithful to Christ. Effectively, the author of Hebrews exegetes this passage as part of his warning against turning away from Christianity and back, presumably, to Judaism.[17] The essence of the argument in Hebrews 4:1–13 is that failure to obey robs the believer of the reward God wants to bring. Challenges will occur. There will be real and trying difficulties we have to face. But turning away from God in times of trial is not the right option. Obedience by clinging to Christ leads to the rest and blessing of the promised land. The use of Psalm 95 in the book of Hebrews runs with the grain of the text. The poem was meant to be heard as a challenge to remain faithful to God, and the author of Hebrews uses it in precisely the same way regarding the Christian community's relationship with Christ. The unfaithfulness of the exodus generation is used as a foil for discussion in both cases: "Let us, therefore, make every effort to enter that rest, so that no one will perish by following their example of disobedience" (Heb 4:11).

Second, the imagery of being "the people of his pasture, the flock under his care" also resonates strongly with Jesus' self-description as the good shepherd in John 10. Just as in Psalm 95 Yahweh fulfills the function of caring Shepherd-King, so also Jesus echoes that role in John 10. The full expression of that divine pastoral keeping of his people becomes apparent in the New Testament where Jesus describes the self-sacrificial nature of God's loving oversight of the covenant community: "The good shepherd *lays down his life* for the sheep" (John 10:11, emphasis added). God's people have always lived under his care. That guardianship is not without cost to God. Psalm 95 explains how Yahweh continued to look after his flock despite their rebellion. John 10 shows just how much the Trinitarian God was prepared to sacrifice out of love for his people.

IDENTITY AND BELONGING. One of the greatest needs in contemporary society is the need to belong. In Abraham Maslow's much-discussed hierarchy of needs, "love and belonging" comprise the third most important need after basic physical needs, such as food, rest, and a sense of safety and security.[18] How many movies have we

---

17. For fuller discussion see Harold W. Attridge, "The Psalms in Hebrews," in *The Psalms in the New Testament*, ed. S. Moyise and M. J. J. Menken (London: T&T Clark, 2004), 205–8. Hossfeld describes this discussion as a midrash on verses 7–11 (Hossfeld and Zenger, *Psalms 2*, 462).

18. A. H. Maslow, "A Theory of Human Motivation," *Psychological Review* 50/4 (1943): 370–96.

watched or books have we read that revolve around the central character's quest for a sense of identity or communal belonging?

Psalm 95, with its strong sense of covenantal theology, speaks clearly to the issue of identity and belonging. The psalm celebrates the community's relationship with Yahweh the Maker ("people of his pasture," "flock under his care" [v. 7]). The people know to whom they belong, and the implication of this psalm is that life is *better* because of that knowledge. The need for identity is properly basic to human existence, so Israel responds in joyous worship *because* they know to whom they belong. There is a sense of inevitability about this joyful response. The logic of covenant is quite inescapable. If Yahweh is God and created humanity for relationship with him, then, inevitably, humanity can only find true fulfillment in that covenantal bond.

This message of belonging is clearly proclaimed in Psalm 95. The declaratory nature of the psalm is not just for the purpose of worship but also serves as proclamation to the nations. As we will see in our discussion of Psalm 96, the Yahweh *malak* psalms proclaim God's true nature to the nations. So, while Psalm 95 serves as a reminder to Israel to be faithful to God, the first part of the psalm also declares God's sovereign rule as Creator of the universe. The declaratory purpose of Psalm 95 reminds us, as it reminded the original hearers, that we have a message to proclaim to all those outside the covenant community, namely, a message of belonging and identity. In a world that is crying out for a sense of purpose, we have a message that speaks of community, identity, and direction in life. The gospel, of course, proclaims a message of redemption and forgiveness, but we have to remember that the good news of Christ is holistic in nature. Redemption is not just about the forgiveness of sins; it is also about the renewal of humanity in its every aspect—spiritual, communal, environmental, and so on. Christ's purpose was to renew relationship with God the Father, and that renewal encompasses much more than just religion. We proclaim a message of community, a message of identity, and a message of holistic future hope. It is important that we never limit our proclamation of God's story to the forgiveness of sins alone. The gospel gives an entirely new sense of belonging and a powerfully renewed sense of human identity. These senses, too, are part of the message that our generation needs to hear and to see modeled in our churches.

Importance of reading church history. This emphasis may seem like a strange area of application to draw from Psalm 95, but the main teaching point of the second part of the psalm (vv. 7d–11) is that we should learn from the mistakes of previous generations. Obviously, we can learn from the errors of God's people that are outlined for us in the Scriptures, but we also have two thousand years of church history at our disposal that can inform our awareness today. The vast majority of theological controversies and questionable practices we presently face in the Christian church have been played out many times in past generations. Reading church history can give us a helpful starting point for addressing such challenges. For example, as I write, the issue of universal salvation or universal reconciliation has been much to the fore following the publication of Rob Bell's book *Love Wins*.[19] Reading from church history shows us that this question has been debated a great deal throughout the life of the church. Origen's contention that all would be saved—though it must be said that his argument was slightly different from Bell's proposals—was rejected by an ecumenical council in Constantinople in 543 CE. Richard Bauckham is able to write on the subject:

> Until the nineteenth century almost all Christian theologians taught the reality of eternal torment in hell. Here and there, outside the theological mainstream, were some who believed that the wicked would be finally annihilated (in its commonest form, this is the doctrine of "conditional immortality"). Even fewer were the advocates of universal salvation, though these few included some major theologians of the early church. Eternal punishment was firmly asserted in official creeds and confessions of the churches.[20]

History helps to frame discussions regarding theology and practice. Looking back, we can see the threads of arguments running through the life of the church. We see why arguments were made, how their implications were worked out, and why they were accepted or rejected. Learning from church history gives us a good grounding to process those discussions that are problematic or controversial in our day. Of course, the church is constantly learning and growing, so we are not bound absolutely by the lessons of previous generations, but there is much wisdom to be found in the lives and debates of our predecessors in the faith. There are many popular-level, readable histories of the church and biographies of significant figures available to us, so let us take seriously Psalm 95's challenge to learn from the past, both from the errors and the examples of those who have gone before us in the faith.

---

19. Rob Bell, *Love Wins: A Book About Heaven, Hell, and the Fate of Every Person Who Ever Lived* (HarperCollins: New York, 2011).

20. Richard Bauckham, "Universalism: A Historical Survey," *Them* 4.2 (1978): 47.

Psalm 96

¹ Sing to the LORD a new song;
　　sing to the LORD, all the earth.
² Sing to the LORD, praise his name;
　　proclaim his salvation day after day.
³ Declare his glory among the nations,
　　his marvelous deeds among all peoples.
⁴ For great is the LORD and most worthy of praise;
　　he is to be feared above all gods.
⁵ For all the gods of the nations are idols,
　　but the LORD made the heavens.
⁶ Splendor and majesty are before him;
　　strength and glory are in his sanctuary.
⁷ Ascribe to the LORD, all you families of nations,
　　ascribe to the LORD glory and strength.
⁸ Ascribe to the LORD the glory due his name;
　　bring an offering and come into his courts.
⁹ Worship the LORD in the splendor of his holiness;
　　tremble before him, all the earth.
¹⁰ Say among the nations, "The LORD reigns."
　　The world is firmly established, it cannot be moved;
　　he will judge the peoples with equity.
¹¹ Let the heavens rejoice, let the earth be glad;
　　let the sea resound, and all that is in it.
¹² Let the fields be jubilant, and everything in them;
　　let all the trees of the forest sing for joy.
¹³ Let all creation rejoice before the LORD, for he comes,
　　he comes to judge the earth.
He will judge the world in righteousness
　　and the peoples in his faithfulness.

MANY MISCONCEPTIONS about the Old Testament are prevalent in the church in the twenty-first century, and one of the most common is that there was no concept of mission before the coming of Christ and the giving of the Great Commission. It would certainly be true to say that the concept of mission changes with the incarnation of Jesus and the sending out of the Twelve and the seventy-two, but Psalm 96 is a poem that is replete with missional themes. The next of the Yahweh *malak* psalms (see Ps 93 for fuller discussion) reminds God's people of *their* responsibility to call the nations into the worshiping community and also gives clear reasons why *Yahweh* should be worshiped above all other gods.

Psalm 96 breaks down into two main sections, and each of these sections consists of two parts. Verses 1–6 give a call to worship (vv. 1–3) followed by a clear rationale as to why Yahweh alone is to be praised (vv. 4–6). The second section, verses 7–13, follows the same pattern with a second call to worship (vv. 7–10[1]) followed by a further set of reasons for praising Yahweh (vv. 11–13). The surprise factor in Psalm 96 is the addressees of the exhortation to worship. Rather than Israel, the established covenant community, the (pagan!) nations are encouraged to join their voices with Israel in bringing worship to the one, true God. If we are going to arrive at a proper understanding of how to read this psalm, it is important that we grasp the amazing significance of the address in Psalm 96. In Book 3 of the Psalter (Pss 73–89), we see that the nations are, by and large, described as the enemies of the people of God and are those who mock the name of Yahweh, Israel's God. It was the nations who destroyed the temple and decried God (Ps 74). The nations invaded Jerusalem and left the bodies of God's people to rot in the streets (Ps 79). The nations are characterized as plotting against Israel and against Yahweh (Ps 83). So, in short and on the one hand, the nations surrounding Israel are presented as the source of opposition, oppression, injustice, and false religion. But even in the darkness of Book 3's lament over the fall of Jerusalem and the exile, we see another minority voice regarding the nations. Both Psalms 86 and 87 point to a future reality in which the nations will join with Israel in worshiping Yahweh (Pss 86:9; 87 *passim*). This perspective on the nations is much less common throughout the Old Testament, but its voice is consistent. The nations are both rebellious but also seen as heirs of God's promise in some future reality. Psalm 96 brings that minority voice front and center by calling on all nations and peoples of the earth to join with Israel in bringing praise and worship to Yahweh as the one God who truly reigns over all the earth.[2]

---

1. The NIV is probably wrong to include verse 10 with the subsequent verses as part of the final section. The vocal command "*Say* among the nations" is better grouped with the preceding commands that call for the vocal and active praise of God in verses 7–9.

2. It should also be noted that Ps 96 is quoted almost in its entirety in 1 Chr 16, thus pointing to a possible role for this psalm in Israel's festal worship.

The First Call to Worship (96:1–3)

Sɪɴɢ ᴛᴏ ᴛʜᴇ Lᴏʀᴅ ᴀ ɴᴇᴡ ꜱᴏɴɢ, ꜱɪɴɢ ᴛᴏ ᴛʜᴇ Lᴏʀᴅ ᴀʟʟ ᴛʜᴇ ᴇᴀʀᴛʜ. Typically, the call to worship is characterized by plural commands of vocal praise and the language of approach and worship. The call to worship in Psalm 96 incorporates these elements (vv. 1–2a) but goes beyond by including commands of proclamation and declaration (vv. 2b–3). As mentioned above, the real surprise is the full extent of the address: *the whole earth* is called to praise Yahweh (i.e., "the Lᴏʀᴅ," Israel's God). Not just Israel but the whole earth, without exception, is called to praise Israel's God.

It is this unusual address that leads to Psalm 96's being described as a "new song" (*shir hadash*). For the Israelite singing Psalm 96, there is little if anything new in terms of content.[3] But a song giving praise to Yahweh as Creator and Ruler of the whole earth would, indeed, be new to the lips of any non-Israelite. As Brueggemann suggests, the newness refers not just to unfamiliar words but also to a "new orientation" reflected in the decision to join the global community of praise that has grown out of Israel.[4] Gerstenberger suggests that the "new" aspect of the song is meant to be read as an expression of hope for a better future:

The criteria for the Old Testament "New Song," consequently, are these:

1. It was intoned against death and evil in order to support and make possible full human life.
2. It was voiced in communities small and great, but never in the privacy of chamber or office.
3. It anticipates boldly, against all evidence, the coming of God's liberation, the new and just world.[5]

This call to praise is also missional in its intent. The nations are invited to join Israel in praising Yahweh, but, of course, the Yahweh *malak* psalms were probably part of Israel's festal worship. The proclamation of Psalm 96 was addressed to the nations, but the primary hearers in the composition's original setting would have been Israelites and, additionally, proselytes (those non-Israelites who had decided to worship Yahweh out of choice

---

3. Alter, *Psalms*, 338.
4. Walter Brueggemann, *The Message of the Psalms: A Theological Commentary*, AOTS (Minneapolis: Augsburg, 1984), 144.
5. Erhard S. Gerstenberger, "Singing a New Song: On Old Testament and Latin American Psalmody," *WW* 5 (1985): 159. Tremper Longman suggests the new song is "a phrase that is normally in warfare contexts and [thus] implies that it is a shout of victory" (Longman, *Psalms*, 341).

rather than because they were born into the covenant community). So, although the whole earth is addressed, the singers and hearers of this new song are primarily Israelites. In that sense, the "newness" of the song is probably twofold: first, those who do not know Yahweh are called to praise him, and second, those who do know Yahweh are reminded that the whole earth is called to join their ranks. So, Psalm 96 may also be described as a "new song" because a minority voice in the Old Testament is given pride of place. The nations are called to sing God's praise alongside Israel. This very notion would have been radically new and extremely challenging to most Israelites, so in that sense Psalm 96's universal address makes this a "new song" for many.[6]

Proclaim his salvation day after day. The language of verse 2b is also interesting. The Hebrew word that is (rightly) translated "proclaim" in the NIV is the command form of the verb *basar*, which seems to provide the Old Testament conceptual root to the idea of "proclaiming good news" in the New Testament.[7] Certainly the same verb is used this way in Isaiah 61:1 in proclaiming Yahweh's daily salvation (i.e., his practical help and engagement in the lives of his people [see the discussion of Ps 74:12 above]). So the good news that Israel proclaims is of a *real* God who is *truly* involved in the lives of his people. This news is, of course, good for the nations because they are invited into relationship with this real God who is actually capable of affecting their reality. Psalm 96:5 makes it clear that the nations' gods are illusory and therefore incapable of effecting salvation.

Declare his glory among the nations, his marvelous deeds among all peoples. "Glory" (*kabod*) and "marvelous deeds" (*nipla'ot*) are characteristics of Yahweh that are entirely absent from the gods of the nations. These terms emphasize God's unquestionably good character and his amazingly

---

6. See Chris Wright's helpful discussion of Ps 96 throughout his *The Mission of God*. Psalm 96 is actually a key text for Wright in the development of a missional reading of the Bible. He comments, for example: "Israel, therefore, as the people who do know the true identity of the living God . . . must bear witness to that knowledge among the nations. . . . [T]he concept is clearly there: this knowledge *is to be* proclaimed to the nations. . . . *How* this would happen is never clearly articulated in the Old Testament, but *that* it would happen is unequivocal. It is celebrated in advance in worship and prophecy." Wright then goes on to cite Ps 96:1–3 and Isa 12:4–5. Psalm 96 has clear missional overtones, yet this focus was something that had become lost in Israel's worldview. So in many ways Ps 96 would have been a stark challenge to the prevailing view of Israel's role among and relationship with the nations.

7. *HALOT* makes it clear that *basar* does not necessarily imply the proclaiming of *good* news, but often the "goodness" of the proclamation may be naturally derived from the context, as in Isa 61 and Ps 96 ("בשׂר," *HALOT* 1:163). As James Mays comments, "The psalm has a definite evangelical cast" (Mays, *Psalms*, 308).

good works. Verse 3 encourages the proclamation of these two features of Yahweh's being among the nations because these characteristics set Yahweh apart from their gods. "Glory" implies that Yahweh is a substantial God: weighty, real, and truly significant in and above the created realm. "Marvelous deeds" is used in the poetic books to refer either to God's work in making and controlling the universe (Job 37:14) or to his amazing works of deliverance in behalf of his people (especially regarding the exodus, see comment on Ps 77:14 above). These characteristics—a God who is real and who works in our reality—stand in marked contrast to the gods of the nations (Ps 96:5), who are neither real nor efficacious.

The First Rationale (96:4–6)

FOR GREAT IS THE LORD AND MOST WORTHY OF PRAISE. The power of the reasons given for the praise of Yahweh is found in their simplicity. "Why should we praise Yahweh?" the nations might ask in response to the call to worship in verses 1–3. "Because Yahweh is great and he is worthy of praise," comes the simple reply from the choir of Israel! His character and his works (v. 3) establish categorically that Israel's God is great. In fact, they establish that he is infinitely greater than all the gods of the nations ("he is to be feared above all gods" [v. 4b]). The language of height used here implies Yahweh's absolute rule and unquestionable authority over the whole of creation, including the gods of the peoples.[8] Why worship Yahweh? Simply because he is worthy of worship—his character and works evidence that fact.

For all the gods of the nations are idols. The psalmist's exercise in the apologetics of comparative religion continues in verse 5. The call to worship Yahweh challenges the peoples to compare their experience of their own gods with the character and works of Yahweh. In verse 5 the poet uses a clever play on words to underline the inadequacies of the gods of the nations compared to the one, true God. Literally, the Hebrew reads: "For all the gods [*'elohim*] of the peoples are worthless things [*'elilim*]." This final world *'elilim* is difficult to capture in English. It is often used to refer to idols (Isa 2:8, 18, 20), but the word is value laden rather than purely descriptive. *'Elilim* is also often used with a pejorative overtone to signify things that are worthless, vain, or insignificant. For example, consider the "worthless physicians" in Job 13:4 or the "worthless shepherd" in Zechariah 11:17. Psalm 96:5 is clearly implying that, while the nations may think

---

8. For fuller discussion of the idea of God and the gods in the Psalms, see the comments on Ps 82 above.

they have gods (*'elohim*), they actually have "worthless idols" (*'elilim*).[9] The psalmist's strategy of poetic proclamation is to encourage the nations to compare the insignificance of their gods with the great weightiness and significance of Yahweh (his *kabod* ["glory"] in v. 3).

But the LORD made the heavens. The significance of this (again straightforward) statement is doubly profound. First, the fact that Yahweh is Creator shows his great power in contrast to the worthlessness of the gods of the surrounding nations. And second, the fact that Israel's god *made* everything implies that he cannot be represented by anything that is part of that creation. If Yahweh created all things, then he is automatically above and beyond whatever object the nations may choose to worship. Here again there is strong polemic that shows the absolute supremacy of Israel's God over the idols of the peoples. As Hossfeld comments,

> In this context the brief reference to YHWH's *creatio prima* of the heavens is also understandable. The gods are things of naught in comparison to YHWH, the Creator. As Creator he cannot be represented by anything that is made, which is why idols are obsolete both in their significance and in their material.[10]

It is probably also significant that it is specifically "the heavens" that are described as being created by Yahweh. As well as referencing God's worth because he is Creator, the expression "the heavens" represented the sphere of existence in which the people of the nations believed their gods lived. The implied polemic then becomes clear: the worthless gods may (or may not) live there, but in either case it was Yahweh who created that dwelling space.

Splendor . . . majesty . . . strength . . . glory. The following verse emphasizes Yahweh's unmistakable right to receive worship by personifying abstract nouns that are attributes of Yahweh's being and imagining them as worshipers in the sanctuary of his own presence. This language is that of temple worship for the Hebrew community, and again the wording stresses the fact that Yahweh is worthy of worship because he *undeniably is* worthy of worship. There is a beautiful circularity in the argumentation here.[11]

---

9. Goldingay's suggested translation of "nonentities" for *'elilim* conveys the essence of the Hebrew very nicely (Goldingay, *Psalms 3*, 103–104).

10. Hossfeld and Zenger, *Psalms 2*, 465.

11. The word "glory" in verse 6b is not from the same Hebrew root that we find in verse 3a and is, perhaps, better translated "radiance" or "magnificence" (see Hossfeld and Zenger, *Psalms 2*, 463).

The Second Call to Worship (96:7–10)

THE SECOND CALL TO WORSHIP echoes the first in terms of its language, ideas, and universal address. But it also goes beyond the initial call to worship by introducing the theme of Yahweh as Judge (vv. 9–10), thus bringing a stronger sense of appeal and urgency to this call. There is clearly an escalation in tone as the psalm approaches its climax.

Ascribe to the LORD, all you families of nations. There is a strong textual link between verses 7–8 and Psalm 29:1–2. The language used is virtually identical except that the "heavenly beings" (probably the angelic host[12]) are addressed in Psalm 29, and here in Psalm 96 it is the "families of nations" who are addressed. Much of Psalm 96 borrows language and concepts from other psalms, but, interestingly, the psalmist takes this familiar language and addresses it to an unfamiliar audience. The call to "ascribe to the LORD" seems to imply a degree of fealty in the response. It is the giving over to Yahweh of all glory and strength that may otherwise have been offered or exerted elsewhere.[13] This call is a summons to declare loyalty and commitment. The psalmist is not interested in the nations' merely offering *words* of praise—he calls for a complete giving over of self, power, and glory to Yahweh and to him alone. This commitment is visualized in the act of bringing an offering or sacrifice (v. 8b). Just as, for example, the bringing of tribute and the offering of a whole burnt offering are acts of complete giving over, so also the ascription of glory and strength called for by the psalmist is an act of conscious and complete giving over of self to Yahweh for his glory and for the fulfillment of his ends.

All you families of nations. This address is of particular significance because it echoes the missional promise made to Abraham in Genesis 12:1–3 that through him "people [the same Hebrew word as in Ps 96:7] on earth" will be blessed. So, from an intertextual perspective the address in Psalm 96:7 is significant. Clearly Psalm 96 has a proleptic, universal perspective—it envisions a time in the future when the praise of God will be sung by all nations. This particular formulation points to a reality in which the Abrahamic promise is fulfilled. Genesis 12:1–3 is a vitally important passage if we are to understand the overall story of salvation that is developed throughout the Scriptures. It is foregrounded in the Bible's salvation-history, and it is significant to many of the major theological concepts that have shaped both Judaism and Christianity (e.g., election, covenant, faith, salvation, etc.). So, it is not by accident that the invitation to join the worshiping community goes out to all the families

---

12. Broyles, *Psalms*, 152.
13. For fuller comment see the interesting discussion in Goldingay, *Psalms 2*, 415.

of the earth. This denominator goes far beyond concepts of nationhood, language groups, or even cultural identity, and it points to an amazingly inclusive worshiping community. Obviously, we see this reality fulfilled in part today, but the address of Psalm 96:7 reminds us that this invitation to worship still needs to be extended to "families of nations" throughout the world today.

Worship the LORD in the splendor of his holiness. In verse 9 the call to "worship" is literally an invitation to "bow down" (cf. Ps 95:6). Just as in Psalm 95:6 Israel is called to "bow down" to Yahweh, so also the families of the nations are called to "bow down." Such a clear act of commitment draws the nations into the flock of Psalm 95—the nations acquire a new sense of belonging and a new communal identity as they offer their allegiance to Yahweh (see the discussion of Ps 95 above). The use of the same terminology in neighboring psalms has an interesting effect: in Psalm 95 Israel is reminded of her rights and responsibilities as the elect people of God, then in Psalm 96 all the nations of the earth are invited to join that community of the elect by offering worship to Yahweh. That the Yahweh *malak* psalms (Pss 93–100) have a decidedly universal and cross-cultural perspective subverts many of the traditional understandings of key theological concepts. Here the concept of election is radically reformed—a theological notion that would often be seen to separate Israel from the nations is transformed into something much more open and inclusive. This transformation is further emphasized by the invitation to bow down to Yahweh in "the splendor of his holiness," a phrase that probably alludes to the priestly attire which had to be worn by the Levites when they served in the tabernacle and temple (cf. Exod 28:2).[14] The nations are reclothed in

---

14. This phrase may seem simple in English, but the correct reading of the Hebrew is actually quite tricky. Literally, the phrase *behadrat-qodesh* is probably best rendered "in the beauty of holiness." There is no possessive "his" in the Hebrew text, though the pronoun was added in the early Greek translation, the Septuagint. So it is not clear whether the reference is then to the beauty of Yahweh's holiness or to the status of the worshipers (the mode in which they should worship Yahweh). The commentators are divided on the question: some read the phrase as a reference to the sanctuary following on from reference to "courts" in verse 8b; others read it as referring to the beautiful holiness in which Yahweh is attired in his majesty and power; and still others see it as pointing to the ceremonial clothing that was sanctified for use by the priests as they served in the tabernacle and temple. In truth, each of these readings is credible to one degree or another. But I see the juxtaposition between the call to "bring an offering" in verse 8b (a priestly act) and the reference to the "beauty of holiness" (the priestly ceremonial clothing) as telling here, and so would suggest that this phrase refers to the complete "rebadging" of the gentile nations. They are reclothed in priestly clothing so that they too can enter the real presence of God.

priestly garb that sets them apart also to worship in the presence of God every bit as much as Israel was set apart for worship before God.

Say among the nations, "The LORD reigns." The call to commitment is further emphasized by the central theme of the Yahweh *malak* collection: Yahweh reigns, and if this statement is true, then it requires a response. The universality of Psalm 96's call to worship is grounded in the simple fact of Yahweh's universal reign as Creator ("the world is firmly established, it cannot be moved" [v. 10b]) and Ruler ("he will judge the peoples with equity" [v. 10c]).[15]

The Second Rationale (96:11–13)

THE FINAL STANZA PROVIDES A VERY DIFFERENT set of reasons why it is important for all peoples to worship Yahweh. Essentially what we see is an environmental rationale that emphasizes the universality of response to the rule and reign of Yahweh.

Let the heavens rejoice. Psalm 96 moves from the imperatives of the second call to worship to a series of jussive verbs that encourage the whole created order to voice its gladness in response to Yahweh's kingship. As Hossfeld observes, "The extrahuman creation is drawn into the act of worship . . . ,"[16] and Schaefer points out that a sevenfold response of praise occurs in verses 11–12 (heavens, earth, the sea and its contents, the fields and their content, and the trees of the forest), thus indicating the completeness of creation's praise of Yahweh.[17] *Everything* in the created order praises Yahweh; therefore, the implied suggestion is that *everyone* should also praise Yahweh! The environmental response in verses 11–13 is interesting and reflects a repeated theme in the Psalms. As Michael Northcott suggests, "In the Hebrew perspective humanity and the cosmos have moral significance, and both are required to make a moral response to the creator, a response which reflects his glory and offers the return of gratitude, praise and worship [Ps 150]."[18]

Effectively, Psalm 96 counteracts two equally erroneous responses to nature and the environment. The first rationale warns against deifying nature. The gods of the nations throughout the ancient Near East were often represented by animals or astral symbols. Verses 4–6 make it clear

---

15. Since the language of "judging" (*din*) was very closely associated with the role of kingship in the ancient Near East, it conveys more the sense of exercising authority than the idea of a courtroom activity.

16. Hossfeld and Zenger, *Psalms 2,* 466.

17. Schaefer, *Psalms,* 239.

18. Michael S. Northcott, *The Environment and Christian Ethics* (Cambridge: Cambridge University Press, 1996), 181.

that deifying the natural realm is empty. But the inclusion of the natural realm in this chorus of praise in verses 11–12 shows the significance of the natural world in God's grand design for humankind. "The environment" realizes something that some people do not—God is absolutely worthy of praise—and as such it plays a sanctified role in the call to worship that goes out to all the nations of the earth. (Paul seems to suggest something similar in Rom 1:18–20.) The environment fulfils a holy purpose within God's plan of salvation for the nations, so clearly its protection and enjoyment is something to be encouraged in the believing community.[19]

Let all creation rejoice before the LORD, for he comes . . . to judge the earth. The final rationale mentioned in Psalm 96 is also the *ultimate* reason for the nations to join in the praise of Yahweh, namely, *Yahweh* will be the one to judge the nations, not any of the illusory idols that are worshiped by the peoples surrounding Israel. Ultimately, all created human beings are answerable to their Creator, and Psalm 96 declares unambiguously that Yahweh alone is the true Originator of all human life; therefore, it is "the LORD" alone who has the right to judge, and he *will* judge according to his standards. So, there is a resonant sense of ultimacy in the final verse of Psalm 96: all peoples should choose to worship God because he is the Judge over all humanity.

The repetition of "for he comes" in verse 13, rather than being the result of a scribal copying error as some suggest, is an example of anadiplosis, the repetition of the end of one line at the beginning of the next line. The net effect of this poetic feature is to draw attention to Yahweh's future theophany.[20] One day he will come, and that appearance will be for the purpose of judgment. As above (see comments on v. 10), the judging probably refers more to rule and governance than it does to judicial punishment,[21] a likelihood stressed by the qualifiers attached to Yahweh's activity on the earth ("in righteousness" [v. 13c] and "in his faithfulness" [v. 13d]). Of course, these qualifiers may also refer to judicial activity, but it seems more likely that the psalmist has in mind a new order of things according to which Yahweh governs the whole earth and all the peoples, not just Israel, in righteousness and truth.[22] Clearly, Psalm 96 sees just such divine rule as

---

19. For a fascinating discussion of God's mission and the earth see Christopher J. H. Wright, *The Mission of God*, 397–420.

20. The verb forms here are participles (*ba'*), which could be equally well translated as "he is coming."

21. Hossfeld and Zenger, *Psalms 2*, 466.

22. The association of the common word for "earth" (*'erets*) in verse 13b and the related term "world" (*tebel*) in verse 13c seems to imply that Yahweh's work of renewal will apply both to the natural order and to humanity (see Goldingay, *Psalms 3*, 107–108).

being a *present* reality, so it is interesting to read this verse—which points to a future appearance of God that will institute a new era of his reign among the nations—from a theological and christological perspective drawn from the Bible.

PSALM 96 IN THE YAHWEH *MALAK* COLLECTION. Psalm 96 continues the thematic consideration of the universal reign of Yahweh that was begun in Psalm 93 and culminates in the benediction of Psalm 100. But there is a clear sense of escalation throughout the collection, with new themes and aspects of Yahweh's reign being brought into focus with the addition of each new psalm.

The new aspect introduced in Psalm 96 is its universal address. We have seen the claim of Yahweh's lordship over the nations and their gods elsewhere in the Psalter (e.g., Pss 2, 72, 82 et al.), but Psalm 96 introduces this element of *invitation* to the nations to join the worshiping community of faith. Adding further interest to this surprising "new" theology is Psalm 96's juxtaposition alongside Psalm 95. As was discussed above, Psalm 95 is a strongly covenantal composition. Israel is called to "bow down" in worship before "the LORD" their maker (v. 6), and then, intriguingly, the nations are called to do exactly the same in verse 9.[23] This connection further stresses the main theme of Psalm 96: the incorporation of the nations into God's community of faith.

It is clear from the addressees of the calls to worship that the pagan nations are called on to join with Israel in the worship of Yahweh. But the way in which this theme is developed in association with Psalm 95 shows that this call extends to full covenantal allegiance between God and the nations. This matter does not just require the pagan peoples to "say the right words." The call on the peoples to bow down to Yahweh, just as Israel must bow down to Yahweh, points to the nations' inclusion in all the rights and responsibilities of intimate and binding relationship with Yahweh. This call to worship is a call to participate in all the privileges of covenantal blessing. The covenant was often seen as a theological concept that separated Israel from the nations (as exemplified by the attitude of Jonah, for example), but it seems that God's purpose for salvation had always intended an inclusive covenantal theology rather than an exclusive one.

---

23. See comments on this verse above. The aspect of "bowing down" in worship is somewhat obscured in the NIV's translation. Robert Alter, for example, translates 96:9a as "Bow to the Lord in sacred grandeur" (*Psalms*, 339.)

Genesis 12:1–3, with its indication that Abraham's election would bring blessing to all the families of the earth, is echoed in the renewal of the covenantal promise with Abraham in Genesis 17:1–8, where he is told that he will be "the father of many nations" (v. 4). But with the passage of time this intercultural and inclusive view of the covenant somehow became lost from Israel's understanding of God's plan for salvation. The juxtaposition of Psalms 95 and 96 reminds Israel that God's salvific plan extends far beyond their own national and cultural bounds. The call to worship invites all nations to bow the knee to Yahweh in covenantal fealty and thus evokes the picture of the nations in the book of Isaiah (e.g., Isa 12 and 19). It is difficult to say how Israel lost that external and inclusive focus—perhaps it was simply the result of the continual opposition of neighboring states. Psalm 96, as part of the Yahweh *malak* psalms, reminds the worshiping community of their responsibilities to those presently outside the body of faith. This reminder was important for Israel. It remains an important reminder for the church.[24] Somehow the Old Testament faith community had lost any real sense of their missional responsibility amid discussions of their own uniqueness and identity. The same can be true in the church. It is vital that missionary songs such as Psalm 96 never become minority voices in terms of our own self-understanding as Christian communities.

God and the gods. For fuller discussion of Israel's God and the gods of the nations, see Psalm 82 above.

Psalm 96 in the New Testament. There may be an allusion to Psalm 96:13 in Revelation 19:11, but the tone is quite different in the respective passages so the similarity between the two verses may be more accidental than purposeful.[25] Nevertheless, the idea of God's future judgment as bringing his intervention into the affairs of humanity is common to both passages, and Hossfeld suggests that wherever there is an allusion to Psalm 96 in the New Testament, "it always retains an eschatological interpretation of the psalm."[26]

Perhaps more telling is the general allusion to a divine theophany that will establish Yahweh's rule on the earth and that will draw the nations into covenantal relationship with him. This theme is, of course, strongly reminiscent of the work and teaching of Jesus as it is outlined for us in the Gospels. Jesus is the physical representation of the invisible God (Col 1:15), and he came bringing a message of the *kingdom* of God. As George Eldon

---

24. For further discussion of the Old Testament's view of the nations, and regarding Israel's "missional" responsibility, see Wright's magisterial work *The Mission of God*.

25. Moyise, "Psalms in Revelation," 244.

26. Hossfeld and Zenger, *Psalms 2*, 467.

Ladd suggests, "The Kingdom is God's kingly rule. It has two moments: a fulfillment of the Old Testament promises in the historical mission of Jesus and a consummation at the end of the age, inaugurating the Age to Come."[27] God's kingship breaks into human reality in a remarkable and new way in the incarnation of Christ. It is that arrival of God on earth that ultimately draws the nations into the worshiping community. And that revelation of God in Christ begins the process of consummation—one day, every single individual will see and acknowledge the absolute rule of Yahweh.

MISSIONAL SONGS, MISSIONAL COMMUNITY. One of the key and unmistakable lines of application from Psalm 96 is the responsibility of the worshiping community to call others to join their ranks. As Christians, we should never forget that we sing a missional song that speaks of a God who reaches out. Equally, we should never forget that ours is a missional identity. Psalm 96 exemplifies for us the right type of praise we should offer in public worship and also the right understanding of our own identity as communities of God's people.

Any song of praise and worship to God that truly reflects his identity will speak of the way he has and does reach out to restore and renew sinful humanity and of how he draws us into a new relationship with him. Our songs should be acts of worship to God that declare his character as a missionary God. They should also proclaim his rule over the whole of the created order. These acts of proclamation are missional in nature. They speak to those who do not know God about his true character and being. So, it is important that our repertoire of worship songs and hymns truly declares the character of God. Whether or not we "like the tune" is neither here nor there. What is much more important is that the songs we sing accurately reflect the character of God to all those who are listening, both "we ourselves" and "others." Our songs are acts of proclamation every bit as much as our sermons are. So, we must think carefully about what our songs of praise say about our God to those who are listening.

Second, the modern church also needs to ensure that our missional responsibility does not become a minority report in terms of our own self-understanding. The age-old question "Why did Jesus create a church?" has often been bogged down in discussions of discipleship and care for

---

27. George E. Ladd, *A Theology of the New Testament*, rev. ed., ed. Donald A. Hagner (Grand Rapids: Eerdmans, 1993), 58.

the flock over against outreach and mission. Of course, this is an entirely false dichotomy. Mission and discipleship, discipleship and mission go absolutely hand in hand. The formation of disciples was an act of outreach for Jesus; equally, outreach involved teaching and instruction. The thing to remember from Psalm 96 is that this missional practice of calling others to join in the praise of Yahweh should never become a minority voice in our setting. In Israel's history, the people's obligation to the nations became lost in their own internal discussions of their uniqueness and identity. Their international and intercultural responsibilities became so neglected that the call for the nations to praise God was described in Psalm 96 as a *new* song. It is vital that our churches remember our own shared responsibility to proclaim the message of a gracious God who reaches out to save people. We should never be so caught up in our own questions that we forget to invite others to join us in bringing praise to God.

Singularity in a pluralistic world. Psalm 96's central theme of the kingship of Yahweh provides an important reminder in another area of missional praxis, namely, the uniqueness of the gospel message we proclaim. In an increasingly pluralistic world, there is great pressure on the church to adapt our message to accommodate a plurality of views and opinions regarding the experience of salvation. It is often asked, especially in the increasingly secular Western scene, "How can you exclude the validity of every other religious experience? How can you exclude others like that?" Words such as "fundamentalism" are easily bandied about.

But Psalm 96 sets absolutely the right tone for the church today. As communities of faith we must be welcoming and inviting and, at the same time, absolutely clear about the uniqueness of our message. Israel invites the nations to sing *Yahweh's* praise (v. 4), and the message of the psalm is absolutely clear about the inadequacies of the gods of the nations (v. 5). This poem gives us the right example to follow. It is a picture of an open and welcoming community that presents an uncompromising message because that message is based on the truth (John 14:6).

Psalm 97

¹ The LORD reigns, let the earth be glad;
   let the distant shores rejoice.
² Clouds and thick darkness surround him;
   righteousness and justice are the foundation of his throne.
³ Fire goes before him
   and consumes his foes on every side.
⁴ His lightning lights up the world;
   the earth sees and trembles.
⁵ The mountains melt like wax before the LORD,
   before the Lord of all the earth.
⁶ The heavens proclaim his righteousness,
   and all peoples see his glory.
⁷ All who worship images are put to shame,
   those who boast in idols—
   worship him, all you gods!
⁸ Zion hears and rejoices
   and the villages of Judah are glad
   because of your judgments, LORD.
⁹ For you, LORD, are the Most High over all the earth;
   you are exalted far above all gods.
¹⁰ Let those who love the LORD hate evil,
   for he guards the lives of his faithful ones
   and delivers them from the hand of the wicked.
¹¹ Light shines on the righteous
   and joy on the upright in heart.
¹² Rejoice in the LORD, you who are righteous,
   and praise his holy name.

PSALM 97 CONTINUES the theme of Yahweh's absolute kingship by celebrating his revelation to all humanity through theophany (appearance) and also through the created realm. The Yahweh *malak* psalms (93–100) stress the absolute lordship of Israel's God, and the particular nuance of Psalm 97 is that God's lordship is established by his self-revelation through dramatic appearance by way of the universe he has created and also through the teaching he has given to his people.

Yahweh has proven himself to be the true God by presenting himself to humanity—something the gods of the nations could never do because they are not real (v. 9). The reality of God's existence and the revelation of his character and being establish his lordship over everything else that would claim ultimate authority in this world. Basically, the message of Psalm 97 is that God *is* and God *speaks*; therefore, he alone is worthy of worship in the market-place of gods that was the reality of the ancient world.

Many of the main themes of Psalm 97 are found in the other psalms of the Yahweh *malak* collection (see consideration of Ps 93 above). So, rather than repeating discussions that have been developed elsewhere in this commentary, we shall simply cross-reference the relevant sections from other psalms where similar discussion has already taken place.

Responding to Yahweh's Rule (97:1)

THE LORD REIGNS, LET THE EARTH BE GLAD; LET THE DISTANT SHORES REJOICE. Picking up where Psalm 96 left off, the psalmist calls for an environmental (cf. Ps 96:11–13b) and international (cf. Ps 96:1–3, 7–10a) response to God's rule. Continuing these emphases from the previous psalm, the poet again extends the benefits of Yahweh's rule far beyond the bounds of Israel—the whole created order ("the earth"), including the foreign and distant nations ("the distant shores"), rejoices in his kingship.

There continues to be some discussion among scholars about how the phrase *Yahweh malak* should be understood. This disagreement is evidenced in the various translations offered by commentators. Goldingay, for example, suggests this phrase should be read as "Yahweh began to reign."[1] Zenger proposes the option, "Yahweh is/has become king."[2] Weiser, apparently following Mowinckel's suggestion, offers: "The Lord is become king."[3] Eaton goes for, "The LORD is King!"[4] More translations abound. The challenge is that these two words in Hebrew carry more nuance than would seem possible at first glance. Zenger comments on the current scholarly opinion: "the newer tendency is to interpret this 'thematic sentence' as ingressive [i.e., a declaration of kingship just begun] *and* durative [i.e., a proclamation of kingship that has continued through the ages regardless of circumstances]: Yahweh became king before all ages (cf. Ps 93:1) and ever since has ruled as king."[5] This understanding leads

---

1. Goldingay, *Psalms 3*, 111.
2. Hossfeld and Zenger, *Psalms 2*, 468.
3. Weiser, *Psalms*, 630.
4. Eaton, *Psalms*, 342.
5. Hossfeld and Zenger, *Psalms 2*, 469.

to Hossfeld and Zenger's somewhat unusual translation, "Yahweh is/has become king."

The discussion of the precise nuance of this phrase is complex, but the theological meaning is clear: Yahweh rules—he always has, he does now, and he always will. Hence the NIV and most contemporary English versions (apart from the NRSV) retain the translation "the LORD reigns." As Alter suggests, "God's grandeur as king of all the world would have been a perfectly appropriate theme for a Hebrew poet,"[6] particularly in terms of Book 4's response to the exile as it is highlighted in (among others) Psalm 89. All the signs of the covenant (temple, city, king) are gone, as we see in the laments of Book 3, but the Yahweh *malak* psalms of Book 4 boldly proclaim that Yahweh *was* King over creation from the beginning (Ps 93), he *is* King now, regardless of how bleak things may look (Ps 94), and he *will* ultimately prove himself to be King at the end of the age (Pss 96; 97). The basic intent of this type of poetry is, obviously enough, to remind the reader of God's control over all things regardless of circumstances.

Revelation by Theophany (97:2–6)

CLOUDS AND THICK DARKNESS SURROUND HIM. The imagery of God's appearance ensconced in cloud and surrounded by darkness is typical of the theophany ("physical" appearance of God[7]) language that we see throughout the Old Testament. We see similar language used to describe God's appearance before Israel at Mount Sinai in Exodus 19–20 (and Deut 5), and Psalm 97:2–6 is typical of the Psalter's representations of Yahweh's miraculous appearance (cf. Ps 18:4–15). The Sinai experience—the primary example of theophany—is intimately associated with the giving of the law (the Ten Commandments and the Covenant Code that follows in Exod 20–23); therefore, with the passage of time the very idea of divine theophany came to be associated with the act of revelation. There is, of course, irony in the fact that clouds and thick darkness actually bring the light of revelation (cf. Ps 97:11). That which would normally obscure one's vision brings clear-sightedness. As Zenger comments:

> The fact that the paired expressions "clouds and thick darkness" surrounding him, that is concealing him, here . . . in Ps 97:2 do not . . . intend to describe YHWH as a god of storm and thunder, but instead characterize him as the God of Sinai (who reveals

---

6. Alter, *Psalms*, 328.

7. See the Bridging Contexts section for further consideration of theophany in the Old Testament.

the Torah, as his order of righteousness, to Israel) and the God of Zion (who from there orders the cosmos and defends it against chaos), is underscored precisely by the "foundation of his throne" motif in v. 2b.[8]

So, the language that is associated with the manifestation of God in these verses points to a God who reigns, who intervenes in human reality (hence his appearance), and who speaks. These themes are developed throughout Psalm 97.

Righteousness and justice are the foundation of his throne. The fact that Yahweh reigns is asserted in verse 1, thus continuing the thrust of Psalm 96, and, again echoing the theology of its preceding psalm, Psalm 97:2b seeks to establish *the nature* of that rule. Just as in Psalm 96:13 God is described as judging in righteousness and truth, so this verse emphasizes that the very basis of Yahweh's rule ("foundation of his throne") is righteousness and justice. Here we have no capricious and nasty god. Yahweh is, rather, a God who embodies in his rule all that is good and fair, hence the joyous response from both Zion (Ps 97:8) and the nations ("distant shores" [v. 1]).[9]

Fire goes before him. Fire and lightning are frequently presented as accompanying the tangible manifestation of God in a theophany. The language here is quite similar to other descriptions of divine manifestation (e.g., see Ps 18:8–12; Exod 19:16–19; Deut 4:11–12). Sometimes God speaks from the fire, or the lightning simply accompanies the real presence of God. But here in Psalm 97, the fire and lightning seem to serve as expressions of God's judgment as well as evidence of his goodness. Yahweh's foes are consumed by the fire, but this occurrence is clearly good news for all peoples in all places (vv. 1, 6). The implication that follows seems to be that these acts of divine judgment illustrate both Yahweh's lordship (note the response of trembling in verse 4) and his righteous goodness (v. 6). God's intervention in spectacular judgment by fire brings evidence of his control over all things and the rightness of his action.

The mountains melt like wax. The picturing of that which is most stable as melting is another common feature found in descriptions of God's tangible presence. It is difficult to be sure of the meaning implied in these descriptions (see also Ps 18:8; Exod 19:18), but it seems likely that the presence of God is more real and substantial than the most real and substantial thing the human mind can imagine. In the created realm there

---

8. Hossfeld and Zenger, *Psalms 2*, 472.
9. Here Ps 97 very much echoes the theology of Ps 82.

is surely nothing more fixed than a mountain. Yet it seems to melt like wax compared to the reality of God himself. His glory (weightiness) is more concrete and tangible than the mountains. All the created order, in some sense, declares the true character of God (Ps 97:6a) and, ultimately, Psalm 97 (like the other psalms in this collection) foresees a day when all peoples will see and acknowledge his true character (v. 6b).

Worship the God of Gods (97:7–10)

ALL WHO WORSHIP IMAGES ARE PUT TO SHAME. The structure of Psalm 97 is difficult to chart with any degree of confidence, but verses 7–10 seem to stand together as a chain of verses that form tricola rather than the typical bicola we find in Hebrew poetry.[10] The thematic focus of these verses revolves around the worship of Yahweh as the one true God. The contrast is between "all those who worship images" (v. 7) and "those who love the LORD" (v. 10). Effectively, these verses call on the peoples of the nations to change their affiliation from worshiping empty idols, which can offer nothing because they are deceptive "ungods,"[11] to loving the true God, who guards and delivers his people.

Worship him, all you gods. Psalm 97 reflects the type of theology that has already been discussed in our consideration of Psalm 82. Israel's monotheism was probably more functional than ontological. All the surrounding nations claimed to be ruled and governed by local, geographically bound gods. We moderns tend to think of monotheism as the abstract concept that the biblical God alone exists and no other gods actually exist in reality. It seems that in the Hebrew mindset the main question was one of worth and value rather than an abstract concept of existence. All societies and cultures in the ancient world would have been theistic, so the type of polemic discussion we witness in these verses does not revolve around questions of existence or nonexistence. The key focus is on the relative merits of Yahweh vis-à-vis the gods of the nations. They are *elilim* (empty and false).[12] He is the Most High, above all gods (v. 9). The univocal claim of the Yahweh *malak* collection is that Israel's God *alone* reigns over the whole of the created order. So the psalmist, in his address

---

10. That is, each verse is made up of three lines that are held together in some sort of creative tension rather than the more normal two lines to a verse.

11. This helpful translation is offered by Robert Alter (*Psalms*, 342). The word used in verse 7 is *'elilim*, echoing verse 5. (See the comment on verse 5 for fuller discussion of the meaning of this word.) The use of this key term in successive psalms is another indication of the linking and interaction that occurs in this collection of poems.

12. See the discussion of Ps 96:5 above.

to the nations, engages in the practice of comparative religion in its most basic form. The question is: whose God/god is actually worth worshiping? The answer is clear. Whether or not the gods of the nations exist, they are false and are subject to Yahweh's lordship. So they too (along with the nations) are called to worship him.

Zion hears and rejoices. Clearly, Yahweh's lordship over all nations and their gods is good news for God's people (Zion and Judah). But the implication of the call to worship in verse 1 and of the international tone of this collection is that this news is also good for the whole world. The modern reader tends not to view "judgment" in a positive light. It may be a necessary exercise, but it is not often viewed with rejoicing. But the implication of these verses is that Yahweh's judgment brings justice to the earth and to human experience. God's judgment (i.e., his intervention into the reality of human affairs), therefore, is good news, for it deals with the oppression and atrocities so often associated with the worship of the gods (cf. Ps 82). Very obviously, divine protection (Ps 97:10) is good news for God's people, but the restoration of justice is good news for the whole created order.

Let those who love the LORD hate evil. As we find so often in Scripture, that which is important to God should also be important to his people. The poetic juxtaposition of opposites emphasizes the right response in both the vertical and the horizontal plane: love for God brings abhorrence to all things that are abhorrent to him.

The Call to Rejoice (97:11–12)

LIGHT SHINES ON THE RIGHTEOUS. The concluding verses of Psalm 97 speak about the benefits that come from devotion to the Lord. The benefits of "light" and "joy" (v. 11) are matched by the calls to "rejoice" and "praise" (v. 12). The interesting aspect, again, is the identity of the recipients of these blessings. Literally, the Hebrew says that "light is sown for the righteous and joy for the upright in heart." Those who receive this light (with the passive verb *zaru'a* implying that it is Yahweh who does the sowing) are characterized by their response of righteousness and uprightness, not by their national or religious identity. It is not the inhabitants of Zion or Judah mentioned in verse 8 who receive light and joy; rather, it is whoever responds to God in righteousness and uprightness of heart. Presumably, therefore—and given the context of this psalm—some of those who so respond will be non-Israelites. Equally, the reader may assume that some Israelites will *not* respond in the way described in verse 11 and will therefore rob themselves of these blessings. It is fascinating that it is the character of the respondent that is key, not his or her national or cultural identity.

Rejoice in the LORD. The psalm ends as it begins. All those who would respond to Yahweh and his expectations are called on to respond with rejoicing and praise (cf. v. 1).

Bridging Contexts

GOD AND THE GODS. For further discussion of concepts of monotheism in the ancient world see Psalm 82 above.

Theophany. Theophany is the term used to describe the appearance of God to his people. The word itself is drawn from two Greek words: God (*theos*) and the verb "to appear" (*phainein*). Strictly speaking, theophany can refer to God's self-revelation in any form—in dreams, visions, or auditory revelation—but most commonly the term is applied to the more physical and tangible appearances of God to his people. We see this type of tangible meeting from the very beginning of the biblical narrative. In Genesis 3:8 we come across the image of God's walking with Adam and Eve in the cool of the day—the physical presence of God as he meets with his people.[13] And this type of encounter between the Creator and his chosen line occurs again and again throughout the Genesis narrative. (For example, Gen 12:7; 15:1; 17:1 and especially chapter 18 outline just some of the theophanies experienced by Abraham.)

As discussed above, the description of a theophany is often accompanied by visual and terrifying storm imagery. For readers in the ancient world, and particularly in the ancient Near East, the storm brought both terror and benefit. The storm could bring great destruction and devastation, but it could also bring the rains, always much needed for crops to grow in an otherwise arid climate. Rudolf Otto suggests that the storm imagery ideally reflects sinful humanity's relationship with an all-holy God. He describes

---

13. Jeffrey Niehaus interestingly argues that the translation "cool of the day" (*leruah hayyom*) is perhaps inaccurate. The Hebrew literally reads that Yahweh was walking in the garden in the "wind/breath of the day," and Niehaus, drawing an analogy from Akkadian (a language related to Hebrew), suggests the noun that is usually translated "day" (*yom*) could actually be an uncommon variant with the same spelling meaning "storm" (see "יוֹם," *HALOT* 1:413–4). The linguistic argument is not strong, as there is insufficient evidence of the use of *yom* in a storm context. But the translation of God's appearance in Gen 3:8 as being "in the wind of the storm" is consistent with the other theophanic accounts of God's self-revelation we encounter throughout the Old Testament. The storm would represent God's judgment on the sin of our human parents, just as the storm of judgment often accompanies other theophanies in the Old Testament, as we see here in Ps 97:2–5. (For fuller discussion see Jeffrey J. Niehaus, *God at Sinai: Covenant and Theophany in the Bible and Ancient Near East*, Studies in Old Testament Biblical Theology [Grand Rapids: Zondervan, 1995], 155–59.)

this relationship as the *mysterium tremendum*—the terrible mystery. We are, at one and the same time, both terrified by God's manifestation and attracted to him because we recognize his gracious intent.[14] We see a similar reaction from the people at Sinai in Exodus 19–20: attraction and the desire to see, hear, and know combine with a sense of terror that led the people to send Moses to speak with God. For many people still today, storms are both attractive and terrifying at the same time.

From Yahweh's remarkable theophany at Mount Sinai onward, divine appearance became linked with the concept of revelation. When God appears, he very often appears in order to speak to his people. Niehaus highlights several activities of God that are associated with his appearance in theophany. Among other reasons, God appears to:

1. Initiate covenant;
2. Instruct (and correct) the community of faith;
3. Call or commission prophets;
4. Bring judgment where necessary.[15]

Psalm 97 *instructs* all people about the true nature of God (v. 1) and also speaks of his impending *judgment* (vv. 2–5, 7 et al.) on all those (regardless of ethnic origin) who reject the things that are important to him. As is common in other theophanic accounts throughout the Old Testament, in Psalm 97 God is presented as both King and Judge:

> As a human figure, God is represented in the biblical theophanies as assuming roles central to the society of ancient Israel. Storm theophanies characterize Yahweh as warrior (Exod 15:3) and king (Pss 97:1–5; 99:1–5) and in the role of king as lawgiver (Exod 19) and judge (Ps 94:1–3).[16]

So, theophany in the Old Testament presents an image of God as one who speaks, as one who rules, and as one who intervenes in the affairs of humanity to work out his justice. We should look for this type of presentation and imagery as characteristic of the psalms that recount divine theophany—such as Psalms 97 and 99.

---

14. Rudolf Otto, *The Idea of the Holy*, trans. John W. Harvey (Oxford: Oxford University Press, 1958).

15. See Jeffrey J. Niehaus, *God at Sinai*; M. F. Rooker, "Theophany," in *Dictionary of the Old Testament: Pentateuch*, ed. T. Desmond Alexander and David W. Baker (Leicester: Inter-Varsity Press, 2003), 860.

16. Theodore Heibert, "Theophany in the OT," in *ABD, Volume 6: Si-Z*, ed. David N. Freedman (New Haven, CT: Yale University Press, 1992), 510.

Psalm 97 in the New Testament. In terms of direct citation, it appears that Hebrews 1:6 is likely to refer directly to Psalm 97:7. In the Septuagint's Greek translation of Psalm 97:7, it appears that the translators struggled with the concept of other gods' being called on to worship Yahweh, so they rendered this verse, "worship him all of his angels." Hebrews 1:6 does not follow the exact wording of the Greek translation of Psalm 97:7, but the verse in the epistle is certainly similar and may well have provided the conceptual root of the author's argument.[17] If so, then it is interesting that the author of Hebrews is clearly implying that Jesus is High King over all creation, since Psalm 97 clearly proclaims this message about Yahweh.

Theophany and Incarnation. The other clear New Testament application of the theophanic presentation in Psalm 97 relates to the ultimate theophany, namely, the human incarnation of God in the person of Christ Jesus. Niehaus makes it clear that the creation first of the tabernacle and later of the temple in some sense regularized the notion of theophany in the habitual religious experience of the people.[18] Entering the tabernacle/temple for worship was effectively coming into the real presence of God. Of course, Old Testament believers fully accepted that God was present everywhere, yet the Zion theology of the psalms shows that the temple represented the presence of God in a heightened way. In some sense, God dwelt in Zion amid his people. This dwelling theophany in the tabernacle/temple is sometimes referred to as the *shekinah* glory of God (based on the Hebrew verb *shakan*, meaning "to dwell"). It is interesting, therefore, that John picks up on this imagery in the prologue to his Gospel by pointing out that "The Word became flesh and made his dwelling among us. We have seen his glory, the glory of the one and only Son, who came from the Father, full of grace and truth" (John 1:14).

The Greek word in the phrase "made his dwelling" uses the same consonants as are found in the Hebrew verb *shakan* ("to dwell"). There has been much scholarly discussion surrounding John's choice of words in John 1:14, but the author seems to be implying that the Word became flesh and *tabernacled* among his people. So, in a very real sense Jesus—God come in human form—is the ultimate theophany of all time. He is the ultimate revelation of the character of God.

---

17. Attridge, "Psalms in John," 201.
18. J. J. Niehaus, "The Theology of Deuteronomy," in *NIDOTTE* 4, gen. ed. W. A. Van Gemeren (Carlisle: Paternoster, 1997), 206–208, 243–44.

THOSE WHO LOVE THE LORD LOVE THE THINGS HE LOVES. In terms of practical application, many of the themes of the previous psalms apply in our consideration of Psalm 97 (e.g., God's absolute lordship over all our realities, the singularity of the gospel as a means of salvation, etc.[19]). But there is at least one theme that is prominent in Psalm 97:10. Our priorities in life should always reflect God's priorities: "Those who love the LORD hate evil."

The challenge for contemporary Christians is twofold and can be summarized in the questions, "What shapes our priorities in life?" and "Do our lifestyle and focus reflect God's priorities?" Psalm 97 issues a clear call that our attitudes should be shaped entirely by the things that are important to God rather than by social or political conventions or by the prevailing currents of the culture in which we live. It is often hard to separate ourselves from the dominant worldviews of our own place and time. But this poem makes it clear that the God of Scripture is King and Judge. His kingdom rule should be our habitual practice. The standards and priorities that he sets should govern our daily living.

So often our attitudes are shaped more by glossy magazines than they are by the Bible. Our perspectives have more in common with the latest hit sitcom than they do with the things that typified the life and ministry of Jesus. The challenge of Psalm 97 is that each and every truth claim must be scrutinized in the light of the priorities of God. It is interesting to note from the Scriptures just how often God's priorities explicitly revolve around care for the poor and marginalized in society, yet, given that that is the case, social engagement does not seem to be as much of a priority in today's church as it ought to be.

As God's people today, we need to be more consciously aware of the catalysts that shape our perspectives. In our thinking, are we more Republican/Democrat/white-collar/blue-collar/middle class/career orientated (etc.) than we are Christian? Our perspective on life should be shaped first and foremost by the things that make God smile—not by the things that make the world happy. If our thought world is shaped by the things of God, then our lifestyle will surely follow.

---

19. See the discussion of Pss 93–96 and 98–100 for other strands of application.

Psalm 98

A psalm.

1 Sing to the LORD a new song,
    for he has done marvelous things;
his right hand and his holy arm
    have worked salvation for him.
2 The LORD has made his salvation known
    and revealed his righteousness to the nations.
3 He has remembered his love
    and his faithfulness to Israel;
all the ends of the earth have seen
    the salvation of our God.
4 Shout for joy to the LORD, all the earth,
    burst into jubilant song with music;
5 make music to the LORD with the harp,
    with the harp and the sound of singing,
6 with trumpets and the blast of the ram's horn—
    shout for joy before the LORD, the King.
7 Let the sea resound, and everything in it,
    the world, and all who live in it.
8 Let the rivers clap their hands,
    let the mountains sing together for joy;
9 let them sing before the LORD,
    for he comes to judge the earth.
He will judge the world in righteousness
    and the peoples with equity.

PSALM 98 CONTINUES the dual themes of the Yahweh *malak* collection (Pss 93–100), namely, the celebration of God's absolute rule and the call for all nations and peoples to join those who worship Yahweh. Many of the themes are similar to those discussed in our consideration of Psalms 93–97 (see especially the discussion of Pss 96 and 97), so we can probably afford to be somewhat brief in our consideration of this poem. But as is true of all of the psalms in this mini-collection, Psalm 98 makes its own presentation of these themes. In particular, this composition

emphasizes the image of God as Judge-King, the importance of exuberant, vocal, and musical response, and the role of the whole created order in bringing worship to Yahweh the Ruler.

The Heading (98:0)

A PSALM. Psalm 98 is the only poem in this collection to begin with a heading. It is the simplest, most basic form of heading (*mizmor*), but, as we have discussed before, the title is appropriate to the psalm because of its emphasis on a musical and vocal response to God.[1] Hossfeld suggests that the inclusion of a title may indicate a "tiny caesura" in the Yahweh *malak* collection that possibly links Psalms 98 and 99 at the end of this collection.[2]

The Call to Worship (98:1–3)

SING TO THE LORD A NEW SONG. Psalm 98 bears a number of linguistic and thematic similarities to Psalm 96, and the first of these similarities is seen in the songs' shared opening line. As with Psalm 96:1, the newness of the song is more connected with its addressees than its content.[3] This song is new for the inhabitants of the "nations" and the "ends of the earth" (vv. 2–3) rather than being entirely new in its content. Longman argues,

> The theme of God the Warrior connects his role as Victor, King and Judge. . . . The song praises God for winning a victory on the battle-field, which recalls his kingly role and his future judgment. . . . "New song" occurs elsewhere in the Psalms (33:3; 40:3; 96:1; 144:9; 149:1), as well as Isaiah (42:10) and the book of Revelation (5:9; 14:3), in contexts connected to warfare. A new song is a hymn of victory sung after God has made all things new by his defeat of the forces of evil.[4]

Psalm 98, with its message of the lordship of a just God, offers hope to nations of people who were subject to the whims of capricious gods and the failures of their earthly representatives.

For he has done marvelous things. Psalm 98 supplements the call to worship with an immediate rationale. All the nations should worship Yahweh because he has done marvelous things. Again, echoing the themes of Psalm 96:3, the Hebrew word for "marvelous things" points to the miracles Yahweh has worked in behalf of his people, especially the miracle of the

---

1. See the discussion of the heading to Ps 73 above. The designation *mizmor* appears to be derived from the root idea of singing or playing music to God's glory.
2. Hossfeld and Zenger, *Psalms 2*, 479.
3. See the discussion of Ps 96:1.
4. Longman, *Psalms*, 345.

exodus. If, as seems likely, Psalm 98 (along with the other Yahweh *malak* psalms) makes up part of the response to the themes of exile that dominate Book 3 of the Psalter (Pss 73–89), then this verse is probably pointing to the return from exile as a second exodus. Already once in the exodus, God has proved his miraculous power over the superpowers of the earth, and he can do so again in Israel's return from exile.[5]

The LORD has made his salvation known. The theme of divine revelation, so prominent in Psalm 97, continues in Psalm 98:2. Once again, what has been revealed is both the character ("righteousness" [v. 2b]) and the works ("salvation" [v. 2a]) of Israel's God (cf. the discussion of Ps 96:3 above).

He has remembered his love and his faithfulness. The language in Psalm 98:3—remember, love, faithfulness, Israel—is reminiscent of the covenant made between God and his people. The interesting part of the equation here is that in remembering his covenantal promises to Israel, God's activity in human history acts as a testimony to the nations. "All the ends of the earth" come to see and recognize the true character and miraculous works of God through his activity in, among, and in behalf of his people. God's dealings with Israel show both that he cares for his people and that he is able to intervene in their behalf.

Participating in Noisy Worship (98:4–6)

SHOUT FOR JOY TO THE LORD, ALL THE EARTH. As we have seen throughout many of the Yahweh *malak* psalms, the focus of the call to worship is universal. The whole earth is called to join in this new song of praise to Yahweh. The "new song" that speaks of God's covenantal faithfulness and all-powerful work in the affairs of humanity gives all people—all the nations—reason to join in the noisy, exuberant praise of God. As we have discussed above, this call to the nations to join in the praise of Yahweh would be a strong paradigm challenge for most in Israel, who would view the nations as being far removed from the holiness of God (see the discussion of Ps 96). The song of the goodness of Yahweh's character and the power of his hand may be new on the lips of the nations, but it gives good *reason* to praise: reason to bring praise that is vocal, praise that is musical, praise that is full of joy.

Shout for joy before the LORD, the King. Emphasizing the main theme of this collection, the poet makes explicit the identity of the God who is to be praised—he is the one, true King of the universe (Ps 98:6).

---

5. It is difficult to know whether this collection was originally exilic or postexilic. If the former, then it celebrates the hope of restoration. If the latter, it celebrates renewal already accomplished.

Longman suggests that this song of praise is a response to the military victory of Yahweh. He points out that much of the language used in these verses often occurs in a holy-war context in the Old Testament. His suggestion is that noisy praise of this type goes into abeyance while the king is at war but is brought back to life when his victory is assured: "Simply stated, while the Divine Warrior wars, music languishes (Isa 24:8ff. . . .), and when the Divine Warrior wins, music is taken up again in a paean of praise."[6] The interesting factor in Psalm 98 and its neighbors is that *the whole earth*—all the nations—are called to respond in praise to the kingship of Yahweh. Normally, Yahweh's victory would mean loss and lament to other nations, but the establishment of God's authority, given his nature, gives the whole earth good cause to rejoice.

The Choir of Creation (98:7–9)

LET THE SEA RESOUND, AND EVERYTHING IN IT. The surprising source of praise in the second stanza (the nations) is echoed by another atypical source of praise in the third stanza, namely, creation itself. The imagery in this final stanza is the recognizing of Yahweh's inherent worth by the whole created order because he is the universal Judge, and the joining of Israel and the nations in bringing praise to God. Ellen Davis notes:

> Thus the world is revealed for what it really is: in fact, not Nature at all but rather Creation, still exquisitely sensitive to the presence and will of its Maker, eager to the point of impatience for the full manifestation of God's will in human life, which is the final goal of judgment (cf. Rom 8:19–22).[7]

Longman suggests that the imagery of creational response to Yahweh continues the presentation of Israel's God as the victorious Warrior-King:

> But, furthermore, the rejoicing of nature in Psalm 98 may be put forward as additional evidence for the Divine Warrior interpretation of the psalm as a whole. L. Greenspoon has most recently delineated the connection between nature and the activity of the Divine Warrior. When the Divine Warrior wars, nature droops, withers, languishes (Isa 24:4–13), but when the Divine Warrior wins, nature is revivified and participates in praising Yahweh.[8]

---

6. Tremper Longman, "Psalm 98: A Divine Warrior Victory Song," *JETS* 27.3 (1984): 270.

7. Ellen F. Davis, "Expository Article: Psalm 98," *Int* 46 (1992): 171.

8. Longman, "Psalm 98," 271, citing L. Greenspoon, "The Origin of the Idea of Resurrection," in *Traditions in Transformation: Turning Points in Biblical Faith*, ed. B. Halpern and J. D. Levenson (Winona Lake, IN: Eisenbrauns, 1981) 247–322.

Let them sing before the LORD, for he comes to judge the earth.
The final stanza concludes with the presentation of Yahweh as Judge, thus
echoing the style of the second stanza (Ps 98:4–6), which concluded with the
presentation of Yahweh as King. The offices of king and judge often combined
in Israel and throughout the ancient Near East. The king was seen as the
ultimate arbiter of justice because he was the ultimate source of power and
authority. In the same way, Psalm 98 suggests that Yahweh's unquestionable
kingship endues him with the right to judge the earth and all its inhabitants.
The fact that the created realm acknowledges Yahweh's right to judge further
emphasizes the inherent and unquestionable nature of that right. Since God
is who he is, that judgment will inevitably be marked by "righteousness" and
"equity" (lit., "uprightness" [v. 9]), but the whole of creation—along with
the whole of humanity (vv. 4–6)—will one day rejoice because of Yahweh's
unquestionable rule over everything and everyone he has made.

JUDGMENT AND JOY. Perhaps one of the most
surprising elements of Psalm 98 is the association between Yahweh's judgment and the
response of joy that is anticipated from all
humanity and all creation. This association is not automatic for us. We
often see judgment as a necessity in response to evil (hence our court
systems, etc.), but judgment would not normally be something in which we
rejoice. Ellen Davis comments on this unexpected response to God's rule:

> Modern Christians . . . are little inclined to rejoice at the prospect
> of judgment, yet the psalm challenges us to examine our preconcep-
> tions and embrace judgment as one of the most positive elements of
> our faith. What makes jubilation the appropriate response to God's
> judgment is the fact that it is characterized by righteousness, that is,
> by the abiding concern to sustain, restore, and enhance relationship.
> The needs of God's relationship with Israel determine the multifarious
> concrete forms that righteousness assumes. Accordingly, the Hebrew
> word *tsedek/tsedakah* is variously translated "righteousness," "salvation,"
> "deliverance," "victory," "vindication"; it denotes healing that takes
> place by rescue (Ps 40:11) as well as by punishment (Ps 119:75; cf.
> Ps 51:15). The righteousness of God's judgment (in contrast to our
> own!) consists in the refusal to answer sin vindictively, in a way that
> robs genuine repentance of its fruitfulness (cf. Matt 3:8).[9]

---

9. Davis, "Psalm 98," 172–73.

From a biblical perspective, the judgment of God is something eminently more holistic than our normal association with the concept. Rather than being about strict restitution, God's judgment is much more about renewal and restoration—therefore both the nations and the created realm are able to rejoice in the judgment of Yahweh. The nations are offered knowledge of the living God, recognition of their Creator, and restored relationship with him—such is God's judgment with righteousness and equity. The earth is offered renovation and renewal. The future promise of God's judgment points to a renewed creation restored to the original promise that was lost in the fall of humanity. The fate of the created order is inextricably linked with the divine-human relationship. Psalm 98 points to a future reality of renewed relationship between God and all the earth. Inevitably, this renewal has a positive impact on the created realm—so creation sings its praise at the very thought of God's righteous judgment.

Psalm 98 in the New Testament. There are a couple of echoes of Psalm 98 reflected in the thoughts of the apostle Paul in his letter to the Romans. First, the language of Romans 1:16–17 picks up on the imagery of Psalm 98. God's "salvation" and "righteousness" are "revealed" in the gospel of Christ Jesus, and this revelation is not just to Israel but also to the gentiles. (In Greek, the word "gentiles" is also used to denote "the nations.") So here there seems to be a clear attempt by Paul to link the eschatological revelation of God's righteousness from Psalm 98 with the person and work of Jesus.[10] Second, Romans 8:18–22 speaks of a creation that is subjected to frustration as a result of human sinfulness and the loss of relationship with God. The same passage pictures the created realm as waiting for the restoration of humanity because with that restoration comes creation's own renewal. The natural world, the environment in all its amazing diversity, is presented as struggling under the weight of decay while waiting for the renewal of humanity. The renewal of the divine-human relationship brings with it the renewal of the world. The same link that is seen in Ps 98 is echoed in the eschatological expectation of Romans 8.

The other main reflection of the themes of Psalm 98 in the New Testament is the image of God as Judge—a frequently repeated presentation in the New Testament. One of the interesting factors of the New Testament's presentation of God as Judge is that often the reference to God's judicial capacity is found in the context of leaving judgment in his hands (e.g., Rom 14:10–11; 1 Cor 4:3–5; Jas 4:11–12 et al.). Herein we find a timely reminder that God is in control and that at the right time he will bring his justice into our reality.

---

10. Keesmaat, "Psalms in Romans and Galatians," 142–43.

WITNESS THROUGH COMMUNITY. One of the key aspects of application from Psalm 98 is the reminder that God works through his people to draw all the nations of the earth back into relationship with him. Psalm 98:3 reminds us that God "has remembered his love and his faithfulness to Israel; all the ends of the earth have seen the salvation of our God." The interesting factor in the dynamic of this verse is that those outside the community of faith are drawn into the praise of God through his dealings with his people. As God's steadfast love and faithfulness are worked out in the church, others are drawn to join that community of faith. As the church experiences the blessings of God openly and without embarrassment, others are drawn to know and love this God who does great things.

Of course, this active witness is only possible when our communities are outwardly focused, welcoming, and open to others. If we ever become too comfortable in our own little groups (dare I say cliques?) to such an extent that we do not offer welcome to others, then we fail to give voice to one of the most powerful testimonies in our arsenal—the testimony of God's gracious and loving dealings with his people through his Son. The truth is that people from outside the church are sometimes uncomfortable. Often they don't think or dress or speak or act the way we would like them to. But surely it is ridiculous for us to expect a Christian morality from those who are not yet Christians. Yes, sometimes it can be uncomfortable to welcome into our midst those who do not share our worldview. It is by doing so, however, that worldviews are changed forever. Allowing people to observe God's grace at work in our communities is one of the most powerful witnesses available to us. It is important for us as communities to be open to those who are still apart from our community.

Exuberant Praise. Psalm 98 is also full of noise! It is loud. It is vocal. It is musical. It is vociferous in its determination to give thanks and praise. Our God is worthy of no less today. He is the great King over all and, as such, is well worth the highest, most melodic, loudest, and most engaged praise we can offer. Nothing reflects the greatness of his character more than the greatest praise we have to offer. Cultural preoccupation should never hold us back. The God of the Scriptures is worthy of the most fulsome praise we can possibly offer. This psalm gives us a clear indication of the type of attitude of heart we should have as we gather to worship God.

Psalm 99

¹ The LORD reigns,
    let the nations tremble;
he sits enthroned between the cherubim,
    let the earth shake.
² Great is the LORD in Zion;
    he is exalted over all the nations.
³ Let them praise your great and awesome name—
    he is holy.
⁴ The King is mighty, he loves justice—
    you have established equity;
in Jacob you have done
    what is just and right.
⁵ Exalt the LORD our God
    and worship at his footstool;
    he is holy.
⁶ Moses and Aaron were among his priests,
    Samuel was among those who called on his name;
they called on the LORD
    and he answered them.
⁷ He spoke to them from the pillar of cloud;
    they kept his statutes and the decrees he gave them.
⁸ LORD our God,
    you answered them;
you were to Israel a forgiving God,
    though you punished their misdeeds.
⁹ Exalt the LORD our God
    and worship at his holy mountain,
    for the LORD our God is holy.

Original Meaning

PSALM 99 CONTINUES the themes of the Yahweh *malak* collection (Pss 93–100) by focusing, once again, on images of kingly rule over the nations and absolute judicial authority. But Psalm 99 adds a priestly element to the presentation of God's sovereignty. This poem adopts the language of the tabernacle/temple by presenting Yahweh as the God who is absolutely holy and, at the same time, hears prayers and forgives sin.

The Rule of the King (99:1–3)

THE LORD REIGNS, LET THE NATIONS TREMBLE. The opening verses of Psalm 99 present a vivid image of Yahweh as reigning over the whole earth from Zion. The language and imagery seen throughout the Yahweh *malak* collection is prominent in these verses: "The LORD reigns," he is exalted, praise to his name is due, and the nations respond in trembling. This language echoes thoughts that dominate Psalms 93–100—Israel's God reigns absolutely, and the whole world should respond accordingly.

He sits enthroned between the cherubim. Although echoing the kingship themes of its neighboring compositions, Psalm 99 adds a more specific emphasis that focuses on Yahweh's residency in Zion. The psalm is full of priestly and temple imagery, as illustrated by a good example in verse 1b. The description of Yahweh as sitting enthroned between the cherubim is a reference to the ark of the covenant that was housed in the most holy place in the temple sanctuary. Cherubim were winged creatures—normally of human appearance but sometimes of animal appearance (Ezek 1:5–28)—that "symbolized the transcendence of God 'enthroned between the cherubim' (1 Sam 4:4) but could also represent his dynamic intervention in human affairs (Ps 18:10[11])."[1] Mounted on the lid of the ark were two cherubim (Exod 25:17–22), and, symbolically, this lid was seen as the throne upon which Yahweh sat in the temple (Ps 99:1b; cf. Exod 25:22). So effectively, Psalm 99:1b connects Yahweh's kingship with his presence in Israel's temple. This connection is further accentuated in verse 2, which also speaks of God's presence in Zion and his lordship over all the earth at the same time. So, the reminder of Psalm 99 is that Yahweh's presence among his people serves a purpose that goes beyond his people alone and extends to the nations. These images remind the original Israelite hearers that God is near but also that his presence in Jerusalem has a significance that goes far beyond Zion, Judah, and Israel.[2]

He is holy. Each of the kingship psalms of this collection focuses on one or another aspect of Yahweh's character, identity, and purpose in creation and the universe. Psalm 99's particular focus is on the holiness of God. This emphatic statement—he is holy—serves as a thematic statement at the end of each stanza of the poem (vv. 3, 5, 9). This emphasis on the holiness of God is consistent with the priestly and temple ideology of Psalm 99. The elaborate structure of the temple visually and physically emphasizes the unique holiness of God. Each stage of progression, from the temple courtyard to the inner court to the holy place to the most holy

---

1. Stephen F. Noll, "כְּרוּב," *NIDOTTE* 2:717.
2. Wright, *The Mission of God*, 480.

place, indicates an increasing level of holiness as one proceeds toward the real presence of God, who sits enthroned on the cherubim above the ark of the covenant. As with Isaiah's vision of Yahweh in the temple (Isa 6), the theology of divine presence in Psalm 99 points the nations, for whom the songs of Yahweh's rule are new (Pss 96:1; 98:1), to the inescapable conclusion that the more they come to know the God of Israel, the more they will be consumed by thoughts of his holiness.[3] The particular flavor of holiness theology in Psalm 99 is interesting, however. With the song's emphasis on intercession and divine speech (vv. 6–8), it seems that the holiness language here is not so much emphasizing the ethical nature of God's character as it is drawing attention to Yahweh's *consistency* of character. He is by definition holy. His being is unchanging; therefore, petitioners can have confidence in approaching God.[4]

The Character of the King (99:4–5)

THE KING IS MIGHTY, HE LOVES JUSTICE. The call to the nations to join in the worship of Yahweh is followed in verses 4–5 by a clear rationale for that declaration of allegiance. What is it that makes Yahweh great? He is a King characterized not just by his might but also by a love of justice and the establishment of equity in all areas under his rule.

Verse 4a is actually quite awkward to translate. Literally, it reads: "And the might of a king, he loves justice." The sentence is unusual because the Hebrew word for strength is expressed as a noun ("might") and not an adjective ("mighty"). For this word (*'oz*) to function as an adjective, we would normally expect the definite article to be attached to the noun "king" (i.e., "*the* king is mighty"), but the article is missing from verse 4a. This lack of clarity is further exacerbated by the fact that, in the verse, this line alone is written in the third person (speaking *about* God) rather than in the second person (speaking *to* God). All these distinctives lead

---

3. Goldingay suggests that the phrase here should be translated "it (the name of Yahweh) is holy" (*Psalms 3*, 128). This translation is, of course, entirely possible, since the Hebrew pronoun rendered "he" in the NIV could also be translated "it," which would make the name of Yahweh the referent. Similarly, Goldingay suggests that the same phrase (*qadosh hu'*) in Ps 99:5 should also be translated "it is holy," this time referring to the footstool of the Lord. In this way there is a build up to the climactic statement of verse 9 that "the LORD our God is holy." Grammatically, this rendering is quite possible; but it seems more likely that the *qadosh hu'* formula is used as a refrain to divide the psalm into three parts (Hossfeld and Zenger, *Psalms 2*, 484–86). So, on balance, it is probably better to stick with the more traditional "he is holy" translation for the statements of verses 3 and 5.

4. We will discuss this idea more fully in the Bridging Contexts and Contemporary Significance sections below.

to several equally valid translation possibilities for this line of poetry.[5] It is impossible to be dogmatic regarding the best translation. Probably the best option, without emending the Hebrew text, is to translate this line thus: "And a King's might is his love of justice."[6] In the remaining lines of this verse the psalmist goes on to verify that Yahweh, as High King, has established equity, justice, and righteousness.

Exalt the LORD our God and worship at his footstool; he is holy. Expressed in the language of exaltation in verse 5, the call to praise God displays a delightful contrast in height imagery. As worshipers, we exalt Yahweh (lit., "lift up on high") while we worship "at his footstool" (i.e., in a position of prostration at Yahweh's feet). So, this call to worship creates a lovely dualism of humble praise lifting God to his rightful place of glorification. This exaltation is fully justified in Psalm 99's thematic statement, which is repeated in this verse: he is holy! We exalt God in humility because of his perfect nature and being.

Pleading with the Holy God (99:6–9)

THE FINAL STANZA OF PSALM 99 focuses in on prayer and intercession, particularly with regard to pleas for mercy.

Moses and Aaron were among his priests. This statement is slightly unusual inasmuch as Aaron was the first Levitical priest, and Moses, although of the priestly clan, is nowhere else in Scripture described as a priest. Samuel is practically unique in the Old Testament in combining the roles of judge, prophet, and priest (1 Sam 6–12). But the emphasis of these verses is not on their roles or offices per se; it is rather on the intercessory activity of these three great leaders of God's people combined with their obedience to the word of God.

They called on the LORD and he answered them. The psalmist highlights the intercessory ministry of these three Old Testament figures of faith. They prayed to Yahweh and he responded to their petitions. Here the most obvious resonance is probably with Moses's intercession on behalf of Israel following the golden calf incident (Exod 32–34). Yahweh had been prepared to destroy the whole nation and to form a new people from Moses's line (Exod 32:9–10), but Moses prayed on behalf of the people and God "relented and did not bring on his people the disaster he had threatened" (Exod 32:14). Aaron, as the first and head of

5. For a fuller discussion of some of the options see John H. Eaton, "Proposals in Psalms XCIX and CXIX," *VT* 18 (1968): 555–58.

6. See Broyles, *Psalms*, 385; Hossfeld and Zenger, *Psalms* 2, 483; and Alter, *Psalms*, 347, all of whom offer similar translations.

the line of Levitical priests, would also be associated with the mediatory role of prayerful intercession. The priests would offer sacrifices morning and evening and pray to God on behalf of the people, thus enabling continuing fellowship (Exod 29). Samuel also had the reputation of being an intercessor who pleaded for forgiveness on behalf of Israel following their rebellion (1 Sam 7:5–9; Jer 15:1). So, the characters chosen here have a strong association with prayer—in particular, prayer for divine mercy in response to the rebellion of God's people (Ps 99:8).

He spoke to them . . . they kept his statutes. Combined with their intercessory role, Moses, Aaron, and Samuel were also associated with the teaching of the torah and obedience to God's revealed word. The priestly office included a teaching role (Lev 10:11; Deut 17:11). God spoke to Moses and Aaron out of the "pillar of cloud" (Exod 33:7–11) to reveal his will, purpose, priorities, and values. These leaders communicated the divine speech to the generation of the exodus and charged them to teach that message to each and every succeeding generation (Deut 4, 6, 11). The psalmist seems to be implying an association between the torah-obedience of Psalm 99:7 and the divine responsiveness in verses 6 and 8 that sandwiches verse 7.

99:6—They prayed, and Yahweh answered them.
99:7—God spoke and they kept his torah.
99:8—The Lord answered them in forgiveness and rebuke.

Placing the statements of divine responsiveness to Moses, Aaron, and Samuel on both sides of this affirmation of their commitment to God's revealed word emphasizes the importance of genuinely seeking to walk in the ways of the Lord. God is gracious and responds to the prayers of his people, but at the same time it is important for them to strive to live out his revealed purpose. As Zenger points out, verse 7 "underscores the saving and healing power of the Torah."[7]

You were to Israel a forgiving God, though you punished their misdeeds. Following the reminder of God's gracious response to the prayers of his leaders, the poet draws attention to God's character once again. Psalm 99 emphasizes God's high kingship within the cosmos and justifies his position by describing the perfection of his character. The repeated statements of divine holiness imply that Yahweh's character, essence, and being are beyond question. He is worthy of worship as High King because he is the perfect Sovereign.[8] Here it is the forgiveness and judgment of God that are brought to the reader's attention. Literally, the

---

7. Hossfeld and Zenger, *Psalms 2*, 490.
8. The psalm is replete with character claims that justify the statement of Yahweh's

Hebrew states: "You were to them a forgiving God yet an avenger of their misdeeds." The focus here broadens from Moses, Aaron, and Samuel specifically to encompass the whole people of God, on whose behalf these men had prayed.[9] Here is the essence of right kingship: a ruler who is merciful, yet one who will always keep his charge from descending into chaos. Once again, this verse resonates strongly with the divine self-presentation in Exod 34:6–7. The stress is on God's grace, but his mercy should never be abused.

For the LORD our God is holy. The closing verse once again draws attention to the perfect nature of Yahweh, which justifies his sovereign rule and cosmic reign. In the context of this collection of psalms (Pss 93–100), there is a clear missional overtone to the concluding call to worship in verse 9: "Exalt the LORD *our God* and worship *at his holy mountain* for the LORD *our God* is holy" (emphasis added). The nations who are explicitly addressed in verse 1 are called to recognize that Yahweh's right to rule is based on his unimpeachable character. No other god is as fundamentally *good* as the God of Israel; therefore, he alone is worthy of worship, exaltation, and rule.

THE HOLINESS OF GOD. Psalm 99 is strongly reminiscent of Isaiah's vision of God in the temple (Isa 6). Both passages present a picture of God's absolute rule over the whole earth, and each of them is strongly focused on the holiness of God. Psalm 99, however, draws the reader's attention to an aspect of the concept of divine holiness that is frequently forgotten in the modern setting but would have been paradigm shattering in the ancient Near East: holiness implies *consistency of character.*

Often the thoughts of contemporary Christians regarding holiness begin and end with reflections on morality and ethics. Holiness implies there are some things we will (or must) do and some things we will (or must) avoid. Of course, the notion of holiness is, indeed, fundamentally rooted in God's absolute perfection, including his moral perfection. Yahweh's ethically upright nature is underlined in verses 3, 4, and 8 in particular. But the psalmist also turns to a ramification of holiness that is less immediately obvious: Since God is holy, his people can approach him in prayer in the knowledge that his character is *unchangingly consistent* (vv. 6–8).

---

absolute reign in verse 1: "Great is the LORD" (v. 2); his name (i.e., being) is "great and awesome" (v. 3); "he is holy" (vv. 3, 5, 9); "he loves justice" (v. 4) et al.

9. Kirkpatrick, *Psalms*, 587.

In the more theologically developed setting of the Christian era, this idea is perhaps not surprising, but in its original setting this psalm was making a claim that would challenge the worldview of the non-Israelite hearers to whom it was addressed. As we have seen above, the Yahweh *malak* collection of psalms makes the claim that Israel's God is the cosmic High King. Each of these eight psalms focuses on different aspects and characteristics of God's universal reign. Through this means, the psalmists are presenting an apology—a genuine work of comparative religion. They are making claims that Yahweh, the God of Israel, is *better* than the gods of the surrounding nations. Here in Psalm 99 the poet makes the attractive claim that Yahweh's holiness means not only that he is morally good but also that he is absolutely consistent and therefore hears and answers the prayers of his people.

The gods of the nations could be fickle, capricious, changeable, and downright nasty. Sacrifices were made to appease the gods in an attempt to prevent them from bringing calamity on the people.[10] Prayer and sacrifice were forms of hopeful celestial bribery. Consistency of character was the very last thing that Israel's neighbors would have expected of their gods.

So, the association that the author of Psalm 99 makes between God's character and his responsiveness to his people's prayers is important. Holiness implies not only that God is morally good and ethically perfect—it also implies that God's character is absolutely consistent. His perfection is matched by his grace (v. 8). He hears the prayers of his people and answers them (vv. 6, 8).

Psalm 99 in the New Testament. There is no direct citation of Psalm 99 in the New Testament,[11] but the intercessory roles of Moses, Aaron, and Samuel are, of course, perfectly fulfilled in the person of Christ. These great leaders of God's people were heard because of their priestly roles, which were characterized by close personal relationship with the Lord and commitment to his word (v. 7). But the author of Hebrews tells us that we can have great confidence to approach the throne of grace because Jesus himself, the Great High Priest, intercedes on our behalf (Heb 4:14–16). In terms of relationship, he is the Son of God. In terms of torah obedience, he is without sin. The implication is clear: if God heard and answered the

---

10. Jamie A. Grant, "'When the Friendship of God Was Upon My Tent': Covenant as Essential Background to Lament in the Wisdom Literature," in *Covenant in the Persian Period: From Genesis to Chronicles*, ed. Richard I. Bautch and Gary N. Knoppers (Winona Lake, IN: Eisenbrauns, 2015), 323–39.

11. Revelation 11:17–18 contains a possible an allusion to Ps 99:1 (Moyise, "Psalms in Revelation," 240).

intercessions of the priests of the Old Testament, how much more will he hear and answer the prayers of his Son on behalf of his people? Robert Murray McCheyne is quoted as having said, "If I could hear Christ praying for me in the next room, I would not fear a million of enemies. Yet the distance makes no difference; He is praying for me."[12]

CONFIDENCE IN PRAYER. Psalm 99's theology of holiness speaks to our own attitude toward prayer as Christians. Often our theology exceeds our experiential practice. Often our life of faith does not match up to what we believe about God. I suspect the same is true of our confidence to approach God in prayer. Theologically, we know that God is loving, kind, gracious, forgiving, and hears and answers our prayers. Experientially, however, aware of our repeated failures, believers are often blighted by doubt: "Surely God can't love me anymore. Surely I have gone too far this time." Our theology is brought down in practice by our own fears and insecurities so that we end up subtly believing in a God of changeable character.

But our God is a holy God, and therefore he is absolutely consistent in his response to his people. Psalm 99:6–8 provides us with an important reminder: When God's people cry to him for mercy, he hears and answers their prayer, regardless of the circumstances. The repeated assurance "he answered them" is designed to give comfort and confidence to the reader of this psalm. If God answered Moses's prayer after the disaster of the golden calf incident; if God answered Aaron's priestly prayers for a continually mutinous people; if God answered Samuel's prayer for a people caught in that downward spiral of rebellion marked out in the book of Judges, then God will hear *our* pleas for mercy as well. He hears because he is gracious and forgiving. He hears because his character is holy, constant, and consistent.

"The Lord reigns" psalms in this collection were probably written in the exilic or early postexilic period, in a time when Yahweh's reign was far from obvious. Israel had been defeated, Jerusalem had fallen, the king was no longer on the throne, and the temple had been destroyed. It did not look like Yahweh was reigning from Zion. Yet the psalmists call us to see with the eyes of faith. Yahweh does reign, and his character is unchanged. Just as he heard the cries of Moses, Aaron, and Samuel, so also will he hear *our* cries.

---

12. Andrew A. Bonar, *The Memoir and Remains of the Rev. Robert Murray McCheyne* (Edinburgh: Oliphant, Anderson and Ferrier, 1984), 158.

Psalm 100

❦

A psalm. For giving grateful praise.

¹ Shout for joy to the LORD, all the earth.
² Worship the LORD with gladness;
   come before him with joyful songs.
³ Know that the LORD is God.
   It is he who made us, and we are his;
   we are his people, the sheep of his pasture.
⁴ Enter his gates with thanksgiving
   and his courts with praise;
   give thanks to him and praise his name.
⁵ For the LORD is good and his love endures forever;
   his faithfulness continues through all generations.

 PSALM 100 CONCLUDES this mini-collection of psalms focusing on the universal reign of God with a strong voice of doxological celebration. The psalm consists of seven commands addressed to the whole earth and two motivation clauses that give clear reasons justifying this resounding call to praise Yahweh!

Psalm 100 exemplifies the slightly unusual dynamic we find in the Yahweh *malak* ("the Lord reigns") collection of psalms (Pss 93–100). These songs are apparently addressed to the nations at large—for example, here in Psalm 100 "all the earth" is called to join in God's praise. But apart from those proselytes who had converted to the Hebrew faith, it was the people of Israel who heard this call to worship rather than the nations. Psalm 100 typifies the tone of this group of songs with a twofold theme: Israel is reminded that their God reigns, despite all appearances to the contrary, and they are reminded of their missional responsibility (the whole earth needs to know of Yahweh's rule).

The psalm describes its purpose as being "For giving grateful praise." The content clearly reflects the title in this case.

Delight in the King! (100:1–3)

SHOUT. Verse 1 highlights the unusual dynamic of particularity and universality in the Yahweh *malak* collection. Israel is called to shout for joy to the

God of the covenant (particular), and the whole earth is invited to join in that proclamation of praise (universal). The Hebrew verb that is used here (*hariy'u*) is strongly *vocal!*[1] There is nothing polite or moderated about this call to praise. The worshiping community—Israel and the whole earth—is to hold nothing back in raising the roof in their praise of Yahweh.[2]

Worship. The second of the seven commands in the list is to "worship the LORD with gladness" (v. 2). English equivalents fail to grasp the fullness of the Hebrew verb *'abad*. The term is perhaps best understood as, in some sense, combining the ideas of "worship" and "service" and blurring the lines between the two.[3] Every act of worship is an act of service, and every act of service done for the Lord is an act of worship. The command used here clearly indicates the connection that exists between praise and lifestyle. There can be no separation of public worship practice from private character and worldview. For the former to be meaningful, the latter must be consistent with the words offered.[4]

Come. The third command is to approach God in worship. This imperative emphasizes the relational nature of worship. It is an act of presence as praise and service are offered "before him" (lit., "before his face"). But both Israel and the nations are able to approach their Creator with "joyful songs" (v. 2) because of the membership of the covenant community; otherwise, approaching the Holy God would be marked by fear and trembling (Ps 2:11, see footnote 4). It is the transformation of relationship with God that turns the act of drawing near to him from terrifying to delightful. Accepting the kingship of Yahweh radically changes the essential experience of the worshiper's approach to God's throne (see Bridging Contexts).

Know. This command is the focal statement of the psalm around which the whole sense of the song coalesces. Three imperatives (shout, worship, come) precede this one and three more (enter, give thanks, praise) follow

---

1. In other contexts the same verb is used of a war cry (Josh 6:10) or a shout of triumph (Isa 44:23).

2. With a degree of understatement, Craig Broyles comments, "**shout**, indicates that Israelite worship was not to be characterized by civilized restraint" (Broyles, *Psalms*, 386).

3. Hence the NIV's translation, "worship"; cf. "serve" in some other versions (ESV, NASB). Both options are perfectly valid in the context of Ps 100.

4. Note also the connection between worship/service and gladness. Psalm 100:2 seems to play on the address to the nations in Ps 2:11. Now is not the place to go into the translational complexities of that verse; however, there the nations are called to "serve the LORD *with fear*" (NIV, emphasis added). Here in Ps 100 the invitation addressed to the nations is to "serve the Lord *with joy*" (v. 2, emphasis added). Becoming part of the worshiping community transforms the nature of that worship. (For a fuller discussion of the command to the nations in Ps 2:11 see Wilson, *Psalms, Volume 1*, 112–14.)

it, thus making the slightly unusual command, "know," the pivot around which the others revolve.[5] The statement "Know that the LORD is God" is the structural and theological heart of Psalm 100.

The nations are invited to join Israel in the exuberant and joyful praise of Yahweh, but that invitation to draw near with confidence *is premised on the realization that he, and he alone, is the one, true God, Creator, and King over the universe.* This command implies much more than simple mental acknowledgment. "To know" here is not simply to assent to the fact that Yahweh is God. This command requires a whole-life affirmation that stems from complete devotion to God and worship of him.

It is he who made us and we are his! The remainder of this verse provides the first rationale and motivation for the exuberant praise of these verses by celebrating the blessings and benefits of the covenant. The most staggering aspect of the covenantal formula in verse 3b–c is the limitless inclusion of the nations along with Israel in its scope. We come across the reference to *Israel* as the sheep of the divine pasture in Psalm 95:6–7, but here in Psalm 100 *all the earth* is given the same honor! In Old Testament terms, this expansion of the covenantal relationship is a mind-blowing one. Jeremias is helpful on this point:

> Here there is, in fact, a universalizing of the "covenant formula." Of course, this reshaping of the "covenant formula" is not carried out in such a way that the promise it contains for Israel (Pss 95:7; 79:13) is simply expanded; rather the nations are called to recognition. . . . The nations are called to recognize and acknowledge their own createdness and, as a consequence, their belonging to the one God and creator and this recognition opens for the nations the gate to an equal sharing in Israel's worship.[6]

It is difficult for us to grasp how these words would challenge the worldview paradigms of the Old Testament community of faith. Access

---

5. In colloquial English we tend not to use the command form of the verb "to know." We either know something or we don't. The command form of the Hebrew verb (*yadab*) is not terribly common either—it occurs in this form only seven times in the Old Testament. Perhaps most enlightening for our understanding of its use in Ps 100:3 is the discussion of the new covenant in Jer 31:34. Here the phrase "know the Lord" is used to illustrate what may, in effect, be described as the evangelistic task ("No longer will they teach their neighbor, or say to one another, 'Know the LORD,' because they will all know me . . ."). The call to give oneself over fully to God is issued in these terms: "Know the LORD!" Similarly, here in Ps 100:3, all the earth is called to "know that the LORD is God," that is, to acknowledge that Yahweh *alone* is God and to declare one's allegiance and devotion to him.

6. Jörg Jeremias, "Ps 100 Als Auslegung von Ps 93–100," *Skrif en kerk* 19 (1998): 612, 614, quoted in Hossfeld and Zenger, *Psalms 2*, 496.

into the presence of the Creator, the particular privilege of Israel, is opened up to people from every national and ethnic identity. All those who recognize Yahweh's cosmic kingship are called to join in this song of praise as full members of the covenant community (the sheep of Yahweh's flock).

Enter with Praise! (100:4–5)

THE STAGGERING INCLUSIVENESS of verses 1–3 is powerfully repeated in the second stanza of the psalm.

Enter his gates . . . and his courts. Verses 1–3 invite the nations to join the pasture of the covenantal flock and to sing songs of praise to Israel's God. The nations' new status as part of the worshiping community of faith is affirmed in the commands "to enter," "give thanks," and "praise" (lit., "bless" [v. 4]). The language here is the language of access into the temple. Normally, of course, non-Israelites would have been excluded from the inner court of the temple, but here they are encouraged not only to "enter his gates with thanksgiving" (i.e., access the temple complex) but also to enter "his courts with praise" (i.e., go beyond the outer court of the temple and enter the inner court with the Israelites). For the nations, this call invites a privileged and unprecedented level of participation in the festal worship of Israel. The final command "to praise his name" further implies a degree of intimacy of relationship with Yahweh that previously would have been unimaginable. As Eaton notes, the command to bless Yahweh has "a note of grateful warmth, a consciousness of having received salvation from the Lord who is kind and gracious, committed in his love, faithful and true forever."[7] The nations have come to realize that Yahweh alone is a truly *good* God, so they praise his name, his very being.

There follow three covenantal statements that voice the realization to which the whole earth has been drawn.

For the LORD is good. This statement gives one of the classic psalmic justifications for the worship of God. Why bring praise? Quite simply, because God is good. This assertion is, in some sense, the most basic but also the most profound character claim that could be made of a deity in the ancient world. The gods were seldom good, loving, or kind. Deities toyed with humans simply because they could do so, or they destroyed humans for the most banal of reasons.[8] So the shared testimony that "the LORD is

---

7. Eaton, *Psalms*, 350.

8. See Grant, "'When the Friendship of God.'" For example, in one of the Sumerian city laments the gods destroy a city simply "in hate," and in another lament they destroy a city because its people had become a nuisance.

good" is a claim that would have been as attractive as it was radical at the time when Psalm 100 was first sung.

His love endures forever. The love that is implied here is the steadfast love (*hesed*) of the God of the covenant. It is not a love that is subject to whims and moods, for God's love for his people and the nations is resolute, never-failing, and never-ending. Schaefer comments, "*Hesed* is part of God's essence, and thus acts of grace are not the expression of some affectionate whim. The people's reliance on God is justified by God's covenant loyalty."[9]

His faithfulness continues through all generations. The third rationale for praise is to be found in the *faithfulness* of God. Once again, this term (*'emunah*) resonates strongly with the Old Testament idea of covenant. God is always faithful to his covenantal promises, and here in Psalm 100 those covenantal promises are extended beyond Israel to all nations. They too will see, know, and experience the unshakable, resolute, and absolute commitment of Yahweh to his people.

So, the second justification for the praise of God is based firmly in his character. God's goodness, love, and faithfulness present people of every nation with good cause to sing his praises and to worship him. The first rationale is relational (v. 3), and the second here is ontological (v. 5). God is *by definition* deserving of human praise just because he is who he is.

Bridging Contexts

THE KINGSHIP OF GOD. The role of Psalm 100 within the Yahweh *malak* grouping is interesting. In fact, because of its worshipful tone and pastoral imagery, some struggle to connect this poem with the remainder of the collection (Pss 93–99). But Psalm 100's links with the rest of the psalms in this group are strong and so should shape our understanding of worship within the community of God's people.

Note first the close ties with the other psalms in "the Lord reigns" grouping. The address in Psalm 100:1 is reminiscent of Psalm 98:4, where the whole earth is also called on to shout for joy to Yahweh. This summons is further echoed by the call for the nations to worship (or serve) Yahweh with gladness (Ps 100:2), in contrast to Psalm 97:7's critique addressed to those who worship idols and its call addressed to the gods of the nations to worship/serve Yahweh. Psalm 100:3 echoes the covenantal formulations of Psalm 95:6–7 with the passages' shared presentation of God's people

9. Schaefer, *Psalms*, 247.

as the sheep of his pasture. The call to praise Yahweh's name in Psalm 100:4 evokes the similar command in Psalm 99:3, and the declaration of the goodness and faithfulness of God, while common in the Psalter, is something the nations have already witnessed in Psalm 98:3. So Psalm 100 is replete with the ideas, imagery, and theology of the other psalms in this collection.

There are two interesting aspects to Psalm 100's inclusion in this collection. First, Erich Zenger sees a strongly missional theme in the Yahweh *malak* psalms. He describes the thread running through Psalms 93–100 as being "Israel and the nations in the world as the royal realm of the God YHWH."[10] He argues that in reading Psalms 93–100 consecutively we witness the nations being drawn ever closer to both Israel and her God. He plots a broad narrative that moves from the declaration of Zion as the foundation of the universe in Psalm 93 (without any indication of the presence of or any call to the nations) through the calls to worship addressed to the nations in Psalms 96–98, the trembling fear of the nations before Yahweh in Psalm 99, and the invitation to enter his gates with thanksgiving and his courts with praise in Psalm 100. There seems to be a dialogue of exclusion followed by invitation, which ultimately leads to inclusion and integration in Psalm 100.

> Psalm 100, as the climax of the composition, integrates the nations of the world in worship before the God of Zion: they should, and they will, shout aloud to Yahweh, serve him (not the idols; cf. 97:7) with joy, and experience his nearness—like Israel and together with it.[11]

The second aspect of the discussion that is interesting is the presentation of the act of worship as an approach to the High King. The language used in Psalm 100 is clearly the language of access and approach, but it is also the terminology of deference to the monarch. For example, the shepherd imagery of verse 3 is classically considered to be a kingship image in the ancient Near East and would certainly have been thought of as such by Hebrew worshipers. While the gates and courts of verse 4 are clearly descriptors of the cultic, temple setting, we should also remember that these words represent the language of entering the royal palace.[12]

---

10. Hossfeld and Zenger, *Psalms 2*, 497.

11. Ibid. Mays also describes the praise of Ps 100 as having "an *evangelical* function. . . . Psalm 100 invites the whole earth to join its doxology, because the great Shepherd has become visible in the story of the people of God" (Mays, *The Lord Reigns*, 68).

12. Hossfeld and Zenger, *Psalms 2*, 494. Of course, this access is the implication of entrance into the temple courts—worshipers come into the presence of the cosmic King.

Most of all, however, verse 2's call to worship/serve Yahweh is a reminder of his kingly role and our proper response to his rule.

Psalm 100 presents worship in terms of approaching the King. The congregation as a corporate body—including both Israel and the nations—is summoned before the King with the expectation that this vibrant and varied community of adherents will "serve" (v. 2; see the discussion above) their Sovereign.[13] Regarding the command to "worship/serve" in verse 2, James Mays notes:

> The form and style of the activity proposed in the imperative sentences is *political;* the language belongs to the monarchical frame of reference and draws its basic meaning from that sphere. . . . A superficial use of lexicons might suggest that "serve" (*'abad*) is no more than "customary cultic language," but a closer inspection of its usage in the Psalter shows that here it specializes in one of its possible functions, denoting conduct appropriate for relation to a royal figure. "Serve Yahweh" is a command that holds the action in the political context and should be heard as an interpretation of the cult, rather than the other way around.[14]

Psalm 100 in the New Testament. There are no direct citations of Psalm 100 in the New Testament. Along with several of the psalms in this collection, however, Psalm 100 resonates strongly with the images of the nations at the heart of the community of faith seen worshiping at the throne of God in the book of Revelation (Rev 5:9–10; 7:9–10). Although the primary intertext is the Song of Moses, Revelation 15 in particular evokes strong associations with the monarchic and worshipful images of this collection that are summed up so well for us in Psalm 100.[15]

Contemporary Significance

DOING WORSHIP WELL. Based on Psalm 100, it strikes me that we are doing worship badly in the contemporary church. Psalm 100 challenges our practices in three particular ways.

Worship has an outward focus. Psalm 100 invites the whole earth to worship God. We tend to think of worship as an internal act—one that is between God and his people. We do not tend to think of worship as a declaratory act of evangelistic proclamation, yet it is. Psalms 93–100 make it clear that

---

13. McKelvey, *Moses, David and the High Kingship of Yahweh,* 158.
14. Mays, *The Lord Reigns,* 76.
15. Moyise, "Psalms in Revelation," 235–36.

the attractive worship of the community of God is an act of proclamation that calls and invites others to join in the praise of the Shepherd King. As Mays comments:

> Praise in the psalms has an *evangelical* function. . . . Over and over again, the hymns in the Psalter summon and invite all nations and peoples of the earth. Over and over again, they announce the reign of the Lord. . . . Praise is proclamation; it witnesses to the present and coming reign of the Lord. It finds in its very content the motive for its openness and outreach.[16]

As a church, we need to consider more carefully our public praise of God as outreach. Do we explain for those who visit our services *why* it is that we want to exalt our God as the King? And do the songs we sing declare his universal kingship in the same way the psalms do?

Worship is a joyful act. Psalm 100 is filled with images of joy, thankfulness, and vibrant praise. Having preached in a wide variety of contexts in Scotland, the UK more broadly, and throughout the world, I sometimes wonder what it is that our worship of God actually communicates to the outside world. Imagine the arch-hypothetical scenario of the alien from space who comes down to visit earth and trucks up to church on a Sunday morning. What does our sung praise communicate about the God we worship? Often our praise is far from exuberant, far from joyful, far from the vibrant, colorful, loud, and captivating image of praise we see in Psalm 100. We stand, our hands in our pockets, mumbling words with little thought or conviction, and such behavior casts our love for God in a very poor light. Is our love for Jesus so weak that we are too shy or inhibited to "shout for joy to the LORD" and to call everyone else in the world to do the same? There is something wrong with our hearts if our praise does not reflect the powerful, joy-filled, vivid, vibrant worship of Psalm 100. Psalm 100 stands as a challenge to us!

In worship we approach the King. Psalm 100 calls on us to serve the King with gladness (v. 2). There is a sense in which our lives should be a continual act of worship to the King (Rom 12:1–2). But there is also a sense in which our public praise is an act of approach to the living King, who reigns over the cosmos. In a spiritual sense, we enter into his palace (temple), we draw near to him in his courts, and we do so with great delight and gladness.[17] On one level, such an act of apparent reverence in approaching

---

16. Mays, *The Lord Reigns*, 68.
17. Speaking of the collection as a whole, McKelvey writes, "In Psalm 100, a climaxing finale of praise occurs as a seven-fold imperative summons [to] all the earth, and Israel in

the King seems incompatible with the loud and exuberant praise pictured in Psalm 100:1. But this view is a construct shaped by our Western ideas of etiquette. In the rituals of the ancient Near Eastern political world, it would be common to direct shouts of acclamation and praise to the king.[18] How much more appropriate is it to direct such shouts of praise to the High King over all the universe as we draw near to him? It is not disrespectful for us to shout out our praise to the King—disrespect occurs when we do so halfheartedly or when we fail to fulfill our covenantal obligations (v. 3; cf. Ps 95:6–11). We are called to engage in loud and lively praise, but we are also called to listen to the voice of the King and to obey his decrees absolutely, as we are enabled to do so through his Son and by the work of his Spirit.

---

particular, to pay homage to the Sovereign of the world" (McKelvey, *Moses, David and the High Kingship of Yahweh*, 164–65).

18. Mays, *The Lord Reigns*, 77.

Psalm 101

Of David. A psalm.
¹ I will sing of your love and justice;
   to you, LORD, I will sing praise.
² I will be careful to lead a blameless life—
   when will you come to me?
I will conduct the affairs of my house
   with a blameless heart.
³ I will not look with approval
   on anything that is vile.
I hate what faithless people do;
   I will have no part in it.
⁴ The perverse of heart shall be far from me;
   I will have nothing to do with what is evil.
⁵ Whoever slanders their neighbor in secret,
   I will put to silence;
whoever has haughty eyes and a proud heart,
   I will not tolerate.
⁶ My eyes will be on the faithful in the land,
   that they may dwell with me;
the one whose walk is blameless
   will minister to me.
⁷ No one who practices deceit
   will dwell in my house;
no one who speaks falsely
   will stand in my presence.
⁸ Every morning I will put to silence
   all the wicked in the land;
I will cut off every evildoer
   from the city of the LORD.

SOMEWHAT SURPRISINGLY, in Psalms 101 and 103 the voice of David returns to Book 4 of the Psalter.[1] The focus so far has been on the kingship of Yahweh and his indisputable rule over the

---

1. The bracketing effect of these two psalms probably indicates that Ps 102 is also

whole earth, regardless of all or any indications to the contrary. The last time we heard the voice *of* David was in Psalm 86, where the psalmist confesses his need for God's help and professes God's abounding love in response to prayer. The last voice *about* the Davidic king came in the poignant and significantly placed Psalm 89, which ends with the rhetorical plea, "where is your former great love [*hesed*]?" (v. 49). Thereafter, Book 4 is silent regarding the human king and focuses on divine kingship and rule. But here in Psalm 101 David returns with determination to sing of Yahweh's covenantal love (*hesed*) and justice (v. 1). In this song the psalmist-king, David, voices his determination to echo the divine priorities in his life and rule.

A Determined Song (101:1–2)

I WILL SING OF YOUR LOVE AND JUSTICE. Following the simple form of the Davidic title, Psalm 101 begins with a voice of determination to sing and to follow. The psalmist will sing of God's "love and justice" (v. 1). These twin ideas of love and justice (*hesed umishpat*) are commonly associated with the covenantal relationship between God and his people or, as here, between God and his chosen servant—the king. The first two verses set the tone for the rest of the psalm in expressing the poet-king's determination to live in accordance with God's standards—his "justice"—and the psalmist expresses this determination in an attitude of praise. Although Psalm 101 appears in a different sub-group of poems, verse 1 firmly grounds this psalm in the theology of the Yahweh *malak* ("Yahweh reigns") collection (Pss 93–100).[2] The theological point of these opening verses seems to be that the poet-king will reflect the ways of Yahweh's rule in his own human and political kingship.[3] The king responds to God's love and justice in praise and with a determination to follow Yahweh's royal model in his own rule.

I will be careful to lead a blameless life. The tone of determination continues in verse 2. There is a "come what may" sense of purpose to these

---

meant to be read as being of Davidic voice. This probability is further emphasized by the fact that so many of the psalms of the individual in Books 1–3 featuring the lament of the "afflicted person" (*'ani*) also bear superscriptions assigning them to David.

2. Yahweh's covenantal love is celebrated in Pss 94:18; 98:3; and 100:5, whereas his justice features in 94:15; 97:2, 8; and 99:4. For a thorough discussion of Pss 101–104 as a group within Book 4 see McKelvey, *Moses, David and the High Kingship of Yahweh*, 169–220.

3. It should be noted that the possessive "your" is not present in the Hebrew text, which reads simply, "I will sing of love and justice." This statement further emphasizes the association between Yahweh's love and justice and the application of these practices in the life of the human king. See Broyles, *Psalms*, 388.

opening verses in which the poet boldly and frankly states how *he* will live *his* life regardless of the standards of the world around him. More literally, the opening statement of this verse could be read as, "I will consider the way of integrity." The first line of verse 2 gives a strong sense of deliberate intent to choose a lifestyle that is pleasing to God. As Kirkpatrick comments helpfully, the psalmist "make[s] whole-hearted devotion to God and perfect uprightness towards men the rule of [his] conduct."[4]

When will you come to me? This plea seems to be a somewhat strange insertion into the flow of the psalm, as the poet's determined statements of intent ("I will") both precede and follow the question. In all likelihood this plea is simply an interjection, an appeal for God's presence and help as the king undertakes to rule in accordance with God's standards.[5] The poet knows that he cannot accomplish such a standard of rule by his own power. To reflect God's ways in the world requires God's help, hence the appeal for the presence of God as his Aide.

I will conduct the affairs of my house with a blameless heart. The idea of "conducting the affairs of my house" is probably a reference to the royal palace and its associated kingly rule. In the ancient Near East, the ruler's palace was often a place of excess on every level—excess that was shrouded from the people by the secrecy of the temple precinct.[6] Here the poet-king declares that even the secret matters of his "house" and his "heart" will be marked by the same integrity that is evident in his public exercise of power.

Turning Toward by Turning Away (101:3–8)

I WILL NOT LOOK WITH APPROVAL ON ANYTHING THAT IS VILE. The remainder of the psalm is an expression of the king's devotion to Yahweh stated largely in terms of the things he will *not* do and the characteristics that will *not* mark his rule. This imagery is, of course, familiar to the reader of the book of Psalms from its introduction. Psalm 1 describes the "blessed" person first in terms of what he or she is *not* like before it goes on to describe this person in positive terms. Although this form of negative expression is perhaps uncommon in the modern world, the significance of the characteristics rejected by the poet-king is quite powerful in the

---

4. Kirkpatrick, *Psalms*, 591.

5. Beat Weber, *Werkbuch Psalmen II: Die Psalm 73 Bis 150* (Stuttgart: Kohlhammer, 2003), 165. Longman sees this cry as indicative of lament, thus implying "that the composer feels distanced from God. He proclaims his innocence in his attempt to draw God close to him" (Longman, *Psalms*, 351).

6. Kirkpatrick, *Psalms*, 591.

context of the Psalms and the Old Testament more broadly. Effectively, what we see in these verses is the declaration of the king that he will not fall foul of the weaknesses of his predecessors that led to the fall of Jerusalem and the demise of the Davidic line.[7] The psalmist-king will not be like the kings before the exile. This king in David's line has learned the lessons of his predecessors' moral failures, and he declares his determination to reject the things that his forebears should have rejected but did not. In order to succeed in this intent, he knows he needs the Lord's help (v. 2b).

Anything that is vile. This expression is a general reference to that which is evil, empty, and worthless.[8] The Hebrew word for "thing" (*dabar*) may refer either to an object or, more conceptually, to matters, ideas, schemes, and perspectives. If taken as an object here, it may be a reference to idols and the associated false worship. But the latter meaning as referring to a wicked and empty lifestyle seems to be more likely in the context of the psalm. Adherence to a lifestyle of integrity (v. 2) necessarily implies the rejection of worthless, wicked, and empty ways of life.

I hate what faithless people do. Echoing the previous line, the poet-king pronounces rejection of the behavioral consequences of a wicked worldview. Surely the wrong attitude of heart will ultimately lead to wrong moral actions. The psalmist rejects these attitudes (v. 3a) *and* the concomitant behaviors (v. 3b). Wicked deeds literally "do not cling to me," the psalmist says. The poet's devotion to Yahweh and his justice has a Teflon effect—the unrighteousness of others just slides right off him because his heart is so captivated by God that he will not consider the ways of the wicked.

The perverse of heart shall be far from me. The rejection of wrong attitudes and actions is, however, insufficient in itself. The king also declares his abhorrence of evil by rejecting *the people* who represent such waywardness. The implication is clear: keeping wrong company will shape the individual, so the psalmist removes himself from their presence in order to protect himself from their influence.

It is, of course, possible to read the Hebrew here as referring to the general attitude of *having* a perverse heart as opposed to *people* of perverse heart.[9] But given the immediate context, which refers to the actions of

---

7. Of course, a Davidic superscription does not necessarily imply that David himself wrote the poem but, rather, that it is associated with the royal court and line that followed David in Jerusalem. See N. T. Wright, *The Case for the Psalms: Why They Are Essential* (San Francisco: HarperCollins, 2013), 4.

8. Allen, *Psalms*, 7.

9. Thus the ESV, NRSV, and NASB, among others.

people ("what faithless people do" [v. 3b] and "whoever slanders their neighbor" [v. 5a]), it seems more likely that the poet here refers to his rejection of people rather than his refusal to adopt a certain attitude. "In the context the supplicant is not declaring a commitment to avoid having a crooked heart; this would in any case be an odd way to say that. Rather the supplicant insists on pushing away people who have a crooked heart (the expression involves synecdoche)."[10]

Whoever slanders their neighbor in secret. Verse 5 voices the psalmist's rejection of those who exhibit two key character failings according to the Hebrew mindset: false testimony and arrogance. Anyone practicing such behaviors is given short shrift by the king. Slander is met with destruction (probably a better rendering of the Hebrew than the NIV's "put to silence") and arrogance will not be tolerated. Slander was, of course, a grave sin because false accusation could ultimately lead to the judicial killing of an innocent person. Arrogance of speech and attitude are often associated with the original sin of Adam, so pride is seen to be a root sin that leads to other immoral behaviors. Perhaps in a way that connection is not made by modern readers, but the original readers of Psalm 101 would have seen these acts as heinous. What is more, both actions are practiced in secret, so it is possible for perpetrators to maintain an outward appearance of moral integrity that masks their iniquity. As we have seen already in this psalm, such duality of practice is abhorrent to the poet-king (v. 2b).

My eyes will be on the faithful in the land. Just as the king rejects those who reject the ways of Yahweh, so also he delights in those who delight in the ways of their God. In contrast to the language of distancing, destruction, and removal in the preceding verses, here with regard to the faithful we see the language of dwelling and ministry, implying closeness and proximity. Just as the poet-king rejects the company of the faithless, here we see that he surrounds himself with the company of the faithful. As we read in Psalm 1, discipleship inevitably involves the rejection of certain behaviors and the regular practice of others. Here in Psalm 101, we see that discipleship is also intimately linked with the rejection of certain groups of people and close communion with others.

For the Old Testament reader the idea of those whose "walk is blameless"

---

10. Goldingay, *Psalms 3*, 143. This distancing, of course, has interesting implications for the standard Christian mantra, "God hates the sin but loves the sinner." On one hand, this claim is perfectly true, yet, conversely, the psalmist makes it perfectly plain that evil deeds cannot be entirely separated from evil people. We will consider this matter further in both the Bridging Contexts and Contemporary Significance sections.

automatically resonates with the characters of Abraham (Gen 17:1) and Job (Job 1:1). Blamelessness does not imply sinless perfection in any way, shape, or form—both Abraham and Job confess their sins; rather, the concept implies an integrity of lifestyle that genuinely seeks to put God first in all things. In many ways Psalm 101 is reminiscent of the theology of Psalm 15, where we are also told that it is the blameless and righteous who, because they speak the truth without slander, can approach the sanctuary of the Lord. Psalm 15:4 summarizes Psalm 101:3–8: "[He] who despises a vile person but honors those who fear the LORD . . . will never be shaken."

No one who practices deceit will dwell in my house. The contrast of the previous verses continues here. The faithful dwell with the king, but those who practice deceit will not be allowed to do so. The blameless minister to the king serves him in his royal court, but those who speak falsehood disqualify themselves from taking a privileged place there. It is godliness of character that marks out the noble advisor, not his or her skill set or political ability. Here there is an obvious line of application for people in leadership of every type: character is key, both with regard to one's own behavior and also in terms of choosing one's advisors.

Every morning I will put to silence all the wicked in the land. This statement probably refers to the king in his judicial role. Typically in the ancient world, the monarch would also embody the court of highest instance. Matters that could not be decided satisfactorily in local and lesser courts were brought before the king for final judgment. The psalmist-king sees his judicial role as echoing the priorities of Yahweh himself. He delights in God's "love and justice" (v. 1) and seeks to apply that justice in his legal office. The verb used in verse 8a is better translated "destroy,"[11] and, as Hossfeld points out, "Only in Psalm 18:40 and twice in Psalm 101 does a human being assume the role of the superior hero, Yahweh" in this most extreme act of judgment.[12] The psalmist's clear desire is to protect justice in the land and city of God (v. 8). These places were chosen by the Lord for the working out of his purposes, so the people dwelling within them are expected to live their lives by the values ingrained by God into his created order.[13]

---

11. See "צָמַת," *HALOT* 2:1035–6.

12. Frank-Lothar Hossfeld and Erich Zenger, *Psalms 3: A Commentary on Psalms 101–150*, Hermeneia, trans. Linda M. Maloney (Minneapolis: Fortress, 2011), 16.

13. For a fuller discussion of the expectation of righteous behavior laid on God's people as stewards of the land, see Walter Brueggemann, *The Land: Place as Gift, Promise and Challenge in Biblical Faith*, Overtures to Biblical Theology (London: SPCK, 1978).

THE KING AS DIVINE REPRESENTATIVE. Some of the language in this psalm is quite alien to the modern mindset. We might be happy enough with the rejection of actions and behaviors as in verse 3 ("I hate what faithless people do"), but we are less comfortable with the rejection *of people* because of their behaviors that we read in verse 8 ("I will put to silence all the wicked in the land"). Normally such acts of judgment are divine acts. For example, we read in Psalm 73:27 that "Those who are far from you will perish; you *destroy* all who are unfaithful to you" (emphasis added).[14] It is unusual for the human king to be described as working out such judgment; however, here we read of God's punishment implemented through the agency of his king.

The law of the king is outlined in Deuteronomy 17:14–20, and the only positive responsibility laid upon the Israelite king is to take the law of the Lord from the Levites, write a copy of it for himself, and then reflect upon and revere the law all the days of his life. The king, in that sense, is "under the law." His rule is to be shaped by his reflection on God's instruction, and that meditation leads inevitably to a keen desire to see the maintenance of social justice in the land under his rule. A desire to see the torah worked out in reality in the land must lead a righteous ruler to oppose evil as well as to promote good. Any other type of rule would be a spiritualized fantasy that bears little relevance to the real world. Psalm 101 emphasizes the king's present responsibility to work for justice on a societal level in real terms.

Psalm 101 in the New Testament. There is no direct citation from Psalm 101 in the New Testament, but the text resonates strongly with the theology of the Lord's Prayer as presented in the Gospels. "Your kingdom come, your will be done on earth as it is in heaven" (Matt 6:10) is a prayer for radical renewal in the social sphere. Jesus teaches his disciples to pray for the radical transformation of the world they inhabited. In Psalm 101 the psalmist-king declares his determination to exercise his rule toward just such an end.

WHEN DOING GOOD IS NOT ENOUGH. The dual themes of Psalm 101 encompass the leader's determination to do good in accordance with God's revealed will and purpose (v. 2) and also

---

14. The same verb (*tsamat*, "to destroy") is used in both Pss 73:27 and 101:8.

his determination *to oppose evil* (vv. 3–5, 7–8). If we believe that the kingdom of God is inaugurated in a radically new way from the incarnation of Christ onward, then we have a real responsibility not only to do good in this world in which we live but also proactively to oppose evil and its impact on the world around us.

Obviously, Christian believers must exercise great caution in terms of how we oppose evil, but oppose evil we must. Zenger is helpful here:

> It may be that the directness of the challenge to God and the certainty it expresses that God must be at work in history and society form the real provocation of these psalms for a Christianity whose belief in God has exhausted its historical potential in soteriology or postponed it to an afterlife by a privatist and spiritualizing attitude. Here the shrill tones of the psalms of enmity can serve to shock Christianity out of the well-regulated slumber of its structural amnesia about God.[15]

It strikes me that part of the "well-regulated slumber" of the contemporary Western church is an unnatural focus on "being nice." We see being non-controversial as an essential part of our witness. Yet our emphasis on "niceness" can lead to the absolute denial of the church's awkward, angular, prophetic office that is so clearly outlined both in the prophets and the teaching of Jesus in the Gospels. Psalm 101 reminds the community of faith of our responsibility to embody the teaching of God's word *both* as exemplars of a good and godly lifestyle *and* as active opponents of evil and injustice.

Faced with the present reality of fascism in his homeland, Dietrich Bohoeffer came to ethical conclusions that resonate strongly with Psalm 101. Douglas Huff writes of Bonhoeffer:

> For Bonhoeffer, the foundation of ethical behavior lay in how the reality of the world and the reality of God were reconciled in the reality of Christ. Both in his thinking and in his life, ethics were centered on the demand for action by responsible men and women in the face of evil. He was sharply critical of ethical theory and of academic concerns with ethical systems precisely because of their failure to confront evil directly. Evil, he asserted, was concrete and specific, and it could be combated only by the specific actions of responsible people in the world. The uncompromising position Bonhoeffer took in his seminal work *Ethics* was directly reflected in his stance against Nazism.[16]

---

15. Zenger, *A God of Vengeance?* 74.

16. Douglas Huff, "Dietrich Bonhoeffer, 1906–45," in the *Internet Encyclopedia of Philosophy* (http://www.iep.utm.edu/bonhoeff/).

Although its source is actually uncertain, a quote often attributed to Bonhoeffer echoes this theology of Psalm 101: "Silence in the face of evil is itself evil: God will not hold us guiltless. Not to speak is to speak. Not to act is to act."[17]

---

17. See, for example, James Cone, "Theology's Great Sin: Silence in the Face of White Supremacy," *Black Theology* 2 (2004), 139–152, among many other sources that attribute this quote to Bonhoeffer.

Psalm 102

*A prayer of an afflicted person who has grown weak
and pours out a lament before the Lord.*

¹ Hear my prayer, Lord;
   let my cry for help come to you.
² Do not hide your face from me
   when I am in distress.
Turn your ear to me;
   when I call, answer me quickly.
³ For my days vanish like smoke;
   my bones burn like glowing embers.
⁴ My heart is blighted and withered like grass;
   I forget to eat my food.
⁵ In my distress I groan aloud
   and am reduced to skin and bones.
⁶ I am like a desert owl,
   like an owl among the ruins.
⁷ I lie awake; I have become
   like a bird alone on a roof.
⁸ All day long my enemies taunt me;
   those who rail against me use my name as a curse.
⁹ For I eat ashes as my food
   and mingle my drink with tears
¹⁰ because of your great wrath,
   for you have taken me up and thrown me aside.
¹¹ My days are like the evening shadow;
   I wither away like grass.
¹² But you, Lord, sit enthroned forever;
   your renown endures through all generations.
¹³ You will arise and have compassion on Zion,
   for it is time to show favor to her;
   the appointed time has come.
¹⁴ For her stones are dear to your servants;
   her very dust moves them to pity.
¹⁵ The nations will fear the name of the Lord,
   all the kings of the earth will revere your glory.
¹⁶ For the Lord will rebuild Zion

---

and appear in his glory.
¹⁷ He will respond to the prayer of the destitute;
  he will not despise their plea.
¹⁸ Let this be written for a future generation,
  that a people not yet created may praise the LORD:
¹⁹ "The LORD looked down from his sanctuary on high,
  from heaven he viewed the earth,
²⁰ to hear the groans of the prisoners
  and release those condemned to death."
²¹ So the name of the LORD will be declared in Zion
  and his praise in Jerusalem
²² when the peoples and the kingdoms
  assemble to worship the LORD.
²³ In the course of my life he broke my strength;
  he cut short my days.
²⁴ So I said:
  "Do not take me away, my God, in the midst of my days;
  your years go on through all generations.
²⁵ In the beginning you laid the foundations of the earth,
  and the heavens are the work of your hands.
²⁶ They will perish, but you remain;
  they will all wear out like a garment.
Like clothing you will change them
  and they will be discarded.
²⁷ But you remain the same,
  and your years will never end.
²⁸ The children of your servants will live in your presence;
  their descendants will be established before you."

PSALM 102 PRESENTS a deeply personal prayer in response to public crisis. It is an interesting response of personal faith to challenges in the geopolitical sphere. All too often people of faith tend to distance themselves from events on the national level. They feel removed from their milieu because they adhere to a very different perspective on life to that held by their peers. But there is a strong Old Testament tradition of the righteous individual's association with the city or the nation in bringing prayers to God (e.g., Isaiah, Jeremiah, Nehemiah). Psalm 102 gives the believer a vocabulary of prayer for the nation in crisis.

The psalm probably divides into three main sections: verses 1–11 outline the poet's lament; verses 12–22 focus on future hope for Zion; and verses 23–28 return to a voice of personal lament. The superscription sets the tone for what follows.

The Personal Lament (102:0–11)

A PRAYER OF AN AFFLICTED PERSON. The Hebrew words translated "afflicted one" and "lament" (*'ani* and *siah*) are stock terms associated with suffering and spiritual complaint. They create a sense of expectation in the mind of the reader, and the psalmist does not disappoint. The section that follows displays all three of the classic types of lament in a single section of the poem: the I-lament (vv. 3–5),[1] the enemy lament (vv. 6–8), and the God lament (vv. 9–10). There is an intensity about the superscription that is borne out in the prayer that follows.

For my days vanish like smoke. Following the standard petitions associated with lament in verses 1–2 ("hear my prayer," "turn your ear to me," "answer me quickly"), the psalmist voices his complaint with the mixed metaphors of a life that is being slowly consumed by fire and withering like grass (vv. 3–4). The graphic images imply suffering to the extent that the poet believes his life is about to be painfully extinguished. There is little left for him, and all seems hopeless. Alter comments, "The haunting image focuses two ideas, ephemerality and suffering."[2] There is an intensely personal potency of expression in this psalm. The reader is drawn to feel the anguished despair of the poet, whose body is failing him (v. 5).

I am like a desert owl. The second aspect of lament is focused on the opposition of enemies and expressed in terms of loneliness and social isolation (vv. 6–8). The sickness and physical decay of the I-lament is exacerbated by the mocking of enemies (v. 8). Not only does the psalmist suffer physically, but that suffering is also compounded by the mockery of his opponents. The enemies in this case are not the cause of the poet's suffering, but their taunting presents him as an apparent example of God's punishment in practice.[3] As a result of the over-easy association between physical illness and the wrath of God in the ancient world, corporeal suffering was often exacerbated by a terrible sense of social isolation and spiritual/moral accusation that would have a traumatic effect on the human

---

1. The I-lament does not necessarily (or often) refer to suffering caused by the self but rather to the impact the circumstances have on the supplicant. These statements are somewhat akin to the impact statements read by victims or their families in contemporary courtrooms.

2. Alter, *Psalms*, 353.

3. Kirkpatrick, *Psalms*, 595.

psyche. We see the effects of both physical and psychological torment in this opening section of Psalm 102 ("my heart is blighted," "I forget to eat," "I lie awake," I "mingle my drink with tears").

For I eat ashes as my food. The third element of this introductory lament section focuses on God as the Prime Mover and ultimate cause of the psalmist's torment (the God lament). The psalms have a high view of God's sovereignty, so even when enemies are the proximate cause of an individual's suffering, Yahweh is always viewed as being ultimately responsible either for causing or failing to prevent the pain that causes lament. Although it is always difficult (if not impossible) to establish the circumstances that lie behind the penning of a particular psalm,[4] it seems likely that the source of the psalmist's suffering here is physical illness.[5] The poet views his affliction as an expression of God's anger (v. 10a) or even God's aggression (v. 10b) toward him. The dual image of "taking me up and throwing me aside" is emblematic of the whirlwind. Akin to Job, the psalmist feels that God has dragged him into the chaos of the storm (Job 30:22). This afflication is the experience mentioned in the superscription.

My days are like the evening shadow. There is a strong time theme that runs throughout the whole of Psalm 102. "Day" and "days" are key words repeated often (vv. 2, 3, 8, 11, 23, 24), and we see repeated signs of the psalmist's awareness of life's slipping away from him (vv. 3, 11, 23). Days "like the evening shadow" is a vivid image of the end of life—darkness approaches. This picture is combined with the repetition of the simile of "withered grass" (cf. v. 4). The passing of the day toward night and the slow death of vegetation in the summer heat are both common images of imminent death.[6] The poet's days are over and his strength is giving out.

National Crisis and Future Hope (102:12–22)

BUT YOU, LORD, SIT ENTHRONED FOREVER. The second section of the poem transitions from personal complaint to an expression of sadness at the

---

4. Grant, "Determining the Indeterminate," 3–5.

5. Note the language of bodily decay in verse 3, loss of appetite in verse 4, weight loss in verse 5, and the mental impact that results (vv. 4a, 5a). The textual indicators suggest that the root of the poet's lament is some form of physical illness (see Mays, *Psalms*, 323). Schaefer describes the psalmist as "a person on the verge of collapse" (Schaefer, *Psalms*, 250).

6. Alter writes: "The similes again are selected with beautiful aptness. The life span races towards its inevitable end like lengthening shadows toward evening (one should remember that sundials were used in ancient Israel). Then the speaker himself, feeling his waning strength, withers like grass, in an appropriately organic image" (Alter, *Psalms*, 354).

demise of Jerusalem but also of hope in the city's future restoration.[7] There is a strong contrast in the Hebrew of verses 11 and 12. More literally, the psalmist says, "and as for me, I wither like grass" (*wa'ani*, v. 11b), which is here contrasted with the emphatic "but as for you, O Yahweh" (*we'attah*, v. 12a). The poet's days pass in the blink of an eye, but the Lord reigns throughout all eternity. "Human frailty encounters divine permanence."[8] On one level, there is hope in this thought—on another, it is daunting for the psalmist. How can he contend with the God who reigns absolutely and forever?[9] This conundrum is part of the great tension of lament.[10]

You will arise and have compassion on Zion. The movement from the individual to Zion is a surprising one, but such a transition is not altogether uncommon. Psalm 102 is often described as one of the seven penitential psalms alongside Psalms 6, 32, 38, (famously) 51, 130, and 143, though it must be said that there is no absolutely clear indication the poet's suffering is rooted in sinful behavior.[11] But if that were the case, then the individual's experience echoes that of the nation and the city. Israel has fallen, Zion is lost, and the great suffering that follows is the result of the people's sinful rebellion. Regardless of the root causes of the individual's complaint, his lament voices the pain of the people at the loss of their locus of worship. Nation, land, king, city, and temple—the external signs of God's covenantal promises—are no more, and the poet's prayer of despair in verses 1–11 voices well the people's sense of tragic loss and suffering that results from the exile ("her stones are dear to your servants" [v. 14]). The fault may have been theirs in the first place, but the pain experienced is no less real.

The appointed time has come. Nevertheless, there is hope! As we have discussed above (see Pss 93–101), one of the main themes of this section of Book 4 of the Psalms is the idea that Israel's God still reigns, despite all appearances to the contrary. Yahweh is the *eternal* King (Ps 102:12), and the psalmist hopes that God will evidence his kingship through the restoration of the city. "For it is time to show favor to her; the appointed time has come" further stresses the importance of the time theme observed in the initial lament section (vv. 1–11). The poet believes that his days are

---

7. How the three parts of the psalm relate to one another is a difficult question and one that we will examine briefly in the Bridging Contexts section.

8. Schaefer, *Psalms*, 251.

9. The psalm returns to this theme in verses 23–28.

10. See comments on Ps 88.

11. Psalm 102:9, with the "eat[ing] ashes as my food" along with the spilling of tears, may well be a reference to penitential rites. But sackcloth and ashes were also used in rituals of mourning in ancient Israel, so this expression is not a conclusive indication that Ps 102 is a prayer of repentance.

passing and that he can cope with no more on the individual level, but here the voice speaks of hope. Maybe the despair and suffering are about to come to an end on the corporate level.

The nations will fear the name of the LORD. The root of this burgeoning hope is missionally grounded. Why is there hope of restoration? Because the nations need to see and realize that Yahweh is in fact King of the cosmos, and they need to make an appropriate response to his sovereignty. How better for the surrounding peoples to recognize Yahweh's undisputed kingship than through the restoration of the city that symbolizes his rule on earth? The response of "fear" is the same response that is expected of Israel (Deut 10:12–13). In seeing Jerusalem restored and the people returned, the nations will be confronted with hard evidence of the lordship of Israel's God, and they will have to respond accordingly. The poet's hope is not based on any sense of the remarkably renewed righteousness of the people. It is rather grounded in a recognition that the *missio Dei* must always move forward.[12]

He will respond to the prayer of the destitute. Verse 17 indicates that the juxtaposition of the two voices (individual lament and corporate restoration) in Psalm 102 is not quite as jarring as some commentators would have us believe. The focus is different, but the resonance with the superscription is poignant. With reference to Zion, the poet expresses his confidence that Israel's God, Yahweh, will hear the prayer of the destitute. It seems likely that this tone of confidence is meant to be read back into the individual despair of the one who prays at the beginning and end of this psalm. If there is hope for Zion in the divine response to prayer, there must also be hope for the individual who prays. This realization is predicated on the reminder that God is a God of compassion (v. 13).[13]

The LORD looked down from his sanctuary on high. Just as this section of Psalm 102 echoes many of the restoration themes of Isaiah 40–66, so also we see resonances of the original escape from exile detailed in the account of the exodus. The image of the Lord looking down from his sanctuary in Psalm 102:19 echoes the divine awareness of his people's suffering in Egypt (Exod 3:7–10). There is something deeply caring and almost incarnational in the concern expressed. That the sentence flows from verse 19 to verse 22 is quite unusual in psalmic poetry, and here the thoughts present Yahweh as being truly attentive to both sights and

---

12. Wright, *The Mission of God*, 482–83.

13. "Clearly, the afflicted one of strand one corresponds in some way to the destitute population of Zion of strand two" (Mays, *Psalms*, 324); therefore, if there is hope for the latter, there must be hope for the former.

sounds and as responsive to the needs of those who are suffering. He not only sees, but he also pays attention to the realities of his people and acts in an efficacious manner. Such knowledge of God's character gives all future generations of believers cause to praise, regardless of their present experience (v. 18).[14] Since God has proven himself to be the God of both exodus and restoration in the past, surely he will be such again.

So the name of the LORD will be declared. There are three clear effects of God's attentiveness to his people: hearing, releasing, and declaring (vv. 20–21). The aim of his observation is to hear the needs of his people *and* to set free those imprisoned *so that* his name (i.e., his true character and being) will be declared in the midst of his people. The revelation of God's perfect character through his perfect actions should always result in a response of praise from his people. The act of liberation must inevitably be met with songs of praise.

When the peoples and the kingdoms assemble to worship the LORD. The inevitable consequence of the revelation of God's character through his intervention in the realities of this world is to attract those who are, as yet, outside the community of faith into the worshiping body. God's works in the world draw people to worship him. Yahweh hears and responds to the prayers of his people, thus leading them to voice their praise of his perfect character and power. This testimony of praise draws others in to find out more about the God who is graciously and effectively at work in the world. In a manner reminiscent of Psalm 126:1–3, testimony to God's goodness draws others to see his true nature and respond to him. "Nations and kingdoms will be gathered not for judgment, as in Psalm 79:6, or for strife among nations, as in Psalm 46:7, but to worship Yhwh, as in Isaiah 2; Micah 4; Isaiah 60."[15]

Passing Life, Eternal God (102:23–28)

IN THE COURSE OF MY LIFE HE BROKE MY STRENGTH. The Hebrew is a little awkward here, as the psalmist returns to a voice of lament, but the implication seems to be that God has cut short the petitioner's life. His days are passing quickly, and there is not much life left for him, so once again he offers his prayer to God (v. 24a). As we have also seen elsewhere in our study of the psalms, this psalm demonstrates the tension of lament: the petitioner believes God to lie at the very root of his suffering, yet God is also his only hope for restoration. The tension is a real and dynamic

---

14. Interestingly, the NIV does not translate the causative *ki* at the start of verse 19. Future generations will praise *"because* the Lord looked down from his sanctuary on high."
15. Hossfeld and Zenger, *Psalms 3,* 25.

aspect of truly biblical spirituality. Although the concluding prayer echoes the despair of the first lament section (vv. 1–11), the reader approaches this closing section slightly differently. The psalmist's prayer may remain unanswered in the here and now, but we have been reminded of a God who hears the groaning of his people's suffering and responds with gracious release (vv. 19–20). Yahweh's response to the prayers of a nation gives the individual hope in his suffering.

Your years go on through all generations. There is a temporal contrast throughout this section of Psalm 102. The fleeting brevity of human life, particularly a life apparently being cut short by illness, is contrasted with the eternal reign of God (vv. 24b–27). In some ways the contrast is stark. The poet decries the abbreviation of his life in juxtaposition with the timelessness of God (v. 24), yet ultimately there is comfort to be found in the eternal reign of the Creator because he is "my God." The personal vocative indicates that there is hope to be found in relationship with God even when one's days are shrouded in darkness and difficulty.

In the beginning you laid the foundations of the earth. The created order reflects the power and control of God (v. 25). In a deliberate echo of Genesis 1, the psalmist paints a picture of a deity of unimaginable ability. Laying the foundations of the earth is completely beyond human understanding, let alone the ability to replicate such action. The reference to the psalmist's God as Creator conjures images of unimaginable power, control, and creativity. The reference is probably meant to imply that the God who made order out of chaos in creation is more than able to order the chaos of a life. The King of the universe, Creator of all things, is surely Lord over the life of the individual as well, sick or not. As we will see below, that hope may be more eschatological than temporal (v. 28).

They will perish, but you remain. The declaration of Yahweh as Creator and Sustainer of the cosmos is common enough in the Old Testament. Discussion of the temporality of the physical order is less frequent but clearly stated here in verse 26 (cf. Isa 51:6). Despite the appearance of permanence, the earth is in reality nothing more than a garment that will wear out in the light of God's actual permanence. It is a good jacket, which has lasted well, but its timespan does not compare to the existence of the God "who was, and is, and is to come" (Rev 4:8).

But you remain the same, and your years will never end. Literally, the Hebrew of Psalm 102:27 reads, "But you are he."[16] The phrase presents the psalmist's God as *sui generis*. He is in a category all his own. No one and

---

16. The formulation resonates with the repeated theme of Ps 99: "Holy is he."

nothing, not even the cosmos, is like him. The cosmic realm will end, but Yahweh's existence, rule, and reign continue forever.

The children of your servants will live in your presence. The psalm ends with a voice of hope for restoration in the future. The enjoyment of God's presence as part of worship in the temple precinct is not a privilege available to the psalmist and his generation.[17] The passage of time is a very relative concept for the eternal King; therefore, there is hope that future generations will see the restoration of the temple and enjoy his presence there. The psalmist's days may be shortened, but God has made covenantal promises to his people, so there is hope for the longer term. God is a God of restoration (v. 16). There is always hope for the future. This optimistic final voice also serves as an *aide-mémoire* for the petitioner: just as there is hope for the future for God's people, so there may well be hope in the poet's own personal circumstance, regardless of how bleak things look now.[18]

HOW MANY POEMS? One of the main points for discussion in the commentaries regarding Psalm 102 is its somewhat unusual structure. As discussed above, the poem moves from personal lament probably in the face of illness (vv. 1–11), to a hymnic expression of hope regarding the restoration of Zion (vv. 12–22), and back to a personal lament regarding the foreshortening of life (vv. 23–28). The unusual collocation of themes leads many commentators to surmise that two originally separate poems have been spliced together into one psalm by a later editor.[19]

In the Psalms, it is not entirely uncommon for the fate of a representative individual to be entwined with the fate of the nation (and vice versa; e.g., see Pss 22 and 69).[20] There is a link between the personal and the corporate in this psalm that encourages two-way reflection. The poet reflects on his own difficult experiences in the light of the fall of Jerusalem, but he also implies the future hope of the restoration of Zion back into his own

---

17. Broyles, *Psalms*, 393.

18. Leslie C. Allen, *Psalms 101–150*, WBC 21, rev. ed. (Nashville: Nelson, 2002), 23.

19. For an excellent analysis of current studies on the redaction of Ps 102 see Hossfeld and Zenger, *Psalms 3*, 20–22. To my mind, it is almost impossible to state conclusively from this historical distance whether or not a psalm was a single composition or the product of later editorial work. Whatever its origins, Ps 102 makes sense as a unitary composition (McKelvey, *Moses, David and the High Kingship of Yahweh*, 182 n. 26).

20. Eaton, *Psalms*, 355.

bleak circumstances. He despairs, just as the nation mourns, but he also finds personal hope in the divine promises to the people as a whole. This interplay between individual and national prayer may seem unusual to the modern Western mindset, but such corporate affiliation was common in the ancient Near East and remains so in other parts of the modern world today.[21]

Psalm 102 in the New Testament. Psalm 102:25–27 is cited in Hebrews 1:10–12 as part of the author's argument that Christ brings a superior revelation than that brought by angels. Unsurprisingly, the author reads the reference to Yahweh's eternal rule as a statement of Jesus' unchanging kingship.[22] Christ is presented as Creator and eternal Ruler. He will remain even though the cosmic order passes away. As is typical throughout this section of the epistle, references to Yahweh's rule are ascribed to Jesus' person and ministry: quite simply, Jesus is the Most High God, the author argues.[23]

PRIVATE PRAYER, *OUR* NATION, AND *THE* NATIONS. It seems to me that the contemporary Christian often has a somewhat ambivalent relationship with the broader society in which she lives. We decry the demise of biblical morality in the formerly Christian West. We distance ourselves from the currents and trends of our countries and cultures because they so often run counter to biblical faith. Yet the psalmist here sets for us an example that entwines deeply personal petition with prayer for the nation and, indeed, for all nations.

Of course, hermeneutically speaking, our home nations cannot be equated with the Israel of the Old Testament. They are not recipients of the promises made to Israel under the old covenant, nor do they hold the same position in God's plans for the world. But the example of prayer that encompasses our own fate and that of the nation(s) is a helpful one. As John Stott so fervently argued, if Christians are meant to be salt and light in the world, then moral decay in our cultures is, at least in part, our fault.[24]

---

21. For further discussion see Trent C. Butler, "Piety in the Psalms," *RevExp* 81 (1984): 385–94 and the Contemporary Significance section below.

22. See Grant, "Cover Versions."

23. Attridge, "Psalms in John," 202–203.

24. "Nevertheless, God intends the most powerful of all restraints within sinful society to be his own redeemed, regenerate and righteous people" (John R. W. Stott, *The Message of the Sermon on the Mount: Christian Counter Culture* [Leicester: Inter-Varsity Press, 1979], 59).

So often our prayers for our own nation complain about its demise rather than lamenting our own ineffectual witness and seeking after God for renewal both of our testimony and of our lands. Stott argues:

> Christian salt has no business to remain snugly in elegant little ecclesiastical salt cellars; our place is to be rubbed into the secular community, as salt is rubbed into meat, to stop it going bad. And when society does go bad, we Christians tend to throw up our hands in pious horror and reproach the non-Christian world, but should we not rather reproach ourselves? One can hardly blame unsalted meat for going bad. It cannot do anything else. The real question to ask is: where is the salt?[25]

There is a good example for us in the prayer of Psalm 102. The poet is not so focused on himself that he fails to see the world around him.[26] Nor is he so focused on his own pain that he forgets the character of God. Remembering God's faithful work in the world brings hope to even the darkest of personal circumstances. All too often our prayers never see beyond ourselves and our nuclear family, though sometimes wider family, friends, neighbors, and our local congregation are drawn in. The psalmist gives us an example of prayer that encompasses deep personal hurt but also goes beyond it with a prayerful vision for his nation (vv. 13–17) and envisions the missional inclusion of all nations into the worshiping community of God's family (vv. 18–22).

Prayer is a deeply personal matter, but Psalm 102 models an attitude to prayer that goes beyond the solely personal. We should follow its example.[27]

---

25. Stott, *The Sermon on the Mount*, 65.
26. Longman, *Psalms*, 355.
27. Mays, *Psalms*, 325–26.

Psalm 103

Of David.

[1] Praise the LORD, my soul;
  all my inmost being, praise his holy name.
[2] Praise the LORD, my soul,
  and forget not all his benefits—
[3] who forgives all your sins
  and heals all your diseases,
[4] who redeems your life from the pit
  and crowns you with love and compassion,
[5] who satisfies your desires with good things
  so that your youth is renewed like the eagle's.
[6] The LORD works righteousness
  and justice for all the oppressed.
[7] He made known his ways to Moses,
  his deeds to the people of Israel:
[8] The LORD is compassionate and gracious,
  slow to anger, abounding in love.
[9] He will not always accuse,
  nor will he harbor his anger forever;
[10] he does not treat us as our sins deserve
  or repay us according to our iniquities.
[11] For as high as the heavens are above the earth,
  so great is his love for those who fear him;
[12] as far as the east is from the west,
  so far has he removed our transgressions from us.
[13] As a father has compassion on his children,
  so the LORD has compassion on those who fear him;
[14] for he knows how we are formed,
  he remembers that we are dust.
[15] The life of mortals is like grass,
  they flourish like a flower of the field;
[16] the wind blows over it and it is gone,
  and its place remembers it no more.
[17] But from everlasting to everlasting
  the LORD's love is with those who fear him,
  and his righteousness with their children's children—

¹⁸ with those who keep his covenant
    and remember to obey his precepts.
¹⁹ The LORD has established his throne in heaven,
    and his kingdom rules over all.
²⁰ Praise the LORD, you his angels,
    you mighty ones who do his bidding,
    who obey his word.
²¹ Praise the LORD, all his heavenly hosts,
    you his servants who do his will.
²² Praise the LORD, all his works
    everywhere in his dominion.
Praise the LORD, my soul.

PSALM 103 GIVES one of the most powerful descriptions of the character and nature of God that we encounter in the Christian Scriptures. It is a statement of theology of the most profound type because it reveals to us the very being of God in a manner that brings us to our knees in grateful praise. Knowing *this* God can only lead to a genuine and heartfelt outpouring of thankfulness. The God of Psalm 103 is not there to be deliberated over. He is there to be delighted in!

The structure of the poem breaks down into four parts. There is the voice of praise at the beginning and end (vv. 1–2 and 20–22), there is consideration of various aspects of God's nature (vv. 3–6), and finally there is focus on the forgiveness and mercy of God (vv. 7–19). The structure illustrates the psalmist's focus:

Blessing Yahweh for his benefits (vv. 1–2);
    Listing the works of God that reveal his nature, with
        forgiveness first on the list (vv. 3–6);
    A poetic celebration of divine forgiveness (vv. 7–19)
Blessing Yahweh in the cosmic realm and in the heart (vv. 20–22)

In many ways Psalm 103 is a poetic reflection on and celebration of Exodus 34:6–7, one of the key statements of Old Testament faith and theology. There Yahweh reveals himself to Moses as a God of unstinting love and extravagant forgiveness, and here the psalmist reflects deeply on that self-revelation and its profound impact on the recipients of such grace.

Blessing Yahweh (103:1–2)

PRAISE THE LORD, MY SOUL. The opening words of the psalm serve as a reminder to one's self. The command is to "bless Yahweh" (v. 1, rightly translated "praise" in the NIV). John Eaton reminds us that the Hebrew verb "to bless" (*barak*) is the "word for praise most warm with gratitude."[1] As always, the Lord is the object of praise, but, unusually, here the addressee is neither Israel nor the nations, for the psalmist is speaking to himself.[2] The reminder to his own "soul" to praise the Lord is a personalized call to worship. Just as the psalmists will frequently call Israel, the priesthood, or Yahweh's followers to give thanks (Ps 118:2–3), or call the nations and peoples to praise him (Ps 117:1), so here the poet addresses his very inner being with the call to praise the Lord (Ps 103:1).[3] The essence of this unusual call to worship is twofold. First, Yahweh is inherently worthy of individual, personal praise, and second, it is easy to forget that truth. The call to bless "his holy name" gives the reader an indication of the basis of that praise. The name (*shem*) in the Hebrew mindset is a reference to the essential being and character of an individual.[4] The poet reminds the reader that Yahweh's essential character is holy. He is different from the rest of the created order, and that uniqueness is celebrated with a particular focus in the remaining verses of the psalm.

Forget not all his benefits. The repetition of the call to praise in verse 2 is cast with the challenge not to forget the "benefits" that life with God brings.[5] The explicit, negative command not to forget affirms

---

1. Eaton, *Psalms*, 358.

2. The address to "my soul" is unique in the Psalms apart from the repeated *inclusio* in Ps 104:1 and 35.

3. The "soul," and especially "my soul" (*napshi*), features quite prominently throughout the Psalter. It is a key word that runs through the second half of Book 1 (Pss 22–27, 30–31, 34–35, 38, 40–41) and links the beginning of Book 2 with the end of the previous section (Pss 42–43). The term is often used in laments as a synonym for the poet's life (e.g., Ps 22:20) but, as here, is also used as shorthand for one's inner life (e.g., Pss 23:3; 24:4). Eaton describes the "soul" used in this context as "the very core of one's being, with all the powers of heart and mind" (Eaton, *Psalms*, 358).

4. See "שֵׁם," *HALOT* 2:1550: "in many cases [name of the Lord] means not only the name but the full being and power of Yahweh." Hossfeld comments quite simply, "The holy name corresponds to Yhwh's holy nature" (Hossfeld and Zenger, *Psalms 3*, 34).

5. Note the repeated use of "all" (*kol*) throughout Ps 103. Schaefer suggests that the psalmist is hinting at the absolute completeness and sufficiency of relationship with God: "Twenty-two lines (verses), the sum of letters in the Hebrew alphabet, hint at a wisdom motif and a comprehensive composition. The repetition of 'all,' *kol*, several times at the beginning and end reinforces the sense of completeness. . . . The initial warning 'do not forget' states the purpose of the psalm, to remember, celebrate, reactualize" (Schaefer, *Psalms*, 254).

---

the implication in the opening verse. The poet addresses his heart with this call to worship because it is easy to forget in our inner being the many reasons we have to praise God. "Benefits" sounds mercenary, yet the psalmist is unashamed in presenting the reader with a vivid reminder that good things result from loving God. The idea of "benefits" can imply "recompense" or "reward," but the focus of the remainder of the psalm is on unmerited blessing received from God's hand.

The Benefits Listed (103:3–6)

THE SECOND SECTION OF THE PSALM (vv. 3–6) gives a powerful rationale for praise. It outlines the character of God by listing his actions through a series of personal participles.[6] The Lord is the one who forgives, heals, redeems, and so on. The catalogue lists five actions that typify the character of God, the first of which focuses on the forgiveness of sins. Often in the Hebrew Bible, first place in a list indicates the priority of the author's emphasis, as is certainly the case in Psalm 103, where the remainder of the poem is so strongly focused on the forgiving love of God toward his people.

Who forgives all your sins. Here we see the primary aspect of God's being that brings benefit to his people and should be a strong motivator toward praise. The poet recognizes that there can be no greater benefit because there can be no relationship with God apart from the forgiveness of sins. All the other benefits are dependent on this initial act of love, which is further unpacked in the third section of the psalm (vv. 7–19).

And heals all your diseases. While in modern interpretations there is a tendency to spiritualize this notion, it is more likely in the ancient world that the poet was actually talking about the healing of physical ailments. In a world before antibiotics, even a tiny cut, if infected, could prove fatal. Childhood illnesses that are thought trivial today could kill, disable, or disfigure. In a world in which the understanding of human anatomy was still relatively primitive, medicines were basic, and illnesses more prevalent, to be alive was a clear sign of God's protection and healing.[7] To live

---

6. There is a fascinating correlation between activity and character in Ps 103. God's actions reflect his essential nature. As the one "who forgives all your sins," he is shown to be a forgiving God; as the one "who redeems your life from the pit," he is shown to be a redeeming God, and so on. We also see the emphasis on God as literally "doing" righteousness and justice for the oppressed (v. 6); as well, his love rests on those who remember to "do" his precepts (v. 18). There is a strong emphasis on consistent living in this poem. Our true nature is not reflected by what we claim to be but rather by what we do—this truth applies to Yahweh, and it is equally true of his people.

7. While Hector Avalos has shown that healthcare in the ancient Near East was not *as* primitive as is often stated, it still must be acknowledged that surviving even basic

into what we would now describe as one's "middle age" was nothing short of miraculous; therefore, continued life was a sign of God's blessing and protection and thus also a reason for praise.

Who redeems your life from the pit. The likelihood that verse 3b refers to physical illness is increased by the benefit that immediately follows in verse 4a.[8] In the Psalms, the pit is a metaphor for the grave (e.g., Ps 30:9), and being redeemed from the grave is a reference to restoration from the very brink of death. Yahweh deserves praise because of his mercy in preserving his people.

And crowns you with love and compassion. Love and compassion are key terms in Psalm 103 (see vv. 8, 11, 13, 17). On one level, the poem is a celebration of the love and compassion God pours out on his people. Such profligate mercy encourages a response of extravagant praise. The terms used (*hesed werahamim*) are covenantal in nature. They would remind the original hearers of God's gracious promises to his people. Any real relationship with God is absolutely dependent on his love and mercy. This is the poet's key idea, and it rings like a *Leitmotif* throughout a musical.[9]

Who satisfies your desires with good things. Such great love and mercy does not just extend to continued existence. The psalmist delights in the God who gives good things (*tov*) necessary for life. This idea is echoed in Psalm 103's twin psalm, Psalm 104, which celebrates God's good provision (cf. Ps 104:14–15, 28).[10]

So that your youth is renewed like the eagle's. The metaphor is either a reference to the eagle's ability to cast off old plumage and replace it with new feathers or simply to the indefatigable strength of the great bird of prey.[11] As in Isaiah 40:27–31, the promise is of a strength that goes beyond our natural health and human abilities. This strength is a gift of God given to his people for the enjoyment of life.

Forgiveness, healing, restoration to life, relationship, a good life to be enjoyed, and one that is marked by strength beyond our own—these are the benefits of life with the Lord, according to the author of Psalm 103. Equally, these actions reflect characteristics of the divine being. God is

---

illnesses was far from guaranteed in the ancient world (Hector Avalos, *Illness and Health Care in the Ancient Near East: The Role of the Temple in Greece, Mesopotamia, and Israel*, Harvard Semitic Monographs [Atlanta: Scholars Press, 1995]).

8. Longman, *Psalms*, 356.

9. Mays, *Psalms*, 326–28.

10. "Yhwh not merely restores and protects but satiates and fills. The verb . . . denotes not merely satisfying but something more like satiating, causing to overflow and run over" (Goldingay, *Psalms 3*, 168).

11. Eaton, *Psalms*, 359.

forgiving, loving, compassionate, generous, and relational. His actions in the cosmos reflect the essence of his being, as summarized in verse 6.

The LORD works righteousness and justice for all the oppressed. This great love, compassion, and generosity are focused in the idea that the God of the covenant will work out what is right and just in behalf of those who have been marginalized, oppressed, and denied a fair voice. The verb used is, more literally, the common verb for "doing." "Yahweh does righteousness and justice for the voiceless," the poet says. As he is, so he does. He is by nature loving—therefore, he will show that love to his people. He is, by nature, just—therefore, one way or another, he will bring about justice for those who have been denied it.[12]

The notion of executing justice for the oppressed seems to trigger an exodus thought in the poet's mind, and he turns to that narrative to continue his reflection on the forgiving mercy of God.

The Loving Forgiveness of God (103:7–19)

HE MADE KNOWN HIS WAYS TO MOSES. The psalmist's reflection on the divine self-revelation in Exodus 34:6 is made explicit by this reference to Moses (Ps 103:7). God's making himself known to the people of Israel through his deeds reflects the accounts of the plagues that secured their release from slavery. During their time of captivity in Egypt, the people had largely forgotten the God of their ancestors, so the first revelation of his character came through their observation of his actions (see Pss 77:12; 78:11, where the same word for "deeds" is used in the context of the exodus). This verse makes the exodus context unmistakable.

The LORD is compassionate and gracious, slow to anger, abounding in love. This direct quotation from Exodus 34:6 continues the poet's focus on God's grace, compassion, and forgiveness. As Alter highlights, "What is left out from the passage in Exodus is God's 'reckoning the crimes of fathers with sons and sons of sons.' Here, on the contrary, the exclusive emphasis is on divine compassion and forgiveness."[13] The language, again, is covenantal: compassionate, gracious, and abounding in steadfast love. God has freely made promises to his people that remain a functioning reality despite the people's repeated inappropriate responses. God is who he is regardless of what his people do. His love is not predicated on obedience—the psalmist is clear that God simply is who he is by nature.[14]

---

12. "'Righteousness' is no static attribute of Yahweh, but it manifests itself in such acts as help, deliverance, healing, forgiveness, etc." (Anderson, *Psalms*, 714).

13. Alter, *Psalms*, 359.

14. This emphasis on divine grace is, of course, an important part of Book 4's response

Of course, the original occurrence of this act of self-revelation would be poignant for the postexilic community of Book 4. Exodus 34:6–7 is God's response to the people's failure in the golden calf incident (Exod 32). The exile was a constant reminder for the poet's community of their own moral culpability. Yet Yahweh revealed himself to be gracious in Moses' day, and the psalmist reminds the people that he remains so in their day.

He will not always accuse. The positive restatement of God's character in Psalm 103:8 is followed by four negated statements meant to indicate clearly what God is not like or ways in which he will not behave. Accusation and anger are, of course, appropriate responses of an all-holy God to the sins of his people (v. 9), but he will sustain neither one indefinitely. Equally, a gracious God does not seek to repay us in accordance with our human fallibility (v. 10). The four statements are almost farcical in the light of the presentation of God's character in Psalm 103—knowing what God is really like means that such thoughts verge on the ridiculous.[15]

For as high as the heavens are above the earth, so great is his love for those who fear him. There follow three similes that beautifully illustrate the extent of Yahweh's grace and love toward his people. The height of the sky above the earth is the only concept that comes close to exemplifying the span of God's steadfast love for his people. In similar terms, only the unending and immeasureable distance between east and west can illustrate the extent of the removal of sin from a forgiven people. The compassionate love of a father for his children is the only human experience that can, however inadequately, approximate God's love for his children. The three images are rich, emotive, and vivid. Anyone can grasp their intent and importance—love that extends beyond our ability to conceptualize; the absolute removal of sins; compassionate care of parents for their own children. Such pictures evoke a powerful insight into the character of God—profound theology in poetic form. As Schaefer comments:

---

to the tragedies of Book 3. Book 3 focuses strongly on the fall of Jerusalem as a result of the people's sinfulness. The response of Book 4 turns to Yahweh's continued reign and also to his continued grace. "For the audience of Book IV, this example of God's kindness to the nation at the beginning of its history serves as a reminder of YHWH's grace toward a sinful people. . . . As he was merciful after the golden calf incident and revealed his way to Moses, so he will show mercy to Israel again and they will see his grace" (McKelvey, *Moses, David and the High Kingship of Yahweh*, 202).

15. Ironically, however, it seems that many Christians subliminally take the view of God that is thoroughly negated in 103:9–10: that he is reluctant to forgive and restore and that he does hold our sins against us. We will consider this further in the Contemporary Significance section.

The poet expounds the theology; God's *hesed*, more durable than his anger at wrongdoing, is why sinners hope for forgiveness. *Hesed* so abounds that it surpasses time and space, as high as the heavens above the earth, the unimaginable distance between east and west, as lasting as eternity (v. 17). . . . God's *hesed*, greater than anything deserved, provides the motive for worship.[16]

Those who fear him. Key to a right understanding of this all-encompassing love is the repeated phrase in verses 11, 13, and 17. The recipients of this great mercy are described using theological shorthand drawn from wisdom literature. Raymond Van Leeuwen describes the fear of the Lord in this way:

> The great phrase "the fear of the LORD" grounds human knowledge and wisdom (cf. 9:10) in humble service of Yahweh. . . . Although this phrase has its origin in the experience of God's numinous majesty (as at Sinai, Deut 4:9–10), *it eventually has come to express the total claim of God upon humans and the total life-response of humans to God.*[17]

The choice of terminology is precise and interesting. Effectively, those who fear the Lord are those who have decided to put Yahweh first in their lives. The terminology does not imply perfection or super-spirituality. This section of the psalm focuses on the universal human need for forgiveness, so the idea of those who fear the Lord clearly does not refer to a spiritual or ethical elite; rather, this wisdom shorthand comes to refer to those who genuinely seek to live their lives for Yahweh in a holistic manner. It is about a fully integrated life of faith that reflects a genuine desire to apply love for God and biblical truths to every area of life. These are not super-believers. They are those who honestly desire to live for God.[18]

For he knows how we are formed. The rationale for the all-encompassing forgiveness extended to those who fear Yahweh has a double root. First, as we have seen, it is based on the great love, mercy, and compassion of God. Second, it is grounded in an act of divine remembrance.

He remembers that we are dust. Psalm 103:14–16 focuses on human weakness, fallibility, and brevity of life. God remembers our finite nature and is, therefore, all the more willing to extend his grace to

---

16. Schaefer, *Psalms*, 256.

17. Van Leeuwen, "Proverbs," 33. Emphasis added.

18. Jamie A. Grant, "'Why Bother with the Vulnerable?': The Wisdom of Social Care," in *Transforming the World? The Gospel and Social Responsibility*, ed. Jamie A. Grant and Dewi A. Hughes (Leicester: Apollos, 2009), 51–67.

us.[19] Remembrance is important to the psalmist. He reminds his own soul to "forget not all his benefits" (v. 2), including the awareness that Yahweh remembers the essence of our human existence even though it is as fleeting as grass whose "place remembers it no more" (v. 16). Since God remembers those who fear him, we should "remember to obey his precepts" (v. 18). Remembering is key to the message of Psalm 103. Mindfulness of God's great grace will surely shape our response to him.

But from everlasting to everlasting the LORD's love is on those who fear him. In verses 17–18 the poet returns to his contemplation of the blessings of covenantal relationship. God's eternal love (*hesed* again) is on those who fear him. His righteousness (see v. 6) extends from generation to generation. Cross-generational blessing is intimately associated with God's covenantal promises from Genesis 12 through to Exodus 34 and 2 Samuel 7. Interestingly, in Exodus 34:7 the reference to Yahweh's anger that might extend to the second or third generation is omitted from Psalm 103's poetic reflection on this key statement of faith, but the continuation of blessing through succeeding generations is celebrated. The emphasis is on bountiful grace.[20]

With those who keep his covenant. Grace is unmerited, but it should always provoke a response in the recipient. Yahweh remembers that people are formed from the dust, so they are weak. His grace extends to those who fear him, that is, to those whose heartfelt desire is to honor him. With this truth in mind, the poet adds a reflection on the reader's response to this great forgiveness. One cannot remain unresponsive to such love. Such love should always be met with a response in kind. There is a beautiful simplicity in the psalmist's conclusion that to love God is to keep covenant with him and to remember to obey (lit., "to do") his precepts. God's people respond to his grace by a commitment to love him through mindfulness of his teaching.[21]

The LORD has established his throne in heaven. In the modern world, love and mercy are often equated with weakness. The same was true among the ancients. Psalm 103:19 testifies to the fact that God's compassion is not a sign of impotence but an expression of merciful kingship.

---

19. As John Goldingay comments, "We are on our way back to the soil. Therefore God does not treat us too hard" (*Psalms 3*, 173).

20. "Yahweh has overcome generational mortality with intergenerational immortality (cf. Gen 3:19–20). This act of common grace guarantees the survival of the people of the covenant, as from generation to generation the same constant relationship with God is handed on" (Allen, *Psalms*, 32).

21. Longman, *Psalms*, 357.

Yahweh has established his throne. He does not need to assert his authority through displays of power. As the undisputed King of the cosmos, he is able to extend mercy to his people because the postexilic generations would never again doubt God's ability to assert his authority in human history. He asserted that authority by delivering his people over to exile *and* by bringing them home from captivity. God's rule is firmly established. He is King over a kingdom. The kingdom image implies an authority that affects every conceivable area of life—the marketplace, finance, leisure, the arts, language, culture, humor, family, the rights of the individual, the obligations of society, and so on— all parts of any kingdom. God's kingdom is a real kingdom. It is not "kingdom lite." The King speaks into every area of life, and the proper covenantal response is to apply his standards to every aspect of our lives and the world around us. Is this not what we declare when we pray, "Your kingdom come, your will be done, on earth as it is in heaven"?[22] Mays is helpful here:

> The Lord's steadfast love can be as great as the heavens are high above the earth, because the Lord's throne is established in heaven (vv. 11, 19). The Lord can remove our transgressions from us as far as the east is from the west because his kingdom rules over all (vv. 12, 19). These are poetic ways of stating one of the fundamental points of psalmic theology: The salvation of the Lord is the manifestation of the reign of the Lord in the world. . . . The grace of the Lord is a sovereignty of grace.[23]

Blessing Yahweh in the Cosmic Realm (103:20–22)

PRAISE THE LORD, YOU HIS ANGELS. The concluding call to praise (the Hebrew command again being "to bless") initially takes something of a surprising turn before reverting to an exact echo of the opening self-exhortation. The initial call to bless Yahweh is addressed to "his angels," who are then described as the "mighty ones who do his bidding," the "heavenly hosts," and "his servants." This call to worship addressed to the angelic armies of the Lord is the logical consequence of his cosmic reign focused on in the previous verse. As throughout the psalm, in these concluding verses the emphasis remains on *doing* the word of God. Alter translates verse 20 in this way:

---

22. For further discussion of a holistic Christian worldview see Bridging Contexts below.

23. Mays, *Psalms*, 330.

Bless the Lord, O His messengers,
  valiant in power, performing His word,
  to heed the sound of His word.[24]

The idea of doing Yahweh's word lies at the very core of angelic existence. The angels do his word in order to heed the sound of his word, thus providing an example for all humans whose desire is to worship God with their lives (v. 18). "There should be and is joyous praise in heaven among the doers in the kingdom of the Lord that there are doers on earth who confirm the love of the Lord by their obedience."[25]

Praise the LORD all his works. There is a sense of building to a crescendo of praise in these concluding verses of Psalm 103. The psalmist moves from charging all the angelic hosts with their responsibility to praise, to calling the whole created order to raise its voice in blessing Yahweh. This shift has a transformative effect on the concluding echo of verse 1. The initial "note to self" has a personal, almost individualistic ring to it, but the final reminder to "Praise the LORD, my soul" (v. 22c) situates the psalmist's voice among the massed chorus of the created order. All creation sings out its praise, and the psalmist raises his voice along with the heavenly armies and all those on earth who fear the Lord. This communion of praise is cosmic.

Everywhere in his dominion. Note also the locative reference in verse 22b. The call for all the works of the Lord to praise him is addressed to "everywhere in his dominion." Praise is due to the King. The picture is of grateful subjects paying homage to their Ruler for all his good works that bring benefit to them.

So, Psalm 103 moves from the poet's self-exhortation to praise to a cosmic call to worship by way of an emotive reminder of God's steadfast love for his creation and, in particular, of the all-encompassing forgiveness he extends to his people.

THEOLOGY AND THE EXPERIENCE OF GOD. The absolute lordship of God is a consistent theme throughout the psalms of Book 4 (Pss 90–106), and, somewhat surprisingly, this theme is repeated here in Psalm 103. In the midst of a poem centered on the steadfast love and powerful forgiveness of God, we come across these focal reminders of his cosmic dominion (vv. 19, 22). Why so?

---

24. Alter, *Psalms*, 360.
25. Mays, *Psalms*, 330.

The idea of the Lord's reign is more than just an abstract theological notion. It is an ontological reality that affects the way the believer views and experiences everything, including the spiritual realm and the "realities" of daily life. The worldview of the psalms is formulated in the combination of two repeated concepts: the Lord reigns (Pss 93–100), and his love endures forever (Ps 136). This combination of beliefs—the absolute sovereignty of God and his relational goodness—is seen clearly in Psalm 103.

First, the ways of the Cosmic King are ingrained in the cosmos he created (v. 19, and more on this point in Ps 104). His instruction speaks authoritatively to *every aspect* of life in creation, so Yahweh's people should live lives shaped by his royal word (v. 18). Second, God's cosmic kingship is intimately linked with the relational expression of his steadfast love toward his people, especially as it is experienced in the forgiveness of sins (vv. 7–18). He forgives because, as King, he alone has the absolute power and the right to pardon offenders.[26]

So, the psalmic idea of an essential worldview is far from being merely an entirely abstract, intellectual concept. Knowing who God is shapes our experience of him. As John Calvin so eloquently points out, if we do not know God in the way that he has revealed himself to us, we will never properly understand ourselves or our place in this world.[27] Yahweh, the King of the universe, reveals himself as a compassionate, forgiving, loving Father. It is important for us never to allow our own hangups and insecurities to blur God's revelation of his true being. In Psalm 103 foundational theology meets the human experience. God's loving compassion is not a concept to be mooted; it is a truth to be celebrated. Theological reflection inevitably invites a response of praise.

Psalm 103 in the New Testament. There are no direct citations of Psalm 103 in the New Testament, but it is not difficult to chart its theological trajectory into the New Testament's theology. "In him we have redemption through his blood, the forgiveness of sins, in accordance with the riches of God's grace that he lavished on us" (Eph 1:7–8).

ACCEPTING GOD'S FORGIVENESS. "Maybe once, but not now." I preach quite a lot "on the circuit," as they say, both here in Scotland and abroad. It would be difficult to estimate how many times

---

26. Raymond Westbrook, *"Vitae Necisque Potestas,"* Historia: *Zeitschrift Für Alte Geschichte* 48 (1999): 203–23.

27. John Calvin, *Institutes of the Christian Religion* I.1.2–3, ed. J. T. McNeil, trans. F. L. Battles (Philadelphia: Westminster, 1960), 35–39.

I have heard these words, or a variation of them, in conversation with Christians who struggle with their own sense of sinfulness. "Maybe God genuinely loved me once . . . but not now," or "Maybe I was forgiven by God at that time I accepted Jesus, but you don't know what I've done since then—surely he cannot forgive me *again*." Awareness of our human failure can blight our experience of relationship with God. Psalm 103 puts to rest this self-told lie in its picture of a love more vast than the cosmos and a forgiveness greater than imagination.

We must allow theology to shape our experience of God rather than allowing our experience of life to shape our theology. Psalm 103 is not an abstract treatise on forgiveness—it is an invitation to *remember* God's all-encompassing, fatherly forgiveness and to praise him for it. It was to this end, after all, that he sent his Son (John 3:16–17). So, the psalmist calls on his soul to "forget not." It is easy to forget or otherwise to limit—consciously or subconsciously—the fullness of God's grace. It is easy to let our constant awareness of failure shape our picture of who God is. Together with the psalmist, we must remind ourselves of God's eternal love for us (v. 17)—a love that will not be tempered by our human weakness (vv. 13–16).

All the sins we committed up to the point of our conversion have been paid for on the cross of Christ. Every failing, from that moment of spiritual transformation until today, is paid for on the cross. Every sin that we will commit, no matter how blatant, from today until that moment when we go to be with God in eternity, is removed from us as far as the east is from the west. Psalm 103 will not allow us to limit God's grace. Yes, we are to be people who fear him and desire to keep his covenant, but the psalmist will permit no notion of a God who is reluctant to forgive. God's essential nature is steeped in steadfast love and mercy. This understanding must be our consistent vision of who he is. "Praise the LORD, my soul, and forget not all his benefits—who forgives all your sins."

Psalm 104

¹ Praise the LORD, my soul.

LORD my God, you are very great;
   you are clothed with splendor and majesty.
² The LORD wraps himself in light as with a garment;
   he stretches out the heavens like a tent
     ³ and lays the beams of his upper chambers on their waters.
He makes the clouds his chariot
   and rides on the wings of the wind.
⁴ He makes winds his messengers,
   flames of fire his servants.
⁵ He set the earth on its foundations;
   it can never be moved.
⁶ You covered it with the watery depths as with a garment;
   the waters stood above the mountains.
⁷ But at your rebuke the waters fled,
   at the sound of your thunder they took to flight;
⁸ they flowed over the mountains,
   they went down into the valleys,
   to the place you assigned for them.
⁹ You set a boundary they cannot cross;
   never again will they cover the earth.
¹⁰ He makes springs pour water into the ravines;
   it flows between the mountains.
¹¹ They give water to all the beasts of the field;
   the wild donkeys quench their thirst.
¹² The birds of the sky nest by the waters;
   they sing among the branches.
¹³ He waters the mountains from his upper chambers;
   the land is satisfied by the fruit of his work.
¹⁴ He makes grass grow for the cattle,
   and plants for people to cultivate—
   bringing forth food from the earth:
¹⁵ wine that gladdens human hearts,
   oil to make their faces shine,
   and bread that sustains their hearts.
¹⁶ The trees of the LORD are well watered,
   the cedars of Lebanon that he planted.

¹⁷ There the birds make their nests;
   the stork has its home in the junipers.
¹⁸ The high mountains belong to the wild goats;
   the crags are a refuge for the hyrax.
¹⁹ He made the moon to mark the seasons,
   and the sun knows when to go down.
²⁰ You bring darkness, it becomes night,
   and all the beasts of the forest prowl.
²¹ The lions roar for their prey
   and seek their food from God.
²² The sun rises, and they steal away;
   they return and lie down in their dens.
²³ Then people go out to their work,
   to their labor until evening.
²⁴ How many are your works, LORD!
   In wisdom you made them all;
   the earth is full of your creatures.
²⁵ There is the sea, vast and spacious,
   teeming with creatures beyond number—
   living things both large and small.
²⁶ There the ships go to and fro,
   and Leviathan, which you formed to frolic there.
²⁷ All creatures look to you
   to give them their food at the proper time.
²⁸ When you give it to them,
   they gather it up;
when you open your hand,
   they are satisfied with good things.
²⁹ When you hide your face,
   they are terrified;
when you take away their breath,
   they die and return to the dust.
³⁰ When you send your Spirit,
   they are created,
   and you renew the face of the ground.
³¹ May the glory of the LORD endure forever;
   may the LORD rejoice in his works—
³² he who looks at the earth, and it trembles,
   who touches the mountains, and they smoke.
³³ I will sing to the LORD all my life;
   I will sing praise to my God as long as I live.

³⁴ May my meditation be pleasing to him,
  as I rejoice in the LORD.
³⁵ But may sinners vanish from the earth
  and the wicked be no more.
Praise the LORD, my soul.
Praise the LORD.

PSALM 104 IS ONE OF THE great declarations of praise in response to God's creative acts. The Psalter often declares God to be the "maker of heaven and earth," but Psalm 104 reminds us that this understanding of God is not just a theological premise—it is cause for the loudest of praises and the deepest joy![1] The structure of Psalm 104 is far from clear but may helpfully be considered in this manner:

1. Praise God, who made the heavens (vv. 1–4);
2. The creation of the earth (vv. 5–23);
   a. The waters (vv. 5–18);
   b. The times (vv. 19–23);
3. A declaration of praise (v. 24);
4. The creation of the sea (vv. 25–26);
5. The Sustainer of life (vv. 27–30);
6. Concluding praise (vv. 31–35).[2]

Praise God Who Made the Heavens (104:1–4)

PRAISE THE LORD, MY SOUL. The psalm begins and ends with the same self-referential reminder to "bless" God as we see in the beginning and ending of Psalm 103.[3] These reminders to self draw together the poems that celebrate God's works of redemption (Ps 103) and creation (Ps 104) into a singular voice of praise. The God who takes away the sins of his people is the God who gives all good things. The voice of praise here sets an important tone of worship and joy that permeates the poem (vv. 1, 15, 24, 26, 33–35). God's creative work is not *just* an abstract matter for

---

1. Psalms 115:28; 124:2; 124:8; 134:3, and 146:5–6 all directly describe Yahweh as the maker of heaven and earth. There are also many other references to God's creative power and acts throughout the Psalter (e.g., Pss 8; 19; 33 et al.).

2. Here I broadly follow Patrick Miller's helpful suggestion regarding the structure of Ps 104 (Patrick Miller, "The Poetry of Creation: Psalm 104," in *The Way of the Lord*, FAT 29 [Tübingen: Mohr Siebeck, 2004], 178–92).

3. See above for further comment.

theological reflection ("I believe in God the Father Almighty Maker of heaven and earth").[4] It is also a truth that brings great joy to those who reflect on it, and it spurs us to praise the Maker of heaven and earth.

Lord my God, you are very great. The initial self-reminder to praise is immediately given a rationale in the ensuing statement of God's greatness. Why praise? Because God is *very* great! The use of the verbal form "to be great" along with the descriptive "very" is relatively unusual in the psalms, where God's greatness is often implied in statements of his character or works. Here the poet provides himself with an immediate justification for praise based on God's ontological nature. He is, quite simply, very great—and therefore worthy of praise. But the statement of ontological reality is matched by a contextualizing address: "Lord *my God*" (emphasis added). The image of the Creator can often seem cold and distant to the human psyche. Such a great Being is far removed from our finite reality. Yet by addressing this Creator as a God of covenantal promise and relationship with his people, the poet immediately prevents the greatness of God from becoming a barrier. "He is great and worthy of praise, and he is *our* God," the poet reminds the reader.

You are clothed with splendor and majesty. The greatness of God is further described in the language of kingship. "Splendor and majesty" are royal terms that we have seen already in Psalm 96:6. They describe the inherent kingly grandeur of Yahweh. When one thinks about God, one cannot help but be struck first and foremost by the awesome power and might of his kingly station. The language of being "clothed" with these features is used to illustrate characteristics so inherent to God's being that they can never be separated from him or, indeed, from our reflections about him.[5]

The Lord wraps himself in light. Just as God is clothed in majesty, so also he "wraps himself in light." We cannot think of God apart from his majestic rule. We cannot think of God without thinking about light. In Old Testament terms, the Creator God is often described as being shrouded in light.[6] In the New Testament, John writes: "God is light; in him there is no darkness at all" (1 John 1:5). Yahweh is a majestic King, bathed in light, and therefore worthy of praise.

---

4. Clearly, the created order does inspire theological reflection (v. 34; see also Jamie A. Grant, "Creation and Kingship: Environment and Witness in the Yahweh *Malak* Psalms," in *As Long as Earth Endures: The Bible, Creation, and the Environment*, ed. Jonathan Moo and Robin Routledge [Leicester: Apollos, 2014], 92–106).

5. See discussion of Ps 93:1 above.

6. Isaiah 60, for example, is dominated by the image of the light of Yahweh's glory (Isa 60:1–3, 19–22). This image culminates in the statement, "the Lord will be your everlasting light" (vv. 19–20).

He stretches out the heavens like a tent. The statement of God's being wrapped in light automatically leads to a consideration of the creative act, for the first act of creation was bringing light into being (Gen 1:3–5). We often think of heaven as the "original" dwelling place of God, yet the Scriptures are clear that "the heavens" were created along with the rest of the cosmos and that they cannot contain God's being (1 Kgs 8:27). Yahweh made the heavenly realm, as though it were a dwelling place for himself. The tense of the verbs is a little awkward here, but, given what follows, past tenses are probably to be preferred to the present tenses seen in the NIV. The psalmist's deliberations are pointing to the original creative work of God in this section of the psalm, and only later does the poet come to consider God's ongoing work of sustaining and preserving the created order.[7]

And lays the beams of his upper chambers on their waters. The concept here is of the stores of water above the heavens from which God sends the rains to water the earth (Gen 1:7; Job 38:25–26). The upper chambers of his cosmic tent reach that high.[8] In psalms dominated by creation imagery, the waters are normally representative of the chaos Yahweh overcame in forming the created realm. But here in Psalm 104, the waters—generally speaking—take on a much more positive characteristic as the life-giving source of fertility.[9]

He makes the clouds his chariot and rides on the wings of the wind. The imagery here is of a deity who is active from his heavenly abode. He does not simply sit in his tent, far removed from the earth below. He strikes out from there to fulfill his purposes throughout the cosmos (cf. Ps 18:7–15).

He makes winds his messengers. Verse 4 links the poem with the preceding psalm (cf. Ps 103:20–21), but here the *malakim* are "messengers" rather than angels. (The same word is used in both passages.) Continuing the image of Yahweh's cosmic kingship using the terminology of God's miraculously powerful appearance in theophany, the psalmist presents him as riding the clouds, commanding the winds as his messengers, and sending out lightning bolts as his servants.[10]

---

7. Miller, "The Poetry of Creation," 180–81 n. 4.

8. See the helpful discussion of cosmic structure in Walton, *ANE Thought*, 165–78.

9. The element of the waters' being put in their rightful place is present in verses 7 and 9, but apart from these verses the waters are seen as a necessary force for good within the created order.

10. Here, as in Ps 18, the reference to clouds as chariots and riding on the wings of the wind may imply an image of Yahweh as riding on the clouds to accomplish his purposes throughout the cosmos. Such metaphors could provide an implied polemic against the

The Creation of the Earth (104:5–23)

a. The Waters (104:5–18)

He set the earth on its foundations. The work of creation is Yahweh's and Yahweh's alone. The earth is not established because it is the earth. The earth is established because it was created and set in place by Yahweh, who is very great (v. 1). The language here ties this poem with Psalm 102:25, which—as we have seen above—indicates the surpassing permanence *of God* even vis-à-vis the immovability of the earth. Miller comments, "The fundamental fact about the earth is its stability. Just as the one who keeps torah and is kept by the Lord is not shaken (e.g., Pss 15:5; 16:8; 17:5), so the earth created by the Lord does not shake or totter."[11] The permanence of the created order results from the stability of God the Creator and Orderer of all things.

You covered it with the watery depths as with a garment. Again, the language here reflects the ancient Near Eastern understanding of the cosmos and the role of the waters in the creative act. In most cosmogonies (stories regarding the origins of cosmos), the waters represented threat and chaos. The waters had to be overcome for ordered creation to come into being. Many scholars read the description of "the deep" in Genesis 1:2 as an Israelite reference to the threatening waters that had to be subdued for order to reign. In the Genesis passage, the deep is simply there as part of the primordial creation with the Spirit of God hovering over it. The image seems to read as a description of God the Creator subduing this potentially destructive power so that order may exist. Psalm 104 presents a yet more impressive image of God's creative power. Yahweh covers the nascent earth with the watery depths. They are not a threat—they are a cloak that shrouds the newborn creation.[12]

---

religious ideologies of Israel's neighbors, in particular, the cult of the storm god Baal, who is often pictured in human form with a helmet of bull's horns and riding on a cloud or holding a thunderbolt. The poet is saying that it is Yahweh who governs all things from his heavenly abode, not any other god (Ps 104:3–4). See Allen, *Psalms*, 45.

11. Miller, "The Poetry of Creation," 180–81.

12. See the Bridging Contexts section for further discussion of ancient Israelite concepts of cosmic structure. As in Ps 104:3, the waters not only take their proper place to form the seas (vv. 8–9), but they also gathered "above the mountains" (v. 6b) in a store from which the rains, snows, and storms come. Robert Alter comments, "This invocation of the waters of the primordial abyss (*tehom*) covering all of the dry land refers in all likelihood not to the flood story . . . but to creation itself. . . . A primordial engulfing of the land by the sea is envisaged, but without personification or mythic imagery. God is the agent controlling the waters and his 'blast' (or 'rebuke') drives the waters back into their appointed bed" (Alter, *Psalms*, 363).

But at your rebuke the waters fled. Psalm 104:7–9 describes Yahweh's control over the uncontrollable.[13] The language is of a defeated foe. The waters flee before Yahweh's great power (v. 7).[14] Allen notes the difference in tone seen in Psalm 104 when compared to other ancient Near Eastern cosmogonies, in which the waters are a great threat. "[T]he hostility of the deep or the waters plays a minor role and serves to underline Yahweh's creative power. . . . The waters simply flee at God's coming. In the light of v 3 they flee in reaction to the theophany of Yahweh (cf. v 32)."[15] The rivers fill the valleys and the seas take their assigned places (v. 8). God sets a border the waters cannot cross, thus reiterating the promise to Noah that the waters will never again cover the earth (v. 9). Far from being a chaotic threat that is barely held in check, the waters are part of Yahweh's sovereign purpose for the earth.[16]

He makes springs pour water into the ravines. According to the psalmist, not only are the waters not a threat, but they also have a vital role to play in God's provision for all the living creatures that populate his earth (vv. 10–18). We must take note of the gratuitousness of the imagery here. The waters are held in check so that the beasts of the field and the wild donkeys do not thirst (vv. 10–11). The waters provide a place for birdsong (v. 12). God subdues the power of the deep so that donkeys will not go thirsty and birds will sing! "The land is satisfied" by the fruit of his work because its satisfaction is also part of the plan (v. 13).[17] Grass grows to feed the animals and human beings can sow and reap crops because of the gift of water (v. 14). Those things that are necessary to life also bring great joy—wine, oil, and bread (v. 15).[18] People need to eat and drink, but these gifts are about more than functionality. We can *enjoy* these good gifts.[19] The trees are watered, even the massive "cedars of Lebanon that

---

13. For fuller discussion of the psalmic imagery of God's sovereign control over the seas see the discussion of Ps 93 above.

14. Interestingly, the Septuagint (an early Greek translation of the Old Testament) uses the same terminology to describe Yahweh's rebuke of the waters in verse 7 as the terminology used to describe Jesus' rebuke of the storm in Matt 8:26.

15. Allen, *Psalms*, 45.

16. The waters have a place "established" (*yasad* [v. 8c]) for them by God, just as the earth is "established on its foundations" (*yasad* [v. 5]).

17. Possibly verse 13 is meant to be read as an animation of the earth that quenches its thirst in drinking the divinely provided waters (see Goldingay, *Psalms 3*, 187).

18. The conjunction of grain, wine, and oil is found in Deut 7:13 and Eccl 9:7–8. These three products were thought to be basic foods in the ancient Near East, but they were also sources of delight and enjoyment (see Hossfeld and Zenger, *Psalms 3*, 53).

19. "God provides for man's enjoyment as well as for his sustenance" (Kirkpatrick, *Psalms*, 610). For more on enjoying God's good gifts, see the Contemporary Significance section.

he planted" (v. 16).[20] These giants provide a home for storks (v. 17) and the hills a home for the wild goat and the hyrax (v. 18). All this beauty and artifice, as well as provision, flows from the life-giving waters instructed as part of God's plan to bless all the inhabitants of the earth with good things, animals and people alike. The imagery is of a Creator who is profligate with his creativity, delights in beauty, and takes joy in good things. Birdsong, wine, and hyraxes are all important to him.[21]

b. The Times (104:19–23)

He made the moon to mark the seasons. The comment about appropriate domiciles in verses 17–18 seems to mark something of a transition in the psalmist's thinking. From right places, he moves on to consider appropriate times and seasons. Just as the cedars of Lebanon provide an appropriate home for the birds of the air, so also the moon marks off appropriate seasons and the sun knows when to rise and set (v. 19). There is a clear picture of order and ordering in this section as well. The previous stanza focused on the right place for the waters in accordance with the divine plan; here the great astral objects also know their role within Yahweh's design for the cosmos.[22] As Patrick Miller comments, "Perhaps more than any other formulation, Psalm 104 conveys the *centrality of order and purpose in the creation*."[23]

You bring darkness, it becomes night. This sense of right and appropriate order continues throughout the ensuing verses of this section

---

20. "Particularly striking is the image of Yahweh as gardener, which indicates his regular intervention in creation. The OT doctrine of creation is not merely about the distant past (the 'beginning'); it is also about the Creator, who personally oversees the promotion of life and order" (Broyles, *Psalms*, 399).

21. "Indeed, the ultimate purpose of fresh water is to nurture the birds so that they may sing! The singing of the birds is one of the more obvious pleasures of the created order available to all and irresistible to the human senses. One of the answers to the why of creation is so that birds can sing and, by inference, the other creatures can enjoy their song" (Miller, "The Poetry of Creation," 188).

22. Interestingly, at the height of the French Revolution in 1793, there was an attempt to create a decimal structure for time and the calendar. But the rhythms of 24 hours in the day and the monthly cycle based on the waxing and waning of the moon were so ingrained that this attempt to secularize time failed spectacularly. Use of the decimal clock was abolished by 1795, and the decimal calendar was removed by Napoleon in 1805. There is, quite simply, an ingrained sense of rhythm to the days, weeks, months, and years of human existence, and this sense is reflected in Ps 104.

23. Italics original. Miller notes, "From the sending of the waters to their appropriate locales to the setting of night and day for animals and human beings, the orderliness of God's creation is underscored" (Miller, "The Poetry of Creation," 186).

(vv. 19–23). First, it is Yahweh, the great Creator and Gardener, who causes the sun to set and the darkness of night to unfold (v. 20a). Second, he does so with purpose: the night gives animals the opportunity to prowl and to seek their sustenance (v. 20b). Third, just as it is Yahweh who provides the waters that irrigate the crops that bring delight to human beings and feed domesticated animals, so also he is the one who supplies food for the predators of the animal kingdom. The whole of the created realm—animals of every type and people alike—is completely and utterly dependent upon God for his provision through his ongoing work of sustaining the earth. Fascinatingly, this acknowledgment leads to the picturing of young lions as praying to God for their prey (v. 21). Yahweh is the Provider-in-Chief. Regardless of our human efforts and attempts to attain autonomy, we are all *completely* dependent on him.[24]

Then people go out to their work. The rhythm of life according to the divine design also leaves scope for the peaceful cohabitation of humans with the predators of the animal world (vv. 22–23). The hunters have their time to roam during the darkness of the night, and humans have their time to work during the light of the day. Work is presented as part of the natural rhythm of life. Just as young lions go out hunting, so people go out to work. This perspective is not always the case in the Old Testament, which can view work and labor as burdensome and pointless (e.g., Eccl 2:17–26). The juxtaposition of Psalm 104:23 with the following verse 24, which celebrates the works of Yahweh, seems to imply that human work is consonant with God's good works. As God has worked in the creation of the universe, and as he continues to work in sustaining power, so also people engage in their labors as part of that ordered reality. We note, too, that work and rest are both ingrained within that natural rhythm of the day. The implication of verse 23 is that there should be a time for rest once the evening comes.

A Declaration of Praise (104:24)

HOW MANY ARE YOUR WORKS, LORD! Verse 24 stands as an exclamation of praise in the middle of the poet's celebration of God's creative power, beauty, and purpose.[25] Reflection on creation gives rise to worship.

---

24. Scholars often make connections between Ps 104 and the fourteenth-century Egyptian poem the Great Hymn of Aton, as both poems draw upon similar creative and cosmological imagery. But these verses reflect a differentiation in the voices of this ancient poem, for in Ps 104 the night is simply a part of the divinely instilled rhythm of life, but in the Egyptian poem, since the main god is the sun god, the night is a threatening reality. For fuller discussion see Hossfeld and Zenger, *Psalms 3*, 53.

25. "With these words, the poet launches on a grand summation of the great hymn to God as master of all creation that he has produced" (Alter, *Psalms*, 366).

The "works" of verse 24a are defined at the end of the verse: "the earth is full of your creatures" (v. 24c). The psalmist contemplates the vast array of God's creation, from the cosmos as a whole to the earth as a spectacular entity, from the primordial seas to the seasons of agriculture, from the vastness of the mountains to the proverbial cedars of Lebanon. But it is the way in which the Lord has populated his earth that provokes this exclamation of praise. Livestock and wild donkeys (v. 11), singing birds and storks (vv. 12, 17), wild goats and hyraxes (v. 18), predatory lions (vv. 20–21), and people who delight in bread, wine, and their own labor (vv. 15, 23) represent the vast array of creatures ("how many") that populate God's earth, and reflection on this diversity rightly provokes a response of praise.

In wisdom you made them all. The association between God's wisdom and his works of creation is a common one in the poetic texts of the Old Testament (see Prov 8; Job 28, 38–41). The creation-wisdom link implies that God's ways are somehow deeply ingrained in the natural order. The rhythms of day and night, passing seasons, sun and moon and constellations all taking their rightful places in the skies—all these phenomena point to a divine decree etched into the cosmos so that everything just works as it should (Job 28:23–28). Here the amazing diversity of created beings—human and animal—is celebrated as an expression of divine wisdom.[26]

The Creation of the Sea (104:25–26)

THERE IS THE SEA, VAST AND SPACIOUS, TEEMING WITH CREATURES. The interlude of praise regarding the amazing variety of creatures on the land and in the air naturally leads to consideration of the vastness and creaturely diversity of the seas. Continuing the theme of the significance of the waters (cf. Ps 104:10–18), the poet reflects on the seas in a different manner from the psalmic norm. Most frequently the seas are a symbol of threat and chaos (e.g., Ps 93). Psalm 104, however, presents the oceans as a playground for ships and sea monsters (v. 26)! It really is a delightful image that continues the sense of purposefulness from the previous stanza (vv. 10–23). The high mountains are *for* the mountain goats. The crags are *for* the hyraxes. Here, quite amazingly, the implication is that the sea is *for* the ships to sail in and *for* Leviathan, the mythic sea monster, to play in. Once again, there is a glorious sense of artifice and delight in the way in which God made the seas.[27]

Living things both large and small. The tiny plankton is food for the gargantuan whale. The smallest of creatures imaginable and the largest on earth both find their home in the same seas, along with millions of others.

---

26. Eaton, *Psalms*, 363.
27. Miller, "The Poetry of Creation," 187.

The psalmist continues the celebration of the amazing diversity of created beings that populate every aspect of creation, first land and air, and now the sea.

The Sustainer of Life (104:27–30)

ALL CREATURES LOOK TO YOU. Continuing the imagery of the rest of the psalm, once again the poet reflects on God's role as the one who sustains all the living beings of creation. Just as the lions have to roar for their prey (v. 21), so also here we see that all of life—animal and human—is absolutely dependent upon divine provision to survive. The images are common enough—God opens his hand and gives food, thus satisfying all living beings with good things. This image demonstrates creaturely dependence on the Creator (vv. 27–28). Alternatively, when the Creator hides his face and takes away their breath, creatures die (v. 29). This observation, too, probably implies the natural rhythms of life and death in the created order. Every living being has its allotted time span before it passes away to be replaced by another living being when God sends forth his creative breath (v. 30; cf. Job 13:5).[28] The message is simple: all living beings, be they animals or people, are completely and utterly dependent on their Creator in each and every moment of life. We often celebrate human "autonomy" and "endeavor"—the things we ourselves achieve. But the truth of the matter is that we cannot demand our next breath. It is a gift from the Sustainer of life. All living beings are completely dependent on him. This dependence, too, is cause for praise (vv. 31–35)![29]

Concluding Praises (104:31–35)

MAY THE GLORY OF THE LORD ENDURE FOREVER. The poet concludes his reflection on creation by echoing the voice of praise with which he begins the psalm. Returning to the language of kingship and majesty (v. 1), the psalmist celebrates the glory of Yahweh the Creator. The wish language ("may the") is a reminder of the reality of God's sustaining power. Do we arrogantly assume that the earth will continue simply because it has done so until today? The earth continues as long as it gives glory to God. This idea, of course, has interesting ramifications for the succeeding line in the parallelism. The implication of the juxtaposed phrases is that "his works" (i.e., creatures, including humans; cf. v. 24) continue as long as they give glory to God. There is a

---

28. *Ruah* can be translated as "spirit," "Spirit," or "breath" in verse 30. Given the image of God's breathing life into the first man in Gen 2:7, the likely connotation here is with the divine breath. See Allen, *Psalms*, 48, and Schaefer, *Psalms*, 258, among others.

29. Eaton, *Psalms*, 364.

prayerful humility in the psalmist's wish-statement that acknowledges the complete dependence of all creation on Yahweh the Sustainer.[30]

He who looks at the earth, and it trembles. Again echoing the beginning of the psalm, the poet returns to the imagery of Yahweh as the God of theophany—the God who appears in majestic and undeniable power. The imagery is drawn from Exodus 19–20 and Deuteronomy 5 and is a frequent subject of poetic reflection in the psalms (e.g., Pss 18; 77; 144 et al.). The language of theophany connotes an interventionist God who enters into the realities of his people in a real way and with awe-inspiring power. Yahweh is not just cosmic Creator and the Sustainer of life; he also visits this earth in power to achieve his glorious purpose. There is warning here as well as assurance.

I will sing to the LORD all my life. Note the psalmist's determination to praise—a determination that results from his reflection on creation. The two acts inevitably go hand in hand. When people of faith reflect on the reality of the created order, it inclines the heart and mind to praise God.

May my meditation be pleasing to him, as I rejoice in the LORD. The language of delight and joy continues with another wish-statement. The psalmist has received a glimpse of the incredible majesty of God the Creator/Sustainer; as a result, all he can do is voice his praise and delight. His expressed wish is that it might be pleasing to God, and the expressed consequence is praise. Here is a model of reflection and response for every human being to follow.

But may sinners vanish from the earth. This third wish-statement seems incongruous but, when viewed in context, is perhaps not as surprising as first seems to be the case. A reflection on creation and the created order (Gen 1–2) inevitably leads the psalmist to a consideration of the fall (Gen 3). The certain consequence of any consideration of the perfections of God's creation consists in lament for the tainting effects of sin. The world as we have it today is amazing, but we cannot escape the consequences of human rebellion that have spoiled the perfection of creation with violence, oppression, greed, inequality, and other pollutions of every type. The psalmist's prayer merely longs for a return to the perfections of Eden (a theme that John develops in Revelation) and echoes the theology of Psalm 1:6. The poet expresses his desire that anything which taints or tarnishes God's glory should be removed from the created order.[31]

---

30. "He expresses a hope that such glorious sustaining power will never cease to be revealed in the natural world (Isa 6:3), praying that God's creation may continue to receive a smile of favor, as Yahweh initially took delight in it (cf. Gen 1:31)" (Allen, *Psalms*, 48).
    31. Kirkpatrick is helpful here: "There is no need to make excuse for this conclusion of

Praise the LORD, my soul. The reminder to the self to praise the Lord brackets the whole psalm (vv. 1, 35). Addressing his own soul, the psalmist reflects on the importance of stopping to think about this world in which we live because such reflection will inevitably lead to praise of the Creator.[32]

HEAVENLY STRUCTURE IN THE ANCIENT WORLD. Some of the imagery in Psalm 104 puzzles modern readers because the ancient understanding of the structure of the cosmos was so different from our own way of understanding the universe. The shared understanding of the ancient world was that the universe consisted of three dome-shaped expanses of existence, sometimes called "vaults."[33] These expanses are often referred to as heaven (or the heavens), earth, and the underworld or netherworld, known as Sheol in the Hebrew worldview. Each sphere of existence had its own population appropriate to that home. For many ancient Near Eastern cultures, the heavens were populated by a kind of government of gods called a pantheon, often headed by a high god *ʾel*.[34] For the Israelites, the heavens hosted—but could not contain—Yahweh and his angelic armies (1 Kgs 8:27).[35] The earth, obviously enough, was the dwelling place of human beings, and the underworld, or Sheol, was a shadowy place that was home to the dead.

The heavens would often be seen as having multiple levels (sometimes three or even seven levels), and the base layer or firmament of the heavens

---

the Psalm. It is not an imprecation but a solemn prayer for the restoration of the harmony of creation by the banishment from it of 'all things that cause stumbling, and them that do iniquity.' The preceding verses (31, 32) have just hinted that there is something in the world which may hinder God from continuing to rejoice in his works. What is it? . . . Modern thought would say, 'May sin be banished': but Hebrew thought is not abstract but concrete, and moreover the form of the prayer reminds us of the solemn truth that sin is a personal thing, which cannot be separated from the sinner" (Kirkpatrick, *Psalms*, 613).

32. "The psalm concludes with the first Hallelujah found in the Psalter. Could a more appropriate place be found?" (Mays, *Psalms*, 336).

33. The Hebrew term is *raqiʿa*, translated "vault" in the NIV's version of Gen 1:6–7.

34. A number of variations of this model existed throughout the region. There were variations in specific details, but the models were broadly similar.

35. There are instances in which psalms seem to imply the existence of a pantheon of gods alongside God in heaven but vastly inferior to him (e.g., see Ps 82). It is unclear, however, whether this idea actually reflects a Hebraic understanding of the heavenly realm or whether such expressions are simply forms of hypothetical polemic. In other words, "Were there to be a pantheon of gods of the nations—and we do not think there is one, but if there were—Yahweh would be vastly superior to them all."

is often presented as being the physical sky with the great celestial lights (sun, moon, and stars). Layers of the heavenly cross-section ascend spatially from there upward in terms of height, with the most powerful god or gods dwelling in the highest levels. (Hence Ps 113:6's figurative presentation of Yahweh as having to "stoop down" even *to see* the heavens, so great is his transcendence.) In Psalm 104 we see this broad perspective of the heavenly realm reflected in the reference to the heavens being "stretched out" like a tent (a dome-like structure) and in the idea of the "beams of his upper chambers" as resting on the waters (vv. 2–3). Here we see the creation of the heavenly dome and a comment on the height of Yahweh's dwelling place.

A further interesting aspect of the presentation of the heavenly realm is the concept of the waters of, or sometimes above, the heavens. Ancient Mediterranean presentations of the cosmos often included the idea of an ocean above and an ocean below.[36] Sometimes the heights of heaven rest on top of the upper ocean; in other representations the waters are either part of or above the heavens. Logically enough, this understanding of the upper waters stems from the fact that precipitation comes from the sky, so there must be a store of water in or above the heavens.[37]

This notion is reflected in verses 3 and 6, where the upper chamber of Yahweh's tent rests on these upper waters, which also stand above the mountains at the time of creation. In each of these ancient Near Eastern cosmogonies, the waters somehow play an important role in the formation of the earth. In Old Testament terms, we see possible references to this idea in Yahweh's sitting enthroned above the flood (Ps 29:10) and in the celestial storehouses of snow and hail with a channel cut for the rains to flow (Job 38:22–28).

While the ancient Israelites did not share their neighbors' understanding of the gods and their often vicious governance over humanity, we can see indications of a shared understanding of cosmic geography and celestial structure in the Old Testament. The primary difference between the view of Israel and her neighbors was theological, not structural.[38] Psalm 104 accepts the basic concept of heavenly structure that was common throughout the ancient Near East but makes clear that the heavens, earth, sea, animal kingdom, and whole of humanity were all created and established by Yahweh and are completely under the control of the one who has done all things well.[39]

---

36. See the helpful images reproduced in Hossfeld and Zenger, *Psalms* 3, 51.

37. Eaton, *Psalms*, 362–63.

38. Izak Cornelius, "The Visual Representation of the World in the Ancient Near East and the Hebrew Bible," *JNSL* 20 (1994): 202–203.

39. Walton, *ANE Thought*, 174–75.

Psalm 104 in the New Testament. Matthew 13:32 may well be an allusion to Psalm 104:12 and uses the imagery of the psalm to emphasize the great effects that will come from the humble beginnings of the gospel message and the new kingdom that it forms.[40] Also, the author of Hebrews seems to use Psalm 104:4 as part of his argument regarding Christ's superiority over the angels.[41] There are other New Testament analogies that can be drawn from Psalm 104. First, Jesus rebukes the waves in the same way that Yahweh rebukes the primordial flood waters (Matt 8:23–27), thus demonstrating his divine control over all creation. Second, in Colossians 1:15–20 Paul describes Jesus as Creator and Sustainer of the universe using very similar language, as does the author of the letter to the Hebrews in Hebrews 1:1–4. These New Testament authors see Jesus as the embodiment of Yahweh's creative and sustaining power. Third, just as Psalm 104 echoes the creation narratives of Genesis 1–3, so also John picks up on this language and imagery of creation in his representation of the new heavens and new earth (Rev 21–22). In this new Eden there is no temple, for God dwells among his people (cf. Ps 104:2), and no sun, for the glory of God gives light (cf. Ps 104:19, 31), and the water of life flows from the throne of God and the Lamb, thus feeding the tree of life, whose leaves bring healing to the nations (cf. Ps 104:10–18).

ENJOYMENT WITHOUT EXPLOITATION. Paul writes to Timothy regarding the wealthy in Ephesus: "Command those who are rich in this present world not to be arrogant nor to put their hope in wealth, which is so uncertain, but to put their hope in God, who richly provides us with everything *for our enjoyment*" (1 Tim 6:17, emphasis added). James describes God as the "Father of heavenly lights" from whom comes "every good and perfect gift" (Jas 1:17). The world is a good gift from God and one that we are to enjoy mightily. Christians often have a hang-up with the whole issue of enjoying God's good creation. In fact, we often have issues with the whole idea of enjoyment period. The concept seems worldly, and we think that is a bad thing. We are often led to believe that the Christian life is all about self-denial and discipline. These practices have their place in the life of faith, of course, but one day the Creator will ask us whether we enjoyed the world he gave us. One day we will

---

40. Martin J. J. Menken, "The Psalms in Matthew's Gospel," in *The Psalms in the New Testament*, ed. S. Moyise and M. J. J. Menken (London: T&T Clark, 2004), 65–66.
41. Longman, *Psalms*, 363.

return to a world that is much like this one, apart from the sin, pain, and hurt that is common to our present experience. That world will be bigger, better, and brighter, but it will be a physical world much like the one we experience today.[42]

In the Western world, which is so influenced by Greek thought, we sometimes fall prey to the false idea that the bodily, physical world is bad or, at the very least, is less important than the spiritual realm. Nothing could be further from the truth. This separation of body and soul, spiritual realm and physical realm, is not derived from the Scriptures. God placed the first people in a garden (earthy in the truest sense of that word) and told them to enjoy the fruit. He made them man and woman so that they might enjoy each other. He provided a world full of creative diversity for them to delight in. God's good gifts are instilled in this world that he gave us, and we are *supposed* to enjoy them.

"Wine that gladdens human hearts, oil to make their faces shine, and bread that sustains their hearts," the psalmist mentions in verse 15. There is a delightful physicality in the images here. These products were staples in the ancient world—staples to be enjoyed. The images inspire us to feel the warming wine, smell the olives, and taste the nourishing goodness of a freshly baked loaf. Physical gifts. Good gifts. They are to be enjoyed. Equally, the world around us has inspired countless beautiful images in the visual arts. Yet none of them *quite* compares with an actual sunset.

God gives human beings a beautiful world and good gifts. It is a human, spiritual, and eschatological tragedy if we do not enjoy these gifts, this world, this life.[43]

We enjoy this created world, but we should *never exploit it.* One of the unusual aspects of Psalm 104 is that it presents humanity as just one of the many works of the Lord in which he delights. Very often the Scriptures point to the distinction that exists between humans and the animal realm (e.g., Gen 1:27–31; 2:19–20). But the poet groups people in among all the other works of the Lord (Ps 104:24, 31), thus emphasizing that our place is within a complex ecosystem and we share this world with a myriad of species.

If Christians have a problem with enjoyment, we often also have a problem with environmentalism. It is often viewed as an ideology associated

---

42. For a fuller discussion of the new earth in Christian hope, see N. T. Wright's excellent *Surprised by Hope* (London: SPCK, 2011).

43. In making this statement I do not mean to demean the sufferings that are also a very real part of life in this world. The sufferings of many are great, yet—as many who have experienced great suffering will testify—the beauties of this world remain.

with New Age movements or radical politics. Again, nothing could be further from the truth. If we truly believe that "the heavens proclaim his righteousness" (Ps 97:6) and "declare the glory of God" (Ps 19:1), or that he plants and waters the cedars of Lebanon (Ps 104:16) and that he made this world to be the appropriate home for animal species of every type (vv. 18, 26), then we should reject *every* action that brings damage to a created order in which the Lord takes delight (v. 31).

Surely if it is true that something of God's being is revealed through creation, we have an apologetic duty to protect that realm so that God's true nature may continue to be seen in it.[44] A world destroyed by human exploitation does not testify to those who do not yet believe as strongly as a world where the beauties of creation remain unspoiled. Every action that does damage to the created order—whether fracking or pollution by heavy industry in the industrial world or industrial logging and the poaching of game in the developing world—should be opposed by all those who take Psalm 104 seriously because of their love for Jesus. Recycling may be occasionally inconvenient, but if it ultimately allows the glory of God to sing out through his creation, is it really too much to ask?

Psalm 104 paints a vivid picture of the diversity of species and of *God's great delight* in each and every one of them (v. 25). Surely the extinction of a species is one of the greatest tragedies of life. If, as Christians, we are uncomfortable with the social or political baggage that goes along with some of the environmental campaign groups prominent today, then we should create our own groups. We should be every bit as vocal in our opposition to the exploitation of the earth, for this world preaches God's glory and we want its voice to ring out clearly. We enjoy the good gifts of this earth, but we do so sustainably and without exploitation.

A creational worldview. Psalm 104 also advocates an understanding of our place within this world from an all-creation perspective. Everything matters to God, from the plankton to the whales to birdsongs and hyraxes. These are all important to him, as is the removal of sin and suffering from this world. Verse 35 seems incongruous within the flow of this poem, yet it makes perfect sense. If Yahweh made this world perfect and everything matters to him, then anything that spoils his glorious design and plan in this world is abominable.

If *everything* matters, then politics and the arts matter. Finance and social governance are important to God. Family relationships and community well-being are important to him. Environmental policy, dance, sports,

44. Grant, "Creation and Kingship," 92–106.

literature, music, work, and church are *all* important to God because they are all vital components of a cosmic order that he has created. The Old Testament is dominated by the idea of *covenant* (a kingship idea), and the New Testament is shaped by Jesus' language of the *kingdom* of God. His rule as Creator affects every single area of the cosmos and every aspect of our interaction with him, with each other, and with this world.

A Christian worldview is a *creational* worldview. *Everything* matters. We should therefore seek to do *everything* consciously for his glory.

Psalm 105

¹ Give praise to the LORD, proclaim his name;
  make known among the nations what he has done.
² Sing to him, sing praise to him;
  tell of all his wonderful acts.
³ Glory in his holy name;
  let the hearts of those who seek the LORD rejoice.
⁴ Look to the LORD and his strength;
  seek his face always.
⁵ Remember the wonders he has done,
  his miracles, and the judgments he pronounced,
⁶ you his servants, the descendants of Abraham,
  his chosen ones, the children of Jacob.
⁷ He is the LORD our God;
  his judgments are in all the earth.
⁸ He remembers his covenant forever,
  the promise he made, for a thousand generations,
⁹ the covenant he made with Abraham,
  the oath he swore to Isaac.
¹⁰ He confirmed it to Jacob as a decree,
  to Israel as an everlasting covenant:
¹¹ "To you I will give the land of Canaan
  as the portion you will inherit."
¹² When they were but few in number,
  few indeed, and strangers in it,
¹³ they wandered from nation to nation,
  from one kingdom to another.
¹⁴ He allowed no one to oppress them;
  for their sake he rebuked kings:
¹⁵ "Do not touch my anointed ones;
  do my prophets no harm."
¹⁶ He called down famine on the land
  and destroyed all their supplies of food;
¹⁷ and he sent a man before them—
  Joseph, sold as a slave.
¹⁸ They bruised his feet with shackles,
  his neck was put in irons,
¹⁹ till what he foretold came to pass,

till the word of the LORD proved him true.
²⁰ The king sent and released him,
 the ruler of peoples set him free.
²¹ He made him master of his household,
 ruler over all he possessed,
²² to instruct his princes as he pleased
 and teach his elders wisdom.
²³ Then Israel entered Egypt;
 Jacob resided as a foreigner in the land of Ham.
²⁴ The LORD made his people very fruitful;
 he made them too numerous for their foes,
²⁵ whose hearts he turned to hate his people,
 to conspire against his servants.
²⁶ He sent Moses his servant,
 and Aaron, whom he had chosen.
²⁷ They performed his signs among them,
 his wonders in the land of Ham.
²⁸ He sent darkness and made the land dark—
 for had they not rebelled against his words?
²⁹ He turned their waters into blood,
 causing their fish to die.
³⁰ Their land teemed with frogs,
 which went up into the bedrooms of their rulers.
³¹ He spoke, and there came swarms of flies,
 and gnats throughout their country.
³² He turned their rain into hail,
 with lightning throughout their land;
³³ he struck down their vines and fig trees
 and shattered the trees of their country.
³⁴ He spoke, and the locusts came,
 grasshoppers without number;
³⁵ they ate up every green thing in their land,
 ate up the produce of their soil.
³⁶ Then he struck down all the firstborn in their land,
 the firstfruits of all their manhood.
³⁷ He brought out Israel, laden with silver and gold,
 and from among their tribes no one faltered.
³⁸ Egypt was glad when they left,
 because dread of Israel had fallen on them.
³⁹ He spread out a cloud as a covering,
 and a fire to give light at night.

⁴⁰ They asked, and he brought them quail;
    he fed them well with the bread of heaven.
⁴¹ He opened the rock, and water gushed out;
    it flowed like a river in the desert.
⁴² For he remembered his holy promise
    given to his servant Abraham.
⁴³ He brought out his people with rejoicing,
    his chosen ones with shouts of joy;
⁴⁴ he gave them the lands of the nations,
    and they fell heir to what others had toiled for—
⁴⁵ that they might keep his precepts
    and observe his laws.
Praise the LORD.

PSALMS 105 AND 106 provide us with a paired message based on the history of Israel. Psalm 105 focuses on the faithfulness of God and his miraculous redeeming works. It is a celebration of God's covenantal promises to the patriarchs, particularly to Abraham, and his powerful intervention in the exodus from Egypt.[1] In Psalm 106 the historical lessons focus on the negative side of things: the forgetfulness and faithlessness of God's people throughout many generations. Historical psalms tend to be didactic. They do not present "history for history's sake"; rather, these poetic accounts of past deeds are designed to teach important lessons to the psalmist's generation and to every succeeding community of God's people. We *learn* from the account of God's faithfulness in dealing with his people and from reflecting on the failures of our forebears.

In terms of structure, Psalm 105 breaks down into five broad sections:

1. The call to praise (vv. 1–7);
2. The covenant with Abraham (vv. 8–15);
3. Providence through trial in the Joseph story (vv. 16–22);
4. Moses and the miracle of the exodus (vv. 23–38);
5. Desert provision and the opportunities of the land (vv. 39–41);
6. Theological commentary and conclusion (vv. 42–45).

---

1. "The psalm's framework is established by **the covenant promise he made with Abraham,** whose goal is **the land** of promise (vv. 8–11, 42–44)" (Broyles, *Psalms*, 402).

The Call to Praise (105:1–7)

GIVE PRAISE TO THE LORD. The opening call to praise consists in eleven commands (vv. 1–5) followed by an address (v. 6) and a rationale (v. 7). The first ten commands focus on the declaration and proclamation of Yahweh's great worth through praise ("give praise," "proclaim," "make known," "sing," "sing praise,"[2] "tell," "glory," "rejoice,"[3] "look to," and "seek"). The eleventh command, in verse 5 ("remember"), introduces the key idea for what follows in Psalms 105 and 106—divine remembrance and human forgetfulness.

The teaching crux of these two linked poems is found in Psalm 105:5: "Remember the wonders he has done, his miracles, and the judgments he pronounced." Remembrance is a key theme in the Psalter.[4] These historical poems are written and were recited as an act of public sharing of vital lessons from the people's common history. Psalm 105 focuses on Yahweh's remembering his covenantal promises to Abraham and shaping human history in response to that oath (vv. 8, 42). Psalm 106 calls to mind Israel's forgetfulness as a people and the negative consequences resulting from that failing (vv. 7, 13, 21 et al.). This theme of remembering God and his faithfulness dominates, and Psalm 105:5 sets the tone for what follows. The call to mindfulness is bifocal: remembering his *works* encourages remembrance of his *word*.[5]

The idea is Deuteronomic in nature.[6] If God's people remember the goodness of his character and the gracious power of his actions in their behalf, then surely they will want to call to mind his instructions and live in accordance with them. Deuteronomy 7 provides a classic example of this

---

2. The Hebrew verb *zamar* can also be translated as "playing music (in praise)." But given the vocalic nature of the surrounding commands the NIV's translation "sing praises" makes better sense of the verb in this context.

3. This form is actually an imperfect rather than an imperative, but in the context it is probably meant to be read as a command.

4. See the discussion of Ps 78 above.

5. The content of the "judgments" of verse 5 is interesting. On the one hand, the tight association with the language of the exodus in this verse might incline us toward seeing these as the "judgments" Yahweh pronounced on Pharaoh in the release of his people (see Kirkpatrick, *Psalms*, 616). But on the other hand, the associated declaration that his "judgments are in all the earth" (v. 7) points to Yahweh's broader activity throughout the whole world (Goldingay, *Psalms 3*, 205–206), thus pointing the reader to the fact that Israel's God rules universally and reminding them that his ways are ingrained in creation in a special way. The focus on the instruction of Yahweh returns toward the end of the psalm (v. 45). So it seems likely that the psalmist is not *solely* referring to the pronouncements against Pharaoh but that he probably has the divine instruction more broadly in mind here.

6. Kirkpatrick, *Psalms*, 616.

type of remembrance. How is Israel to prepare for the conquest of Canaan in the face of peoples much mightier than they? Deuteronomy 7:18 tells them to "remember well" God's works in the exodus, his victory over what was arguably the greatest superpower of the day.[7] Calling to mind God's power in their miraculous escape from Egypt gave the people courage to face new challenges. But Deuteronomy 7 makes it clear that the real challenge is not military but spiritual. Yahweh will secure the land for them (Deut 7:17–24). The key challenge is how the people are going to live their lives in that land. "Therefore, take care to follow the commands, decrees and laws I give you today," Moses challenges the people (Deut 7:11). The second generation after the exodus is charged not to make the same mistakes their ancestors made. Remembering God's saving works would give them courage for the future. Remembering God's laws would enable them to live that future well and under his blessing (Deut 7:11–14).

Herein lies the message of Psalm 105, encapsulated in verse 5. Remembering God's miracles gives the downtrodden postexilic community courage to face an uncertain future. Remembering God's instructions gives them a model to live life well, without repeating the failings of past generations.[8]

Make known among the nations what he has done. There is a fascinating missional element to the call to praise in verses 1–7, where the act of praise is also seen as an act of proclamation to the nations (vv. 1b, 2b).[9] Praise declares God's character and great worth; therefore, such public proclamation inevitably becomes an act of comparative religion. In offering praises, the psalmist makes it clear that God's people are effectively stating to anyone watching that their God, Yahweh, is better than any other god or any other worldview. There is a clear link between praise and proclamation, worship and mission.

You his servants, the descendants of Abraham. The addressees of the call to worship are described in terms of the covenantal promises as "the descendants of Abraham" and the "children of Jacob" (v. 6).[10] This address is contextualizing. Those hearing and reciting Psalm 105 would

---

7. The emphatic repetition of the verb "to remember" in Hebrew (*zakor tizkor*) emphasizes the importance of the action: "make sure you remember."

8. See Goldingay, *Psalms 3*, 203–206, for a helpful discussion of some of the linguistic indicators that point to this psalm's being particularly relevant for a struggling postexilic community of faith.

9. For fuller consideration of missional themes in the Psalms see the discussion of Ps 96 above. Wright points out the significance of Israel's "celebration of the past" as a constitutive part of the nation's missional identity (Wright, *The Mission of God*, 56–57).

10. Alter, *Psalms*, 370.

associate Abraham with the original covenantal promise by God to form a nation and give them a land.[11] This promise was restated and continued during the life of Jacob, who ended up giving his name to a nation (Israel). So, the address of the call to worship frames the hearers' thinking in terms of the covenantal promises of God.[12]

He is the LORD our God. The rationale for the praise and proclamation of verses 1–5 is grounded in the idea of covenant in its most basic form: the promise that Yahweh would be God to Israel and that they would be his people (Gen 17:7–8; Lev 26:11–12). Why praise? Because Yahweh is *our* God of the covenant. This statement brings with it an awareness of the fundamental goodness of his character and works and also a recognition of the promise of blessing that comes with the covenantal relationship (Gen 12:1–3). The second aspect of the rationale for praise is that "his judgments are in all the earth." This statement recognizes the universal nature of God's design and instruction. He may well be Israel's God, but—as is so clearly stated in Ps 104—he is the Creator God over the entire universe, so his rules and laws are instilled into the created order as a matter of design and are, to some extent, visible for all to see.[13]

The Covenant with Abraham (105:8–15)

HE REMEMBERS HIS COVENANT FOREVER. This statement is key to the psalmist's didactic intent in Psalm 105. After the initial call to worship, the idea of divine remembrance appears at the beginning and end of the remainder of the psalm. Verse 7 pronounces the eternal, cross-generational nature of God's covenantal mindfulness, and verse 42 contextualizes the practical ramifications of covenant in the events of the exodus. How was it that Israel was born out of oppression? It was possible because "he remembered his holy promise given to his servant Abraham." This is the message that underpins the whole psalm: in diverse ways and through terrible circumstances, God has always been faithful to his people because of the promise he made to Abraham.[14] God *always* remembers that covenant, and he is

---

11. Interestingly, and somewhat surprisingly given his significance in the history of Israel, Abraham is mentioned by name only four times in the Psalter—here in Ps 105:6, 9 and 42, and also in Ps 47:9. Isaac, so often the forgotten figure of the patriarchs, is mentioned by name in the Psalms only here in Ps 105:9.

12. James Mays titles his discussion of Ps 105 as "The Power of Promise" (Mays, *Psalms*, 337).

13. See the discussion of creational norms in the consideration of Ps 104 above.

14. As Mays point out regarding Pss 105 and 106, "the first calls for trust and the second for repentance," (Mays, *Psalms*, 337). The tone here is of trust in God's power despite all indicators to the contrary.

always working the circumstances around his people in accordance with that promise of blessing, even when this case does not appear to be so. It is not difficult to imagine how such a message would communicate powerfully in the straitened setting of Second Temple Israel.[15]

The covenant he made with Abraham . . . swore to Isaac . . . confirmed . . . to Jacob. The patriarchal narratives are brought to mind in the poet's reflection on the covenant.[16] A whole complex set of associations would be conjured up in the minds of the hearers, from the call of an idolater from Ur through the crises of childlessness to a miraculous revelation at Bethel. The associations with the patriarchal narratives of Genesis would also bring to mind the weaknesses and folly of the recipients of the covenantal promise, from Abraham's doubts to Jacob's manipulative machinations.

To Israel as an everlasting covenant. Delineating the covenant in its historical origins reminds the hearers that covenant is not an abstract theological concept but a real promise made to real people in real life—and that God was faithful even when these people were weak. That promise made with Abraham is every bit as valid for the psalmist's generation as it was for the patriarchs. That promise of blessing included the promise of a land (v. 11), which would, again, have been a comforting assurance for those living in the fragile setting of the return from exile.

They wandered from nation to nation. Verses 12–15 reference that period of the promise when the patriarchs were in the land but not owners of it. In this section of Psalm 105 we once again see echoes of Deuteronomy, particularly Deuteronomy 26:5–10:

> Then you shall declare before the LORD your God: "My father was a wandering Aramean, and he went down into Egypt with a few people and lived there and became a great nation, powerful and numerous. But the Egyptians mistreated us and made us suffer, subjecting us to harsh labor. Then we cried out to the LORD, the God of our ancestors, and the LORD heard our voice and saw our misery, toil and oppression. So the LORD brought us out of Egypt with a mighty hand and an outstretched arm, with great terror and with signs and

---

15. In the context of this section of Book 4 of the Psalter, the reference to God's remembering the covenant "for a thousand generations" connects Ps 105 with the powerful message of forgiveness in Ps 103:7. In the original text of Exod 34:6–7 cited in Ps 103:7, God declares his love to a thousand generations also.

16. "The psalm views Israel as a people whose identity and destiny come to them from their forefathers. . . . Their identity as people of the Lord (v. 24, 25, 43) is rooted in God's relation to these ancestors" (Mays, *Psalms*, 338).

wonders. He brought us to this place and gave us this land, a land flowing with milk and honey; and now I bring the firstfruits of the soil that you, LORD, have given me." Place the basket before the LORD your God and bow down before him.

As the writer of the epistle to the Hebrews reminds us, Abraham was one of those heroes of the faith who believed but never witnessed the complete fulfillment of the promises made to him. He did receive great blessing and the promised heir, but a land and nationhood remained distant realities (Heb 11:8–16). The psalmist reminds his hearers of the great fragility of the early days of covenantal reality. A single family, living as migrants dependent on the good graces of their host—in the ancient world such an existence was, indeed, a fragile one. Yet the poet makes the point that the patriarchal family was not, in fact, dependent on the favor of the nations where they wandered because they were under the protection of the divine promise. It was not just circumstances that saw the patriarchs survive. Yahweh protected them to the point of rebuking kings and declaring his people to be anointed ones and prophets.[17]

Providence through Trial in the Joseph Story (105:16–22)

HE SENT A MAN BEFORE THEM—JOSEPH, SOLD AS A SLAVE. Verses 16–22 continue this poetic take on the early stages of the covenantal history by giving a brief rendering of the Joseph narrative. Tellingly, the psalmist's emphasis in recounting this part of the story is that God's plan is still at work even during periods of great hardship. Famine destroys the food supply for the patriarchal family (v. 16),[18] *but* Yahweh sent a man before them (v. 17).

---

17. The idea of rebuking kings is probably a reference to Abraham's misadventures with the pharaoh in Egypt when he tried to pass Sarah off as his sister (Gen 12:10–20) and the staggeringly similar account with Abimelek (Gen 20). Abraham's victories over the confederation of kings in Gen 14 also come to mind. The idea of the patriarchs as "anointed ones" and "prophets" (Ps 105:15) brings an additional nuance to the picture of the patriarchs we are familiar with from the Genesis accounts. The psalmist seems to be implying that the presence of Abraham, Isaac, and Jacob among the nations fulfilled a proclamatory role regarding the nature of their God, Yahweh, as the idea of the anointed one (often the priest) and the prophet are both associated with an intermediary function. In some sense, according to the poet, the patriarchs proclaimed God's presence among the nations where they sojourned. "They were his 'anointed ones' and 'prophets' in the sense that they were his intimates, specially called to his service and favoured with his converse and self-revelation (cf. Gen 20:7)" (Eaton, *Psalms*, 368).

18. Literally, "he broke the whole staff of food." This metaphor is uncommon in Hebrew but seems to be a reference to the loss of food supply in the area the patriarch inhabited at that time.

Joseph was put in the chains of a slave that scarred both feet and neck (v. 18),[19] *but* he was a part of Yahweh's plan for his people and the world around (v. 19). Famine puts the fragile existence of the nascent community of God at risk, so he formulates a plan involving Joseph. Joseph is enslaved and later imprisoned, but he is part of the divine plan and the recipient of a divine promise (v. 19).[20] The repeating theme is that even when things look bleak, Yahweh has a plan for the good of his covenant people.

He made him master of his household. The efficacy of the divine plan comes to the fore with the declaration that the "slave" of verse 17 has become "master" and "ruler" by verse 21. The massive irony shows that Yahweh's plan ("the word of the LORD" [v. 19]) is always effective, even when that plan is shrouded in mystery and hardship for those who participate in it. The ironies continue in verse 22a where Joseph, who was bound as a slave in verse 18, now "instructs his princes as he pleases" (literally, "binds his rulers by his will").

Moses and the Miracle of the Exodus (105:23–38)

THEN ISRAEL ENTERED EGYPT. The play on words here is deliberate. Israel is, properly, to be read as Jacob, who did indeed go down into Egypt with his family, but, somewhat anachronistically, there are inevitable resonances with the nation of Israel. The latter is certainly implied by the former.[21] This section of Psalm 105 begins and ends with the language of entrance and exit. Israel came to Egypt (v. 23), but it was the Egyptians who rejoiced when they departed (v. 38).

Jacob resided as a foreigner in the land of Ham. Two key indicators appear here. First, Egypt was never going to be Israel's permanent residence—he sojourned there as a foreigner, a resident alien, a migrant; second, the description of Egypt as "Ham" brings to mind shared origins. The Egyptians were sons of Noah just as much as the Israelites were (Gen 5:32, 1 Chr 1:8). Shared origins remind Israel that their election is from

---

19. The psalmist takes some poetic liberties in the description of Joseph's captivity inasmuch as in the patriarchal period shackles would have been crafted from bronze, yet he appears to adopt the practice common at the time of his writing in describing the bonds of slavery.

20. There is some debate regarding the tenor of verse 19b. The NIV translates the verb used (*tsarap*) as "proved him true" apparently in the sense of vindication. But other versions translate the same verb as "tested him" (as in "refined him"; see ESV, NRSV et al.). It may well be that a metaphoric use of the verb implies vindication. As Alter points out, "the use of the verb [purged him] . . . is cryptic. The idea seems to be that God's word or promise now exonerates Joseph of the crime of which he had been accused" (Alter, *Psalms*, 371).

21. Hossfeld and Zenger, *Psalms 3*, 72.

among their brothers. They are no better or stronger or more righteous than any other nation (Deut 7). They were chosen by God not because of any sense of inherent value in and of themselves; rather, they were chosen for a particular task (Ps 105:43–45).[22]

The LORD made his people very fruitful. The language of entry into Egypt followed by reference to the fruitfulness of the people would immediately resonate with the historical account of Exodus 1. The exodus was the ultimate salvation narrative of the Old Testament and was inextricably linked with the identity of the nation. The Passover was a tangible, annual reminder of God's miraculous release, and here we have a poetic commemoration of Israel's central miracle. The exodus reminds the reader of God's faithfulness to the covenant: the departure from Egypt happened because Yahweh remembered his promises to Abraham. It also reminds the reader of a miracle that requires a response: the exodus led to the covenant at Sinai.[23]

He sent Moses his servant, and Aaron, whom he had chosen. What follows in Psalm 105:25–38 is essentially a brief summary of the exodus events beginning with Egypt's turning against Israel and going on to the call of Moses and Aaron through eight out of the ten plagues outlined in the exodus account.[24] Most of the content in these verses is self-explanatory, but one or two verses merit some brief comment. First, it is interesting that the psalmist begins the plague accounts with the second to last one of them: the plague of darkness (v. 28). This order is emblematic inasmuch as darkness often represents divine judgment in the Old Testament imagery of the day of the Lord; therefore, rebellion against God and his plan is tantamount to a self-destructive act by placing oneself under his judgment.[25] Second, a literal reading of the Hebrew text of 10:28b states

---

22. See the discussion on Psalmic Election in the Bridging Contexts section below.

23. Interestingly, the historical record of Ps 105 does not include a specific reference to Sinai as such, but the fact that the exodus requires a response from God's people—a response of obedience to his word—is nonetheless made explicit in verse 45.

24. The smiting of the cattle and the painful rash are both missing, and the order of the plagues is changed by the poet.

25. As W. Dennis Tucker Jr. points out, "In the attempt to stress the significance of land, the psalmist has employed much of the language and theology of Deuteronomy. This overt stress on land also explains the alterations performed on the plague narrative by the psalmist, and the significance of 'land' in the presentation of the plagues. The land of Egypt is presented as a place of 'catastrophe, loss of land, and death,'—the type of land that might be inhabited by a disobedient people. In recounting the plagues, the psalmist has presented the land of Egypt as a foil to the land of Israel" (W. Dennis Tucker Jr., "Revisiting the Plagues in Psalm CV," *VT* LV [2005]: 410).

---

that "they did not rebel against his word." In the most natural reading of the text, "they" here refers to the Egyptians (see vv. 29ff.). But the meaning then becomes somewhat opaque, for the plagues resulted from Egypt's disobedience to the word of Yahweh. The NIV resolves this tension by turning the statement into a question: "for had they not rebelled against his words?" This solution is certainly possible, but more likely these words constitute a specific reference to the ninth plague, in which Yahweh defeats Egypt's sun god and Pharaoh finally seems to acknowledge fleetingly his claims of rule in response to the plague of darkness (Exod 10:24).[26] Third, it is important to note the strong presentation of divine sovereignty and involvement in human affairs on every level. Throughout this section, Yahweh is the subject of almost all the verbs, ensuring that his will and purpose are done through "sending" (vv. 26, 28), "speaking" (vv. 31, 34), and "striking down" (vv. 33, 36), among other activities.

Egypt was glad when they left. This does not quite grasp the fullness of the Hebrew expression. The verb *samah* is often used in psalms for rejoicing in God and all he has done. Such is the level of delight in Egypt at the departure of the Israelites. Yahweh has so thoroughly proven himself victorious over Pharaoh and the gods of Egypt that a great dread had fallen on the country.[27]

Desert Provision and the Opportunities of the Land (105:39–41)

HE SPREAD OUT A CLOUD AS A COVERING AND A FIRE TO GIVE LIGHT AT NIGHT. The psalmist begins his take on the plague account with darkness; he transitions into the wilderness experience with light where darkness is expected (v. 39b). Interestingly the cloud, which is normally presented as going before the people in leadership (Exod 13:21–22), is here presented as covering the people in protection (v. 39a).[28] The psalmist continues with reference to the miraculous provision of food and water in the desert before drawing his didactic conclusions in the final stanza.

---

26. See Kirkpatrick, *Psalms*, 621; Hossfeld and Zenger, *Psalms 3*, 65.

27. John D. Currid, *Ancient Egypt and the Old Testament* (Grand Rapids: Baker, 1997), 104–20. Currid argues that the plague accounts, as described in Exodus, are effectively "decreative"—that is, God's judgment is described as being opposite to his life-giving creation—and Archie Lee argues similarly with regard to the plague references in Ps 105 (Archie Lee, "Genesis I and the Plagues Tradition in Psalm CV," *VT* XL [1990]: 257–63).

28. Perhaps the psalmist is picking up on the protection by the angel of the Lord and the pillar of cloud in the Red Sea narrative—protectors that come between the Israelites and the Egyptian armies (Exod 14:19–25).

Theological Commentary and Conclusions (105:42-45)

FOR HE REMEMBERED HIS HOLY PROMISE GIVEN TO HIS SERVANT ABRAHAM. The psalmist ends the main section of the psalm (following the introductory call to worship) by recounting Yahweh's mindfulness of his covenantal promise once again (v. 8; cf. 42). Yahweh remembers his holy promise in a relational sense.[29] Covenantal faithfulness is not just a point of principle—it is also an indication of God's great love for his chosen people. The motivation for his covenantal faithfulness is as much an expression of God's love as it is an expression of his thoroughly consistent character. The relational motivation behind God's remembrance is expressed first with regard to Abraham in verse 42 and then the nation in verse 43. This progression itself shows the Lord's faithfulness to the covenant. He responds faithfully to the cries of his people, who are themselves the product of his promise. Yahweh is always faithful to his promise because he is who he is and because he loves as he does.

He gave them the lands of the nations. Once again, the particular expression of the covenant that draws the psalmist's attention is the land (cf. v. 11).[30] This interest is not surprising in a message to the postexilic community. The land is a stump of what it once was, all sense of sovereignty is gone, and the nation is subject to the whims of its powerful neighbors and masters. Yet, the poet says, Yahweh remains true to his promise, and that promise includes the land. The people have to remember, however, what the promise of the land is all about. The land is not an end in itself or a possession by right. The land is a trust to the people and was always intended to be no more than a forum in which the torah could be practiced and where the benefits of such a lifestyle would be observed by those who look on.

That they might keep his precepts and observe his laws. The influence of Deuteronomy is seen again in the poet's closing remarks. Patrick Miller is absolutely correct to observe:

> So out of the graciousness and love of God, Israel hears and receives the divine offer of a pleasant life in this place of abundance. But Deuteronomy repeatedly insists that all of this is completely and totally contingent upon the character of Israel's response to her giving Lord, upon her love for Yahweh and obedience to his commandments. Ultimately, therefore, it is not possible to speak of the gift of the land apart from obedience to Yahweh and his law.[31]

---

29. The idea of a *holy* promise indicates that God's covenant is reflective of his character. Just as God himself is holy, so also his spoken word is holy.

30. Longman, *Psalms*, 367-68.

31. Patrick D. Miller, "Gift of God: Deuteronomic Theology of the Land," *Int* 23 (1969): 458.

But Deuteronomy also goes on to outline a rationale for that link between torah obedience and the gift of the land that is also reflected in Psalm 105. Note the words of Deuteronomy 4:5–9:

> See, I have taught you decrees and laws as the LORD my God commanded me, so that you may follow them in the land you are entering to take possession of it. Observe them carefully, *for this will show your wisdom and understanding to the nations,* who will hear about all these decrees and say, "Surely this great nation is a wise and understanding people." What other nation is so great as to have their gods near them the way the LORD our God is near us whenever we pray to him? And what other nation is so great as to have such righteous decrees and laws as this body of laws I am setting before you today? Only be careful, and watch yourselves closely so that you do not forget the things your eyes have seen or let them fade from your heart as long as you live. Teach them to your children and to their children after them. (emphasis added)

"[F]or this will show your wisdom and understanding to the nations . . ." (Deut 4:6). Deuteronomy makes it clear that the gift of the land to Israel is a missional act. The land becomes an open forum in which God's chosen people are to live in accordance with his instruction. In so doing, they live lives so different, so godly, that the surrounding nations look on and are attracted to the ways of Yahweh. The nations realize that he is by nature better than their gods and that a lifestyle devoted to him is the best way of life available to humanity.[32]

This missional tone resonates throughout Psalm 105. Note the commands to proclaim Yahweh's worth among the peoples (vv. 1–2), the fact that his judgments are in the whole earth (v. 7), the disciplining of kings (v. 14), Joseph's instruction of the princes and elders of Egypt (v. 22), the reminder that Egypt too is a son of Noah (vv. 23, 27), Yahweh's miraculous deeds during the plagues (v. 27), ultimate victory in the exodus (v. 38), and conquest over the nations in giving Israel the land (v. 44). All these mentions speak to the missional purpose of God that worked out in granting the land to his people as a trust. The poet's conclusion in verse 45 offers the clear reminder that the covenantal promise of the land is linked to the covenantal identity of the people of God. Their purpose and identity is missional, so if God's people fail morally, they fail missionally. If they fail in their commitment to God's word, they fail in their calling and purpose as his chosen people.[33]

---

32. Christopher J. H. Wright, *Deuteronomy,* 47–49.

33. We will discuss the idea of election in the Old Testament more fully in the Bridging Contexts section.

Psalm 105 is about God's faithfulness to the covenant. It ends with a reminder of the people's responsibilities under the covenant and with a call to praise this faithful God, thus setting the reader up for what follows in Psalm 106.

PSALMIC ELECTION. The idea of election is often seen as a contentious doctrine among Christians and a problematic barrier to faith for non-Christians. But the way in which the systematic doctrine of election is presented often fails to take account of the nuance of the biblical text. Richard Clifford points out the significance of the repeated terms "land," "servant," and "chosen one" in understanding the meaning of Psalm 105.[34] The combination of these terms takes us to the very heart of the Old Testament's teaching regarding God's choice (or election) of a chosen people. All too frequently, election is understood as a reference to a privileged status, which can result in an attitude of arrogance. But what we see in the Old Testament, and what is reflected here in Psalm 105, points to election as *an expression of God's calling in the setting apart of his people for a missional purpose.* God chooses a people not because they are in any way better than anyone else in this world. He chooses a people to serve his purposes in drawing others into the community of faith.[35]

Note the repetition of the phrase "Abraham, his servant" in Psalm 105:6 and 42.[36] This phrase is accompanied by the description of Jacob and the Israelites as his "chosen ones" (vv. 6, 43). This combination of election and service go hand in hand in the Old Testament's presentation of the divine choice. Let's briefly take note of two key passages that illustrate the connection between election and service, and in particular, service in terms of drawing others to know God. First, Genesis 12:1–3 is seen by many to be the foundational text in terms of understanding the idea of divine election. The Lord had said to Abram, "Go from your country, your people and your father's household to the land I will show you. I will make you into a great nation, and I will bless you; I will make your name great, and you will be a blessing. I will bless those who bless you, and whoever curses you I will curse; and all peoples on earth will be blessed through you."

---

34. Richard J. Clifford, "Style and Purpose in Psalm 105," *Bib* 60 (1979): 420–27.

35. Wright, *Deuteronomy*, 111–15.

36. See the 1984 version of the NIV. Note also the description of Moses as "his servant" and the Israelites as "his servants" in verses 25–26.

God chooses Abram to be his representative on this earth. Abram receives the promises of land, nationhood (i.e., progeny), and blessing—that is, one could say, Abram acquires a new status through the promises of God. But it is also clear that Yahweh is going to use him to be a blessing to all the peoples (lit., "families") on earth—that is, a new calling accompanies Abram's new status. There is no change in status apart from this new calling. Abram will become Abraham, the father of many nations, but this new identity is a purposeful one. The choice of Abraham is to serve Yahweh's ultimate end of bringing blessing to all the families of the earth.

Second, we need to take note of Israel's setting apart as a nation in Exodus 19:3–6:

> Then Moses went up to God, and the LORD called to him from the mountain and said, "This is what you are to say to the descendants of Jacob and what you are to tell the people of Israel: 'You yourselves have seen what I did to Egypt, and how I carried you on eagles' wings and brought you to myself. Now if you obey me fully and keep my covenant, then out of all nations you will be my treasured possession. Although the whole earth is mine, you will be for me a kingdom of priests and a holy nation.' These are the words you are to speak to the Israelites."

In Genesis 12, God chooses for himself *a family* and sets it apart to serve his purposes. In Exodus 19, God chooses for himself *a nation* and sets it apart to serve his purposes. Once again we see the dual concepts of a new status ("treasured possession") and a new calling ("kingdom of priests and a holy nation"). Israel becomes Yahweh's prized possession but also his representatives on earth (Exod 19:5–6). Priests represent God to the people and the people to God. Israel—as a whole kingdom of priests—is meant to fulfill an intermediary role between Yahweh and the nations. They represent the voice of Yahweh to the nations, and they are also meant to intercede with Yahweh on behalf of the nations, for intercession is a key part of the priestly function.

We can see in these two formative texts that the concept of election implies a new status *and* a new representative, missional calling. This idea is echoed in the Deuteronomic voice of Psalm 105. Jacob and the Israelites are Yahweh's "chosen ones," yet their calling as "servants" is clear: "Make known among the nations what he has done" (v. 1b). They do so by keeping "his precepts and observ[ing] his laws" in the land (vv. 44–45). Election is about being the missional people of a missionary God.

Psalm 105 in the New Testament. As a truncated history of Israel, it seems that the New Testament writers pick up on this poetic narrative when a summarized salvation history is required. Luke 1:72–73 in Zechariah's *Benedictus*—his account of God's covenantal faithfulness—echoes the form of expression in Psalm 105:8–9, 42. Similarly, Stephen's rendering of the Joseph narrative in Acts 7:10 seems to borrow from Psalm 105:20–21.[37] Equally, Paul's so-called midrash on the exodus in 1 Corinthians 10:1–5 has the Israelites "under the cloud," as is the case in Psalm 105:39.

But the most significant overlap with the New Testament probably comes in Acts 2:42–47, where the nascent church lives out the torah of Yahweh together with such vibrancy and power that they draw others in the observing crowd to join the community of faith, as is the expectation in Psalm 105:1, 45.[38]

THE CHURCH BEFORE THE WATCHING WORLD. Francis Schaeffer wrote a short book under this title back in the 1970s.[39] His basic argument is that the lifestyle and behavior of people in the church always has had and always will have an important impact on the mission of the church to the world around us. Schaeffer picks up on Jesus' teaching during the Last Supper that people will know we are his disciples by our love for one another (John 13:34–35). He contended that Jesus effectively gives the watching world the right to decide, on their own, whether you and I are believers by our practice of love for each other. Of course, their assessment may be wrong, but it remains the measure Jesus makes available to the world to assess the genuineness of our faith. The way we live our lives is key to the mission of the church to a lost world.

Psalm 105 makes it abundantly clear that the community of faith has an obligation to declare God's great worth to the world (v. 1) and that we do so through our actions as well as our words (v. 45). It is often noted that there is no mission in the Old Testament, but Psalm 105 strikes the tenor of Old Testament mission: Yahweh's great worth is declared by lives lived out openly in community, according to the standards of his torah, for everyone else to see. Living in this way will lead to such an attractive way of being that others will see Jesus in us and be drawn to his message.

---

37. There may also be echoes of Ps 105, verses 24 and 27, in Acts 7, verses 17 and 36, respectively.

38. See the discussion of Centripetal Mission in the Contemporay Significance section below.

39. Francis A. Schaeffer, *The Church before the Watching World: A Practical Ecclesiology* (Downers Grove, IL: InterVarsity, 1971).

Chris Wright, Mike Goheen, and others refer to this lifestyle as *centripetal mission.*[40] Centrifugal mission, which sends people out from the center, is what we typically think of as mission. But as discussed above, the theology of Deuteronomy 4 as it is represented in Psalm 105 points to this other type of mission: outreach by way of open community living that is so shaped by the beauty and justice of God's word that it draws others in to the core—centripetal mission. Open, attractive, godly, community living *will* draw people to Jesus.

It strikes me that in a secular and postmodern world saturated by media messages, be they political or marketing or campaigning communications, we are all becoming more skeptically positioned toward pronouncements. We do not, by and large, believe our politicians. We are doubtful about the excessive claims of commercials. Even campaigns for good causes are questioned because we are unsure of the facts and wary of being manipulated. Public pronouncements wash over us today with little or no impact. The same thing, of course, can also happen with the gospel in the world we live in. To many hearers, the gospel is just one more media message to be ignored.

But *lifestyles* of self-denying love lived out in local communities in which all are welcomed and people seem somehow different from the rest of the world—*that* is a truly powerful message in this cynical world in which we live. Following the lead of Psalm 105, the church today must find ways to live out Scripture-shaped, local expressions of community that are so vibrant, attractive, and welcoming that they draw people in and point them to the Jesus who truly changes lives and who is truly worthy of praise.

---

40. For fuller discussion, see, for example, Wright, *The Mission of God;* Michael W. Goheen, *A Light to the Nations: The Missional Church and the Biblical Story* (Grand Rapids: Baker Academic, 2011).

Psalm 106

¹ Praise the LORD.

Give thanks to the LORD, for he is good;
   his love endures forever.
² Who can proclaim the mighty acts of the LORD
   or fully declare his praise?
³ Blessed are those who act justly,
   who always do what is right.
⁴ Remember me, LORD, when you show favor to your people,
   come to my aid when you save them,
⁵ that I may enjoy the prosperity of your chosen ones,
   that I may share in the joy of your nation
   and join your inheritance in giving praise.
⁶ We have sinned, even as our ancestors did;
   we have done wrong and acted wickedly.
⁷ When our ancestors were in Egypt,
   they gave no thought to your miracles;
they did not remember your many kindnesses,
   and they rebelled by the sea, the Red Sea.
⁸ Yet he saved them for his name's sake,
   to make his mighty power known.
⁹ He rebuked the Red Sea, and it dried up;
   he led them through the depths as through a desert.
¹⁰ He saved them from the hand of the foe;
   from the hand of the enemy he redeemed them.
¹¹ The waters covered their adversaries;
   not one of them survived.
¹² Then they believed his promises
   and sang his praise.
¹³ But they soon forgot what he had done
   and did not wait for his plan to unfold.
¹⁴ In the desert they gave in to their craving;
   in the wilderness they put God to the test.
¹⁵ So he gave them what they asked for,
   but sent a wasting disease among them.
¹⁶ In the camp they grew envious of Moses
   and of Aaron, who was consecrated to the LORD.
¹⁷ The earth opened up and swallowed Dathan;

it buried the company of Abiram.
¹⁸ Fire blazed among their followers;
a flame consumed the wicked.
¹⁹ At Horeb they made a calf
and worshiped an idol cast from metal.
²⁰ They exchanged their glorious God
for an image of a bull, which eats grass.
²¹ They forgot the God who saved them,
who had done great things in Egypt,
²² miracles in the land of Ham
and awesome deeds by the Red Sea.
²³ So he said he would destroy them—
had not Moses, his chosen one,
stood in the breach before him
to keep his wrath from destroying them.
²⁴ Then they despised the pleasant land;
they did not believe his promise.
²⁵ They grumbled in their tents
and did not obey the LORD.
²⁶ So he swore to them with uplifted hand
that he would make them fall in the wilderness,
²⁷ make their descendants fall among the nations
and scatter them throughout the lands.
²⁸ They yoked themselves to the Baal of Peor
and ate sacrifices offered to lifeless gods;
²⁹ they aroused the LORD's anger by their wicked deeds,
and a plague broke out among them.
³⁰ But Phinehas stood up and intervened,
and the plague was checked.
³¹ This was credited to him as righteousness
for endless generations to come.
³² By the waters of Meribah they angered the LORD,
and trouble came to Moses because of them;
³³ for they rebelled against the Spirit of God,
and rash words came from Moses' lips.
³⁴ They did not destroy the peoples
as the LORD had commanded them,
³⁵ but they mingled with the nations
and adopted their customs.
³⁶ They worshiped their idols,
which became a snare to them.

³⁷ They sacrificed their sons
    and their daughters to false gods.
³⁸ They shed innocent blood,
    the blood of their sons and daughters,
whom they sacrificed to the idols of Canaan,
    and the land was desecrated by their blood.
³⁹ They defiled themselves by what they did;
    by their deeds they prostituted themselves.
⁴⁰ Therefore the LORD was angry with his people
    and abhorred his inheritance.
⁴¹ He gave them into the hands of the nations,
    and their foes ruled over them.
⁴² Their enemies oppressed them
    and subjected them to their power.
⁴³ Many times he delivered them,
    but they were bent on rebellion
    and they wasted away in their sin.
⁴⁴ Yet he took note of their distress
    when he heard their cry;
⁴⁵ for their sake he remembered his covenant
    and out of his great love he relented.
⁴⁶ He caused all who held them captive
    to show them mercy.
⁴⁷ Save us, LORD our God,
    and gather us from the nations,
that we may give thanks to your holy name
    and glory in your praise.
⁴⁸ Praise be to the LORD, the God of Israel,
    from everlasting to everlasting.
Let all the people say, "Amen!"
Praise the LORD.

PSALM 106 FLIPS THE MESSAGE of Psalm 105 on its head.[1] The reader moves from a vivid picture of the mindfulness and faithfulness of God to a powerful warning grounded in poetic reflection on the forgetfulness and faithlessness of Israel's forefathers. In this second twin-psalm, the themes of remembrance and forgetfulness are continued

---

1. Note Broyles's comment: "Like Psalm 105, this psalm rehearses Israel's early history,

as an instruction to the people to reflect on the power and goodness of their Lord, even as they face a decidedly uncertain future.[2] The warning of the text is plain: "Do not be forgetful of God's goodness and might as your predecessors were. Do not be forgetful of the covenant, because consequences inevitably follow."

Like Psalm 105, Psalm 106 presents itself as a poetic reflection on the history of Israel. The previous poem focuses on Yahweh's faithfulness to the covenantal relationship throughout the beginnings of Israel's national history in the exodus and the desert experience. Psalm 106 picks up the story from there with a hymnic record of the failings of Israel from the Red Sea to the exile. As God was faithful, the people were faithless. As Yahweh was true to his covenant, Israel forgot. Psalm 105 reminds the people of their call to be distinctive as part of God's broader, missional purposes for the nations. Psalm 106 recounts the failure of Israel to be a holy, covenant people—distinctive in the eyes of the watching world—and it begins and ends with a cry for saving grace. Surely there is something to learn from Psalm 106 that is an appropriate reminder for every community of God's people throughout all generations.

Psalm 106 seems to break down into nine stanzas:

1. Introductory call to praise and intercession (vv. 1–5)
2. Forgetfulness from the beginning (vv. 6–12)
3. Hurrying to forget in the desert (vv. 13–18)
4. Forgetting God at Sinai (vv. 19–23)
5. Failing to believe the promise of a land (vv. 24–27)
6. Provoking Yahweh through idolatry (vv. 28–33)
7. Polluting the land with blood (vv. 34–39)
8. Punishment and grace in exile (vv. 40–46)
9. Intercession, praise, and conclusion to Book 4 (vv. 47–48)

Introductory call to praise and intercession (106:1–5)

GIVE THANKS TO THE LORD, FOR HE IS GOOD; HIS LOVE ENDURES FOREVER. The opening call to praise is justified by one of the standard psalmic

---

but the differences between the two psalms could not be more striking—they are so divergent, in fact, that one might call them contradictory" (Broyles, *Psalms*, 405). Quite poetically, Kidner describes Ps 106 as "the dark counterpart to its predecessor, a shadow cast by human self-will in its long struggle against the light" (Derek Kidner, *Psalms 73–150*, TOTC [Leicester: Inter-Varsity Press, 1973], 377).

2. On the idea of twin-psalms, see the introductory comments on Ps 105 above; Walther Zimmerli, "Zwillingspsalmen," in *Wort, Lied und Gottesspruch, II: Beiträge zu Psalmen und Propheten*, ed. Joseph Schreiner (Würzburg: Echter, 1972), 105–13; and McKelvey, *Moses, David and the High Kingship of Yahweh*, 270–80.

confessions of faith: Yahweh is by nature good, and he is forever faithful to his covenant (see Pss 118:1; 136:1). Hossfeld describes this formula as "indispensable in Psalm 106," since the remainder of the poem entirely presupposes the goodness and grace of God.[3] The poet's intercessions at the beginning and end of the psalm (Ps 106:4–5, 47) and his account of Israel's continuing history are completely predicated on the awareness of Yahweh's fundamental goodness and his loving commitment to his people. The psalmist could not offer his prayers apart from belief in a God of grace. The history of the nation would never have continued for as long as it did apart from God's steadfast love even for a rebellious people.

Who can proclaim the mighty acts of the LORD? Continuing his focus on the goodness of God, the psalmist asks a question that is not entirely rhetorical—one that forces reflection on Yahweh's historical interventions in Israel's behalf.[4] It compels the hearer to think about all God has done to preserve, protect, and prosper his people. The question inherently implies the impossibility of the task. Just as it is impossible to express fully or even adequately God's worth in praise, so also it is impossible to give an account of all God's activity in human history for the benefit of the covenant community. But the question is as much leading as it is rhetorical, for it is actually answered in verse 3. Effectively, verse 2 functions as a bridge in the progression of the psalmist's thought. It provides further rationale for the opening statement of praise by expanding on verse 1. It also carries with it the question of appropriate response to such a God, as is developed in verse 3. *Why* give thanks (v. 1)? Because of the list of God's innumerable actions. *Who* can give account (v. 3)? Those who maintain justice and constantly do what is right.[5]

Blessed are those who act justly, who always do what is right. The sense of covenantal expectation is heightened in verse 3. Covenantal background is implied by the link with Psalm 105 and reinforced by the opening statement of God's character (Ps 106:1, where his covenantal love "endures forever"). Justice and righteousness are the covenantal responsibilities of God's people. He promises his steadfast love (*hesed*) and peace (*shalom*) and expects his people to practice justice (*mishpat*) and righteousness (*tsedaqah*).[6] The blessing statement (cf. Ps 1:1) contextualizes the discussion that follows. Those who delight in God's justice and

---

3. Hossfeld and Zenger, *Psalms 3*, 87.
4. Alter, *Psalms*, 375.
5. For fuller discussion of the role of the question in verse 2 see Goldingay, *Psalms 3*, 224–25; Hossfeld and Zenger, *Psalms 3*, 87.
6. See the discussion of Ps 103:6 above and note the link between the two psalms.

righteousness live their lives under his blessing. But that is the requirement of the covenantal relationship. The desire of God's people should be to live their lives consistently ("always" in the NIV; "at all times" in the Hebrew) in accordance with his ways and standards. Such is the clear expectation of the God of the covenant, and the psalmist goes on from here to show just how far the people fell short of that anticipated response.[7]

Remember me, LORD. This intercession comes as something of a surprise in the opening flow of the psalm. If anything, one would expect the continuation of the call to worship or transition into the body of the psalm. But the poet's prayer for divine remembrance and blessing is a fitting introduction to his ensuing reflections on human failure and forms an *inclusio* around the body of the psalm with the concluding prayer of verse 47. Once again, picking up on imagery derived from Psalm 105, the psalmist prays that God would "remember" him. Inevitably, divine remembrance of the individual implies that Yahweh will be faithful to his covenantal promises.[8]

Come to my aid when you save them. The prayer is for God's intervention in the psalmist's present realities. The psalmic language of salvation seeks God's intervention in historic, real-world circumstances. Seeking Yahweh's saving work implies that the poet does not see his God at work in the temporal realities of the world around him.

That I may enjoy the prosperity of your chosen ones. That "chosen ones," "rejoice/glad," "nation," and "portion" of inheritance also appear in Psalm 105 emphasizes the connections between the two poems.[9] Interpretations vary with regard to the object of the poet's prayer. Some people see this petition as the prayer of a proselyte asking to receive the blessing of a true Israelite.[10] Others see it as the prayer of an exile unable to access the benefits of the "chosen ones" who had enjoyed their own land, city, and temple prior to the fall of Jerusalem.[11] Either view could be consistent with the text. But the prayer could simply be read as the earnest appeal of an individual believer to experience God's saving power for himself as part of the believing community. We should note the language of "remembering" (*zakar*) and "visiting" (*paqad*, translated "come to my aid" in the NIV). These verbs are strongly linked with the exodus in the mind of the

---

7. "At v. 3 the theme of human response is introduced, its positive tone contrasting with what is to be unfolded" (Eaton, *Psalms*, 372).

8. See the discussion of Ps 105 above.

9. In Ps 105, "chosen ones" (vv. 6, 43); "rejoice/glad" (vv. 3, 38); "nation" (vv. 13, 44); "portion" of inheritance (v. 11).

10. Hossfeld and Zenger, *Psalms 3*, 88–89.

11. Alter, *Psalms*, 376.

Hebrew reader (Exod 2:24; 3:15–16). Yahweh *remembered* his covenant with Abraham and as a result *visited* his people in their suffering to bring them release. The psalmist prays that he personally (along with the rest of God's people) might experience just such an act of redemption. Regardless of the individual's status (proselyte) or historical location (Babylonian exile), the prayer simply seeks God's saving grace and renewal.

Forgetfulness from the Beginning (106:6–12)

WE HAVE SINNED, EVEN AS OUR ANCESTORS DID. It is always easy to point the finger at others—particularly at past generations of people who are remote from us and not here to defend themselves. The arrogance of the modern can lead us to assume that we will not make the mistakes of our forebears. Jesus had just the same conversation with the Pharisees and teachers of the law (Luke 11:47–51). But the writer of Psalm 106 does not fall prey to the same temptation and confesses the sinfulness of his own generation alongside the sins of his fathers.[12] Clearly, reflection on the events of the exile led the people to a sober understanding of their own failings.[13] The attitude reflected in verse 6, however, is exemplary for every generation and community of faith. When we see ourselves as better than others, we place ourselves at great spiritual risk, and awareness of failings serve us better, spiritually speaking, than any false confidence in our own abilities.

We have done wrong and acted wickedly. Here is the polar opposite of the blessed person of verse 3. The vocabulary of "sinned," "done wrong," and "acted wickedly" is contrary to "acting justly" and "doing what is right." This confession shows a realistic awareness on the part of the psalmist of just how dependent he and his peers are on the grace of God in response to his prayer for salvation (vv. 4–6).

They gave no thought . . . they did not remember . . . they rebelled. Once again we return to the familiar theme of this section of Book 4—the theme that forgetfulness of God's character and activity in our behalf will inevitably lead to sin. Carelessness of thought is the first stepping stone to rebelliousness of action. The initial verb is found most

---

12. James Mays suggests that the confession of sin in verse 6 shows a strong sense of connection with the failings of Israel's forefathers. "Both of the exilic prophets, Jeremiah and Ezekiel, said that the guilty character of their contemporaries was rooted in the character and conduct of Israel's earlier generations (e.g., Ezekiel 16; Jeremiah 2). . . . The stories about the ancestors are also about contemporary Israel" (Mays, *Psalms*, 341–42).

13. Deuteronomy 28:64–68 makes it clear to a people recently freed from foreign captivity that exile is the ultimate corrective God will bring upon his people and, even then, only if all measures fail to bring a change of heart and behavior. So the fact that the people found themselves in exile was a sure indication of their covenantal failings.

typically in the wisdom literature and indicates an attitude of reflection or contemplation that leads to insight and understanding.[14] Failure to reflect on God's miraculous works in behalf of his people combined with their failure to remember the *many* kindnesses he had shown to them led to their rebellion in a time of stress.[15] The irony of this record of rebellion, of course, is that the Red Sea[16] becomes synonymous with God's mighty acts of salvation in behalf of his people (Exod 14:13–14). Yet immediately prior to the miraculous parting of the waters and the destruction of the armies of the greatest superpower of the day, the people who had just witnessed the amazing feats of the exodus assume the worst and whine against God, thus calling his good character into question.[17] The warning is clear: the root of this rebellion is found in the failure to reflect on and remember the character of God.[18]

Yet he saved them for his name's sake, to make his mighty power known. Verse 8 suggests that God's saving activity is predicated on his character rather than his people's actions and what they deserve. Yahweh saved Israel because he was true to himself, not because the people responded well to the threat they faced. Being true to his own character means that God will be true to his nature as a missionary God.[19] Rebuking the Red Sea not only saved his people but also revealed his great power to Egypt and the surrounding nations (Num 22–23). Yahweh's actions in behalf of his people communicate to the world more about him than they do about us.

---

14. Psalm 14:2–3, for example, uses the same verb (*sakal*) to imply that right attitude will lead to right action and that failure to reflect appropriately will inevitably lead to behavioral failure: "The LORD looks down from heaven on all mankind to see if there are any who understand (*sakal*), any who seek God. All have turned aside, they have together become corrupt; there is noone who does good, not even one."

15. "EVV [English Versions] have the ancestors not thinking about these wonders, and no doubt they did not, but *sakal* (*hiphil*) usually means more than that (cf. 94:8; 119:99). They did not draw the right implications from their awareness of these wonders. 'They saw and yet they did not see'" (Goldingay, *Psalms 3*, 227).

16. Properly, although traditionally rendered "Red Sea," the text actually refers to the Sea of Reeds (*yam sup*), one of the northern arms of the Red Sea.

17. I would suggest that there is probably a fairly direct line of application to the Christian community in the modern world here. With little time to stop and call to mind the things God has done for us in the past or to consider the goodness of his character, it becomes easy to react wrongly when stresses come to bear on our lives. Often these challenges, with the passage of time, turn into testimonies of God's goodness, grace, power, and love.

18. Eaton, *Psalms*, 372.

19. Kirkpatrick, *Psalms*, 627.

Then they believed his promises and sang his praise. The miraculous parting of the Red Sea, revisited in Psalm 106:9–11, showed the folly of the people's initial response to the threat they faced and ultimately led them to a more appropriate reaction (v. 12). But the change of heart was not lasting.[20] The conjunction is probably telling here—"*then* they believed his promises" (emphasis added). The psalmist's point is that, had they reflected properly on the character and works of God in the first place, they would have believed *prior to* their great water trial, and as a result their praise would have been all the more heartfelt.

Hurrying to Forget in the Desert (106:13–18)

BUT THEY SOON FORGOT WHAT HE HAD DONE. Verse 13 could be translated more literally, "They hurried to forget what he had done and did not wait for his counsel." The clear implication is that the change of heart and mind in verse 12 was not lasting, and indeed, looking back, it is as though the people put some real effort into their forgetfulness. All too soon after the experience of God's mighty deliverance at the Red Sea, the people's selective amnesia returns and they rebel.[21]

And did not wait for his plan to unfold. The idea of waiting for God's counsel is also borrowed from the wisdom corpus. The plan (*'etsah*) of God can be his "advice" or "guidance" (Job 12:13), but the same word can also be used in reference to God's broader "design" or "plan" for life (Ps 20:4; Job 38:2).[22] If we read *'etsah* in this way, as the NIV does, then it implies that the people were too quick to complain against God, and in rejecting his plan they question the goodness of his character or ability. Having seen what Yahweh is like, the people should have remembered his goodness and waited for the outworking of his providence in their behalf, but instead they hurried to forget and rebellion soon followed.

In the desert they gave in to their craving. Verses 14–15 probably refer to the almost absurd rebellion in Numbers 11:4–35, where the people complain about the miraculous provision of food in the desert and start whining about the lack of meat. Of course, all they had to do was ask for meat and God would have provided, but the absurdity arises in their memory of Egypt (Num 11:4–6).[23] They present it as a place full of

---

20. Hossfeld and Zenger, *Psalms 3*, 89.
21. "The basic failure underlying all particular sins is the failure to take the words and the deeds [of the Lord] as the basis of life (vv. 7, 13, 21–22, 24)," (Mays, *Psalms*, 342).
22. Goldingay translates this verse as: "They quickly ignored his deeds, they did not wait for his plan," (*Psalms 3*, 229).
23. Leslie Allen points out that it was always Yahweh's intention to supply the Israelites' material needs in the desert (*Psalms*, 71).

fresh produce rather than a place of slavery, torture, and brutality. What difference does garlic make when people are being beaten to death? In revising their history in Egypt, the people also revise their understanding of Yahweh. Instead of being their Redeemer, he becomes a killjoy. Instead of saving them from oppression, he has simply robbed them of fresh fish and cucumbers. This revising trivializes the miraculous work of God. The exodus was impossible, humanly speaking, yet it was accomplished by God. Feeding thousands of people in the desert was impossible, yet it too was accomplished by God. But lack of meat ("craving") led them to "put God to the test" (i.e., effectively to reject Yahweh; Num 11:20).[24]

The earth opened up and swallowed Dathan. The second desert rebellion reprised by the psalmist (Ps 106:16–18) is found in Numbers 16, where Dathan and Abiram are among a group that leads a rebellion against Moses and Aaron. Once again the essence of the issue is right relationship with Yahweh—"these men have treated the LORD with contempt" (Num 16:30). The rebellions called into question the goodness of God's character and his design for the people.

Forgetting God at Sinai (106:19–23)

AT HOREB THEY MADE A CALF AND WORSHIPED AN IDOL CAST FROM METAL. There is an implied sense of absolute incredulity in Psalm 106:19–20. The actions are unbelievable and the location even worse. Making an idol from metal and declaring that inanimate thing to be the living God is farcical enough, but doing so at Sinai, the place of ultimate revelation prior to the incarnation, exacerbates the crime.[25] The pathetic truth laid out by the psalmist is that God's people "exchanged their glorious God for an image of a bull, which eats grass." Could there possibly be anything more absurd? To have seen the miracles worked in their own historical reality (plagues, Passover, passage through the Red Sea, water from a rock, supply of manna and quails, theophany on Sinai) and then to make an idol from metal that they themselves knew full well had *nothing* to do with their release from Egypt combined, as far as the psalmist is concerned, to make the ultimate absurdity. Exchanging the glory of the invisible but living God for a piece of metal fashioned after a creature that eats grass[26]—what was the point? Had the people just stopped to think, surely they would have realized for

---

24. Note here the similarity with Ps 78, which frequently refers to the testing of Yahweh by Israel (Ps 78:18, 41, 56).

25. "Horeb" is the name for Sinai commonly used in the Deuteronomy and Deuteronomic writings (Deut 5:2).

26. Schaefer, *Psalms*, 263.

themselves the stupidity of such behavior, but forgetfulness had stepped in once again.

They forgot the God who saved them. The essence of the issue once more is forgetfulness of the works of God in behalf of his people (vv. 21–22). Had the people reflected for a moment on all that Yahweh had done for them in getting them out of Egypt, the calf would never have been made.[27]

So he said he would destroy them—had not Moses . . . stood in the breach. The intercessory role played by Moses saved the people more than once, but his mediation following the golden calf incident led to one of the most profound revelations of God's character in Exodus 34:6.[28] Moses's prayers saved the exodus generation.[29] The psalmist's hope seems to be that the intercession of the current generation will lead to a similar expression of divine mercy (Ps 106:4–5, 47).

Failing to Believe the Promise of a Land (106:24–27)

THEN THEY DESPISED THE PLEASANT LAND. The next failing highlighted by the psalmist is the people's response to the report of "the ten faint-hearted spies sent to scout out the land" (Num 13–14).[30] The verb used in Psalm 106:24a (*ma'as*) is a strong one and implies, again, the rejection of the divine plan.[31] The root cause of this rejection is failure to believe (v. 24b). Similarly, verse 25 begins with an action resulting from a failure to do what was expected of them. The desert generation grumbled in their tents (cf. Deut 1:27) rather than "obey[ing] [Hebrew "listening to"] the voice of the LORD." Failure to believe and obey led to negative consequences for that generation of God's people.

So he swore to them with uplifted hand. The people's failure to believe and obey led Yahweh to make with them a covenant of an altogether different type: he promised they would all die in the desert because

---

27. Again the line of application seems fairly direct here. The psalmist reminds the reader of the importance of reflecting on the biblical accounts of God's faithful action and on our own experiences of God's help so that these reflections shape our current outlook on the events and challenges of life.

28. See the discussion of these verses in the consideration of Ps 103 above.

29. Anderson points out the military overtones of the prayer metaphor here: "Moses is depicted as a fearless warrior, standing in the breech of the city wall (cf. Ezek 22:30) and facing the enemy" (A. A. Anderson, *The Book of Psalms, Volume I, Psalms 1–72*, NCB [London: Marshall, Morgan & Scott, 1972], 743). With the present threat of divine annihilation, it took great courage for Moses to intercede on Israel's behalf.

30. Alter, *Psalms*, 379.

31. The same verb is used in Num 14:31 to describe the people's action.

of their inability to believe in and follow him. The physical gesture of swearing with uplifted hand indicates a solemn vow.[32]

Make their descendants fall among the nations. Psalm 106:27 telescopes the effects of the fathers' failings and focuses on the impact in the psalmist's generation. The desert generation's failure to believe and obey had significant consequences not only for them but also for their heirs. Faithlessness has a cross-generational impact that resonates through the ages from exodus to exile.[33]

Provoking Yahweh through Idolatry (106:28–33)

THEY YOKED THEMSELVES TO THE BAAL OF PEOR. As in the book of Judges, just when the reader thinks that things could not possibly get any worse, events nosedive further. Five of the six verses in this stanza begin with the *waw*-conjunction ("then," "and," or "but") and the sixth with the causative *ki* ("for"). Their "yoking" leads to a string of events that shows the ups and downs of a community's unraveling and veering away from its true identity. "*Then* they yoked themselves . . . ," "*and* they ate . . . ," "*but* Phineas stood up . . . ," "*and* this was credited. . . ," "*but* they angered the LORD . . . ," "*for* they rebelled. . . ." Even the actions of the best of Israelites (Phineas and Moses) could not save that generation from their rebellion. The lack of belief and obedience highlighted in the previous stanza ultimately manifests itself in idolatry. Verse 28b refers, literally, to the "sacrifices to the dead"—possibly offerings made on behalf of dead ancestors (a practice prohibited in Deut 26:14), but the NIV's translation is probably to be preferred here. Following on from the reference to the golden calf as a metal image of a thing that eats grass (Ps 106:19–20), the psalmist reminds the reader that these gods are dead, "sacrifices offered to lifeless gods."[34]

But Phineas stood up and intervened. The events of Numbers 25 describe an idolatrous orgy of cultic prostitution quelled only by the radical intervention of Phineas. The language echoes the actions of Moses in Psalm 106:23 and presents Phineas as an intermediary who is zealous for God's purposes to be fulfilled (Num 25:13). His intervention stayed the immediate punishment but was not enough to secure obedience on the part of the people. Just as Moses' prayer saved them from destruction

---

32. Longman, *Psalms*, 371.

33. See the comments on verse 6 above and note the echo of Ezek 20:23. Just as the faithfulness of Abraham is seen as having a lasting and far-reaching impact throughout many generations (Isa 51:1–2), so also here the failings of the nascent nation are seen as having long-term resonances.

34. Allen, *Psalms*, 72; Hossfeld and Zenger, *Psalms* 3, 90.

(Ps 106:23), so Phineas' intervention saved them from the plague, but neither of these representative actions was enough to bring a change of heart and behavior on the part of the people.

By the waters of Meribah they angered the LORD. The place name Meribah is a byword for the failure of God's people (Exod 17:1–7; Num 20:1–13; Ps 95:8). As we have already seen above regarding food in the desert (Ps 106:13–15), it is the revisionist take on their shared history in Egypt and the associated aspersions cast regarding God's good character and good plan that provoke God's anger. The addition of "and trouble came to Moses because of them" refers to Numbers 20:9–12 and adds the image of communal sin's bringing down even a leader of great faith and obedience. Faithlessness has repercussions.

For they rebelled against the Spirit of God. As footnoted in the NIV, there is a translational issue here. The text simply alludes to the fact that "they rebelled against *his* spirit." So, the question becomes, Is this a reference to Yahweh's Spirit or to Moses' spirit? Either option is possible, but the latter is more likely. Note the flow this understanding gives to Psalm 106:32–33: they troubled Moses by rebelling against his spirit—therefore he spoke rashly. The action for which Moses is punished is rooted in the constant, vexing rebellion of the people.[35]

Polluting the land with blood (106:34–39)

THEY DID NOT DESTROY THE PEOPLES AS THE LORD HAD COMMANDED THEM. Disobedience first crosses generations in this stanza. Following the disobedience and disbelief of the desert generations, now their children—the first generation to live in the land—fail to meet the command to drive out the Canaanite tribes from the land (Deut 7:1–11). For contemporary readers, the conquest command itself can seem difficult to understand. It was not rooted in any sense of ethnic cleansing. It was, rather, a moral imperative to prevent the pagan worship practices that resulted in the slaughter of innocents through the habitual sacrifice of children. As with the previous generation, the issue boils down to one of simple obedience. They knew that mingling with the Canaanites meant running the risk of adopting their abhorrent religious practices (Deut 7:4; cf. Ps 106:35–36).

They sacrificed their sons and their daughters to false gods. The unbelievable once again became "normal" practice. The failure to drive the nations out led, as predicted by Moses, to religious syncretism, which inevitably led to the practice of child sacrifice in the land *by Yahweh's*

---

35. For further discussion see Hossfeld and Zenger, *Psalms 3*, 91; Goldingay, *Psalms 3*, 235; Allen, *Psalms*, 73.

own people. They polluted the land by performing the same act that had originally provided part of the motivation for God's promising the land to Abraham (Gen 15:12–16). The Canaanite tribes were spewed out of the land because their toxic slaughter of their own children polluted the very ground they inhabited.[36] Yet Israel, not long after their conquest of Canaan, was practicing the same abhorrent acts and desecrating the land in the same manner. What fate could they reasonably expect other than the same one that befell the Canaanites? The people had been warned from the outset that they would face the same fate as the original inhabitants if they failed to live life *differently* in the land (Deut 4, 7, and 28).[37]

They defiled themselves by what they did. Verse 39 makes a clear statement concerning the realities of covenantal identity. Being called by God and being the recipients of a particular promise grants Israel no special privileges with regard to the behaviors he expects of all humanity. Israel's covenantal status does not change or lessen the moral obligations placed on the nation. If anything, their obligation to follow God's paths is increased by the privilege of being recipients of his instruction (Deut 4). The people were meant to be distinctive from all the other tribes and nations. "By what they did, by their deeds," God's people—though recipients of all the blessings of the covenant—proved themselves unworthy of their calling, so the punishments of Deuteronomy 28 were bound to unfold as promised by God. As people, we are defined by what we do rather than by any identity we might claim for ourselves. Israel may have claimed to be "a nation apart," but the psalmist says their deeds proved them otherwise.

---

36. On the land as the arbiter that vomits out inhabitants because their moral failings pollute its very being, see Lev 18:24–30; 20:22–26. Von Waldow summarizes helpfully: "Because of their conduct, even though they did not know what they were doing, the original inhabitants of Canaan defiled the land, so that it 'vomited them out,' and the people of God entered it to fulfill its destiny. The same fate could easily befall Israel and, as a matter of fact, it did (Lev 26:32f). The same idea is widely expressed by both the Deuteronomic-Deuteronomistic literature and the pre-exilic prophets" (H. E. von Waldow, "Israel and Her Land: Some Theological Considerations," in *A Light Unto My Path: Old Testament Studies in Honor of Jacob M. Myers*, ed. H. N. Bream, R. D. Heim, and C. A. Moore [Philadelphia: Temple University Press, 1974], 506). For fuller discussion see also Miller, "Gift of God"; Brueggemann, *The Land*.

37. The reference to sacrificing their children to "false gods" (lit. "demons") seems to allude to Deut 32:17, where the demons are described as being "not God" (NIV) but should, more likely, be read as "no gods at all!" (J. Gordon McConville, *Deuteronomy*, AOTC [Leicester: Apollos, 2002], 445). The verse strikes a tone of abject futility. The people go through the pain and horror of committing such a repulsive act in a sacrifice to something that is not god at all and can bring no benefit to them.

Punishment and Grace in Exile (106:40–46)

THEREFORE THE LORD WAS ANGRY WITH HIS PEOPLE. The rhetoric of the psalmist is clear. Given the truncated history recounted to this point, the conclusion of Psalm 106:40 is absolutely inevitable. By summarizing the history of Israel in this manner—focusing on the many and repeated failures of the nation—the psalmist makes it plain that Yahweh could respond in no other way. The exile was the inevitable consequence of the nation's action.[38]

He gave them into the hands of the nations. Exile is, in effect, a reversal of the exodus. Yahweh freed his people from the control of a mighty and oppressive power with the warning that they are to live differently in the land. Failure so to do will result in a return to such oppressive control, and this consequence is recounted in verses 41–42. The language of "oppression" (*lahats*) in verse 42 is borrowed from the exodus narratives to make the point clear that the people, by their deeds, have placed themselves back in the very scenario of suffering that Yahweh saved them from in the first place (Exod 3:9). There is further irony in the use of the verb "ruled over them" (*kana'*). This was meant to be the fate of the Canaanite nations under Israel's hand because of their abhorrent practices (Deut 9:3). But the psalmist tells the reader, poignantly, that the tables are turned because Israel's deeds were as bad as those of the original inhabitants of the land.

Many times he delivered them, but they were bent on rebellion. Verse 43 is, effectively, a summary of the covenantal relationship throughout the history of Israel. Many times Yahweh extended grace to his people despite their failure to maintain their covenantal obligations, yet the people "were bent on rebellion" (lit., "rebellious in their intent/purpose"). Acts of forgiveness, restoration, and renewal were ultimately met with further acts of rebellion. The verb used in the statement "they wasted away in their sin" (*makak*) is an unusual one and probably implies "sinking lower." The image conveys the idea that the people's constant return to sinful patterns of behavior was not just repetition but was debasement. Through their choices God's people sank lower and lower.

Yet he took note of their distress when he heard their cry. Despite this image of decay and decline, once again grace triumphs over rebellion (vv. 44–46). Even having disobeyed for so long and with such determination that they incurred the ultimate covenantal curse of exile (cf. Deut 28:64–68), yet God's people experience his mercy. The imagery of verse 44 is akin to the first exodus: God notices the suffering of the people, hears

---

38. Note the language of abhorrence in verse 40b: by failing "utterly [to] detest" the foul practices of the nations (Deut 7:26), Israel has made itself abhorrent to God.

their cry, and responds with mercy (cf. Exod 2:23–25). Yahweh's grace is expressed in staying the hand of Israel's captors from the worst excesses of oppression (Ps 106:46). As seen in the covenantal curses of Deuteronomy 28, exile would normally be a painful and anxious experience (Deut 28:65–66), but, even after all that has gone before, God mitigates his people's punishment by causing their captors to show them mercy.[39]

For their sake he remembered his covenant. In an echo of Psalm 105:8, even in the disaster of the people's exile Yahweh remembers his covenantal promise.[40] It is the motivation for this remembrance that strikes a poignant chord in Psalm 106:45. It is not for his own name's sake that he remembers the covenant (v. 8), nor is it because of Abraham (Ps 105:42). Yahweh remembers his promise for *their* sake simply because he wanted to be true to the people despite their failures. His desire was to show love to *them* (Ps 106:45b) despite their lack of love for him.

Intercession, Praise, and Conclusion to Book 4 (106:47–48)

SAVE US, LORD OUR GOD, AND GATHER US FROM THE NATIONS. The prayer for salvation places the psalmist with the people in the exile. Whether exile is his literal or metaphorical location is difficult to say.[41] But the prayer resonates through all generations and communities of faith. Troubled by the burden of our own repeated sins, we all often feel exiled from God and, together with the poet, we cry out for his mercy and help.[42] In an echo of verse 4, the psalmist voices the realization that it is only in prayer and by the response of grace that we can ever change and find release from our own determination to rebel. God's grace despite our sin is our only hope.

That we may give thanks to your holy name and glory in your praise. The expectation of divine help brings with it the expectation of praise.[43] The only appropriate response to the grace of salvation is to praise and delight in the one who saves us.

Praise be to the LORD, the God of Israel, from everlasting to everlasting. The concluding call to praise serves as a doxology that indicates

---

39. Schaefer, *Psalms*, 264.

40. Yahweh's remembrance, of course, stands in marked contrast to the forgetfulness of the Israelites reprised throughout this poem.

41. It makes sense to read this poem as the prayer of one experiencing the exile (Longman, *Psalms*, 373). But it is difficult to be absolutely definitive, for many of those experiencing the inadequacies of postexilic Israel also saw themselves as living among the nations because of the continuing political control of other nations.

42. "The line of argument is that God has always been merciful in the past, mitigating the punishment that Israel's sin deserves. May God do so again" (Schaefer, *Psalms*, 264).

43. Goldingay, *Psalms 3*, 238–39.

the close of Book 4 of the Psalter as well as the logical conclusion of the psalm. The message of both the psalm and the book (Psalms 90–106) is met with a call to communal praise. Despite the rebellion of the people (Psalm 106), God is gracious. Despite the exile and the loss of all the trappings of covenant (Book 4), Yahweh is still King; therefore, "Let all the people say, 'Amen!' Praise Yahweh." What other possible conclusion could one draw from the poems of Book 4?

PSALMIC HISTORY. History, despite modern protestations to the contrary, is never neutral. There is an expectation with modern works of history that the author should strive after some sense of neutrality and balance. Doing so is, of course, an impossibility because all history is inevitably selective and, therefore, to a greater or lesser extent, will reflect the biases, presuppositions, preferences, and predilections of the historian doing the writing. For contemporary historians there is an expectation that they will try, as far as they are able, to rein in these personal biases and to reflect as objectively as possible on the events under their gaze. Anything else is seen as preachy or agenda driven.

In the ancient world there was no such expectation. History was *never* intended to be unbiased, and it was *always* didactic in intent. Biblical history always *intends to be* preachy and agenda driven! Take, for example, the major histories of the Old Testament canon—the so-called Deuteronomistic History (Joshua–2 Kings) and the Chronicler's history. In the main they cover the same period of Israel's history and many of the same events, but their "take" on these matters is quite different. David, for example, is presented as politician, warrior, king, lover of Bathsheba, murderer of Uriah the Hittite, and the one who could not build the temple because he had blood on his hands in the Deuteronomistic History. Yet, at the same time, he is a devoted friend to Jonathan, fair and gracious where other kings would not have been, and passionate in his love for Yahweh. It is a "warts-and-all" presentation. David could be the best of Hebrews and commit the worst of sins.

The Chronicler's presentation of David, however, is quite different. His text very much centers on the temple as the focal point of Israel's worship. It is a history that desires to communicate the importance of right worship of Yahweh. The Chronicler's David is, perhaps, best described as the great sponsor of the temple and the one who orders its worship. Bathsheba is only mentioned as the mother to David's children and Uriah in a list of his mighty men. This David is psalmist, musician, and worship leader.

The figure is the same man. The events are the same events. But each author puts David to a different use in his history. Here we see the way of ancient histories in general; they are driven by the rhetorical agendas of the author.[44]

History in the book of Psalms tends to function in much the same manner. Historical psalms are inherently selective; they telescope large tracts of history and, broadly speaking, tend to focus on relatively singular rhetorical purposes.[45] The three classic examples of historical psalms are Psalms 78, 105, and 106. Psalm 78 is a lengthy account of the people's rebellions that ends with a note of hope rooted in the worship of the temple and in a future king like David. Psalm 105 focuses on the great faithfulness of God in calling a people to himself and establishing them as a nation. Psalm 106, as we see above, focuses on the covenantal faithlessness of the people despite repeated grace, forgiveness, and restoration from Yahweh.

Psalm 78:1–8 illustrates well how the historical psalms work:

> My people, hear my teaching;
>   listen to the words of my mouth.
> I will open my mouth with a parable;
>   I will utter hidden things, things from of old—
> things we have heard and known,
>   things our ancestors have told us.
> We will not hide them from their descendants;
>   we will tell the next generation
> the praiseworthy deeds of the LORD,
>   his power, and the wonders he has done.

---

44. The classic example of this approach is probably the Israelite King Ahab, who becomes a watchword for apostasy in 1 Kings, yet who was, as far as we can tell from archaeological and extrabiblical accounts, a progressive, modernizing builder, a great political mover, and active monarch on the international stage in his day. But from the biblical perspective he was the archexample of an unbelieving and apostate ruler who rejected the ways of Yahweh. From the perspective of the biblical writer(s), nothing else mattered. Their intent was not to give Ahab a fair hearing. Their intent was to show his rejection of Yahweh and examine its negative consequences as a warning to every reader not to become like Ahab. See Jerome T. Walsh, *Ahab: The Construction of a King*, Interfaces (Collegeville, MN: Liturgical Press, 2006) and the various histories of Israel for fuller discussion.

45. It is interesting to note the recent plea of two eminent professors of history, Jo Guldi (Brown University) and David Armitage (Harvard University), in their work *The History Manifesto* (Cambridge: Cambridge University Press, 2014), that historians should write studies which encompass longer sweeps of time and can thus "speak truth to power." The implication is that the task of the historian is not entirely "neutral" and that history done properly can have desirable and powerful rhetorical effects.

He decreed statutes for Jacob
  and established the law in Israel,
which he commanded our ancestors
  to teach their children,
so the next generation would know them,
  even the children yet to be born,
  and they in turn would tell their children.
Then they would put their trust in God
  and would not forget his deeds
  but would keep his commands.
They would not be like their ancestors—
  a stubborn and rebellious generation,
whose hearts were not loyal to God,
  whose spirits were not faithful to him.

Note the language of teaching, listening, parables, hidden and ancient truths, things heard and known, teaching the next generation, and so on. To what end? Verses 7–8 make the rhetorical intent of the psalmist clear, that the next generation would:

1. Put their trust in Yahweh;
2. Not forget his deeds;
3. Keep his commands; and
4. Not be disobedient like their forefathers.

There is a strong sense in which psalmic history is always and explicitly designed *to teach*. The lessons tend not to be subtle but instead obvious and emphasized through repetition. So, it is important to remember when encountering a historical psalm in personal reading or corporate study that a particular agenda is being driven by the psalmist. To get to the heart of the poem, then, we must ask ourselves the questions, "What is that agenda?" and "How, then, should I respond?"

Psalm 106 in the New Testament. Psalm 106 is alluded to a few times in the New Testament. Perhaps unsurprisingly, verse 20 seems to provide the basis for Paul's teaching on the sin of idolatry in Romans 1:23.[46] Similarly, we see repetitions of Psalm 106 in Paul's historical précis and

---

46. "What is surprising is that Paul takes an injunction laid out against Israel and expands that to the nations as well. 'You too,' he says, 'should have known better than to exchange the glory of the Creator for an image made from metal.' However, it is probably also an indicator to the Hebrew-background believers in Rome that they have no heightened moral status vis-à-vis their gentile-background brothers" (Keesmaat, "Psalms in Romans and Galatians," 143).

accompanying conclusions in 1 Corinthians 10 (Ps 106:14 in 1 Cor 10:6; Ps 106:37 in 1 Cor 10:20). But perhaps the most telling resonance from Psalm 106 in the New Testament is the theological conclusion to be drawn from this psalm. As human beings we are given to sin repeatedly, and we are thoroughly dependent on God's grace both if we are to enjoy continued relationship with him and if any change is going to occur in our character and behavior (Rom 3).[47]

REFUSING TO LIMIT GOD'S GRACE. Walter Brueggemann makes a helpful observation with regard to the conclusion of Psalm 106:

The world proposed in these psalms [Pss 105–106] is dialogically open. Each partner can do new things and neither partner is simply fated by past action. . . . Even when the psalms seem to have reached their rhetorical conclusion and their point of covenantal extremity, matters are kept open for new possibility. Thus after the long recital of sin, Psalm 106 nonetheless petitions for rescue. After the long recital of joy in Psalm 105, the concluding assertion is a summons to obedience. In both Psalm 105 and 106, the final statement moves boldly against the grain of the preceding extended argument. . . . The recital, in both cases, is not aimed at a conclusion, but at a fresh starting point in which new decisions are made.[48]

As Christians it is important for us to remember that we are not "fated by past action." We can feel beaten down by a strong sense of our own moral failure. We have failed God. Repeatedly. And this despite our frequent protestation that we will do better in the future and will not fall prey to the same sins again. Most Christians, at some point in their lives, just feel condemned by the weight of their own sinfulness and dismayed by the repeating pattern of seeking forgiveness followed by sudden relapse in the same area of life. All too often, if we are honest, it seems as though our spiritual reality resembles that of the Israelites who "soon forgot what [God] had done for them" (Ps 106:13).

---

47. Psalm 106:48 may provide the backdrop to Rev 19:4. But to my mind these terms are common and appropriate to any setting of praise; therefore, it is difficult to argue that John had Ps 106 specifically in mind here (Moyise, "Psalms in Revelation," 240).

48. Walter Brueggemann, *Abiding Astonishment: Psalms, Modernity, and the Making of History*, Literary Currents in Biblical Interpretation (Louisville: Westminster John Knox, 1991), 23–24.

The psalmist's prayer should be an example for us (v. 48). Just think about it. He lived long before the ultimate revelation of God's grace in his Son—centuries before the cross. Yet the psalmist could recount a long list of the people's failings, some of them horrible, and still conclude his poem with a prayer for salvation that seeks God's grace *once again*. Therein lies the essence of the life of faith. We can *always* make a fresh start in the Lord Jesus. "But where sin increased, grace increased all the more, so that, just as sin reigned in death, so also grace might reign through righteousness to bring eternal life through Jesus Christ our Lord" (Rom 5:20–21).

The poet was able to believe that God's grace was bigger and more determined than the often-repeated sins of the people. How much more should we, having seen what he has done for us in Jesus, be able to trust in God's great love? What is more, as Brueggemann points out, even the psalmist and his community were not fated to fail repeatedly. How much more is this true for those who experience not only the cleansing of the cross but also the empowering of the Holy Spirit (Rom 5:1–11; 8)? As Paul instructs in Romans 6:11–14:

> In the same way, count yourselves dead to sin but alive to God in Christ Jesus. Therefore do not let sin reign in your mortal body so that you obey its evil desires. Do not offer any part of yourself to sin as an instrument of wickedness, but rather offer yourselves to God, as those who have been brought from death to life; and offer every part of yourself to him as an instrument of righteousness. For sin shall no longer be your master, because you are not under law, but under grace.

Could there be a better way for the psalmist to finish Book 4 of the Psalter? As a book that responds to the crisis of loss and the trauma of exile, Book 4 answers the pain of Book 3 with a message of Yahweh's continued kingship and his people's continued hope. Book 3 ends with the bitterest of questions: "Lord, where is your former great love?" Book 4 ends with the joint message of Psalms 105 and 106. God's love is at work in our history and experience right here and right now, just as it always has been (Ps 105). What is more, God's grace is available to us (even us!), despite the depth of our failings, just as it always has been (Ps 106).

There was hope for those in exile.
There is hope for us.

> Let all the people say, "Amen!"
> Praise the LORD. (Ps 106:48b)

Psalm 107

¹ Give thanks to the LORD, for he is good;
   his love endures forever.
² Let the redeemed of the LORD tell their story—
   those he redeemed from the hand of the foe,
³ those he gathered from the lands,
   from the east and west, north and south.
⁴ Some wandered in the desert wastelands,
   finding no way to a city where they could settle.
⁵ They were hungry and thirsty,
   and their lives ebbed away.
⁶ Then they cried out to the LORD in their trouble,
   and he delivered them from their distress.
⁷ He led them by a straight way
   to a city where they could settle.
⁸ Let them give thanks to the LORD for his unfailing love
   and his wonderful deeds for mankind,
⁹ for he satisfies the thirsty
   and fills the hungry with good things.
¹⁰ Some sat in darkness, in utter darkness,
   prisoners suffering in iron chains,
¹¹ because they rebelled against God's commands
   and despised the plans of the Most High.
¹² So he subjected them to bitter labor;
   they stumbled, and there was no one to help.
¹³ Then they cried to the LORD in their trouble,
   and he saved them from their distress.
¹⁴ He brought them out of darkness, the utter darkness
   and broke away their chains.
¹⁵ Let them give thanks to the LORD for his unfailing love
   and his wonderful deeds for mankind,
¹⁶ for he breaks down gates of bronze
   and cuts through bars of iron.
¹⁷ Some became fools through their rebellious ways
   and suffered affliction because of their iniquities.
¹⁸ They loathed all food
   and drew near the gates of death.
¹⁹ Then they cried to the LORD in their trouble,

and he saved them from their distress.
²⁰ He sent our his word and healed them;
    he rescued them from the grave.
²¹ Let them give thanks to the LORD for his unfailing love
    and his wonderful deeds for mankind.
²² Let them sacrifice thank offerings
    and tell of his works with songs of joy.
²³ Some went out on the sea in ships;
    they were merchants on the mighty waters.
²⁴ They saw the works of the LORD,
    his wonderful deeds in the deep.
²⁵ For he spoke and stirred up a tempest
    that lifted high the waves.
²⁶ They mounted up to the heavens and went down to the depths;
    in their peril their courage melted away.
²⁷ They reeled and staggered like drunkards;
    they were at their wits' end.
²⁸ Then they cried out to the LORD in their trouble,
    and he brought them out of their distress.
²⁹ He stilled the storm to a whisper;
    the waves of the sea were hushed.
³⁰ They were glad when it grew calm,
    and he guided them to their desired haven.
³¹ Let them give thanks to the LORD for his unfailing love
    and his wonderful deeds for mankind.
³² Let them exalt him in the assembly of the people
    and praise him in the council of the elders.
³³ He turned rivers into a desert,
    flowing springs into thirsty ground.
³⁴ and fruitful land into a salt waste,
    because of the wickedness of those who lived there.
³⁵ He turned the desert into pools of water
    and the parched ground into flowing springs;
³⁶ there he brought the hungry to live,
    and they founded a city where they could settle.
³⁷ They sowed fields and planted vineyards
    that yielded a fruitful harvest;
³⁸ he blessed them, and their numbers greatly increased,
    and he did not let their herds diminish.
³⁹ Then their numbers decreased, and they were humbled
    by oppression, calamity and sorrow;

⁴⁰ he who pours contempt on nobles
made them wander in a trackless waste.
⁴¹ But he lifted the needy out of their affliction
and increased their families like flocks.
⁴² The upright see and rejoice,
but all the wicked shut their mouths.
⁴³ Let one who is wise heed these things
and ponder the loving deeds of the LORD.

PSALM 107 BEGINS BOOK 5, the final book in the Psalter. Although the psalm represents the start of a new book (Pss 107–50) in the Psalter, Psalm 107 shares much in common with the two preceding psalms, especially Psalm 106.[1] The two earlier psalms provided a historical recital of significant moments in Israel's history. Psalm 105 retraces God's intervention in the life of his people, beginning with the patriarchs and culminating with the entrance into Canaan. Psalm 106, however, offers a more comprehensive rehearsal of Israel's history beginning with the events in Egypt (vv. 6–12), rehearsing the wilderness period (vv. 16–33), alluding to the idolatry in the land (vv. 34–39), and culminating with the exile. In verse 47 the community cries out, "Save us, LORD our God, and gather us from the nations." As explained below, Psalm 107 serves, in some sense, as the response to the petition in Psalm 106. Those who have been gathered to Jerusalem are instructed to look back "to the end of the exile and in hope of the still unaccomplished complete restoration of Israel."[2]

The structure of the psalm includes an introduction (vv. 1–3), followed by four sections of uneven length (vv. 4–32) but with two common refrains.

---

1. On the numerous semantic and conceptual links between Psalms 106 and 107 see Frank-Lothar Hossfeld and Erich Zenger, *Psalms 3*, Hermeneia (Minneapolis: Fortress, 2011), 101–2.

2. Ibid., 102. John Goldingay argues that the shared semantic and conceptual terms between the three psalms indicates that the "division between Books IV and V is rather artificial . . . it is another indication that the division of the Psalter into books . . . is not a major key to their interpretation" (Goldingay, *Psalms 3*, BCOTWP [Grand Rapids: Baker Academic, 2008], 247). While the three psalms do have much in common, Psalm 107 appears to provide a shift in orientation from the preceding two psalms. Psalms 105 and 106 recall key scenes from Israel's canonical history, while Psalm 107 alludes to scenes of deliverance from exile. These scenes are meant as instructional (v. 43) for those gathered back to Israel.

In each perilous situation described, once the people had realized they have no hope, the psalmist recounts: "Then they cried out to the LORD in their trouble, and he delivered them from their distress" (vv. 6, 13, 19, 28). Following an assurance of deliverance, the psalmist invites them to thank God for his steadfast love (*hesed*) for his people. The repetition of both themes in each section creates a rich theological confession in this psalm, as suggested below. Each section in verses 4–32 follows a similar pattern: description of trouble, a cry to Yahweh for help, Yahweh's saving intervention, and an exhortation to public thanksgiving. Although some writers have attempted to link the four scenes in verses 4–32 to the four "scenes" in verses 2–3, these kinds of connections seem forced. Instead, as John Goldingay has noted, the scenes in verses 4–32 reflect "states or types of experiences."[3] It is even conceivable to believe that these four scenes are more metaphorical in meaning and meant to represent larger theological ideas, not simply specific instances of deliverance.[4] Even the arrangement of the four scenes appears to point to such a reading. The two inner scenes attribute this distress to sin and disobedience, while the two outer scenes speak of people on a journey but interrupted due to the desert and the sea. Or as Jorge Mejía has noted, the "two acts of salvation from sin are framed by two acts of salvation from chaos."[5] Following these four scenes, verses 33–41 serve as a hymn meant to praise the power of God at work in all aspects of creation in behalf of his people, with verses 42–43 invoking wisdom language. The NIV separates verse 43 from the remainder of the text, thus suggesting that the final verse provides a conclusion to the psalm. As noted below, the wisdom language in the verse provides "a final exhortation to give heed to the lesson" found within the psalm.[6]

The Steadfast Love of God (107:1–2)

HIS LOVE ENDURES FOREVER. The psalmist instructs the community to "give thanks" to the Lord and then provides a rationale for giving thanks. The NIV renders the Hebrew term *hesed* as "love" in this verse. While not incorrect, such a rendering may fail to convey the full meaning of the term being employed in this context. The covenantal and enduring commitment of Yahweh to his people may not be fully captured with the word "love,"

---

3. Goldingay, *Psalms* 3, 249. Leslie Allen also prefers to understand these scenes as "types" (Allen, *Psalms 101–150*, rev. ed. WBC 21 [Waco, TX: Word, 1983], 63–64).

4. Hossfeld and Zenger, *Psalms* 3, 104.

5. Jorge Mejía, "Some Observations on Psalm 107," *BTB* 5 (1975): 58, 66.

6. Erhard Gerstenberger, *Psalms, Part 2, and Lamentations*, FOTL XV (Grand Rapids: Eerdmans, 2001), 249.

particularly given our own culture's penchant for use of the term. Martin Leuenberger suggests that the opening line of Psalm 107 introduces one of, if not the, dominant theme for Book 5 of the Psalter.[7] The *hesed* of the Lord shapes the community's understanding of their own history (cf. Pss 106:1; 136:1) and God's faithful, covenantal commitment throughout it, but the term also reminds the community that the *hesed* of the Lord remains the foundational hope for deliverance, both in the past and in the future (cf. Pss 107:1; 118:1).

Let the Redeemed of the LORD tell their story. The psalmist invites the community to testify to the steadfast love of the Lord mentioned in verse 1. The word "redeemed" comes from the root *g'l*, which elsewhere alludes to the deliverance from Egypt (Exod 6:6; 15:13; Pss 74:2; 77:16). When the term is appropriated in the book of Isaiah, the exodus imagery is invoked but with a clear reference to the exodus out of exile (e.g., Isa 41:14; 44:6; 47:4; 48:17; 60:16; 63:16). In the Isaiah texts, the term serves as a title for God (i.e., "Redeemer"). He was the redeemer for those exiled in Babylon. Similarly, the psalmist joins in the proclamation that Israel's God has redeemed his people from captivity. In Psalm 107, however, the passive participial form of *ga'al* appears. The NIV correctly translates the phrase as "the redeemed of the LORD." While such a translation acknowledges the relationship between the people and their God (i.e., they are the redeemed ones of God), it may fail to capture the connection between the redemption of the people and the active work of the Redeemer. A more explicit reading of the relationship might be rendered, "Those redeemed *by* the LORD." The four scenes depicted in verses 4–32 illustrate the need the people had for God to do his redemptive work on their behalf because "there was no one to help" (v. 12).

Those he gathered from the lands. In verses 2–3 the psalmist calls upon the people to confess that they have been gathered "from the lands, from east and west, from north and south" (NIV). The four cardinal points are mentioned in Isaiah 49:12, a text that also alludes to Israel's being brought back from the lands. In Psalm 107, however, the last term in verse 3 is actually *yam*, "sea." When used directionally, this term typically refers to the west, but almost never to the south. Some scholars have attempted to interpret *yam* in a way that retains the four cardinal points, but these efforts seem largely unconvincing.[8] Such a reading fails to capture the

---

7. Martin Leuenberger, *Konzeptionen des Königtums Gottes im Psalter: Untersuchungen zu Komposition und Redaktion der theokratischen Bücher IV–V im Psalter*, ATANT 83 (Zürich: Theologischer Verlag Zürich, 2004), 284.

8. For example, Allen has attempted to retain the term by understanding that the

more metaphorical and symbolic language invoked in Psalm 107.[9] The term *zaphon*, "north," is imbued with considerable theological and metaphorical meaning in the Old Testament. The term often alludes to the enemies from the north (i.e., Assyria and Babylon), while also equating those locations with the more metaphorical understanding of the term as a place of disaster and chaos (cf. Ezek 38:15; 39:2). Similarly, the term *yam* ("sea") appears throughout the Psalter and much of the Old Testament, where it often functions as a metaphor for pending chaos or chaos overcome (e.g., Pss 33:7; 65:7; 74:13). To limit the interpretation of verse 3c to a geographic understanding alone fails to capture the full range of possible meanings. The people are to give thanks to the Lord because he has gathered them from the lands, from the east to the west, but also because he has delivered them from the "north" and the "sea," from places that threatened to unleash chaos into the lives of God's people.

Deliverance from the Desert Wasteland (107:4–9)

THE FIRST SCENE DEPICTS A GROUP lost in the wilderness with no hope of delivering themselves. Their only hope rests in the God to whom they call.

Wandered in desert wastelands. The psalmist goes to great lengths to present a dire scenario for those mentioned in this scene. The people are not traveling; they are "wandering." The verb *ta'ah*, which means "to wander," suggests much more than simply to meander. Perhaps more ominously, *ta'ah* means to wander because one has erroneously left the path or, worse yet, to wander because there is no longer a path to follow.[10] So far off the beaten path are they, the psalmist says, that they cannot even find a city in which to dwell. Instead of following the path, these people are in the *midbar*, "the desert," a place further described as the "waste places" (*yeshimon*). Beyond the threat of attack by humans, the waste places of the desert prove deadly because they lack roads or a clearly marked road system.[11] In short order, those wandering aimlessly will be overtaken by hunger and thirst.

---

people were gathered from the east and the west, and from the north and from "overseas" (Allen, *Psalms 101–150*, 58 n. 3b). Citing 2 Chr 8:17, where *yam* appears to refer to the Gulf of Aqabah, Mitchell Dahood understands *yam* as antithetic parallelism to *zaphon* ("north"), thus referencing the "motif of the four cardinal points" (Mitchell Dahood, *Psalms III: 101–150* AB 17A [New York: Doubleday, 1970], 81). See also, John Jarick, "The Four Corners of Psalm 107," *CBQ* (1997): 270–87.

9. Hossfeld and Zenger, *Psalms 3*, 104.

10. Goldingay, *Psalms 3*, 250.

11. Othmar Keel, *The Symbolism of the Biblical World: Ancient Near Eastern Iconography and the Book of Psalms*, trans. T. J. Hallett (Winona Lake, IN: Eisenbrauns, 1997), 76.

They cried out to the LORD. In each scene of deliverance the psalmist recounts how the people cried out to God and how they were delivered (vv. 6, 13, 19, 28). The verb "to cry out" (*tsa'aq*) appears repeatedly in the Old Testament, especially in contexts associated with the exodus. The cry of the people stirs God to act on their behalf by bringing deliverance (Exod 2:23).

Give thanks to the LORD for his unfailing love. Central to all four scenes is the repeated refrain, "Let them give thanks to the LORD for his unfailing love; and his wonderful deeds for mankind" (vv. 8, 15, 21, 31). The NIV's translating *hesed* in these verses as "unfailing love," while translating the same term as "love endures" in verse 1, inadvertently severs the opening verse from the remainder of the psalm, thus preventing the reader in English from seeing the theological thread that has been woven throughout the poem. The entire psalm, from beginning (v. 1) to end (v. 43), confesses the *hesed* of Yahweh, his unfailing love to his people. Deliverance from the wastelands (and the deliverance articulated in each of the three other scenes) is described as a "wonderful deed" deserving of thanksgiving to Yahweh. In describing each event as one of Yahweh's "wonderful deeds" (*nipla'ot*), the psalmist employs a term rife with historical, confessional, and theological overtones. Frequently in the Psalter, *nipla'ot* recalls the major events in Israel's redemption (cf. Pss 78:4, 11, 32; 105:5; 106:7, 22). Even outside the Psalter the poetic use of the term is appropriated (e.g., Neh 9:17; 1 Chr 16:9, 12). With the use of *nipla'ot*, the poet folds these episodes of redemption, these "wonderful deeds," into the larger narrative of Israel's encounter with her Redeemer God. Because of the Lord's steadfast love and his capacity to perform "wonderful deeds," the people are delivered from "their trouble" and "their distress." They are given a city to live in, and their appetites are satiated (v. 7b, 9).

Deliverance from Prison (107:10–16)

THE SECOND SCENE DEPICTS individuals suffering in captivity. Unlike the first scene, however, those in prison make a correlation between their dire circumstances and their lack of faithfulness to God (v. 11).

Some sat in darkness. The psalmist explains that some sat in "darkness, in utter darkness" (*hoshek wetsalmawet*). The depths of their peril are captured in particular with the latter term. Rather than being rendered as "utter darkness," *tsalmawet* can be rendered as "deathly shadow" or "shadow of death," a phrase emphasizing threat to human life.[12] Elsewhere in the

---

12. The Septuagint makes clear its understanding of the Hebrew term with the Greek translation *skias thanatou* ("shadow of death"). See also the use of the same term in Ps 23.

Old Testament the two terms appear in reference to the Babylonian exile (Isa 42:7, 22; 49:9; Jer 13:16; Lam 3:2), which is likely the meaning in Psalm 107 as well, particularly given the overall thrust of the psalm. Although the images in verse 10b only enhance the image of the imprisoned Israelite, the same phrase "darkness, in utter darkness" (*hoshek wetsalmawet*) appears five times in Job (3:5; 10:21; 12:22; 28:3; 34:22), but in that context the meaning is associated with "the sphere of death and destruction" more broadly.[13] In Psalm 107, even as those who had wandered in the desert wasteland teetered on the edge of life and death, those imprisoned under foreign powers found themselves in the "sphere of death and destruction" and in need of divine intervention.

Because they rebelled against God's commands. As mentioned above, the psalmist provides no rationale for the suffering endured in the desert wastelands. In the second scenario, however, the poet is explicit as to the reason for their plight: "they rebelled against God's commands, and despised the plans of the Most High." In Hebrew poetry, writers often make subtle wordplays based on the sound of Hebrew words—a connection that, unfortunately, gets lost in English translation. Frequently these wordplays make a significant contribution to the meaning of the text. In verse 11 the psalmist explains that the punishment came because the people had rebelled (*himru*) against the very words (*'imre*) of God.

There was no one to help. Similar to the hopelessness in verses 4–9, the psalmist now notes "there was no one to help" those "subjected . . . to bitter labor." Consequently, they cried out to Yahweh (v. 13), and he delivered them out of "darkness, . . . utter darkness" (*hoshek wetsalmawet*) and broke the chains that bound them (v. 14). And in the final verse of the section the psalmist refers to Yahweh's breaking the bronze doors. In Isaiah 45:2 the prophet announces that Cyrus, the anointed one of Yahweh, will break down the doors of bronze and cut in two the bars of iron. As Hossfeld and Zenger note, the image could refer to the barred doors of a prison, but it could easily represent the doors of the city more generally. In Isaiah the reference was to Cyrus's deliverance of those in exile in Babylon. In Psalm 107, however, Cyrus has been replaced by Yahweh; it is Yahweh alone who delivered his people from "darkness, . . . utter darkness" (*hoshek wetsalmawet*). Because of this act of covenantal faithfulness, the people are invited to give thanks for the steadfast love (*hesed*) of Yahweh.[14]

---

13. Walter Beyerlin, *Werden und Wesen des 107. Psalms*, BZAW 153 (Berlin: de Gruyter, 1979), 45.

14. Hossfeld and Zenger, *Psalms 3*, 105–106.

Deliverance from Sheol (107:17–22)

SOME BECAME FOOLS THROUGH THEIR REBELLIOUS WAYS. Questions concerning the precise meaning of verse 17a have led to a number of different renderings of this verse. The NIV follows the Hebrew text closely: "Some are fools [*ewilim*] through their rebellious behavior." The text-critical apparatus in the *Biblia Hebraica Stuttgartensia* (BHS) proposes "languishing" (*'umlalim*) or perhaps "sickness" (*holim*), with the latter reading having been adopted in the NRSV.[15] The subsequent verse's mention of nearing the "gates of death" provides some rationale for such a reading of the text, as does the presupposed connection between illness and sin, mentioned elsewhere in the Psalter (cf. Pss 32; 38; 39). Despite the presumed logic of such suggested changes, the Hebrew text should be retained (cf. NIV). From the perspective of the psalmist, those who were foolish and turned aside or rebelled (*peshah;* cf. Ps 107:17a) from the ways of God followed a pathway that appeared to lead to the gates of death (v. 18b). Later in this section (v. 20), these gates of death are referred to as "the pit" or "the grave" (*shehit*).[16] Strikingly however, the psalmist personalizes the term by adding a third person masculine plural suffix to the end of the word—an ending that would result in rendering the word "their pit." In other words, their iniquities have led to their pit. The connection between cause and effect appears rather explicit. Nonetheless, those sick under the weight of sin cry to Yahweh for deliverance (v. 19), and he delivers them from their oppression or distress.

He sent out his word and healed them. Yahweh sends his word to heal those near to the pit. Elsewhere in the Old Testament, Yahweh sends forth his word. In Isaiah 55:11, for example, Yahweh sends forth his word to accomplish his purposes for his people (i.e., delivering and restoring those in exile). In Psalm 147 the sending forth of Yahweh's word alludes to Yahweh's governance over all creation (vv. 15, 18), which ensures the presence of God with his people (v. 20). Goldingay, however, has suggested that Psalm 107:20 "presupposes . . . things do happen when a powerful person speaks. Yhwh only has to say the word and a person gets healed."[17] Perhaps the text is working at a much deeper level theologically. Yahweh's word operates as a surrogate for Yahweh himself. Those who are sick due to rebellion and iniquity run the risk of separation from God; those who

---

15. The *Biblia Hebraica Stuttgartensia* is the only complete scholarly edition of the Codex Leningradensis Hebrew text. This edition includes significant textual variants and proposals for correction in the critical apparatus.

16. On the images associated with the pit or the grave, see Keel, *The Symbolism of the Biblical World*, 62–72.

17. Goldingay, *Psalms 3*, 253.

were ill in this psalm "drew near the gates of death" (v. 18b). Yet Yahweh heard their cries, overcame the perceived distance (i.e., "sent his word"), and remedied their affliction.

Deliverance from the Sea (107:23–32)

SOME WENT OUT ON TO THE SEA. This narrative section is longer than the previous three, with added attention to the crisis itself. As Hossfeld and Zenger suggest, this added attention "shifts the accent of God's intervention more strongly toward the miraculous demonstration of YHWH's power, which is transparent to the fundamental message that YHWH can defeat the sea's chaos."[18] Three times the psalmist refers to the sea in terms that are metaphorically rich in meaning: "mighty waters" (v. 23b); "deep" (v. 24b); and "depths" or "primeval floods" (*tehom* [v. 26a]). Frequently these terms connote chaos and the threat of death (cf. Ps 69:1, 2, 15). Similar imagery is employed in the book of Jonah as well (Jonah 2:3, 5).

He spoke and stirred up a tempest. Unlike the two previous scenes, which explained disaster in the light of the people's rebellion, the final scene attributes both the cause of the storm and its solution to God (Ps 107:25, 29). Yet in claiming God as both the cause *and* remedy of the storm, the psalmist does not imply a certain level of capriciousness for Israel's God. Instead, the poet invokes a much richer theological tradition—that of the Divine King. Mastery over the sea is evidence of divine rule.[19] The psalmist goes to considerable lengths to describe the destructive nature of the storm. Waves reached to the heavens and down to the depths of the "primeval floods" (*tehom*). So great was the storm that the sailors were "at their wits' end." Literally the Hebrew reads, "all their wisdom was swallowed up"—perhaps another allusion to Jonah. McCann suggests that "true wisdom is to cry out to God, to acknowledge one's utter dependance upon God," and to recognize that God's steadfast love (*hesed*) is "sufficient for even the worst possible scenario."[20]

A Hymn on the Power of God (107:33–41)

FOLLOWING THE FOUR NARRATIVE PORTIONS of the psalm, the psalmist offers a poem that celebrates the awesome power of God over all aspects of creation.

He turned rivers into a desert. Verses 33–34 open the final hymn with a stark reminder of Yahweh's power. In the fourth scene (vv. 23–32) the psalmist portrayed God as God over the sea, in effect declaring his

---

18. Hossfeld and Zenger, *Psalms 3*, 107.
19. Ibid., 108.
20. McCann, "Psalms," 1118.

power as divine king. The recognition of Yahweh's power continues in the opening lines of the final hymnic portion of the psalm. In the second (vv. 10–16) and third (vv. 17–22) scenes, the disastrous circumstances were connected to human sinfulness and rebellion, and similarly in verses 33–34 this particular exercise of Yahweh's power is a response to the wickedness (*ra'*) of those who dwell in the land. According to the psalmist, sources of continuous water ("rivers" and "springs") can be dried up by Yahweh, and land that is fruitful can be made nothing more than a "salt waste."[21] Such imagery is meant to highlight Yahweh's role as "master of life and death."[22]

There he brought the hungry to live. Although the first two verses in the hymn provide a general claim regarding Yahweh's power, verses 36–38 recall Israel's settlement in the land as further evidence of Yahweh's transformative power. Just as God has the power to turn rivers into a desert and fruitful land into salty wastes, so also he has the power to transform that which is dead into that which is alive and flourishing. Into such a land, the psalmist affirms, Yahweh brought his people so that they might enjoy the benefits of his blessings (v. 38).

He lifted the needy out of their affliction. The theology of the poor plays a significant role in the theology of the Psalter as a whole, and elements of such a theology are reflected in verses 39–41.[23] The land that had been transformed from a desert into pools of water, a place where their numbers "greatly increased" (v. 38), became a place that suffered because of the oppression, calamity, and sorrow that had overtaken it. As Goldingay correctly notes, the conditions of oppression and calamity are not necessarily impositions by an outside force; rather, these conditions more likely reflect "the affliction [the community imposed] on others, or the affliction that characterizes the life of the community."[24] Consequently, the nobles, the ones with the power in the community and the ones tasked with maintaining justice within the community, are condemned to "wander in a trackless waste" (v. 40b). Literally the text says they will wander "in waste places [*tohu*] without a path." While the word *tohu* appears to refer to the unformed chaotic space prior to creation in Genesis 1, it also refers to

---

21. Perhaps the psalmist alludes here to the story of Sodom and Gomorrah (Gen 19), in which a land was turned into a salty waste because of the wickedness of the inhabitants.

22. Hossfeld and Zenger, *Psalms 3*, 109.

23. For an overview of the poor in the Psalms, see Hans-Joachim Kraus, *Theology of the Psalms*, CC (Minneapolis: Fortress, 1992), 150–54.

24. Goldingay, *Psalms 3*, 259. A number of commentators follow the suggestion in the critical apparatus of *BHS* to switch verses 39 and 40, presumably to make better sense of the text. Kraus goes so far as to call this section of the psalm a "senseless text" as it presently stands (Kraus, *Psalms 60–150*, 325).

empty, desert-like regions. The latter, more mundane meaning, however, is certainly infused with the more cosmic overtones of the former. For those who wandered in *tohu*, there was little hope. For the needy (*'ebyon*), however, this was hope. Yahweh lifted them out of their affliction and blessed them by increasing their families. Hossfeld and Zenger suggest that with this claim of deliverance and blessing, Yahweh intended to make the poor "a great people with whom he will shape the history of the post-exilic restoration."[25]

Wisdom Conclusion (107:42–43)

THE FINAL TWO VERSES MAKE CLEAR the paraenetic-didactic purpose of the psalm. The upright are instructed to "see" and learn from the stories of deliverance and the testimonies of Yahweh's transforming work in the world. Should they do so, they will be led to rejoicing, while those engaged in wickedness will have their mouths shut in the light of Yahweh's power. The final verse refers to "the one who is wise." Who are the wise? They are those who "heed" (*shamar*) these things. The word *shamar*, however, means much more than simply to "heed," as in pay attention to, but instead implies "keeping," "protecting," and "preserving."[26] Only as the images and theology constructed in Psalm 107 are kept and preserved by the wise will the psalm's meaning seep into their lives and prove to be formative. The opening verse in Psalm 107 implores the community to praise Yahweh because of his steadfast love (*hesed*). The psalm concludes by returning to the same idea (v. 43b). Those who consider or understand (*bin*) the *hesed* of Yahweh will not only have reason to give thanks (v. 1a); they will also be well on their way to becoming wise (v. 43b).

Bridging Contexts

THE STEADFAST LOVE OF GOD. As suggested above, the steadfast love (*hesed*) of God functions as the foundational theme for the entire psalm from beginning to end. Within the book

---

25. Hossfeld and Zenger, *Psalms 3*, 109. On the condemnation of power in Book 5, see W. Dennis Tucker Jr., *Constructing and Deconstructing Power in Psalms 107–150*, AIL 19 (Atlanta: SBL Press, 2014).

26. Goldingay understands the question in verse 43a to be, "Who is the wise person who notes these things?" (Goldingay, *Psalms 3*, 259). The NIV appears to capture better the structure of the verse. The question is limited to the initial verbless clause (*miy hakam*). The next two clauses begin with *waw* + *yiqtol* forms, and both are better rendered as jussives ("Let"). In an attempt to create two parallel cola, the NRSV sets aside the verbless clause in verse 43a and prefers instead to assimilate it into the entire colon ("Let those who are wise give heed to these things").

of Psalms the term appears 125 times. No other book in the Old Testament uses the term with such frequency. The next closest is 2 Samuel, with only twelve occurrences! The affirmation of and dependence upon the steadfast love of God was foundational to the language of piety expressed in the Psalter. In Psalm 107 the people are called to give thanks for the steadfast love of God in verse 1; it was this love that provided the redemption of his people. Throughout the four scenes in verses 4–32, the community is asked to testify to the steadfast love of God in light of their deliverance (vv. 8, 15, 21, 31), and the psalm concludes by defining the wise as those who consider the steadfast love of God (v. 43). As James Mays suggests, Psalm 107 not only exalts the notion of God's steadfast love, it is also "an exposition" of the term itself.[27] The very actions of God are predicated on God's love for his people. This same theme resonates throughout the New Testament. Both 1 John 4:9–10 and the oft-quoted John 3:16 explain that it was the love of God—the one who loved us first—that prompted him to send Jesus as the Reconciler (1 John 4:10). In both testaments redemption is the result of divine love, steadfast love.[28] The acknowledgment of God's steadfast love for his people yields two additional themes in this psalm.

The incomprehensible reach of God. The Babylonian exile not only resulted in physical and economic devastation that led to considerable human suffering, but it also threatened to undercut many of Israel's foundational theological claims concerning Yahweh and Yahweh's relationship with his people. Despite the challenge of the exile to Israel's theology, Israel's faith "did not disappear in the wake of the catastrophe that struck Judah and Jerusalem, as was the standard outcome in comparable situations in the ancient Near East."[29] On the contrary, Israel reaffirmed her belief in Yahweh's steadfast love in certainty that their only hope was in the faithfulness of this God. The request at the end of Psalm 106 for Yahweh to gather all those who have been scattered among the nations was grounded in that hope. That text suggests a continued faith in Yahweh to act in behalf of his people despite their unfaithfulness to him (e.g., Ps 106:34–39). Psalm 107 functions as a theological response to the plight of a sinful

---

27. James L. Mays, *Psalms*, Interpretation (Louisville: Westminster John Knox, 1994), 343.

28. Reinhard Feldmeier and Hermann Spieckermann note that the affirmation made in 1 John 4:8, "God is love," is "not a general religious statement characterizing love as divine in an equation." Instead, with this formula the author of the letter explains that the act of God's revealing himself in Jesus is in fact an explication of God's love for his people (Reinhard Feldmeier and Hermann Spieckermann, *God of the Living*, trans. Mark E. Biddle [Waco, TX: Baylor University Press, 2011], 126).

29. Konrad Schmid, *The Old Testament: A Literary History*, trans. Linda Maloney (Minneapolis: Fortress, 2012), 107.

nation scattered among the nations as a result of their own covenantal faithlessness.

Following the opening celebration of the steadfast love of God in Psalm 107, the psalmist implores those redeemed by Yahweh (v. 2a) to give thanks because he has gathered them from the lands (v. 3a) and because he has in fact responded to their earlier plea in Psalm 106:47. The testimony in Psalm 107:3 counters any claim that their sin has reduced them to a people literally exiled from the land forever, or worse yet, a people exiled from their God. Instead the psalmist claims that from the east to the west, God's reach extends in pursuit of his people, and neither human threats from the "north" (*zaphon*) nor the chaotic waters of the sea (*yam*) can cut short that reach. The four scenes in Psalm 107 give graphic testimony to the incomprehensible reach of God as a result of his steadfast love. Whether wasting away in foreign prisons (v. 10) or clinging to life at the gates of death (v. 18), God heard their cry and delivered them because of his steadfast love. Whether tracking aimlessly in the desert or tossed about upon the stormy waters, God heard their cry and delivered them because of his great love for them.

The God who responds. Scenes of Israel crying out to Yahweh appear repeatedly in the Old Testament but especially in Exodus 1–15 (e.g., Exod 2:23; 3:7, 9; 5:8, 15; 8:12; 11:6; 12:30; 14:10, 15) and throughout the book of Judges. In these instances, the people cry out to the Lord because they are incapable of overcoming the forces that threaten them, whether it be Pharaoh and the Egyptian empire or the strong kingdoms that threaten them in the promised land. In the exodus story and the stories found in Judges, the cries of the people do not go unheeded by Israel's God. Instead, Yahweh, the God of the covenant, responds by delivering them from the oppressive forces that have threatened them. To cry out to God is to invoke memories of a redeeming God who has faithfully responded to the cries of his people before and to believe this God is inclined to do so again because of his steadfast love. In Psalm 107, those in the first scene are said to have cried out to their God in the belief that he can redeem them from the "desert wastelands" in which they have found themselves. Davidson notes the obvious connections between the language and imagery in these psalms and that associated with the exile in Isaiah.[30] Yet because these scenes are "types," Davidson acknowledges that "anyone in the community . . . who had gotten lost while traveling across barren terrain" could identify with the scene in a "profoundly personal way."[31] Even further, this

---

30. Davidson, *Psalms*, 355. On similar imagery in Isaiah, see Isa 40:3; 43:18–20; 55:1–3.
31. Ibid.

psalm and the scenes depicted in verses 4–32 make a much more fundamental claim about Israel's God. It is because of Yahweh's steadfast love
that he responds again and again to his people. Unlike other ancient Near
Eastern religions that demote the role and relationship of humankind to
the gods, Israel confesses that Yahweh, the God of the covenant, takes this
relationship seriously.[32] God's response to Israel's cry is evidence of that
seriousness and, even more, is evidence of the steadfast love undergirding
that commitment.

EXILED COMMUNITIES. Psalm 107 may appear to
be too historically located for contemporary
application. After all, when is the last time
you've heard people describe themselves as
"exiles" needing to be "gathered in from the lands"? But nightly there are
tragic news stories of people groups around the world for whom the threat
of becoming exiled is no longer metaphorical—it is existential and real.
In those contexts exile and the threat of exile remain daily realities. In
many industrial countries, however, such stories seem a world away, and
the thought of being exiled and alone seems inconceivable. For many in
the congregations where I preach, the thought of literally being lost in the
wilderness or being threatened upon the stormy seas likely never crosses
the mind.

Yet if exile by definition means to be forced from one's homeland,
from the place that creates both memory and meaning, then there are
many who know something of exile in its metaphorical sense. The four
scenes in Psalm 107 remind us all of the "essential weakness, neediness,
and sinfulness of humanity."[33] Those essential qualities of our human condition remind us that we stand at some distance from God. Those essential
qualities remind us that we are a long way from home. At times our lives
feel as though the north (*zaphon*) has come crashing down upon us and the
waters (*yam*) have threatened to overtake us. We need for God to gather
us back to himself again.

Even in our technological age, people are falling into exile in new
and more sophisticated ways. In her book *Alone Together*, Sherry Turkle, a
social psychologist at Massachusetts Institute of Technology, argues that

---

32. For a helpful overview of such issues, see John H. Walton, *Ancient Israelite Literature in
its Cultural Context* (Grand Rapids: Zondervan, 1989). See especially his analysis concerning
similarities and differences between the various cultures and their literature (pp. 229–48).
33. McCann, "Psalms," 1119.

people have started to use social technology as a means of a self-imposed exile.[34] When circumstances become challenging or conversations become difficult, people resort to social media as a means of escape. Rather than engaging others, people withdraw into a sophisticated form of isolationism. Ironically, for many people deliverance is associated with being exiled from others—a concept foreign to the psalmist and to the church.

Whether through wandering, confinement, sickness, or sinfulness, each one of us knows the truth of the claim that to be exiled means one is not at home. The psalmist does not minimize the threat of exile, and neither should we. Exile has the capacity to undo us all—and it would, "if the LORD had not been on our side" (Ps 124:1). The psalmist is clear: God alone is our source of deliverance from such desperate circumstances.

The faithful God. Psalm 107 takes seriously the plight of exile, but perhaps even more it takes seriously the only remedy, Yahweh. As noted above, the Hebrew word *hesed* appears throughout the psalm, thus declaring to all who were in exile *and* to all who are in exile that the steadfast love of God is a source of deliverance. The psalmist makes clear that this steadfast love manifests itself not as an emotion but instead through the power of God. To announce to those in our congregations who are enduring the "essential weakness, neediness, and sinfulness of humanity" that God loves them may not be enough. "Love" has become so stripped of its meaning in our culture that, regrettably, such a claim may be little more than an "empty metaphor" for some. They likely need more.

Those who occupy our pews know something of the "hunger and thirst" mentioned by the psalmist, and, even more, they know something of what it feels like when life seems to be ebbing away (v. 5). Some have sat in darkness and felt the weight of the shadow of death (v. 10). And many, if not all, have felt both their courage and their hope melt away amid calamity (v. 26). To tell a person that she or he is loved in those moments does little to extinguish the pain and angst associated with those times. Instead, people long to know of a faithful God who refuses to let exile have the final word. They want to know of a God who has performed "wonderful deeds" for his people in the past, even lifting up the needy out of affliction (v. 41), and they want to know that this God will act again even in their behalf. The final verse of the psalm instructs us in this way. If we are wise, we will give "heed" to these things and we too will consider the steadfast love of God (v. 43).

---

34. Sherry Turkle, *Alone Together: Why We Expect More from Technology and Less from Ourselves* (New York: Basic Books, 2011).

Psalm 108

A song. A psalm of David.

¹ My heart, O God, is steadfast;
    I will sing and make music with all my soul.
² Awake, harp and lyre!
    I will awaken the dawn.
³ I will praise you, LORD, among the nations;
    I will sing of you among the peoples.
⁴ For great is your love, higher than the heavens;
    your faithfulness reaches to the skies.
⁵ Be exalted, O God, above the heavens,
    let your glory be over all the earth.
⁶ Save us and help us with your right hand,
    that those you love may be delivered.
⁷ God has spoken from his sanctuary;
    "In triumph I will parcel out Shechem
    and measure off the Valley of Sukkoth.
⁸ Gilead is mine, Manasseh is mine;
    Ephraim is my helmet,
    Judah is my scepter.
⁹ Moab is my washbasin;
    on Edom I toss my sandal;
    over Philistia I shout in triumph."
¹⁰ Who will bring me to the fortified city?
    Who will lead me to Edom?
¹¹ Is it not you, God, you who have rejected us
    and no longer go out with our armies?
¹² Give us aid against the enemy,
    for human help is worthless.
¹³ With God we will gain the victory,
    and he will trample down our enemies.

Original Meaning

FOLLOWING PSALM 107, the first collection in Book 5 is a trilogy of psalms associated with David (Pss 108–10). In Book 4 of the Psalter (Pss 90–106) David is mentioned in the superscriptions of only two psalms (Pss 101 and 103), thus reducing significantly the role of David in that collection. In Book 5, small collections associated with David appear at the beginning of the collection (Pss 108–10) and at the end (Pss 138–45), thus creating a frame around Book 5. Some contend this renewed interest in David in the final book of the Psalter suggests an expression of hope in the postexilic period for "a restoration of the Davidic 'founding era.'"[1] Others suggest that David serves as a model for those who pray the psalms. The king was always seen as the "first citizen" or the "model citizen," and in Book 5 the image of David serves as model of piety for the psalmists.[2]

Psalm 108 is the first psalm in this short trilogy and is well known for its appropriation of two earlier psalms. Psalm 57:7–11 (an individual psalm of thanksgiving) and Psalm 60:5–12 (a communal lament) have been joined together in that order to create a new, composite psalm. Hans-Joachim Kraus once remarked that "it is . . . difficult, if not impossible to shed light" on the reasons for this composition.[3] The difficulty in determining such a rationale has often led to the neglect of Psalm 108 and the powerful testimony created by a psalmist. Phil Botha suggests that this style of psalm (an anthological style) was likely created in the postexilic period, when psalmists "made extensive use of texts which had already assumed a kind of canonical status" for the community.[4] The psalmist, however, did much more than simply "cut and paste" from earlier psalms. To the contrary, the psalmist adopted and adapted the earlier psalms to create a theological confession for the community at that point in Israel's history.

Close attention to the structure of Psalm 108 aids the interpreter in understanding the argument being constructed in the psalm. In the first strophe (vv. 1–4) the psalmist offers a song of praise celebrating God's love (*hesed*), which extends "higher than the heavens." In the second strophe (vv. 5–6) the psalmist pleads with Yahweh to demonstrate his glory cosmically and, in so doing, bring deliverance to his people. The psalmist has carefully constructed this section from *both* psalms. Verse 5 comes from Psalm 57, while verse 6 comes from Psalm 60, yet the psalmist has created a seamless connection, both grammatically and theologically, between the two psalms. The third strophe (vv. 7–9) contains a divine oracle in which God, as the Divine Warrior, declares a coming military triumph. The shift

---

1. Hossfeld and Zenger, *Psalms 3*, 118.

2. Wilson, *The Editing of the Hebrew Psalter*, 221; Wilson, "The Structure of the Psalter," 235–36. On the portrayal of David as the "poor servant" of Yahweh, see Tucker, *Constructing and Deconstructing Power in Psalms 107–150*, 181–83.

3. Hans-Joachim Kraus, *Psalms 60–150*, CC (Minneapolis: Fortress, 1993), 333.

4. Phil Botha, "Psalm 108 and the Quest for Closure," *Old Testament Essays* 23 (2010), 574.

to interrogative questions in verses 10 and 11 indicates another strophe in the psalm. In these verses, the psalmist pleads for Yahweh to act in behalf of people in their struggles with Edom. (The use of Edom as a cipher will be explored below.) The final strophe appears in verses 12–13. The psalm closes with a communal plea for God to deliver his people from their foes.

Although Psalm 108 is comprised of two earlier psalms this poem does possess a certain sense of unity. A common thread is woven throughout all five strophes. In each strophe the word for "God" (*'elohim*) appears. It is found in the first line of each of the first three strophes and appears twice in verse 11 in response to the questions raised in that strophe. In the final strophe (vv. 12–13) of the psalm, *'elohim* is the first word in verse 13. The frequent use of *'elohim* throughout the psalm suggests that it is thoroughly theocentric in orientation, thus driving the interpreter to consider what the psalmist is confessing about Israel's God.

The Heading (108:0)

THE HEADINGS OR SUPERSCRIPTIONS found in Psalms 57 and 60 both associate the psalm with events in the life of David. Psalm 57 alludes to the scene in which David escapes Saul by hiding in a cave (1 Sam 24), and Psalm 60 references the occasion when David fought with Aram-naharaim and with Aram-zobah (2 Sam 8).[5] Regarding these types of historical superscriptions, Clinton McCann explains that "these references should be not construed as historically accurate, but neither should they be dismissed as irrelevant. Rather they provide an illustrative narrative context" for interpreting the psalms.[6] Strikingly, however, in Psalm 108 the psalmist has omitted both historical superscriptions and prefers, instead, a much simpler heading, "A song. A psalm of David." The omission of the two previous headings and the introduction of a new category, "a song" (*shir*), in the superscription suggests that the psalmist was, in fact, creating a new psalm altogether and that it was meant to be understood as such.

A Song of Praise to God (108:1–4)

THE PSALM OPENS WITH A CALL to praise God in verses 1–3, followed by a rationale in verse 4. Verses 3 and 4, in particular, hint at the psalmist's interest in celebrating the universal and cosmic scope of Yahweh's kingship.

I will sing. The psalmist is prepared to "sing and make music" (v. 1b) because his heart is *nakon*, his heart is "steadfast" (NIV). In Psalm 107:1 the

---

5. There are thirteen psalms in total that connect a psalm with an incident in the life of David (Pss 3; 7; 18; 34; 51; 54; 56; 57; 59; 60; 63; 142).

6. McCann, "Psalms," 656.

psalmist declared that Yahweh's commitment to him was "steadfast," but in that context he used the term *hesed* clearly to reference the covenantal commitments Yahweh has made to his people. In Psalm 108, however, the psalmist opts for a different Hebrew term, *nakon*, to speak of himself as steadfast. The term can also mean "firm" or "set." The psalmist can sing of God because his heart remains firm or loyal despite the apparent challenges of the "enemy" mentioned later in verses 12–13.[7]

Phil Botha has suggested another interpretation of the term *nakon* in this context. In Hebrew's *niphal* verb stem, the term can also mean "to be ready." In Exodus 34:2 *nakon* is connected to the morning, as it is here in Psalm 108. In Exodus, Moses is told to be ready in the morning for the coming of Yahweh. Botha surmises that the use of *nakon* in conjunction with the morning imagery in Psalm 108 might refer to the psalmist's readiness to meet Yahweh as the morning dawns.

Awake, harp and lyre! In verse 2 the psalmist employs images and language that are suggestive of the early morning hours. Twice the psalmist uses the verb "awake" (*'ur*). In the first part of verse 3 the psalmist calls for the harp and lyre to awaken from their slumber. With the harp and lyre awake, the psalmist explains that he will awaken the dawn. The precise meaning of "waking the dawn" has yielded a number of suggestions. Perhaps most obviously, the phrase may refer to the psalmist's desire to start praising God even before the sun has risen. In other words, as the sun rises on the psalmist, he will already be in full praise of his God. Alternatively, the term can function metaphorically in the ancient Near East. Dawn signals the first light of the day, followed by sunrise. In the ancient Near East, sunrise signaled the appearance of the "god-king," who manifests himself with the rising of the sun. With his appearance, he provided sustaining life to all of creation.[8] This observation is not to suggest that Israel actually perceived God as the sun—only that the psalmist may have employed a frequent metaphorical image invoked in the ancient Near East in an effort to speak of the cosmic rule of Israel's God—God's rule extends over the world even as the sun rays do the same.[9] In short, while the former interpretation seems the most straightforward, the emphasis on the cosmic rule of God over all creation may warrant serious consideration.

---

7. See Botha, "Psalm 108 and the Quest for Closure," 576.

8. Hossfeld and Zenger, *Psalms 3*, 119.

9. In other postexilic texts the mention of the sun was in reference to God's saving presence with his people. On the larger issue of solar imagery in the Psalter, see William P. Brown, *Seeing the Psalms: A Theology of Metaphor* (Louisville: Westminster John Knox, 2002), 81–99.

I will praise you, LORD, among the nations. In verse 3 the psalmist says that he will "praise" Yahweh among the peoples. The dominant word for praise in the Psalter is *halal*. In Psalm 108 the word is *yadah*, which can be correctly translated as "praise." The term does, however, have another meaning that might be more suggestive in this context. The verb *yadah* can also mean "to confess." The psalmist is announcing that he will make a confession concerning all that God has done in behalf of his people—and that he will make that confession among the peoples and the nations.[10] By confessing God among nations, the psalmist also stakes out the claim that Yahweh is much more than a regional or tribal deity; this God is the Great King over all creation. The psalmist provides an explicit rationale to this claim in verse 4.[11] God's steadfast love is so great that it reaches above the heavens and his faithfulness (*'emet*) extends to the clouds. These defining features of the fidelity of Yahweh permeate the entire cosmos; there is no place on earth, in heaven, or even above the heavens to which God's faithfulness does not extend.

The Divine King is Mighty to Save (108:5–6)

IN VERSE 5 THE PSALMIST IMPLORES GOD to "be exalted" over the heavens.[12] This request continues the image suggested in verse 4—that of God's presence throughout the cosmos. Konrad Schmid has identified the diverse ways in which the writers of the Old Testament speak about the relationship between God and heaven and the implications of this kind

---

10. The second line of verse 3 reads *bal-'ummim*, which is often simply translated as "among the nations." The spelling of the phrase is somewhat unusual; it appears elsewhere only in Pss 44:15 and 149:7 (and the donor text, Ps 57:10). Raymond J. Tournay contends that this spelling is meant to be understood pejoratively and might be better translated as "among the *non*-nations." In other words, the psalmist was suggesting that these so-called nations are not really such and will not be until they acknowledge the universal King. See Raymond J. Tournay, "Psaumes 57, 60 et 108. Analyse et Interprétation," *RB* 96 (1989), 25. Hossfeld and Zenger follow Tournay in suggesting that "the nations will achieve their authentic politico-social form only when they acknowledge and accept YHWH as the world's king" (Hossfeld and Zenger, *Psalms 3*, 139). See also Botha, "Psalm 108 and the Quest for Closure," 579–80.

11. Verse 4 begins with the particle *ki*, which has a causal function in this context ("for," "because"). The psalmist makes his confession among the nations *because* the claims made in verse 4 are in fact true.

12. The verb *rum*, "be exalted," has an extensive range of meanings in the Old Testament and in verse 5 could be easily rendered as "arise" or "rise up." As Hossfeld and Zenger explain, the psalmist is requesting that "Yahweh should arise (from his throne) in order to put his royal glory into action" (Hossfeld and Zenger, *Psalms 3*, 120). With both translations, "be exalted" or "rise up," however, the emphasis remains on Yahweh's rightful place as Sovereign.

of metaphorical language.[13] Some texts, such as Psalm 108, portray God as above or beyond the heavens: "Be exalted, O God, above the heavens; let your glory be over all the earth" (v. 5). In such instances, the entire cosmos actually appears to serve as the sanctuary of God. Such an image reinforces the notion that God is king over all of the created order, both heaven and earth. Yet despite being enthroned above the heavens, with all creation as his sanctuary, God remains closely bound to this world. God sends out his steadfast love and faithfulness (v. 4) along with his glory (v. 5b) to fill the created order, thereby ensuring his felt presence in the world.[14] To be sure, God's presence above the heavens does not signal God's absence from his people; rather, it stresses his role as the Sovereign God over all creation.

Both the NIV and NRSV invert the order of the two clauses in verse 6. Following verse 5, the Hebrew text actually reads, "so that those you love may be delivered; Save with your right hand and answer me." The initial word in verse 6 is the Hebrew particle *lema'an*. This term often introduces a purpose clause, "so that" or "in order that." The purpose clause ("that those you love may be delivered") relates directly to the plea in the rest of verse 6 ("Save us and help us with your right hand").

In addition to the connection between verse 6a and 6b, the relationship between verses 5 and 6 should not be overlooked. The psalmist's request for God to rise up and be exalted over the heavens in verse 5 establishes the ground for the petition that follows in verse 6. Because Yahweh has assumed his rightful place over the heavens as Sovereign over the created world, the psalmist has confidence that God, and God alone, will deliver his people.

The Response of God (108:7–9)

IN THE HEBREW, VERSE 6 CONCLUDES with the petition for Yahweh to "answer me." As Marvin Tate has noted, the verb in this instance means "more than a verbal answer"; it means a response that announces both help and impending victory.[15] Or put differently, the psalmist desires more than simply a word from God; he yearns to see God act in behalf of the petitioner in distress. The anticipated response to the psalmist's request follows in

---

13. Konrad Schmid, "Himmelsgott, Weltgott, und Schöpfer: 'Gott' und der 'Himmel' in der Literatur der Zeit des Zweiten Tempels," in *Der Himmel*, ed. D. Sattler and S. Vollenweider (Neukirchen-Vluyn: Neukirchener Verlag, 2006), 111–48.

14. In other texts, God sends out his "word" to the world to ensure his presence with his people (cf. Ps 147:15, 18).

15. Tate, *Psalms 51–100*, 102.

the next section of the psalm, verses 7–9. While this "divine oracle" does provide a "verbal answer," it indicates much more; the response suggests God's intent to act on behalf of his people by bringing deliverance. This oracle resembles the kind given to a king just before a battle—an oracle ensuring the king's victory because Yahweh will fight for his people.[16]

God has spoken. The divine oracle is pregnant with metaphorical language and imagery, particularly those of a great king who is dividing up his spoil following a victory. The mention of Shechem and Sukkoth (v. 7) refers to the lands on both sides of the Jordan, with Shechem representing the lands to the west of the Jordan and Sukkoth the lands to the east. The geographical imagery continues in verse 8. Both Gilead and Mannasseh, clans associated with east of the Jordan, are declared to be the Lord's, as are Ephraim and Judah, the two major clans identified with west of the Jordan. Ephraim and Judah receive a special designation. Ephraim will function as the helmet for Yahweh, while Judah will serve as the scepter. The helmet mentioned in verse 8 likely refers to the impressive headgear of the king, while the scepter invokes images of royal rule.[17]

While Gilead, Manessah, Ephraim, and Judah receive positions of respect, Moab, Edom, and Philistia will become part of the conquered regions of Yahweh, and in their defeat they will be shamed. Although the entire geographical region identified marks out a territory reminiscent of the Davidic empire, the focus of the oracle remains upon Yahweh as a warrior in overcoming the powers that threaten the people of God. The oracle, then, is not primarily a "map" referring to the boundaries of a restored community but, instead, an affirmation that hostile forces can and will be overcome by the Divine Warrior with the goal of establishing a new order.[18]

Prayer for Help against the Enemies (108:10–13)

THE CONFIDENT CLAIM made in the divine oracle stands in grave tension with the realities articulated in verses 10–13. Although the divine oracle promises victory over the enemies and a restoration of order, the psalmist closes the psalm with the confession that things remain otherwise. The reference to Moab, Edom, and Philistia in verse 9, and to Edom again in verse 10, helps to highlight the threat being experienced by the psalmist.

---

16. Hossfeld and Zenger, *Psalms 3*, 120.

17. The image of a helmet (in Hebrew, literally the "protection of the head") could also figuratively represent the "place from which [Yahweh] will fend off all enemy attacks" (i.e., Ephraim), while the scepter represents the locus of divine rule (Judah). See Hossfeld and Zenger, *Psalms 3*, 120.

18. *Contra* Hossfeld and Zenger, *Psalms 3*, 123.

The literal place names mentioned first in Psalm 60 are now likely understood as symbolic aggressors in Psalm 108. The language in verses 3 and 5, and in particular the psalmist's location "among nations [and] the peoples," suggests that the psalmist has adapted this language. Although he mentions Edom in verse 10b, the ideas associated with Edom as the enemy have been extended. As Tournay explains, "the perspectives have been universalized. Edom has become the symbol of all the enemies of God and God's people."[19] The threat of enemies poses serious issues related to protection and deliverance, but equally so, if not more, the threat of the enemies generates serious theological questions.

Is it not you, God, who have rejected us . . . ? The threat of the enemy raises several questions in verses 10–11. In verse 10 both questions begin with the interrogative *mi* ("who"), and both questions simply inquire whether there is anyone to lead them against the enemy threats. The question in verse 11, however, is far more pointed and aimed directly at God. The psalmist returns to second-person language ("you") in addressing his question to God. The fundamental question in verse 11 is whether God has abandoned his people altogether and left them alone to face their enemies, whether God has "rejected" (*zanah*) his people. The events of the exile seemed to have prompted this kind of question elsewhere in the Psalter. The verb *zanah* appears in Psalm 74:1 as the people lament the destruction of their temple, and the word appears again in Psalm 89:38 as the people lament the apparent rejection of the Davidic covenant in the light of the exile.[20] This fear that God has rejected them and will not go forth in battle with his people likely explains the psalmist's request in Psalm 108:5 that God "be exalted" or "rise up" to his proper place in the heavens. The perception that God is not going out with his people (v. 11) inspires the psalmist to plead with God to return to his rightful place in the cosmos so that he might act again and deliver his people.

He will trample down our enemies. The community pleads in verse 12 for Yahweh to help against "the enemy" (*tsar*) and concludes the psalm with an affirmation that "it is he who will tread down our enemies [*tsar*]." This term appears in the previous poem (Ps 107:2), where it references

---

19. Tournay, *Seeing and Hearing God with the Psalms*, 181. Oracles against Edom were common in the prophetic literature (cf. Isa 34:1–17; 63:1–6; Jer 49:7–22; Ezek 25:12–14; 35:1–15; and Obad 1–15). The vitriolic rhetoric reserved for Edom shortly after the exile, however, was later applied to other nations. The use of Edom, in particular, as a cipher for an empire can be found extending down to the Targum Psalms, where both the "wicked city of Rome" and "Constantinople" are mentioned in connection with Edom.

20. See also Lam 3:31 for a similar usage.

geopolitical powers. The location of the psalmist among the peoples and the nations in Psalm 108:3 coupled with the plea for God to manifest himself "over all the earth" (v. 5) suggests that the foe (*tsar*) in Psalm 108, like in Psalm 107:2, must in fact be geopolitical powers capable of continuing to threaten the people of God. Earlier in Psalm 108:10, the psalmist asked who would go up with him against the enemy. In verse 12b, he confesses that the help of humans is "worthless."[21] The psalmist concludes with a plea that God will come to the aid of his people followed by a confession (v. 13b) that God and God alone can tread down Israel's foes.

THE STEADFAST LOVE OF GOD. In Psalm 107 the psalmist celebrated God's faithfulness and steadfast love in returning the dispersed people of God to Jerusalem. Psalm 108 continues the theme of the steadfast love of God, but in this instance the psalmist explores its implications for the people of the postexilic community who face threats from those around them. In verse 4 the psalmist praises God for his *hesed* ("love") and his *'emet* ("faithfulness"), thus declaring that God's covenantal commitments are not only present but have also filled the cosmos. Through such metaphorically rich language the psalmist affirms that God's covenantal commitments remain valid, true, and ever present. This conviction prompts the psalmist to sing aloud praises to God despite the presence of nations and peoples (v. 3). Rolf Jacobson contends that the dominant theological confession of the Psalter is, "the Lord is faithful."[22] These two Hebrew terms *hesed* ("steadfast love") and *'emet* ("faithfulness") are part of a larger semantic field he identifies with the term "fidelity."[23]

The psalmist exhorts Yahweh to assume his rightful place "above the heavens" (v. 5). While the language concerning God's presence "above the heavens" may sound somewhat strange in an age of science, such language should not be too quickly dismissed as pre-scientific speculation or simply as rhetorical flare; rather, the psalmist is making a fundamental, theological

---

21. Various psalms in Book 5 of the Psalter portray human power as inefficacious in warding off impending threats. See Tucker, *Constructing and Deconstructing Power in Psalms 107–150*, 169–74.

22. Rolf A. Jacobson, "The Faithfulness of the Lord Endures Forever': The Theological Witness of the Psalter," in *Soundings in the Theology of Psalms: Perspectives and Methods in Contemporary Scholarship*, ed. R. A. Jacobson (Minneapolis, MN: Fortress, 2011), 111.

23. Ibid., 113. Other terms in this word field include: "righteous/righteousness" (*tsedeq/tsedaqah*); "deliverance/salvation" (*yeshu'ah*); "mercy" (*rehem*); "grace" (*hanan*); "justice" (*mishpat*); "good/goodness" (*tov/tovah*); and "faithfulness" (*'emunah*).

claim concerning the kingship of God. God stands over all creation as the Divine King, whose "glory" fills the earth (v. 6). And because he is the Divine King who rules from on high, the psalmist pleads for the right hand of Yahweh to give him aid.[24]

While God had been faithful to bring the community back home, the question remained whether God would be faithful to protect his people in the face of dire threats. The question is further complicated by God's apparent silence or failure to act as suggested in verse 11. In that verse the psalmist toys with the question of whether God has ultimately rejected his people and will no longer go with them into battle. While this verse may look out of place in a psalm focused on the fidelity of Yahweh, it actually contributes to the nature of the psalm itself. Patrick Miller has remarked that, while the "structure of faith does not *require* questions concerning the presence and power of God, the prayer of faith *permits* such questions and usually cannot avoid them."[25] In this instance, however, the description of such dire circumstances actually functions as grounds for the expectation of help from God.[26] This is surely the case in Psalm 108 given that the following verses plead for God's assistance (v. 12) and confess the certainty of his power (v. 13).

God as Divine Warrior and source of power. The image of Yahweh as a Divine Warrior appears throughout the Old Testament with varied meanings and nuances.[27] These descriptions are laden with poetically rich language and imagery. In Exodus 15, for example, God appears as the dreaded warrior (v. 3) who piled up the waters with the blast of his nostrils (v. 8) and drove Pharaoh's armies into the heart of the sea with his right hand. In Habakkuk 3 the imagery only grows richer. Yahweh comes from Teman with rays of light flashing forth from his hands and plagues following after him (v. 5). In Psalm 68 Yahweh appears as the Warrior King riding across the heavens presumably in a chariot en route to battle (v. 33). These and other similar texts help populate the image of "God as warrior" with rich and textured meanings.

---

24. On the reference to Yahweh as the "God of heaven," see Tucker, *Constructing and Deconstructing Power in Psalms 107–150*, 142–53.

25. Patrick D. Miller, *They Cried to the Lord: The Form and Theology of Biblical Prayer* (Minneapolis, MN: Fortress, 1994), 133. Emphasis added.

26. The question asked in verse 11 is an example of what can be termed a "motive clause" in biblical prayer. As Miller explains, "the description of the plight of the petitioner, the lament over trouble and affliction, can be understood as evoking or eliciting the sympathetic response of God" (ibid., 114).

27. Tremper Longman III and Daniel G. Reid, *God is a Warrior*, Studies in Old Testament Biblical Theology (Grand Rapids: Zondervan, 1995).

In Psalm 108, however, the imagery remains rather reserved. When the psalmist announces the divine oracle in verses 7–9, God self-describes as the Warrior King prepared to lay waste to Israel's enemies. The only images invoked are those of the helmet and scepter (v. 8), along with Yahweh's battle cry (v. 9). Beyond that, the psalmist remains restrained in his description of the Divine Warrior. The crisis for the psalmist, however, is not the image itself but the fact that God no longer appears to go out with Israel's armies as the Warrior King (v. 11). The striking move in Psalm 108 is that despite God's perceived absence as the Warrior King, the community remains steadfast in their commitment to this God. Repeatedly throughout the psalm, the psalmist or the community confesses that their hope for deliverance remains with God and God alone (vv. 1, 6, 12–13). As suggested above, the community refuses to put their trust in human help (v. 12b); such help remains worthless in the face of such grave threats. True help can only come from Israel's God, the Divine Warrior, who is enthroned in the heavens.

FIRM CONVICTION. In Psalm 108 the psalmist is resolute in his belief that God remains faithful to his covenant people. As noted above, in the opening line the psalmist indicates that his heart is steadfast or firm. Because such a declaration of God's faithfulness is not altogether surprising in the Psalter, we are prone to read over the opening line, since it does appear so formulaic. Yet if we keep reading Psalm 108, we discover that the psalmist remains in need of deliverance, that the enemies continue as a threat, and that God does not appear to be coming on the immediate horizon. Despite these realities, the psalmist seeks to awaken the dawn (v. 3a) in anticipation of God's work. He believes the steadfast love of God fills the cosmos *even if* circumstances may suggest otherwise. The psalmist implores God to be exalted and to rise up above the heavens in order to deliver "those you love." And in the end—even when it seems God no longer goes out with the psalmist's army—the poet confesses that it is God alone who can deliver his people. From beginning to end the psalmist remains firm in his commitment and steadfast in his conviction concerning the faithfulness of Yahweh. In so doing, the writer models for us the kind of deeply rooted faith that permeates the Psalter.

Like the psalmist, circumstances in everyday life, both expected and unexpected, crowd in upon our lives and often threaten to define life for us. Worse yet, such circumstances frequently threaten to define God for us. It is not so much that we want such circumstances to define God or our lives—we just seem inclined to allow it to happen. But it does not occur without serious consequences. In his small classic treatise, *Your God is Too Small,* J. B. Phillips reminds us all of the danger this poses for the life of faith. Phillips explains, "the conception of the character of God which slowly forms in our minds is largely made by the conclusions we draw from the 'providences' and 'judgments of life.' We envisage 'God' very largely from the way in which He appears to deal with (or not to deal with) His creatures."[28] Phillips then explains that if we allow such events to define God, then we are "likely to find ourselves with a second-hand god who is quite different from the real one."[29] The psalmist refuses to believe in a second-hand god because he refuses to allow the circumstances that surround him to define God. Had the psalmist done so, he would have arrived at a very deficient view of God—one that is theologically at odds with the faithful God to whom all of Scripture witnesses.

---

28. J. B. Phillips, *Your God is Too Small* (New York: Macmillan, 1961), 44.
29. Ibid.

Psalm 109

❦

For the director of music. Of David. A psalm.

[1] My God, whom I praise,
    do not remain silent.
[2] for people who are wicked and deceitful
    have opened their mouths against me;
    they have spoken against me with lying tongues.
[3] With words of hatred they surround me;
    they attack me without cause.
[4] In return for my friendship they accuse me,
    but I am a man of prayer.
[5] They repay me evil for good,
    and hatred for my friendship.
[6] Appoint someone evil to oppose my enemy;
    let an accuser stand at his right hand.
[7] When he is tried, let him be found guilty,
    and may his prayers condemn him.
[8] May his days be few;
    may another take his place of leadership.
[9] May his children be fatherless
    and his wife a widow.
[10] May his children be wandering beggars;
    may they be driven from their ruined homes.
[11] May a creditor seize all he has;
    may strangers plunder the fruits of his labor.
[12] May no one extend kindness to him
    or take pity on his fatherless children.
[13] May his descendants be cut off,
    their names blotted out from the next generation.
[14] May the iniquity of his fathers be remembered before
    the Lord;
    may the sin of his mother never be blotted out.
[15] May their sins always remain before the Lord,
    that he may blot out their name from the earth.
[16] For he never thought of doing a kindness,
    but hounded to death the poor
    and the needy and the brokenhearted.

¹⁷ He loved to pronounce a curse—
  may it come back on him.
He found no pleasure in blessing—
  may it be far from him.
¹⁸ He wore cursing as his garment;
  it entered into his body like water,
  into his bones like oil.
¹⁹ May it be like a cloak wrapped about him,
  like a belt tied forever around him.
²⁰ May this be the LORD's payment to my accusers,
  to those who speak evil of me.
²¹ But you, Sovereign LORD,
  help me for your name's sake;
  out of the goodness of your love, deliver me.
²² For I am poor and needy,
  and my heart is wounded within me.
²³ I fade away like an evening shadow;
  I am shaken off like a locust.
²⁴ My knees give way from fasting;
  my body is thin and gaunt.
²⁵ I am an object of scorn to my accusers;
  when they see me, they shake their heads.
²⁶ Help me, LORD my God;
  save me according to your unfailing love.
²⁷ Let them know that it is your hand,
  that you, LORD, have done it.
²⁸ While they curse, may you bless;
  may those who attack me be put to shame,
  but may your servant rejoice.
²⁹ May my accusers be clothed with disgrace
  and wrapped in shame as in a cloak.
³⁰ With my mouth I will greatly extol the LORD;
  in the great throng of worshipers I will praise him.
³¹ For he stands at the right hand of the needy,
  to save their lives from those who would condemn them.

Original Meaning

FOR MANY CHRISTIANS Psalm 109 remains problematic. Often termed an imprecatory or "cursing" psalm, this poem employs language and imagery that appears to stand outside the bounds of what many readers would consider to be appropriate content for a prayer. As indicative of its treatment, or lack thereof, by Christians, Psalm 109 is one of the very few psalms that does not appear in the three-year lectionary cycle. Its exclusion might give the modern reader cause for dismissing this psalm altogether, yet the very nature of this challenging poem invites the reader into a prayer that recognizes the reality of violence humans may do to one another. While this psalm probes the dark side of human relationships, it performs a pastoral function as the psalmist is required to lean fully into a just God.

Psalm 109 can be divided into three main strophes: verses 1–5, 6–19, and 20–31. Scholars are agreed that the first and last sections of the psalm appear to be the prayer of the psalmist. The middle section, verses 6–19, has received the bulk of attention. In verses 1–5 the psalmist refers to the enemy using third-person plural language ("they") and returns to the use of plural language in the third section. In the middle section, however, the enemy is referred to in the first-person singular (i.e., "my enemy" [v. 6]). This shift in person has led some writers to contend that the middle section includes the charges labeled against the psalmist by the enemies. In other words, according to this interpretation verses 6–19 represent the words the enemies used against the psalmist himself. This interpretation helps explain why the NRSV inserts the words, "They say," at the beginning of verse 6. In the Hebrew text, however, no introductory formula is present. The text simply begins with the imperative "appoint" (*hapqed*). The Septuagint follows similarly (i.e., no introductory formula and the presence of an imperative). The NIV renders the text accordingly by beginning with the imperative "appoint." Regarding the switch to the singular in verses 6–19, several suggestions are possible options. James Mays has suggested that these verses are along the lines of a "formulaic curse used against each of the enemies."[1] More likely is Bernd Janowski's contention that the singular form is often used in Hebrew to describe a type, such as an enemy.[2] In short, the middle section of the psalm contains a series of curses spoken by the psalmist, who is using language often invoked against any enemy.

In an attempt to understand the purpose of Psalm 109, scholars have typically focused on the *Sitz im Leben*, or "setting in life," of the psalm. The general consensus is that at some point this psalm would have been used within the temple complex, where an innocent person would appear before

1. James L. Mays, *Psalms*, Interpretation (Louisville: Westminster John Knox, 1994), 349.

2. Bernd Janowski, *Arguing with God: A Theological Anthropology of the Psalms*, trans. Armin Siedlecki (Louisville: Westminster John Knox, 2003), 106.

the priestly judges in the hope of rebuffing false accusations. This position is argued most notably by Hans Schmidt.[3] Although Ps 109 is an individual rather than communal petition, Sigmund Mowinckel noted that there are a number of "I-Psalms," which are quite personal but in reality are national or congregational psalms, and among those, he includes Psalm 109.[4] Others have proposed a similar reading. Mowinckel's student Harris Birkeland connected Psalm 109 with a number of other psalms in which war appears to be a dominant theme; he thus concluded that a collective reading of such psalms seems preferable.[5] More recent interpreters such as John Eaton and Michael Goulder have adopted a collective or national understanding of the psalm as well.[6] While intriguing, the evidence marshaled by Mowickel, Birkeland, Eaton, and Goulder ultimately proves unconvincing. Rather than claiming the psalm was *composed* with the community in mind, Croft suggests that a collective understanding of the psalm was imposed only secondarily.[7] The theological claims in the psalm that proved relevant for the individual psalmist likely found resonance with the later and larger community of faith.

The Complaint (109:1–5)

IN MANY WAYS PSALM 109 follows the general pattern of a lament psalm with the first five verses including an appeal to Yahweh for assistance amid threatening circumstances.[8] That both the direct appeal and a general description of the crisis are explicated in these opening lines sets the tone for the curses to follow and a second plea for help later in the psalm (vv. 21–29), followed by a vow of praise (vv. 30–31).

---

3. The classic formulation of this position is found in Hans Schmidt, *Das Gebet der Angeklagten im Alten Testament*, BZAW 49 (Berlin: Alfred Töpelmann, 1928). Although more recent studies have set aside Schmidt's initial claim regarding detention and imprisonment, they have retained the emphasis on the psalm as a prayer of an unjustly accused individual. See, for example, Allen, *Psalms 101–150*, 76, and Klaus Seybold, *Introducing the Psalms* (Edinburgh: T&T Clark, 1990), 162–64.

4. Sigmund Mowinckel, *The Psalms in Israel's Worship*, 2 vols. (Oxford: Basil Blackwell, 1962),1:219.

5. Harris Birkeland, *The Evildoer in the Book of Psalms* (Oslo: Jacob Dybwad, 1955), 31–33.

6. John Eaton, *Kingship and the Psalms*, The Biblical Seminar 3 (Sheffield: JSOT Press, 1980), 81; Michael D. Goulder, *The Psalms of the Return: Book V, Psalms 107–150*, JSOTSup 258 (Sheffield: Sheffield Academic, 1998), 133–34.

7. Steven J. L. Croft, *The Identity of the Individual in the Psalms*, JSOTSup 14 (Sheffield: JSOT Press, 1987), 32, 77, 134, and 180.

8. Noticeably absent from Ps 109 are two features that frequently appear in lament psalms: (1) complaints or accusations against God; and (2) questions such as "How long?" or "Why, O Lord?"

Do not remain silent. The first five verses refer repeatedly to acts of speaking. In verse 1 the psalmist announces that he praises God, while a few verses later he explains that those around him continue to assault him with lying words. In the midst of this context, the psalmist pleads with Yahweh not to remain silent. The verb *ḥrsḥ* can mean "to keep silent," but it can also mean "to be deaf." The nominal form of the verb *ḥeresḥ* actually refers to someone who is deaf (Isa 42:18). The plea for Yahweh not to remain silent is actually a plea for Yahweh not to remain deaf to the cry of the petitioner. The psalmist's ears have been filled with false accusations from the enemy; having heard those accusations, the psalmist cannot remain silent any longer, and he calls upon Yahweh to do the same. The psalmist associates action with having been heard, so the fact that nothing has changed in his present circumstance suggests to the psalmist that Yahweh has not heard, that he remains silent.

Words of hatred. In verses 2–5 the psalmist rehearses the situation that has prompted this prayer. Verses 2–3a refer to acts of speech. In verse 2 the Hebrew reads literally, "a wicked mouth and a deceitful mouth" are against the psalmist. This claim is amplified in the following cola as the psalmist complains about the "lying tongues" and the hateful words that surround him (v. 3a). The chief complaint of the psalmist is that these individuals "attack" him "without cause" (v. 3b). Military metaphors are frequently employed in laments psalms (cf. Pss 35:1–3; 56:1–2; 120:1–7), and the pictures of being "surrounded" and "attacked" only heighten the imagery in this text. This imagery may serve as a corrective for those who cannot understand why the psalmist is so vexed by a little gossip ("lying tongues"). For him, such "words of hatred" are life-threatening.[9] The social relationships of the psalmist have been skewed as loyalty and friendship (vv. 4a, 5b) have given way to accusation and hatred.

Request for an Accuser (109:6–7)

GIVEN THE SERIOUSNESS OF HIS PREDICAMENT, the psalmist turns to God for help in the form of an extended request. Nearly every verse in this section contains an imperative or a jussive verbal form ("May"), with the accuser as the recipient of that plea.

Let an accuser stand at his right hand. In verse 6 the psalmist makes a request. As he has been charged by a wicked person (*rasḥaʿ* [v. 2]), the

---

9. See Robert Davidson, *The Vitality of Worship: A Commentary on the Book of Psalms* (Grand Rapids: Eerdmans, 1998), 360. Davidson contends that a possible outcome for the psalmist could have been a death sentence. More striking is Ryan Stokes's contention that the Hebrew word for "accuse" actually could mean "to attack with lethal intent" (Ryan Stokes, "Satan: Yahweh's Executioner," *JBL* 133 [2014]: 251–70).

psalmist requests that a wicked person be appointed over those who have made false claims. In the second half of verse 6 the psalmist requests that an accuser, or *satan*, stand against the enemy. Although the word *satan* accrues additional meaning in later biblical texts, the meaning here suggests a prosecutor. The entire request by the psalmist is meant as a mockery of the judicial process under which he has been tried.

The psalmist requests that once the enemy is tried, "let him be found guilty." The Hebrew word for "guilty" is *rasha'*; those with wicked mouths (*rasha'* [v. 2a]) will be declared *rasha'*, "wicked" or "guilty." And even if the enemy offers up a plea to Yahweh, the psalmist requests that such a prayer would be considered something like "sin" (*hata'ah*; NIV "condem him") or, better yet, that such a prayer would simply "miss the mark."[10]

Request for a Just Sentence (109:8–19)

LET HIM BE FOUND GUILTY. Following the psalmist's request for a trial and, even further, that the enemy be found guilty, the psalmist then provides a lengthy list of presumed punishments that should be exacted upon the enemy. Such an unadulterated list of curses challenges the modern reader. May his life be cut short (v. 8). May his wife and children endure a meager future as beggars (v. 10). May all his property be seized and his descendants blotted out (v. 13). The psalmist even requests that this curse be retroactive and that the enemy's mother and father have their sins "be remembered before the LORD" (v. 15). The apparent vitriol in verses 8–15, however, may best be understood if the reader considers the psalmist's claim in verses 16–19.

He . . . hounded to death the poor. The psalmist offers a rationale for why the enemy is deserving of such a harsh sentence. In verse 16 the enemy is chastised for having never remembered to show *hesed* ("kindness") to the "poor and the needy" or the brokenhearted but, instead, hounded them to death. To those in need the enemy showed no compassion. Not only did the enemy fail to show compassion to the most vulnerable, he actually thrived on the cursing of others (v. 17). To be more precise, the Hebrew in verse 17 actually says, "He loved cursing and it entered him."[11] The psalmist then offers an extended simile to illustrate how deeply seated this propensity to curse others was for the enemy.[12] He wore cursing like

---

10. McCann, "The Book of Psalms," 1126.

11. The NIV and NRSV repoint the second verb in verse 17 so that it reads like a jussive, "may it come back on him" (NIV). The Hebrew, however, has a *waw consecutive* attached to an imperfect, or *yiqtol*, verb suggesting an action that has already occurred (i.e., "it entered him").

12. Anne Marie Kitz, "Effective Simile and Effective Act: Psalm 109, Numbers 5, and *KUB* 26," *CBQ* 69 (2007): 440–56.

a garment that wrapped about him. Like water and oil that soaks into the body, so too had curses saturated this enemy. Yet unlike water that can be lost through normal bodily functions or like oil whose effects gradually dissipate, for this enemy the proclivity to cursing is like a "belt tied forever around him."

Request for Deliverance (109:20–25)

IN THIS SECOND REQUEST FOR DELIVERANCE the psalmist invokes two images, one for Yahweh and the other for the psalmist. The first image references Yahweh as the covenantal partner of the psalmist. He cries out in verse 21, "But you, Sovereign LORD," which invokes both Yahweh's covenantal name as well as his position within the covenantal relationship. In addition, the psalmist pleads with Yahweh for the sake of Yahweh's name or, better yet, for the sake of his reputation. In patron-client relationships, the failure of the patron to act would certainly have brought shame and discredit to the patron.[13] The psalmist then requests that Yahweh deliver him "out of the goodness of your love." The word *hesed* ("love") appears again in this psalm, and once again it suggests covenantal faithfulness and loyal love. The psalmist pleads with Yahweh, his lord, to do his good work by demonstrating his faithfulness to the psalmist amid such dire circumstances.

The second image is that of the psalmist. Whereas Yahweh is depicted as the master, capable of delivering the psalmist (v. 21b), the psalmist describes himself as the servant, one of the "poor and needy." The enemy was chastised for hounding the poor and needy to death earlier in the psalm (v. 16), but in this section Yahweh's faithfulness to the poor and needy is foundational to the psalmist's claim. By declaring himself among the poor and needy, the psalmist invokes the royal responsibility of Yahweh to act on behalf of the poor and needy, including the psalmist himself. The subsequent metaphors in verse 23 suggest that the life of the psalmist is gradually being extinguished; it is fading away like an evening shadow. The image of the locust could be interpreted in one of two ways. Like a locust easily shaken off one's garments, so too is the life of the psalmist. Peter Riede, in his study of metaphors in the psalms, suggests that this metaphor might allude to the practice of rising early in the morning to shake the locusts off the trees or other structures to be boiled or fried.[14] The implication is that without the aid of Yahweh, life is quickly coming to a disastrous end.

---

13. W. Dennis Tucker Jr., "Is Shame a Matter of Patronage in the Communal Laments?" *JSOT* 31 (2007): 465–80.

14. Peter Riede, *Im Netz des Jägers: Studien zur Feindmetaphorik der Individualpsalmen*, WMANT 85 (Neukirchen-Vluyn: Neukirchener Verlag, 2000), 315–26.

The psalmist shifts from metaphorical language about the psalmist's life and the nearness of its end in verse 23 to a more graphic description of his body in verse 24. The psalmist appears as an emaciated figure, worn down and weary. Although the NIV explains that his knees "give way from fasting," the meaning of the text is captured better in John Goldingay's translation, "My knees have collapsed from hunger."[15] The psalmist has grown thin and emaciated; his very appearance invokes the scorn of others.

Request for Deliverance (109:26–29)

THE PREVIOUS PETITION IN VERSES 21–25 gave attention to the plight of the psalmist with the intent of stirring Yahweh to action. The third petition of the psalmist appears in verses 26–29, where attention turns to the enemy. In verse 26 the psalmist pleads for Yahweh to save him "according to your unfailing love" (*hesed*). The same word appears in the first verse of the previous petition (v. 21) as well. The NIV, however, translates *hesed* as "love" in verse 21 and "unfailing love" in verse 26, thus, unfortunately, missing the intended connection seen between the two petitions.[16] Both petitions begin by laying claim to the significance of Yahweh's *hesed*; Yahweh will act for the sake of his name (v. 21); his action is rooted in his covenantal loyalty (vv. 21, 26).

The psalmist draws heavily from the language of cursing and blessing as well as honor and shame. The cursing of the psalmist by the enemies has led to great shame. The psalmist acknowledges that the enemies have the power to curse (v. 28), but he also believes that Yahweh has the power to bless—a power that is greater than that of the enemy. The psalmist, therefore, requests that Yahweh bless him (v. 28b) while clothing the accusers in shame (v. 29). At first glance such a request may appear retaliatory, but in a culture dominated by honor and shame, if Yahweh shows his "hand," delivers the psalmist, and clears the psalmist of any wrong, then the enemies have lost face. They are "wrapped in shame as in a cloak" (v. 29). Even as the enemies had worn cursing as a garment (v. 18), their garments of cursing (and presumed power) will be replaced with a garment of shame (v. 29) once Yahweh acts.

Promise of Praise (109:30–31)

THE POEM CONCLUDES IN A MANNER typical of a lament psalm by promising worship of Yahweh and declaration of his name in the presence of others.

---

15. Goldingay, *Psalms 3*, 286.

16. Hossfeld and Zenger suggest that the presence of *hesed* in both sections of the psalm creates an "arc" of meaning between them. Although each petition is addressing different issues, they are both grounded in the covenantal faithfulness of Yahweh (Hossfeld and Zenger, *Psalms 3*, 135).

In the final verse the psalmist concludes by claiming that Yahweh "stands at the right hand of the needy" to deliver them. This declaration appears to function as a response to the opening claim in the psalm. In verse 1 the psalmist pleads for Yahweh to remain silent no longer (v. 1). For the poet, the silence of God appears inextricably linked to the inactivity of God. In the opening of the psalm he suggests that God's perceived inactivity and silence suggest something of God's apparent absence in the midst of the situation of great suffering and unjust accusation. Despite this apparent silence, the psalmist can do nothing else but confess what he knows to be true, namely, that God stands at the "right hand" of the needy. In the end, the psalmist does not allow injustice and the resulting despair to define his world. On the contrary, he declares that God will stand alongside those unjustly accused, including the psalmist himself. According to him, this God will stand "at the right hand of the needy." Earlier in the psalm the poet self-describes as "poor and needy" (v. 22). By declaring in the final verse that Yahweh stands at the right hand of the needy, the psalmist asserts his belief that God must be standing alongside him as well.[17]

GOD OF JUSTICE. The rhetoric of Psalm 109, and particularly the language found in verses 6–19, can become a stumbling block for many readers. The explicit requests by the psalmist for God to destroy the enemy and make the enemy's family vulnerable leaves the modern reader uneasy at best, if not theologically flummoxed. Instead of reflecting on this challenging text more deeply in an effort to explore the theological claims found in such a psalm, many readers understandably ignore it, thus jettisoning it from their own "canon within a canon." Yet even on such a challenging psalm as this, extended reflection is profitable.

Within Psalm 109 there are theological strands that remain consistent with the larger witness of Scripture. One of the theological strands that spans both testaments is the notion of justice, and in particular the notion of Yahweh's role as the God of justice. In the case of Psalm 109, the psalmist does not bring his complaint to God because he believes God is "on his side" or because he believes God is a vindictive or even vengeful god.

---

17. Although the use of the "hand" metaphor earlier in the psalm (v. 27) relates to the power of God, the use of another hand metaphor in verse 31 is meant to reinforce the image of the presence of God. See Tucker, *Constructing and Deconstructing Power in Psalms 107–150*, 149–53.

Instead, the psalmist brings his petition to God because he understands God as the God of justice, the one who seeks to make things right. Erich Zenger and Frank-Lothar Hossfeld actually reject the claim that this psalm should be labeled "a psalm of cursing and vengeance." On the contrary, they suggest that this psalm should be called a "justice psalm" because of the psalmist's reliance upon God to provide justice.[18]

This theological tenet (i.e., Yahweh is the God of justice) is found repeatedly in the prophetic literature. The prophet Amos, for example, alludes specifically to injustice in the courts in Amos 5:1–17. Amos roundly condemns those who lie in court (v. 10), those who take bribes, and those who deprive the poor (v. 12). At the center of this lengthy indictment, Yahweh announces, "I know how many are your offenses and how great your sins" (v. 12). As a result of such injustice, Yahweh announces that he will pass through their midst in judgment (v. 17). In short, the prophet Amos announces to those in the Northern Kingdom that injustice will not and cannot go unobserved by the God of justice. Not only will God see it—he will also respond to it.

Not surprisingly, this theme appears in the New Testament. James indicts the rich for egregious displays of wealth while failing to pay fair wages to those who worked for them. Worse yet, the rich oppressors condemn and murder those who are innocent (Jas 5:6). James warns the wealthy oppressors that the cries of the victims have "reached the ears of the Lord Almighty" (Jas 5:4). Similar to the message communicated by the prophet Amos and the writer of Psalm 109, the message of James assumes that because God hears the cries of the oppressed, God will act.

In the opening strophe of Psalm 109, the psalmist outlines the injustice before him. He has been falsely accused, his enemies have spoken with "lying tongues," and they have uttered "words of hatred" (vv. 2b–3a). As a result of such injustice and its effects, the psalmist refers to himself three times, each time using a verbless clause. In such clauses the first-person pronoun "I" is used plus a description of the "I" but without using a verb. These references tell us something about the psalmist's sense of identity. Two are worth noting in particular. In verse 22, the psalmist confesses, "I am poor and needy." In verse 25 he declares that, as a result of the unjust accusations, he has become an "object of scorn." These labels position the psalmist as one without power, one unable to right this wrong. Because of his powerlessness in the face of injustice, the psalmist calls upon the God of justice to help him (vv. 21, 26) and to save him (v. 26).

---

18. Hossfeld and Zenger, *Psalms 3*, 128.

GIVEN THE CHALLENGING NATURE of this psalm and its exclusion from the lectionary, the modern reader might question whether there is, in fact, any "contemporary significance" at all for a psalm such at this one. If, however, all Scripture is indeed "useful for teaching, rebuking, correcting and training" (2 Tim 3:16), then Psalm 109 must have some word for the communities of faith that still understand it as part of its Scripture. To communicate rightly the contemporary significance of this psalm requires sound exegesis and careful theological construction. In biblical interpretation it is always possible to make interpretive moves that are less than desirable and often lead to troubling theological conclusions. Likewise, it is possible to choose interpretive moves that can and should be made—moves that allow the interpretive conclusions to remain consistent with the larger witness of Scripture. An example of each approach is considered below.

Praying people to death. Regrettably, in the history of the Christian tradition this psalm has often been used to "pray someone to death." In other words, this psalm has been understood as a "curse psalm" in every sense of the word. In particular, Psalm 109:8–9 has been prayed against others to ask that a person's "days be few," thereby making his children orphans and his wife a widow. John Calvin, in his commentary on the Psalms, notes this frequent use of the psalm in his own time. He explains:

> All the more to be condemned is the sacrilege committed by the monks, especially the Franciscans, when they desecrate this psalm. For it is no secret that anyone who has a deadly enemy he [or she] wants to ruin employs one of these villains to recite the psalm daily against him [or her].[19]

During the eighteenth century some people believed one needed only to pray this psalm for an entire year plus nine days in order to have its mortal effect upon a person's enemy. Erich Zenger notes this type of usage was prevalent in Switzerland, Bavaria, and Swabia well into the ninteenth century.[20] Such uses of the Scriptures were rooted in local superstition and a clear misunderstanding of the function of the biblical text.

One would like to hope that congregations and Christians no longer fall prey to such misuse of this psalm, but in an overly politicized and radically polemicized culture, such as the type found in the United States

---

19. Zenger, *A God of Vengeance? Understanding the Psalms of Divine Wrath*, 58.
20. Ibid.

in the first decades of the twenty-first century, Christians are invited into this kind of misreading. Sadly, Psalm 109 has made its way into the headlines as pastors and other religious leaders have invited persons to pray its verse 8 against the President of the United States and other leaders. Bumper stickers ask for people to pray for our leaders, and then they include Psalm 109:8. When asked, most of those advocating for such use of these psalms have acknowledged that they are indeed praying for the death of another person.

Regardless of one's view of another person, responsible biblical interpretation cannot allow such use of the psalm to go unchecked. As Zenger suggests, to pray someone to death collides with the overall meaning of the psalm itself.[21] Moreover, such a reading fails to consider verse 8, and Psalm 109 as a whole, within the larger canonical witness of Scripture. As some have suggested, such use of this verse is tantamount to making it a talisman. The complexities of our world, however, demand a much richer and far more profound reading of this psalm.

Praying for justice amid injustice. How then does Psalm 109 assist the modern reader in thinking about such weighty matters as justice and injustice? In his book *Evil and the Justice of God*, N. T. Wright wrestles with the question of evil and injustice in the world. In the second chapter of the book, Wright teases out four ways in which the Old Testament attempts to wrestle with this notion. In the conclusion to that chapter Wright explains:

> The Old Testament never tries to give us the sort of picture the philosophers want, that of a static world order with everything explained tidily. At no point does the picture collapse into the simplistic one which so many skeptics assume must be what religious people believe, in which God is the omnicompetent managing director of a very large machine and ought to be able to keep it in proper working order. What we are offered instead is stranger and more mysterious: a narrative of God's project of justice within a world of injustice.[22]

Psalm 109 confronts us with the injustice of which Wright speaks. For most readers of this commentary, however, personal exposure to injustice is limited at best. Or put differently, few of us understand this psalm fully because few of us understand the impact of life-altering injustice. Rarely have we seen the kind of raw injustice that leaves a person fading away like an evening shadow or feeling shaken off like a locust (v. 23). Few of

---

21. Ibid.
22. N. T. Wright, *Evil and the God of Justice* (Downers Grove, IL: InterVarsity, 2006), 73.

us have witnessed a person waste away beneath the oppressive weight of injustice. Only on rare occasions have we sat with a person whose world has become so consumed by the sounds of injustice that the silence of God seems deafening. But if we have seen such a person, or if we ourselves have been that person, then a psalm like Psalm 109 makes more sense. This psalm invites the reader into a world filled with injustice. The jarring nature of the psalm itself is meant, in some sense, to replicate the jarring, life-altering, life-taking nature of injustice. To speak of injustice in docile and hushed terms, as perhaps we may prefer, only masks the devastating work of injustice in the world. The language of this psalm strips away such a veneer, thus exposing the inhumanity experienced by one trapped by injustice.

This psalm is about justice and injustice. Those who seek to "pray someone to death" are asking the wrong question. They seem to be asking, "Who is my enemy?" and "Against whom should I pray this psalm?" Those who desire to pray for justice, however, are asking a far different question. Those who desire justice are asking, "In whom can I trust and in whom can the oppressed person trust amid the scorn of injustice?" In the first instance, the person praying appears focused on the enemy. In the second, the prayer is focused on the Deliverer. In short, the hope of the psalmist, and the hope of all who endure injustice, is rooted in God's *hesed* ("unfailing love"). This psalm asks us to acknowledge injustice but then to declare that injustice does not have the final word. Our prayers are meant to be joined with all those seeking justice so together we might proclaim that the God we serve is indeed a God of justice.

Psalm 110

Of David. A Psalm.

¹ The LORD says to my lord:
"Sit at my right hand
　　until I make your enemies
　　a footstool for your feet."
² The LORD will extend your mighty scepter from Zion saying,
　　"Rule in the midst of your enemies!"
³ Your troops will be willing
　　on your day of battle.
Arrayed in holy splendor,
　　your young men will come to you
　　like dew from the morning's womb.
⁴ The LORD has sworn
　　and he will not change his mind:
"You are a priest forever,
　　in the order of Melchizedek."
⁵ The Lord is at your right hand;
　　he will crush kings on the day of his wrath.
⁶ He will judge the nations, heaping up the dead
　　and crushing the rulers of the whole earth.
⁷ He will drink from a brook along the way,
　　and so he will lift up his head high.

FORM CRITICALLY, PSALM 110 can be classified as a royal psalm. Royal imagery appears throughout the song, including references to footstools, scepters, battle, nations, kings, and rulers—imagery found in other royal psalms as well (e.g., Pss 2; 18; 20; 21; 72; 101). While scholarship remains uniform in its recognition of the royal themes within Psalm 110, there is considerable divergence of opinion related to the date and use of the psalm as well as to its interpretation. Some scholars have posited that the poem reflects a royal coronation of a king in the temple at Jerusalem, thus suggesting a preexilic setting for the psalm.[1] It may in fact

---

1. For example see Th. Booij, "Psalm CX: 'Rule in the Midst of Your Foes,'" *VT* 41 (1991): 396–407.

have had a "previous life" in the preexilic period; its language and imagery may have been drawn from the royal psalms during that period. Nevertheless, this psalm does deviate in notable ways from the other royal psalms. For example, in Psalms 18 and 21 the king himself plays a prominent role. In Psalm 18 the king announces that he pursued the enemies and crushed them (vv. 37–38), beat them like fine dust and trampled them like mud (v. 42). In Psalm 110, especially in the latter portion of the psalm, Yahweh moves to the fore and remains the central focus. Yahweh wages war against the enemies, makes the enemies a footstool (v. 1), and crushes the kings and rulers of the earth (vv. 5b, 6b).

Other scholars have pushed the date of the psalm well into the Second Temple period, even down to the time of the Maccabean revolt. Still others have suggested that the poem is likely postexilic and may reflect the community's desire to see another person assume the throne of David.[2] Such an interpretive move would reflect a messianic reading of the psalm. John Goldingay, however, has argued, "there is no indication that it speaks of a future king, nor any necessity to reckon that it would be interpreted messianically by the time the Psalter reached its final form" (on the New Testament's use of Ps 110, however, see Bridging Contexts below).[3] The psalm, rather, serves as a confession of God's faithfulness to his people amid a challenging social and political context.[4] Martin Leuenberger has suggested that the figure of "David" appears in the psalm "as the identification figure for the prayer/reader of the Psalter."[5] Thus, while parts of the psalm may have been spoken to a king in an earlier period, the poem in its present (canonical) context provides a theological confession for individuals and communities who would have prayed this psalm much later.

---

2. The book of Haggai makes a similar move with Zerubbabel (cf. Hag 2:20–23).

3. Goldingay, *Psalms 3*, 292.

4. Allen, *Psalms 101–150*, 87. Markus Saur notes that in this psalm, royal ideology, priestly concepts, and prophetic speech have been linked with the "war against the nations" motif to create a new theological claim. Saur argues correctly that the royal themes in this psalm must be read in light of the circumstances present in the postexilic period. Under Persian rule, those in Jerusalem had little prospect of a Davidic kingdom's being restored. By combining royal themes and priestly claims, the psalmist appears to announce that the new kingdom, a priestly kingdom, will be established for God's people (Markus Saur, *Die Königpsalmen: Studien zur Entstehung und Theologie*, BZAW 340 [Berlin: de Gruyter, 2004], 221, 224).

5. Martin Leuenberger, *Konzeptionen des Königtums Gottes im Psalter* (Zurich: Theologischer Verlag Zürich, 2004), 290. Similarly, see Ballhorn, who contends that "The poor from Psalm 109 are enthroned as king in Psalm 110" (*Zum Telos des Psalters: Der Textzusammenhang des Vierten und Fünften Psalmenbuches*, Bonner biblische Beiträge 138 [Berlin: Philo, 2004], 156).

As explained below, the psalm presents a number of key theological themes that would have addressed the concerns of a postexilic community. Hebrew poetry frequently combines themes and images from across Israel's literary and theological traditions in order to craft a message for the intended audience. These theological themes continue to have relevance for those who read the psalms as Scripture. The contemporary reader has the responsibility of not only recognizing and teasing out the allusions to the various traditions but also of considering the theological force of these images that have now been joined together into a whole.

The structure of the poem itself provides guidance in understanding the movement of the psalm, which can be divided into two strophes: verses 1–3 and 4–7. Divine speech is recorded in the first verse of each strophe (vv. 1, 4), followed by verses that offer further commentary on the declaration of Yahweh. What unites both sections, however, is their common theme announcing the destruction of the king's enemies by Yahweh himself. For some, such rhetoric may prove theologically problematic (i.e., Yahweh's involvement in the destruction of others), but before the contemporary reader jettisons the psalm entirely because of that kind of rhetoric, the reader must realize that the psalmist, by making such a claim, is actually making a fundamental claim regarding Yahweh and his governance of the world. The rule of the Persians (and other empires) may have led some to question God's rule in the world, but the claims in Ps 110 and elsewhere in the Psalter concerning God's capacity to put down the nations affirm Israel's belief in the universal kingship of their God. Yahweh is not a tribal deity, but the God who reigns supreme over all nations.

The Announcement of Victory over Enemies (110:1–3)

THE LORD SAYS TO MY LORD. In the Hebrew, the opening phrase of verse 1 actually reads, "Utterance of Yahweh [*ne'um yhwh*] to my lord." The phrase "utterance of Yahweh" appears frequently in the prophetic literature (cf. Jeremiah; Ezekiel) but nowhere else in the Psalter. In the prophetic literature the phrase appears at the end of an oracle or embedded within the oracle, but in Psalm 110 it appears at the beginning. The unusual placement is merely meant to emphasize that what follows is indeed "a word from the LORD" for the person being addressed as "my lord." The term "my lord" suggests a hierarchical relationship between the person speaking and the one being addressed. Likely the poet is a court priest or prophet and, based on the remainder of the psalm, the "lord" mentioned in verse 1a refers to a king or political figure particularly given the language and imagery employed throughout the remainder of the psalm.

Sit at my right hand. The actual oracle follows in the remainder of verse 1: "Sit at my right hand until I make your enemies a footstool for your feet." The king being addressed in verse 1a is invited to sit at the right hand of Yahweh. While the reference to the "right hand" of Yahweh is entirely metaphorical, and as such implies a position of honor, it does connote something of a symbolic world that the psalmist seeks to convey. As scholars have noted, Egyptian iconography frequently depicts the "co-enthronement" of the king with the deity.[6] The language of the "right hand" is suggestive of a symbolic world in which the king participates in the rule of Yahweh over the world. Or put differently, the psalmist envisions the king of Zion as a "throne companion" of Yahweh. Yet the psalmist is clear: it is Yahweh who will route the nations and make them a footstool (v. 1c).

The LORD will extend your mighty scepter from Zion. The image and implications of Yahweh and the king as his co-ruler are spelled out in verse 2a. The word "scepter" operates as a synecdoche, a single term that implies a much larger idea (in this instance kingship). Yahweh instructs the king that he will "rule in the midst of the enemies." The word translated as "rule" (*radah*) contains a more nuanced meaning than other similar terms. As John Goldingay has explained, *radah* "indicates a rule imposed on a people even if they resist it."[7] In addition, the term appears frequently in contexts that celebrate the king's rule over a considerable area (cf. Ps 72:8).

Arrayed in holy splendor. A comparison of various English translations will result in a number of different and quite divergent translations due to the difficult and somewhat unusual imagery employed in Psalm 110:3. The opening phrase literally reads, "your people, freewill offerings, in the day of your power." Rather than simply making a claim about the voluntary nature of those who will fight for the king, perhaps the psalmist wants to imbue the entire event with a certain sense of sacredness. This sense continues in the second half of verse 3 with the claim that the young people serving the king will be arrayed in holy splendor (*hadar*). Although a number of translations read "on the holy mountains," following several manuscripts that have "mountains" (*harar*) instead of "splendor" (*hadar*), the NIV should be followed.[8] Verse 2 promises that the king will rule over the enemies; verse 3a indicates that the king will not approach the day of battle without sufficient support from his troops.

---

6. Hossfeld and Zenger, *Psalms 3*, 147. Keel, *The Symbolism of the Biblical World*, 263.

7. Goldingay, *Psalms 3*, 294.

8. See William P. Brown, "A Royal Performance: Critical Notes on Psalm 110:3ay–b," *JBL* 117 (1998): 96 n. 21.

The final line in verse 3 employs several metaphors (dawn, womb, and dew) in a very tight construction. The syntax of the Hebrew is challenging, as suggested by the various attempts at translation. The text literally reads, "from the womb of the dawn belong to you the dew of your young people." The phrase "from the womb of the dawn" resembles the imagery and language in Isaiah 14:12, another text associated with kingship. In Isaiah 14 the poet applies the imagery of being a "son of the dawn" to a Babylonian king, thus resulting in a negative assessment of that king. In Psalm 110, however, the imagery possesses a much more positive connotation, implying the rise to power of a great king. As Robert Davidson has correctly suggested, the imagery in verse 3b symbolizes "the dawning light which shatters the darkness of night."[9] To ensure the success of the king, God will grant the king young persons who will come with vigor and vitality ("dew") to join in subduing the enemies.

A Priest Like Melchizedek (110:4–7)

IN THE FIRST STROPHE OF THE PSALM (vv. 1–3) the psalmist announces that he has received an oracle from the Lord. The second strophe opens with more emphatic language declaring Yahweh's faithfulness.

The LORD has sworn and will not change his mind. In 2 Samuel 7 the Lord swore to David that he will establish a kingdom for David, and, despite circumstances that may challenge that promise, Yahweh affirms that he will not change his mind.

You are a priest forever. Following the Babylonian exile and the loss of a monarchy, the community may have wondered about whether another Israelite king would emerge. In verse 4a Yahweh affirms that he has not changed his mind; God would still honor his promise, but perhaps in a way different from before. The oracle in verse 4 claims that the king will be a priest in the order of Melchizedek. The promise invokes the somewhat enigmatic story of Melchizedek, the Jebusite priest-king who ruled in Jerusalem (Gen 14). In many ancient Near Eastern cultures the king exercised certain priestly functions, and while Israel's king may have led in worship or offered up prayers to Yahweh, the king never appeared to function formally as a priest. The realms of monarchy and priesthood remained relatively separate. But similar to Melchizedek, the king in Psalm 110 will serve as mediator between Yahweh and his people even as he fends off the military aggression of the nations.

The Lord is at your right hand. In verses 5–6 the psalmist refers to the routing of the nations and rulers of the earth. Whereas in verse 1 the

---

9. Davidson, *The Vitality of Worship*, 365.

king was invited to sit at the right hand of Yahweh, in verse 5 the king is informed that Yahweh will appear at his right hand when he engages in battle. In the former instance, sitting at the right hand of Yahweh is a sign of honor; in the latter instance, Yahweh's appearance at the right hand of the king implies protection and support. In this role, however, Yahweh is not a passive observer. On the contrary, it is Yahweh who will exact judgment upon the nations and their kings on the day of his wrath (*'ap*). The same term for "wrath" appears in Psalm 2:5 when Yahweh brings judgment against the kings who plot against him. Hossfeld and Zenger explain the larger sense of wrath suggested in this text. They contend that it "is not an emotional category but a philosophical one signaling YHWH's action in defending and accomplishing the world order he has established, above all against kings and rulers who flout this universal order of justice."[10] This theme is reinforced with the opening verb in Psalm 110:6, *din*, "to execute judgment." In the ancient world, the true king is the one who executes judgment (*din*) over his empire and against those who would dare to thwart royal rule. By standing at the right hand of the king, Yahweh will do more than simply support the king in battle—Yahweh will act as the universal king. He will vanquish those who resist his vision for a rightly ordered creation, and he will prepare the way for his king to establish God's rule over the whole earth (v. 6b).

He will drink from a brook. In the final verse the subject appears to shift. Although Yahweh has been the primary actor in verses 5b–6, the king now appears in view in verse 7. Miriam von Nordheim interprets the final verse in the light of the honor-shame continuum. She contends that drinking "from a brook along the way" implies the victors are "drinking foreign water," and such an act would be considered a hostile and provocative move meant to indicate the superiority of one group over another.[11] For von Nordheim, then, "lift high his head" is a sign of the final triumph over the defeated foes.[12] With this action the king signals that he is the beneficiary of Yahweh's judgment against the nations.

---

10. Hossfeld and Zenger, *Psalms 3*, 150.

11. Miriam von Nordheim, *Geboren von der Morgenröte: Psalm 110 in Tradition, Redaktion und Rezeption* (Neukirchen-Vluyn: Neukirchener Verlag, 2008), 110–11. Hossfeld and Zenger conclude similarly in suggesting that "the closing verse of the psalm accordingly signals the definitive and universal victory of YHWH over the hostile kings and so the accomplishment of YHWH's universal royal rule" (Hossfeld and Zenger, *Psalms 3*, 152).

12. William van der Meer understands the final line in a manner somewhat consistent with von Nordheim's suggestion that the image implies final victory. See William van der Meer, "Psalm 110," in *The Structural Analysis of Biblical and Canaanite Poetry*, JSOTSup 74, ed. W. van der Meer and J. C. de Moor (Sheffield: Sheffield Academic, 1988), 207–34.

DELIVERANCE IN A HOSTILE WORLD. The first royal psalm in the Psalter, Psalm 2, introduced the theme of a hostile world. In that psalm the reader is told that "nations conspire," that "peoples plot in vain," and that kings and rulers take their stand in opposition to God and his anointed one (vv. 1–2). The psalmist painted a vivid picture of a world gone awry but, even more, a world at odds with its rightful King. As Gerald Wilson explains, "Since the 'kings' and 'rulers' of the earth do not acknowledge Yahweh, they have no allegiance to him and are depicted here as fomenting rebellion to cast off his overlordship."[13] In Psalm 2 the psalmist explains that those nations, kings, and rulers who fail to acknowledge the kingship of God will face grave consequences.

Psalm 110, another royal psalm, returns to the theme of God and his anointed in the face of a hostile world. Like many psalms, this poem speaks candidly about enemies and powers that stand in opposition. The apparent threat posed by enemies, kings, and nations (vv. 1–2, 4–5) signified that kings and rulers failed to heed the injunction in Psalm 2 that they should "Serve the LORD with fear." Their continued opposition suggested that not all was right with the world; they were a constant threat, both literally and theologically. The continued presence of such hostile forces could have thwarted Israel's theological confession about Yahweh and his reign in the world and perhaps even led them to wonder, "If there are still enemies, then perhaps God is less than we thought." The psalmist, however, rejected any such claim and instead moved in a very different direction. While he recognized those forces that threaten God's vision for the world, he also held firmly to the conviction that Yahweh was still king. Israel's acknowledgment of a hostile world, however, was always countered by the nation's certainty of the kingship of God. One is as real as the other, but in the end only one prevails.

Psalm 110 and Jesus. The writers of the New Testament quote or allude to Psalm 110 more than any other text in the Old Testament. Without question, the theological claims in this psalm proved important to early Christians in developing a robust theological confession about Jesus. In several instances Psalm 110:1 is quoted directly (Mark 12:36; Luke 20:42–43), and in each case the psalm is used to validate Jesus' identity as the Messiah. The motif of sitting at the right hand of God (v. 1) appears in Mark (14:62; 16:19) but is found with greater frequency in the epistolary

---

13. Wilson, *Psalms, Volume 1,* 109.

literature of the New Testament (Acts 2:34; cf., Rom 8:34; Eph 1:20; Col 3:1; Heb 1:3; 8:1; 10:12; 12:2; 1 Pet 3:22). In each instance the New Testament writer refers to Psalm 110:1 in announcing Jesus' post-resurrection exaltation to the right hand of God. As in Psalm 110, the reference to Jesus as sitting at the "right hand" reinforces Jesus' kingship over all creation and, perhaps more importantly, over all foes that may seek to thwart the ways of God (Rom 8:31–39). The writer of Hebrews attempts to connect the messianic role of Jesus with his priestly function by combining Psalm 2:7 ("You are my son, today I have become your father") with Psalm 110:4 ("You are a priest forever, in the order of Melchizedek"). Some may want to understand Psalm 110 and its use in the New Testament within the framework of "promise and fulfillment," with Psalm 110 functioning as a prophetic witness to the coming of Jesus. Robert Davidson, however, has suggested an alternative interpretive approach. He contends, "We are not asked to see Jesus as the literal fulfillment of the words of this psalm or any psalm. Rather we are invited to look back at this psalm in light of what we know of Jesus and to see *how the vision of the psalm is transformed* in his life, death and resurrection."[14] As we speak of Jesus as the Messiah, the Son of God, we are saying all that this psalm can say—and even more.

THE LANGUAGE OF KINGS and rulers, nations and enemies, rings strangely odd to our ears as we read Psalm 110 and seek to make sense of it in our contemporary world. To be sure, there are kings and rulers in our world, and any map, whether interactive or paper, reminds us of the plethora of nations that exist. Given the political complexity of our world, it is understandable why some might approach Psalm 110 with a sense of consternation about how best to read, interpret, and even preach such a psalm.

Frank-Lothar Hossfeld and Eric Zenger remind us, however, that this psalm is a "political text that, as a counterproposal to the foreign powers oppressing Israel, asserts that Yahweh's royal rule will be established."[15] We should not pass too quickly over the word "counterproposal" in their assessment. The psalms, while laden with the language of prayer and petition, root their claims in a decidedly theological commitment that is indeed a counterproposal to the ways of the world, and this rooting is no less true with Psalm 110. In attempting to interpret Psalm 110, we would

---

14. Davidson, *The Vitality of Worship*, 367.
15. Hossfeld and Zenger, *Psalms 3*, 154.

do well to be reminded that this song is offering a counterproposal in that it redefines both power and hope. Those who stand in opposition to the work of God and who appear to have power in and over this world in fact do not; those powers are not our source of hope.

We would also do well to be reminded that contemporary readers of Scripture are looking for a counterproposal. Most people are awash in a dominant cultural narrative that has little room for serious engagement with faith. "For centuries now, secularism has been defining and constructing the world. It is a world in which the theological order is either discredited or turned into a harmless leisure-time activity of private commitment."[16] Neither of those options will do for the psalmist in Psalm 110. Instead, Psalm 110 calls us to declare our belief in the confession that "the LORD reigns" (cf. Pss 93; 95–99). This confession, however, cannot and should not lead us to devolve into a faith that is a "harmless leisure-time activity of private commitment," nor should our confession allow us to slip into some form of religious escapism.

The author of Hebrews reminds us that we have great hope as the people of God because we serve the one who endured the cross, scorned its shame, and "sat down at the right hand of the throne of God." And as we consider him, our priest and king, we "will not grow weary and lose heart" (Heb 12:2–3). On the contrary, we will be emboldened by our conviction that, "Since we are receiving a kingdom that cannot be shaken, let us be thankful, and so worship God acceptably with reverence and awe" (Heb 12:28).

---

16. John Milbank, Catherine Pickstock, and Graham Ward, "Suspending the Material: The Turn of Radical Orthodoxy," in *Radical Orthodoxy*, ed. J. Milbank et al. (London: Routledge, 1999), 1.

Psalm 111

¹ Praise the LORD.

I will extol the LORD with all my heart
    in the council of the upright and in the assembly.
² Great are the works of the LORD;
    they are pondered by all who delight in them.
³ Glorious and majestic are his deeds,
    and his righteousness endures forever.
⁴ He has caused his wonders to be remembered;
    the LORD is gracious and compassionate.
⁵ He provides food for those who fear him;
    he remembers his covenant forever.
⁶ He has shown his people the power of his works,
    giving them the lands of other nations.
⁷ The works of his hands are faithful and just;
    all his precepts are trustworthy.
⁸ They are established forever and ever,
    enacted in faithfulness and uprightness.
⁹ He provided redemption for his people;
    he ordained his covenant forever—
    holy and awesome is his name.
¹⁰ The fear of the LORD is the beginning of wisdom;
    all who follow his precepts have good understanding.
    To him belongs eternal praise.

PSALMS 111 AND 112 belong together. They resemble each other in form, with each being an acrostic. (Each half verse in the English versification of the psalm begins with a successive letter in the Hebrew alphabet.) The two psalms share additional similarities in form. The first eight verses of each poem have two lines, while the final two verses (vv. 9–10) each have three lines. Thematically, the two psalms allude to righteousness, but in differing ways. Psalm 111 refers to divine righteousness, while Psalm 112 focuses on human righteousness. As Erich Zenger has observed, "Psalm 111 presents theology and Psalm 112 presents anthropology. Psalm 111 sketches out the acts of YHWH, Psalm 112 sketches out the acts of humanity in response to the acts of

YHWH."[1] Or, put differently, Psalm 111 praises the works of Yahweh and calls for the appropriate posture of piety (i.e., "fear of the LORD" [v. 10]), while Psalm 112 builds upon Psalm 111 by outlining the appropriate way of life for those who do indeed take seriously the call to fear God.

As explained more fully below, the theme of the Psalm 111 concerns the works of God. Of primary interest for the psalmist are both the exodus (vv. 3–6) and the law of the Lord (vv. 7–9). Both subjects are perceived and understood as the works of the Lord. The association of the exodus with the works of the Lord is not unusual. Other psalms (Pss 78; 105; 106) rehearse the events of Israel's salvation history, with the exodus story functioning as a, if not *the*, primary component of that history. The association of the law with the works of the Lord in this psalm, however, is striking. Other psalms ponder the law, but in differing ways. Psalm 19:1–6, for example, juxtaposes the law of the Lord with the testimony of creation. In Psalm 111, however, the law of the Lord stands in tandem with the events of the exodus story, and both are construed as the "works of the LORD."

This dual emphasis on the exodus and the law in Psalm 111 provides additional insight into the psalm's current location within the Psalter. The poem's opening words, *halelu yah*, "Praise God," are set apart both in the Hebrew text and in the NIV and function as a title, or superscription, for the psalm. This same superscription or title can be found also in Psalms 112 and 113, thus creating a link between Psalms 111 and 112 and the subsequent collection (the Egyptian Hallel) in Psalms 113–18. Beyond linguistic links, there are also thematic links. Psalms 113–18 are recited at Passover and meant to recall God's deliverance from the land of Egypt. The giving of the law at Sinai represents the decisive moment in the exodus story when God established a covenant with all those gathered at Sinai. With this moment in mind, the editors of the Psalter likely positioned Psalms 111 and 112 (two psalms focused on the torah of the Lord) alongside a string of psalms that refer back to the deliverance out of Egypt. The connection of these two themes is further verified by the location of Psalm 119, the magisterial torah psalm, which follows the Egyptian Hallel. So, beginning with Psalm 111 and running through Psalm 119, a deliberate association is developed between history and torah. These are the works of God; indeed, they are the foundational works of God that have the capacity to shape the identity of those who pray these psalms.

The structure of Psalm 111 reinforces the importance of these two themes for the poem. Following an introduction in verses 1–2, verses 3–6

---

1. Erich Zenger, "Psalmenexegese und Psalterexegese," in *The Composition of the Book of Psalms*, BETL 238, ed. Erich Zenger (Leuven: Peeters, 2010), 38.

allude to the exodus tradition, while verses 7–10 focus on the law of the Lord for the people of God.

Introduction (111:1–2)

THE FIRST TWO VERSES FUNCTION as an introduction to the psalm. Together they introduce both the purpose of the psalm as well as its primary theme.

Praise the LORD. The opening imperative stands outside the acrostic structure of the remainder of the psalm. As suggested above, the imperative functions as a title announcing the intent of the psalm and likely connecting it to subsequent psalms. The psalmist implores the audience to "praise the LORD" (*halelu yah*). The opening words suggest that Psalm 111 is a song of praise. The theme of praise, however, is defined further in the second line of the psalm. The poet announces that he will "extol the LORD with all my heart." The verb "extol" (*yadah*) can mean to praise, but it can also mean "confess" or "proclaim."[2] While the difference between praise and confess may appear minimal, it proves instructive for understanding the purpose of the psalm. John Goldingay consistently renders the term *yadah* as "confess" or "make known," thus leading him to label this psalm a confessional hymn.[3] The language throughout the psalm confirms Goldingay's claim. Throughout the poem the psalmist refers to God in the third person. This poem is not spoken *to* God by the psalmist; instead, it is a psalm spoken *about* God *to* the congregation (v. 1).

The works of the LORD. In verse 2 the psalmist introduces the theme: the "works of the LORD." The term "works" (*ma'asim*) and the larger semantic domain associated with that term appear throughout the psalm. The works of the Lord are mentioned in verses 3, 4, 6, and 7. In response to the works of the Lord, the people are called in verses 8b and 10b to "do" the law of the Lord.

In verse 2b the psalmist announces that the works of the Lord, writ large, are "great." In the ancient Near East, the term "great" was a descriptive term reserved primarily for the divine king.[4] Thus verse 2a does far more than simply announce that the works of the Lord were spectacular ("great"). By invoking the term "great," the psalmist actually attributes these works to Israel's Divine King, the one about whom he is confessing and the one to whom praise belongs. The royal metaphor appears elsewhere in the psalm as well.

---

2. Leslie Allen suggests that the opening line of the psalm might be best understood as "an announcement of praise" (Allen, *Psalm 101–150*, 89).

3. Goldingay, *Psalms 3*, 302.

4. Hossfeld and Zenger, *Psalms 3*, 164.

They are pondered by all who delight in them. For those who study the works of the Lord and seek them out, there is great delight and profit to be gained. The word "delight" (*ḥepets*) also appears in Psalm 1:2. There the psalmist refers to the "blessed" person "whose delight [*ḥepets*] is in the law of the LORD and who meditates on his law day and night." Even as Psalm 1 calls for the blessed person to meditate on the law of God and to find delight in it, the psalmist in Psalm 111 offers similar counsel, but with the object of such study being the larger works of God. Verse 2 and the reference to the "works of the LORD" in no way precludes the law but, as suggested above, includes both the great acts he has carried out in Israel's history as well as the giving of his precepts and laws for instruction.

The Works of God in History (111:3–6)

GLORIOUS AND MAJESTIC ARE HIS DEEDS. The phrase "glorious and majestic" occurs elsewhere in the book of Psalms (cf. Pss 21:5; 96:6; 104:1; 145:5), with the two terms typically functioning as a hendiadys. They refer to the royal attributes of the Divine King. In this instance, however, the usage differs somewhat because the two terms modify the work or "deeds" (*poʾal*) of the Divine King. These deeds represent the righteousness of God, which will stand forever (Ps 111:3). The word for righteousness (*tsedaqot*) signals the "giving and establishment of a life-sustaining world order and social order."[5] Thus verse 3 functions as an introduction to the first major section in the psalm. Through its language the verse invokes the image of Yahweh as Divine King while in verses 4–6 describe the works as constitutive of a life-sustaining world established by God.

He has caused his wonders to be remembered. The next three verses provide an abbreviated rehearsal of the central works of God in Israel's history. In verse 4 the psalmist refers to the "wonders" (*niplaʾot*) that God caused to be remembered. While the term *niplaʾot* contributes to the larger thematic thread in Psalm 111 concerning the works of the Lord, the term appears elsewhere in the Old Testament with specific reference to the exodus (cf. Exod 3:20; 34:10; Pss 78:4; 105:5; 106:22; 136:4). The Hebrew in verse 4 reads, "he has made a memorial [or 'a commemoration'] for his deeds." In other words, these saving deeds cannot be forgotten because Yahweh has established that they be remembered. Hans-Joachim Kraus explains the significance of this claim by suggesting that "worship is not a matter of human remembering, but of God's founding."[6]

---

5. Ibid.
6. Hans-Joachim Kraus, *Psalms 60–150*, CC, trans. Hilton Oswald (Minneapolis: Augsburg, 1989), 358.

The references to the central works of God continue in Psalm 111:4b with the claim that Yahweh is both "gracious and compassionate." The two terms appear in Exodus 34:6 in a grand statement of self-disclosure by Yahweh following the golden calf incident. The works or deeds of Yahweh are more than impressive demonstrations of divine power; they are in fact evidence that Yahweh is the God he claims to be—the God of the covenant who is "compassionate and gracious . . . , slow to anger, abounding in love and faithfulness" (Exod 34:6).

Verses 5 and 6 recount two subsequent scenes in the history of God's dealing with his people. The mention of "food" in verse 5 recalls God's provision of quail and manna in the wilderness.[7] In verse 6 the psalmist refers to the "power of his works." That the word "power" (*koah*) can be found in Exodus 9:16 and 15:6 once again reminds those who pray this psalm of the Divine King, the one with power, who acted in their behalf by bringing them out of slavery and "giving them the lands of other nations" (Ps 111:6b). Erhard Gerstenberger notes that verse 6 stands in the very center of the psalm, with ten lines of poetry appearing before and after this verse. According to Gerstenberger, this positioning of verse 6 implies that "the celebration of Yahweh's power and glory revolves around the gift of the (holy) land."[8] Whether verse 6 actually functions as the center of the psalm is difficult to determine, but Gerstenberger is correct to note the significance of that theme, particularly given the imperial constraints under which those in Yehud (i.e., Judah) lived during the postexilic period.

The Torah as the Work of God (111:7–10)

FOLLOWING THE REHEARSAL OF GOD'S WORK in Israel's history, the psalmist shifts the focus of the psalm. While maintaining the larger theme of the works of God, the poet introduces the theme of torah as the work of God.

All his precepts are trustworthy. Verse 7a announces that the "works of his hands are faithful and just." The mention of the "works" of God in verse 7a echoes the references to the works and deeds of God in verses 3a, 4a, and 6a, thus leading some to consider verse 7a as the concluding line to the first section (vv. 3–6). But the second line in verse 7 redirects the reader's attention to God's covenant law. As Clinton McCann has

---

7. The word for "food" (*terep*) typically refers to food that was prey, but in later texts (Mal 3:10; Job 24:5; Prov 31:15) the term has a more general meaning of food. In addition, *terep* is the first word in verse 5a and was intentionally chosen based on the structure of the acrostic.

8. Erhard S. Gerstenberger, *Psalms, Part 2 and Lamentations*, FOTL XV (Grand Rapids: Eerdmans, 2001), 272.

suggested, verse 7a likely serves as an intentional transition linking the "saving works of God and God's works that take the form of instruction."[9] In verse 7b the word "precepts" (*piqudim*) functions as a synonym for torah (cf. Pss 19:9; 103:18 and throughout Ps 119). In Hebrew the verse has a chiastic structure, thus making the connection between "works of his hands" and the precepts of God even more apparent.

A	B
The works of his hands	are faithful and just;
B'	A'
trustworthy	are all his precepts.

The precepts of God are reliable—they can be trusted—because they introduce a world filled with faithfulness and justice. Even as the works of God in Israel's history demonstrated the faithfulness and justice of God, so too the precepts of God are reliable in carrying out the will and ways of God in the world. Yet for this working out of God's will to occur, these precepts must be "enacted in faithfulness and uprightness" (Ps 111:8).[10] In verse 2 the psalmist called for the works of God to be studied, to be pondered, but in verse 8 he calls for the people to move from reflection to action, from observation to implementation.

He provided redemption for his people. The word "redemption" (*pedut*) calls to mind more generally the notion of redemption from slavery, in this instance, Israel's redemption from slavery in Egypt. The first section of the psalm (vv. 3–6) recounted the exodus, Israel's deliverance out of the land of Egypt, and into the land that was Israel's inheritance. Verses 7–9 press further by introducing the covenant of the Lord, thus suggesting that redemption culminates in the covenant he has ordained (v. 9b). Even as deliverance from Egypt signaled God's love for and commitment to his people, the covenant represents the same. The work of God's hands reflects his design for his people and the world in which they live.

Verse 9c concludes by affirming that God's name is "holy and awesome." The latter term comes from the root *yr'*, "to fear" or "to hold in reverence." The first two lines in verse 9 are in the perfect, or *qatal*, form in Hebrew, which usually refers to a past action (i.e., God *sent* redemption and God *ordained* his covenant). In the final line of verse 9, however, the verse

---

9. McCann, "The Book of Psalms," 1134.

10. The Hebrew word for "enacted" (*'suyim*) is a passive participle but likely has the force of a gerund. See Allen, *Psalms 101–150*, 89; Ruth Scoralick, "Psalm 111—Bauplan und Gedankengang," *Bib* 78 (1997): 190–205, esp. 199.

is verbless: "holy and awesome [is] his name." The verbless clause helps to define who God is, then and now. What has happened in the past is because of who God is—the one who is holy and awesome—and what has happened in the past should draw the community into proper worship of the Divine King, even now.[11]

The fear of the LORD is the beginning of wisdom. The opening line of verse 10 invokes a verse found elsewhere in wisdom literature (Prov 1:7; 9:10; Job 28:28). While it may be possible that the psalmist simply included the wisdom saying here because the acrostic required a word that begins with the letter "r" (the line opening in Hebrew is the word *reshit*, "beginning"), its placement in the final verse of the psalm appears more significant. The wisdom saying provides a theological lens through which to interpret the entire psalm.

For this psalmist, the fear of the Lord is connected to living out the torah of God. In Psalm 111:10b the text reads literally, "good [*sekel*] [is] to all those who do them." The word *sekel* can mean "understanding," but the term can also refer to reward or success. Hossfeld and Zenger note that the wisdom tradition frequently highlights the cause-and-effect relationship: correct actions lead to beneficial gain. Such an understanding of *sekel* might suggest that a "good reward" is the preferable interpretation.[12] Understood in this way, verse 9b would indicate that if one carries out the precepts of God, then there will be a reward (cf. Prov 3:4); they will be rewarded with insight and understanding.

CONFESSING GOD. In the opening line of Psalm 111 the psalmist announces that he will confess the Lord with all of his heart. Perhaps because it is the opening line of the psalm, the reader may simply pass over such a comment in order to move to what may be perceived as "weightier matters." But in making such a move the reader misses the significance of the opening claim: confession and testimony are central to the community of God's people (v. 1b). This significance is not only true of Psalm 111 but is equally true elsewhere in the Psalter.

---

11. Walter Brueggemann and William H. Bellinger Jr. add that "the holiness and awesomeness of God are intended not to create a distance from the congregation [and the presence of God], but to call people to acknowledge and explore these acts of salvation in both worship and living" (Walter Brueggemann and William H. Bellinger Jr., *Psalms*, NCBC [New York: Cambridge University Press, 2014], 483).

12. Hossfeld and Zenger, *Psalms 3*, 158.

Other psalmists frequently recount the "works of God," or the "deeds of God," and promise to *yadah* ("praise" or "confess")—to make those deeds known in the congregation or to all people.[13] These confessions function didactically in that they shape and inform those who hear them.

The connection between the works of God and confession was not lost on the New Testament writers either. The New Testament includes a number of texts aptly labeled "christological hymns." These hymns recounted the works of God in and through Jesus Christ (e.g., Phil 2:5–11; Col 1:15–20); they were "reflexive and expressive of gratitude to God for all he had done for the world's reconciliation and the church's salvation."[14] But these texts were much more than recitals of history. Similar to Psalm 111, these texts were not *to* God, but *about* God and God's way in the world; they were confessions in the truest sense of the word. As these texts were read, heard, and confessed, they shaped the theology of a formative Christian community seeking to maintain its identity amid a world of competing ideas and religious claims.

The Hebrew Psalter was likely compiled in the postexilic period under Persian rule, or perhaps even later; it was a time in which the Jewish community in Yehud (i.e., Judah) sought to maintain its identity amid a world of competing ideas. In response to that need, the psalmist makes a confession of praise. The psalm merges hymnology and theology, poetry and confession, thus drawing together the chief theological traditions in Israel's history in didactic praise of their God.

The Work(s) of God. From beginning to end, Psalm 111 remains focused on the "works of God," here interpreted as the deliverance from Egypt and the establishment of God's law. These two works, however, have a singular focus: the faithfulness of God in the creation of his people. The fidelity of God to humanity, which is reflected throughout all Scripture, and more narrowly identified in these two great works of God in Psalm 111, creates the ground for our theological claims about God. Harry Nasuti has observed that in the book of Psalms we rarely find a description of God that is in isolation *from* the world.[15] God can be described only as God is known *in* the world. Psalms that have a wisdom bent frequently explore

---

13. Cf. 9:1; 35:18; 52:9; 75:1; 88:10; 105:1; 107:8, 15, 21, 31; 142:7.

14. Ralph P. Martin, "Some Reflections on New Testament Hymns," in *Christ the Lord: Studies in Christology Presented to Donald Guthrie*, ed. H. H. Rowdon (Leicester: Inter-Varsity Press, 1982), 45.

15. Harry P. Nasuti, "God at Work in the World: A Theology of Divine-Human Encounter in the Psalms," in *Soundings in the Theology of the Psalms: Perspectives in Contemporary Scholarship*, ed. Rolf A. Jacobson (Minneapolis: Fortress, 2011), 30.

God and God's ways in the world with humanity. Rolf Jacobson contends that wisdom psalms typically "rest at the intersection between communal experience and testimony regarding the Lord's fidelity."[16] Because this connection between experience and testimony is so vital, the psalmist calls the people of God to ponder, study, and delight in the stories of God's faithful work for and in relationship with his people.

Although the allusions to the exodus and the wandering period in Psalm 111 are not overt, they are certainly present, as indicated above. The events of the exodus and the giving of the land represented the creation of God's people formally. The significance of these events for the subsequent biblical tradition cannot be underestimated. The fact that the exodus tradition appears in various genres of exilic and postexilic texts suggests that this singular event represented a foundational moment in Israel's history. Consequently, the foundational moment became a cipher for the moment when deliverance and fidelity converged. Out of God's fidelity, Israel was delivered. This convergence of fidelity and deliverance yielded important theological claims about God, and these claims shaped (and continue to shape) the identity of those who prayed these psalms. The psalmist's claim is straightforward: The work of God *then*, at that moment, remains the hope of the people *now*. Those who were living in the aftermath of the exile were reminded that they *too* were the people of God; that story was their story, that deliverance, theirs. There was, once again, reason to lift their voice in praise and confession (v. 1).

The psalmist mentions the law as the second "work of God." Although the giving of the law occurred in association with the deliverance from Egypt, the emphasis in Psalm 111 is not on the *process* of giving the torah to his people, it is on torah itself (cf. vv. 7b, 8a, and 9b). The psalm juxtaposes salvation history (i.e., deliverance from Egypt) with *covenantal instruction*— and considers both of them the work of God. While the first work created a people, the second work offered the means to shape a people. In the exilic and postexilic period, torah obedience became a central marker in identifying those who sought to live in fidelity to God. In Isaiah 56:6, for example, God announces who will be identified as his people: "all who keep the Sabbath . . . and who hold fast to my covenant." The emphasis on torah obedience during this period should not be construed as legalism but, instead, understood as a response of fidelity to an ever-faithful God who created his people and sustains them by his word.

---

16. Rolf A. Jacobson, "'The Faithfulness of the Lord Endures Forever': The Theological Witness of the Psalter," in *Soundings in the Theology of the Psalms: Perspectives in Contemporary Scholarship*, ed. Rolf A. Jacobson (Minneapolis: Fortress, 2011), 116.

AS NOTED ABOVE, Psalm 111 is an acrostic. Throughout the psalm, from beginning to end, from *aleph* to *tav*, the psalmist repeatedly makes theological claims about God. These claims, however, are rooted in God's story with Israel and, in turn, make certain claims upon God's people both then and now. In his classic work *After Virtue*, Alasdair MacIntyre wrote, "I can only answer the question 'What am I to do?' if I can answer the prior question: 'Of what story or stories do I find myself a part?'"[17] MacIntyre understands well the power of story. Stories have the capacity to root ourselves into something that is much bigger than any one individual. For example, most every nation I know has stories about its founding, of key moments that proved decisive. But why remember those events? What power do such events have for those who are living hundreds of years later? Such stories place claims upon people, and they provide a framework that interprets reality and continues to shape reality in profound ways.

So what kind of story is being communicated in Psalm 111, and to what end? Although the redemption from Egypt and the giving of the law are rarely combined in this fashion in the Old Testament, the mention of these acts together here invites us into a certain knowledge about God. This God is the God who has called out his people, saved them, and redeemed them. But their identity is not simply rooted in a past event. The story continues. Through the giving of the law, God provides a way for each generation to live into their identity as the people of God. These laws provide a framework that interprets reality for the people of God— even more, it helps to shape reality. But this shaping does not happen by accident. We must choose to live into the ways of God in faithfulness and uprightness (v. 8), and we must choose to "follow his precepts" (v.10).

The works of God call us, even now, to root our lives in the story of God *and* in the values and commitments expressed in his word. There is no hint of legalism in this kind of commitment to the work and word of God; rather, such a life reflects a proper "fear of the LORD" (v. 10).

17. Alasdair MacIntyre, *After Virtue: A Study in Moral Theology* (Notre Dame, IN: University of Notre Dame Press, 1981), 250.

Psalm 112

¹ Praise the LORD.
Blessed are those who fear the LORD,
    who find great delight in his commands.
² Their children will be mighty in the land;
    the generation of the upright will be blessed.
³ Wealth and riches are in their houses,
    and their righteousness endures forever.
⁴ Even in darkness light dawns for the upright,
    for those who are gracious and compassionate and
      righteous.
⁵ Good will come to those who are generous and lend freely,
    who conduct their affairs with justice.
⁶ Surely the righteous will never be shaken;
    they will be remembered forever.
⁷ They will have no fear of bad news;
    their hearts are steadfast, trusting in the LORD.
⁸ Their hearts are secure, they will have no fear;
    in the end they will look in triumph on their foes.
⁹ They have freely scattered their gifts to the poor,
    their righteousness endures forever;
    their horn will be lifted high in honor.
¹⁰ The wicked will see and be vexed,
    they will gnash their teeth and waste away;
    the longings of the wicked will come to nothing.

Original Meaning

PSALMS 111 AND 112, both wisdom psalms, have long been recognized as a "pair" of psalms with considerable similarities both in form and function.[1] While not readily obvious in English, both psalms appear in the form of an acrostic, with each line beginning with the subsequent letter in the Hebrew alphabet. Beyond their common literary form, the two psalms share a number of words, further creating an intertextual relationship between the two psalms.

---

1. Walther Zimmerli, "Zwillingpsalmen," in *Wort, Leid, und Gottespruch: Festschrift für Joseph Ziegler,* ed. J. Schreiner (Würzburg: Echter, 1972), 5–13.

The idea of the "fear of the LORD" functions as a bridge theme between the two psalms. While the final verse in Psalm 111 reminds the reader that "the fear of the LORD is the beginning of wisdom," the opening verse of Psalm 112 exclaims that "Blessed are those who fear the LORD," thus seamlessly connecting the end of one psalm with the beginning of the next. There are additional linguistic features that connect the two psalms. For example, each psalm begins with the call to praise the Lord (*balelu yah*). Further, eleven words or phrases are shared between the two psalms. Some of the terms are repeated, with similar meaning and usage in each psalm.

"fear"	Ps 112:1	Ps 111:5, 10
"delight"	Ps 112:1	Ps 111:2
"upright"	Ps 112:2, 4	Ps 111:1
"good"	Ps 112:5	Ps 111:10

In other instances, however, the usage has noticeably shifted. There are seven terms that relate or are applied to Yahweh in Psalm 111, but in Psalm 112 they are appropriated differently, with each term applying instead to the righteous.[2] The precise meaning of the shift in usage will be explored below in the Bridging Contexts section.

"righteousness endures forever"	Ps 112:3b, 9b	Ps 111:3b
"gracious and compassionate"	Ps 112:4b	Ps 111:4b
"justice/just"	Ps 112:5b	Ps 111:7a
"remembered"	Ps 112:6b	Ps 111:4a
"secure/established"	Ps 112:8a	Ps 111:8a
"provides/gifts"	Ps 112:9a	Ps 111:5a
"forever"	Ps 112:6b	Ps 111:5, 8, 9

The differing application of these terms (i.e., to Yahweh or to the righteous) further validates the earlier commentary on Psalm 111 (see above). In Psalm 111 the psalmist focused on the works of God, thus providing a rationale for the fear of God; Psalm 112 begins with the fear of God and then considers the shape of human life in the light of a proper relationship

---

2. While not identical terms, "commandments" in Ps 112:1b and "precepts" in Ps 111:7b certainly function as synonyms, so suggesting further the relationship between the two psalms. While not a linguistic link, the final verse in each psalm also reflects the connection between the two poems. Psalm 111:10 recounts the fate of those who fear the Lord, while Ps 112:10 focuses on the fate of the wicked. The juxtaposition of the upright and the wicked in the two psalms recalls the comparison made in Ps 1:6.

with God. While Psalm 111 is thoroughly theological in orientation, Psalm 112 maintains an anthropological orientation.

Introductory Beatitude (112:1)

PSALM 112 BEGINS WITH A CALL to praise the Lord (*halelu yah*). The opening line does not figure into the acrostic structure of the psalm but functions more as a heading to the entire psalm, thus explaining why the NIV has set the call to praise apart from the rest of the psalm.[3]

Blessed are those who fear the LORD. The acrostic structure of the psalm begins in verse 1b with the beatitude. The Hebrew word *'ashre* ("blessed") appears with considerable regularity in the wisdom literature of the Old Testament, where it introduces conduct and attitudes that the faithful of God should embody.[4] These actions and attitudes, however, are not arbitrary commitments but ones signaling that our lives are congruent with the larger purposes of God. Contrary to contemporary society's fixation with self-fulfillment, the psalmist rightly knows that the blessed life is the one that is oriented towards God and God's purposes in the world. The psalmist calls those blessed who "fear the LORD" and "delight in his commands." In Psalm 111 the psalmist calls people to delight in the *works* of God, while here in Psalm 112 the emphasis shifts to the *words* of God.

Markers of a Blessed Life (112:2–5)

IN THE NEXT SECTION THE PSALMIST provides several markers of a life that takes seriously the fear of the Lord while delighting in his purposes. These markers contain both a familial and a societal component, thereby enriching and extending what the psalmist means by *'ashre*.

Their children will be mighty in the land. A blessed life, one lived in fear of God and in delight of his word, yields benefits for one's family. Verse 2a suggests that this person's offspring will become "mighty" (*gibbor*) in the land. While the term *gibbor* typically occurs in reference to military might or power, its metaphorical use suggests a person who is powerful or influential, one similar to the person who sits at the city gate in Proverbs 31:23. While Old Testament writers relied on a sense of cause and effect for understanding much of reality, caution is in order in that regard when reading a text

---

3. In the Hebrew a *paseq* (a vertical accent mark) sets it off from the remainder of the poetic line.

4. Cf. Job 5:17; Prov 3:13; 8:32, 34; 14:21; 16:20; 20:7; 28:14; 29:18; Eccl 10:17. The term appears repeatedly in the Psalter, with considerable use in Books 4 and 5. Cf. Pss 1:1; 2:12; 32:1, 2; 33:12; 34:8; 40:4; 41:1; 65:4; 84:4, 5, 16; 89:15; 94:12; 106:3; 112:1; 119:1, 2; 127:5; 128:1, 2; 137:8, 9; 144:15; 146:5.

such as this one. Psalm 112 does not suggest that "mighty" offspring are a *reward* for faithful living; rather, they are the *result* of faithful living.

Wealth and riches are in their houses. Although the words "wealth" (*hon*) and "riches" (*'osher*) rarely appear in the Psalter, they occur repeatedly in the book of Proverbs (eighteen times and nine times, respectively).[5] Despite their infrequency throughout the book of Psalms, their appearance in a wisdom psalm seems fitting. Phil Botha has suggested that Psalm 112:3 likely alludes to Proverbs 1:13.[6] In Proverbs 1 the sagacious father warns his son of the enticing words of the "sinful men" who promise to "get all sorts of valuable things [*hon*]" in order to fill their houses with plunder. Such wealth is the result of their violence against others. The psalmist provides a counter to such claims by linking wealth with a life that delights in the laws of the Lord. Although at first glance Psalm 112:3 appears to buttress contemporary claims of a "prosperity gospel"—the fear of the Lord will yield material wealth—such an interpretation would be a serious misreading of the verse. Verse 3 does not promise that wealth will come to those who fear the Lord—it merely functions as the premise for what occurs in verse 4 and especially verse 9. Those who have wealth and riches have received them *from God*, but they are to be used *for the community*.

Even in darkness light dawns. The translation of verse 4 into English has generated considerable scholarly discussion. The verse begins with the verb *zarah*, "has risen." The chief interpretive question concerns the subject of verse 4a. The NIV understands "light" to be the subject of the sentence, a choice that is grammatically possible. Understood as such, "even in darkness light dawns" functions as a metaphor for deliverance. Other scholars agree that light functions as the subject, but they maintain that light functions as a metaphor for God. Numerous texts refer to God as light, thus again making this option equally plausible (cf., Pss 27:1; 37:6; Mic 7:8). This line of argumentation is supported further by the use of "gracious and compassionate" in Psalm 112:4b, terms used to characterize God in Exodus 34:6. The third option, and the one adopted here, suggests that the subject of verb *zarah* in Psalm 112:4a is actually the "blessed" person mentioned in verses 1–3. Following this reading, the verse could be translated as:

---

5. Outside Ps 112, the word "wealth" appears in Psalms only in Pss 44:13 and 119:14, and "riches" only in Pss 49:7 and 52:9.

6. Phil J. Botha, "'Wealth and Riches are in His House' (Ps 112:3): Acrostic Wisdom Psalms and the Development of Anti-materialism," in *The Shape and Shaping of the Book of Psalms: The Current State of Scholarship*, ed. Nancy L. deClaissé-Walford (Atlanta: SBL Press, 2014), 105–28.

He will rise as a light in the darkness for the upright ones,
  he is gracious, compassionate, and just.[7]

In verses 2–3 the psalmist outlines the blessings that will come to those who live in the fear of the Lord and delight in his purposes (v. 1b). Beginning in verse 4, however, there are social implications for how one conducts his or her life. The blessed life is marked both by what it receives and by what it does. The blessed person acts for the sake of others, thus securing the good of the community of the upright (v. 4a). In this way the blessed person does indeed take on the qualities of God (i.e., gracious and compassionate; Exod 34:6) while also exemplifying God's commitment to a just world.

Conduct their affairs with justice. Psalm 112:5 provides another social marker of a blessed life. Even though the blessed person apparently has attained stature in the land (v. 2a) and a measure of wealth (v. 3a), one who truly delights in the ways of God is generous, lends freely, and carries out his or her business with justice. Although the theme of antagonism between the rich and the poor and the subsequent oppression of the poor run throughout the Old Testament, these issues became particularly acute during the Persian period, especially with the development of coinage during that time.[8] Nehemiah 5 reflects the grave social and economic conditions of that period. Without question, the system of interest in the ancient Near East had long been "one of the principal causes of the pauperization of broad classes of the population" and the rapid growth of debt slavery.[9] Israel's law codes prohibited the charging of interest and the taking of sureties (Exod 22:24–26; Deut 24:6, 10–14). Leviticus 25:35–38 also forbids charging interest or selling people "food at a profit." Strikingly, in Leviticus 25:36 the community is told to fear God and refrain from such injustice.

The Fear of God and the Absence of Fear (112:6–9)

IN THE SECOND MAJOR SECTION the psalmist claims that those who fear Yahweh have no reason to fear anything in life. Nothing can occur that will unseat the one who fears Yahweh. If Psalm 112 was composed during the postexilic period, as many suggest, then the psalm was likely addressing

---

7. Author's translation. For a similar assessment of the issue, see Goldingay, *Psalms 3*, 311; Hossfeld and Zenger, *Psalms 3*, 168–69.

8. Pierre Briant, *From Cyrus to Alexander: A History of the Persian Empire* (Winona Lake, IN: Eisenbrauns, 2002), 406–10; Erich Zenger, "Geld als Lebensmittel? Über die Wertung des Reichtums im Psalter (Psalmen 15.49.112)," *JBTh* 21 (2006): 73–96.

9. Hossfeld and Zenger, *Psalms 3*, 174.

the uncertainty and fear that may have paralyzed many within the community in Yehud.

The righteous will never be shaken. The verb *mot* can mean to sway or to totter as a sign of instability and impermanence. In Psalm 46, for example, the psalmist announces that the nations are tottering (*mot* [v. 6]), yet he confesses that the city of God remains immovable; it cannot totter (*mot* [v. 5]). Like the city of God, the blessed person cannot be moved or shaken by the affairs of the world.

They will have no fear. Psalm 112:7–8 addresses two issues that likely would have produced anxiety and fear: bad news and the presence of enemies. Despite the reality of both threats, those who fear God have no need to fear (*yara'*). The absence of fear, however, does not come from the denial or dismissal of such threats; rather, the absence of fear stems from the psalmist's trust in the Lord. Those who fear and trust in God possess hearts that are firmly established (*nakon* [v. 7a]) and unflinching (*samuk* [v. 8a]). And in the end, they will watch in triumph over their enemies.

Their horn will be lifted high. Although "horn" (*qeren*) can be associated with altars elsewhere in the Old Testament (Exod 27:2; Lev 8:15; Ps 18:3), its use in Psalm 112 refers to the horn of an animal and functions as a metaphor for power and strength. The metaphor is pressed further in many contexts and refers to military might (1 Sam 2:10; Lam 2:17). The horn metaphor serves as an apt conclusion to this section (vv. 6–9). Those who could have been brought low by their own angst and fear concerning daily affairs will instead be lifted high because their hearts are firmly established and unflinching in their fear of the Lord.

The Fate of the Wicked (112:10)

PSALM 112 CONCLUDES WITH an assessment concerning the fate of the wicked. In verse 8 the psalmist explains that the righteous will "look" (*ra'ah*) upon their foes in triumph, while, in contrast, the psalmist contends in verse 10 that the wicked will look (*ra'ah*) and be "vexed" (*ka'as*) to the point of irritation. The anger of the wicked will result in their gnashing of teeth, like that of a wild animal on the attack (cf. Pss 35:16; 37:12). The imagery, however, does little to enhance the ferocity of the enemy, for, as the psalmist quickly adds, the wicked "waste away" (*masas*). Elsewhere in the Old Testament the term *masas* often appears in contexts related to a struggle or a military engagement (e.g., Josh 2:11; 5:1; 7:5; Ezek 21:7; Mic 1:4). In each instance, the heart or courage of one participant is said to have "melted away" in the light of the apparent strength and vigor of the opponent. According to Psalm 112, while the wicked may gnash their teeth, ultimately they will melt away in the light of the one with greater strength.

The final line of the psalm sums up the fate of the wicked: "the longings of the wicked will come to nothing." The word for "longings" (*ta'awah*) can also be translated "desires," which is preferable is this context and likely references the desires of the wicked to bring harm to the righteous.[10] The psalmist has spent the previous nine verses outlining the "desires" of the righteous person—desires that will bring good both to one's family (vv. 2–3) and the larger community (vv. 4–5, 9). These desires stem from a fear of God and a delight in God's ways. As a result of such faithfulness, this person's righteousness "endures forever" (v. 9). Not so with the wicked. The longings of the wicked will perish or come to an end (*'abad*). Thematically and linguistically, the fate of the wicked in Psalm 112:10 mirrors the fate of the wicked in Psalm 1:6—both will come to an end (*'abad*).

A STRONG ANTHROPOLOGICAL focus runs throughout Psalm 112. Firmly rooted in the wisdom tradition, this psalm leads to two fundamental claims about what it means to be human. The first concerns human action, the second, human identity.

Fear of the Lord and reality. Interpreters of wisdom literature have frequently associated the teaching of the sages with a type of philosophic idealism that transcends time and space. As Leo Perdue has aptly noted, this kind of idealism "understands the teachings of the sages as disconnected ideas that are seen as eternal thoughts the [sages] understood to be true."[11] Consequently, the notion of the "fear of the LORD" often remains an abstract concept for most readers of Scripture; the intersection between that sort of piety and human life seems vague at best.[12]

Although Psalm 112 may be classified as a wisdom psalm, it resists the temptation to move toward philosophical idealism and instead grounds the psalm in the reality of human life. The psalmist opens with a beatitude praising the "those who fear the LORD, who find great delight in his commands" and then moves to trace in some detail the contours of just such a life. The promise of prominent children coupled with wealth and riches (vv. 1–2)

---

10. Hossfeld and Zenger, *Psalms 3*, 174.

11. Leo Perdue, *The Sword and the Stylus: An Introduction to Wisdom in the Age of Empires* (Grand Rapids: Eerdmans, 2008), 1.

12. Obviously, wisdom literature as a genre remains keenly focused on observation in an attempt to understand life and how it is meant to be lived well. In Prov 6 the author references the behavior of a number of animals in the world in an attempt to illustrate how life is meant to be lived. Despite such earthy illustrations, interpreters have allowed a certain type of idealism to dominate how wisdom literature is read and appropriated.

may cause some to bypass this psalm on the assumption that such language appears too closely aligned with the more recent movements promoting a "prosperity gospel." Yet the content of the remainder of the psalm holds in check such unbridled thinking. In verse 4, the "blessed" person functions as a light to those who are in darkness and in need of compassion and justice. The mention of the psalmist to be generous and to lend freely is suggestive, implying there are many within that society in desperate need of assistance.

In the next section of the psalm, the challenging circumstances surrounding the psalmist are magnified. Verse 6 says the righteous will not be shaken; they will not be moved by the adverse circumstances that surround them. Further, they will not fear bad news (v. 7), nor will they have any fear of their foes (v. 8). One could even consider the mention of the poor in verse 9 as another indication of the difficult circumstances faced by the "blessed" person.

Hossfeld and Zenger note that "the psalmist's optimism is not as naïve as it seems to some interpreters. On the contrary, the psalm is intended to be an encouragement, in terms of wisdom theology, to live Yahweh's torah in the midst of a hostile and godless world and to seek happiness of one's life in it."[13] But I would suggest that the psalmist calls for even more. Despite the circumstances of the day, the psalmist suggests that the blessed person is also the one who uses his prosperity (vv. 1–2) for the sake of others (vv. 4, 9). His piety shapes his morality. Psalm 112 serves a reminder that piety and morality belong together and that both are manifestations of the same commitment to God (v. 1).

In the New Testament, the book of James (also strongly influenced by wisdom theology) reflects on this same theme. James suggests that while wisdom comes "from heaven," this wisdom is "peace-loving, considerate, submissive, full of mercy and good fruit, impartial and sincere" (Jas 3:17). James argues that the wise person understands the inherent connection between faith and works—piety and morality: "Do not merely listen to the word . . . . Do what it says" (1:22). Later in his letter he makes the connection even clearer: "As the body without the spirit is dead, so faith without deeds is dead" (2:26).

The book of James condemns those who have hoarded wealth for themselves and "lived on earth in luxury and self-indulgence" while turning a deaf ear to those in need (5:5). That type of person is the antithesis of a wise person, and that kind of life is the antithesis of the "blessed life" articulated in Psalm 112 and reiterated in the book of James.

---

13. Hossfeld and Zenger, *Psalms 3*, 174.

Human life as a reflection of God. Psalm 112 invites the reader to consider the shape of human life—more specifically, the shape of human life when lived in the fear of God and in alignment with his purposes in the world. The location of Psalm 112 immediately after Psalm 111 invites further thought about human life. The linguistic and thematic connections that exist between the two psalms do far more than simply provide a rationale for the present location of the "twin psalms"; they invite the reader to reflect theologically on human life in relation to God.

As suggested in the introductory material to this psalm, Psalms 111 and 112 share a number of terms. These terms are applied to God in Psalm 111, while in Psalm 112 the psalmist has shifted the referent by applying the terms to the blessed person instead. God's kingship is celebrated in Psalm 111:3a, followed by the declaration that God's righteousness will endure forever (v. 3b). Similarly, the righteousness of the person who delights in God's commands will also endure forever (Ps 112:3b). In Psalm 111:4b the psalmist alludes to Exodus 34:6 when calling God gracious and compassionate, while in Psalm 112:4b the person who lives in the fear of the Lord is labeled "gracious and compassionate," thereby taking on the characteristics of Israel's God. God will be remembered for his mighty works (Ps 111:4a), while the righteous person will be remembered for his unyielding commitment to God and God's ways (Ps 112:6a).[14] The righteous person remains secure and unflinching (*samuk*; Ps 112:8a) because he delights in the law of the Lord, which is also said to be established (*samuk*) forever and ever (Ps 111:8a). Even as God gives food to those who fear him (Ps 111:5a), the psalmist gives to the poor (Ps 112:9a).[15]

By placing these two psalms adjacent to one another, the psalmists suggest that the works of God in Psalm 111 become the works of the wise human being in Psalm 112. In "fear[ing] the LORD" and "find[ing] great delight in his commandments" (v. 1), the blessed person does much more than simply earn the good will of the deity in hopes of securing an easy life. Worshipers associated with the religions surrounding Israel sought to placate their gods in the hope of ensuring a blessing for themselves. In such

---

14. Psalms 111:4a and 112:6b include the noun *zeker*, which comes from the verb "to remember" and refers to the mention or utterance of a name. The implication is that the name of God and the name of the righteous will continue to be remembered; because of what they have done, they will not be forgotten.

15. These connections might be easily overlooked because the translators of the NIV have opted to replace the singular language (i.e., his/he) with plural language (i.e., they/their) based upon their translation technique. The decision to make this shift makes sense given their aims for the translation, but such a shift also makes these subtle connections between the psalms less evident.

an arrangement, the human-divine interaction looks more like a transaction and less like a relationship. These two psalms together suggest that as human beings choose to fear God and delight in his commandments, we not only participate in God's ways in the world—we also discover that our lives begin to resemble the God we serve.

Likewise, the Sermon on the Mount in the Gospel of Matthew performs a similar function by outlining the aspects of a faithful life of obedient service to God. But these texts do much more than simply list acceptable behaviors; these texts invite disciples into a new way of life. We are told that those who mourn and are meek, those who hunger and thirst for righteousness will participate in the kingdom of heaven (Matt 5:3b, 10b). This new way of life is patterned on God's ways in the world. To live out the Sermon on the Mount is to embody God's will in the world. Those who are called blessed, who choose to live out God's will in the world, will become known as "children of God" (5:9)—their life resembles that of God, the giver of life.[16] The beatitudes leave little doubt that such a life will come amid persecution and "all kinds of evil" (5:11), yet true disciples are to live in such a way to "let your light shine before others, that they may see your good deeds and glorify your Father in heaven" (5:16).[17]

The blessed person in Psalm 112 redefines human life. When lived well, human life is a reflection of the divine life. Through our relationship to God and his word, we are reminded that the shape of our lives is meant to reflect that of God's. To live thus is wisdom indeed.

THE BLESSED LIFE. Psalm 112 invites the reader to consider the nature of the blessed life. Our culture offers a seductive and persistent message as to what comprises the happy or blessed life—a message that affects most all of us, in one way or another, despite our willful objections to the core principles of that message. In his book *Shiny Objects: Why We Spend Money We Don't Have in Search of Happiness We Cannot Buy,* James Roberts explores our fascination with such messaging and the deleterious effects that it has on our lives as individuals, families, and communities.[18]

---

16. Charles H. Talbert, *Reading the Sermon on the Mount: Character Formation and Decision Making in Matthew 5–7* (Grand Rapids: Baker Academic, 2006), 57–58.

17. In many ways Jesus' call for his disciples to be a light echoes the call in Ps 112:4 for the righteous to be a light for the upright in the midst of darkness.

18. James A. Roberts, *Shiny Objects: Why We Spend Money We Don't Have in Search of Happiness We Cannot Buy* (New York: HarperCollins, 2011).

Throughout his book, one of the underlying claims is that most people chase after "shiny objects" because they are not sure what constitutes a meaningful life. He explains:

> In our rush, rush world, a common way we tell others who we are (or would like to be) is through our use and display of material possessions. He drives a Mercedes, so he must be a captain of industry. A truck and he must be a cowboy or at least a rugged individualist. . . . This tendency to define ourselves by the products we consume results in what researchers call the "extended self"; in other words, our possessions become an *extension* of who we are.[19]

Our failure to understand what constitutes a meaningful life suggests that we have a deficient theological anthropology and, to compensate, we are forced to create our own identity, created in our own wishful image.

Psalm 112, however, seeks to redirect us from such misguided attempts by grounding us in a biblical view of the blessed life—one that is rooted in a relationship and embodied in action. If the fundamental question of our day, and any day, is, "What does it mean to be human?"—and further, "What does it mean to have a meaningful life?"—then Psalm 112 offers a response. In the previous psalm (Ps 111), the poet celebrated the work of God through redemption and the provision of his law. These works of God are directed at humans for the sake of relationship. God has acted so that humanity might respond. Psalm 112 provides one such response to the work of God by acknowledging what a blessed life should entail. According to the psalmist, this blessed life is one that lives in relationship with God ("fear the LORD") and one that finds "great delight" in the purposes of God in the world (v. 1). Yet the psalmist continues by suggesting that the meaningful life, the blessed life, requires a commitment to others that is exhibited through meaningful action: to be a light in darkness, to be generous in lending, and to provide for the poor. In short, one's actions are driven by one's understanding of a meaningful life, and one's understanding of life is driven by one's fundamental commitment. If a person's fundamental commitment derives from his or her relationship with God, then his or her actions should follow from that relationship. In the end, that person will resemble the God we serve. That life will be more properly the "extended self" that Roberts mentions. Rather than our possessions defining this extended self, God and God's ways in the world will do so. And in the process we will know fully the meaning of a blessed life.

---

19. Ibid., 6.

Psalm 113

¹ Praise the LORD.

Praise the LORD, you his servants
    praise the name of the LORD.
² Let the name of the LORD be praised,
    both now and forevermore.
³ From the rising of the sun to the place where it sets,
    the name of the LORD is to be praised.
⁴ The LORD is exalted over all the nations,
    his glory above the heavens.
⁵ Who is like the LORD our God,
    the One who sits enthroned on high,
⁶ who stoops down to look
    on the heavens and the earth?
⁷ He raises the poor from the dust
    and lifts the needy from the ash heap;
⁸ he seats them with princes,
    with the princes of their people.
⁹ He settles the childless woman in her home
    as a happy mother of children.

Praise the LORD.

PSALM 113 IS A PRAISE psalm opening and closing with the call to praise the Lord (*halelu yah*). The NIV has rightly set verses 1a and 9b apart from the remainder of the psalm—a move that highlights their role as a framing device (*inclusio*) for the entire poem. The appearance of *halelu yah* at the beginning of Psalm 113 connects it with the two previous psalms, thus creating a linguistic arc across the three psalms. There are other verbal parallels that connect Psalm 112 with Psalm 113. For example, in Psalm 112:2 the upright will be blessed (*barak*), while in Psalm 113:2 the name of God will be blessed (*barak*). In Psalm 112:9a the righteous person gives freely to the poor (*'ebyon*), and in Psalm 113:7b God lifts up the poor (*'ebyon*). In Psalm 112:9c the blessed person is exalted (*rum*) in honor (*kabod*), while in Psalm 113:4 God's glory (*kabod*) is lifted high (*rum*) above the nations. Just as the verbal links between Psalm 111 and

Psalm 112 signal the connection between God and the God-fearer, so too do the links between Psalm 112 and Psalm 113.

Although Psalm 113 serves as the final psalm in an arc from Psalms 111–113, Psalm 113 also serves as the first psalm in the next collection, Psalms 113–118. This collection is frequently labeled the Egyptian Hallel or the Passover Hallel because of its references to the exodus in Psalms 114 and 118. Although Psalm 113 does not reference the exodus event, the text's reference to Yahweh's cosmic kingship over the nations and his commitment to deliver the poor serves as an apt thematic introduction to the entire collection. In contemporary Jewish life, these psalms are recited in conjuection with the Passover meal.

The body of Psalm 113 is comprised of three evenly divided sections. Verses 1–3 open the psalm with a call to praise the Lord, but more specifically to praise the *name* of the Lord (see below). In the second and third sections of the psalm the psalmist registers two fundamental reasons that justify praise of God. The second section, verses 4–6, celebrates God's enthronement in the heavens over the nations; and in the final section, verses 7–9, the psalmist recounts the work of God in behalf of the poor and needy.

Praise the Name of the Lord (113:1–3)

THE PSALMIST OPENS WITH AN EXTENDED CALL for the servants of the Lord to praise him. Poetically, this call to praise is reinforced through the repetition of language and imagery.

Praise the LORD. As noted above, verse 1a calls for the people to praise the Lord (*halelu yah*). Following this initial exhortation, the psalmist extends his invitation by using the verb "to praise" (*halal*) three more times in the first three verses (vv. 1b, 1c, 3b). The theme of praising God appears as well in verse 2a, with the psalmist opting for the verb "to bless" (*barak*), a term that can mean bless in the sense of worship or honor.[1]

The Name of the LORD. In addition to the threefold call to praise God, there is a threefold mention of the name of the Lord (vv. 1c, 2a, 3b). The focus on the name of God in verses 1–3 functions in tandem with the claim in verses 4–6 that Yahweh is the exalted one who is "enthroned on high." In such instances, the phrase "the name of the LORD" functions as a cipher for the real and felt presence of God.[2] Although God is enthroned in the

---

1. Goldingay translates Ps 113:2a as, "May Yhwh's name be worshipped" (*Psalms 3*, 315).
2. Kraus explains that the "name" stands "as a substitute term in place of the person and becomes the embodiment of the presence and power of God" (Kraus, *Psalms 60–150*, 1993], 368). On the relationship between "name and presence" see Tryggve N. D. Mettinger,

heavens as the cosmic King, Israel's God was present with and accessible to his people because his name dwelled among them. Earlier psalms also connect the name of the Lord with the certainty of his presence. In Psalm 75:1, for example, the psalmist declares, "We praise you, God, we praise you, for your Name is near."[3]

Using both temporal and spatial imagery, the writer of Psalm 113 highlights the durative nature of the praise of the Lord. In verse 2b he states that such praise should continue "both now and forevermore." The phrase suggests the "limitless continuity of God's praise," a dominant theme throughout the remainder of the Psalter.[4] The psalmist couples this call for unceasing praise with a call for universal praise of God. The phrase "from the rising of the sun to the place where it sets" may at first appear to be a temporal reference—"from sun up until sun down"—yet upon further investigation the spatial dimension is clearly in view. The emphasis is not on *time* but location—the praise of the Lord's name should extend from one horizon to the other. Similar usage of the same phrase also appears in Psalm 50:1, where the psalmist declares,

> The Mighty One, God, the LORD,
> speaks and summons the earth
> from the rising of the sun to where it sets.

The final line, "from the rising of the sun to where it sets," modifies "earth" and thereby clarifies the expansive rule of the Mighty One. The psalmist concludes the first section of Psalm 113 with a similar call. The praise of the Lord's name should fill the entire earth, from horizon to horizon.

The Lord is Exalted (113:4–6)

WHILE THE CALL FOR THE PRAISE of God to extend from horizon to horizon (v. 3) serves as a fitting conclusion to the opening strophe of the psalm, the verse also functions as a transition to the second strophe in the poem and the spatial imagery that dominates in that section. All three verses point to Yahweh as the exalted Lord who reigns on high.

The psalmist makes three claims about God in this strophe: he is exalted

---

In Search of God: The Meaning and Message of the Everlasting Names (Minneapolis: Fortress, 1988); Sandra L. Richter, *The Deuteronomistic History and the Name Theology: leshakken shemo sham in the Bible and the Ancient Near East*, BZAW 318 (Berlin: de Gruyter, 2002).

3. The reference to the name of the Lord can be found in a number of the Asaphite psalms. Cf. Pss 74:7; 76:1; 79:8b; 80:18b; 83:16.

4. Hossfeld and Zenger, *Psalms 3*, 182. Cf. Pss 115:18; 121:8; 125:2; 131:3.

---

over the nations, his glory is above the heavens, and he is enthroned on high. Each spatial statement builds on the previous one, thus providing additional theological depth to Israel's confession about her God. In verse 4a Yahweh is acknowledged as exalted over the nations, so suggesting his reign as Divine King over all other earthly rulers and powers.[5] In the second claim the psalmist extends Yahweh's rule to "above the heavens," thus securing Yahweh's position as Divine King over earth *and* heaven. The final claim makes clear what has been suggested in the two previous claims: Yahweh occupies his rightful place as the Divine King who is enthroned on high.

As divine king, Yahweh stoops down to look over the heavens and the earth. Whereas some psalms that appear earlier in the Psalter (Books 1–3) employ the same image (i.e., the enthroned Yahweh looking down from the heavens), the imagery in those psalms has a much more foreboding sense implying that this divine glance is reserved primarily for the testing of the people of God (Pss 11:4; 14:2; 17:2–3). In Psalm 113, however, the motive appears altogether different. In this instance, Yahweh's enthronement above the heavens reinforces his supremacy over all powers, both earthly and heavenly (v. 6b). Yet Yahweh's exaltation above the heavens does not suggest the hiddenness of God, or, worse yet, abandonment by God. To the contrary, his location above the heavens ensures the faithfulness of God and his capacity to deliver.[6] Verse 6a holds in tension the immanence and transcendence of God; God is exalted above the heavens yet cognizant of his people as he "stoops down to look."

The Lord Delivers the Weak (113:7–9)

THE CLAIMS OF RADICAL TRANSCENDENCE in verses 4–6 are met with claims of radical immanence in verses 7–9. Yahweh is worthy of Israel's praise because he is in fact the Divine King enthroned on high, but also because he is the Divine King who acts as a king by delivering the most vulnerable.

He raises the poor. The psalmist proclaims that the Divine King will raise up the "poor" (*dal*). There are many terms for the "poor" in the Psalter, and each term has a degree of elasticity to it based upon its context.[7]

---

5. Harry P. Nasuti, "'Who is Like the Lord our God?' Relating Theology and Ethics in Psalm 113," in *The Psalter as Witness: Poetry, Theology, Genre*, ed. W. Dennis Tucker Jr. and W. H. Bellinger (Waco, TX: Baylor University Press, 2017), 27–45.

6. Beate Ego, "'Der Herr blickt herab von der Höhe seines Heiligtums.' Zur Vorstellung von Gottes himmlischen Thronen in exilisch-nachexilischer Zeit," *ZAW* 110 (1998): 556–69.

7. On the various terms for the poor in the Psalter, see W. Dennis Tucker Jr., "A Polysemiotic Approach to the Poor in the Psalms," *PRSt* 31 (2004): 425–39.

Of all the terms for the poor, *dal* remains the most consistent in meaning both in the Psalter and across the Old Testament. The term connotes economic deprivation; the *dal* have no financial and economic resources and consequently are subject to exploitation and oppression. The *dal* have no capacity to deliver themselves; their survival is contingent upon Yahweh's faithfulness to raise them up.

The second half of verse 7 employs a second term from the "poor" wordfield: *'ebyon*. Frequently this term is translated as "needy" and suggests those who live a meager, subsistent existence. The fact that the *'ebyon* have been relegated to the ash heap (*ashpot*) suggests acute material poverty and, even further, acute social ostracism. Like the *dal*, the hope of the *'ebyon* rests entirely with the work of God.

The wordplay between verses 4a and 7a is lost in the English translation, which is unfortunate because it highlights the theological strand that connects the second and third strophes. Both verses contain the verb "to raise up" or "to be exalted" (*rum*). In the first instance (v. 4a), it is God who is raised up or exalted; in the second, the poor and needy are raised up. The implication is clear: the one who is raised up (v. 4a) is the only one who *can* raise up the poor (v. 7a). Not only will he raise them up, but he will also sit them with the princes of his people. Because of the work of God, the poor have moved from the margins of society into the very heart of the community. God's position as the exalted one gives hope to those awaiting their deliverance, those waiting to be lifted up out of the dust and the ash heap.

He settles the childless woman. The psalmist concludes the third strophe by declaring that God will make the childless woman the joyous mother of many children (v. 9). In the ancient world, barrenness created a social stigma for women, one that marginalized such women and prevented them from enjoying the benefits of participation in the community. Despite that stark reality, the psalmist asserts that there is hope with Yahweh. The text reads literally, "he causes the barren woman of the family to dwell [*yashab*] as a joyous mother of children." Similar to the wordplay with *rum* mentioned above, *yashab* ("to sit") creates another wordplay between the second and third strophes. In verse 5 Yahweh "sits" (*yashab*) on high. The God who "sits" (*yashab*) on high is in fact the only one who can make a place for the barren women to dwell or sit (*yashab*) in a house surrounded by children.

Praise the LORD. The psalm closes where it began, namely, by calling people to praise God. Having confessed that God sits enthroned in the heavens as the Divine King, and having confessed that God will deliver the poor and oppressed, the community can do no other than praise God.

STANDING AT THE CENTER of Psalm 113 is verse 5. Nine poetic lines appear before verse 5 and nine appear after it. In that verse the psalmist queries, "Who is like the LORD our God, the One who sits enthroned on high?" One could argue that the remainder of the psalm is a reflection of and response to that question. Taken as a whole, the psalm does more than offer a negative response to the question (i.e., "no one is like our God")—it actually creates a justification for such a claim based on who God is and what he does.

The transcendence and immanence of God. Given the destruction of Jerusalem by Babylon, the subsequent exile, and even the rather bleak circumstances that greeted the people of God when they returned home, one might not blame a psalmist had he tamped down his cosmic claims about the universal rule of God. After all, in the ancient Near East, military success and the well-being of a nation were often associated with the might of a national deity. Given the structure of such a worldview and given Israel's recent demise, there were potential grounds for calling into question the faithfulness of Yahweh, much less, Yahweh's might. Yet difficulties not withstanding, the psalmist presses forward with a radical confession of the incommensurability of Israel's God: "Who is like our God?" The implied answer is clear: there is none.

The psalmist emphasizes the incommensurability of God by acknowledging that Israel's God is no regional deity—he is not confined to regional worship centers, nor is his identity fashioned by the success or failure of his people; rather, this God, Israel's God, is in fact exalted over the nations and enthroned above the heavens as the Divine King on high. Psalm 113 is not unique in this claim. Despite the exile and the potential implosion of Israel's theological worldview, numerous texts from the exilic period and beyond posed a similar rhetorical question or made an affirmation of the same: there is no god like Yahweh. Frequently these confessions acknowledge Yahweh's place in the heavens, or even above the heavens, as a means of signaling the *sui generis* character of Israel's God.[8] In Isaiah 44:7, for example, the prophet places this question on the lips of God:

---

8. Konrad Schmid has explained that the loss of the first temple, in particular, likely "triggered" a greater emphasis on Yahweh as the God of heaven. Schmid also traces the various ways biblical writers attempted to articulate the relationship between Yahweh and the heavens. See Konrad Schmid, "Himmelgott, Weltgott, und Schöpfer: 'Gott' und der 'Himmel' in der Literatur der Zeit des Zweiten Tempels," in *Der Himmel*, ed. D. Sattler and S. Vollenweider (Neukirchen-Vluyn: Neukirchener Verlag, 2006), 111–48.

"Who then is like me?" The presumed rhetorical question is followed up by a series of direct responses, including "there is no other Rock" (v. 8) and "there is no other god" (Isa 45:14; see also Isa 45:18, 21; 22). How can the prophet make such a claim given the destruction of Jerusalem and the reailty of exile? Earlier, in Isaiah 40:22–23, the prophet declares that

> [Yahweh] sits enthroned above the circle of the earth,
>   and its people are like grasshoppers.
> He stretches out the heavens like a canopy,
>   and spreads them out like a tent to live in.
> He brings princes to naught
>   and reduces the rulers of this world to nothing.

God sits above the earth and the heavens as the enthroned king. The prophet attempts to capture the spatial distance by suggesting that the people appear as mere grasshoppers when viewed from God's throne above the heavens. Such language suggests that God is utterly transcendent—so high, in fact, that he must stoop down to look upon the earth and the heavens (v. 6). Yet the image of a transcendent God as presented in Isaiah and Psalm 113 does not suggest a God utterly removed from the affairs of the world but a God who stands over all creation as its king, incapable of being thwarted by the machinations of the world. The enthroned king cannot be unseated.

This image of a fully transcendent God in Psalm 113, however, is juxtaposed with the image of a God who remains utterly involved in the lives of his people. As suggested above, the mention of God's name in the opening strophe (three times) suggests something of the immanence of the Divine King. In Solomon's prayer of dedication in 1 Kings 8, Solomon prays,

> LORD, the God of Israel, there is no God like you in heaven above or on earth below. . . . But will God really dwell on earth? The heavens, even the highest heaven cannot contain you. How much less this temple I have built [vv. 23, 27].

Immediately after this acknowledgment of the exalted nature of Israel's God, Solomon pleads with God and makes explicit reference to the nearness of God.

> Hear the cry and the prayer that your servant is praying in your presence this day. May your eyes be opened toward this temple night and day, this place which you have said, "My Name shall be there," so that you will hear the prayer your servant prays towards this place [vv. 28–29].

The sense of God's presence is coupled with the traditional claim that Yahweh's name is to dwell in the temple. In 1 Kings 8 Solomon holds in tandem the transcendent nature of Israel's God while simultaneously acknowledging the presence of God in the place where his name dwells. Similarly to the claims in 1 Kings 8, Psalm 113 suggests that the distance of God in no way precludes the nearness of God, and equally, the nearness of God in no way precludes his divine kingship. Although the two notions stand in considerable tension, it is precisely this inexplicable set of claims that justifies Israel's belief that their God, Yahweh, is like no other; he is the one who stands over all creation yet remains capable of intervening in the lives of his people.

Theology of poor. Because Israel's God is the God who stands over all creation yet is fully present with his people, the psalmist can claim that this God intervenes in the lives of individuals. In Psalm 111 the psalmist references the works of God and, in particular in the first half of the psalm, alludes to the events surrounding the exodus. Immediately following Psalm 113, Psalm 114 makes explicit reference to the events of the exodus. In both instances the nation as a whole is in view as God demonstrates his faithfulness to his people through their deliverance. Psalm 113, however, shifts from a national or corporate identity and narrows the scope to focus on the poor (*dal*), the needy (*'ebyon*), and the barren. Although such language could be applied to the nation as a whole, Psalm 113 seems bent on praising God for his "transformative interventions in the lives of the powerless."[9] The juxtaposition of transcendence and immanence could be not starker: the enthroned God on high is intervening in the individual lives of those relegated to the ash heap.

 PSALM 113 CALLS THE FAITHFUL to praise God, and through this call to praise the psalm constructs a picture of God—or more precisely, through the images and language in Psalm 113 a more robust theological vision of God emerges. This picture, or vision, is one that resonates across Scripture but does not always comport with contemporary constructions of God.

The Institute for the Study of Religion at Baylor University conducted a comprehensive study titled "American Piety in the 21st Century: New Insights to the Depth and Complexity of Religion in the United States."[10]

---

9. Goldingay, *Psalms 3*, 319.

10. The findings from the study and its significance can be found in Paul Froese and Christopher Bader, *America's Four Gods—What We Say about God and What that Says about Us* (Oxford: Oxford University Press, 2015).

Based on the participants' responses to a series of questions, the researchers identified four "models" of God that seemed most prevalent in the United States. The first model is that of the Authoritarian God. Those who held to this model believed that God is highly involved in their daily lives and world affairs. They also tended to believe that God is quite angry and capable of meting out punishment. In the second model, the Benevolent God, individuals also believed that God was very active in their daily lives but is less angry and, instead, is a positive influence in the world. With the third model, the Critical God, individuals contended that God does not really interact with the world at all. While God may see the world and even have an unfavorable opinion of the world, any judgment or divine response will be meted out in the next life. In the last model, the Distant God, individuals contended that God is not active in the world but instead functions more as a "cosmic force which set the laws of nature in motion. As such, God does not 'do' things in the world and does not hold clear opinions about our activities or world events."[11]

The four models or images of God that emerged from the study reflect considerable diversity of opinion about God and God's way in and with the world. The first two models stress the nearness of God in human life, while the latter two models place emphasis on the distance of God. While these models reflect a commitment to the immanence and transcendence of God, each model emphasizes one element over the other.

Psalm 113, however, invites us to reflect on a God who seemingly defies any of these models. This psalm reminds us that a biblically grounded and theologically informed view of God asks us to hold both models in tension—the kind of tension that yields praise, not consternation. How do we not break out in unfettered praise when we consider that our God is enthroned on high as the Divine King? Yet how can we not be humbled deeply by a God who lifts people from the ash heap and creates life from barrenness? The capacity of this God, our God, to move from the highest realms of the heavens to the lowest rungs of earth is stunning. Perhaps that is why the early church forged another psalm, a confession that bore witness to a God who moved in such ways in the life, death, and resurrection of Jesus Christ. Although he became a slave (*doulos*), "obedient to death even death on a cross,"

> God exalted him to the highest place
>> and gave him the name that is above every name,
> that at the name of Jesus every knee should bow,

11. Ibid., 26.

in heaven and on earth and under the earth,
and every tongue acknowledge that Jesus Christ is Lord,
to the glory of God the father. (Phil 2:9–11)

This God is to be praised "from the rising of the sun to the place where it sets" (Ps 113:3) and "in heaven and on earth and under the earth" (Phil 2:10). Although he reigns on high, he has come among us. Praise the Lord—hallelujah.

Psalm 114

¹ When Israel came out of Egypt,
　　Jacob from a people of foreign tongue,
² Judah became God's sanctuary,
　　Israel his dominion.
³ The sea looked and fled,
　　the Jordan turned back;
⁴ the mountains leaped like rams,
　　the hills like lambs.
⁵ Why was it, sea, that you fled?
　　Why, Jordan, did you turn back?
⁶ Why, mountains, did you leap like rams,
　　you hills, like lambs?
⁷ Tremble, earth, at the presence of the Lord,
　　at the presence of the God of Jacob,
⁸ who turned the rock into a pool,
　　the hard rock into springs of water.

PSALM 114 IS FREQUENTLY categorized as a song of praise despite the glaring absence of many features normally present in such a song (e.g., an opening call to praise in the form of an imperative; participial phrases that describe the activities or qualities of God worth praising).[1] Despite the absence of certain features, the psalm celebrates Yahweh's victory over the primeval powers and his creation of a people, as well as his coming in glory (vv. 3–6). These events in the history of Israel merit the praise of the people of God. Although the references to the exodus and Israel's crossing of the Jordan demonstrate a certain affinity with the historical psalms, especially Psalms 105 and 135, the succinct nature of Psalm 114 and its larger focus on the theophanic presence of God differentiates it from the more extended recitals of Israel's past in the historical psalms. Erhard Gerstenberger suggests that Psalm 114 is a communal hymn characteristic of exilic-postexilic theological reflection in Judah with the dual purpose of praising God and instructing the people.[2]

---

1. Only one participial phrase appears in Ps 114:8a.

2. Gerstenberger, *Psalms, Part 2, and Lamentations*, 283. On the didactic function of the psalm, see Goldingay, *Psalms 3*, 321.

Psalm 114 is comprised of four strophes of two verses each (vv. 1–2, 3–4, 5–6, 7–8). Taken together, they form a concentric or chiastic pattern. The first strophe (vv. 1–2) and the last strophe (vv. 7–8) focus on God and God's work in the world, while the middle two strophes (vv. 3–4 and 5–6) focus on the reaction of the sea, the Jordan, mountains, and hills in the light of the larger work of God, both past and present, in behalf of his people. The parallelism within each verse is carefully structured, thus creating a sense of symmetry throughout the psalm.[3]

Deliverance and Election (114:1–2)

IN THE OPENING STROPHE THE PSALMIST recounts the decisive moment in Israel's history in verse 1 and then draws theological conclusions from that event in verse 2.

When Israel came out. The psalmist begins his psalm of praise by noting God's deliverance in bringing Israel out of Egypt, out from a people of a "foreign tongue [*lo'ez*]." Although the term *lo'ez* appears only here in the Old Testament, there are numerous other texts that refer to the speech of those in foreign lands as "strange and incomprehensible" (Isa 33:19; cf. Deut 28:49; Jer 5:15). The stress on the "foreign tongue" or "incomprehensible speech" of the captor highlights the sense of powerlessness experienced by the Israelites and, even more, emphasizes their sense of alienation in a foreign land. Typically, one would expect the text to connect deliverance from Egypt with the deliverance from slavery (cf. Deut 6:21), but in this instance the imagery has shifted, as has the emphasis. The opening verse references "Israel" and the "house of Jacob" but locates them in Egypt, estranged and alienated from those in that land because of the "foreign tongue." In Egypt, Israel was not a nation in the most basic sense but a homeless and threatened people in a foreign land when God called them out to be his people.

God's sanctuary. In Psalm 114:1 the psalmist refers to "Israel" and "the house of Jacob," but both labels are applied to the same people group. In verse 2, however, the language shifts to "Judah" and "Israel," thus raising a question as to whom these labels refer. The reference to Judah and Israel could be understood as signaling the Southern Kingdom and the Northern Kingdom, respectively. Although this understanding is possible, other biblical texts from the exilic and postexilic periods make reference

---

3. For example, verse 1 parallels "Israel" and "house of Jacob," as well as "Egypt" and "people of a foreign tongue." The second verse places "Judah" and "Israel" in parallel construction, as well as "sanctuary" and "dominion." Each verse in the psalm contains similar parallel constructions.

to "Judah" but also apply the label "Israel" to Judah. For example, Ezra 7:7 refers to all those living in Yehud in the postexilic period as "Israelites" and verse 6 refers to God as the "God of Israel." Other postexilic texts, such as Isaiah 58:1 and 65:9, refer to "Jacob" or the "descendants of Jacob" when referencing those living in Yehud during the same time. While varied, the labels used in Psalm 114:1–2 all refer to those living in Yehud in the postexilic period; they are the people of God.[4]

Verse 2 explains that when God brought Israel up from Egypt, he made them his "sanctuary" (*qodesh*) and his "dominion" (*memshalah*). Rather than understanding these two terms as different spheres of operation, the terms likely stand in parallel construction and "refer to the same matter, but from different perspectives."[5] In Exodus 19:6 Israel is referred to as "a kingdom of priests" and a "holy nation." Obviously, the text in Exodus is not referring to two different nations or two different entities but, instead, is using different ways of characterizing Israel's identity. Similarly, the psalmist explains that when God brought Israel up from the land of the "foreign tongue," he gave them an identity (see below, Bridging Contexts). Israel/ Judah/the house of Jacob were the people with whom God has chosen to "sanctuary." They were no longer strangers in a foreign land but the place from which the Divine King ruled and from whence he exercised his reign. Israel, as the people of God, became "the place where the God-king Yahweh is present on the world stage."[6]

Nature's Response to God's Work (114:3–4)

IN PSALM 114:3–4 THE PSALMIST rehearses the response of nature to God's awesome work of deliverance and election of his people. While terse and succinct, these verses draw from and build on the images and language associated with the exodus and the entry into the promised land.

The sea looked and fled. In verse 3 the psalmist alludes to the two stories of Israel's crossing a body of water. Verse 3a makes reference to the crossing of the Red Sea as recounted in Exodus 14–15. In the Song of Moses (Exod 15), the seas are said to have piled up like a wall and the deep waters to have "congealed in the heart of the sea [*yam*]" (15:8). In Exodus 15, nature was under the sovereign rule of Israel's God and was a means of deliverance for his people. In the second half of Psalm 114:3 the psalmist references the crossing of the Jordan in Joshua 3–5 and

---

4. Allen, *Psalms 101–150*, 103. Allen contends that "the fall of the Northern Kingdom is presupposed and Judah is the sole heir of the cultic designation 'Israel.'"
5. Hossfeld and Zenger, *Psalms 3*, 195.
6. Ibid.

couples the tradition of the crossing of the Red Sea with that tradition. The connection between the two crossings appears elsewhere in the Old Testament: "The LORD your God did to the Jordan what he had done to the Red Sea" (Josh 4:23). Similarly to the waters of the Red Sea, the waters of the Jordan "piled up in a heap" (Josh 3:16), once again signaling God's rule over creation. While Psalm 114 refers to the sea (*yam*) and the Jordan River, the imagery has shifted. Both bodies of water no longer "pile up"—they "flee" (*nus*) and "turn back" (*sabab*). These Hebrew words, *nus* and *sabab*, regularly refer to military struggles and the retreat of the defeated forces. For example, in Exodus 14, as the waters converged upon the Egyptians, the soldiers "fled" (*nus*). The battle scene in Psalm 114, however, appears to be between Yahweh and waters. In the ancient Near East, water functioned as a cipher for the larger threat of the chaotic forces in the world. Neighboring traditions refered to the deity as battling the waters of chaos in an effort to secure the orderliness of creation. The defeat of chaotic waters in these other traditions signaled the identity of the divine king. Psalm 114 draws from this larger tradition in suggesting that God has appeared (i.e., a theophany) and that when the waters "looked" (*ra'ab*) at God leading his people out of Egypt, they fled. Yahweh's defeat of the waters signals his rightful role as the Divine King.

The mountains leaped. When a theophany occurs and God's presence breaks into the world, all nature responds. The psalmist announces that the mountains and hills leap like rams and lambs. Some interpreters understand the mountains and hills as an allusion to the giving of the law at Sinai and the accompanying earthquake there. While this interpretation is possible given the reference to the exodus tradition in verse 3, the reference appears to have shifted. The only other place where the word "leap" (*raqad*) occurs in connection with mountains is in Psalm 29:6. Although the image of young animals as leaping about seems to convey a certain sense of playfulness and celebration, the metaphorical image is meant to convey that the power of God's cosmic kingship is recognized by all creation.[7] The use of *raqad* in Psalm 29 and the images in the surrounding verses appear to support this understanding. According to the psalmist,

---

7. Hossfeld and Zenger suggest that verse 4 differs markedly from verse 3 both in meaning and focus. While both verses focus on theophany, verse 3 highlights Yahweh's defeat of the chaotic forces. Verse 4, the authors contend, shows the land in full exuberance as Yahweh and his people return from a foreign land (Hossfeld and Zenger, *Psalms 3*, 197). While the verb "leap" (*raqad*) can mean "to dance," the idea of leaping as in fright or alarm seems better suited for the overall context of the psalm (cf. v. 8, "tremble").

> The voice of the LORD is over the waters;
>> the God of glory thunders,
>> the LORD thunders over the might waters . . . .
> The voice of the LORD breaks the cedars;
>> the LORD breaks in pieces the cedars of Lebanon.
> He makes Lebanon leap like a calf,
>> Sirion [Mount Hermon] like a young wild ox.
>> (vv. 3, 5–6)

Even as the sea and the Jordan fled at the sight of Israel's God, the mountains and hills leaped with alarm at the sight of this awesome God. The fleeing of the seas and the leaping of the mountains signal not only God's sovereignty over all creation, but even more, these reactions signal that all creation declares that this God, the one who brought his people up out of Egypt, is indeed the Divine King over all.

The Questioning of Nature's Response (114:5–6)

IN PSALM 114:5–6 THE PSALMIST references the same four elements that appeared earlier in verses 3–4 (sea, Jordan, mountains, hills), but in the latter verses he has made two fundamental changes in his comments. The psalmist has modified the narrative report in verses 3–4 so that the same information now reads as rhetorical questions directed at each of the four elements (i.e., "Why was it, sea . . . ?"). The second modification pertains to the type of verbal form used in each strophe. In strophe 2 (verses 3–4) the psalmist uses the perfect (*qatal*) form of the verb in reference to events at the Red Sea and the Jordan River (vv. 3a, 4a). Typically, this verbal form refers to action in the past or action that has been completed. In strophe 3 (vv. 5–6), however, the psalmist opts for the imperfect (*yiqtol*) form of the verb, thus shifting the discourse from the past to the present.[8] The NIV's translators opted not to recognize the shift in the verbal forms in verses 5–6, consequently locating the interrogation of the four elements in Israel's past. Unfortunately, this translational decision reduces the force of the questions. By shifting the questions to the present, the psalmist inquires

> Why is it, O sea, that you flee?
>> O Jordan, that you turn back?
> O mountains, that you leap as rams,
>> O hills, as lambs?

---

8. Richard D. Nelson, "Psalm 114," *Int* 63 (2009): 172.

As Richard Nelson suggests, "the distant past of the exodus and creation are made present for the reader."[9] The powers of chaos and false gods that threatened Israel when God brought them out of Egypt remain the same forces that continue to threaten the people of God. And just as God's theophanic presence caused them to flee and leap in fear in "the distant past," so too will his presence hold such powers in check even now.

The Presence of the Lord (114:7–8)

THE FINAL STROPHE CALLS ALL CREATION to acknowledge God as the Divine King. Although verses 1–6 have referenced the *work* of God, the *name* of God does not appear until the final strophe. The delayed identification of God by name only serves to heighten the significance of the last two verses, thus creating in the psalm a crescendo of sorts.

Tremble, earth, at the presence of the Lord. The rhetorical questions in verses 5–6 find their answer in verse 7. The seas, Jordan, mountains, and hills flee and leap because of "the presence of the Lord." The psalmist suggests that the very presence of God should cause all the earth, and in particular all people, to stop and tremble in his presence. While the word "tremble" (*hil*) can refer to writhing or being in pain, the context suggests that the proper response to the Divine King is fear and trembling, pure awe. A parallel text is located in Psalm 97:3–4. In describing the presence of the Divine King, the psalmist there explains that "fire goes before him" and that "his lightning lights up the world." He then records that the earth sees this God "and trembles" (*hil*)—the mountains all melt like wax before the presence of God.[10] In Psalm 114 the psalmist likely has similar images in mind.

Rock into a pool. The psalmist concludes by declaring that God is the one who "turned the rock into a pool, the hard rock into springs of water." The image invoked in this verse recalls God's provision of water for his people in the wilderness (Exod 7:1–7; Num 20:2–13). As the last line in the psalm, verse 8 reminds the reader of God's transformative power as well as his gracious provision. God's cosmic rule is balanced by his attentive care for his people. Even as he can turn rocks into pools of water, so also can God turn a people into his sanctuary.

---

9. Ibid., 174.

10. On the proposal that *hul* and *hil* are actually a single root, see Hossfeld and Zenger, *Psalms 3*, 197. Also see "חוּל," *HALOT* 1:297 and "חִיל," *HALOT* 1:310.

THEOPHANY. In alluding to the exodus tradition, the psalmist does much more than simply retell the narrative features of Israel's story—he celebrates God's breaking into Israel's world. Such appearances, while considerably diverse in description, are labeled "theophanies." The word itself comes from two Greek words, *theos* ("God") and *phainein* ("to appear"), and refers to God's appearance to individuals or groups of people. Although the writers of the Old Testament understood God as wholly other, independent of creation, they also believed that God broke into the world at significant moments in Israel's history. A reported theophany in the Old Testament conveyed the sense that Israel's God was at work in the world in visible ways. Frequently theophanies occurred by bodies of water (e.g., rivers, seas) or on mountains (e.g., Mount Sinai), a point not to be lost on the interpreter of Psalm 114. And while a precise description accompanied some accounts of a theophany, other accounts simply report that God "appeared" to an individual or community. Regardless of the precise form of the appearance, the reporter is nonetheless certain that God has made himself known in the world.

The more memorable accounts of theophanies occur in narrative texts. Immediately following the call to Abram in Genesis 12:1–3, God appears to him, and this theophany prompts Abram to build an altar on the site. Several chapters later a smoking firepot with a blazing torch passes through a sacrifice as further confirmation of God's commitment to Abram and his future. In Exodus 3 God appears as a burning bush. From that bush God calls Moses to a task and then communicates his name to Moses as a pledge of divine faithfulness to him. In Exod 19 God appears at Sinai in the form of a storm, and from that mountain he communicates his covenantal expectation in the form of the torah. Throughout the wilderness period God appears as a pillar of cloud by day and a pillar of fire by night to guide his people through the wilderness; he even speaks to them out of the cloud (Num 12:6–8). In many of the theophanic accounts in narrative texts, the intent seems to be communication. God appears in varied forms and in varied contexts to bring a word to his people. In these texts, theophanies function as mediators of God's communications to his people.

Theophanies are not limited to narrative texts, however. Images of God breaking into the world appear in poetic and prophetic texts as well. Because these texts frequently use language that is highly stylized and metaphorically laden, the description of the theophany can differ considerably from that found in a narrative. For example, in Habakkuk 3 the prophet announces the coming of God as the divine warrior.

> God came from Teman,
> > the Holy One from Mount Paran.
> His glory covered the heavens
> > and his praise filled the earth.
> His splendor was like the sunrise;
> > rays flashed from his hand,
> > where his power was hidden. . . .
> He stood, and shook the earth;
> > he looked, and made the nations tremble.
> The ancient mountains crumbled
> > and the age-old hills collapsed—
> > but he marches on forever. (vv. 3–4, 6)

Similarly, the description of God in Psalm 18 contains highly charged language. In that psalm, the poet describes the appearance of God as a response to the king's plea for deliverance from his enemies (vv. 2–3). God parted the heavens and came down, with dark clouds under his feet. He mounted his cherubim and flew on "the wings of the wind" (vv. 9–10). Smoke rose from the nostrils of God (v. 8a), and a consuming fire poured forth from his mouth (v. 8b) even as he shot forth arrows and bolts of lightning (v. 14).

While theophanies in many of the narrative texts primarily provide divine communication to the individual or group of individuals, theophanies in poetic texts appear to function somewhat differently, generally speaking. In texts such as Habakkuk 3 and Psalm 18, the message is not in what is said but in what is described. The images and metaphors employed in these texts construct an image of God, and that image is meant to convey to the reader something about this God of Israel. Thus, when God speaks out of the burning bush in Exodus 3, the reader learns something about God as a result of what God said. In Habakkuk 3 and Psalm 18, however, the reader learns something about God by how God is described. The theological force of those texts lies in their descriptive power. In the latter two texts, the writer describes God as the divine warrior—a metaphor that is linked to the images of God as king and judge.[11] Israel's hope rests with this God, the one who breaks into the world as the great king but who is also judge and warrior. All nature yields at the appearance of this God.

The truncated language and imagery in Psalm 114 fails to describe God with the graphic language used above, but the response of the seas and the Jordan signal that Israel's God is indeed the Divine Warrior-King

---

11. Walter Brueggemann, *Theology of the Old Testament: Testimony, Dispute, Advocacy* (Minneapolis: Fortress, 1997), 241.

who comes in behalf of his people. Israel's God causes waters to flee and mountains to bolt in alarm, and, as the psalmist suggests, all the earth should tremble in his presence. Theophanies are not intended as fanciful descriptions; instead, they are reminders that God breaks into our world in profound ways—then and now. And we would do well to recover that sense of awe.

Transformation and election. In Psalm 114 the psalmist connects election with God's transformative power. Other psalms (Pss 106; 135; 136) recount the events of the exodus and celebrate God's deliverance from the "enemy." These psalms rehearse the key features of the story as reminders of God's intervention in behalf of the nation. In Psalm 114, however, explicit references to Israel's deliverance have been pressed into the background, and the two main "characters," Israel and God, have been moved to the foreground of the psalm. The stress is not on what happens to Egypt (cf. Ps 105:38) but on what has happened to the people of God. They have not simply been delivered from the hands of a formidable imperial power— they have been transformed into a sacred nation in service to the Divine King. Hans-Joachim Kraus notes, "the joy that the exodus brought was due to the fact that those rescued from Egypt had been taken to the side of their deliverer and had entered into a incomparable realm of his might. *This gave the people a completely new basis for their existence.*"[12] For the psalmist, the story of Israel's exodus does not move along a line from captivity to freedom, from enslavement to liberation; rather, the story of Israel involves the movement from captivity to purpose, from slavery to service. God does more than simply rescue people; he delivers them so that they might be transformed, so that they might "have a completely new basis for their existence." God elects Israel, he transforms the house of Jacob, so that they might become the sanctuary of God, the dominion of the living God.

Psalm 114 opens by acknowledging God's transformative power and then returns to this theme in the final verse. The psalmist reminds Israel of God's capacity to turn rock into pools of water and hard rock into springs of water. He acknowledges not simply the provision by God but the impossibility of the act. No one turns water into pools of water, and springs of water do not suddenly pour forth from hard rock—unless they have been transformed utterly. As noted above, the events that transpired in the wilderness period likely stand in the background of this verse, but the transformative power of God is not locked into a singular moment within Israel's history; rather, God's capacity to transform becomes part of Israel's testimony.

---

12. Hans-Joachim Kraus, *Theology of the Psalms*, trans. Keith Crim (Minneapolis: Fortress, 1992), 52. Emphasis added.

In Isaiah, for example, the prophet announces that the Babylonian captivity is nearing its end and that God will bring his people out from Babylon. The making of this confession returns to the theme of God's transformative power, his capacity to do what seems utterly impossible. In order to make this point, the prophet returns to these same images from Israel's past as evidence of God's capacity to deliver. In Isaiah 43:19 the prophet announces,

> See, I am doing a new thing! . . .
> I am making a way in the wilderness,
> and streams in the wasteland.

And elsewhere the prophet indicates that the "burning sand will become a pool" and "thirsty ground bubbling springs" (Isa 35:7).

How could those exiled in Babylon actually believe that they would return home? Such a proposal seems impossible. Yet the prophet is clear. The power of God to transform his people, and even nature, suggests that with this God nothing is impossible (Luke 1:37).

The New Testament writers also seized on the theme of transformation and election. In 1 Peter 2:9–10 Peter calls on his audience to "declare the praises of him who called you out of the darkness into his wonderful light." Much as Israel was taken from Egypt and transformed, much as the exiles were taken from Babylon and given a new life, so too, Peter explains, Christians were brought out by the mighty acts of God to find life in the light. But Peter adds more. He tells the Christians that not only were they brought out of darkness and into the light, they were also called out to be a "royal priesthood, a holy nation" (1 Pet 2:9). Then Peter reminds them, "once you were not a people, but now you are the people of God" (v. 10). They were brought out *so that* they might be transformed into the people of God. While God is a God who delivers, he is even more the God who transforms.[13] He has made us what we were not—a work that he alone can do. We can do little more than tremble before such a God.

AWE. Of the psalms that comprise the Egyptian Hallel (Pss 113–18), Psalm 114 provides the most explicit reference to Israel's deliverance out of Egypt; yet in the Hebrew text, "Egypt"

---

13. As Kraus reminds, transformation and election were and are creative events in the work of God in the world (Kraus, *Theology of the Psalms*, 52).

appears as the third word in the psalm and is mentioned no more. The focus on the psalm remains thoroughly theocentric. The psalmist invites the reader to consider God more fully. Through the mention of God's presence and his power to transform, the psalmist calls the reader, and all creation, into a deep sense of awe.

In a world that seems to place humans and their significance at the center, we have little room for a deepened sense of awe. In a "can-do" culture, the assumption is that human beings have the capacity to do anything, that we are limited only by our imagination—yet Scripture reminds us differently. We are not the center—God is—and Scripture calls us to live in awe before this God. Psalm 114 returns us to Israel's story and reminds us of the Power that is even greater than the story. The psalmist asks us to pause and to lift our eyes to God so that we might consider again what it means to be the people of God in the presence of God.

In recent years I attended a conference at the University of Münster in Germany. Across from the seminary dormitory in which we were housed was the majestic St. Paulus Dom, the Catholic cathedral for the diocese. The original cathedral was built on that site in 805 CE. While that date alone was enough to give me pause, it was what I saw as I entered the south side of the cathedral that left me standing speechless. Jutting out from the cathedral was one of the entrances that has been traditionally labeled, "Paradise." Beveled stonework runs from wall to wall, all filled with images of vines, animals, and persons tilling the earth and no doubt simultaneously invoking images of paradise and the German countryside. In order to walk into the nave of the cathedral, you must pass through two large wooden doors. Between the two doors is a massive statue of St. Paul, Scripture in hand, and just above Paul is Jesus sitting upon his throne, hand held high to bless all who enter. On each side of the doors are the apostles, six to a side. My German colleague who accompanied me to the cathedral explained that those statues had been there since 1200 CE. And I stood there. For more than 800 years, Christians had passed through that same hallway on the south side of a cathedral in Münster, Germany. My feet were crossing the paving stones that the feet of countless numbers before me had crossed, and my eyes had lit upon the same statues that their eyes had seen. I was standing silently where no doubt many others had stood, they too in silence. And in that moment I felt very small. The statues were imposing, indeed, but even more imposing was the thought that I belonged to a story, a long story—a story so compelling that for more than eight centuries people had passed through these doors as they made their way to worship the living God. I was in awe.

In his treatment of Psalm 114, Robert Davidson suggests that "the congregation is left contemplating the miracle of God's grace, the foundation of Israel's life in the past and their continuing hope in the present and the future. This is where every act of worship should end, as we bow before the mystery of the God who unites past and present, and therefore bathes the future in hope."[14] Tremble, O earth—tremble indeed.

---

14. Davidson, *The Vitality of Worship*, 375.

Psalm 115

¹ Not to us, LORD, not to us
   but to your name be the glory,
   because of your love and faithfulness.
² Why do the nations say,
   "Where is their God?"
³ Our God is in heaven;
   he does whatever pleases him.
⁴ But their idols are silver and gold,
   made by human hands.
⁵ They have mouths, but cannot speak,
   eyes, but cannot see.
⁶ They have ears, but cannot hear,
   noses, but cannot smell.
⁷ They have hands, but cannot feel,
   feet, but cannot walk,
   nor can they utter a sound with their throats.
⁸ Those who make them will be like them,
   and so will all who trust in them.
⁹ All you Israelites trust in the LORD—
   he is their help and shield.
¹⁰ House of Aaron, trust in the LORD—
   he is their help and shield.
¹¹ You who fear him, trust in the LORD—
   he is their help and shield.
¹² The LORD remembers us and will bless us:
   He will bless his people Israel,
   he will bless the house of Aaron,
¹³ he will bless those who fear the LORD—
   small and great alike.
¹⁴ May the LORD cause you to flourish,
   both you and your children.
¹⁵ May you be blessed by the LORD,
   the Maker of heaven and earth.
¹⁶ The highest heavens belong to the LORD,
   but the earth he has given to mankind.
¹⁷ It is not the dead who praise the LORD,
   those who go down to the place of silence;

¹⁸ it is we who extol the LORD,
  both now and forevermore.
Praise the LORD.

 **PSALM 115 CONTAINS ELEMENTS** found in various types of psalms. For example, within this psalm the reader encounters language associated with laments, hymns, and divine oracles, as well as exhortations to trust in God, and it concludes with a final call to praise God. The complexity of the psalm is furthered by the shifting language and perspective in it. The psalm opens by addressing God in the second person (v. 1) but then refers to God in the third person for the remainder of the poem. The congregation speaks first in the psalm (vv. 1–8), followed by another speaker (a priest?) who exhorts the congregation to trust in God. The congregation responds in verses 12–13 with a confession in light of that exhortation. In verses 14–15 another voice (a priest?) prays for a blessing upon the people, and the psalm concludes with a communal confession. Based on the antiphonal nature of the psalm, most commentators have suggested that it originally had a liturgical use. The precise occasion, of course, cannot be discerned with any degree of certainty. Frank-Lothar Hossfeld and Eric Zenger contend that the reader is best served not by determining the supposed liturgical events behind the text but instead by observing "the guidance of the reader discernible *within the text itself.*"[1]

The variety of outlines proposed by commentators suggests that the structure of the psalm is not entirely obvious. Although the outline below deviates from the structure suggested above in the NIV, this outline attempts to capture the inherent connection that exists between the various strophes in the psalm.

A—vv. 1–3 Petition to the God of Heaven
  B—vv. 4–8 The Impotence of Other Gods
    C—vv. 9–11 Call to Trust in Israel's God
    C'—vv. 12–13 Communal Assurance of Blessing
  B'—vv. 14–15 The Power of Israel's God
A'—vv. 16–18 Vow of Praise to the God of Heaven

---

1. Emphasis added. Following the work of Walter Beyerlin, Hossfeld and Zenger have suggested that Ps 115 might best be understood as "learned psalmography" or "poetic theology." See Hossfeld and Zenger, *Psalms 3,* 205. See also Walter Beyerlin, *Im Lichte der Traditionen: Psalm LXVII und CXV. Ein Entwicklungszusammengang,* VTSup 45 (Leiden: Brill, 1992). On the larger issue of "learned psalmography" see Sigmund Mowinckel, *The Psalms in Israel's Worship* (Oxford: Basil Blackwell, 1962), 2:104–25.

The two middle sections (C, C') refer explicitly to Israel, the house of Aaron, and those who fear the LORD. In verses 9–11 someone (perhaps a priest) calls on the three groups to trust in the Lord. In response, the people acknowledge that God "remembers us" and "will bless us," that he will bless the people of Israel, the house of Aaron, and those who fear the Lord. Sections B and B' provide a stark contrast between the impotence of the gods of the nations (vv. 4–8) and the power of the living God (vv. 12–13). The opening and closing sections of the psalm proclaim the preeminence of Israel's God, the one deserving of praise (v. 18).

Psalm 115 appears in a collection known as the Egyptian Hallel (Cf. Ps 113). Although there is no reference to Egypt or Israel's deliverance from Egypt, the psalm does acknowledge that Israel's God is the living God who responds to the cries of his people (Ps 115:1–2; Exod 2:23). Psalm 115 contends that whatever power the foreign nations (*goyim*) think they possess, those powers are illusory. The feigned power of their gods stands in stark contrast to the power of the God who made the heavens and earth and who now resides in the heavens.

Petition to the God of Heaven (115:1–3)

THE OPENING STROPHE OF PSALM 115 presents the theological crisis that confronted the people of God (v. 2). In response, the psalmist offers a short confession in verse 3. This confession functions like a thesis statement by presenting the community's primary response to the crisis articulated in verse 2. The remainder of the psalm explores the meaning and implications of their confession.[2]

Not to us, LORD, not to us. No other psalm opens with a similar phrase. The uniqueness of the opening line indicates that the emphasis is thrown fully upon Yahweh, but in a manner distinct from other psalms. The crisis concerns the glory of God's name, or his reputation, and leads the congregation to pray that Yahweh will restore glory and honor (*kabod*) to his name.

The language used in the opening verse recalls the book of Ezekiel. There the prophet reminds the people that, because of their sinfulness and the exile which followed, God's name has been "profaned in the eyes of the nations" (Ezek 20:9). According to Ezekiel, Yahweh must act for his name's sake (Ezek 20:9; 36:22). The current plight of Israel—the apparent "Godforsakeness" suggested by the mocking cry of the nations in Psalm

---

2. Kraus notes, "Even though the post-exilic community . . . is still in deep affliction and Godforsakenness, it praises the God of Israel as the living one in high hymnic effusions" (Kraus, *Psalms 60–150*, 381).

115:2—suggests that God's glory has faltered. The psalmist calls for God to act—not so that Israel might be justified or increase her stature in the land but so that the name of God might receive the glory due it. Despite all appearances, the psalmist knows that God's name deserves glory because Yahweh had kept *hesed* ("steadfast love") with his people and remained faithful. Current circumstances do not dissuade the psalmist from acknowledging who God is and what he has been to the people of God.

Where is their God? Throughout its pages the Old Testament calls the people to be firmly aniconic—to refrain from having images of deities. In this way, Israel does not resemble her ancient Near Eastern neighbors and their proclivity toward idols and idol worship. According to verse 2b, the foreign nations (*goyim*) mock Israel by asking, "Where is their God?" The question drips with irony. Since Israel is aniconic, there is no chance that God can be seen or visualized through an idol. By asking "where," the nations mock the very form of Israel's concept of God, or, more properly, its formlessness—there is no idol or god to be seen, so perhaps there is no god at all. The attention to idols in verses 4–8 extends the discourse on them.[3] While they may function as the meaning at one level, the question cuts much deeper.

With the exile and the apparent Godforsakenness signified by that event, the question concerning the presumed absence of God becomes much more acute. Questions concerning the presumed absence of God can be found in other poetic texts (Pss 42:3; 79:10; Joel 2:17; Mic 7:10). These kinds of taunting questions are often found within the context of war and conflict, with one nation challenging the efficacy of the other nation's god. For example, in Isaiah 36:13–20 the Rabshekeh, an Assyrian high official, calls out to those in the walled-up city of Jerusalem, "Who of all the gods of these countries have been able to save their lands from me? How then can the LORD deliver Jerusalem from my hand?" The assumption is that the other nations have fallen because their gods were no match for the gods of Assyria.

Following the exile, the period of restoration provided little visible evidence to counter the claims of the nations. Although the Jewish community had been returned to Yehud by the Persian king Cyrus, little else signaled a return to a thriving community under the blessing of God. The mocking question once posed by the nations may in fact have become a lingering question in the minds of those living under Persian imperial rule.[4]

He does whatever pleases him. The community provides two responses to the question posed by the nations. In response to the question

---

3. Hossfeld and Zenger, *Psalms* 3, 206.
4. Goldingay, *Psalms* 3, 329.

of where God is (given that Israel has no idols), the community confesses that their God is in heaven. (On the significance of God as the God of heaven, see the comments on Psalm 113, "Original Meaning.")

The community also responds to the taunting claim that Israel's God has no power by contending that their God "does whatever pleases him." Variations of this claim appear in Psalm 135:6, Isaiah 46:10, Jonah 1:14, and in reference to a human king in Ecclesiastes 8:3. At first blush this claim appears to refer to God's omnipotence—God's power to do whatever he wants to do. Upon closer investigation, however, the meaning is more nuanced and, frankly, more theologically profound.

The Hebrew text reads *kol 'asher-hapets 'asah*, literally, "everything which he desires, he does." Avi Hurvitz understood the meaning of this phrase in the light of an Aramaic legal formula, which held that the owner or heir of a specific item (e.g., slave, land) could do with that item whatever he chose to do.[5] For Hurvitz, the phrase in Psalm 115 signaled God's unlimited power. Klaus Seybold differed from Hurvitz in suggesting that the phrase highlights the *freedom* of God to act as he pleases. This freedom would also include God's right not to act, thus perhaps explaining the perceived absence of God.[6] More recently, Judith Krawelitzski has provided another reading of the phrase.[7] She notes that the verb *hapats*, "to desire," appears fifty times in the Old Testament with God as the subject. Krawelitzski notes that, within those fifty usages, some texts mention objects or values in which God takes delight (i.e., right sacrifices). Other texts mention that there are certain people in which God does or does not take delight, and still others refer to certain actions (i.e., "justice") in which God takes delight. Beyond these three categories, she notes a number of texts that refer more broadly to what God desires, and these texts are found generally in Isaiah 40–55 and the psalms. According to Krawelitzski, the phrase in Psalm 115:3b falls in latter category, and she argues that the meaning is not so much about the attributes of God (i.e., almighty, omnipotence), or even an abstract notion of power; rather, as she explains,

> Even though the first part of the sentence explicitly states that God can do everything (*kol*), the relative clause, "that he pleases," immediately provides a firm reference point qualifying the meaning of

---

5. Avi Hurvitz, "The History of a Legal Formula," *VT* 32 (1982): 257–67.

6. Klaus Seybold, *Die Psalmen*, HAT 1/15 (Tübingen: Mohr Siebeck, 1996), 451.

7. Judith Krawelitzski, "God the Almighty? Observations in the Psalms," *VT* 64 (2014): 434–44.

"everything"—not as a limitation on God's power, but rather as a specification of how God chooses to act . . . *kol*, "everything," has to be understood as God's acting in favor of his people. . . . They are the beneficiaries and recipients of God's redeeming power.[8]

With this foundational idea present, verses 9–11 call upon the people to "trust in the LORD," and verse 14 reminds the community that God will cause them to flourish. God can do whatever he pleases to redeem his people. The question posed by the nations, "Where is their God?" is answered in their confession that they serve a God who acts mightily to redeem his people. The two preceding psalms in the Egyptian Hallel testify to the same confession.

The Impotence of Other Gods (115:4–8)

IN THE SECOND STROPHE THE PSALMIST invites a comparison between "our God" (v. 3) and "their idols" (v. 4). The Septuagint (LXX) further defines the "idols" by adding *tōn ethnōn*, "of the nations." Thus the comparison is with more than just idols; the idols function as representatives of the gods of other nations. The juxtaposition of the living God, who acts in behalf of his people, with the other nations' impotent idols/gods, which are incapable of action, reinforces Israel's monotheistic claim. Israel's God is not *better than* the gods of the other nations; Israel's God *is* the only God. Hossfeld and Zenger suggest that these kinds of invectives against idols are about the "de-divinization" of the gods of the nations.[9] Their gods are not gods. In this strophe the psalmist makes three claims about the impotence of the foreign idols/gods.

Made by human hands. Despite the attention given to the construction of idols and the inclusion of idols in ancient Near Eastern religions, the psalmist reduces idols to their most basic terms. The idol is constructed of silver and gold, metals used by other ancient Near Eastern religions to represent the heavenly realm.[10] In the prohibition against Israel's making of idols, however, silver and gold are mentioned as explicitly forbidden (cf. Exod 20:23; 32:2–3; Isa 2:7). Israel's confession is clear: Earthly matter, even precious metals, cannot capture the image of the God of heaven.

The mockery of the idols intensifies in the second half of Psalm 115:4. The verb *'asah* ("to make" or "to do"), which appeared in the first strophe,

---

8. Ibid., 438.
9. Hossfeld and Zenger, *Psalms 3*, 207.
10. See Jeffrey Jay Niehaus, *Ancient Near Eastern Themes in Biblical Theology* (Grand Rapids: Kregel, 2008), 83–115.

reappears in verse 4b, thus highlighting the difference between Israel's God and the gods of the nations. In verse 3b the psalmist affirmed that God can "do" or "make" whatever he pleases, but in verse 4b the poet explains that these images were "made [*'asah*] by human hands." Thus the psalmist implicitly poses the question, "What kind of power can an idol/god made by human hands and comprised of earthly material actually have?"

They have mouths, but cannot speak. The idols mentioned in verse 4 are described in verses 5–7 with anthropomorphic characteristics. In rapid-fire succession, the psalmist lists seven faculties of the idols/gods. Use of these faculties would suggest that such gods should be fully inter-active in the world, even as humans are, yet after listing each faculty the psalmist replies *welo'*, "but not." For example, verse 5 reads literally, "they have mouths, *but not* can they speak." The activity of the god is listed first and then immediately negated by the psalmist.

The final reference, in verse 7c, mentions the idol's inability to speak. In constructing idols in Mesopotamia, the final step in the process included a two-day ritual called the *mis pi*, or "mouth washing" ritual. In this ceremony the idol was purified of all associations with the human world with a final, symbolic "opening of the mouth." With the idol purified and its mouth open, the image was ready to speak, eat, hear, see, and smell.[11] But as the psalmist notes, idols can do none of these things because they are lifeless creations made by human hands. While the foreign nations can see their idols/gods, the idols fail to act in any way. The nations' experience with respect to their gods contrasts with Israel's; while Israel cannot see their God, they confess that he sits enthroned in the heavens with the power to act decisively in behalf of his people.

Those who make them will be like them. The final statement in this strophe functions as a malediction with its roots in older curses or judg-ments.[12] The Septuagint shifts the verbal form (jussive) so that it expresses a strong desire and functions as a wishful prayer: "May those who make them become like them." The NIV, however, reflects the reading of the Hebrew text and should be retained. The psalmist is making a declarative statement: those who make idols are indeed like them.

The root *'sh* ("to do," "to make") appears for the third time in this psalm. In verse 3b God does (*'asah*) whatever he desires; in verse 4b idols are the works (*me'aseh*) of human hands; and in verse 8 the term appears in reference to those who make them (*'osehem*). The repetition of the term creates an

11. Christopher Walker and Michael Dick, *The Induction of the Cult Image in Ancient Mesopotamia* (Helsinki: Neo-Assyrian Text Corpus Project, 2001), 8–14.

12. Kraus, *Psalms 60–150*, 381.

implied comparison between the work of God and the works of human hands. The first use suggests divine power, the second, the lack thereof. All those who trust (*batah*) in such lifeless images will become like them. The use of *batah* ("trust") serves as a linking word to the third strophe.

Call to Trust in Israel's God (115:9–11)

THE THIRD STROPHE APPEARS as a litany with a threefold call for each group to trust in the Lord and to acknowledge that he is their help and shield. The use of "trust" (*batah*) in these verses connects this strophe to the previous strophe (v. 8b). Those who trust in lifeless idols have no hope, but those who trust in Yahweh have a deliverer and a protector.[13]

The first and second groups represent the people and the priesthood, respectively, but opinions concerning the identity of the third group ("those who fear God") differ. Hossfeld and Zenger have proposed that the label "those who fear God," or the "God fearers," likely represents proselytes, or converts from foreign nations.[14] Though intriguing, this suggestion must be rejected for several reasons. While other texts in the Hebrew Bible assume that foreigners can join themselves to Israel (e.g., Isa 56), they are never referred to as "God fearers." Second, the term "God fearers" does in fact appear in subsequent Second Temple literature, but always in reference to the piety of a Jewish individual, not a foreign convert.[15] Were "God fearers" a recognizable term for proselytes in the early Second Temple period, some mention of this group in the subsequent literature would be expected. The use of the term elsewhere in the Hebrew Bible, however, refers to those who trust in Yahweh (Pss 40:3; 115:11; 2 Chr 19:9) or are obedient to the commands of Yahweh (Deut 10:12; 13:4; 31:12; Pss 112:1; 119:73–74), thus suggesting that the use of the term in Psalm 115 likely refers to devout and pious Israelites (similarly to its use in later Second Temple literature), not to converts from among the nations.

Communal Assurance of Blessing (115:12–13)

THE THREEFOLD CALL TO TRUST in the Lord in verses 9–11 is met with a communal response, "The LORD remembers us." As the opening strophe suggests, those praying this psalm find themselves in a situation in which

---

13. On the role of shields and their metaphorical meaning see Othmar Keel, *The Symbolism of the Biblical World: Ancient Near Eastern Iconography and the book of Psalms* (Winona Lake, IN: Eisenbrauns, 1997), 222–25.

14. Hossfeld and Zenger, *Psalms 3*, 226.

15. For example, see Jdt 11:17; 4 Macc 15:28; 16:12; Jos. Asen. 4:9; 8:5–7; 20:18; 23:9, 10; 28:4; 29:3; T. Jos. 6:7; T. Naph. 1:10; T. Ab. 4:6; Let. Aris. 179.

the honor of God's name needs to be restored. The circumstances are such that the nations are questioning the presence of Israel's God. Some might interpret the opening line in this strophe as a reminder that God has not forgotten his people. While that reminder is certainly present, the act of divine remembering in the Old Testament invokes a much more powerful image. The act of remembering is always accompanied by an act of deliverance. For example, in Genesis 8 God remembered Noah and sent a wind to dry up the waters. In Genesis 30 God remembered Rachel and opened her womb. God tells Moses in Exodus 6 that he has remembered his covenant with his people and will bring them out of Egypt. The assertion that God has remembered his people signals that deliverance is on the way.

The Power of Israel's God (115:14–15)

AGAIN, THE SPEAKER CHANGES in this strophe. In Psalm 115:9–11 the speaker (priest) calls the people to trust in the Lord. In next strophe (vv. 12–13) the people reply with a communal confession affirming that God has remembered them and will bring blessings upon them. In verses 14–15 the speaker (priest) replies to the communal confession by issuing a prayer for the people.

This speaker requests that the Lord "add to you" or "increase you." The NIV's translation of verse 14a as "May the LORD cause you to flourish" quite possibly carries additional connotations that may not actually be intended in the present context. During the Persian period the population of Yehud was small, and survival remained a challenge. The exilic and postexilic prophets recognized this threat and promised that God would increase his people (cf. Isa 54:1; Zech 10:10). The prayer here is not for abundance or "prosperity," as is often construed in our own culture; rather, the prayer focuses on a much simpler request, namely, that God would increase his people and that the present generation and those to follow would be the beneficiaries.

In Psalm 115:15 the speaker refers to Yahweh as the "Maker of heaven and earth," the one who will issue forth blessings. The language of blessing and creation recalls the Priestly writer's theology in Genesis 1 and, in particular, the claim that God stands sovereign over all creation. As the outline above suggests, verses 14–15 are a response to the statements made in verses 4–8. There the psalmist reports that the idols are works (*me'aseh*) of human hands (cf. v. 8a, "make" ['*oseh*]), so they are impotent to act. They have no power to speak, see, hear, or smell, much less act in behalf of those who created them. Verse 15, however, claims that Israel's God is the one who has made ('*oseh*) the heavens and earth. While this God does not look like the idols of foreign nations, he does not act like them either.

The prayer of blessing (vv. 14a–15a) is guaranteed by the power of this God, the one labeled "maker of heaven and earth."

Vow of Praise to the God of Heaven (115:16–18)

HAVING ACKNOWLEDGED THE FUTILITY of the foreign gods and the power of Israel's God, in the final strophe the community makes a vow to praise God. The twofold confession returns to the theme of God as the creator to whom belongs all creation while also introducing a new theme, that of the vocation of praise.

Highest heavens belong to the LORD. The previous strophe concluded with the affirmation that Yahweh is the maker of heaven and earth. The language of heaven and earth in verses 15b and 16 refers back to the claim made in verse 3 that Yahweh is in heaven and "does whatever pleases him." While all three verses highlight the cosmic rule of Israel's God over creation, they also signal his power to act in that creation.

The psalmist notes that, while the highest heavens belong to the Lord, he has given the earth to humanity. While subtle, the language of verse 16 alludes to Genesis 1. In both Psalm 115 and Genesis 1 God is said to have given (*nathan*) the earth to humans (Gen 1:28–29; Ps 115:16b). Although God rules on high and the "highest heavens" belong to him, he has entrusted the earth to humans so that they might carry out their vocation as his "vicegerents." While Genesis 1 stresses humanity's responsibility to exercise dominion over the earth, Psalm 115 suggests humanity's role includes the responsibility to praise. The community acknowledges that their vocation includes unfettered praise of the maker of heaven and earth. The earth is the place where humans are meant to live out that vocation of praise and, in so doing, enjoy the blessings of God.

It is not the dead who praise the LORD. Verse 17 stands in antithesis to verse 16. Those who are dead cannot praise the Lord. In referring to the dismal plight of the dead and their inability to praise God, the community seeks to create another comparison: to be alive is to praise God, to be dead is to be silent. Compared to the silence of the dead in verse 17, the community confesses in verse 18 that they will praise the Lord both now and forevermore. As Hossfeld and Zenger suggest, "praise simply becomes the most elementary characteristic of one who is alive."[16] To reinforce this point, the Septuagint adds a participial phrase to modify "we" in verse 18. The text reads, "but we *who are alive* will bless the Lord." In this final strophe the writer of the Septuagint wanted to ensure that the reader understood the inherent comparison

---

16. Hossfeld and Zenger, *Psalms 3*, 210.

being made between the vocation of the living and the silence of the dead. So long as there is life, the community should "Praise the LORD" (v. 18c).

ALTHOUGH THE DECALOGUE linked the prohibition of idols with the prohibition concerning the worship of foreign gods (Exod 20:2–4), later texts collapsed the two ideas in some ways to suggest that the gods of foreign nations were in fact nothing more than mere idols and constructions of human hands. By making this move, the biblical writers stripped both foreign gods and idols of any perceived power. As most scholars contend, participants in ancient Near Eastern religions would not have claimed that an idol "housed" its god anymore than an Israelite would have said that the temple "housed" Yahweh. Yet the point of Israel's rhetoric was not to provide an objective report on religious practices in the ancient Near East; it was to make a theological confession concerning the nature of their own God. Richard Clifford correctly observes that the "relationship between the nations and their idols acts as a foil between Yahweh and Israel."[17] The power and efficacy of the God of the heavens is compared to the power and efficacy of handmade objects, and the latter are found wanting.

The events of the exile could have prompted Israel to rethink their confession. The destruction of Jerusalem at the hands of the Babylonians and the sacking of the temple could have prompted Israel to reconsider the power of their God in the face of the Babylonians' gods. Yet rather than retreating from their theological convictions, Israel pressed them further by celebrating the reality of their God and the illusory nature of all other so-called gods. In making this move, Israel intensified its rhetoric concerning the reality of foreign gods and the efficacy of the nations' idols. In Psalm 96:5 the psalmist explicitly announces, "For all the gods of the nations are idols, but the LORD made the heavens." The gods of the nations are nothing. The spatial dimensions in this declaration are central to its theological claim. The Lord stands over the heavens as its creator, while the gods of the nations are nothing more than idols upon the earth—the former as Creator, the latter as creation. Psalm 96 is one of several texts labeled "the LORD reigns" psalms or Yahweh *malak* psalms (Pss 93 and 96–99). Each of these psalms proclaims the kingship of Yahweh

---

17. Richard Clifford, "The Function of Idol Passages in Deutero-Isaiah," *CBQ* 42 (1980): 464.

despite the events of the exile; Yahweh and Yahweh alone is the divine king who "sits enthroned between the cherubim" (Ps 99:1).

Four texts in Isaiah 40–55 also lampoon the creation of idols and their efficacy for delivering their worshipers.[18] The mocking tone of these prophetic texts is unmistakable. In Isaiah 41:22–24 God challenges the idols,

> Tell us, you idols,
>> what is going to happen. . . .
> tell us what the future holds
>> so we may know that you are gods.
> Do something, whether good or bad,
>> so that we will be dismayed and filled with fear.
> But you are less than nothing
>> and your works are utterly worthless;
>> whoever chooses you is detestable.

The prophet implores, "tell us, you idols . . . so we may know that you are gods." The silence of the idols presumes the powerlessness of the gods. Such idols are "less than nothing." Beyond the explicit challenge issued to the idols in Isaiah 41, other texts address the impotence of the idols in differing ways. For example, Isaiah 44 provides an extended reflection on the detailed craftsmanship involved in creating an idol, yet the fact that the idol is the result of human hands is precisely the point. What kind of god is made by human hands? Does such a god deserve worship, or is it mere folly to bow down to worship it (Isa 44:17)? The prophet concludes that these works of human hands are "gods that cannot save" (Isa 45:20; 46:17).

In Psalm 115:2 the nations disparage Israel by asking, "Where is your God?" But similarly to Paul, Israel claims that we live by faith and not by sight (2 Cor 5:6–7). The idols and their gods have no power, but the God of Israel, whose name deserves glory, is the one to whom belong the highest heavens, the one who "does whatever pleases him" (Ps 115:3).

DISAPPOINTMENT, DISASTER, and crisis can lead a person, or an entire community, to ideas that appear expedient or justifiable but in the end reveal a failure of understanding. How does a person respond when life unfolds in ways perhaps not fully anticipated? To whom does one turn in the face of brokenness and uncertainty? All of us

---

18. Isa 41:21–29; 44:9–20; 45:20–25; 46:1–13.

likely have stories, both great and small, of moments when our own lives have felt "undone." The exile created a true existential and theological crisis for the people of God, and much of the postexilic literature reflects an ongoing struggle to make sense of their reality.

Although Psalm 115 quotes the question posed by the nations, "Where is your God?" this question was likely raised in the minds of those who had returned from exile and were now living in the land. They too likely wondered, "Where is our God—now?" Psalm 115 was not actually written to respond to the nations—to those who did not believe; it was meant to address those in Yehud who had believed but now wondered in the light of their own disappointment.

Such situations, however, are not reserved only for those who survived the Babylonian exile. There are moments of existential and theological crisis in all our lives and in the lives of those to whom we minister. One response may be to ask "Why?"—the question of theodicy. Another question may be simply to ask, "What next?" How does one respond when such questions echo in our own heads and cause our hearts to ache, and like our forbearers in ancient Yehud we wonder about the presence *and* the promise of our God. In such moments we may be inclined to strike out on our own, to forge the next steps, and in so doing to secure a good future.

Psalm 115 reminds us, however, that our way forward is through God and with God. To find hope in other places is to fall short. Augustine referred to these kinds of pursuits as "disordered love"—and for him it was sin in its most base form. He explains in *On Christian Doctrine*, "But living a just and holy life requires one to be capable of an objective and impartial evaluation of things: to love things, that is to say, in the right order, so that you do not love what is not to be loved, or fail to love what is to be loved."[19]

In the face of disappointment and disaster the temptation is to "love what is not to be loved" and not to love what should be loved. In the apparent absence of God, Israel's temptation was to succumb to the question posed by the nations and, in so doing, turn to those idols that are more readily at hand. Stories of idol making and idol worship fill the pages of Scripture—and our own lives—and we should not be surprised. John Calvin reminds us that "the human mind is, so to speak, a perpetual forge of idols," and he explains further that in creating idols we

substitute vanity and an empty phantom in the place of God. To these evils another is added. The god whom man has thus conceived

---

19. Augustine, *Teaching Christianity (De Doctrina Christiana)*, trans. Edmund Hill; ed. John E. Rotelle (Hyde Park, NY: New City Press, 1996), 27–28.

inwardly he attempts to embody outwardly. The mind, in this way, conceives the idol, and the hand gives it birth. That idolatry has as its origin in the idea which men have, that God is not present with them unless the presence is carnally exhibited. . . . In consequence of this blind passion men have, almost in all ages since the world began, set up signs on which they imagined that God was visibly depicted to their eyes.[20]

In answer to this need for a visible depiction of God the psalmist calls us to "trust in the LORD." We are to trust in him because he is not the absentee God, but the God enthroned in the heavens (v. 3). We need no idols when the God of the heavens has agreed to be our help and shield. His "apparent" absence in our world must be countered by our continual confession that "The LORD remembers us." And he will answer our needs (v. 14).

So how do we move forward when facing the existential and theological crises that will no doubt come our way? Strikingly, in the opening verse of Psalm 115 the psalmist gives us the proper starting ground for our reflection on such matters: *lo'lanu*—"not to us." Our reflection begins not on us but on God, the one whose name deserves glory. And as we move through our reflections and are reminded of God's faithfulness, we discover that our next step begins as we fully embody our vocation of praise (vv. 16–18).

---

20. John Calvin, *Institutes of the Christian Religion*, ed. J. T. McNeil; trans. F. L. Battles (Philadelphia: Westminster, 1960), 1:3.8.

Psalm 116

¹ I love the LORD, for he heard my voice;
   he heard my cry for mercy.
² Because he turned his ear to me,
   I will call on him as long as I live.
³ The cords of death entangled me,
   the anguish of the grave came over me;
   I was overcome by distress and sorrow.
⁴ Then I called on the name of the LORD:
   "LORD, save me!"
⁵ The LORD is gracious and righteous;
   our God is full of compassion.
⁶ The LORD protects the unwary;
   when I was brought low, he saved me.
⁷ Return to your rest, my soul,
   for the LORD has been good to you.
⁸ For you, LORD, have delivered me from death,
   my eyes from tears,
   my feet from stumbling,
⁹ that I may walk before the LORD
   in the land of the living.
¹⁰ I trusted in the LORD when I said,
   "I am greatly afflicted";
¹¹ in my alarm, I said,
   "Everyone is a liar."
¹² What shall I return to the LORD
   for all his goodness to me?
¹³ I will lift up the cup of salvation
   and call upon the name of the LORD.
¹⁴ I will fulfill my vows to the LORD
   in the presence of his people.
¹⁵ Precious in the sight of the LORD
   is the death of his faithful servants.
¹⁶ Truly I am your servant, LORD;
   I serve you just as my mother did;
   You have freed me from my chains.
¹⁷ I will sacrifice a thank offering to you
   and call on the name of the LORD.

¹⁸ I will fulfill my vows to the LORD
  in the presence of all his people,
¹⁹ in the courts of the house of the LORD—
  in your midst, Jerusalem.
  Praise the LORD.

THANKSGIVING SONGS traditionally include the following elements: lament, petition, expression of trust, and thanksgiving. While each of the traditional elements is present in Psalm 116, the order of the elements, and even the structure of the psalm itself, appears "haphazard" at best.[1] For example, reports concerning the past threats to the psalmist appear in verses 3, 10, 11, and 16a, while hymnic confessions appear in verses 5, 6a, and 15, and the announcement of a thank offering appears in verses 12–14 and 17–19.

The lack of order and structure is complicated further by the fact that in the Septuagint and the Latin Vulgate, Psalm 116 was divided into two separate psalms at some point in its transmission history (vv. 1–9 = Ps 114; vv. 10–19 = Ps 115). Despite the apparent lack of structure in the psalm and its division into two psalms in the Septuagint and the Vulgate, there is considerable evidence of Psalm 116's overall unity. Repeated terms bind the two halves of the psalm together. For example, the word "call" (*qara'*) appears in verses 2, 4, 13, and 17. The repetition of "death" occurs throughout the psalm (vv. 3, 8, 15), and the terms associated with the word *gamal*, "bounty," and *shub*, "return," appear in each half of the psalm (vv. 7, 12). While the appearance of similar terms alone cannot justify the unity of the psalm, their frequency does lend further support to that claim.

A number of scholars have offered proposals regarding the overall structure and movement of the entire psalm. Michael Barré suggests that Psalm 116 contains two main sections, verses 1–9 and verses 10–19, based on the "traditional" division of the psalm (e.g., Septuagint; Vulgate) as well as the structural markers he identifies in the psalm.[2] Leslie Allen,

---

1. Gerstenberger, *Psalms, Part 2 and Lamentations*, 291. Klaus Seybold suggests that the structure has been damaged by additions and overlays that were likely introduced into the original psalm (Klaus Seybold, *Die Psalmen*, HAT 1/15 [Tübingen: Mohr Siebeck, 1996], 454).

2. Michael Barré, "Psalm 116: Its Structure and Its Enigmas," *JBL* 109 (1990): 61–79. Barré notes the symmetry of the two halves of the psalm based on word count and cola. As further evidence of the symmetry, he also notes that the name of God appears eight times in each half of the psalm.

James L. Mays, J. Clinton McCann, and Walter Brueggemann and William H. Bellinger have opted to divide the psalm into three strophes: verses 1–7, verses 8–14, and verses 15–19.[3] They contend the psalmist's repeated promise to fulfill his vows in verses 14 and 18–19 appears to close out the last two strophes, while the self-exhortation in verse 7 appears to close out the first strophe. Alternatively, Bernd Janowski makes a compelling case for dividing the psalm into two main sections: verses 1–11 and verses 12–19. He terms the first section a thanksgiving song and suggests that the latter section refers to a thanksgiving sacrifice.[4] Hossfeld and Zenger follow similarly in suggesting that verses 10–11 occupy a liminal position, pointing back to the first section while also transitioning the psalm to verses 12–19.[5] This commentary follows the proposal of Janowski and Hossfeld and Zenger. In the first major section (vv. 1–11) the psalmist recounts the threatening circumstances of his past and then gives thanks for what Yahweh has done for him. In the second major section (vv. 12–19) the poet shifts the focus of the psalm by talking about what he will do for Yahweh in the light of his deliverance. The theological implications of this structure will be explored below.

Declaration of Trust (116:1–2)

THE OPENING LINES OF PSALM 116 provide the fundamental reason for the psalmist's song of thanksgiving: God has heard his prayer. The word order for verse 1 is unusual in that it literally reads in Hebrew, "I love ['ahab] because Yahweh has heard my cry, my plea." Typically, one would expect the verb 'ahab to be followed by a direct object indicating the object of the psalmist's affection. A number of English translations have sought to remedy the somewhat awkward phrase by inserting "the LORD" immediately after the verb. Els correctly notes that there was an "undoubted hesitancy" to make Yahweh the direct object of a verb, even the verb 'ahab.[6] In other texts, psalmists would mention their love of objects related to Yahweh (i.e., "your name," "your commandments," "Jerusalem"). In verse 1 the object of the psalmist's affection is that "the LORD . . . heard my voice." Rather than simply attributing such a phrase to circumlocution or pleonasm, the

---

3. Allen, *Psalms 101–150*; Mays, *Psalms*; McCann, "Psalms"; Brueggemann and Bellinger, *Psalms*.

4. Bernd Janowski, "Dankbarkeit: Ein anthropologischer Grundbegriff im Spiegel der toda-Psalmen," in *Ritual und Poesie: Formen und Orte religiöser Dichtung im Alten Orient, im Judentum und im Christentum*, ed. Erich Zenger, HBS 36 (Freiburg: Herder, 2003), 91–136.

5. Hossfeld and Zenger, *Psalms 3*, 215–16.

6. P. J. Els, "אהב," *NIDOTTE* 1:277–99, see esp. 288–89.

focus of the psalmist's love is aptly put: the psalmist loves "that the LORD has heard his voice." Yahweh's faithful action in the past (vv. 1b, 2a) prompts the psalmist to respond in the future, "I will call [*qara'*] on him as long as I live."[7] Allen renders the verb *qara'* as "proclaim" and suggests that what follows in the remainder of the psalm is the testimony or proclamation of the psalmist.[8]

Recollection of Deliverance (116:3–6)

FOLLOWING THE DECLARATION OF TRUST, the psalmist recounts the scene of deliverance that prompted the song of thanksgiving. He recounts the depths of his plight in verses 3 and 6b, thereby creating an *inclusio* around the verses that deal with Yahweh's capacity to deliver.

The cords of death entangled me. Although the psalmist alludes to the impending threat of death, he refers to his plight using highly metaphorical and stylized language. Søren Holst, drawing from work in cognitive linguistics, argues convincingly for a metaphorical motif in the Old Testament connected with the idea of being in a tight place, being constricted, or being confined.[9] The more concrete idea of being in a tight place or being caught conveys metaphorically the sense of being in need. In Psalm 116:3 the psalmist explains that the "cords of death" had entangled him (*'apap*). Rather than "entangled," the verb might better be understood as "encompassed" or "surrounded." Cords of death that surrounded a victim are part of the "hunt" metaphor frequently employed in the Old Testament. The language and imagery used in this metaphor signal the entrapment of the victim and its impending death or destruction.[10] Here in verse 3a, the psalmist confesses that the cords of death had surrounded him and that death was impending.

The second colon in verse 3 continues the same imagery. The NIV reads, "the anguish [*metsare*] of the grave came over me," but such a rendering misses

---

7. The Hebrew *beyami*, "in my days," appears only here in the Hebrew Bible.

8. Allen, *Psalms 101–150*, 112, 115.

9. Søren Holst, "Psalmists in Cramped and Open Spaces: A Cognitive Perspective on the Theology of the Psalms," *SJOT* 28 (2014): 266–79.

10. Keel notes that in ancient Sumerian the sign for hunt designated an enclosed space and originally meant "to surround." The association between hunting and entrapment was extended metaphorically into the political sphere by means of kings' frequently associating the capture of enemies with the casting of a hunting net. Eannatum reports his military conquest over the citizens of Umma by proclaiming, "Over the people of Umma, I, Eannatum, threw the net of the god Enlil." The stele depicts Enlil holding a large net with the inhabitants of Umma closed within it. The presence of Imdugud, the lion-headed bird of death, at the top of the net signals the fate of those entrapped (Keel, *The Symbolism of the Biblical World*, 89–90).

the metaphorical imagery suggested above. The word *metsare* comes from the root *tsrr*, which in the intransitive sense means "to be narrow" and in the transitive, "to tie up." The nominative forms of the root suggest "narrowness, constriction, physical and/or mental claustrophobia," idiomatically rendered quite often as "distress."[11] The connection is rather apparent: even as the ropes of death surround him, so too do the straits or restraints of Sheol. The threat is far more ominous than the NIV's translation suggests. The Hebrew suggests that the straits of Sheol had found (*matsa'*) the psalmist; death had hunted him down.

Then I called on the name of the LORD. In verse 3c the psalmist admits that, from the midst of his confining, entrapped, near-death existence, all he can find are sorrow and constraint. There is no relief. As a result, the psalmist's only recourse is to plead with God for deliverance (v. 4). To call on the name of Lord is to invoke God and all that he is in an attempt to find relief from the current constraints. The desperation of the psalmist's plea is captured with the use of the particle of entreaty *'annah* ("please" or "I pray") along with the verb *malat*, "to save." Some translators opt not to translate *'annah*, but in doing so they fail to communicate the despair of the psalmist: "O LORD, save me, I pray."

The LORD is gracious and righteous. Having just called upon the name of Yahweh, the psalmist recounts the characteristics of God that warrant the psalmist's trusting in him for deliverance. Verses 5a–6a contain three verbless clauses meant to reinforce the claims about this God. The psalmist has modified what Janowksi calls "the grace formula" (Exod 34:6–7). While use of the larger formula is seen most clearly in Psalms 103:8 and 145:8–9, portions of the formula appear in Psalm 116 as descriptors of Yahweh.[12] Variations of this grace formula appeared earlier in Psalms 111:4 and 112:4.

The LORD protects the unwary. In addition to being a gracious and righteous God, full of compassion, the psalmist celebrates that God protects the unwary (*peta'im*). The word *peta'im* refers to the simple or naïve ones, those who are still learning their way. The term often elicits negative connotations in the book of Proverbs (cf. Prov 1:32; 14:15, 18; 22:3), but elsewhere the word can refer to those who simply remain in need of instruction (cf. Pss 19:7; 119:130). Because they have yet to receive proper instruction, they are likely to walk in the wrong paths and consequently need the protection of God. The psalmist contends that surely the God

---

11. Ignatius Swart and Robin Wakely, "צרר (ṣrr I)," *NIDOTTE* 3:853.

12. Bernd Janowski, *Arguing with God: A Theological Anthropology of the Psalms*, trans. Armin Siedlecki (Louisville: Westminster John Knox, 2013), 283.

who cares for the *peta'im* would also care for him. Like the *peta'im* who need protection, so too does the psalmist. In Psalm 116:6b he explains that he had been brought low (*dalal*). Other texts in the Old Testament indicate that the *dal* are those who are materially poor and socially estranged, those who cannot contend for themselves.[13] The psalmist reports, however, that from his helpless estate Yahweh saved him.

Self-Exhortation in the Light of Deliverance (116:7–9)

FOLLOWING THE RECOLLECTION of deliverance in verses 3–6, the psalmist turns to reflect on his own condition in the present. The earlier verses mentioned the sense of confinement experienced by the psalmist. In this section such oppressive, life-threatening conditions have been abated and replaced by conditions of hope.

Return to your rest, my soul. As noted above, the psalmist uses the metaphor of being confined or in a tight place as a means of indicating his need. Having been delivered (v. 6b), he reminds himself that he no longer lives under the threat of such circumstances but instead can return to his rest. Rather than understand rest as meaning the absence of activity, the usage here likely is meant to suggest a place of rest. The psalmist has been delivered *from* Sheol and the grave (v. 3) and delivered *to* a place of rest.

You, LORD, have delivered me from death. In verse 4a the psalmist used *malat* ("to save") in his plea for deliverance, and he employed a different term for deliverance (*yasha'*) in verse 6b. In the first instance he called on Yahweh for deliverance, and in the latter the psalmist recounts that deliverance. The use of "save" both times in the NIV obscures the variety of language used by the poet. In verse 8a he mentions God's capacity for deliverance yet a third time. In this instance, however, the psalmist praises God for having been delivered but uses the verb *halats*, which often connotes the idea of being pulled out of something (i.e., "deliverance"). The psalmist celebrates that he was pulled out of death, out of the constricting and confining sense of impending death and distress. The verb *halats* appears in 2 Samuel 22:20, where deliverance and being brought out into an open space are clearly connected ("[Yahweh] brought me out into a spacious place; he rescued [*halats*] me because he delighted in me"). Arguably, the psalmist has opted for this verb to underscore the idea of "open spaces" as a metaphor for deliverance (cf. Ps 116:9b). The remainder of verse 8 uses a merismus. His being delivered has removed the tears from

---

13. On the language of the poor in the Psalter see Tucker, "A Polysemiotic Approach to the Poor in the Psalms," 425–39.

his eyes and prevented his feet from stumbling. From head to toe the life of the psalmist has been changed.

In the land of the living. Whereas the psalmist's life had once been lived under the threat of Sheol and the grave, he is now free to walk before the Lord. The verb *halak* (in the *hithpael* stem) can mean literally "to walk about" (Gen 13:17), but it also has a figurative sense that indicates a particular way of living, in this case, living in the presence of God. The image once again is that of release—of freedom of movement—to live fully before the Lord. The psalmist indicates that he has been freed so that he might walk in the land of the living (Ps 116:9b) once more. The grave and Sheol had their hold on the psalmist and threatened to pull him down to the grave, but God has delivered him and brought him back to the community in which he lives so that he might dwell in the presence of God and enjoy the fellowship of community.[14]

Confession of Trust (116:10–11)

THE CONFESSION OF TRUST IN VERSES 10–11 links back to the declaration of trust in verses 1–2. In essence, these two sections create an *inclusio* around verses 3–9 by opening and closing the thanksgiving song with affirmations of the psalmist's trust in God's capacity to deliver. Verses 1–2 recount his call to God amid his distress, and verses 10–11 recount the severity of the plight amid that call. For the casual reader who expects a smooth linear or narrative sequence of events in a text, the location of verses 10–11 may seem unusual at best, if not a misplacement. Yet verses 10–11 serve as a recapitulation of the thanksgiving song by highlighting the psalmist's belief in God and the hopelessness of his situation.

I trusted. The verb *'aman* in the *hiphil* means "to believe" or "to put trust in something." Similar to verse 1, the syntax of verse 10a has a verb but no direct object. While many translations render verse 10a as "I trusted in the LORD," the prepositional phrase does not actually appear in the Hebrew; the text reads "I believed/trusted when I said." As noted in verse 1 above, there was some hesitancy to make Yahweh the object of a verb, and this hesitancy also appears to surface with respect to verse 10a. Perhaps for the psalmist the object need not even be mentioned—after all, in whom else would one believe?

I am greatly afflicted. The psalmist affirms that he maintained his belief even when he was "greatly afflicted." The verb *'anah* means to "be bowed down," but in the sense of forced subjugation by another. Other Semitic

---

14. Brueggemann and Bellinger, *Psalms*, 500–1.

languages carry a similar meaning for this root. For example, the ninth-century Moabite Inscription (i.e., The Mesha Stele) uses this root in the opening lines, referring to the oppression experienced by the Moabites at the hands of King Omri of Israel (lines 5, 6). In Psalm 116 the use of the term *'anah* likely suggests the affliction experienced by the psalmist was external. The fact that in verse 6 the psalmist praises God as a "protector" may provide additional support to this claim. In verse 6 the poet describes his condition as having been brought low (*dalal*), and in verse 10b he refers to himself as being "bowed down." These images correspond well to the other metaphorical images in verse 3 in which the cords of death and the ropes of Sheol appear to be trapping him in his own grave (v. 3b). The figurative descriptions of being beaten down and being trapped in the grave signal a person who is powerless to overcome the external threat that is before him. The psalmist confesses in verse 10 that when he was in this position, he remained firm in his belief that God would deliver him.

Everyone is a liar. This generalized assessment that "every person" (*kol 'adam*) is a liar may appear puzzling given the scope of the psalm thus far. The verb *kazab* means "to lie" or "to deceive," but the term can also imply deception or worthlessness. Hossfeld and Zenger contend that *kazab*, in this instance, is not an ethical qualification (i.e., "people tell lies") but a metaphysical qualification ("humans are unreliable").[15] Because humans are unreliable, they cannot be the source of deliverance or the ultimate source of hope. In this second confession of trust (vv. 10–11) the psalmist acknowledges that he has only one source of hope, and it is in that one source that he believes (v. 10a).

Act of Thanksgiving (116:12–14)

FOLLOWING THE SONG OF THANKSGIVING for the psalmist's deliverance in verses 1–11, the poet considers his response to God: "What shall I return to the LORD for all his goodness to me?" in the context of the subsequent verses 13–14 and 17–19 refers to the psalmist's participation in a sacrificial thanksgiving meal. His expression of praise is manifested in action before the people of God. As evidence of thankfulness, the psalmist raises a "cup of salvation." Cups were used in various worship events and sacrifices, so the precise meaning of the "cup of salvation" remains difficult to determine. Yet, as Janowski has observed, the fact that the deliverance of the psalmist is linked to the raising of a cup suggests that the cup had a symbolic meaning; it is "understood as an elementary symbol of salvation from death

---

15. Hossfeld and Zenger, *Psalm 3*, 116.

and the continued existence of the one who has been saved."[16] In raising the cup, the psalmist also calls upon "the name of the LORD," the very name he called upon from the depths of Sheol (v. 4).

Confession of Trust (116:15–16)

AS PART OF THE ACT OF THANKSGIVING, the psalmist offers up the third confession of trust in Psalm 116:15–16. In both verses he explains why God has sought to deliver him.

Precious in the sight of the LORD. The translation of *yaqar* as "precious" has resulted in a number of interpretations of this text. Some believe that God sees the death of his beloved ones ("faithful servants") as precious or beautiful in the eyes of God. Such a reading would explain why Psalm 116 was mentioned in tandem with martyrdom, especially in the early church.[17] While more popular uses of this verse today do not make the association with martyrdom, they do continue the idea that the death of a godly person is considered beautiful or esteemed in the eyes of God. Such a reading, however, would run counter to how the rest of the Old Testament viewed death. Death is never viewed as positive, even for the righteous ones. Further, in Psalm 116 the psalmist has pleaded repeatedly for God to deliver him from the "cords of death" and for God to prevent the "anguish of the grave" from overcoming him. It would seem inconsistent that in this third confession of trust the psalmist would refer to death in such affirming ways.

In light of the larger context in Psalm 116, a better rendering of *yaqar* might be "costly." The death of a righteous one is "costly in the eyes of God." Janowski suggests it is costly in that Yahweh loses a witness when a devout one dies.[18] Rather than stressing that "death" is precious, the psalmist is really try to affirm that it is the *life* that is precious; death is costly because it takes life away. Because these lives matter to God, when he hears the psalmist's request for deliverance (v. 4) he acts upon it to deliver him from death.

You have freed me from my chains. The psalmist returns to the imagery of confinement as a way of speaking about his distress. He refers to his chains or bonds (*moser*), a term that evokes images of a yoke around the neck of a slave, and the use of *moser* accords well with his self-description

---

16. Janowski, *Arguing with God*, 282.

17. For representative examples see Quentin F. Wesselschmidt, ed., *Psalms 51–150*, Ancient Christian Commentary on Scripture, VIII (Downers Grove, IL: InterVarsity, 2007), 292–96.

18. Janowski, *Arguing with God*, 261 n. 261.

as a slave in the first part of the verse.[19] In describing himself, however, the psalmist admits to his powerlessness. He calls himself a "servant" but then extends that claim. The Hebrew literally says, "I am your servant, the son of your handmaiden." This latter phrase is legal terminology that refers to a slave born into a household (Exod 23:12). Such a child has neither power to free himself nor legal rights to claim such freedom. He is "the lowliest servant and slave."[20]

In using this second image the psalmist holds two contrasting ideas in tension. In Psalm 116:15 he confesses that the life of a godly one is important to God, and in verse 16 freely admits that his life is not worth much, that he is like a lowly slave. Yet God's zealous concern to deliver people from death overrides whatever status they may hold. Out of his abundant desire for his people to walk in the land of the living (v. 9), God frees the psalmist from his chains.

Thanksgiving Sacrifice (116:17–19)

THE POEM CONCLUDES with the psalmist's promising to give a thanksgiving offering while once again calling on the name of the Lord (v. 17). The poet announces that he will make good on this promise "in the presence of all [God's] people," in the court of the temple in Jerusalem. Then his deliverance will be full and complete. The one who had been brought low and was greatly afflicted was the one who had felt the cords of death wrapping about him. This one cried out to God, who not only enabled him to walk among the living (v. 9) but also raised him up to stand in the temple with God's people. Such deliverance is worthy of the psalm's final admonition: *hallelu yah,* "Praise the LORD."

THE THREAT OF DEATH. The language and imagery of death pervades Psalm 116. In recounting his plight, the psalmist mentions the word "death" (*mawet*) three times (vv. 3, 8, 15), and the mention of Sheol in verse 3b introduces yet another reference to death.[21] The explicit mention of Sheol and the repeated references to "death" (*mawet*) in Psalm 116 may seem overdrawn in a thanksgiving psalm, and perhaps their appearance would be more at home in a lament psalm, yet as

---

19. Cf. Isa 28:22; 52:2; Jer 27:2. The feminine form of the noun carries the same meaning. Cf. Jer 2:20; 5:5; Nah 1:13; Pss 2:3; 107:14.

20. Kraus, *Psalms 60–150*, 389.

21. Mays, *Psalms*, 369.

Christoph Barth and others have noted, the opposite is in fact the case. Language and imagery associated with death and the underworld appear with greater frequency in the thanksgiving psalms than in the lament psalms, with lament psalms rarely even mentioning Sheol by name.[22] While death can have positive connotations in the Old Testament, especially in reference to the death of one who was "full of years" (e.g., Abraham [Gen 25:8]; David [1 Chr 29:28]), quite often the idea of death carries a more foreboding sense. The mention of death and Sheol in thanksgiving psalms suggests this latter sense by drawing attention to the acute crisis faced by the psalmist in the past.

This foreboding sense of death often can carry with it the sense of being confined or constrained, as noted above. The sense of confinement and powerlessness captures the angst associated with the tenuous life-and-death experiences confronted by the psalmist. Seemingly, the threatened individual has little power against the deathly grasp of Sheol or the fate that awaits him. In Psalm 18:4–5 the psalmist writes:

> The cords of death entangled me;
> > the torrents of destruction overwhelmed me.
> The cords of the grave coiled around me;
> > the snares of death confronted me.

Human beings, understanding that death follows life, are well aware of their own mortality. Yet the psalmist's angst over death does not stem from his inability to confront his own mortality; rather, it stems from the intrusion of the forces of death into the sphere of the living and his inability to hold such forces at bay.

As the cords of death reach into the sphere of the living, one of the chief threats is that death has the capacity to separate the psalmist from God. Death does much more than simply end life. More devastatingly for the psalmist, death threatens to take him to a place removed from the presence of God. In Psalm 88 the psalmist uses death language to describe his crisis, but even in its metaphorical sense the existential crisis created by death is clear. In verse 5 the psalmist bemoans,

> I am set apart with the dead,
> > like the slain who lie in the grave,
> whom you remember no more,
> > who are cut off from your care.

---

22. Christoph Barth, *Die Errettung vom Tode in den individuellen Klage—und Dankliedern des Alten Testaments* (Zollikon: Evangelischer, 1947), 111.

In response, a contemporary reader might be quick to cite Psalm 139 and exclaim that God is present everywhere, or perhaps refer to the book of Revelation and suggest that, through death, one experiences God in new and more profound ways. In 1 Corinthians 15:55 Paul cites Hosea 13:14, "Where, O death, is your victory? Where, O death, is your sting?" Yet such quick rejoinders dismiss too easily the theological crisis articulated by both the psalmist and the New Testament writers. The psalmist is not afraid of death for death's sake; rather, he fears the possibility of no longer being in the presence of God—a fate even worse than death. Paul acknowledges a similar fear among the early Christians and reminds those at Corinth that there is "victory through our Lord Jesus Christ" in the hope of the resurrection; death will not separate the people of God from the God they serve.

For the psalmists, death signals much more than simply a cessation of life; death signals an absence from God and his provision. Such a perspective on death explains the psalmist's exuberance in Psalm 116:8–9 that God had delivered him, so he could once more "walk before the LORD in the land of the living" (cf. Ps 56:12–13).

Thanksgiving and testimony. Individual psalms of thanksgiving frequently include the psalmist's promise to bear witness to God's act of deliverance. In the first half of Psalm 116 the poet recounts the crisis he faced and the deliverance granted to him by God. In those verses (vv. 1–11) the psalmist addresses himself ("my soul") in verse 7 and addresses Yahweh in verse 8, but the remaining verses function as a report, of sorts, referring to God in the third person. In verse 5b the psalmist includes a first-person plural pronoun, "[and] our God [*we'lohenu*] is full of compassion," thus suggesting that this report of deliverance and song of thanksgiving have moved from the realm of privatized faith to their rightful setting in the context of the larger community.

In the second half of the psalm, twice the psalmist pledges, "I will fulfill my vows to the LORD in the presence of all his people" (vv. 14, 18). Other individual thanksgiving psalms include similar promises to bear witness to the work of God. For example, in Psalm 66:16 the psalmist invites all those who fear God to come near and he will tell them "what he has done for me." Similar promises of testimony appear elsewhere in the Psalter (e.g., Pss 52:9; 118:17). Some may ask why testimony accompanied thanksgiving. Was it not enough simply to utter a song of thanksgiving to God? Why involve the community? To what end? Patrick Miller explains that:

> The deliverance of *one* of God's afflicted is cause for rejoicing by *all*. It is not only the thanks of one saved. This act is a pointer to the way that God always acts. The salvation of one who cried out creates a

community of praise and thanksgiving, of worship and the fear of the LORD. The voice of the one becomes a choir of many.[23]

A song of thanksgiving is ultimately never about the one who has been delivered but instead about the God who intervenes in those tenuous places between life and death. Such songs of testimony give proper praise to God, but in so doing they also confirm and perhaps even reorient the community's confession about this God. To give thanks without testimony is to diminish the significance of deliverance itself, and worse yet, to minimize the fullness of its power for the people of God.

SPIRIT OF GRATITUDE. TESTIMONY OF HOPE. Hermann Gunkel, one of the leading Psalms scholars at the turn of the twentieth century and the pioneer of the form-critical approach to the Psalter, reflected on the concept of thanksgiving in the Psalter. In particular, Gunkel considered the celebrations in which the psalmists would have uttered their poems of thanksgiving within the context of the community. He suggests that such moments must have been among "the most beautiful hours in the life of the pious."[24]

In one of my interim pastorates I served a church that had been through a particularly challenging season, and the church had not weathered that season well. The church had a center aisle that divided the sanctuary cleanly in two, and the building's architecture reflected its present climate. Worship was strained; even more was conversation between members. I was asked by many if I thought that church would survive, and if so, how? I honestly did not know.

I announced one Sunday morning that beginning the following week there would be a testimony each Sunday. I approached one of the lay leaders and tasked him with lining up one person for each week. The people were to come from various age groups, from various Sunday School classes, and from different "sides" in the congregation. I gave each of them a prompt for sharing that simply read, "I saw God this week because he did [blank]. And for that I am thankful."

Week after week individuals made their way to the pulpit and identified where they had seen God at work in their lives, and week after week

---

23. Patrick Miller, *They Cried to the Lord: The Form and Theology of Prayer* (Minneapolis: Fortress, 1994), 192.

24. Gunkel, *Introduction to the Psalms*, 200.

they concluded by saying, "And for that I am thankful." Because of the controversy and conflict in that church, it had been some time since many people had sensed God at work in that community, and longer still since anyone had said, "For that I am thankful." But together, as the people of God, they listened to one another despite their differences, and they were reminded that God remains at work among his people; each testimony became a "pointer to the way that God always acts."

Gunkel was right; such experiences can create beautiful moments in the life of the pious. Regrettably, however, in our need to manage time, stay on message, and control quality, the notion of testimony has become a vestige of the past in most of our worship services. There is no room for thanksgiving, no room for testimony. For some these are antiquated practices of another generation. Yet the truth is that some people in the pews before us sense that "the cords of death" are surrounding them. Some feel trapped and "overcome by distress and sorrow" and they are weary from stumbling. They are less concerned about time management, messaging, and quality control in the worship service because they simply need to know there is still hope. They need to know God is still at work.

The writer of Psalm 116 testifies to those gathered around him that "our God is full of compassion" (v. 5). Perhaps there are others, even now, who need to know the same truth about *our* God. And while ministers can climb into the pulpit weekly to make that proclamation, what most people really want to hear is a testimony—a testimony grounded in unadulterated thanksgiving.

Psalm 117

¹ Praise the LORD, all you nations;
    extol him, all you peoples.
² For great is his love toward us,
    and the faithfulness of the LORD endures forever.
Praise the LORD.

PSALM 117 IS THE SHORTEST of all the psalms and, despite its brevity, contains the classical elements of a hymn. The poem opens with an imperative calling all nations and peoples to praise God and acknowledge him. Following the introductory call to praise God, the psalmist offers a rationale in verse 2 for the imperatival call to praise God.[1] The psalm concludes with another exhortation, one that dominates Psalms 113–18: *hallelu yah.*

The brevity of Psalm 117 resulted in a number of textual traditions either making verses 1–2 the final two verses of Psalm 116 or the first two verses of Psalm 118. For example, there are thirty-six Hebrew manuscripts that have combined Psalms 116 and 117. Additionally, two significant medieval printed Bibles combined the two psalms.[2] Despite these textual traditions, the two psalms are best understood as discrete units and should be interpreted as such. A cursory reading of the two poems suggests they have different functions. Psalm 116 is a thanksgiving psalm in which the psalmist appears to have the congregation in focus (vv. 5, 18–19), while Psalm 117 is a pure hymn, with the nations as its hypothetical audience.

Call to the Nations (117:1)

THE HYMN OPENS WITH A CALL to praise the Lord, but the directive is given to the "nations" (*goyim*). While *goyim* is applied to Israel as a political entity (cf. Num 14:12), the term typically refers to non-Israelite nations and people groups (cf. Zech 2:15; 12:3; Ps 79:1; 2 Chr 32:15). Psalm 117:1b parallels the

---

1. The first word in verse 2, *ki* ("for"), introduces the rationale for praise and is a constituent part of most hymns. See Gunkel, *Introduction to the Psalms,* 29.

2. Of the two medieval Bibles to follow this tradition is the *edition princeps* on the Masoretic Bible in Venice (1525). See the brief discussion in Hossfeld and Zenger, *Psalms 3,* 222 n.1a.

first colon with the psalmist's calling on the "peoples" (*ha'ummim*) to extol the Lord. The unusual form *ha'ummim* has generated considerable discussion and prompted a number of proposals.[3] Because this term does not appear elsewhere in the Old Testament, scholars have emended the text to read *le'ummim*, "peoples," a term frequently paired with *goyim*.[4] Hossfeld and Zenger suggest that *ha'ummim* could be an Aramaism, a claim that is further substantiated by the presence of *shabah* ("extol"), an Aramaism in that same colon.

While the nations and peoples are addressed in the opening lines of Psalm 117 and in fact appear to be the recipients of the commands, they are not the *intended* audience. Psalm 117 is best understood as a "rhetorical imperative," which suggests that the intended audience is not really the nations, rather, the speakers themselves.[5] On this point, see below, Bridging Contexts.

Reason for Praise (117:2)

IN VERSE 2 THE PSALMIST PROVIDES the reasons why the nations should praise and extol Israel's God. Given the exhortation for the nations to praise God, one might anticipate that the psalmist will offer a rationale similar to that found Psalm 86:9—that God has made all the nations of the earth. Strikingly, however, the reasons indicated in Psalm 117 have nothing to do with the nations themselves and everything to do with God's relationship with Israel. Verse 2a suggests as much in explaining that "great is his love toward us." The fullness of that statement, however, is somewhat lost in translation. The psalmist refers to Yahweh's "love," his *hesed*, and while *hesed* can be translated "love," it often connotes a sense of loyalty and covenantal fidelity. Consequently, the psalmist points to God's fidelity or covenantal loyalty to his people as reason enough for why the nations should recognize Yahweh as worthy of praise. To make the point even more emphatically, the psalmist employs the verb *gabar*, which can refer to the might or power of a military conqueror.[6] Verse 2a could be translated, "Because his commitment has been strong over us."[7] The prepositional phrase *'alenu* can

---

3. Note that *'ummim*, absent the definite article, appears in Ps 108:4.

4. Kraus, *Psalms 60–150*, 390. While *ha'ummim* does not appear elsewhere in the Old Testament, the word *'ummim*, which is missing the definite article, does appear in Ps 108:4.

5. Hossfeld and Zenger, *Psalm 3*, 223.

6. McCann, "The Book of Psalms," 1150. In 2 Sam 11:23, for example, the term appears in connection with military imagery. In Isa 42:13, Yahweh is described as a "mighty warrior" or "champion" (NIV) who prepares for battle with his enemies, and in Zech 10:6 and 10:12 the verbal form appears with God's strengthening his people so that they will become like mighty warriors.

7. Goldingay, *Psalms 3*, 350.

be translated "toward us," with the NIV, but the preposition could also be rendered "over us."[8] Understood in this way, the psalmist contends that because of his *hesed*, God's steadfast love, God has stood strong and been mighty "over us," so suggesting that God has stood over Israel in protecting her despite all that has occurred.

This claim is extended in the second half of verse 2 with the psalmist's assertion that Yahweh's faithfulness (*'emet*) will be forever. Both terms in verse 2, *hesed* and *'emet*, are part of the "grace formula" found in Exodus 34:6. Fanie Snyman suggests that the reference to Exodus 34 likely provided an assurance that would have been critical "in a time when there would be some doubt as to whether Yahweh's love and faithfulness are indeed still present in the life of the people."[9] According to the psalmist, it will be the very fact of Yahweh's love and faithfulness that will elicit praise from the nations.

THE NATIONS. In Psalm 115:2 the nations mockingly inquired, "Where is your God?" Two psalms later, in Psalm 117, the psalmist calls on the very same nations to offer up praise to Israel's God. Assuming that *goyim* and *ha'ummim* in verse 1 refer to foreign nations, the question that remains concerns the role of the "nations" in Psalm 117. A number of scholars have followed the Briggses' initial assessment that Psalm 117 is "of an entirely different temper towards the nations," meaning that the nations no longer stand in opposition to Israel.[10] As evidence of this "different temper" in Psalm 117, scholars such as Artur Weiser have suggested that the mention of the nations in verse 1 implies the participation of the nations in the worship of God. Weiser writes,

> The meaning and purpose of life, for nations as well as individuals, finds its fulfillment in praising God. In the presence of God, the political and national barriers disappear, and across the frontiers of countries and states, [humans] are linked together in a bond which unites them in God in fellowship with one another.[11]

---

8. Hossfeld and Zenger understand the suffix on *'alenu* to refer to both Israel and the nations (Hossfeld and Zenger, *Psalms 3*, 224). "The nations are called on by Israel here to praise YHWH because he has proved his love for Israel *and* for the nations" (italics original). Such a reading seems unlikely.

9. Fanie Snyman, "Reading Ps 117 against an Exilic Context," *VT* 61 (2011), 116.

10. Charles A. Briggs and Emilie G. Briggs, *A Critical and Exegetical Commentary on the book of Psalms*, vol. 2 (Edinburgh: T&T Clark, 1909), 402.

11. Artur Weiser, *The Psalms*, OTL (Louisville: Westminster John Knox, 1962), 721–22.

This somewhat generous reading of Psalm 117 appears most recently in the work of Hossfeld and Zenger. They contend that the psalm "is a call to praise directed to the nations and to Israel, and to bring them together in *common* praise of YHWH."[12] While appealing, such an intepretation appears somewhat forced. The Psalter is replete with examples of the nations' being summoned to praise Yahweh, the God of Israel, regarding his work in behalf of Israel; but as Robert Martin-Achard has noted, "The nations are most often called to sing the deeds of God in favor of Israel. They are witnesses to the goodness of God to his people but they do not benefit directly."[13] The position of Weiser and that of Hossfeld and Zenger attempts to read the psalm as an invitation to the nations to join with the people of God, but as Kraus has rightly cautioned, "this 'universalism' has its roots neither in a prophetic idea nor in a poetic exuberance, nor finally in an eschatological view of history"; rather, the call to the nations is rooted in the claim that Yahweh is indeed God Most High.[14] In other words, the psalmist calls the nations to praise God and recognize Israel's God as God alone. Whereas the nations apparently mocked the God of Israel in Psalm 115:2, in Psalm 117 they are now, rhetorically, a witness to the very same God and his faithfulness to his people. The psalmist declares that when the nations see the faithfulness of *this* God, Israel's God, they will be compelled to lift their voices to the only true God. The psalmist does not call the nations to praise God because he has shown his love *for* the nations; rather, the nations are called to praise God because he has proven himself *gabar* ("mighty") in behalf of Israel.

Although in its original context Psalm 117 did not possess the missiological thrust that many Christian readers might infer, the text did become part of Paul's argument in Romans 15:7–11 regarding the inclusion of the gentiles. Paul writes, "Christ has become a servant of the Jews on behalf of God's truth so that the promises made to the patriarchs might be confirmed and, moreover, that the gentiles might glorify God for his mercy" (vv. 8–9). In many ways Paul has simply restated the idea present in Psalm 117: God will be faithful to his people and the nations will recognize the mercy of God. But Paul then extends the interpretation of the text by citing Psalm 117 and three other Old Testament texts (Deut 32:43; Ps 18:49; Isa 11:10) as evidence of God's desire that all people recognize

---

12. Hossfeld and Zenger, *Psalms 3*, 226. Italics original.

13. Robert Martin-Achard, *Israël et les nations. La perspective missionaire de l'Ancien Testament*, Cahiers théologiques 42 (Paris: Delachaux & Niestlé, 1959), 52.

14. Kraus, *Psalms 60–150*, 391. See also Hans-Peter Mathys, *Dichter und Beter: Theologen aus spätalttestamentlicher Zeit*, OBO 132 (Göttingen: Vandenhoeck & Ruprecht, 1994), 292–97.

Israel's God. Most telling is the final line in Romans 15:12, where Paul writes, "in him [Jesus], the Gentiles will hope." The nations have moved from being passive observers to active participants. In the original context of Psalm 117, the nations were merely meant to serve as choristers, as those who give testimony of what they see and know. But as Leslie Allen has reminded, "Israel's would-be hired choristers were destined eventually to become [Israel's] partners in faith in the international religion of the New Testament."[15]

PSALM 117 WAS A CALL to worship Israel's God because of his *hesed* and *'emet* ("steadfast love" and "faithfulness"). As suggested above, the psalm likely addressed a serious concern among those who had experienced the exile and returned home to less-than-idyllic circumstances. This psalm reminded them that despite their circumstances, God had remained faithful to his people—so faithful in fact, that even the nations would testify to that truth.

Psalm 117 calls us to celebrate, even now, this "steadfast love" and "faithfulness" of our God. While some wring their hands over comments suggesting the demise of the church, Psalm 117 invites Christians to look again and to ponder the faithfulness of the God we serve. His faithfulness is indeed everlasting (*'olam*). So faithful is this God that all nations shall lift their voices in recognition. As James Mays rightly notes, praise "is not complete, not what it should and must be, until all are drawn into its faith and joy. Until the answer of praise arises from every people on the globe, the LORD is not recognized as the one and only God."[16] Until then, we remain steadfast in our proclamation, *hallelu yah*. This God is the hope of us all (Rom 15:12).

---

15. Allen, *Psalms 101–150*, 118.
16. Mays, *Psalms*, 372.

Psalm 118

¹ Give thanks to the LORD, for he is good;
   his love endures forever.
² Let Israel say:
   "His love endures forever."
³ Let the house of Aaron say:
   "His love endures forever."
⁴ Let those who fear the LORD say:
   "His love endures forever."
⁵ When hard pressed, I cried to the LORD;
   he brought me into a spacious place.
⁶ The LORD is with me; I will not be afraid.
   What can mere mortals do to me?
⁷ The LORD is with me; he is my helper.
   I look in triumph on my enemies.
⁸ It is better to take refuge in the LORD
   than to trust in humans.
⁹ It is better to take refuge in the LORD
   than to trust in princes.
¹⁰ All the nations surrounded me,
   but in the name of the LORD I cut them down.
¹¹ They surrounded me on every side,
   but in the name of the LORD I cut them down.
¹² They swarmed around me like bees,
   but they were consumed as quickly as burning thorns;
   in the name of the LORD I cut them down.
¹³ I was pushed back and about to fall,
   but the LORD helped me.
¹⁴ The LORD is my strength and my defense;
   he has become my salvation.
¹⁵ Shouts of joy and victory
   resound in the tents of the righteous.
"The LORD's right hand has done mighty things!
   ¹⁶ The LORD's right hand is lifted high;
   the LORD's right hand has done mighty things!"
¹⁷ I will not die but live,
   and will proclaim what the LORD has done.
¹⁸ The LORD has chastened me severely,

but he has not given me over to death.

¹⁹ Open for me the gates of the righteous;
   I will enter and give thanks to the LORD.

²⁰ This is the gate of the LORD
   through which the righteous may enter.

²¹ I will give you thanks, for you answered me;
   you have become my salvation.

²² The stone the builders rejected
   has become the cornersone;

²³ the LORD has done this,
   and it is marvelous in our eyes.

²⁴ The LORD has done it this very day;
   let us rejoice today and be glad.

²⁵ LORD, save us!
   LORD, grant us success!

²⁶ Blessed is he who comes in the name of the LORD.
   From the house of the LORD we bless you.

²⁷ The LORD is God,
   and he has made his light shine on us.
With boughs in hand, join in the festal procession
   up to the horns of the altar.

²⁸ You are my God, and I will praise you;
   you are my God, and I will exalt you.

²⁹ Give thanks to the LORD, for he is good;
   his love endures forever.

PSALM 118 IS TRADITIONALLY classified as a thanksgiving psalm. The psalm opens and closes with the imperative, "Give thanks to the LORD, for he is good," and as similarly in other thanksgiving psalms, the psalmist recounts a situation of deliverance. In many ways, however, this psalm is unique both in its orientation and structure. A number of scholars have suggested that Psalm 118 reflects a type of liturgical procession, with verses 1–18 taking place outside the temple complex. The first half of the psalm has virtually no reference to the temple court; verses 19–29, however, shift the focus decidedly, with several explicit references to the temple suggesting that the procession has moved inside the temple court.[1]

---

1. See, for example, Allen, *Psalms 101–150*, 122. Allen includes verse 19 with the former grouping given the psalmist's request for the gates to be opened.

In addition to the spatial shift in the psalm, the shift in speakers adds further complexity to this poem. While in verses 5–18 an individual recounts the circumstances from which he was delivered, the psalm is far from a "private ceremony"; rather, it has its home in communal worship. The psalm opens with the voices of the worshipers and the psalmist celebrating the *hesed*, "love," of Yahweh in verses 1–4. Verses 5–18 recount Yahweh's deliverance of the psalmist (and perhaps also the larger community; see below). Within this section focused on deliverance, the language appears to shift yet again in verses 8–9 and 15–16. The first instance includes a double wisdom saying and the latter a song of victory.[2] John Goldingay suggests that these "interludes" are comments made by the congregation in response to the testimony of the psalmist.[3] Others have suggested that the claims may represent the psalmist's reflections on his own situation.[4] Whether one understands verses 8–9 and 15–16 to be the words of the psalmist or those of the congregation, their rhetorical force remains the same: reflection on past deliverance results in theological confession. The final section, verses 19–28, contains the grateful praise of both the psalmist and the community. Embedded within this litany of thanksgiving in verses 19–28 is the request, "Lord, save us," suggesting that the cause for thanksgiving has become the cause for hope amid a distressing situation in the present. The psalm concludes (v. 29) by repeating the opening line, thereby creating an *inclusio* around the entire psalm.

Because Psalm 118 is an individual psalm of thanksgiving, the identity of the individual petitioner has garnered much attention. The general consensus is that the psalm may have been composed originally as a royal song of thanksgiving for a military victory, thereby implying that the "I" of the psalm was in fact the king. The present location of the psalm in Book 5 of the Psalter, however, suggests that it was read and understood in a postexilic context when there was no king. McCann builds on this notion by suggesting that the recollection of God's past deliverance would have offered "a perspective from which to face the reality of continuing oppression" during the postexilic period.[5] A similar move is made in Psalm 144. The plural request in Psalm 118:25 for Yahweh to "save us" and "grant us success" suggests that the community seeks the same kind of deliverance once experienced by the psalmist.

---

2. Ibid., 122.
3. Goldingay, *Psalms* 3, 355.
4. See, for example, McCann, "The Book of Psalms," 1154.
5. McCann, "The Book of Psalms," 1154.

Call to Thank God (118:1–4)

THE PSALMIST OPENS BY INTRODUCING the principle theme for the psalm: "Give thanks to the LORD, for he is good; his love endures forever." Verse 1 is identical to the opening verse in Psalms 106:1, 107:1, and 136:1. The repeated use of this language in the introductory verse of all four psalms is likely not accidental and appears to signal a compositional arc that connects all four psalms.[6] The verb *hodu*, "give thanks," appears in verse 1 and is repeated in verses 19, 21, 28, and 29. Thus the psalm opens with a call to give thanks and closes with a fourfold use of the term in the final section.

Give thanks. The NIV translates *hodu* as "give thanks," and Hossfeld and Zenger render the term the same way, given the nature of the psalm itself and the *toda* (thanksgiving) liturgy that appears later in the psalm (vv. 19–28). As noted earlier regarding Psalm 111, Goldingay argues that the term is better rendered "confess." The Septuagint translates *hodu* as *exomologeisthe*, which can mean "confess" or "profess," in the sense of praise. Thus, the opening verse in Psalm 118 calls the people to do more than simply have a thankful attitude; their giving thanks carries with it the sense of giving testimony about Yahweh's goodness and steadfast love.

His love endures forever. Verses 2–4 contain a short litany in which the psalmist invites Israel, the house of Aaron, and those who fear God to make a confession: "his love endures forever." On the identity of those groups, see the commentary on Psalm 115:9–11.

Deliverance from Peril (118:5–18)

IN THE SECOND MAJOR SECTION OF THE PSALM, the poet shifts from a call to give thanks in verses 1–4 to recounting his past deliverance. This section provides the rationale for the call to give thanks found in the opening and closing sections of the psalm. The psalmist recounts how "all the nations" had surrounded him (v. 10), but Yahweh had brought him into a "spacious place"(v. 5) and delivered him. Within this section there are two interludes (vv. 8–9, 15–16); both play a critical role in the theology of the section. The first interlude makes use of language from the wisdom tradition, while the second one invokes imagery associated with the exodus.

Spacious Place. The psalmist explains that he was "hard pressed" (*hammetsar*). The word *hammetsar* comes from the root *tsrr*, which in the intransitive sense means "to be narrow" and in the transitive, "to tie up." The nominative forms of the root suggest "narrowness, constriction, physical and/or mental

---

6. W. Dennis Tucker Jr., "The Role of the Foe in Book 5: Reflections on the Final Composition of the Psalter," in *The Shape and Shaping of the Book of Psalms*, AIL 20, ed. Nancy L. deClaissé-Walford (Atlanta: SBL Press, 2014), 186.

claustrophobia," idiomatically rendered quite often as "distress" in some translations (e.g., NRSV).[7] The person feels a sense of distress from feeling hemmed in and constrained by circumstances beyond his or her control. The theme of narrowness, or of being constrained and confined, appears repeatedly in the psalm and serves as the dominant metaphorical image for the plight faced by the psalmist (cf. vv. 10–12).

A more literal understanding of the word *hammetsar* makes the parallel construction more apparent in the verse. The sense of confinement and constraint mentioned in verse 5a is placed in antithetical construction to God's work of bringing the psalmist into an open place (*merhab*). Because of God's work, the psalmist has moved from narrowness to wideness. Søren Holst argues that salvation and deliverance are frequently construed by terms related to wide open places. The dominant terms employed in this connection are verbal forms related to the root *rhb* and the nominal form *merhab* (as used in v. 5b). As Holst contends, these two conceptual metaphors, narrowness (*hammetsar*) and wideness (*merhab*), create an even larger "motif cluster" that he terms "narrowness-as-problem" and "wideness-as-solution."[8] Verse 5 contains both motifs, narrowness ("hard pressed," NIV) and wideness ("spacious place"), signaling both the psalmist's dilemma and God's deliverance.

In verses 6–7 the psalmist acknowledges he is not alone when he experiences distress in the face of enemies and external threats. Both verses open with the phrase, "the LORD is with me" (vv. 6a, 7a). Because Yahweh is with the psalmist, he queries, "What can mere mortals do to me?" Whatever the enemies can do to confine and constrain the psalmist, he boldly asserts that because Yahweh is "with me" those contraints will be ripped asunder and the psalmist will be led to wide open places where he can look in triumph on his enemies (v. 7b).

Take refuge in the LORD. Verses 8 and 9 function as the first interlude in the psalm. These verses are identical in form and represent what is often referred to as a "better . . . than" saying. These sayings function as proverbial statements and, not surprisingly, appear most often in the books of Proverbs and Ecclesiastes. Goldingay has suggested that the presence

---

7. Ignatius Swart and Robin Wakely, "צרר (tsrr I)," *NIDOTTE* 3:853.

8. Søren Holst, "Psalmists in Cramped and Open Spaces: A Cognitive Perspective on the Theology of the Psalms," *SJOT* 28 (2014) 266–79. Janowski has argued similarly, particularly in texts related to life and death. According to him, "deliverance from death is described as an elementary freedom of movement, as 'wideness' or 'wide open space,' which was given back by Yahweh to the supplicant in the midst of his life-threatening narrowness" (Bernd Janowski, *Die Welt als Schöpfung*, Beiträge zur Theologie des Alten Testament 4 [Neukirchen-Vluyn: Neukirchener Verlag, 2008], 3–38).

of such sayings in this psalm reinforces the didactic aspect of the poem in its entirety.[9]

In verses 6–7 the psalmist confessed that because Yahweh was with him "mere mortals" could not harm him. Verses 8–9 extend the theme of the impotence of human power, but with a different conclusion in view. Both verses consider in whom one should take refuge and trust in the midst of challenging times. In each instance, those who hear this psalm are called to take refuge in Yahweh rather than trusting in human beings (*'adam;* v. 8b). This theme is extended in verse 9b by encouraging the audience not to trust in princes. Whether the psalmist is referring to foreign rulers or perhaps leaders within his own community is not entirely clear, but either way the resulting conclusion remains the same: in the midst of crisis, true security can be found only in Yahweh. No human, not even a prince with considerable power, can provide the kind of security found in Yahweh.

All the nations surrounded me. In verses 10–12 the psalmist returns his thought to the plight from which he was delivered. While individual thanksgiving psalms typically rehearse the deliverance of the psalmist from a particular threat, this psalm broadens the nature of that threat by explaining that the nations were in fact the source of the threat (vv. 10–14).[10] The frequent allusions to the book of Exodus (see below) confirm the significance of the nations in this psalm. The intertextual references to exodus recall the flight out of Egypt, an enemy nation that threatened the existence of the people of God. In referring to the nations explicitly in verses 10–14 and in alluding to the nations implicitly, the psalmist creates a "world political horizon" for the psalm. The psalmist seeks to recall moments when God has delivered his people out of the hands of foreign powers.[11] McCann suggests that allusions to both

> the exodus and deliverance from exile served as a basis for hope that future deliverance would also occur. This gives Ps 118 an open-endedness that would have made it particularly relevant to

---

9. Goldingay, *Psalms 3*, 357.

10. Although verses 10–14 are in the singular, the individual and the collective are quite often merged in the Psalter, especially when the king or a leader appears to be speaking. See Mowinckel, *The Psalms in Israel's Worship*, 1:45–46. Several recent commentators suggest the psalmist is that of the king or community leader. See Goldingay, *Psalms 3*, 354; Allen, *Psalms 101–150*, 122–23; Brueggemann and Bellinger, *Psalms*, 506–507. Michael Goulder argues for the psalm's significance within the larger context of the postexilic period (Michael Goulder, *The Psalms of the Return: Book V, Psalms 107–150*, JSOT 258 [Sheffield: Sheffield Academic, 1998], 182–91).

11. Hossfeld and Zenger, *Psalms 3*, 231.

the post-exilic era, during which the aftermath of the exile persisted and the people continued to be dominated by the nations.[12]

Earlier in the psalm the poet had described his deliverance with the metaphor of being brought out into an open space (v. 5). In this section he describes his predicament with more precise imagery by explaining that "all the nations" had trapped or surrounded him. In the Persian period these groups would have likely included those peoples who put pressure on Jerusalem as the Hebrews sought to rebuild the city (cf. Neh 6). The nature of the threat is reinforced with the repetition of the verb *sabab* ("to surround"), which appears in all three verses of Psalm 118:10–12. In verse 12 the NIV translates *sabab* as "swarm," which captures well the metaphorical image in the verse; but this translation also causes the reader of the English text to miss the repetition of the verb in each verse. The psalmist laments that he was surrounded by the nations (v. 10) and that the nations surrounded him on every side (v. 11). Their presence was comparable to that of swarming bees, which surround their victim (v. 12). The image of swarming bees as a metaphor for an attacking military force is not unique to Psalm 118—compare Deuteronomy 1:44 and Isaiah 7:18.[13]

The image of the lone psalmist surrounded by "all the nations" creates a rather bleak picture—one that certainly appears to hint at the psalmist's demise. Yet the threefold repetition of the verb *sabab* ("to surround") is matched by the thrice repeated declaration of the psalmist that "in the name of the LORD I cut them down" (Ps 118:10b, 11b, 12c). As Hans-Joachim Kraus suggested, the "name" (*shem*) not only refers to the "salvific presence of Yahweh" but in many ways also functions "like a weapon, a shield, that enfolds him who is surrounded by the rage of the enemy."[14] In Isaiah, the prophet references the power of the "name" similarly. He announces the coming judgment on Assyria by proclaiming, "See, the Name of the LORD comes from afar, with burning anger and dense clouds of smoke; his lips are full of wrath and his tongue is a consuming fire" (Isa 30:27).[15]

The psalmist contends that in the name of the Lord he "cut down" the nations. The verb used in each of the three phrases is *mul*, which is normally translated "to circumcise." Mitchell Dahood suggested that the reference

---

12. McCann, "The Book of Psalms," 1153.

13. See Peter Riede, *Im Netz des Jägers: Studien zur Feindmetaphorik der Individualpsalmen*, WMANT 85 (Neukirchen-Vluyn: Neukirchener Verlag, 2000), 254–66.

14. Kraus, *Psalms 60–150*, 397–98.

15. For similar uses of the phrase "the name of the LORD" see Deut 28:10; Isa 59:19; Joel 2:2; Zeph 3:12; Pss 102:15; 124:8.

to circumcision in Psalm 118:10–12 implied a militaristic context similar to the one portrayed in 1 Samuel 18:25–27.[16] In that context, David killed two hundred Philistines and removed their foreskins. For Dahood, the association of circumcision with a successful military campaign against the enemies fits the overall context of Psalm 118. Of the many neighboring enemies of Israel in the Hebrew Bible, the Philistines garnered the most attention as an "uncircumcised people," thus leading Israel in many ways to equate uncircumcision with a barbarous people. More recently, however, a second root for *mul* has been suggested—one meaning "to fend off."[17] The second root accords well with the image of swarming bees in verse 12 and likely functions as a homonym with the other root form of *mul* meaning "circumcision." The contextual meaning of the verb in Psalm 118 involves Israel's having fended off the enemy, but secondarily (as a homonym) was meant to evoke an association with the object of Israel's actions, the "uncircumcised."

In verse 13 the psalmist depicts his plight using a different image. In the previous three verses he compared his plight to being surrounded or trapped; but in verse 13 the psalmist turns to another well-used image in the Psalter to depict the nature of his threat, namely, the image of being pushed down (cf. Pss 145:14; 146:8).[18]

The LORD is my strength. Psalm 118:14 quotes verbatim from Exodus 15:2 to invoke the Song of Moses, which celebrates Israel's deliverance from Egypt (Exod 15). The direct quotation in Psalm 118:14 is followed up by the second interlude in the psalm (vv. 15–16). The first interlude (vv. 8–9) exhorted the congregation to trust in Yahweh, not human beings. In the second interlude the psalmist attributes his deliverance to Yahweh alone by affirming the power of God that was on display. The thrice-repeated reference to Yahweh's right hand in Psalm 118:15c, 16a, and 16b echoes the threefold reference to Yahweh's right hand in Exodus 15 (vv. 6a, 6b, 12).[19]

---

16. Mitchell Dahood, *Psalms 3:101–150*, AB (New York: Doubleday 1970), 157.

17. "מוּל," *HALOT* 1:555–6.

18. That the Hebrew text actually reads "you pushed me" apparently refers to Yahweh as the cause of the psalmist's fall. The Septuagint, Jerome, and the Peshitta all have a first-person passive verb, "I was pushed," similar to the translation provided by the NIV. Goldingay (*Psalms 3*, 358–59), as well as Hossfeld and Zenger (*Psalms 3*, 239), follow the Hebrew text, with the latter suggesting the psalmist attributes his fall to Yahweh. Allen notes that Yahweh is not addressed repeatedly in the second person until verse 21, thus making it seem unlikely that a second-person form would appear (Allen, *Psalms 101–150*, 121). The first-person form aligns with the frequent first-person references (i.e., "I, me, my") used in verses 10–12 and appearing in verses 13–14.

19. A fourth reference to the hand appears in Exod 15:9, but there the Hebrew word is *yad*, which is simply translated "hand." In Ps 118 and in the three other instances in Exod 15, however, the Hebrew term is *yemin*, which specifically designates the right hand.

The right hand of God on display in the exodus has been revealed again in the life of the psalmist and, by extension, the life of the congregation.

The LORD has chastened me severely. The lengthy section in verses 5–18 closes with a theological assessment of the threat posed to the psalmist but matched by God's deliverance. Hans-Joachim Kraus terms this a "theocentric understanding of suffering."[20] The psalmist understands his previous situation to be one of divine chastisement. The verb *yassar* can mean "to discipline" or "to chastise" and often has an educative connotation. The *piel* form of the verb (as seen in Ps 118) can also mean "to teach" or "to bring up" (Deut 8:4; Prov 31:1; Job 4:3). The use of the verb in Psalm 118 more nearly resembles the nuance expressed in the book of Jeremiah. According to Jeremiah, the Babylonian invasion was chastisement executed by Yahweh (Jer 2:30; 5:3; 30:11; 31:18), a view seen across the prophetic corpus and throughout the Deuteronomistic History as well. In Psalm 118:18b the psalmist confesses that divine chastisement was not the final word; Yahweh did not hand him over to death. (See also the claims made in verse 17.)

Thanksgiving Celebration (118:19–28)

THE FINAL SECTION OF THE PSALM rehearses a thanksgiving or *todah* ceremony that would have probably taken place near or within the temple precinct. The participants in this liturgy likely included the individual psalmist (vv. 19, 21, 28), the temple priests or ministers (vv. 20, 26–27), and the worshiping community (vv. 22–25).

Open for me the gates. With the imperative "open" in verse 19, the psalmist shifts from his lengthy recitation of deliverance in verses 5–18 and begins a new section in the psalm. The precise nature of the exchange between the psalmist (vv. 19, 21) and the temple ministers (v. 20) remains elusive, but at a minimum there seems to be an inquiry concerning the individual's legitimate right to participate in cultic worship. Psalm 15 contains another entrance liturgy focused on the petitioner's right to enter the temple. That psalm opens with a question, followed by a response (vv. 1–2b):

> LORD, who may dwell in your sacred tent?
> Who may live on your holy mountain?
> The one whose walk is blameless,
> who does what is righteous . . .

The remainder of Psalm 15 describes the actions of one whose way is blameless and righteous. But in Psalm 118 the focus has shifted slightly.

---

20. Kraus, *Psalms 60–150*, 398.

Here the psalmist desires to enter the "gates of the righteous" so that he might offer his thanksgiving praise and *todah* sacrifice (v. 19). In response to the psalmist's request to enter the gates of righteousness, the temple ministers remind him, "this is the gate of the LORD through which the righteous may enter." So, in what sense is "righteousness" being understood in Psalm 118:19? In the Old Testament, distress often implied a sense of distance and separation from God and sometimes was even interpreted as divine punishment.[21] The psalms of lament frequently record sentiments of anguish at the apparent distance of God in the midst of such circumstances, for such distance could be interpreted as a breach in the relationship. In Psalm 118, however, the psalmist has already recounted his plight and even confessed that the Lord had chastened him—but not to the point of death. For the psalmist, his rescue by Yahweh has changed everything. As Hossfeld and Zenger explain,

> Rescue from the crisis meant restoration of the disturbed relationship with God and so was celebrated in the *todah* sacrifice as a demonstration of Yahweh's righteousness (in technical theological language: justification): the person who had been rescued enters as a righteous person . . . in order to give thanks to his divine savior.[22]

Without drawing too fine a distinction, one might say that, whereas Psalm 15 spoke about the righteous actions of the person seeking entrance into the temple, Psalm 118 appears to be addressing whether the person has been made righteous (i.e., placed in right relationship) with Yahweh. This understanding explains the response of the psalmist to the statement by the temple ministers. They remind him that the gate he seeks to enter is the gate of the Lord, through which those made righteous may enter.

The stone the builders rejected. In response to the psalmist's declaration that Yahweh has heard him and saved him, the community speaks in verses 22–25. In verse 22 they assess the psalmist's plight, both past and present, by citing what many assume was a proverbial saying: "The stone the builders rejected has become the cornerstone." Because Israelite houses and structures were composed of stone, the literal meaning of the proverb, as well as its metaphorical meaning, would have been obvious to the original audience. In the construction of homes, builders would have regularly thrown aside stones that appeared to be worthless or useless in construction; yet in this proverb it is precisely such a stone that becomes

---

21. Hossfeld and Zenger, *Psalms 3,* 241.
22. Ibid.

the cornerstone.[23] The Hebrew *ro'sh pinah* can be translated literally as "head of the corner," which explains the frequent translation "cornerstone," as in the NIV. In Job 38:6 the phrase is associated with the foundation, thus leading some to translate the phrase as "foundation stone" (e.g., CEB). Hossfeld and Zenger, citing a similar phrase in Zechariah 4:7, propose the image more likely refers to a capstone that would have signaled the completion of a building.[24] While the precise meaning of the particular phrase may be in debate, the meaning of the proverb is clear: someone who was once considered marginalized and of little value has now been placed back into the "structure," the community of the righteous, by the Builder. The worshiping community "treats the saved one as a rehabilitated, important member."[25]

The LORD has done this. The community provides further analysis of the situation in Psalm 118:23–24. They attribute the deliverance of the psalmist to Yahweh and none other, not even the psalmist himself. In verse 23a the community confesses, "the LORD has done *this*" (emphasis added)—a reference to God's faithful act of deliverance and restoration. In addition to attributing these acts to Yahweh, the psalmist places this act of deliverance in the broader context of God's salvific acts in history. In verse 23b the poet says, "it is marvelous [*niplat*] in our eyes." The nominal form, *pele'*, and the participial form, *nipla'ot*, are frequently translated "wonder," as seen in Exodus 15:11 and 34:10, respectively. The significant moments in Israel's history in which God delivered his people are frequently termed the "wondrous works" of God. The community understands the victory over the foreign nations mentioned in Psalm 118:5–18, as well as the psalmist's presence in the community (vv. 19–21), as "wondrous works" of Yahweh that stand in continuity with Israel's deliverance at the Red Sea (Exod 15).

Psalm 118:24 extends the claim made in the prior verse. Traditionally, verse 24a has been rendered, "This is the day that the LORD has made." The NIV, however, has rendered the Hebrew, "The LORD has done it this very day," a translation that fits better contextually. The community is not celebrating the creation of that day but instead is celebrating the miraculous work that Yahweh "has done" (*'asah*) on that day. Earlier in the psalm, the root *'sh* appears three times (vv. 15–17) as the psalmist recounts the deliverance brought about by the right hand of the Lord. In verse 24a the community is echoing the testimony of the psalmist by affirming that Yahweh indeed has acted on this day.

---

23. Ibid., 242.
24. Ibid.
25. Erhard S. Gerstenberger, *Psalms, Part 2, and Lamentations*, FOTL XV (Grand Rapids: Eerdmans, 2001), 306.

LORD, save us! In verses 22–24 the community celebrates the psalmist's deliverance. In verse 25, however, the community turns to Yahweh and makes a communal request. The strongly worded petition in verse 25 is unexpected in a song of thanksgiving.[26] Both lines in verse 25 open with the interjection *'anna'*, which normally begins a request and adds a sense of pleading to it. Each line closes with another interjection, *na'*, and likewise reinforces the sense of pleading in the verse.[27] Typically, English translations truncate the translation (as with the NIV) by leaving out the additional interjections. Rendered literally, the verse reads, "Please, O LORD, save us, we beg! Please, O LORD, make us prosper, we beg!" The structure of the verse signals the desperation of the community for Yahweh to act in their behalf even as he has done in behalf of the psalmist. This request suggests that the community remains in need of deliverance from some kind of crisis, but even more it signals their firm conviction that Yahweh remains the sole source of hope.

Blessed is he who comes in the name of the LORD. The priests or temple ministers appear to be speaking to those who will be coming into the temple precinct.[28] Hebrew poetry does not always identify the various speakers in a psalm, so modern attempts to do so are tentative proposals at best. Because the speakers are "from the house of the LORD" and because they provide liturgical instruction in verse 27a, the suggestion that the priests are speaking in verses 26–27 appears plausible. The language of verse 26 recalls the language in verse 19. In that verse the psalmist explains that he will "enter" (*bo'*) the house of the Lord and give thanks. The same verb is used in verse 26, which declares that those who come or enter (*bo'*) the house of the Lord will be blessed. The community's request that Yahweh save them amid turmoil (v. 25) is met with the promise "from the house of the LORD" that all who enter in the name of the Lord receive the blessing of God. That the "you" in verse 26b is actually a plural form perhaps implies the meaning that *any of you* who come in the name of the Lord will be blessed by God from the house of the Lord.

Despite whatever turmoil or threat that may be behind the plea in verse 25, the priests are confident the Lord will bless those who come to him (v. 26). This confidence is predicated on their confession in verse 27 that "The LORD is God." Exodus 15 stands in the background of this psalm once more. In verse 11 of that text the question is asked, "Who among the

---

26. Allen, *Psalms 101–150*, 121 n. 25a.

27. The verbs in both lines of verse 25 have an additional *he*, commonly referred to as a *paragogic he*, placed at the end of each verb. While the precise function of the *paragogic he* is debated, it is thought that it can provide additional emphasis to the imperatival request.

28. See Kraus, *Psalms 60–150*, 400. Hossfeld and Zenger (*Psalms 3*, 242–43) contend that the community is still speaking in verses 26–27.

gods is like you LORD?" The claim in Exodus 15 and the response in Psalm 118:27a is clear: Yahweh alone is God. Yahweh's victory over the nations in Exodus 15 and his victory recorded in Psalm 118:5–18 reinforce the claim that Yahweh, our God, is God indeed.

You are my God, and I will praise you. Following the declaration by the priests in verse 27 that Yahweh is God, in verse 28 the psalmist speaks again in affirming not only that Yahweh is God but also that Yahweh is *his* God, that there is a relationship between Yahweh and the psalmist. The language in verse 28 follows closely the language in Exodus 15:2b by declaring the psalmist's intent to praise or confess (*yadah*) God and magnify him.

Concluding Verse (118:29)

THE PSALM CONCLUDES BY REPEATING the opening verse of the psalm. The psalm opens with this affirmation, but the deliverance recounted in verses 5–18 and the events of the thanksgiving celebration in verses 19–28 give reason anew for the call to give thanks.

THE DELIVERANCE OF THE LORD. As noted in the exegetical treatment above, the psalmist repeatedly alludes to Yahweh's deliverance of Israel from Egypt. The Song of the Sea in Exodus 15 is a poetic remembrance of that deliverance and fertile soil for the poetic reflections of the later psalmist. The opening and closing lines of Psalm 118 refer to the *hesed* ("steadfast love") of Yahweh, as does the repeated refrain in verses 2–4. In Exodus 15:13, it is because of God's *hesed* that Israel will be guided into God's presence, even as the psalmist is brought into God's presence in Psalm 118:19–21. Both the Song of the Sea and Psalm 118 acknowledge the power of the nations, but both songs assuredly assert that even such nations can be overcome through the power of Israel's God (Exod 15:14–15; Ps 118:10–12). In addition to the textual relationship evidenced in these references, the connection between the two poetic texts appears elsewhere in Psalm 118. In verse 14 the psalmist quotes directly from Exodus 15:2a, and later in Psalm 118 (v. 28) Exodus 15:2b is recalled. The repeated references to the right hand of the Lord in Psalm 118 recall similar language in the exodus event (cf. Exod 15:6, 12). The psalmist may have also been aware of the verses just prior to the Song of the Sea (Exod 14:30–31), given the shared vocabulary between those verses and Psalm 118.[29]

---

29. "Save" (Exod 14:30 // Ps 118:14, 21, 25); "day" (Exod 14:30 // Ps 118:24); "saw" (Exod 14:30 // Ps 118:7).

With the repeated references and allusions to Exodus 15, the writer of Psalm 118 does much more than simply use "cut-and-paste" language, imagery, and thought from a previous poetic text in Israel's tradition; rather, the psalmist makes a critical theological move—one that speaks to the identity of God and the hope of his people. Psalm 118 is a song of thanksgiving. The bulk of the poem (vv. 5–18) focuses on God's deliverance of the psalmist. This portion of the psalm illustrates above all God's *hesed*, his faithful love for the people of God. God's *hesed*, which was on display at the Red Sea (Exod 14–15), is likewise on display in the life of this psalmist. By the nature of the faithful love of God, his deliverance is not whimsical or arbitrary, but constant. The God who delivered the Israelites from the Egyptians is the same God who delivered the psalmist from the nations (Ps 118:10–12). Because of this kind of faithful love on God's part, the psalmist confesses that it is better to take refuge in the Lord than in any human deliverer.

While the first half of Psalm 118 confesses that in the past God has proven his faithfulness as refuge and deliverer, the second half of the psalm suggests that such knowledge leads to hope. In verse 25 (as translated above), the community confesses the plea, "Please, O LORD, save us, we beg! Please, O LORD, make us prosper, we beg!" The people of God plead for deliverance not because this God is their last and only hope but because this God has proven faithful from generation to generation. Put otherwise, their hope is grounded in the witness of God's consistent desire to deliver his people. The community in Psalm 118 turns to God (v. 18) because they know of his faithful acts in the past to deliver his people, and they trust that his faithful love will extend to them even now. In the New Testament Paul reminds those at Ephesus of this God who faithfully loves his people and seeks to deliver them: "But because of his great love for us, God, who is rich in mercy, made us alive with Christ even when we were dead in transgressions" (Eph 2:4–5). The faithful love of God, seen throughout the pages of the Old Testament but made most manifest in the life, death, and resurrection of Jesus Christ, assures us that this God has loved us with a great love and continues to demonstrate that love as he makes us "alive with Christ."

Psalm 118 in the New Testament. The New Testament writers made considerable use of the language and imagery of Psalm 118 as "a means of understanding and articulating the significance of Jesus."[30] Given that Psalm 118 celebrated the faithful love (*hesed*) of God to deliver his people,

---

30. McCann, "The Book of Psalms," 1156.

it is not surprising that the psalm was frequently cited in the New Testament. Among the uses of Psalm 118 in the New Testament, all four Gospels cite its verse 26 and declare that Jesus is the one "who comes in the name of the Lord" (Matt 21:9; Mark 11:9–10; Luke 19:38; John 12:13). In each instance the citation occurs in the context of Jesus' entrance into Jerusalem. As suggested above, the verse in its original context refers to the person who enters the temple precinct to worship God. Given that Psalm 118 is often labeled a royal psalm, some readers assume that the person mentioned in 118:26 is a king. In the passion narratives, the Gospel writers make a similar connection and declare that Jesus comes into Jerusalem as a king (e.g., Matt 21:5) and, consequently, is the long-awaited one "who comes in the name of the LORD."[31] In Mark, Matthew, and John, the announcement that Jesus comes in the name of the Lord is preceded by the shout, "Hosanna." That word is also derived from Psalm 118 (v. 25), where the people pray, "Save us" (*hoshi'ah na*). Although many interpreters suggest that the word "hosanna" had morphed in meaning and likely was used as a cry or exclamation of praise, it might be possible that the Gospel writers intended the word as a double entendre. Indeed, the crowds shouted in praise as Jesus, the Messiah-King, made his way into Jerusalem, but even in the exclamation itself they were declaring this king's purpose.

In the parable of the tenants (Matt 21:33–46; Mark 12:1–12; Luke 20:9–19), Psalm 118:22–23 ("the stone the builders rejected") functions as the interpretive key. Jesus weaves the story of a man who plants a vineyard and rents it to some farmers. The farmer sends a number of servants to the tenants, but each one is killed. In a final act the farmer sends his son, but he too meets with the same fate. Jesus refers to the fate of the son in the parable, and by extension his own fate, in the light of Psalm 118. Jesus is the stone the builders rejected—even as the tenants exercised their rejection—but the rejected stone will become the chief cornerstone. James Mays notes that Psalm 118 furnished "a scriptural warrant for taking the very rejection of Jesus as a moment of messianic disclosure."[32] Interestingly, after referring to the rejected stone Jesus cites Psalm 118:23, "the LORD has done this, and it is marvelous in our eyes." The purpose is clear. The New Testament writers wanted to affirm that the establishment of the crucified Lord as the cornerstone had nothing to do with the work of humans; rather "the LORD has done this." And "this" was not a messianic plan gone awry—it was the very work of the living God.

---

31. Kraus, *Psalms 60–150*, 193.
32. Mays, *Psalms*, 380.

THANKSGIVING. Psalm 118 invites the reader to two acts of spiritual formation. The first is an act of praise comprised of recitation—the heart of thanksgiving. At times thanksgiving has been reduced simply to the act of saying "thank you." As such, the expression is merely the final statement made in a series of exchanges between two or more parties. For example, you enter a store to make a purchase. The salesperson rings up the purchase and you slide your card through the card reader. The salesperson punches a few keys on the computer, hands you a receipt, and says "thank you." He hands you your purchase and you reply "thank you" in return. Such exchanges are perfunctory; they are statements of common courtesy made with little thought and likely no real sense of gratitude.

The lengthy recitation in Psalm 118:5–18, however, poses a different model for thanksgiving. Had the psalmist sought brevity, he could simply have said, "I was in trouble. God delivered me. Thanks be to God." But such a statement reduces what happened to a transaction, at best. Yet the psalmist opted to recount at length the depths of his trouble and the reality of his helplessness. In this section of the psalm such images are juxtaposed with God's intervention in the psalmist's life. Rather than simply offering a perfunctory "thank you" to God, we also might do well to describe the depths of our own trouble and the reality of our own helplessness. Perhaps we are too self-reliant and too ashamed of our inability to save ourselves, but when we confess the depths of our need, we are confronted above all with our need for God. As we make this recitation-turned-confession, we are also reminded of the greatness of God's deliverance. It is in those moments that we may find ourselves overwhelmed with a sense of true thanksgiving.

God's narrative. Our narrative. The reality of biblical illiteracy, both in our larger society and in our congregations, has been well documented. In a blog post for *Christianity Today*, Ed Stetzer labeled such illiteracy an "epidemic" and noted that only 45 percent of those who regularly attend church read the Bible more than once a week. More than 40 percent of the people attending read their Bible occasionally—maybe once or twice a month—while almost 1 in 5 churchgoers say they *never* read the Bible.[33] This problem is more than simply an issue of information: Does a person know who King Hezekiah was or in which testament he appeared? The real

---

33. Ed Stetzer, "The Epidemic of Biblical Illiteracy in our Churches," *Christianity Today*, July 6, 2015, http://www.christianitytoday.com/edstetzer/2015/july/epidemic-of-bible-illiteracy-in-our-churches.html.

issue is more than whether we know enough to win a game in Bible trivia; rather, at its root this issue concerns our own formation, or lack thereof. In Psalm 118 the psalmist links his own narrative with God's narrative. As suggested above in Bridging Contexts, the poet makes extensive use of Exodus 14–15, a central story in God's narrative with his people, and he understands his deliverance as an extension of that story. His narrative has been enfolded into the larger narrative of God's work in the world, while no doubt informing and forming his own view of his deliverance *and* his Deliverer.

When we make thanksgiving solely about what God has done *for me and me alone*, we run the risk of skewing our view of the Deliverer and jettisoning any sense of God's greater narrative in the world. But when we understand our stories of deliverance and our reasons for thanksgiving in the light of God's ways with those who have gone before us, we are connected to a narrative—a narrative that gives us reason for thanksgiving in the present and hope for the future.

Perhaps we need to invite those in our congregations to consider how our narrative might be enfolding into God's greater narrative. For example, perhaps we should consider the particular ways God has been at work in our lives to demonstrate his *hesed*, his faithful love, in the midst of the things that press in upon us and surround us. Are there biblical stories on which we might draw to assist us in telling our own story and thereby connect us to the long narrative of God's redemptive work in the world? In connecting our narrative with God's narrative, we might be compelled to say to those around us: "Give thanks to the LORD, for he is good; his love endures forever"—and truly mean it.

Psalm 119

א Aleph

¹ Blessed are those whose ways are blameless,
   who walk according to the law of the LORD.
² Blessed are those who keep his statutes
   and seek him with all their heart—
³ they do no wrong
   but follow his ways.
⁴ You have laid down precepts
   that are to be fully obeyed.
⁵ Oh, that my ways were steadfast
   in obeying your decrees!
⁶ Then I would not be put to shame
   when I consider all your commands.
⁷ I will praise you with an upright heart
   as I learn your righteous laws.
⁸ I will obey your decrees;
   do not utterly forsake me.

ב Beth

⁹ How can a young person stay on the path of purity?
   By living according to your word.
¹⁰ I seek you with all my heart;
   do not let me stray from your commands.
¹¹ I have hidden your word in my heart
   that I might not sin against you.
¹² Praise be to you, LORD;
   teach me your decrees.
¹³ With my lips I recount
   all the laws that come from your mouth.
¹⁴ I rejoice in following your statutes
   as one rejoices in great riches.
¹⁵ I meditate on your precepts
   and consider your ways.
¹⁶ I delight in your decrees;
   I will not neglect your word.

ג Gimel

¹⁷ Be good to your servant while I live,
   that I may obey your word.
¹⁸ Open my eyes that I may see
   wonderful things in your law.
¹⁹ I am a stranger on earth;
   do not hide your commands from me.
²⁰ My soul is consumed with longing
   for your laws at all times.
²¹ You rebuke the arrogant, who are accursed,
   those who stray from your commands.
²² Remove from me their scorn and contempt,
   for I keep your statutes.
²³ Though rulers sit together and slander me,
   your servant will meditate on your decrees.
²⁴ Your statutes are my delight;
   they are my counselors.

ד Daleth

²⁵ I am laid low in the dust;
   preserve my life according to your word.
²⁶ I gave an account of my ways and you answered me;
   teach me your decrees.
²⁷ Cause me to understand the way of your precepts,
   that I may meditate on your wonderful deeds.
²⁸ My soul is weary with sorrow;
   strengthen me according to your word.
²⁹ Keep me from deceitful ways;
   be gracious to me and teach me your law.
³⁰ I have chosen the way of faithfulness;
   I have set my heart on your laws.
³¹ I hold fast to your statutes, LORD;
   do not let me be put to shame.
³² I run in the path of your commands,
   for you have broadened my understanding.

ה He

³³ Teach me, LORD, the way of your decrees,
   that I may follow it to the end.

³⁴ Give me understanding, so that I may keep your law
    and obey it with all my heart.
³⁵ Direct me in the path of your commands,
    for there I find delight.
³⁶ Turn my heart toward your statutes
    and not toward selfish gain.
³⁷ Turn my eyes away from worthless things;
    preserve my life according to your word.
³⁸ Fulfill your promise to your servant,
    so that you may be feared.
³⁹ Take away the disgrace I dread,
    for your laws are good.
⁴⁰ How I long for your precepts!
    In your righteousness preserve my life.

ו Waw

⁴¹ May your unfailing love come to me, LORD,
    your salvation, according to your promise;
⁴² then I can answer anyone who taunts me,
    for I trust in your word.
⁴³ Never take your word of truth from my mouth,
    for I have put my hope in your laws.
⁴⁴ I will always obey your law,
    for ever and ever.
⁴⁵ I will walk about in freedom,
    for I have sought out your precepts.
⁴⁶ I will speak of your statutes before kings
    and will not be put to shame,
⁴⁷ for I delight in your commands
    because I love them.
⁴⁸ I reach out for your commands, which I love,
    that I may meditate on your decrees.

ז Zayin

⁴⁹ Remember your word to your servant,
    for you have given me hope.
⁵⁰ My comfort in my suffering is this:
    Your promise preserves my life.
⁵¹ The arrogant mock me unmercifully,
    but I do not turn from your law.

⁵²I remember, LORD, your ancient laws,
   and I find comfort in them.
⁵³Indignation grips me because of the wicked,
   who have forsaken your law.
⁵⁴Your decrees are the theme of my song
   wherever I lodge.
⁵⁵In the night, LORD, I remember your name,
   that I may keep your law.
⁵⁶This has been my practice:
   I obey your precepts.

ח Heth

⁵⁷You are my portion, LORD;
   I have promised to obey your words.
⁵⁸I have sought your face with all my heart;
   be gracious to me according to your promise.
⁵⁹I have considered my ways
   and have turned my steps to your statutes.
⁶⁰I will hasten and not delay
   to obey your commands.
⁶¹Though the wicked bind me with ropes,
   I will not forget your law.
⁶²At midnight I rise to give you thanks
   for your righteous laws.
⁶³I am a friend to all who fear you,
   to all who follow your precepts.
⁶⁴The earth is filled with your love, LORD;
   teach me your decrees.

ט Teth

⁶⁵Do good to your servant
   according to your word, LORD.
⁶⁶Teach me knowledge and good judgment,
   for I trust your commands.
⁶⁷Before I was afflicted I went astray,
   but now I obey your word.
⁶⁸You are good, and what you do is good;
   teach me your decrees.
⁶⁹Though the arrogant have smeared me with lies,
   I keep your precepts with all my heart.

⁷⁰ Their hearts are callous and unfeeling,
　　but I delight in your law.
⁷¹ It was good for me to be afflicted
　　so that I might learn your decrees.
⁷² The law from your mouth is more precious to me
　　than thousands of pieces of silver and gold.

י Yodh

⁷³ Your hands made me and formed me;
　　give me understanding to learn your commands.
⁷⁴ May those who fear you rejoice when they see me,
　　for I have put my hope in your word.
⁷⁵ I know, Lord, that your laws are righteous,
　　and that in faithfulness you have afflicted me.
⁷⁶ May your unfailing love be my comfort,
　　according to your promise to your servant.
⁷⁷ Let your compassion come to me that I may live,
　　for your law is my delight.
⁷⁸ May the arrogant be put to shame for wronging me without
cause;
　　but I will meditate on your precepts.
⁷⁹ May those who fear you turn to me,
　　those who understand your statutes.
⁸⁰ May I wholeheartedly follow your decrees,
　　that I may not be put to shame.

כ Kaph

⁸¹ My soul faints with longing for your salvation,
　　but I have put my hope in your word.
⁸² My eyes fail, looking for your promise;
　　I say, "When will you comfort me?"
⁸³ Though I am like a wineskin in the smoke,
　　I do not forget your decrees.
⁸⁴ How long must your servant wait?
　　When will you punish my persecutors?
⁸⁵ The arrogant dig pits to trap me,
　　contrary to your law.
⁸⁶ All your commands are trustworthy;
　　help me, for I am being persecuted without cause.
⁸⁷ They almost wiped me from the earth,

but I have not forsaken your precepts.
⁸⁸ In your unfailing love preserve my life,
　　that I may obey the statutes of your mouth.

ל Lamedh

⁸⁹ Your word, LORD, is eternal;
　　it stands firm in the heavens.
⁹⁰ Your faithfulness continues through all generations;
　　you established the earth, and it endures.
⁹¹ Your laws endure to this day,
　　for all things serve you.
⁹² If your law had not been my delight,
　　I would have perished in my affliction.
⁹³ I will never forget your precepts,
　　for by them you have preserved my life.
⁹⁴ Save me, for I am yours;
　　I have sought out your precepts.
⁹⁵ The wicked are waiting to destroy me,
　　but I will ponder your statutes.
⁹⁶ To all perfection I see a limit,
　　but your commands are boundless.

מ Mem

⁹⁷ Oh, how I love your law!
　　I meditate on it all day long.
⁹⁸ Your commands are always with me
　　and make me wiser than my enemies.
⁹⁹ I have more insight than all my teachers,
　　for I meditate on your statutes.
¹⁰⁰ I have more understanding than the elders,
　　for I obey your precepts.
¹⁰¹ I have kept my feet from every evil path
　　so that I might obey your word.
¹⁰² I have not departed from your laws,
　　for you yourself have taught me.
¹⁰³ How sweet are your words to my taste,
　　sweeter than honey to my mouth!
¹⁰⁴ I gain understanding from your precepts;
　　therefore I hate every wrong path.

נ Nun

105 Your word is a lamp for my feet,
    a light on my path.
106 I have taken an oath and confirmed it,
    that I will follow your righteous laws.
107 I have suffered much;
    preserve my life, LORD, according to your word.
108 Accept, LORD, the willing praise of my mouth,
    and teach me your laws.
109 Though I constantly take my life in my hands,
    I will not forget your law.
110 The wicked have set a snare for me,
    but I have not strayed from your precepts.
111 Your statutes are my heritage forever;
    they are the joy of my heart.
112 My heart is set on keeping your decrees
    to the very end.

ס Samekh

113 I hate double-minded people,
    but I love your law.
114 You are my refuge and my shield;
    I have put my hope in your word.
115 Away from me, you evildoers,
    that I may keep the commands of my God!
116 Sustain me, my God, according to your promise, and I will live;
    do not let my hopes be dashed.
117 Uphold me, and I will be delivered;
    I will always have regard for your decrees.
118 You reject all who stray from your decrees,
    for their delusions come to nothing.
119 All the wicked of the earth you discard like dross;
    therefore I love your statutes.
120 My flesh trembles in fear of you;
    I stand in awe of your laws.

ע Ayin

121 I have done what is righteous and just;
    do not leave me to my oppressors.

¹²² Ensure your servant's well-being;
   do not let the arrogant oppress me.
¹²³ My eyes fail, looking for your salvation,
   looking for your righteous promise.
¹²⁴ Deal with your servant according to your love
   and teach me your decrees.
¹²⁵ I am your servant; give me discernment
   that I may understand your statutes.
¹²⁶ It is time for you to act, LORD;
   your law is being broken.
¹²⁷ Because I love your commands
   more than gold, more than pure gold,
¹²⁸ and because I consider all your precepts right,
   I hate every wrong path.

פ Pe

¹²⁹ Your statutes are wonderful;
   therefore I obey them.
¹³⁰ The unfolding of your words gives light;
   it gives understanding to the simple.
¹³¹ I open my mouth and pant,
   longing for your commands.
¹³² Turn to me and have mercy on me,
   as you always do to those who love your name.
¹³³ Direct my footsteps according to your word;
   let no sin rule over me.
¹³⁴ Redeem me from human oppression,
   that I may obey your precepts.
¹³⁵ Make your face shine on your servant
   and teach me your decrees.
¹³⁶ Streams of tears flow from my eyes,
   for your law is not obeyed.

צ Tsadhe

¹³⁷ You are righteous, LORD,
   and your laws are right.
¹³⁸ The statutes you have laid down are righteous;
   they are fully trustworthy.
¹³⁹ My zeal wears me out,
   for my enemies ignore your words.
¹⁴⁰ Your promises have been thoroughly tested,

and your servant loves them.

¹⁴¹ Though I am lowly and despised,
    I do not forget your precepts.
¹⁴² Your righteousness is everlasting
    and your law is true.
¹⁴³ Trouble and distress have come upon me,
    but your commands give me delight.
¹⁴⁴ Your statutes are always righteous;
    give me understanding that I may live.

ק Qoph

¹⁴⁵ I call with all my heart; answer me, LORD,
    and I will obey your decrees.
¹⁴⁶ I call out to you; save me
    and I will keep your statutes.
¹⁴⁷ I rise before dawn and cry for help;
    I have put my hope in your word.
¹⁴⁸ My eyes stay open through the watches of the night,
    that I may meditate on your promises.
¹⁴⁹ Hear my voice in accordance with your love;
    preserve my life, LORD, according to your laws.
¹⁵⁰ Those who devise wicked schemes are near,
    but they are far from your law.
¹⁵¹ Yet you are near, LORD,
    and all your commands are true.
¹⁵² Long ago I learned from your statutes
    that you established them to last forever.

ר Resh

¹⁵³ Look on my suffering and deliver me,
    for I have not forgotten your law.
¹⁵⁴ Defend my cause and redeem me;
    preserve my life according to your promise.
¹⁵⁵ Salvation is far from the wicked,
    for they do not seek out your decrees.
¹⁵⁶ Your compassion, LORD, is great;
    preserve my life according to your laws.
¹⁵⁷ Many are the foes who persecute me,
    but I have not turned from your statutes.
¹⁵⁸ I look on the faithless with loathing,
    for they do not obey your word.

¹⁵⁹ See how I love your precepts;
    preserve my life, LORD, in accordance with your love.
¹⁶⁰ All your words are true;
    all your righteous laws are eternal.

ש Sin and Shin

¹⁶¹ Rulers persecute me without cause,
    but my heart trembles at your word.
¹⁶² I rejoice in your promise
    like one who finds great spoil.
¹⁶³ I hate and detest falsehood
    but I love your law.
¹⁶⁴ Seven times a day I praise you
    for your righteous laws.
¹⁶⁵ Great peace have those who love your law,
    and nothing can make them stumble.
¹⁶⁶ I wait for your salvation, LORD,
    and I follow your commands.
¹⁶⁷ I obey your statutes,
    for I love them greatly.
¹⁶⁸ I obey your precepts and your statutes,
    for all my ways are known to you.

ת Taw

¹⁶⁹ May my cry come before you, LORD;
    give me understanding according to your word.
¹⁷⁰ May my supplication come before you;
    deliver me according to your promise.
¹⁷¹ May my lips overflow with praise,
    for you teach me your decrees.
¹⁷² May my tongue sing of your word,
    for all your commands are righteous.
¹⁷³ May your hand be ready to help me,
    for I have chosen your precepts.
¹⁷⁴ I long for your salvation, LORD,
    and your law gives me delight.
¹⁷⁵ Let me live that I may praise you,
    and may your laws sustain me.
¹⁷⁶ I have strayed like a lost sheep.
    Seek your servant,
        for I have not forgotten your commands.

WITH 176 VERSES, Psalm 119 is the longest psalm in the Hebrew Psalter. The massive size of this poetic work, coupled with its seemingly repetitive emphasis on the law, or the instruction, of God (see below), however, has not always garnered the appreciation of interpreters. At the beginning of the twentieth century, noted German scholar Bernard Duhm puzzled over the need for 176 verses and concluded that this psalm is the "most empty [*inhaltsloseste*] product that has darkened a piece of paper."[1] Some forty years later, the psalm did not fare much better. Artur Weiser castigated the psalm by deriding it as an "artificial product of religious poetry."[2] More recent interpreters have come to appreciate the highly stylized form of the psalm as well as its orientation toward torah piety.[3] Rather that viewing Psalm 119 as a poem with needless repetition, modern interpreters have argued that the psalm presents to the reader the "model of a Yahweh believer and student of the Torah."[4]

The most distinguishing feature of Psalm 119 is its tightly configured literary structure. The psalm is an alphabetic acrostic containing twenty-two strophes (one strophe for each letter in the Hebrew alphabet), with eight verses in each strophe. This form of Hebrew poetry can be found in other psalms as well (e.g., Pss 34 and 145), but in those psalms there is only one verse assigned to each letter in the Hebrew alphabet. In Psalm 119, however, the form of the acrostic is extended with the first letter of each verse in every eight-verse strophe beginning with the same Hebrew letter. For example, in the first strophe, Aleph, the first word in each verse begins with the letter *aleph*. While this poetic form is impressive, it is "not mere 'scholastic gamesmanship,' but was deliberately chosen by the author of the psalm as appropriate to his theological intention" for the poem.[5] Among the intentions of the psalmist, two seem most apparent. By structuring

---

1. Bernard Duhm, *Die Psalmen*, Kurzer Hand-Kommentar zum Alten Testament, ed. D. Karl Marti (Tübingen: J. C. B. Mohr, 1922), 727.

2. Artur Weiser, *The Psalms*, OTL, trans. Herbert Hartwell (Philadelphia: Westminster, 1962), 739.

3. See, for example, Erich Zenger, "Torafrömmigkeit. Beobachtungen zum poetischen und theologischen Profil von Psalm 119," in *Freiheit und Recht. Für Frank Crüsemann zum 65. Geburtstag*, ed. Christof Hardmeier, Rainer Kessler, and Andreas Ruwe (Gütersloh: Kaiser, 2003), 380–96.

4. Gerstenberger, *Psalms, Part 2, and Lamentations*, 315. For a more recent and expanded argument of this position see Kent Aaron Reynolds, *Torah as Teacher: The Exemplary Torah Student in Psalm 119*, VTSup 137 (Leiden: Brill, 2010).

5. Hossfeld and Zenger, *Psalms 3*, 257.

the psalm as an acrostic that uses the entirety of the Hebrew alphabet, the psalmist signals the range of the subject matter, or more specifically the comprehensiveness of the subject matter. English speakers would use the idiom "from A to Z" to suggest the full range of meaning provided by a word, phrase, or expression (i.e., "That document spells out everything from A to Z"). Psalm 119 provides a comprehensive reflection on torah as the guiding principle in all aspects of human life.

The acrostic structure of the psalm also signals order. The psalm repeatedly mentions the threats of the enemies against the psalmist. Although these threats suggest that the world is *disordered*, hostile, and menacing, Psalm 119 invites the petitioner to commit to a different world—one that has been rightly ordered by God's instruction. Through careful reflection on Psalm 119, the student is guided into the ways of God.

As noted above, each strophe contains eight verses (comprised of a bi-cola)—a feature that distinguishes the Psalm 119 from all other acrostics in the Old Testament. The choice of eight as the number of verses per strophe was likely not arbitrary but intentional. Hossfeld and Zenger have noted the significance of the number eight in narrative and cultic traditions.[6] Following the completion of the tabernacle in Exodus 40, the writer of Leviticus says that Moses gathered Aaron and all the people of Israel together to worship Yahweh on the eighth day. Equally instructive is the comparison between Psalm 119 and Nehemiah 8:1–18 in the light of the Festival of Booths. For seven days the torah was read aloud publicly, and on the eighth day the festival ended in joyous celebration; they had heard the torah of Yahweh, and the shaping of their lives by it led them into worship. Attention to the torah results in worship and joyous celebration.

In addition to each strophe's having eight lines, eight terms associated with torah are used throughout Psalm 119. The word *torah* itself occurs twenty-five times, and though one might expect the use of this word to overshadow the synonymous terms also employed, the words are actually distributed quite evenly. Because these words all function synonymously, they are rendered differently from translation to translation. (The English translation provided here comes from the NIV, but as a reference point a text is provided in parentheses following each word to allow readers to compare translations.) The word *'edut*, "statute," occurs twenty-three times (v. 2). The word *mishpat*, "law," occurs twenty-three times (v. 7). The word *hoq*, "decrees," occurs 22 times (v. 5). The word *dabar*, "word," occurs 22 times (v. 9). The word *mitsvah*, "commandment," occurs twenty-two times (v. 6). The word

---

6. Ibid., 257–58.

piqqud, "precepts," occurs twenty-one times (v. 4), and the word *'imrah,* "word," occurs nineteen times (v. 11). The distribution of these eight terms across the entirety of Psalm 119 proves yet again the artistic construction of this psalm. These terms appear an equal number of times (eighty-eight) in strophes 1–11 and in strophes 12–22. With the exception of verses 3, 37, 90, and 122, every verse in Psalm 119 contains one of these eight terms.[7]

Although the repeated emphasis on the instruction of God dominates the entirety of the psalm, another theme plays a significant role throughout (see Bridging Contexts). Repeatedly in this psalm the poet refers to enemies and their disordering presence in his life.[8] Although the enemies are a present threat to the psalmist, he confesses that they will not deter him from focusing on torah.[9] He trusts that God will deliver him from his present circumstance (v. 122).

Because of the repeated references to the enemies and the threat they posed to the psalmist, some scholars have suggested that Psalm 119 is actually a lengthy and complex individual lament psalm. William Soll has argued that the psalm actually moves from complaint to praise, with the zenith of the psalm occurring in the Lamed strophe (vv. 89–96).[10] The diversity of genres throughout the psalm, however, calls into question Soll's suggestion of a well-structured psalm that follows the contours of the lament psalm. Goldingay contends that there is no discernible structural principle in the psalm at all—"no argument or development."[11] As with many issues, the truth is likely somewhere in the middle. Goldingay is correct that the psalm contains a wide array of genres, including elements of hymns, thanksgiving songs, and wisdom teachings. Yet Soll is also correct in that the traditional elements of a lament psalm can be found in this psalm as well; his argument that the entire poem is structured as a lament, however, is less likely. Taken as a whole, the psalm may be correctly labeled a torah psalm, but embedded throughout is "a petition for rescue from a multifaceted threat."[12] Despite the threats assailing the psalmist, he pledges to remain faithful to the torah (e.g., vv. 23, 51, 61, 141, 161).

---

7. Even among these four verses it is worth noting that the word *derek,* "way," appears in verses 3 and 37. While *derek* is not necessarily a synonym of *torah,* it is an associated term.

8. In Ps 119 the terms from the enemy word field include: *sarim,* "rulers" (vv. 23, 161); *zedim,* "arrogant" (vv. 21, 51, 69, 78, 85, 122); and *resha'im,* "wicked" (vv. 53, 61, 95, 110, 119, 155).

9. Cf. verses 23, 38, 49, 65, 76, 84, 91, 122, 124, and 135.

10. William M. Soll, *Psalm 119: Matrix, Form and Setting,* CBQMS 23 (Washington, DC: Catholic University of America Press, 1991).

11. Goldingay, *Psalms 3,* 377.

12. Hossfeld and Zenger, *Psalms 3,* 262.

Prior to examining each strophe, one question remains to be addressed: What does the psalmist mean by "torah"? As noted above, the psalmist employs eight different words in an attempt to capture the full range of the intended meaning. The diversity of terms used in Psalm 119 suggests that the term "torah" cannot be limited to a single notion (i.e., the Mosaic law) but instead is far more expansive. In his insightful analysis of Psalm 119, Jon Levenson notes that there were three sources of torah for the psalmist.[13] The first was "received tradition," which would have included the instruction of teachers but also material from earlier biblical texts (e.g., vv. 97–98). In particular, scholars have noted the presence of Deuteronomic language and theology in Psalm 119.[14] The second source of torah was divine instruction taken from nature (i.e., natural law; cf. vv. 89–91), and the third source was what Levenson referred to as "unmediated divine teaching" (vv. 33, 124),[15] by which, Levenson suggested, the psalmist sought the continued instruction of God for the present moment. Taken together, these sources reflect the complex notion of torah adopted in Psalm 119. The psalmist relies on the instruction (*torah*) passed on to him both in verbal and written forms, but even further he trusted in God's ongoing work of instruction to provide guidance for his life. The psalm is not simply about the content of torah; instead, it is a prayerful search for refuge in God's instruction in the midst of a hostile and threatening world.[16]

Aleph (119:1–8)

PSALM 119 BEGINS WITH THE SAME WORD that begins Psalm 1: *'ashre*, "blessed." The term also appears in the first verse of Psalm 112. As explained in the comments on that psalm, the term *'ashre* appears with considerable regularity in the wisdom literature of the Old Testament to identify conduct and attitudes the faithful of God should embody.[17] These actions and attitudes,

---

13. Jon Levenson, "The Sources of Torah: Psalm 119 and the Modes of Revelation in Second Temple Judaism," in *Ancient Israelite Religion*, ed. Patrick D. Miller Jr., Paul D. Hanson, and S. Dean McBride (Philadelphia: Fortress, 1987), 559–74.

14. On the influence of Deuteronomic language in Ps 119 see Michael D. Goulder, *The Psalms of the Return (Book V, Psalms 107–150)*, JSOTSup 258 (Sheffield: Sheffield Academic, 1998), 204–6.

15. Levenson, "The Sources of Torah," 568.

16. Zenger, "Torafrömmigkeit," 394.

17. Cf. Job 5:17; Prov 3:13; 8:32, 34; 14:21; 16:20; 20:7; 28:14; 29:18; Eccl 10:17. The term appears repeatedly in the Psalter, with considerable use in Books 4 and 5. Cf. Pss 1:1; 2:12; 32:1, 2; 33:12; 34:8; 40:4; 41:1; 65:4; 84:4, 5, 16; 89:15; 94:12; 106:3; 112:1; 119:1, 2; 127:5; 128:1, 2; 137:8, 9; 144:15; 146:5.

however, are not arbitrary commitments but ones that signal that our lives are congruent with the larger purposes of God. In Psalm 119 the poet acknowledges that the ways of the "blessed" are blameless because they walk in the ways of the torah of Yahweh and seek instruction with their heart. In this instance the psalmist holds up the "blessed" one as a person who takes seriously God's torah. Whenever the psalmist refers to the torah, it never stands alone (i.e., the torah); rather, the term appears as either the "torah of the LORD" or as "your torah," thus once more stressing the importance of the covenantal relationship. In the first half of the strophe (vv. 1–4) the psalmist describes the blessed life as one rooted in the torah of Yahweh. In the second half of the strophe he refers to the tumultuous circumstances that appear to threaten him. The psalmist worries about being put to shame (v. 6) and left forsaken (v. 8). Thus, the opening strophe holds in tandem the desire to live a blessed life that is rooted in the torah of Yahweh and the reality of a threatened existence. The psalmist eschews trite platitudes that suggest that faithfulness to the torah of Yahweh rids one of challenging circumstances. To the contrary, Psalm 119 reminds the reader of the need to root one's life in the instruction of God amid such challenging circumstances in life.

Beth (119:9–16)

THE SECOND STROPHE BEGINS with the question, "How can a young person stay on the path of purity?" In the Aleph strophe the psalmist mentions his "ways" (*derek*), but in this strophe the image shifts to that of a "path" (*'arah*), a term that refers metaphorically to one's way or journey in life. The response to this question involves the repetition of the word *dabar* in this strophe. In verse 9b the psalmist explains that a person must live according to God's word (*dabar*). The term itself can refer either to the written revelation of God, as in the case of the "Ten Words [*debarim*]" mentioned in Exodus 34:28 and Deuteronomy 4:13 and 10:4, or it can refer to God's direct communication to his people (cf. Jer 1:4; Ezek 1:3). The entire strophe is bracketed by the term "word" (*dabar*). In the strophe's opening verse (v. 9b) the psalmist announces that the pure path is reached by choosing to live according to God's word, and in the final verse the psalmist pledges not to forget God's *dabar*. In verse 11 the poet declares that he has "hidden your word" in his heart so that he might not sin against God. The word "hidden" (*tsapan*) in this instance means "to store up" rather than simply "to hide." As a result, the heart of the blessed person becomes a storehouse of God's words; they too help him pursue the path of purity. In the final line of the Beth strophe the psalmist declares, "I will not neglect [lit., 'forget'] your word [*dabar*]."

Gimel (119:17–24)

IN THE OPENING (ALEPH) STROPHE of Psalm 119 the psalmist alluded to the difficult circumstances he faces (v. 6). The Gimel strophe makes clear the impact this threat has had upon him. In the second half of the strophe the psalmist refers to those who are plaguing him—the "arrogant," "the accursed," and the rulers. Together they slander the psalmist and rain down on him scorn and contempt. He explicitly defines them in verse 21 as "those who stray from your commands." The threat has become so significant that the psalmist declares, "I am a stranger on earth" (v. 19, NIV). In the NIV's rendering, this verse seems to make a cosmic claim (i.e., that psalmist no longer feels at home on the earth). The verse would be better rendered, "I am a stranger [or 'sojourner'] in the *land*." The word *'erets* can indeed be translated as "earth," but in the light of the psalmist's declaration that he is a sojourner, the word seems best understood as reference to the land where he dwells. The very place that should feel like home indeed does not.[18] Over against the threatening group, the psalmist self-identifies as "your servant" in verses 17 and 23. In the first instance he is the servant who obeys God's word (*dabar*), and in the latter, he is the one who will meditate on God's decrees (*hoq*). The verb "to meditate" recalls the Psalter's opening psalm, in which the poet declares that the blessed person meditates on the torah of Yahweh day and night.[19] Although the psalmist feels pressure from his enemies, he longs for God's laws (v. 20), for they are his counselors (v. 24); they provide the needed and necessary guidance amid the challenges he confronts.

Daleth (119:25–32)

THE LAMENT UTTERED IN THE GIMEL STROPHE continues in this strophe. The opening line indicates the depths of the psalmist's complaint: "I am laid low in the dust." In other psalms the word "dust" can refer to death or Sheol (Pss 7:5; 22:15; 44:26). While the NIV's translation makes sense, a more literal rendering of the Hebrew offers an instructive mental picture. In verse 25a, the verb *dabaq* means "to cling to something," in this case, the dust. The subject of the verb is *nepesh*, that equivocal term which can be rendered "soul," "life," or even simply used as a replacement for the pronoun "I." Thus the psalmist describes his plight by saying, "my life clings to the dust." This plight is

---

18. Like the widow and the orphan, the sojourner was vulnerable to oppression by those in power. Israel was warned to care for the sojourner because they too were once sojourners in Egypt (Deut 10:18).

19. In Ps 1:2 the verb is *hagah*, while the verb is *siah* in Ps 119:23. Although the verbs differ, the language in the latter clearly alludes to the image in Ps 1.

juxtaposed with his confession in verse 31: "I hold fast [*dabaq*] to your statutes, LORD." Although his life is "laid low [clings] in the dust" (v. 25), he confesses that he clings to the statutes of God (v. 31). Repeatedly in this strophe the psalmist implores Yahweh to guide him through instruction: "preserve my life according to your word" (v. 25b); "teach me your decrees" (v. 26b); "cause me to understand the way of your precepts" (v. 27a); and "strengthen me according to your word" (v. 28b). As a result of Yahweh's instructing the psalmist, he can exclaim, "you have broadened my understanding" (v. 32). Frequently, distress or trouble conveys the spatial image of a tight or confined space (see the comments on Pss 116 and 140). Just as trouble is imagined as being in a tight spot, so deliverance is imagined as being in an open space (*rahaq*). Thus, the final verse in the Daleth strophe functions metaphorically in two different directions. On the one hand, the psalmist suggests that by following the paths of Yahweh's instruction, his understanding will be enlarged. On the other hand, the reference to paths and open spaces in this verse suggests deliverance.

He (119:33–40)

THE PREVIOUS STROPHES INDICATED the threats experienced by the psalmist. The He strophe shifts the focus to petition. Every line in this strophe begins with an imperative addressed to Yahweh. The symmetry is further extended in the first seven lines with each verb appearing in the *hiphil* form (based upon the guiding letter for the strophe, *he*). Even more deliberately than in previous strophes, Yahweh is depicted as the teacher for his pupil, the psalmist. In the two middle verses, the psalmist asks God to remove those things that can prove distracting: "selfish gain" (v. 36) and "worthless things" (v. 37). Both terms are meant to suggest that the value of Yahweh's torah surpasses all things. In verse 38 the psalmist refers to the covenantal relationship that defines his life with Yahweh. As similarly seen in verses 17 and 23, the psalmist self-describes as "your servant." On the covenantal imagery present with this image, see the comments on Psalm 123.

Waw (119:41–48)

THE OPENING VERSE OF THE WAW STROPHE binds it with the previous strophe. That strophe (He) contains a number of imperatives directed at Yahweh; the Waw strophe opens with another petition directed at Yahweh but uses a jussive rather than an imperative. In this initial petition the psalmist requests that Yahweh's "unfailing love" (*hesed*) and salvation (*teshu'ah*) come to him. The taunting of the enemies has prompted this plea (v. 42). Throughout the Psalter the enemies have asked mockingly, "Where is your God?" (e.g., Pss 42:4, 11; 115:2), and this kind of taunting ridicule appears to stand in the background of the petition (cf. Ps 3:3). The coming of Yahweh's *hesed* would signal God's covenantal loyalty to the psalmist and, further, would rebut the claim of the enemy that the psalmist has been abandoned. Moreover, the arrival of Yahweh's salvation (*teshu'ah*) or deliverance would signal that Yahweh has demonstrated his loyalty through action. The psalmist declares that he will trust and hope in God's torah; he will remain faithful to it "forever and ever." Because the psalmist trusts in God's word (*dabar*), he declares that he can "walk about in freedom [*rehabah*]." The adjective *rehabah* functions substantively and refers to a wide, open space. (The verbal form of the word appears in Ps 119:32.) He is no longer under the mocking taunts of the enemies. So certain is the psalmist of God's promises (*'imrah* [v. 41]) that he pledges to speak of Yahweh's statutes (*'edut*) in the presence of kings. They will not be able to put him to shame (v. 46b) when they hear what the psalmist has declared, presumably because they will acknowledge who Yahweh is. On the worship of Yahweh by the kings of the nations see Psalms 72:11 and 138:4–6. The strophe closes with the psalmist's professing his "love" (*'ahab*) for the commands of Yahweh (vv. 47–48), a clear demonstration of his loyalty to Yahweh.[20] In the opening verse of the strophe the psalmist asks for God's *hesed*, his unfailing love, to come to him. The strophe draws to a close with the psalmist's confessing his loyal love to the ways of Yahweh.

Zayin (119:49–56)

THE FOCUS OF THE ZAYIN STROPHE is the thrice repeated word *zakar*, "to remember." In verse 49 the psalmist implores Yahweh to remember his word (*dabar*) to his servant (cf. vv. 17, 23) in the midst of the arrogant and mocking throng. In this context the psalmist declares that he "remembers" Yahweh's ancient laws (v. 52). The instruction of Yahweh provides comfort (vv. 50a and 52b) to him and preserves his life (v. 50). The nature of his plight is also evident later in the strophe. In verse 54 the Hebrew literally says, "Your decrees [*hoq*] have been my songs in the house of my sojourning." Earlier in the psalm (v. 19) the poet self-described as a sojourner (*gur*)—a theme to which the psalmist returns in this strophe. Despite the sense of being "without a land," the psalmist confesses that the decrees of Yahweh have been a comfort and a source of joy. They have been his song (Exod 15:2; Ps 118:14). In the midst of his sense of dislocation, the psalmist

---

20. The verb *'ahab* appears repeatedly in the book of Deuteronomy in reference to the covenantal relationship between God and his people. In Deuteronomy the particular emphasis falls on the covenantal obligations of the people in response to the God of the covenant (e.g., Deut 5:10; 7:6–8; 10:12–13).

confesses that at night he "remembers" the name of Yahweh (Ps 119:55). Although the Zayin strophe recalls the plight faced by the psalmist, the strophe concludes by affirming his regular practice of obeying the precepts (*piqqud*) of Yahweh. As with previous strophes, the psalmist holds in tension the reality of his world with his tenacious commitment to the torah of Yahweh.

Heth (119:57–64)

IN THE PREVIOUS STROPHE (v. 54) and the Gimel strophe (v. 19), the psalmist declares that he is a sojourner, a person without a land. In response to that assessment of his condition, the psalmist opens the Heth strophe by describing Yahweh as his "portion" (*heleq*). Elsewhere the word "portion" (*heleq*) refers to the division or apportionment of land.[21] The book of Joshua explains that all Israelites are to receive a "portion" (*heleq*) when they enter the land (Josh 15:13; 18:7; 19:9). The psalmist shifts that imagery by suggesting that, while he feels like an alien, he is not without a home. Yahweh will be his portion. The psalmist confesses that he has not only a home but also a community (Ps 119:63). Until this point in the psalm the image has been that of the lone, faithful psalmist against his godless enemies; but in the Heth strophe the image shifts. The wicked remain a present danger (v. 61), but that threat is not faced in isolation.

Teth (119:65–72)

IN THE TETH STROPHE the operative word is "good" (*tov*). The word begins the first two verses of the strophe and, likewise, is the first word in the last two verses, thus serving as a framing device. Beyond these four uses the word *tov* begins verse 68, and the verbal form of the term appears later in the verse. In the book of Deuteronomy *tov* represents the life-sustaining gifts or blessings of Yahweh, particularly as related to Israel's faithfulness to the covenant (cf. Deut 10:13). In Psalm 119 the poet explains in verses 67 and 71 that, like the enemies, he too had gone astray, but his affliction "brought him back to an understanding of Torah and a corresponding life."[22] What he learned from his affliction is that Yahweh is "good" (*tov*) and that he brings about good (v. 68). Rather than continuing to go astray, the psalmist has become obedient to Yahweh's word (v. 67) and even delights in it (v. 70). The arrogant, however, have not changed. They continue to malign the psalmist because their hearts have become callous to the ways of God. Whatever gain he may have achieved by following the

---

21. Cornelis van Dam, "חלק," *NIDOTTE* 2:162–63.
22. Hossfeld and Zenger, *Psalms 3*, 273.

ways of the arrogant, the psalmist now concludes that the only source of value is the law (torah) that proceeds from God's mouth (v. 72).

Yodh (119:73–80)

THE OPENING LINE OF THE YODH STROPHE refers to human creation, thus leading Robert Davidson to suggest that perhaps the psalmist had Genesis 1–3 in view when he penned this strophe.[23] Whether the psalmist is alluding specifically to that text or to the creation motif more generally is difficult to determine. What is not difficult to discern is the rationale for invoking creation language. The psalmist declares that he was fashioned by God and, consequently, designed to live out God's commandments. Human life and faithful obedience are intertwined in this strophe with the larger truth that true life, as fashioned by God, includes faithfulness to God's instruction. The psalmist indicates that it is God's *hesed* ("unfailing love") and mercy that provide comfort to him so that he may live (Ps 119:77). Yahweh is not only the creator of human life, but by his very nature (Exod 34:6) he is also the sustainer of those who delight in his law (Ps 119:77a).[24]

Kaph (119:81–88)

THE KAPH STROPHE AND THE STROPHE to follow (Lamed) function as the center of Psalm 119, both literally and figuratively. The Kaph strophe provides the most explicit account of the psalmist's plight and serves to anchor the lament element of the psalm. Hossfeld and Zenger have suggested that the strophe has a chiastic structure.[25] The verb "to finish" or "to complete" (*kalah*) occurs three times (vv. 81, 82, 87) in the psalm and serves to frame the poem. In all three instances the psalmist laments that he is nearly "finished" because of all that has occurred. In the intervening verses, the psalmist acknowledges his need (vv. 83–84; 85–86). Each pair of verses contains a metaphor, followed by a reference to the persecution (*radap*) being experienced by the psalmist. In the Teth strophe the psalmist indicated that he had been afflicted in the past because he had gone astray (v. 67). In this strophe, however, he confesses that everything happening now is "without cause" (v. 86). Consequently, he can do nothing other

---

23. Davidson, *The Vitality of Worship*, 396.

24. The language in the remainder of the strophe harkens back to the previous strophe. That the Teth and Yodh strophes share a number of lexical terms serves to create a thematic subunit within the larger psalm. The terms include: "servant" (*'ebed* [vv. 65, 76]); "to afflict" (*'anah* [vv. 67, 75]); "proud" (*zedim* [vv. 69, 78]); "falsehood" (*sheqer* [vv. 69, 78]); and "delight" (*sha'ashu'im* [vv. 70, 77]).

25. Hossfeld and Zenger, *Psalms 3*, 275.

than to petition Yahweh for help (v. 86b). The strophe concludes with the psalmist's citing Yahweh's *hesed*, "loyal love." The NIV translates the verse, "In your unfailing love preserve my life." The preposition attached to *hesed* is a *kaph*, which can be translated as "according to." Thus, the psalmist is asking that Yahweh preserve his life "according to [his] *hesed*," or "based upon [his] *hesed*." With his life preserved, the psalmist explains, he will be able to obey the words of Yahweh's mouth (v. 86; cf. v. 72).

Lamed (119:89–96)

THE KAPH STROPHE HIGHLIGHTED the conditions that prompt the psalmist's lament; the Lamed strophe emphasizes the psalmist's cause for hope, namely, the faithfulness of Yahweh and the enduring strength of his torah. Throughout Book 5 of the Psalter God is depicted as being in the heavens or above the heavens.[26] Yahweh's enthronement in the heavens secures his rightful place as the cosmic king over all creation. Similarly, the psalmist contends that Yahweh's word stands firm in the heavens. Whatever political and social machinations may occur on earth, they do not undermine the authoritative power of Yahweh's word or his faithfulness; it "endure[s] to this day." According to verse 93b, the enduring power of God's word has preserved the life of the psalmist thus far, and it is because of that enduring power that in verse 94 the psalmist confesses, "I am yours." With this declaration the psalmist recognizes God as his patron and seeks the deliverance that only he can bring.[27]

Mem (119:97–104)

THE MEM STROPHE CONTINUES the praise of Yahweh's torah. As with the author of Psalm 1:2, the writer of Psalm 119 confesses that he meditates on Yahweh's laws all day long. In Psalm 1:2, the verb "to meditate" is *hagah*, but in Psalm 119:97 it is *siah*. Although the terms differ, they are synonymous. In Psalm 1:2 the psalmist employs a merismus ("day and night") to capture the sense of continual meditation on God's word. In Psalm 119:97a the poet confesses that he meditates "all day long," thus conveying a similar meaning. In the first half of the strophe (vv. 97–100), the psalmist employs three terms associated with Israel's wisdom tradition: "wiser" (v. 98); "insight" (v. 99); and "understanding" (v. 100). Even though he has teachers and elders who teach him (vv. 99–100), he confesses that he is the recipient of this wisdom because he has received instruction from Yahweh himself

---

26. Tucker, *Constructing and Deconstructing Power in Psalms 107–150*, 142–49. See Pss 113:5–6; 115:3; 123:1; 136:26; 144:5–7.

27. Hossfeld and Zenger, *Psalms 3*, 276.

(v. 102). On Yahweh as the teacher of the psalmist, see verses 26, 27, 33, 66, and 68. Twice the psalmist acknowledges that the torah of Yahweh has allowed him to keep his feet from walking on evil paths ('orah [vv. 101, 104]), thus implying that the instruction of Yahweh has kept him walking in the ways of God. Like honey, Yahweh's instruction has been life giving and life sustaining (v. 103). It is because of all these things that the psalmist begins the strophe with his declaration, "Oh how I love your law!"

Nun (119:105–12)

THE NUN STROPHE OPENS WITH WHAT may arguably be the most well-known verse in Psalm 119. More popularly, this verse is applied to a broader understanding of Scripture, but it actually serves to bind the Mem and Nun strophes together around the idea of "path." In the previous strophe the psalmist referred to evil paths by using the Hebrew 'orah (vv. 101, 104), but in the Nun strophe the psalmist opts for the Hebrew word *netibah*. Both terms have a similar meaning, with the latter likely having been chosen primarily because of its first letter (*nun*).[28] The psalmist needs a lamp to light his way because of the darkness that threatens the path. This darkness is the result of the affliction he is enduring (v. 107) and the traps being set by the wicked to snare him (v. 110). While traps are often set along the well-worn paths, the light of God's word (v. 105) will enable to the psalmist to see such snares and avoid them altogether. He feels his existence is so tenuous that he concludes, "I constantly take my life in my hands" (v. 109). Yet the psalmist does not allow those elements of his life to define his existence, nor does he allow them to take him off the path determined by God. Instead, he confesses that his life is focused on keeping the decrees of Yahweh.

Samekh (119:113–20)

THE STROPHE OPENS WITH THE PSALMIST'S announcement of his antipathy for "double-minded" people. The word *se'ep* occurs only here in the Old Testament and means "divided," referring in this instance to people with divided commitments. Throughout the Samekh strophe the psalmist signals that he remains single-minded in his commitment to Yahweh: "I love your law" (v.115b); "I may keep the commands of my God" (v. 113b); and "I love your statutes" (v. 119b). Those who remain double-minded and stray from God's instruction, however, will be rejected by Yahweh (v. 118a) and ultimately cast aside like dross. The final verse in the strophe reiterates his posture of

---

28. The conventions of the acrostic require that the first word of each line begin with the appropriate letter, in this case, a *nun*. Verse 105a begins with *ner*, "lamp," but also ends with *netibah*, "path."

piety before Yahweh. In verse 120a the Hebrew reads literally, "My flesh trembles because I fear you," and the verse concludes with his confession that he stands "in awe of your laws."

Ayin (119:121–28)

IN THE AYIN STROPHE THE PSALMIST stresses the urgency of his situation. The first two verses (vv. 121–22) refer to the oppression he is experiencing at the hands of the arrogant (cf. vv. 21, 51, 69, 78, 85)—an oppression so great that his eyes have started to fail and grow weary in watching for deliverance (v. 123). In the final verse of the strophe the psalmist acknowledges the reality of the wrong paths that exist, but he remains firm in his resolve to reject those paths despite his weariness. The entire situation leads the psalmist to register his formal complaint in verse 126a: "your law is being broken [*hepar*]." The word *hepar* occurs regularly in texts that report the breaking of the covenant, but in this instance it is the torah of Yahweh that has been abrogated.[29] The actions of the arrogant reflect their wanton disregard for Yahweh's torah—a choice that has had a deleterious effect on the psalmist. As a result, the poet announces, "It is time for you to act, LORD" (v. 126). The psalmist can make such a demanding claim on Yahweh because already in this strophe he has declared himself "your servant" three times (vv. 122, 124, 125). Yahweh is the master/patron and the psalmist, his servant. Based on this relational arrangement, the psalmist appeals to his patron to act in behalf of his servant. The psalmist affirms that he has done what is "righteous and just" (v. 121); he has honored his commitments to Yahweh. In return, the psalmist requests that God respond.

Pe (119:129–36)

IN THE PREVIOUS STROPHE THE PSALMIST insisted that it was time for Yahweh to act (v. 126). In the opening line of the Pe strophe, the psalmist refers to Yahweh's statutes as "wonderful" (*pele'*), a term used in connection with the exodus events (i.e., "wonderful works"; cf. Exod 15:11). This strophe highlights the "wonder-working" power of the torah.[30] In the light of the language of the opening verse, Hossfeld and Zenger suggest that the entire strophe is shaped by the ideas and concepts associated with Israel's salvation history.[31] For example, Yahweh's instruction provides light in the darkness (Ps 119:130), satisfies the thirsty (v. 131), and directs the paths of

---

29. For the use of *hepar* in connection with covenant breaking, see Gen 17:14; Lev 26:15; 26:44; and Deut 31:16.
30. Hossfeld and Zenger, *Psalms 3*, 279.
31. Ibid.

God's people (v. 133). While the allusions are indirect, they arguably point to events associated with the wilderness wandering, as does the request that Yahweh make his face shine upon his servant (cf. Num 6:25). The psalmist also pleads with Yahweh to turn to him (v. 132) and, even more, to redeem (*padah*) him from human oppression. The verb *padah*, "to redeem," appears in the book of Deuteronomy in reference to Israel's deliverance from oppression in Egypt (e.g., Deut 7:8; 13:5; 15:15; 24:18). In the concluding verse of the Pe strophe the psalmist weeps, not because of his own dilemma but because of the rampant disobedience that characterizes his society.

Tsadhe (119:137–44)

THE RECCURRING ROOT IN THE TSADHE STROPHE is *tsdq*, "righteous(ness)," which appears five times in these verses (vv. 137, 138, 142 [2x], 144).[32] Broadly speaking the root *tsdq* refers to "the policy that God wills and enacts as ruler of the universe."[33] The psalm opens with the declaration that God is righteous (*tsaddiq*) and then repeatedly contends that Yahweh's instruction is righteous (vv. 138, 142, 144). Although the enemies ignore God's words (v. 139), the psalmist confesses his love for those words (v. 140). He also acknowledges the reality of his plight: he is lowly and despised, and his life is marked by trouble and distress (v. 143). The strophe concludes by declaring God's statutes as "righteous." They are the psalmist's source of life.

Qoph (119:145–52)

IN THE PREVIOUS STROPHE THE PSALMIST referred to the trouble and distress that threaten him (v. 143). In the Qoph strophe he uses language typical of a lament psalm: "I call out," "answer me," "save me," and "hear my voice." The psalmist longs for the coming deliverance of Yahweh. In verse 148 he declares that through the watches of night he meditates on God's promises, perhaps in anticipation of the morning. On the association between morning (dawn) and God's deliverance, see Psalm 130:6. Verses 150 and 151 of Psalm 119 both begin with the root *qrb*, "to be near." The psalmist declares that, although the godless who devise evil schemes remain near, "you are near, LORD" (v. 151). While in the present moment the psalmist is harangued by the enemy, he takes heart that the justice of God has been from "long ago" and is meant to "last forever" (*'olam*). The nearness of the enemy is momentary, but the enduring justice of God, as evident in his torah, remains the psalmist's hope.

---

32. In verse 137b the NIV reads, "your laws are right," but in this instance the adjective is *yashar*, a synonym of *tsaddiq*, "righteous."

33. McCann, "The Book of Psalms," 1173.

Resh (119:153–60)

THE LANGUAGE OF COMPLAINT in the previous strophe continues in the first two lines of the Resh strophe: "look on my suffering," deliver me," "defend my cause," and "redeem me." Three times the psalmist recounts his faithfulness to God's law (*torah* [vv. 153a, 157b, 159a]), and twice the psalmist observes the insolence of the enemies against it (vv. 155b, 158b). Matching the three times the psalmist confesses his commitment to God's instruction, three times (vv. 154, 156, 159) he asks for Yahweh to "preserve his life" (NIV) or "give me life" (NRSV). The psalmist's faithfulness and his claim to deliverance are linked. His desire for deliverance is not wishful thinking; rather, it is rooted in God's "promise" (v. 154), God's "compassion" (v. 156), and God's "love" (*hesed*).

Sin and Shin (119:161–68)

THIS STROPHE INITIALLY ECHOES the complaint of previous strophes but then quickly turns to claims of joy and declarations of faithfulness. The strophe opens with a reference to the "rulers" or "princes" (*sarim*) who persecute the psalmist—a complaint uttered earlier in the Gimel strophe (v. 23). And while one should shudder or be in fear (*pahud*) of such worldly powers, the psalmist confesses that his heart trembles before the word of Yahweh. The military metaphor appears elsewhere in the strophe. While military victors may collect the "spoils of war" following a successful battle, the psalmist declares that he has found a "great spoil" in the instruction of God (v. 162). Those who are victorious in battle may find "great peace" (v. 165), but the psalmist announces that "great peace" awaits those who love the law (*torah*) of God. The poet refers to loving (*'ahab*) two additional times, thus making the threefold repetition of this claim a central motif in the strophe (vv. 163, 165, 167). His love of the law is so great, in fact, that he praises God seven times a day (v. 164). Here the psalmist's metaphorical speech indicates that his life is one of continuous praise of God because of God's "righteous laws."[34]

Taw (119:169–76)

THE FINAL STROPHE IN THE PSALM opens with a series of four petitions, including language associated with lament (vv. 169, 170) and concluding with language of praise and thanksgiving (vv. 171, 172). In the second half of the

---

34. The Benedictine tradition, among others, understood the verse literally and established the liturgy of the hours accordingly. For a brief but helpful historical survey of this practice, see Phyllis Tickle, *The Divine Hours: Prayers for Autumn and Wintertime* (New York: Doubleday, 2000), x–xiv.

strophe the psalmist turns to the actions requested of God (vv. 173–75). What binds both sections of this strophe together, however, is the relationship between faithfulness to the torah of Yahweh and the sheer gift of life that it brings. Rather than viewing the torah as onerous or burdensome, the psalmist concludes this majestic work of poetry by stressing that the torah is an extension of Yahweh's life-giving work among his people. Given the poet's resolve throughout this psalm to follow the torah of Yahweh, verse 176 may seem incongruent with the poem as a whole. In this final verse, the psalmist declares that he "has strayed like a lost [*'abad*] sheep." The verb *'abad* appears in Psalm 1 in reference to the wicked ("the way of the wicked will perish"). Throughout the entirety of Psalm 119 the psalmist acknowledges that his hope rests with the work and word of God. Even though the psalmist remains faithful to God's word and leans into its promises, the psalmist remains in need of God's work of redemption from the travails of life. He concludes the psalm by confessing that, while he has not forgotten the commandments of God, he is a frail creature of dust, a "lost sheep" who stands in need of the mercy of God. Robert Davidson aptly notes, "Always it is those who are closest to God who are most aware of their own need for confession."[35] The psalmist remains committed to God until the end in the certainty that the same can be said of God's commitment to him, and even more.

DUE TO THE SHEER LENGTH of Psalm 119, theological analysis of the poem can prove daunting. Any attempt at a synthetic analysis will likely fall short due to the richness of the language and its comprehensive scope. Despite that disclaimer, the observant reader will discern a number of key themes that prove instructive for the life of faith.

The torah and life with God. In his work *The Message of the Psalms*, Walter Brueggemann suggests that the "*torah* becomes an entry point for exploring the whole range of interactions with Yahweh."[36] Because Psalm 119 is labeled a "torah psalm," some may mistakenly assume that the poem is simply "torah-centric" and meant to call people to rigorous obedience to torah instruction. Upon closer examination, however, such an assessment of the psalm falls short. Although the concept of torah is central to the psalm, it is not torah-centric. According to the psalmist,

---

35. Davidson, *The Vitality of Worship*, 404.

36. Walter Brueggemann, *The Message of the Psalms: A Theological Commentary* (Minneapolis: Fortress, 1984), 41.

obedience to the torah is never the telos, or ultimate goal, of the faithful person; rather, obedience to the torah is the *point of departure* for a faithful life lived in relationship with God. In other words, the psalm is not *torah*-centric—it is, like the rest of the Old Testament, properly *theo*-centric. As with nearly all the psalms, this psalm includes second-person pronouns; it is a prayer to God about life *with* God. In the Beth strophe, for example, the words "you" or "your" appear in every verse, with several verses including the pronoun in both lines (vv. 10, 11, 12, 15, 16). Further, in that same strophe (Beth) the psalmist declares, "I seek you with all my heart" (v. 10). Terms from the torah word field appear nine times in that strophe, but they serve as the avenue to finding God and enjoying his presence. The psalmist pledges to recount the laws of God, rejoice in his statutes, meditate on his precepts, and delight in his decrees. He concludes with the promise not to neglect God's word. He acts thus because he seeks God (v. 10). Because he remains faithful in his torah obedience, he confesses certain claims about God: "You are my portion, LORD" (v. 57), "You are righteous, LORD" (v. 137), and "You are near, LORD," (v. 151). Adherence to the torah of God invites one into life with God, and in that fellowship one discovers the fullness of his presence.

Torah as preserver of life. Throughout Psalm 119 the verb *hayah* ("to live") occurs with considerable regularity; it appears sixteen times in the psalm.[37] The verbal form repeatedly occurs in the *piel* stem. Historically that stem has been defined in elementary Hebrew grammars as the "intensive" stem, but that explanation has been replaced by a more nuanced understanding of the *piel* in recent grammars.[38] Grammarians have suggested that the *piel* form is associated with causation, and more particularly with causing a state of existence.[39] Thus in the case of the verb *hayah*, the *qal* means simply "to live" (e.g., "Do this and you will live, for I fear God" [Gen 42:18]), but the *piel* means "to cause to be alive" (e.g., "Preserve my life according to your promise" [Ps 119:154]). Throughout Psalm 119 *hayah* appears in connection with the various terms associated with the torah word field. The meaning of that association is twofold. As illustrated above in Psalm 119:154, the psalmist believes that God's torah contains promises that include God's commitment to preserve the life of his servant.

---

37. Cf. verses 17, 25, 37, 40, 50, 77, 88, 93, 107, 116, 144, 149, 154, 156, 159, 175.

38. See Bruce K. Waltke and Michael O'Connor, *An Introduction to Biblical Hebrew Syntax* (Winona Lake, IN: Eisenbrauns, 1990), 396–400; Bill T. Arnold and John H. Choi, *A Guide to Biblical Hebrew Syntax* (Cambridge: Cambridge University Press, 2003), 41–45.

39. Some grammarians refer to this function as the "factitive" use of the *piel*. See Waltke and O'Connor, *An Introduction to Biblical Hebrew*, 400–4.

When the psalmist senses his life is ebbing away, he calls on Yahweh and reminds him of his promises, which include "causing [the psalmist] to be alive" (v. 25). The second implication is more straightforward than the first. In the first instance, the promises of God include a commitment to preserving the psalmist's life. In the second instance, faithfulness to the torah itself yields life. In associating terms from the torah word field with the *piel* form of *hayah*, the psalmist is declaring that obedience to God's torah "causes one to be alive." In short, God's instruction ushers one into the life that God intended.

Torah obedience amid a hostile world. Psalm 119 jettisons any Pollyanna notion that whoever declares fidelity to the ways of God and continuously gives attention to his torah should experience a "blessed life," one absent the threat of a hostile world. Instead, the psalmist refers to his affliction and laments the shame, scorn, and even persecution wrought upon him by the enemy.[40] He refers to these enemies as the "arrogant" (vv. 21, 51, 69, 78, 85, 122), "the rulers" (vv. 23, 161), "the wicked" (vv. 53, 61, 95, 110, 119, 155), and even the "oppressors" (vv. 121, 122, 134). At times he feels as though they are the hunters and he is their prey (cf. vv. 61, 110). Those who classify Psalm 119 as a lament psalm have good reason—it is filled with types of complaints and petitions found in other, shorter lament psalms.

Despite the presence of the enemies, the psalmist does not dispense with torah obedience. Instead, trusting that God will "preserve [his] life according to [his] word" (v. 25), the poet redoubles his commitment to being a faithful servant of Yahweh. In Psalm 119 this trust is manifested in hope. Although the world remains hostile, the psalmist "waits" and "hopes" for the intervention of Yahweh (vv. 49, 81, 84, 114, 147, 166). Clinton McCann contends that, ultimately, "the perspective of Psalm 119 is eschatological. Life is entrusted to the sovereign God in circumstances that seem to belie God's sovereignty."[41] While the psalmist waits and hopes, he chooses to align his life with the ways of God, thereby redefining both the parameters and content of the blessed life (vv. 1–2). For the psalmist, torah obedience does not nullify the presence of a hostile world; rather, it provides him the means with which to navigate through that world as the faithful servant of the Living God.

---

40. On the "affliction" experienced by the psalmist see verses 28, 50, 67, 71, 75, 92, 107, and 153, and on feelings of shame, scorn, and persecution see verses 6, 22–23, 39, 42, 46, 51, 69, 80, 84–87, 95, 110, 121, 134, 141, 150, 157, and 161.
41. McCann, "The Book of Psalms," 1167.

CHRISTIANS TEND TO HEAR or read the word "law" or *torah* through a decidedly Pauline lens. When one calls to mind Paul's words from the book of Galatians, "by the works of the law no one will be justified" (Gal 2:16), or his comments later in that letter that we were "held in custody" under the law and "locked up," one understandably develops a negative association with the word "law." As a result, a person experiences some cognitive dissonance when she or he comes to Psalm 119, a psalm that lauds the torah and torah observance. How can people overcome that perceived dissonance as they read Psalm 119?

Reading Psalm 119 and the Beatitudes intertextually, or in conversation, may offer some hermeneutical clues for overcoming that dissonance and appropriating Psalm 119. Although some New Testament scholars have suggested that the Beatitudes were entrance requirements or ethical demands that one must adopt and exhibit prior to entrance into the kingdom of heaven (per the Matthean account), others understand the Beatitudes as promises of eschatological blessings on those "who have responded positively to God's saving initiative in Jesus."[42] In the Beatitudes Jesus called his disciples to adopt a particular way of living, a certain posture of piety—a posture rooted in the eschatological vision of God and his kingdom. Similarly, the focus on torah observance in Psalm 119 is not to pass an "entrance test" or gain divine approval but, instead, a reflection of a particular posture of piety adopted by a servant in response to his lord (Lord).

Both the Matthean beatitudes and Psalm 119 reflect the perilous circumstances faced by followers of God. In both texts the faithful encounter persecution (Ps 119:86, 157, 161; Matt 5:10, 11), and in both texts they experience the derisive insults of the ungodly (Ps 119:23; Matt 5:11). Yet each of the Matthean beatitudes begins with "Blessed," even as Psalm 119:1–2 opens with "Blessed." The "blessed life" stands front and center, although in a nuance far richer than expected. The blessed life is possible when understood in the light of the proleptic reign of God. Both texts describe the life of the faithful as they await the fullness of God's work in the world. Waiting and hoping involves living in and living into the ways of God in the here and now. But even more, these texts remind us that *our work* is that of faithfulness; *his work* is that of deliverance (Ps 119:173–76). And so we wait—in abiding faithfulness and with much hope, we wait.

---

42. Charles H. Talbert, *Reading the Sermon on the Mount: Character Formation and Decision Making in Matthew 5–7* (Columbia, SC: University of South Carolina Press, 2004), 47.

Psalm 120

A song of ascents.

¹ I call on the LORD in my distress,
   and he answers me.
² Save me, LORD,
   from lying lips
   and from deceitful tongues.
³ What will he do to you,
   and what more besides,
   you deceitful tongue?
⁴ He will punish you with a warrior's sharp arrows,
   with burning coals of the broom brush.
⁵ Woe to me that I dwell in Meshek,
   that I live among the tents of Kedar!
⁶ Too long have I lived
   among those who hate peace.
⁷ I am for peace;
   but when I speak, they are for war.

PSALM 120 IS THE FIRST poem in the Songs of Ascents (Pss 120–34), and as such this psalm introduces one of the primary themes that appears throughout the collection: the psalmist's desire for divine protection and refuge in the midst of a hostile world.[1] Like nearly all the poems in the Songs of Ascent, Psalm 120 is relatively brief and rather singular in focus.

Scholars are divided on whether Psalm 120 should be classified as a thanksgiving psalm or a lament psalm. The debate centers primarily on the verbs in the opening verse. The two verbs in verse 1b are a perfect or *qatal* form of a verb ("I called"), followed by a *waw*-consecutive imperfect or *wayy-iqtol* form ("and he answered me"); both forms regularly point to a completed or past action. The verbs in verses 2–3 and 7, however, do not point in that direction. To remedy this inconsistency, Kraus suggests that the entire psalm

---

1. Hossfeld and Zenger, *Psalms 3*, 296.

720

is actually a recollection of the psalmist's deliverance some time in the past.[2] Read in this way, the poem functions as a psalm of thanksgiving that was likely read by a petitioner who had found safety in the temple precinct. The psalmist mentions his past deliverance in verse 1 and then rehearses the specifics of that deliverance in the remainder of the psalm.

Taking a different tack, and recognizing the unusual structure of the psalm, the NIV (as well as the NRSV) has opted to translate both verbs in verse 1 in the present tense: "I call on the LORD . . . and he answers me." Rendered in this way, verse 1 suggests that the call to Yahweh, as well as Yahweh's answer, pertains to the same crisis necessitating the plea for deliverance in verse 2.[3] Unfortunately, neither option appears entirely satisfactory given the Hebrew of the text.

The perfect and imperfect forms of the verb in verse 1 suggest that the psalmist has the past in view. Rather than understanding the remainder of the psalm as a retelling of that past event, as does Kraus, it appears that the past event mentioned in verse 1 functions differently. God's faithfulness in the past provides the rationale for the request articulated by the psalmist in the remainder of the psalm.[4] Laments frequently include a statement of conviction signaling the psalmist's belief that God will hear his cry. In this instance that conviction is rooted in God's past response to such a cry.

Although Psalm 120 is brief, it contains four very distinct sections. Verse 1 is a recollection of a past answered prayer, while verse 2 introduces a new plea by the psalmist. Verses 3–4 include a rhetorical question posed by the psalmist to the enemy, while the final three verses contain the psalmist's lament concerning his situation.[5] Read in this way, Psalm 120 may be classified as a psalm of lament, albeit one that differs in structure from a traditional lament.

Recollection of the Past (120:1)

THE WORD ORDER IN THE OPENING LINE of the psalm is often lost in English translations. Verse 1 reads literally, "To Yahweh in my distress, I called and

---

2. Kraus, *Psalms 60–150*, 423.

3. A number of interpreters suggest the psalmist announces in verse 1 that he has cried to the Lord and even received an answer related to the current crisis. In the remainder of the poem, however, the psalmist seems to indicate that the situation has not been remedied, thus necessitating the plea for deliverance in the remainder of the psalm. See Allen, *Psalms 101–150*, 147–48; McCann, "The Book of Psalms," 1177–78.

4. For similar interpretations see Davidson, *The Vitality of Worship*, 404–5; Cuthbert C. Keet, *A Study of the Psalms of Ascent: A Critical and Exegetical Commentary upon Psalms CXX to CXXXIV* (London: Mitre, 1969), 18–19; Hossfeld and Zenger, *Psalms 3*, 303–5.

5. For similar structure see Goldingay, *Psalms 3*, 448.

he answered." By moving the indirect object ("to Yahweh") to the beginning of the verse, the psalmist has fronted the most critical information in the poetic line.[6] Typically, fronting signals that the object mentioned is the focus of the utterance. In other words, by structuring the psalm in this manner the psalmist is confessing that he is calling "to Yahweh" (and no other).[7] The emphasis in this verse does not fall on the one who cries but on the one to whom the cries are made.

The psalmist characterized his previous situation as "distress" (NIV). The root *tsrb* implies a narrow place or a "tight" situation that confines the psalmist. In Psalm 118:5 the psalmist uses a cognate of the verb and contrasts being in a tight place, which connotes threat, with being in the wide, open places, suggestive of God's deliverance. In Psalm 120 the poet recalls a similarly constricting circumstance from which God delivered him. God's capacity to deliver him from a previous threat provides the assurance that God can redeem him from another context.

Plea for Deliverance (120:2)

EVEN AS VERSE 1 OPENS WITH MENTION of Yahweh, so the plea for deliverance in verse 2 begins by mentioning Yahweh and actually uses the vocative, "O Yahweh." English translations typically move the imperative verbal form to the front (i.e., "Save me, O LORD"), but the psalmist has placed the vocative ("O Yahweh") first, perhaps in an attempt to structure the second verse similarly to the first one. In Hebrew, the vocative can occur after the verb ("Save me, O king" [2 Sam 14:4]), or it can appear before the verb, as in Psalm 120 (cf. 1 Kgs 1:17). Consequently, the location of the vocative in Psalm 120:2a does not necessarily suggest a deviation from expected word order but, more likely, signifies an attempt to create parallelism between verses 1a and 2a.

The nature of the distress currently experienced by the psalmist appears initially in verse 2 ("lying lips" and "deceitful tongues"). On first glance, the mention of lying lips and deceitful speech may seem only mildly threatening, but other psalms reinforce the gravity of deceitful speech for the life of the psalmist. For example, in Psalm 59 the psalmist compares the enemy and his deceitful words to wild dogs that prowl the city, prepared to devour their victim.[8] Arguably, a similar usage appears in Psalm 120.

---

6. For a brief explanation of fronting in biblical Hebrew see Christo H. J. van der Merwe, Jackie A. Naudé, and Jan H. Kroze, *A Biblical Hebrew Reference Grammar*, Biblical Languages: Hebrew 3 (London: T&T Clark, 2002), 344–50.

7. Hossfeld and Zenger, *Psalms 3*, 305.

8. Göran Eidevall has tracked numerous occurrences in the book of Isaiah in which

As the psalm progresses, the threatening overtones increase in intensity, culminating in the psalmist's final claim: "They are for war" (v. 7b).

Rhetorical Challenge of the Foe (120:3–4)

BEGINNING IN VERSE 3 THE DISCOURSE shifts and the psalmist turns to address the enemy rhetorically.[9] The psalmist links verses 2 and 3 by repeating "deceitful tongue" from 2b and using it as a vocative ("you deceitful tongue") in verse 3b. In poetry, a synecdoche is a figure of speech in which the part represents the whole. In this instance the psalmist uses "deceitful tongue" to indicate the enemy.

The statement in verse 3 adapts a self-cursing formula meant to suggest that something is unquestionably true. In an attempt to reinforce claims of veracity, a person would have pledged, "May Yahweh do so to me and more as well if I do not do this or that."[10] Such a self-cursing vow can be found in the book of Ruth when Ruth vows to Naomi, "May Yahweh do thus to me and even more if death parts me from you."[11] A variation of the formula also appears in an exchange between David and Jonathan in 1 Samuel 20:12–13. In each instance the speaker (e.g., Ruth or Jonathan) invites God's punishment upon her or him should the individual fail to live up to the oath. In Psalm 120, however, the relationship between the psalmist and the enemy is not evident, so the context of the oath remains obscured. Goldingay contends that the psalmist may be recalling an oath the enemy had uttered previously but had failed to honor; his failure would result in the curses that follow in verse 4.[12] While this understanding is possible, it may be that the psalmist has simply reworked the self-curse formula as a rationale for God's judgment on the enemy. The enemy's deceitful words will result in punitive actions by God.

Verse 4 answers the question in verse 3a: "What will he do to you, and what more besides?" The psalmist's response is simply to mention two items: the warrior's sharp arrows and burning coals of the broom brush. The sharp arrows and coals of the broom brush were actually used

---

the prophet associates the use of arrogant and deceitful language with the behavior of empires. See Göran Eidevall, *Prophecy and Propaganda: Images of Enemies in the Book of Isaiah*, ConBOT 46 (Winona Lake, IN: Eisenbrauns, 2009), 23–131.

9. While it is possible that the enemy was actually in the audience as the psalmist spoke, it is more likely that this address is meant rhetorically, as when the prophets address the nations (cf. Joel 3:4–8).

10. Hossfeld and Zenger, *Psalms 3*, 306.

11. Author's translation. See also 1 Sam 14:44; 20:13; 25:22; 2 Sam 3:9, 35; 19:13; 1 Kgs 2:23; 2 Kgs 6:31.

12. Goldingay, *Psalms 3*, 450.

in battle to lay waste to a city and its inhabitants, as is well attested both in textual and iconographic evidence. In this instance the reference to such devastating weapons of war is used figuratively to express divine punishment.[13] In an attempt to provide greater clarity, the NIV interjects the phrase, "He will punish you with," at the beginning of verse 4 but the Hebrew simply mentions both items without attributing them directly to the action of Yahweh.[14] While not made explicit, such an association appears understood in the psalm. The two images mentioned in verse 4 could function metaphorically to imply that Yahweh will return the false words of the enemy upon them. In Proverbs 26:18–19 spoken words are compared to burning arrows: "Like a maniac shooting flaming arrows of death is one who deceives their neighbor and says 'I was only joking!'" Both items of war are used metaphorically in the Old Testament, and particularly in the Psalter, to describe the "life-destroying power of lies, betrayal and calumny through 'tongue' and 'lips.'"[15] For example, in a manner similar to the allusion in Psalm 120, the writer of Psalm 57:4 incorporates the image of wild animals, mouths, and weapons of war:

> I am in the midst of lions;
> I am forced to dwell among ravenous beasts—
> Men whose teeth are spears and arrows,
> Whose tongues are sharp swords.

The plea for deliverance in Psalm 120:2 and the foreboding sense of war in verse 7 suggest that the psalmist perceives his life to be in danger because of the deceitful tongue of the enemy. In the light of his circumstances, the psalmist pleads with God in verse 2 for deliverance and then later, in verse 4, announces God's punishment on the perpetrators of such lies: their lives will be laid waste even as cities were last waste by arrows and flames of fire.

Lament Regarding Crisis (120:5–7)

IN THE FINAL STROPHE OF THE POEM the psalmist provides further explication concerning the situation that has prompted the lament. While verse 2 suggests that the enemy has "deceitful tongues," verses 5–7 suggest that the one with a deceitful tongue has a proclivity toward violence, presumably against the psalmist.

Woe to me that I dwell in Meshek. The psalmist compares his present circumstance to living in a foreign land. Both place names can be located

---

13. Keet, *A Study of the Psalms of Ascents*, 21.
14. For example, see the translation in the NRSV.
15. Hossfeld and Zenger, *Psalms 3*, 307.

on a map and appear to allude to warring people groups. Those from the tribes of Kedar are first mentioned in Genesis 25 and are recognized elsewhere for their skills in battle, especially with the bow (Isa 21:13–17). Geographically, Kedar would have been associated with the tribes in the Arabian Desert to the southeast. Although more difficult to locate, Meshek has generally been associated with a region in the far north, where a warlike people group lived south of the Black Sea.[16] Despite the ability to locate these people groups more specifically, the place names are here functioning metaphorically for hostile peoples generally.[17] Similar to the move made in Psalm 108, the apparent historical references in Psalm 120 have been loosened from their historical moorings in an effort to heighten the drama of the text. Mention of these locations is what Hossfeld and Zenger refer to as "theological topography."[18] These terms are not meant to provide actual locations of where the psalmist is; rather, they are meant to reinforce the isolation he experienced and his utter reliance on Yahweh for deliverance.

Too long have I lived among those who hate peace. The final two verses encapsulate the struggle of the psalmist. In verse 6a he announces, "Too long have I lived." The phrase carries with it a note of exasperation in that the psalmist is confessing his circumstance has become more than he can bear.[19] He seeks what he does not have, *shalom* or "peace" (v. 7a). By using *shalom* he is invoking the full range of meanings associated with the word. James Mays suggests that *shalom* "in the psalmic vocabulary is the hopefulness and wholeness of life when living is knit into the fabric of relatedness to God and others and world."[20] In the experience of the psalmist, however, such wholeness remains altogether absent. Rather than peace, he is met by those who seek war. Given that the psalm centers on

---

16. Ibid., 309. The Septuagint and Vulgate failed to identify the word "Meshek" and opted instead to render the word based on the same three consonants (*mshk*), which can mean "to draw out," "to endure," "far away"; hence the Septuagint's translation, "that my place of sojourn was placed far away" (NETS).

17. David C. Mitchell, *The Message of the Psalter: An Eschatological Programme in the Book of Psalms*, JSOTSup 252 (Sheffield: Sheffield Academic, 1997), 118. See also Gerstenberger, *Psalms, Part 2, and Lamentations*, 319.

18. Hossfeld and Zenger, *Psalms 3*, 309. Michael Goulder rejects a symbolic reading of Meshek and Kedar and instead attempts to connect the activity of Sanballet with Meshek and Geshem with Kedar. Such a move is consistent with his larger project of reading the Psalms of Ascents in light of the fourteen testimonies of Nehemiah, an approach that has yet to win significant support (Goulder, *The Return of the Psalms*, 37–39).

19. On the construction *rabat . . . lah*, "more than they can bear," in verse 6a, see Hossfeld and Zenger, *Psalms 3*, 310.

20. Mays, *Psalms*, 388.

speech, and in particular false speech, the reference to war may have been meant metaphorically (i.e., "a war of words"); yet in using the language of "war," the lament of his own social location (vv. 5–6) and the response he has received (v. 7) suggest that words have given way to threatening action that further necessitates deliverance by God.

DISORIENTATION. In his volume *The Message of the Psalms*, Walter Brueggemann sought to provide a new paradigm for considering the psalms—a paradigm that broke with the form-critical categories posited in traditional historical-critical studies.[21] Modifying the Hegelian dialectic, Brueggemann suggested that there were three types of psalms in the Old Testament: psalms of orientation, psalms of disorientation, and psalms of new orientation. The first category, psalms of orientation, reflects the community's claims to certain fundamental truths about God, the world, and God's ways in the world (e.g., Pss 8, 33, 145). These claims lead to the praise of God. The second category, psalms of disorientation, contains poems that lament the "incoherence" between the faith claims of the psalmist and his experience in the world (e.g., Pss 1, 22, 88). The third category, psalms of new orientation, reflects the psalmist's experience as he discovers a new understanding of reality after being delivered by God (e.g., Pss 30, 138).

Following Brueggemann's paradigm, Psalm 120 can be understood as a psalm of disorientation. In many ways this label seems particularly well suited for Psalm 120 and is far more instructive than the more generic label of "lament." Psalm 120 speaks of the disorienting experiences of the psalmist. Another psalm of disorientation, Psalm 12, reflects concerns similar to Psalm 120 and serves to highlight the intensity of the psalmist's disorientation in Psalm 120. In Psalm 12 the poet mentions his travails and, as in Psalm 120, makes reference to the "lips" and "tongues" of the wicked (Ps 12:2–3, 8). His situation has devolved into such a state that the psalmist confesses "no one is faithful anymore; those who are loyal have vanished from the human race" (v. 1). Yet at the end of Psalm 12 the psalmist asks for God to protect "us" (v. 7).[22] While this poet laments the alleged disappearance of faithful and godly people, he does nevertheless

---

21. Brueggemann, *The Message of the Psalms*.

22. In the Masoretic text the first verb, *shamar* ("to guard"), does not have the first-person plural suffix ("us") added to the end of the word. Other Hebrew manuscripts and the Septuagint include the suffix, likely in an attempt to create tighter parallelism in the verse.

appear to be part of a presumably faithful and godly group ("us") who are suffering at the hands of the wicked.

Although Psalm 120 shares with Psalm 12 the imagery of "lips" and "tongues," the poet in Psalm 120 never makes the shift from singular to plural when referring to himself. The psalmist speaks throughout of an "I-they" struggle, never a "we-they" encounter as in Psalm 12. The last three verses of Psalm 120 highlight the isolation, both physical and psychological, experienced by the psalmist. Six times in the last three verses some form of the first-person pronoun appears, yet the repeated references to "I" stand over against the plural references related to the enemy (i.e., the "tents of Kedar," "those who hate peace," and those who are for war). The disorientation experienced by the psalmist results from his isolation and his location.

The focus on isolation and location may also explain why Psalm 120 appears as the opening poem in the Songs of Ascent. The collection begins with a psalmist's crying for help while ensconced in a foreign land amid a hostile world. As the reader prays through the Songs of Ascent, the psalms move from the threats experienced in a foreign land to God's dwelling in Zion (Ps 132:13–14), where one enjoys living in unity with his people (Ps 133:1) and receiving the blessing of Yahweh (Ps 134:3).

 **LOSS OF PLACE.** Although the twenty-first century continues to be marked by a sense of globalization and transnational identity, a number of writers have returned to the concept of "place" and even lamented what seems to be the loss of place.[23] For many people, the loss of place is not by choice but by forced migration. The Syrian refugee crisis in recent years serves as but one of many examples. Due to political instability in the region and military threats posed by ISIS, nearly eleven million Syrian refugees were displaced; half of them children. Perhaps like this psalmist, they too lament that they have lived too long in a place that is not their own. And they too have sensed the threats surrounding them.

---

23. Craig G. Bartholomew, *Where Mortals Dwell: A Christian View of Place Today* (Grand Rapids: Baker Academic, 2011); John Inge, *A Christian Theology of Place* (Burlington, VT: Ashgate, 2003); Philip Sheldrake, *Spaces for the Sacred: Place, Memory and Identity* (Baltimore: The Johns Hopkins University Press, 2001). For a comprehensive investigation of "place" in the Western tradition, see Edward S. Casey, *The Fate of Place: A Philosophical History* (Berkeley: University of California Press, 1997).

Other people find themselves in loss of place because of the mobility and movement associated with modern culture. As Craig Bartholomew laments, in our society "every person constantly 'on the move' suffers from placelessness in one form or another."[24] While it may seem that such movement leads to the threat of social instability, Edward Casey suggests that our culture does not suffer from anomie (social instability) as much as it does from atopia, placelessness.[25] Nearly four decades ago, Walter Brueggemann first raised this concern about the loss of place and its significance for human life. In his classic study on land in the Bible, Brueggemann suggests that a sense of place is a "human hunger."[26] Psalm 120 captures well the notion that place is indeed a human hunger. Some commentators suggest that perhaps the psalmist is speaking metaphorically—he feels so isolated that it is *like* living in a foreign country. Others suggest that the language in verses 3–4 suggests a social context among a hostile people. Whether the psalmist is physically or socially removed from his society, it is clear that he has no sense of place—the kind of place that makes sense of God, his world, and God's interaction with the world. As a result, the psalmist can only cry out to God for deliverance (v. 2).

The human hunger for place is not resolved in this poem. Psalm 120 remains open-ended. As one reads the Songs of Ascent, however, one discovers a move from placelessness to a sacred place—to Zion. It is a journey of faith that orients life to the place of life. As we minister among people experiencing atopia from frequently moving every few years due to job demands and other commitments, we would do well to remember that, despite all appearances of "upward mobility," they too likely suffer from the human hunger for a place that makes sense of God and his world. Psalm 120 invites them—and us—to give words to that human hunger for place (v. 5b), and the Songs of Ascent invite us on a journey toward God.

24. Bartholomew, *Where Mortals Dwell*, 3–4.

25. Edward S. Casey, *Getting Back into Place: Toward a Renewed Understanding of the Place-world* (Bloomington, IN: Indiana University Press, 1993), xi.

26. Walter Brueggemann, *The Land: Place as Gift, Promise, and Challenge in Biblical Faith* (Philadelphia: Fortress, 1977).

Psalm 121

A song of ascents.

¹ I lift up my eyes to the mountains—
    where does my help come from?
² My help comes from the LORD,
    the Maker of heaven and earth.
³ He will not let your foot slip—
    he who watches over you will not slumber;
⁴ indeed, he who watches over Israel
    will neither slumber nor sleep.
⁵ The LORD watches over you—
    the LORD is your shade at your right hand;
⁶ the sun will not harm you by day,
    nor the moon by night.
⁷ The LORD will keep you from all harm—
    he will watch over your life;
⁸ the LORD will watch over your coming and going
    both now and forevermore.

PSALM 121 IS CLASSIFIED as a psalm of confidence meant to celebrate God's providential care and is the second psalm in the Songs of Ascent (see Ps 120). The psalm can be divided into four strophes (vv. 1–2; 3–4; 5–6; 7–8), as illustrated in the NIV's translation above. The first strophe provides an overarching thematic claim for the entire psalm, namely, the Lord will be the psalmist's helper. Since the language in the first two verses is put in the first person, this opening strophe appears as a confession by the psalmist. Beginning in verse 3, however, the language shifts to the second person ("you"). The claims made in verses 3–8 serve as a response to the confession made by the psalmist in the opening strophe.[1]

---

1. Interpreters have put forward a number of proposals regarding the possible setting in life (*Sitz im Leben*) for this psalm and, in particular, who might be speaking in verses 3–8. Some have suggested that the psalm reflects an actual dialogue or verbal exchange between two parties: the psalmist (vv. 1–2) and another person or persons (vv. 3–8). This conversation may have taken place as the psalmist began a journey to Jerusalem and involved persons

The psalm exhibits a poetic technique frequently employed in the Songs of Ascent. Anadiplosis occurs when a word or phrase at the end of one line is picked up and used in the subsequent line, often near the front. Some interpreters refer to this literary device as a "stair-step" technique—the vocabulary connects each line as the reader moves through the psalm. For example, verse 1b concludes with a reference to Yahweh as "my help," and the same Hebrew word ("my helper") appears as the initial word in verse 2a. The participle "watch" or "guard" (*shomer*) appears near the end of verse 4 ("watches over Israel") in reference to God, and then the participle appears at the beginning of verse 5 ("the LORD watches over you"). The parallelism between the two lines is tighter if the Hebrew in verse 4b is translated as "the one who keeps Israel" and in verse 5a as "Yahweh is the one who keeps you." The same verb, "to guard" or "to watch" (*shamar*), functions similarly at the end of verse 7b and the beginning of verse 8a.

In addition to the sense of cohesiveness provided by anadiplosis, a thematic thread binds the psalm together as well. In verses 3–8 the theme of Yahweh as the "guardian" of Israel or the one who keeps watch (*shamar*) over Israel is the fundamental claim in the psalm, as suggested below. In verses 1–2 the psalmist looks for a helper and refers to Yahweh as "my help" (*'ezri*). The image of God in verses 1–2, however, shifts from "helper" to that of "guard" or "keeper" in the subsequent verses. Various forms of the verb *shamar* ("to guard," "to keep") appear six times in verses 3–8, all in reference to the work of Yahweh.

Confidence in the Lord (121:1–2)

THE OPENING STROPHE IN PSALM 121 contains the psalmist's confident assertion that God will be his helper. In verse 1 the psalmist announces, "I lift up my eyes to the mountains." Some interpreters have suggested that the idea of the "mountains" has a negative connotation and perhaps refers to the treacherous and dangerous path through the mountains; or perhaps the reference to the mountains alludes to the places at which false gods were worshiped.[2]

---

from his community, or it may have taken place once the psalmist arrived in Jerusalem and involved fellow pilgrims or perhaps priests. Others have suggested that Ps 121 is an "internal dialogue." Rather than representing a script with different speaking parts, Ps 121 may have been more akin to a journal. The psalmist poses the question and confession in verses 1–2 and then provides a response in verses 3–8. For an expanded discussion of the options, see Hossfeld and Zenger, *Psalms 3*, 317–20. Ultimately, the inability to identify with precision the speaker or even the setting of the psalm does not prevent the interpreter from appreciating the poetic quality of Ps 121 or its meaning.

2. See Kraus, *Psalms 60–150*, 429; A. A. Anderson, *The Book of Psalms: Volume II, Psalms 73–150*, NCB (Grand Rapids: Eerdmans, 1981), 852.

Alternatively, some have understood the "mountains" in verse 1a to refer to Zion, or the hills that surround Zion, so suggesting a more positive interpretation of the action.[3] The first part of the colon may prove decisive in attempting to decide between the two options. In both Hebrew and Akkadian, the action of "lifting the eyes" implies looking at something longingly or with desire rather than looking at something with dread.[4] This meaning is clearly evident in another psalm in the Songs of Ascent. Psalm 123 opens, "I lift up my eyes to you, to you who sit enthroned in heaven." In Psalm 121 a similar action may be in view. Understood in this way, "mountains" likely refers to the mountains of Zion, thereby creating an "emphatic confession of YHWH as the God present" on Zion, the mountain of God.[5]

The second half of verse 1 has also received considerable scholarly attention, in particular, its interrogative phrase *me'ayin*, "from where." Some translations have understood the phrase to have a relative sense—that is, the phrase in verse 1b modifies the "mountains" in verse 1a. For example, the King James Version reads, "I will lift up mine eyes unto the hills, from whence cometh my help."[6] Linguistically, however, *me'ayin* typically functions as an interrogative, not a relative particle. Thus, verse 1b should be understood as a rhetorical question. The NIV attempts to render this sense nicely: "I lift up my eyes to the mountains—where does my help come from?" In other words, the psalmist sees the mountains of Zion and asks rhetorically about the location of his help, with the question serving as a foil to his confession following in verse 2.[7]

The psalmist answers his own question in verse 2a: "My help comes from the LORD." The word "help" in English fails to capture the fullness of the meaning implied by the Hebrew term *'ezer*. The English word "help" can be understood as mere "assistance," but such an understanding falls short of the claim being made by the psalmist. In its nominal form, "help" occurs twenty times in the Old Testament, with thirteen of those occurrences referring to Yahweh's ability to save and deliver. Further, when combined with the word for "shield," the terms together indicate Yahweh's divine protection over Israel (Deut 33:29; Pss 33:20; 89:19–20; 115:9–11).[8] While the word "shield" is absent from Psalm 121, this latter meaning (i.e., divine

---

3. Most recently see Mitchell, *The Message of the Psalter*, 118; Goldingay, *Psalms 3*, 456.

4. See also Gen 39:7; Ezek 18:6; Jer 3:2.

5. Hossfeld and Zenger, *Psalms 3*, 322.

6. Luther's translation in the 1545 Luther Bibel translates the phrase similarly: "*Ich hebe meine Augen auf zu den Bergen von welchen mir Hilfe kommt*" ("I lift my eyes to the mountains from which my help comes").

7. Mays, *Psalms*, 389.

8. Allan H. Harman, "עֹזֶר," *NIDOTTE* 3:378–79.

---

protection) appears in view in verses 1b and 2a. Both the language and imagery in the remainder of the psalm extend this understanding of *'ezer*. In the following verses (vv. 3–8) the psalmist refers to God's watchful care over him, and in the fourth strophe he even confesses that "the LORD will keep you from all harm" (v. 7). God provides this kind of "help" because he is "the Maker of heaven and earth."[9]

The Watchful Care of Yahweh (121:3–4)

IN THE SECOND STROPHE THE PSALMIST employs a different word to describe the protection afforded by Yahweh while also introducing a new metaphorical concept. The verb *shamar* ("to guard," "to protect," or "to watch") occurs six times in the final three strophes, with its first occurrence in verse 3b. Throughout the psalm the NIV translates the Hebrew as "watch," but the watchful care of Yahweh must not be limited to passive observation; rather, Yahweh "watches" over Israel by providing protection. This image is heightened further in verse 4a. In that verse the verb appears as a participle (*shomer*) and stands in a construct relationship with "Israel." Most English translations render this unit as a participial phrase, "he who watches over Israel" (NIV). The placement of the two terms together in a construct relationship, however, could suggest something closer to a title. The psalmist may have sought to label Yahweh as "the Guardian of Israel."[10]

To highlight the watchful and attentive care of Yahweh, the psalmist invokes a metaphorical image—that of the sleeping deity. Within the larger ancient Near Eastern tradition, the gods were frequently depicted as sleeping. This activity on the part of the deities was not considered exceptional or unusual but simply necessary. Even as humans need sleep to perform their daily activities, so too do the deities. In the Atrahasis Epic (1800 BCE) the god Enlil is awakened from his restful slumber by the humans, and he demands that they be cut off from food as punishment for waking him (II:1–9).[11] In the Enuma Elish the god Apsu also complains about his lack of sleep because of the noise made by his offspring (I:35–50). Neither text records outrage or shock that a deity was asleep—only that a sleeping deity had been disturbed.

The image of Yahweh in Psalm 121 subverts the claims about deities in the literature of the broader ancient Near East. As the "Guardian of Israel," Yahweh remains on watch to protect his people because God will not "slumber nor sleep." While the two words may appear synonymous, the

---

9. On the title "Maker of heaven and earth," see the comments on Ps 115:15.
10. Hossfeld and Zenger, *Psalms 3*, 326.
11. For a more extensive treatment of deities and the role of sleep, see Manfred H. E. Weippert, *Jahwe und die anderen Götter*, FAT 18 (Tübingen: Mohr Siebeck, 1997), 99–107.

first Hebrew term, *num*, refers to drowsiness or light sleep, while the second term, *yashan*, may be understood as sleep in the more traditional sense. In using both words the psalmist confesses that the Guardian of Israel never "nods off" or dozes, much less falls into a deep sleep, but rather remains attentive and keeps continual watch over his people so that not even a foot of theirs will slip from the path (v. 3a).

The Lord is your Shade (121:5–6)

IN THE THIRD STROPHE THE PSALMIST introduces two additional metaphorical images meant to illustrate Yahweh's watchful care over him. The psalmist collapses the notion of standing at the right hand with that of the shade. Because the soldier carried his shield in his left hand, the right side of his body remained exposed and vulnerable. Consequently, one always sought to have a friend or ally at his "right hand" to provide protection. The image of Yahweh as standing at the right hand of the psalmist and fending off potential threats can be found elsewhere in the Psalter (e.g., Pss 16:8; 109:31; 110:5).

Adding to the claim that Yahweh will station himself at the right hand of the psalmist, verse 5 suggests that Yahweh will be for him a protective shade or shadow (*tsel*). This image of Yahweh is not unique to Psalm 121. Frequently individuals are invited into the "shadow of the wings" of Yahweh (cf. Pss 17:8; 36:7; 57:1; 63:7; Isa 30:2–3). In that space the psalmists find relief from the forces that threaten them. In Psalm 121 the poet speaks figuratively in claiming that, as shade, Yahweh will protect him from the searing heat of the sun by day and the dangers of the moon by night.[12] While the threats associated with the sun seem readily apparent, those associated with the moon are less so. The Babylonians attributed to the moon god, Sîn, a number of illnesses, including fever and leprosy.[13] By the time of the New Testament, there remained some thought of a connection between illness and the effects of the moon. (For example, the word *selēniazomenous*, translated as "seizures" in Matt 4:24; 17:15, means "to be moonstruck.") The mention of the sun by day and the moon by night, however, has a rhetorical force that supersedes its literal meaning. The two concepts create a merismus, a literary device in which two contrasting

---

12. The NIV translates verse 6a as "the sun will not harm you by day" and verse 7a as "The LORD will keep you from all harm." The reader might conclude that there is an inherent lexical connection between the two words translated "harm," but they are in fact different. In verse 6a the word is a verb, *nakah*, which is normally translated "strike" or "smite," as in the rays of the sun or moon striking the pilgrim. In verse 7a the word is an adjective functioning substantively—the adjective *ra'*, which means "bad, evil, disaster" or "harm" (cf. Jon 1:7; 3:10). While the terms are not lexically related, they do function as near synonyms in this instance.

13. Kraus, *Psalms 60–150*, 429.

ideas or objects are mentioned in an effort to capture the sense of the whole. By noting the threats by day and the threats by night, the psalmist acknowledges that God stands as the protective shade over all life.

The Lord Will Protect Your Life (121:7–8)

IN THE FINAL STROPHE THE PSALMIST reinforces and extends the theme of Yahweh's attentive and protective care. The verb *shamar* ("to guard," "to watch," "to keep"), which governs Psalm 121, appears in verses 7a, 7b, and 8a. The NIV translates verse 7a as "the LORD will keep you from all harm," while in the two latter cola the verb is translated as "watch." The repetition of the verb in all three cola should not be missed, however. As the psalm draws to a close, the thrice-repeated word creates a sort of crescendo celebrating Yahweh as the guardian and keeper of all life.

In verse 8a the psalmist acknowledges that "the LORD will watch over your coming and going."[14] The phrase "going out and coming in" functions elsewhere in the Old Testament as a metaphor for going to war, yet the context of the psalm, particularly as a pilgrim psalm, seems to warrant against such a narrow interpretation.[15] Elsewhere the phrase functions as a merismus referring simply to the general activity of life (e.g., 1 Kgs 3:7; 2 Kgs 19:27; Jer 37:4). The latter understanding appears to be in view in Ps 121. The poem may have been included in the Songs of Ascent because of the image evoked by the phrase "going and coming."

 IN HIS TREATMENT OF PSALM 121, James Limburg labels this psalm "A Psalm for Sojourners."[16] Its placement within the Songs of Ascent certainly justifies such a label, and the explicit "journey" imagery present in the psalm itself reinforces his claim: lifting up one's eyes to the hills (v. 1); the potential for feet to slip (v. 3); the mention of the sun and

---

14. While the Hebrew reads literally, "your going out and your coming in," the NIV has sought to capture the phrase idiomatically in English by reversing the order.

15. See Num 27:21; Deut 31:2; 1 Sam 18:13; 1 Kgs 15:17; 2 Chr 16:1 for representative examples of this phrase in a military context. Kraus provides a cultic interpretation of the phrase, thus suggesting that these words would have been those of the priest as he dismissed the worshiper. The priest promises that God will watch over the worshiper from the time he goes out of the temple (to his home) until he returns to the temple (Kraus, *Psalms 60–150*, 430). The Septuagint reverses the order ("coming in and going out") from its likely understanding of the text as a pilgrim psalm meant to be used as the worshiper makes his or her way to the temple, only later to return home.

16. James Limburg, "Psalm 121: A Psalm for Sojourners," *Word and Way* 5 (1985): 180–87.

moon (v. 6); and the final image of "coming and going" (v. 8). The images in the last three strophes of the psalm function as reminders that such sojourns are fraught with peril, whether it is getting lost along the way (v. 3a), being beaten down by natural forces (v. 6), or simply the more generalized notion of "harm" (v. 7a) that could beset any traveler. Throughout the Songs of Ascent collection, the world is depicted as a hostile and threatening place.[17] The writer of Psalm 121 understands well that the journey to God and the journey with God never occur in a vacuum, but rather in the context of a life that at times feels more like a tempest than a solitary walk down a quiet pathway. Yet, in response to the challenges referenced in Psalm 121 and those in life more generally, the psalmist exudes a certain sense of confidence based on his convictions concerning the character of Yahweh.

Helper and Maker. In the opening verses of Psalm 121, the poet describes Yahweh by using two labels—"my help" and and "the Maker of heaven and earth." Each of these appellations for God can be found elsewhere in the Old Testament, but they appear together only here in Psalm 121 and in one other poem (Ps 124:8) in the Songs of Ascent. The unique appearance of these labels together in this collection may relate to another thematic thread that permeates these fifteen psalms. James Mays has suggested that one of the recurring themes in the Songs of Ascent is "dependence upon the LORD in a hostile world."[18] Such dependence on God, however, must be predicated on a proper understanding of this God. Amid a threatening and hostile world, having a God who desires to help but whose power is not sufficient provides little hope. Conversely, a God who stands over all as Creator yet fails to intervene personally remains equally problematic. The psalmist rejects what is sometimes labeled as a "false dilemma" in logic—that there are only two solutions to the problem. Instead, the psalmist provides a "third way" that offers a much more powerful affirmation about the God of Israel. The God who will deliver the psalmist is the God who stands over all creation as its Maker, and the God of all power who stands over all creation as its Maker seeks to intervene in the life of the psalmist to ensure that not even his foot will slip (v. 3).

Guardian and keeper. In verses 1–2 the psalmist adopts language from creation theology to affirm that Israel's God can and will protect the psalmist because God is the Maker of heaven and earth. In the remaining verses of Psalm 121 the poet shifts the imagery and language. As noted above, the verb *shamar* occurs six times in verses 3–8. In translating *shamar*,

---

17. This theme is especially present in the first two major sections of the Songs of Ascent (Pss 120–24; 125–29). See Pss 123:3–4; 124:4–5; 125:3; 126:4; 129:1–5.

18. Mays, *Psalms*, 390.

the NIV alternates between "watch over" and "keep"; but regardless of which translation is chosen in English, the meaning remains the same: Israel's God keeps faithful watch over his people. In Psalm 121 the notion of keeper or guardian is cast within the context of a journey: God guards his people, who face uncertain times while on journey. A similar connection is made in Joshua 24:17. As the book comes to a close, the people respond to Joshua's call to "serve the LORD" by pledging their own faithfulness to this God, who brought them "out of Egypt, from that land of slavery." But they extend the idea of God's faithful deliverance by claiming that "he protected [*shamar*] us on our entire journey and among all the nations through which we traveled." Yahweh, the God of Israel, not only delivered Israel from captivity in Egypt, but he also accompanied them as Keeper and Guardian on their sojourn from Egypt to Canaan.

Elsewhere in the Old Testament, the metaphor of God as Guardian for those on a journey is extended to refer to any difficult or challenging circumstance, whether or not on a literal journey. The psalmists often invoke the image of the "slipping foot" in an effort to capture the danger that is present (cf. Pss 38:16; 94:18). The psalmists lament the peril of their own situation, and they cry out to God to steady their feet lest they stumble. Even closer to the assertion made in Psalm 121, other texts suggest that God can keep the petitioner's feet from stumbling altogether. In Hannah's prayer she confesses that God "will guard [*shamar*] the feet of his faithful servants" (1 Sam 2:9a), and in Psalm 91 the psalmist explains that God will "guard [*shamar*] you in all your ways . . . so that you will not strike your foot against a stone" (vv. 11b, 12b). In the cries to God because of "slipping feet" and in the confident assertions that God will guard the feet of his people, there is a presupposition at work. The images or claims are only effective if the speaker perceives the nearness of God. God cannot steady the slipping feet or protect the steps of his servants from a distance. God travels with his people and consequently will "keep [*shamar*] you from all harm" (Ps 121:7).

Similarly, the New Testament writers refer to the protective care of God for his people. In John 17:12, Jesus prays that God would protect his disciples because, "While I was with them, I protected them and kept them safe [*phylasso*] by that name that you gave me."[19] And later in the chapter Jesus explains, "My prayer is not that you take them out of the world but that you protect them from the evil one" (17:15). Those who journey in this world are assured that God journeys with them and protects them.[20]

---

19. The Septuagint uses the verb *phylasso* to translate the Hebrew word *shamar* ("to keep, protect") in Ps 121.

20. On God's protective care in the New Testament see also John 10:28; Phil 4:7; 1 Pet 2:25.

Contemporary Significance

THE SONGS OF ASCENT were likely used as the people of God made their way to Jerusalem on a pilgrimage. Most of us have taken trips on which the people traveling together sing songs. Typically, these songs are silly, nonsensical, and designed primarily to entertain as the time passes ever so slowly. The Songs of Ascent may have been intended to help pass the time, but the collection had a much larger theological purpose. These psalms were confessional. Together as people recited these psalms, they were making claims about God, themselves, and the world in which they lived.

Psalm 121 invites those who recite this psalm to consider "from whence" comes their help. The correct answer is God, of course, but to speak it is one thing, to believe it is another. The psalmist assures those who pray this psalm that we do not walk alone—the Maker of heaven and earth journeys with us as our helper. John Ortberg reminds us that "Scripture alternates between hair-raising risks and assurances of impregnable security. And when we look at the lives of great followers of God, we see this combination of breath-taking risks with an almost brazen confidence of being safe in God's hands."[21]

Ortberg mentions those moments in biblical history when people journeyed with God amid the risks. Moses defied Pharoah. Israel occupied the promised land. David challenged Goliath. A poor band of disciples followed Jesus. Paul sat in a Roman prison. None of these actions make sense unless the actors all understood "from whence" came their help—unless they understood that they were "in the watch-care of a great big God."[22] And the same is true for us. The risk-taking, journey-making paths we walk as Christians are informed by the claims in Psalm 121. While the paths we walk and the lives we live may be fraught with challenges, we are not forced to confront them alone, for we know that there is nothing that can separate us from the love of God (Rom 8:39). We have confidence that the Maker of heaven and earth stands as Guardian "watch[ing] over [our] coming and going both now and forevermore."

---

21. John Ortberg, *Love Beyond Reason* (Grand Rapids: Zondervan, 1998), 172.
22. Ibid.

Psalm 122

A song of ascents. Of David.

¹ I rejoiced with those who said to me,
  "Let us go to the house of the LORD."
² Our feet are standing
  in your gates, Jerusalem.
³ Jerusalem is built like a city
  that is closely compacted together.
⁴ That is where the tribes go up—
  the tribes of the LORD—
to praise the name of the LORD
  according to the statute given to Israel.
⁵ There stand the thrones for judgment,
  the thrones of the house of David.
⁶ Pray for the peace of Jerusalem:
  "May those who love you be secure.
⁷ May there be peace within your walls.
  and security within your citadels."
⁸ For the sake of my family and friends,
  I will say, "Peace be within you."
⁹ For the sake of the house of the LORD our God
  I will seek your prosperity.

PSALM 122 IS THE THIRD PSALM in the Songs of Ascent, but interestingly, given the explicit references to Jerusalem in verses 1, 2, and 6, it is the only psalm in the collection that may be classified form critically as a Song of Zion.[1] In the Songs of Zion, often the term "Zion" signals a larger complex of theological ideas associated with the city.[2] For example, these psalms often celebrate Zion as the "dwelling place" of Yahweh (Pss 46:4; 48:9; 84:1; 87:2) and its inviolability, while also invoking other themes: Zion as the highest mountain (Ps 48:2), the presence

---

1. Other Songs of Zion include Pss 46, 48, 76, 84, and 87.
2. See the classic treatment by Ben C. Ollenburger, *Zion the City of the Great King: A Theological Symbol of the Jerusalem Cult*, JSOTSup 41 (Sheffield: JSOT Press, 1987).

---

of the paradisiacal river within the precinct of Zion (Ps 46:4), and Yahweh's ultimate victory over the nations and their kings (Ps 48:4–7).[3] But in Psalm 122, the focus remains on the actual city and its physical features.[4] For example, references to the house of Yahweh (vv. 1, 9) and the house of David (v. 6), as well as references to the "walls" and "citadels" of the city (v. 7), reinforce the psalm's focus on the physical city of Jerusalem.[5] Even the mention of the city's structure in verse 3 and the historical remembrances in verses 4 and 5 provide a certain sense of physicality to the description of Jerusalem. Yet, as will be suggested in Bridging Contexts, the "thick descriptions" of Jerusalem still reflect the ideas more directly associated with Zion theology.

With the emphasis on the city of Jerusalem and travel to it (v. 1), Psalm 122 is the only psalm within the Songs of Ascent that may truly be labeled a "pilgrimage psalm."[6] As such, its placement as the third psalm within the larger collection (Pss 120–34) appears intentional. Psalm 120 opens the collection with the psalmist's lamenting his status as a sojourner far from home among the nations. Psalm 121 contains the prayer of a person en route to Jerusalem and in need of Yahweh's protective care. Psalm 122 reflects the joyous celebration of the one who has arrived in Jerusalem (v. 2).[7]

As suggested by the NIV's translation, Psalm 122 can be divided into three strophes, verses 1–2, 3–5, and 6–9, with each strophe making explicit mention of Jerusalem by name. The first strophe refers to the pilgrimage up to Jerusalem, and the next two strophes contain four poetic

---

3. For the most recent assessment of the complex of theological ideas associated with Zion, see the exhaustive study on Zion by Corinna Körting, *Zion in den Psalmen*, FAT 48 (Tübingen: Mohr Siebeck, 2006).

4. Goldingay, *Psalms 3*, 462.

5. Although Ps 122 does refer to the "house of the LORD" (vv. 1, 9), and thus could be seen as invoking the theme of Zion as the dwelling place of Yahweh, the rhetorical force of verse 1 appears to be on the "house of the LORD" as a place to which one makes pilgrimage more than on the larger complex of Zion ideas.

6. Although the final three poems in the Songs of Ascent (Pss 132–34) make explicit reference to Zion, they do not contain the imagery or vocabulary typically associated with pilgrimage.

7. Though pilgrimages to Jerusalem occurred well before the exile, Ps 122, which reflects on a pilgrimage, is likely postexilic. Loren Crow suggests that the psalm as it currently stands is a postexilic composition. The mention of "the tribes of Yah" and of the Davidic throne have a "nostalgic" ring to them as the psalmist looks to the past (Loren D. Crow, *The Songs of Ascents [Psalms 120–134]: Their Place in Israelite History and Religion*, SBLDS 148 [Atlanta: Scholars Press, 1996], 47). Linguistic clues also point to a postexilic dating: a periphrastic genitive (v. 5), a *lamed* for the direct object in verse 4b, and the use of the *shin* for the relative pronoun. Further, the spelling of David's name in verse 5b is the standard spelling in Chronicles, while it is all but absent from the earlier Deuteronomistic history.

lines each, with each strophe beginning with a reference to Jerusalem. Hossfeld and Zenger have adopted the threefold division of the psalm and noted a temporal shift with each strophe. Verses 1–2 refer to the present moment for the pilgrim as he enters the city, while verses 3–5 provide historical remembrances of the city, and verses 6–9, with their petitionary language, look to the future.[8]

Joy in the Pilgrimage (122:1–2)

IN THE OPENING STROPHE OF THE PSALM the poet quickly shifts from recollection of a past moment to present experience. In verse 1 he announces that he rejoiced (*samah*) at the invitation to go to the house of the Lord. Some translations render *samah* as "be glad" (e.g., ESV, NRSV, KJV), but such a rendering places the emphasis on the emotional state of the psalmist and perhaps implies that the psalmist is "happy" or "glad" at hearing this news. While this understanding is not entirely incorrect, the verb *samah* can suggest much richer overtones. The use of *samah* in this pilgrimage psalm is likely meant to capture the connection made elsewhere in the Old Testament between *samah* and the celebration of cultic festivals and feasts. For understanding this connection between the feasts and *samah*, the book of Deuteronomy is particularly instructive (cf. Deut 12:12, 18; 14:26; 16:11; 27:7). In Deuteronomy and elsewhere, *samah* appears within the larger phrase "rejoice before the LORD."[9] Thus, as John Goldingay somewhat humorously explains, "The basis for rejoicing is indeed that it means not merely a visit to the big city, but a visit to the house where Yahweh lives."[10] The psalmist may be pleased to receive this invitation to journey to the house of Yahweh, but the real source of joy remains being in the presence of God himself.

Verse 1 recounted the moment when the psalmist was invited to make the pilgrimage to Jerusalem; verse 2 records his arrival at the gates of the city. Some translations and commentaries prefer to render verse 2b in the past ("our feet were standing"), which would suggest that the entire strophe is a remembrance of the past—both the call to pilgrimage and the entrance into Jerusalem. The decision to render verse 2b as a completed action in the past is because the verb is a *qatal* form, which quite often in

---

8. Hossfeld and Zenger, *Psalms* 3, 335. As noted below, the difficulty in translating the verbs in Ps 122, particularly the *qatal* forms in verses 2a, 3b, and 4a, has resulted in a number of proposals in the secondary literature. The proposal by Hossfeld and Zenger remains convincing.

9. See also Lev 23:40; 1 Sam 11:15; Ps 68:4.

10. Goldingay, *Psalms* 3, 464.

English would be rendered in the past tense. Yet, as Graham Ogden has suggested, *hayah* in direct speech can have a stative sense, as it appears to here in Psalm 122:2.[11]

Descriptions of Jerusalem (122:3–5)

THE SECOND STROPHE OF PSALM 122 is connected to the first one by virtue of the operative word for the entire psalm, "Jerusalem." Both in the NIV's translation and in Hebrew, the word "Jerusalem" is the last word in verse 2 and the first word in verse 3—a perfect example of anadiplosis.[12] The psalmist offers a description of Jerusalem more generally, followed by two recollections associated with the importance of the city in Israel's history. Whether the words in verses 3–5 were uttered by the psalmist and his colleagues on the pilgrimage, or were uttered perhaps by a priest at the temple, does little to detract from the meaning being conveyed in this suggestion. Rhetorically, the second strophe is meant to explain why Jerusalem is the "real symbol of the presence of God in a hostile world."[13]

Built like a city. Jerusalem is the "real symbol" of God's presence because it provides protection to the people of God; it is a refuge. In verse 3 the psalmist refers to Jerusalem itself and confesses that it was built "like a city." The Hebrew word for "like" is *ki*, and in this instance the particle appears to function less like a comparison or simile (i.e., "like" or "as") and instead more as a confirmation of what has been said.[14] Thus Jerusalem is not built *like a* city but *as a true* city. Verse 3b attempts to explain what is meant by "a true city." The subsequent language in this line is difficult, however. Literally the line reads, "which was bound [*habar*] to her together." The verb *habar* is a technical building term that reflects how a building has been constructed or put together ("bound together"). The term could also suggest "bound together" in reference to the design of the city itself; that is, the city is bound together in a way that provides ample protection for its inhabitants. This meaning appears to lie behind the NIV's translation, "closely compacted together." Unlike the rural areas in and around Jerusalem, the city serves as a place of refuge due to its fortifications. When a region came under threat, people in the surrounding countryside would find shelter within the city (Josh 10:20; Jer 4:5; 35:11).

---

11. Graham Ogden, "Time and the Verb היה in OT Prose," *VT* 21 (1971): 453.
12. See Ps 121 for a discussion on anadiplosis. For a helpful guide to understanding various poetic, linguistic, and syntactic features in the Old Testament, see Todd J. Murphy, *Pocket Dictionary for the Study of Biblical Hebrew* (Downers Grove, IL: InterVarsity, 2003).
13. Hossfeld and Zenger, *Psalms 3*, 338.
14. This function is sometimes referred to as a *ki veritatis* ("in truth").

Where the tribes go up. Jerusalem was more than simply a fortified city that offered protection for those threatened by external forces; Jerusalem functioned as a centralizing and unifying place for the entire nation of Israel (i.e., "tribes of the LORD"). Texts in the Pentateuch ("the statute given to Israel") indicate that all Israel was to appear in Jerusalem three times each year (Exod 23:17; 34:23; Deut 16:16).[15] The primary purpose of such festivals was to "confess" or "praise" (*yadah*) the name of Yahweh. This accent on the name of Yahweh in Psalm 122:4b reflects the Deuteronomic notion that, while Yahweh is the God of the heavens, he has made his name to dwell among his people. The close association between the name of Yahweh and Jerusalem is evident in the oft-repeated reference to Jerusalem as "the place the LORD your God will choose as a dwelling for his Name" (Deut 12:5, 11; 16:2, 6; 26:2). The tribes gathered in Jerusalem to confess the name of Yahweh and, in so doing, to enjoy his very presence.

There stand the thrones. In Psalm 122:5 the poet recalls another significant feature of Jerusalem: the thrones for judgment and for the house of David. For most readers, the mention of a throne for the house of David will be of little surprise; but they may not have the same sense of familiarity with the "thrones for judgment." "A throne of judgment" occurs elsewhere in the Old Testament, most notably in 1 Kings 7:7. In that text Solomon orders that within the royal palace there should be built "the Hall of Justice where he was to judge." The precise role that any king played in the "Hall of Justice" remains speculative at best, but reference to the hall in conjunction with the throne of David does emphasize the role of Jerusalem (and the thrones therein) in the judicial and political affairs of the nation. Even more, the verdicts rendered at these thrones secured the social stability of the nation. As evident in an earlier psalm (Ps 72), the role of the king was to bring about peace and prosperity for his people.[16] The rule of the king was based on the premise that "God is the source of right rule, and those monarchs who allow themselves to be so empowered will rule so that the defenseless are protected, the oppressor crushed, and the whole land experiences *shalom*."[17] The psalmist remembers and celebrates

---

15. Psalm 122:4b reads "a statute of Israel, to confess the name of Yahweh" (author's translation). The reference to a "statute" (*'edut*) likely refers to the Pentateuchal texts mentioned above. The Qumran text (11QPsa) has been changed to *'dt*, "assembly." A similar move is made in Symmachus with *ekklesia*, "assembly." Both changes likely represent the desire of the copyists to create a poetic parallel to "tribes of Yah," which appears at the end of Ps 122:4a.

16. On Ps 72 see Wilson, *Psalms, Volume 1*, 983–95.

17. Ibid., 987.

these thrones even as he appears to long for renewed *shalom* for Jerusalem (see below, vv. 6–9).

The first strophe ends with the psalmist's feet standing in the gates of Jerusalem. The second strophe, which opens with explicit mention of "Jerusalem," recounts all the ways in which the city has remained the central place for God's presence. The city remains a safe refuge for those fleeing oppressive forces (v. 4). Further, those who travel to Jerusalem on a pilgrimage follow in the pathway of the "tribes of the LORD" who have repeatedly journeyed to Jerusalem to enjoy the presence of Yahweh. Finally, the psalmist claims that from the thrones in Jerusalem go forth the decisions that can lead to peace, *shalom*, for the land.

Pray for Peace (122:6–9)

THE THEME OF PEACE OR *SHALOM* dominates the final strophe of Psalm 122. In verses 6–8 the word "peace," or *shalom*, appears once in each verse, thereby repeatedly invoking the theme of this section of the psalm. Even the appearance of the name "Jerusalem" itself in this section (v. 6a) reinforces the theme of peace, given that the Hebrew root for "peace," *shlm*, comprises part of the city's name, "Jerusalem." Other terms in this strophe function alliteratively with the word *shalom*. For example, in the strophe's opening line, the Hebrew word for "pray," *sha'al*, appears in verse 6a. In addition, the verb *shalah*, "to be secure," occurs in verse 6b, and the related nominal form, *shalwah*, "security," appears in verse 7b. These words replicate the initial letters in *shalom*, thus leading Clinton McCann to suggest that this section may be "the most striking example of alliteration in the whole Psalter; the effect is to emphasize even further the concept of 'peace.'"[18]

May there be peace. In verses 6–7 the psalmist offers an invitation for others to pray for the peace of Jerusalem. He continues by suggesting a prayer that should be prayed. In verse 6b the psalmist notes that those who love Jerusalem will be *shalah*. The verb *shalah* in the *qal* stem usually means "to be at rest" or "to be undisturbed." A number of English translations render this verb "to prosper" (NRSV, KJV, NASB); unfortunately, this rendering may result in a skewed reading of the text. Read in this way, verse 6b seems to suggest that those who love Jerusalem should expect to prosper, as though there is a causal relationship between loving and prospering. The issue in the final strophe of Psalm 122, however, has nothing to do with doing well or "prospering." Instead, the psalmist invites those in his presence to pray that one day the city will be at rest, secure

---

18. McCann, "The Book of Psalms," 1184.

from the political and social upheaval that currently plagued it. Verse 7 follows a similar logic by requesting peace (*shalom*) within the walls and security (*shalwah*) within the citadels. Similar to the verbal form above, the nominal form here is rendered by some translations as "prosperity," but this rendering disrupts the poetic parallelism and likely invites a similar, unintended conclusion.

While God is not directly invoked in this proposed prayer, God is obviously the one to whom the prayer is directed and the only one capable of granting peace for the city.[19] Although the reader could point to numerous occasions in the preexilic period when Jerusalem was under attack, the postexilic period when Jerusalem was under Persian rule is likely in view.[20] In Nehemiah 1:3 the narrator records this period in Israel's history: "They said to me, 'Those who survived the exile and are back in the province are in great trouble and disgrace.'" The social and political conditions confronted by those in Yehud were untenable. Nehemiah 5 records the bleak circumstances experienced by the people living in Jerusalem and the larger region of Yehud during this time. Those living under such dire circumstances likely were not focused on "prosperity" as much as they were focused on living a peaceful, undisturbed existence.

I will seek your prosperity. In Psalm 122:8–9 the psalmist makes his own confession. The language is in the second person and is spoken directly to Jerusalem. The psalmist calls for peace (*shalom*) within the city and then concludes with a promise to seek Jerusalem's "prosperity." The NIV translates the word *tov* as "prosperity," but in its most basic sense the word means "good." In effect, the psalmist commits to seeking the good of the city and to doing so for the sake of "the house of the LORD our God." Ultimately, the poet does not seek the good of Jerusalem simply because of a nostalgic love for the city or for the religious history that it holds; rather, his love for Jerusalem rests solely on his belief that it is the place where he encounters most fully the presence of God.

The fact that the psalm concludes with petitions in verses 6–7 and a commitment to work for the good of Jerusalem in verse 9 suggests that such hopes have yet to be fulfilled. The pilgrimage to Jerusalem is a reminder for the psalmist that this city, and perhaps the world, remains at unrest—but there is always hope—a hope that is grounded in the presence of the living God.

---

19. Hossfeld and Zenger, *Psalms 3*, 341.

20. Regarding the Persian imperial ideology and its potential impact upon those living in Judah (or Yehud), see Tucker, *Constructing and Deconstructing Power in Psalms 107–150*, 19–53.

 PSALM 122 IS ONE OF THE Songs of Ascent, and as a piece of pilgrimage literature it has a certain liturgical function—it invites the community to celebrate their arrival in Jerusalem, to recall the defining features of the city, and to pray for God's unfolding future for the city. While perhaps Psalm 122 may not represent a "liturgy" in the narrowest of definitions, it does show certain liturgical characteristics. The Greek word for liturgy is *leitourgia* and derives from two root words—*laos*, "the people," and *ergon*, "work." Consequently, some have rendered the term "liturgy" as "the work of the people," and indeed Psalm 122 reflects something of the "work of the people" as they made their way to and into Jerusalem.

Eugene Peterson, in his small volume *Answering God: The Psalms as Tools for Prayer*, considers the role of liturgy and offers a brief but suggestive claim concerning its purpose.[21] Peterson writes that "liturgy can be elaborate or simple, baroque or bare, but it always provides these three things: space, time, order."[22] In many ways Psalm 122 invites those who pray this poem to make certain claims about God and his interaction with the world. These claims are structured around the themes of space, time, and order, and they resonate with the larger witness of Scripture.

Jerusalem as sacred space. Psalm 122 celebrates the city of Jerusalem. From beginning to end, the psalmist celebrates the features of Jerusalem and its history, and he prays for its future. Nearly every verse refers to Jerusalem or some aspect related to the city. The reader of Psalm 122 is inundated with repeated images of and references to Jerusalem—far more than any other of the Songs of Ascent. Given that Jerusalem is the goal of the pilgrimage, perhaps the celebratory fixation on the city is in order. Yet to assume the celebratory tone of the psalm can be attributed simply to reaching the journey's destination is to miss the interpretation of Jerusalem as sacred space.

As suggested in the Original Meaning section above, a cluster of theological claims developed around the notion of Zion, but none perhaps more important than the belief in the centrality of Jerusalem. To refer to the "centrality of Jerusalem" is to comment on more than its geographical or topographical features—such a claim involves much more than mere cartography. Melody Knowles has explained that in the biblical tradition

---

21. Eugene Peterson, *Answering God: The Psalms as Tools for Prayer* (New York: Harper One, 1989).

22. Ibid., 85.

"centrality incorporates sacrality."[23] After Jerusalem's defeat at the hands of the Babylonians, however, one would not have been surprised if Jerusalem's importance had been diminished, not only politically but also ideologically and theologically. Despite that possibility, the exilic prophets moved in the opposite direction by imbuing an even greater sense of "sacrality" to the city and reinforcing its centrality. In the book of Ezekiel, for example, Yahweh announces that he has made Jerusalem the "center of the nations" (Ezek 5:5), and later in the book Jerusalem is called the "center [*tabbur*] of the land" (Ezek 38:12). Yet the importance of those claims is not evident until the final verse of the book. In that context the prophet recognizes Jerusalem by announcing that its new name will be "The LORD is there." Jerusalem stands at the center of the nations and functions as the navel of the earth because the presence of God is there.[24] Psalm 122 captures this same sense by opening and closing with a reference to the house of the Lord. Centrality is indeed defined by sacrality in Psalm 122—the house of the Lord is Jerusalem, the Lord is there. The desire to visit Jerusalem is driven by the desire to enter sacred space and enjoy the presence of the Lord.

Jerusalem and the notion of time. As Peterson explains in *Answering God*, prayer and liturgy take place in "time and space."[25] As noted above, Psalm 122 takes place "in space"—in Jerusalem—while also invoking the sense of the significance of that place. This "work of the people," however, does not occur in a vacuum, removed from the vicissitudes of daily life; it only makes sense as daily life becomes connected to a history. The psalmist is also keenly aware of his present moment; it is a moment filled with joy (vv. 1–2) tempered by the apparent threats that stand in the background of verses 6–9. In response to his present moment, the psalmist places his life within the larger context of the tribes of the Lord (v. 4). Just as they had made their journeys to Jerusalem, so too had this psalmist. The same well-worn roads had carried countless pilgrims before as they made their way to these festivals in Jerusalem. Throughout Israel's history these festivals marked time, but even more they marked identity. As seasons changed

---

23. Melody Knowles, *Centrality Practiced: Jerusalem in the Religious Practice of Yehud and the Diaspora in the Persian Period*, ABS 16 (Atlanta: SBL Press, 2006), 5. On Knowles's observations concerning the rich notion of centrality in Jerusalem, see pages 121–28.

24. The postexilic prophets express this theme in similar fashion. For example, the book of Zechariah associates the centrality of Jerusalem with the very presence of God. Following a vision in which the four horns (i.e., the leaders of the nations [Zech 1:18]) are struck down by four blacksmiths (v. 21), Yahweh promises Judah that many nations will come to Jerusalem and join his people (2:11) and that Yahweh will dwell in their midst.

25. Peterson, *Answering God*, 85.

and as festivals rolled around, the people made their way to Jerusalem because doing so was a "statute given to Israel" (v. 4b)—making pilgrimage to Jerusalem is what the people of God did. In these moments of time, Jerusalem was the place where the people of God were to be.

Jerusalem and the call for order. Psalm 122 also reminds the pilgrims that because God is present in Jerusalem, the city is a place from which the judgments of God pour forth (v. 5). In the postexilic period, when the thrones of judgment and of the house of David may have had a limited function at best, this verse reminds those traveling to Jerusalem that because God is in the city, there is hope that God's orderly intentions for creation will be carried out. James Mays suggests that "pilgrimage is a journey in search of justice."[26] He imagines that people with fundamental disagreements and legal disputes in that day would have used these festivals as an opportunity to receive a hearing concerning such matters. While that may in fact have been the case, the poet in Psalm 122 has shifted the focus from his own legal disputes to the *dis*order that threatened Jerusalem (vv. 6–9). By asking those who had accompanied him on the pilgrimage to pray for the peace of Jerusalem, the psalmist was acknowledging the *lack of order*. Equally, however, he was also acknowledging the *source of order*. The God who had issued forth judgments and decisions through the thrones of judgment and of David was still the one who could act decidedly to bring peace to the city of Jerusalem.

IN BIBLICAL INTERPRETATION there is always the temptation to be reductionist—to reduce the meaning of the text, *prima facie*, to its most basic idea. Such an approach is not always incorrect, but at times it can deprive us of the rich tapestry of ideas present in the text. Based on verses 1–2, the interpreter may interpret Psalm 122 as a joyous call to go to church. While the psalm does speak of the joy the psalmist feels as he receives the invitation, the psalm actually invites us to consider much more. These yearly treks to Jerusalem were much more than weekend excursions or annual vacations to a celebrated site, much like family summer vacations or annual skiing trips. As valuable as those experiences are, they are altogether different. The practices reflected in the Songs of Ascent are practices that have been instituted within the life of the community—practices that invite those pilgrims to lift their eyes

---

26. Mays, *Psalms*, 393.

(cf. Pss 121:1; 123:1) and see beyond the mundane.[27] Dorothy Bass and Craig Dystra remind us of the sacred role such practices play in our lives. These authors explain that such practices help us weave together a particular way of life that

> becomes visible as ordinary people search together for specific ways of taking part in the practice of God, as they faithfully perceive it in the complicated places where they really live. It is like a tree whose branches reach out toward the future, even when the earth is shaking, because it is nourished by living water.[28]

The annual pilgrimages to Jerusalem no doubt took place amid the "complicated places where they lived," yet they returned annually because they were nourished by the living water they experienced in Jerusalem. Although Psalm 122 begins with joyous celebrations, the promise of Jerusalem as a place of protection (v. 3) and the request for peace in the city intimate a reality far more complex. Yet they made their way to Jerusalem because, as Clinton McCann reminds, Jerusalem "is not just place but a symbol of God's presence in space and time."[29] These pilgrims continued to come in order to celebrate a way of life that was much bigger than they themselves—a way of life that was rooted deeply in the presence of God.

---

27. On the formative role of Christian practice see Dorothy C. Bass, ed., *Practicing Our Faith: A Way of Life for a Searching People* (San Francisco: Jossey Bass, 1997).

28. Dorothy Bass and Craig Dystra, "Growing in the Practices of Faith," in *Practicing Our Faith: A Way of Life for a Searching People*, ed. Dorothy C. Bass (San Francisco: Jossey Bass, 1997), 203.

29. McCann, "The Book of Psalms," 1185.

Psalm 123

A song of ascents.

¹ I lift my eyes to you,
    to you who sit enthroned in heaven.
² As the eyes of the slaves look to the
    hand of their master,
as the eyes of the female slave look to the
    hand of her mistress,
So our eyes look to the LORD our God,
    till he shows us his mercy.
³ Have mercy on us, LORD, have mercy on us,
    for we have endured no end of contempt.
⁴ We have endured no end
    of ridicule from the arrogant,
    of contempt from the proud.

Original Meaning

ALTHOUGH PSALM 123 does not contain the same vivid pilgrimage imagery as does Psalm 122, the poem nevertheless does play an important role within the Songs of Ascent collection by reinforcing the community's struggle amid a hostile environment. The structure of Psalm 123 suggests a communal lament despite the fact that verse 1 is in the first person singular ("I"). The first two verses contain an expression of trust, followed by a petition for mercy in verses 3–4. Laments typically include an expression of certainty that the psalmist will be heard or a statement of confidence that Yahweh will intervene, but strikingly, Psalm 123 does not include such an affirmation. Like Psalm 120, this psalm contains a lament that is left "unanswered,"[1] thus leading some scholars to conclude that the expected affirmation and praise occurs in the subsequent psalm.[2]

The governing metaphor of the psalm appears in verse 1b—the psalmist looks to the one enthroned in the heavens. The poet and his audience,

---

1. Loren D. Crow, *The Songs of Ascents (Psalms 120–134): Their Place in Israelite History and Religion*, SBLDS 148 (Atlanta: Scholars Press, 1996), 50.
2. McCann, "The Book of Psalms," 1187; Hossfeld and Zenger, *Psalms 3*, 346.

much like male and female slaves, approach the Divine King as slaves would approach their master (v. 2). The use of the second metaphor to explicate the first extends the metaphorical imagery in the psalm and makes claims about Yahweh as well as his relationship with his people. Frank-Lothar Hossfeld and Erich Zenger explain, "On the one hand, as the one enthroned in heaven, YHWH has a universal and unlimited effective power, but, on the other hand, as the God of the petitioners ('our God'), he has a specific relationship to them that properly obligates him to intervene to save them."[3] The precise nature of this relationship, as articulated in this psalm, will be explored below.

Although Psalm 123 is one of the shorter Songs of Ascent (with only Pss 131, 133, and 134 being shorter), the psalm does exhibit considerable structure through the repetition of vocabulary. The repetition is structured in such a way as to connect the adjacent lines in the psalm—a technique known as anadiplosis (see Ps 120). That the noun "eyes" occurs four times in the first two verses serves to bind the two claims made in the opening expression of trust. The image of the hand connects verse 2a with verse 2c. Twice the psalmist mentions looking toward Yahweh ("to you" [v. 1a]; "to the LORD" [v. 2e]). The word "mercy" appears as the final word in verse 2f and begins verse 3a—and then is repeated again in that same line. The phrase "we have endured no end" in the NIV translates a Hebrew term that means "to be full," or "satiated." This term serves as the linking word between verse 3b and 4a. The concept of shame or contempt also is repeated in verses 3b and 4c. The repetition of imagery and vocabulary does more than show the poetic dexterity of the psalmist, notwithstanding that it does do so; but this repetition also signals a tightly configured psalm that leads the reader to a particular theological confession.

Expression of Trust (123:1–2)

THE PSALM BEGINS WITH A STRONG expression of trust. Embedded within this expression are two images. The first metaphor serves to justify the psalmist's trust and the second to illustrate the posture of trust.

I lift up my eyes to you. The NIV has rearranged the Hebrew word order in an effort to create a translation that reflects a more traditional English word order: "I lift up my eyes to you." The Hebrew structure is worth considering, however. The Hebrew text begins "to you," referring to Yahweh. Psalm 120 also opens the psalm with a similar prepositional phrase, "to Yahweh." As noted in that psalm, by moving the indirect

---

3. Hossfeld and Zenger, *Psalms 3*, 345.

object to the beginning of the verse, the psalmist has fronted important information in the poetic line.[4] Typically, fronting signals that the object mentioned is the focus of the utterance. In other words, by structuring the psalm in this manner the psalmist is confessing that the focus of this poelm is on the one "who sit[s] enthroned in heaven."

Beyond its similarity to Psalm 120, Psalm 123 also takes up the opening line in Psalm 121:1: "I lift up my eyes to you." The vocabulary is identical in both psalms—"to lift" (*nasa'*) and "eyes" (*'enim*). As mentioned in the commentary on Psalm 121, the action of "lifting the eyes," both in Hebrew and in Akkadian, implies looking at something longingly or with desire.[5] Such is the case in Psalm 123, even though the necessity or rationale for the glance heavenward to Yahweh is not fully revealed until the latter half of the poem (vv. 3–4). The act of lifting the eyes to Yahweh is interpreted metaphorically in verse 2 (see below) via the relationship between the male and female slaves and their master. On the attribution "you who sit enthroned in heaven" and its theological significance, see Bridging Contexts below.

The eyes of slaves look to the hand of their master. The language of "lifting the eyes" first mentioned in verse 1 appears in the extended metaphor in verse 2. Phil Botha notes that verse 2 includes one of the poem's most striking features, "delayed identification."[6] The metaphorical comparison extends across three poetic lines and delays the concluding force of the comparison until the very end of verse:

> As the eyes of slaves look to the hand of their master,
> > as the eyes of a female slave look to the hand of her mistress,
> So our eyes look to the LORD our God,
> > till he shows us his mercy.

Botha opines that the delay "is probably done to emphasize the prolonged suffering of Yahweh's people and to heighten the focus on the expected intervention which is (linguistically) reached in the last words of the strophe."[7] Whether Botha is correct in the first part of his analysis (i.e., that the delay has to do with suffering) is debatable, but he is

---

4. For a brief explanation of fronting in biblical Hebrew see van der Merwe, Naudé, and Kroze, *A Biblical Hebrew Reference Grammar*, 344–50.

5. See also Gen 39:7; Ezek 18:6; Jer 3:2.

6. Phil J. Botha, "Social Values and the Interpretation of Psalm 123," *OTE* 14 (2001): 189–98.

7. Ibid., 191.

undoubtedly correct in the second part of his assessment. Just as fronting "to you" in verse 1 draws attention to Yahweh, so the delayed identification in the extended metaphor "heightens the focus" on Yahweh.

In this extended metaphor the psalmist mentions male slaves and a female slave and their relationship with their respective masters. The term *shiphah* can be understood as "slave girl," or "female slave," and likely would have represented the lowest position in the household, while *'abadim* can be rendered "servants." Given the larger context in verse 2, however, the term is better understood as "male slave." Hossfeld and Zenger explain that "the petitioners compare themselves to slaves—those with no real power and no capacity to protect themselves, much less defend themselves. They are literally at the mercy of their masters."[8] This image of the petitioner as a powerless slave comports well with the imagery that appears earlier in the psalm—that of Yahweh as the Divine King enthroned in the heavens. Kings in the ancient Near East had the responsibility of caring for the weak in society. For example, in the opening line of the Code of Hammurabi the king refers to himself as "the pious prince" whose job it is "to make justice prevail in the land, to abolish the wicked and the evil, and to prevent the strong from oppressing the weak."[9] Thus the relationship between slave and master anticipates the lament that follows in verses 2b–4. The psalmists stretch out their hands to the Divine King in a time of great travail, much as slaves do to their mistresses or masters.

The poem does not initially indicate what it means to "look to the hand" of a master or mistress, the psalmist explains in the final line of verse 2 that they are waiting for the Lord to show mercy. The term *hanan* is often translated as "mercy" as the NIV, NRSV, and other translations, and it often appears in texts in which one party pleads for favor in the face of great adversity. Put differently, *hanan* "expresses the disposition and action of a superior to be for those who are related as dependants."[10] Thus in the context of this psalm, even as the slave would wait for any signal from the hand of the master, those who were enduring hardship were looking to the hand of Yahweh in the face of their current plight.[11]

---

8. Hossfeld and Zenger, *Psalms 3*, 347.

9. "The Laws of Hammurabi," *COS* 2:336. See also the analysis of royal power by Dale Launderville, *Piety and Politics: The Dynamics of Royal Authority in Homeric Greece, Biblical Israel, and Old Babylonian Mesopotamia* (Grand Rapids: Eerdmans, 2003).

10. Mays, *Psalms*, 395.

11. Botha, "Social Values and the Interpretation of Psalm 123," 195. Botha casts the relationships in verse 2 in light of patron-client relationships in the broader ancient Near Eastern context.

Petition for Mercy (123:3–4)

IN THE FINAL TWO VERSES THE PSALMIST shifts from the metaphorically rich language employed in verses 1–2 and addresses the issue that necessitates this prayer. The poet makes a petition for mercy (v. 3a) and gives the rationale for the petition in verses 3b–4. Verse 3 begins with *hanan*, the same verb that concludes verse 2. The language employed in these two verses remains general, thus precluding any easy idenfication of the social context. Given that the pronouns are plural, the references could signify a small group of the faithful who have been shamed, or the "we" group could signify "Israel," scorned and humiliated by its conquerers (Ps 44:13–16). The next Song of Ascents (Ps 124) also includes plural pronouns and leaves little doubt that all Israel is in view. While not determinative, the references in Psalm 124 are suggestive for how to read Psalm 123.

Psalm 123:3b introduces the basis for this request with a *ki* clause ("*for we have endured no end of contempt*"). *Ki* clauses usually begin with the English word "for" and follow a main clause; they serve to provide the rationale for the earlier request (v. 3a). Verse 3b connects with verse 4a through the repetition of the word *saba'*, which means "to be full" or "satiated." Literally, the community is confessing that they have had their fill of shame and contempt, or more precisely they have had *more than* their fill of shame and contempt.[12] In verse 4a the psalmist adds *nepesh* with a pronominal suffix, "our"; the result could be rendered as "our throat" or "our life," thus leading to verse 4a's translation as "our lives have had more than their fill"; or *nepesh* could be translated literally as "throat" in an effort to create another metaphor (i.e., eating): "Too long has our *throat* been sated."[13] As mentioned in the comments on Psalm 122, however, the pronominal suffix attached to *nepesh* more nearly functions as an independent personal pronoun in most contexts (i.e., in this instance, "we"), thus making any such metaphorical imagery only secondary at best.

In the final two verses the psalmist invokes language from the "shame" word field.[14] The term *buz*, "contempt," frequently reflects the derisive attitude of rich people or those in power toward the needy and unfortunate.[15] In verse 4b the term *la'ag*, "ridicule," functions as a synonym of *buz*. The terms *buz* and *la'ag*, along with the verbal form of *la'ag*, occur in Nehemiah 4. In that

---

12. The use of *rab* and *rabbat* in verses 3b and 4a creates something akin to a comparative statement in these verses (i.e., "we have had *more than* our fill").

13. Dahood, *Psalms 101–150*, 208–10.

14. On the use of shame language in the Psalter see W. Dennis Tucker Jr., "Is Shame a Matter of Patronage in the Communal Laments?" *JSOT* 31 (2007): 465–80.

15. Michael A. Grisanti, "בוז," *NIDOTTE* 1:618.

context Sanballet, Tobiah, and Geshem all mock and deride the people of God; those in power mock the weak and needy. Although the context of Psalm 123 cannot be determined, its references to "ridicule" and "contempt" suggest that verbal threats were levied against the community, thereby creating a context that necessitated a communal lament. The mention of verbal threats in Psalm 123 also recalls the cause of vexation in the opening psalm in the Songs of Ascent, namely, the cries for war (Ps 120:3–4, 7). As a result, Psalm 123 extends the motif of "living in a hostile world"—a motif that appears throughout the Songs of Ascent collection.

THE GOD OF THE HEAVENS. In Psalm 123:1b the poet refers to Yahweh as the one "who sit[s] enthroned in heaven." The phrase might easily be overlooked in reflecting on the larger psalm, but this metaphorical reference anchors the remainder of the poem. During the postexilic period, in particular, Yahweh was frequently described in relation to the heavens.[16] The destruction of the temple and subsequent exile created acute theological tensions. If the house of God had been destroyed, what more could they say about God? Rather than conceding any weakness on the part of God, the Jewish community affirmed that in fact their God was not just *a* god who was known in Jerusalem but in fact *the* God who stands over all creation. As the God of the heavens, he was sovereign over all.

The metaphorical depictions of God in relation to the heavens varied to some degree. Konrad Schmid has identified the different models employed in the Old Testament to depict the one enthroned in the heavens. Two are worth mentioning in relation to Psalm 123.[17] One model, labeled the "cosmos-theistic" concept, can be found in other texts, such as Amos 9, Deuteronomy 3, and Isaiah 66, but within the Psalter the clearest example is found in Psalm 104. God is praised for being "clothed with splendor and majesty" (v. 1), and then in verses 2–3 the psalmist explains that

> The LORD wraps himself in light as with a garment;
> he stretches out the heavens like a tent

---

16. On the enthronement of Yahweh in the heavens in Book 5 of the Psalter see Tucker, *Constructing and Deconstructing Power in Psalms 107–150*, 142–49.

17. Konrad Schmid, "Himmelsgott, Weltgott, und Schöpfersgott: 'Gott' und der "Himmel' in der Literatur der Zeit des Zweiten Tempels," in *Der Himmel*, ed. Martin Ebner and Irmtraud Fischer (Neukirchen-Vluyn: Neukirchener Verlag, 2005), 111–48.

and lays the beams of his upper chambers on their waters.
He makes the clouds his chariot
and rides on the wings of the wind.

Clearly, the entire cosmos is associated with the throne room of Yahweh, but interestingly, even the elements found *within* the cosmos play a role in his royal rule. This view does not associate Yahweh with creation, as in some kind of panentheism, but instead attempts to recognize the "otherness" of Israel's God. As Schmid explains, "the cosmos corresponds to the heart of the sanctuary, namely its throne and footstool."[18] Even though the temple in Jerusalem was destroyed, the throne of God in the cosmos was not—God remains God over all.

Beyond the cosmos-theistic concept, Schmid identifies another model, the "heavenly [*Uranisierende*] concept." In this model, the biblical writer locates the dwelling of God in the heavens, or even above the heavens. In Psalm 113, for example, the psalmist explains that the glory of God is "above the heavens" (v. 4) and that from that position, he "stoops down to look on the heavens and the earth" (v. 6). Yahweh's kingship is also associated with the "heavens" in Psalm 115. In this model, the heavens, or "above the heavens," serve as the location for God's dwelling place, but unlike in the cosmos model, in the heavenly model elements of creation are usually not part of God's royal retinue.

As noted above, in the postexilic period Yahweh was frequently depicted as the one enthroned in the heavens. At first glance this affirmation regarding Yahweh's location may imply that a great chasm existed between Yahweh and his people, particularly following the destruction of the temple. To the contrary, just the opposite should be inferred. Schmid explains that the heavenly enthronement of Yahweh stressed the reign of Yahweh over the universal kingdom of God and should be understood soteriologically. Because he is the ruler of the world, "unchallengable and in a constant state of readiness for his own," he is always prepared to intervene in behalf of his people.[19] In Psalm 121 the eyes of the psalmist were turned to the hills of Zion in the hope of finding deliverance, but in Psalm 123 the psalmist's gaze has turned heavenward to the one enthroned on high. The ridicule and contempt being experienced by the psalmist and his community could no longer be endured; they needed the king on high to "stoop down" from his royal throne and bring deliverance to his people.[20]

---

18. Ibid., 20.
19. Ibid., 13–14.
20. See also the Bridging Contexts section on Ps 113.

The household metaphor. A number of the Songs of Ascent contain imagery associated with the family or a small community. For example, Psalms 127 and 128 refer to the rearing of children, and Psalm 131 employs the metaphor of a weaned child. Other familial or communal references include such activities as farming (Ps 129:3–4) and house construction (Ps 127:1). Both Psalm 123 and Psalm 130 refer to the relationship between household slaves and their master or mistress, thus again suggesting a household context. Even the motif of the "house of the LORD" mentioned in the opening and closing verses of Psalm 122 appears to take on a slightly different nuance given the repeated references to family and community life throughout the collection.[21] These references and allusions to family and communal life are subsumed under the greater theme of the household of God.

The psalmist holds these two metaphors in tension. The God we serve is the God enthroned in the heavens, but the God of the heavens also invites us into his household. While the language of domestication in Psalm 123 signals the closeness between the two parties, it functions more importantly as a reminder of the obligations incumbent upon the "master of the house." Hossfeld and Zenger note that because the petitioners perceive themselves to be part of the household of God, any shame or scorn that comes on them ultimately falls on the master of the house. This potential provides additional incentive for the one enthroned in the heavens to hear the request and respond.[22]

The use of household imagery to describe the relationship between God and his people is not unique to the Old Testament. Paul makes frequent references to familial imagery. In Galatians 4:1–7, for example, the apostle uses inheritance language to describe redemption. He reminds those at Galatia that they are heirs in the household of God, but as heirs they are still minors. This reminder must be understood in the light of the Roman legal view of minors. As minors, the Galatians are really no better off than household slaves (Gal 4:1). Both they and the property they will inherit remain under the oversight of the father until the appropriate day, when the inheritance will be distributed. Paul says that day came "when the set time had fully come" when the Son of God was born to a woman (Gal 4:4). He extends the imagery with another household metaphor (that of adoption) to emphasize what has happened through redemption. Under Roman law, children who were adopted received the same legal status and inheritance rights as biological children—upon adoption, the status of

---

21. Hossfeld and Zenger, *Psalms* 3, 349.
22. Ibid., 348.

the child was changed. According to Paul, our status has been changed because of the work of Jesus Christ. Rather than assuming only some were adopted, Paul appears to conclude that we are *all* adopted children (Gal 4:5–6), thus leading us to cry out to God, "Abba! Father!" Because we are in the household of God, we "are no longer a slave, but God's child; and since you are his child, God has made you also an heir" (Gal 4:7).[23]

DESPITE ITS BREVITY PSALM 123 offers a great word of hope to those who "have endured no end of contempt." Although the psalm appears to refer to verbal assaults levied against the psalmist and the larger community, its applicability extends well beyond images of verbal sparring or insults, beyond the kinds of exchanges one might imagine on a playground or in a boardroom. The real issue is shame. The experience of shame for the ancients in Israel, however, is vastly different from contemporary notions of embarrassment. Shame "leads to the fear of psychological or physical rejection, abandonment, expulsion, or loss of social position.[24] Shame of this sort does result in blushing cheeks and the downward glancing of the eyes, but even more, this kind of shame makes one feel powerless in the face of the other.

The community grieves over the contempt (Ps 123:3b, 4c) and ridicule (v. 4b) that has come to define their reality—they have grown weary of their own sense of powerlessness. If we translate verse 4 literally, it reads, "our throats [*nepesh*] have been filled to no end." The image here is similar to that in Numbers 11:30, where those in the wilderness are told that quail will come out of their noses. In Psalm 123 the problem is that shame has become so acute and pervasive that they are "filled to the brim" with shame, and it has left them devastated. What makes matters more troubling is that such shame does not appear to be the doing of the psalmist or the community. In other psalms, the community is not averse to establishing a causal relationship between their shame and their failures. In Psalm 79, for example, the community laments the destruction of the temple (Ps 79:1), and they bemoan that they have become objects of shame, contempt, and derision (v. 4). Yet they understand that their present plight is tied to "the sins of past generations" (v. 8). Such is not the case in Psalm 123, however. The community does not perceive itself to be the cause—shame

---

23. Paul makes similar use of household imagery in Rom 4:1–18 and 8:12–29.

24. Lyn M. Bechtel, "Shame as a Sanction of Social Control in Biblical Israel: Judicial, Political, and Social Shaming," *JSOT* 49 (1991): 47–76.

has come upon them and powerlessness has overtaken them in ways that have overwhelmed them and threatened to choke out their very lives.

There are people we serve and to whom we minister who know something of this kind of shame. They too feel rejected and abandoned and know something of the bitter taste of losing social position. It used to be, at least, that when small boys wrestled one another, they would keep at it till one of them yelled "uncle." It was a sign of having had enough. There are many people who are at the point of screaming "uncle" due to the vicissitudes of life that have befallen them. The community in Psalm 123 has yelled "uncle"; they have had enough of their shame (vv. 3–4). As a result, they turn to God as the only one who can redeem them from such a desperate plight. The psalmist's hope is our hope. We are called to turn to God and plead, "Have mercy on us, LORD, have mercy." As noted above, the word for "mercy" is *hanan*. We may readily conceive of this term in an emotional sense, that is, that God looks on people "sympathetically"; but in many places in the Old Testament the plea for mercy extends well beyond a "spiritual matter" and refers to God's addressing, or better yet, God's redressing of all areas of life.[25] Like the community in Psalm 123 we must turn to God as dependents—not for his sympathy but for his active intervention in our lives.

The two metaphors mentioned in verses 1–2 (and discussed in Bridging Contexts) provide the rationale for why we can cry out to God for mercy. The God we serve is the one enthroned in the heavens, the Sovereign King over all. Because he is the king and we are his servants, we lift our eyes and look to his hand for a sign of deliverance. And because of who he is (Exod 34:6–7), we wait with anticipation and certainty that the King over all will stoop down and pick us up from the ash heap (Ps 113:7).

---

25. Terence E. Fretheim, "חנן," *NIDOTTE* 2:203–206.

Psalm 124

A song of ascents. Of David.

¹ If the LORD had not been on our side—
  let Israel say—
² If the LORD had not been on our side
  when people attacked us,
³ they would have swallowed us alive
  when their anger flared against us;
⁴ the flood would have engulfed us,
  the torrent would have swept over us,
⁵ the raging waters
  would have swept us away.
⁶ Praise be to the LORD,
  who has not let us be torn by their teeth.
⁷ We have escaped like a bird
  from the fowler's snare;
the snare has been broken,
  and we have escaped.
⁸ Our help is in the name of the LORD,
  the Maker of heaven and earth.

GIVEN THE REPEATED use of the first-person plural in every verse of the Psalm 124, it is traditionally labeled a communal psalm of thanksgiving. As most interpreters observe, Psalm 124 is unique in its structure and does not follow the expected patterns of a communal thanksgiving psalm. Most thanksgiving psalms attempt to narrate the cause of distress, the cry to Yahweh, and the deliverance experienced by the psalmist. Further, the psalmist typically gives thanks for deliverance and then concludes with a pledge to provide a thank offering. Many of these elements are absent from Psalm 124, and those that are included do not follow the anticipated order. In addition, the imagery and language in the psalm are interesting, given its present form as a communal thanksgiving. As Crüsemann observed, "not a single idiom, not a single word or figure of Psalm 124 is typical of psalms of the people or the community."[1] John Goldingay provides the most logical explanation for this tension: the psalmist may have "recycled" the imagery of individual thanksgiving psalms in order to speak to the experience of the larger community.[2] Regardless of the psalm's history or the origin of its images, the poem as presently constructed is meant to be heard as a communal psalm ("let Israel say" [v. 1a]).

The poem itself can be divided into two strophes. In verses 1–5 the community reminds itself of what *could have happened* had not God delivered them. Most communal psalms of thanksgiving narrate how God delivered his people out of a dire circumstance, as is evident in Psalm 118:5–14, but Psalm 124 begins differently. The community starts by acknowledging what never came to fruition thanks to God's intervention—a thought that should generate a spirit of thanksgiving. Verses 3–5 employ various metaphors in an attempt to capture the dire nature of the threat that was thankfully avoided. Each of the three lines begins with *'azay*, "then," thus connecting the images linguistically.

Whereas the first section in the psalm celebrates what God prevented from coming to fruition, the second section of the psalm (vv. 6–8) calls for the praise of Yahweh for what he has done in behalf of his people. As explained below, the metaphorical imagery in these verses likely alludes to the devastation experienced by Israel at the hands of other nations or people groups.

As in the other Songs of Ascent, the repetition in Psalm 124 binds the various lines together, thereby creating a strong sense of unity within the poem, and in some ways the repetition groups the major themes and images of the psalm into clusters. As mentioned above, verse 2a repeats verse 1a verbatim, while verses 3–5 all begin with the same word, *'azay*, "then." The phrase *'abar 'al napshu* ("swept us away" or "pass over us") functions as a transition, with the words appearing as the final phrase in verse 4 and the opening phrase in verse 5.[3] In addition, the word *pah*, "snare" or "trap," appears in verses 7a and 7b, as does the term *nimlat* "escaped."

The God Who Is For His People (124:1–5)

THE FIRST STROPHE IN THE PSALM considers how dire the people's circumstances would have been were God not on their side. Using conditional

---

1. Frank Crüsemann, *Studien zur Formgeschichte von Hymnus und Danklied in Israel*, WMANT 32 (Neukirchen-Vluyn: Neukirchener Verlag, 1969), 166.

2. Goldingay, *Psalms 3*, 477.

3. The English translation obscures this repetition. Verse 5 literally reads in the Hebrew, "then, sweeps us away, the raging waters."

"if . . . then" language, the psalmist creates an imagined scenario. The first two verses function as the protasis and provide the condition ("if the LORD had not been on our side"); the final three verses function as the apodosis, introducing the result.

If the LORD had not been on our side. The opening word in verses 1a and 2a is *lule* ("if," "perhaps," or "except") and introduces a negative unreal condition or a situation that runs counter to reality.[4] The idea of an "unreal situation" might be better construed in English as "it was Yahweh (who acted), but if he had not," then this is what would have happened (the "unreal situation"). The use of the "if [*lule*] . . . then [*'azay*]" construction in verses 1–5 is understood as "a narrative about what might have occurred without Yahweh's aid" rather than a true "if . . . then" clause as often expressed in Greek.[5] The word "if" (*lule*) occurs in a number of texts in the Old Testament in which the speaker attributes some form of unexpected deliverance to Yahweh (cf. Gen 31:42; 43:10; Deut 32:29; 1 Sam 25:34; 2 Sam 2:27; 2 Kgs 3:14; Ps 94:17). This deliverance is rooted in Israel's claim that Yahweh is "for us." The phrase that Yahweh is "for us" or "for me" appears frequently in texts that refer to military and hostile threats (Gen 31:42; 1 Sam 17:46; Pss 56:10; 118:6–7).[6] The language in Psalm 124 points in a similar direction. The NIV translates the second half of verse 2 as "when people attacked us." The word "attack" is derived from the Hebrew phrase "to rise up against" (*qum 'al*), which often connotes the aggressive, warlike imagery of human enemies (cf. Ps 84:14). In Psalm 124 the threat to the psalmist is identified by the general term *'adam*, "people." On the power of humans in the Psalter, see Bridging Contexts below.

Swallowed us alive. The verb *bala'*, "swallow up," provides a visually graphic image—that of being devoured alive. The most memorable use of this term occurs in Numbers 16:34. The text explains that, in response to the challenges and taunts against Moses by Korah, Dathan, and Abiram, the earth opened up and swallowed the three men and their families. While that scene may be the most memorable, there are other texts in which the verb and the image of the devouring of the victim appear in scenes associated with war and conflict. In the Song of the Sea, for example, the Israelites explain that the Egyptians were defeated when Yahweh stretched out his hand and the earth swallowed the enemies (Exod 15:12). A similar expression is used by the prophets who refer to Israel's defeat at the hands of Nebuchadnezzar as being "swallowed up" by the enemy

---

4. van der Merwe, Naudé, and Kroeze, *A Biblical Hebrew Reference Grammar*, 304.

5. Crow, *The Songs of Ascents*, 52–53.

6. Hossfeld and Zenger, *Psalms 3*, 355.

(Isa 49:19; Jer 51:34). The writer of Lamentations also invokes imagery of being swallowed up in reference to military defeat (Lam 2:16).

The flood would have engulfed us. Psalm 124:4–5 employs a second metaphor in an attempt to portray the kind of devastation that could have come upon the community had not Yahweh been on their side: devastating floods. Othmar Keel explains that devastation can be wrought from the kind of flash flooding that plagues the region:

> The inhabitants of Palestine had special opportunity . . . to experience the destructive power of the proud floods of Chaos: the numerous dry wadis can in the space of a single hour become engorged with water. The rain itself often falls somewhere in the mountains or far out in the desert. The waters gather in the dry beds; then suddenly, perhaps even under a fair sky, the flood appears in a place remote from the area of precipitation and carries off with it both man and beast.[7]

In Psalm 124 the imagery of floods, torrents, and raging waters as sweeping over the community confirm human powerlessness by invoking images of a watery grave and certain death. The final image employed, "raging waters," is particularly noteworthy. The word "raging" (*zedon*) is used to describe the waters, but in other texts related forms of the word are translated as "arrogant" or "insolent." While the psalmist is no doubt referring to the rising or seething waters that would have swept the community away, the use of *zedon* provides a subtle allusion to the arrogance that often characterizes the enemies in the psalms (cf. Ps 123:4).

An interesting parallel text occurs in Psalm 69, which includes imagery and vocabulary similar to that found in Psalm 124:3–5. In Psalm 69 the psalmist weaves together the language of *bala'* ("to swallow") with "water" and "being engulfed." (Both terms appear in each of the two texts.) In addition, Psalm 69:15 adds an explicit reference to Sheol ("the pit").

> Do not let the floodwaters engulf me
> or the depths swallow me up
> or the pit close its mouth over me.

The explicit reference to "the pit" in Psalm 69 is instructive for interpreting verses 3–5 in Psalm 124. While there the word "pit" or "Sheol" is not mentioned specifically, the image is certainly present. Leslie Allen

---

7. Keel, *The Symbolism of the Biblical World*, 73.

contends that the enemies in Psalm 124 are compared with the watery monster, which he suggests "implicitly stands for Sheol."[8] Had not Yahweh been on the side of Israel, they would have met with death.

Thanksgiving for God's Deliverance (124:6–7)

THE PSALM SHIFTS FROM WHAT DID *NOT* HAPPEN (vv. 1–3) to what *did* happen in the deliverance of the community. In verse 1b the community was invited to confess: "let Israel say." This attitude of confession continues in verses 6–7.

Praise be to the LORD. Verse 6 opens with a doxological formula, *baruk* + "the LORD." The phrase appears repeatedly in the Psalter (Pss 72:18; 89:52; 103:20, 21, 22; 106:48; 135:21; 144:1) with the primary aim of acknowledging "someone in his position of power and in his claim to greatness."[9] The NET captures the sense of the phrase: "the LORD deserves praise." In addition to denoting that Yahweh's greatness should be acknowledged, this phrase also appears in texts in which the people celebrate what God has done for them (Pss 28:6; 31:21; 66:20).[10] In Psalm 124 both senses may be in view. God's acts of deliverance demonstrate his power and greatness, and together they substantiate why Yahweh deserves praise.

Who has not let us be torn by their teeth. The second half of verse 6 explains part of the rationale for the praise that is due Yahweh. A more literal rending of the Hebrew in verse 6b explains that it was Yahweh who "did not give [*natan*] us over as prey to their teeth." As Hossfeld and Zenger have noted, in such contexts the verb *natan* "plays on the well-known formula according to which YHWH 'gives' Israel or Jerusalem 'into the hands' of the enemies."[11] For example, in Psalm 106:41 the psalmist recalls that, following Israel's disobedience in the land, "He gave them into the hand of the nations." In the first strophe of that psalm, allusions to "being swallowed" signaled political or national threats. The reference to political or national threats occurs in this verse as well.

The reference to the "teeth" is another frequently occurring metaphor in the Hebrew Bible, as apparent in Psalm 35:15b–16, and can signify a threat imposed by foreigners.[12] More specifically, in Ezekiel 22:25 the

---

8. Allen, *Psalms 101–150*, 162. See also Jonah 2:2, 3. In that context, references to water (i.e., "the depths," "seas," "waves and breakers"), Sheol, and the pit (v. 6) are intermingled, with all the references signaling a place of death.

9. Kraus, *Psalms 60–150*, 441.

10. Claus Westermann, *The Living Psalms*, trans. J. R. Porter (Grand Rapids: Eerdmans, 1989), 52.

11. Hossfeld and Zenger, *Psalms 3*, 357. See 2 Kgs 18:30; 19:10; Jer 20:4–5; 34:20–21.

12. The image of being caught in the teeth of a wild animal appears with great regularity

Babylonians are said to be "like a roaring lion tearing its prey; they devour people." The image constructed in Psalm 124:6, like that constructed in verses 3–5, is meant to convey a sense of certain death had not Yahweh been on their side.

We have escaped like a bird. The most politically overt metaphor in Psalm 124 appears in verse 7: "We have escaped like a bird from the fowler's snare [*pah*]." The imagery of the hunting metaphor signals the entrapment of the victim and its impending death or destruction. The "snare" (*pah*) is reserved primarily for the capture of birds and small prey. The trap or snare closes upon the bird, thus ensnaring it and making its escape impossible.[13] In some ancient Near Eastern texts, the image of a bird caught in a snare serves as a metaphor for death more generally, but its use in Psalm 124 reflects the more narrow, militaristic sense.

When the metaphor of a bird trapped in a cage or snare appears to have a collective sense, as in Psalm 124, the image seems to be a stock metaphor for a city under siege in the ancient Near East.[14] The *Annals of Sennacherib* make use of this ornithological metaphor when recounting the siege of Jerusalem: "As for Hezekiah, the Judean, I besieged forty-six of his fortified walled cities and surrounding towns. . . . He himself, I locked up within Jerusalem, his royal city, like a bird in a cage."[15]

The celebration of having escaped such a snare as mentioned in Psalm 124:7 presumably refers to the lifting of a siege or some other kind of deliverance from a foreign occupier. All three images in Psalm 124—water, teeth, and snare—suggest the presence of a force so menacing that it could snuff out the lives of the inhabitants of the city. In Psalm 124 the community celebrates their deliverance from such a dire fate.

Declaration of Trust (124:8)

IN THIS PSALM THE COMMUNITY gives thanks and confesses that Yahweh has been on their side. As a result, the threat of death has been averted (vv. 1–3) and deliverance has been granted (v. 6–7). Yet the community acknowledges this outcome was only possible because Yahweh was their help. The noun '*ezer*, "help," occurs often in the Old Testament, where it

---

in the Hebrew Bible (and the larger ancient Near Eastern context). See Peter Riede, *Im Netz des Jägers: Studien zur Feindmetaphorik der Individualpsalmen*, WMANT 85 (Neukirchen-Vluyn: Neukirchener Verlag, 2000), 150–94; Brown, *Seeing the Psalms*, 139.

13. Riede, *Im Netz des Jägers*, 341–43.

14. Such a statement appears in the El Armana letters as well as in Hittite literature. See the comments by Crow, *The Songs of Ascents*, 53 n. 39. The metaphor does not appear to relate to the return from exile, *contra* Satterthwaite, "Zion in the Psalms of Ascents," 120.

15. *COS*, 2:302–303.

frequently "refer[s] to the majestic 'help' of God in some sort of military situation (Exod 18:4; Deut 33:26; Ps 33:20)."[16] In Psalm 124 the stakes appear to have been quite high. The community was about to be swept away and their lives snuffed out like a bird in a snare. The concluding verse in Psalm 124 stands in stark relief to verse 2b. In verse 2 the community remembers "when people ['adam] attacked us." The threat posed by the 'adam, however, is little match for the "Maker of heaven and earth."

PSALM 124 EMPLOYS various metaphors to describe the enemy: raging waters, wild animals, and snares. These images capture the sense of helplessness experienced by the community, but even more they reflect a certain sense of powerlessness, eventuating in death. The psalmist does not identify the enemy by name or even leave any interpretive clues; the enemy is simply labeled 'adam, "people." While the term 'adam invokes idyllic scenes from the Genesis creation stories in which the breath of God enlivened human beings so that they might participate in tending to a well-ordered creation, such an idyllic image has no place in this psalm. On the contrary, the world looks like anything but a well-ordered creation—and it would have been much worse had God not been on the community's side. In referring to the enemies as 'adam, "people," the psalmist holds in tension two concepts regarding the human enemy faced by individuals and the community—themes that reverberate across the entirety of the Psalter. The enemies are at once both strong and weak, powerful and frail, arrogant and timid.

Many psalms confess that human enemies have the power to wreak havoc in the world—and that they do so. The psalmists do not shy away from mentioning the threat that comes to them in the form of other humans. A simple analysis of the Hebrew word for "enemy," 'oyeb, indicates that the term occurs seventy-four times in the book of Psalms—three times more than in any other book. This disparity only increases as words and images associated with the "enemy" word field are included, thereby indicating the prominence of the enemies in the language of the Psalter.[17] The frequency of this language suggests that the threats levied against

---

16. Nancy deClaissé-Walford, Rolf A. Jacobson, and Beth LaNeel Tanner, *The Book of Psalms*, NICOT (Grand Rapids: Eerdmans, 2014), 825.

17. On the enemy in the psalms more generally, see Hans-Joachim Kraus, *The Theology of the Psalms*, CC, trans. Keith Crim (Minneapolis: Fortress 1992), 125–36. See also the classic study by Harris Birkeland, *The Evildoers in the Book of Psalms* (Oslo: Jacob Dybwad, 1955).

the psalmists and the concomitant actions carried out against them were indeed proper subject matter for prayer—the human enemies represented a real threat to life. In Psalm 10, for example, the psalmist refers to the enemy as the *'adam* and explains that they devise schemes against the righteous, murder the innocent, and revile God.[18] In similar fashion to Psalm 124, Psalm 10 contains various hunting metaphors comparing the enemy to a lion who lies in wait or to a human on the hunt who "catches the helpless and drags them off in his net" (v. 9). Both metaphorical images signal the utter powerlessness of the psalmist in the face of great peril. Perhaps most damning, however, is the admission made by the wicked person in verse 11: "He says to himself, 'God will never notice.'" These psalms take seriously the destructive capacities of humans and nations—and even more, of their arrogance in thinking that such behavior will escape the gaze of the Divine King.

While the psalms do recognize the destructive capacity of the enemies, the psalms also acknowledge that human power is ultimately ineffectual. In Psalm 56:11 the poet confesses: "In God I trust and am not afraid. What can man [*'adam*] do to me?" And again in Psalm 118 the psalmist queries, "The LORD is with me; I will not be afraid. What can mere mortals [*'adam*] do to me?" So how does the interpreter balance this apparent tension in the text? Which view is correct? Are humans truly destructive, or is their threat only illusory? Psalm 124 seems to respond in the affirmative to both questions. The various metaphors in this poem suggest that death seemed imminent and the destructive power of the enemy was real. Yet the psalm is a song of thanksgiving; it is such because it confesses that all *human* power is ultimately illusory when compared to the help that comes from the Maker of heaven and earth. This claim takes on even greater significance when considered in the light of the congregation's confession in verses 1a and 2a. In those opening verses the congregation confesses that Yahweh was "for us" (*lanu*). With this short prepositional phrase, the community makes a profound theological claim by acknowledging that while destructive human power is real, it is not ultimate, and more importantly, while such power is real, the community has not been abandoned to face it alone. Thus, the rationale for thanksgiving is not simply that Israel's God is the Maker of heaven and earth (v. 10) but, much more significantly, that the Maker of heaven and earth is *for us*.

This claim finds its counterpart in the New Testament with Paul's assertion that "If God is for us, who can be against us?" (Rom 8:31). Paul is

---

18. In Ps 10 the Hebrew word is *'enosh*, "man," but like *'adam*, "people," it can be used in reference to the nations or people groups. See also Ps 9:19–20.

not remiss to mention those things that threaten to destroy life and separate us from the love of Christ: "trouble or hardship or persecution or famine or nakedness or danger or sword" (Rom 8:35). He understands well the same tension that existed for the community in Psalm 124, the tension between powers that seem simultaneously to be truly destructive and entirely illusory. According to Paul, all such perceived powers will be thwarted and overcome by the power and love of God, and "we are more than conquerors through him who loved us."

 ONE NEED DO LITTLE MORE than turn on the television or scan news sites on the Internet to be reminded that we live in a hostile and violent world. Even as I write the commentary on this psalm, news sources report of a double suicide bombing in Baghdad with more than seventy-five people killed in a market square. Death swallowed people up and they were swept away by the torrents of hate and despair. And in the same region of the world the innocent citizens of Syria remain like a bird in a fowler's cage as a result of political infighting, violence, and terrorism. But such violence is not just "there"; it is around us all, regardless of our address, nationality, or station in life. The destructive capacity of human beings is staggering—so staggering, in fact, that people could begin to despair. This is part of the power of the psalms. Their beautiful and artistic poetry is matched only by their unfettered realism about the brokenness of the world in which we live. The Songs of Ascent were meant to be sung by pilgrims as they made their way to Jerusalem. If there were ever a reason to become Pollyannaish about the world around us and to sweep aside the concerns of daily life, surely a holy pilgrimage would be sufficient grounds. And yet these psalms invited pilgrims to lean into the tension expressed in Psalm 124, the tension caused by humans who are, at once, strong and weak, powerful and frail, arrogant and timid.

How do we invite people to live in a world fraught with danger and violence, both explainable and unexplainable? Perhaps we remind them of another familiar text, Psalm 23. I have read this psalm at countless graveside services and alongside hospital beds of those preparing to close their eyes for the final time. But in many ways Psalm 23 is not for the dead and dying but for those living and trying to live. The bucolic images of shepherd, sheep, lush grass, and running water are abruptly interrupted by the reality of verse 4: "Even though I walk through the darkest valley, I will fear no evil, for you are with me." We need not remind people of dark valleys or impending evil—not because we have become Pollyannaish ourselves but because people are acquainted with these things all too well. The true question is whether they know the confession made in Psalms 23 and 124, the confession that claims God is "with me," God is "for us."

The community in Psalm 124 remembered well the reality of human violence in their lives and even the threat of death that seemed all but certain, yet they gave thanks for their deliverance—a deliverance achieved only because God was "for us." Amid a world of swirling waters and fowler's snares, the Maker of heaven and earth stands watch. He is our help. He is for us.

Psalm 125

A song of ascents.

¹ Those who trust in the LORD are like Mount Zion,
   which cannot be shaken but endures forever.
² As the mountains surround Jerusalem,
   so the LORD surrounds his people
   both now and forevermore.
³ The scepter of the wicked will not remain
   over the land allotted to the righteous
for then the righteous might use
   their hands to do evil.
⁴ LORD, do good to those who are good,
   to those who are upright in heart.
⁵ But those who turn to crooked ways
   the LORD will banish with the evildoers.
Peace be on Israel.

THE APPARENT DISTRESS mentioned in Psalm 125 has prompted some interpreters to suggest that this Song of Ascents is a communal complaint.[1] Although the poem does address a perilous situation, the psalm lacks a characteristic feature of communal complaints: explicit petitions to God for deliverance (cf. Ps 123:3). As a result, a number of scholars have labeled this poem a psalm of confidence or psalm of trust.[2] In explaining the rationale for this labeling of Psalm 125, Erhard Gerstenberger explains that such songs "betray an atmosphere of calmness and security . . . the words spoken are directed more to the participants in worship, praising Yahweh's trustworthiness rather than to the deity" directly.[3] The only direct petition uttered to God is found in verse 4a, but even that request differs somewhat from the kind of complaints or pleas

---

1. Allen, *Psalms 101–150*, 167; Carol Bechtel Reynolds, "Psalm 125," *Int* 48 (1994): 272–75. On the Songs of Ascent, more generally, see Ps 120.

2. deClaissé-Walford, Jacobson, and Tanner, *The Book of Psalms*; Kraus, *Psalms 2*; Gerstenberger, *Psalms, Part 2*.

3. Gerstenberger, *Psalms, Part 2*, 338.

uttered in traditional communal complaints. To suggest that Psalm 125 is a psalm of confidence does not diminish the crisis addressed in the psalm but rather indicates the posture of faith in which the psalmist confronts the reality of the crisis.

A Declaration of Trust (125:1–2)

THIS PSALM OF TRUST OPENS WITH two comparisons meant to encourage confidence on the part of those who pray the psalms. In the first example the community is compared to Mount Zion, and in the second Yahweh is compared with the mountains that encircle Jerusalem.

Those who trust in the LORD. Although this verse contains the first occurrence of the word "trust" (*batah*) in the Songs of Ascent, its rarity in this collection is not matched in the remainder of the Psalter. The word *batah* occurs more often in the Psalter than in any other book in the Old Testament, with the term frequently appearing in tandem with language and imagery that suggests God's vindication or deliverance.[4] The plural participial form of the verb (i.e., "those who trust") in verse 1a indicates that this psalm has a communal orientation, "those" refers to the community. Further, the reference to Israel in verse 2 as "his people" reinforces the communal focus of this psalm,[5] as do other terms it contains. The substantival use of the adjective in the plural ("the righteous" [v. 3]; "those who are good" [v. 4]; "those who are upright" [v. 4]) has a collective sense that sets up the comparison between "those who trust" (referring to the members of the community) versus the evildoers and those who are crooked in their way (on their identity, see below).

Are like Mount Zion. Those who trust in the Lord in the face of perilous circumstances are compared to Mount Zion, "which cannot be shaken but endures forever." In the Songs of Zion (e.g., Pss 46; 48; 87) the psalmists celebrate the stability and security of Mount Zion, and in Psalm 125:1b the poet reiterates this theme by claiming that Zion "cannot be shaken" (*mot*). The verb *mot* typically connotes something much stronger than just being "shaken" or "disturbed." More often the word means "to totter" or "to fall," as in the sense of being destroyed or falling apart (cf. Ps 60:2). In Psalm 46:5–6 the psalmist refers specifically to the security of Zion by claiming that "God is within her, she will not fall" (*mot*); despite the travails she faces, Zion will not be destroyed. Zion's security, however, is juxtaposed to the instability of the nations in Psalm 46: "Nations are

---

4. R. W. L. Moberly, "בטח," *NIDOTTE* 1:646.

5. Gerstenberger suggests that the initial participial phrase is similar to a beatitude (cf. Ps 1:1) in both form and meaning (Gerstenberger, *Psalms, Part 2*, 337).

in uproar, kingdoms fall" (*mot*). In Psalm 125 the psalmist compares the community of those who trust in Yahweh to Zion, and like Zion they too will not fall (*mot*) in the face of impending threats; rather, the community will continue to dwell in the land.[6] Goldingay aptly notes that while the comparison in verse 1 can be labeled a simile, "there is a substantial link, and not merely a figurative one, between Yahweh and Zion, and thus between the people and Zion, as well as between the people and Yahweh."[7] The simile invites theological reflection on the inherent connections that exist between Zion, Yahweh, and his people, particularly in light of the threat mentioned in verse 3.

The LORD surrounds his people. The Songs of Ascent employ a common technique by connecting one verse to the subsequent verse through the use of shared vocabulary (anadiplosis; see Ps 121). In Psalm 125:2 the psalmist makes a second comparison, and in doing so he takes the word for "mount" or "mountain" in verse 1 and makes it the operative image in verse 2. Whereas the word *har* ("mountain") was used in verse 1 in reference to Mount Zion proper, its use in verse 2 alludes to the mountains that surround Jerusalem. Although both the Old and New Testaments refer to going "up to Jerusalem," Mount Zion is not the highest point in the area. The Mount of Olives stands sixty-six meters higher than Zion, and Mount Scopus towers more than seventy-six meters above Zion, with other peaks standing higher than Zion as well.[8] The surrounding mountains function as a wall around Zion—a wall that keeps invading forces at bay. In a similar fashion Yahweh surrounds "his people" (v. 2b), thereby warding off that which threatens them. The term "surrounds" (*sabib*) is rarely used in reference to God's protective care, but in this instance it captures well the thrust of the metaphoric claim.

A Declaration of Trust Regarding the Enemy (125:3)

IN VERSES 1–2 THE PSALMIST EMPLOYS two comparisons that provide a positive declaration of trust. Both verses state positive circumstances that justify a sense of security. In verse 3, however, the psalmist provides what might be labeled a "negative" declaration of trust.[9] Here the psalmist explains

---

6. See the interesting parallel in Prov 10:30, "The righteous will never be uprooted [*mot*], but the wicked will not remain in the land."

7. Goldingay, *Psalms 3*, 485.

8. The reference to "going up" could refer to the change in elevation as people made their way from Jerusalem "up to" the Solomonic temple, an increase in elevation of more than one hundred meters (Keel, *The Symbolism of the Biblical World*, 116).

9. Goldingay, *Psalms 3*, 485.

what Yahweh will do to eradicate the threat that is before the people. This "negation" of the threat provides an additional reason for a sense of security.

The scepter of the wicked will not remain. The "scepter [*shebet*] of the wicked" mentioned in verse 3 invokes the language of an oppressive rule at the hands of a foreign power. The term "scepter" (*shebet*) itself functions metonymically and is value neutral; it simply refers to the ruler of a nation. For example, in Psalm 45:7 the word "scepter" (*shebet*) appears in the phrase "the scepter of justice" (Ps 45:6), a phrase meant to symbolize the just rule of Israelite kings. The term's connotation in Psalm 125, however, is far more ominous. Hossfeld and Zenger suggest that the phrase implies both "a political and social system," as well as the type of injustice practiced by the oppressive nations.[10] Although not precisely identical to this phrase in language, similar phrases appear in the Old Testament in reference to the nations that oppressed Israel. In Isaiah 9:4, for example, the phrase "the rod [*shebet*] of their oppressor" is used in reference to the rule of Assyria. Similarly, in referring to the king of Babylon, the writer of Isaiah 14:5 places "the scepter [*shebet*] of the rulers" in apposition to "the rod [*mateh*] of the wicked."

In Psalm 125:3 the psalmist states that the "scepter of the wicked will not remain [*nuah*] over the land allotted to the righteous." Since the verb *nuah* can mean "to rest," its use in this context could suggest that the scepter of wickedness has yet to "rest" upon the land. While this meaning is possible, the preferred meaning seems to be "to remain."[11] Later in the psalm (v. 5), the poet asserts that those within the community who turn aside to wicked ways will be led away with the "evildoers." As Allen avers, the psalmist makes "a plea for Yahweh to deal with renegades who have broken the covenant and forfeited their share in the land by expelling them and their foreign patrons."[12] By implication, the "evildoers" are already in the land, thus suggesting that the "scepter of the wicked" has already exerted its influence.[13]

The land allotted to the righteous. In verse 3 the psalmist suggests two reasons why the scepter of the wicked should not remain. He explains that the scepter currently rules over the "land allotted to the righteous."

---

10. Hossfeld and Zenger, *Psalms 3*, 366.

11. Allen, *Psalms 101–150*, 166.

12. Ibid.

13. Erhard Gerstenberger suggests that the first two Hebrew words in verse 3 (*ki-lo*) serve to introduce a negative wish formula: "May the scepter of wickedness not remain" (Gerstenberger, *Psalms, Part 2 and Lamentations*, 337).

The expected word for "land" (*'erets*) does not appear in this context; instead, the psalmist refers to a "lot" or an "allotment" (*goral*). This word has its greatest concentration in the book of Joshua—twenty-six appearances, or more than twice the appearances found in any other book in the Old Testament—and in that context the term refers to the allotment of the land to the people of Israel upon their entry into it. By using this term in Psalm 125, the poet seeks to construct an important argument. The "scepter of the wicked" cannot remain in the land because this land does not belong to them; this land belongs to the ones to whom it was allotted, "the righteous."

The psalmist also provides a second, more explicit rationale for why the wicked cannot remain in the land: if they do, the faithful ones might use their hands for evil. Other postexilic texts suggest that, under the influence of the occupying Persians, the community in Yehud turned upon itself and its members carried out injustice toward one another, as in Nehemiah 5. That chapter recounts how Nehemiah chastised the Jewish leaders in Jerusalem for charging interest on their own people (v. 7) despite the prohibitions in Exodus 2:25, Leviticus 25:35–37, and Deuteronomy 23:19–20. In Leviticus the community is commanded, "Do not take interest or any profit from [the poor], but fear your God, so they may continue to live among you. You must not lend them money at interest or sell them food at a profit" (Lev 25:36–37). Apparently these torah requirements were being ignored, thus causing some people in the post-exilic community to sell their sons and daughters into slavery (Neh 5:5). Such behavior was surely understood as evil. Whether or not this matter is the one in view in Psalm 125:3 is impossible to determine, but the scope of verse 3 certainly would have encompassed this action and others like it.

The Petition (125:4–5)

IN THE LIGHT OF THE CIRCUMSTANCES recounted in verse 3 (i.e., the presence of "the scepter of the wicked" upon the land), the psalmist contends that the members of the community must choose one of two paths. Either they can align themselves with those who choose to do good, or they can align themselves with those who "turn to crooked ways." The contrast of the "two ways" of living appears first in Psalm 1 but reappears repeatedly in the Psalter (cf. Ps 37:8–11). Each "way" reflects a particular orientation in life, and each orientation leads to a certain end. In Psalm 1, for example, the life of the righteous person is oriented toward the law of Yahweh; such a person delights in God's law and meditates on it. As a result, the Lord watches over his way (Ps 1:6)—but "not so the wicked" (v. 4a). Their life is oriented away from God; consequently, their path leads to destruction.

In Psalm 125 the poet petitions Yahweh to act in behalf of those who are "upright in heart." The word "upright" comes from the root *yshr*, which has as its root meaning "to be straight." The word's use in texts such as Ezekiel 1:7 and Isaiah 40:3 retain this nuance of being straight, as in a straight leg or a straight way in the desert. Proverbs 3:6 invokes the same root but in a metaphorical sense. There the sage writes, "In all your ways submit to him, and he will make your paths *yashar* ['straight']." In Psalm 125:4 the writer refers to those who are "*yashar* ['straight'] of heart," those who have willingly chosen the ways of God. The language of being "straight of heart" stands in contrast to those mentioned in verse 5a, "those who turn to crooked ways." The word for "crooked ways" (*'aqalqal*) is rare in the Old Testament and suggests a twisting or winding path (cf. Judg 5:6). Thus, the psalmist lifts up two images: the one who remains "straight of heart" and the one who turns to a twisted or crooked path.

The poet also assures the community that toward each kind of person, Yahweh acts with justice. In verse 4 the psalmist requests that Yahweh will do good to those who are straight of heart. The certainty of his petition is matched by the certainty of his statement in verse 5. Those who make their ways crooked will be led away with the "evildoers." In this case the evildoers are the foreigners associated with the scepter of the wicked in verse 3, and the "crooked ones" are those who have chosen to align themselves with them. In orienting their lives with the evildoers, the crooked ones can anticipate the same fate—they will be banished (v. 5b).

The psalm concludes with a benediction: "Peace be upon Israel." Although many recognize the final phrase as a gloss, Kraus is correct in his assessment that it serves as the "real theme of the psalm."[14] The poem announces the end of the evildoers and those who desire to be like them. That will bring to the land peace, *shalom*, in all its fullness.

PSALM 125 REMINDS WORSHIPERS of two fundamental truths central to the Christian faith: the world can be a dangerous place, and Yahweh can be a sure refuge. The psalmist seeks to hold both truths in tandem from his understanding that a proper view of both leads to true worship and faithful living.

Living in a troubled world. Like many of the Songs of Ascent, this psalm speaks candidly about a troubled and troubling world that threatens

---

14. Kraus, *Psalm 60–150*, 446. See also Crow, *The Songs of Ascents (Psalms 120–134)*, 130–36.

the faithful. The kinds of threats posed in Psalm 125 are more than existential threats, although they are surely that as well. The scepter of the wicked lords it over them, thereby destabilizing their world and tempting the righteous to "do evil." The last verse of the psalm suggests that some people have already capitulated to the temptation to do evil, so their lives can only be described as "crooked ways." The presence of such threats, however, does not seem surprising to the psalmist—such menacing circumstances appear to be the norm in a broken world. Contrary to the views of Karl Marx and many others, Christianity has little room in its theology for an escapist ideology. Like the psalmist in Psalm 125, the Christian faith does not ignore the world, nor does it seek to escape the trouble inherent to it. Christianity readily accepts that such is life in a broken creation (Rom 8:20–22). In 1 Peter 4:12 Peter instructs the community, "Dear friends, do not be surprised at the fiery ordeal that has come on you to test you, as though something strange were happing to you." If the Christian faith is not an escapist religion, and if such "fiery ordeals" are not surprising, then how should a Christian live in such times? The response involves a mixture of right belief and right praxis, or perhaps better said, right belief that issues in right action. Peter returns to this theme later in 1 Peter 4 when he exhorts the community by saying, "So then, those who suffer according to God's will should commit themselves to their faithful Creator and continue to do good" (1 Pet 4:19). Peter contends that trials and struggles should not lead people away from God; instead, such realities should drive believers toward God by compelling them to commit (or recommit) themselves to God, which in turn, should lead to right action.

A more explicit parallel to this theme in Psalm 125 appears in 2 Timothy 3:12–15. There Paul refers to his own sufferings in the world and then explains that all followers of Christ can expect persecution and trouble in this life (v. 12). In the midst of such trying circumstances there will be two paths, two orientations. Some people will fail to orient themselves to the ways of God (v. 13). He labels that group as "evildoers and imposters" and suggests that they will "go from bad to worse, deceiving and being deceived" in the face of such trials. They will "turn to crooked ways" (Ps 125:5). But there are others who still desire to orient their lives toward God. To those persons he gives encouragement and exhorts them to "continue in what you have learned and have become convinced of" (2 Tim 3:14).

For the community in Yehud, and any community, the gravity associated with the reality of life could have provided a "reasonable excuse" for people to jettison their fundamental commitments of faith. Similarly, the gravity associated with the reality of life could provide a "reasonable excuse" for any person to escape into a religious cocoon and assume that such an existence is truly authentic life. The biblical witness, however, rejects both extremes and instead invites believers to live fully in this world with lives oriented toward God

Protection of God. Psalm 125 continues to reinforce a repeated theme in the Songs of Ascent: the protection of God. To be more specific, these psalms are variations on this theme. Some psalms celebrate the protection that has already been afforded by God, while others turn to God in supplications which ask that this kind of protection be granted now. Psalm 120 pleads with Yahweh for protection and deliverance (v. 2) due to the lying lips and threats of war that surround the psalmist. Psalm 121 celebrates that, as the Maker of heaven and earth (v. 2), God watches over his people and will keep them from all harm. Psalm 122 refers to Jerusalem and the "house of the LORD" present within the city—both are images of security and safety in a troubled time. Psalm 123 pleads with God to have mercy on his people by bringing an end to the shame that their enemies have brought on them; the psalmist seeks the kind of protection a master would provide for his household. Psalm 124 celebrates that, because God was on the people's side, they escaped the perils of foreign threats. This psalm, Psalm 125, returns to the theme of a foreign threat with the reference to the "scepter of the wicked." Whereas the first five poems in the Songs of Ascent allude to the hostile world in which the psalmists live, Psalm 125 is the first psalm to make explicit reference to the nature of the threat. Hossfeld and Zenger have suggested that Psalms 125 and 129 serve as a framing device in the middle section of the Songs of Ascent collection (Pss 125–29).[15] Both poems contain an overt political reference, and both mention the "righteous" and the "wicked." In fact, these psalms are the only two poems in this collection that mention both groups.

As suggested above, all these psalms suggest that the world in which the poets live contains threats that are real, dangerous, and omnipresent. Despite the seemingly omnipresent nature of these enemies, the psalmists are quick to assert the certainty that the enemies are not omnipotent. While these enemies do pose threats, they are no threat to God. In Psalm 48 the psalmist declares that the kings all joined forces to come against Jerusalem, but when they saw God in the city's fortress they "were astounded; they fled in terror. Trembling seized them there, pain like that of a woman in labor" (vv. 4–6). Because the enemies pose no threat to God, the community can trust (Ps 125:1) that God is their refuge. He encircles them as their protector, even as the mountains encircle Jerusalem.

---

15. Hossfeld and Zenger, *Psalms 3*, 367.

PSALM 125, AND TEXTS LIKE IT, both comfort us and challenge us, assure us and compel us. The psalm begins by noting the kind of protection afforded by the God we serve and shifts in verse 4 to challenging us to remain "straight of heart." To complicate matters, however, surrounding the challenge to remain upright of heart is the previous verse, which refers to the scepter of the wicked (v. 3), and the following verse, which alludes to those who have abandoned their faith commitments (v. 5). The call to remain faithful is "hemmed in," if you will, with texts that remind us of the reasons why faithfulness is difficult, and trust in God even more so. There are many people to whom we minister and with whom we live and work who feel hemmed in. While the names and identities may differ from those mentioned in Psalm 125, the crisis does not. The reality of the wicked and the temptation of crooked ways both before us and behind us makes it seem as though God is no longer present, much less our protector. What we all long to know is that we are not alone in such circumstances, and even more, that perhaps, just perhaps, we might encounter the protective presence of God amid such trials. In his work *The Magnificent Defeat*, Frederick Buechner writes:

> For what we need to know, of course, is not just that God exists, not just that beyond the steely brightness of the stars there is a cosmic intelligence of some kind that keeps the whole show going, but that there is a God right here in the thick of our day-to-day lives who may not be writing messages about himself in the stars but in one way or another is trying to get messages through our blindness as we move around down here knee deep in the fragrant muck and misery and marvel of the world. It is not objective proof of God's existence that we want but the experience of God's presence. That is the miracle that we are all really after and that is also, I think, the miracle that we really get.[16]

The psalmist invites those who pray this psalm to make a confession. The admission that not all is right with the world is only part of this confession, albeit an important part. The greater confession concerns the protective care of the pray-ers' God. As certain as they are of wicked rulers, evildoers, and those who have chosen crooked paths, they are to be equally assured—no, even more assured—of the presence of their God.

---

16. Frederick Buechner, *The Magnificent Defeat* (San Francisco: Harper and Row, 1985), 47.

As noted above, the Songs of Zion suggest that when God is present in Jerusalem the city is inviolable, her people secure. God's presence and God's protection prove sufficient in a world that appears unruly and unstable. The psalmist invites the community to look around and see—to see the hills 'round about Jerusalem and to remember. They are to be reminded that, as sure as the mountains surround the city, so too can they be sure that God surrounds them.

In a world that appears both unruly and unstable, people today still wonder whether God is sufficient to be our protector. Because we have become blinded, as Buechner suggests, we have lost sight of his presence. And when we lose sight of his presence, it is far easier to choose the crooked paths offered by seductive powers than to remain straight of heart and choose to do *his* good will. In such moments we need the good news of Psalm 125; we need to be reminded that God indeed surrounds his people.

Psalm 126

A song of ascents.

¹ When the LORD restored the fortunes of Zion,
    we were like those who dreamed.
² Our mouths were filled with laughter,
    our tongues with songs of joy.
Then it was said among the nations,
    "The LORD has done great things for them."
³ The LORD has done great things for us,
    and we are filled with joy.
⁴ Restore our fortunes, LORD,
    like streams in the Negev.
⁵ Those who sow with tears
    will reap with songs of joy.
⁶ Those who go out weeping,
    carrying seed to sow,
will return with songs of joy,
    carrying sheaves with them.

Original Meaning

PSALM 126 IS THE SEVENTH of the Songs of Ascent (see Ps 120) and may be divided into two strophes: verses 1–3 and 4–6. Although some interpreters argue for a three-part division of the psalm (vv. 1–3, 4, 5–6), the twofold division seems preferable for a number of reasons.[1] Most noticeably, the perspective of time in verses 1–3 shifts in verses 4–6. The preposition *bet* + infinitive ("when the LORD restored") in verse 1a followed by the perfect form of the verb ("we were") in verse 1b points to a past event. The remaining verses in the first strophe point back to subsequent events in the past. The second strophe begins with an imperative ("Restore") in verse 4a and refers to a desired future. In addition to the changing perspective of time, the two strophes change the locus of the action in each section. In the first strophe the action takes place on the world stage; the action culminates in the confession of the

---

1. Those who argue for a threefold division include Kraus, *Psalms 60–150* and Anderson, *Introduction and Psalms 1–72*.

nations in verse 2b and of the Jewish community in verse 3. In the second strophe the psalmist returns to the agricultural imagery consistent with the familial context found in other Songs of Ascent (i.e., sowing and reaping; vv. 5–6).[2] With these strophes taken together, the psalm functions as a communal lament. The first three verses recall Yahweh's earlier action of restoration; this remembrance provides the rationale for the subsequent plea for restoration and deliverance in the second half of the psalm.[3]

Remembering Yahweh's Return to Zion (126:1–3)

IN THE FIRST THREE VERSES OF PSALM 126, the community looks back and remembers when Yahweh returned to Zion. This remembrance provides the impetus for the plea in the latter half of the psalm.[4]

The LORD restored the fortunes of Zion. The opening phrase in verse 1, *shub shibat* ("restored the fortunes of"), has generated considerable debate among interpreters. In particular, the Hebrew word *shibat* has proven challenging to interpret. The word *shibat* does not appear elsewhere in the Old Testament, thus making its precise meaning even more difficult to determine.[5] Translators have understood the term to derive from the Hebrew root *shbb*, "to take captive." This move appears to have been the one made in the NIV's 1984 translation, "When the LORD brought back the captives to Zion." The NIV's 2011 translation, however, reads noticeably differently: "When the LORD restored the fortunes of Zion." The change in translating *shibat* from "brought back the *captives* to Zion" to "restored the *fortunes* of Zion" likely stems from two observations. First, an Aramaic contractual text from Sifre (eighth century BCE) has been found; it contains the two terms, *shub* and *shibat*. In this text, the deity is mentioned as the subject, and the context appears to be that of restoration, not captivity.

---

2. For an extended discussion concerning the twofold division of the psalm, see Hossfeld and Zenger, *Psalms 3*, 374–75.

3. While many interpreters classify this psalm as a communal lament, Gerstenberger classifies the psalm as one of communal thanksgiving based on the celebratory tone of the first three verses (Gerstenberger, *Psalms, Part 2*, 338).

4. Not all interpreters read Ps 126 in this manner. Most notably is Walter Beyerlin. In his monograph on Ps 126, Beyerlin argues that the first three verses are in fact not about the past; rather, they point to the future. For Beyerlin these verses refer to the coming restoration of Zion, an event that was revealed to the people in a dream (v. 1b). Beyerlin's position has failed to garner considerable support among subsequent interpreters, due in large part to the language and structure of the first three verses, which, as suggested above, appear to point to a past event. See Walter Beyerlin, *We are Like Dreamers: Studies in Psalm 126* (Edinburgh: T&T Clark, 1982).

5. The Septuagint renders the term *aichmalōsia*, "captivity," hence the translation, "the LORD returned the captivity of Zion."

The phrase is translated "the gods brought about the restoration of my father's house." This translation suggests that the term *shibat* need not be limited to the notion of captivity and may also include the larger meaning of "the restoration of a previous situation."[6] Second, the imperative phrase in verse 4a, *shub shebut*, "Restore our fortunes," is the more expected form and normally refers to the returning of possessions (cf. Pss 14:7; 85:2).[7] This same phrase in verse 4a (*shub shebut*, "Restore our fortunes") appears in the prophetic literature associated with the exile (cf. Jer 32:44; 33:26; Ezek 16:53) and seems to refer to the restoration of Zion. Thus, the phrase in verse 1a, *shub shibat*, and the phrase in verse 4a, *shub shebut*, function synonymously and serve to introduce the two main sections of the psalm. The first section recalls when God did restore the fortunes of Zion, and the second pleads with Yahweh to act once more in Zion's behalf.

We were like those who dreamed. In remembering when Yahweh restored the fortunes of Zion, the psalmist says the community was "like those who dream." While the verb *halam* can mean "to dream," there are occurrences in which the term can also mean "to be strong" (Job 39:4) or even "to restore to health" (Is 38:16).[8] While the latter two definitions may be intriguing, the reference to dreaming seems most apparent. Hossfeld and Zenger are correct to caution that to refer to a group as "like those who dreamed" does not imply that they were "only" dreaming, or that they were deceiving themselves, or worse yet, that "they had experienced something that later proved to be a 'mere dream.'"[9] Rather, the idea of a dream in the ancient Near East was understood as a medium for divine revelation—a means for communicating what was about to happen or what was in fact already happening.[10] Thus when the community declared that they were dreamers at that time, they were not invoking "pie-in-the-sky" language or some hoped for but yet unrealized expectation. To the contrary, as dreamers they were announcing that Yahweh's work of restoration was at hand.

6. See Herbert Donner and Wolfgang Röllig, *Kanaanäische und aramäische Inschriften*, 3 vols. (Weisbaden: Harrassowitz, 1971), 3:24. See also the interpretive discussion in Hossfeld and Zenger, *Psalms 3*, 370–71. See also the assessment of the matter in Dahood, *Psalms 101–150*, 217–18; and more recently, Crow, *The Songs of Ascents (Psalms 120–134)*, 59–63.

7. To complicate matters further, the Qere reading in verse 4 reads *shibat* in place of *shebut*. This is likely an attempt by those compiling the Masoretic text to make the two forms parallel—a move that is ultimately unnecessary.

8. "חלם," *HALOT* 1:320–21. The Septuagint obviously understood *halam* along the lines of the last definition in translating the term as *parakeklēmenoi*, "we became like people comforted."

9. Hossfeld and Zenger, *Psalms 3*, 375.

10. Ibid., 375–76.

Our mouths were filled with laughter. Language of joy and celebration in light of God's work of restoration appears repeatedly in Isaiah
40–55 and Jeremiah 30–33 (i.e., the Book of Consolation). In Isaiah 51:11,
for example, those returning home to Zion shall come with "singing," and
they shall obtain "gladness and joy." Perhaps more analogous to Psalm 126
is Jeremiah 30:19. In that context Yahweh announces that he will "restore
the fortunes of his people" (*shub shebut*), and then the nation will return
home with thanksgiving and with the "sound of rejoicing." The word for
rejoicing, *tsahaq*, in Jeremiah 30 is the same word in Psalm 126:2. Similarly,
the word for joy, *rinnah*, in Psalm 126:2b ("our tongues with songs of joy")
also occurs in Isaiah 51:11. These intertextual references are not meant to
suggest that the psalmist borrowed this language from one or both of the
prophetic books but instead are meant to suggest that these references do
signal a certain continuity of thought among those who had endured the
exile. In Isaiah and Jeremiah, as well as in Psalm 126, the restoration of
God's people is always followed by joy, evidenced by laughter and singing.

The theme of joy or rejoicing (*rinnah*) occurs in both halves of Psalm
126 (vv. 2, 5, 6) and serves as the unifying theme of the psalm.[11] In the first
half of the psalm, *rinnah* appears in reference to God's restorative work in
the past; in the second half, the word follows God's restorative work yet
to come.

The LORD has done great things. God's work of restoration yielded
two confessions—one by the nations and the other by the community.
Throughout the Psalter the nations stand in opposition to the people of
God. Frequently this opposition comes in the form of mocking questions
concerning the apparent absence of Israel's God from the world stage.
Following the exile, this kind of mockery no doubt became even more
acute. According to the various psalmists the nations would ask derisively,
"Where is your God?"[12] In Psalm 126, however, the derisive and mocking
tone of the nations gives way to their confession: "The LORD has done great
things for them." The community reports that God's act of restoration
proved so decisive that even the nations had to recognize Israel's God as
supreme. Prophetic texts from the exilic period connected God's activity
with the turning of the nations to God and his people. In Isaiah 49:7 the
prophet clams that kings and princes alike will fall prostrate because of the
faithfulness of Israel's God (cf. Isa 49:23).

---

11. deClaissé-Walford, Jacobson, and LaNeel Tanner, *The Book of Psalms*, 915.
12. See for example Pss 42:3; 79:10; 115:2. For matters related to quotations of the
enemy in the Psalter see Rolf A. Jacobson, *"Many are Saying:" The Function of Direct Discourse
in the Hebrew Psalter*, LHBOTS 397 (New York: T&T Clark, 2004).

This confession was not reserved for the nations alone. The confession made by the nations in verse 2b now appears on the lips of the community in verse 3. In light of God's work of restoration, and perhaps even in light of the confession by the nations, the community was filled with "joy." The word "joy" appears in verses 2b and 3b, both times on the mouths of the community. Despite the translation's use of the same English word, however, the Hebrew actually employs two different terms, *rinnah* and *sameah*. Strikingly, both terms appear in Isaiah 51:11. There the prophet announces that God will bring back his people to Zion with singing (*rinnah*) and everlasting joy (*sameah*). The prophet looked forward in announcing that joy would follow restoration; the community in Psalm 126 looked backward in confessing that restoration had begun because joy had filled their lives. The NIV translates the last phrase in verse 3 as "we are filled with joy," but the perfect form of the Hebrew verb would imply that this final phrase should also be understood in the past—"we were filled with joy."

Petition for God's Work of Restoration (126:4–6)

THE FIRST HALF OF THE PSALM recalled when Yahweh returned the fortunes of the people to Zion. In the second half of the psalm the community pivots to request that Yahweh restore them once more. Whereas the first three verses suggest that Yahweh demonstrated his power on the "world stage" (i.e., the confession of the nations), the second half of the psalm concentrates solely "on the effective power and nearness of YHWH to be experienced in everyday life by the community."[13] The simple agricultural images prove powerfully rich metaphors of hope.

Restore our fortunes, LORD. The community's petition in verse 4 nearly repeats the language used in verse 1. The opening words in verse 1a, *shub shibat*, are similar to the phrase in verse 4a, *shub shebut*, with both phrases suggesting "to restore the fortunes."[14] Allen proposes that the variation in terms may be understood as "a pointer to a new beginning at verse 4 and as a means of differentiating the changes of fortune as separate events."[15] While verses 1 and 4 refer to the restorative work of Yahweh, the community clearly envisions two separate moments in the life of Israel. In verse 1 the community recalls how Yahweh had restored the fortunes of Zion at some

13. Hossfeld and Zenger, *Psalms 3*, 377.

14. The Qere reading of the verse suggests reading *shibat* in the place of *shebut*, thus explaining the alternative reading provided in the NIV's note for verse 4a: "Bring back our captives." Likely the scribes sought to emend the text in verse 4 so that it would correspond to the form in verse 1.

15. Allen, *Psalms 101–150*, 174.

point in the past. The restoration at that moment was significant enough to warrant a confession by the nations (and the community of Israel) that what occurred should be listed among the "great things" or great deeds of Yahweh in behalf of his people. Despite this restoration and the celebratory singing that followed, full restoration apparently remained lacking.[16] As a result, the community pleads in verse 4, "Restore our fortunes, LORD."

Like streams in the Negev. During the summer months, the wadis (or riverbeds) of the Middle East become dry and appear as little more than gashes in the landscape. But with the winter rains these riverbeds fill quickly with water, and the once barren landscape comes to life. With the request in verse 4 the community acknowledges that they were experiencing a "dry season" and were in desperate need of the fructifying presence of God once more. The point of comparison is the suddenness with which the wadis swell during a rain, as well as the depth and power of these raging waters. In Psalm 124 the psalmist referred to the raging waters and lamented over their life-*threatening* power. In Psalm 126, however, the psalmist acknowledges their life-*giving* power. The community desires a sudden display of divine favor in which God overwhelms them with blessings.

Those who sow with tears. The agricultural metaphors continue in the final two verses of the psalm with a basic juxtaposition between planting and gathering. The former involves much weeping, the latter much joy. Most interpreters have noted the similarities between these verses and the religious myths in Ugarit and Egypt related to agriculture. In those cultures, the planting of seed in the ground was associated with burying the fertility god(s). As a sign of grief, sowing was equated with weeping and sorrow. According to these traditions, when the "dead" seed comes to life and when it has arrived at full stature, there is reason for joyful celebration at the harvest. While these myths circulated within the larger framework of ancient Near Eastern thought, they need not be pressed too far in the interpretation of Psalm 126. Mays is correct in saying that the images likely functioned as a cultural idiom associating sowing with weeping and harvesting with joy.[17] While the original meaning of the phrase may have been applied strictly to agriculture, its use in this psalm

---

16. The restoration promised by the exilic prophets appears wanting in the postexilic period. Several of the postexilic prophets allude to the impoverished conditions faced by the community in that period. See Hag 1:3–11 and Mal 1:2–5. While both prophetic books attribute the community's struggle to their continued sin, they both also illustrate the less-than-idyllic circumstances faced by the community.

17. Mays, *Psalms*, 400. Gerstenberger suggests that the agricultural imagery drawn from everyday life can likely also be associated with Israel's wisdom traditions (Gerstenberger, *Psalms, Part 2*, 340–41).

has expanded—what began in weeping will end in rejoicing. God will come and restore the fortunes of his people such that a present moment defined by barrenness and sorrow will be transformed into a future filled with shouts of joy and arms full with the harvest.

 THE LANGUAGE OF PSALM 126 suggests something of the lingering trauma associated with the exile and the subsequent return. Not surprisingly, this psalm explicitly mentions the restoration of Zion, an event placed on par with the "great things" Yahweh has done for his people (vv. 2d, 3a). Contemporary readers of Scripture tend to think of the exile solely in political terms, and understandably so. Under the leadership of Nebuchadnezzar II the Babylonians laid siege to Jerusalem in 597 BCE and deported King Jehoiachin, his wives, the king's mother, and a number of "officials and the prominent people" in the land (2 Kgs 24:15). Zedekiah was placed on the throne as a Babylonian puppet king, but after his attempts to create an alliance with the Egyptians failed, the Babylonians invaded Jerusalem in 586 BCE and laid waste the entire city. The walls were destroyed, the city plundered, and the temple razed to the ground.[18]

While the political implications are significant, the biblical witness also mentions the devastation this event brought upon the actual land of Israel itself. The events of 586 BCE were not limited to the city of Jerusalem— the countryside was also devastated, as were the surrounding towns and cities. Jeremiah refers to the utter destruction that would come upon the land itself as a result of the exile. In Jeremiah 4:23–26 he writes:

> I looked at the earth,
>   and it was formless and empty;
> And at the heavens,
>   and their light was gone.
> I looked at the mountains,
>   and they were quaking;
>   all the hills were swaying.
> I looked, and there were no people,
>   every bird in the sky had flown away.
> I looked, and the fruitful land was a desert.

---

18. The destructive work of the Babylonians in and around Jerusalem is recorded in 2 Kgs 25:8–21.

Because of the exile, Jeremiah explains that the created order would become "uncreated"—all that was once pronounced good would no longer be so. In summative fashion Yahweh announces that "the whole land will be ruined" (Jer 4:27). Walter Brueggemann opines that "the exile of Israel concerns not just geographical displacement, but the cessation of life possibilities, the withdrawal of fruitfulness."[19] In reading Psalm 126 we would do well to remember the fullness of the trauma associated with the exile. The deportation of the royal family and the officials to Babylon coupled with the destruction of Jerusalem and the temple would have removed any hope of a future for God's people.

Despite the seeming impossibility of restoration, however, verses 1–3 recall how Yahweh had restored the fortunes of Zion through returning those in exile back to Jerusalem. Undoubtedly, this event was momentous, as the confession of both the nations and the community suggests. But beginning in verse 4 the reader is reminded that not all has been restored. In verse 1 the community speaks of the continuing need for the restoration of Zion's fortunes. In verse 4 the community pleads for Yahweh to "restore *our* fortunes" (emphasis added). The images invoked in the second strophe of the psalm all have to do with the land—perhaps understandably so, given the devastation wrought upon the land as a result of the Babylonian occupation. Loren Crow suggests that the agricultural imagery reflects the concerns of "individual Israelite landowners whose fate is almost wholly determined by whether crops will be abundant or scarce."[20] For Crow, this psalm is focused on "concerns of a more mundane sort."[21] Without question, such mundane matters would have occupied the thoughts of the community, but the imagery in Psalm 126 suggests that they may also have had loftier thoughts in view.

A number of biblical texts refer to the "re-fructification" of the land following the exile; what was once a desert (Jer 4:26) will be restored to full life. This idea is seen most clearly in Isaiah 51:3, where the prophet announces that, upon Israel's return to the land, Yahweh will "look with compassion on all her ruins; he will make her deserts like Eden, her wastelands like the garden of the LORD." In similar fashion, Ezekiel reports that, following the exile and the return of the presence of God, the waters from the temple will flow, thereby turning the hyper-saline water of the Dead Sea into fresh water. There will be abundant aquatic life in it, and people will be able to feed off the fruit-bearing trees that will grow along its shores.

---

19. Brueggemann, *Theology of the Old Testament*, 542.
20. Crow, *The Songs of Ascents*, 64.
21. Ibid.

Although these prophetic announcements have a certain hyperbolic ring to them, they are meant to suggest the life-giving, life-transforming impact of God's restoration. The request in verse 4 for Yahweh to restore the fortunes of his people refers to agricultural prosperity, but not because agricultural prosperity is the ultimate good. Songs of joy and armloads of harvest signal the fullness of God's restorative work among his people— they are signs of a much larger work among them. By confessing that Yahweh has restored the fortunes of Zion, the community understands that the restoration has started. By requesting that God "restore our fortunes," they acknowledge that restoration has not come fully. The community leans into a proleptic sense of restoration—it is already here, but not yet.

 LIKE MANY OF THE Songs of Ascent, Psalm 126 is deceptive in its brevity. While only six verses in length, the language and imagery of the psalm speaks powerfully to our human condition and our divine hope.

Joy amid weeping. As noted above, the theme of joy pervades this psalm. The Hebrew terms *rinnah* ("songs of joy") and *sameah* ("joy") appear in verses 2 and 3, respectively, and *rinnah* appears again in verses 5 and 6. Yet the language of joy in this psalm must be heard amid the weeping, lest joy be mistaken for happiness. The first strophe (vv. 1–3) does not record weeping; it simply picks up the story once Zion has been restored. If one did not know the "backstory," he or she might think the references to their mouths as filled with laughter (v. 2) and the repeated mentions of joy seem overdrawn and excessive. The book of Lamentations, however, provides a sobering backdrop to the jubilatory language in Psalm 126:1–3. In the opening verses of the book, the poet speaks of Daughter Zion: "Bitterly she weeps at night, tears are on her cheeks" (Lam 1:2). Later in the chapter Daughter Zion references her eyes that "overflow with tears" (v. 16). The celebratory language in the first part of Psalm 126 comes out of such weeping. The community remembers fondly that it was Yahweh who turned their mourning into dancing (Ps 30:11).

The second half of the psalm also serves as a reminder that joy must be heard amid weeping. The agricultural imagery of planting is coupled with tears and weeping. It is the harvest that will bring shouts of joy, but the harvest will come only if the seed has been planted—weeping and all. To plant anything is an act of faith. The end cannot be known, only trusted. The community in Psalm 126 trusted that the end was safely and securely in the hands of Yahweh, so they prayed, "Restore our fortunes, LORD."

As Henri Nouwen reminds us, "By inviting God into our difficulties we ground life—even in its sad moments—in joy and hope."[22] Weeping does not have the last word.

Memory and hope. The request to "Restore our fortunes, LORD" in verse 4 has a long history, or perhaps better stated, the request itself is the *result* of a long history between Yahweh and his people. Within the Psalter there are historical psalms (e.g., Pss 78; 105; 106) meant to recount the mighty deeds of God. More than simply preserving a historical record, these psalms are meant to prescribe a particular identity. They remind each generation that its identity is embedded in a story. But even more, these historical recollections remind people that, in their acts of faithful remembering, they discover the grounds for an expectant hope.

In the Christian calendar, Psalm 126 is read during the seasons of Advent and Lent. In these seasons memory and hope play a powerful role. We read and reread the birth narratives of Jesus, thus grounding our identity in a story and hearing the good news of an expectant hope. As we make our way through the season of Lent, we "sow with tears" and "go out weeping" as we are reminded of our own stories of frailty and waywardness. Yet in Lent we are also reminded that we are a people of hope because our tears will give way to an empty tomb. We remember that story so that we might hope, so that we too might return with songs of joy.

---

22. Henri Nouwen, *Turn My Mourning into Dancing* (Nashville: Nelson, 2001), xv.

Psalm 127

A song of ascents. Of Solomon.

¹ Unless the LORD builds the house,
  those who build it labor in vain.
Unless the LORD watches over the city,
  the guards stand watch in vain.
² In vain you rise early
  and stay up late,
toiling for food to eat—
  for he grants sleep to those he loves.
³ Children are a heritage from the LORD,
  offspring a reward from him.
⁴ Like arrows in the hand of a warrior
  are children born in one's youth.
⁵ Blessed is the man
  whose quiver is full of them.
They will not be put to shame
  when they contend with their opponents in court.

PSALM 127 IS A WISDOM POEM, as evidenced by both its rhetorical features and its thematic concerns.[1] Although short, Psalm 127 contains three different types of wisdom sayings: the truth saying or proverb (v. 1), the comparison (v. 4), and the beatitude (v. 5). Hossfeld and Zenger suggest that verse 2 is also a proverbial saying, even though the final line of that verse breaks with traditional wisdom thought.[2] Thematically, the psalm advises on everyday conduct—a theme echoed in other wisdom texts (cf. Prov 5–7). Although elsewhere in Scripture (cf. Prov 10–22) a number of wisdom sayings involve a comparison between the righteous and the wicked, Psalm 127 says nothing of the wicked and only obliquely references the righteous life. The implication, however, is that by heeding the wisdom of this psalm, individuals will discover life.

---

1. Psalm 127 is the first of three wisdom-influenced psalms in the Songs of Ascent. See also Pss 128 and 133. On the Songs of Ascent as a collection, see Ps 120.
2. Hossfeld and Zenger, *Psalms 3*, 384.

The wisdom features of Psalm 127 also likely explain the reference to Solomon in the superscription. Many of the rhetorical forms present in Psalm 127 are found in the books of Proverbs and Ecclesiastes, both of which are associated with Solomon in various ways. Beyond the literary features of the Psalm 127 itself, the poem may have been associated with Solomon because of the mention of "those he loves" in verse 2d. In 2 Samuel 12, following the death of their firstborn, David and Bathsheba have a second son, Solomon. Nathan the prophet instructs the couple to name the child "Jedidiah," which means "beloved of Yahweh." The reference to the "beloved one" in verse 2d creates an association between Solomon and this label. A third reason for associating Solomon with this psalm involves the subject matter of the psalm itself: the building of a house and the guarding of a city. Within Israel's tradition Solomon is honored for having built the temple of Jerusalem and secured the city (cf. 1 Kgs 6–7).

Psalm 127 can easily be divided into two strophes, verses 1–2 and 3–5. The clear division between the two sections, both in form and content, has led some interpreters to suggest that the two halves of the poem were originally two different proverbial sayings that were later combined to create a composite psalm.[3] More recent interpreters, however, have argued that despite the differences between the two sections, a unity can be observed. Konrad Schaefer contends that both strophes invoke familial imagery. The building of a house (v. 1) relates to the building of a family (v. 4) even as the protection afforded by a city gate (v. 2) resembles the defense provided by children in the city gate.[4] Similarly, John Goldingay notes that Psalm 127 is comprised of two four-line poems. Each poem begins with a reference to God's involvement in human life and concludes with a statement concerning the implications of that claim for human life. While both strophes in the psalm do appear to diverge in both content and form, they work together to create a coherent whole. In reflecting on the question of success in daily life, the psalmist contends that life, much less success, can be rightly understood only in the light of Yahweh's cooperation in daily life. The emphasis on work and daily life also functions as the primary subject matter in the subsequent Psalm 128. The connections between these two poems as "twin psalms" will be explored in the treatment of the latter psalm.

---

3. See, for example, C. C. Keet, *A Study of the Psalms of Ascents: A Critical and Exegetical Commentary upon Psalms CXX to CXXXIV* (London: Mitre, 1969), 54–55.

4. Konrad Schaefer, *Psalms*, Berit Olam (Collegeville, MN: Liturgical Press, 2001), 307.

The Involvement of the Lord in Life (127:1–2)

THE FIRST STROPHE OF THE PSALM explains the necessity of God's involvement in human life by alluding to two spheres of it: the home and the city. To live one's life apart from the involvement of God would be to run the risk of engaging in activity that, in the end, proves unsuccessful and meaningless. The opening verse of the strophe is highly structured. Verses 1a and 1b begin with *'im YHWH lo'* ("Unless the LORD . . ."), followed by an imperfect verb ("to build," "to guard") in the first half of the line. Normally, an *'im lo'* ("if . . . not") construction appears in oaths or oathlike statements with the intent of expressing an affirmative declaration. For example, in Jeremiah 15:11 Yahweh exclaims, "Surely [*'im lo'*] I will deliver you for a good purpose."[5] In Psalm 127, however, the use of *'im lo'* funtions differently. Much like in Psalm 124:1–2, the psalmist refers to possible or irreal situations.[6] The second half of the line begins with the noun *shawe'* ("vain"), followed by a perfect verb ("to labor," "to stand watch"). The highly stylized form of the opening verses suggests they are meant to be read together, but even more, that they point to a common conclusion.

Unless the LORD builds the house. The word "house" (*bayit*) occurs more than two thousand times in the Old Testament and, similarly to its use in English, the Hebrew term covers a wide range of meanings. The term *bayit*, in its most basic sense, can refer to a home or a family dwelling (cf. Gen 44:14), or more symbolically to the household in general (cf. Gen 45:11), to a family line (Exod 6:14), or to a dynasty (cf. 2 Sam 7:16). The term can also refer to an entire nation (Ruth 4:11). If the proverbial sayings in verse 1 had an "earlier life" as independent proverbs, their use of *bayit* likely referred to the actual construction of a home, and the same referent is likely in view in the psalm. The use of the verb "labor" (*'amal*) in the second half of the line supports this reading, given that *'amal* can refer to strenuous, manual labor (Deut 26:7; Ps 107:12). Further, the subject of the verb, "builders," normally refers to those constructing something (i.e., a house, temple, or wall).[7] Yet because of the polyvalent nature of the term and the penchant for writers of proverbs to play on such polyvalence, the precise meaning here of *bayit* remains open to a number of interpretations.

As similarly in the first line, the second line of verse 1 presents a possible or irreal situation. The image shifts from that of the home to that of the city, with a particular focus on the city as a place of security.

---

5. van der Merwe, Naudé, and Kroze, *A Biblical Hebrew Reference Grammar*, 296. In English, the sense of the affirmative for *'im lo'* is expressed with the word "surely."

6. Erhard S. Gerstenberger, *Psalms, Part 2*, 345.

7. For example, see 1 Kgs 5:18, 32; 2 Kgs 12:11; Ezra 3:10; Neh 4:5; 2 Chr 34:11.

The implication is that any human attempt to protect the city remains vain unless Yahweh watches over it. Together, the images of "the building of houses and keeping watch over a city evoke the human preconditions for a happy and carefree life together, for a family and a society."[8]

In vain. In the opening strophe the word "vain" (*shawe'*) occurs three times and thus serves to link the proverbial statement in verse 1 to the claim made in verse 2. Although the English does not reflect the word order, the word "vain" (*shawe'*) appears as the first word in three different lines: "In vain [*shawe'*] the builders toil over it" (v. 1b); "in vain [*shawe'*] the guards stand watch" (v. 1d); "in vain [*shawe'*] you rise early" (v. 2a). The translation of *shawe'* as "vain" calls to mind the dominant term in the book of Ecclesiates: "vanity" (*hebel*). Upon closer analysis, however, the terms connote very different meanings in their respective contexts. In Ecclesiastes the writer employs the word "vanity" (*hebel*) to suggest that, while persons may be successful in their undertakings, their activities may still prove to be pointless, ephemeral, and worthless. The psalmist, however, is not assessing a value on building a house or guarding a city; rather, the psalmist is claiming that the success of such work is contingent on whether God is involved in the activity. If God is not involved, such activity remains deceptive, delusional, and ultimately unsuccessful.[9]

The theme of vain or deceptive activity continues in verse 2. The verse opens literally, "it is vanity to you," followed by three participial phrases meant to describe the person the psalmist has in mind: those who "rise early," those who "stay up late," and those "toiling for food to eat." The first two participial phrases function as time markers that signal a long work day.[10] The third participial phrase does not refer to the duration of the activity but, intead, assigns a particular value to that activity. The poet refers to "the bread of toil" (*'ezeb*). Elsewhere in the Psalter (Ps 80:5), the psalmist

---

8. Hossfeld and Zenger, *Psalms 3*, 386. This statement stands in tension with Dan Fleming's contention that the word pair "house/city" is a stylized reference to the temple and Jerusalem (Daniel Fleming, "House/City: An Unrecognized Parallel Word Pair," *JBL* 105 [1986]: 689–93). Fleming cites a number of narrative biblical texts in which the two terms reference the temple and Jerusalem, and he offers several extrabiblical texts to suggest that the word pair is used similarly in those contexts. He notes, however, that Psalm 127:1 is the only poetic text in the Hebrew Bible to make use of this word pair. I would argue that the two proverbial sayings reference actual cities and homes, but with the inclusion of Psalm 127 in the Songs of Ascent and the use of the word pair elsewhere to refer to the temple and Jerusalem, it is likely that this meaning was a secondary one applied to the psalm in light of its literary context. See the brief discussion below under Bridging Contexts.

9. Goldingay, *Psalms 3*, 500.

10. Hossfeld and Zenger, *Psalms 3*, 387.

refers to eating "the bread of tears" as a cipher for suffering in life. The noun "toil" (*'ezeb*) in Psalm 127 refers to strenuous labor or pain and always has a negative connotation. Consequently, the "bread of toil" does not refer to the bread earned from toil (as suggested in the NIV); instead, the phrase reflects a particular way of life, one filled with the hardship of labor. Texts that reflect the tenets of wisdom theology typically extol the virtue of work (cf. Prov 6:6–11; 10:4–5; 12:24; 24:30–34), yet in Psalm 127 this kind of toil—relentless work from sunup to sundown—proves deceptive and useless (*shawe'*).

He grants sleep to those he loves. The first three clauses of verse 2 recount the harried activity of humans attempting to secure their own lives. This image of such a laborious life is placed alongside the image of sleep in verse 2d.[11] Although based upon the structure of the verse and, even more, human experience, one might infer that hard work leads to sleep, the psalmist invites the reader to think otherwise. In verse 1 he confesses that all human activity is useless unless God is actively involved. In verse 2 he confesses that the toilsome life depicted in the first three lines of the verse likewise is vain or useless; it does not secure one's life. The psalmist does not dismiss the value of hard work, only the assumption that hard work is all one needs to succeed. Like in verse 1 the psalmist reminds the reader that God's involvement in human life is what leads to success and satisfaction. The claim that God grants sleep to his beloved ones means that human beings "can afford to relax and sleep because Yhwh continues to be active."[12] Human effort alone is not sufficient to create a meaningful life, but when divine involvement intersects with human effort, the fear of a vain and useless (*shawe'*) life is erased.

Children are a Heritage from the Lord (127:3–5)

BEGINNING IN VERSE 3 THE PSALM shifts to a different subject matter. This shift is evident in the use of the particle *hinneh*, a term meant to signal the start of a new stanza or pericope. Not all English translations opt to translate the term, however. The NIV and NRSV, for example, do not supply a corresponding term in English, while the NASB and ESV render the term as "Behold." Whether a translation renders the term in English or not, its presence in the Hebrew text signals the start of the next section in the text.

---

11. The noun *shena'*, "sleep," is the Aramaic spelling for *shenah* in Hebrew. The meaning of "sleep" in this context has elicited a number of proposals. See the overview of the various options in Hossfeld and Zenger, *Psalms 3*, 386–92.

12. Goldingay, *Psalms 3*, 502.

In the second half of Psalm 127 the poet turns to familial matters and, in particular, considers the blessings associated with a larger family. Similar to the claims made in verses 1–2, the latter strophe in the psalm focuses on the activity of God in human life.

Heritage from the LORD. In the opening line of the second strophe, the psalmist describes children as "the heritage from the LORD." The Hebrew word *nahalah*, often translated as "heritage" or "inheritance," typically refers to the land given to Israel by Yahweh. The term appears repeatedly in the book of Joshua (50x) with reference to the land apportioned among the tribes (e.g., Josh 14:9, 13; 15:20; 16:5). Although the land belongs to God, he apportions it to his people, thereby securing their future. The psalmist makes a similar move in declaring that children are the *nahalah* of Yahweh. Children are a free gift *from* God, even as the land was, and as similarly with the land, children secure the future of God's people.[13]

In Psalm 127:3b the psalmist explains that children are a reward from God—they are valuable. Although the word *tsakar* can mean "wages," the meaning should not be taken literally. The term in Psalm 127 does not imply that fathers have "earned" children because of their work or that they are being given children as a "reward" for some particular act. Similar to *tsakar* in Isaiah 40:10; 62:11, *tsakar* in Psalm 127:3b is something that belongs to God but is given as a gift. The use of *tsakar* in verse 3b parallels the language of *nahalah* in verse 3a.[14] Much as the first strophe suggests that nothing humans do can be successful apart from God's active involvement in the human sphere, the second strophe begins with the declaration that it is precisely because of God's active involvement in life (in the form of giving children) that humans can in fact be successful.

Like arrows in the hand of a warrior. In verses 4 and 5a the psalmist compares children to arrows by suggesting that the blessed man has a quiver full of "arrows." Earlier in the Songs of Ascent arrows were mentioned (Ps 120:4), but with a negative connotation. In Psalm 120 the term refers to the injurious comments of the taunting enemies who threaten the psalmist, who himself seeks peace. By contrast, the poet in Psalm 127 invokes the image of arrows in an effort to signal the strength and protection that comes from having children in one's youth (v. 4a). To contextualize this thought, the psalmist refers to the gate (*sha'ar;* NIV "court") in verse 5b, suggesting that a quiver full of children will prevent the father from experiencing shame in that public forum. The gate was the place of

---

13. Kraus, *Psalms 2*, 455.

14. Joseph Blenkinsopp, *Isaiah 56–66*, AB 19B (New York: Doubleday, 2003), 241–44; Cornelius Van Dam, "שכר," *NIDOTTE* 3:1244–46.

---

public assembly but also the location for business and commercial activity, as well as the location for settling legal disputes. In the book of Ruth, for example, the question concerning the next of kin (*go'el*) is resolved at the city gate. Because the gate funtioned as the center of the community, it was also a prime location for injustice, abuse, and corruption, thus leading the prophet Amos to exhort those in the Northern Kingdom to establish justice in the gates (Amos 5:15). The psalmist explains that although the gate holds the potential for injustice and false accusations, the blessed man and his quiver full of children will thwart any forms of injustice or abuse attempted by his enemies.[15]

IN READING PSALM 127, the overarching theme unfolds: dependence on Yahweh. The language and imagery of the psalm considers this theme in the light of events associated with everyday life: building, protecting, working, and even procreating. The psalm also must be considered within the larger collection of the Songs of Ascent. The emphasis on Zion and the temple in Psalm 120–34 provides an additional level of interpretation to the psalm. The mention of building a house in verse 1a recalls the mention of the "house of the LORD" in Psalms 122:1, 9 and anticipates the reference in Psalm 134:1. The references to a "city" in Psalm 127:1b recall the mention of Jerusalem (or Zion) in Psalms 122:2; 125:2; 126:1; 128:5; 129:5; 132:13; 133:3; and 134:3. Even the language associated with "watching" or guarding recalls language from Psalms 121:3–8 and 130:6. Further, the focus on offspring or "children" in the second half of Psalm 127 is used explicitly in reference to the offspring of David in Psalm 132:12. The connections between Psalm 127 and its larger context may explain the psalm's inclusion within the larger collection, but it does not necessarily drive the poem's interpretation at the level of the individual psalm.

As noted above, Psalm 127 has been traditionally recognized as a wisdom psalm. Broadly construed, the theological underpinnings of the wisdom tradition are rooted in a system of retributive justice. Hard work and

---

15. The NRSV and ESV translate Ps 127:5b in the singular: "He will not be put to shame when he speaks with his enemies in the gate." The referent of "he" in verse 5b is apparently the "blessed" man mentioned in verse 5a. Both verbs in verse 5b are plural, thus suggesting that both the man and his children are in view in verse 5b. Because the man has children, he is not left alone to face the potential challenges, and perhaps even shame, associated with the gate. The Septuagint follows the plural forms found in the Hebrew text.

faithfulness to the ways of Yahweh result in blessings, while apathy and improper behavior result in a diminished existence. Although Leo Perdue's assessment is correct that retributive justice was not "some infallible system that was inevitably true" (cf. the books of Job and Ecclesiates), the claims associated with retributive justice certainly established a mechanistic worldview that operated from the assumption that retributive justice was more true than not.[16] Many of the proverbs provide counsel about everyday life predicated on a system of retributive justice. Virtues of diligence and hard work receive praise, while sloth and wickedness, condemnation. In Proverbs 6:6–8 the sage extols the ant as an exemplary model of wisdom: the ant works hard during the summer and at harvest in order to secure its future. The sage continues in that chapter by chastising the "sluggard" and asking, "When will you get up from your sleep? A little sleep, a little slumber, a little folding of the hands to rest—and poverty will come on you like a thief" (Prov 6:9b–11a). Texts such as these might lead one to conclude that the theology associated with wisdom texts appears overly anthropocentric, that it appears to suggest everything rests on whether humanity does enough or does the right thing, and only then do the blessings of God follow.

Psalm 127 invokes another stream of thought within the wisdom tradition. This stream does not stand in tension with Proverbs 6 and related texts but instead seeks to make more explicit the triangular relationship that exists beween God, humans, and everyday life.[17] In texts such as Proverbs 6, the assumption is that God is in the "background," so to speak, ensuring that retributive justice unfolds as appropriate. In Psalm 127, however, God moves to the foreground. There is an inherent connection between the work of God, the work of humans, and the unfolding of everyday life. The goodness of life and the certainty of the future cannot be fully secured by humans alone; fully securing them is the work of God. Other wisdom texts echo this strain of thought. For example, in Proverbs 21:31 the sage writes, "The horse is made ready for the day of battle, but victory rests with the LORD." The people may prepare for battle, as well they should, but ultimately it is the work of God that remains decisive. Security does not come from human effort alone, but only as humans recognize their utter dependence on God. The language of the second strophe (vv. 3–5) reinforces this assertion. The psalmist acknowledges that children are a heritage "*from* the LORD" and they are a reward "*from* him" (emphasis added).

---

16. Perdue, *The Sword and the Stylus*, 7.

17. Dirk Human, "Ethical Perspectives from the *Sîrê Hamaʿalôt* Psalm 127," in *The Composition of the Psalter*, ed. Erich Zenger, BETL 238 (Leuven: Peeters, 2010), 531.

Beyond building a house, securing a city, and working the land, humans remain dependent on Yahweh even for the giving of a family. The triangular relationship between God, humans, and everyday life extends into every facet of life, thus necessitating a sense of humility in those very same places of life.

In the first strophe of Psalm 127 humans are referred to as builders, guards, and laborers; yet, despite their dedicated efforts, vigilant attention, and exhausting toil, none of their actions ensure success. Worse yet, all of them remain vain (*shawe'*) *unless* God is involved. In verse 2d, however, the psalmist reminds us that, because God is involved, he gives sleep to his beloved. The image of giving sleep proves instructive. As noted above, Proverbs 6:9–11 includes a derisive statement about sleep, as though sleep is inherently bad, but in Psalm 127 sleep fares much better. The psalmist encourages a rhythm between work and rest, but this kind of rhythm only comes *after* the laborer's faithful submission to God.[18] This kind of rhthym only comes after we have "rested" in the belief that God is at work in our daily lives.[19] For the psalmist, the ability to sleep implies recognition that all his efforts cannot do what God alone can do. The psalmist does not call for the cessation of building, guarding, or toiling, but only recognition of our limitations. Although Psalm 8 reminds us that God made humans a little lower than God (or "the angels," NIV), Psalm 127 reminds us that we are not God. Gratefully, this psalm reorients us with a proper theological anthropology in light of everyday life and, more significantly, in light of God.

PSALM 127 PROVIDES Christians in the twenty-first century with a powerful corrective concerning our own abilities to "make something of ourselves." Those of us who live in the United States are well acquainted with the rhetoric of the "American dream." Historians trace the first use of that phrase to James Truslow Adams in his 1931 book *The Epic of America*.[20] In that volume Adams contends that, because of this dream, "each man and woman shall be able to attain to the fullest stature of which they are innately capable, and be recognized by others for what they are."[21] There is an inherent assumption in this claim that is

---

18. Augustine writes, "You have made us for yourself, O Lord, and our hearts will remain restless until it finds its rest in you" (Augustine, *Confessions* 1.1).

19. Human, "Ethical Perspectives from the *Sîrē Hama'alôt* Psalm 127," 532.

20. James Truslow Adams, *The Epic of America* (Boston: Little, Brown, and Co., 1931).

21. Ibid., 415.

thoroughly anthropocentric. As David Platt suggests, the American dream teaches us that "our greatest asset is our own ability."[22] Out of this belief, we may fall prey to two lines of thought, neither of which is life giving.

First, because we believe success is contingent upon effort, we are compelled to work harder. Prior to the invention of electricity, most of our ancestors lived according to the rhythm of the day. So long as there was sunlight, they would work. As the day ebbed into evening and transitioned to night, their work slowed and finally came to a halt. Some may have worked by candlelight or lantern for a time, but because these were precious commodities they too were held in reserve. Such a life stands in stark contrast to our own. Because our computers travel with us and artificial light is always available, we now can work late into the evening and through the night—darkness never falls upon us. Cell phones allow us to remain on call and accessible 24/7. And worse yet, this capacity to work continuously has become a source of pride for us. We assume that we "will attain to the fullest stature of that which we are innately capable," to borrow from James Truslow Adams, if we not only work hard but work even harder than that. Yet as Eugene Peterson admonishes, "Relentless, compulsive work habits ('the bread of anxious toil') which our society rewards and admires are seen as a sign of weak faith and assertive pride, as if God could not be trusted to accomplish his will, as if we could rearrange the universe by our own effort."[23] Psalm 127 invites us to reconsider our lives and the work that has been placed in our hands. We are invited to depend on God and not on ourselves. Surely the God who "stretches out the heavens like a canopy" (Isa 40:22) is worthy of our trust. So long as we depend on ourselves, we are resigned to eating the "bread of anxious toil."

Second, Psalm 127 goes so far as to suggest that *unless* God is part of *our work*, or perhaps better stated, *unless* we are part of *God's work*, our efforts are in vain. In John 15:5 Jesus instructs his disciples, "I am the vine; you are the branches. If you remain in me and I in you, you will bear much fruit; apart from me you can do nothing." In our own hubris and out of our own sense of self-reliance, we may become convinced that we, in fact, are the vines—that all life springs from us. But such thinking is misguided and an affront to the work of God in the world. As a reminder of God's work in the world, the psalmist refers to children in the second half of Psalm 127. If ever humans could look at something and declare, "We made that," surely

22. David Platt, *Radical: Taking Back Your Faith from the American Dream* (Colorado Springs: Multnomah, 2010), 46.

23. Eugene Peterson, *A Long Obedience in the Same Direction: Discipleship in an Instant Society* (Downers Grove, IL: InterVarsity, 1980), 106.

that would be the case with children. We could assume that we, in fact, are the vines—and that all life, especially the life of our children, springs from us. And yet . . . the psalmist confesses that children are "from the LORD" and "from him" (v. 3). When one watches the birth of his or her own child, one becomes keenly aware that this work is much bigger than either the husband or the wife, and even the two together. In some way that cannot be explained, God has invited human beings into his ongoing creative work in the world. He has allowed the branches to experience something of what the Vine already knows. And in those moments, our hubris and self-reliance should give way to utter humility.

Psalm 128

A song of ascents.

¹ Blessed are all who fear the LORD
   who walk in obedience to him.
² You will eat the fruit of your labor;
   blessings and prosperity will be yours.
³ Your wife will be like a fruitful vine
   within your house;
your children will be like olive shoots
   around your table.
⁴ Yes, this will be the blessing
   for the man who fears the LORD.
⁵ May the LORD bless you from Zion;
   may you see the prosperity of Jerusalem
   all the days of your life.
⁶ May you live to see your children's children—
   peace be on Israel.

PSALM 128 IS PART OF a larger collection of psalms entitled the Songs of Acents (see Psalm 120). The language of this psalm, particularly verses 1–4, exhibits characteristics associated with Israel's wisdom tradition. Among the vocabulary employed in the psalm, the words "blessed" (*'ashre*) and "fear" (*yare'*), as in "fear of the LORD," are key indicators of the wisdom influence. In addition to these signature terms, the repeated counsel concerning matters associated with everyday life also point to the wisdom tradition. Terms such as "walk," "obedience," "house," "table," "wife," and "children" appear repeatedly in other wisdom texts. Although Psalm 128 contains a number of wisdom motifs, its placement within the Songs of Ascent, coupled with the benediction in the final two verses, suggests that this poem likely had its place in the cultic or worship life of ancient Israel.

The NIV breaks the psalm into two strophes: verses 1–4 and 5–6. Some interpreters divide the strophes differently by opting for a twofold division that consists of verses 1–3 and 4–6.[1] Supporting the argument

---

1. Allen, *Psalms 101–150*, 184; Goldingay, *Psalms 3*, 508.

for this division is the fact that the first verse in each strophe refers to the "fear of the LORD" as a characteristic of the blessed person. Further, in this arrangement each strophe begins with a verse in the third person (vv. 1 and 4), followed by two verses in the second person. While such a division is plausible, this commentary will follow the division reflected in the NIV and supported by many interpreters.[2] Based on this understanding of the structure, verse 1 opens with a general wisdom saying about the blessed (*'ashre*) person who fears the Lord. Verses 2–3 provide a threefold blessing on the type of person mentioned in verse 1. The final verse in the first strophe (v. 4) provides a summary statement concerning the blessed life. The repetition of "fear the LORD" and the reference to the blessed life (*'ashre* in v. 1; *barak* in v. 4) create an *inclusio* around the opening strophe. The final strophe (vv. 5–6) contains a benediction that is rooted in Zion theology and concludes with a prayer for the peace of Israel (cf. Ps 125:5).

Psalm 128 and the immediately preceding Psalm 127 have much in common. Both psalms can be classified broadly as wisdom psalms. Portions of each psalm likely reflect the kind of wisdom that had its origins in family and clan life.[3] More specifically, each psalm contains a beatitude (verse 5 in Ps 127; verses 1 and 2 in Ps 128), and each refers to the blessings associated with work and family. While these two wisdom psalms share many features, they also differ somewhat in purpose. Psalm 127 instructs the reader along the pathway to a blessed life. The verses in that poem outline a proper structuring of life as a means to experiencing the blessed life. Psalm 128, however, "articulates a theology of blessing as it celebrates the daily realms of work and family as gifts from God."[4] Psalm 127 points the way to the blessed life; Psalm 128 calls for the acknowledgment and celebration of the same.

A Blessed Life (128:1–4)

THE FIRST STROPHE IN PSALM 128 begins and ends with a reference to the fear of the Lord (vv. 1a, 4b). In the Hebrew word order, verse 1 opens with the macarism "blessed" (*'ashre*), which is then followed by the phrase, "all who fear the LORD." In the Hebrew, as in the English, the final phrase in the

---

2. A number of scholars follow this same division. See Davidson, *The Vitality of Worship*, 420–21; Kraus, *Psalms 60–150*, 458–59; Mays, *Psalms*, 403. Hossfeld and Zenger argue for dividing the strophes as verses 1–3 and 4–6, but they then contend that verse 4 actually functions as the summary verse to the first strophe. See Hossfeld and Zenger, *Psalms 3*, 396. The NRSV actually divides the psalm into three strophes: verses 1–2, 3–4, and 5–6.

3. See the discussion in Crow, *The Songs of Ascents (Psalms 120–134)*, 70–71.

4. McCann, "The Book of Psalms," 1201.

strophe is "fear the LORD." This phrase creates an *inclusio* around the entire first strophe and governs its reading.

Blessed are all who fear the LORD. The term *'ashre*, "blessed," appears with considerable regularity in the literature of the Old Testament.[5] Frequently this term appears in conjunction with conduct and attitudes the faithful of God should embody. These actions and attitudes, however, are not arbitrary commitments; rather, they are commitments that signal that a person's life is congruent with the larger purposes of God. To reinforce this understanding, the writer of Psalm 128 further describes the "blessed" person as one who "walk[s] in obedience" to the Lord (v. 1b). Thus, the term *'ashre* could be translated as "truly happy" or "content," in the sense that as one aligns her life with the ways of God, she discovers a blessed life, a life that is truly happy and fulfilled. Contrary to contemporary society's fixation with *self*-fulfillment, the psalmist rightly knows that the blessed life is the life that is oriented toward God and God's purposes in the world.[6]

This kind of life is marked by a sense of the "fear [of] the LORD" (v. 1a). Within the wisdom tradition, the fear of the Lord might best be described as "a foundational trust in YHWH as the good, life-promoting creator God who, despite all disturbances and dangers, rules the universe and brings success on the path of life to those who seek to recognize the proper order of life and act in accordance with it."[7] One does not "fear" the Lord because of what he can do in the sense of judgment, but of what he can bring: life in all its fullness.

Blessing and prosperity will be yours. The psalmist spoke in the third person in the opening verse and provided something of a universal claim concerning the blessed or truly happy life. In shifting to the second person in verses 2–3, however, the universal claim made in verse 1 is meant to be appropriated in the lives of the readers or hearers. Beginning with verse 2a, the psalmist outlines the blessings to be enjoyed in the lives of those who fear the Lord. First among them is the claim that people will "eat the fruit of [their] labor." At first reading, this claim may seem to stand in tension with the previous poem, Psalm 127. In that psalm, the poet cautioned people against rising early and staying up late in order to toil for food. Yet in

5. Cf. Job 5:17; Prov 3:13; 8:32, 34; 14:21; 16:20; 20:7; 28:14; 29:18; Eccl 10:17. The term appears repeatedly in the Psalter, with considerable use in Books 4 and 5. Cf. Pss 1:1; 2:12; 32:1, 2; 33:12; 34:8; 40:4; 41:1; 65:4; 84:4, 5, 16; 89:15; 94:12; 106:3; 112:1; 119:1, 2; 127:5; 128:1, 2; 137:8, 9; 144:15; 146:5.

6. On the place of *'ashre* within the semantic domain of "blessing" (*barak*), see Simon Chi-Chung Cheung, *Wisdom Intoned: A Reappraisal of the Genre "Wisdom Psalms,"* LHBOTS 613 (London: Bloomsbury, 2015), 128–37. See also Michael L. Brown, "ברך," *NIDOTTE* 1:763–64.

7. Hossfeld and Zenger, *Psalms 3*, 400.

Psalm 128 the psalmist acknowledges the value of labor and the good it produces (i.e., food). How could one psalm caution against too much work and the other laud it? The different approach to work in the two psalms stems from the larger presupposition operative in each psalm. In Psalm 127 individuals are cautioned, if not outright chastised, for working too hard out of the belief that they can secure their own future. Psalm 128 begins with the universal claim concerning the blessed person. This person lives in the "fear [of] the LORD" and consequently understands, as Hossfeld and Zenger explain (see above), that it is the Lord who "brings success on the path of life to those who seek to recognize the proper order of life and act in accordance with it." Psalm 128 provides no hint of self-reliance but instead receives all "blessings and prosperity" (v. 2b) as a gift from God.

Like a fruitful vine . . . like olive shoots. In verse 3 the psalmist recounts additional markers of the blessed life. These markers, namely a wife and children, recall the imagery present in Psalm 127. In Psalm 128:3a, however, the psalmist mentions the wife specifically and celebrates that she will be "a fruitful vine." The word "fruitful" (*parah*) recalls the command in Genesis 1:22 for the man and woman to be "fruitful" (*parah*) and multiply (*rabah*). This pairing of terms echoes throughout the remainder of Genesis, first regarding Noah and his sons and then in terms of the patriarchs (e.g., Gen 9:1, 7; 28:3; 35:11). The reference to the wife as a "fruitful vine" obviously celebrates the fertility of the wife and her capacity to bear children, but it may implicitly signal that the male referent and his family are experiencing the fullness of life as commanded at creation and as fulfilled subsequently by God's people.

The second familial image involves children, another theme shared with Psalm 127. In that psalm the poet celebrated the gift of children as "a heritage from the LORD" and a "reward" (v. 3). Moreover, the psalmist recognized and celebrated the protection afforded to parents by their children in the court. In Psalm 128 the psalmist also invites the reader to recognize children as a blessing from God. And as in Psalm 127, the writer of Psalm 128 recognizes the benefits of children. In this psalm children are compared to "olive shoots." Olive trees are not cultivated from seed; rather, new trees come from the shoots that grow around older olive trees. Biologically, the new shoots are identical copies of the source tree; they are the new life that stems from the older tree. As Helga Weippert has suggested, in a culture in which the notion of an afterlife was unknown, one's life continued only through the lives of his or her children.[8] In Psalm 128

---

8. Helga Weippert, "'Deine Kinder seien wie Schösslinge von Ölbäumen rund um deinen Tisch!' Zur Bildsprache in Psalm 128,3," in *Prophetie und Psalmen: Festschrift für Klaus*

the psalmist invokes the image of the olive shoots as a means of celebrating the new life represented in these "shoots" but also and equally as a means of celebrating the permanency of the life of his family through them.

Yes, this will be the blessing. The final verse in the first strophe (v. 4) returns to third-person language: "Yes, this will be the blessing for the man who fears the LORD." The word for "blessing" in verse 4 differs from the word used in the first verse of the psalm. In verse 1 the psalmist used *'ashre*, which means "truly blessed" or "content," as suggested above, and describes a state of existence. In verse 4, however, the psalmist uses the *pual* form of the verb *barak*, "to bless." The *pual* stem is passive, suggesting that the subject of the sentence is acted upon by another. Unfortunately, the NIV does not clearly capture this sense. A better rendering might be, "Thus, shall the man be blessed who fears the LORD," as in the NRSV and ESV. Read in this way, the text provides another universal claim: The man who fears the Lord will be blessed by that very God.[9] Whereas *'ashre* ("blessed") refers to a state of existence or contentment, *barak* ("to bless") signals that the source of that blessing is not the person himself or herself. As in Psalm 127, the psalmist acknowledges that God is the one "from whom all blessings flow."

Blessings from Zion (128:5–6)

THE LANGUAGE OF BLESSING (*BARAK*), which concluded the first strophe, appears in the first line of the second strophe. The repetition of terms from one line to the next (anadiplosis) is a characteristic feature of the Songs of Ascent. In verse 4 God is rightly presumed as the subject of the passive verb *barak*, but in verse 5 the psalmist is much more explicit. Yahweh is the agent of the blessings to come.[10]

Psalm 128 closes with a benediction that announces blessings upon the pilgrims who are making their journey from their homes to Jerusalem, to Mount Zion. As suggested above, the first four verses of the psalm have as their focus the household, with references to food production and family life, both of which are perceived as blessings from God. The final two verses in the psalm, however, shift the focus through explicit references to Zion and Jerusalem in verse 5. The first four verses highlight the blessings that come to those who fear the Lord and walk in his ways, but verse 5

Seybold zum 65. Geburtstag, AOAT 280, ed. Beat Huwyler (Münster: Ugarit Verlag, 2001), 163–74.

9. A similar sentiment is expressed in Ps 115:13. In that context the Lord blesses (*brk*) those who "fear the LORD."

10. Goldingay, *Psalms 3,* 511.

specifies not only the source of blessings but also those blessings yet to come. Unlike Psalm 127, Psalm 128 invokes elements of Zion theology (cf. Pss 46; 48). In particular, the psalmist asserts that blessings come from Zion because that is the place where Yahweh dwells. The language and theology invoked in this benediction resonate with that found in the well-known Zion psalm, Psalm 46. In verse 4 of that psalm, the poet explains that "there is a river whose streams make glad the city of God, the holy place where the Most High dwells." These streams pour out into the city and region, and thus pour forth the blessings of Yahweh upon his land and upon his people (cf. Ezek 47). The writer of Psalm 128 prays similarly that God's blessings would pour forth from Zion upon his people (v. 5a).

The NIV translates verses 5–6 as a series of three blessings or wishes. The first verbal form, *yebareka,* "he will bless you," is an imperfect with a pronoun attached. The imperfect form often functions with a jussive sense and expresses to the hearer the wish or desire of the speaker. The NIV and NRSV translate the next two phrases similarly, "May . . . you . . . ," thus creating a series of three blessings. Upon closer inspection, however, the structure of the subsequent sentences (vv. 5b, 6a) suggests an alternative translation. Following the imperfect with a jussive in verse 5a ("May the LORD bless you"), the next two lines begin with the imperative: "see" (*ra'ah*). In Hebrew, whenever a jussive is followed by another sentence with an imperative, the following sentence expresses a sense of purpose ("May X happen so that Y will happen").[11] Thus a preferred translation of verses 5–6 would be:

> May the LORD bless you from Zion,
>> *so that* you may see the prosperity of Jerusalem
>> all the days of your life.
> *So that* you may live to see your children's children.
>> Peace be upon Israel.

The implications of this alternative reading are significant to the theology of the psalm itself. The psalm does not conclude with three benedictory wishes, as though all three statements are equal. The psalmist is clear: the benediction is, "May the LORD bless you from Zion." This blessing will result in what follows: enjoying the goodness of Jerusalem and living a long life. The word "propersity" (*tov*) in verse 5b often functions as a synonym

---

11. In such constructions there is typically a change in person. In verse 5a Yahweh is the operative subject, whereas in the remaining two statements "you" functions as the subject. Van der Merwe, Naudé, and Kroeze, *A Biblical Hebrew Reference Grammar,* 171.

for *shalom*, "peace," "wholeness," or "goodness" (Isa 52:7; Jer 8:15). In Psalm 128 the psalmist asks the Lord to bless the hearer from Zion so that he may experience the peace and wholeness of Zion. In turn, the peace and wholeness of Jerusalem will allow the hearer to live a long life—"to see your children's children." The last line in the psalm reiterates the desire for peace upon Israel, a desire expressed elsewhere in the collection (Pss 120:7; 122:6–9; 125:5).

RETRIBUTIVE JUSTICE AND BLESSINGS. As noted in Psalm 127, texts associated with the wisdom tradition typically operate within a system of retributive justice; the righteous receive blessings but the wicked, punishment. The contrast between the life of the righteous and that of the wicked appears repeatedly in Proverbs 10–22. In Proverbs 10:27, for example, the sage writes, "The fear of the LORD adds length to life, but the years of the wicked are cut short." Such language is not reserved for the book of Proverbs, however. A nearly identical statement occurs in Psalm 37:9: "For those who are evil will be destroyed, but those who hope in the LORD will inherit the land." A cursory reading of texts such as these might lead one to construct an image of God as one who "takes names" and metes out punishment or reward as appropriate. Constructing this image would be to reduce the idea of retributive justice simply to a forensic notion.[12] Such a view underestimates the depths of the worldview that is foundational to the concept of retributive justice. The sages averred that God had structured the created order, but even more, as Kenneth Kuntz has explained, they believed that the "structure of reality is essentially good and that man's well-being is contingent upon his conforming to that unseen, yet efficacious order."[13] In the Old Testament, "conforming to that unseen, yet efficacious order" cannot occur apart from the torah of God, the ways of God. That worldview explains why the psalmist calls "blessed" those who "walk in obedience" to God (Ps 128:1b)—they are participating in the "efficacious order" that has been established and is sustained by God. But what of the verses that follow, particularly those that mention food, a wife, and offspring? Are food and family nothing more than incentives offered by God to coax his people to faithfulness? Is he buying the faithfulness of his people (Job 1:9)? The psalmist refuses

---

12. See the classic analysis by J. Kenneth Kuntz, "The Retribution Motif in Psalmic Wisdom," *ZAW* 89 (1977): 223–33.
13. Ibid., 226.

such reductionistic thinking and asks us to do the same. Those who fear the Lord and walk in his ways understand something of the structure of the created order (Ps 19), but even more, through their relationship with God and their commitment to his ways, they are conforming their lives to that order. In Psalm 128:2–3 the psalmist suggests that those who remain committed to that order (v. 1) may discover life in all of its fullness (i.e., food, family, and community). The fullness of life is not a "reward," so to speak, but a gift. And as verse 5 reminds, these blessings are not an "automatic 'receipt of retribution,' but a free gift of the God of Israel, who is present with his people."[14]

Blessings of life. In verses 2–3 the psalmist invites the readers or hearers to celebrate three aspects of life that are gifts from God: food, a wife, and children. Throughout the Songs of Ascent there is a focus on the ordinary—and perhaps even more mundane—aspects of life. Yet these aspects of life are lifted up and "accorded a high level of dignity."[15] In verse 2b the psalmist explains that to those who fear the Lord, "blessings and prosperity" will come. In this psalm, blessings and prosperity have nothing to do with wealth or power. As noted above, the Hebrew word *tov*, translated "prosperity" in the NIV (vv. 2, 5), can function as a synonym for *shalom* ("peace," "wholeness"). Thus, verse 2b could be translated as "how blessed you will be and it shall go well with you." The translation of *tov* as "prosperity" in the NIV is unfortunate and may lead readers in ways not intended. In North American culture, the terms "prosperity" and "prosperous" are generally associated with affluence, which could lead some people to assume that a proper fear of Yahweh (v. 1a) and a proper life of obedience (v. 1b) should necessarily lead to prosperity in its most materialistic forms. Psalm 128, however, is not concerned with the accumulation of wealth but with the fullness of life, with *tov* and *shalom*. In the postexilic period, life was anything but *tov* and *shalom*. Those living in Yehud were faced with numerous challenges: taxation imposed on the region by the Persians, tensions between those returning from exile and those who remained in the land, crop failure, famine, and poverty, to name but a few.[16] In the face of such daunting social and economic circumstances the psalmist reframes the issue. According to Psalm 128, food and family, as simple at they may seem, signal a full life. They are blessings from God and are meant to be received as such.

---

14. Kraus, *Psalms 60–150*, 459.

15. Hossfeld and Zenger, *Psalms 3*, 400.

16. For an extensive analysis of postexilic life see Samuel L. Adams, *Social and Economic Life in Second Temple Judea* (Louisville: Westminster John Knox, 2014).

PSALM 128 OPENS BY UNITING the "fear of the LORD" with walking in obedience. The psalmist does not suggest that this is an "either . . . or" option, as though a person could choose one at the expense of the other. Instead, to fear the Lord *is* to walk in obedience; to walk in obedience *is* to know the fear of the Lord. The claim is not merely tautological, however, as though one concept simply repeats the other by using different language. To the contrary, the psalmist invites us into a way of life, one that is predicated on relationship and manifested through daily life. That way of life is the blessed life.

This reframing of the blessed life is the gift of wisdom theology to the contemporary reader. The choices in life are manifold, from the most basic to the deepest and most profound. Yet, because these choices are legion, we are left paralyzed. When we have so many choices to make, how can we make any choice? And if we do not choose correctly, how can we be assured of a blessed life, a life filled with *tov* and *shalom*? And if we are not sure life can be filled with *tov* and *shalom*, then can we be sure there is any order whatsoever in the world in which we live? These questions present vexing issues to which the psalmist provides a sure response. He does not instruct the reader to "choose wisely" among the myriad options; instead he points the reader, novice and experienced alike, down a pathway. The psalmist knows that those on the pathway, those who seek to order their lives rightly, after the ways of God and in the fear of God, will see the world differently. Those individuals will soon realize that the goal of life is not to *earn* divine blessing but to *receive* the simple elements of life *as* divine blessing, as an assurance that life is indeed filled with *tov* and *shalom*.

Psalm 129

A song of ascents.

¹ "They have greatly oppressed me from my youth,"
   let Israel say;
² "they have greatly oppressed me from my youth,
   but they have not gained the victory over me.
³ Plowmen have plowed my back
   and made their furrows long.
⁴ But the LORD is righteous;
   he has cut me free from the cords of the wicked."
⁵ May all who hate Zion
   be turned back in shame.
⁶ May they be like grass on the roof,
   which withers before it can grow;
⁷ a reaper cannot fill his hands with it,
   nor one who gathers fill his arms.
⁸ May those who pass by not say to them,
   "The blessing of the LORD be on you;
   we bless you in the name of the LORD."

Original Meaning

PSALM 129 IS THE TENTH psalm in the Songs of Ascent (see Ps 120). Similar to other psalms in this collection, Psalm 129 relies on agricultural imagery, in this instance, plowing (v. 3) and harvesting (v. 7). Unlike the more literal reference to the "fruit of your labor" (v. 2a) in the immediately preceding Psalm 128, the images in Psalm 129 function metaphorically by using everyday imagery in graphic illustrations of the political and militaristic threats, both past and present, faced by the community. In attempting to discern the structure of the psalm, the careful reader will observe that the agricultural imagery mentioned above actually governs the two major sections of the poem. In verses 1–4 the image of plowing dominates the strophe, while in verses 5–8 the image of harvesting functions as the operative metaphor. Typically, images of planting and harvesting create positive associations, as is evident in the earlier Psalm 126, where those who had planted in weeping will return "carrying sheaves with them" (v. 6). The imagery in Psalm 129 is altogether different. The image of planting evokes remembrances of oppression from times past; the image of harvesting alludes to the destruction of the enemy.

The precise genre or "form" of this psalm remains difficult to establish because the psalm contains elements that warrant labeling the text a thanksgiving psalm (vv. 1–4), a psalm of lament (vv. 5–8), or perhaps even a psalm of vengeance or imprecation.[1] The psalm might be best understood as a mixed form of poetry, with the elements of thanksgiving in the first strophe providing the foundation for the imprecations that follow. The language throughout verses 1–4 appears in the first-person singular form (i.e., "I," "me," "my"), yet the poem should be understood as a collective or communal psalm. The invitation, "Let Israel say," in verse 1 suggests that a corporate identity is intended, as does the reference to "my youth" in verses 1a and 2a (see below). Elsewhere in the Songs of Ascent, the psalms are marked by a strong collective sense through their frequent shifting from singular to plural language. For example, Psalm 123 opens, "I lift up my eyes to you," but then goes on to plead, "Have mercy on us" (v. 3). Psalm 130 begins with an individual reflection but then extols the community in the final two verses (vv. 7–8), a phenomenon seen also in Psalm 131. Other psalms in the collection simply refer to the community (Pss 124; 125; 126; 133; 134). The repeated references to Israel and Zion throughout the collection remind those who pray these psalms that their identity is inseparable from the identity of the larger community.[2]

Recalling Israel's History of Oppression (129:1–4)

IN THE FIRST STROPHE THE COMMUNITY recalls Israel's oppression at the hands of the nations. Yet despite the repeated episodes of oppression, the community gives thanks because God has consistently delivered his people.

They have greatly oppressed me from my youth. A number of the Songs of Ascent contain lines that begin with the same word or even phrase (Pss 124:1–2, 3–5; 121:7–8; 122:8–9; 126:2a–b; 127:1a–b; 132:3–4). This feature serves to link lines (anadiplosis; see Ps 121) and reinforce key themes in the psalm. In Psalm 129 the first two verses begin with the same declaration: "They have greatly oppressed me from my youth." Both lines begin with the Hebrew word *rabbat*, which comes from the root that means "many" or "numerous." The NIV's translators understood the term to refer to the degree to which Israel was oppressed, that is, "greatly" or "severely." More likely, the word functions adverbially with reference

---

1. See the discussion in Erhard Gerstenberger, *Psalms, Part 2*, 352–53.
2. The repeated references to Israel include Pss 122:4; 124:1; 125:5; 128:6; 129:1; 130:7–8; 131:3. On Zion, see Pss 125:1; 126:1; 128:5; 129:5; 132:13; 133:3; 134:3.

to time (i.e., "often"). The term *rabbat* appears earlier, in Psalms 120:6 and 123:4, and in both instances the implication is that oppression has happened "too often." While this grammatical point may appear to be minor, it does inform the reading of the text. The community is not recalling the *severity* of oppression that marked their past; rather, the community is recalling the oppression that has *repeatedly* marked that past—it has been "too often."

In referring to the oppression that has come "too often" on the community, the psalmist uses the verb *tsarar*, "to oppress." Although the verb *tsarar* can refer both to individual attacks and to hostility, *tsarar* can also refer to political and even military threats at the hands of foreign powers.[3] The use of *tsarar* in the opening lines of Psalm 129 recalls the first psalm in Book 5 of the Psalter—Psalm 107. In that psalm the "hand of the foe" (*yad-tsar*) is mentioned in verse 2 as a clear reference to the nations that had dispersed Israel to the four corners of the world (v. 3). Although the use of first-person language in Psalm 129:1–2 might warrant interpreting the verb as referring to personal or individual attacks, the context of the psalm suggests that Israel's larger history of oppression is in view. The reference to "my youth" (*ne'urim*) in both verses further validates this claim. In the books of Hosea and Jeremiah the prophets refer to the "youth" (*ne'urim*) of Israel. In both instances the prophets allude to the time in which Israel came out of Egypt and wandered in the wilderness (Hos 2:17; Jer 2:2).[4] The poet in Psalm 129 explains that from that time, from Israel's youth in the wilderness, Israel's history has been marked "too often" by oppression at the hands of foreign powers.

Plowmen have plowed my back. The use of "plowmen" (*horshim*) in verse 3a underscores the theme of foreign oppression.[5] The psalmist

---

3. For the use of verb in reference to military battle see Num 10:9; 25:17; Isa 11:13. The participial form of *tsarar* is used frequently in reference to national enemies, "foes" (cf. Exod 23:22; Ps 74:4; Esth 3:10).

4. Although the wilderness period is often remembered as a time of sinful rebellion (cf. Ps 95:7b–11), that association does not carry over in Hosea and Jeremiah. These prophets refer to Israel's "youth" with fondness. God announces in Jer 2:2, "I remember the devotion of your youth [*ne'urim*], how as a bride you loved me." Similar betrothal imagery occurs in Hos 2:17 as well.

5. In verse 3a the Septuagint reads *hamartōloi*, "the sinners." Apparently the translators read *resha'im*, "the wicked ones," in the place of *horshim*, "the plowmen." That the two terms have the same consonants, save one, perhaps explains the alternative translation. In addition, the Septuagint's translators may have sought to align verse 3a with the reference to the wicked/sinners in verse 4a. The Hebrew text should be retained. Hossfeld and Zenger attempt to explain the altered reading in the Septuagint: "While in the [Hebrew text], the metaphors for plowing, sowing, and harvesting, drawn from the world of farm life, shape the whole psalm—as images for exploitation by foreign powers—the LXX changes the image world in the first section of the psalm (vv. 1–4), probably because in its urban

cries out, "Plowmen have plowed my back and made their furrows long." Metaphorically, the language suggests heavy oppression at the hands of enemy. With the use of the verb *harash* ("to plow"), the psalmist "invokes the image of a work animal whipped while laboring," thus likening Israel's experience under foreign oppression to that of a beaten animal.[6] In the prophetic corpus the image of plowing can also function as a metaphor for total destruction (cf. Mic 3:12; Jer 26:18). Elsewhere in the Old Testament similar agricultural imagery appears in reference to oppression at the hands of foreign powers. In Isaiah 9:4 the prophet writes, "For as in the days of Midian's defeat, you have shattered the yoke that burdens them, the bar across their shoulders, the rod of their oppressor." Although the word "yoke" is absent from Psalm 129, the image of plowing infers the larger metaphorical field that suggests forced labor. The scene in a relief from a tomb at Edfu (ca. 1500 BCE) depicts a plow being pulled by human slaves, a scene similar to the one envisioned in Psalm 129:3.[7] In short, the imagery of pulling a plow in verse 3 no doubt functioned metaphorically, but its meaning was likely one not too removed from reality itself.[8]

The LORD is righteous. In the first three verses the psalmist recounted Israel's troubled past at the hands of its oppressive neighbors. Over against these powerful forces the psalmist recognizes Israel's one source of hope, its lone source of power: Yahweh. Verse 4a is terse in its announcement of Israel's hope: *Yahweh tsadiq.* The word *tsadiq*, when used of Yahweh, refers to "righteousness" in the sense of "being just" (cf. Ps 7:12) or establishing justice (Ps 119:137; Zeph 3:5). Yahweh, the just God, the one committed to establishing justice, was the one who intervened in Israel's past and thwarted the oppressive rule of Israel's enemies. Continuing the agricultural metaphor, the psalmist announces that Yahweh "has cut me free from the cords of the wicked" (v. 4b), thereby implying that, at some point in the past, Israel was freed from those who had oppressed her. The cord would have tethered the animal or human to the plower, the oppressed to the oppressor. As a remedy, however, Yahweh "cut" the cords. The verb "cut" (*qatsats*) appears elsewhere in the Old Testament to describe graphically the cutting off of hands (2 Sam 4:12), the cutting off of thumbs and toes

---

cultural context that imagery was foreign and perhaps incomprehensible" (Hossfeld and Zenger, *Psalms* 3, 418).

6. Allen, *Psalms 101–150*, 187.

7. Hossfeld and Zenger, *Psalms* 3, 415

8. The whole process, including the yoking and plowing, function as a "metaphor for compulsion and foreign rule, for oppression, exploitation, forced labor, and slavery" (Hossfeld and Zenger, *Psalms* 3, 415).

(Judg 1:6–7), and the destruction of weapons of war (Ps 46:10). Its usage in Psalm 129 suggests "the disempowerment of the wicked/enemies."[9] The affirmation that Yahweh has cut the cords of the wicked in times past provides the necessary foundation for the imprecations that follow.

Imprecations against the Enemy (129:5–8)

IN THE SECOND STROPHE OF THE PSALM the poet turns to a series of curses or imprecations. The curses in verses 5–8 suggest that a persistent threat remains—a threat that must be redressed by Yahweh. The psalmist shifts metaphors and language in verse 5, where he employs overt militaristic images and momentarily suspends the agricultural theme before returning to that imagery in verses 6–7.

May all who who hate Zion be turned back. The psalmist refers to the enemies as "all who hate Zion," thus pitting all Israel (v. 1b) against "all who hate Zion" (v. 5). The desire of the psalmist is that the enemies of Zion be shamed (*bosh*) and turned back (*sug*).[10] Both verbs, which appear to function as a hendiadys in this context, can allude to militaristic and political upheaval.[11] Frequently the idea of shame (*bosh*) appears in texts related to warfare and signals the shame endured by those routed or yet to be routed in battle (cf. Isa 20:5; Jer 2:26, 36; 51:51; Zech 10:5). When used in the *niphal* elsewhere, *sug* suggests the repelling of an attacking force (cf. Pss 35:4; 40:15; 70:3). Just as the community had experienced deliverance from the oppressing foes (vv. 1a, 2a) in the past, the psalmist implores Yahweh to mount up and rout the forces that threaten the community.

May they be like grass. In the remaining verses the psalmist returns to agricultural imagery, but of the type that undermines the perceived power and strength of the enemy. In the first strophe the agricultual imagery presented the enemy as the "plowmen" (v. 3) who hold tightly to the reigns of oppression (v. 4). The agricultral imagery in the second strophe of the psalm reverses the images of power. The "grass" that withers is here understood as the grass seed that blows onto the rooftop and begins to take root. Because there is no fertile soil on the roof, such weeds can only develop shallow roots and hence, under an oppressive sun, are prone to wither. The agricultural metaphor in verse 6 also depicts more militaristic imagery, thus connecting verses 5 and 6. In Isaiah 37:27 Yahweh explains how he has used the Assyrians to accomplish his purposes. He recounts how God

---

9. Ibid., 407.

10. On the role of shame in the Psalter see W. Dennis Tucker Jr., "Is Shame a Matter of Patronage in the Communal Laments?" *JSOT* 31 (2007): 465–80.

11. Goldingay, *Psalms 3*, 518.

caused the Assyrians to invade cities (Isa 37: 26–27) and overwhelm their populations and, in so doing, make their habitants "like grass sprouting on the roof, scorched before it grows up." The psalmist requests that God act again—and in this instance, wither up the rootless grass that plagues Israel.[12]

In Psalm 129:6b the poet apparently opts for another term that appears to have an agricultural meaning in the present context, but one that also carries with it military connotations. The word *shalap* can mean to "pull up" or "uproot," agriculturally speaking, but in texts related to battle and military struggle *shalap* refers to the act of pulling out a sword in battle (cf. Num 22:23, 31; Josh 5:13; Judg 3:22; 8:10, 20; 9:54; 20:2, 15, 17, 35, 46; 1 Sam 17:51; 31:4; 2 Sam 24:9; 2 Kgs 3:26; Job 20:25). In the present context the term no doubt refers to the uprooting of a plant. Read in this way, the psalmist requests that the enemy wither up before there is even time for it to be uprooted. If the term functions as a *double entendre*, however, the psalmist may be requesting that the enemies wither up before they have the opportunity to pull out the sword again in military conquest.

A reaper cannot fill his hands with it. In the Old Testament, harvesting signals a time for celebration, joy, and thanksgiving (cf. Ps 126:6; Ruth 2). Although the writer of Psalm 129 extends the agricultural metaphor in verse 7 by appropriating the language of harvesting, he alters the nuance of the image. Typically, celebration is associated with an abundant harvest, and the abundant harvest is indicative of God's intervention in Israel's life—an assurance of his provision. In Psalm 129, however, the psalmist explains that the grass grown on the rooftop will wither, thus resulting in nothing to harvest—not even enough to fill one's hands with the yield (v. 7a). After the work of God against those who hate Zion (v. 4), the remaining threat will be reduced to nothing more than a handful. Consequently, and ironically, the *absence* of sufficient yield for the harvest is cause for celebration by the community.

We bless you in the name of the LORD. Psalm 129 concludes with an *irreal* situation—a situation that will *not* occur given the imprecations already announced (vv. 5–7). As the book of Ruth suggests, during the harvest season passersby and those harvesting in the field would exchange greetings (e.g., Ruth 2:4). Although the exchange of greetings may seem perfunctory, and perhaps was so, the greetings do convey the notion that in the act of harvesting God was at work blessing his people. Yet the psalmist

---

12. Verses 5 and 6 remain connected through paronomasia. The opening word in verse 5 is *yeboshu* ("shame"), and the final word in verse 6 is *yabesh* ("withers"). In reading both verses together, the implication is clear: "All who hate Zion" will be a people put to shame, a people withering under the might of Yahweh, the Righteous One (v. 4).

announces that once God has exacted his punishment upon those who "hate Zion" (v. 5a), there will be nothing to harvest (v. 7), and consequently there will be no need for passersby to issue a greeting. In ironic fashion, the lack of harvest in Psalm 129 is reason for hope and celebration for the community. The absence of the enemies, represented by the meagerness of the harvest, suggests that Israel's God remains righteous (v. 4) in once again thwarting the ways of the oppressive peoples that have plagued the nation of Israel since her youth (vv. 1–2).

 **REALITY OF SUFFERING.** From beginning to end Psalm 129 exposes the reality of oppression that had so defined Israel's experience. Suffering had been there from the beginning (vv. 1–2) and apparently remained before them still (vv. 5–8). Psalm 129 does little to hide the reality of suffering. With the aid of the agricultural images associated with plowing (vv. 3, 4b), the psalmist acknowledges the gravity associated with oppression. The image of a "plowed . . . back" (v. 3) leaves little to the imagination, nor does the idea of a yoked animal forced into labor (v. 4). Rather than denying or "spiritualizing suffering," this psalm joins the chorus of biblical texts that compel us to acknowledge the reality of suffering.

Throughout the Old Testament, prophets and scribes alike offered explanations for Israel's suffering at the hands of foreign nations. In the book of Amos, for example, the prophet understood the impending destruction of the Northern Kingdom by the Assyrians as a consequence of rampant social sin (Amos 5:1–17). Jeremiah characterized the arrival of the Babylonians as a consequence of Judah's breach of covenant with God (Jer 2:4–8), and Ezekiel explained the same event by referring to Judah as a "rebellious people" that had committed abominations (Ezek 2:1–10; 8:6). Even some psalmists connect their suffering with sinfulness. The same types of connections are also made in various poems in the Psalter. In Psalm 79:2 the people remind God that the maurading invaders have "left the dead bodies of your servants as food for the birds of the sky; the flesh of your own people for the animals of the wild." Later in the psalm the community pleads with God, "do not hold against us the sins of past generations" (v. 8). These texts, and others, imply that there is a causal relationship between suffering and sin, destruction and disobedience— the kind of connection that makes the modern reader uneasy at times. Although one might simply wish to set aside these kinds of connections, the covenantal promises in Deuteronomy 28–30 prevent one from doing so. These chapters remind the community of the devasting consequences of disobedience and of the glorious blessings associated with faithfulness.

The covenantal framework associated with Deuteronomy casts a long shadow. The paradigm outlined in Deuteronomy, and references in the texts above, may lead some interpreters to associate all suffering with sin and disobedience. Although *some* texts do make that association based on the covenantal framework that governed Israel's relationship with God, not all suffering was associated with sin in the Old Testament—sometimes suffering was just that, suffering. Within the Songs of Ascent, in particular, the psalmists acknowledge suffering, both past and present, as a reality. None of these psalms, however, associate sin with suffering. Instead, those who recited these psalms acknowledged that they lived among a people "who hate peace" (Ps 120:6) and seek to "swallow" the people of God (Ps 124:3). They confessed that the "scepter of the wicked" rested over the land (Ps 125:3), and they longed for God to restore the fortunes of his people (Ps 126:4). None of these psalms associate suffering with sin, destruction with disobedience. In Psalm 129 the community reviews its history, and, consistently with the other Songs of Ascent, this psalm refuses to attribute suffering to sin. The poet simply acknowledges the reality of suffering in a broken world and then brings that suffering into the sphere of worship.

Cursing the enemy and the worship of God. A psalm with such a raw analysis of Israel's plight, both past and present, may seem questionable in a collection of psalms intended to accompany pilgrims as they make their way to worship and festal life in Jerusalem. Perhaps one could argue that the recounting of Israel's deliverance in the first four verses seems understandable; it provides a rationale for worship and thanksgiving. Even if that point is granted, however, the remaining verses, filled with images of cursing or imprecation, prove more daunting to explain. Is such language appropriate for worship? Admittedly, other psalms contain imprecatory language that is far more graphic than the language employed in Psalm 129 (cf. Pss 18; 58; 83; 109; 137), yet all these psalms were retained in the Psalter and deemed suitable for use, both private and communal. Even subsequent communities recognized these imprecatory psalms as part of the witness of the Psalter. Both the Septuagint and the various psalms manuscripts among the Dead Sea Scrolls retained the imprecatory psalms, thus suggesting their continued use by communities of faith. Had these communities considered the imprecatory psalms inconsistent with Israel's larger scriptural witness, they might have opted to jettison the poems. But they did not do so. These psalms remained part of the Psalter, part of "Our words to God and God's word to us."

Although these psalms were retained in the Psalter, the thought of their use as worship texts remains difficult to imagine. Few people today would attend a church in which the congregation identified enemies and then prayed that those people would wither up and die. Consequently, some may assume these psalms are pre-Christian or sub-Christian and, hence, not appropriate them for use in the church.[13] This kind of dismissive move operates from the hermeneutic that the modern reader has the right to determine what is truly authoritative and what is not. Rather than jettisoning certain psalms or verses from the canon based on their incompatibility with our "modern" notions of civility, perhaps we would do well to consider the larger theological confession being made in Psalm 129. For the community who prays Psalm 129, the reality of suffering is juxtaposed with the reality of a just God (v. 4). The community leans into the latter reality but is no less cognizant of the former. These kinds of prayers are not analogous to a schoolyard fight between two children with each child hurling threats at the other until a scrum breaks out. The reality presented in Psalm 129 is far more ominous, one-sided, and ill fated for the people of Israel. Their history of being oppressed is like having had their backs plowed into long furrows—only it was much worse. The book of Lamentations provides shocking and graphic imagery meant to illustrate the devastation brought about at the hands of the Babylonians. Lamentations 4 records that the tongues of children stuck to the roofs of their mouths due to thirst (v. 4) and that mothers had to boil their own children for food (v. 10). Texts such as these suggest that Israel's struggle with the nations was never between equals. Consequently, Israel's only hope was her God. The cries of imprecation in Psalm 129 are Israel's last hope and only confession. These cries are acts of worship lifted up to God in the hope that he will hear their cries and be moved to respond (Exod 2:23–25).

IN HIS VOLUME *Evil and the Justice of God,* N. T. Wright reminds us that the "Old Testament never tries to give us the sort of picture the philosophers want, that of a static world order with everything explained tidily." The Old Testament presents little of a "static world order" and even less of a tidy explanation. As Wright explains,

---

13. See Erich Zenger, *The God of Vengeance: Understanding the Psalms of Divine Wrath,* trans. Linda Maloney (Louisville: Westminster John Knox, 1996). In the opening chapter Zenger traces this negative assessment of the imprecatory psalms particularly among scholars within the last two centuries.

"What we are offered instead is stranger and more mysterious: a narrative of God's project of justice within a world of injustice."[14] In preaching and teaching Psalm 129 we may be inclined to "explain away" or "justify" the presence of the imprecations in the psalm. In doing so, however, we take attention away from the psalm's great theological claim—a just God is present in the midst of an unjust world. For many of us living in North America, the notion of injustice may seem foreign. We may think it unjust because we can't afford to buy the house we always dreamed of or drive the car we desire. We may think it unjust because our pay raise was not as high as we had hoped. Perhaps we consider it unjust when we get pulled over for speeding and others do not. These inconveniences do not merit the label "injustice," nor do they signal an unjust world—at least not the kind envisioned in Psalm 129. But there are those who know something of the world envisioned by the psalmist. Children and women who have been trafficked in the sex industry know something of the oppression referenced in Psalm 129. Christian communities experiencing persecution at the hands of those around them have experienced the kind of power-lessness understood by those confessing in Psalm 129. Workers in foreign countries who are making pennies on the hour so that companies can sell cheaper goods in first-world countries know something of having their backs plowed. Rather than ignoring Psalm 129 in our preaching and teaching, perhaps we would well to invite our congregations into what Wright termed "God's project of justice within a world of injustice." We should acknowledge the injustice—the true injustice—in the world and long for God's redeeming and redemptive work that will overturn this injustice. Such an approach to injustice can be heard again in the teaching of Jesus: "Blessed are those who hunger and thirst for righteousness, for they will be filled" (Matt 5:6).

---

14. N. T. Wright, *Evil and the Justice of God* (Downers Grove, IL: InterVarsity, 2006), 73.

Psalm 130

A song of ascents.

¹ Out of the depths I cry to you, LORD;
 ² Lord, hear my voice.
Let your ears be attentive
 to my cry for mercy.
³ If you, LORD, kept a record of sins,
 Lord, who could stand?
⁴ But with you there is forgiveness,
 so that we can, with reverence, serve you.
⁵ I wait for the LORD, my whole being waits,
 and in his word I put my hope.
⁶ I wait for the Lord
 more than watchmen wait for the morning,
 more than watchmen wait for the morning.
⁷ Israel, put your hope in the LORD,
 for with the LORD is unfailing love
 and with him is full redemption.
⁸ He himself will redeem Israel
 from all their sins.

Original Meaning

PSALM 130 IS THE ELEVENTH psalm in the Songs of Ascent (Pss 120–34). Within the Christian tradition Psalm 130 may be best known as one of the seven penitential psalms. In the sixth century CE, Cassiodorus penned his commentary on the psalms and labeled this poem (along with Pss 6; 32; 38; 51; 102; 143) a penitential psalm.[1] While that label does not represent one of the traditional types of form-critical categories established by Hermann Gunkel (e.g., lament, thanksgiving, praise), the label "penitential" does capture well the theological force of the psalm.[2] Form critically, however, the psalm does contain a number of elements associated with a lament psalm: invocation

---

1. Not all the penitential psalms deal with sin as overtly as Ps 130 (cf. Pss 6; 102).
2. Several texts outside the Psalter (Ezra 9; Neh 9; Dan 9) suggest that penitential prayers emerged as an important development in postexilic Israel. See Richard J. Bautch,

of God (vv. 1, 2); complaint (v. 1); petition (v. 2); and expression of trust (vv. 4–6).

As suggested by the divisions in the NIV, Psalm 130 can be divided into four strophes of two lines each. The first two strophes address God, while the latter two strophes address the congregation. Within each strophe the psalmist employs repetition, parallelism, and ellipsis, thereby creating a tightly constructed and poetically sophisticated psalm. Each strophe references God twice. In the first three strophes the name of Yahweh, or the shortened form Yah, appears, followed by 'adonay, "Lord." In the final strophe the name of Yahweh is mentioned twice. Other examples of repetition include the mention of the psalmist's voice (qol) in verse 2a and 2c, as well as the reference to "sins" ('awonot), which occurs in the second and last strophes (vv. 3a, 8b). That the idea of waiting dominates the psalm is evident from the repetition of terms and phrases. The psalmist uses two terms, qawah and yahal, from the same lexical word field referring to waiting and hoping. The verb qawah occurs twice in verse 5a, and the verb yahal appears as the last word in verse 5b and the first word in verse 7a. In the Hebrew verse 6a does not contain the verb "to wait," but its lack is due to ellipsis, with its meaning therefore inferred in the line. The final word in verse 7b, "redemption" (pedut), and the first verb in verse 8a, "will redeem" (padah) bind the final strophe together. Even less overt examples of repetition occur in the psalm. The psalmist repeats the Hebrew term nepesh ("life," "soul," "neck"), but the term is translated in the NIV as "my whole being" in verse 5a and "I" in verse 6a. In verse 3a the psalmist refers to Yahweh as having "kept" (shamar) a record of sins. The participial form of the verb is repeated in verse 6b–c, "watchmen" (shomrim). The frequent repetition within strophes and across the strophes serves to bind the entire psalm together into an organic whole.

Each strophe differs from the others both in focus and content. The first strophe is a direct plea to God for his attentiveness. In the second strophe (vv. 3–4) the psalmist still addresses God directly, but the intent of his speech has shifted. In the first strophe he highlighted his own need, but in the second strophe he shifts to a more generalizing tone and considers the larger issue of the forgiveness of sin. The third strophe returns to first-person language, but Yahweh is no longer addressed directly ("you"); instead, the psalmist speaks of God only in the third person. The theme of waiting dominates this strophe. In the final strophe the psalmist addresses the congregation and assures them of God's unfailing love for his people.

Developments in Genre between Post-Exilic Penitential Psalms and the Psalms of Communal Lament, AcBib 7 (Atlanta: SBL Press, 2003).

Cry to God (130:1–2)

IN THE OPENING STROPHE OF THE PSALM 130 the psalmist makes a direct appeal to Yahweh for deliverance. Although the spatial distance between the poet and God is highlighted in this portion of the psalm, the potential for such distance to be overcome is also signaled in the reference to Yahweh's capacity to hear.

Out of the depths. The opening word of the psalm locates the psalmist and highlights his helpless estate. As Walter Brueggemann aptly explains, "this psalm is the miserable cry of a nobody from nowhere."[3] The term "depths" (*mimma'amaqqim*) occurs five times in the Old Testament, each time with a negative connotation implying death and destruction.[4] In Isaiah 51:10 and Ezekiel 27:34 the prophets refer to the "depths of the sea" and understand them to constitute a watery grave—an image more fully reflected in Jonah 2. While Psalm 130 does not include the full phrase (i.e., "depths of the sea"), the imagery is intended; the image of the watery grave and chaotic abyss remains.[5] In Book 5 of the Psalter, in particular, Yahweh is depicted as the God of the heavens (e.g., Pss 113:5–6; 115:3; 123:1; 136:26; 144:5), and in Psalm 130 the poet seems worlds apart from this God. The spatial distance between God and the psalmist appears nearly insurmountable.

I cry to you, LORD. In verses 1b–2 the psalmist cries out to God in the hope of gaining an audience with him. These lines are structured chiastically.

A I cry to you, LORD;
  B Lord ['*adonay*], hear my voice.
  B' Let your ears be attentive
A' to my cry for mercy.

The cries of the psalmist bracket the two requests for Yahweh to hear the psalmist's voice. Numerous prayers from the ancient Near East refer to a "listening god," and a number of stele and stamps from Egypt and Mesopotamia include pictures of ears to represent the listening ear of the deity.[6] Within the Psalter, selected psalms also employ the language of

---

3. Brueggemann, *The Message of the Psalms*, 104.

4. Bernd Janowski refers to the "depths" (*mimma'amaqqim*) as an "abysmal place . . . where the antiworld of chaos begins" (Janowski, *Arguing with God*, 33).

5. Alastair Hunter suggests that the use of "depths" without the modifying prepositional phrase ("of the sea") may refer to sinfulness, particularly given the reference to sin in verse 3. (Alastair Hunter, *Psalms*, Old Testament Readings [London: Routledge, 1999], 218).

6. Hossfeld and Zenger, *Psalms 3*, 429–32. See also Keel, *The Symbolism of the Biblical World*, 192–93.

calling out (*qara'*) to God alongside a reference to the "listening ear" of the deity (e.g., Pss 102:2; 141:1). To gain the listening ear of God is predicated on the psalmist's having gained the attention of God (Ps 130:2b) and, more importantly, God's favor.

While the covenant name of God was used in verse 1b, the word *'adonay* ("lord") appears in verse 2a. Martin Rösel has argued that *'adonay* ("lord") introduces laments or confessions of trust when the petitioner seeks to highlight the personal relationship the psalmist has with God.[7] Put differently, the use of this language invokes a particular image, namely, that of a servant approaching his or her master.[8] The servant is coming, request in hand, fully understanding that the only one with the power to fulfill the request is the "lord." The use of such language, however, is not simply to strike a deferential tone, but more importantly to signal that the petitioner is subordinate to, and in need of, the other. Another Psalm of Ascents, Psalm 123, illustrates this idea of piety:

> As the eyes of slaves look to the hand of their master,
>> as the eyes of a female slave look to the hand of her mistress,
> So our eyes look to the LORD our God
>> till he shows us his mercy [*hanan*].

As in Psalm 123, the petition requested by the psalmist in Psalm 130 is mercy (*hanan*) from God.

A Statement of Confidence (130:3–4)

IN THE OPENING STROPHE OF PSALM 130, the psalmist locates himself in the "depths" but neglects to acknowledge the cause. In the second strophe the psalmist introduces the concept of sin but does not make explicit the connection between his plight (v. 1) and the problem of human sinfulness. Although the connection is not overt, the proximity between the circumstance and the condition (i.e., the depths and sinfulness) in these verses presumes a causal relationship between the two. To remedy his plight, the psalmist confidently asserts that there is forgiveness with Israel's God.

If you, LORD, kept a record of sins. Verse 3 opens with a rhetorical question: "If you, LORD, kept a record of sins, Lord [*'adonay*] who could

---

7. Martin Rösel, *Adonaj—warum Gott "Herr" genannt wird*, FAT 29 (Tübingen: Mohr Siebeck, 2000), 193–201.

8. See Ps 86, in which the language of *'adonay* ("lord") is coupled with that of "servant"—a more explicit example of the relationship noted by Rösel. That, similarly to Ps 130, Ps 86 also opens with the request, "Let your ears be attentive," once again stresses the desire of the psalmist to have an audience with God.

stand?" Once again the psalmist invokes both names of God—the covenantal name (*Yahweh*) followed by *'adonay*, meaning "Lord" or "Master." As suggested above, the use of both names implies a relationship between the psalmist and God, but in this strophe the psalmist emphasizes that the relationship may be jeapordized by sin. In referring to human sinfulness, the psalmist uses the term *'awon*, a word with a root meaning of to "bend," "curve," "turn aside," or "twist."[9] In reference to sin, the term carries with it a complex meaning, as it encompasses not just the action deemed "sin" but also the "damage it creates *and* the consequences it threatens."[10] Consequently, the term is rendered "inquity" or "sin" in some contexts (Ps 130:3; Prov 5:22), but elsewhere it appears to refer more nearly to the guilt associated with sin (Zech 3:4), and still elsewhere, even the punishment resulting from iniquity (Ezek 44:10). James Mays captures this complex image poetically by describing *'awon* as "the flood of wrong and its consequences that sweeps life along and from which there is no escape apart from a liberating, rescuing redemption."[11] In Psalm 130:3 the term *'awon* appears in the plural form, which frequently can function as a summary word for all the sins committed against God.[12] The psalmist is not confessing to *a* sin but rather to all sins that leave him broken, estranged from God, and in need of forgiveness.

The psalmist contends that if God did track the sins of humans, then no one would be able to "stand" (*'amad*). The term *'amad* can mean literally "to stand," or more figuratively "to stand in the presence of" a king or deity (Ps 76:7). In the latter instance, one would expect the prepositional phrase *lepane*, literally "before the face of," but the absence of the prepositional phrase from Psalm 130 suggests an alternative interpretation. In addition to the more literal meaning of "to stand," *'amad* can also mean "to endure" (e.g., Pss 102:26; 111:3, 10; 112:3, 9; 119:90, 91). If Yahweh "kept a record of sins," then no one would survive the judgment of God, no one would endure.

But with you there is forgiveness. The nominal form of forgiveness, *selihah*, appears only here and in Daniel 9:9 and Nehemiah 9:17—the verbal form occurs forty-six times. In every instance, however, Yahweh is named as the subject—Yahweh is either the subject who forgives, or, as suggested in Psalm 130, forgiveness is named as part of God's identity (i.e., forgiveness is "with you"). In making this statement the psalmist acknowledges

9. Rolf Knierem, "עָוֹן," *TLOT* 2:863.
10. Hossfeld and Zenger, *Psalms 3*, 434.
11. Mays, *Psalms*, 406.
12. Alex Luc, "עָוֹן," *NIDOTTE* 3:351.

that Yahweh and Yahweh alone has the authority to forgive sins, but even more, he has the disposition to do so.

As suggested above, sin damages the relationship between God and humanity. Were it not for God's disposition to forgive, humanity would have no hope of enduring (v. 3a). But Israel's history has demonstrated otherwise. From the time in the wilderness to the Hebrews' settlement in the land, and even during the time of the monarchy, Israel's history was riddled with sin. Despite their proclivity to sin, however, they endured.

The psalmist confesses in verse 4b that the forgiveness of sins has as its proper end fear or "reverence." The NIV attempts to render verse 4b more fully, "so that we can, with reverence, serve you," but in doing so strips some of the poignancy of the text. The Hebrew reads simply, "so that you may be feared." Forgiveness does not enable us to *serve* God better, as suggested by the NIV's rendering; instead, forgiveness enables us to *see* God better. The relationship once broken by sin is restored, not by us but by the God with whom there is forgiveness. Consequently, the psalmist asserts that forgiveness leads to fear and a renewed faith, which *then* results in faithful service.

Waiting for the Lord (130:5–6)

IN STROPHE 2 THE PSALMIST EXPLAINED the reality of human sinfulness and the necessity of forgiveness in order to live a life fully restored and in relation to God. In the third strophe the poet highlights his current posture in the light of the previous claim—he waits, but not in vain. In verse 5 he uses the words *qawah* and *yahal* three times. Both words mean "waiting," but waiting with a sense of hopeful expectation. In the book of Psalms, such anticipatory waiting is reinforced because God is nearly always the object of the verb. Because God is the object of waiting, such a posture is never in vain. In Psalm 130:5a the psalmist waits for God, and in verse 5b the poet waits for "his word," presumably an oracle of salvation.[13] In the opening line of verse 6a the text reads literally, "my soul [*nepesh*] for the Lord [*'adonay*]." The verb is absent from the verse due to ellipsis, but it is clearly understood nevertheless (i.e., "my soul waits for the Lord"); the absense of the verb may in fact heighten the force of the claim.

The final two lines in verse 6 prove illustrative of this posture of waiting. The psalmist waits for the Lord "more than watchmen wait for the morning." As similarly in verse 6a, the verb "wait" does not actually appear in the Hebrew, but it is implied based on its threefold use in the previous

---

13. Kraus, *Psalms 60–150*, 467.

verses. In ancient cities, guards were stationed on the city walls to keep watch over the city during the night. Just as the guards await the morning, so too does the psalmist wait on God.

The image of the morning in verse 6b–c may be set in contrast to the mention of the "depths" in verse 1, thus creating a contrast between darkness and light, the absence of God and the presence of God. Elsewhere in the Psalter the morning symbolizes the time of God's intervention in the lives of his people. In Psalm 30:5 the psalmist explains that "weeping may stay for the night, but rejoicing comes in the morning." Similarly, in Psalm 143:8 the psalmist says, "Let the morning bring me word of your unfailing love." In Psalm 5:3 the connection between the morning and waiting is made explicit: "in the morning I lay my requests before you and wait expectantly."[14] Similarly, the psalmist waits expectantly for the forgiving God, assured that his waiting is not in vain.

The Redemption of Israel (130:7–8)

THE FIRST-PERSON LANGUAGE that has dominated the first three strophes is absent from the final one. That "I" has been replaced by "Israel" (vv. 7a, 8a) could suggest that the final strophe was spoken by a priest or other worship leader and addressed to the people. By necessity, this understanding would imply that the "I" of the first three strophes should be understood collectively as the nation. While this interpretive move is possible, given that "I" does represent the community in other psalms, an alternative reading seems preferable. The final two verses are likely an exhortation to the community (i.e., "Israel") by the same person who spoke in verses 1–6. The "I" in verses 1–6 turns and exhorts the community to adopt the same posture of waiting that he himself has adopted (vv. 5–6). This connection to the previous strophe is made explicit with the opening word in the fourth strophe, *yahal*, "to wait" or "to hope," the same word used in verse 5b. Just as the psalmist waits and hopes, so too should the community.

With the LORD is unfailing love. Following the imperative to "put your hope in the LORD" (v. 7a), the psalmist introduces a causal clause (*ki*, "for") to explain why Israel should hope in the Lord. This causal clause introduces two distinct claims as descriptors of the character of God. In verse 7b the psalmist refers to the "unfailing love" (*hesed*) of Yahweh. As suggested above, the repeated use of *'adonay* ("lord") in reference to Yahweh serves as reminder of the master-servant relationship that exists between God and the psalmist. The use of *hesed* in verse 7b reiterates this claim, thus even

---

14. See also Pss 59:17; 88:14; 90:14; 143:18.

intensifying it. Although the term can rightly be rendered "unfailing love" (NIV), a more contextually appropriate rendering might be "loyalty" or "solidarity," or perhaps even "faithfulness." The multivalent sense of "love" in English distorts the particular meaning intended here. The sense is captured best in Deuteronomy 7:9: "Know therefore that the LORD your God is God; he is the faithful God, keeping his covenant of love [*hesed*] to a thousand generations of those who love him and keep his commandments." In Deuteronomy 7 the use of *hesed* suggests covenantal loyalty and unflinching faithfulness on the part of Yahweh. In Psalm 130 the psalmist contends that it is for *this reason*, the covenantal loyalty of Yahweh to his people, that the people can adopt a posture of waiting and hoping.

With him is full redemption. In the second half of the causal clause the psalmist refers to "full redemption" (*pedut*). The noun in verse 7c, *pedut* ("full redemption"), and the verb found in verse 8a, *padah* ("to redeem") derive from the same root and invoke a particular idea. The verbal form means "to buy the freedom" of something or "to pay an atonement price" for something.[15] Frequently this langauge is applied to Israel's liberation out of Egypt.[16] In other texts the word more generally means to buy someone out of slavery (e.g., Exod 21:8). In both instances the one with the power must act in behalf of the other to bring about deliverance.

Like the reference to God's loyal love, the references to God's capacity for redemptive work provide Israel with the necessary rationale for hoping in the Lord. The psalmist and Israel alike apparently find themselves in a similar plight. In the second strophe the psalmist implies that "iniquities" or "sins" (*'awon*) are what has brought the psalmist down to the depths (v. 1). In verse 4 he contends that with Yahweh there is forgiveness. This claim of forgiveness is expanded in verse 8 and extended to the full community of Israel. According to the psalmist, God does more than forgive; his loyalty is so great that he is willing to "buy the freedom" of his people "from all their sins." There is hope for those who wait.

Bridging Contexts

FROM THE DEPTHS OF THE SIN that has isolated him from God, the psalmist cries out. As suggested above, the reference to the "depths" is meant to highlight the perceived spatial distance between the praying sinner and the faithful God. The only remedy for addressing this need and closing the "gap" rests with God. Near the center

---

15. Hossfeld and Zenger, *Psalms 3*, 438.
16. See, e.g., Deut 7:8; 9:26; 13:6; 15:15; Pss 78:42; 111:9

of the psalm is the declaration, "But with you there is forgiveness" (v. 4a). The concept of forgiveness and its place within the cultic life of ancient Israel appears regularly in the books of Leviticus and Numbers. In those books, the root *slh*, "to forgive," is paired with, *kpr*, "to atone," thereby creating what Klaus Koch has deemed the *kipper . . . wenislah* formula, "to make atonement . . . to forgive." [17] For example, in Leviticus 4:13–21 the narrative acknowledges the sins of the community, followed by the prescribed actions for both the people and the priests. This text, like others in Leviticus and Numbers, concludes with the phrase, "In this way the priest will make atonement [*kipper*] for the leader's sin, and he will be forgiven [*nislah*]." [18] While the first portion of this formula highlights the activity of the priests, it is only in the second half of the formula that forgiveness is announced. Worth noting, the verb *salah*, "to forgive," appears in the *niphal* stem, which indicates a passive sense. While the priests may perform the *kipper* ritual, the assumption is that forgiveness remains the work of God— forgiveness is received.

Psalm 130 does not include the *kipper . . . wenislah* formula, but it does retain the claim that forgiveness remains the work of God because of God's "unfailing love" (*hesed*) for his people. Earlier in the Psalter the psalmist described God similarly as "forgiving and good, abounding in *hesed*" (Ps 86:5). The psalmists are clear: Forgiveness is the work of God precisely because *hesed* is the character of God. Together, Psalm 130:4, 7–8 reveal something of this God. Patrick Miller explains that the "three fundamental characteristics—forgiveness, steadfast love or grace, and redemption—are set forth almost as intimate friends and companions of God. Wherever the Lord goes, they are there accompanying and going with God. To encounter this god is also to meet with grace and forgiveness and abundant redemption." [19] For the psalmist, this is the face of hope amid the darkness of the depths.

Other texts from the postexilic period reinforced this claim concerning the very character of God (e.g., 1 Kgs 8:30–53; Jer 31:31–33). The "depths" of the exile no doubt served as a perpetual reminder of the gravity of sin. That singular event bolstered their conviction that, should Yahweh keep a record of sins, surely no one would endure (Ps 130:3). The only explanation for the end of the exile is that Israel's God is one characterized

---

17. Klaus Koch, "Sühne und Sündenvergebung um die Wende von der exilischen zur nachexilischen Zeit," *EvT* 26 (1966): 217–339; see p. 233.

18. For this and similar phrases, see Lev 4:26, 31, 35; 5:10, 13, 16, 18; 19:22; Num 15:25–28.

19. Patrick D. Miller, *Interpreting the Psalms* (Philadelphia: Fortress, 1986), 142.

by forgiveness, prompted by *hesed*. This conviction led to the confession in Nehemiah 9:17 that Israel's God is *'eloah selihot*, the "God of forgiveness."

In addition to its signficance in the Old Testament, the theme of divine forgiveness plays a central role in the confession of the early church as the various New Testament writers employed different metaphors and images to capture the richness of this concept.[20] The God identified by forgiveness, steadfast love, and redemption in Psalm 130 is the same God in view in these latter texts. In the Gospel narratives, for example, Jesus often heals, but the healing event is coupled with the announcement concerning the forgiveness of sins. Not surprisingly, the announcement of the forgiveness of sins by Jesus leaves the religious officials apoplectic and declaring, "Why does this fellow talk like that? He's blaspheming! Who can forgive sins but God alone?" (Mark 2:7). Ironically, the declaration issued by the religious officials represents a fundamental tenet in the Christian faith— that indeed it is God alone who can forgive sin. In extending this claim, Paul repeatedly asserted that it was God *through Christ* who has forgiven sin. In his letter to the church at Rome, Paul reminded the community that "God demonstrates his own love for us in this: While we were still sinners, Christ died for us" (Rom 5:8). And further, Paul indicates that "while we were God's enemies," while we were in the depths, far removed from God, "we were reconciled to him." The work of reconciliation, forgiveness, and restoration was indeed the work of God, but it was a work predicated on the faithful love of God.

 PSALM 130 CONFRONTS each of us with the reality of human sinfulness—our own sinfulness. Perhaps it would be easier to assume the "depths" mentioned in verse 1 refer only to difficult times, challenging circumstances, or unwanted threats, but the psalmist invites us to plumb the depths of our human condition. To refer to that condition, to our own sinfulness, is rarely if ever in vogue today; such thoughts are assumed to be from another generation when tent revivals and pulpit pounding held sway. Regrettably, we deprive ourselves of the richness of faith when such dismissive and even infantile attitudes guide our thoughts. Throughout the history of the church, faithful saints before us read Psalm 130, and they understood well the power of its words.

---

20. On the New Testament claims concerning forgiveness and reconciliation, see Reihard Feldmeier and Hermann Spieckermann, *God of the Living: A Biblical Theology*, trans. Mark Biddle (Waco, TX: Baylor University Press, 2011), 319–37.

Luther called it one of the "Pauline Psalms" because it articulated so well Paul's thought on the reality of sin and the grace that remedied it.[21] John Wesley had just heard an anthem on Psalm 130 being sung at St. Paul's Cathedral on the day he made his way to the room at Aldersgate where he claims his heart was "strangely warmed" as he thought about the grace of God in the face of his own sin.[22] Countless other nameless saints have poured over Psalm 130 in confronting their own sinfulness, confessing their own depths, and waiting on this faithful God to do his good work.

As we reflect on our own sinfulness we might be inclined to turn away from God. We know our own brokenness and failures—they are both profoundly disruptive and thoroughly destructive. The psalmist would say that such turning away is akin to living in the depths. And yet in those disruptive and destructive moments, when the darkness of the depths threatens to have the last word, the psalmist turns to God—directly to God—and cries out. And we are invited to do the same.

The point of Psalm 130 is not to remind people of their sinfulness—my hunch is that most if not all of us are keenly aware of our brokenness and sinfulness. The point of Psalm 130, rather, is to remind people that the darkness of the depths is not life as God intended it—that such darkness is not the end of our story (v. 3). In his book *Embodying Forgiveness: A Theological Analysis*, Greg Jones acknowledges the reality of sin but then reminds us of a greater reality still:

> To be forgiven by God, to be initiated in the life of God's kingdom, is to be transferred from one narrative—the narrative of death-dealing sin—to the narrative of God's reconciliation in Christ. And in the latter narrative, we are forgiven of our sin so that we can learn to become holy through lifelong repentance and forgiveness.[23]

One narrative exchanged for another—darkness for light, death for life. Despite the darkness, the psalmist leans forward toward the God he knows—the one who chooses to love us, redeem us, and forgive us . . . the one who invites us all into a new narrative, a narrative marked by grace.

---

21. Edward Henry Lauer, "Luther's Translation of the Psalms in 1523–24," *The Journal of English and Germanic Philology* 15 (1915): 1–34 (6).

22. Rowland E. Prothero, *The Psalms in Human Life and Experience* (New York, NY: E. P. Dutton and Co., 1903), 141.

23. Greg Jones, *Embodying Forgiveness: A Theological Analysis* (Grand Rapids: Eerdmans, 1995), 159.

Psalm 131

A song of ascents. Of David.

¹ My heart is not proud, LORD,
   my eyes are not haughty;
I do not concern myself with great matters
   or things too wonderful for me.
² But I have calmed and quieted myself,
   I am like a weaned child with its mother;
   like a weaned child I am content.
³ Israel, put your hope in the LORD
   both now and forevermore.

Original Meaning

PSALM 131 IS THE TWELFTH psalm in the Songs of Ascent and the second shortest poem in the entire Psalter. Loren Crow argues that the brevity of Psalm 131 might suggest that the material in it was likely a fragment of a larger poem. Unlike many psalms, this one fails to fit the traditional form-critical categories.[1] The psalm begins with a series of three negatives in verse 1. Normally, the psalmist would utter a series of petitions in response to the negative claims in verse 1, but instead of petitions the poet utters confessions of trust in Yahweh. Consequently, this brief psalm is best understood as a psalm of confidence (cf. Pss 16; 23; 62).

Thematically, the entire psalm focuses on an attitude of humility before Yahweh. The literal and figurative posture of humility involves the entire body: the heart (*leb*), the eye (*'ayin*) and the throat/soul (*nepesh*). These individual parts represent the whole person, or aspects of the whole person (synecdoche). Although the metaphor is lost in the English translation, another image associated with the body also appears in Psalm 131:1c. In the NIV the line begins, "I do not concern myself," but the verb employed is *halak*, which means literally "to walk." Hence the psalmist's heart, eyes, body, and even feet participate in this posture of piety. These images and their meanings, along with the mother-child image and the image of being quiet

---

1. Crow, *The Songs of Ascents (Psalms 120–134)*, 94. To say so is not to suggest that the psalm itself lacks elements associated with particular forms or genres. For example, Mitchell Dahood observes that the psalm has elements of a royal psalm (Dahood, *Psalms 101–150*, 180).

before God (v. 2), demonstrate the affinity of Psalm 131 with other wisdom texts, including Job, Proverbs, and selected psalms (Pss 37; 39; 73; 139).[2]

Declaration of Humility (131:1)

PSALM 131 BEGINS WITH A VOCATIVE, "LORD," followed by three negated statements, each meant to indicate the piety of the psalmist. The first two statements refer to the psalmist's relationship with others, while the last statement, to God.

My heart is not proud. The verb, *gabah*, translated as "proud" in the NIV, means to be high. The term itself is value neutral and can have a positive connotation. In Isaiah 52:12, for example, the prophet refers to the servant of Yahweh who shall be lifted high, hence suggesting a positive assessment of the servant; but when *gabah* appears with "heart" (*leb*), as in Psalm 131:1, a negative assessment is frequently expected. Perhaps this sense is no more strongly worded than in Proverbs 16:5a. In that proverb, the two words from Psalm 131:1a—*gabah* ("high") and *leb* ("heart")—appear. The Hebrew text reads literally, "every heart that is lifted high ['arrogant'] is an abomination [*to'abah*] to the LORD."

My eyes are not haughty. The language used in reference to the psalmist's eyes is similar to the language associated with the psalmist's heart—both refer to being lifted up or high. In verse 1b the verb is *rum*, which means "exalted" or "lifted up," but with a negative connotation. For a similar use of "lifted up" (*rum*) with "heart" (*leb*) see Hosea 13:6. Twice before in the Songs of Ascent the "lifting up" of eyes has been mentioned. In Psalms 121:1 and 123:1 the psalmist lifts up his eyes. In those instances, however, the verb was *nasa'* ("lifted up"), whereas in Psalm 131:1 the verb differs (*rum*). The former usage (*nasa'*, "lifted up") suggests a posture of piety; the latter suggests arrogance.

I do not concern myself with great matters. As noted in the introductory comments, the English translation in the NIV fails to capture the image conveyed in verse 1c–d. The verb employed is *halak*, which means literally "to walk," but in the *piel* form the verb could be rendered "to walk about." Like the words mentioned above, to walk about is not a particularly negative activity. William Brown has convincingly argued that the "pathway" metaphor functions as one of the major images throughout the Psalter, and subsumed within that image is that of walking.[3] What matters, however, is where one walks and in what posture. The opening lines of Psalm 1

2. Walter Beyerlin, *Wider die Hybris des Geistes: Studien zum 131. Psalm*, SBS 108 (Stuttgart: Katholisches Bibelwerk, 1982), 71–80.

3. Brown, *Seeing the Psalms*, 31–54.

exhort the psalmist not to walk in the counsel of the wicked or the way of sinners. Such wisdom should lead one down the right pathway. In Psalm 131 the psalmist invokes the image of pathway but in a nuanced manner. He explains that he has not attempted to walk (*halak*) in a way that concerns himself with "great matters or things too wonderful" for him. The phrase "great matters" or "wonderful things" (*gedolot wenipla'ot*) appears elsewhere in the Psalter typically to refer to God's salvific acts in Israel's history (e.g., Pss 86:10; 136:4; 145:5–6). Even when used individually, these terms refer to moments in Israel's savlation history.[4] Lest the interpreter misunderstand, the psalmist is not advocating that the humble person refrain from seeking to understand the world (i.e., "great matters"); rather, he is confessing that he is not God, nor does he try to do the things of God. Such attempts are little more than vain ambition.[5] The humble walk otherwise.

Declaration of Trust in God (131:2)

AS SUGGESTED ABOVE, Psalm 131:1a–d included three negations (*lo'*) as part of a threefold declaration that indicated the behaviors rejected by the psalmist. In verse 2 the word *lo'* appears again, but this time as part of the first phrase in the line, *'im-lo'*, which often functions as an asserveration and is translated "indeed" or "surely" (cf. NASB, JPS). Alternatively, the term can be translated "but," as rendered in the NIV. The latter usage captures well the the distinction between verses 1 and 2. In verse 1 the psalmist explains his posture of piety by highlighting what he is not (*lo'*) doing. By contrast, in verse 2 the psalmist explains his piety in the light of what he is doing.

I have calmed and quieted myself. The verb *shawah* means "to even out" or "to level" ground (Isa 28:25), or figuratively, "to settle down."[6] The second verb, "quieted," comes from the root *dmm*, which means "to be silent." The idea of "quieting oneself" or "being still" occurs elsewhere in the Psalter, though synonymous terms are employed in those contexts (e.g., Pss 46:11; 76:8). This language and imagery comports well with the larger concept of "abasing oneself," or humbling oneself, in the presence of God. As Loren Crow suggests, perhaps this language refers to the "cultic postures intended to secure the divine favor" for the psalmist.[7]

---

4. Crow, *The Songs of Ascents*, 95.

5. H. Stephen Shoemaker, "Psalm 131," *RevExp* 85 (1988): 89–94.

6. John Goldingay translates that the verb *shawah* as "conformed" based on the *qal* form of the verb, which means "to be the same." According to Goldingay, the psalmist has "conformed" his spirit to be like or to resemble the image that appears in the latter half of the verb, the nursed child (Goldingay, *Psalms* 3, 536 n. 13). In Ps 131:2, however, *shawah* appears in the *piel*, not the *qal*, thus making the preferred translation "to even out" or "to settle down."

7. Crow, *The Songs of Ascents*, 95.

I am like a weaned child. The metaphors in Psalm 131:1–2a provide a contrast between the posture of pride and that of a proper petitionary stance. In verse 2b–c the psalmist introduces the final image in this comparison, the mother-child relationship. Although the image appears obvious enough upon first reading, two questions have dominated scholarship on this psalm: the meaning of *gamul* ("wean") and the sense and object of the preposition *'al* ("upon"). The verb *gamul* can refer to the time when a child has finally become weaned from her or his mother's breast, typically around three years of age. This moment in the life of the family was marked with a family feast. Genesis 21:8 records the time at which Isaac was weaned from Sarah—and a "great feast" was held. Later, in 1 Samuel 1:20–23, the narrator refers to the time Hannah intends to take Samuel to Shiloh as soon as he is weaned.[8] These passages could suggest that the metaphor of the weaned child in Psalm 131:2b would be beyond the age of three and consequently one "who no longer cries out in hunger for the mother's breast, but who seeks out the mother for her warm embrace and nurturing care."[9] The preposition *'al* appears in the clause and is translated "with" in the NIV. More often, however, the preposition would be rendered "upon," which would slightly alter the reading of the clause: "like a weaned child *upon* its mother." If the above-mentioned proposal for the weaned child is adopted, then the preposition would imply a young child that is being carried by its mother (i.e., "upon its mother"). The image of trust is evident in this image.

While such a reading remains plausible, the image in Psalm 131 seems to point the interpreter in a different direction. The image of the weaned child likely refers to an infant who has just come off the breast, still resting upon (*'al*) its mother.[10] The child has received all that is necessary for life and physically enjoys the close bond between mother and child; the young child rests peacefully, assured that her life has been cared for and will continue to be so. Even as the young child trusted that her mother was the source of life, so too the psalmist trusts that his life is being cared for by God.

---

8. In 2 Macc 7:27 the mother speaks to her youngest son prior to his murder at the hands of Antiochus Epiphanes. In the course of her exhortation, she mentions having nursed her son for three years.

9. Suggested by Nancy deClaissé-Walford in deClaissé-Walford, Jacobson, and LaNeel Tanner, *The Book of Psalms*, 931.

10. Brueggemann and Bellinger, *Psalms*, 553; Goldingay, *Psalms 3*, 537; Keet, *A Study of the Psalms of Ascent*, 84–85.

Exhortation to All Israel (131:3)

IN THE FINAL VERSE OF PSALM 131 the poet repeats Psalm 130:7a, "Israel, put your hope in the LORD." (On the meaning of "hope," see the comments on Ps 130:7.) Further, the psalmist reminds Israel that they are to hope and wait "both now and forevermore." Goldingay suggests that this final line has a more immediate application to the audience. He writes:

> the psalm commends a quietism that lasts forever. Israel needs to be prepared to settle down for the long haul with circumstances such as those of the Persian period described in Ezra and Nehemiah and forgo any attempt to bring in the kingdom of God, which is the venture of a lofty heart and eyes that look high. It needs to be prepared to wait forever.[11]

The first two verses of Psalm 131 refer to a proper posture of trust, and the same posture seems to constitute the rhetorical force of the final verse as well. The issue is not simply how long Israel will wait (i.e., "now and forever") but that, as long as they do wait, they do so with a proper posture of trust. Like the infant child resting upon its mother, all Israel is called to trust in God, with the assurance that its collective life will be cared for "both now and forever more" (v. 3b).

Bridging Contexts

INTERPRETERS HAVE SUGGESTED that perhaps Psalm 131 was composed by an Israelite woman. Verse 2, in particular, is suggestive of this possibility. The Hebrew in verse 2c literally reads, "My soul is like the weaned child upon me." Could the author be an Israelite woman carrying a child while on a pilgrimage to Jerusalem? Without question, women did compose prayers that were recorded. Miriam utters a prayer in response to Israel's deliverance at the hands of the Egyptians (Exod 15:20–21), and Hannah utters two prayers in her desire for a child (1 Sam 1:10–11; 2:1–10). Other prayers by women appear elsewhere in the Old Testament (Judg 5:1–31; Ruth 4:14). In the apocryphal literature the prayers of women appear as well. For example, Sarah prays in Tobit 3:11–15, and Judith prays repeatedly in the book that bears her name (Jdt 9:2–14; 16:1–17). Perhaps best known is Mary's *Magnificat* in Luke 1:47–55. This evidence suggests that the prayers of women, or scenes that reflected women at prayer, were collected as part of canonical or deuterocanonical Scripture.

---

11. Goldingay, *Psalms 3*, 538.

When the interpreter turns to Psalm 131, however, there is not sufficient evidence to determine the gender of the psalmist either way.[12]

While the psalmist's gender may be difficult to determine, the presence of feminine imagery is not. The imagery in Psalm 131 is that of an infant being comforted by its mother, with the psalmist self-describing as an infant and presumably God as the comforting mother. The use of feminine metaphorical imagery for God is not unique to Psalm 131. Although metaphors such as king, judge, and warrior appear with much greater regularity throughout the Old Testament, there are a number of texts that use feminine imagery to capture a particular understanding of God. In Isaiah 49:15, for example, God inquires, "Can a mother forget the baby at her breast and have no compassion on the cild she has borne? Though she may forget, I will not forget you!" Similarly, in the final chapter of Isaiah God explains, "As a mother comforts her child, so I will comfort you" (Isa 66:13). In the book of Jeremiah, following the anguished cry of Israel to God concerning their desperate estate, God announces, "Is not Ephraim my dear son, the child in whom I delight? Though I often speak against him, I still remember him. Therefore, my heart yearns for him; I have great compassion for him" (Jer 31:20). While other texts use feminine imagery in different ways, the texts from Isaiah and Jeremiah employ feminine imagery to draw attention to the very compassion of God.[13] This connection may inform our reading of Psalm 131. The psalmist portrays himself as an infant on the lap of his mother. His future is not secured by arrogance, "haughty" eyes (v. 1a–b), or an obsession with "great matters" (v. 1c). To the contrary, his future rests with the nourishing, consoling, life-sustaining God, whose care for his people is marked by his compassion. The psalmist can rest easy in the certain care of God, and likewise, all Israel can "hope" (v. 3) in the same.

AS SUGGESTED IN THE introductory material, this psalm can rightly be labeled a psalm of confidence. In this poem the psalmist confesses his trust in God. Trust is a frequently employed term throughout both the Old and New Testaments, yet despite its frequency, its precise definition remains elusive for most modern readers.

---

12. For a similar assessment see Hossfeld and Zenger, *Psalms 3*, 448; deClaissé-Walford, Jacobson, LaNeel Tanner, *The Book of Psalms*, 932.

13. For other uses of feminine imagery associated with God see Deut 32:11–12, 18; Hos 11:3–4; 13:8; Isa 42:14; Ruth 2:12.

Regrettably, because the term is so difficult to define, it has become minimized at best, if not altogether trivialized. For many people, a posture of trust simply signals a passive stance—the individual waits for God to do something. Such a definition of trust, however, grossly misunderstands all that trust involves. Trusting requires us to reject some things so that we might receive other things, as is particularly true in the midst of challenging and uncertain times. In the most difficult of circumstances we are prone to believe that we must save ourselves, and that, if anything, we must work harder, faster, and with greater determination to secure our future. Thus far the Songs of Ascent have included several poems that recount the troubling circumstances plaguing the lives of those who prayed these prayers (cf. Pss 120; 124; 125; 126; 129; 130). In light of the frequent references to difficult circumstances, we might anticipate that the final psalms in this collection would invite us to push back, to work harder, and to do more in the face of such trials. The psalmist does indeed call for us to take action, but this action comes in the form of relinquishment. We are called to relinquish our sense of self-reliance, hubris, and pride, and in its place to adopt a posture similar to that of a child—a posture that positions us so that we might experience the fullness of God's compassion. James Mays explains this posture further by suggesting that "the stance adopted is that of a calm and patient soul, calm because ultimately it does not have to depend upon itself and patient because it does not believe that the present time is a prison."[14] Such a posture, however, runs counter to the reality that we know; we are anything but calm and patient, and we have been lulled into thinking that we can deliver ourselves. In such moments of delusional thinking we need the compassion of God to sweep over us, thus calming us, reassuring us, saving us. In that moment and every moment we need the posture of a child, the very model of the one invited into the kingdom of God (Matt 18:1–4).

---

14. Mays, *Psalms*, 408.

Psalm 132

A song of ascents.

¹ LORD, remember David
  and all his self-denial.
² He swore an oath to the LORD,
  he made a vow to the Mighty One of Jacob:
³ "I will not enter my house
  or go to my bed,
⁴ I will allow no sleep to my eyes
  or slumber to my eyelids,
⁵ till I find a place for the LORD,
  a dwelling for the Mighty One of Jacob."
⁶ We heard it in Ephrathah,
  we came upon it in the fields of Jaar;
⁷ "Let us go to his dwelling place,
  let us worship at his footstool, saying,
⁸ 'Arise, LORD, and come to your resting place,
  you and the ark of your might.
⁹ May your priests be clothed with your righteousness;
  may your faithful people sing for joy.'"
¹⁰ For the sake of your servant David,
  do not reject your anointed one.
¹¹ The LORD swore an oath to David,
  a sure oath he will not revoke:
"One of your own descendants
  I will place on your throne.
¹² If your sons keep my covenant
  and the statutes I teach them,
then their sons will sit
  on your throne for ever and ever."
¹³ For the LORD has chosen Zion,
  he has desired it for his dwelling, saying,
¹⁴ "This is my resting place for ever and ever;
  here I will sit enthroned, for I have desired it.
¹⁵ I will bless her with abundant provisions;
  her poor I will satisfy with food.
¹⁶ I will clothe her priests with salvation,

and her faithful people will ever sing for joy.
¹⁷ "Here I will make a horn grow for David
and set up a lamp for my anointed one.
¹⁸ I will clothe his enemies with shame,
but his head will be adorned with a radiant crown."

PSALM 132 IS THE THIRTEENTH psalm in the Songs of Ascent collection (Pss 120–34), but its length distinguishes it from the other, shorter psalms in this group.[1] In length alone, the eighteen verses of Psalm 132 are double those of the next longest psalm in the collection (Ps 122), perhaps indicating the importance of Psalm 132 for the collection as a whole.[2] While the length of the poem is suggestive of this probability, the theological foci of the psalm (Zion and David) confirm its importance for the Psalms of Ascents collection. While previous psalms in the group refer to Zion or Jerusalem by name (Pss 122; 125; 126; 128; 129; 133; 134), this psalm articulates most clearly the rationale for the pilgrimage to Zion: it is the dwelling place of Yahweh. And though David appears in the superscriptions of four of these psalms (Pss 122; 124; 131; 133), he is mentioned in the body of only one other psalm (Ps 122).

Psalm 132 draws heavily from two previous traditions, one associated with the ark and the other with the Davidic dynasty. According to 2 Samuel 6:1–19, David brought the ark of God, "which is called by the Name, the name of the LORD Almighty, who is enthroned between the cherubim on the ark" (v. 2), from Kiriath-Jearim to the City of David. In Psalm 132 the association of the ark with the dwelling place of Yahweh becomes a central theme, one that is expanded in the latter half of the poem. In 2 Samuel 7 the prophet Nathan comes to David and announces that David would not be the one to build the temple, but Yahweh would build a house (i.e., dynasty) for David. In Psalm 132, references to a dynastic promise appear in verses 11–12 and 17–18. The references to David in Psalm 132 have led some scholars to classify it as a royal psalm similar to Psalm 2 or Psalm 89; yet the heavy emphasis on Zion throughout Psalm 132 has led

---

1. Psalm 132 also differs linguistically from other psalms in the larger collection. In Psalm 132, for example, the relative pronoun is spelled in full (*'asher*) rather than in the shortened form (*she*), which appears elsewhere in the collection (e.g., Pss 122:4; 124:1, 2, 6). In addition, Ps 132:9, 16 refer to "priests" and "faithful people," terms that are absent from the other fourteen psalms in the collection.
2. McCann, "The Book of Psalms," 1210.

others to suggest that it may have more in common with the Zion psalms (Pss 46; 48). Given the placement of Psalm 132 in the Songs of Ascent—a collection of psalms focused on Zion—its primary emphasis should be on Zion as the eternal dwelling place of Yahweh. The references to David serve to reinforce that theme, as explained below.

Psalm 132 can be divided into two major sections, verses 1–10 and 11–18, with each division containing twenty lines. The two divisions are also bound together by a number of repeating terms: "to David" (*ledavid* [vv. 1, 11a]); "he swore" (*nishba* [vv. 2, 11a]); "if" (*'im* [vv. 3, 4, 12a]); "until" (*'ad* [vv. 5, 12b]); "resting place" (*menuhah* [vv. 8, 14]); and "anointed one" (*meshiah* [vv. 10, 17]). In addition to the repetition of terms, the two divisions follow a similar structure:

David vows to God (vv. 1–5)	God vows to David (vv. 11–12)
Allusion to the ark story (vv. 6–8)	God's response to the ark story (vv. 13–15)
Prayer for the priests and people (v. 9)	Prayer for the priests and people (v. 16)
Prayer for David (v. 10)	Response to prayer for David (vv. 17–18)

Both divisions are structured around oaths. In the first division David utters an oath in verses 3–5, and the "we" group utters an oath in verses 7–9. In contrast, the entire second half of the psalm consists of two oaths by Yahweh (vv. 11–12, 14–18). The first half represents the petitions and sworn oaths of the people, while the second signals Yahweh's response to the petitions (vv. 2–5//vv. 11–12; vv. 7–10//vv. 14–18). It is the response of Yahweh that provides the enduring hope for those who read and prayed Psalm 132. Earlier in the Psalter Psalm 89 announced the end of the Davidic monarchy in light of the exile. The fall of Jerusalem and the demise of royal rule signaled a new era for Israel, one filled with considerable uncertainty. In the face of this uncertainty, the two poems preceding Psalm 132 in the Songs of Ascent collection invited God's people to "put your hope in the LORD" (Pss 130:7; 131:3). Psalm 132 likely serves as a response to that invitation; it is a reminder of God's oath to his people and of their hope for a future.

David Vows to God (132:1–5)

THE STROPHE OPENS WITH A PETITION for Yahweh to remember David. The oath that David made to Yahweh (vv. 3–5) anchors the first strophe by providing a rationale for God's remembrance.

LORD, remember David. The opening strophe highlights David's role as the founder of the Jerusalem temple. The psalm begins with a request or a petition for God to remember David because of his "self-denial" or "hardships."[3] Although the Hebrew root for "self-denial," *'nh* II, means "to be afflicted" or "to suffer" in the *qal* stem, in the *pual* stem the verb refers to being degraded or humiliated, or in this case, deprived.[4] The deprivation was not externally imposed; rather, it was the result of David's earnest desire to build a sanctuary for Yahweh. David spared no effort in ensuring that there were proper resources available for the construction of Yahweh's temple. He assembled workers, stonecutters, masons, and carpenters to ensure the completion of the project (1 Chr 22:15) and to ensure that it was properly funded he collected "one hundred thousand talents of gold, one million talents of silver," and quantities of bronze and iron that were "too great to be weighed."

In 1 Chronicles 22:14 David declares, "I have taken great pains [*'onyi*] to provide for the temple." Terms associated with the root *'nh* are applied to David only in Psalm 132:1 and 1 Chronicles 22:14. Because Chronicles was written after Psalm 132, the Chronicler was likely familiar with, and perhaps even dependent upon, the psalm. While the additional details provided in 1 Chronicles 22 do not appear in Psalm 132, they do serve to explain and amplify the claim made in Psalm 132:1.

He swore an oath. In addition to remembering David's extensive preparation for the rebuilding of the temple, the speaker also recalls the vow David made to "the Mighty One of Jacob," a title used of Yahweh only in this psalm (vv. 2, 5), Genesis 49:24, and Isaiah 49:26; 60:16. The title recalls the scene in Israel's early history when Jacob blessed his twelve sons. In referencing this title, those praying the psalm emphasize that David swore an oath with the God who had been with the nation, the entire nation, from its very beginning. David's zeal to build a house for Yahweh alludes to another scene in the Jacob cycle, namely, Jacob's sworn oath to Yahweh in Genesis 28:10–20. Upon waking from his dream, Jacob makes a vow to Yahweh declaring that the stone he erected will be "God's house."[5]

---

3. Those who are uttering this petition are likely the "we" group mentioned in verses 6–7. The precise identity of this group is difficult, if not impossible, to determine. Hans-Joachim Kraus opines that the speaker in verse 1 may have been a king or perhaps a group of priests (Kraus, *Psalms 60–150*, 480). While either option is possible, the psalm's inclusion within the larger Songs of Ascent collection likely creates a third option, namely, the pilgrims themselves. Other psalms throughout this collection include first-person singular and plural language meant to reflect the prayers and petitions of the pilgrims.

4. "II עָנָה," *HALOT* 1:852–4.

5. Hossfeld and Zenger, *Psalms 3*, 461.

Both Jacob and David, the founder of the nation and the founder of the temple, make oaths regarding the dwelling place of God among his people.

While the vow placed on the lips of David in Psalm 132:3–5 does not appear in the narrative accounts in 2 Samuel 6–7, it does reflect the zeal expressed by David in 2 Samuel 7:1–2.[6] In that account, the narrative explains that after "the king was settled in his palace" (v. 1) he spoke to Nathan, "Here I am, living in a house of cedar, while the ark of God remains in a tent" (2 Sam 7:2). David's realization is followed by a vision that came to Nathan, which the prophet subsequently relayed to David—a vision concerning the building of a "house" in which Yahweh would dwell. David's comparison between his own "house of cedar" and Yahweh's tent reflects not only David's awareness but also his resolve. This resolve is manifested in Psalm 132 with the emphasis on David's self-denial and deprivation. David's commitment to "self-denial" and deprivation, mentioned first in verse 1, continues in verses 3–5 with his refusal to return home or sleep until he finds a "place" (*maqom*) and "dwelling" (*mishkan*) for Yahweh (v. 5). Both terms, *maqom* and *mishkan*, also refer to the temple elsewhere (e.g., Deut 12:5, 11; Pss 24:3; 26:8; 43:3; 84:1), thereby merging elements of the ark narrative with those of the temple tradition. The account in 2 Samuel 6 recalls David's bringing the ark to Jerusalem, the site of his newly conquered capital, with the primary intent of finding a resting place for the ark. While that narrative stands in the background of Psalm 132, the focus in this psalm shifts entirely to Zion and the temple, as is evident in verses 11–18.

Allusion to the Ark Story (132:6–10)

THE SECOND STROPHE OF PSALM 132 recounts the movement of the ark from Kiriath-Jearim to Jerusalem, as well as the words uttered by those who accompanied the ark into Jerusalem. Rather than using the third person to speak of those involved, as though merely recounting history objectively, the community uses the first-person plural, "we," and in doing so they place themselves within the story. As Goldingay has suggested, "it is as if they were themselves involved when their ancestors undertook this action with David."[7] What occurred in the past continues to shape the present.

We heard it in Ephrathah. Verse 6 presents two interpretive questions. The first one concerns the pronoun "it," used twice in the verse: "We heard *it* in Ephrathah, we came upon *it* in the field of Jaar." To whom or to what does "it" refer? Normally, pronouns refer to something mentioned

---

6. McCann, "The Book of Psalms," 1211.
7. Goldingay, *Psalms 3*, 549. See also McCann, "The Book of Psalms," 1212.

previously in a text (an anaphoric reference). In this instance, however, the pronoun is cataphoric, referring to another word later in the text. Because the pronoun is feminine singular, the likely referent appears in verse 8: "ark" (*'aron*). Although *'aron* is typically masculine, it does appear as a feminine noun in several texts (e.g., 1 Sam 4:17; 1 Chr 13:6).[8]

The second question concerns the locations mentioned in the verse. Ephrathah is traditionally associated with the area around Bethlehem in the Old Testament (Ruth 4:11; Mic 5:2), but the region is not mentioned by name in either of the Samuel narratives devoted to the ark (1 Sam 4–6; 2 Sam 6). The second location, Jaar, is likely a poetically shortened reference to Kiriath-Jearim, the place where the ark rested prior to its eventual relocation in Jerusalem (2 Sam 6:2; 1 Chr 13:6). Taking both interpretive questions together, the community in Psalm 132 is confessing that those in the region of Ephrathah heard that the ark of God was in Kiriath-Jearim, and that upon arriving in Kiriath-Jearim they found "it" (i.e., the ark). Although Ephrathah is not mentioned by name in other texts, the Chronicler does indicate that David assembled "all Israel" to go retrieve the ark from Kiriath-Jearim (1 Chr 13:5). Given the prominence of David in Psalm 132, the assumption that the region of Ephrathah, a region associated with David, would have been instrumental in this effort seems logical.

Let us go to his dwelling place. Having heard about the ark while in Ephrathah and having found it in Kiriath-Jearim, in verse 7 they approach "his footstool" to bow down in worship. The phrase "his footstool" (*hadom raglayw*) also appears in Psalm 99:5 and 1 Chronicles 28:2, both times in reference to the ark. The worshipers appear before the ark and offer up their petitions in Psalm 132:8–10. As rendered in both the NIV and NRSV, the first petition appears to be a request for God to come and meet them at his "resting place" above the ark, yet the Hebrew does not contain the word "come." The rhetorical force of the petition might be better understood by rendering the Hebrew as "Rise up, O LORD [*qumah YHWH*], for the sake of your resting place."[9] This petition echoes the story of the ark in the book of Numbers. Whenever the ark set out, Moses would cry, "Rise up, LORD" (*qumah YHWH*), and petition Yahweh to scatter all the enemies of Israel (Num 10:35). In similar fashion to the request uttered in the wilderness, the petitioners in Psalm 132 seek the protective presence of Yahweh, thus likely explaining the reference in verse 7b to the "ark of your might." The second petition concerns the priests and the

---

8. The NIV understands the first "it" anaphorically, that is, as referring back to the oath sworn by David in verses 3–5.

9. McCann, "The Book of Psalms," 1212.

"faithful ones." They request that God establish righteousness, or a rightly ordered world, for his priests; the establishment of such a world will result in singing or shouting for joy by all the people of God (v. 9).[10]

Do not reject your anointed one. The mention of David in verse 10 recalls verse 1 and his mention there. Together the two verses create an *inclusio* around the first half of the psalm. Verse 10a provides the rationale for the request by the "we" group. The request made, however, is not for David but for "your anointed one." Some have cited the democratization of the Davidic covenant in Isaiah 55:3–5 and suggested that the "anointed one" in Psalm 132 must likewise be a reference to the nation as a whole, not a specific member of the Davidic line. Although other texts, even within the Psalter, appear to apply Davidic ideology to the nation (e.g., Ps 149:5–9), Psalm 132 seems to retain its focus on the Davidic line. The emphasis on future progeny in verses 11–12 suggests that the psalmist has David and his line in view. In other texts that appear to collectivize or democratize the Davidic tradition, the issue of progeny is not referenced. Further, as noted above, Chronicles makes use of Psalm 132. In the closing of Solomon's dedicatory prayer for the temple, 2 Chronicles 6:41–42 quotes Psalm 132:9–10 specifically. Clearly, the Chronicler had David's progeny in view in his use of this psalm.

God's Vow to David (132:11–12)

JUST AS THE NAME "DAVID" PROVIDED an *inclusio* in the first half of the psalm (vv. 1, 10), so too does it in the poem's second half. References to David appear in the first strophe and final strophe (vv. 11, 17). David's name functions as a "bookend" of sorts. The second half of the psalm places the focus on Yahweh's fidelity both to the Davidic dynasty and to Zion, the place of Yahweh's dwelling (v. 13).

The LORD swore an oath. David's oath to God in verses 2–5 is matched by Yahweh's oath to David in verses 11–12. Both swear or pledge an oath (*nishba*) to one another. Other vocabulary terms link this opening strophe in the second half of the psalm with previous lines in the first half. Most notably, in the final line of the first section the petitioners ask of Yahweh, "do not reject [*shub*] your anointed one" (v. 10b). Their concern is addressed in verse 11b with the statement, "a sure oath he will not revoke [*shub*]." The verb *shub* means to "to turn"—in this case to turn away from either a person or a promise. The culminating concern in the first half of the psalm is whether Yahweh will literally "turn away the face of his

---

10. In several of the Yahweh-is-king psalms (cf. Pss 95; 96; 98) the people are called to participate by singing and shouting for joy.

anointed." The second half of the psalm counters by declaring that Yahweh will not "turn [*shub*] away from it [the oath]." The remainder of the psalm serves to illustrate Yahweh's fidelity to the oath.

If your sons keep my covenant. The oath made to David in 2 Samuel 7:14–16 does not contain the type of condition uttered in Psalm 132:12. According to 2 Samuel 7, kings who do wrong will be punished by human hands. In Psalm 132, however, the connection between covenantal faithfulness and the promise of a Davidic dynasty is made much more explicit. To ensure that David's progeny remain faithful to Yahweh's statutes and covenantal expectations, Yahweh declares that he himself will teach them (cf. Ps 119:2). So long as they remain obedient, David's sons will remain on the throne. The statement assumes, conversely, that disobedience will result in the end of the monarchy in Jerusalem. If Psalm 132 was written or collected in the postexilic period, then the conditional statement in verse 12 serves to explain the fall of Jerusalem in 586 BCE and the exile of the Judean king (2 Kgs 25).[11] Yet, as Psalm 132:11b affirmed, Yahweh's commitment to David and his progeny remains "sure" or "certain" (*'emet*). This pledge is explicated in the final strophe of the psalm (vv. 17–18).

The LORD has chosen Zion. In the background tradition for this text (2 Sam 6–7), it is David who chooses Zion. From Hebron (2 Sam 5) David and his men march into Jerusalem, attack the Jebusites, and establish the city as his new capital, "The City of David." Beginning with Solomon, however, the language shifted to introduce the claim that it was not David but Yahweh who actually chose (*bahar*) Zion.[12] Psalm 132 reflects the latter tradition of Yahweh's choosing Zion. This point is reinforced in verses 13b and 14b with the use of the word "desired" (*'iwwah*).

The traditional Zion psalms describe the city in cosmic terms by referring to the paradisiacal river that pulses through the city (Ps 46:4) and its inspiring height, which rivals that of Mount Zaphon (Ps 48:2), perhaps thus offering a rationale for God's choice of this city. Psalm 132 explains simply that Zion is the place he deeply desires to be. The "we" group testifies to this desire in verse 13b, and Yahweh himself declares it in verse 14b. For those in the postexilic community wondering about God's presence with his people, these verses affirm his desire, his deepest desire, to make Jerusalem his dwelling place, where he will sit enthroned as the Divine King (v. 14b).

I will bless her. In verses 8–10 the people uttered several petitions. God answered the first one by declaring Jerusalem to be his resting place (vv. 8a, 14a). The second petition expressed their desire to see God bless

---

11. Hossfeld and Zenger, *Psalms 3*, 465.
12. See in particular 1 Kgs 8:44, 48; 11:13, 32, 36.

the priests and his "faithful people" (v. 9), as promised in verse 16. In verse 15 he promises to satisfy the poor (*'ebyon*) with food. Although the poor were not mentioned in the oath uttered by the "we" group in verses 8–10, their mention here is important to note. In verse 14b Yahweh announces that he will sit enthroned in Zion as the Divine King. As King, he is under obligation to see to the well-being of the poor, and with his oath he affirms his commitment to fulfilling that role. In addition, the mention of the poor signals that the entire society—the priests, the laity, and even the poor— are the beneficiaries of Yahweh's blessings from Zion.

Yahweh's Blessing upon David (132:17–18)

THE FINAL PETITION IN THE FIRST HALF of the psalm urged Yahweh not to turn from or reject the anointed one (v. 10). The final strophe in the psalm answers this petition by confirming Yahweh's faithfulness to the line of David. Despite the failure of previous kings to "keep my covenant and . . . statutes," the dynasty has not reached its full and final end. Just as Yahweh will bless the priests, the laity, and the poor, Yahweh will bless "David" and his progeny; he will make a "horn" grow for David. The horn symbolizes royal power (1 Sam 2:11; Pss 18:3; 89:18) and suggests that, while the dynastic line may appear to have diminished during the postexilic period, it will "grow," or "sprout up" (*tsamah*) yet again. Several exilic and postexilic texts associate the verb *tsamah* with the restoration of Davidic rule (Jer 23:5; 33:15; Zech 3:8; Isa 11:1), thus demonstrating a use of the word similar to that in Psalm 132.

In verse 17b Yahweh also promises to set up a lamp for the anointed one. The metaphor of the lamp refers to the oracle of Ahijah in 1 Kings 11:36. There the prophet announces that while Jeroboam will take ten tribes and form a new kingdom (i.e., the Northern Kingdom), Yahweh will "give one tribe to [Solomon's] son so that David my servant may always have a lamp before me in Jerusalem." The oracle of Ahijah links the presence of Yahweh in Jerusalem with the promised continuation of the Davidic dynasty. A similar move is made in Psalm 132. According to verse 14, Yahweh chooses and desires to dwell in Zion; this choice is a harbinger of good things to come for the line of David. Once more the head of the anointed one will be adorned with a crown (v. 18b). The Hebrew literally reads, "Upon him, I will *yatsits* his crown." The root of *yatsits* can refer to something that gleams, such as the plate crafted by Moses in Exodus 28:36, but the term more often means "to blossom" or "to flourish" (Ps 103:15–17). Thus, the final strophe begins and ends with images that signal hope concerning the future of the Davidic line: the sprouting up of royal power and the blossoming or flourishing of the anointed one.

FROM BEGINNING TO END, Psalm 132 remains focused on two topics: Zion and David. Both themes are intertwined and carefully laced together in this psalm, even as they are throughout the Old Testament. In the lengthy historical Psalm 78, for example, the psalmist recounts Israel's history from its inception but concludes with Yahweh's choice of Mount Zion and selection of David, his servant. In Psalm 78 these two events represent the zenith in Israel's history. God's selection of a king and choice of a sanctuary bear witness to God's desire to be present with Israel in palpable ways. Psalm 132 returns to these intertwined and interlaced themes to celebrate once more God's presence among his people.

Zion. In the first two collections in the Songs of Ascent (Pss 120–24; 125–29), the community repeatedly confesses the conditions that plague them. They live among people who seek to stoke the fires of unrest (Pss 120; 122). They endure contempt and ridicule and remain in need of God's watchful care (Pss 121; 123). Wicked rulers lord it over and threaten them (Pss 125; 129). The people whose existence has been filled with tears and weeping (Ps 126) long to sing for joy.

The final collection in the Psalms of Ascents responds to these crises by articulating Israel's hope. Psalms 130 and 131 call on Israel to "put your hope in the LORD" (Pss 130:7; 131:3). Psalm 132 provides the most explicit articulation of that hope—one grounded in Yahweh's faithful presence in Zion and evident in his faithful promise to the dynasty of David. Psalm 132 explains through remembrance and confession why Zion is the *telos* of their pilgrimage.

This psalm also highlights the intertwining and interlacing of the human and the divine in the establishment of God's living and active presence in the world. Perhaps surprisingly, the poem begins with David's initiative to create a home for God. There is no thunderous clap from the heavens with a deity demanding his human pawns to construct a majestic temple for the divine; rather, illustrating his commitment to God and moved by covenantal faithfulness, David declares his desire to build a dwelling place for his God. And God, out of his commitment to his people and his covenantal faithfulness, chooses Zion and desires to make it the place of his enthronement. This intertwining of the human and the divine continues in the discussion of the Davidic dynasty. Yahweh promises to continue the dynasty of David provided that the members of the dynastic line remain faithful to Yahweh's covenantal statutes. To suggest that the relationship between God and his people, or between God and the Davidic dynasty, has devolved into some form of *quid pro quo* ("this for that") is gravely to misunderstand the true nature of covenant. John Goldingay equates these kinds of covenantal relationships with the relationship of marriage or an abiding friendship, such as with Jonathan and David. Goldingay suggests that when we say relationships are covenantal, "those relationships presuppose a mutual commitment, but they are not exactly conditional or unconditional or contractual. They are more personal than such categories imply."[13] As pilgrims made their way to Jerusalem, with their eyes lifted to the mountains, they were making their way to the place where God has chosen to dwell among his people. And, as his people, they were choosing to abide there also, if only for a season of life. In making their way to Zion, they were confessing that their lives remained intertwined with the life of God and that, together, the living and active presence of God in the world will be realized.

David. As noted above, the name of David opens and closes each major section of the psalm (vv. 1, 10, 11, 17). It is David's oath to Yahweh that initiates the action of the psalm, and it is Yahweh's oath to David (vv. 17–18) that consummates the hope of the psalm. If Psalm 132 is about the intertwining of the human and the divine, it is most clearly expressed in Yahweh's commitment to David. Yet the depiction of David throughout the poem advances two particular themes. Verse 1 acknowledges David's "self-denial" or, as suggested above, his humiliation and deprivation. Throughout the Psalter the image of David suggests one who is humble, persecuted, and in great need. The thirteen historical superscriptions spread across the Psalter depict David not as the glorious king of a bygone gilded age but as one desperate for God's intervention (e.g., Pss 51; 142).[14] A similar image of kingship appears in Psalm 132. In the poem's latter half, it is Yahweh who acts. Yahweh the Divine King, not the human king, promises to care for the poor and ensure that there are provisions for Jerusalem (v. 15a). Even in the final strophe, in his promise to the line of David, Yahweh declares that it will be he who clothes the enemy with shame and not the human king. The decisive action by Yahweh over against the humble spirit of the human king does not mean the king is without task, however. The second theme in Psalm 132 concerns the relationship between torah and kingship.[15] According to Deuteronomy 17:14–20, torah obedience was

---

13. Goldingay, *Psalms 3*, 560.

14. See Tucker, *Constructing and Deconstructing Power in Psalms 107–150*, 179–85.

15. See the discussion in Jamie Grant, "The Psalms and the King," in *Interpreting the Psalms: Issues and Approaches*, ed. David Firth and Philip S. Johnston (Downers Grove, IL: InterVarsity, 2005), 113–18. See also his earlier work, *The King as Exemplar: The Function of Deuteronomy's Kingship Law in the Shaping of the Book of Psalms*, AcBib 17 (Atlanta: SBL Press, 2004).

central to the life of an Israelite king. He was meant to be the "paradigmatic Israelite believer" by embodying the fullness of God's ways in the world.[16] In Psalm 132 David is the paradigmatic servant who makes Yahweh the central focus of his reign, as is evident in his oath (vv. 3–5). Yahweh's oath to David's dynastic line concerns their capacity to live as paradigmatic Israelite believers by integrating kingship and torah faithfulness (v. 12).

Even as Zion is the embodiment of Yahweh's presence on earth, the king is the embodiment of Yahweh's design for the world. Psalm 132 declares that God's faithfulness to both—Zion and David—endures. The threats rehearsed earlier in the Songs of Ascent do not detract from the reality of God's faithfulness or the certainty of his promises.

THE PSALMS OF ASCENTS call people to a journey. This journey is rooted in the past but points to the future. Those living in Jerusalem and the outlying areas of Yehud were well aware of the bitter taste of disappointment—the kind of disappointment that might lead to despair. "Why make *another* pilgrimage to Jerusalem?" they may have wondered. "Why go yet *again*?" Despite the disappointment, those first pilgrims in Yehud leaned into hope. To do so, they moved effortlessly between the past and the future while jettisoning romantic notions of the past and opting instead for remembrances that secured their hope for the future. They were not pessimists, nor were they optimists; they were Yahwists who believed in the God who chose to dwell among them and who provided a royal line to embody the ways of God in the world. Jürgen Moltmann asks, "what is more primal and more profound, joy or pain, life or death? And we reply: existence is more primal than nonexistence, life is more than death: first of all comes love, then grief, and hope runs ahead of despair."[17] Psalm 132 reminds those first pilgrims, and us, that indeed "hope runs ahead of despair." Grief and loss dot our existence often with a frequency we struggle to bear, yet grief and loss are countered by love and hope.

Hebrews living in the postexilic period continued to return to Zion, festival after festival, certain that grief and loss would soon be shouted down by love and hope (v. 16b). To be clear, such faith is not rooted in foolish naiveté that closes its eyes to the world about us; rather, such faith

---

16. Grant, "The Psalms and the King," 115.

17. Jürgen Moltmann, *The Living God and the Fullness of Life*, trans. Margaret Kohl (Louisville: Westminster John Knox, 2015), 100.

"cultivates our memory and nurtures our hope."[18] Psalm 132 invites us to think more deliberately about how we cultivate that memory, how we nurture that hope. Pilgrimages do not happen by accident, nor do cultivated memory and nurtured hope, but they are necessary. They are necessary for those who seek to walk in the Way (Mark 8:27; 9:33–34; 10:17).

18. Peterson, *A Long Obedience in the Same Direction*, 166.

Psalm 133

❧

A song of ascents. Of David.

¹ How good and pleasant it is
  when God's people live together in unity!
² It is like precious oil poured on the head,
  running down on the beard,
running down on Aaron's beard,
  down on the collar of his robe.
³ It is as if the dew of Hermon
  were falling on Mount Zion.
For there the LORD bestows his blessing,
  even life forevermore.

PSALM 133 IS THE NEXT-TO-LAST poem in the Songs of Ascent collection (see Ps 120). Although brief, the psalm contains a number of poetic features that reveal the complexity of the poem itself and, further, the challenges this complexity may present to the interpreter. The psalm opens in verse 1 with an aphorism, or wisdom saying, followed by two similes that connect the language of family with the larger sphere of cultic or festal worship on Zion.[1] Interpreters have debated the meaning of the wisdom saying itself as well as its social context, and they have labored to determine what association, if any, the following similes have with verse 1. One interpreter candidly claimed that Psalm 133 is "a psalm that starts but never really ends. Its point . . . is made in the first verse and then it chases a chain of similes into a verbal whirlpool and stops, never really clarifying itself."[2] While Psalm 133 does present a certain set of interpretive challenges, such an estimation of the poem is overdrawn, to be sure.

The repetition of vocabulary in this short psalm is considerable and serves to create a tightly configured poem despite the apparent dissonance

---

1. William H. Bellinger, Jr., "Poetry and Theology: Psalm 133," in *The Psalter as Witness: Poetry, Theology and Genre*, ed. W. Dennis Tucker, Jr. and William H. Bellinger, Jr. (Waco, TX: Baylor University Press, 2017), 3–14.

2. Ziony Zevit, "Psalms at the Poetic Precipice," *HAR* 19 (1987): 351–66; see p. 356.

created by the various images (i.e., family, oil, dew). The opening and closing lines of the psalm contain a wordplay that creates an *inclusio* around the entire psalm. Verse 1b refers to "brothers" *'ahim,* and in the final line of the psalm (v. 3b) the poet refers to "life," *hayim.* The two words *'ahim* and *hayim,* "brothers" and "life," point to an overarching theme that governs this psalm. Together the people of God receive the blessings of life from the God of Zion.

As well as *'ahim* and *hayim,* additional examples of repetition appear in the psalm. The word "good" (*tov*) is used in verses 1a and 2a ("precious," NIV) thus linking the wisdom saying with the first simile. The word "beard" (*zakan*) appears as the final word in verse 2b and the first word in 2c (in the Hebrew). Verses 2a–3b are connected by the threefold repetition of the phrase "running down upon" or "goes down upon" (*yored 'al*). The NIV's translation fails to capture this feature because it adds the word "running down" in the line that mentions Aaron's beard, when in fact the verb does not appear in the Hebrew, likely due to ellipsis. In addition, the NIV translates *yored 'al* as "were falling on Mount Zion," thus obscuring the third occurrence of the phrase. The two verses can be translated literally as,

> It is like precious oil poured on the head
>   that goes down upon the beard,
> Upon the beard of Aaron
>   that goes down upon the collar of his robe.
> It is as if the dew of Hermon
>   that goes down upon Mount Zion (133:2a–3b).[3]

The phrase *yored 'al,* however, is more than merely ornamental. It actually moves the psalm from one image to the next, from Aaron to his robe and finally to Mount Zion.

Because Psalm 133 begins with an aphorism, or a wisdom saying, some would contend that this poem is a wisdom psalm.[4] Admittedly, the language associated with family life accords with a number of the aphorisms found in the book of Proverbs (e.g., Prov 4:1–8; 11:29; 13:24; 17:6); further, the word "good" (*tov*) found in Psalm 133:1 also appears with considerable regularity in Proverbs, particularly in the "better than" sayings (e.g., Prov 3:13–14). Although these similarities might suggest that the poem is a wisdom psalm, the references to Aaron, Hermon, and Zion in verses 2–3

---

3. Author's translation.

4. See, for example, deClaissé-Walford, Jacobson, and LaNeel Tanner, *The Book of Psalms,* 937.

temper that claim, given that this language would be foreign to the wisdom texts in the Old Testament. John Goldingay is correct in his assessment that if this psalm "links with wisdom thinking, it does so by applying wisdom thinking to some aspect of worship life and utilizing worship life to illumine an aspect of wisdom thinking; it is hardly a wisdom poem."[5]

Wisdom Saying (133:1)

AS SUGGESTED ABOVE, PSALM 133 begins with a wisdom saying that clearly could stand alone and perhaps did at some point in its history. The saying commends a particular way of life, namely, that of familial unity. Because the term *'ahim*, literally "brothers," can connote a variety of relationships, the precise meaning of the opening aphorism has received considerable treatment and demands our attention prior to addressing the similes that follow.

How good and pleasant it is. The NIV does not translate the Hebrew term that begins verse 1a: *hinneh*, "behold, look." The NASB, NRSV, and JPS translate the opening line, "Behold, how good." The addition of the word to the English translation does not fundamentally alter the meaning, but its presence in the Hebrew text is suggestive of the type of saying found in verse 1. William Bellinger has rightly noted that, while the saying begins with *hinneh* rather than *'ashre* ("blessed"), the opening line of Psalm 133 has the feel of a beatitude similar to that found in Psalms 1 and 128, which are both considered wisdom texts.[6] The subsequent terms in the opening line, "good" and "pleasant," appear repeatedly in wisdom texts and contribute to the verse's beatific sense.[7] The word "pleasant," *na'im*, refers to something that is attractive or desirable; fraternal unity was something to be valued, prized, and pursued. As a beatitude of sorts, the opening verse commends a certain understanding of life.

When God's people live together in unity. Although the NIV mentions "God's people" in Psalm 133:1b, the Hebrew term is *'ahim*, which literally means "brothers." Rendered literally, the line reads, "when brothers live together in unity." The precise identity of the *'ahim* and the meaning of their unity have received considerable discussion, but the options can be reduced to three. The first one is familial. Some interpreters note the

---

5. Goldingay, *Psalms* 3, 564.

6. Bellinger, "Poetry and Theology: Psalm 133," 6. See also Gerstenberger, *Psalms, Part 2 and Lamentations*, 371. He proposes that the exclamatory opening suggests there is some form of "educational quality" associated with the saying in verse 1b–c.

7. For additional uses of *tov*, "good," in wisdom texts, see Prov 15:23; 16:16; Job 34:4; Eccl 6:12. For the use of *na'im* see Prov 2:10; 24:25; Job 36:11.

---

similarities in language between Psalm 133:1b and Deuteronomy 25:5. In the latter text, the situation involves brothers who have reached manhood and have married, yet they have remained part of the larger family household and choosen to live on the ancestral land. Thus, the phrase "when brothers live together in unity" may have its origin as a wisdom saying that extols "the value of fraternal harmony and extended family life."[8]

Other interpreters have noted that while verse 1b may have had its origin in a familial context, it has been appropriated differently in Psalm 133. Given that this psalm mentions both Zion and blessing and, further still, that it appears in a pilgrimage collection suggests the poem has in view a festal gathering in Jerusalem. The reference to 'ahim, "brothers," no longer applies solely to a familial context but instead refers to a "festal fraternity," the kind experienced amid jubilant festal celebrations.[9] The NIV's translation of 'ahim as "God's people" no doubt reflects this interpretive option.

The third option, posited by Adele Berlin, is that the image of unified brothers has in view the unification of the entire country, the Northern and Southern Kingdoms.[10] Although the two kingdoms split many centuries earlier (922 BCE), later writers indeed envisioned the possibility of a United Kingdom once more (cf. Ezek 37:15–28). Berlin contends that the imagery of oil flowing down or flowing together likely suggests such a reunification. In addition, she explains that the mention of Hermon in the North and Zion in the South provides overt references to both kingdoms. Although this thesis is appealing, a simpler interpretive explanation seems preferable. Likely the saying, or something similar, had its origin in the family setting but was later adapted for use in the postexilic community to highlight the importance of communal unity.[11]

Explanatory Similes (133:2–3b)

IN THE SECOND STROPHE OF THE PSALM 133 the poet employs two similes to illustrate the claim articulated in verse 1: oil and dew. The first simile, that of the pouring of oil on the head, suggests a festal setting, while the second

---

8. Brian Doyle, "Metaphora Interrupta: Psalm 133," *ETL* 77 (2001): 5–22; see p. 6. Hans-Joachim Kraus further explains that "it is probably correct to think of family order and family law in Israel and the ancient Near East. In many instances, the family estate remains undivided in the possession of the sons after the death of the father. Grazing rights too in the area of transhumance are often willed to the descendants without dividing them. So it happens that brothers must live together and dwell together" (Kraus, *Psalms 60–150*, 485).

9. On "festal fraternity" see Doyle, "Metaphora Interrupta," 7.

10. Adele Berlin, "On the Interpretation of Psalm 133," in *Directions in Biblical Hebrew Poetry*, JSOTSup 40, ed. E. R. Follis (Sheffield: JSOT Press, 1987), 141–48.

11. For a similar assessment see, among others, Gerstenberger, *Psalms, Part 2*, 372–73.

simile concludes with a reference to the mountains of Zion. Both images, the festal event and mountains of Zion, shift the setting of the psalm from the familial in verse 1 to the festal—the type envisioned for a group of pilgrims en route to Jerusalem for a sacred celebration.

Like precious oil poured on the head. With the first comparison, the psalmist likens the unity of God's people to the pouring of oil on the head of a person at a banquet. The application of oil to the head was not medicinal, in this instance, but suggestive of the celebratory nature of the banqueting event. In Ecclesiastes 9:7–8 the sage commends the reader, "Go, eat your food with gladness, and drink your wine with a joyful heart. . . . Always be clothed in white, and always anoint your head with oil." In such settings the oil would have been mixed with spices to add a pleasurable smell to the experience. The Septuagint translates "precious oil" as *muron*, "perfume," thereby making clear that a central feature of this oil would have been its aromatic qualities. The psalmist explains further that this oil would run down onto the beard of the banqueting guest. The beard itself has no particular significance other than to suggest the abundance of oil being poured out.

Running down on Aaron's beard. The psalmist focuses the comparison more narrowly in the second half of Psalm 133:2. The image of oil being poured upon the head and running down onto the beard is extended in verse 2c–d with the focus placed on Aaron and the high priesthood.[12] Given that this psalm celebrates the unity of brothers who live well together, perhaps the psalmist had in mind Leviticus 8. In that text, Moses anoints his own brother Aaron to consecrate him as a priest for the people: "Then Moses took the anointing oil and anointed the tabernacle and everything in it. . . . He poured some of the anointing oil on Aaron's head and anointed him to consecrate him" (Lev 8:10, 12).

In Psalm 133:2 the reference to Aaron's beard brings the cultic life of Israel into sharp focus. Several texts in the Pentateuch refer to the anointing of Aaron or the high priest (Exod 29:7; 30:30–32; Lev 8:12, 30), and central to this anointing of the high priest was the power to bless the people (Lev 9:22). According to Psalm 133:2d, the oil of blessing that is poured

---

12. Wilfred G. E. Watson contends that these lines represent yet another simile entirely (Wildred G. E. Watson, "The Hidden Simile in Psalm 133," *Bib* 60 [1979]: 108–109). Rather than functioning as another simile, the reference to Aaron's beard appears to extend the meaning of the "oil simile" in verse 2a–b in moving the focus from the individual person at the banquet to the community as a whole. Verses 2a and 3a each begin with particle *ke*, "like," but the line that refer to Aaron's beard does not include a comparative particle, thus suggesting that the reference to Aaron's beard remains part of the first comparison (v. 2a).

out on the head of "Aaron" drips down across his beard and onto his robe. Continuing with this imagery, the oil would have then spilled down on the high priest's ephod and breastplate, where the names of the twelve tribes of Israel were inscribed. The image is suggestive: the oil of blessing poured out on the high priest in worship at the temple symbolically extends to the entire community. Together they embody the unity referenced in verse 1.[13]

As if the dew of Hermon. The first and second similes are bound together by the phrase "running down on" (*yored 'al*). The first simile refers to the oil "running down on" the beard, and the second one refers to the dew that "goes down upon Mount Zion." As noted above, the NIV translates this phrase (*yored 'al*) differently in verse 3a ("falling on"). As a result, the interpreter might be led to miss the lexical connection between the two images in the psalm. In verse 3a the Hebrew reads, "It is like the dew of Hermon which falls on the mountains of Zion." Mount Hermon, located in the northern region of ancient Israel (northeast of Dan), towers some 9,100 feet above sea level and receives more than 60 inches of precipitation annually. The interpretive challenge concerns the dew of Hermon and its relation to Mount Zion, given that Zion is more than 200 miles south of Mount Hermon. In the critical apparatus to the *BHS*, the editors attempt to remedy this geographical conundrum by proposing that "Zion" should be read as "Ijon," located at the foot of Mount Hermon (1 Kgs 15:20; 2 Kgs 15:29).[14] Obviously, this change would overcome the geographical challenge to understanding this verse, but that reason alone is not sufficient grounds for such an emendation. Given the complete lack of manuscript evidence to suggest that the Hebrew name should be altered to "Ijon," the text as it stands should be retained and the meaning of the image reevaluated.

Frank-Lothar Hossfeld and Erich Zenger have argued that the meaning of this image is not rooted in geography but, instead, in "theological topography."[15] As noted above, Hermon was blessed with considerable precipitation, but the emphasis in Psalm 133:3a is not on Hermon but on the abundance of the dew there. Repeatedly in the Old Testament the writers refer to the life-giving capacity of dew. In Genesis 27:28 the giving of dew is mentioned alongside "earth's richness" as well as grain

---

13. The reference to Aaron, and by extension the priesthood, suggests his role as a "key figure" in the cultic life of the entire Israelite community (Goldingay, *Psalms 3*, 567).

14. For a more extensive discussion of the proposals offered in the history of scholarship see Crow, *The Songs of Ascents (Psalms 120–134)*, 114–16, esp. n. 170.

15. Frank-Lothar Hossfeld and Erich Zenger, *Psalms 3*, Hermeneia (Minneapolis: Fortress, 2011), 481.

and wine (cf. Deut 33:28; Hos 14:5). The prophet Haggai notes that the earth has withheld its produce because the heavens have withheld their dew (Hag 1:10). In Isaiah 26:19 the idea of dew takes on a much deeper metaphorical meaning related to the resurrection of life. There the prophet announces that the dew of God will come in the morning and "the earth will give birth to her dead." In these texts and others, the arrival of "divine dew" (i.e., dew from the heavens) suggests divine blessing and the fructi-fication of all life.

The metaphor of abundant dew must then be applied to the wisdom saying that begins Psalm 133. The association seems clear: the unity of God's people is as life giving as the abundance of fructifying dew. But even more, the psalmist stresses, the life-giving unity found among God's people is understood most fully as emanating from Zion.

The Centrality of Zion (133:3c/d)

THE FINAL LINE IN PSALM 133 REINFORCES two themes that appear repeatedly in the last poems (Pss 132–34) in the Songs of Ascent: blessing and Zion. Psalm 133:3b does not actually mention Zion by name but simply states "for *there*" God will pour forth his blessings. The word "there" can be clas-sified as deictic, meaning that we cannot know the word's definition apart from the larger context. Given the centrality of Zion in the final three poems in the Songs of Ascent, clearly Zion is in view. The blessings of God pour forth from Zion because that is the place where he has chosen to dwell (Ps 132:13–14). But these blessings are best received and best realized when God's people gather in unity in festive celebration before the God of Zion—the source of all blessed life.

Bridging Contexts

IMMEDIATE FAMILY AND CONFLICT. In one sense, Psalm 133:1 can be read at the level of the immediate family. In modern parlance, we might think of the "immediate family" in terms of the "nuclear family," but that concept would be too restrictive in relation to Psalm 133. The idea of the family in the Old Testament is embodied best in the concept of the "father's house" (cf. Gen 24:38; 47:12; Num 1:4; Judg 19:3). This familial unit included the patriarch and his wife, unmar-ried children, married sons and grandsons with their families, as well as slaves and their families, and sojourners. This extended family could easily approach well over seventy-five members. Given the complexity of such a family arrangement, the threat of conflict was not only possible but likely. Scripture recounts numerous familial conflicts, particularly those between brothers (*'ahim*). The first brothers, Cain and Abel, demonstrated from the outset that family unity would always be tenuous at best in the narrative of Scripture. The patriarchal stories of Jacob and Esau as well as Joseph and his brothers confirm this claim. And such tensions did not subside with the rise of the monarchy, as the sons of David demonstrated well. In their book, *Flawed Families of the Bible*, Drs. David and Diana Garland remind the reader that family life in the ancient world was anything but serene and copacetic. As they note, the "stories of the families in the Bible are raw and uncensored, bitter reminders of how awful family life can become."[16] As suggested above, the wisdom saying in Psalm 133:1 may have had its origin in the midst of the type of family life described by the Garlands. The unity of the larger family, the father's household, was indeed something to be valued as "good and pleasant."

Family and identity. In agricultural and nomadic cultures, the immediate family played a critical role in matters related to economics, as one might expect; but the immediate family was also critical in establishing and cultivating religious identity. In Deuteronomy 6, most notably, the family is instructed to recite the teachings of the torah to their children (v. 7) and to explain the primary narratives of their faith to them (v. 20). This admonition had two purposes: (1) to shape the faith of the family members; and (2) to connect the faith of the family members with the larger identity of God's people. In Psalm 133 the poet appears focused on the second of these two purposes. In the light of the entire psalm and its inclusion in the Songs of Ascent, the focus appears to be on God's people and the blessings bestowed on them by the God of Zion. While the psalmist is not attempting to discount the immediate family, the "father's house," he is reframing the discussion. The "brothers" (*'ahim*) mentioned in verse 1 must now be understood as all those gathering in Jerusalem for festal celebration—the very same ones who together will enjoy the blessings of God.

Similarly, the New Testament reconfigures the notion of family in the light of God and God's people. When Jesus is told that his mother and brothers are outside looking for him, he responds, "Who are my mother and my brothers?" Then he answers his own question: "Here are my mother and brothers! Whoever does God's will is my brother and sister and mother" (Mark 3:31–35). The importance of the immediate family is not discredited by Jesus, but its meaning is transformed. The place of identity is now understood in the light of the larger community of faith. This understanding is made even clearer in Jesus' prayer in John 17, where Jesus

---

16. David Garland and Diana Garland, *Flawed Families of the Bible: How God's Grace Works through the Imperfect* (Grand Rapids: Brazos, 2007), 13.

prays for "those who will believe in me . . . , that all may be one." This prayer for unity does not result from Jesus' presumed aversion to conflict (cf. John 2). Instead, this desire for unity is rooted in a deep theological claim. Jesus prays,

> that all of them may be one, Father, just as you are in me and I am in you. May they also be in us so that the world may believe that you have sent me . . . . I in them and you in me—so that they may be brought to complete unity. Then the world will know that you sent me and have loved them even as you loved me. (John 17:21, 23)

Jesus prays for their unity so that, just as God is in him, Jesus would be in us. And out of that unity—each of us with one another, and all of us together with Jesus—the world will know that God sent Jesus. That thought is a particularly stunning one—that out of our unity in Christ Jesus, the world will indeed know the content of the gospel. Just as God's people gathered around Zion and looked to the God from whom all blessings flow, so also do Christians gather as a unified body around Jesus so that the blessing may pour forth and the world may come to know of the one who has been sent.

 A SIMPLISTIC (and entirely unsatisfactory) understanding of Psalm 133:1 would be that the psalmist simply calls for everyone to get along and that unity is the chief end. Granted, the oft-repeated stories of church conflict and congregational division reinforce our need to reconsider our unity. But as I have attempted to suggest above, the entirety of the psalm invites us to think deeper about the nature of such of unity and its implications for all God's people.

In his classic work *Life Together*, Dietrich Bonhoeffer begins by citing Psalm 133:1.[17] Bonhoeffer's slender volume recounts his experience in Finkenwalde living in community with twenty-five vicars even as Hitler and the Third Reich advanced their cause by crushing all those in their way, including the Confessing Church in Germany. In such a destructive environment, one could have been forgiven if he or she gave little attention to matters such as common worship, personal prayer, Christian service, and confession to one another, to name but a few of the practices addressed by Bonhoeffer. Yet he understood well that it was not the practices *themselves*

---

17. Dietrich Bonhoeffer, *Life Together* (New York: HarperCollins, 1954), 17.

that created the community's bond of unity; rather, it was the community's life lived together in the presence of Christ. Bonhoeffer writes, "Christianity means community through Jesus Christ and in Jesus Christ. No Christian community is more or less than this. . . . We belong to one another only through and in Jesus Christ."[18] Those ministers of the Confessing Church who gathered in Finkenwalde were unified in their belief in Jesus, and their common belief in him created their unity.

The Songs of Ascent witness to the throngs of pilgrims who made their way to Jerusalem. As sisters and brothers, as God's people, they recounted the threats existing in the world around them and longed for the blessings that can come from God alone. Amid real threats and anticipated hopes, the pilgrims leaned into their identity as the people of God. And we are invited to do the same. In doing so, we will confess with Bonhoeffer that "we belong to one another through and in Jesus Christ."

18. Ibid., 21.

Psalm 134

A song of ascents.

¹ Praise the LORD, all you servants of the LORD
   who minister by night in the house of the LORD.
² Lift up your hands in the sanctuary
   and praise the LORD.
³ May the LORD bless you from Zion,
   he who is the Maker of heaven and earth.

Original Meaning

PSALM 134 IS THE FINAL POEM in the Songs of Ascent (see Ps 120). In this last song in the collection, the worshipers have made their way to Jerusalem and now find themselves in the sanctuary and prepared to worship before they depart and return home. Frank-Lothar Hossfeld and Erich Zenger contend that Psalms 132–34 shift the rhetoric of the entire collection. The focus turns away from the hostile world that threatens God's people and turns instead toward Zion, the place of divine blessing for God's people.[1] In Psalm 132 the psalmist celebrates that Zion is the place where Yahweh dwells and from whence he blesses his people (vv. 13, 15). Similarly, Psalm 133 concludes with the declaration that from Zion go forth the blessings of God (v. 3), a theme to be repeated in this psalm. Psalm 134 invites those gathered in Zion to praise the Lord— the very reason for their pilgrimage to Jerusalem—and then concludes with a priestly blessing, thereby reinforcing the role of Zion as the place of blessing for God's people. The final verse serves as a benediction as the pilgrims depart from Jerusalem having received the blessing of the Lord.[2]

Call to Praise the Lord (134:1–2)

VERSES 1–2 CONTAIN THREE IMPERATIVES addressed to the "servants of the LORD" (v. 1a). The first and last imperative are identical, "Praise [*baraku*]

---

1. Hossfeld and Zenger, *Psalms 3*, 487. Hossfeld and Zenger contend that Ps 134 (like Ps 133) may not have actually been used in the temple liturgy by individuals but instead was composed for its literary role within the larger Songs of Ascent collection. While this idea is intriguing, there is not sufficient evidence to validate or invalidate such a proposal.
2. McCann, "The Book of Psalms," 1216.

the LORD," thus creating a framing device in the first strophe (vv. 1a, 2b). Between the two calls to praise the Lord, the psalmist situates the action of the people within the temple ("house of the LORD," "sanctuary").

Praise the LORD. The Hebrew word for "praise" comes from the root *brk*, a term which occurs more than four hunderd times throughout the Old Testament. Depending on context, usage, and form, the Hebrew term can mean "to praise," "to bless," or even "to greet." *Barak* can refer to encounters between human beings (Gen 27:30; Deut 33:1; 2 Sam 6:20), but more often it is God who dispenses blessings to his people or his creation. For example, God blesses humans in Genesis 12:2, Exodus 20:24, and Psalm 115:22, but he also blesses elements of the created order in Genesis 1:22; 2:3 and Exodus 23:25. Although our contemporary culture tends to discount the notion of a blessing, in the ancient Near Eastern world "there was nothing more important than securing the blessing of God in one's life or nation."[3] Clearly it is this meaning that appears to be inferred in the final verse (v. 3) of Psalm 134. In verse 1a and 2b, however, the psalmist exhorts the community to "bless" Yahweh. While the idea of God's blessing his people seems logical, the reverse—the people's blessing God—seems counter-intuitive. Other ancient Semitic traditions expressed similar reservations about who could bless whom and decided that the deity was the one who granted blessing but never the one who received blessing. By contrast, Yahweh in the Old Testament not only appears as the subject of the verb "to bless" but also can function as the object of the verb, as evidenced in this psalm. Obviously *barak* functions differently depending on whether Yahweh is the subject or the object of the verb. The NIV has attempted to capture this difference by rendering *barak* as "to praise" whenever Yahweh is the object of the verb and humans are the subject (as in Ps 134:1a, 2b). The Septuagint understood the different nuance being communicated in this use of *barak* and so rendered the Hebrew term with *eulogeō*, "to speak well of," as a servant would speak well of his or her superior.[4] Within the framework of a covenant, or even a patron-client relationship, the master or lord would bestow favor on the servant, and in return the servant would speak well of, or "bless," the master. In the Old Testament, God bestows blessings upon his people, and in return his people speak well of God; they bless or praise God for the good he has brought to them.

Servants of the LORD. The servants of the Lord mentioned in verse 1a appear to refer to the larger worshiping community and not more specifically to priests or Levites. As Leslie Allen has rightly noted, the plural

---

3. Michael L. Brown, "ברך," *NIDOTTE* 1:758.
4. For a similar use of the term *eulogeō* in the New Testament see Jas 3:9.

---

form of "servant" does not refer to priests or Levites in other texts.[5] In Isaiah 54:17 the phrase refers to the entire worshiping community, as it does in Psalms 113:1 and 135:1. In Psalm 134:1b, the NIV's rendering of the verb 'amad ("to stand") as "to minister" might lead some interpreters to assume the priestly class is in view in both lines of verse 1. While the verb 'amad is used to refer to cultic personnel (cf. Deut 10:8; 18:7; 1 Chr 23:20), the term can also refer to the activity of the larger worshiping community (cf. Lev 9:5; Jer 7:10). The communal references in the previous psalms provide further justification for interpreting this language communally.[6]

Lift up your hands. In addition to praising Yahweh, the servants are called to "lift up" their hands. The NIV and NEB render the full line, "Lift up your hands *in* the sanctuary." In the Hebrew, the preposition "in" does not appear prior to the word "sanctuary." Allen suggests the word functions accusatively and should be translated "towards the sanctuary."[7] Elsewhere in the Psalter a similar meaning appears, but in those instances the preposition 'el ("to" or "toward") occurs in contexts that refer to the lifting of hands toward the sanctuary or temple (cf. Pss 5:7; 28:2; 135:2). Although the preposition is absent from Psalm 134, the imagery and meaning remain consistent with those of the other texts. The worshipers are not lifting their hands in the air in celebration—they are lifting their hands *toward* the one being exalted or honored, the one who is the source of blessing (i.e., the God who dwells in the sanctuary). In Egyptian iconography, the palms of the worshiper are not lifted up, as though to the sky, but instead turned forward in the direction of the one being worshiped.[8]

Blessings from Zion (134:3)

IN THE FINAL VERSE THE PRIESTS pronounce a blessing on those who have gathered "in the house of the LORD" (v. 1b). The verb *barak* appears for the third time in the psalm. As noted above, its meaning in verses 1a and 2b is better understood as "to praise" or "to exalt." In verse 3, however, *barak* means "to bless" in the more traditional sense of the word. The concluding blessing recalls the blessing offered by Aaron in Numbers 6:24, "The LORD

---

5. Allen, *Psalms 101–150*, 216. For similar conclusions see also Egbert Ballhorn, *Zum Telos des Psalters: Der Textzusammenhang des Vierten und Fünften Psalmenbuches*, BBB 138 (Berlin: Philo, 2004), 245–46. Ballhorn notes that the word "servant" is applied to David in Ps 132:10, but the plural form in Ps 134 suggests that the term has been democratized to include all God's people.

6. Cf. "Israel" (Pss 130:7a; 131:3a); "God's people" (Ps 133:1b).

7. Allen, *Psalms 101–150*, 216. The Septuagint interprets the Hebrew similarly by inserting the preposition *eis*, "to" or "toward."

8. See the Egyptian iconography in Keel, *The Symbolism of the Biblical World*, 315–16.

bless you and keep you."[9] In the Songs of Ascent, the form of the blessing found both here and in Psalm 128:5 does not include the final phrase ("and keep you") from the Aaronic benediction but prefers instead the addition of the phrase "from Zion." Yahweh issues forth his blessings from Zion.

The shift from plural to singular in the psalm is also suggestive. In verse 1a the noun is plural, "servants," and each of the imperatives in that strophe is plural. In verse 3, however, the singular form of "you" appears. The use of the singular "you" in verse 3 corresponds to the use of the singular in Numbers 6:24. The singular form used in Numbers 6 as well as in Psalms 128 and 134 suggests that while God's blessings do extend to the community as a whole, they also extend to the individual worshipers.

Maker of heaven and earth. The guarantor of the blessings that are to come upon Israel is none other than the Creator, the one who has made heaven and earth. On the phrase, "Maker of heaven and earth," see the discussion on Psalm 115:15.

ALBEIT BRIEF, PSALM 134 proves to be a fitting conclusion to the Songs of Ascent. Martin Leuenberger has noted that much of the vocabulary in this short psalm can be found in earlier psalms in Songs of Ascent collection.[10] Various forms of the word *barak*, "bless," appear in verses 1a, 2b, and 3a, but they also appear earlier—in Psalms 124:6; 128:5; 129:8; 132:15; and 133:3. The verb "stand" (*'amad*) appears in Psalm 134:1 and earlier in Psalm 122:2. The phrase "house of the LORD" in Psalm 134:1b appears earlier in Psalm 122:1. As noted above, the reference to "servant" or "servants" appears earlier in Psalms 123:1 and 132:10. The final line in Psalm 134, "Maker of heaven and earth," appears earlier in Psalms 121:2 and 124:8. Because of the similarities between Psalm 134 and the other psalms that comprise the larger collection, Leuenberger has suggested that perhaps Psalm 134 was created specifically for its "literary place" in the collection (i.e., the conclusion).[11] Whether this poem was created specifically as a conclusion to the Songs of Ascent or was used earlier as a separate psalm is difficult, if not impossible, to determine with

---

9. Other texts that report a priestly blessing on the people include Deut 21:5 and 1 Sam 2:20.

10. Martin Leuenberger, *Konzeptionen des Königtums Gottes im Psalter: Untersuchungen zu Komposition und Redaktion der theokratischen Bücher IV–V im Psalter*, ATANT 83 (Zürich: Theologischer Verlag, 2004), 305 n. 129.

11. Ibid., 305

certainty. Nevertheless, Leuenberger's observations concerning the repetition of key words and phrases in Psalm 134 merits the interpreter's attention. The temptation for the interpreter might be to read Psalm 134 in isolation, simply as a call to praise God; yet to do so is to miss the rich intertextuality found in the poem. Psalm 134 is indeed a call to praise and bless God, but the theology of that call is grounded in the prayers that precede this psalm.

The opening poems in this collection refer to the troubled circumstances surrounding those who opted to make a pilgrimage to Zion. Their world was not idyllic and serene, but a world fraught with those who spoke often of violence (Ps 120), threatened to sweep away God's people (Ps 124), and oppressed God's people (Ps 129); there were evildoers all around (Ps 125). In such a context, making a pilgrimage seems like an unwise choice. Yet the threatening circumstances mentioned in the Songs of Ascent were matched by declarations of God's faithfulness to his people. The psalmists refer to lifting up their eyes to Yahweh for help (Pss 121; 123), and they declare that those who trust in God are immovable, like Mount Zion (Ps 125). The God to whom they cry is the "Maker of heaven and earth" (Pss 122:2; 124:8; 134:3), the one enthroned in the heavens (Ps 123:1). The reality of the threats around them was held in check by the certainty of their confession, the certainty of their God. In Psalm 134 the poet calls on the people to bless God and lift up their hands toward the temple. As suggested above, by this lifting up of their hands to or toward the temple, the people are acknowledging Yahweh as the source of power, the true Maker of heaven and earth—the one who will bless his people from Zion.

THE FIRST QUESTION in the Westminster Shorter Catechism is, "What is the chief end [primary purpose] of man?" The answer is, "to glorify God and enjoy him forever." The Songs of Ascent invite worshipers to consider the question posed in the Catechism, a question that is profoundly theological and deeply existential. What is our end? What is our purpose? Psalm 134 invites worshipers into this larger purpose, that of glorifying God. But the invitation to bless God, to lift our hands toward him, must be heard in the light of the poems that precede this concluding psalm. The call "to glorify God and enjoy him forever" is not a form of escapism from a reality fraught with "dangers, toils and snares"; rather, it is a form of confession declaring that such powers, while real, do not measure up to the God whom we confess. We lift our hands to God, the Maker of heaven and earth, assured that from him "all blessings flow."

Psalm 135

¹ Praise the LORD.

Praise the name of the LORD;
    praise him, you servants of the LORD,
² you who minister in the house of the LORD,
    in the courts of the house of our God.
³ Praise the LORD, for the LORD is good;
    sing praise to his name, for that is pleasant.
⁴ For the LORD has chosen Jacob to be his own,
    Israel to be his treasured possession.
⁵ I know that the LORD is great,
    that our Lord is greater than all gods.
⁶ The LORD does whatever pleases him,
    in the heavens and on the earth,
    in the seas and all their depths.
⁷ He makes clouds rise from the ends of the earth;
    he sends lightning with the rain
    and brings out the wind from his storehouses.
⁸ He struck down the firstborn of Egypt,
    the firstborn of people and animals.
⁹ He sent his signs and wonders into your midst, Egypt,
    against Pharaoh and all his servants.
¹⁰ He struck down many nations
    and killed mighty kings—
¹¹ Sihon king of the Amorites,
    Og king of Bashan,
    and all the kings of Canaan—
¹² and he gave their land as an inheritance,
    an inheritance to his people Israel.
¹³ Your name, LORD, endures forever,
    your renown, LORD, through all generations.
¹⁴ For the LORD will vindicate his people
    and have compassion on his servants.
¹⁵ The idols of the nations are silver and gold,
    made by human hands.
¹⁶ They have mouths, but cannot speak,
    eyes, but cannot see.
¹⁷ They have ears, but cannot hear,

nor is there breath in their mouths.
¹⁸ Those who make them will be like them,
    and so will all who trust in them.
¹⁹ All you Israelites, praise the LORD;
    house of Aaron, praise the LORD;
²⁰ house of Levi, praise the LORD;
    you who fear him, praise the LORD.
²¹ Praise be to the LORD from Zion,
    to him who dwells in Jerusalem.
Praise the LORD.

PSALM 135 IS A HYMN that calls the community to praise God. The call is based on who God is and what he has done for his people. The psalm opens and closes with the phrase *halelu yah*, "Praise the LORD," thereby creating an *inclusio* around the entire psalm. The poem in its entirety alternates between the call to praise and the reasons that justify that call. Psalm 135 is frequently listed as a historical psalm, along with its "twin psalm," Psalm 136, but the poem does much more than simply recount Israel's history—the poem acknowledges the power of the God of Zion who has shaped Israel's history. Similar to the writer of the Asaphite psalms in Book 3 of the Psalter (e.g., Pss 74; 77; 78; 80; 81; 83), this psalmist sought to integrate Israel's canonical history with the theological claims associated with Zion theology.[1]

The opening strophe of Psalm 135 (vv. 1–4) exhorts the community to praise God and then gives two reasons justifying this initial call to praise. In the second strophe (vv. 5–7) the psalmist acknowledges God's sovereignty over all creation—a claim, with political implications, that supports the subsequent verses in the psalm. The third strophe (vv. 8–14) recalls God's victory over the nations in behalf of his people. Verses 15–18 taunt the idols of the nations by lampooning their impotence to save. The final strophe (vv. 19–21) invites the entire community to praise God.

The name "Yahweh" in both its full and shortened version ("Yah") appears eighteen times in this psalm, but its use is not evenly divided across the various strophes. To the contrary, its usage seems quite selective based on the subject matter of the verse. The psalmist uses "Yahweh" or "Yah" whenever he refers to God's direct activity with his people (vv. 1–6, 13–14,

---

1. Hossfeld and Zenger, *Psalms* 3, 496.

19–21), but verses in which the psalmist refers to God's activity against other nations or objects (i.e., idols) lack the name of God. For example, in the verses that recount God's victory over the nations (vv. 7–12), the covenantal name of God is not present, nor is it employed in the discussion of the idols.[2] The selective use of God's covenantal name appears to stress the relationship that exists between Yahweh and his covenant people, those whom he has chosen (v. 4).

One of the defining features of Psalm 135 is its repeated use of earlier texts throughout the psalm. Leslie Allen suggests that readers find themselves "assailed by a conglomeration of snatches" from other texts in the Old Testament.[3] Nearly every verse in Psalm 135 contains either implicit or explicit references to earlier texts:

Verses 1–2	Pss 113:1; 134:1–2; 116:19
Verse 3	Pss 133:1; 147:1
Verse 4	Deut 7:6; 14:2
Verse 5	Exod 18:11
Verse 6	Ps 115:3
Verse 7	Jer 10:13
Verse 8	Exod 12:29
Verse 9	Deut 6:22; 34:11
Verses 10–12	Ps 136:17–22[4]
Verse 13	Exod 3:15
Verse 14	Deut 32:36
Verses 15–18	Ps 115:4–8
Verses 19–21	Ps 115:9–11
Verse 21	Pss 133:3; 134:3

The use of texts from across the canon suggests that this psalm was written fairly late, but John Goldingay correctly cautions that we should not imagine the psalmist in Psalm 135 as pouring over scrolls in order to

---

2. J. P. Fokkelman, *Major Poems of the Hebrew Bible: At the Interface of Prosody and Structural Analysis, Volume II: 85 Psalms and Job 4–14*, Studia Semitica Neerlandica (Leiden: Brill, 2000), 298.

3. Allen, *Psalms 101–150*, 224. See also Leuenberger, *Konzeptionen des Königtums Gottes im Psalter*, 314–15.

4. Psalm 136 is considered by most scholars to have been written prior to Ps 135, and there is even the possibility that the writer of Ps 135 may have been using Ps 136 as a type of template. See Hossfeld and Zenger, *Psalms 3*, 496. For a short overview of the relationship between the two psalms see W. Dennis Tucker Jr., *Constructing and Deconstructing Power in Psalms 107–150*, 110–19.

"lift out" a precise word or phrase.[5] More likely, the parallels stem from the psalmist's (and the community's) familiarity with earlier texts and traditions. By invoking earlier texts and traditions, the psalmist grounds the community's hope for the future in its confessions from the past.

The Call to Praise God (135:1–4)

THE CALL FOR THE PEOPLE TO PRAISE GOD dominates the initial strophe, with the verb *halelu* ("praise") appearing four times, and a related term, *zamar*, which means to make celebratory music, appears once. Following the repeated call to praise God in the opening verses, the psalmist puts forth two reasons justifying this imperatival call to praise.

Servants of the Lord. As noted in the chart above, the opening verses of Psalm 135 echo the vocabulary found in the preceding psalm, Psalm 134. The references to "servants" (Ps 135:1b) and "ministering" or "standing" (Ps 135:2a) recall the use of the same terms in Psalm 134:1–2. As noted there, the plural form of "servant" does not refer to priests or Levites in other texts, but more generally to the worshiping community.[6] While the immediate context of Psalm 135:1–2 is not determinative, the final strophe is suggestive. In those verses the psalmist invites "all you Israelites" (v. 19)—priests and non-priests alike—to praise God. The reference to the entire community in the final strophe makes plausible the claim that the "servants of the LORD" in verse 1 has the same, more expansive understanding in view.

For the LORD is good. Verse 3 provides the first of two reasons meant to justify the call to praise God. In this verse God is celebrated as "good" (*tov*). In Psalm 133:1, the word "good" (*tov*) appeared in reference to the blessedness of communal unity. In Psalm 135, however, attention turns back to God, and more specifically, to the character of God. Consequently, in verse 3a the congregation is exhorted to praise God, "for the LORD is good"—a phrase that functioned as a common formula in postexilic temple liturgy (e.g., Jer 33:11; 1 Chr 16:34; Pss 118:1; 136:1). In Psalm 135:3b the community is encouraged to "sing praise" or "make music" (*zmr*) to his name. In communal hymns, the verb frequently appears at the beginning of the psalm and serves to introduce the call to praise God (e.g., Pss 33:2; 66:2; 81:2; 95:2; 147:1).

For the LORD has chosen Jacob. Psalm 135:4 provides the second reason for God's praise: God's election of his people. The verb *bahar*, "to choose," appears 170 times in the Old Testament, with the most

---

5. Goldingay, *Psalms 3*, 578.

6. Leslie C. Allen, *Psalms 101–150*, WBC 21 (Waco, TX: Word, 1983), 216. For similar conclusions see also Egbert Ballhorn, *Zum Telos des Psalters: Der Textzusammenhang des Vierten und Fünften Psalmenbuches*, BBB 138 (Berlin: Philo, 2004), 245–46.

occurrences appearing in the book of Deuteronomy. On the use of *bahar* in reference to the election of Israel as God's people, see Deuteronomy 4:37; 7:6–7; 10:15; 14:2. In these verses Israel is reminded that their election is not based on their status—their election comes as a result of God's gracious act. According to Deuteronomy 7:6–7, "the LORD your God has chosen [*bahar*] you out of all the peoples on the face of the earth to be his people, his treasured possession [*segullah*]. The LORD did not set his affection on you and choose [*bahar*] you because you were more numerous than the other peoples, for you were the fewest of all the peoples. But it was because the LORD loved you."

In addition to using *bahar* in Psalm 135:4, the psalmist also explains that Israel, in being elected or chosen, became God's "treasured possession" (*segullah*), a term that can also be translated as "crown jewel" and have royal connotations.[7] Hossfeld and Zenger suggest that the reference to a "crown jewel" may be a subtle reference to the notion of Yahweh as the Divine King.[8] The reference to the kingship of Yahweh in verse 4 presages the more explicit references to Yahweh's kingship in the following verses.

God's Kingship over All Creation (135:5–7)

BEFORE INTRODUCING THE HUMAN KINGS overthrown by Yahweh (vv. 8–14), the psalmist pauses to acknowledge the royal rule of God over all creation. The claims asserted in this portion of the psalm serve to substantiate the claims made in the latter verses.

Our Lord is greater than all gods. In verse 5 the psalmist gives testimony. In Hebrew syntax, a personal pronoun does not have to be used in conjunction with a verb; the gender, person, and number are built into the structure of most verbs. In this verse, for example, the verb is *yada'ti*, "I know." Although not necessary, the personal pronoun may be inserted in the sentence, thereby potentially shifting or altering the meaning. In verse 5a the personal pronoun "I" (*ani*) appears prior to *yada'ti*, "I know." The NIV's translation does not account for the addition of the pronoun, but the use of the pronoun is likely meant to create a reflexive sense: "I myself know that the LORD is great."[9] This translation reflects the testimonial nature of these verses.

The confessional tone of this verse continues in the second line of verse 5. Here, however, the psalmist makes a subtle shift from singular

---

7. Eugene Carpenter, "סְגֻלָּה," *NIDOTTE* 3:224.

8. Hossfeld and Zenger, *Psalms 3*, 496.

9. Author's translation. On the reflexive use of the pronoun see van der Merwe, Naudé, and Kroeze, *A Biblical Hebrew Reference Grammar*, 252.

to plural in confessing that *"our* Lord is greater than all gods" (emphasis added). The psalmist makes a confession about God in verse 5a but then adds a collective bent to his confession with the reference to "our Lord" in verse 5b. This shift has a rhetorical function similar to Joshua's declaration before the people in Joshua 24. In both Psalm 135 and Joshua 24, the speaker makes a claim with the assumption that the community would join him in his claim (cf. Josh 24:15, 18).[10]

In Psalm 135:5b the psalmist confesses that "our Lord is greater than all gods." While this line of the poem clearly acknowledges the supremacy of Israel's God, the choice of words adds texture to this claim. The Hebrew word for "Lord" used in this verse is not "Yahweh," as might be expected, but *'adon,* which literally means "lord" or "master." In Psalm 123:2 the psalmist uses this term in the context of the master servant relationship, thereby highlighting the covenantal relationship between God and his people. This understanding may inform our reading of Psalm 135. In verse 1 of this psalm the people are referred to as the "servants" of the Lord; in verse 5 the psalmist mentions "the Lord" (*'adon*) of Israel and compares him with the "gods" (*'elohim*) of the nations. The psalmist confesses the glory of Israel's God because Israel's Lord or Master (*'adon*) is greater than all the other gods of the nations. The master-servant relationship mentioned in Psalm 123:2 appears once more in Psalm 135 and affirms the covenantal relationship between God and his people, and even more, affirms this God's preeminence in the face of other gods.

The Lord does whatever pleases him. The first line of Psalm 135:6 is drawn from Psalm 115:3. The Hebrew text reads literally, "everything which Yahweh desires, he does" (*kol 'asher-hapets yehwah 'asah*). As noted in the commentary on Psalm 115, the verb *hapats,* "to desire," appears fifty times in the Old Testament with God as the subject. Judith Krawelitzski notes that in those fifty uses some texts mention objects or values in which God takes delight (i.e., right sacrifices).[11] Other texts mention certain people in whom God does or does not take delight, and still others refer to certain actions (i.e., "justice") in which God takes delight. Krawelitzski notes that beyond these three categories are a number of texts that refer more broadly to what God desires, and these texts are generally found in Isaiah 40–55 and the psalms. The use of this phraseology in Ps 135 appears to fall in the latter category. Israel's God can do whatever he pleases in any realm—heaven, earth, sea, and the deeps—because he is greater than all

---

10. Goldingay, *Psalms 3*, 580.

11. Judith Krawelitzski, "God the Almighty? Observations in the Psalms," *VT* 64 (2014): 434–44.

---

other gods. Verse 7 extends this thought by providing a rationale for why God can do whatever he pleases in these realms, namely, not only does Yahweh stand over them as the Divine King, but he also manifests his rule within them. Although perhaps strange to our modern ears, the mention of storm clouds, wind, and rain in verse 7 likely evoked the images of the Canaanite god of storms and weather—Baal. The point, however, was not to compare Yahweh to Baal but to declare that Yahweh alone reigns in, through, and over creation. These phenomena are "the demonstration of the disempowerment of all false gods and God-resistant powers."[12] By making these claims in verses 5–7 the psalmist prepares the way for the confessions concerning human power in the subsequent verses.

The Power of God against the Nations (135:8–14)

IN THE THIRD STROPHE OF THIS POEM, the psalmist turns to consider the display of God's power among the nations. The use of names and actions recorded in Psalm 135 presupposes that the readers had a general familiarity with Israel's canonical history as expressed in the Pentateuch. As a result, the psalmist has no need to rehearse the entirety of this history, nor does he provide considerable detail. Relating history for the sake of history is not the psalmist's intent. To the contrary, these truncated accounts serve to substantiate the poet's larger claim concerning the power of Israel's God.

He struck down the firstborn of Egypt. Verses 8–9 recount Yahweh's decisive victory over Pharaoh. The psalmist mentions the "signs and wonders" that were "sent" by Yahweh. In the book of Deuteronomy, the words "signs and wonders," which appear together, function more nearly as a hendiadys in reference to the acts of God against the Egyptians (e.g., Deut 6:22; 26:8; 29:2). Of the ten signs and wonders, however, only the last one is referenced specifically, the plague affecting the firstborn. Yahweh's act of striking down Egypt's firstborn demonstrated the potency of his power versus the power apparatus of the Egyptians.[13]

He struck down many nations. Yahweh's victory over kings and imperial powers continues in Psalm 135:10–12 and culminates in the giving of the land as an inheritance. In recounting not only the victory in Egypt but also the subsequent victories, the psalmist employs the verb *nakab* ("to strike"), a verb found frequently in texts referring to battles between political or military powers, in verses 8a and 10a.[14] As seen in verse 10a,

---

12. Hossfeld and Zenger, *Psalms 3*, 498.
13. Ibid.
14. For example, see Gen 14:7, 15, 17; 36:35; Num 14:45; Deut 29:6; Josh 11:10–12. See also the repeated use of the verb throughout Exod 2–15.

the verb is used in conjunction with the Sihon and Og traditions but with one significant alteration. In the Pentateuch and the book of Joshua, Israel and Moses are traditionally given credit for the slaying of Sihon and Og (cf. Num 21:24, 35; Deut 1:4; 3:2; 4:46; 29:6; Josh 2:10; 21:1).[15] In nearly every account the narrator credits either Israel or Moses for having struck down the two kings. In Psalm 135, however, the psalmist has reworked the tradition to ensure that Yahweh is credited with the victory over Pharaoh, the mighty kings Sihon and Og, and "all the kings of Canaan" as well. Yahweh deserves Israel's praise because he has overturned political powers and empires to ensure that the people of Israel receive their inheritance.[16]

Your name, LORD, endures forever. Having just recounted Yahweh's primacy over all other gods (v. 5), as evidenced in his victory over all nations (vv. 8–12), the psalmist moves to consider the significance of these claims for the present and future generations. In verse 13a he declares that the name (*shem*) of Yahweh endures forever. By referring to the name (*shem*) of Yahweh, the psalmist refers to the very nature and character of God. The Hebrew term *shem* ("name") stands in parallel construction with the Hebrew word *zeker* in verse 13b. The latter term generally means "remembrance" or "memorial" (cf. Ps 6:6), but when *zeker* and *shem* stand in a parallel relationship, the former term often carries the meaning "reputation," or as the NIV translates the term, "renown." The nature and reputation of God did not cease with the giving of the land—they remain available "through all generations."

Verse 14 extends the thought expressed in verse 13 by indicating how God will relate to his people. The verb in verse 14a, *shapat*, means "to judge," but here the implied meaning is "to judge in behalf of" or "to vindicate." This language alludes to the image of kingship, in this case divine kingship. The role of the human king in the ancient Near East was to execute judgment in behalf of his people, thus ensuring the well-being of society. What was expected of the human king (cf. Ps 72) was expected even more of the Divine King (cf. Ps 144). The psalmist contends that even as Yahweh has vindicated his people in the face of human power before, he will do so again—his name and reputation guarantee it (v. 13).

---

15. The only two exceptions are Deut 31:4 and Josh 9:10. In those instances Yahweh is given credit for the victory. On the Sihon and Og traditions elsewhere in the Hebrew Bible see Rolf Rendtorff, "Sihon, Og, und das israelitische 'Credo,'" in *Meilenstein: Festgabe für Hebert Donner zum 16. Februar 1995*, ed. Manfred Weippert and Stefan Timm (Wiesbaden: Harrassowitz, 1995), 198–203.

16. Ruth Scoralick explains that this language is meant to show "the superior power of God over against the potency of other nations and their rulers" (Ruth Scoralick, "'Hallelujah für einen gewalttätigen Gott?': Zur Theologie von Psalm 135 und 136," *BZ* 46 [2002]: 257).

The Powerlessness of Idols (135:15–18)

IN THIS STROPHE THE PSALMIST ADOPTS an abbreviated form of Psalm 115:4–6, 8. (See the comments on Ps 115 for an extended analysis of that text.) While the poet appears to draw principally from Psalm 115, he does make one significant modification to the earlier text—a modification that contributes to the larger topic concerning the power of Yahweh. In Psalm 115, as in Psalm 135, the psalmists lampoon the idols for their inability to speak, see, and hear. In Psalm 115:7b the writer extends this line of thinking by claiming that the idols cannot even "utter a sound with their throats," but in writing Psalm 135:17b he omits the phrase altogether and instead inserts a text from Jeremiah's critique of idols: "nor is their breath in their mouths" (see Jer 10:14). The lack of breath in their mouths suggests that there is no life in them (Gen 2:7). Because the idols are lifeless, they have no power and are ineffectual. So too are those who make them and rely on them (Ps 135:18).[17]

Invitation to Praise God (135:19–21)

IN THE FINAL STROPHE OF THE PSALM THE POET RETURNS once more to Psalm 115 and models the final section of Psalm 135 after the langauge found in Psalm 115:9–11. In Psalm 115 the poet calls on all Israel, the house of Aaron, and those who fear the Lord to trust in God. In adapting this earlier material, the writer of Psalm 135 alters it in two notable ways. First, he adds a fourth group to the list, namely, the house of Levi.[18] Thus the names of those being invoked include "all the Israelites" (the laity), the house of Aaron (the priests), the house of Levi (the temple singers and temple personnel), and those who fear God (the entire nation).[19]

In addition to including the house of Levi, the psalmist also exhorts the people to a particular action. In Psalm 115 all three groups were invited to

---

17. John Goldingay contends that this material does not constitute a polemic against idols but rather a victory song over the powerlessness of idols. This assumption is predicated on the claim that the psalm comes from a time "when victory has been won by a commitment to worship Yhwh alone (worship of other deities is not the problem in the later postexilic period that it was in earlier centuries)" (see Goldingay, *Psalms* 3, 584). As a victory song, the point of the text is not to convince the audience of the correct choice between two options; rather, it is to remind the people of the power they have already witnessed in the actions of Yahweh—power entirely lacking in lifeless idols.

18. Regarding the differentiation between the Aaronid priests and the Levites, see Num 3:6–9; Ezek 44:10–16; Neh 7:63–65.

19. Hossfeld and Zenger contend that this final group, "the fearers of the LORD," is actually comprised of foreign people who have converted to Yahwism—they are similar to the "God-fearers" in the New Testament (Hossfeld and Zenger, *Psalm* 3, 500). The evidence, however, does not support this claim. See the discussion on Ps 115:9–11 for the arguments against this position.

trust in Yahweh. In Psalm 135, however, the four groups are instructed to *barak* Yahweh, or "praise Yahweh." The word *barak* is frequently translated "to bless." On the meaning of *barak*, "to praise" or "to bless," see the comments on Psalm 134.

Although Psalm 135 traces the early history of Israel up to the point of their entry into the land, verse 21 references Zion as the place where God dwells. The emphasis on Zion in the concluding verse serves to create an arc back to the Songs of Ascent (Ps 132:13; 133:3; 134:3).

 As a hymn of praise, Psalm 135 invites the worshiper to make confessions that are central to the biblical witness of the God who has made himself known to his people. These confessions, however, are more than simple platitudes directed at a deity in the hope of placating that deity. Instead, as Sigmund Mowinckel has correctly noted, these kinds of prayers and confessions can be labeled "world-making." In confessing God, one encounters God, and in doing so the world is shaped and reshaped—as are those who pray these psalms.[20] Although Walter Brueggemann affirms Mowinckel's notion of the world-making capacity of hymns, he also offers what I would argue is an unwarranted negative assessment of psalms of orientation (i.e., hymns).[21] He contends that these psalms exhibit a high degree of certitude and that "such a satisfied and assured assertion of orderliness probably comes from the well-off, from the economically secure and the politically significant . . . . such religious conviction comes from those who experience life as good, generous and reliable."[22] Yet much of the Psalter was likely compiled after the exile, when social and political circumstances strained the theological claims of Israel. Consequently, the confessions collected in the Psalter and prayed by those

---

20. See the excellent discussion by Harry Nasuti, "God at Work in the World: A Theology of the Divine-Human Encounter in the Psalms," in *Soundings in the Theology of the Psalms: Perspectives and Methods in Contemporary Scholarship*, ed. Rolf Jacobson (Minneapolis: Fortress, 2011), 27–48.

21. Brueggemann includes the larger category of "Hymns of Praise" under the rubric "Psalms of Reorientation" but then quickly equivocates, explaining that he is not "sure whether, in the pattern of orientation-disorientation-new orientation which we have pursued, these psalms should all be placed at the very end of the process as surprising, glad statements of a new ordering of life, or whether they should be treated as the very deepest and established statements of the old orientation that is firm, settled and nonnegotiable" (Brueggemann, *The Message of the Psalms*, 158).

22. Ibid., 26–27.

in Yehud likely served to declare what they knew to be true about their God. Hymns of praise were not attempts at social control by the elite, as Brueggemann intimates; rather, such hymns were theological anchors that tethered the people of Israel to the central tenets of their faith.[23]

Encountering the living God. In his description of the hymn of praise, Sigmund Mowinckel writes,

> The core of the hymn of praise is the consciousness of the poet and congregation that they are standing face to face with the Lord himself, meeting the almighty, holy and merciful God in his own place, and worshiping him with praise and adoration. He is in their midst and they owe him everything.[24]

Psalm 135 is not simply a historical recitation of events in Israel's past; rather, the poem is a call to confession that eventuates in unfettered praise of the God who encountered his people and encounters them still. This psalm begins and ends with the same phrase, *halelu yah*, "praise the LORD." Further still, three more times in verses 1b–3 (and perhaps four times, if ellipsis is assumed in verse 2a) the psalmist calls the people to praise (*halelu*) God, and once he calls them to "sing praise" (*zamar*). The psalm then concludes with a fivefold call to praise or bless the name of Yahweh (vv. 19–21a). Thus the entire poem is bounded by the well-structured call to praise:

Verse 1: *halelu yah*
    Verses 1b–3: Fivefold call to praise God (if ellipsis is assumed)
    . . .
    Verses 19–21a: Fivefold call to praise God
Verse 21b: *halelu yah*

When the references to natural phenomena (vv. 5–7) and historical events (vv. 8–14) are rehearsed, they are processed through the lens of praise. And through the lens of praise, the congregation both recognizes and celebrates this powerful God who has encountered them and encounters them still. His name endures forever (v. 13), and he continues to vindicate those who declare themselves to be his servants.

The election of Israel. After issuing the opening call to praise God, the psalmist roots this hymn of praise in the election of Israel. Joel Kaminsky has helpfully traced the modernists' critique against the biblical concept

---

23. On Brueggemann's claim that these psalms reflect a type of social control, see ibid., 27–28.

24. Mowinckel, *The Psalms in Israel's Worship*, 1:81.

of election and has concluded that what is needed is a reclamation of this central theological claim in Scripture, both for Jews and Christians. He writes, "I do not think either tradition can sidestep, marginalize, or jettison election theology without severing its connections to its biblical roots, a move that would greatly impoverish or perhaps even destroy both of these venerable faith traditions."[25] The writer of Psalm 135 understood the centrality of election in the faith of Israel, a tradition that reaches back to the calling of Abraham and the assembling of God's people at Sinai. These events cast a long shadow. Prior to tracing the work of God in the world at large in Psalm 135, the psalmist roots his praise in the work of God in "choosing" (*bahar*) Jacob/Israel as his people. In calling a people, God ensured their inheritance and promised his continued presence with them (v. 13). Election results in praise (Ps 135:1b–3, 19–21a). Paul makes similar use of the notion of election in the New Testament. In Ephesians 1:3–14 he suggests that those in Christ have an inheritance (vv. 11, 14). As the adopted children of God (v. 5), we receive the riches of his grace and are called to a life of unfettered praise (vv. 6, 12, 14). This act of God in "choosing" and electing his people appears across the New Testament in varying ways and gives an explanation for the salvific acts provided by God.[26]

The testimony of the power of God against human power can only be understood correctly in the light of election and the call to praise the God who has encountered his people. The recitation of these key moments in Israel's history reflects a theological claim that is far deeper than some form of triumphalism. The psalmist is doing more than simply recalling the "good old days" when Israel's enemies were thwarted. Instead, these stories of God's victory over human power give testimony about Israel's covenantal partner. The God who has chosen them has been at work to secure their future—and he remains so. Even as he has done in the past, he will continue to "vindicate his people and have compassion on his servants" (v. 14). When they realize that this God is the God they are encountering, they can do nothing else than lift their voices in praise.

IN TEACHING AND PREACHING on Psalm 135, the temptation can be to focus primarily on the historical allusions in verses 8–12 and highlight how God strikes down any foe. We know these

---

25. Joel Kaminsky, *Yet I Loved Jacob: Reclaiming the Biblical Concept of Election* (Eugene, OR: Wipf & Stock, 2007), 10.

26. For example, see John 15:16; Rom 8:30; Eph 2:8–9; 2 Tim 1:9; 1 Pet 2:9.

stories well, and such an approach might feed into our own insecurity about the future and the world in which we live. Or one might be tempted to focus primarily on the powerlessness of idols (vv. 15–18) and lampoon those who trust in idols. While both of these themes appear in this psalm and can be found elsewhere in Scripture, they are not the focal point of the poem—they buttress the larger claim.

The point of the hymn is to confess what we know about God, and what we know about God begins with election (v. 4). It is only because God has made us his treasured possession that we come to understand that "our Lord is greater than all gods" (v. 5). It is only because God has chosen us that we understand and believe that "the LORD does whatever pleases him" (v. 6). And it is because God has chosen us as his covenantal partners that he has acted in our behalf to secure our future. The defeating of the enemies in verses 8–12 and the lampooning of the idols in verses 15–18 serve to support the claim that our covenantal partner is "great" (v. 5). He is the God of all power.

Psalm 136

¹ Give thanks to the LORD, for he is good.
   His love endures forever.
² Give thanks to the God of gods.
   His love endures forever.
³ Give thanks to the Lord of lords:
   His love endures forever.
⁴ to him who alone does great wonders,
   His love endures forever.
⁵ who by his understanding made the heavens,
   His love endures forever.
⁶ who spread out the earth upon the waters,
   His love endures forever.
⁷ who made the great lights—
   His love endures forever.
⁸ the sun to govern the day,
   His love endures forever.
⁹ the moon and stars to govern the night;
   His love endures forever.
¹⁰ to him who struck down the firstborn of Egypt
   His love endures forever.
¹¹ and brought Israel out from among them
   His love endures forever.
¹² with a mighty hand and outstretched arm;
   His love endures forever.
¹³ to him who divided the Red Sea asunder
   His love endures forever.
¹⁴ and brought Israel through the midst of it,
   His love endures forever.
¹⁵ but swept Pharaoh and his army into the Red Sea;
   His love endures forever.
¹⁶ to him who led his people through the wilderness;
   His love endures forever.
¹⁷ to him who struck down great kings,
   His love endures forever.
¹⁸ and killed mighty kings—
   His love endures forever.
¹⁹ Sihon king of the Amorites

 His love endures forever.
²⁰ and Og king of Bashan—
 His love endures forever.
²¹ and gave their land as an inheritance,
 His love endures forever.
²² an inheritance to his servant Israel.
 His love endures forever.
²³ He remembered us in our low estate
 His love endures forever.
²⁴ and freed us from our enemies.
 His love endures forever.
²⁵ He gives food to every creature.
 His love endures forever.
²⁶ Give thanks to the God of heaven.
 His love endures forever.

PSALM 136, LIKE ITS "TWIN" (Ps 135), is a hymn that exhorts the people to praise God. Together these two psalms create an appendix to the Songs of Ascent. Worshipers would recite the Songs of Ascent as they made their way to Jerusalem and once in the city itself (Ps 134). In the psalms' present location in the Psalter, Psalms 135 and 136 function as culminating invitations for Israel to worship the God who dwells in Zion. Central to this call to worship is a truncated recitation of Israel's history as presented principally in the Pentateuch.[1] The purpose of these psalms, however, is not simply historical but hortatory. God's acts in Israel's past serve as a guarantor of God's faithfulness to his people in the present and the future

Psalms 135 and 136 share a number of themes. Both psalms celebrate the goodness of God (Pss 135:3; 136:1), and each psalm opens with a comparative confession concerning God's supremacy over all other gods (Pss 135:5;

---

1. See the analysis by Dirk J. Human, "Psalm 136: A Liturgy with Reference to Creation and History," in *Psalms and Liturgy*, ed. D. J. Human and C. J. A. Vos, JSOTSup 410 (London: T&T Clark, 2004), 76–82. Among the comparisons listed by Human are the following: Ps 136:7–9 with Gen 1:14–16; Ps 136:11 with Exod 7:5; 18:1; 20:1; Ps 136:12 with Exod 6:1, 6; Ps 136:13 with Exod 14:16–17, 21; Ps 136:14 with Exod 14:22; Ps 136:15 with Exod 14:27; Ps 136:17–22 with Num 21:21–24, 33–35; Ps 136:2 with Deut 10:27; Ps 136:11 with Deut 1:27; 4:20; 5:15; Ps 136:12 with Deut 4:34; 5:15; 7:19; 9:29; 11:2; 26:8; Ps 136:16 with Deut 8:15; 32:10; Ps 136:19 with Deut 2:33; Ps 136:22 with Deut 32:36 (Human, "Psalm 136," 76 nn. 5, 6, 7).

136:2–3). The historical recitation offered by both psalmists follows the same historical events. Creation is mentioned in both psalms (Pss 135:6–7; 136:4–9), as are the events associated with the exodus (Pss 135:8–9; 136:10–15). Both poems recount the wilderness period and Israel's settlement in the land (Pss 135:10–12; 136:16–22). And both psalms conclude by affirming God's care for his people (Pss 135:13–14; 136:23–25). As in Psalm 135, the language and imagery present in Psalm 136 gives considerable attention to God's victory over human kings. Christian Malchoz, noting the political and militaristic dimensions throughout Psalm 136, contends that the community understood "holy history" in terms of the "militant acts of the power of Yahweh."[2] These victories signaled the power of God to thwart all threats against Israel. The legitimation of such threats in Israel's past *and* the legitimation of Yahweh's power over them provide the necessary theological underpinnings for the claims made in verses 23–24.

The similarities between Psalms 135 and 136 have been well noted and have led to considerable diversity of opinion regarding which psalm, if either one, has priority (i.e., came first). Frank-Lothar Hossfeld and Erich Zenger argue that Psalm 135 was written well after Psalm 136 and drew heavily from it.[3] Both Leslie Allen and Klaus Seybold argue likewise, as does Han-Peter Mathys, among others.[4] Michael Goulder works in a different direction of influence in suggesting that the same individual wrote both psalms, with Psalm 136 expanding the themes in Psalm 135.[5] Dirk Human contends that neither psalm drew from the other—instead, both drew from a common source of tradition.[6] At present, the weight of scholarly opinion considers Psalm 136 to have been the earlier psalm, with Psalm 135 written much later in the Perisan period but drawing heavily from Psalm 136. That said, because of the difficulty in dating psalms precisely, one cannot be dogmatic on this matter.

Psalm 136 does differ from Psalm 135 in two notable ways. First, the governing verb in Psalm 136 differs from its counterpart in Psalm 135. The latter opens and concludes with the verb *halelu yah*, "Praise the LORD." Throughout the psalm the congregation is called to remember the manifold

---

2. Christian Malchoz, "Psalm 136: Exegetische Beobachtungen mit methodogischen Seitenblicken," in *Mincha. Festgabe für Rolf Rendtorff zum 75. Geburtstag*, ed. E. Blum (Neukirchen-Vluyn: Neukirchener Verlag, 2000), 186.

3. Hossfeld and Zenger, *Psalms 3*, 496.

4. Allen, *Psalms 101–150*, 224; Klaus Seybold, *Die Psalmen*, HAT I/15 (J. C. B. Mohr: Tübingen, 1996), 503–504; Hans-Peter Mathys, *Dichter und Beter: Theologen aus spätalttestamentlicher Zeit*, OBO 132 (Göttingen: Vandenhoeck & Ruprecht, 1994), 259–62.

5. Goulder, *The Psalms of the Return*, 221.

6. Human, "Psalm 136," 79.

ways in which God has demonstrated his power in their history. These recollections should result in unfettered praise of God (Ps 135:19–21). In Psalm 136 the operative verb is *hodu,* translated "give thanks" in the NIV. The verb *hodu* comes from the Hebrew root *ydh,* which can mean "to praise" or "to give thanks" but can also mean "to confess" or "to proclaim." While the difference between "praise" and "confess" may appear minimal, that difference may prove instructive for understanding the intent of Psalm 136. Throughout this text the psalmist refers to God in the third person. The psalmist is not imploring the community to speak *to God* but instead to speak *about God.* In doing so the community confesses what it knows to be true about the God of heaven (v. 26)—that he is the God who stands over all creation, who unseats the powers of this earth and secures the protection of his people.

Psalm 136 differs substantially from Psalm 135 in one additional way: its highly structured form. The psalm opens with a call to confess Yahweh (vv. 1–3) and concludes with a call to confess Yahweh as the God of heaven (v. 26). The intervening section is composed of twenty-two lines, the number of letters contained in the Hebrew alphabet. Although this section is not constructed in the form of an acrostic, the use of twenty-two lines suggests a highly stylized form of poetry. A quick scan of the psalm reveals that the dominant verbal form in the poem is the participle (vv. 4–10, 13, 16–17, 25). In Hebrew, the participle is often used attributively to make claims about a noun, and normally the participle stands in apposition to the noun it modifies. In Psalm 136, however, this case does not apply. The noun ("Yahweh") is introduced in verses 1–3, followed by an intermittent series of participles modifying Yahweh.[7]

Beyond the number of lines and the dominant verbal form, the principle structuring element in this psalm is the refrain, "his *hesed* endures forever." The repetitive use of this refrain suggests that the psalm was used antiphonally in a worship setting. The priest or worship leader would read the first portion of each line—those lines that describe or confess Yahweh in some way—and the people would respond with the refrain. The paramount question that remains is the meaning of *hesed*—moreover, its precise meaning in this psalm. The NIV translates the term as "love," which, while not incorrect, may fail to capture the richness of the term in the Old Testament. The term itself occurs 246 times in the Old Testament,

---

7. In the central section of the psalm other verbal forms do appear, including the *wayyiqtol* (*waw* consecutive + imperfect) and *weqatal* (simple *waw* + perfect). Both verbal constructions are used to recount Yahweh's activity in the past. For example, see verses 11, 14, 15, 18, 21, 24,

with more than half those occurrences appearing in the book of Psalms. In nearly all those instances, the term *hesed* refers to God's covenantal relationship with his people. In an effort to capture the covenantal sense of the term, Erhard Gerstenberger has rendered the repeated refrain in Psalm 136 as, "yes, his solidarity forever."[8] Other renderings of *hesed* in this psalm include "commitment" and "loyal love."[9] These translations make explicit the claim that the actions of God are predicated on his covenantal commitment to his people. God stands over against the powers of the world because "his commitment is forever."[10]

Call to Confess Yahweh (136:1–3)

PSALM 136 OPENS WITH A CALL FOR ISRAEL to confess that Yahweh is good—a claim appearing in Psalm 135:3 as well. The reference to the divine name in verse 1 is the only appearance of the term in the psalm. Other appellations are used in referring to Yahweh, most notably in the first strophe (vv. 2–3) and in the last verse. In verse 2 the psalmist refers to Yahweh as the "God of gods" (*'elohim*), and in the subsequent verse as the "Lord of lords." The repetition of a term in a construct relationship ("X of X") typically expresses the superlative. The only other text where these two titles ("God of gods" and "Lord of lords") occur together is Deuteronomy 10:17. In that text the writer also refers to God as the God of the heavens (v. 14), a title repeated in the final verse of Psalm 136. Together the appellations that frame this psalm in verses 2–3 and verse 26 reinforce a central claim of Psalm 136: Yahweh is supreme over all other gods (i.e., "God of gods")—a claim similarly made in Psalm 135:5.

Yahweh's Mighty Works in Creation (136:4–9)

FOLLOWING THE OPENING CALL for the people to "confess" their faith in Yahweh, in the second strophe the psalmist turns to consider Yahweh's work as Creator. The focus of the strophe is not cosmological in nature (i.e., how the universe came to be), but decidedly theological. What does the creative work of God reveal concerning Israel's covenantal partner? In rehearsing Yahweh's role as Creator of all, the psalmist declares concomitantly that Yahweh is the Divine King.

Who alone does great wonders. Three of the six verses in this strophe begin with the participial form of the verb *'asah*, often translated as "to make" or "to do." The verb appears frequently as a synonym of *bara'*, "to create,"

---

8. Gerstenberger, *Psalms, Part 2*, 388.
9. Goldingay, *Psalms 3*, 588–89; Allen, *Psalms 101–150*, 228–29.
10. Goldingay's translation (Goldingay, *Psalms 3*, 588–89).

and clearly carries that connotation in this strophe: God "made" or "created" great works (v. 4); God "made" or "created" the heavens (v. 5); and God "made" or "created" the great lights (v. 7). A fourth verb is invoked, and it too carries associations with creation. In verse 6 the psalmist declares that Yahweh "spread out the earth upon the waters." The verb *raqa'* means "to beat" or "to hammer out." In several texts the verb refers to the "hammering out" or "spreading out" of the earth (Isa 42:5; 44:24) or the heavens (Job 37:18). The word "firmament," found in Genesis 1, comes from this same root.

The word *nipla'ot*, "wonders," appears frequently in Old Testament texts that refer to Yahweh's creating, liberating, and redeeming work in behalf of Israel.[11] Admittedly, many of these texts have the exodus event in view, but other texts (e.g., Ps 89:5) associate the larger theme of redemption with the work of God in creation. In this strophe the psalmist makes a similar move by associating *nipla'ot* with creation. He also echoes the earlier claims of Yahweh's supremacy (Ps 136:2–3) by declaring that Yahweh "alone" has created the world; the reputed creator gods of the other nations proved powerless, as Yahweh "alone" performed his wonders (*nipla'ot*) in creation.

Made the heavens . . . spread out the earth. As suggested above, the language in this strophe has close associations with the language found in Genesis 1.[12] Psalm 136 mentions the creation of the heavens and the earth but also alludes to the sun, moon, and stars. According to the psalmist, these are the bodies that "govern" (from the root *mshl*, "to rule") the day and night. In Genesis 1 these celestial bodies were not identified by name; instead, they were called the "greater light" and the "lesser light." Babylonian religion had deified these celestial bodies and attributed to them power over the created world. Their deification perhaps explains why the writer of Gen 1 opted to omit their particular names and preferred, instead, more generalized terms. Apparently, and particularly given the claims about God in verses 2–3, the psalmist no longer shared this concern and felt liberated to use the more specific terms associated with each heavenly body. No celestial body could "govern" the world that was created by Israel's God, the Divine King; to the contrary, it was God who exercised his power in bringing them into existence.

---

11. Hossfeld and Zenger, *Psalms 3*, 506. For example, see Exod 3:20; 34:10; Josh 3:5; Job 5:9; Pss 72:18; 78:4, 11; 86:10; 96:3; 98:1; 105:5; 106:22; 107:15; 111:4.

12. Malchoz opines that the writer of Ps 136 likely knew the Priestly creation story found in Gen 1 and had a written copy of that text before him (Malchoz, "Psalm 136," 178). Whether the psalmist had an actual written text before him remains impossible to verify. Malchoz's initial claim that the poet was well aware of the Gen 1 creation account seems all but certain based on the repetition both in language and imagery.

Yahweh's Victory of the Powers of Egypt (136:10–15)

IN THE THIRD STROPHE THE PSALMIST turns to God's demonstration of power against the Egyptians. Similar to the psalmist's appropriation of the Genesis 1 text, verses 10–15 follow closely the language and imagery of the Pentateuchal tradition. Susan Gillingham has identified the core elements of the exodus tradition as rehearsed in the literature within the Old Testament.[13] She suggests that, at minimum, the exodus tradition consists of three component parts: (1) the escape from Egypt; (2) the role of Moses in leading the people out of Egypt; and (3) the crossing of the Red Sea. While these components typically appear together, other references to other events may appear as well, including the sojourn in Egypt, the plagues, the death of the firstborn, and the wilderness wanderings, among others.[14] In Psalm 136 the poet refers to the smiting of the firstborn in Egypt (v. 10), the coming out of Egypt (v. 11), and the crossing of the Red Sea (vv. 13–14)—all constituent elements within the exodus tradition. In verse 15, the final reference to this tradition, the psalmist praises Yahweh for having "swept Pharaoh and his army into the Red Sea."

To him who struck down the firstborn of Egypt. The opening line in the third strophe highlights the nature of the encounter between Yahweh and Pharaoh. Because the verb "to strike down" (*nakah*) is frequently found in texts that recount battles between political powers, the psalmist understands the exodus event as the routing of one power by another power.[15] The decisive act in this battle between human kingship and divine kingship occurred with the tenth plague. By striking down the firstborn of Egypt, Yahweh demonstrated the potency of his power versus the power apparatus of the Egyptians.[16]

The psalmist also references the power of God in verses 11–12. Both verses use language associated with Israel's deliverance from Egypt. The verb "to bring out" (v. 11) appears repeatedly in referring to Israel's departure from the land (Exod 12:17, 51), and the reference to a "mighty hand and an outstretched arm" in verse 12 suggests the active role Yahweh played in delivering Israel. The pairing of the hand and the arm with the verb "to bring out" occurs repeatedly in the book of

---

13. Susan Gillingham, "The Exodus Tradition and Israelite Psalmody," *SJT* 52 (1999): 19–46.

14. Ibid., 21. To these events Gillingham adds the theophany at Sinai and the settlement of the land.

15. Cf. Gen 14:7, 15, 17; 36:35; Num 14:45; Deut 29:6; Josh 11:10–12; and repeated references in Exod 2–15.

16. Hossfeld and Zenger, *Psalms* 3, 498.

Deuteronomy, where it highlights God's role in securing the deliverance of his people.[17]

To him who divided the Red Sea asunder. The psalmist follows the Pentateuchal tradition in explaining that God's power was on display in the crossing of the Red Sea. The language of verse 13, however, suggests that the psalmist may have incorporated another tradition from the ancient Near Eastern world. Commentators have noted that the verb *gazar*, "to divide asunder," in Psalm 136:13 also appears in the Ras Shamra texts in recounting the battle waged against the "dragon" in Ugaritic literature.[18] As Ruth Scoralick has contended, this language of cutting into pieces "carries mythological overtones of the warring enforcement of Yahweh against the sea, suggesting the powerful enforcement of Yahweh not only against the nations, but against all powers."[19] For the psalmist, the confession that Yahweh cut the Sea in two is indicative of the comprehensive scope of his power against all forces in creation, both human (Pharaoh) and non-human (chaos).

Yahweh's Defeat of the Kings (136:16–22)

THE FOURTH STROPHE BEGINS WITH ISRAEL'S departure from Egypt and culminates in their arrival in the land. The principle focus, however, is not on the journey itself but on the demonstration of Yahweh's power in defeating the kings who threatened Israel's entrance into the land.

Who led his people through the wilderness. Verse 16 provides a notably truncated account of the wilderness period. The brevity of this report, however, should not be construed as lack of access to that tradition in Israel's history. In Psalm 136 the brief reference to the wilderness tradition has a rhetorical function—it serves principally as a bridge between the accounts of Yahweh's battle with human power in Egypt and his battle with human power in Canaan. Despite the brevity of the verse, the focus on kingship is suggested by the choice of verb. The psalmist explains that Yahweh "led" his people through the wilderness. The verb for "led" is a

---

17. For example, see the declaration made in Deut 4:34: "Has any god ever tried to take for himself one nation out of another nation, by testings, by signs and wonders, by war, *by a mighty hand and an outstretched arm*, or by great and awesome deeds, like all the things the LORD your God did for you in Egypt before your very eyes?" (emphasis added).

18. See Kraus, *Psalms 60–150*, 499; Human, "Psalm 136," 81. See also, René Dussaud, *Les Découvertes de Ras Shamra (Ugarit) et l'Ancien Testament* (Paris: Geuthner, 1941), 84. On depictions of chaos more generally in the ancient Near East, see Keel, *The Symbolism of the Biblical World*, 47–56.

19. Ruth Scoralick, "'Hallelujah für einen gewalttätigen Gott?': Zur Theologie von Psalm 135 und 136," *BZ* 46 (2002), 253–72; see p. 262.

hiphil participle from the root *hlk*, "to go out." The participial form is *molik*, which shares the same consonants with the Hebrew word for king, *melek*. Yahweh leads his people out (*molik*) as he prepares to defeat the kings (*melakim* of Canaan (vv. 17–20).

To him who struck down great kings. In staccato fashion the psalmist reports Yahweh's victory over the kings east of the Jordan by using a fourfold structure: great kings, mighty kings, Sihon king of the Amorites, and Og king of Bashan. Joshua 12:24b records that, in total, thirty-one kings were killed in the settlement of the land—a number that is somewhat obscured by the fourfold list in Psalm 136. Obviously, the list in the psalm is not meant to be comprehensive, as verses 17–18 suggest, but those on the list do function as "exemplary prototypes of enemies in Israel's history," perhaps with an eye to the great kings of Babylon and Persia faced more recently by Israel.[20] All kings, whether great Pharaohs of Egypt, those ruling east of the Jordan, or presumably even the monarchs of the empires presently standing (Persia), will be struck down (*nakah*) by Yahweh (vv. 10, 17).

Gave their land as an inheritance. The giving of the land as an "inheritance" or "possession" (*nahalah*) to Israel may seem only tangentially related to the claims of Yahweh's power as Divine King. Yet the giving of "their land" (i.e., the land of the kings) to his servants reinforces Israel's confession of the sovereignty of Yahweh in international history. As the Divine King, Yahweh is sovereign over all nations, and his victory over "great kings" and "mighty kings" validates his claim of supremacy. Further, as the Divine King Yahweh has the right to parcel out a possession or inheritance to his servants, namely, those with whom he stands in a covenantal relationship (cf. Ps 123).

God's Deliverance of the Present Generation (136:23–25)

THE PREVIOUS STROPHES INCLUDED third-person descriptions of Yahweh's victorious power over human kingship. In the final strophe the psalmist breaks with the previous strophes by introducing first-person plural language (i.e., "our low estate," "our enemies"). The subtle shift in person and number suggests the hermeneutical move being made by the psalmist. The story of a people plagued by kings and political powers becomes, for the present community, the operative lens through which to view its own history; the story is "not merely of a generation dead and gone, but of 'us.'"[21]

---

20. Human, "Psalm 136," 82; Gerstenberger, *Psalms, Part 2 and Lamentations*, 387. For a similar use of the nations or people groups as a "prototype," see Ps 108.
21. Macholz suggests that "the community speaking here emphasizes its own historical

The connection between past and present, however, extends beyond simply the use of first-person language. The psalmist refers to the community's most recent threat as "our enemies" (*mitsarenu*), a term that appears repeatedly in Book 5, beginning with Psalm 107, and one that typically refers to political and military enemies. The term *mitsarenu* (Ps 136:24) is no doubt a partial homophone with the Hebrew term for Egypt, *mitsrayim* (v. 10). With the use of *mitsarenu*, the psalmist connects the most recent oppressive threat with the empire of old.[22] But unlike the particularities reported in the previous two strophes (vv. 10–22), the community reports its deliverance without providing specific details.[23] These concluding verses affirm that the power of the Divine King, evidenced throughout Israel's history, remains alive and active with the present generation. Yahweh's commitment indeed endures forever.

The final verse in this strophe extends God's care to all creation: "He gives food to every creature." Because God's work in behalf of Israel has dominated the entire psalm, such a universal declaration may appear misplaced. Yet prior to the rehearsal of God's work in Israel's history (vv. 10–22), the psalmist recounts God's work for the sake of all creation. Verse 25 returns to this very theme. The theological implications of this confession are considered below in Contemporary Significance.

A Concluding Call to Confess Yahweh (136:26)

THE PSALM CONCLUDES BY REPEATING the opening exhortation to give thanks (*hodu*) to Yahweh. Having rehearsed Israel's history and recounted Yahweh's decisive acts in Israel's behalf, the community can do nothing less than confess or praise this God. That the designation used for God in this verse, "God of heaven," appears repeatedly in later texts from the Persian period (cf. Ezra 1:2; 5:11; 6:9; 7:12; Neh 1:4; 2:4; 2 Chr 36:23), perhaps suggests a possible setting for this psalm. But this designation is not found in narrative texts alone. The reference to Yahweh's abode in the heavens or above the heavens also occurs in the Psalter, and with some regularity in Book 5 of the Psalter (e.g., Pss 113:5–6; 115:3; 123:1; 144:5–7). The idea of Yahweh as the God of the heavens emphasizes Yahweh's role as Divine King and disqualifies any human king's claim to supremacy.

---

experiences as the acts of God in line with the acts of God of the earlier *Heilsgeschichte*" (Christian Macholz, "Psalm 136: Exegetische Beobachtungen mit methodogischen Seitenblicken," in *Mincha. Festgabe für Rolf Rendtorff zum 75. Geburtstag*, ed. E. Blum (Neukirchen-Vluyn: Neukirchener Verlag, 2000], 186).

22. J. F. J. van Rensburg, "History as Poetry: A Study of Psalm 136," in *Exodus 1–15: Text and Context*, ed. J. J. Burden, P. J. Botha, and H. F. van Rooy, OTWSA/OTSSA 29 (Pretoria: V & R Printing, 1987), 87. See also Human, "Psalm 136," 83.

23. Seybold, *Die Psalmen*, 508.

Bridging Contexts

DIVINE KINGSHIP. In the center of Book 4 of the Psalter, Psalms 93 and 95–99 draw attention to the kingship of Yahweh. These psalms, frequently labeled as Yahweh *malak* ("the LORD reigns") psalms, announce the kingship of Yahweh in clear and unequivocal terms.[24] Four of the psalms begin with the declaration Yahweh *malak* or include it within the body of the psalm (Pss 93; 96; 97; 99), and other psalms in this collection simply refer to Yahweh as "king" (Pss 95; 98; 99). Some of the language and imagery reflects the metaphor of kingship: "throne" (Ps 97:2); "footstool" (Ps 99:5); "bow down" (Ps 95:6); judge of the world (Ps 96:13). Beyond these overt references to kingship, the psalms in this small collection affirm that Yahweh rules over the gods (Ps 95:3) and that all other gods must acquiesce to his authority as the one true God over all creation (Ps 97:7, 9). Moreover, these psalms declare that God stands over creation and that the "earth sees and trembles. The mountains melt like wax before the LORD" (Ps 97:4b–5a). Even more, as king over creation Yahweh holds in check the chaotic waters that threaten the stability of the world (Ps 93:3–4). As king, Yahweh will execute justice in behalf of his people, thus thwarting the ways of the wicked (Pss 97:10; 99:4). And the Yahweh *malak* psalms refer to God's reign over the nations and the peoples of the world (Pss 96:10; 97:9b; 99:2); even more, Yahweh will "consume his foes on every side" (Ps 97:3b).

While Psalm 136 does not contain the more overt references to kingship (e.g., thrones and footstools), the psalm does include many of the themes present in the Yahweh *malak* psalms. To say so is not to suggest that Psalm 136 was derived from the Yahweh *malak* psalms—only that the themes related to divine kingship, evident most clearly in the Yahweh *malak* psalms, provide a helpful lens through which to view Psalm 136. According to verses 2–3, Yahweh is greater than all other gods—he is "God of gods" and "Lord of lords." As Divine King, he fashioned creation and ordered it (vv. 4–9), and he even controls the menacing waters (v. 13–14). In the final strophe the psalmist refers to the Divine King's willingness to execute justice for the lowly. Most notably for Psalm 136, Yahweh as Divine King reigns over the nations (vv. 10–22) and will strike those who seek to threaten his covenant people (vv. 10; 17).

His love endures forever. The repeated refrain in Psalm 136 serves as a bedrock confession of the people of God: God's *hesed* is without end.

---

24. For an overview of this theological theme see James L. Mays, "The Center of the Psalms: 'The LORD Reigns' as Root Metaphor," in *The Lord Reigns: A Theological Handbook to the Psalms* (Louisville: Westminster John Knox, 1994), 12–22.

Israel's history cannot be understood apart from God's commitment to his covenantal relationship with his people. If the governing verb for Psalm 136, *hodu*, is indeed understood as "to confess" or "to proclaim," then the claims made by the priest in the first part of each verse, as well as the refrain uttered by the people in the second half, function as confession. The speaker confesses the *work* of God and the people confess the *faithfulness* of God. The two cannot be easily separated, nor should they be. One informs the other. God's faithfulness is made evident in his activity, and his activity demonstrates his faithfulness.

MODERN READERS MAY WORRY that the language that dominates Psalm 136 smacks of nationalistic rhetoric, or worse yet, political propaganda. To read the psalm in this highly reductionistic manner, however, is to miss the larger theological confession altogether. The rhetoric of Psalm 136 does not point to Israel, nor to Israel's own strength as a nation; rather, the rhetoric points to the Divine King to which all Scripture testifies. The confession that Yahweh is King "involves a vision of reality that is the theological center of the Psalter," and indeed, the center of all Scripture.[25] This vision of reality is rooted in God's *hesed* ("steadfast love") toward all creation. Creation is ordered properly (vv. 4–9) because of Yahweh's *hesed*. God acts to redeem and deliver his people because of that same *hesed*. And out of his *hesed* he cares for the lowly (v. 23). Repeatedly, Scripture confesses that this God is the one who takes down the mighty only to lift up the humble (e.g., 1 Sam 2; Luke 1). Yet the next-to-last verse of the psalm returns to God's larger commitment to creation. To all his creation he grants provisions out of his *hesed* (cf. Ps 145:14–16). This truth is the vision of reality at work in Psalm 136, the vision of a world rightly ordered. This work is indeed the work of the God of heaven, the God of gods and Lord of lords.

As suggested in the introduction to the comments on this poem, Psalm 136 is hortatory in nature. It exhorts us to confess what we know to be true about this God. We do more than simply recall a story—we confess a truth and lean into a vision. God's faithfulness to us in the past compels us to hope in a future in which God's vision of reality continues to unfold, a future in which God's *hesed* shapes us and the world. Because of that past, because of that hope, we have much to confess, much to proclaim.

---

25. Ibid., 22.

Psalm 137

¹ By the rivers of Babylon we sat and wept
    when we remembered Zion.
² There on the poplars
    we hung our harps,
³ for there our captors asked us for songs,
    our tormentors demanded songs of joy;
    they said, "Sing us one of the songs of Zion!"
⁴ How can we sing the songs of the LORD
    while in a foreign land?
⁵ If I forget you, Jerusalem,
    may my right hand forget its skill.
⁶ May my tongue cling to the roof of my mouth
    if I do not remember you,
if I do not consider Jerusalem
    my highest joy.
⁷ Remember, LORD, what the Edomites did
    on the day Jerusalem fell.
"Tear it down," they cried,
    "tear it down to its foundations!"
⁸ Daughter Babylon, doomed to destruction,
    happy is the one who repays you
    according to what you have done to us.
⁹ Happy is the one who seizes your infants
    and dashes them against the rocks.

Original Meaning

DESPITE ITS RELATIVE BREVITY, Psalm 137 has received considerable attention, both from those in the academy as well as those in worshiping communities. As with most biblical texts, such attention has focused on the historical context of the psalm and its meaning for its intended audience. But with Psalm 137, much attention has also been given to the theological claims of this poem, particularly verses 7–9 (see below, Bridging Contexts). Although Psalm 137 is not the only psalm to issue the kind of invective found in the final strophe (cf. Ps 58:6–8), it may be the most well known. The question concerning its theological claims, however, cannot be properly addressed until matters concerning the historical context of the psalm and its intended meaning are considered.

As suggested in the treatment of the two previous psalms (Pss 135 and 136), both of them functioned as an appendix to the Songs of Ascent. Both psalms celebrated the supremacy of God over all other gods (Pss 135:5; 136:2–3) and recounted God's power as manifested in the deliverance of Israel against the nations. The historical recitation in each psalm ended with Israel's entrance into the land. These remembrances provided ample reason for the psalmists' call for all Israel to praise and confess God (Pss 135:1, 21; 136:1, 26). While Psalm 137 differs in scope from the two previous psalms, the theological confession remains the same. The psalm pleads for Yahweh's judgment against the Babylonians and, in doing so, once more affirms the community's belief that Israel's God "is greater than all gods" (Ps 135:5), that the nations have no power against the "God of heaven" (Ps 136:26).

Psalm 137 shows affinities with the Songs of Zion (Pss 46; 48; 76; 84), particularly in its focus on Zion in the opening strophe (vv. 1–4). Psalm 137:3 even references this genre of psalm. The exiled community is demanded to "sing us one of the songs of Zion." Yet, as John Goldingay has correctly observed, Psalm 137 is better understood as an "inverted version of a Zion psalm."[1] Remembering Zion should invoke joy, not bitter weeping; it should invoke celebratory singing rather than silence, as symbolized by the hanging of the harps on the trees. The Songs of Zion celebrate the inviolability of the city of Zion in acknowledgment that Yahweh will be her fortress (Ps 48:3) and that all nations will be astonished at this God who protects his city (Ps 48:5). Yet the writer of Psalm 137 ponders how they can sing such songs on foreign soil—a sure sign not only of their captivity and the fall of Zion, but even more, of the apparent failure of their theological claims. Given all three (their captivity, the destruction of Jerusalem, and the failure of their theological claims), the claims in Psalm 137 are remarkable and demonstrate a theological depth that outstrips the veneer of reality. Despite all that has happened, the psalmist remains devoted to Jerusalem (vv. 5–6) and convinced of God's capacity to rout the nations (vv. 7–9).

Traditionally, the scene and events depicted in verses 1–4 have led scholars to suggest that Babylon may have been not only the locus of the action but in fact the provenance of the psalm itself.[2] More recently,

---

1. Goldingay, *Psalms 3*, 601. See also the discussion in Ulrich Kellerman, "Psalm 137," *ZAW* 90 (1978): 43–58, esp. 50–55. Kellerman notes that the "song of the Temple singers should be a Song of Zion, but given the poor conditions and particular circumstances of their singing" the song does not come so easily from their lips (50).

2. Klaus Seybold, *Die Psalmen*, HAT 1/15 (Tübingen: J. C. B. Mohr, 1996), 509–10.

however, a growing number of interpreters have argued that the psalm was likely written as a retrospective reflecting on an event in exile, yet done so at some distance, both chronologically and physically, from the original event.[3] Among the evidence marshaled to support such a claim, the primary rationale concerns the use of adverb "there" (*sham*) in verses 1 and 3. A literal translation of verses 1–3 reads:

> By the canals of Babylon,
>> there [*sham*] we sat down and wept
>> when we remembered Zion.
> Upon the poplar in her midst [*betokah*]
>> we hung our lyres.
> For there [*sham*] our captors required of us a song,
>> And our tormentors, songs of joy,
>> "Sing to us one of the Songs of Zion."

The NIV's translation differs slightly in omitting "there" from verse 1 and actually adding "there" at the beginning of verse 2, even though *sham* does not appear in the Hebrew of verse 2. As the rendering above suggests, the use of *sham* frames the opening three lines. Even more, the use of the prepositional phrase "in her midst" (*betokah*) in verse 2 complements the adverb "there." Everything that happened in verses 1–3 happened "there," in Babylon, "in her midst." These linguistic clues suggest that the psalmist is no longer in Babylon but instead back in Jerusalem, likely sometime in the postexilic period.

This understanding of "there" (*sham*) also informs our interpretation of the structure of the psalm itself.[4] Verses 1–4 constitute the opening strophe of the psalm and, as suggested above, look back to the community's experience in exile; it has a past orientation. In addition to the use of *sham*, the repeated use the perfect (*qatal*) verbal forms in the opening strophe reinforce the claim that the poet is referring to events in the past.

Seybold considers the psalm likely to be "early exilic," perhaps as early as the initial deportation in 598 BCE, and absolutely no later than 539 BCE. Hans-Joachim Kraus explains matter-of-factly that "Psalm 137 is the only psalm in the Psalter that can be dated reliably" (Kraus, *Psalms 60–150*, 501). Based on his translation of verse 8a, Kraus suggests that Babylon was still in power when the psalm was written.

3. Hossfeld and Zenger, *Psalms 3*, 513–14; Goldingay, *Psalms 3*, 600–601; Goulder, *Psalms of the Return*, 224–25. See also Birgit Hartberger's assessment of the various proposals related to dating (Birgit Hartberger, *"An den Wassern von Babylon--": Psalm 137 auf dem Hintergrund von Jeremia 51, der biblischen Edom-Traditionen und babylonischer Originalquellen*, Bonner Biblische Beiträge 6 [Frankfurt am Main: Peter Hanstein Verlag, 1986], 4–7).

4. See Hossfeld and Zenger, *Psalms 3*, 514.

The middle strophe, verses 5–6, contains a present orientation with the psalmist's making an oath never to forget Jerusalem. The final strophe, verses 7–9, is an imprecation, or curse, with a future orientation and concluding with a call for God to exact judgment on Babylon (vv. 8–9).

Recalling the Experience in Exile (137:1–4)

A NUMBER OF TRANSLATIONS end the first strophe at verse 3, but the strophe should be extended to include verse 4. Understood in this way, the opening and closing lines in this strophe refer to Babylon, and together they create an *inclusio* around the entire strophe. The opening line of verse 1 refers to being "by [*al*] the rivers of Babylon," and the final three words in verse 4 refer to being "in [*al*] a foreign land." From start to finish verses 1–4 recall the events associated with Babylon. In addition to the *inclusio*, further evidence can be marshalled to justify this divison. For example, the reference to "songs" in verse 4 repeats the language found in verse 3a–c.[5]

By the rivers of Babylon. Here the psalmist recalls life in exile—according to him, the people "sat" (NIV) or "dwelled" by the rivers of Babylon. The Hebrew word *yashab* can mean either "to sit" or "to dwell," but in this instance the preferred meaning appears to be the latter. Ezekiel 3:15 recalls a similar scene: the prophet "came to the exiles who lived [*yashab*] at Tel Aviv near the Kebar River." The image in Psalm 137:1 is not that of a group who decided to sit down by a river one day to weep but rather of a community whose home in exile was there by the rivers. The word "rivers" likely refers to the system of canals in Babylon that connected the Tigris and the Euphrates. Shimon Bar-Efrat suggests that this opening line paints a stark contrast between the conditions faced by those in exile and the conditions that characterized life in Zion.[6] He proposes that the Hebrew word "Zion" has its etymology in the root *tsyh*, "a dry region."[7] Thus the exiles have left their homeland, a dry region, and have been forcibly settled in a region flowing with water. As Bar-Efrat explains, "from a material point of view, the exiles' condition had improved. . . . They could build houses and plant fruit trees (Jer 29:5) and start a new life. But the material point of view is not the only one."[8] Regardless of their new life

---

5. Unique in her treatment of Ps 137, Nancy deClaissé-Walford isolates verse 4 and treats it as a separate strophe that is altogether independent of verses 1–3 and 5–6. See deClaissé-Walford, Jacobson, and LaNeel Tanner, *The Book of Psalms*, 953.

6. Shimon Bar-Efrat, "Love of Zion: A Literary Interpretation of Psalm 137," in *Tehillah le-Moshe*, ed. Moshe Greenberg et al. (Winona Lake, IN: Eisenbrauns, 1997), 3–4.

7. *HALOT* 2:1022 lists, as one of three options, the etymological connection between *tsiyya*, "dry land," and Zion as suggested by Bar-Efrat.

8. Bar-Efrat, "Love of Zion," 5.

in Babylon, Babylon was not Jerusalem. So they wept as they remembered Zion. The opening strophe does not mention Yahweh, nor are their comments directed toward Yahweh; the exiles are not worshiping or lifting up their communal laments to Yahweh, they are simply remembering (*zakar*) Zion, but remembering in the fullest sense of the word.[9]

On the poplars. The Hebrew word for this particular tree is *'arabah*, which can be translated "willow tree" (NRSV) or "poplar tree" (NIV); but the tree is likely the *Populus euphratica*, the Euphrates poplar that is often found alongside rivers in arid regions and can grow to a height of some fifteen meters. The psalmist explains that the community "hung" their lyres on these trees. Elsewhere in the Old Testament the lyre is often associated with songs of praise and festal celebration. In Nehemiah 12:27 the lyre is played along with the cymbals and harps in the dedication of Jerusalem's wall. Similarly, the lyre is played as others sing and celebrate (Job 21:12). And throughout the book of Psalms the lyre is connected with songs of praise (e.g., Pss 98:5; 147:7). But by the rivers of Babylon the lyre was not needed. Songs of praise were replaced with weeping, and dancing with mourning.

Our captors asked us for songs. In Psalm 137:3 the poet recalls the taunting nature of those who held the exiles captive. Such imagery highlights the oppressive power of the Babylonian Empire. In verse 3 the psalmist refers to the Babylonians as "our captors" and "our tormentors." The word "captors" comes from the verb *shabah*, "to take captive," and carries with it heavy political and militaristic overtones elsewhere in the Old Testament (e.g., 1 Kgs 5:2; Jer 41:10, 14; 1 Chr 5:21; 2 Chr 6:36). The oppressive connotations continue with the label "our tormentors" (*tolalenu*). Although the term itself is a *hapax legomenon*, the most likely root is *yll*, meaning "to wail" or "to howl."[10] The "tormentors" are those who cause others to wail. The two terms together highlight the challenge of living under foreign oppression. Bob Becking has suggested that, in labeling the Babylonians "our captors" and "our tormentors," the Jewish community

---

9. Goldingay translates *zakar* as "to be mindful." The meaning of the word does not refer to "an accidental remembering, but a deliberate focusing of attention and thought" (Goldingay, *Psalms* 3, 603).

10. Hossfeld and Zenger, *Psalms* 3, 512. Alfred Guillaume understands *tolal* in Ps 137:3 in light of the Arabic word *talla*, which refers to the driving of animals. Guillaume alludes to the Assyrian and even Achaemenid iconography, which frequently depict humans bound by the neck as they are driven into captivity. Guillaume concludes, "Thus it is clear beyond all doubt that the תוללל were the harsh, pitiless slave-drivers who drove the prisoners they had plundered hundreds of miles eastward to distant Babylon" (Alfred Guillaume, "The Meaning of *twll* in Psalm 137:3," *JBL* 75 [1956], 144).

offered a particular view of the cause of the exile. Becking explains that, to the Jewish community, "the Exile was not a neutral event in history, nor a punishment by YHWH in view of their sins, but a brute act of a cruel enemy."[11] This assessment of exile informs our understanding of the final strophe in this psalm and the imprecations contained therein.

How can we sing the songs of the LORD. As suggested above, verses 1 and 4 of Psalm 137 create an *inclusio* for the first strophe. Verse 1 refers to being "by [*al*] the rivers of Babylon," and verse 4 concludes with a reference to being "in [*al*] a foreign land." The word "foreign" (*nekar*) in verse 4 establishes both geographical *and* theological claims. Having been taken to Babylon, the exiles were clearly on foreign soil. They were no longer enjoying the land that was their "inheritance," as that land was referenced in the two preceding psalms (Pss 135:12; 136:21).

In addition to the geographical meaning of *nekar*, the term can also carry a theological claim. Although *nekar* occurs thirty-six times in the Old Testament, nearly half of those occurrences refer to "foreign gods."[12] In the ancient worldview, when one nation conquered another nation, the victor's god was considered more powerful. The destruction of Jerusalem and its temple would have signaled to the Babylonians that Marduk indeed was the superior deity. To have been led away to Babylon was indeed to live "in a foreign land," but even more, it was to live in the land where Marduk was worshiped as the god of gods. Understandably, the psalmist looks back at that moment and asks, "How could we sing the songs of the LORD upon foreign soil?"[13] Could the exiles have sung a song? Nothing prevented them from singing, but as Hossfeld and Zenger note, "a Yahweh song, sung by the conquered and deported Yahweh musician for the entertainment of the adherents of Marduk, in the midst of Babylon, was simply impossible— especially if the deportees wanted to hold fast to their faith."[14] To hang their harps on the poplars and refuse to sing was not a sign of resignation or hopelessness, but one of active resistance.

---

11. B. Becking, "Does Exile Equal Suffering: A Fresh Look at Psalm 137," in *Exile and Suffering: A Selection of Papers Read at the 50th Anniversary Meeting of the Old Testament Society of South Africa OTWSA/OTSSA, Pretoria August 2007*, ed. B. Becking and D. Human (Leiden: Brill, 2009), 198.

12. Gen 35:2; 35:4; Deut 31:16; 32:12; Josh 24:20; 24:23; Judg 10:16; 1 Sam 7:3; Jer 5:19; 8:19; Mal 2:11; Pss 81:9; 137:4; Dan 11:39; 2 Chr 33:15.

13. Author's translation. The verb in verse 4 (*nashir*, "we sing") is an imperfect (*yiqtol*) form. In this instance the imperfect indicates a non-indicative (modal) form. The psalmist is looking back and, in light of the current condition of the exiles, is suggesting the impossibility of actually singing a song.

14. Hossfeld and Zenger, *Psalms 3*, 516.

An Oath to Jerusalem (137:5–6)

IN THE SECOND STROPHE THE PSALMIST continues the theme of remembering that dominated the first strophe. The very structure of the second strophe itself reinforces this theme and its significance, as evidenced by the chiasm formed in verses 5a/b and 6a/b. The two outer lines (vv. 5a, 6b) highlight the word pair "forgetting" and "remembering," while the two inner lines (vv. 5b, 6a) include a self-curse, highlighting the punishment to be meted out for failure to remember.

In verses 1–4 the psalmist speaks on behalf of the community ("we," "our"), but in verses 5–6 he shifts to first-person singular language ("I," "my") and issues three oaths. The shift from communal to individual language in these verses recalls a similar rhetorical move made in Psalm 135:5. Both Psalms 135 and 137 open with a communal focus, which is interrupted by an individual who makes a confession or oath (Pss 135:5; 137:5–6). The intent of the confession is to state one's own commitment or belief, but even more, to invite the community to believe similarly.

As suggested above, Psalm 137:1–4 looked back to the time of the exile, when those in Babylon remembered Zion. In remembering Zion while living on foreign soil, the only response was silence. In the second strophe, however, the poet shifts from a recollection of the past to an oath in the present. Although the psalmist has returned from exile to the homeland, he pledges never to forget Jerusalem, the place of his "highest joy" (v. 6d).

Swearing an oath. In verses 5a/b and 6a/b, the psalmist begins each oath with the conjuction "if" (*'im*). In addition to its other functions, *'im* can introduce the protasis of a sworn oath, thereby marking a process or event that the speaker claims will not occur.[15] In this instance the psalmist swears that he will not forget Jerusalem, nor will he fail to remember Jerusalem, lest his hand and tongue become useless. The oath formula suggests the resolve of the speaker to remember.

My right hand . . . my tongue. In his oath the psalmist issues a self-curse involving both his right hand and tongue. He imprecates that if he forgets (*shakah*) Jerusalem, his right hand may forget (*shakah*). The Hebrew text does not indicate what the right hand might forget, so the NIV has provided a likely suggestion: "its skill." Understood in this way, the psalmist is declaring that if he forgets Jerusalem he should no longer to be able to play his harp (first self-curse) or sing the songs of Zion (second self-curse). Other scholars have offered alternative interpretations of these self-curses. Bar-Efrat has

---

15. Van der Merwe, Naudé, and Kroeze, *A Biblical Hebrew Reference Grammar*, 296. For example see 2 Sam 11:11. The point is not that the sworn item cannot occur but rather that the individual swears it will not be so.

suggested that both elements actually refer to the act of making an oath.[16] If the psalmist failed to remember Jerusalem, then the hand that was raised in the oath and the tongue that uttered the oath would be cursed. Hossfeld and Zenger have argued the hand and tongue are metonymns for action and speech, the "fundamental aspects of life."[17] As central as action and speech are to life, so too is remembering Jerusalem; the failure to remember Zion is a sign of the ebbing away of life.[18] While intriguing, both proposals seem to press the imagery too far, with Hossfeld and Zenger doing so more than Bar-Efrat. If the oath refers to temple singers, as they say it does, then the prior explanation seems preferable. Those who sing and play instruments in the temple area declare an oath to remember Jerusalem, and they issue a self-curse as part of this oath. The self-curse strips them of the very tasks they are meant to do in service to God.

My highest joy. In verse 6c–d the psalmist adds one final oath, "If [*'im*] I do not consider Jerusalem my highest joy." A more literal (and wooden) rendering of the Hebrew reflects the spatial imagery invoked in this verse: "If I do not cause Jerusalem to go up over my highest joy." The verb "to go up" (*'alah*) appears regularly in the Old Testament in reference to a person or persons "going up" to Jerusalem (cf. 2 Sam 19:34; 1 Kgs 12:27, 28; 2 Kgs 23:9; Isa 2:3//Mic 4:2; Zech 14:16). In this instance, however, the image has been inverted. The psalmist is not "going up" to Jerusalem but instead figuratively lifting up Jerusalem.[19] He swears that he will lift up Jerusalem over (*'al*) his chief joy, thereby making it his quintessential joy, his "highest joy." As in the two other oaths, the protasis includes the conjunction *'im* ("if"), but unlike in the other two there is no apodosis, no self-curse. Consequently, one may assume that verse 6c–d actually functions more as summary of the two previous oaths. Refusing to forget Jerusalem (v. 5a) and swearing to remember the city (v. 6b) signals that the psalmist has made Jerusalem his highest joy.

Imprecatory Plea against Edom and Babylon (137:7–9)

THE THEME OF REMEMBERING CONTINUES in the final strophe. Whereas verses 1–4 recall how those in exile remembered Zion and verses 5–6 announce the psalmist's oath never to forget, the final strophe turns attention away

---

16. Bar-Efrat, "Love of Zion," 7–8.

17. Hossfeld and Zenger, *Psalms 3*, 518.

18. Ibid. They provide a paraphrase of verses 5–6 based on this reading of the text: "If I do not make Jerusalem the center of my life, I would be better off dead."

19. The *hiphil* form of the verb communicates the causative action, i.e., "causing to go up" versus "going up."

---

from the psalmist and his community and instead calls on Yahweh to remember. In particular, the psalmist implores Yahweh to remember, or call to mind, the actions of the Edomites and the Babylonians.

Remember, LORD, what the Edomites did. The book of Obadiah (verses 10–14 in particular) recounts the actions of the Edomites as the Babylonians laid waste to Jerusalem. The psalmist provides his own account of the taunting suffered by the Israelites at the hands of the Edomites. Psalm 137 reports that the Edomites cheered the Babylonians with the cry to "tear it down." The verb *'arah* in the *piel* stem means "to expose" and can refer literally to exposing the nakedness of another person (Lev 20:19). Figuratively, however, the term can be used in reference to a city, and, given that cities are personified as feminine, the verb may refer to a city about to be "exposed" or put to shame (Isa 3:17; Lam 4:21; Ezek 16:35–42). The repetition of the call to "expose" the city in Psalm 137:7d moves from the figurative to the literal by adding the descriptive phrase, "down to its foundations" (cf. Hab 3:13). The Babylonian destruction razed Jerusalem to its foundations, and according to Obadiah the Edomites "stood aloof" (Obad 11) and "rejoice[d]" over what was happening to the people of Judah (v. 12). Because the eponymous ancestor of the Edomites was Esau, the outrage against the Edomites stemmed from a perceived violation of kinship norms. In Obadiah, twice the prophet admonishes the Edomites for mistreating "your brother" (vv. 10, 12). This perceived violation of kinship norms and the hostility that resulted against the Edomites is not unique to Psalm 137 (cf. Ezek 25:12–14; Jer 49:7–22).

Daughter Babylon, doomed to destruction. Psalm 137:8 begins with a vocative, "Daughter Babylon," signaling that the psalmist is no longer addressing Yahweh (v. 7) but the city of Babylon itself. Following "Daughter Babylon," the word *hashshedudah*, the one "doomed to destruction," stands in apposition. Although the word is pointed as a passive participle in the Hebrew text, a number of interpreters follow a Greek translation (Symmachus) and render the term as an active participle, "the devastator."[20] Other scholars, however, have recognized the Hebrew text as the more difficult reading and opted instead to retain the passive construction.[21] As a passive participle the term could be rendered, "the one devastated,"

20. Kraus, *Psalms 60–150*, 501 n. 8e; Allen, *Psalms 101–150*, 251 n. 8b; Seybold, *Die Psalmen*, 509 n. 8a; Becking, "Does Exile Equal Suffering?" 193.

21. David N. Freedman, "The Structure of Psalm 137," in *Near Eastern Studies in Honor of W. F. Albright*, ed. H. Goedicke (Baltimore: Johns Hopkins, 1971), 202–3; Kellerman, "Psalm 137," 45–46; Norbert Rabe, "'Tochter Babel, die verwüstete!'(Psalm 137,8)—textkritisch betrachtet," *BN* 78 (1995), 84.

implying that Babylon has already fallen, or it could be rendered passively but implying a future devastation of Babylon—"O Daughter Babylon, the one condemned to devastation." The subsequent curses in verses 8a–9 suggest that the psalmist longs for future action that will utterly and finally devastate the city of Babylon, thus making retribution complete. Although the Achaemenid dynasty under Cyrus defeated the Babylonians, the city of Babylon itself apparently suffered little under the hands of the new empire.[22] Based on the principle of *lex talionis*, the psalmist desired to see the city of Babylon devastated even as Jerusalem had been (v. 8).

Happy is the one who repays you. Verses 8b and 9 contain two curses or imprecations against Babylon. Both imprecations begin with the word *'ashre*, regrettably translated as "happy" in both the NIV and NRSV. It is this notion of being "happy" juxtaposed with doling out judgment and dashing babies against rocks that creates such cognitive dissonance for most readers. DeClaissé-Walford has suggested that rather than translating *'ashre* as "happy," perhaps the word "content" captures better the sense of peace that will be realized once judgment is enacted.[23]

Both imprecations must be read in the light of *talion*, a concept developed in early Babylonian law codes but also found throughout Scripture. Based on this legal principle, criminals should receive as punishment what they carried out against their victims. Two words that appear in verse 8 operate as technical terms for *talion*. The verb "repays" (the *piel* form of the root *shlm*) in verse 8b and two uses of the root *gml* ("to reward" or "to repay") in verse 8c underscore the importance of this concept in interpreting these verses.[24]

The admittedly disturbing language and imagery in verse 9 is rooted in the tactics of warfare as practiced in (but not limited to) that cultural setting. In addition to the murder of children, other Old Testament texts mention the murder of pregnant women and the elderly in the contexts of battle (Deut 32:25; 2 Kgs 8:12; Hos 14:1; Amos 1:12; Nah 3:10). Walter Brueggemann and William Bellinger explain the logic of the psalmist's

---

22. According to the Nabonidus Chronicle (ll. 15–16, 18–19), "On the sixteenth day of Ug, Gubaru, governor of Gutium, and the army of Cyrus without battle entered Babylon . . . Cyrus entered Babylon. They filled the *haru*-vessels in his presence. Peace was imposed on the city" (A. Kurht, ed., "The Nabonidus Chronicle," in *The Persian Empire: A Corpus of Sources from the Achaemenid Period* [London: Routledge, 2010], 51).

23. deClaissé-Walford, Jacobson, and LaNeel Tanner, *The Book of Psalms*, 956.

24. The Septuagint translates both *shalam* and *gamal* with the Greek verb *antapodidōmi* and the nominal form, *antapodoma*. Both terms refer to the recompense and retribution handed out as punishment for bad bahavior. See Jdt 7:15, where both the nominal and verbal forms are used together. See also LXX Ps 27:4 and LXX Joel 4:7.

focus on the killing of Babylonian children. They contend that the murder of the children would have "destroyed the next generation of warriors."[25] While no doubt such an act would certainly have destroyed a generation of warriors, the action called for in verse 9 is better understood based on the concept of *talion*. The psalmist was calling for punishment to be carried out against the Babylonians based on the treatment the Israelites had received, particularly as it related to their children. In recording the fall of Jerusalem, Jeremiah 52 cites that Zedekiah was captured on the plains of Jericho and that there the king of Babylon executed all the sons of Zedekiah in front of him prior to putting out his eyes. But the death of Israel's children was not limited to royal families. The book of Lamentations records the horrors of war and, in particular, refers to the deaths of children during the final seige. Their dead children "became their food when my people were destroyed" (Lam 4:10; cf. 2:20). The imprecation in Psalm 137:9, then, is not the result of some unchecked vitriol; instead, it is a call to enact the concept of *talion*, even if carried out at the level of nations.

THE REALITY OF POWER. Like the two previous poems, Psalm 137 confronts those who pray this psalm with the very real issue of power. Psalms 135 and 136 named several world and territorial powers—Pharaoh, Sihon, Og, and the mighty kings—and each psalm records how Yahweh dismantled them one by one, thus confirming his rightful title as Divine King. Psalm 137, however, explores the issue of power in a decidedly different manner. In the first four verses, the world-altering power of the Babylonian Empire comes to the fore. Existence as a refugee and exile is nothing if not "world-altering."[26] Along with the temple and city walls, everything that those in Judah knew and believed about the world came crashing down in 586 BCE. Rather than confidently asserting the inviolability of Zion, the exiles sat weeping on foreign soil. As a result, Psalm 137 serves as a stirring reminder of the devastating effects of oppressive power on human life.

Psalm 137 confronts the reader, both ancient and modern, with the reality of unchecked power in the world—a problem that did not end with the fall of Babylon in 539 BCE. If the psalm is postexilic, as suggested

---

25. Walter Brueggemann and William H. Bellinger Jr., *Psalms*, NCBC (Cambridge: Cambridge University Press, 2014), 575.

26. For more on this topic see the collection of essays edited by Stanley Porter, *Rejection: God's Refugees in Biblical and Contemporary Perspective* (Eugene, OR: Pickwick, 2015).

above, then it was likely written from Jerusalem when Yehud was under the thumb of another empire, the Persians.[27] As Goldingay has noted, any "imperial authority that controls and oppresses [Yehud] after the exile could be thought of as Babylon," and indeed was thought so, as recorded in other postexilic texts (e.g., Ezra 5:13; Neh 13:6).[28] Thus the problem of unchecked power continued, as did the theological challenges that it posed, thereby making the claims of Psalm 137 timeless and necessary for subsequent generations. Understood as such, this imprecatory psalm is much more than a historical relic meant solely to capture the trauma and angst endured during one particular experience in Israel's history; instead, the psalm now stands as a testimony to the potentially devastating reality of power on human life.

The acknowledgment of power in the world appears across the biblical witness.[29] In his letter to the church at Rome, Paul acknowledges the powers of the world but confesses he is "convinced that neither death nor life, neither angels nor demons, neither the present nor the future, nor any powers, neither height nor depth, nor anything else in all creation, will be able to separate us from the love of God that is in Christ Jesus our Lord" (Rom 8:38–39). In its own way Psalm 137 makes a similar confession. The psalmist does not diminish the reality of power or its devastating effects, but he is persistent in his claim that the presence of power in the world does not diminish his confession in the God of Israel.

The justice of God. If the opening strophe (Ps 137:1–4) serves as a reminder of the effects of power, the final strophe testifies to the justice of God. The two previous psalms both declared that Yahweh was the God of gods, greater than all other gods (Pss 135:5; 136:2). Those psalms celebrated the power of God over all other powers while rightfully concluding that Israel's God is indeed the God of heaven (Ps 136:26). In Psalm 137 the psalmist adds to that description of Yahweh. The request in verse 7, and the two imprecations that follow, announce that violence will not go unchecked by God. Frequently interpreters will attempt to temper the language of the final three verses by claiming that the psalmist, while he had anger, gave his desire for revenge over to God. In some ways this claim reduces the prayer of the psalmist to little more than a therapeutic exercise.

---

27. On a response to Persian royal ideology see Tucker, *Constructing and Deconstructing Power in Psalms 107–150.*

28. Goldingay, *Psalms 3,* 601. The use of "Babylon" as a cipher for any world power extends into the New Testament, as is evident in the book of Revelation, throughout which Babylon functions as a cipher for Rome.

29. See J. P. M. Walsh, *The Mighty from Their Thrones: Power in the Biblical Tradition,* OBT (Philadelphia: Fortress, 1987).

Such an explanation fails to address fully the confession being articulated by the poet. In short, he is declaring that God reigns, and because of that claim God can be trusted to right all injustice and thwart all powers that stand in opposition to his vision for the world. While the language and imagery in these verses strains our imagination, they are rooted in a concept of *talion*, as suggested above; but even more, they are rooted in the confession of the reign of God.

In his book *Exclusion and Embrace*, Miroslav Volf refers to an ethic of divine justice. His comments come in reference to his discussion on the rider on a white horse in the book of Revelation (Rev 19:11–21). In that text, the rider is said to have coming out of his mouth a sharp sword with which to strike down the nations (v. 15). Volf addresses those who might object to any image of a sword-wielding God. He writes, "It would not be worthy of God *not* to wield the sword; if God were *not* angry at injustice and deception, and did not make a final end to violence, God would not be worthy of our worship."[30] The images in Revelation 19 and Psalm 137 are not the musings of a disgruntled minority projecting their anger on God— rather, both texts confess that God takes injustice and oppressive power seriously and that in his reign as Divine King he can be trusted to eradicate them as he moves to establish things on earth as they are in heaven.

HOW DOES THE READER of Scripture appropriate such a challenging text? The truth is that some readers will not. The hermeneutical challenges posed by such a psalm are significant. Consequently, some readers of Scripture will simply turn elsewhere. Others, out of moral protest, will refuse to read or preach such a text while contending that such words are unfit for use in worship. As one writer argued,

> [That is] what the psalms really are: in large part, and to a degree seldom encountered otherwise, a text dominated by primitive and uncontrolled feelings of hatred, desire for vengeance and self-righteousness. . . . In spite of all apparent "matters of fact" that seem to deny it, I must acknowledge that for a long time I have not read any text so marked by excessive and unbridled hatred and thirst for revenge.[31]

---

30. Miroslav Volf, *Exclusion and Embrace: A Theological Exploration of Identity, Otherness and Reconciliation* (Nashville: Abingdon, 1996), 303. Italics original.

31. Franz Buggle, *Denn sie wissen nicht, was sie glauben. Oder warum man redlicheweise nicht mehr Christ sein kann. Eine Streitschift* (Reinbek: Rowohlt Verlag, 1992), 79–80. English translation from Zenger, *A God of Vengeance*, 22.

Although both treatments are perhaps understandable, neither option is satisfactory for those who receive Scripture as the "word of God for the people of God." Admittedly, some texts prove easier to exegete than others. But to disqualify a text based on our own assessment of it is to place ourselves above Scripture rather than under its authority. We must wrestle with texts such as these to hear God's word anew.

Psalm 137 invites us to think seriously about God, the world, and our place in it. As Erich Zenger has opined, "the shrill tones of the psalms of enmity can serve to shock Christianity out of the well-regulated slumber of its structural amnesia about God."[32] Psalm 137 reminds us of the reality of oppressive power that exists in the world, even today. "Babylon" now has many faces and goes by many names. Its presence in our world is legion, and we have come to accept it as reality—as the norm. A "shrill" psalm such as Psalm 137 seems oddly out of place for many of us because we have been lulled into a certain slumber that has made us accustomed to oppression in this world. But for those who live under oppression today, for those who this very day sit by the banks of a river and weep because they have hung up any thought of singing again, this psalm is far from shrill. This psalm reminds us that we should be less concerned about how this psalm fits neatly into "our world" and more concerned about those for whom this psalm describes their world.

As Zenger suggests, this psalm also calls us out of our amnestic view of God. Most of us prefer a domesticated view of God, one in which God looks strangely similar to ourselves. But such a view makes God little more than a household deity reserved for our own personal needs. The God of Scripture, however, resembles nothing of the sort. Psalms 135 and 136 invited us to remember this God who acted in history to thwart the powers that inhibited the unfolding of his kingdom. This God is no household deity—he is the God of heaven. And it is in this God that those who pray Psalm 137 hope. The psalmist invites God into the very warp and woof of the human condition and prays "with an understanding of the reign of the Lord that looks for its manifestation in the affairs of people and nations."[33] Oppression does not escape the view of God—he "remember[s]" (v. 7).

32. Zenger, *A God of Vengeance*, 74.
33. Mays, *Psalms*, 423.

Psalm 138

Of David.

¹ I will praise you, LORD, with all my heart;
   before the "gods" I will sing your praise.
² I will bow down toward your holy temple
   and will praise your name
   for your unfailing love and your faithfulness,
for you have so exalted your solemn decree
   that it surpasses your fame.
³ When I called, you answered me;
   you greatly emboldened me.
⁴ May all the kings of the earth praise you, LORD,
   when they hear what you have decreed.
⁵ May they sing of the ways of the LORD,
   for the glory of the LORD is great.
⁶ Though the LORD is exalted, he looks kindly on the lowly;
   though lofty, he sees them from afar.
⁷ Though I walk in the midst of trouble,
   you preserve my life.
You stretch out your hand against the anger of my foes;
   with your right hand you save me.
⁸ The LORD will vindicate me;
   your love, LORD, endures forever—
   do not abandon the works of your hands.

PSALM 138 IS TRADITIONALLY labeled a song of thanksgiving, but a more precise label might be a song of testimony.[1] The verb *yadah* appears three times in Psalm 138 (vv. 1a, 2b, 4), and although the term can mean "to give thanks" or "to praise" (cf. NIV), "the notion of acknowledgment or confession is fundamental to its meaning."[2] The structure of the psalm as a whole becomes readily apparent when

---

1. Goldingay, *Psalms 3*, 616.
2. Christoph Buysch, *Der letzte Davidpsalter: Interpretation, Komposition, und Funktion der Psalmengruppe Ps 138–145*, SBB 63 (Stuttgart: Katholisches Bibelwerk, 2009), 24.

yadah is understood as "confess." In verses 1–3 the psalmist confesses his faith in Yahweh in the presence of the gods. In the second strophe (vv. 4–6) he announces that the kings of the earth will praise Yahweh; and in the final strophe (vv. 7–8) he makes his confession of faith in the presence of his enemies.

The theology of Psalm 138 builds on the theological claims present in the preceding run of psalms (Pss 135–37). Psalms 135 and 136 recounted God's supremacy over the other gods as manifested in his routing of the nations when delivering Israel out of Egypt and as the Hebrews made their way into the promised land. While Psalm 137 provides a clear reminder that nations continue to oppress the people of God, Psalm 138 answers that challenge. In Psalm 137 the tormentors demand that the people sing a song, but in Psalm 138 it is the "kings of the earth" who will confess Yahweh (v. 4) and sing of his ways (v. 5a). In Psalm 137 the psalmist refers to the captors and tormentors who overwhelmed God's people, but Psalm 138 confesses that God will "stretch out [his] hand against the anger of my foes" (v. 7). Psalm 137 prays for Yahweh to "remember" what the nations did to his people; Psalm 138 celebrates that Yahweh will vindicate his people because of his love (v. 8).

Psalm 138 appears to draw heavily from earlier psalms, as evidenced in the following parallels: verse 1a//Psalm 9:1; verse 2a//Psalm 5:7; verses 4–5//Psalm 102:15; verse 6//Psalm 113:5–6; verse 8a//Psalm 57:2; verse 8b// the refrain in Psalm 136. The implied kingship of Yahweh over all gods and all nations has much in common with Isaiah 40–55, but precise verbal links between these chapters and Psalm 138 are more difficult to establish.

Heading (138:0)

PSALM 138 BEGINS THE FINAL Davidic collection in the book of Psalms (Pss 138–45). The superscription in each of the eight psalms includes the phrase "Of David" (*ledawid*). There are three other "David collections" in the Psalter. Books 1 and 2 contain two large collections that include David's name in the psalms' superscriptions (Pss 3–41; 51–72) and culminate with a reference to the "prayers of David" in 72:20. David is largely absent from the superscriptions in Books 3 and 4 of the Psalter.[3] In Book 5 (Pss 107–45), however, the name "David" reappears in the superscription of two collections. The first one, Psalms 108–10, begins Book 5; the second one,

---

3. Book 3 is dominated by psalms of Asaph and psalms associated with the Sons of Korah. David is mentioned only in Ps 86. In Book 4 Moses is mentioned in the superscription to Ps 90, but most psalms in that book do not contain a superscription. David appears in only two superscriptions of Book 4—Pss 101 and 103.

Psalms 138–45, concludes it. As I have argued elsewhere, the reemergence of David in the superscriptions in Book 5 signals that David has become emblematic of the poor servant who depends entirely on Yahweh for deliverance.[4] In Book 5 David is not the warring king seen in earlier psalms (e.g., Ps 18) but instead the one in need of God's deliverance, as is certainly true in Psalm 138 (vv. 6–8). In this way David functions as a model of piety for all who pray these psalms.

Pledge to Confess God (138:1–3)

THE FIRST STROPHE IN THE PSALM includes the psalmist's pledge to confess God (v. 1) and spells out the content of that confession (vv. 2–3).

I will praise you. As noted above, the verb *yadah* can mean "to praise" and also "to confess" or give testimony. The psalmist vows to confess God with his whole person. Not only does the poet mention his heart (i.e., "his will") but also his mouth ("I will sing" [v. 1b]) and his body ("I will bow down" [v. 2a]).[5]

Before the "gods." In verse 1b the psalmist vows to sing praises to Yahweh "before the 'gods'" (*neged 'elohim*). At first glance the reference to the *'elohim* in Psalm 138 appears to differ markedly in tone from the rhetoric found in Deutero-Isaiah. In that collection the idols are mocked relentlessly as vacuous creations of human hands (e.g., Isa 41:29; 44:9–20; 46:1–7)—a claim similarly made elsewhere in Book 5 of the Psalter (cf. Pss 115:4–8; 135:15–18). In Psalm 138, however, the psalmist speaks not of idols but of *'elohim*, "gods." While Deutero-Isaiah mocked the idols, the author of Psalm 138, by using the phrase "before the 'gods'" (*neged 'elohim*), promises to sing the praises of Yahweh "in defiance [of the gods]."[6] Rather than mocking the ineffectiveness of idols or gods, the psalmist opts to testify about Yahweh's *hesed* ("covenantal loyalty") and *'emet* ("faithfulness"). The very character of God, his "name" (*shem*), has been proven by his *hesed* and *'emet* toward his people.

The act of confessing Yahweh "before the 'gods'" (*neged 'elohim*) asserts Yahweh's supremacy over all other presumed deities. In making such a claim the psalmist also posits a political claim. As similarly in Psalms 86:8

---

4. Tucker, *Constructing and Deconstructing Power in Psalms 107–150*, 181.

5. Hans Walter Wolff explains that the "heart [*leb*] undoubtedly embraces the whole range of the physical, the emotional and the intellectual, as well as the functions of the will, yet must clearly hold on to the fact the Bible primarily views the heart as the centre of the consciously living [person]" (Hans Walter Wolff, *Anthropology of the Old Testament*, trans. Margaret Kohl (Philadelphia: Fortress, 1974], 55).

6. Goulder, *The Psalms of the Return*, 231. Similarly, Clinton McCann suggests the phrase creates a polemical tone (McCann, "The Book of Psalms," 1232).

and 96:4, the referent for *'elohim* in Psalm 138 is clearly the gods of the nations. Because gods and nations were so closely associated in the ancient Near East, the psalmist's defiant claim of Yahweh's faithfulness "before" the gods (*'elohim*) also implies a certain rejection of the claims of supremacy by the surrounding nations.

When I called, you answered me. The NRSV translates the beginning of verse 3 as "on the day I called," but the opening prepositional phrase *beyom* ("in a day") lacks the kind of specificity suggested in the NRSV. The phrase *beyom* likely has a temporal frame of reference and is better translated as "when" or "whenever" (cf. Jer 34:13; Pss 20:10; 56:9). In Psalm 138:2 the poet praises God for his unfailing love and faithfulness. In verse 3 he makes a general statement to support that claim, namely, that whenever he called on Yahweh, the Lord proved himself faithful and answered. The psalmist confesses that Yahweh's faithfulness "greatly emboldened me."

Kings Will Confess God (138:4–6)

IN THE SECOND STROPHE THE PSALMIST declares that the world powers, the "kings of the earth," will join with the psalmist in making a confession about Israel's God.

May all the kings of the earth praise you, LORD. In verse 4 the psalmist prays that the kings of the earth will confess or praise (*yadah*) Yahweh and sing (*shir*) of his ways. The kings of the earth will join the people of God in their praise, thus participating joyously in the ways of God. This portion of the Psalter was likely collected during the Persian period. According to the royal imperial ideology of Persia's Achaemenid dynasty, their empire was a worldwide one in which nations participated joyously in the Achaemenid rule because, under this dynasty, the world was well ordered. The claim made by the poet in Psalm 138, however, reverses such imagery and thereby pictures an entirely reordered world. According to the psalmist, the empires of the world will participate joyously in the praise and confession of Yahweh.

The ways of the LORD. The psalmist explains that the kings will make their confession once they "hear what you have decreed." The second half of verse 4 provides the precondition for what is announced in the first half of the verse. In his translation of verse 4, Leslie Allen captures well this relationship between the two halves: "Let all the kings in the world give you thanks *in reaction to* hearing of the promises of your mouth."[7] The kings

---

7. Allen, *Psalms 101–150*, 243. Emphasis added.

will not confess Yahweh *until* they have first heard "what you have decreed," or, more literally, until they have heard "the words of your mouth" (*'imre-pika* [v. 4b]). The emphasis, however, is not simply on God's making a pronouncement *ex cathreda*, so to speak, but on the content of his speech. The kings of the earth shall recognize the intended order of the world as outlined in the "ways of the LORD" when they hear the words of his mouth (*'imre-pika*). Buysch has noted that *pika* ("your mouth") occurs seven times in the Psalter. Of these seven occurrences, three appear in Ps 119 (vv. 13, 72, 88). In each of the three instances, *pika* stands in a construct relationship with terms such as "law," "justice," and "testimony." All three words are considered "technical terms" for the torah.[8] The psalmist declares that once the kings of the earth hear the "words of Yahweh's mouth," his torah, they will realize who serves as the true king and will join Israel in singing of his ways.

For the glory of the LORD is great. The final line of the second strophe reinforces the psalmist's claim of Yahweh's universal rule as Divine King. The word "glory" (*kabod*) occurs in texts that acknowledge God's divine reign (cf. Isa 6:1–8; Pss 97:1, 6; 145:10–13), as does the declaration about the "greatness" of Yahweh (cf. Pss 48:1; 95:3).[9] The kings of the earth hear the words of Yahweh's mouth, thus leading them to confess him and sing his praises while acknowledging that he reigns as the King on high.

The LORD is exalted. The NIV associates verse 6 with the final strophe; but while doing so is syntactically possible, the verse seems better understood as the final verse in the second strophe. Grammatically speaking, verses 4–5 both begin with imperfects (*yiqtols*), which here should be translated as jussives (i.e., "May all the kings") expressing the desire of the psalmist to see the kings praise God and sing of him (v. 6a). Verse 6 begins with the evidential use of the particle *ki*, "for." The claims made in verse 6 are "evidence" for the statements made in verses 4–5; put differently, the oblique reference to kingship in verse 6 serves to explicate the claims made in verses 4–5. As King, Yahweh stands on high, but he sees the lowly—the care of the poor is the responsibility of all kings in the ancient Near East. A similar confession is made in Psalm 113. There the psalmist declares that Yahweh is "exalted over the nations, his glory above the heavens" (v. 4), but as Divine King "he raises the poor from the dust" (v. 7). Thus, the declaration in Psalm 139:8 by the kings of the earth concerning Yahweh's kingship (i.e., "the glory of the LORD is great") is predicated on both the words of his mouth and the actions of his hands.

---

8. Buysch, *Der letzte Davidpsalter*, 32.
9. McCann, "The Book of Psalms," 1232.

God Preserves the Lowly (138:7–8)

IN VERSE 6 THE PSALMIST RECOUNTS Yahweh's commitment as Divine King to lift up the lowly. That declaration serves not only as evidence for the anticipated confession of the kings in verses 4–5 (as suggested above) but also as the ground of hope for the psalmist in verses 7–8. In this final strophe the psalmist moves from the general to the particular, from a general claim about Yahweh to its significance for his own predicament.

I walk in the midst of trouble. The psalmist's allusion to the threats that confront him indicates he is in "the midst of trouble." The word for "trouble" is *tsarah* and derives from the root *tsr*, which often refers to enemies.[10] Although the image of walking "in the midst of trouble" portrays a more abstract notion of trouble (i.e., "distress"), in reality, the image is much more concrete. The psalmist is referring to the individuals who are threatening him, as confirmed by the parallel lines of verse 7c–d and the mention of the psalmist's "foes."

Your hand. Three times in the final two verses the psalmist makes reference to Yahweh's hand or hands. Metaphorically, they signal the deliverance initiated by Yahweh and made manifest in the life of the psalmist. In verse 6 the psalmist confessed that Yahweh is the Divine King, the one "exalted" and "lofty." Repeatedly in Book 5 of the Psalter Yahweh is depicted as the God of the heavens, yet his enthronement in the heavens in no way precludes the possibility of his active intervention in the life of his people. Frequently, the "hand of God" signals his work of deliverance, particularly against those who threaten the people of God. In Psalm 136, for example, the poet declared that Yahweh defeated the forces of Pharaoh with "a mighty hand and an outstretched arm" (v. 12). Similarly, in verse 7c the psalmist confesses that Yahweh "stretch[es] out his hand" against the psalmist's enemies; it is by God's "right hand" that the Lord will deliver the beleaguered poet (v. 7e).

In the final line of Psalm 138 the psalmist makes the third reference to "hand," but the image has shifted. The poet implores Yahweh not to "abandon the works of your hands." Although the phrase "works of your hands" can refer to creation (cf. Ps 102:26), the phrase appears frequently in Book 5 of the Psalter in reference to Yahweh's acts of deliverance (Pss 107:22, 24; 111:2, 6; 118:17; 143:5; 145:4, 9, 10, 17). In Psalm 138, however, a third possibility exists. The "works of your hands" may in fact refer to the psalmist or community as the pray-ers of this psalm. The parallel construction of the first and last lines of verse 8 confirms this possibility:

---

10. "II צָרָה," *HALOT* 2:1058–59. According to *HALOT*, II צָרָה is derived from II צָר, "enemy" or "foe."

A	B	C
The LORD	will vindicate	me (v. 8a)

A'	B'	C'
(ellipsis)	do not abandon	the works of your hands.

The first-person references in verse 7 strengthen this argument further by drawing attention to the psalmist and his community.

The verb *rapah* in the final line of the psalm can be translated as "abandon" (NIV), but the term invokes the image of something being dropped or let go (Josh 10:6). In Psalm 138 the psalmist implores Yahweh not to drop or let go of his people, the works of his hands. This request is rooted in the Deuteronomic promise that Yahweh would not forsake (*rapah*) his people (Deut 4:31; 31:6, 8; Josh 1:5).[11] The psalm comes to a close with the assurance of God's vindication—an assurance predicated on the *hesed* of Yahweh (v. 8b) and grounded in the Deuteronomic promise of God's faithfulness (v. 8c).

Bridging Contexts

AS A PSALM OF CONFESSION Psalm 138 invites us to consider a number of declarations made about God and his work in the world.

The supremacy of Yahweh. In all three strophes the psalmist confesses that Yahweh alone is the true God. The mention of "gods" (*'elohim*) in verse 1b invites a comparison of Psalm 138 with Psalm 82. In Psalm 82:4 the "gods" are chastised by Yahweh for failing to "rescue the weak and the needy," as well as for failing to deliver them "from the hand of the wicked"; further, in 82:7 Yahweh declares that these deities are not true gods and will "die like mere mortals." In Psalm 138, however, Yahweh is declared as the one enthroned on high, the one characterized by *hesed*, "covenant loyalty," and *'emet*, "faithfulness." And unlike the "gods" mentioned in Psalm 82, Yahweh delivers the lowly.

The writer of Psalm 138 moves from the realm of the "gods" to the realm of empires and human kings, and there, too, Yahweh proves his supremacy, but perhaps in an unexpected way. In Psalms 135 and 136 the psalmist recounted Yahweh's decimation of nations and kings, thereby leading one to surmise that any nation or king subsequently mentioned

---

11. Hossfeld and Zenger contend that the reference to the "works of your hands" does indeed refer to creation and that in the final line the psalmist is asking God to remain true to his creation, his people (Hossfeld and Zenger, *Psalms 3*, 531).

in the Psalter would meet with the same fate at the hands of Israel's God. Yet Psalm 138 prays for a fate far different for the "kings of the earth." When those in positions of power hear what Yahweh has done and see the greatness of God's glory (i.e., his reign), they can do nothing other than confess and sing to the Lord. They will shrink back as they pay homage to the one true king.

The final strophe of Psalm 138 affirms the supremacy of Yahweh as manifested in the deliverance of his people. As noted above, this psalm reflects the conditions of the restored community during the postexilic period, and it is likely that the supplicant is either a "person who speaks in the identity of the people or is the personified community" itself.[12] The psalmist and the community affirm that because Yahweh is the Divine King, his people have hope for their vindication. Were Yahweh not the supreme God, any hope in him would be tenuous at best; but because they confess what they know to be true (i.e., Yahweh is God alone), they look forward to his acts of deliverance renewed and revealed for a new generation.

Immanence and transcendence. Psalm 138 juxtaposes the immanence and transcendence of God without needing to clarify or resolve the ambiguity inherent in that juxtaposition. Yahweh is the God of the heavens, yet he is fully active in creation. See Bridging Contexts on Psalm 113 for an extensive reflection on the immanence and transcendence of God.

PSALM 138 CONFESSES to the proleptic reign of God—the kingdom of God has come already, but it is not yet fully realized. The psalmist confesses to the supremacy of God and notes the work of God already in his life (v. 3), yet he also acknowledges that the world is not as it should be. When the world is not as we had hoped and when powers seem to rise up all around us, our human inclination is to push back and fight. In Psalm 138 the psalmist does indeed push back and resist the claims of his world, but his resistance begins and ends in worship and prayer. Such suggestions may appear naïve at best, and superficial at worst, yet the work of worship and prayer is rooted in a fundamental confession that the kingdom of God has come and is coming still. Moreover, our work of worship and prayer reflects our tenacious belief that only one God sits on high—and despite the circumstances of the world, he "looks kindly on the lowly" still.

---

12. Mays, *Psalms*, 424. For a similar example see Isa 12:1–6.

The belief in the proleptic reign of God offers a response to the questions posed in the dystopian vision of our modern culture. Dystopian literature provides nightmarish visions of a future in which human power goes unchecked and impotent individuals suffer under the oppressive rule of authorities.[13] The disquieting *Hunger Games* trilogy by Suzanne Collins and the haunting work of Lois Lowry (*The Giver*) capture well this dystopian view of the future. Regrettably, audiences assume this literature is written primarily for "young adults," and consequently they miss the existential themes evoked in it. These works reflect the angst that frequently plagues all ages of our society. The underlying assumption is that the crisis of the present will yield a sense of powerlessness and hopelessness for the future.

Although God had earlier answered the prayers of the psalmist, kings remained in power and enemies still assailed him. When we as individuals and communities confess our belief in God's reign, we are resisting the urge to believe in a dystopian vision of reality. We are declaring that the reign of God compels us to see the world differently. In his work on the book of Revelation, Richard Bauckham writes:

> The effect of John's visions, one might say, is to expand his readers' world, both spatially (into heaven) and temporally (into the eschatological future), or to put it another way, to open their world to divine transcendence. . . . it is not that the here-and-now are left behind in an escape into heaven or the eschatological future, but that the here-and-now look quite different when they are opened to transcendence.[14]

To borrow Bauckham's language, Psalm 138 invites us to "expand our world" both spatially and temporally. The psalmist worships in the temple but claims that God is enthroned on high. The psalmist confesses what God has done (v. 3) but longs for all that God will do. To see the world differently necessitates a proper view of "divine transcendence," a divine transcendence that is capable of reaching into the present moment while also pointing to the divine future.

---

13. See Suzanne Collins, *The Hunger Games* (New York: Scholastic, 2006); Suzanne Collins, *Catching Fire* (New York: Scholastic, 2008); Suzanne Collins, *Mockingjay* (New York: Scholastic, 2010); Lois Lowry, *The Giver* (New York: Houghton Mifflin, 1993).

14. Richard Bauckham, *The Theology of the Book of Revelation* (Cambridge: Cambridge University Press, 1993), 7–8.

Psalm 139

For the director of music. Of David. A psalm.

¹ You have searched me, LORD,
   and you know me.
² You know when I sit and when I rise;
   you perceive my thoughts from afar.
³ You discern my going out and my lying down;
   you are familiar with all my ways.
⁴ Before a word is on my tongue
   you, LORD, know it completely.
⁵ You hem me in behind and before,
   and you lay your hand upon me.
⁶ Such knowledge is too wonderful for me,
   too lofty for me to attain.
⁷ Where can I go from your Spirit?
   Where can I flee from your presence?
⁸ If I go up to the heavens, you are there;
   if I make my bed in the depths, you are there.
⁹ If I rise on the wings of the dawn,
   if I settle on the far side of the sea,
¹⁰ even there your hand will guide me,
   your right hand will hold me fast.
¹¹ If I say, "Surely the darkness will hide me
   and the light become night around me,"
¹² even the darkness will not be dark to you;
   the night will shine like the day,
   for darkness is as light to you.
¹³ For you created my inmost being;
   you knit me together in my mother's womb.
¹⁴ I praise you because I am fearfully and wonderfully made;
   your works are wonderful,
   I know that full well.
¹⁵ My frame was not hidden from you
   when I was made in the secret place,
   when I was woven together in the depths of the earth.
¹⁶ Your eyes saw my unformed body;
   all the days ordained for me were written in your book

before one of them came to be.
¹⁷ How precious to me are your thoughts, God!
How vast is the sum of them!
¹⁸ Were I to count them,
they would outnumber the grains of sand—
when I awake, I am still with you.
¹⁹ If only you, God, would slay the wicked!
Away from me, you who are bloodthirsty!
²⁰ They speak of you with evil intent;
your adversaries misuse your name.
²¹ Do I not hate those who hate you, LORD,
and abhor those who are in rebellion against you?
²² I have nothing but hatred for them;
I count them my enemies.
²³ Search me, God, and know my heart;
test me and know my anxious thoughts.
²⁴ See if there is any offensive way in me,
and lead me in the way everlasting.

PSALM 139 IS THE SECOND psalm in the final Davidic collection of the Psalter (Pss 138–45) and arguably the most familiar within that collection. In the previous psalm (Ps 138), the psalmist referred to his lowly status (v. 6) and explained that he was walking "in the midst of trouble," yet he took solace in the fact that his God stands as the Divine King over all gods (v. 1) and all the kings of the earth (v. 4). As in Psalm 138, the writer of Psalm 139 announces the threats that befall him and pleads for God's action (Ps 139:19–22). In this poem, however, the psalmist's hope rests entirely with the God who knows him, the God with whom he is in relationship. The verb *yada'*, "to know," occurs seven times in the poem (vv. 1, 2, 4, 6, 14, 23 [2x]), thereby repeatedly reinforcing the "I-Thou" relationship between the psalmist and God. This "I-Thou" relationship serves as the "unifying thread" throughout the psalm.[1]

As suggested by the NIV's translation, the psalm can be divided into four strophes: verses 1–6; 7–12; 13–18; and 19–24. The language adopted in the first two strophes underscores the dominance of the "I-Thou" relationship in the poem. In the first strophe "you" serves as the subject of nearly

1. Jan Holman, "The Semiotic Analysis of Psalm CXXXIII (LXX)," *OtSt* 26 (1990): 93.

all the verbs, while in the second strophe, "I" dominates throughout. The first three strophes praise God for his comprehensive knowledge of the psalmist, the fullness of his presence in the world, and his power as Creator. The final strophe, however, shifts both in focus and tenor. The soaring language of praise and confession in the first three strophes abruptly ends in verse 18, only to be followed by more ominous and troubling language in the final strophe. Beginning in verse 19, the psalmist turns his attention to the enemies and the "bloodthirsty" in requesting that God eradicate or slay those who "hate" the Lord (v. 21a). The imprecatory nature of this final strophe has plagued interpreters. The radical departure in imagery and language in the fourth strophe led Hans Schmidt to conclude that verses 19–24 were likely a later addition to the psalm.[2] The disjuncture between the first three strophes and the fourth strophe is noted in communities of faith as well, as evidenced by the omission of the final strope from the lectionary readings.

Although verses 19–24 differ from the preceding three strophes, the final strophe remains an integral part of the psalm's structure. A number of terms in that strophe also appear in the first strophe of the psalm: *derek* ("way" [vv. 3, 24]); the divine name (vv. 1, 4, 21); *qum* ("rise" [vv. 2, 21]); *baqar* ("search" [vv. 1, 23]); and *yada'* ("to know" [vv. 1, 23]). Although two different Hebrew terms are used (*re'a* and *sarap*), the reference to the psalmist's "thoughts" also binds together the first and last strophe. The repetition of vocabulary in the first and last strophes serves to create an *inclusio* around the psalm, thus confirming that the final strophe should be understood as an integral part of the psalm itself.

The precise genre of this psalm has generated considerable debate and discussion. The hymnic nature of the first eighteen verses seems to support the claims of Hermann Gunkel and Claus Westermann, among others, that the poem is best understood as a psalm of praise or a hymn.[3] Taking their cue from the final strophe, others have understood the psalm as a prayer of an unjustly accused person.[4] Still others have suggested, more broadly, that the psalm is a complaint uttered by a psalmist in the midst of a hostile context. Leslie Allen, championing this view, suggests that the final strophe functions like a "demarcated climax." The complaint

---

2. Schmidt, *Die Psalmen*, 246.

3. Gunkel, *An Introduction to the Psalms*, 40, 46; Claus Westermann, *The Praise of God in the Psalms* (Richmond, VA: Knox, 1965), 139.

4. Most famously Ernst Würthwein, "Erwägungen zu Ps 139," *VT* 7 (1957): 165–82; Seybold, *Die Psalmen*, 513–18; Robert B. Coote, "Psalm 139," in *The Bible and the Politics of Exegesis*, ed. D. Jobling et al. (Cleveland: Pilgrim, 1991), 33–38.

in the final strophe is prefaced by a lengthy discourse that praises the attributes of Yahweh that pertain to his own crisis.[5] Others however, note the wisdom themes present throughout Psalm 139, and prefer instead to label it a "meditation" or "wisdom meditation."[6] Gerstenberger contends that the psalm "is meditating on human destiny before God in general, doing so somewhat in analogy to complaining prayers."[7] This mediating position takes seriously the view of Allen that the final strophe plays a vital role in the psalm by emphasizing the plight of the psalmist, but it also takes seriously the claims of the first three strophes concerning human life, and in particular the psalmist's life. The blending of wisdom themes with a complaint appears later in this collection, in Psalm 141, thereby suggesting that this type of mixed form is not unique to Psalm 139 in the final Davidic group of poems in the Psalter.

Heading (139:0)

SIMILAR TO THE OTHER PSALMS in this final Davidic collection, this psalm includes the superscription "Of David" (*ledawid*). On the figure of David in the final Davidic collection see the comments on Psalm 138, "Heading." The superscription also includes the notation, "For the director of music" (*lamnatseah*), a term likely referring to a worship or liturgical leader. The frequency of this directive in superscriptions across the Psalter indicates its importance in Israel's cultic affairs. The precise role of that person, however, remains unclear. Other forms of the verb (*natsab*) appear in Ezra and 1–2 Chronicles in reference to those who supervise the affairs of the temple. The last term in the superscription, *mizmor*, "a psalm," refers to a song likely to be sung with instrumental accompaniment.[8] In Book 5 the title is assigned to Psalms 108–10, the first Davidic collection in the book, as well as to Psalms 139–41 and 143 in the final Davidic collection.

God's Examination of the Psalmist (139:1–6)

THE OPENING STROPHE OF THE PSALM considers Yahweh's comprehensive knowledge of the psalmist. The poet captures the fullness of God's knowledge through several examples of merism. A merism is a poetic technique that expresses a totality by mentioning two parts, typically polar opposites. For example, Psalm 139 includes "when I sit" and "when I rise" (v. 2a),

---

5. Allen, *Psalms 101–150*, 257. For a similar assessment, see deClaissé-Walford, Jacobson, and LaNeel Tanner, *The Book of Psalms*, 962.
6. Gerstenberger, *Psalms, Part 2*, 405–406; Hossfeld and Zenger, *Psalms 3*, 539.
7. Gerstenberger, *Psalms*, 405.
8. "מִזְמוֹר," *HALOT* 1:566.

"my going out and my lying down" (v. 3a), and "behind and before" (v. 5a). Poetically speaking, a merism provides vivid images that are meant to replace more abstract concepts such as "all," "every," or "always." Given this intended usage, a merism is meant to be understood figuratively or metaphorically, but not literally.[9] Thus the psalmist's contention that Yahweh hems the psalmist in "behind and before" is best understood figuratively: Yahweh completely surrounds the psalmist.

You have searched me . . . and you know me. The psalm begins with the divine name, "you LORD," which constitutes an invocation in the truest sense of the term—one invoking Yahweh to search the psalmist. The verb "to search" (*baqar*) can refer to searching out land (Judg 18:2) or searching out a city (2 Sam 10:3), but often, especially in the wisdom literature, the verb means "to search" in the sense of "to examine" (Prov 18:17; 28:11; Job 13:9). As noted above, the verb "to know" (*yada'*) appears seven times in Psalm 139—four of them in this strophe. Because Yahweh has "examined" the psalmist, God "knows" him fully.

You know when I sit. Verses 2–3 begin with a merism in the first line, followed by a summative statement in the second. The merisms recount the psalmist's actions and inaction. Taken together, they appear to be chiastically structured: inaction ("sit"); action ("rise"); action ("going out"); inaction ("lying down"). Four verbs of perception reflect Yahweh's attentiveness to the fullness of the psalmist's life: "to know" (*yada'*); "to perceive" (*bin*); "to discern" (*zarah*); and "to be familiar with" (*sakan*). None of the terms imply a critical, hostile, or even scrutinizing attitude toward the psalmist; instead, they reveal the depth of Yahweh's knowledge.[10] This depth of knowledge is held in tension with the claim that Yahweh knows these things "from afar" (v. 2b). Particularly throughout Book 5 of the Psalter, Yahweh is depicted as the God of the heavens, a claim meant to reinforce Yahweh's cosmic kingship, yet his position in the heavens in no way precludes his capacity to be fully observant of his people and cognizant of their lives.

Before a word is on my tongue. Although the pattern evident in the two preceding verses (a merism followed by a summative statement) breaks down in verse 4, the emphasis on the comprehensive nature of Yahweh's knowledge remains in view. Verses 2–3 suggest that Yahweh is fully aware of the psalmist's *actions*; verse 4 extends the reach of his knowledge by claiming that Yahweh knows even the psalmist's *thoughts*. The Hebrew term

---

9. For an extended review of merism in the Old Testament see Jože Krašovec, "Merism—Polar Expression in the Hebrew Bible," *Bib* 64 (1983): 231–39.

10. Hossfeld and Zenger, *Psalms 3*, 540.

for "word" (*millah*) is a synonym for the traditional Hebrew term for "word" (*dabar*), with no real differentiation in meaning. The use of the term *millah* does, however, reflect the penchant for wisdom language in Psalm 139. Of the thirty-eight occurrences of the term, the vast majority appear in texts associated with Israel's wisdom tradition (Prov 23:9; Job 4–38 [34x]; Ps 19).

You hem me in behind and before. The verb "to hem in" (*tsur*) or "to bind" is an equivocal term that at times refers simply to the binding or tying up of items (Exod 32:4; 2 Kgs 5:23), while in other texts a more ominous meaning is implied. For example, the word can mean to "hem in" in the sense of laying siege to a city (Deut 20:12; 2 Sam 11:1; Ezek 4:3). The question is whether Yahweh is making the psalmist secure or is "laying siege" to him. Is the comment meant to be construed as a comforting thought or one that induces fear? The second half of verse 5 offers little help in making this determination. "The hand of the LORD" can signal judgment (e.g., 1 Sam 5:6; Ps 75:8), but equally it can also indicate the fullness of God's presence (e.g., Ezek 8:1; 37:1; 40:1). To suggest it must mean one or the other creates a false dilemma. Even as the merisms in Psalm 139:2–3 used polar-opposite images to construct a much greater truth, so too does the language used here invite the reader to think beyond the dichotomy of meanings. As Goldingay has commented, "the person who has nothing to hide has nothing to fear of Yhwh's binding or the touch of Yhwh's hand."[11] Yahweh is indeed close enough to bind him up (in support) but also "to lay siege" to him, should doing so be warranted. In verse 5 of Psalm 139 the stress is on God's attentive presence. The psalmist confesses that Yahweh is fully cognizant of his life because Yahweh can be found on "all sides" of him.

Such knowledge is too wonderful for me. The word "wonderful" translates the rare Hebrew term *pili'*, appearing only here and in Judges 13:18. The more commonly occurring verb *pala'* can refer to things that are puzzling to understand or too difficult to comprehend, and that nuance is likely intended in Psalm 139:6 as well. The psalmist is not celebrating how "wonderful" God's knowledge is, nor is he celebrating God's "omniscience" (see Bridging Contexts). Instead, the psalmist is confessing that God's ability to be fully cognizant of his life is a thought too difficult to grasp fully. The NET more nearly captures the sense of verse 6: "Your knowledge is beyond my comprehension; it is so far beyond me, I am unable to fathom it." In his conclusion of the first strophe, the psalmist is awestruck at the fullness of God's knowledge of his life.

---

11. Goldingay, *Psalms 3*, 630.

The Psalmist's Thoughts on Fleeing from God (139:7–12)

THE SECOND STROPHE CONTINUES the theme of God's pervasive presence. The strophe opens with a set of rhetorical questions followed by a series of hypothetical, or irreal, queries meant to suggest the fullness of God's presence in the world.

Where can I flee from your presence? Verse 7 contains two rhetorical questions placed in parallel. Both questions concern the scope of God's spirit or presence. Both terms, "Spirit" and "presence," also appear together in Psalms 51:11 and 104:29–30. While the verb in the first question, "go" (*halak*), appears innocuous enough, the verb in the second question, "flee" (*barah*), typically suggests the action of a person under duress and in need of escaping a probable threat. Often the verb is followed by the prepositional phrase "from the face of" (*mippane*) or "from the presence of," indicating the cause of the threat. In Genesis 35:1, for example, Jacob flees (*barah*) from the presence of (*mippane*) Esau. In Psalm 139:7 the psalmist refers to fleeing (*barah*) from the presence of (*mippane*) Yahweh. Similar to the use of the verb "to hem in" (*tsur*) in verse 5, the verb *barah* appears to suggest a negative connotation, i.e., the psalmist is fleeing from the threatening presence of God. But also like *tsur, barah* ("flee") is meant to suggest the comprehensive and pervasive sense of God's presence—it is coming at him all the time.

You are there. In verses 8–9 the psalmist returns to the use of merisms to convey the spatial sense, both vertical and horizontal, of God's presence. In verse 8 he acknowledges that if he goes up to the heavens or makes his bed in the depths, "you [God] are there." Although the NIV refers to the "depths" in verse 8b, the Hebrew actually reads "Sheol," in reference to the underworld. Traditionally, Yahweh is not associated with Sheol, much less does he make his presence known there; the heavens are considered his domain (cf. Ps 115). As with the merisms mentioned earlier, this one should also be understood figuratively, not literally. Although the statement does reflect the ancient three-tiered worldview (heavens, earth, and under the earth), we should not follow Hossfeld and Zenger in their claim that with this verse "we may be on the threshold of resurrection in the Old Testament."[12] Instead, we should understand the psalmist as speaking figuratively and as once more suggesting the all-encompassing and inescapable presence of God.

The second merism functions horizontally. The "wings of the dawn" refers to the east, from where the sun rises, and to the "far side of the sea," which refers to the distant horizon in the west. Even as God's presence

---

12. Hossfeld and Zenger, *Psalms 3*, 541.

is inescapable vertically (from the heights to the depths), so too is his presence inescapable from the east to the west.

Your right hand will hold me fast. The psalmist confesses that, regardless of his location, God's hand will guide him and hold (*'ahaz*) him. As similarly with "to hem in" (*tsur*) and "to flee" (*barah*), the verb "to grasp" or "to take hold of" (*'ahaz*) is equivocal. The term can refer to grasping someone or something like a trap (Job 18:19) or a lion (Isa 5:29), and hence can have a negative connotation (Pss 119:53; 137:9). Alternatively, the word can refer to Yahweh's grasping the psalmist's right hand as a sign of his continual presence, as in Psalm 73:23. Regardless of where the psalmist flees, he can escape neither the grasp nor the notice of Israel's God.

The darkness will hide me. The final two verses in this strophe appear to contain another merism, this one involving darkness and light; but in reality these terms function differently. The psalmist proposes another possible scenario for escaping the presence of God. In the ancient Near East light was typically associated with divine presence (Num 6:25–26), while darkness was associated with chaos and death.[13] The writer of Psalm 139 suggests that if he were in the darkness, the place of chaos and death, the place that is absent of light, then perhaps finally he would find a place apart from God. The psalmist quickly recognizes the fault in his own logic, however, because "even the darkness will not be dark to [God]" (v. 12). The darkness quickly ceases to be darkness because of the radiant light of God. His very presence casts out all darkness (John 1:5).

God's Presence from the Beginning of Life (139:13–18)

IN THE THIRD STROPHE OF PSALM 139 the poet continues his reflection on God's presence by highlighting God's involvement in the life of the psalmist from its very beginning. The focus on his birth, however, is not an afterthought but actually serves to buttress the claims made in the first two strophes. As evidence of this logic, verse 13 begins with the causal use of the particle *ki*, translated as "for" or "because."[14] The first strophe concentrates on the comprehensive nature of God's knowing presence, and the second highlights the psalmist's inability to escape the pervasive

---

13. See the brief explanation in Bernd Janowski, *Arguing with God*, 69–70. On the connection between light and Yahweh, see Brown, *Seeing the Psalms*, 84–89. See especially page 84, where Brown notes that "the *deus praesens* is typically depicted as an effulgence of light" and again that light "bears an intimate association with God."

14. Leslie Allen contends that the particle should be read as an affirmative one, "Indeed" (Allen, *Psalms 101–150*, 251 n. 13a).

presence of God. These claims make sense "because" (*ki*) God has been with the psalmist from the beginning of his life.

For you created my inmost being. In verse 13 the psalmist attributes his creation to God. Rather than using more traditional creation language (*bara'*, "to create," or *'asah*, "to make"), the psalmist uses the verb *qanah*, which normally means "to acquire by purchase" (cf. Gen 47:19; 49:30; Lev 22:11; Jer 32:7).[15] Although the transactional nature of the term remains its dominant meaning throughout the Old Testament, the word does appear in contexts that clearly refer to creation. For example, in Genesis 14:22 Yahweh is referred to as the "Creator [*qanah*] of heaven and earth," and in Deuteronomy 32:6 the verbs *qanah* and *'asah*, "to make," appear together in reference to the creation of the nation. The second line of Psalm 139:13 develops the creation motif further by indicating that the psalmist was knit together in his mother's womb. Other texts in the Old Testament make reference to the mother's womb; most notably for the present context is Psalm 22:10, "from my mother's womb you have been my God." Both Psalms 22 and 139 confess God's presence with the psalmist from the very beginning of existence.

I am fearfully and wonderfully made. In Psalm 139:14 the psalmist describes his own creation using two words frequently employed in reference to God's great acts in Israel's history. In other psalms these terms appear in parallel when discussing events associated with God's deliverance of Israel (cf. Pss 45:5; 65:6; 106:22). Thus, the birth of a human is described in terms reminiscent of the birth of the nation, with both being awe inspiring. While the NIV's translation captures the general sense of the Hebrew, a more literal rendering places the stress on the mystery of human creation. In Hebrew there is no conjunction ("and") between the two terms; and to complicate matters further, neither does the Hebrew have the verb "made," though it has been supplied in the NIV. The Hebrew simply reads, "for I am fearfully wonderful." The emphasis in Psalm 139 is not simply on the quality of the workmanship ("fearfully and wonderfully made"), but instead on the mystery of human creation itself. The psalmist acknowledges that human creation, from its beginning, is a mystery and a wonder known only to God.[16]

My frame was not hidden from you. Verses 15–16a intensify the claims made in the preceding verses. The psalmist confesses that although Yahweh is the God of the heavens, the one who "perceive[s] my thoughts

---

15. The Septuagint retains the transactional meaning of *qanah* by translating it with the verb *ktaomai*, "to gain possession by purchase, procure."

16. Davidson, *The Vitality of Worship*, 448.

from afar" (v. 2b), God is also the one who was fully present in the psalmist's formation. In verse 16a the poet indicates that Yahweh looked on his "unformed body" (*golem*). The Hebrew word *golem*, a *hapax legomenon*, appears only here in the Old Testament. In Babylonian Aramaic, the term refers to a formless mass or an incomplete vessel.[17] The word's later use in the Talmud suggests the term could be construed as meaning "embryo" or something that was formless or shapeless. In this context *golem* is better understood as parallel to "my frame" (*'otsem*) in verse 15a, with both terms referring to a human in its embryonic state.[18] In both instances the psalmist affirms God's watchful presence over his life.

I was woven together in the depths of the earth. In verse 15b the psalmist employs more traditional creation language in declaring that he was "made" (*'asah*). In the parallel line (v. 15c), however, the psalmist returns to the language of needlecraft (cf. v. 13b). The verb "woven together" (*radam*) appears elsewhere in Scripture in reference to the embroidery work carried out for the tabernacle. Threads of blue, purple, and scarlet were intertwined in the making of the curtain (Exod 26:36; 27:16; 28:39; 35:35; 36:37; 38:18–23). The intricate work of embroidery, the weaving of varied strands, is meant to parallel the intricate work of human creation as each person is woven into a tapestry.

In Psalm 139:15b–c the psalmist refers to the formation of the human as taking place "in secret" and "in the depths of the earth," respectively. The "secret place" likely refers to the mother's womb, already mentioned in verse 13b.[19] The latter phrase, however, has received considerable treatment concerning its meaning. The reference to the earth and fertility has led some to suggest the influence of foreign myths associated with a "mother earth."[20] But the association between the mother's womb and the depths of the earth can be more easily explained based on references to both images (womb and earth) elsewhere in the Old Testament. Job confesses, "Naked I came from my mother's womb, and naked I shall return there" (Job 1:21). In Job's confession, the womb and the earth are treated as though they are identical, yet when people die they do not return literally to their mother's womb. The presumed association likely stems from Genesis 2:7. There the narrator explains that humans were formed from the "dust of the ground," thus implying that, at some primeval level, all humans have their origin of life in the "depths of the earth." The question for the psalmist,

---

17. "גֹּלֶם," *HALOT* 1:194.
18. Hossfeld and Zenger, *Psalms 3*, 542.
19. Wolff, *Anthropology of the Old Testament*, 97.
20. See the discussion in Kraus, *Psalms 60–150*, 517.

however, does not concern the location of the origins of life as much as it does whether God was present *even there*. He concludes in the affirmative.

All the days ordained for me. The psalmist indicates that all the days ordained for him are written in "your book." Other texts in the Old Testament refer to a scroll or book; many of these texts (e.g., Exod 32:32–33; Pss 56:8; 69:28; Dan 12:1; Mal 3:16) serve various functions but none imply that they contain the preordained affairs of humans. Hossfeld and Reuter have suggested that the book mentioned in Psalm 139 likely stems from the Mesopotamian idea of tablets or books of fate in which the deities would write the preordained life of humans.[21] By making this claim immediately after using the womb imagery, the psalmist declares that no part of his life, from his formation in the "secret places" even until now, has escaped the watchful gaze of Yahweh.

How precious to me are your thoughts. Verses 17–18 provide a conclusion to the third strophe and arguably to the entire hymnic section (vv. 1–18). The verb *yaqar* can mean "precious" (NIV), as in the sense of "valued," but the term also can mean "difficult" or "weighty."[22] Given the larger context of verses 1–18, the verse is better translated as, "How difficult it is for me to fathom your thoughts about me, O God" (NET). Understood in this manner, verse 17 is a reprise of verse 6. The psalmist confesses a sense of awe at the vastness of God's thoughts about him.

The psalmist concludes by confessing, "When I awake, I am still with you." Since in the psalm the poet has not referenced falling asleep, the first verb ("awake") is problematic. A number of interpreters have followed the critical apparatus in the *BHS* in suggesting that the Hebrew term translated "awake" actually comes from the similar root *qtsts*, which means "to come to an end." Rendering the verb accordingly, the line could be translated, "When I come to the end—I am still with you" (NRSV). The psalmist could be referring to the end of his life or simply the end of all God's thoughts. Either way, he confesses that, while he cannot know the vast sum of God's thoughts, he does know that God is with him, whether at the end of his inquiry or the end of his life.

The Threat of Enemies (139:19–24)

THE FINAL STROPHE ABRUPTLY SHIFTS from the hymnic language of the first three strophes to more petitionary language in the final strophe. In these six verses the psalmist utters a petition (vv. 19–20), a declaration

---

21. Frank-Lothar Hossfeld and Eleonore Reuter, "ספר," *ThWAT* 5:942–43.
22. "יקר," *HALOT* 1:431–2.

of commitment (vv. 21–22), and a concluding plea (vv. 23–24).[23] Verse 18 ended the third strophe with the psalmist's affirmation that he remained in the presence of God. In verses 19–24 he introduces the presence of yet another party, the enemies. Through his petitions the psalmist aligns himself with God and asks for God to redress his present circumstances.

The wicked . . . you who are bloodthirsty. The psalmist describes the enemies as the "wicked" and the "bloodthirsty," or literally, "men of blood." The latter phrase, "men of blood" (*'anshe damim*), appears repeatedly in the laments found in the first two Davidic collections (Pss 1–41; 42–72), where it refers to violent persons and murderers.[24] In the book of Proverbs, the threat of the bloodthirsty is made evident. There the sage announces that the men of blood seek out the life of the upright and blameless (Prov 29:10). These labels prove critical in understanding the image being presented in this strophe and the imprecatory language involved. The labeling of the enemy as "wicked" and "bloodthirsty" is not petty name-calling by the psalmist; instead, it is indicative of the grave threat he perceives. The psalmist has no recourse against such violent power but to turn to the God who is present with him.

Do I not hate those who hate you? The psalmist's petition in verse 19 is not rooted in personal animosity or desire for revenge; rather, the poet petitions God to act because these people are against *him* (i.e., God). Although the word "hate" (*sone'*) can refer to an emotion or feeling, it is often used in the context of a relationship. In those instances, "hating" does not connote a negative emotion but, instead, a lack of relationship (cf. Mal 1:2–5; Luke 14:26). Through their misuse of God's name and rebellion against God (vv. 20, 21b), the "haters" have demonstrated not only their proclivity to sin but also, and even more, their desire to abrogate any relationship with God. Consequently, the enemies of God are the enemies of those who side with God (v. 22). While such language may appear harsh, the psalmist affirms that "there can be no moral or spiritual neutrality."[25]

Search me, God, and know my heart. The psalmist concludes the poem with the same request from verse 1, "search me . . . and know me." In verse 23, however, the psalmist extends this request by asking God to test him concerning "my anxious thoughts" (*sar'appay*).[26] In the Old Tes-

23. Goldingay, *Psalms 3*, 636.

24. Cf. Pss 5:6; 26:9; 55:23; 59:2.

25. Davidson, *The Vitality of Worship*, 449.

26. The noun can also be spelled *se'ippim*. In Ps 139 the noun appears, but with an epenthetic *resh*. See John E. Hartley, "שַׂרְעַפִּים," *NIDOTTE* 3:1261.

tament, "anxious thoughts" can be the result of night visions (Job 4:13) or defamatory rhetoric (Job 20:2), as well as the fear of being mistreated by others (Ps 94:19). In Psalm 139 the psalmist's anxieties are due to the threat posed by the enemies mentioned in verses 19–22. The psalmist's only hope is God; thus, the purpose of God's searching, knowing, and testing is to determine whether there is "any offensive way in me."[27] Because the psalmist desires the presence of God, he seeks to eradicate anything in his own life that might vitiate that life-giving relationship. Earlier in the strophe the psalmist established that the enemies of God are defined by their arrogant speech and rebellious behavior; they are "haters of God." Rather than becoming like the enemies, the psalmist desires nothing more than to walk in the "everlasting way" (v. 24).

IN TURNING TO PSALM 139, readers of Scripture often refer to God's omniscience, omnipresence, and omnipotence, but as Howard Neil Wallace muses, "the psalm does not want to make a statement about the Lord's omni-this or that. The psalm is not a philosophical or theological treatise on the nature of God."[28] Instead, this psalm confesses both God's constant presence *with* the psalmist as well as his comprehensive knowledge *of* the psalmist. The psalm is intimately personal, as is the God to whom the psalm testifies.

The constant presence and comprehensive knowledge of God appears to evoke for the psalmist both "flight" and "fascination," both comfort and fear.[29] As noted in the exegetical comments above, several verses use language that seems to suggest the weightiness that comes with the nearness of God's presence. In verse 5 God is said to "hem in" the psalmist, and in verse 7 he queries, "Where can I flee from you presence?" Both images (being hemmed in and fleeing) nearly always carry a negative connotation. Similarly, the reference to Yahweh's "grasp" of the psalmist in verse 10b leaves open whether this action is positive or negative, a comfort or cause for fear. Yet as the poem draws to a close, it is the psalmist's nearness to God (v. 18b) that gives him cause for hope even in the face of impending threats.

---

27. The Hebrew term *'otseb* in verse 24a is derived from *'otseb* I, meaning "grievous" or "hurtful," hence "offensive" in the NIV.

28. Howard Neil Wallace, *Words to God, Word from God: The Psalms in the Prayer and Preaching of the Church* (Burlington, VT: Ashgate, 2005), 182.

29. On the reference to "flight" and "fascination" in Ps 139, see Feldmeier and Spieckermann, *God of the Living*, 159.

The image of God's hand in the psalm illustrates further this "flight and fascination" with God's presence in the psalm. In verses 13 and 15, the poet invokes images of knitting and weaving to explain the care with which God created him. Wallace contends that both verbs, knitting and weaving, are evidence of "manual dexterity"; the hands of God were at work in the creation and formation of the psalmist's life.[30] Earlier in the poem the hand of God is said to guide the psalmist (v. 10a), thereby suggesting once more the formative work of God in his life. Yet in verse 5 he confesses that God laid his hand upon him. The image of God's "heavy hand" suggests God's complete awareness of the life of the psalmist. No reason is provided or justification offered for the divine hand that has befallen the psalmist. He simply understands that even God's corrective action is expressive of his pervasive presence. Therein lies the challenge of worshiping a God who remains intimately personal with his creation, who takes seriously the "I-Thou" relationship. The God who is near to us is the God who knows us—who knows even those parts of our lives we would prefer to remain hidden (cf. Ps 90:8b).

Throughout Scripture this tenuous balance between "flight" and "fascination" exists. Because God is pervasively present, the comfort of his presence is juxtaposed with the very threat of the same. The God who appears to Israel on Mount Sinai in a theophany is the same God who exacts judgment moments later at the base of that very mountain. The God who calls David from the fields to be his anointed king is the same God who chastens David for his pursuit of Bathsheba. Neither moment escapes his gaze; both confirm his presence.

IN THE OLD TESTAMENT, far greater attention is paid to the people of Israel as a corporate entity than to individuals. Indeed, individuals played key roles within the life of Israel, but the primary relationship explored in the Old Testament is of that between God and his people. Psalm 139, however, proves to be an exception to that observation. In this text the psalmist reflects on the human condition—in particular, on God's interaction within *individual* human experience.

Many of the great hymns of the Christian faith give considerable attention to the personal relationship between God and the individual. The chorus of one hymn ("In the Garden") reads, "And he walks with me

---

30. Wallace, *Words to God, Words from God*, 182.

and he talks with me, and he tells me that I am his own." The refrain of another hymn reads, "Just a closer walk with Thee / grant it, Jesus, is my plea / daily walking close to Thee / Let it be, dear Lord, let it be." Hymns such as these tend to highlight the "fascination," or the comfort, gained from God's presence. Rarely do hymns remind us of the kind of pervasive presence of God in our lives that might prompt a sense of holy fear. We are content with having God near us, but preferably not *too* near. As one writer explained, "We are reluctant to be known so well. There are things in our lives we keep hidden from others, even God. But if God is really the one we believe God to be then it follows that we are never out of the presence of God nor [are we] unknown to God."[31] Like the psalmist, the thought of God's pervasive presence should inspire us, yet give us pause. The God who has known us from our very beginnings is the God who has watched us all along. He has seen our comings and goings, our faithfulness and faith*less*ness. Yet he has remained present with us (v. 18). Because God has known us, fully known us, we can trust in him when the world goes awry and seems to be in open rebellion against his ways (vv. 19–22). And because God has known us, fully known us, we should be compelled to ask God to search us to see whether there is any offensive way in us (vv. 23–24). By living in the tension between comfort and fear, we acknowledge anew the presence of God; we acknowledge anew our desire to walk in "the way everlasting."

---

31. Wallace, *Words to God, Word from God,* 183. In a sermon on Ps 139, Paul Tillich incisively explained, "Man cannot stand the God who is really God" ("The Escape from God," in *The Shaking of the Foundations* [London: SCM Press, 1949], 45.

Psalm 140

For the director of music. A psalm of David.

¹ Rescue me, LORD, from evildoers;
  protect me from the violent,
² who devise evil plans in their hearts
  and stir up war every day.
³ They make their tongues as sharp as a serpent's;
  the poison of vipers is on their lips.
⁴ Keep me safe, LORD, from the hands of the wicked;
  protect me from the violent,
  who devise ways to trip my feet.
⁵ The arrogant have hidden a snare for me;
  they have spread out the cords of their net
  and have set traps for me along my path.
⁶ I say to the LORD, "You are my God."
  Hear, LORD, my cry for mercy.
⁷ Sovereign LORD, my strong deliverer,
  you shield my head in the day of battle.
⁸ Do not grant the wicked their desires, LORD;
  do not let their plans succeed.
⁹ Those who surround me proudly rear their heads;
  may the mischief of their lips engulf them.
¹⁰ May burning coals fall on them;
  may they be thrown into the fire,
  into miry pits, never to rise.
¹¹ May slanderers not be established in the land;
  may disaster hunt down the violent.
¹² I know that the LORD secures justice for the poor
  and upholds the cause of the needy.
¹³ Surely the righteous will praise your name,
  and the upright will live in your presence.

Original Meaning

PSALM 140 IS THE THIRD PSALM in the Psalter's final Davidic collection (Pss 138–45). The collection opens with two psalms of thanksgiving (Pss 138; 139) but then shifts to four lament psalms calling on Yahweh to deliver the psalmist from the oppressive actions of the enemies and the wicked (Pss 140–43).

Psalm 140 is a highly stylized lament psalm containing five strophes (vv. 1–3; 4–5; 6–8; 9–11; 12–13) of nearly identical length.[1] The first strophe (vv. 1–2) contains twenty-three Hebrew words plus the word *selah;* the second strophe (vv. 4–5) contains twenty-three Hebrew words plus *selah;* verses 6–8 contain twenty-four Hebrew words plus *selah;* and verses 9–11 contain twenty-three Hebrew words.[2] The word count in the final strophe (vv. 12–13) differs considerably from the first four, but this difference may serve to highlight its role as a closing statement of trust.

On closer examination, the structure of the first three strophes provides another example of the stylized form of the psalm. In verses 1–3 and 4–5, the psalmist begins with a petition to God for deliverance, followed by a relative clause that describes the enemy and supplemented by an additional descriptive statement of their threat. Both strophes end with *selah.* In the first two strophes, the psalmist characterizes the behavior of the enemy, but in the third strophe he shifts to focus on Yahweh as a source of deliverance. The shift in subject matter (enemies to Yahweh) is reinforced by the shift in structure. Rather than beginning with a petition (as in strophes 1 and 2), the third strophe concludes with a petition (v. 8); the strophe begins with descriptive claims about God. It also ends with *selah,* perhaps to reinforce its intended comparison with the first two strophes.

Embedded in the stylized structure of the poem are the traditional elements of a lament psalm: a lament proper (vv. 3, 5), petitions (vv. 1, 4), confession (vv. 6–7, 12), and vow of praise (v. 13).

Heading (140:0)

THE SUPERSCRIPTION INCLUDES THE SAME three words found in Ps 139 but arranged differently. The first term is a directive, "For the director of music" (*lamnatseah*), a term likely referring to a worship or liturgical leader. The frequency of this directive in superscriptions across the Psalter indicates its importance in Israel's cultic affairs. The precise role of the person it refers to, however, remains unclear. Other forms of the verb (*natsah*) appear in Ezra and 1–2 Chronicles in reference to those who supervise the affairs of the temple. The second term, *mizmor,* "a psalm," refers to a song likely to be sung with instrumental accompaniment. In Book 5 the title is

---

1. Richard Clifford, *Psalms 73–150,* AOTC (Nashville: Abingdon, 2003), 284.

2. Although *selah* was likely used as musical term, its precise meaning remains speculative. As a result, the NIV's translation team opted to include that word in a footnote rather than in the body of the text.

assigned only to psalms found in the two Davidic collections.[3] As similarly with all the poems in this final Davidic collection, this psalm includes the superscription "Of David" (*ledawid*). On the figure of David in the final Davidic collection see Psalm 138, "Heading."

Lament over the Enemies (140:1–5)

THE FIRST TWO STROPHES BEGIN WITH petitions pleading for deliverance from the enemies. The gravity of the threat posed by the enemies is expressed through a series of metaphors.

Rescue me, LORD, from evildoers. The verb *halats* ("to rescue") suggests delivering someone by pulling that person out of a dangerous situation. In Psalm 18:19, for example, the psalmist announces that Yahweh "brought me out into a spacious place; he rescued [*halats*] me because he delighted in me." Frequently, trouble or distress is characterized as a "narrow space" or a "tight spot," so deliverance entails being pulled out of that situation. In Psalm 140 the psalmist stands in need of deliverance because of the life-threatening actions of the enemy that have closed in on him.

In the Hebrew, the enemy is described using singular terms: "a man of evil" and "a man of violence." Although both terms are singular, they function as collective nouns; hence the NIV's translation "evildoers" accurately represents the collective aspect implied. The language associated with the enemies in Psalm 140 alternates between the singular and plural, thus resisting any attempt to identify the enemy or enemies. Instead, the collective references in verse 1 and the shifting language throughout simply highlight the pervasive nature of the hostility faced by the psalmist—the hostility from which he needs to be extracted (*halats*).[4]

The structure of verse 1 creates an ABA'B' chiastic structure: "rescue," "evil doers," "protect," "violent." Thus, poetically and structurally speaking, the psalm opens with the call to Yahweh for deliverance from the sources of hostility that stand at the heart of this verse and at the heart of the poet's plea.

Devise evil plans in their hearts. Verses 2–3 describe the nature of the threat posed by the hostile "other." The "evildoers" plan in their heart, and the "violent" stir up war. The word for "war" (*milhamah*) typically refers to military engagement, but twice already in Book 5 of the Psalter the term has referred to hostile speech (cf. Pss 109; 120). The hostility engendered

---

3. The term *mizmor* appears in the superscriptions of Pss 108–10 as well as those found in the latter Davidic collection (cf. Pss 139–41; 143).

4. Hossfeld and Zenger argue that the "tendency to generalize indicates the wisdom tone of the psalm from the outset" (Hossfeld and Zenger, *Psalms 3*, 551).

by the enemy was neither accidental nor incidental but, instead, carefully planned out and then carried out "every day." The psalmist cries out both because of the nature of the threat and, even more, because of its relentless presence in his life.

Tongues as sharp as a serpent's. In verse 2 the psalmist noted the careful planning and execution of the enemy's verbal assault, and in verse 3 he uses two metaphors to assess its lethal force. The reference to war in the previous verse is extended with a reference to a sharp tongue. Elsewhere in the Old Testament, the tongue is compared to military weaponry. For example, in Jeremiah 9:8 the tongue is referred to as a "deadly arrow," and in the book of Psalms the tongue is compared to "a sharpened razor" (Ps 52:2) and "swords" (Ps 64:3). In Psalm 140, however, the psalmist has modified the metaphor slightly by suggesting that the deadly words of the enemy are sharp like a serpent's tongue. The second line of verse 3 reinforces this claim by noting the lethal poison of the viper. The word for "viper" (*'akshub*) occurs only here in the Old Testament. In the largest extant Dead Sea Scrolls text of Psalms (11QPs[a]) the verse reads *'akbish*, "spider," with the transposing of the *bet* and the *shin*. Goldingay's translation follows 11QPs[a] in rendering the line, "a spider's poison is under their lips," but the rejection of the Masoretic text is unnecessary.[5] The Septuagint translates *akshub* as *aspidon*, "asp," thus supporting the reading offered in the Masoretic text (and the translation offered in the NIV). A similar comparison between the speech of the enemies and the lethal poison of a snake appears in Psalm 58:4–5.

Keep me safe, LORD, from the hands of the wicked. The second strophe opens similarly to the first with a petition to Yahweh for protection. The opening verb, *shamar*, means "to guard" or "to keep watch" (cf. Ps 121), and verse 4b repeats verse 2b, "protect me from the violent." In the first strophe the psalmist referred to the heart, tongue, and lips of the enemies, and to that list the psalmist adds the "hands of the wicked." From planning to execution, from heart to hand, the enemies are working toward the downfall of the petitioner. To highlight the gravity of the situation and the threat of the enemies, the psalmist refers to the enemies by another name, "the wicked" (*rasha'*), a term that implies godlessness. To find protection from the godless, the psalmist implores God to keep watch over him.

The arrogant have hidden a snare for me. The psalmist employs images from the "hunt" metaphor to signal his entrapment and potential death or destruction.[6] Verse 5 uses an array of terms from the hunt metaphor

---

5. Goldingay, *Psalms 3*, 641.

6. Othmar Keel notes that in ancient Sumerian the sign for "hunt" designated an enclosed space and originally meant "to surround." The association between hunting and

word field: "snare" (*pah*), "cords" (*habalim*), "net" (*reshet*), and "traps" (*moqshim*). The "snare" (*pah*) and "traps" (*moqshim*) are reserved primarily for the capture of birds and small prey. Once the trap or snare closes up on the prey, its escape becomes impossible.[7] The other term used in Psalm 140, *reshet*, refers to a net that would have been cast on the ground and hidden from sight. As soon as an animal's feet had crossed the net, the cords would have been pulled and the animal immediately entangled. The reference to nets and traps in Psalm 140 presents a dark reality for the psalmist. These images "work together to bring before our eyes a vivid picture of the mortal danger to the petitioner's body and soul."[8] They graphically illustrate the plight of the psalmist as one caught, or potentially caught, in a "tight spot" and in need of God's power to "rescue" him (v. 1a).

Confession of Trust (140:6–8)

IN THE THIRD STROPHE THE PSALMIST utters a confession of trust predicated on his relationship with God (v. 6). His hope for deliverance is grounded in his affirmation of God's protective care in the midst of battle, whether literal or figurative (v. 7).

You are my God. With this declaration the psalmist affirms his covenantal relationship with God and God alone, but his declaration is rooted in Israel's larger covenantal confession. Beginning in Exodus 6:7 God announces, "I will take you as my own people, and I will be your God," a promise repeated elsewhere, including in exilic texts such as Jeremiah 11:4; 30:22; Ezekiel 36:28. The declaration, "You are my God," appears in Psalms 31:15 and 63:1, and in both instances the psalmist faces threats by the enemies.[9] The psalmist's hope for deliverance is founded on God's faithfulness to the covenantal relationship.

Sovereign LORD, my strong deliverer. The covenantal language present in verse 6 continues in verse 7 with the reference to Yahweh as a "master" or "lord." The Hebrew in verse 7a reads literally, "Yahweh, my lord [*'adon*], is my strong deliverer." The servant, or psalmist, acknowledges the

---

entrapment was extended metaphorically into the political sphere with kings frequently associating the capture of enemies with the casting of a hunting net over them. Eannatum reports his military conquest over the citizens of Umma by proclaiming, "Over the people of Umma, I, Eannatum, threw the net of the god Enlil." The stele depicts Enlil as holding a large net with the inhabitants of Umma closed within it. The presence of Imdugud, the lion-headed bird of death, at the top of the net signals the fate of those entrapped. See Keel, *The Symbolism of the Biblical World*, 89–90.

7. Ibid., 89–91.
8. Hossfeld and Zenger, *Psalms 3*, 552.
9. See also Isa 44:17.

role of Yahweh as lord and master (cf. Ps 123:2). As lord, Yahweh serves as the "strong deliverer" for the "servant" (i.e., the psalmist), and Yahweh's faithfulness to this role has been evident in the past. At some point Yahweh shielded or covered the head of the psalmist during battle (cf. Ps 91:4).

Do not grant the wicked their desires. In verse 6b the psalmist pleaded for Yahweh to hear his cry. Verse 8 provides greater specificity as to the nature of that cry. In the light of the covenantal relationship mentioned in verses 6a and 7a, the psalmist requests that God act as his deliverer. In strophes 1 and 2 the poet outlined the ways the enemy was planning and scheming against him. In verse 8 he refers to the enemy as the "wicked" (v. 4), who, as mentioned above, can be understood as the "godless." In the mind of the psalmist the battle lines are drawn: God and the psalmist stand on one side, "the wicked" (*rasha'*) or "godless" on the other. For the psalmist, God has not arbitrarily chosen sides; rather, God stands with his covenantal partner to "cover his head" in battle. The language of verse 8 alludes back to the imagery in the first two strophes. The poet petitions God to intervene and disrupt the plotting of the wicked.

The second line of verse 8 proves challenging for interpreters. The final word in verse 8b, *rum*, "to rise up," actually appears at the beginning of the next line, followed by the word *selah*. Were this a narrative text, the "wrapping" of the text from one line to the next would not be unusual, but poetry very rarely "wraps" a text in this way; the features of Hebrew poetry generally preclude this occurrence.[10] Because of its unusual position, many translations have suggested that *rum* ("to rise up") should be undertood as part of verse 9. Both the NIV and NRSV have made this interpretive decision, resulting in the translation "Those who surround me proudly rear their heads."

Although the position of *rum* is unusual, it should be retained as part of the previous verse (v. 8) for three reasons. First, the verb appears prior to *selah*, the term that concludes the first three strophes in this psalm. The use of *selah* as a structuring device in this psalm argues for reading the verb with the third strophe. Second, the Septuagint translates *rum* ("to rise up") with the third strophe, followed by *selah*. The Septuagint renders verse 8b as "do not abandon me, that they may not be exalted." Finally, and perhaps most importantly, the Hebrew text makes sense and does not require the suggested changes. Verse 8b should be translated, "Do not let their plans succeed, so that they might rise up. Selah." In the first two strophes, the enemies have been plotting to crush the psalmist, and in verse 8b the

---

10. For an extensive discussion on the layout of Hebrew poetry in various Hebrew manuscripts, see F.W. Dobbs-Allsopp, *On Biblical Poetry* (Oxford: Oxford University Press, 2015), 29–42.

psalmist pleads with Yahweh, his covenantal partner, to frustrate their plans lest they rise up and overtake him.

Curse on the Enemies (140:9–11)

THE FOURTH STROPHE CONTAINS a series of three curses levied against the "the wicked" (*rasha'*). The psalmist prays that the scheming plans of the enemies mentioned in strophes 1 and 2 be turned back upon them. Each curse includes a jussive form of the verb (i.e., "May . . ."). Goldingay has suggested that "the use of jussives rather than pleas underlines the conviction that there is a process of justice built into the structure of reality."[11] Thus the fourth strophe is not an unfiltered "rant" against the enemy but a request for justice to be enacted.

May the mischief of their lips engulf them. As noted above, the verb "rise up" or "rear" (NIV) belongs with verse 8. As a result, verse 9 begins by fronting the object of the first curse, "the head of those who surround me, may the mischief of their lips cover them."[12] The issue is not whether the head of the enemy will rise up, but what will come down on the heads of the enemy. The NIV translates the verb *kasah* as "engulf," but the *piel* form of the verb means literally "to cover." The psalmist prays that the heads of the enemy would be covered with the very trouble they had planned for him.

May burning coals fall on them. The second curse actually alludes to images from the first two strophes—the images of war and the hunt. According to verse 2a, the evildoers "stir up war every day." In response the psalmist asks that "burning coals" fall on the enemy (v. 10a–b). The image invoked is similar to that of Psalm 120, where burning coals refer to the burning arrows that would rain down on a city during war, thereby creating a conflagration consuming everything in its path.

The second image, "miry pits," while apparently inconsistent with the image of the fiery scene in the first half of the verse, alludes back to the image of the hunt in Psalm 140:4b–5. In the earlier verses the enemy set out traps and snares to capture the psalmist, but in verse 10 the psalmist refers to the pit used to trap large animals. The prey would fall into the pit and, unable to climb out, could be easily killed. Because of this association between the image of the pit and death, the "pit" metaphor often referred to the grave.[13]

---

11. Goldingay, *Psalms 3*, 648.

12. Author's translation. For a brief explanation of fronting in biblical Hebrew see van der Merwe, Naudé, and Kroze, *A Biblical Hebrew Reference Grammar*, 344–50.

13. Philip Johnston, *Shades of Sheol: Death and Afterlife in the Old Testament* (Downers Grove, IL: InterVarsity, 2002), 69–84, esp. 83–84.

May slanderers not be established in the land. In the final imprecation the psalmist places in parallel two descriptions of the enemy. In Hebrew, the first words in verse 11a are "a man of tongue" ("slanderer," NIV), and the first words of verse 11b are "a man of violence" ("the violent," NIV). The implication is clear: slander and violence go hand in hand. As a result, the one who practices slander and violence cannot remain in the land. They should receive the treatment they had planned to enact upon the psalmist, "blow for blow" (*lemadhepot*).

Declaration of Faith (140:12–13)

IN THE FINAL STROPHE THE PSALMIST expresses his confidence in Yahweh's capacity to deliver. Although deliverance has yet to occur, its delay is only temporary. God is the one who "secures justice for the poor and upholds the cause of the needy" (v. 12). Frequently, "poor" (*'ani*) and "needy" (*'ebyon*) appear together in the Old Testament to create a hendiadys (i.e., the expression of single idea by two words connected with "and"). Hans-Joachim Kraus has suggested that the terms are not a formula of "pious phraseology" but instead reflect concrete reality.[14] Similarly, Marvin Tate translated these terms "needy-poor" or "truly poor."[15] In Psalm 140 the poet understands his plight as one of powerlessness and true need. In the ancient world it was the responsibility of the king to care for the poor and render justice and equity in their behalf (cf. Ps 72:12–14). In Psalm 140 the psalmist looks to his "lord," the Divine King, in confidence that Yahweh will defend the poor (i.e., the psalmist) from all threats.

Because of Yahweh's action in behalf of the poor, the righteous will confess or praise Yahweh's name, and the upright will enjoy his presence (cf. Ps 107:41–42). Following the action of God, the world will be rightly ordered once more.

LIKE MANY LAMENT PSALMS, Psalm 140 reflects the reality of a world gone awry. As Walter Brueggemann and William Bellinger explain, this psalm "makes it unmistakable that evil and opposition to justice and faith pervade all of life."[16] The "unmistakable" nature of this reality can be observed more easily in some genres than in others. For example, through the power of story, narrative texts in the

---

14. Hans-Joachim Kraus, *The Theology of the Psalms* (Minneapolis: Augsburg, 1986), 153.
15. Marvin Tate, *Psalms 51–100*, WBC 20 (Waco, TX: Word, 1990), 203.
16. Brueggemann and Bellinger, *Psalms*, 588.

Hebrew Bible provide an explicit context for understanding the "opposition to justice and faith" in the world. Out of jealousy and rage, Cain lashes out against Abel (Gen 4). Out of lust and unchecked power, David has Uriah killed so that the king might have Bathsheba as his own (2 Sam 11). Out of greed, Ahab and Jezebel plan the demise of Naboth (1 Kgs 21). Narrative texts typically introduce the reader to characters, and often even to their motivations (2 Sam 11:16); in doing so, such texts construct a "world" for the reader to enter. These "worlds" give readers a glimpse of a world gone awry.

Poetic texts, however, can prove more challenging. Often the "personal" situation and the "ideological" situation merge in Hebrew poetry, thus making it difficult to determine the event or events associated with the petitions uttered by the poet.[17] But it is precisely this merging of the personal and ideological that allows the language of any one psalm to transcend its particular context. One must not assume, however, that the ideological or metaphorical language adopted by the psalmist is disconnected from the world of reality itself. As Bernd Janowski explains,

> Why doesn't the supplicant say directly and straight-forwardly how he is doing? He actually says it bluntly—but in images! These images are not an illustration of intellectual content, an aesthetically-poetic embellishment of reality that might as well be absent, but they are an expression of an understanding of reality.[18]

In Psalm 140 the petitioner employs metaphors associated with serpents, war, and the hunt in an effort to describe his reality. While one of those metaphors alone would have communicated the sense of threat experienced by the psalmist, together all three portend a world that has been overrun by injustice and evil, a world that can only be righted by the Divine King. The psalmist petitions God directly in verses 1, 4, and 8, and then in a final declaration he confesses his hope in the faithfulness of God.

The New Testament writers quote or allude to the book of Psalms more than any other Old Testament book. In Romans 3:9–20 the apostle Paul appropriates Psalm 140:3 in his discussion of the pervasive nature of sin. But unlike the psalmist, who limits his discussion to the enemies, Paul expands the reach of sin by declaring that all people, Jews and gentiles alike, are under its power (v. 9). To construct his argument, Paul cites

---

17. Martin R. Hauge, *Between Sheol and Temple: Motif Structure and Function in the I-Psalms,* JSOTSup 178 (Sheffield: Sheffield Academic, 1995), 36.

18. Bernd Janowski, "Dem Löwen gleich, gierig nach Raub. Zum Feindbild in den Psalmen," *EvT* 55 (1995): 155–73, 168. Author's translation.

a series of Old Testament texts that reflect generally on the failure of humanity to "do good"—they prefer instead to turn away (Pss 14:1–3; 53:1–3; Eccl 7:20). In Romans 3:13–17 Paul structures his argument in a manner very similar to that in Psalm 140 by referring to the speech and action of all humans as indicative of their sinfulness. Their mouths are "open graves" that practice deceit. And quoting from Psalm 140:3, Paul says the "poison of vipers is on their lips." The apostle shifts from speech to action in arguing that human conduct matches the depravity of our speech. Paul says that, like "the violent" who hunted down the psalmist (Ps 140:4–5), we are all "swift to shed blood" and that "the way of peace" is foreign to us (Rom 3:17).

In Psalm 140 the hope of the poet rests fully in the covenantal faithfulness of God to redeem him from "the pit." Paul's confession in Romans 3 reiterates that same claim. The opening section in the chapter (Rom 3:1–8), as well as the concluding section (vv. 21–31), refer to God's faithfulness. In structuring the chapter in this manner, Paul affirms that the pervasive nature of sin can be matched and overcome only by the pervasive nature of God's faithfulness. Paul both begins and ends the chapter by assuring readers of God's faithfulness and our hope (vv. 3–4a; 24–25).

IN THE OPENING PAGES of his book *Divine Discourse: Philosophical Reflections on the Claim that God Speaks*, Nicholas Wolterstorff wonders:

> It remains part of the liturgy of many branches of the Christian church for the listeners to respond to the public reading of Scripture with some such words as, "This is the Word of the Lord". . . . What is one saying in that? How would one go about interpreting the words read to discover what God said? And is it rationally acceptable to say, and mean it, that when sitting one morning in St. Mary's church, or some evening in Oriel chapel, one heard something God had said—or something that God was saying?[19]

How does one hear the word of God in a text such as Psalm 140, a text described as "one of the less pleasing examples of a lamenting prayer?"[20]

---

19. Nicholas Wolterstorff, *Divine Discourse: Philosophical Reflections on the Claim that God Speaks* (Cambridge: Cambridge University Press, 1995), 18.

20. William R. Taylor, "The Book of Psalms," in *The Interpreter's Bible*, ed. George Buttrick (Nashville: Abingdon, 1955), 4:718.

Perhaps it is the unusual mix of metaphors that troubles the reader, or more likely it is the request that the enemies should receive on their own "heads" the evil they had planned that gives the reader pause. Regardless, this psalm reminds us of the highly disruptive nature of sin, evil, and injustice in the world. But even more, in the midst of such a disrupted world this psalm calls us to lean into our covenantal relationship with God, the one we have confessed as our "strong deliverer" and our shield.

Our society remains attuned to issues of injustice in the world, but frequently the accompanying rhetoric suggests that we alone must remedy sin, evil, and injustice. To be sure, there are biblical texts that call people to remedy injustice (Isa 58), but Psalm 140 is not one of them. Instead, this psalm invites us to turn to God fully, and with certainty, in the belief that God will once more "secure justice" and "uphold the cause of the needy." In addition, this psalm provides us with an "understanding of reality," as Janowski explained. We are reminded of the reality of evildoers and the presence of violent people in the world. We are reminded of the pervasive nature of sin and injustice. But even more, we are reminded that these evils do not have the last word. Our hope rests fully in the one to whom we have said, "You are [our] God" (v. 6), the one who hears our cries for mercy.

Psalm 141

A psalm of David.

¹ I call to you, LORD, come quickly to me;
  hear me when I call to you.
² May my prayer be set before you like incense;
  may the lifting up of my hands be like the evening sacrifice.
³ Set a guard over my mouth, LORD;
  keep watch over the door of my lips.
⁴ Do not let my heart be drawn to what is evil
  so that I take part in wicked deeds
along with those who are evildoers;
  do not let me eat their delicacies.
⁵ Let a righteous man strike me—that is a kindness;
  let him rebuke me—that is oil on my head.
My head will not refuse it,
  for my prayer will still be against the deeds of evildoers.
⁶ Their rulers will be thrown down from the cliffs,
  and the wicked will learn that my words were well spoken.
⁷ They will say, "As one plows and breaks up the earth,
  so our bones have been scattered at the mouth of the grave."
⁸ But my eyes are fixed on you, Sovereign LORD;
  in you I take refuge—do not give me over to death.
⁹ Keep me safe from the traps set by evildoers,
  from the snares they have laid for me.
¹⁰ Let the wicked fall into their own nets,
  while I pass by in safety.

Original Meaning

PSALM 141 IS THE FOURTH psalm in the Psalter's final Davidic collection (Pss 138–45). The collection opens with two psalms of thanksgiving (Pss 138; 139) but then shifts to four lament psalms calling on Yahweh to deliver the psalmist from the oppressive actions of the enemies and the wicked (Pss 140–43). Psalm 141 shares a number of lexical terms with the previous psalm, thus perhaps explaining vits present location in the collection.[1] In Psalm 140 the poet petitions God

---

1. Cf. "hear me" (*'azan* [Pss 140:6; 141:1]); "guard" (*shamar* [Pss 140:4; 141:3, 9]); "keep

to deliver him from the "violent" who threaten to do him harm (v. 1). Those people have tongues like snakes and seek to do him harm both verbally and physically (vv. 3, 5). As similarly in Psalm 140, the psalmist in Psalm 141 acknowledges the presence of the wicked (v. 6) and even petitions God for deliverance from the traps set by the evildoers (v. 9). Yet unlike in Psalm 140 the principle danger to the psalmist comes from "within." He petitions for God's aid so that he might turn aside from participating in the work of the wicked (vv. 3–5).[2] Clinton McCann argues that this latter theme in Psalm 141 contributes to the theology of Book 5 and its response to the ongoing crisis initiated by the exile. As McCann explains, "this crisis involved not only the need for protection against powerful enemies but also the persistent temptation to conclude, in effect, 'if you can't beat them, join them.'"[3] While that conclusion may have been the "persistent tempta-tion" during this period, the final verse in the psalm signals the psalmist's desire to overcome that temptation and be differentiated from the wicked.

Identifying the structure of Psalm 141 is complicated by verses 5–7. The textual challenges in these three verses are considerable. The uncertainty around them prompted Artur Weiser, in his commentary, to leave verses 5c–7 altogether untranslated, thus suggesting that they are essentially incomprehen-sible.[4] A survey of several translations (e.g., NIV, NRSV, NAS, CEV) reveals the considerable divergence among interpreters. Despite the challenges, however, we will not follow Weiser's lead but instead understand these verses as vital to the message of the psalm. Psalm 141 can be divided into three strophes:

Petition to be heard (vv. 1–2)
Request for aid in resisting temptation (vv. 3–6)
Plea for deliverance (vv. 7–10)

While this proposed structure does not fully remedy the challenges pre-sented in verses 5–7, it does provide a way to interpret them within the larger movement of the psalm.

Heading (141:0)

THE SUPERSCRIPTION IN EACH OF THE PSALMS in this collection (Pss 138–45) includes the phrase "Of David" (*ledawid*). There are three other "David"

---

watch" (*natsar* [Pss 140:4; 141:3]); "lips" (*sapah* [Pss 140:3, 9; 141:3]); "evil" (*ra'* [Pss 140:1, 2, 11; 141:4]); "wicked" (*rasha'* [Pss 140:4, 8; 141:4, 10]); "righteous" (*tsaddiq* [Pss 140:13; 141:5]); "Sovereign LORD" (*YHWH 'adonay* [Pss 140:7; 141:8]); "trap" (*pah* [Pss 140:5; 141:9]); "snare" (*moqesh* [Pss 140:5; 141:9]).

2. Buysch, *Der letzte Davidpsalter*, 210–11.
3. McCann, "The Book of Psalms," 1243.
4. Artur Weiser, *The Book of Psalms*, OTL (Louisville: John Knox, 1962), 811.

collections in the Psalter. Its Books 1 and 2 contain two large collections that include David in the superscription (Pss 3–41; 51–72) and culminate with a reference to the "prayers of David" in 72:20. The third "David" collection is comprised of Psalms 108–10. Similar to the other psalms in this final Davidic collection, this psalm includes the superscription "Of David" (*ledawid*). On the figure of David in the final Davidic collection see Psalm 138, "Heading." The superscription also includes the term *mizmor*, "a psalm," which refers to a song meant to be sung with instrumental accompaniment.[5] In Book 5 the title is assigned to Psalms 108–10, the first Davidic collection therein, as well as to Psalms 139–41 and 143 in the final Davidic collection.

Petition to be Heard (141:1–2)

IN THE OPENING STROPHE THE PSALMIST uses standard petitionary language. The request in verse 1b for Yahweh to "hear me" (literally, "give ear to me") frequently stands in the opening line of psalms (e.g., Pss 5:1; 17:1; 55:1; 78:1; 80:1). The opening phrase "I call to you" (first-person singular form of *qara'*) occurs in a number of texts in the Psalter but almost never in the opening line of a psalm (e.g., Pss 17:6; 31:17; 86:7; 88:9). The only place where this exact same form of the verb (first-person singular form of *qara'*) appears in a psalm's opening line is in Psalm 130:1, another psalm in which the psalmist is concerned about matters "within."

In Psalm 141:1 the psalmist asks that Yahweh "come quickly to me." The verb *hus* means "to hasten" or "to hurry," and in the Psalter this verb often appears together with *'ezrah* ("help") plus the first-person singular suffix. Thus, the phrase typically reads, "Come quickly to help me" (cf. Pss 22:19; 38:22; 40:13; 70:1; 71:12). In Psalm 141, however, the noun *'ezrah*, "help," is absent. The psalmist simply pleads, "Come quickly to me." Psalm 140 concluded with the confession that the upright will (eventually) live in God's presence (v. 14). In Psalm 141 the psalmist acknowledges the challenges that remain, including the sense that he remains apart from the presence of God. The call to God and the request that God "give ear" to the psalmist, coupled with his plea for Yahweh to "come quickly" *to him*, suggests that the psalmist perceives a spatial distance, a chasm between himself and God. To overcome that perceived chasm "the transcendent God is asked to become a God of presence."[6]

---

5. "מִזְמוֹר," *HALOT* 1:566.
6. Hossfeld and Zenger, *Psalms 3*, 558.

Request for Aid in Resisting Temptation (141:3–6)

IN THIS STROPHE THE PSALMIST REQUESTS three things—two provided by God, and a third by a fellow community member. The poet's request consists in the divine guarding of his mouth and keeping of his heart from following evil so that he will not act accordingly. Then in verse 5a–b he asks that someone correct his paths. The section concludes with the affirmation that the ways of the wicked shall be met with God's just judgment (v. 6).

Set a guard over my mouth. The language of Psalm 141:3 echoes the language found in Psalm 140. In Psalm 140:4 the psalmist asks God to keep watch (*shamar*) over him and to protect (*natsar*) him from the "hands" of the wicked. In Psalm 141:3 the poet uses both verbs once more, but this time the action is directed toward the psalmist himself. He asks God to keep him from falling under the influence of those around him (i.e., the evildoers [v. 4c]). In verse 3b the psalmist refers to the "door" (*dal*) of his lips.[7] The use of *dal* in this verse, however, may serve two functions. According to *HALOT*, *dal* I means "door," but *dal* II means "poor" or "helpless," with *dal* II being one of the primary terms in the "poor" word field.[8] Thus *dal* I and *dal* II are homophones but with vastly different meanings; yet here, as Buysch has suggested, both meanings may be in view.[9] Clearly the psalmist is referring to his lips as the "door" to his mouth, as inferred from the parallel claim in verse 3a, but the reference to *dal* in verse 3 also serves to establish a connection with the theological claims made in Psalm 140:12—claims associated with a theology of the poor.[10]

Do not let my heart be drawn to what is evil. In Psalm 140:2 the psalmist lamented how the wicked devise evil plans in their hearts and stir up war every day. In Psalm 141:4 the poet petitions Yahweh to keep his heart from being drawn to participation in wicked deeds with the evildoers even though the temptation is great. In verse 4d the writer mentions their "delicacies" (i.e., fine food). The "evildoers" seem to have the persuasive power to beckon others to join them in evil deeds; their fine foods and luxurious living are evidence of their social privilege. The psalmist implores

---

7. This Hebrew root, *dl*, occurs only here in the Old Testament; but based on its usage in Phoenician texts and its apparent connection with the Hebrew feminine noun *delet*, translations are nearly unanimous in rendering the term as "door." Note also the use of *thuran* ("door") in the Septuagint.

8. On the "poor" word field see Tucker, "A Polysemiotic Approach to the Poor in the Psalms," 425–39.

9. Buysch, *Der letzte Davidpsalter*, 211–12.

10. This point is not to suggest that Ps 141 was written after Ps 140 as some kind of response but instead simply to assert that these close verbal links may help to understand it's *Sitz im Literatur* (i.e., it's canonical location within the book).

Yahweh to aid him in resisting such alluring circumstances. Goldingay suggests that the language in verses 3 and 4 "point[s] to a strong understanding of the way Yhwh is involved in our moral life."[11] From planning in his heart to speaking with his mouth and, finally, to carrying out his actions, the psalmist requests that God be at work to guide him in the right way.

Let a righteous man strike me. In verse 5a–b the psalmist extends his wish for correction and guidance but shifts his focus to the community as a source of corrective wisdom. The "righteous man" (*tsaddiq*) is a collective noun referring to any righteous person from the community who can provide instruction. Repeatedly in the wisdom literature the sage recommends that the naïve and puerile be struck with sticks as a corrective measure (e.g., Prov 10:13; 13:24; 26:3). In Proverbs 19:25 the sage suggests that the scoffer deserves a lash in order to learn prudence, while the discerning should receive a rebuke. (The same word is used in Ps 141:5b.) While such actions appear shockingly severe to the modern reader, they do illustrate the seriousness with which the community took wise living.

Their rulers will be thrown down from the cliffs. Here the psalmist refers to the leaders of the evildoers and suggests that their waywardness shall be judged. The word "thrown down" (*shamat*) means to "let loose" or "fall" in the *qal* stem; the *niphal* form occurs only here in the Old Testament. While the *niphal* is commonly rendered as a passive, it can be used to communicate a causative-reflexive sense (e.g., Exod 6:3; Ruth 3:3).[12] In these instances the subject causes the action to happen to himself. For example, Isaiah 19:21 reads, "So the LORD will make himself known." Thus Psalm 141:6a might be better rendered literally, "Their rulers will make themselves fall into the hands of the rock [*sela'*]." In the Psalter the term *sela'*, "rock," typically functions as a metaphor for God (cf. Pss 18:2; 31:3; 42:9; 71:3).[13] Thus Psalm 141:6a may actually resemble a wisdom saying: "their rulers will make themselves fall into the hands of the Rock [i.e., God]." The foolish actions of the rulers, that is the evildoers and the wicked (v. 4), will lead them into the hands of God for judgment. Verse 6b suggests that, as a result, they will learn that God's words are true: "the wicked will not stand in the judgment" before God (Ps 1:5). The closing verse of the psalm appears to confirm this reading (a causative-reflexive sense) as well.

---

11. Goldingay, *Psalms 3*, 656.

12. Waltke and O'Connor, *An Introduction to Biblical Hebrew*, 390–91 (§23.4h).

13. The term also appears in Ps 41:2 as a metaphor for a safe place and in Pss 78:16 and 104:18 as part of the historical recital in those psalms. Only in Ps 137:9 does *sela'* refer to an actual rock.

Plea for Deliverance (141:7–10)

IN THE FINAL STROPHE THE PSALMIST acknowledges the desperate plight of the faithful while confessing that their hope rests solely with God.

As one plows and breaks up the earth. The NIV adds "they will say" at the beginning of verse 7, presumably to suggest that the verse represents the words of the "rulers" mentioned in verse 6. The Hebrew does not include these words, and their insertion actually confuses the flow of the psalm rather than resolving it. Typically, when a psalm moves from singular first-person pronouns ("I," "my") to plural forms ("we," "our"), the move signals a shift in referent from the individual to the community. Rather than interpreting verse 7 as a statement by the rulers, the verse should be understood as coming from the community as they recount the torment experienced at the hands of the wicked. The community laments that, like freshly plowed soil that has clods scattered about, so too have the bones of the righteous been scattered "at the mouth of the grave." Goldingay notes the image constructed in verse 7: "it is as if the people have been swallowed up by Death, who has then spat out their bare bones and left them."[14] The dire circumstances require the intervention of one greater than the psalmist—or even the community.

But my eyes are fixed on you. In the midst of these bleak circumstances, the psalmist confesses that his eyes are on *Yahweh 'adonay,* "Sovereign LORD." In Psalm 123 the poet made a similar confession in referring to God as *'adonay.* As there, so here in Psalm 141 the term *'adonay* invokes covenantal language. Rather than siding with the community of evildoers, the psalmist has opted to side with God. The psalm opened with his request for God to "come quickly," and it concludes with the poet's affirmation that his eyes are fixed on the God who has come near. Because the God of the covenant has come near, the psalmist can take "refuge" in him.

In verse 8b the NIV reads, "do not give me over to death." The verb *'arah* means "to expose," and as similarly in English usage, "expose" can refer to "nakedness," or the term can allude to being "laid bare" or "poured out," with both referring to death. The latter seems to be the intent of the image in Psalm 141; the psalmist pleads with Yahweh for deliverance so that he would not die from exposure. Because the God of the covenant is his "refuge," the psalmist has hope. *Yahweh 'adonay,* the "Sovereign LORD," will provide his shelter against those who assail him.

Keep me safe. In the final two verses the psalmist invokes the language associated with the hunt metaphor by referring to the traps, snares,

---

14. Goldingay, *Psalms 3,* 659.

and nets also mentioned in Psalm 140:4–5. (On the terms and images associated with the hunt metaphor see the comments on those verses.) Although the opening strophe of the psalm refers to danger "within" (i.e., succumbing to the ways of the wicked), the final strophe highlights the danger "without" (vv. 7, 9).

Let the wicked fall into their own nets. As suggested above, verse 6a can be read, "their rulers will make themselves fall into the hands of the Rock." Verse 10 expands that reading with the request that the wicked fall into their own nets. The notion of an enemy or wicked person's falling into a pit or trap laid by that person himself is not unique to Psalm 141 (cf. Ps 9:15). While the wicked writhe in their nets, the psalmist asks to pass by safely.

 In his book *Seeing the Psalms*, William Brown argues that the two defining metaphors of the Psalter are those of "refuge" and "pathway."[15] Both metaphorical images possess a didactic function meant to assist the petitioner in negotiating life amid a complex world. Brown notes that the image of "pathway" is frequently linked with that of torah, thus suggesting to the observant reader that Israel's way in the world (i.e., the people's moral conduct) and God's ways (i.e., torah) are inextricably linked (e.g., Pss 119:29, 105).[16]

Yet as the psalms testify, to walk faithfully as the people of God is never easy in a world fraught with danger. The lament psalms give voice to this challenge. Brown explains that the metaphor of the pathway

> lends itself to conveying the struggles the prayer faces within a world ravaged by chaos in all its manifestations as he or she seeks a way through, as well as a way out, a way to preserve one's dignity, hope, sanity and even one's life amid demoralizing and debilitating forces.[17]

Living *in* the way (torah) of God is complicated by what one encounters *on* the way. In Psalm 141 the psalmist stresses his desire to live in the way of God while also acknowledging those matters which bedevil that pursuit. In verses 3–5 the psalmist confesses that the temptation is great, very great, to turn from the way of God and "take part in wicked deeds."

---

15. Brown, *Seeing the Psalms*, 15–53..
16. Ibid.
17. Ibid., 38.

The temptation to "eat their delicacies" is rich indeed. The psalmist needs the instructive care of God (v. 4) and his covenant community (v. 5) to turn aside from such temptations.

These temptations, however, stem not from apathy or simple distraction but from the vagaries of life that threaten to destabilize one's perception of reality. Clearly the psalmist perceives that the wicked ones and evildoers have power. They clutter the paths with traps and snares (v. 9) that threaten to capture the psalmist or the community. Moreover, as the ones with power they have brought the community dangerously close to death and Sheol (v. 7).

So how does a person stay on the way amid such complicated and complicating factors? As suggested above, the metaphors of pathway and refuge are inextricably linked in the Psalter, but they are not interchangeable; rather, as Brown has explained, "the direction of the 'pathway' is set resolutely toward 'refuge,' the locus of divine protection."[18] In verse 8 the psalmist turns his eyes upon God and declares, "in you I take refuge." One resists the temptations to turn from the pathway by acknowledging the refuge offered by the God of the covenant. One perseveres amid the obstructions on the pathway by recognizing that her or his hope rests in the protective care found only in God's refuge.

AS IN THE PSALTER, the image of the way plays a central role in the writings of the New Testament, particularly the Gospels. From the opening lines of the Gospel of Mark, the image of the "way" weaves throughout the remainder of the book. In Mark 1:2–3 the writer quotes Isaiah twice in reference to John the Baptist's preparing the "way for the Lord." In the center of the book (chs. 8–10) the writer recounts stories of Jesus and the disciples "on the way" (*en tē hodon*), thus suggesting that the way of Jesus and the way of his disciples are to be inextricably linked.[19] This connection between the way of Jesus and the way of discipleship was not lost on the early church. Six times in the book of Acts the followers of Jesus are referred to as the people of "the Way" (Acts 9:2; 19:8, 23; 22:4; 24:14, 22). The church understood well that our way is his way, or perhaps framed differently, his way is meant to *become* our way.

---

18. Ibid., 41.

19. Mark 8:3, 27; 9:33; 10:32; 10:52. In this section "the way" (*hodon*) is also mentioned in Mark 10:17, 46; 11:8.

In the Gospel of John, Jesus refers to himself as the "Way" in the sixth of his seven "I Am" declarations. Eugene Peterson opines that this statement "is among his most memorable and frequently quoted statements." To that rather optimistic assessment Peterson responds, "it is also among the most frequently dismissed in the present-day culture of North America."[20] How can both evaluations be true—that Jesus' statement is both the most memorable and the most dismissed? If we know Jesus is the Way, then why does *his* way not *become* our way?

Perhaps in the twenty-first century we are not so different from the psalmist in Psalm 141. The challenge to walk in the way of God remains before us; this challenge is so great that at times the choice to enter the wide gate seems preferable to negotiating our way through the narrow one (Matt 7:13–14). Like the psalmist, on any given day we may perceive there is a chasm that exists between God and us; the vagaries of life have overwhelmed us, and we feel as though God stands at a distance. We feel lost and awash in uncertainty. And so we wonder. We wonder whether the wide gate really does "lead to destruction," and we ponder whether it is all that necessary to choose the narrow gate to find life.

In those moments we would do well to reflect on Psalm 141. For the psalmist, temptation and despair have mingled to create a perfect storm. In those stormy moments, the choice to "take part in wicked deeds" (v. 4) and choose the wayward path seems almost intuitive. Yet the psalmist chooses otherwise. Although his pathway is littered with traps and snares, temptations and despair, he fixes his eyes upon God and musters the courage to declare, "in you I take refuge" (v. 8).

For those of us who truly desire for his way to *become* our way, we must do likewise. We must forsake the wide gate by setting aside the temptations and despair that threaten to overwhelm us and set our eyes upon God.

---

20. Eugene Peterson, *The Jesus Way: A Conversation on the Ways that Jesus is the Way* (Grand Rapids: Eerdmans, 2007), 21.

Psalm 142

A maskil of David. When he was in the cave. A prayer.

¹ I cry aloud to the LORD;
    I lift up my voice to the LORD for mercy.
² I pour out before him my complaint;
    before him I tell my trouble.
³ When my spirit grows faint within me,
    it is you who watch over my way.
In the path where I walk
    people have hidden a snare for me.
⁴ Look and see, there is no one at my right hand;
    no one is concerned for me.
I have no refuge;
    no one cares for my life.
⁵ I cry to you, LORD;
    I say, "You are my refuge,
    my portion in the land of the living."
⁶ Listen to my cry,
    for I am in desperate need;
rescue me from those who pursue me,
    for they are too strong for me.
⁷ Set me free from my prison,
    that I may praise your name.
Then the righteous will gather about me
    because of your goodness to me.

PSALM 142 IS THE FIFTH psalm in the Psalter's final Davidic collection (Pss 138–45). The collection opens with two psalms of thanksgiving (Pss 138; 139) but then shifts to four lament psalms calling on Yahweh to deliver the psalmist from the oppressive actions of the enemies and the wicked (Pss 140–43).

As suggested by the divisions in the NIV, Psalm 142 can be divided into four strophes. In the opening strophe (vv. 1–2) the psalmist describes his intent to offer up lamentations and announces to whom his lament is directed. The four verbs in this strophe are standard terms from the "lament vocabulary": "I cry aloud," "I lift up my voice," "I pour out before him," "I tell." In the Hebrew, all four verbs are in the imperfect or *yiqtol*. The NIV translates these verbs as present tense, but the verbal forms could also be translated as future tense, i.e., "I will cry aloud." Either way, the opening strophe in the poem reinforces the psalmist's intent to lift up a prayer to Yahweh. The two previous lament psalms in this collection (Pss 140; 141) began with direct addresses to Yahweh in the second person, but in Psalm 142 the opening strophe refers to Yahweh in the third person.

In the second strophe (vv. 3–4) the language shifts as Yahweh is addressed directly by the psalmist, who describes his plight in a series of images (see below). Verse 5 stands alone as the third strophe and represents the traditional "confession of trust" found in other lament psalms. The final strophe, verses 6–7, includes three petitions and a closing word of assurance.

The trouble that afflicts the psalmist is twofold. As in many laments, enemies threaten the poet's life. They have placed a snare in his path (v. 3d) in their attempt to trip him up in his "way" (v. 3b). Further, he has grown weary from being pursued by those who "are too strong for me" (v. 6c–d). In addition to the threats posed by the enemy, the psalmist laments the isolation he feels amid such travails. This feeling of despair is most evident in verse 4, where the psalmist mentions not once, but four times, his sense of isolation. From his angle of vision, "no one cares for my life" (v. 4d). This desperate sense of solitude is remedied in verse 7c–d.

Heading (142:0)

OF THE POEMS IN THIS FINAL DAVIDIC COLLECTION (Pss 138–45), Psalm 142 has the most complex superscription. The psalm is described as a "maskil" and a prayer. Psalm 142 is the only poem in Books 4 and 5 of the Psalter (Pss 90–150) with the label "maskil." The term itself describes a type of poetry that might best be understood as instructional in nature; it has much in common with Israel's wisdom tradition (cf. Ps 32; 52). The second term, "a prayer" (*tephillah*), refers to the petitionary nature of the psalm (cf. Ps 90; 102).

Similar to the other psalms in the final Davidic collection, this psalm includes the phrase "Of David" (*ledawid*) in the superscription.[1] In addition

---

1. There are three other "David collections" in the Psalter. Its Books 1 and 2 contain two large collections that include David in the superscription (Pss 3–41; 51–72) and culminate with a reference to the "prayers of David" in Ps 72:20. David is largely absent from the superscriptions in Books 3 and 4, but in Book 5 (Pss 107–45) David reappears in the superscriptions of two smaller collections, Pss 108–10 and Pss 138–45. Book 3 is

to the attribution to David, the superscription also includes a "historiciz-ing link" to David's biography.[2] A total of thirteen psalms contain some form of allusion to the life of David. Strikingly, other than Psalm 142, the remaining twelve psalms appear in Books 1–2 of the Psalter—collections with a heavy emphasis on David.[3] As Brevard Childs has argued, these headings were likely added after the composition of the psalms and served an exegetical or midrashic function in interpretation.[4] In other words, the reader is meant to hear Psalm 142 in concert with an event in the life of David; the biographical reference is meant to provide a hermeneutical key for faithful reflection.

The superscription to Psalm 142 refers to a time when David was in a cave (*me'arab*). Christoph Buysch argues that the mention of a cave likely refers to the events in David's life at the cave at En Gedi when he was pur-sued by Saul.[5] As evidence, Busch contends that Psalm 142 and 1 Samuel 24 share several words or images: *qol*, "voice" (Ps 142:1; 1 Sam 24:17); *nepesh*, "soul" or "life" (Ps 142:4; 1 Sam 24:12); and the image of the enemies on the path (Ps 142:3; 1 Sam 24:20). Although the linguistic parallels between the texts are minimal, the scene in 1 Samuel 24 does provide an interpre-tive backdrop for reading the psalm. David appears not as the powerful monarch but as the poor servant in need of God's deliverance amid hostile threats. In this way the figure of David serves as the prototypical person of piety for all who pray this psalm.

Declaration of Lament (142:1–2)

IN THE OPENING STROPHE THE PSALMIST employs four verbs in declaring his intent to utter a lament to Yahweh. Unlike the opening strophe in Psalm 141, this strophe remains in the third person, thus perhaps suggesting that the psalmist is making his declaration in the presence of the congregation or a smaller group within the community.[6]

My voice. The NIV obscures the parallel structure of the two lines in verse 1. In the Hebrew, each line opens, "With my voice to the LORD" (*qoli 'el-YHWH*) followed by a verb. In verse 1a the psalmist declares his intent

---

dominated by psalms of Asaph and psalms associated with the Sons of Korah. David is mentioned only in Ps 86. In Book 4 Moses is mentioned in the superscription to Ps 90, but most psalms in that book do not contain a superscription. David appears in only two superscriptions, those to Pss 101 and 103.

2. Hossfeld and Zenger, *Psalms 3*, 565.

3. Pss 3; 7; 18; 34; 51; 52; 54; 56; 57; 59; 60; 63; 142.

4. Brevard Childs, "Psalm Titles and Midrashic Exegesis," *JSS* 16 (1971): 137–50.

5. Buysch, *Der letzte Davidpsalter*, 237.

6. Goldingay, *Psalms 3*, 665.

"to cry aloud" (*za'aq*), a verb found in texts associated with oppression. In Exodus 2:23 the Israelites cried out (*za'aq*) to God for deliverance, as they did in similar circumstances throughout the book of Judges (Judg 3:9, 15; 6:6–7). In the second half of verse 1 the psalmist declares, "With my voice to the LORD [*qoli 'el -YHWH*] I make supplication [*hanan*]" (author's translation). The verb *hanan* plus *'el* ("to") suggests pleading (cf. Deut 3:23), thus replicating the language and intensity found in the opening line.

Before him. The opening verse of the psalm contains tightly constructed parallel lines, as noted above. The second verse, however, shifts in structure and in the Hebrew, reflects a well-constructed chiastic parallelism.

> I pour out
> > before him
> > > my complaint;
> > > My trouble
> > before him
> I tell.

At the center of the chiasm are terms that describe the circumstances of the psalmist: complaint and trouble. Surrounding those two elements is the phrase "before him," or literally, "before his face." It is "before him" that the psalmist can both pour out and declare the matters that plague him. The psalm does not suggest that during those difficult moments God is absent from the psalmist's life; to the contrary, the psalm confesses that those moments are surrounded, both literally and figuratively, by the presence of God.

Both verses make clear that the psalmist has sought an audience with God. He lifts his voice *to God* in verse 1, and in verse 2 he pours out and declares his trouble *before God*. His best, last hope is God. The emphasis on God's presence in the opening two lines prepares the reader for the psalmist's direct address of God in the remainder of the psalm.

The Complaint of the Psalmist (142:3–4)

IN THE FIRST STROPHE THE PSALMIST described his plight in more obliquely descriptive terms: "complaint" and "trouble." In the second strophe the poet expands the description of his current situation.

My spirit grows faint. The psalmist opens this strophe with a confession of trust, or more precisely, a statement of confidence.[7] The circumstances that surround the psalmist have caused his spirit to grow faint (*'atap*) and

---

7. Gerstenberger, *Psalms, Part 2*, 418.

become exceedingly weak—a confession similarly made in Psalm 77:4. Despite his bleak circumstances, however, he has confidence in God. The NIV translates verse 3b as, "It is you who watch over my way," but a literal rendering of the Hebrew reads simply, "But you know [*yada*] my way." The verb *yada* implies that a relationship exists between the two parties (cf. Ps 139:1–3), and it is because of this relationship that the psalmist can offer a statement of confidence.

People have hidden a snare. In verse 3c–d the psalmist describes his current circumstances with images from the hunt metaphor. Such images signal the entrapment of the psalmist and his potential death or destruction.[8] In verse 3 the poet refers to the "snare" (*pah*), a small device reserved primarily for the capture of birds and small prey. The snare closes up on the animal and makes its escape impossible.[9] With this image the psalmist stresses his vulnerability and powerlessness in the face of his enemies.

There is no one at my right hand. The hunt metaphor (v. 3) implied that the psalmist was threatened or in a threatening circumstance and in need of help. Verse 4 reinforces his need for assistance by highlighting his vulnerability and isolation. He calls to Yahweh and invites God to "look and see" his situation.[10] The two verbs "look" (*nabat*) and "see" (*ra'ah*) appear in other contexts (Isa 63:19; Ps 80:14) in which the poet appeals to the God of heaven to look down and see his plight. The intent is to move Yahweh to action.

In verse 4a the psalmist shifts metaphors from that of a hunt to that of a military setting. Because the soldier carried his shield in his left hand, the right side of the body remained exposed and vulnerable. Consequently, one always sought to have a friend or ally "at [his] right hand" to provide protection. The image of Yahweh as standing at the right hand of the psalmist and fending off potential threats can be found elsewhere in the Psalter (e.g., Pss 16:8; 109:31; 110:5; 121:5), but in this instance the psalmist laments that no person stands on his right to protect him or defend him.

I have no refuge. In verse 4b–d the psalmist makes three additional claims concerning his isolated existence. Lines 4b and 4d begin with the Hebrew particle of negation, *'en*, "there is not," or in this case, "there is no one." The psalmist is doubly emphatic: there is no one (*'en*) who takes note

---

8. Keel, *The Symbolism of the Biblical World*, 89–90.
9. Ibid., 89–91.
10. In the first line of verse 4 the Hebrew text contains the imperative, "Look." The textual witnesses (11QPsa, LXX, Jerome, Tg) have rendered the verb as a first-person singular, "I look," but the reading in the Hebrew text (MT) is the *lectio difficilior* (the more difficult reading) and should be retained.

(*nakar*) of his condition, and there is no one (*'en*) who cares for him. In the latter instance, the Hebrew word is the participial form of the verb *darash*, which means "to seek after" or "to inquire." In the psalmist's time of need, no one bothered to inquire about his condition. In addition to having no one to take note of him or inquire about his condition, the poet confesses that he has no refuge (*manos*), or better yet, his place of refuge "has perished" (*'abad*). The word *manos* comes from the Hebrew word that means "to flee" (*nus*), thus *manos* is the place where those fleeing find refuge (cf. Jer 25:35; Amos 2:14; Job 11:20). Thus, in verse 4 the psalmist self-describes as a fugitive with no one at his right hand to protect him and no place to flee for protection.

Confession of Trust (142:5)

HAVING RECOUNTED HIS DESPERATE PLIGHT in the second strophe (vv. 3–4), the psalmist cries to Yahweh in verse 5 with his confession of trust. His confession is predicated on his understanding of God. Once more the psalmist shifts the metaphorical field in order to communicate two seemingly different claims about Yahweh but claims that, in fact, function as one.

You are my refuge. In verse 4 the psalmist lamented that his refuge (*manos*), the place where he could flee, had perished. In verse 5, however, he responds by claiming that Yahweh is his "refuge" (*mahseh*). Although certain types of refuge (*manos*) had disappeared, the psalmist confidently asserts that Yahweh remains a refuge for the faithful. In the Psalter the term *mahseh* is the more traditional word for refuge, particularly when referring to Yahweh (cf. Pss 2:12; 46:2; 62:7–8; 71:7; 91:2; 94:22).

My portion in the land of the living. Elsewhere in the Old Testament the word "portion" (*heleq*) refers to the division or apportionment of land.[11] For example, the book of Joshua explains that every Israelite is to receive a "portion" (*heleq*) when the people enter the land (Josh 15:13; 18:7; 19:9). Yet, as Kathrin Liess has argued, the term *heleq* has morphed into the language of personal piety in texts described as confessions of trust (Pss 16:5–6; 73:26; 142:6; Lam 3:24).[12] As these texts reflect, the epithet "You are my portion" or "Yahweh is my portion" occurs within the context of life-and-death situations. Thus, in these texts the language of "portion" (*heleq*) shifts in meaning and resembles more nearly that of "refuge" (*mahseh*). The poet no longer has a portion (*heleq*) of his own, no place to flee for protection, and instead must rely on Yahweh as his *heleq* if he wants to remain in the land of the living (cf. Ps 116:9).

---

11. Cornelis van Dam, "חלק," *NIDOTTE* 2:162–63.

12. Kathrin Liess, *Der Weg des Lebens: Psalm 16 und das Lebens-und Todensverständnis der Individualpsalmen*, FAT 2/5 (Tübingen: Mohr Siebeck, 2004), 183–84.

Both images, that of "refuge" (*mahseh*) and that of "portion" (*heleq*), combine to affirm God's capacity to rescue the psalmist from death. A similar confession is made in the previous poem (Ps 141:8).

Petition for Yahweh to Act (142:6–7)

IN THE FINAL STROPHE THE PSALMIST petitions Yahweh for deliverance. In verse 6 a complaint follows each petition: verse 6a, petition; verse 6b, complaint; verse 6c, petition; verse 6d, complaint. The complaint is meant to justify the petition.[13] Verse 7a contains a petition but breaks the pattern by issuing a promise to praise God instead of a complaint (v. 7b).

Listen to my cry. Although the English translation of verse 6a seems to reflect the rhetoric of other lament psalms, there is a subtle difference implied in the choice of Hebrew vocabulary. The verb "to listen" is *qashab*, not the more frequently occurring word *shama'* (cf. Deut 6:4). Like *shama'*, the verb *qashab* can mean "to listen," but it can also mean "to give attention to." In addition, the psalmist requests that Yahweh give attention to his "cry" (*rinnah*). The word *rinnah* frequently refers to shouts of praise or joy (cf. Isa 14:7; 35:10; Pss 42:5; 47:2; 105:43) but can also be used in petitionary language. In those contexts the term seems to retain the sense of shouting out or wailing aloud (cf. Pss 17:1; 106:44). Even though the psalmist is wailing aloud, perhaps the psalmist remains unsure of God's attentiveness to his plight. Rather than simply asking God to "listen" to his cry, he pleads with God to give attention to his cry and, concurrently, to the circumstances which have produced that outcry.

In verse 6b the psalmist utters his complaint. He pleads with God to pay attention to his plight because he is in "desperate need" (*dalal*). The verb *dalal* means "to be brought low" and suggests one who is weak and powerless. The psalmist cries out to God because he has no other recourse—he has grown faint (v. 3a); the enemies have placed snares in his path (v. 3d); and there is no one at his right hand (v. 4a). He is powerless to respond.

In verse 6c–d the psalmist follows the same pattern: a petition followed by a complaint. Both the petition and the complaint reinforce the "desperate need" of the psalmist. He pleads for deliverance from those who are pursuing or persecuting him (*radap*); he cannot overcome them—they are too strong for him.

---

13. Both clauses begin with the particle *ki*, "for." Although *ki* has a variety of functions in Hebrew, here the evidential use of the particle best describes its function. The information in the *ki* phrase serves as the evidence of the motivation that lies behind a particular statement (in this instance, the preceding petition). See Arnold and Choi, *A Guide to Biblical Hebrew Syntax*, 149–50.

Set me free from my prison. The psalmist petitions God yet again in verse 7. The verb "to set free" (*yatsa'*) appears in the language associated with the exodus. Not only does this language appear in the book of Exodus (e.g., Exod 18:1; 20:2), but also Jeremiah repeatedly employed the term in reference to God's work in bringing Israel out of Egypt (e.g., Jer 7:22; 11:4; 34:13). Like Jeremiah, Ezekiel uses this term in reference to the exodus (Ezek 20:6) but then presses the image further and applies it to their situation in the exile (Ezek 34:13). The psalmist invokes the same term in the light of his own circumstances. Even as God set Israel free in the exodus and set them free from the Babylonian exile, the psalmist needs God to set him free from his present circumstances.

The psalmist refers to being in "prison" (*masger*). Although the term could be construed literally (i.e., an actual prison or dungeon), the term more likely refers metaphorically to the plight of the poet and the circumstances that have figuratively trapped or confined him.[14] The metaphorical connection between prison and death is reinforced by the supplicant's earlier claim that Yahweh is his portion (*heleq*) in "the land of the living" (v. 5c). Whatever the psalmist is enduring, he feels trapped, like one imprisoned, with no hope of deliverance.

That I may praise your name. Unlike verse 6a–d, in which a complaint followed each petition, a vow to praise God follows the petition in verse 7a. The psalmist petitions God to free him from "prison" so that he may praise God. The verb "praise" (*yadah*) can also mean "to confess," a meaning that appears more appropriate in this context. Thus, the poet actually pleads for deliverance from prison *so that* he can confess Yahweh's name. When he confesses Yahweh's name, he explains, the righteous will surround him, thus reversing the circumstances lamented in verse 4. Earlier the psalmist bemoaned the isolation he experienced amid his suffering. A sense of community will replace this sense of isolation as the people celebrate God's "goodness" toward the psalmist.

Bridging Contexts

PSALMS 138–45 COMPRISE the final Davidic collection in the Psalter. The opening and closing psalms create an *inclusio* that celebrates the kingship of God over the world. The collection concludes with an unreserved and universal call for all flesh to bless Yahweh's holy name (Ps 145:21). Amid this language of praise are

---

14. Goldingay, *Psalms 3*, 668. Although the Septuagint does render the term literally as "prison" (*phulakēs*), two Greek traditions, Aquila and Symmachus, use words that suggest "a more figurative confinement."

four individual lament psalms (Pss 140–43). Their presence in this final collection may prove puzzling. After all, many have noted that the Psalter in its entirety moves from lament to praise. Books 1–3 of the Psalter are dominated by lament psalms, but beginning with Psalm 90 the Psalter turns toward praise. Yet, in a collection bounded by claims of Yahweh's kingship (Pss 138; 145) and standing just before the final run of Hallelujah psalms (Pss 146–50), the four lament psalms appear to anchor the collection found in Psalms 138–45. Together these four psalms make theological claims about God in the light of the human condition in the world.

Hossfeld and Zenger contend that these lament psalms are bound together by two threads that are woven throughout.[15] First, these psalms confess God's care for the poor and lowly. The Psalter as a whole possesses a strong "theology of the poor" and repeatedly emphasizes God's care for the poor and destitute, the weak and powerless (cf. Pss 9–10; 34; 82). This concern, however, is not rooted in some sense of divine humanitarianism; rather, the concern is rooted in God's covenantal commitment as the Divine King. He establishes justice even for the most marginal—or perhaps *especially* for the most marginal—because that is the work of a king. In Psalm 142 the psalmist aligns himself with the marginal and the marginalized in the hope of securing divine aid. Using the language from the "poor" word field, he declares himself in desparate need (*dalal*), unable to fend off the powerful advances of the enemy (v. 6b/d). Most disturbing, however, is the psalmist's sense of utter isolation (v. 4). Yet in the midst of such distressing circumstances the poet turns to God. Claus Westermann argues that the proper "yes" to God "is not primarily to be found when someone says something about God or about his relationship to God, but when he *turns* to God."[16] In Psalm 142 the psalmist confesses that he has no refuge, no hope, save God alone. He can do nothing other than to turn to God, his refuge and portion.

The second thread that weaves throughout Psalms 140–43 is God's attention to the "way" of the psalmist. Despite the work of the enemies to trip him up (Pss 140:1–6; 141:9–10; 142:3) and crush him (Ps 143:3), he confesses that God will provide the guidance necessary to navigate through such oppressive circumstances. In Psalm 142 the poet confesses that even when his spirit grows faint, the one thing he knows is that God watches "over [his] way" (v. 3). The way is fraught with dangers, and the psalmist makes no pretense as to his own abilities to overcome them. He is

---

15. Hossfeld and Zenger, *Psalms 3*, 524.
16. Claus Westermann, *Praise and Lament in the Psalms*, trans. Keith Crim (Atlanta: John Knox, 1961), 7. Emphasis added.

cast down and overpowered (v. 6), hedged in on every side, like one confined to a prison. No one is concerned for him. Yet he is not resigned to utter hopelessness. God knows the psalmist's way and the psalmist longs for the day when he can confess the name of God (v. 7b) and acknowledge him as his deliverer. Even more, the psalmist longs for the day when he will be surrounded once again by the community of the righteous.

I ONCE READ AN ONLINE POST in which the person commented on religious belief in general: "crutches are for people with broken bones." That assumption is rather commonplace in our culture—that religion is for the weak. Those who operate with such a skewed perspective on religion, and Christianity in particular, fail to understand that their analysis is only half right, if that much. At first glance Psalm 142 does indeed refer to someone who is weak and broken, but that admission is in no way a crutch. To confess that we are weak is, instead, to acknowledge how God works in the world. Paul exhorts the community at Corinth by reminding them that "God chose the foolish things of the world to shame the wise; God chose the weak things of the world to shame the strong" (1 Cor 1:27). Scripture reminds us that our troubled existence is always intermingled with our assurance in a God who has worked, and is working still, for the redemption of his people. Psalm 142 "portrays the simultaneity of trouble and assurance" in the life of those who believe.[17] Consequently, true faith is not a crutch for those with a broken bone but a way of living that allows us to acknowledge the reality of the human condition while also believing in the ongoing work of the Divine King. The power of this psalm is that it invites us to confess openly *our plight*, while leaning fully into *his hope*.

Dr. Chuck Poole was the pastor of First Baptist Church in Macon, Georgia, for many years. The church is located not far from the interstate in downtown Macon. He once had a friend ask why that church seemed to have so many people from all walks of life just drop in on a Sunday morning. Without thinking much, he said, "Our church sits on this high hill, and from the interstate you can see the church and the towering steeples. I guess some just come because they saw the steeples."[18] In reflecting on that comment some time later, he wrote:

---

17. McCann, "The Book of Psalms," 1248.
18. Charles E. Poole, *Don't Cry Past Tuesday* (Macon, GA: Smyth and Helwys), 8–9.

People come to the steeples because they assume that wherever there is a steeple at the top there is a sanctuary at the bottom. People come to the steeples to find beneath the spires a place where fears can be voiced, sins can be confessed, tears can fall, questions can rise and grace can accept. . . . We come to the steeples yearning for a sanctuary and listening for the enduring hope of the Gospel. We come to the steeples, dragging behind us all the regret that drags us down. We come to the steeples, pulling in our wake all the fatigue that pulls us under.[19]

Psalm 142 invites us to "come to the steeples" and discover the God who is our refuge and our portion. The sanctuary beneath the steeples is for those fainting and those faint of heart, for the downcast and those overpowered, for those hedged in and those who have been kept out. In this place our troubled existence is intermingled with the enduring hope of the gospel. In this place there is no mention of crutches, but only of hope.

19. Ibid.

Psalm 143

A psalm of David.

¹ LORD, hear my prayer,
  listen to my cry for mercy;
in your faithfulness and righteousness
  come to my relief.
² Do not bring your servant into judgment,
  for no one living is righteous before you.
³ The enemy pursues me,
  he crushes me to the ground;
he makes me dwell in the darkness
  like those long dead.
⁴ So my spirit grows faint within me;
  my heart within me is dismayed.
⁵ I remember the days of long ago;
  I meditate on all your works
  and consider what your hands have done.
⁶ I spread out my hands to you;
  I thirst for you like a parched land.
⁷ Answer me quickly, LORD;
  my spirit fails.
Do not hide your face from me
  or I will be like those who go down to the pit.
⁸ Let the morning bring me word of your unfailing love,
  for I have put my trust in you.
Show me the way I should go,
  for to you I entrust my life.
⁹ Rescue me from my enemies, LORD,
  for I hide myself in you.
¹⁰ Teach me to do your will,
  for you are my God;
may your good Spirit
  lead me on level ground.
¹¹ For your name's sake, LORD, preserve my life;
  in your righteousness, bring me out of trouble.
¹² In your unfailing love, silence my enemies;
  destroy all my foes,
  for I am your servant.

PSALM 143 IS THE SIXTH psalm in the Psalter's final Davidic collection (Pss 138–45). This poem is one of four lament psalms that comprise the heart of the collection (Pss 140–43). The psalm contains a number of features characteristic of lament psalms, including an invocation (v. 1), a formal complaint (vv. 3–4), a petition (vv. 7–11), an imprecation (v. 12a/b), and a confession (v. 12c). Some interpreters have sought to provide a particular setting in life (*Sitz im Leben*) for the psalm by suggesting that the poet faced some type of unjust judicial process, one that might potentially lead to his death.[1] While this suggestion is intriguing, the psalm contains few if any specifics regarding a particular setting. More recent interpreters have jettisoned attempts to identify a specific setting; they have preferred instead to argue that lament psalms in general are better understood as stereotypical language, or "forms," meant to give expression to the psalmist's misery, persecution, and anguish.[2] The lack of specificity actually creates a certain open-endedness to the psalm, thus allowing for its application in a multiplicity of settings.

Structurally, Psalm 143 can be divided into two strophes: verses 1–6 and 7–12. The first strophe contains a number of elements associated with lament psalms, as noted above (e.g., invocation, complaint, expression of confidence [v. 5]), while the second strophe is comprised entirely of petitions. These strophes are bound together linguistically and thematically by their shared vocabulary. The opening verse in each strophe begins with the appeal for Yahweh to "answer" the psalmist (vv. 1, 7). Although the NIV translates verse 1d as "come to my relief," the Hebrew term is *'anah* ("to answer"), the same term that appears in verse 7. Other terms that appear in each section include: "your servant" (vv. 2, 12); "enemy/enemies" (vv. 3, 9); "in your righteousness" (vv. 1, 11); and "ground" (vv. 3, 10). In several instances the terms used in the first strophe figure prominently in the petitions found in the second one. For example, in verse 3 the psalmist refers to the "enemy" that crushes him, and then later in verse 9 he asks Yahweh to deliver him from his enemies. Even when the term itself does not repeat but the image or metaphor does, a similar phenomenon can

---

1. According to this view, in verse 2 the psalmist faces judgment, apparently brought about by the actions of his enemies (v. 3). As a result of their actions, the psalmist appears to be in a dungeon (vv. 3c, 7d) awaiting an oracle of deliverance in the morning (v. 8). Those adopting this interpretive approach include: Goulder, *The Psalms of the Return*, 265–70; Kraus, *Psalms 60–150*, 535–36; Seybold, *Die Psalmen*, 527–28.

2. Gerstenberger, *Psalms, Part I*, 425; Hossfeld and Zenger, *Psalms 3*, 572.

be observed. In verse 3c the psalmist refers to dwelling in the "darkness" (*mahshak*) and then requests that Yahweh deliver him from the "pit" (*bor;* v.7)

Heading (143:0)

THE SUPERSCRIPTION IN EACH of the psalms in this collection (Pss 138–45) includes the phrase "Of David" (*ledawid*). There are three other Davidic collections in the Psalter. Books 1 and 2 contain two large collections that include "David" in the superscription (Pss 3–41; 51–72) and culminate with a reference to the "prayers of David" in Ps 72:20. The third Davidic collection appears in Psalms 108–10. On the figure of David in the final Davidic collection see Psalm 138, "Heading." The superscription also includes the term *mizmor,* "a psalm." The term refers to a song meant to be sung with instrumental accompaniment. Within Book 5 the title is assigned to Psalms 108–10, the first Davidic collection in Book 5, as well as to Psalms 139–41 and 143 in the final David collection.

Opening Petitions (143:1–2)

THE PSALM OPENS IN VERSE 1 with three petitions meant to move Yahweh to action in the poet's behalf. By contrast, verse 2 calls Yahweh to *inaction.* The petitions both for action and inaction reflect the psalmist's longing for the mercy of God.

LORD, hear my prayer. The first two verbs, "hear" (*shama'*) and "listen," or literally, "give ear" (*'azan*), are common terms in the language of lament. One and sometimes both terms frequently appear in the opening lines of a psalm (Pss 4:1; 28:2; 40:1; 61:1; 64:1; 65:2; 102:1); in several texts the two terms stand together (Pss 4:1; 17:1; 49:1; 54:2). The third petition asks that Yahweh answer (*'anah*) the psalmist (Ps 143:1d). In making this request, the poet does more than seek a verbal response from God—he petitions Yahweh to act. In Psalm 65:5 the connection between "asking" and "acting" is even more explicit: "You answer us with awesome and righteous deeds."

Cry for mercy. In verse 1b the psalmist asks that God give ear to his cry for mercy. The word "mercy" comes from the verbal root *hanan* and plays an important role in petitionary texts. (More than half the occurrences of the verb appear in the book of Psalms.) The term itself implies granting favor or being gracious, hence the translation "mercy" in the NIV. In Exodus 34:6 Yahweh self-describes as compassionate (*rahum*) and gracious/merciful (*hannun*). This "graciousness formula" in Exodus 34 testifies that God's nature "is such that he is disposed to respond in merciful ways to the world."[3] In short, *hannun*

---

3. Terence E. Fretheim, "חנן," *NIDOTTE* 2:204.

is part of God's identity. Thus, the psalmist's cry for mercy in Psalm 143:1 is much more than a desperate plea for help—it is a request for God to be God.

Do not bring your servant into judgment. Some lament psalms include a protestation of innocence (e.g., Ps 7), but in Psalm 143 the poet attempts no such argument. He acknowledges human sinfulness. While other psalms refer to sin, its context seems localized in referring to the actions of the particular psalmist (Pss 25:7; 51:6–7). In contrast, Psalm 143 appears to be talking about human sinfulness writ large: "no one living is righteous before you." The psalmist understands that he, like all humans, has done nothing to garner God's aid, only God's judgment. Nonetheless, he implores Yahweh to withhold his judgment and instead deliver him from his enemies (vv. 3–4). The request for Yahweh's aid and his withholding of judgment points back to the psalmist's initial cry in verse 1b for the mercy of God.

Formal Complaint (143:3–6)

FOLLOWING THE PETITIONS IN VERSES 1–2, the psalmist outlines the threats that currently plague him. The language of threat involves metaphors and imagery associated with death (vv. 3–4), thus indicating the perceived gravity of the situation. The rehearsal of the threats is followed by a recollection of the past (v. 5) and then a brief description of the psalmist's posture of prayer in the present (v. 6).

The enemy pursues . . . crushes. By making explicit use of the "grave" metaphor in verse 3, the psalmist signals the severity of the threat. In verse 3a he laments that the enemies have pursued him (*radap*). His use of *radap* recalls the same word used in reference to the enemies in Psalm 142:6b. This verbal parallel between the two psalms further connects the two texts and their emphasis on powerlessness and death. The second line in Psalm 143:3 reinforces the nature of the threat with the use of the verb "to crush" (*daka'*). Kathrin Liess has argued that the verb refers to the "crushing power" of the enemy and serves as a typical image of death in other contexts (e.g., Ps 94:5; Job 4:19; 5:4; Lam 3:34).[4]

The clearest references to death occur in verse 3c–d of Psalm 143 with the mention of darkness (*mahashakkim*) and the dead (*metim*). In this verse

---

4. Kathrin Liess, "Von der Gottesferne zur Gottesnähe: Zur Todes-und Lebensmetaphorik in den Psalmen," in *Metaphors in the Psalms*, BETL 231, ed. P. van Hecke and A. Labahn (Leuven: Peeters, 2010), 169–70. Phillip Johnson argues to the contrary that "the verb 'crushed' hardly suggests removal to Sheol" or death (Johnson, *Shades of Sheol*, 106). If Johnson intends to suggest that there are contexts in which *daka'* does not refer to death, then he is correct (e.g., Jer 44:10), but that observation in no way undermines the validity of Liess's claim.

the word "darkness" occurs in the plural form, a form that typically implies a reference "to the realm of the dead . . . as a place of darkness."[5] The reference to the "dead" at the end of verse 3 further confirms the association of "darkness" with death. The image in verse 3 is clear: the psalmist is being pursued, crushed to the ground, and relegated to the confines of the dead. Verse 3c–d appears verbatim in Lamentations 3:6, another context associated with death and destruction.

My spirit grows faint within me. Understandably, the circumstances explained in verse 3 have caused the spirit of the psalmist to grow faint (*'atap*) and become exceedingly weak, a confession similarly made in Psalms 77:4 and 142:3. The psalmist explains in verse 4b that his heart is "dismayed." The verb translated as "dismay" (*shamam*) actually has a much stronger connotation. In the English language "dismay" typically refers to being shocked or surprised, or more narrowly to being concerned or distressed. In Hebrew, *shamam* can refer to being "horrified" or "appalled."[6] The oppressive nature of the enemies has done far more than leave the psalmist feeling faint and dismayed; the psalmist feels weak and powerless (*'atap*) and utterly horrified (*shamam*) at his present state. This helplessness stands as a backdrop to the psalmist's posture of prayer in verse 6 and the petitions that comprise the entirety of the second strophe.

I remember the days of long ago. The language in verse 5 echoes the language in Psalm 77:5–6, 12–13. In both psalms (Pss 77 and 143) the poet recalls the past and takes solace in it. He mentions the "works" (*po'al*) of God, a reference to the exodus event, as well as the "deeds" (*ma'aseh*) of his hands, a reference to God's creative work. These remembrances of the past do more than simply recall a glorious time—they also inform the present and anticipate the future.[7] God's work in the past prefigures the salvific work yet to come in behalf of the psalmist. This act of remembering has a certain durative sense; it is not confined to a singular moment. Thus, in verse 5b the psalmist indicates that he will meditate (*hagah*) on God's work. The same verb, *hagah*, also appears in Psalm 1, in which the blessed person "meditates on his law day and night." In that spirit, the writer of Psalm 143 continually reflects on God's past works.

I spread out my hands to you. The spreading out of the hands is mentioned in the Psalter as an appropriate posture for praying (Pss 28:2;

---

5. Liess, "Von der Gottesferne," 170. Othmar Keel notes that the plural form *mahashakkim* is frequently used in the psalms "to express the intensity of the gloom which prevails in the grave and in the realm of the dead" (Keel, *The Symbolism of the Biblical World*, 65). Cf. Ps 88:7.

6. "שָׁמַם," *HALOT* 2:1563. For a similar use of the *hithpolel* form of *shamam*, see Isa 59:16; 63:5.

7. Wolff explains that the "Israelite sees former times as the reality *before* him," not behind him (Wolff, *Anthropology of the Old Testament*, 88).

77:2; 88:9; 141:2). Although the lifting of hands in contemporary settings often implies joy and celebration, the same act in the Psalter signals the psalmist's deep desire for God's intervention. The metaphorical image of a thirsty person in a parched land (Ps 143:6b) intensifies the nature of the psalmist's desperation (cf. Isa 63:2).

Petitions (143:7–12)

THE SECOND STROPHE IN THE PSALM contains what Leslie Allen labels an "urgent, breathless series of appeals."[8] Verses 7–10 contain a series of seven imperatives and jussives, with each calling on Yahweh to act in particular ways in behalf of the psalmist. The final two verses contain the volitional use of the imperfect verb (*yiqtol*). Although the form is an imperfect, the volitional use approximates the force an imperative verb. As the use of an imperative would similarly communicate, the speaker "imposes an obligation on the subject addressed" (i.e., God in Ps 143).[9]

Answer me quickly. The opening lines in the second strophe repeat vocabulary from the first strophe, thus highlighting the desperate plight of the psalmist. With the request to "answer me," the psalmist implores Yahweh to act with haste. As suggested above (cf. v. 1), when the psalmist calls for Yahweh to "to answer" (*'anah*) him, he expresses his desire to see God act. As further evidence of the psalmist's sense of despair, he implores God not to hide his face from him (v. 7c). In the Old Testament, when God turns his face toward someone the act implies blessing and life. This implication is seen mostly clearly in the priestly blessing found in Num 6:25–26: "the LORD make his face to shine on you and be gracious to you; the LORD turn his face toward you and give you peace [*shalom*]." The converse was assumed as well. If God "hid" his face from the psalmist, then his life would remain under threat, potentially leading to death, as inferred in Psalm 143:7d. In the final line of verse 7 the psalmist explains that unless God turns his face toward him, he will "be like those who go down to the pit." In the Old Testament, the "pit" (*bor*) functions as a frequent metaphor meant to conjure up images of confinement and death. Hermann Gunkel noted that surprisingly "the sinister word for 'sheol' is avoided" in the individual laments, and instead the psalmists opts for "suggestive images for sheol: the grave, the pit, the cistern."[10] Although the word "pit" (*bor*) can be used as a hunting metaphor, its association with Sheol is clearly in view

---

8. Allen, *Psalms 101–150*, 285.

9. Waltke and O'Connor, *An Introduction to Biblical Hebrew Syntax*, 509.

10. Gunkel, *An Introduction to the Psalms*, 131.

in verse 7. The psalmist asks for God to answer him quickly and make his face shine upon him so that he may not taste death.

Let the morning bring me word of your unfailing love. Previous interpreters argued that the psalm was uttered by someone unjustly imprisoned (as suggested above) and that the reference to morning points to the time at which the psalmist would receive an oracle concerning his fate. Supporting this line of argumentation, Michael Goulder explains that "trials often took place at dawn in the ancient world to allow time for execution."[11] While this interpretation is possible, the reference to the morning need not be restricted to such a narrow explanation; the psalmist is likely alluding to a broader theme. In the ancient Near East, the night was considered a dangerous place, one fraught with numerous mythological threats (e.g., demons). The Old Testament adopts this notion but replaces the mythological threats with historical threats (i.e., the wicked). According to the broader ancient Near Eastern worldview, the arrival of the morning signaled the end of darkness and the dangers associated with it. The clearest appropriation of this motif occurs in Job 38:13, in which the wicked are associated with the darkness. When the sun rises the wicked are scattered. In Psalm 143 the psalmist longs for the morning out of certainty that it will bring God's "unfailing love," his *hesed* love, and in turn it will bring the psalmist's deliverance from the pit. The motif of God's attentive care in the morning appears repeatedly in the Psalter (e.g., Pss 5:3; 30:6; 59:16) and serves as a cause for both hope and celebration.

I hide myself in you. In Psalm 143:9 the psalmist petitions Yahweh to rescue him from the enemies mentioned in verse 3. As evidence of his trust in Yahweh the poet confesses, "I hide [*kasah*] myself in you." The Hebrew word translated "hide" in the NIV is typically translated "to cover" elsewhere. The Hebrew line reads literally, "to you I covered (myself)."[12] Because of the awkwardness of that line, the critical apparatus in the *BHS* suggests that we follow the Septuagint and other manuscripts in reading the verb as *nasti*, "to flee," rather than *kissti*, "to hide."[13] Several translations have followed the suggested emendation (NRSV, HCSB, NET). The NIV,

---

11. Goulder, *The Psalms of the Return*, 268.

12. The Hebrew does not include an object for "hide" (*kasah*). The reference to *napshi* ("my life") at the end of verse 8 and the first-person pronoun in verse 9a ("me,"-*ni*), however, appears to justify in verse 9b the use of the reflexive pronoun "myself" (absent perhaps due to ellipsis).

13. In support of this emendation, text critics have noted that the initial letters in each word, *nun* (נ) and *kaph* (כ), were often confused.

however, has correctly retained the Hebrew text despite its unusual formulation. The psalmist appears to create a juxtaposition between verses 3 and 9. In the former he laments that his dwelling place is with the dead, but in the latter he confesses that his only hope is to be covered by Yahweh. The covering of darkness has been replaced by the covering of Yahweh; death has been replaced by life.

Teach me to do your will. In verse 8 the psalmist asks Yahweh "to show me the way I should go," and in verse 10 he returns to this theme, "Teach me to do your will." Both verses contain vocabulary associated with the wisdom tradition, especially "way" (*derek* [v. 8]) and "teach" (*lamad* [v. 10]). The request for Yahweh to "teach me" occurs eight times in Psalm 119 (vv. 12, 26, 66, 68, 108, 124, 135, 171), and in every case but one the psalmist implores Yahweh to teach him "his decrees," a synonym for *torah*. By referencing the "way" in Psalm 143:8 and "your will" in verse 10, the psalmist is making a similar request. The ways and will of God are found in his decrees. The psalmist seeks this instruction because, as explained in Psalm 143:2, humans are fallible and remain in need of God's instruction.

The request for instruction must also be understood within a covenantal context. Twice the psalmist confesses that he is the servant of God (vv. 2a; 12c), and in verse 10b he announces, "you are my God." Both comments suggest that the psalmist perceives his relationship with God within a covenantal framework. As with all such arrangements, there are expectations and obligations inherent to the relationship. Both parties obligate themselves to each other and agree to certain expectations. As Goldingay notes, "the fact that I am Yhwh's servant means Yhwh has accepted an obligation to me; the fact that Yhwh is my God means I have accepted an obligation to Yhwh."[14] Psalm 143 places this covenantal framework within the context of petitionary language.

For your name's sake, LORD, preserve my life. The final set of petitions is predicated on two claims: the name of Yahweh (*shem* [v. 11a]) and his righteousness (v. 11b).[15] Rather than appealing to his own righteousness, which he has already confessed is inadequate (v. 2), the psalmist appeals to a concern for Yahweh's reputation. As Walter Brueggemann and William Bellinger explain, "YHWH gains 'points' in the presence of the nations and the other gods for committing a powerful act of rescue."[16] Throughout the book of Ezekiel the concern for God's honor, particularly given the devastation of the exile, remains paramount. Repeatedly

---

14. Goldingay, *Psalms 3*, 677.
15. Kraus, *Psalms 60–150*, 538.
16. Brueggemann and Bellinger, *Psalms*, 597–98.

Yahweh announces that he will act "for his name's sake" before the nations (Ezek 20:9, 44; 36:22, 32). Although the book of Ezekiel is dealing with corporate loss and disaster and the writer of Psalm 143 is presumably dealing with loss on the individual level, the concern for God's honor in both passages is similar. In Psalm 143 the poet argues that Yahweh should indeed act in his behalf because, in doing so, God's name will be honored.

Bring me out of trouble. In verse 11b the psalmist asks Yahweh to bring him out of his trouble (*tsarab*). Søren Holst, drawing from work in cognitive linguistics, argues convincingly for a metaphorical motif in the Hebrew Bible that connects the idea of being in a tight place or being confined with that of being weak, powerless, and in great need.[17] The word *tsarah* ("trouble") is certainly included in that word field. The verbal root *tsrr* means in the intransitive sense "to be narrow" and in the transitive, "to tie up." The nominative forms, *tsar* in the masculine and *tsarah* in the feminine, suggest narrowness and constriction, quite often idiomatically rendered as "distress." The connection is rather apparent: the person is in distress because of his confining circumstances. The psalmist petitions for Yahweh to bring him out of the "tight spot" in which he finds himself.

Lest one assume the psalmist's use of "trouble" (*tsarah*) merely implies that the poet has fallen on hard times, he clarifies his situation in verse 12: "in your unfailing love [*hesed*], silence my enemies; destroy all my foes [*tsorarim*]." While the words "trouble" (*tsarah*) and "foes" (*tsorarim*) come from different roots, together they participate in the larger conceptual domain mentioned above (i.e., "confinement"). Rather than viewing the two terms as altogether different, Holst contends that "enemies on the one hand, and suffering and distress on the other, are not concepts which are all that different."[18] Circumstances of suffering and distress are often caused by enemies, and correspondingly, the presence of enemies typically portends the possibility of suffering and distress.

In the face of "trouble" (*tsarah*) and mounting threats from "foes" (*tsorarim*), the psalmist leans into his covenantal relationship with Yahweh by asking God to act in his behalf based on Yahweh's "unfailing love" (*hesed*). In the final line (v. 12c) the poet declares himself the servant of God and so reinforces the rationale for divine action: coventantal faithfulness.

---

17. Holst, "Psalmists in Cramped and Open Spaces," 266–79.
18. Ibid., 267.

Bridging Contexts

COVENANTAL FAITHFULNESS. Psalm 143 begins and concludes with references to God's covenantal faithfulness, a faithfulness that is manifestly active in the world. In the opening verse the psalmist petitions Yahweh to answer him "in your faithfulness" and "righteousness." Both phrases begin with the preposition *be*, often translated in a locative sense (e.g., "I have heard that there is grain *in* Egypt," Gen 42:2). Were the preposition understood similarly in Psalm 143:1, God would be "depicted as clothed, dwelling or subsisting *in* faithfulness and righteousness"[19] Rather than a locative sense, the preposition should be understood instrumentally. God demonstrates his covenantal commitment *by* or *through* his faithfulness and righteousness. These terms are not merely static characteristics or traits—they are commitments borne out in action. It is for this reason that the psalmist remembers "the days of long ago" (v. 5a); they are filled with the works of God, the very evidence of his covenantal faithfulness.

The ending of Psalm 143 mirrors its beginning with two prepositional phrases, both also beginning with *be*. The first phrase repeats verse 1c, "by your righteousness," and the second phrase incorporates the explicitly covenantal term *hesed*, "by your unfailing love." As similarly in the opening of the psalm, both prepositional phrases are associated with God's action. In verse 11b the psalmist petitions to be brought out of trouble, and in the second he petitions God to silence his enemies. All four prepositional phrases (vv. 1, 11, 12) suggest that the psalmist does not envision covenantal faithfulness in terms of passive acknowledgment but instead in terms of active presence.

As mentioned in the Original Meaning section, two additional phrases—or more precisely, confessions—reinforce the significance of covenantal faithfulness in this psalm. The poem concludes with the psalmist confessing, "I am your servant," and that confession is matched by his earlier confession in verse 10b, "you are my God." Although the poet is likely writing in the postexilic period, his confessions echo those made throughout Israel's history. In Exodus 6:7 Yahweh declares that he will take Israel as his people and he will be their God. The more formulaic confession, "I will be your God and you will be my people," appears repeatedly in the Old Testament, but particularly in the writings of the exilic prophets (Jer 7:23; 11:4; 24:7; 30:22; 31:1; 31:33; 32:38; Ezek 11:20; 14:11;

---

19. Richard B. Hays, "Psalm 143 and the Logic of Romans 3," *JBL* 99 (1980): 114.

34:30; 36:27–28; 37:23, 37). In the face of perilous circumstances, the need for such a confession became particularly acute. Whether being carried off to exile in shackles or being crushed to the ground (Ps 143:3), such moments render one utterly powerless. Yet the covenantal God renders such dispair null and void. By invoking this covenantal confession and calling on Yahweh to act in righteousness, the psalmist leans forward in hope and in the belief that Yahweh will act once more to redeem his people from the pit (v. 7).

Human sinfulness. Psalm 143:2b makes a declarative statement concerning human sinfulness: "no one living is righteous before you." The statement is striking on two fronts: the reference to individual judgment and the sweeping assessment of human sinfulness. Generally speaking, judgment in the Old Testament tends to be corporate, whether issued on a household (Josh 7), a tribe (Judg 20), the nation of Israel (2 Kgs 21), or greater still, the foreign nations. There are only a few Old Testament texts in which God judges an individual (Job 9:32; 14:3; 22:4), with the closest parallel text occurring in Eccl 11:19, "know that for all these things God will bring you into judgment" (cf. 12:14).

Second, Psalm 143:2 clearly implies that not one person can be considered righteous before God. A nearly identical claim occurs in Psalm 130:3–4. In that psalm the poet asks, "If you, LORD, kept a record of sins, LORD, who could stand?" Both texts refer to the pervasive nature of human sinfulness. Later Jewish writings appear to allude to this notion as well, particularly as formulated in Psalm 143. In 1 Enoch 81:5 the seven holy ones command Enoch to explain to his children that "no flesh is righteous before the Lord," and among the Dead Sea Scrolls the Hymns offer a similar assessment of the human condition.[20] In addition to its use in the earlier literature in the Second Temple period, Psalm 143:2b also appears in the New Testament. Paul makes significant use of the psalm in his letter to the church at Rome. Following a lengthy catena of Old Testament texts alluding to human sinfulness (Rom 3:10–18), Paul offers this summary conclusion in verse 20: "Therefore no one will be declared righteous in God's sight." Paul's paraphrase of Psalm 143:2b serves to reinforce his claim concerning human sinfulness, a claim central to his theological argument in the book of Romans.

The reference to human sinfulness in Psalm 143:2b must be heard in the light of the emphasis on covenantal faithfulness mentioned above.

---

20. 1QH 9:14 reads, "for there is no one righteous in your judgment," and in 1QH 12:19, "there is no one righteous before you." See also 1QH 13:16–17 and James P. Ware, "Law, Christ, and Covenant: Paul's Theology of Law in Romans 3:19–20," *JTS* 62 (2011): 513–40.

The psalmist does not make this confession simply to acknowledge the waywardness of humanity; instead, he declares that because "no one living is righteous before" God, humans cannot make demands on God to act in their behalf. Were humans carefully scrutinized before God, they would be found wanting as covenantal partners and certainly not in a position to make demands. Whatever action God chooses to take is the result of his mercy carried out through his faithfulness and righteousness (v. 1).

Thankfully, human sinfulness does not have the final word for the psalmist or for Paul. For the psalmist, not all hope is lost. Although righteousness proves impossible apart from God, for those faithful to the covenant, there is always the promise of mercy.[21] Neither is hope lost for Paul. He boldly proclaims that righteousness is impossible apart from God—but it is "given through faith in Jesus Christ to all who believe" (Rom 3:22).[22]

 ALTHOUGH PSALM 143 uses language traditionally associated with a lament (e.g., "hear," "cry," "answer me"), the psalm also employs two images worth considering, namely, those of confinement and open spaces. Each year research firms will release surveys and statistics explaining why people no longer choose to go to church or participate in a faith tradition. Among the many responses reported, some will express people's frustration over the church's "rules" and complain that "religion" is too confining or restricting for them. They want to be free to do as they choose.

Interestingly in Psalm 143, confinement comes not from the demands of God but rather from the crushing demands of the world that cause our spirits to faint. Regardless of the source, these kinds of experiences can leave our hearts "dismayed" (v. 4b) and our lives in darkness (v. 3c). The psalmist is clear that the desire to be "free" can only be realized in relationship to God. Those who live fully into that relationship with God (v. 10b) will be led onto "level ground." While the notion of level ground signals the absence of hills and rugged terrain, it also conjures up images of wide open spaces. A person does not know this kind of freedom apart from God.

---

21. Ware, "Law, Christ, and Covenant," 539.

22. The phrase *dia pisteōs Iēsou Christou* in verse 22 can also be translated "through the faithfulness of Jesus Christ." Understood in this way, it is the faithful work of Christ that has secured humanity's right relationship with God. Such a reading would accord well with the emphasis on God's action in Ps 143. See Hays, "Psalm 143 and the Logic of Romans 3," 108–9.

The very environment that we think frees us actually confines us, while our only hope for true freedom is found in our willingness to enter into a relationship with God—a relationship initiated and sustained by God. It is in this relationship that we discover a hopeful word for our lamenting cries. It is in this relationship that we replace a vision of life in the pit with that of a pathway on level ground. Ultimately, it is in this relationship that we experience both mercy and freedom. As Paul confesses, "It is for freedom that Christ has set us free" (Gal 5:1).

Psalm 144

Of David.

¹ Praise be to the LORD my Rock,
　　who trains my hands for war,
　　my fingers for battle.
² He is my loving God and my fortress,
　　my stronghold and my deliverer,
my shield, in whom I take refuge,
　　who subdues peoples under me.
³ LORD, what are human beings that you care for them,
　　mere mortals that you think of them?
⁴ They are like a breath;
　　their days are like a fleeting shadow.
⁵ Part your heavens, LORD, and come down;
　　touch the mountains, so that they smoke.
⁶ Send forth lightning and scatter the enemy;
　　shoot your arrows and rout them.
⁷ Reach down your hand from on high;
　　deliver me and rescue me
from the mighty waters,
　　from the hands of foreigners
⁸ whose mouths are full of lies,
　　whose right hands are deceitful.
⁹ I will sing a new song to you, my God;
　　on the ten-stringed lyre I will make music to you,
¹⁰ to the One who gives victory to kings,
　　who delivers his servant David.
From the deadly sword ¹¹ deliver me;
　　rescue me from the hands of foreigners
whose mouths are full of lies,
　　whose right hands are deceitful.
¹² Then our sons in their youth
　　will be like well-nurtured plants,
and our daughters will be like pillars
　　carved to adorn a palace.
¹³ Our barns will be filled
　　with every kind of provision.

Our sheep will increase by thousands,
by tens of thousands in our fields;
¹⁴ our oxen will draw heavy loads.
There will be no breaching of walls,
no going into captivity,
no cry of distress in our streets.
¹⁵ Blessed is the people of whom this is true;
blessed is the people whose God is the LORD.

PSALM 144 IS THE SEVENTH psalm in the Psalter's final Davidic collection (Pss 138–45) and contains a "curious mixture" of various psalmic forms, including praise, blessing, petition, complaint, and vow.[1] The complexity of the psalm is evident not only in its array of literary forms but also in its repeated allusions to earlier psalms. Several verses find their parallel or nearly parallel text elsewhere in the Psalter: Psalms 144:3//8:4; 144:4//39:5–6; 144:9//33:2–3; 144:15//33:12. Most striking, however, is the psalmist's extensive use of Psalm 18 throughout (Pss 144:1, 2//18:1, 2, 3, 4, 46, 47; 144:5//18:9; 144:6//18:14; 144:7, 11//18:16, 45, 46; 144:10//18:0 [superscription]). While the parallels in language prove instructive regarding the possible sources behind Psalm 144, it is the variations that prove most illuminating. The psalmst has taken indicative statements present in Psalm 18 and created petitions with the force of an imperative in Psalm 144. For example, in Psalm 18 the king gives thanks for having been "rescued . . . from my powerful enemy" (v. 17), yet in Psalm 144 the psalmist pleads for Yahweh to "deliver me and rescue me" (vv. 7, 11). In Psalm 18:9 the psalmist recounts how Yahweh "parted the heavens and came down," but in Psalm 144:5 he cries out, "Part your heavens, LORD, and come down." Yahweh is praised for having stretched forth his hand to deliver the psalmist from the many waters in Psalm 18:16, while in Psalm 144:7 the psalmist craves for such action. The earlier poem, Psalm 18, is generally labeled a royal psalm of thanksgiving.[2] In Psalm 144, however, the song of thanksgiving has been transformed. In Psalm 18 the threat has been resolved, thus prompting thanksgiving; in Psalm 144 the threat lingers, thus prompting petition.

The texts referenced above, including the royal Psalm 18, come from Book 1 of the Psalter (Pss 1–41), but they have been adopted and adapted

1. Gerstenberger, *Psalms, Part 2*, 427.
2. DeClaissé-Walford, Jacobson, and LaNeel Tanner, *The Book of Psalms*, 191.

in the light of concerns in the postexilic period.[3] More so than with any of the other texts, it is the use of Psalm 18 that proves most critical in ascertaining the hermenuetical move being made in Psalm 144. James L. Mays explains that "by repraying Psalm 18 in a new version, the writer appealed to the Lord to do what the Lord had done for his servant David."[4] As similarly with the claim made in Isaiah 55:3, the psalmist operates under the assumption that the promises made to David now in fact are to be applied to the community as a whole, the faithful ones who comprise the postexilic community. The shift from singular pronouns in Psalm 144:1–11 to plural pronouns in verses 12–14 reinforces this interpretive move.[5]

Heading (144:0)

AS WITH EACH OF THE PSALMS in the Psalter's final Davidic collection (Pss 138–45), the superscription includes the phrase "Of David" (*ledawid*). There are three other Davidic collections in the Psalter: its Books 1 and 2 contain two large collections that include "David" in the superscriptions (Pss 3–41; 51–72) and culminate with a reference to the "prayers of David" in Psalm 72:20. In Book 5 (Pss 107–45) David reappears in the superscription of two collections. The first one (Pss 108–10) begins Book 5, and the second (Pss 138–45) serves as a concluding collection. The reemergence of David in the superscriptions in Book 5 signals that David has become emblematic of the poor servant who depends entirely on Yahweh for deliverance.[6] In Book 5 David is not the warring king seen in earlier psalms (e.g., Ps 18); instead, he is the one in need of God's deliverance. In the Septuagint the superscription to Psalm 144 has been expanded to include the phrase "against Goliath," thus connecting this psalm with the heroic story in 1 Samuel 17. Yet, even in that text, David is portrayed as a "boy, glowing with health and handsome" (v. 42)—surely no match for a Philistine giant. In that scene, David appears not as the mighty warrior but as the faithful servant (vv. 34–37).

---

3. The significant number of Aramaic terms in the psalm coupled with its anthological style points to its postexilic dating. (See Hossfeld and Zenger, *Psalms 3*, 583–84.)

4. Mays, *Psalms*, 436.

5. Moreover, as Marko Martilla has observed, there are characteristic features of psalms that reflect a "collective theology," one intended to address the complaints or hopes of the people. The comments made in verses 12–14 accord well with Martilla's observations, thus further strengthening the claim that this psalm is not about a single royal figure, whether past or future, but about the people of God (Marko Martilla, *Collective Reinterpretation in the Psalms*, FAT 2/13 [Tübingen: Mohr Siebeck, 2006], 212–13).

6. Tucker, *Constructing and Deconstructing Power in Psalms 107–150*, 181.

The Psalmist Praises God (144:1–2)

THE PSALM OPENS WITH A SERIES of descriptive statements meant to highlight the relationship between the psalmist and his God. The relational nature of the comments is emphasized by the repeated use of first-person singular language ("me," "my"); the terms together appear nine times in the opening two verses, not counting the first-person form of the verb in verse 2c ("I take refuge"). The psalmist draws much of his imagery from Psalm 18. The opening line, "Praise be to the LORD my Rock," is drawn from Psalm 18:2, 46. The phrase "who trains my hands for war" in Psalm 144:1b is drawn from Psalm 18:34, and much of the remainder of the language in Psalm 144:2 compares to that found in Psalm 18:2.

Praise be to the LORD. The Hebrew word for "praise" comes from the root *brk*, a term that occurs more than four hundred times throughout the Old Testament. Depending on the context, usage, and form, the Hebrew term can mean "to praise," "to bless," or even "to greet." *Barak* can refer to encounters between humans (Gen 27:30; Deut 33:1; 2 Sam 6:20), but more often it relates to God's dispensing of blessings to his people or his creation (cf., commentary on Ps 134).[7] In Psalm 144:1a and 2b the psalmist exhorts the community to "bless" Yahweh. While the idea of God's blessing his people seems logical, the reverse—the idea of the people's blessing God— seems counterintuitive. Other ancient Semitic traditions expressed similar reservations about the idea of who could bless whom and decided that the deity was the one who granted blessing but never the one who received blessing. By contrast, in the Old Testament Yahweh not only appears as the subject of the verb "to bless" but also can function as the object of the verb, as evidenced in this psalm. Obviously, *barak* functions differently depending on whether Yahweh is the subject or the object of the verb. The NIV has attempted to capture this difference by rendering *barak* as "to praise" when Yahweh is the object of the verb and humans are the subject (as in Ps 134:1a, 2b). The Septuagint understood the different nuance being communicated in this use of *barak* and so rendered the Hebrew term with *eulogeō*, "to speak well of," as a servant would speak well of his or her superior. Within the framework of a covenant, or even a patron-client relationship, the master or lord would bestow favor on the servant, and in return the servant would speak well of, or "bless," the master. The use of *hesed* in Psalm 144:2a underscores the covenantal nature of this relationship.

---

7. Recipients of God's "blessing" include humans (Gen 12:2; Exod 20:24; Ps 115:22) and the created order (Gen 1:22; 2:3; Exod 23:25). In other contexts, priests, acting on behalf of God, pronounce blessings upon the people of God, as evidenced in the priestly blessing in Num 6:24–26.

In the Old Testament, God bestows blessings on his people and, in return, his people speak well of God; they bless or praise God.

"My people" or "peoples." Verse 2d contains a text-critical note that does shape the interpretation of the opening strophe and explains the difference in translations. The Masoretic Text reads, "who subdues my people ['*ammi*] under me." Hossfeld and Zenger read with the Hebrew text and contend that verse 2d refers to some type of internal unrest among those in Yehud.[8] This reading raises two issues. Thematically, the psalm is not concerned with internal unrest but with the oppression experienced at the hands of foreign peoples (vv. 7, 11). The second issue involves the relationship between Psalms 144 and 18. The phrase found in Psalm 144:2b is also found in Psalm 18:47, but in that instance the word '*ammim* ("peoples") appears instead of '*ammi*, "my people." The use of '*ammim* ("peoples") in that context clearly refers to external threats. Several Hebrew manuscripts, Aquila's Greek translation, the Dead Sea Scrolls (11QPs[a]), the Syriac, and the Targum all read '*ammim* ("peoples"). The NIV's translation follows these textual witnesses.

Reflection on the Human Condition (144:3–4)

IN THE SECOND STROPHE THE PSALMIST turns to consider the nature of the human condition. In verse 3 he borrows language from Psalm 8:4, but in that psalm the answer to the question is vastly different. In Psalm 8 God is mindful of humans and cares for them because he has "made them a little lower than the angels and crowned them with glory and honor" (v. 5). That claim is followed in verse 6 with the statement that God has made them to rule over creation, he has "put everything under their feet." In short, Psalm 8 praises humans both for their position and their power. In Psalm 144, however, the answer to the same question differs considerably. Rather than drawing from Psalm 8 and celebrating the status of humans, the writer of Psalm 144 turns to a different motif found in Scripture. He confesses that human life is like a "breath" (*hebel*), the same word that appears throughout the book of Ecclesiastes (cf. Eccl 1:2) and a word that stresses the ephemerality of life. Psalm 144:4b echoes that assertion by likening human life to a shadow (*tsel*).[9] Together these claims provide a rationale for the confession in verses 1–2 and the petitions that follow in verses 3–8. Because humans are little more than a breath and a shadow, they must rely fully on another as their fortress and stronghold. And similarly, because humans are little more than a breath and a shadow, they do not posses the strength

---

8. Hossfeld and Zenger, *Psalms 3*, 584–85.
9. On the motif of life as a shadow see Job 8:9; 14:2; 17:7, as well as Pss 102:11; 109:23.

or vigor to withstand the aggression of hostile forces (vv. 3–8). In such circumstances, neither a breath nor a shadow can offer the protection and strength found in a rock (v. 1a).

Petitions to Yahweh (144:5–8)

GIVEN THE HUMAN CONDITION, as expressed in verses 3–4, the psalmist petitions Yahweh for deliverance from the present threat (i.e., "the hands of foreigners"). In these verses the language and imagery draws considerably from Psalm 18, but they have been adapted to address the current plight.

Part your heavens, LORD, and come down. In light of the present threat, the psalmist petitions for a theophany, for the inbreaking of God's manifest presence in the world. In Book 5 of the Psalter the poets have repeatedly referred to God's locale as being in the heavens or even above the heavens (e.g., Pss 113; 115), a claim meant to reinforce Israel's confession that Yahweh is the Divine King over all creation. In Psalm 144 the psalmist envisions Yahweh as the God of the heavens, but he seeks to close that spatial distance by calling upon Yahweh to part the heavens and come down (v. 5). The descriptive language that follows clearly invokes imagery associated with the Sinai theophany in Exodus 19. When Yahweh appeared on Sinai, "smoke billowed up from it like smoke from a furnace" (v. 18).[10] The sending forth of lightning coupled with images of archery is frequently employed in other theophanic texts (cf. Hab 3). Together the images signal that not only has Yahweh made himself present with his people, but he has also come as the Divine Warrior prepared to defend them.

Reach down your hand. The image in verse 7a reinforces both the perceived spatial distance as well as Yahweh's capacity to "come down" (v. 5a). Although the NIV follows a number of English translations by rendering the word "hand" as singular, the Hebrew is plural, "hands."[11] This change may seem innocuous enough not to warrant a comment, but the shift from the expected singular to the plural in Hebrew suggests an important theological move being made by the psalmist. Typically, the noun "hand" appears in the singular when referring to God's capacity to help his people, and in this sense the noun functions as a cipher for the power of God (cf. Deut 5:15). But when the *hands* (plural) of God are

---

10. Although the reference to "mighty waters" later in Ps 144:7 alludes to the foreign enemies, the mountains do not (contra deClaissé-Walford, Jacobson, and LaNeel Tanner, *The Book of Psalms*, 987). In Ps 18:7b the mountains are mentioned in reference to the theophanic presence of God.

11. The *BHS*'s critical apparatus indicates that several Hebrew manuscripts show a singular noun.

mentioned, reference is being made to God's creative work (cf. Pss 8:6; 143:5), and even more to God's creative power to bring order out of chaos. In making this slight change (i.e., from singular to plural), the psalmist sought to "represent the theophanic YHWH also as the creator God."[12]

Hands of foreigners. In Psalm 18 the poet asked Yahweh to rescue him from his enemies and those who "hate him." In Psalm 144 the psalmist has narrowed the terminology considerably in explaining that the threat is *miyyad bene-nekar*, literally, "from the hand of the sons of the foreigner." The word *nekar* ("foreign") occurs with great regularity in the Hebrew Bible and most often functions adjectivally with *'elohim*, "foreign gods." The phrase that appears in Psalm 144:7, 11 ("sons of a foreigner," *bene-nekar*) occurs only eighteen times in the Hebrew Bible, with the highest concentration appearing in Isaiah 56–66, frequently with overt political connotations (e.g., Isa 60:10).[13] The threat facing the psalmist, and arguably the entire community (cf. Ps 144:12–14), comes from foreign powers that oppress them.

Mighty waters. The phrase "from the hands of the sons of a foreigner" (*miyyad bene-nekar*) stands in parallel to the previous phrase *mimmayim rabbim*, literally, "from the many waters." The direct allusion to foreign powers, then, is filtered through the first image of the "many waters." As similarly to the imagery in Psalm 124, the writer of Psalm 144 employs the metaphor of "many waters" in an effort to recast the present threat in cosmological terms. As J. J. M. Roberts has suggested, such cosmological themes are fundamental to Israel's construction of the identity of Yahweh. These cosmological themes articulate Yahweh's rule over the world. Roberts explains, "It is these primeval, cosmogonic victories of Yahweh that the psalmist cites, not the exodus or the conquest of Canaan, as a motivation to stir Yahweh to act against the historical enemies that now threaten the people of God."[14] The cosmological language employed reinforces the significance of the threat and once more affirms that Israel's only hope against such powers rests with Yahweh alone.

Praise and Petition (144:9–11)

THE FOURTH STROPHE CONTAINS a vow of praise followed by a petition. The reason Yahweh deserves praise (v. 10a–b) provides the warrant for the petition offered in verses 10c–11.

---

12. Hossfeld and Zenger, *Psalms 3*, 585.
13. See also Gen 17:12; 17:27; Exod 12:43; Lev 22:25; 2 Sam 22:45, 46; Isa 56:3, 6; 60:10; 61:5; 62:8; Ezek 44:7, 9; Ps 18:45, 46; Neh 9:2.
14. J. J. M. Roberts, "God's Imperial Reign According to the Psalter," *HBT* 23 (2001), 217.

I will sing a new song. The reference to a "new song" occurs only seven times in the Old Testament (Isa 42:10; Pss 33:3; 40:3; 96:1; 98:1; 144:9; 149:1). The psalmist's vow to sing a new song has little to do with his song being a "new" composition; instead, his vow appears to point to a particular understanding or confession about Israel's God (see below, Bridging Context; see also the comments on Ps 96:1).

Who gives victories to kings. In Psalm 144:10a–b the psalmist describes Yahweh as "the one who gives victory to kings, who delivers his servant David." Hossfeld and Zenger, as well as Christoph Buysch, argue that with the use of "kings" in verse 10a the psalmist claims that Yahweh provides victory to all the kings of the world.[15] Further, they contend, the psalmist refers to the kings of the nations in verse 10a while verse 10b refers to David and the Davidic dynasty. In support of such a claim, scholars have suggested that the plural form of *melek* ("king") appears frequently in the Psalter (e.g., Pss 2:10; 72:10; 102:23; 138:4), and in such contexts the word refers to the kings of earth, thus necessitating a similar rendering in Psalm 144.[16] Those following this line of reasoning also point to Psalm 138:4 ("may all the kings of the earth praise you") and contend that, just as the kings turned to Yahweh in Psalm 138, so also is Yahweh turning to the kings of the earth in Psalm 144 and guaranteeing victory to them. The context of Psalm 144 itself and its intertextual relationship with Psalm 18, however, suggest a different, albeit more straightforward interpretation. Psalm 144:10 draws from Psalm 18:50, and there the psalmist places David in parallel with "his [Yahweh's] king." The poet makes a similar move in Psalm 144. The psalmist sings a new song to Yahweh celebrating the victories he has provided for David and the other kings of Israel.

Psalm 144 depicts a crisis at the hands of the "sons of a foreigner," *bene-nekar*, a crisis that necessitates the "part[ing] of the heavens" and the direct intervention of Yahweh. The two figures used in verse 10a–b—David and the kings of David's lineage—serve as a reminder of Yahweh's faithful intervention in behalf of his people in the past. Yahweh's faithfulness in the past provides the rationale for the petitions that follow in verses 10c–11.

Communal Statement of Confidence (144:12–14)

THE PRECISE FUNCTION OF VERSES 12–15 within Psalm 144, including whether they were an original part of the psalm, has received considerable attention. In the first eleven verses of the poem, the language and imagery

---

15. Hossfeld and Zenger, *Psalms 3*, 586; Buysch, *Der letzte Davidpsalter*, 291–92.

16. See Christoph Rösel, *Die messianische Redaktion des Psalters: Studien zu Entstehung und Theologie der Sammlung Psalm 2–89*, CThM 19 (Stuttgart: Calwer, 1999), 188–89.

---

from Psalm 18 were employed with a dual emphasis on the serious threat of foreign power and the community's utter reliance on Yahweh for deliverance. Although appropriation of previous traditions does not occur with the same regularity in verses 12–15, the function of the final verses nevertheless appears consistent with that of verses 1–11, namely, the challenging of foreign kings.

The psalm also shifts from first-person singular language ("I," "me") to first-person plural language ("we," "us"). In these verses the community describes their life once Yahweh has rid the land of the oppressive enemies. The postexilic period was marked by famine and hardship; some of the conditions may have been natural (e.g., see Isa 58:11–12; Hag 1:6–11), but others were clearly the result of imperial oppression (e.g., Neh 5:1–5). Jon Berquist, in his work on imperialization, has suggested that central to the formation, administration, and continuation of an empire is its ability to extract resources. Berquist argues that an empire can be decribed as

> a large-scale social unit that extracts resources (including labor) from other social units, the colonies. . . . An empire is not a static social unit or a category that a social unit attains once it reaches a certain size and power as compared to its neighbors, or once its military defeats another empire.[17]

Berquist suggests there are "multiple modes of extraction," but included among such resources would be food, products, and human capital. In addition, empires may extract resources through taxation, thereby "leading to a decreasing colonial ability to survive."[18] The scarcity of resources and the threat of survival due to mistreatment at the hands of the "sons of a foreigner" (*bene-nekar*) stand behind the imagery present in Psalm 144:12–14. The psalmist longs for sons and daughters to grow to full stature, like full-grown plants, and to become like beautiful corner pillars on a palace. Likewise, the psalmist wishes that the storehouses, now empty, would provide for the people "with every kind of provision"; that the sheep and cattle would be prolific in their reproduction; and finally, in verse 14c, that there would be "no cry of distress in our streets." The word *tsewahah*, "cry of distress," occurs elsewhere only in Isaiah 24:11 and Jeremiah 14:2; 46:12. In all three instances the meaning is connected to community destruction and situations of depravity at the hands of others.

---

17. Jon L. Berquist, "Postcolonialism and Imperial Motives for Canonization," *Semeia* 75 (1996), 16–17.
18. Ibid., 17.

Closing Beatitude (144:15)

THE PSALM CONCLUDES WITH two beatitudes concerning the people. In the first one the psalmist announces that "blessed" (*'ashre*) are the people whose lives reflect that which is described in verses 12–14. The second beatitude (v. 15b) suggests that such a "blessed existence" is only possible because Yahweh is Israel's God. This second beatitude provides the "crucial lesson" for those who read and hear this psalm: the covenantal faithfulness of God to his people will lead him to put down their enemies (vv. 5–11) and restore their land to prosperity and peace (vv. 12–14).[19]

HEAVENLY DIVINE WARRIOR IMAGERY. The motif of the divine warrior appears repeatedly throughout the Old Testament (cf. Exod 15), as does the motif of Yahweh as the God of heaven (Ps 115). Each metaphor captures a sense of Yahweh that words alone cannot. By referencing Yahweh as the God of heaven, the author confesses Yahweh as the God who stands over all creation (and all powers); he is no regional deity with limited authority but the Creator King enthroned in the heavens, where he stands over his kingdom (i.e., the world) and exercises his reign. This metaphor clearly alludes to the transcendent nature of Israel's God. The divine-warrior imagery, however, often appears alongside theophanic imagery meant to highlight Yahweh's salvific immanence—Yahweh comes as the Divine Warrior to deliver his people. As God marches across the earth, the mountains crumble before him, and the nations tremble as he comes to deliver his people (Hab 3:6, 13). A number of texts, particularly in the Psalter, have melded the two images into one by describing Yahweh as the heavenly Divine Warrior, the one enthroned in the heavens yet who acts decisively to deliver his people. The frequency of this metaphor in the Psalter is somewhat surprising, with nearly 25 percent of all metaphors in the Psalter alluding to heavenly divine-warrior imagery.[20] Clearly the psalmists found in this metaphorical image a rich vein from which to draw their theological confessions.

---

19. Hossfeld and Zenger, *Psalms* 3, 588.

20. See Martin Klingbeil, "Metaphors that Travel and (Almost) Vanish: Mapping Diachronic Changes in the Intertextual Usage of the Heavenly Warrior Metaphor in Psalms 18 and 144," in *Metaphors in the Psalms*, BETL 231, ed. Pierre van Hecke and Antje Labahn (Leuven: Peeters, 2010), 132. Klingbeil has tracked the use of this metaphor across the Psalter. In Book 1 (Pss 1–41) the image occurs fifty-eight times, and in Book 2 (Pss 42–72) it appears thirty-six times. In Books 3 and 4 (73–89; 90–106) the metaphor appears only

New song. As noted above, the mention of a "new song" occurs relatively infrequently in the Old Testament, where the phrase appears only seven times (Isa 42:10; Pss 33:3; 40:3; 96:1; 98:1; 144:9; 149:1). As similarly in Psalm 144, the theme of a new song and the metaphor of the heavenly divine warrior appear together in the other six texts, thus suggesting a close association between the two elements. A "new song" must always be heard in the light of Israel's confession of Yahweh as the heavenly Divine Warrior. It is Yahweh's role as such that even makes this singing possible. In Psalm 33, for example, the psalm begins with a threefold call to praise, with the last call instructing the community to "sing to him a new song." In the remainder of the poem the psalmist confesses that Yahweh looks down "from heaven" (Ps 33:13) and sees all mankind. But the heavenly Divine King is at work foiling the plans of the nations and thwarting those of the peoples (v. 10). No king is safe from the heavenly Divine King/Warrior when he comes to deliver his people (v. 16, 19). Similarly, in Psalms 96 and 98 the call to sing a new song appears in connection with Israel's praise of Yahweh as the Divine King who stands over all creation, yet both psalms confess that Yahweh comes to "judge the earth" (Pss 96:13; 98:9). And likewise in Isaiah 42:10, the prophet calls the people to sing "a new song" but then announces that Yahweh will "march out like a champion, like a warrior he will stir up his zeal" (v. 13).

When analyzed together, several characteristics pertaining to the "new song" emerge from these seven texts. Erhard Gerstenberger catalogs three signficiant "criteria" for the "new song" in the Old Testament. More than comprising merely form-critical observations about the structure of the psalms themselves, Gerstenberger's analysis reminds us of the theological heft found in the concept of the "new song." According to Gerstenberger, the "new song" was "intoned against death and evil in order to support and make possible full human life."[21] Second, these psalms were voiced within the lives of communities rather than as individual meditations. What was confessed within the new songs had implications for all God's people and the nations writ large (e.g., Pss 96; 98; 149). And third, the "new song" "anticipates boldly, against all evidence, the coming of God's liberation, the new and just world."[22]

The phrase "new song" occurs twice in the New Testament, both times in the book of Revelation (Rev 5:9; 14:3). The meaning associated with

---

twenty times and twelve times, respectively. In the final (and largest) book, Book 5, the metaphor appears only six times and only in three psalms (Pss 113:5, 6; 123:1; 144:5, 6, 7).

21. Erhard Gerstenberger, "Singing a New Song: On Old Testament and Latin American Psalmody," *WW* 5 (1997): 155–67; see p. 159.

22. Ibid.

a "new song" in the Old Testament extends into these New Testament texts, but through the filter of Jesus Christ. According to Revelation 5, a new song is to be sung because of the one who sits upon the throne and the Lamb who was slain (Rev 5:13). Through his victory a "new and just world" will be experienced, one in which people from "every tribe and language and people and nation" will become "a kingdom and priests to serve our God" (vv. 9–10).

As noted in the Original Meaning section above, when referencing a "new song," the authors are not referring to a "new" composition or a freshly composed work. Instead, by declaring a "new song" they are making a fundamental claim about God and his ways in the world. The God of the "new song" is the heavenly Divine Warrior, the one who comes to make all things new.[23]

 AS WE HAVE NOTED ABOVE, Psalm 144 makes considerable use of earlier psalms, most notably Psalms 8, 18, and 32. This use and reuse of earlier psalms reflects the elasticity of psalmic poetry; its language and themes are malleable to a myriad of contexts. In Psalm 144 the poet has taken elements of Psalms 8 and 18 and reworked them to address the theological and existential crises faced by the postexilic community. Yet, among the goals of biblical interpretation, merely identifying the sources used by the psalmist is not enough. We must ask, why and to what end did he use them? Here with respect to the use of both Psalms 8 and 18, the writer of Psalm 144 has adapted earlier psalmic texts to create a thoroughly theocentric perspective. As noted above, Psalm 8 actually praises humanity's creation, yet in Psalm 144 the psalmist has borrowed the same question from that psalm and arrived at a negative assessment of human power. In arriving at that conclusion, the poet is also conversely asserting the necessity for a demonstration of God's power. Verses 5–8 allude to that display of power as the psalmist adapts specific elements from Psalm 18 and makes them part of his petition—part of his plea for Yahweh to act.

Psalm 144's use of both Psalms 8 and 18 feeds into the larger concern related to the "new song." While humans have no power, God does. Those in the postexilic period understood well their own plight, and they understood well the source of their redemption. If the members of the Jerusalem

---

23. See also Tremper Longman III, "Psalm 98: A Divine Warrior Hymn," *JETS* 27 (1984): 267–74.

community understood that they were little more than a "breath" or "fleeting shadow," then they recognized well that there was no hope for them. But if their confession of hope rested fully and entirely with the heavenly Divine Warrior, the very God of Israel, the one who could deliver them from the "hands of foreigners," then there was hope indeed. There was reason to sing a "new song" and to believe that the world as experienced is not the world as intended.

When we read and sing Psalm 144, we are invited to make that same claim. We are asked to renounce our sense of self-sufficiency and the hubris associated with claims of self-deliverance. We are asked to acknowledge what we know to be true—we are mere "fleeting shadows." Because we know what *we are*, we must lean fully into who *he is*—the Divine King (Ps 145), the heavenly divine warrior, our Rock and Shield. Because he is that God, because he is our God, we have reason to sing a new song.

Psalm 145

A psalm of praise. Of David.

¹ I will exalt you, my God the King;
   I will praise your name forever and ever.
² Every day I will praise you
   and extol your name forever and ever.
³ Great is the LORD and most worthy of praise;
   his greatness no one can fathom.
⁴ One generation commends your works to another;
   they tell of your mighty acts.
⁵ They speak of the glorious splendor of your majesty—
   and I will meditate on your wonderful works.
⁶ They tell of the power of your awesome works—
   and I will proclaim your great deeds.
⁷ They celebrate your abundant goodness
   and joyfully sing of your righteousness.
⁸ The LORD is gracious and compassionate,
   slow to anger and rich in love.
⁹ The LORD is good to all;
   he has compassion on all he has made.
¹⁰ All your works praise you, LORD;
   your faithful people extol you.
¹¹ They tell of the glory of your kingdom
   and speak of your might,
¹² so that all people may know of your mighty acts
   and the glorious splendor of your kingdom.
¹³ Your kingdom is an everlasting kingdom,
   and your dominion endures through all generations.
The LORD is trustworthy in all he promises
   and faithful in all he does.
¹⁴ The LORD upholds all who fall
   and lifts up all who are bowed down.
¹⁵ The eyes of all look to you,
   and you give them their food at the proper time.
¹⁶ You open your hand
   and satisfy the desires of every living thing.
¹⁷ The LORD is righteous in all his ways

and faithful in all he does.
¹⁸ The LORD is near to all who call on him,
   to all who call on him in truth.
¹⁹ He fulfills the desires of those who fear him;
   he hears their cry and saves them.
²⁰ The LORD watches over all who love him,
   but all the wicked he will destroy.
²¹ My mouth will speak in praise of the LORD.
   Let every creature praise his holy name
   forever and ever.

 PSALM 145 IS THE CONCLUDING psalm in the Psalter's fourth and final Davidic collection (Pss 138–45). The superscription labels the psalm as a "psalm of praise" (*tehillah*), a title unique to this psalm. Its appearance in the opening verse creates an *inclusio* with the final verse in the psalm, where the word appears once more (the "praise [*tehillah*] of the Lord"). The kingship of Yahweh remains the dominant theme throughout the psalm and constitutes a theological claim that merits the praise of his people.

Psalm 145 is one of several acrostic poems in the Psalter (cf. Pss 25; 34; 37; 111; 112; 119). In an acrostically structured psalm, each line begins with the subsequent letter in the Hebrew alphabet (*aleph, bet, gimel,* etc.). Noticeably absent from the Hebrew text of Psalm 145, however, is a line that begins with *nun*. Verse 13 begins with a *mem* (*malkutka,* "your kingdom"), followed in verse 14 by a *samek* (*somek,* "upholds"), thus altogether bypassing the intervening letter *nun*.[1] Other important textual witnesses, including the Septuagint, Dead Sea Scrolls (11QPsª), Vulgate, and Syriac, include a *nun* line, as does a Hebrew manuscript (Kennicott ms. 142). The NIV reads with the textual witnesses and includes the *nun* line provided in those versions: "The LORD is trustworthy in all he promises and faithful in all that he does."[2] Some interpreters remain unconvinced by the textual witnesses

---

1. According to the Babylonian Talmud, the *nun* strophe is omitted because the psalmist did not want to speak of the "fall" (*napal*) of Jerusalem (m. Ber. 4b).

2. Similarly to Ps 145, the other acrostic psalms ascribed to David in the Psalter (Pss 25; 34; 37) are not "complete" acrostics either, as each poem lacks lines that begin with one or two Hebrew letters. It is possible that the Masoretic Text may reflect the original reading or at least another textual version that differed from the one adopted by the Septuagint and Dead Sea Scrolls. For additional analysis see Reuven Kimelman, "Psalm 145: Theme, Structure, and Impact," *JBL* 133 (1994): 37–58, esp. 50–51.

and prefer instead to allow the absence of the *nun* to stand.[3] Given that other acrostic psalms (Pss 25; 34) lack lines that begin with certain letters, it is not unreasonable to believe the same may be true in Psalm 144. Nevertheless, whether one includes the *nun* line or not, the psalm remains properly classified as an acrostic.

While this poetic form is impressive, it is "not mere 'scholastic gamesmanship,' but was deliberately chosen by the author of the psalm as appropriate to his theological intention."[4] By structuring Psalm 145 in this manner, the psalmist highlights the comprehensiveness of the poem and its claims concerning the kingship of God. Analogously, English speakers might choose the idiom "from A to Z" in everyday language when referring to the comprehensive scope of a word, phrase, or expression (i.e., "That document spells out everything from A to Z"). The comprehensive claims concerning the kingship of God, those that run from *aleph* to *taw*, are meant to compel the reader to unadulterated praise.

The comprehensive nature of the acrostic psalm is buttressed by the repeated use of the word "all" (*kol*) throughout the psalm. The word appears seventeen times in the poem; sometimes it refers to God and God's actions (e.g., vv. 10, 13c, 13d, 17), and at other times it refers to those who are the recipients of his actions (e.g., vv. 9a/b, 12a, 18a/b). The psalm celebrates "all" that God has done and is doing for "all" his people. The poem even concludes by acknowledging that God will destroy "all" the wicked. From beginning to end, the psalm celebrates Yahweh as the Divine King, and the repeated references to "all" serve to amplify that claim. He is "all" and he stands over "all."

In addition to the repeated use of "all," terms associated with the vocabulary of praise appear with considerable regularity in Ps 145. The frequency of their appearance in the first half of the poem is stunning. Verses 1b, 2a/b, 3a, 4a/b, 5b, 6a/b, 7a/b, 10a/b, 11a/b, and 12a all contain vocabulary of praise. The theme also reappears twice in the final verse of the psalm (v. 21a/b), thus providing an apt conclusion to this psalm of praise. The poet employs a variety of Hebrew terms across these 18 occurrences, with each referring to praising, speaking, or singing praise.[5] Those involved in the act of confessing and praising include: the psalmist (v. 1b); the "generation[s]" (v. 4a); Yahweh's works (v. 10a); the "faithful people" (v. 10b); and every creature (v. 21b). While they appear unrelated,

---

3. Hossfeld and Zenger, *Psalms 3*, 593.
4. Hossfeld and Zenger, *Psalms 3*, 257.
5. In addition to these uses, two other occurrences appear in verses 18b and 19a. Both instances refer to crying to God in need rather than to praising God.

the frequent occurrences of "all" (*kol*) and the many and varied uses of terms from the vocabulary of praise highlight the claim of Psalm 145: all creation is enjoined to praise the Divine King (v. 1).

From start to finish the psalm celebrates the kingship of Yahweh, a theme that resounds throughout the entirety of the Psalter but that is evident most clearly in the Enthronement Psalms of Book 4 (Pss 93; 95–99). The opening verse in the final psalm of Book 5 (Ps 145:1) returns explicitly to this theme by referencing Yahweh as "My God the king." The kingship theme is not restricted to the opening line—this theme appears again in verses 11–13a. Although other verses make less overt claims concerning the kingship of Yahweh, taken together they reinforce the central claim of the psalm.

Perhaps due to the acrostic form of the psalm, or perhaps even the repetition of language and motifs, Psalm 145 does not divide as easily into strophes as do other psalms—hence the considerable variations in structure proposed in other studies (and even in the English translations). Reuven Kimelman has observed that the outline is marked by a threefold use of the word "praise" (*barak*) in verses 1, 10, and 21. He posits that these verses function as a prelude, interlude, and postlude for the poem as a whole.[6] The psalm begins with the poet's vowing to praise Yahweh (vv. 1–2). In verse 10 the "faithful people" are mentioned—they too will "praise" (*barak*) Yahweh. In the final verse the psalmist extends the angle of vision and declares that "every creature" will "praise" (*barak*) Yahweh. Thus, the psalm moves from individual to corporate and finally to universal praise of Yahweh. The intervening verses alternate between focusing on God's character and offering statements of praise. Verse 3 offers a sweeping statement on the nature of God, followed by statements of praise in verses 4–7. Verses 8–9 return to the character of God. Verse 10 serves as an interlude, followed by additional statements of praise (vv. 11–13b). Beginning in verse 13c and extending through verse 20, the psalmist provides a thorough description of God's character.[7]

Heading (145:0)

As with each of the poems in the final Davidic collection in the book of Psalms (Pss 138–45), the superscription includes the phrase "Of David" (*ledawid*). There are three other Davidic collections in the Psalter. Books 1 and 2 in the Psalter contain two large collections that include "David"

---

6. Kimelman, "Psalm 145," 40–41. Goldingay structures the psalm similarly, particularly regarding the role that verses 1–2, 10, and 21 play. See Goldingay, *Psalms 3*, 695–96.

7. McCann, "The Book of Psalms," 1259.

in the superscriptions (Pss 3–41; 51–72) and culminate with a reference to the "prayers of David" in Psalm 72:20. In Book 5 (Pss 107–45) David reappears in the superscription of two collections. The first collection, Psalms 108–10, begins Book 5, and Psalms 138–45 serve as a concluding collection. The reemergence of David in the superscriptions in Book 5 signals that David has become emblematic of the poor servant who depends entirely on Yahweh for deliverance.[8] As noted above, the other word in the superscription, *tehillah* ("psalm of praise"), is unique to this psalm.

Vow to Praise God (145:1–2)

IN THE OPENING LINE THE PSALMIST confesses Yahweh as "My God the king." Although kingship language is frequently used to describe Yahweh, only here and in Psalm 98:6 is Yahweh declared "*the* king" (the noun with the definite article). Some interpreters understand both terms as vocatives and translate the phrase as "My God and King" (cf. NRSV), but it should be understood as a truncated nominal clause, "My God (is) the king."[9] Understood in this way, the statement is univocal: there is no king but the God of the psalmist. The NIV interprets the phrase similarly.

In the light of his confession the psalmist commits to three actions: "exalt," "praise," and "extol." The verb "exalt" comes from the root *rum*, meaning "to lift high" or "to raise up." The psalmist pledges to "lift high" Yahweh, even as servants might literally lift high a king in honor. The next two verbs (vv. 1b, 2a) come from the root *brk*, "to bless." The psalmist vows to "bless" Yahweh. For an extended discussion of the meaning of the root *brk*, "to bless," see the comments on Psalm 134. The final verb in the opening strophe is *halal*, "to praise" or "to extol." All three verbs in the opening strophe are part of the vocabulary of praise that dominates the first half of the psalm.

In the first two verses the psalmist refers to the name (*shem*) of God twice (vv. 1b, 2b); the psalmist pledges to bless and extol the name of God. In this instance the "name" (*shem*) of Yahweh is "metonymical for the nature of the Lord."[10] Thus, in pledging to bless or extol the *shem* of God, the psalmist is actually vowing to celebrate the defining characteristics of his God, the King. This association between the character of God and the name of God is clearly evident in Exodus 34:5–7. In that context the name of God is mentioned first, followed by a list of attributes meant to describe God. Similarly, in Psalm 145 the psalmist mentions the *shem* of

---

8. Tucker, *Constructing and Deconstructing*, 181.
9. Hossfeld and Zenger, *Psalms 3*, 594.
10. Allen P. Ross, "שֵׁם," *NIDOTTE* 4:148.

Yahweh in verses 1–2 and then celebrates the character of God in the subsequent verses. The psalm concludes with a third reference to the *shem* of Yahweh—all creation will celebrate the *shem* of Yahweh and bless him for who he is.

Praise of God (145:3–7)

IN THE OPENING STROPHE THE PSALMIST vows to praise God, the only King. This vow is predicated on the psalmist's understanding of God and his work in history. The second strophe begins with a succinct statement about the character of God in verse 3, followed by the praise of God uttered by all generations.

Great is the LORD. To declare Yahweh "great" is to do far more than make a subjective assessment about the nature of God. In the ancient Near East, the label "great" was applied to deities in combination with their role as kings. Examples of this practice abound in ancient texts, stela, and iconography. In ancient Mesopotamia the prologue to the Lipit-Ishtar law code begins "Anu, the great, the father of the gods."[11] In Egypt the god Resheph is declared "the great god, lord forever, ruler of eternity and lifetime" on a stela found at Deir el-Medina.[12] And the Cyrus Cylinder, so named for the Persian king, refers to Marduk explicitly as the "king of the gods" and "the great lord."[13] The connection between kingship and the label "great" also appears in the Psalter. In Psalm 95:3 the poet declares that Yahweh is "the great God, the great King above all gods." The declaration that Yahweh is great in Psalm 145:3 complements the earlier confession that he is *the* King (v. 1a).

One generation commends your works to another. The confession that Yahweh is the "great God" is not a static confession locked into a moment in Israelite history; instead, the claim is one that transcends time as each generation confesses the works of Yahweh to the next. The vocabulary of praise referenced above spills over into verses 4–6 as each generation speaks, confesses, and proclaims what they know to be true of Yahweh. In these verses the psalmist uses four different words to convey the magnitude of Yahweh's greatness. In verse 4a he refers to the "works"

---

11. S. N. Kramer, trans., "Lipit-Ishtar Lawcode," in *Ancient Near Eastern Texts Relating to the Old Testament*, ed. James B. Pritchard, 3rd ed. with supplement (Princeton, NJ: Princeton University Press, 1969), 159.

12. Maciej M. Münnich, *The God Resheph in the Ancient Near East*, Orientalische Religionen in der Antike 11 (Tübingen: Mohr Siebeck, 2013), 83–84.

13. "The Cyrus Cylinder," in *The Persian Period: A Corpus of Sources from the Achaemenid Period*, ed. Amélie Kuhrt (London: Routledge, 2007), 71.

(*ma'aseh*) of Yahweh. *Ma'aseh* comes from the root *'sh*, "to make" or "to do," and often refers to acts of creation (cf. Ps 104:13, 24) but can also refer to God's creative power in delivering his people (Ps 66:3). The second word, "mighty acts," is the plural form of the noun *geburah*, a term used to refer to God's strength and power. His "mighty acts" are demonstrations of his power as the "great King." In Psalm 145:5b the psalmist refers to Yahweh's "wonderful works" (*nipla'ot*). While the term *nipla'ot* contributes to the larger thematic thread in verses 4–6 concerning the works of the Lord, the term appears elsewhere in the Old Testament with a specific reference to the exodus event (cf. Exod 3:20; 34:10; Pss 78:4; 105:5; 106:22; 136:4). In that moment of deliverance Yahweh indeed proved himself the great King, as expressed in the confession of the people in the Song of Moses (Exod 15:18). In Psalm 145:6a the community will tell of Yahweh's "awesome works." The Hebrew term is a *niphal* participle from the root *yr'*, "to fear." Thus Yahweh's "awesome" works are in fact those works that should inspire fear and awe in both the recipients and the beneficiaries of Yahweh's faithful acts (cf. 2 Sam 7:23).

Confession of Yahweh's Character (145:8–9)

FOLLOWING THE REHEARSAL OF GOD'S faithful action in behalf of Israel in verses 4–6, the psalmist returns to explicit statements concerning the character of God. In celebrating God's character, the poet references the "graciousness formula" of Exodus 34:6–7 in which Yahweh self-describes. Psalm 145:8 quotes the Exodus text nearly verbatim but with one notable change. The NIV translates the last phrase in verse 8b as "rich in love [*hesed*]." In the Exodus text the phrase is "abounding [*rab*] in love," but in Psalm 145 the poet has changed the phrase to read, literally, "great [*gadol*] in love [*hesed*]." The Hebrew word *hesed*, "love," is often translated as "steadfast love" or "covenant love" and has the sense of abiding commitment and loyalty. To say that Yahweh is "great in love" is to declare that he is "fiercely loyal" to his people. Thus, both Yahweh and his covenantal faithfulness (*hesed*) are "great [*gadol*]" (vv. 3a, 8b); they are marks of *the* King (v. 1a).

Interlude (145:10)

AS NOTED IN THE INTRODUCTION ABOVE, verses 1, 10, and 21 each contain the verb "bless" (*barak*) and facilitate the movement of the psalm. In verse 1 the psalmist pledges to "praise" (NIV) or "bless" Yahweh (v. 1b). In verse 10a the poet explains that all God's works will "praise" (*yadah*) him. The Hebrew term *yadah* can also be rendered "confess" or "make known" (cf. Pss 111; 118). While the difference between praise and confess may appear minimal, it proves instructive for understanding the interlude. The psalmist pauses to claim that all God's works "confess" who he is; they bear witness to his identity as the great King who is "gracious and compassionate, slow to anger," and "rich in love" (i.e., "great in covenantal faithfulness"). In verse 10b the psalmist shifts to declare that the faithful people of Yahweh will "extol" him. God bestows blessings upon his people, and his people in return speak well of God; they bless or praise God for the good he has brought to them.

In Praise of Yahweh's Kingdom (145:11–13)

WITHIN THIS SHORT SECTION of the psalm, the word *malkut* ("kingdom") appears four times, each time referencing Yahweh, the Divine King. In his outline of the psalm, Barnabas Lindars contends that these verses function as the center of an extended chiastic structure and together reinforce the psalm's primary theme.[14] In addition to the repetition of *malkut* in these lines, another structural device confirms the emphasis on kingship. Lindars, following the earlier suggestion of Watson, observes that the three Hebrew letters that begin each of these lines are *kaph*, *lamed*, and *mem*. Rearranged in reverse, the three letters *mem*, *lamed*, and *kaph* are the root letters for "king" (*melek*) and "kingdom" (*malkut*).[15] Some interpreters have attributed this occurrence to mere happenstance based on the order of the Hebrew alphabet itself; but given the heavy emphasis on *malkut* ("kingdom") in these three verses and the emphasis on kingship throughout the psalm, there seems to be more at work than coincidence.[16] Likely the arrangement reflects the artistic work of a skilled poet seeking to join form and meaning in order to reinforce a particular theme.

Characteristics of Yahweh's Just Rule (145:14–20)

IN THE FINAL STROPHE THE PSALMIST builds on the fourfold reference to Yahweh's kingdom in verses 11–13. In this lengthy strophe the psalmist confesses Yahweh's sovereign care over all creation (vv. 14–16), and in particular over those who call on him (vv. 18–20).

The LORD upholds all who fall. Yahweh's concern for the poor, marginalized, and oppressed appears throughout the Old Testament and

---

14. Barnabas Lindars, "The Structure of Ps CXLV," *VT* 29 (1989): 23–30.

15. Ibid., 29. Wilfred G. E. Watson, "Reversed Rootplay in Ps 145," *Bib* 62 (1981): 101–102.

16. Hossfeld and Zenger dismiss the suggestions of Lindars and Watson, as does Egbert Ballhorn. See Hossfeld and Zenger, *Psalms 3*, 594; Egbert Ballhorn, *Zum Telos des Psalters: Der Textzusammenhang des Vierten und Fünften Psalmenbuches (Ps 2)*, BBB 138 (Berlin: Philo, 2004), 286.

is clearly on display in the Psalter. God holds up those who are falling and "lifts up [*zaqap*] all who are bowed down [*kapap*]." The latter verb, *kapap*, "bowed down" or "discouraged," is a passive participle and implies that another person is causing the psalmist to be bowed down and discouraged; the psalmist is not just "down" but has been brought down by the activity of another. Thus, the psalmist confesses that Yahweh the King will act in their behalf. The reference to Yahweh's lifting up the poor appears elsewhere, in 1 Samuel 2:8 and Psalm 113:7, though these texts use a different verb from that in Psalm 145:14.

You open your hand. Verses 15–16 refer to God's sustaining care for his creation; "all" (*kol*) eyes look to God for their provision. The verb "look" is the Hebrew word *sabar*, which means "to wait for" or better yet, "to hope for." The verb suggests that all creation waits to see whether God will satisfy their needs, whether he will act beneficently toward a creation that stands in need. He will. As nearly identical to Psalm 104:27, Psalm 145:15b confesses that God gives food at the appropriate time, and rather than clenching his fist, Yahweh responds to his creation with an open hand (v. 16a). Yahweh's beneficence is neither ill-timed nor begrudgingly parceled out, but instead reflects his character—gracious, compassionate, and good (vv. 8–9a).

Both images, care for the poor and the sustaining of creation, reflect kingship motifs. The prologue to the Code of Hammurabi reflects this motif, as does the extended reflection on kingship in Psalm 72. Thus, the language in Psalm 145:14–16 portrays Yahweh as the model king. In addition to noting Yahweh's royal prerogatives toward creation, the psalmist also notes the nature of Yahweh's kingdom. The word "all" (*kol*) appears four times in the three verses (vv. 14a/b, 15a, 16b), thus reinforcing the scope of Yahweh's royal rule—he rules over "all."

The Lord is righteous in all his ways. Verses 14–16 noted the universal scope of Yahweh's concern as the Divine King, yet lest the community be concerned that Yahweh has reordered his commitments and lost sight of the Israelites, the psalmist confesses that Yahweh is "just" or "righteous" in his ways and "faithful" (*hasid*) in what he does. The latter word, *hasid*, might better be translated as "loyal"; Yahweh's action for all creation in no way undermines his loyalty to his people. Thus, with verses 17–20 "we move from universal providence to the dependable way in which the Lord meets the needs of his own people."[17] Although Yahweh is the Divine King who stands over "all" creation as provider and sustainer, his nearness

---

17. Davidson, *The Vitality of Worship*, 468.

is reserved for those who "show themselves loyal" to Yahweh (v. 18).[18] In verses 18–20 the people of God are described as those who call on him in truth, those who fear him, and those who love him. In accord with the confessions made in Psalm 121, Yahweh watches over his people, but the way of the wicked he will destroy (cf. Ps 1:6).

Postlude (145:21)

THE PSALM CONCLUDES BY REPEATING three words from verse 1: "praise" in verse 21a, and "name" and "praise" (*barak*, "to bless") in verse 21b. In verse 21 the psalmist expresses his desire for "every creature" (lit., "all flesh") to praise or bless God, thus bringing the psalm to a fitting conclusion. Psalm 145 opens with the psalmist's vow to bless (*barak*) God, moves to the declaration that the faithful people of God will bless (*barak* [v. 10]) him, and concludes with the desire that all creation bless (*barak*) God's holy name. From beginning to end Psalm 145 declares Yahweh's kingship and indicates that his kingship demands our response. Even as his kingdom is everlasting (v. 13), so too must our praise be "forever and ever" (v. 21c).

BOOK 5 OF THE PSALTER (Pss 107–45) was composed well after the exile and, in many ways, functioned as a response to the crises produced from that experience, crises that prompted questions that were both theological and anthropological—who is God and who are we? Although the collection opens with a remembrance of how God gathered his exiled people from all regions (Ps 107:3), that celebration is tempered by the reality the postexilic community experienced. While Yahweh led Israel out of Babylon, the world remained far from idyllic. Throughout the Psalter's Book 5, the psalmists lament the persistent threat of enemies. While the precise identity of these enemies proves challenging to determine, there are instances where it appears that the psalmists are referring to the powers that dot the political landscape around them (e.g., Pss 108; 124; 125; 129; 144). In the face of such challenges, however, the book of Psalms affirms the reign of God in the world. Yet to be clear, this struggle is not a struggle among equals. Israel's declaration sets Yahweh apart as the Divine King, the one who rules over all nations and all peoples. In Psalm 113 the poet announces that this God

---

18. Hossfeld and Zenger, *Psalms 3*, 600.

is exalted over all the nations,
    his glory above the heavens.
Who is like the LORD our God,
    the One who sits enthroned on high? (vv. 4–5)

Because Israel's God reigns, the nations tremble and the earth shakes (Ps 99:1); "the mountains melt like wax before the LORD . . . of all the earth" (Ps 97:5). Such language is not meant to be hyperbolic or escapist but instead truly confessional. The psalmists are keenly aware of the threats before them, but they make their confession in "My God the king," thus declaring that the Lord is near to all who call on him (145:18).

In the New Testament, the kingship of God is central to the preaching of Jesus. The phrase "kingdom of God" appears fifty-three times in the Gospels, and the synonymous phrase, "kingdom of heaven," another thirty-two times in Matthew. In the majority of instances it is Jesus who references the kingdom, but there are others who also declare the fullness of its arrival. In the opening chapter of Mark, for example, John the Baptist announces that "the kingdom of God has come near" (Mark 1:15). The description of the kingdom permeates the preaching of Jesus. Thus, through both parables and pronouncements, Jesus attempts to communicate to his disciples the reality of the kingdom and its nearness.[19]

Yet to speak of the kingdom of God (whether in the Old Testament or the New) is not to refer to a region or a domain, as though "kingdom" signaled a defined area, rather, "kingdom" refers to God's rule, to his power and authority over all creation.[20] To declare God as "King" (Ps 145:1) or to refer to his kingdom (v. 13; Mark 1:15) is to suggest that God's power and authority are being made manifest and that all other claims to authority are denuded. All those who call on him, fear him, and love him (Ps 145:18–19) will find their home in this kingdom, a kingdom ruled unlike any other. This psalm reminds us that we are invited "to live in the world of God's reign, the world where the fundamental reality and pervasive power is the gracious, compassionate and faithful love of God."[21] Knowledge of that truth should lead to unbridled praise of God.

---

19. In the prayer that Jesus taught the disciples to pray, the language of God's kingdom has much in common with the announcement in Ps 145. See the brief discussion in Goldingay, *Psalms 3*, 705.

20. Even in Ps 145:11 the connection between the "kingdom" and "might" is made evident.

21. McCann, "The Book of Psalms," 1261.

PSALM 145 IS A PRAISE PSALM. From beginning to end, from *aleph* to *taw*, the psalm calls us to praise God. Central to the praise of God is our capacity to bear witness to who God is, and central to understanding the identity of God is remembering his activity. Beginning in verse 4 of Psalm 145, the psalmist instructs those who pray to tell of God's mighty acts, to speak of his majesty, to meditate on his wonderful works, to tell of his awesome works, and to proclaim his great deeds. But to do all of those things requires *remembering*.

The psalmist explains that a people of praise are those who remember and tell, recall and proclaim. The majority of terms in verse 4–6 appear in the story related to Israel's deliverance from Egypt. These same terms are used repeatedly in other texts to point back to that moment in Israel's past. That moment was emblazoned in their collective mind as a perpetual remembrance of the God they serve: God the King, God the fiercely loyal one. That story and every story of deliverance since then was seared into their memory. To recall those stories was to proclaim God. To recall those stories was to be shaped as a people.

Most of us are controlled by the immediacy of the present. Our schedules are busy, life seems full, and we have little time to breathe, much less remember. But if we desire to live a life of praise in the presence of the Divine King, then remember we must. Our history, both our individual histories and our histories as communities of faith, are marked with moments that remind us that God is still at work. The psalmist calls us to the task of remembering those moments. We do so not to be nostalgic and "remember the good ol' days," or worse yet to wax on about returning to those days; rather we recall those moments so that we will remember the faithfulness of the God we serve as we lean into the future. We remember those moments so that we will be reminded of our hope. In our moments of weakness and powerlessness, fear and dread, when it seems as though the powers of the world hold sway, we remember and confess that God the King, the one enthroned over the heavens, has the power to act. And in our moments of brokenness and waywardness, apathy and disillusionment, when we are not sure who we are, the compassionate God who is fiercely loyal steps toward us in love. And in those moments our voices join with the voice of the psalmist in declaring, "the LORD is near."

Psalm 146

¹ Praise the LORD.

Praise the LORD, my soul.
² I will praise the LORD all my life;

I will sing praise to my God as long as I live.
³ Do not put your trust in princes,

in human beings, who cannot save.
⁴ When their spirit departs, they return to the ground;

on that very day their plans come to nothing.
⁵ Blessed are those whose help is the God of Jacob,

whose hope is in the LORD their God.
⁶ He is the Maker of heaven and earth,

the sea, and everything in them—

he remains faithful forever.
⁷ He upholds the cause of the oppressed

and gives food to the hungry.

The LORD sets prisoners free,
⁸ the LORD gives sight to the blind,

the LORD lifts up those who are bowed down,

the LORD loves the righteous.
⁹ The LORD watches over the foreigner

and sustains the fatherless and the widow,

but he frustrates the ways of the wicked.
¹⁰ The LORD reigns forever,

your God, O Zion, for all generations.

Praise the LORD.

Original Meaning

PSALM 146 IS THE FIRST of five psalms that comprise the concluding collection in the Psalter. The collection, often termed the "Final Hallel," consists of five hymns. Instead of being bound together by a superscription like the one used in the previous collection (i.e., "to David"), each psalm in the Final Hallel begins and ends with the phrase *halelu-yah*, "Praise the LORD." These ten occurrences of the expression suggest the "totality and perfection" of the praise of God exhibited in this hymnic collection.[1] That theme is reinforced and expanded in the final psalm.

---

1. Hossfeld and Zenger, *Psalms 3*, 605.

In Psalm 150 the verb *halal*, "to praise," occurs another ten times within the main body of the psalm, where the totality of praise is on display yet again.

In addition to the verbal and structural elements that bind this final collection together, these psalms share a common theological outlook. The psalmists repeatedly return to elements of creation theology, Zion theology, and the theology of the poor. By invoking themes associated with creation theology, the psalmists affirm that Yahweh not only created the world but also, as its maker (Ps 146:6), governs it and maintains its life-sustaining order (Pss 146:9; 147:8–9). The references to Zion theology invoke Yahweh's rightful position as the Divine King, "who is present in Zion/Jerusalem, who chooses and saves the poor of Israel as his people."[2] While each of the psalms in the Final Hallel differs in its emphasis on these three theological themes (i.e., creation theology, Zion theology, theology of the poor), together the poems create a unified collection that elicits the praise of the faithful.

The structure of Psalm 146 adopted here differs from that found in the NIV. The proposed structure highlights the rhetorical features of the psalm while also giving attention to the theological contours of the text.

Opening (vv. 1–2)
Wisdom theme (vv. 3–4)
The Divine King as Creator and Redeemer (vv. 5–9)
Conclusion (v. 10)

The core of the psalm (vv. 5–9) focuses on God's role as both Creator and Redeemer, themes that are in accord with the larger confession of Yahweh's kingship. This confession is preceded by a reflection on the powerlessness of human rulers. The psalm is bounded on both ends with an invocation to praise God.

Introductory Call to Praise the Lord (146:1–2)

PRAISE THE LORD. The psalm opens with an exhortation to "Praise the LORD" (*halelu-yah*) in verse 1a, an exhortation that repeats at the close of the psalm in verse 10c. The two together create an *inclusio* around the entire psalm, as is characteristic of all the psalms in the Final Hallel. In verse 1b the psalmist exhorts himself to praise God: "Praise the LORD, my soul." A variation of this call to praise appears in Psalms 103 and 104, both of which poems open and close with the call to "Praise the LORD, my soul." In these two earlier psalms the operative verb is *barak*, which can mean "to bless" and also "to praise." (See the discussion related to

---

2. Ibid. For explicit references to Yahweh as the Divine King, see Pss 146:10; 147:12; 149:2.

barak in the commentary on Ps 134.) In Psalm 146, however, the verb "to praise" is *halal*. The two earlier psalms focus on Yahweh's role as redeemer of the oppressed (Ps 103) and king of creation (Ps 104)—themes whose reappearance in Psalm 146 perhaps explains the intertextual reference.

I will sing praise to my God as long as I live. In verse 2a the psalmist vows to praise (*halal*) the Lord all his life, a vow reiterated in the parallel statement in verse 2b. In the latter line the psalmist promises to "sing praise" (*zamar*) as long as he lives. Elsewhere in the Psalter psalmists have equated the capacity to praise God with being alive. Conversely, being dead prevents one from singing the praises of God (cf. Pss 6:5; 30:9; 118:17). Simply put, to be alive is to sing the praises of God and to sing the praises of God constitutes what it means to be alive.

Wisdom Reflection on the Human Condition (146:3–4)

INDIRECTLY, PSALM 146:3–4 PROVIDES a rationale for the call to praise God in the first strophe. The psalmist emphasizes the ephemerality of humans and human power. Elsewhere in Book 5 of the Psalter (Pss 108:13–14; 116:10–11) the psalmists have acknowledged the inefficacy of human power against the enemy. For example, in Psalm 118 the poet implores the community in times of need to trust in Yahweh rather than "humans" (*'adam*) and "princes" (*nedibim*). Yet here in Psalm 146, rather than simply forbidding the people to trust in human leaders, the psalmist provides a rationale based on the ephemeral nature of "humans" (*'adam*) and "princes" (*nedibim*). Invoking language and imagery from Genesis 3, the psalmist explains in verse 4 that, upon death, the human (*'adam*) returns to the "ground," the *'adamah*. Whatever plans humans have made or power they have assumed (Ps 2:1–3) will come to naught.

The Divine King as Creator and Redeemer (146:5–9)

AFTER ACKNOWLEDGING THAT ALL HUMAN power is frail and ephemeral, the psalmist places the focus on Yahweh, the Divine King. Beginning with a beatitude (Ps 146:5), followed by nine participial phrases and two additional statements (v. 9b–c), the psalmist recounts the activity of this God who merits our praise.

Blessed are those whose help is the God of Jacob. The NIV places the beatitude as the final line in the previous strophe, but typically beatitudes "were the preferred form for introducing lessons about life, especially those that call for loyalty or obedience."[3] Consequently, the

---

3. Hossfeld and Zenger, *Psalms 3*, 613. This claim bears out in the New Testament as well. Note the collection of beatitudes that begin the Sermon on the Mount (Matt 5–7).

beatitude likely belongs with the following strophe. According to verse 5, the blessed person is the one whose "help is the God of Jacob." This title (*'el ya'akob*) alludes to the claims associated with Zion theology and reinforces the claim that Yahweh alone is King. In Psalm 46, for example, amid a world that appears to be overrun with chaos and warring nations, the psalmist confesses that "The LORD Almighty is with us; the God of Jacob is our fortress" (vv. 7, 11). Later in the same psalm Yahweh is celebrated as the one enthroned over all the earth (v. 10c). The use of this language is not limited to Psalm 46 alone but appears in other Psalms of Zion as well (e.g., Pss 76:6; 84:8; 132:5), thereby once more affirming the connection between this title and kingship language.

Maker of heaven and earth. This appellation appears four other times in the Psalter, all in Book 5 (Pss 115:15; 121:2; 124:8; 134:3), and nowhere else in the Old Testament. The participial form of the verb "to make" or "to do" (*'asah*) accents the idea of *creatio continuata*, suggesting that, as Creator, Yahweh remains fully attentive to the world he has made and continues to make as he both sustains and protects it.[4] In this iteration of the title in Psalm 146, the psalmist has expanded the phrase also to include "the sea [*yam*], and everything in them." Metaphorically, the sea (*yam*) can represent the chaotic forces that seek to assail the orderly creation of God (cf. Ps 65:7), but in this instance its inclusion likely refers to the three-tiered understanding of the cosmos: heaven-earth-waters.[5] The God of Jacob is able to provide help (Ps 146:5a) because he is the Creator and Sustainer of all creation.

The final line in verse 6 connects the claims in verse 6a–b with what follows in verses 7–9. The psalmist confesses that Yahweh "remains faithful [*'emet*] forever," or more literally, "he is the one who keeps [*hashshomer*] faith forever." Israel's God does not remain aloof from the created order but instead "keeps faith" by remaining committed to that which he has created (cf. Ps 117:2). The subsequent participial phrases (Ps 146:7–9a) provide demonstrable evidence of Yahweh's faithfulness (*'emet*).

He upholds the cause of the oppressed. Verse 7a is a truncated form of the confession made in verse 6 of Psalm 103, a psalm that also references the kingship of Yahweh (v. 19). With its reference to Israel's deliverance out of Egypt (vv. 7), the psalm explicitly identifies the oppressed with the nation of Israel. Beyond Psalm 103 there are other examples in which the passive participle *'ashuqim* ("oppressed") also refers

---

4. Ibid., 323.

5. On the triadic vision of the created order in the ancient Near East see Keel, *The Symbolism of the Biblical World*, 35–47.

to the nation of Israel (e.g., Deut 28:29, 33; Jer 50:33).[6] In Psalm 146:7 the psalmist affirms that the Divine King, out of his faithfulness (*'emet* [v. 6c]), will execute justice for his people. Admittedly, this statement seems to break with the confession made in the previous psalm. In Psalm 145:14–16 the poet appeared to acknowledge God's care for all people, as well as God's concern for Israel specifically (vv. 17–20). To remedy this apparent tension, Hossfeld and Zenger aver that the entirety of the Final Hallel functions at the "universal, world-political" level.[7] While this view may be theologically appealing, a closer reading of Psalm 146 does not support such a claim. In the Final Hallel the language associated with the theology of the poor is applied specifically to Israel (Pss 146:7–9; 147:2–3, 12–14; 149:4). Yahweh's faithfulness as Divine King to his people dominates the final five psalms.[8]

Verses 7c–8b allude to God's redemptive work of delivering those enslaved and in captivity. As similarly in the previous line, and contrary to the position of some interpreters, Israel seems to be in view rather than the enslaved writ large. Use of this imagery elsewhere in the Old Testament supports a more narrowly defined group (i.e., Israel). The language in Psalm 146 parallels that of Isaiah 49:9 and 61:1, two texts that refer specifically to God's work of bringing his people out of Babylonian captivity and providing sight to the blind. The latter act refers not to healing *per se* but to freeing those once in darkness so that they might see light again.[9] There are other instances of Yahweh's "opening" the eyes of the blind in Isaiah, and each occurrence also has Israel in view (Isa 35:5; 42:7, 17; 43:8).

The LORD loves the righteous. The reference to the "righteous" in Psalm 146:8c may appear misplaced. Prior to this line the psalmist refers to the poor, and then, following the mention of the righteous, the psalmist names individuals and categories that comprise the larger "poor" word field (i.e., foreigner, widow, orphan).[10] The label "righteous" may seem to have little in common with the other descriptive phrase, yet throughout the

---

6. Norbert Lohfink, *Lobgesänge der Armen: Studien zum Magnifikat, den Hodajot von Qumran und einigen späten Psalmen*, SBS 143 (Stuttgart: Katholisches Bibelwerk, 1990), 112.

7. Hossfeld and Zenger, *Psalms 3*, 614.

8. Donatella Scaioloa, "The End of the Psalter," in *The Composition of the Book of Psalms*, BETL 238, ed. Erich Zenger (Leuven: Peeters, 2010), 701–10. Scaioloa explains that at the end of the Psalter is "a people, an assembly of faithful which we see as an alternative community amongst other nations" (p. 707).

9. Goldingay, *Psalms 3*, 712.

10. On the various terms that comprise the "poor" word field, see Tucker, "A Polysemiotic Approach to the Poor in the Psalms," 425–39.

Psalter the righteous ones are in fact those who "are constantly besieged, assaulted and oppressed"; their lives in fact do resemble the lives of the poor and needy.[11]

The use of the word "righteous" (*tsaddiq*) in verse 8c stands in contrast to the "wicked" (*resha'im*) in verse 9c. Based on the two terms "righteous" and "wicked," John Kselman argues that verses 8c–9c actually represent a separate strophe that has much in common with the wisdom tradition.[12] Admittedly, the righteous and the wicked frequently stand in comparison in the book of Proverbs (e.g., Prov 10:3, 6, 7, 30; 11:8, 10, 18), but the structure of Psalm 146 appears to argue against the notion of a separate strophe, since it would disrupt the flow of thought in the psalm. In Psalm 146:6 the psalmist announces that God is the Maker of heaven and earth and then proceeds to describe how God enacts his divine reign. If we understand the "righteous" as part of the "poor" word field, as explained above, then verses 7–9b celebrate the Divine King's proclivity for delivering the poor. The final line, verse 9c, references the destruction of the wicked (cf. Ps 1:6), thereby providing further evidence of God's power and authority as the Divine King.[13] As such, Yahweh enacts his rule, which involves delivering the weak and needy while decimating the wicked (cf. 2 Sam 2:3–8b).

Conclusion (146:10)

THE FINAL LINE OF PSALM 146 STANDS in contradistinction to the statement made in verse 4 concerning human power (i.e., human kings die and their plans come to naught). By comparison, the psalmist confesses that Yahweh reigns forever, a likely allusion to the confession made in Exodus 15:18.[14] The hope for all generations in Zion rests fully with the Divine King, the one who demonstrated his dominion over human power in the exodus and stands poised to do so once more (v. 10b).

The psalm concludes as it began, with the confession, "Praise the LORD" (*halelu-yah*).

---

11. McCann, "The Book of Psalms," 1264.

12. Kselman, "Psalm 146," 591. He mirrors the language in verses 8c–9c with that of verses 3–4 and argues that both strophes reflect the language and thought of the wisdom tradition. While verses 3–4 appear to function as an independent strophe rooted in wisdom themes, the same cannot be said of verses 8c–9c. Although the psalmist does use the word pair "righteous" (*tsaddiq*) and "wicked" (*resha'im*) in verses 8c–9c, the comparison appears "interrupted" by a reference to the foreigner, widow, and orphan, thus making the comparison strained.

13. Lohfink, *Lobgesänge der Armen*, 113–14.

14. This claim is not limited to Exod 15. See also Pss 29:10; 96:10; 97:1.

Bridging Contexts

AS THE FIRST PSALM in the fivefold conclusion to the Psalter (Pss 146–50), this psalm connects the Final Hallel with earlier confessions in the book of Psalms. These connections highlight a number of important theological strands present in the Psalter.

Divine kingship. Psalm 146 extends the hymnic imagery from Psalm 145 and celebrates the royal rule of Yahweh. Psalm 145 opened with the declaration that Yahweh is "the King" (v. 1), and the final verse of Psalm 146 affirms that "The LORD reigns forever." In addition, both psalms celebrate the enduring nature of God's rule (Pss 145:1, 13; 146:10). Both psalms celebrate the work of the Divine King, a work that both sustains creation and redeems the poor and oppressed (Pss 145:14–16; 146:6–9).

Divine power. In addition to its connection with Psalm 145, Psalm 146 invokes another theme from Book 5 of the Psalter—a theme related to the kingship of Yahweh. The psalmist confesses that Yahweh is the "Maker of heaven and earth," a claim meant to highlight the sovereignty of Yahweh over all creation. Because he is indeed the "Maker of heaven and earth," Yahweh's power and authority not only subvert but also dwarf any human claims to the same. Human power is derided (v. 3) as ineffective and ephemeral, thus offering no hope for those seeking deliverance. That hope rests with the God of Jacob (v. 5) alone.

Human life and divine rule. In addition to its linguistic and thematic connections to Book 5, Psalm 146 also recalls the language and imagery present in the Psalter's two introductory psalms.[15] Psalm 1 opens with a reference to the blessed person, defined as the one whose life is oriented toward God. In similar fashion, the blessed person in Psalm 146 orients his life toward God by acknowledging Yahweh as his only help and hope. Beyond its connection with Psalm 1, Psalm 146 also shares a thematic link with Psalm 2 in that both poems attend to the question of human power. Although the kings of the earth may rise up against Yahweh and his anointed (Ps 2:2), these kings will be terrified by God's wrath and utterly routed by his power (2:12). While the rulers ("princes") in Psalm 146:3 do not pose the same threat as those in Psalm 2:2, they prove equally impotent in light of the Divine King.

The righteous. Psalm 146:8c mentions that Yahweh "loves" the righteous. Generally speaking, the righteous are "those who have a right relationship with God and whose relationships with other people are governed by God's expectations for human community."[16] The description of

---

15. McCann, "The Book of Psalms," 1264.
16. Jerome Creach, *The Destiny of the Righteous in the Psalms* (St. Louis: Chalice, 2008), 3.

---

the righteous is quite often expanded in the Psalter to include the poor, the oppressed, and the needy. In fact, in many texts the righteous are assumed to *be* the poor and needy. This situation is particularly true in Book 1 of the Psalter (e.g., Pss 5:12; 11:3; 14:5; 15:2). In Psalm 146 the "righteous" are mentioned in a rather lengthy list of those deemed destitute and poor: the oppressed, the hungry, the prisoner, the "blind," those bowed down, the foreigner, the orphan, and the widow. Clearly the writer of Psalm 146 understands the righteous as part of that larger class of individuals, and because they lack the power to redeem themselves, they must depend fully upon the Divine King. As Clint McCann argues, "by determining the 'righteous' as being oppressed and hungry, and impoverished and so on (vv. 7–9), Psalm 146 conveys the eschatological perspective of the Psalter: God's reign is proclaimed amid circumstances that seem to deny it."[17]

THE FOURTH STANZA of the hymn "O Worship the King, All Glorious Above" reads,

> Frail children of dust and feeble as frail
> In Thee do we trust, nor find Thee to fail;
> Thy mercies how tender, how firm to the end,
> Our maker, defender, redeemer and friend.[18]

The words of this hymn echo the theological confessions expressed in Psalm 146. The psalmist associates himself with those are who down and out, weak and weary, poor and impoverished. The psalmist reminds those of us in such circumstances that our only hope, our only help, is the God of Jacob (v. 5). We cannot save ourselves. There is no room for self-aggrandizement, much less self-delusion. We are all frail children of dust, and lest we look to those around us who feign power to save us, we are reminded that they too will "return to the ground" (v. 4a). Such a bleak outlook could lead us to a growing sense of despondency and despair, yet the psalmist declares, "I will praise the LORD all my life." Despite the conditions that surround us and at times overwhelm us, we can spend our life singing praises because "he remains faithful forever" (v. 6c), he is "firm to the end," as Robert Grant asserts in his hymn. God indeed is our maker and defender, redeemer and friend, because he is the God who reigns forever.

---

17. McCann, "The Book of Psalms," 1264.
18. Robert Grant, "O Worship the King, All Glorious Above," 1833.

Psalm 147

¹ Praise the LORD.

How good it is to sing praises to our God,
how pleasant and fitting to praise him!

² The LORD builds up Jerusalem;
he gathers the exiles of Israel.

³ He heals the brokenhearted
and binds up their wounds.

⁴ He determines the number of the stars
and calls them each by name.

⁵ Great is our Lord and mighty in power;
his understanding has no limit.

⁶ The LORD sustains the humble
but casts the wicked to the ground.

⁷ Sing to the LORD with grateful praise;
make music to our God on the harp.

⁸ He covers the sky with clouds;
he supplies the earth with rain
and makes grass grow on the hills.

⁹ He provides food for the cattle
and for the young ravens when they call.

¹⁰ His pleasure is not in the strength of the horse,
nor his delight in the legs of the warrior;

¹¹ the LORD delights in those who fear him,
who put their hope in his unfailing love.

¹² Extol the LORD, Jerusalem;
praise your God, Zion.

¹³ He strengthens the bars of your gates
and blesses your people within you.

¹⁴ He grants peace to your borders
and satisfies you with the finest of wheat.

¹⁵ He sends his command to the earth;
his word runs swiftly.

¹⁶ He spreads the snow like wool
and scatters the frost like ashes.

¹⁷ He hurls down his hail like pebbles.
Who can withstand his icy blast?

¹⁸ He sends his word and melts them;

he stirs up his breezes, and the waters flow.
¹⁹ He has revealed his word to Jacob,
his laws and decrees to Israel.
²⁰ He has done this for no other nation;
they do not know his laws.
Praise the LORD.

PSALM 147 IS THE SECOND of five psalms that comprise the concluding collection in the Psalter. The collection, often termed the "Final Hallel," consists of five hymns. Instead of being bound together by a superscription like the one used in the previous collection (i.e., "to David"), each psalm in the Final Hallel begins and ends with the phrase *halelu yah*, "Praise the LORD." These ten occurrences of the term suggest the "totality and perfection" of the praise of God exhibited in this hymnic collection.[1]

Despite the arrangement proposed in the NIV's translation, this communal hymn may be divided into three strophes. Each strophe (vv. 1–6, 7–11, 12–20) opens with a call to praise Yahweh: "Praise the LORD" (v. 1); "Sing to the LORD" (v. 7); "Extol the LORD" (v. 12). Each hymnic exhortation is then followed by a series of predicates, or descriptive phrases, which serve to justify the preceding call to praise. In the first two strophes (vv. 1–6, 7–11) these descriptive phrases derive from claims associated with creation theology and the theology of the poor, as well as from a theological reflection on Israel's history (v. 2). Although creation imagery is present in the third strophe (vv. 13–18), the emphasis in this strophe is on the "word" of Yahweh (vv. 15, 18–20). In many ways this final strophe shows much in common with the theology present in the book of Nehemiah: the restoration of Jerusalem followed by the promulgation and proclamation of the Torah.

Given the shift in theological emphases between the first two strophes and the third strophe, scholars have suggested that Psalm 147 may consist in two originally separate psalms. Supporting evidence for this claim can be found in the Septuagint. In its Greek translation of the Psalter, Psalm 147 is divided to form two separate psalms comprised of verses 1–11 and verses 12–20. The first verse of each psalm in the Greek (vv. 1, 12) contains the world *Allelouia*, followed by a reference to Haggai and Zechariah

1. Hossfeld and Zenger, *Psalms 3*, 605.

(a feature not found at all in the Hebrew text). The reference to the two prophets suggests that the compilers understood these texts in the light of the events associated with the postexilic period. Although the two halves may have circulated independently at some point in their history, in their present context they should be read as a diptych or double hymn.[2] The two alleged psalms are now bound together by their reference to Jerusalem in verses 2 and 12, as well as by the reference to Israel in verses 2 and 19. If indeed Psalm 147 was originally two separate psalms, in their present context these poems create a rather coherent narrative from beginning to end. After the initial call to praise, the psalm begins by referencing the reconstruction of Jerusalem and the return of the exiles (v. 2), followed by Yahweh's care and concern for the brokenhearted and wounded (vv. 3, 6). The poem celebrates Yahweh's fortification of Jerusalem (v. 13a), followed by his blessings of provision and prosperity (vv. 13b–14). The psalm concludes by noting the provision of God's law (vv. 19–20). Interspersed in the movement of this psalm are references to Yahweh's creative power (vv. 4–5, 8–9, 16–18)—the power and might that make all else in the psalm possible.

Praise the God Who Cares for His People (147:1–6)

FOLLOWING THE INITIAL CALL to praise God (v. 1a), in verse 1b the psalmist provides an initial justification (or what Goldingay terms "an interim rationale") for doing so prior to offering a more comprehensive rationale in verses 2–6.

Praise the LORD. The psalm opens with an exhortation to "Praise the LORD" (*halelu yah*) in verse 1a, an exhortation that repeats at the close of the psalm in verse 20c. The two together create an *inclusio* around the entire psalm, as is characteristic of all the psalms in the Final Hallel. The rationale provided in verse 1b/c contains two parallel lines that are identically structured. Each line includes a particle *ki* ("for" or "because") followed by an adjective, an infinitive, and an object. The NIV understands the particle *ki* as having an asserverative function, i.e., the particle serves to emphasize the claim found in the clause it modifies (i.e., "How good"). While this understanding is certainly defensible, one could also understand the particle to serve a causal function with the meaning "because." The comments in verses 1b–c provide the rationale; they explain why the people should "Praise the LORD."

The LORD builds up Jerusalem. Verses 2–3 introduce two images, those of builder and shepherd. In verse 2a Yahweh "builds up" the city.

---

2. Ibid., 622.

The references to the reconstruction of the city have led Hans-Joachim Kraus, among others, to suggest that Psalm 147 originated after the completion of the city walls during the time of Nehemiah (Neh 12:27).[3] The verb "to build" (*banah*) appears as a participle, thus suggesting the ongoing work of reconstruction and restoration. The reference to strengthening the gate (Ps 147:13a) further supports Kraus' claim. While dating the psalms with any precision remains a tenuous task, at minimum one can conclude that Psalm 147, as presently arranged, likely reflects the social, historical, and theological crises associated with the events of the fifth century.

In addition to his ongoing work of building up the city, Yahweh is to be praised for gathering up the exiles of Israel. The Hebrew does not use the traditional word for "exiles" but instead the word *nidhe*, a *niphal* participle from the verbal root *ndh*, meaning "scattered." In Ezekiel 34:12–13 Yahweh promises that like a shepherd he will gather his scattered flock, and in verse 16 the same root (*ndh*) appears in reference to the scattered sheep. The two texts (Ps 147 and Ezek 34) provide a striking image of Yahweh as the Great Shepherd of his people.

He heals the brokenhearted. The Great Shepherd does more than simply bring back the scattered—he also heals the brokenhearted and the wounded. Similar language occurs in Ezekiel 34:16 and Isaiah 61:2, and in both texts the images refer to the people of Israel who have endured much as a result of the exile and its aftermath. The language in Psalm 147:2–3, which is similar to other postexilic writings, suggests the community perceived that the exile had not yet ended, or at a minimum that the effects of the exile still cast a long shadow on the community.

He determines the number of the stars. The psalmist appears to make a rather abrupt shift in verses 4–5 by moving from the language of deliverance to that of creation. The poet declares that Yahweh determines the number of the stars and then names them—a clear reference to the confession in Isaiah 40:26 (Yahweh "brings out the starry host one by one and calls forth each of them by name"). The act of naming the stars indicates Yahweh's dominion over them and once more highlights his sovereign power over all the elements of creation.

Great is our LORD and mighty in power. Psalm 147:4 illustrates Yahweh's power through an image rooted in creation; verse 5, however, celebrates his power through explicit confession. The confession in verse 5 echoes the confession made earlier in Psalm 145:3. To declare Yahweh as "great" is to do far more than make a subjective assessment about the

3. Kraus, *Psalms 60–150*, 556.

nature of God. In the ancient Near East, the label "great" was applied to deities in combination with their role as kings (for examples, see comments on Ps 145). This connection between the label "great" and kingship can also be found in other texts in the Psalter (e.g., Ps 95:3). Thus, the Divine King, Yahweh, is "great" and stands over all creation (Ps 147:4). The magnitude of his power in these arenas of creation justifies Israel's hope (vv. 2–3) for his salvific work within their own community.

The Lord sustains the humble. The psalmist employs the same form of the verb used in Psalm 146:9, "to sustain" (the *polel* form of *'wd* I). The verb means more precisely "to help up" or "to support," a nuance that better aligns with the image of the brokenhearted and wounded in Psalm 147:2. The noun "humble" often has a "religious" connotation, hence the NIV's translation; yet the word belongs to the larger word field associated with the poor and can refer to those suffering under social, economic, and political duress as well.[4] The latter seems to fit better the context of the psalm. Rather than being "sustained," those who have been scattered need to be lifted up. This image stands in contrast to the fate of the wicked in verse 6b, whom Yahweh "casts . . . to the ground."

Praise the God Who Sustains the World (147:7–11)

SIMILAR TO FIRST STROPHE, the second strophe opens with a call for the community to praise Yahweh with both voice and lyre. In particular, the community is invited to sing in a spirit of thanksgiving (*todah*). The remaining verses in the strophe identify the things for which they have reason to give thanks.

He supplies the earth. The first strophe alluded to Yahweh's kingship by employing several images; this theme is continued in the second strophe with an emphasis on Yahweh as the "beneficent world king."[5] Verses 8–9 allude to the imagery found in Psalm 104:13–14, that of Yahweh's providing food for his creation—a theme that receives extended treatment in Psalm 104. The sequence of events is quite logically constructed: Yahweh establishes the clouds, which produce the rain, which nourishes the earth and thereby produces the grass, which provides the food for the cattle and ravens. The reference to ravens seems unusual, particularly given that ravens are identified elsewhere in the Old Testament as unclean and consequently of little worth (Lev 11:15; Deut 14:14). Hossfeld and Zenger, following the work of Siegfried Risse, suggest that perhaps the

---

4. On the "poor" word field, see Tucker, "A Polysemiotic Approach to the Poor in the Psalms," 425–39.

5. Hossfeld and Zenger, *Psalms 3*, 625.

---

ravens functioned "as an outstanding example of YHWH's generous and compassionate care."[6] Even as God cares for the unclean and lowly raven, Yahweh will lift up the poor of his people and provide for them.

His delight is not in the legs of the warrior. As similarly in strophe 1, the imagery in strophe 2 switches unexpectedly. The psalmist shifts from picturing the Divine Provider (vv. 8–9) to picturing the Divine Protector (vv. 10–11). In the previous psalm (Ps 146) the poet referred specifically to human leaders with power (i.e., "princes"), but in Psalm 147 the language is more opaque in referring only to horses and the legs of warriors.[7] Although such images of warring steeds and armored foot soldiers can be found in Assyrian reliefs, the Persians were also well known for their use of horsemen and footsoldiers to quell uprisings and expand their territorial holdings.[8] At one point Artaxerxes II employed 20,000 horses with riders and another 100,000 footsoldiers of Persian nationality, along with tens of thousands of Greek mercenaries, in an effort to put down a potential threat. With the language in Psalm 147:10 the psalmist conjures up impressive, if not terrorizing, images of imperial war machines that would have been familiar to those living in Jerusalem and the surrounding area during this period under Persian rule.

Despite the impressive power associated with such military might, the psalmist confesses that Israel's God takes no delight in such matters. Yahweh the "Great" God (v. 5) does not choose his people based on *their* demonstrable power but instead on their willingness to trust in his. He delights not in those who masquerade as powerful but in those who know well where true power lies—he delights in those who "fear him" and hope in his "unfailing love" (*hesed*).

Praise the God Who Gives His Word (147:12–20)

IN SIMILAR FASHION TO THE TWO previous strophes, the final strophe opens with a call for the community to praise Yahweh, followed by a lengthy justification for this call. Unlike the two previous strophes, this strophe is directed at Jerusalem and Zion (v. 12), thus explaining the rationale offered in verses 13–14 (see below). The remainder of the strophe focuses on the "word" of God.

He strengthens the bars of your gates. In verses 13–14 the psalmist identifies four ways in which Yahweh demonstrates his concern for

---

6. Ibid.

7. Othmar Keel notes that admiration for the horse "was based primarily on its military capabilities" (Keel, *The Symbolism of the Biblical World*, 239).

8. Pierre Briant, *From Cyrus to Alexander: A History of the Persian Empire* (Winona Lake, IN: Eisenbrauns, 2002), 796–97.

Jerusalem: strengthening the city's defenses ("gates"); blessing its citizens; establishing peace in the land; and providing ample food. At their most basic level these actions suggest that the distress and anguish associated with the exile is coming to a close, that Yahweh is working to restore his city and bless his people. At another level, however, the language of these verses recalls the poetic language and imagery found in Isaiah 54. There Yahweh promises that Zion would once more become a place where his people would gather (v. 7), but even more, it would be a city rebuilt "with precious stones" (v. 12c) and "sparkling jewels" (v. 12b). Zion would become a place marked by peace (v. 13b) and fully protected by Yahweh (v. 14). In Psalm 147 the psalmist comments on the events of his day, including the gradual restoration of Jerusalem, but he understands those events in light of what God had promised earlier in Isaiah 54. While the language in Psalm 147:13–14 celebrates restoration as a gift from God, it also serves as a reminder of God's faithfulness to his earlier word.

His word runs swiftly. Just as the restoration of Jerusalem revealed the power of God's word, so too do the meteorological phenomena observed by all people. The psalmist likely had in mind Psalm 33, another psalm that celebrates the creative power of God's word. By his "word" (*dabar*) the heavens and the "starry host" were made; he spoke and "it came to be" (v. 6). Only this God, the one who stands above the heavens as the Divine King, can speak a world into being. In Psalm 147:15–18 the psalmist refers to God's word three times. God sends his "command" (*'imrah*) to the earth, where his "word" (*dabar*) runs swiftly. The same term, "word" (*dabar*), appears once more in verse 18a: "he sends his word [*dabar*] and melts them." A final reference to God's "word" appears in the second line of verse 18: "he stirs up his breezes, and the waters flow." Rendered more literally, verse 18b reads, "he blows his breath [*ruah*], the waters flow." In Psalm 33:6 the psalmist declares that the starry host was made by the "breath [*ruah*] of his mouth," so suggesting that as God spoke, creation came into being (cf. Gen 1). Although the psalmist omits from Psalm 147:18b the reference to "his mouth," the use of the word *ruah* in that line points back to Psalm 33 and was likely intended as a double entrendre. The frozen precipitation melts due to the winds that blow over them, but even those "winds" must be correctly understood as the breath (*ruah*) that blows from the mouth of God as he speaks. Snow, frost, and hail serve as visual and vivid reminders that God's rule remains active and present in the world.

He has revealed his word. The final two lines of Psalm 147 shift the focus from the role of God's word in ordering the world (vv. 15–18) to the role of God's word in governing his people (vv. 19–20). In addition to "word" (*dabar*), the psalmist also refers to the "laws" (*hoq*) and "decrees" (*mishpatim*) in this section; all three terms function as synonyms for *torah* in Psalm 119 (cf. Ps 119:5–8, 9). Although they were scattered exiles (Ps 147:2b) who were wounded, broken, and poor (vv. 3, 6), their world is not *dis*ordered. To the contrary, the psalmist reminds them, God has given his "word" (*dabar*) to Israel, and it is that word which will order their lives. Even as God's word orders the meteorological phenomena around them, so God's "laws" (*hoq*) and "decrees" (*mishpatim*) structure their world. More than simply reminding Israel of her covenantal obligations, God's "word" (*dabar*) reminds them of the one with whom they are in covenant, namely, the Divine King.[9]

HUMAN POWER DOES NOT IMPRESS GOD. The second strophe concludes with a comment related to human power (vv. 10–11). The psalmist confesses that Yahweh is the one who names the stars (v. 4) and overseas the phenomena of creation (vv. 8–9, 15–18); he is the one who stands over all creation as the Divine King. Given his status as all-powerful, one might assume that Yahweh seeks followers who exhibit a similar characteristic and, in some way, reflect that type of dominant power. Yet Yahweh explicitly rejects power for power's sake. The "strength of the horse" and the legs of the mighty do little to impress Yahweh. To the contrary, Yahweh has chosen the humble and poor (v. 6), the brokenhearted and wounded. He has chosen those who fear him and place their hope in him, not themselves.

God's choice of the humble and poor is not limited to the Old Testament. In Matthew 11 Jesus explains to the disciples that God has hidden things from the "wise and learned" and instead revealed them to the "little children." In referring to the "little children," Jesus uses the Greek word *nēpios*, which often refers to infants (Matt 11:25). In the ancient Greco-Roman world, infants were considered expendable and of little worth, while the most valued people were the wise and the learned—those with power. Jesus declares that God did not choose the wise and learned to accomplish his work in the world but instead chose those of seemingly little worth, yet in that choice the nature of God is revealed.

Paul also knew something of this counter-cultural surprise. In his first letter to the church at Corinth he declared, "For the message of the cross

---

9. John Goldingay argues similarly by suggesting that "laws" (*hoq*) and "decrees" (*mishpatim*) are a "reference to Yhwh's own acts rather than acts Yhwh expects of the people. The laws are decrees about what should happen to Israel (Ps 2:7; Mic 7:11; Zeph 2:2)." See *Psalms 3*, 725.

is foolishness to those who are perishing, but to us who are being saved it is the power of God" (1 Cor 1:18). Later in that same chapter (vv. 26–28a) Paul says to the church,

> Brothers and sisters, think of what you were when you were called. Not many of you were wise by human standards; not many were influential; not many were of noble birth. But God chose the foolish things of the world to shame the wise; God chose the weak things of the world to shame the strong. God chose the lowly things of this world.

Although not a formal "hymn of praise," Paul's words echo such a sentiment. God is to be praised because his logic runs counter to that of the world. God in his power chose that which is weak to proclaim Christ crucified, "a stumbling block" to some, but testimony of the very power and wisdom of God (vv. 23–24).

God's power in the world. Psalm 147 weaves together three prominent themes in Israel's theological confession: God's power in creation, God's power in deliverance, and God's power through his word. Other psalms give considerable attention to God's work in creation (e.g., Pss 19; 104), and others still to his power to deliver in Israel's history (e.g., Pss 107; 135–36); frequently, these two themes are wedded. God delivers because he is the "Maker of heaven and earth," and because he stands over all creation as its maker, he intervenes in history to deliver his people. To these two themes Psalm 147 adds a third—Yahweh's word.

In the postexilic period Israel likely pondered God's presence in the world and, much more, his governance of the same. The events of the exile and the subsequent restoration likely called into question much of what Israel had confessed regarding God's sovereignty over the world. In response, the postexilic community sought to reaffirm the power of God by declaring him the "the God of heaven" (cf. Ps 115), the one who stands over all creation. Yet in doing so they also ran the risk of declaring Yahweh an absentee potentate who was only marginally, if at all, interactive with his creation and his people. Psalm 147 silences this concern by declaring that God remains intimately involved in the world via his word. God's word orders all creation (vv. 8–9, 15–18), but even more, his word shapes his people (vv. 19–20).

These three themes—God's power in creation, God's power in deliverance, and God's power through his word—find their counterpart in the New Testament. In the prologue to the Gospel of John, creation, deliverance, and the word are intermingled anew, thereby declaring God's power and, even more, reinforcing God's redemptive activity both in the world and in its behalf. In his classic work *Evangelical Theology: An Introduction*, Karl Barth writes of God,

> He exists neither *next* to man nor merely *above* him, but rather *with* him, *by* him, and most important of all, *for* him. He is *man's* God not only as Lord, but also has father, brother, friend and this relationship implies neither diminution nor in any way a denial, but instead confirmation and display of his divine essence. "I dwell in the high and holy place, and also with him who is of a contrite and humble spirit . . ." (Isa 57:15). This he does in the history of his deeds. A God who confronted man simply as exalted, distant and strange, that is, a divinity without humanity, could only be the God of *dysangelion*, of "bad news," instead of "good news."[10]

The Gospel of John explains that "in the beginning was the Word" and that, through the Word, "all things were made" (John 1:3). But the Word did not remain "exalted, distant and strange"; instead, "the Word became flesh and made his dwelling among us" (v. 14). This is the God of *euangelion*, the God of good news.

IN COMMENTING ON THE Final Hallel (Pss 146–50), Eugene Peterson declares that these psalms "put all the acts of God's salvation and deliverance, his creation and providence on display and festoon them with hallelujah garlands."[11] Psalm 147 invites us to pause and think deeply on these matters—God's salvation, his deliverance, his creation, and his providence. Because these labels capture so well the warp and woof of God's ways in and with the world, nearly the entire biblical story falls under one or more of these headings. And this observation is no less true of Psalm 147, even as the psalmist narrows the parameters of his reflection by pausing to consider God's warp and woof in the light of the postexilic experience. The psalmist declares God's power by detailing moments and places in time when and where that power has been or is being manifested, whether at creation (v. 4), in creation (vv. 8–9), or among God's people (vv. 2–3). Yet God's exhibitions of power are far more than a divine "flexing of the muscles" meant to cause his creation to cower in

---

10. Karl Barth, *Evangelical Theology: An Introduction*, trans. Grover Foley (Grand Rapids: Eerdmans, 1963), 11.

11. Eugene Peterson, *Answering God: The Psalms as Tools for Prayer* (New York: Harper-Collins, 1989), 127.

fear; to the contrary, these acts are a form of *euangelion*, of good news. God's power always leans toward the restoring, sustaining, and shaping of his creation.

The psalm was likely written and, likelier still, to have been read in a time when restoration seemed all but impossible, yet the psalmist confesses that nothing is impossible with God (Jer 32:27; Luke 1:37). Jerusalem was being rebuilt, the city gate being strengthened, and the land returning to its fecundity. And the exiles who returned, those who were brokenhearted and wounded—they too would experience the restorative work of God in their lives; through his power he would bind them up and sustain them. Yet this restorative work of God among his people is always heard alongside God's sustaining work in creation. God provides the rain that waters the earth that feeds the animals, and God guides the meteorological events in nature, yet all without fanfare and with little notice. James Mays suggests that these confessions of God's care for his people and the world appear to create an "indiscriminate montage," but in fact, together, they are much more.[12] Although they seem only tangentially related, they are in reality inextricably linked. The God who cares for creation is the same God who binds up the wounded and rebuilds the city. And the God who faithfully sends his word (Ps 147:15b) so that nature might fulfill its God-appointed task is the God who sends his word so that his people might also fulfill their role as God's covenantal partner: "He has done this for no other nation" (v. 20a).

The God who sends his word to order and sustain creation is the God who continues to come to us in his word, and in the Word, so that we too might be ordered and sustained by the very power of God that is at work in the world. Because he continues to come to us, because he continues to sustain us, and because he continues to shape us, we are invited to praise the Lord.

12. Mays, *Psalms*, 442.

Psalm 148

¹ Praise the LORD.

Praise the LORD from the heavens;
    praise him in the heights above.
² Praise him, all his angels;
    praise him, all his heavenly hosts.
³ Praise him, sun and moon;
    praise him, all you shining stars.
⁴ Praise him, you highest heavens
    and you waters above the skies.
⁵ Let them praise the name of the LORD,
    for at his command they were created,
⁶ and he established them for ever and ever—
    he issued a decree that will never pass away.
⁷ Praise the LORD from the earth,
    you great sea creatures and all ocean depths,
⁸ lightning and hail, snow and clouds,
    stormy winds that do his bidding,
⁹ you mountains and all hills,
    fruit trees and all cedars,
¹⁰ wild animals and all cattle,
    small creatures and flying birds,
¹¹ kings of the earth and all nations,
    you princes and all rulers on earth,
¹² young men and women,
    old men and children.
¹³ Let them praise the name of the LORD,
    for his name alone is exalted;
    his splendor is above the earth and the heavens.
¹⁴ And he has raised up for his people a horn,
    the praise of all his faithful servants,
    of Israel, the people close to his heart.
Praise the LORD.

Original
Meaning

PSALM 148 IS THE THIRD of five psalms that comprise the concluding collection in the Psalter. The collection, often termed the "Final Hallel," consists of five hymns. Instead of being bound together by a superscription like the one used in the previous collection (i.e., "to David"), each psalm in the Final Hallel begins and ends with the phrase *halelu yah*, "Praise the LORD." These ten occurrences suggest the "totality and perfection" of the praise of God exhibited in this hymnic collection.[1]

Within Psalm 148 itself a similar structuring principle occurs. Other terms appear ten times (or in factors of ten), thus serving to reinforce the "totality" of praise. As suggested above, the first and last *halelu yah*, "Praise the LORD," should be understood as a framing device, but in the intervening verses the verb "to praise" (*halal*) occurs ten times—eight times as an imperative and two times as a jussive ("Let them praise" [vv. 5, 13]).[2] In addition to the repetition of the dominant verb in this psalm, the word "all" (*kol*) appears ten times. The term's meaning, as well as its repetition, contributes to the larger theme of the psalm: *all* creation is meant to praise God. Further, there are thirty (3 × 10) addressees called upon in this psalm to praise God—the same number of addressees as there are lines in the body of the psalm itself, provided that the two framing lines are not counted. Although modern readers of Psalm 148 might dismiss such observations out of hand, Hossfeld and Zenger caution us that "none of this is a game; it is a stylistic means of impressing the fundamental conviction of the psalm in poetic fashion, namely, that the multiple forms of creation are governed by a skillfully planned order by the creator God" and that, together, this creation is called upon to praise the God of Israel.[3]

The psalm can be divided into two sections, verses 1b–6 and 7–14. In the first half of the psalm the heavenly sphere and all that inhabits it are called to praise Yahweh; in the second half all inhabitants of the earthly sphere are called to do likewise. Together, the two sections suggest that all creation, from the highest heavens (v. 4a) to the ocean depths (v. 7b), is called upon to praise Yahweh. The ancient Near Eastern worldview typically operated with a three-tiered understanding of reality: heaven, earth, and under the earth ("Sheol"). In Psalm 148, however, only the first two tiers are referenced; Sheol is omitted. But this omission is not surprising, given the claims elsewhere in the Old Testament that "It is not the dead

---

1. Hossfeld and Zenger, *Psalms 3*, 605.

2. Hossfeld and Zenger contend that by combining the calls to praise God in the framing device with the ten occurrences in the "body" of the psalm, "we have the number twelve as the symbol for the twelve tribes of Israel who are to recite this psalm as, indeed, a praise of the creator God YHWH that will fill out the twelve months, that is the whole year" (ibid., 632). Although the suggestion that the use of the verb twelve times points toward the twelve tribes of Israel seems plausible, the suggestion that it also alludes to the twelve months in the Jewish calendar year seems less so.

3. Ibid.

who praise the LORD, those who go down to the place of silence" (Ps 115:17; see also Ps 6:5; Isa 38:18).

Although the structure of this praise psalm is rather uncomplicated, it remains unique in its final arrangement. Hymns typically begin with a call to praise Yahweh, followed by a series of statements justifying the initial invocation. The explanatory statements are often preceded by the word "for" or "because" (*ki*). (For an example of a typical hymn, see Ps 30.) In Psalm 148, however, the psalmist alters the format with a call to praise Yahweh that is considerably longer than the actual rationale. For example, verses 1b–5a contain the extended call to praise Yahweh, followed by the particle *ki* ("for") and the shorter rationale for the praise of Yahweh (vv. 5b–6b). The second strophe proceeds similarly: verses 7–13a contain the extended call to praise Yahweh followed by the particle *ki* ("for") and the shorter rationale for the praise of Yahweh (vv. 12b–13).

Exhortation for the Heavens to Praise Yahweh (148:1–6)

THE PSALM OPENS WITH AN EXHORTATION to "Praise the LORD" (*halelu yah*) in verse 1a, an exhortation that repeats at the close of the psalm in verse 14. The two together create an *inclusio* around the entire psalm. Verses 1b–5a call on the heavens and all that inhabit them to praise Yahweh. The strophe concludes with a threefold acknowledgment of the creative power of Yahweh's spoken word (vv. 5b–6).

Praise the LORD from the heavens. In the Old Testament, the relationship between God and the heavens is construed principally through three different models.[4] The first model ("the heavenly model") depicts the heavens, or "heaven of heavens," as the very dwelling place of Yahweh (Pss 115:3; 136:26), and it is from there that Yahweh sits enthroned (Ps 123:1) and from there that he looks down upon creation. His sovereignty over all creation, including other gods and earthly powers, is accentuated in this model. In other texts a different model is suggested. God is depicted as enthroned in the heavens while remaining closely bound to his creation ("the cosmos model"). The language frequently invoked in the Old Testament for this model is that of a throne and footstool. The biblical writer contends that all creation serves as the very sanctuary of the Divine King, the one enthroned in the heavens but fully present in his creation (cf. Isa 6). The third model understands God as entirely separate or completely distinct from all creation. As envisioned in Psalm 148, God is not in the heavens or even in the heavens of heavens; rather, he is over all parts of

---

4. Schmid, "Himmelsgott, Weltgott, und Schöpfer," 111–48.

---

creation, the heavens included. All creation, from the highest heavens to the ocean depths and everything between those realms, are called upon to participate in the rightful worship of the one true God. More specifically, the psalmist invites the beings ("angels" and "heavenly hosts") that inhabit the heavenly realm to lift their voices in praise of God. In addition to these beings, the inanimate objects in the heavens (e.g., sun, moon, stars) are invited to do likewise. In other ancient Near Eastern traditions these objects are divinized and associated with particular deities (i.e., Shamash the sun god or Sin the moon god), but the writers of the Old Testament explicitly reject this interpretation of reality.[5] In Genesis 1 these objects in the heavens are not deities themselves, but rather creations of the one true God. And in Psalm 148 these created objects are not worthy of worship themselves, but instead, like all creation, are called upon to join in the chorus of praises offered to Yahweh.

At his command they were created. Verses 1b–5a call upon all inhabitants of the heavenly sphere to praise God. The rationale for this comprehensive call to praise occurs in verses 5b–6. The particle *ki* ("for" or "because") is the first word in verse 5 and signals that the rationale is to follow. Psalms 147 and 148 both refer to the "word" of God in the world. In Psalm 147 the psalmist celebrated the power of God's word both to create life (v. 4) and sustain it (vv. 15–18), while in Psalm 148 the poet celebrates the generative power of God's command. God spoke, and they were created (*bara'*)—the same word used in Genesis 1. The emphasis is not simply on God's "potent" speech that can bring things to life; it is much greater. God's capacity to bring things to life through his word signals his sovereignty over all he created. In other ancient Near Eastern religions the structure and order of creation is established through theomachy—a battle between the gods for supremacy.[6] Generally speaking, Ancient Israel jettisoned any notion of a divine battle and declared instead that Yahweh, and Yahweh alone, remains responsible for all that inhabits the created order. And by his decrees, that which he has established "will never pass away" (v. 6). No power on earth or in the heavens can thwart what Yahweh has created and established.

---

5. In the second strophe the psalmist refers to the "stormy winds" (v. 8b). In the Neo-Assyrian pantheon of the gods, Adad was the storm god (cf. Set in Egypt; Baal in the Ugaritic tales, among others). Typically, this god was depicted with a bolt of lightning in his hand. Yet, as similarly in the reference to the sun and stars in the first strophe, the psalmist suggests that stormy winds are not gods in and of themselves but creations of Yahweh and subject to his directives.

6. See Walton, *Ancient Near Eastern Thought and the Old Testament*, 179–201.

Exhortation for the Earth to Praise Yahweh (148:7–14)

IN THE FIRST HALF OF PSALM 148 the poet called upon the heavens and its inhabitants to praise Yahweh. In the second half he turns his attention to the inhabitants of the earth and calls on them to do the same. As similarly in the first strophe, references to Genesis 1 and traditions associated with Israel's creation theology inform these verses.

Praise the LORD . . . you great sea creatures and all ocean depths. Psalm 148:7b begins the second strophe with a reference to the waters of the earth. Genesis 1:7 explains that Yahweh created the firmament and separated the waters above from the waters below. In the first strophe of Psalm 148, the last element of the heavens referenced was the "waters above the skies" or, better yet, "above the heavens" (*shamayim*); in verse 7 the psalmist continues his treatment of creation by referencing that which inhabits the "waters under." Contained within the waters of the earth are the "sea creatures" (*tanninim*) and the "ocean depths" (*tehomot*). In the larger conceptual world of the ancient Near East, these objects appeared alongside other mythical monsters such as the Leviathan, Rahab, the mythical crocodile, Tanninim, and the Behemoth. These creatures inhabited the primeval chaotic waters and sought to disrupt the ordered world of the gods. Within the literature of ancient Israel, vestiges of the larger cultural tradition remain present. For example, the Leviathan as a source of chaos is mentioned in Psalm 74:14 and Job 41:1–34, and Rahab the dragon (*tanninim*) is mentioned in Isaiah 51:9 and Psalm 89:10. The Behemoth, as a menacing threat, appears in Job 40:15–24. Yet in Psalm 148 the roles of the "sea creatures" (*tanninim*) and the "ocean depths" (*tehomot*) have been altered considerably. The psalm not only "deprives the monsters of chaos and the primeval floods of their menace but on the contrary exhorts them, through their praise of Yahweh, to make a constructive contribution to the world of Yahweh's creation."[7] The objects of chaos have been stripped of their alleged power and have been set alongside the snow and the clouds, the mountains and hills, as parts of creation exhorted to raise their voices in praise to the one God over all.

Lightning and hail, snow and clouds. These four meteorological phenomena, along with the reference to the wind in verse 8b, recall similar imagery in Psalm 147:15–18. At first glance these phenomena might appear better suited for the first strophe, with its emphasis on the heavens. Yet, in one form or another, all these phenomena refer to precipitation, with the chief beneficiary being the earth. The psalmist declares that the winds

---

7. Hossfeld and Zenger, *Psalms 3*, 637.

that blow and the storms that rise up are the results of "his bidding" (Ps 148:8c). Even as Yahweh called the objects of heaven into existence (v. 5), so too are these objects called into being and tasked by the Creator God.

Nature and animals. Verses 7b–8a include three pairs of objects: sea creatures and ocean depths; lightning and hail; snow and clouds. Verses 9–12a continue the pairing of terms, beginning with nature. The "mountains and all hills" refer to earth and its rugged features, and the fruit trees and cedars represent the vegetation that fills those domains. Although in the Ugaritic texts the mountains are understood as the home of the gods, the psalmist demythologizes that terrain and declares that it too will sing of Yahweh. "Fruit trees" likely refers to the cultivated vegetation, pruned and preserved by humans, while the reference to "cedars" invokes images of the wild cedars (*Cedrus libani*) that tower some 130 feet over the landscape in Lebanon. Together they are meant to represent all vegetational life.

The taxonomy of creatures, both wild and tame, that participate in the praise of God continues in verse 10: "wild animals" (*hayyah*) and "cattle" (*behemah*); "small creatures" (*remes*) and "flying birds" (*tsippor*). This same sequence of terms (wild animals, cattle, small creatures, and flying birds) occurs in Genesis 7:14 in reference to the animals to be preserved within the ark. In Genesis 7 these labels represent animal life in its totality, both wild and domesticated. The poet employs the same terms in Psalm 148:10 with a similar meaning in view.

Humans. Thus far in Psalm 148 the psalmist has called upon the highest heavens (v. 4a), the earth (v. 7a), the ocean depths (v. 7b), and every created object that inhabits those spheres to join in the chorus of praise to Yahweh. Humans are not mentioned, however, until verses 11–12. As similarly in the structure of Genesis 1, Psalm 148 mentions humans last (cf. Gen 1:28). And as with the other pairings, these pairings encompass the totality of creation invited to praise God. The reference to kings, nations, judges, and rulers in verse 11 has a geopolitical connotation referring to those *in* power and those *with* power, both near and far; even they are called upon to praise the God of Israel. Verse 12 extends the comprehensive sweep of humanity invited to praise God. Verse 12a focuses on gender, both male and female, or better yet, *all* men and women. The NIV translates the second line in verse 12 as "old men and children," but this reading suggests that "old women" are not referenced. In verse 12b the Hebrew text includes the adjective "old" (*zaqen*) with a masculine plural suffix, thus the rendering "old men." In this instance, because the masculine plural ending likely functions collectively, a better translation of the term would be the "elderly," inclusive of both genders. The emphasis is not on "old men" and young children but on every human being, from the elderly to the young.

Praise the name of the LORD. The second section of Psalm 148 concludes as the first section did, that is, with a jussive verb calling the people to praise the name of Yahweh, followed by a rationale meant to justify the call to praise. As with verse 5b, so also does verse 13b begin with the particle *ki* ("for" or "because"), which signals the rationale is to follow. Whereas verses 5b–6 explain that God's power to call things into existence merits his praise, verse 13b–c focuses entirely upon the kingship of Yahweh. Yahweh is to be praised because he is "above the earth and the heavens." The word "exalted" (v. 13b) comes from the root *shgb*, which means in the *qal* stem "to be fortified" or "to be inaccessibly high."[8] In Psalm 148:13 the verb appears in the *niphal* and is often translated as to be "high" or "exalted," but even in that rendering, the sense of being fortified or inaccessibly high is not far beneath the surface of the meaning. Rather than making a simple "spatial statement" affirming that God's name is lifted high or exalted, the psalmist makes a much stronger claim, namely, that Yahweh himself is lifted high—he is unassailable and impregnable to the forces of creation because he is the Divine King.

The royal motif continues in verse 13c with the word "splendor" or "majesty" (*hod*). The term appears elsewhere in describing the majesty of human kingship (Ps 21:5) as well as divine kingship (Ps 145:5). In this instance "splendor" (*hod*) is a figure of speech known as a metonymy. Rather than declaring Yahweh a king, the psalmist opts to use a closely related term to communicate that thought; Yahweh's "splendor" signals his kingship. To suggest that Yahweh's "splendor" or majesty is "above the earth and the heavens" is in fact to declare that Yahweh reigns from on high as king.

He has raised up for his people a horn. The psalm opened with directives aimed first at the heavens, followed by the earth and all that inhabit it. Among those that inhabit the earth is humanity, from the most powerful to the least (Ps 148:11–12). The final verse of the psalm narrows the anthropological focus further by referencing Israel. The psalmist declares that Israel should praise God because "he raised up [*rum*] for his people a horn [*qeren*]." In the broader cultural context of the Old Testament, the horn (*qeren*) refers to strength and might (e.g., Pss 74:4; 75:10; 89:17). Although the term could be applied to kings and nations as emblematic of their military and political might (1 Kgs 22:11; Jer 48:25), its usage in Psalm 148 appears to have the covenant community in view.[9] Israel, God's faithful servants (v. 14b), has reason to praise God because he has endowed his

---

8. Keith N. Schoville, "שׂגב," *NIDOTTE* 3:1216.
9. Brueggemann and Bellinger, *Psalms*, 613.

---

people with the strength necessary to endure the trying events of the exile and the subsequent challenges associated with restoration to the promised land in the postexilic period.[10]

CREATOR AND KING. Psalm 148 stands at the center of the Final Hallel, with two psalms coming before and two after it. In addition to its literary placement at the center of the collection, Psalm 148 functions as the theological center of the collection as well. Although creation language and imagery permeate the entirety of Psalm 148, the fundamental theological claim that undergirds this text is that of the kingship of Yahweh. Yahweh, the covenantal God of Israel, is presented as the Creator King. To substantiate this claim, the psalmist takes great pains to establish the nature of the "Creator-creation" relationship. In Psalm 148 Yahweh is not embedded *within* creation but, instead, is differentiated *from* creation. The Creator stands *apart* from his creation because he stands *over* it as the Divine King (v. 13c).

This tradition of Yahweh as the Creator King is not limited to Psalm 148 but can be found in other texts that carefully weave together the concept of kingship with that of creator. This interweaving is most clearly on display in Psalms 93 and 95–99, poems that announce the reign of God. Psalm 95 declares that Yahweh is the "great King" (v. 3b) and then invites all worshipers to "kneel before the LORD our Maker" (v. 6). Other psalms in the same collection declare Yahweh's kingship but then recount creation's participation in praising the Creator King. Psalm 96 explains that the heavens and the earth, the sea, the fields, and all that are in them will rejoice and sing for joy, and in Ps 98:8 even the rivers will "clap their hands" at the coming of the Divine King. All creation, humans and nature alike, create what Clinton McCann terms "a symbiosis of praise."[11] Together they testify to the work of the Creator King in the world.

The Old Testament confesses that the work of the Creator King is not limited to a singular act of creation. While some biblical texts certainly allude to *creatio prima*, God's initial act of creation in the world (Gen 1;

---

10. In the Hebrew the verb is *wayyarem*, a *hiphil* imperfect third-person masculine singular with a *waw* consecutive. This form, labeled by some grammarians as a *wayyiqtol*, is used in reference to a past event (cf. NIV). The Septuagint changes the verb to a future indicative form, *hupsōsei*, "he will exalt," perhaps suggesting that the strength of God has yet to appear for the people of God.

11. McCann, "The Book of Psalms," 1272.

Ps 104:5–9), others refer to *creatio continua*, God's ongoing creative power in the world (Pss 93:1; 96:10b; 104:10–30). It is the power exhibited in the former that grounds Israel's belief in the latter.

Humanity's place within creation. Given humanity's capacity to create so much on our own, we sometimes fall prey to misguided thoughts concerning our sense of place within the created order. At times we speak as though God *and* humanity together stand differentiated from the rest of creation. We speak as though in some way we too stand *with* God over and apart from all creation. Psalm 148, however, redirects and refashions our thoughts. Like the sun, moon, and stars—all elements of the created order—we too are called to the act of praise. We stand alongside the wild animals, cattle, small creatures, and birds as we confess that "his name alone is exalted; his splendor is above the earth and the heavens" (v. 13). And despite the considerable diversity found in the human race itself, Psalm 148 reminds us that the call to praise flattens out such differences. In fact, "Praise makes myths of all our rationalizations and distinctions. Our shared humanity is never so evident as it is when we lower our heads, bow our knees, and praise the Lord."[12] Psalm 148 reminds us that regardless of our station in life, our gender, age, or ethnicity, we are part of the heavens and the earth that are meant to praise God.

In similar fashion, Psalm 100 calls for "all the earth" to shout for joy to the Lord. In addition to worshiping him, this psalmist calls us to "Know that the LORD is God. It is he who has made us, and we are his" (v. 3). Rather than lamenting our "creatureliness," the psalmists in both Psalms 100 and 148 invite us to embrace our place within the created order—we are part of the creation that praises its Creator King. By accepting our place within the created order, we announce that God is God and we are not, and because God is God and we are not, we are compelled to sing for joy and praise God. Bernd Janowski reminds us that "the praise of God is a fundamental expression of theology, and is, according the Old Testament, even the reason for human existence."[13] In other words, we are most human when we are praising the only true God, the Creator King.[14]

---

12. Duane Warden, "All Things Praise Him (Psalm 148)," *Restoration Quarterly* 35 (1993): 107.

13. Janowski, *Arguing with God*, 250.

14. See Wolff, *Anthropology of the Old Testament*, 228–29. Wolff writes, "In praise . . . the destiny of man finds its truly human fulfillment. Otherwise, man becoming his own idol, turns into a tyrant" (p. 229).

FROM BEGINNING TO END Psalm 148 calls us to praise God. To praise God rightly, however, requires that we understand God rightly, and to understand God rightly means that we deny all other claims that mar our understanding of God and his way in the world. In trying to make sense of ourselves and the world around us we often fall prey to idols, both those that we construct and those that have been constructed for us. Question 95 in the Heidelberg Catechism (1563) inquires, "What is idolatry?" to which the catechism responds, idolatry is "having or inventing something in which one trusts in place of or alongside of the only true God."[15] Frequently our mind (and our preaching) associates idols with money and power, among myriad other objects that occupy our thoughts and sometimes guide our living. Yet beyond these things, a far more subtle and perhaps more damaging form of idolatry is that of "false or distorted concepts about God."[16] Using the language of faith, we construct images of God that stand at odds with the biblical witness. We fashion God after ourselves so that his values match ours—his ways, our ways.

In the call to praise God in Psalm 148, the psalmist is doing much more than asking all creation to sing a song—he is asking us to declare what is true and right about the Creator King. John Witvliet explains, "The world loves to worship the stuff it has made, but the church proclaims a God who made us. The world lives to worship the ideas it has thought up, but the church points to a vision of God far greater than we can ever imagine on our own."[17] Psalm 148 invites us to reorient our worship and our words, and yes, even our very lives. We are asked to dispense with our own idolatrous constructs about the nature of God, and even ourselves, and instead we are called to find our rightful place in a chorus comprised of all creation as we lift our voices to the one true God who indeed stands over the entirety of earth and heaven.

---

15. Zacharias Ursinus, *The Commentary of Dr. Zacharias Ursinus on the Heidelberg Catechism,* trans. G. W. Willard (Grand Rapids: Eerdmans, 1956), 509. For additional discussion on the document itself see Margit Ernst-Habib, *But Why Are You Called a Christian? An Introduction to the Heidelberg Catechism* (Göttingen: Vandenhoeck & Ruprecht), 2013.

16. John D. Witvliet, "Isaiah in Christian Liturgy: Recovering Textual Contrasts and Correcting Theological Astigmatism," in *Touching the Altar: The Old Testament for Christian Worship,* ed. Carol M. Bechtel (Grand Rapids: Eerdmans, 2008), 76.

17. Ibid., 84.

Psalm 149

¹ Praise the LORD.
Sing to the LORD a new song,
    his praise in the assembly of his faithful people.
² Let Israel rejoice in their Maker;
    let the people of Zion be glad in their King.
³ Let them praise his name with dancing
    and make music to him with timbrel and harp.
⁴ For the LORD takes delight in his people;
    he crowns the humble with victory.
⁵ Let his faithful people rejoice in this honor
    and sing for joy on their beds.
⁶ May the praise of God be in their mouths
    and a double-edged sword in their hands,
⁷ to inflict vengeance on the nations
    and punishment on the peoples,
⁸ to bind their kings with fetters,
    their nobles with shackles of iron,
⁹ to carry out the sentence written against them—
    this is the glory of all his faithful people.
Praise the LORD.

PSALM 149 IS THE FOURTH of five psalms that comprise the concluding collection in the Psalter. The collection, often termed the "Final Hallel," consists of five hymns. Instead of being bound together by a superscription like the one used in the previous collection (i.e., "to David"), each psalm in the Final Hallel begins and ends with the phrase *halelu yah*, "Praise the LORD." These ten occurrences of *halelu yah* across the five psalms suggest the "totality and perfection" of the praise of God exhibited in this hymnic collection.[1]

As its language suggests, Psalm 149 is a communal hymn calling on the entire nation to break out in praise of Yahweh. Although the references to "Israel" and the "people of Zion" in verse 2 make explicit the communal

---

1. Hossfeld and Zenger, *Psalms 3*, 605.

orientation of the psalm, additional terms appear throughout the poem that reinforce this orientation. For example, the community is referred to as the *hasidim*, the "faithful people," in verses 1, 5, and 9; the repetition of this term provides a framing device for the entirety of the psalm.[2] Other communal terms include "his people" in verse 4a and "the humble," or "the humble ones," in verse 4b.

Judging from verses 1–3, the psalm was designed for use by the "assembly" (*qahal*) in a cultic setting—another indication of its communal orientation. The precise occasion and specific purpose of this psalm has received considerable scholarly attention, but attention that has generated little consensus. Among the occasions proposed is one suggested by Mitchell Dahood, namely, that the psalm was composed for use on the night prior to a battle against the enemy nations.[3] In the light of verse 6, some have suggested that Psalm 149 was associated with a "sword dance" that would have been performed in association with military occasions.[4] More recently, however, a number of psalms scholars have classified Psalm 149 as an "eschatological hymn."[5] Accordingly, the community affirms the sovereignty of their God over the entire world, but even more they anticipate the day when justice shall be executed against those powers that rise up against God and his work in the world. To that end Psalm 149 invokes a number of theological traditions. The psalmist harkens back to Psalm 2, a poem that affirms the kingship of Yahweh but acknowledges the threatening reality of the nations.[6] Psalm 2 recalls the rebellious nations and their leaders, who "conspire" and "plot" against Yahweh and his anointed (v. 1–3).

---

2. Norbert Lohfink, *Lobgesänge der Armen: Studien zum Magnifikat, den Hodajot von Qumran, und einigen späten Psalmen*, SBB 143 (Stuttgart: Katholisches Bibelwerk, 1990), 121–22.

3. Dahood, *Psalms 101–150*, 356. Similarly, Hans-Joachim Kraus argues that the people have gathered in Jerusalem in preparation for the "revolt of the nations," but he contends that the imagery and theology of Ps 149 is derived principally from Israel's cultic traditions (cf. Pss 2; 9; 46; 48). See Kraus, *Psalms 60–150*, 566–67.

4. For example see Goulder, *The Psalms of the Return: Book V, Psalms 107–150*, 299–300. Others yet have suggested that the psalm has less to do with preparations for battle and more to do with Israel's confession concerning the kingship of Yahweh. Artur Weiser suggested that perhaps the psalm was part of a liturgy used to celebrate Yahweh's kingship in light of Israel's salvation history (Weiser, *Psalms*, 839–40). See also Anderson, *Psalms II*, 952.

5. Allen, *Psalms 101–150*; Hossfeld and Zenger, *Psalms 3*; McCann, "The Book of Psalms"; Mays, *Psalms*, Interpretation (Louisville: Westminster John Knox, 1994). Hermann Gunkel also spoke of Psalm 149 as eschatological, but with a greater weight placed on the destruction of the nations and "the world domination of YHWH's people" (*An Introduction to the Psalms*, 260).

6. See the extended discussion of Pss 2 and 149 in Derek Wittman, "'Let Us Cast Their Ropes from Us'; The Editorial Significance of the Portrayal of the Foreign Nations

In light of their insubordinate and unruly behavior, the psalmist calls on all kings and rulers to "serve the LORD with fear" (v. 11). Should they choose to do otherwise, they will be met with destruction (v. 12). Throughout the Psalter, different psalms have highlighted the oppressive actions of foreign nations and their kings, thereby suggesting that indeed they have chosen otherwise and opted not to serve Yahweh in fear. Psalm 149 aids in concluding the Psalter much as it began, namely, by affirming the kingship of Yahweh and the waywardness of the nations; but in this next to last psalm the impending judgment that is to come upon the nations moves to the fore. References in Psalm 149 to other biblical texts, including Psalms 96–98 and Isaiah 40–66, reinforce the kingship of Yahweh and the ultimate demise of the nations.[7]

The structure of Psalm 149 contains both expected and unexpected elements in a hymn. Some scholars have attempted to divide the psalm into three strophes (vv. 1–3, 4–6, 7–9), based principally on the thematic unity in the first strophe and the syntactic unity in the third strophe.[8] Proponents of this view note that the term *hasidim* appears three times in the psalm, once in each of the proposed strophes.[9] The NIV has also divided the psalm into three strophes, but the breaks between strophes differs. Verse 1b–c appears as an opening strophe, followed by two additional strophes of equal length (eight lines each).

Alternatively, Psalm 149 can be divided into two strophes, verses 1b–4 and 5–9b. Read in this way, each strophe begins with an extended call to praise (vv. 1–3, 5–6), followed by a motivation for that call to praise. In the first strophe, the motivation clause follows a typical hymnic device and begins with the particle *ki*, "for" or "because." The community is called to praise Yahweh because (*ki*) he "takes delight in his people; he crowns the humble with victory" (v. 4). In the second strophe the psalmist shifts rhetorical devices and uses the infinitive construct form of the verb in verses 7–9a to create a purpose clause (i.e., "in order to inflict vengeance on the nations" [v. 7a]). The distinction between the rationale for the motivation clause in verse 4 differs from that found in verses 8–9b. In the first instance

---

in Psalms 2 and 149," in *The Shape and Shaping of the book of Psalms*, AIL 20, ed. Nancy deClaissé-Walford (Atlanta: SBL Press, 2014), 53–69.

7. On the use of Isa 40–66 in Ps 149 see Allen, *Psalms 101–150*, 319–20.

8. Verses 1–3 are thematically bound by the first word in verse 1b, "sing" (*samah*), and the final word in verse 3b, "make music" (*zamar*). Each line of the final strophe (vv. 7–9) begins with an infinitive construct ("to inflict," "to bind," "to carry out"), thus creating a syntactically parallel strophe.

9. For example see Raymond J. Tournay, "Le psaume 149 et la 'vengeance' des Pauvres de YHWH," *RB* 92 (1985): 349–58.

(v. 4) the motivation clause "speaks of an event affecting God's people," while in the second (vv. 7–9b), the motivation "looks to an event in the world of the nations."[10]

The Divine King and His Care for His People (149:1–4)

THE FIRST STROPHE INVITES the congregation to sing praises to God based on the community's relationship with God in the present (v. 4a) and their belief in the work that is yet to come (v. 4b).

A new song. The reference to a "new song" occurs only seven times in the Old Testament (Isa 42:10; Pss 33:3; 40:3; 96:1; 98:1; 144:9; 149:1). The psalmist's vow to sing a new song has little to do with his song's being a "new" composition but, instead, appears to point to a particular understanding or confession about Israel's God. As noted in the commentary on Psalm 144, the theme of a new song remains closely connected to the metaphor of the divine warrior. In Isaiah 42:10 the prophet calls the people to "sing . . . a new song," but then he announces that Yahweh, the Divine Warrior, will "march out like a champion, and like a warrior he will stir up his zeal" (v. 13)—a confession quite similar to Psalm 149. Although many other texts refer to Yahweh as the Divine Warrior, texts that refer to a new song "anticipate boldly, against all evidence, the coming of God's liberation," these songs announce the coming of "a new and just world."[11]

The assembly of his faithful people. The psalmist indicates that the praise of God should take place within the "assembly" (*qahal*) of the faithful. The term *qahal* may simply refer to the community or people of Israel more broadly (e.g., Lev 4:14; Deut 23:1–3), or it may refer more specifically to those gathered for worship (e.g., Joel 2:16; Ps 22:22). In addition to these meanings, the term can also have military connotations (e.g., Judg 20:2; Ezek 17:17; 23:24; Jer 50:9). The psalmist may have opted for "assembly" (*qahal*) rather than "congregation" (*'adah*) in Psalm 149 given the military imagery present in the psalm.[12]

Maker . . . King. The community is called to praise Yahweh because he is both Creator and King. Four other times in Book 5 of the Psalter (Pss 115:15; 121:2; 124:8; 134:3) and once in the Final Hallel (Ps 146:6), the psalmist refers to Yahweh as the Maker of heaven and earth. In referencing God as Maker, the psalmists highlight Yahweh's rightful place as ruler over all creation, but even more they highlight his creative power that can be

---

10. Hossfeld and Zenger, *Psalms 3*, 644.
11. Gerstenberger, "Singing a New Song: On Old Testament and Latin American Psalmody," 159.
12. Hossfeld and Zenger, *Psalms 3*, 648.

unleashed *against* the forces of chaos *in behalf* of his people. To the image of God as Creator, the writer of Psalm 149 adds the image of Yahweh as King (v. 2b). The tradition of Yahweh as the Creator King is not limited to this psalm—the tradition can be found in other texts that carefully weave together the concept of kingship with that of creator. The previous psalm (Ps 148) acknowledges Yahweh as Creator King out of confidence that his role in that capacity will produce blessings for the "people close to his heart" (v. 14). The Creator King image is most clearly on display in Psalms 93 and 95–99, psalms that announce the reign of God. Psalm 95 declares that Yahweh is the "great King" (v. 3b) and then invites all worshipers to "kneel before the LORD *our Maker*" (v. 6). In Psalms 96 and 98 the people are called to sing a "new song" in the light of their confession that it is Yahweh, the Divine King, who stands over all creation, the one who comes to "judge the earth" (Pss 96:13; 98:9).

Dancing and make music. Following Israel's confession of Yahweh as the Creator King, the psalmist invites the people to dance (*mahol*) and make music with the timbrel, or tambourine, and the harp. Although the noun *mahol* is the most frequently used term for dancing in the Old Testament, its usage is reserved primarily for military contexts involving hostile forces.[13] Following Israel's crossing of the Red Sea and the defeat of the Egyptians, Miriam and the women danced with tambourines and sang. Following the young David's slaying of Goliath, the women of the city greeted King Saul and the army with dancing and the playing of timbrels (1 Sam 18:7–6). Jeremiah announces that once Yahweh returns his people from the hands of the Babylonians, the people will take up timbrels and dance once more (Jer 31:4, 13). See also Judges 11:34 and the story of Jephthah.

Other texts refer to dancing and singing in a proleptic, anticipatory sense. In Psalms 96 and 98, singing and dancing signal "the inbreaking of the universal royal reign" of Yahweh.[14] Both psalms declare that Yahweh will judge the peoples of the earth and, in doing so, restore the world to its right order under the reign of God. The call to dance and make music in Psalm 149 functions similarly—that is, it functions proleptically. Those in the assembly of the faithful are invited to sing and dance before the Creator King in anticipation of the work he will accomplish (vv. 5–9).

The LORD takes delight in his people. With the use of the particle *ki* ("for"), verse 4 provides the rationale for the call to praise in verses 1–3. The verb "takes delight" (*ratsah*) appears as a participle in verse 4a and is

---

13. David S. Dockery, "מָחוֹל," *NIDOTTE* 2:46. The verb can mean to "whirl about," thus leading some to call this form of dance a "round dance" or "whirling dance."

14. Hossfeld and Zenger, *Psalms 3*, 649.

---

often translated in English in the present tense.[15] The psalmist suggests that Yahweh's delight in his people, his acceptance of them, is enduring. This claim may appear as an innocuous comment worthy of little note, but in fact the claim addresses a much deeper and much darker concern of the community. The trauma of exile and its immediate aftermath no doubt raised serious questions concerning the relationship between God and his people, as evident in the closing verses of Lamentations:

> Why do you always forget us?
> Why do you forsake us for so long?
> Restore us to yourself, LORD, that we may return;
>   renew our days as of old
> unless you have utterly rejected us
>   and are angry with us beyond measure. (5:20–22)

Because the restoration of Yehud in the postexilic period did not unfold as the community had anticipated, they could have assumed that God had forsaken them. Yet, in Psalm 149, the community rejects such thinking, choosing instead to lean into the belief that Yahweh was pleased with his people and took delight in them. That thought alone merits their praise.

He crowns the humble. Psalm 149:4b adds further reason for the people to praise Yahweh. Although they are the poor and oppressed (*'anawim*, the "humble"), Yahweh crowns them with victory. Because of this victory their status will change from their being poor and oppressed to their being crowned and adorned.[16] To be clear, the poor are not celebrating a victory already achieved; instead, they are celebrating "an attitude of Yahweh that will issue an action in the future."[17]

The word "to crown" (*pa'ar*) can refer to royalty (Esth 1:4) and, in particular, the Davidic monarchy (Zech 12:7). In Isaiah 60:9, however, the prophet announces that the entire nation has been crowned (*pa'ar*) with splendor. This shift in crowning—from the monarch to the people—can be explained based on Isaiah 55:3. In that text the prophet declares that the covenant given to David has been transferred to the entire nation. Whereas Psalm 2 had assigned the task of "asserting God's sovereignty in the world" to the monarchy, Psalm 149 declares that this work will become that of the *'anawim*, the oppressed and powerless people of God.[18]

---

15. In the first Servant Song, Yahweh declares that in Israel is the one "in whom I delight" (*ratsah*; Isa 42:1), another indicator of the intertextuality between Isaiah 40–55 and Ps 149.

16. In the second Servant Song, Yahweh promises to deliver (*yeshu'ah*) his servant (Israel) from the threats that surround them (Isa 49:8; cf. 51:5–7).

17. Goldingay, *Psalms 3*, 740.

18. McCann, "The Book of Psalms," 1274.

God's Royal Rule (149:5–9)

THE SECOND STROPHE RESUMES the call to praise in verses 5–6. A series of statements concerning the demonstration of Yahweh's rule over the world follows in verses 7–9.

Let his faithful people rejoice. In verse 5 the NIV reads, "Let his faithful people rejoice in *this* honor" (emphasis added). The Hebrew does not include the demonstrative pronoun "this," but its inclusion in the translation helps to clarify the claim being made. "This" honor points forward to the work of the people mentioned in verses 5–9. Within this section, verses 5a and 9b function as an *inclusio* that opens and closes the final strophe. Both lines mention the "faithful people," and both lines include synonyms meant to describe the people's participation with God in the establishment of his reign (*kabod*, "honor" [v. 5a]; *hadar*, "glory" [v. 9b]). The intervening verses in the final strophe describe the work of the people in the establishment of God's reign.

Sing for joy on their beds. Because the meaning of verse 5b is not immediately clear, this line has been given considerable attention, which has resulted in a number of suggestions. As mentioned above, verse 1 called on the people to rejoice in the "assembly of his faithful people," thereby suggesting that the psalm may have been set in the temple. Some have postulated, therefore, that the "beds" mentioned here refer to cots that worshipers would have used if they slept overnight in the temple (cf. Ps 139:18). Others have suggested that the text means more generally, "the places where they lie prostrate" in the temple, perhaps in reference to mats or prayer rugs. More likely, "beds" refers to the private beds or couches upon which people would meditate and reflect while in their homes (Ps 4:5). Here, however, the reference to beds is not intended literally; instead, it functions metaphorically to mean "in private," even as their own beds or coaches are private places.[19] The call to praise God in private (Ps 149:5b) corresponds to the call to praise God in public ("in the assembly" [v. 1]).

A double-edged sword in their hands. Without question, the most troubling line in the psalm is verse 6b. Verse 6a continues the reference to praise that started in verse 5: "May the praise [*romam*] of God be in their mouths." The word for "praise" in verse 6a (*romam*) differs from that used in verse 1c (*tehillah*). The former word, *romam*, comes from the root *rum*, which refers to being high or exalted; the psalmist calls for the exaltation of Yahweh, the lifting high of God through the people's praises.

---

19. See Willem S. Prinsloo, "Psalm 149: Praise Yahweh with Tambourine and Two-edged Sword," *ZAW* 109 (1997): 395–407, esp. 402–3.

Verse 6b then reads, "and a double-edged sword in their hands." The jarring imagery of weaponry has resulted in a number of alternative readings. These readings focus principally on the conjunction that opens the line. The conjunction "and" (*waw*) in this text has been rendered in a number of ways. For example, Raymond. J. Tournay contended that the conjunction is best understood as a *waw* of comparison (*waw adaequationis*).[20] Understood in this way, the verse would read, "let the praises of God in their throats *be like* a two-edged sword in their hand." In a simliar vein, Erich Zenger has suggested that the conjunction is best understood as a *waw* of explication (*waw explicativum*)—the second line explicates or explains the first line. Read in this way, the verse would state, "let the praises of God be in their throats and *let that be* a two-edged sword in their hand."[21] In other words, let the praise of God be as sharp as a two-edged sword. Admittedly, there are numerous texts in the Old Testament that associate the power of words with swords (e.g., Isa 59:2; Pss 57:4; 59:7; 64:3), so the suggestions proferred by Tournay and Zenger are not without warrant. Further, either reading would certainly soften the imagery present in verse 6b. Speaking of a sword as a metaphor for praise presents far fewer theological challenges than does a more literal reading. In the end, however, the readings suggested by Tournay and Zenger must be rejected based on the larger context of the second strophe. The actions that follow in verses 7–9 (i.e., inflicting vengeance, binding kings and princes) appear far from figurative and seem to imply the work of God's people against the nations. The more literal reading of verse 6b does not stand in tension with the call to lift high their voices. John Goldingay suggests that "verse 6b makes one reread verse 6a and wonder whether that [line] refers to the kind of acclamation of Yahweh that an army would give in battle."[22] Given the context of the psalm, this latter reading, while troubling for modern readers, seems preferable nevertheless.

To inflict vengeance on the nations. Verses 7–9a include a series of statements that outline the activity of God's people en route to the victory referenced in verse 4b. In verse 7 the psalmist explains that the people will "inflict vengeance" (*neqamah*) on the nations. The term *neqamah* does not refer to some form of revenge or irrational vengeance but refers, instead, to the "legitimate exercise of political authority" that a person or group can assume "for the benefit of the individual or the community

---

20. Tournay, "Le psaume 149," 350.
21. Erich Zenger, *Mit meinum Gott überspringe ich Mauern: Einführung in das Psalmenbuch*, 7th ed. (Freiburg: Herder, 2007), 54.
22. Goldingay, *Psalms 3*, 742.

whose existence or well-being is at risk."[23] In other words, the people of God, the "humble" (v. 4), will challenge the powerful nations that have mocked Israel's God (Ps 115) and oppressed his people. By their actions, the nations have created a world that stands in tension with the vision of God's kingdom, a vision articulated in the previous psalms in this collection (Pss 146–48).

In the second line of Psalm 149:7 the psalmist refers to this action as "punishment" (*tokehah*). The term also implies a rebuke, thus implying that there is an educative connotation to the term.[24] The psalmist is not calling for the people of God to destroy or annihilate the nations and peoples but instead to rebuke and chastise them for their attitudes. In this moment the nations "will see the truth about their position in the world and before Yahweh."[25]

To bind their kings with fetters. Verse 8 narrows the focus from the "nations and peoples" to the "kings" and "nobles." Those who sit in powerful places and those who exert considerable influence will find themselves fettered and shackled. The irony in the text is unmistakable. Earlier in the psalm (v. 4) the people of God are called the "humble" ('*anawim*), yet in verse 8, those who wield great power will be rendered powerless by a group considered poor and oppressed according to the standards of the world. This turn of events can only happen because Israel's God is the Divine King over all. Hossfeld and Zenger posit that the psalmist may have had Isaiah 24:21–23 in mind. There the prophet announces, "in that day the LORD will punish the powers in the heavens above and the kings on the earth below." The kings will be bound up and placed in prison, and as a result the world will know that Israel's God reigns. A similar scene appears in Isaiah 45:14.

To carry out the sentence written against them. The reference to a written sentence to be carried out is unclear. It may refer to the declaration in Deuteronomy 32:39–43 in which Yahweh promises to take his "flashing sword" (v. 41) and exact vengeance on the nations (v. 43).[26] Alternatively, it may simply be a figure of speech implying that Yahweh has passed

23. Notker Füglister, "Ein garstig Leid—Ps 149," in *Freude an der Weisung des Herrn: Beiträge zur Theologie der Psalmen. Festgabe zum 70. Geburtstag von Heinrich Groß*, SBB 12, ed. Ernst Haag and Frank-Lothar Hossfeld (Stuttgart: Katholisches Bibelwerk, 1987), 100.

24. Cf. Prov 1:23, 25, 30; 3:11; 5:12; 6:23; 10:17; 12:1; 13:18; 15:5, 10; 27:5; 29:1.

25. Goldingay, *Psalms 3*, 742.

26. This suggestion was proposed by Qimchi but has been more recently adopted by Robert Alter, *The Book of Psalms: A Translation with Commentary* (New York: Horton, 2007); see page 514, where Alter also suggests that the text may refer to "some notion of a divine book of destiny, an idea that occurs in several ancient cultures."

judgment on the nations. The intent is clear: What is to come will not be by historical accident—it will be because of the decree issued by Yahweh, the Divine King.

This is the glory of all his faithful people. As suggested above, verse 9b forms an *inclusio* with 5a, thereby bracketing the second strophe. Both lines mention the "faithful ones" and both lines include synonyms (*kabod*, "honor" [v. 5a]; *hadar*, "glory" [v. 9b]). In the Psalter, both terms, *kabod* and *hadar*, are royal attributes of Yahweh (e.g., Ps 96:6) and of the human king (e.g., Ps 45:4–5). Here, however, the psalmist extends the language to the entire community by declaring that the "faithful people" will participate with God in the establishment of his reign and thereby have a share in his royal glory.[27]

ECHOES OF EXODUS AND CONQUEST. Many psalms make explicit use of earlier traditions and texts. In some instances the references are overt and easily identifiable, such as the use of the "graciousness formula" (Exod 34:6–7) in Psalm 145:8–9. Other psalms, however, contain references that are more suggestive; they "point" to other texts in much more subtle and nuanced ways. Anthony Ceresko has suggested that the two strophes in Psalm 149 refer to two signature events in Israel's history—events that were foundational to Israel's theological confession, namely, the exodus and the conquest of the promised land.[28] In the first strophe of this poem, the most explicit reference to the exodus occurs in verse 3 with the words "dancing" (*mahol*) and "timbrel," or tambourine. As noted above, the language in verse 3 recalls the language of Exodus 15:20: "Then Miriam the prophet, Aaron's sister, took a timbrel in her hand, and all the women followed her, with timbrels and dancing." Beyond this subtle allusion to the exodus out of Egypt, the first strophe also invokes the language associated with Isaiah 40–55 and the exodus out of Babylon. In Psalm 149:2 Yahweh is declared "Maker," from the root *'sh*. The root means "to make" or "to do," but it frequently appears as a synonym of the verb *bara'*, "to create." In Isaiah 40–55 various forms of *'asah* appear twenty-seven times, each time in reference to God's work in creating this "second" exodus to bring his people out of exile.[29]

---

27. Hossfeld and Zenger, *Psalms 3*, 652.

28. Anthony Ceresko, "Psalm 149: Poetry, Themes (Exodus and Conquest) and Social Function," *Bib* 67 (1986): 177–94.

29. Ceresko also notes the presence of *'asah* ("to make" or "to do") in the exodus story (cf. Exod 14:31–15:1). Ibid., 183.

The second strophe of Psalm 149 appears to allude to the wars and struggles that occurred in the period of the judges. The image of the "double-edged sword" in verse 6 occurs in only two other places in the Old Testament: Judges 3:16 and Proverbs 5:4. In the book of Judges the reference occurs in the context of the story of Ehud and Eglon. Ehud, a judge for Israel, ran his two-edged sword through Eglon, the king of Moab. The story is emblematic of the conquest in general: God's people proved victorious over the nations. In addition, the phrase "edge of the sword" appears elsewhere in Joshua and Judges in reference to the settlement of the land. Ceresko suggests that, of the thirty-three uses of the phrase "edge of the sword" in the Old Testament, twenty-six appear in Genesis through Judges, with the primary focus being that of the exodus and conquest.[30]

Whereas the first strophe of Psalm 149 recalls God's work as Creator in bringing his people out of exile, the second strophe recalls Israel's participation in God's work in the world. This latter point is confirmed by the use of 'asab, "to make" or "to do," in verses 7 and 9. In verse 2 the term referred to Yahweh as "Maker," but in the second strophe it refers to the work of Israel as "doer." In verse 7 Israel is to "do" ('asab), or inflict, vengeance on the nations, and in verse 9 they are to "do" ('asab), or carry out, the judgment written about the nations and kings. Thus, as God did in the exodus, so also is he at work creating his kingdom anew; and as his people did in the conquest, so also are they to participate in the creation of this new reality.[31]

Psalm 149 in the light of the Final Hallel. Hossfeld and Zenger argue that the Final Hallel forms a tightly constructed unit that together creates a theologically unified composition. Were Psalm 149 to be lifted from its literary context, the psalm may sound terribly militaristic, nationalistic, and even xenophobic. But when read in the context of the Final Hallel, the poem's language and imagery seem less discordant. In a separate article, Zenger suggests that the psalm in this final collection focuses on the meaning of the coming kingdom of God amid a world filled with unrighteousness and violence.[32] Read in light of that reality, the psalms in the Final Hallel offer a vision of a restored world order, one that both reflects and exhibits the expectations of the Divine King. In addition, these psalms address the question of earthly power in light of the reality of divine power. In Psalm 146 the poet declares that humans should not

---

30. Ibid., 189–90.

31. Ibid., 194.

32. Erich Zenger, "Die Provokation des 149. Psalms: Von der Unverzichtbarkeit der Kanonischen Psalmenauslegung," in *Ihr Völker alle, klatscht in die Hände?*, ed. R. Kessler, et. al. (Münster: LIT Verlag, 1997), 191.

trust in princes or those in power; instead, people are called to trust in the Maker of heaven and earth (vv. 3, 6). In Psalm 148 the kings, nations, and princes of the earth are invited to join with all creation in singing praises befitting the Divine King. Psalm 149 concludes this run of psalms by declaring that all human power will be eviscerated in light of God's divine rule (cf. Pss 96:13; 98:9). Further, Psalm 149 celebrates "poor" Israel as the instrument of Yahweh for the establishment of this order. The final psalm in this collection, Psalm 150, reflects the unadulterated praise that shall come from all creation once the reign of God is fully realized.[33] In short, Psalm 149 is not about the destruction of "them"—those not like us—but instead it is a celebration of the Divine King and his initiative to order and reorder the world.

IN PSALM 149, the juxtaposition of the call to praise God (vv. 1–3) with the call for the "humble" to arm themselves against the nations (v. 6b) leaves most readers understandably unsettled. The psalm appears to carry with it the risk of unchecked nationalism and divinely sanctioned violence. Such usage sadly, and repeatedly, dots Christian history. As a result, some interpreters might avoid this psalm altogether for fear of veering off into such rhetoric. Yet, as Hans-Joachim Kraus suggests, "the psalm . . . can be understood correctly when we take the praise of God in vv. 1–4 as the basis of all interpretations."[34] The psalm begins with an invitation to the community to sing a "new song" to God. As noted above, the mention of a "new song" occurs relatively infrequently—the phrase appears only six other times in the Old Testament (Isa 42:10; Pss 33:3; 40:3; 96:1; 98:1; 144:9), each time with an emphasis on Yahweh as the heavenly Divine Warrior. These psalms declare that the heavenly Divine King is at work foiling the plans of the nations and thwarting those of the peoples (Ps 33:10). In Psalm 149 Yahweh stands over all creation as the Maker (v. 2) and Divine King. What proves notable in this psalm, however, is the role of God's people. In the other psalms listed above, Yahweh the Divine King thwarts the nations as he delivers his people; his people are the beneficiaries of his salvific work. In Psalm 149, however, God invites his people to join him in establishing his kingdom.

As suggested above, Psalm 149 is a natural extension of Psalm 2. In Psalm 2 it is the king who will "break [the nations] with a rod of iron"

---

33. Hossfeld and Zenger, *Psalms 3*, 653.
34. Kraus, *Psalms 60–150*, 568.

(v. 9). In Psalm 149 it is the people who will place the kings of the earth in shackles of iron (v. 8). The latter psalm explains that God's people have replaced the king, that the "faithful people" have been invited to share in God's reign. Yet similarly to the militaristic language referenced above, the mention of "reign" seems equally troubling. Dallas Willard is correct, that "reign is no doubt wording that is a little too grand for the contemporary mind," yet it is precisely the language and imagery employed in Psalm 149: God's people reign with God.[35] That kind of life, that kind of work, can only come through prayer, however. Perhaps that is why Psalm 149 appears as the next-to-last psalm in the Psalter. Much prayer and much formation have come prior to arriving at this psalm and at this understanding. As we pray the Psalter, we learn of God and his ways in the world. *His* vision of the kingdom slowly becomes *our* vision of the kingdom. As we pray, and as the Maker slowly remakes us, we take our place among the faithful ones crowned with victory (v. 4b), those prepared to do (*'asab*) the work of God in the world. Willard explains that "kingdom praying is an arrangement explicitly instituted by God so that we as individuals may count, and count for much, as we learn step by step how to govern, to reign with him in his kingdom."[36] That understanding seems to be the central claim of the psalm—that as God's people we have been entrusted with a share in this work. To pray and live in such a way is indeed the "glory of all his faithful people."

---

35. Dallas Willard, *The Divine Conspiracy: Rediscovering our Hidden Life in God* (New York: Harper Collins, 1998), 250.
36. Ibid.

Psalm 150

¹ Praise the LORD.
   Praise God in his sanctuary;
   praise him in his mighty heavens.
² Praise him for his acts of power;
   praise him for his surpassing greatness.
³ Praise him with the sounding of the trumpet,
   praise him with the harp and lyre,
⁴ praise him with timbrel and dancing,
   praise him with the strings and pipe,
⁵ praise him with the clash of cymbals,
   praise him with resounding cymbals.
⁶ Let everything that has breath praise the LORD.
Praise the LORD.

PSALM 150 IS THE FINAL PSALM in the concluding collection in the Psalter. The collection, often termed the "Final Hallel," consists of five hymns (Pss 146–50). Instead of being bound together by a superscription like the one used in the previous collection (i.e., "to David"), each psalm in the Final Hallel begins and ends with the phrase *halelu yah*, "Praise the LORD." These ten occurrences of the term suggest the "totality and perfection" of the praise of God exhibited in this hymnic collection.[1]

Although Psalm 150 is indeed a hymn, or a praise psalm, it does deviate from the expected form. Other hymns often begin by invoking God ("LORD"), followed by a call to worship. In addition, hymns normally contain a series of statements that explain the rationale for the worship that is due God (cf. Ps 47:2–9). Often these statements, typically expressed in participial phrases, refer to the works of God, his actions, or his qualities (i.e., "the one who delivers," "the one who creates"). Unlike other hymns, however, Psalm 150 does not begin with an invocation and only provides the briefest of rationales in verse 2. The entirety of the psalm is an extended call to worship. The opening and closing lines in the psalm contain the phrase *halelu-yah*, "Praise the LORD," and from beginning to end the verb

---

1. Hossfeld and Zenger, *Psalms 3*, 605.

halal, "to praise," dominates the poem. Every line in the psalm contains the word. In verses 1b–5b the verb appears ten times as an imperative, and then once more as a jussive in verse 6 ("let . . . praise"). The varying uses of *halal* are reflected in the structure proposed in the NIV (vv. 1a, 1b–5b, 6a, 6b).

Praise the Great King (150:1–2)

THE FIRST TWO VERSES FOCUS ON THE God who is to be praised, and in particular on his role as the Sovereign over all creation. The language employed in these verses appears elsewhere in the Psalter in association with the reign of God.[2] Given the dominance of this theme (i.e., the kingship of Yahweh) throughout the Psalter, its presence in the book's final psalm is hardly surprising.[3]

Praise God in his sanctuary. Although verse 1b/c refers to spatial locations ("sanctuary," "heavens"), its purpose is to identify the God who is to be praised. Elsewhere in the Psalter the word "sanctuary" can refer to the Jerusalem temple (cf. Pss 74:3; 134:2), and it is likely in view in Psalm 150 as well. Yet the reference to the earthly sanctuary is extended to the heavenly realm with the subsequent line. In verse 1c creation is called to praise God "in his mighty heavens [*raqi'a*]." The word *raqi'a* means "dome," and according to Genesis 1 it is that which holds in place the "waters above." In other texts (cf. Ezek 1:25; Ps 19:1) the term refers to the heavenly realm more generally—the apparent connotation in this verse. Hossfeld and Zenger explain the image being constructed in verse 1 in light of Israel's larger tradition of the divine sanctuary:

> While in pre-exilic Temple theology the Jerusalem Temple functioned as the *axis mundi* that gives stability to the cosmos by being the foundation of YHWH's throne, which extends upward to the heavens (cf. Isa 61:1–4; Ps 93), post-exilic theology distinguishes between a heavenly sanctuary where YHWH dwells and an earthly sanctuary, the image of the heavenly one, to which he descends, where his Name dwells, and from which he acts.[4]

Psalm 150 merges the references to the two sanctuaries and, by doing so, declares that Yahweh is the one who rules over all, both in heaven and on earth.

---

2. McCann, "The Book of Psalms," 1278.

3. See James L. Mays' discussion concerning the reign of God as the "root metaphor" for the book of Psalms in *The Lord Reigns: A Theological Handbook to the Psalms* (Louisville: Westminster John Knox, 1994), 12–22.

4. Hossfeld and Zenger, *Psalms 3,* 658.

Praise him for his acts of power [and] greatness. The reference to Yahweh's "acts of power (*geburah*)" occurs elsewhere in the Psalter in reference to Yahweh's kingship and rule over all creation (cf. Pss 65:6; 66:7; 106:2, 8). The clearest example of this association can be found in Psalm 145:11, which declares, "They tell of the glory of your kingdom and speak of your might [*geburah*]." The might (*geburah*) of Yahweh is understood only in light of his kingship. Similar associations are found in Psalm 145:4, 12.

Psalm 150 continues the association of Yahweh's "acts of power" (*geburah*) and his kingship by referencing the greatness of Yahweh in verse 2b. To declare Yahweh "great," or to refer to his greatness, is to do far more than make a subjective assessment about the nature of God. In the ancient Near East the label "great" was applied to deities in combination with their role as kings, as abundantly reflected in ancient texts, stela, and iconography. In ancient Mesopotamia, the prologue to the Lipit-Ishtar law code begins, "Anu, the great, the father of the gods."[5] In Egypt, the god Resheph is declared "the great god, lord forever, ruler of eternity and lifetime" on a stela found at Deir el-Medina.[6] And the Cyrus Cylinder, so named for the Persian king, refers to Marduk explicitly as the "king of the gods" and "the great lord."[7] In the Psalter, the connection between kingship and the label "great" can be found well beyond Ps 150 (cf. Pss 95:3; 145:3; 147:5).

Offer Praise to the Divine King (150:3–5)

IN VERSES 3–5 THE PSALMIST DECLARES that the praise of God as the great King begins in the context of celebratory worship. Even though the instruments listed in these verses were used in temple worship, their purpose has likely been expanded in Psalm 150. As suggested below, the language and imagery used in these verses allude to "everything the biblical tradition knows about celebrating the appearance and majesty of a king, or a god-king."[8] Thus verses 3–5 do not comprise simply a call to make music before God; instead, they suggest that celebratory music and dancing are demonstrable evidences of the people's confession concerning the kingship of Yahweh.

---

5. S. N. Kramer, trans., "Lipit-Ishtar Lawcode," in *Ancient Near Eastern Texts Relating to the Old Testament*, ed. James B. Pritchard, 3rd ed. with supplement (Princeton, NJ: Princeton University Press, 1969), 159.

6. Maciej M. Münnich, *The God Resheph in the Ancient Near East*, Orientalische Religionen in der Antike 11 (Tübingen: Mohr Siebeck, 2013), 83–84.

7. "The Cyrus Cylinder," in *The Persian Period: A Corpus of Sources from the Achaemenid Period*, ed. Amélie Kuhrt (London: Routledge, 2007), 71.

8. Hossfeld and Zenger, *Psalms 3*, 659.

The trumpet. The Hebrew term for "trumpet" is *shofar,* a term that makes its way into the English vocabulary as well ("shofar"). Rather than being a polished brass instrument, the *shofar* is the horn of an animal and lacks any type of mouthpiece. Because the *shofar* lacks a mouthpiece to govern sound, it is not designed to serve as a melodic instrument. Instead, in the Old Testament world the *shofar* was simply blown to signal that certain events were impending, including war (Josh 6:4–20; Judg 3:27) and festal events such as the Day of Atonement (Lev 25:9).[9] In Exodus 19 the *shofar* is sounded at Sinai to signal to the people the coming presence of Yahweh. In other words, the *shofar* served as "the acoustic signal of the theophany" of Yahweh, the Divine King.[10] Similarly, the *shofar* was used as a signal to announce God's royal rule (Pss 47:6; 98:6).[11]

The harp and lyre. Both terms refer to stringed instruments, although the word for "harp," *nebal,* is more difficult to identify with precision.[12] It is possible that *nebal* simply refers to a different type of lyre (a standing lyre versus a hand lyre). The books of Chronicles explain that the harp and lyre were the instruments played by the Levites for temple music (cf. 1 Chr 15:16). In addition to making music, these instruments were understood to have something of a "numinous effect." The playing of the harp and lyre drove the evil spirit out of Saul (1 Sam 19:9–10), and according to 2 Chronicles 5, the harp and lyre were played prior to the arrival of the glory of Yahweh (see below, Bridging Contexts).[13]

Timbrel and dancing. As noted in the commentary on Psalm 149, dancing and the playing of the timbrel can function in a proleptic, anticipatory sense. In Psalms 96 and 98 the making of music and dancing signaled "the inbreaking of the universal royal reign" of Yahweh.[14] Both psalms declare that Yahweh will judge the peoples of the earth and, in doing so, will restore the world to its right order under the reign of God. As similarly in Psalm 149, the call to dance and make music in Psalm 150 functions proleptically. The psalmist invites "everything that has breath" to sing and dance before the Divine King in praise of who he is and in anticipation of what he will do.

Clash of cymbals. Verse 5 mentions cymbals (*tseltselim*) twice: "clash of cymbals" and "resounding cymbals." The Hebrew could also be translated

---

9. Ivor H. Jones, "Music and Musical Instruments," *Anchor Bible Dictionary,* ed. David Noel Freedman (New Haven, CT: Yale University Press, 1992), 4:930–39.

10. Ibid., 660.

11. Hossfeld and Zenger, *Psalms 3,* 659.

12. See the brief overview in Jones, "Music and Musical Instruments," 937.

13. Hossfeld and Zenger, *Psalms 3,* 660.

14. Ibid., 649.

as "cymbals of sound [*shema*]" and "cymbals of a loud blast [*teru'ah*]." While the translation provided by the NIV attempts to be descriptive of their sounds, the alternative translation provided here attempts to capture their purpose. The word *teru'ah*, "loud blast," has a considerable range of meaning, but included in that range is reference to a war cry that would have been shouted prior to battle. Such a cry would have accompanied the blowing of the *shofar* (cf. Zeph 1:16). Elsewhere the loud "blast" or shout was used in cultic settings (Lev 23:9) to announce the great feast. Additionally, the "shout" was lifted up in celebration of the coming of the Divine King (Pss 47:5; 81:2; 95:1). Thus, as John Goldingay explains, the first reference to cymbals ("cymbals of sound") was meant to encourage "the people to listen to what is about to happen," and the second reference ("cymbals of a loud blast") tells them that it is "time to shout in acclamation."[15] Understood in this way, verse 5 does not imply the loud, frenetic clanging of cymbals, as might first be imagined, but instead may reflect the liturgical use of musical instruments to guide the people toward anticipatory worship and unfettered praise of their God.

Exhortation to Universal Praise of God (150:6)

FOLLOWING A SERIES OF TEN IMPERATIVES exhorting the people to praise God, the psalmist concludes with a final exhortation in the form of a jussive, "Let everything that has breath [*kol-neshamah*] praise the LORD." The line is meant to parallel Psalm 145:21, "Let every creature [*kol-basar*] praise his holy name." The word for "breath," *neshamah*, can refer to that which God breathed into humans (Gen 2:7) or, more generally, to all creation (Gen 7:22), even as *kol-basar*, "all flesh," can refer to all living creatures (Gen 6:12, 17). With this final exhortation the psalmist extends the summons beyond the temple to all creation, thus inviting all creation to praise God.

PSALM 150 SERVES as a fitting conclusion to the Final Hallel (Pss 146–50) and, equally so, to the entire Psalter. The psalm affirms the kingship of Yahweh, and throughout the preceding 149 psalms, references to Yahweh's kingship have dominated the language and imagery of these poetic texts. Thus, taken together, the entire Psalter confesses that Israel's God is not a tribal or regional deity associated with a particular group of people; instead, Israel is a particular group of

---

15. Goldingay, *Psalms 3*, 749. See also Jones, "Music and Musical Instruments," 935.

people in covenant with the Divine King who stands over the cosmos. The one whose throne reaches from the earth to the heavens (and over the heavens) is the God of Israel (Ps 150:2). His commitment to his people is evident in his great acts of power (v. 3a). These acts are manifestations of his "greatness" and further evidence of his royal rule over the world. Because this is the God whom Israel worships, Psalm 150 breaks out into full-throated praise. From the beginning to end of this poem, the psalmist calls for praise.

In the first two verses of Psalm 150 the psalmist identifies the God who is the object of the praise. In verse 3–5 he turns to the means of that praise. In addition to dancing, the people are called upon to play musical praise on seven different instruments. Yet in dancing and celebrating, in blowing the shofar and clashing the cymbals, they are doing much more. Hossfeld and Zenger explain the significance of the instruments by declaring that, when "Psalm 150 begins the series of instruments that are to sound with the *shofar,* the coming and the presence of the God-King Yahweh are both signaled and effected."[16] The connection between liturgical music and the coming of God is clearly on display in 2 Chronicles 5:11–14, a text that references many of the instruments listed in Psalm 150:

> The priests then withdrew from the Holy Place. All the priests who were there had consecrated themselves, regardless of their divisions. All the Levites who were musicians . . . stood on the east side of the altar, dressed in fine linen and playing cymbals, harps and lyres. They were accompanied by 120 priests sounding trumpets. The trumpeters and musicians joined in unison to give praise and thanks to the LORD. Accompanied by trumpets, cymbals, and other instruments, the singers raised their voices in praise to the LORD and sang:
> "He is good; his love endures forever."
> Then the temple of the LORD was filled with the cloud, and the priests could not perform their service because of the cloud, for the glory of the LORD filled the temple of God.

The people played instruments and offered up a confession—and they experienced the fullness of God's glory on display. The psalmist invites the congregation, and even all creation, to do likewise.

In his treatment of Psalm 150, Walter Brueggemann notes the relationship between Psalms 1 and 150. The former is an apt introduction because of its emphasis on torah faithfulness. The latter psalm is a fitting conclusion

---

16. Hossfeld and Zenger, *Psalms 3*, 649

because "it states the outcome of such a life under *torah*. *Torah*-keeping does arrive at obedience, yet obedience is not the goal of *torah*-keeping. Finally such a life arrives at unencumbered praise."[17] For Brueggemann, the "expectation of the Old Testament" is not obedience but *adoration*. Yet it seems that the language of Psalm 150 presses us even beyond adoration to *expectation*. We are called to sing, dance, and make music because we are offering up praise to the one who is and is to come. Praise is indeed grounded in adoration, but it compels us to lean forward in expectation.

MOST ANY INTRODUCTION to the book of Psalms will observe that the Psalter, from beginning to end, moves from lament to praise. The first three books of the Psalter (Pss 1–89) are comprised chiefly of lament psalms and the latter two books (Pss 90–150) of psalms of praise and thanksgiving. Regrettably, in reflecting on lament and praise, some people revert to analogs that are simple but incorrect. They equate lament with sadness and praise with happiness. In making such claims, however, they fundamentally miss the rich theological move that takes place in the Psalter. People utter a lament not simply because they are sad, but more significantly because their world is broken and disordered. A lament confesses that the world they know, their own world and the world writ large, stands in need of restoration and redemption. The psalms of praise, however, move us in a very different direction. To suggest that one who utters praise can be equated with one who is happy is to misunderstand grossly the confessional nature of praise. When we praise God, we are doing far more than simply listing all the good qualities God possesses—we are uttering a confession about the reality of that God. We are declaring that the God who is worthy of praise is the God who will redeem the brokenness of our lamenting world. We are declaring that our wailing will be turned into dancing by this God (Ps 30:11). We are declaring that the Divine King is coming still. And for that, we have no other words to utter but

Hallelujah—Praise the Lord.

---

17. Brueggemann, *The Message of the Psalms*, 167.

Scripture Index

Genesis

1 . . 558, 649–50, 883–84,
    1011, 1019–21, 1040
1–2 . . . . 93, 94, 149,
    265, 503
1–3 506
1:2 . . . . 93, 497
1:3–5 496
1:6–7 504
1:7 . . . . 496, 1020
1:21 903
1:22 . . . . . 803, 861, 975
1:27–31 507
1:28 1021
2:3 . . . . 861, 975
2:7 . . . 336, 502, 873, 884,
    922, 1043
2:19–20 507
3 . . . . 163, 232, 380, 503
3:4–5 220
3:8 431
3:19 336
4 936
5:12–16 560
5:32 518
6:5 391
6:12 1043
7:14 714
7:15 1021
7:22 1043
8 649
9:1 803
9:7 803
9:8–17 89
12 . . . . 231, 487, 524
12:1–3 . . . . 232, 327, 381,
    417, 422, 515, 523, 635
12:2 . . . . 861, 975
12:7 . . . . 91, 431
12:10–20 517
13:17 661
14 . . . . 255, 517, 593
14:7 . . . . 871, 884
14:15 . . . . 871, 884

14:22 921
15 . . . . 232, 270
15:1 431
15:14–16 155
17:1 464
17: 7–8 515
20 517
21:8 803
25 724
25:8 665
27:28 855
27:30 . . . . 861, 975
28:3 803
28:10–20 840
30 649
31:42 761
35:1 919
35:11 803
36:36 . . . . 871, 884
39:7 751
42:18 718
44:14 791
45:11 791
47:19 921
49:24 . . . . 150, 840
49:30 921

Exodus

1 519
1–15 561
2:23 . . . . . . 554, 643, 951
2:23–25 . . . . . . 175, 542
2:24 . . . . 302, 533
2:25 773
3 . . . . 380, 635, 636
3:7–10 473
3:9 541
3:13–15 99
3:15 867
3:15–16 533
3:19–20 318
3:20 . . . . . 601, 883, 991
4:22 355
6 649

6:1 318
6:2–3 247
6:3 943
6:5 302
6:6 552
6:7 . . . . 932, 968
6:14 791
7:1–7 634
9:16 602
10:1–2 85
10:24 520
12:17 884
12:29 867
12:43 978
13 134
13–17 147
13:3 154
13:18 188
13:21–22 520
14 . . . . 129, 632
14–15 631
14:11 148
14:13 . . . . 134, 402
14:13–14 534
14:16–17 879
14:19–25 520
14:22 879
14:27 879
14:30–31 686
15 . . . . 143, 286, 373,
    631, 681, 684, 686,
    687, 981, 1002
15:2 . . 375, 385, 402, 681,
    686, 709
15:3 432
15:5 261
15:6 . . . . 86, 127, 318,
    602, 686
15:6–12 129
15:11 . . . . . 143, 217, 280,
    684, 714
15:12 . . . . 686, 761
15:13 . . 83, 130, 552, 686
15:14–15 686

15:15 236
15:18 . . . . 991, 1002
15:20 1035
15:20–21 834
15:22–27 206
16 . . . . 148–50, 154, 164
16–17 149
16:2–3 148
16:8 150
17 405
17:1–7 . . . . 206, 405, 539
17:3 405
17:2 206
17:7 148
18:1 955
18:4 765
18:11 867
19 . . . . . . 236, 432, 524,
635, 977, 1042
19–20 . . . . 203, 427, 427,
432, 503
19–24 232
19:3–6 524
19:5–6 . . . . . . 327, 524
19:6 631
19:16–19 428
20 367
20–23 427
20:1–3 207
20:2 . . . . 207, 955
20:2–4 651
20:3 207
20:5 171
20:18–21 . . . . . 129, 236
20:23 646
20:24 . . . . 861, 975
22:21–24 390
22:24–26 612
23:12 664
23:17 742
23:22 811
23:20–23 351
23:25 . . . . 861, 975
25:17–22 443
25:22 443
26:30–37 380
26:36 922
27:2 612
27:16 922
28:2 418
28:39 922

29 446
29:7 854
30:30–32 854
31:8 379
32–34 . . . . 262, 334,
342, 445
32:2–3 646
32:9–10 . . . . . . 157, 445
32:11 272
32:11–14 262
32:14 445
32:15 379
32:32 293
33:1–3 157
33:2 351
32:4 918
33:7–11 446
34 487
34:2 567
34:6 . . . . . 279, 484, 537,
602, 611, 612, 616,
671, 711, 961
34:6–7 . . . 125, 153, 173,
339–40, 447, 480,
485, 516, 659, 758,
991, 1035, 989
34:7 487
34:10 684
34:12 191
34:14 . . . . 156, 171
34:23 742
35:35 922
36:37 922
38:18–23 922
40 703

Leviticus
4 170
4:13–21 827
4:14 1029
8:10 854
8:12 854
8:15 613
9:5 852
9:22 854
10:11 446
11:15 1011
18:24–30 540
19:2 287
20:19 898
20:22–26 540

22:25 978
23:9 1044
23:10 740
23:23–25 201
23:24 203
23:33–43 201
25:9 1042
25:35–37 773
25:35–38 612
25:36 612
25:36–37 773
26 237
26:11–12 515
26:15 714
26:40–45 393
26:44 714

Numbers
1–3 293
1:4 856
5 581
6:22–27 187
6:24 . . . . 862, 863
6:25 714
6:25–26 920
10:9 811
10:10 203
10:35 842
11 . . . 148, 149, 154, 164
11:4 150
11:4–5 148
11:4–6 . . . 149, 164, 535
11:4–35 535
11:20 536
12:6–8 635
13–14 537
14 405
14:3 405
14:12 669
14:18 . . . . 173, 279
14:20–25 148
14:45 . . . . 871, 884
15:25–28 827
15:38–41 134
16 535
16:30 535
18:10 72
20 405
20:2–13 634
20:4 405
21 405

20:1–13 539
20:9–12 539
21:5 405
21:21–24 879
22–23 534
22:23 814
25 538
25:13 538
25:17 811
27:21 734
29:1 201
29:12–40 201
31 234
35:19 175

Deuteronomy

1:27 537
2:3 879
3:23 951
4 . . . . 446, 526, 540
4:1–14 327
4:5–9 522
4:7–8 144
4:9 144
4:9–10 . . . . 266, 486
4:10 134
4:11–12 428
4:14 239
4:31 910
4:34 885
5 . . . . 367, 427, 503
5:1 404
5:2 536
5:9 171
5:9–10 173
5:15 . . . . 134, 977
5:22–27 129
6 354
6:4 954
6:4–5 . . . . 142, 207, 282
6:7 144
6:8 134
6:14–15 156
6:16 354–55
6:19–25 144
6:21 . . . . 154, 630
7 . . . . 513, 519, 540
7:1–11 539
7:7 366
7:11 514
7:13 498

7:17–24 514
7:18 . . . . 134, 514
8 . . . . 134, 155, 185
8–9 382
8:2 134
8:15 879
8:18 134
9:3 541
9:7 134
9:26–29 169
10:9 72
10:12 648
10:12–13 . . . . . 266, 473
10:15 366
10:17 882
11:2 134
12:4–14 99
13:4 648
14:10 294
14:14 1009
15:15 134
16 91
16:1–7 . . . . 201, 374
16:3 134
16:12 134
16:13–16 244
17:11 446
17:14–20 . . . . . 326, 465
19:12 175
20:12 918
23:1–3 1029
24:6 612
24:8 134
24:9 134
24:22 134
25:17 134
26:5–10 516
26:12 390
26:14 538
26:17–19 403
28 . . . 321, 326, 540, 542
28–29 337
29:29 1001
28:49 630
28:64–68 . . . . . 174, 208,
    533, 541
29:6 884
29:21 337
29:22–29 151
29:26 169
30:11–14 144

31:6 910
31:6–8 393
31:12 648
31:16 895
31:16–18 171
32 . . . . 221, 402
32:4 . . . . 366, 402
32:6 921
32:7 134
32:8 . . . . .217, 221
32:8–9 . . . . . . 221, 223
32:10 879
32:11 366
32:12 895
32:15 402
32:16 171
32:25 899
32:36 879
32:39–43 1034
33:1 975
33:17 364

Joshua

1:5 910
2:10 872
2:11 613
3 186
3–5 631
3:16 632
4 133
4:19–24 134
4:23 632
5:1 613
5:13 814
6 . . . . 8, 202
6:4–20 1042
6:10 451
7 969
7:5 613
9:10 872
10:6 910
10:20 741
11:10–12 . . . . . . 871, 884
12:24 886
14:4–5 72
14:9 794
14:13 794
15:13 . . . . 710, 953
15:20 794
16:5 794
18:7 953

18:17. 710
19:9. . . . . 710, 953
21:1. 872
24 870
24:15. 870
24:16–18. 403
24:17. 736
24:19. 171
24:20. 895
24:23. 895

Judges
1 146
3:9. 951
3:16. 1036
3:22. 814
3:27. 1042
4–8 234
4:17–24. 234
5:10–31. 834
6–8 . . . . 234, 236
6:6–7 951
7 202
8:10. 814
8:20. 814
9:54. 814
10:16. 895
11:34. 1020
13:18. 918
18:2. 917
19:3. 856
20 969
20:2 . . . . 814, 1029
20:15. 814
20:17. 814
20:35. 814
20:46 814

Ruth
2 814
2:4. 814
2:12. 835
3:3. 943
4:11 . . . . 791, 842
4:14. 834

1 Samuel
1:11–20. 82
1:20–23 833
2 889
2:1. 107

2:8. 993
2:9. 736
2:10. 613
2:11. 845
2:12–36. 158
4–6 . . . . . 146, 154, 842
4:1–11 158
4:17. 842
5:6. 918
7:1–17 26
11:15 740
14:44. 723
17 974
17:46. 761
17:51 814
18:7. 1030
18:13. 734
18:25–27. 681
19:9–10. 1042
20:12–13. 723
20:13. 723
24 . . . . 566, 950
25:22. 723
25:34. 761
31:4. 814

2 Samuel
2:308b 1002
2:27. 761
3:9. 723
3:35. 723
4:12. 812
5 844
5:2. 184
5:23. 249
6 841–42
6–7 . . . . 841, 844
6:1–19. 838
6:20 . . . . 861, 975
7 . . 160, 232, 320–21, 487,
    593, 838, 841, 844
7:7. 184
7:16. 791
7:23. 991
8 566
10:3. 917
11 936
11:1 918
11:11 896
14:4. 722
19:13 723

19:34. 897
21:10. 169
22:26–28 63
22:45–46 978
24:9. 814

1 Kings
1:17. 722
2:23. 723
3:6 173
3:7. 734
4 314
5:2. 894
5:18. 791
6 366
6–7 790
7:7. 742
8 625–26
8:15–21. 99
8:22–66 90
8:27. . . . . . 90, 496, 504
8:27–30. 92
8:30–53 827
8:44 844
11:13 844
11:32 844
11:36 845
12:27. 897
15:17. 735
15:20. . . . . 272, 855
16 363
21 936
22:11 1022
22:17. 184

2 Kings
3:14. 761
3:26. 814
5:23. 918
6:31. 723
8:12. 899
12:11 791
15:29. 855
17 146
18–19 . . . . .112, 119
18:30. 763
19:19. 763
19:27. 134
19:35–36. 114
21 969
23:9. 897

24:15 785
25 844
25:8–21 785

1 Chronicles

1:8 518
5 1042
5:21 894
6:16–47 244
7:20–24 146
9:17–22 244
13:5 842
13:6 842
14:13–16 249
15:16 1042
15:21 98
16:4–7 59
16:34 868
22–29 251
22:14 840
22:15 840
23:20 862
26 251
28:2 842
29:28 665

2 Chronicles

2:1–6 91
5 1042
5:11–14 1044
6 248
6:36 894
6:41–42 843
8:17 553
16:1 734
19:9 648
20:19 244
34:11 791
36:23 887

Ezra

1:2 887
3:8–9 98
3:10 791
5:11 887
5:13 901
6:9 887
6:22 234
7:7 631
7:12 887
8:31 193

9 819

Nehemiah

1:3 744
1:4 887
2:4 887
4 753
4:5 791
5 . . . . 744, 773
5:1–5 980
5:5 744
6 680
8:1–18 703
9 819
9:2 978
9:17 . . . . . 173, 279, 553,
                   823, 828
12:27 . . . . 894, 1008
13:6 901

Job

1–2 . . . . 216, 303
1:1 464
1:6 216
1:21 922
2 225
2:1 216
3:5 555
4:6 145
4:13 925
4:19 962
5:9 883
5:17 705
8:9 976
9:32 969
10:21 555
11:20 953
12:13 535
12:22 555
13:5 502
13:9 917
14:2 976
14:3 969
17:7 976
18:19 920
20:2 925
20:25 814
21:12 894
22:4 969
24:5 602
28 501

28:3 555
28:23–28 501
28:28 604
30:19–23 308
30:22 471
33:1 141
34:2 555
34:4 852
36:11 8528
37:14 415
37:18 883
38–41 501
38:1 206
38:2 535
38:22–28 505
38:25–26 496
39:4 781
40:11–12 488
40:15–24 1020
41:1–34 1020

Psalms

1 . . . . 61, 726
1–2 24
1–41 23
1:1 . . . . . . 392, 531, 802
1:1–3 31
1:2 601
1:3 . . . . 25, 365
1:4–5 364
1:5 943
1:6 . . . 24, 25, 34, 74, 392,
         503, 773, 994, 1002
2 . . . . . . 26, 31, 295, 315,
          328, 382, 421, 589,
          595, 838, 1027, 1037
2–72 . . . . 25, 325
2–89 . . . . 25, 26
2:1–3 . . . . 238, 999
2:2 1003
2:5 . . . . 236, 594
2:6–9 25
2:7 1012
2:10 . . . . 25, 979
2:10–12 238
2:11 451
2:12 . . . . . 802, 953, 1003
3–41 . . . . 21, 25
3 983
3:1 35
3:3 254

3:6 306	17:7 193	26:8 841
3:7. 35	17:8 . . . . 33, 733	26:9. 924
4:1 961	18 . . . . . . 236, 315, 589,	27:1 . . . . 252, 611
4:5 . . . . 35, 1032	636, 816, 983	27:2. . . . . 35, 36
5:3. 825	18:1 253	27:3. 35
5:5. 102	18:1–2. . . . . 72, 152	28:2. . . . . 862, 961, 963
5:7. . . . . 862, 905	18:2. . . . . 107, 402, 943	28:5. 863
5:12 . . . . 253, 1004	18:3. . . . . 613, 845	28:9. 184
6 . . . . 472, 819	18:4–15 428	29 632
6:3. . . . . 170, 323	18:7. 503	29:1. 216
6:5 . . . . 999, 1018	18:7–15 . . . . . 129, 496	29:1–2. 417
6:6 872	18:8. 428	30 726
6:10. 35	18:8–12. 428	30:7–8 825
8:6 978	18:10. 443	30:9 . . . . 306, 483, 999
9:12 175	18:19. 930	30:11. 1045
9:15. 35	18:31. 402	31:3. 943
7:5. . . . . 35, 707	18:35. 193	31:13. 981
7:6. 272	18:46. . . . . >. . 402	31:15. 932
7:10. 253	18:47. 96	31:17. 941
7:11. 272	18:49. 672	32 . . . . . . 472, 556, 819
7:12. 812	19 . . . . . .807, 918, 1013	32:1–2. 802
7:15. 392	19:1 . . . . 508, 1040	32:8. 81
8 . . . . 59, 494, 983	19:7. . . . . 183, 380, 659	33 494
8:4. 192	19:9. 603	33:3. . . . 436, 1029, 1037
9 1027	19:14 152	33:6. 1011
9:1. 905	20 589	33:7. 553
9:10. 486	20–21 382	33:12. 802
9:15. 392	20:6 193	33:20. 731
10 766	20:10. 907	34:8 802
10:4. . . . . 238, 283	21 589	34:10. 152
10:6 35	21:1 375	35:1–3. 580
11:3. 1004	21:5 . . . . 601, 1022	35:4. 813
11:4. 622	22 . . . . 476, 726	35:7–8 . . . . 35, 392
12:1. 748	22:1. . . . . 76, 105	35:10. 217
12:3. 708	22:10. 921	35:16. 613
13 59	22:12–13. 36	35:17. 323
13:1. . . . . 170, 323	22:15. 707	35:18. 605
13:4. 35	22:19. 941	36:7. . . . . 33, 733
13:7. 35	22:22. 1029	36:9. 252
14:2. 622	22:27. . . . . 152, 152	37 986–87
14:2–3. 534	23 . . . . . . 267, 767, 830	37:6. 611
15 34	23:1. 105	37:8–11 773
15:1. 35	23:3. 481	37:9. 806
15:2. 1004	23:4. 131	37:12. 613
15:5. 497	23:5. 35	38 . . . . . . 472, 556, 819
16:4–7 59	24:3. . . . . 35, 841	38:16. 736
16:8. . . . . 497, 733, 952	24:4. 481	38:22. 941
17:1. 954	24:10. 188	39 556
17:2–3. 622	25 986–87	39:11. 39081
17:5. 497	25:7. 962	40 59
17:6. 941	26:5 35	40:1. 961

40:3 . . . . .436, 648, 1029, 1037
40:4 802
40:11. 440
40:13. 941
40:15. 813
41:2. 943
41:3. . . . . 23, 324
41:4. 802
42–49. 21
42–72. 23
42:3. 644
42:4. 708
42:9. 943
42:11. 7
43:3. . . . . 252, 841
44:13. 611
44:13–16. 753
44:15. 568
44:26 707
45:7. 772
46 . . . . . 33, 83, 191, 267, 289, 293, 382, 613, 770, 1027
46:2 953
46:4 . . . . . . 90, 738, 739
46:4–7 739
46:5 770
46:7 . . . . 188, 474
46:8–10 116
46:11. 188
47:1 201
47:2–9. 1039
47:4. 160
47:6. 1042
47:9. 281
48 . . . . . . 33, 83, 91, 191, 267, 289, 293, 382, 770, 776, 1027
48:1. 908
48:1–3. 290
48:2. . . . . 103, 738
48:3. 33
48:4–7 116
48:5 236
48:8 188
48:9. 738
49:7. 611
50 . . . . . 21, 90, 100, 200
51 . . . 267, 472, 819, 847
51:6–7. 962

51:11 919
51:15 440
51–72 . . . . 21, 25
52:9. . . . . 605, 611
53:1–3. 937
55:3. 924
55:18. 35
56:1–2. 580
56:8 923
56:9. 907
56:12–13. 666
57:1 733
57:2. 905
57:4. . . . . 724, 1033
57:7–11 565
57:10 568
58 816
58:4–5 931
59:2. 924
59:17. 825
60:2 770
60:5–12 565
61:1 961
62 830
62:6–7 32
62:7. 123
63:1. 932
63:7. 733
64:1. 961
64:3 . . . . 931, 1033
65:4. 802
65:5. 375
65:7. 553
65:9. 192
66:1. 201
66:4 . . . . 281, 740
67:7–8. 953
68:18. 281
68:29. 281
69 . . . . .317, 476
69:1–2. 557
69:5. 76
69:15. 762
69:28. . . . . 923, 924
70:3. 813
71:3. . . . . 335, 943
71:19. 217
72 . . . . . 21, 26, 315, 382, 421, 589, 872
72:1–2. 326
72:2 318

72:8–11. 116
72:10. 979
72:11. 710
72:12–14. 935
72:18. . . . . 763, 883
72:18–19. 23
72:20 . . . . 326, 949, 989
73 . . . . 58, 59, 61, 67, 90, 122, 179, 362, 436
73–83. . . . . . 21, 90, 244
73–89. . 23, 59, 277, 330, 353, 367, 412, 333, 437
73:1. . . . . . 60, 61, 68, 74
73:2. 72
73:2–17. 61
73:3. 102
73:5. 65
73:7. 63
73:11 . . . . 74, 283
73:12. 65
73:13. 68
73:13–14. 66
73:14. 65
73:14–16. 65
73:15–17. 66
73:16. . . . . . . 65, 66, 78
73:17. 363
73:18. 65
73:18–20. 68
73:21–22. 67
73:22. 69
73:23. 920
73:23–24 71
73:27. . . . . 72, 465
73:28. . . . . . . 74, 77, 99
74 . . . .26, 59, 88, 90, 94, 104–5, 111, 220, 238, 297, 313, 412
74:1. . . . . 82, 99, 155
74:1–3. 83
74:1–11 86
74:2. . . . . 82, 552
74:3. 1040
74:4. . . . . .101, 811
74:4–7 169
74:4–9 . . . . 84, 112
74:10. .111, 215, 323, 1022
74:10–11 . . . . 84, 98, 109
74:11 . . . . . 103, 109, 113
74:12. . . . . 264, 402
74:12–17. . . . . . . 86, 88

74:12–21 86
74:12–14 93
74:13 553
74:13–17 87
74:14 1020
74:18 . . . . 98, 215
74:18–23 89
74:20 105
74:22 . . . .90, 98, 111, 215
74:22–23 109
75 . . . . 97, 105, 378
75:1 . . . . . . 99, 605, 621
75:2 . . . . .98, 101, 113
75:2–5 . . . . 100, 101
75:3 101
75:4 . . . . 98, 102
75:4–5 106
75:5 107
75:6 103
75:6–8 102
75:7 98
75:7–8 98
75:8 . . . 108, 111, 113, 918
75:9–10 104
75:10 105–7,
76 . . . . . . 105, 210, 289
76:1 111–12
76:1–2 118
76:1–3 111
76:2 113
76:3 112–13,
76:3–10 118
76:4–6 112
76:5 . . . . 113, 150
76:6 1000
76:7 823
76:7–10 113
76:8 . . . . 113, 832
76:9 115
76:10 . . . . .114, 117
76:11 117
76:11–12 116
76:12 117
77 . . . . 119, 132, 317, 503
77:1–2 206
77:1–9 . . . . 122, 124, 132
77:2 123
77:3–6 123
77:4 . . . . . . 124, 952, 963
77:5–6 . . . . . . 124, 963
77:7–9 . . . . 125, 127

77:10 126
77:10–12 131
77:11 . . . . 143, 152
77:11–15 127
77:12 484
77:12–20 131
77:14 143
77:16 552
77:16–20 143
77:17–18 129
77:20 . . . . . 130, 155, 184
78 . . . . 81, 132, 210, 513,
599, 846
78:1 . . . . 81, 170
78:1–2 141
78:1–8 . . . . .141, 161, 533
78:2 141
78:4 . . 142, 554, 883, 991
78:5 380
78:7 144
78:8 145
78:8–9 . . . . . . 171, 187
78:9 148
78:9–16 145
78:10–11 146
78:11 . . . . 484, 554
78:12–16 147
78:12–43 140
78:13 147
78:17–21 150–51,
78:18 . . . . 164, 536
78:19–20 148
78:21–22 149
78:23–25 149
78:24 . . . . 150, 163
78:27 150
78:29 150
78:30–31 151
78:32 554
78:32–39 151
78:35 153
78:37 152
78:40–55 154–55
78:41 536
78:42 826
78:56 . . . . 156, 536
78:56–64 . . . . . 140, 156
78:57 156
78:58 156
78:60 157–58,
78:61 158

78:62–63 158
78:64 158
78:65 159
78:65–72 162
78:68 291
78:72 160
79 . . . . 26, 210, 211, 238,
297, 313, 412, 757
79:1 176
79:1–2 669
79:1–4 . .168, 174, 176, 179
79:2 . . . . 177, 815
79:3 170
79:4 215
79:5 . . . . . .171, 177, 323
79:6 . . . . 177, 474
79:6–7 172
79:7 172
79:8 172
79:9 . . . . 36, 172
79:10 . .170, 215, 230, 644
79:11 175
79:12 . . . . . .170, 177, 215
79:13 . . . . 177, 452
80 . . .21, 81, 132, 210–11
80:1 . . . 82, 155, 183, 186
80:1–2 . . . 184, 185, 206
80:3 . . . . . 186, 187, 198
80:4 . . . . . 197, 245, 323
80:6 . . . . 215, 231
80:7 . . . . . 186, 187, 198
80:8–11 189
80:8–18 189
80:10 215
80:12–13 190
80:14 . . . . 198, 245
80:16 192
80:17 195
80:19 . .186, 187, 198, 245
81 . . . . 100, 132, 235
81:1–3 . . . . . .201–2, 212,
81:1–5 200
81:2 1043
81:3 201
81:4–5 203
81:6–7 . . . . 205, 207
81:7 205
81:9 207
81:10 207
81:11–16 208
81:12 . . . . .208, 209

81:13 . . . . 205, 210
81:14 231
81:15 209
82 . . . . 32, 100, 211, 235,
238, 415, 421, 430,
431, 504, 909
82:1 215
82:2 . . . . .217, 323
82:3–4 218
82:5 219
82:6 225
82:6–7 219
82:7 220
82:8 . . . . . . 220–21, 230
83 . . . . .81, 412, 816
83:1 230
83:1–7 230
83:1–8 229
83:3–5 231
83:4 . . . . . . 231, 235–36
83:5 232
83:6–8 . . . . . . 233, 237
83:7 231
83:8 234
83:9 234
83:9–15 237
83:9–18 . . . 229, 233, 234
83:10 234
83:13 236
83:14–15 235
83:17 239
84 . . . . 33, 155, 289
84–85 21
84–88 244
84:1 . . . . 738, 841
84:1–4 245
84:3 246
84:4 . . . . 319, 802
84:5–7 248
84:8 1000
84:8–9 250
84:10–12 251
84:11 . . . . 253, 319
85:1–3 . . . . 260, 264
85:2–3 271–72
85:3 269
85:4–7 263
85:5 220
85:8 145
85:8–9 264
85:9 338

85:10–13 267
85:11 268
86 . . . . 244, 822
86:1–7 . . . . 272, 277
86:8 216
86:8–10 . . . . . 280, 288
86:9 . . . . . 288, 412, 941
86:11 283
86:11–17 281
86:15 283
87 . . . . 33, 293, 770
87:1–3 290
87:2 . . . . . . 160, 290, 738
87:4 291
87–88 21
88 . . . . 21, 726
88:1–5 301
88:4–6 306
88:5 666
88:6–8 303
88:9 941
88:9–12 304
88:10 605
88:13–18 305
88:14 825
89 26
89:1–18 314
89:1–37 330
89:5 883
89:5–18 316
89:8 217
89:10 . . . . 291, 1020
89:14 . . . . 219, 326
89:15 . . . . 337, 802
89:17 1022
89:18 845
89:19–20 731
89:19–37 . . . . . 314, 319
89:24 320
89:32 321
89:33–35 322
89:38–51 . . 314, 322, 330
89:44 26
89:46 170
89:50–51 26
89:52 . . . . . 23, 324, 763
90 . . . . 21, 353, 906, 949
90–106 . . . . . 23, 31, 333
90:1 334
90:8 926
90:10 377

90:11 338
90:12–17 338–39
90:13 342
90:14 825
91 . . . . 267, 605
91:1–2 348
91:2 . . . . 355, 953
91:3 . . . . 335, 357
91:3–13 349
91:9 335,355
91:13–16 352
92:11–13 360
93 . . . . . 22, 28, 317, 372,
378, 380, 498, 501,
888, 988
93–100 . . . 131, 238, 372,
380, 395, 418, 435, 442,
447, 455, 490, 988
93:1 . . . . . .32, 372, 395,
426, 495, 1024
93:5 379
94 412
94:1–3 . . . . 388, 432
94:3 323
94:4–7 391
94:5 962
94:8–11 391
94:11 394
94:12 802
94:13 393
94:14 394
94:15 460
94:17 761
94:18 736
94:20–23 394
95 200
95–99 . . . . 22, 28
95:1 1043
95:1–5 402
95:1–7 405
95:3 . . . .31, 216–17, 1009
95:6 . . . . . . 32, 404, 918
95:6–7 452
95:7 . . . . . . 184, 404, 452
95:7d-11 . . 407, 409, 811
95:11 404
96 . . . . 292, 888
96:1 . . . . 436, 444,
1029, 1037
96:3 . . . . . 436, 437, 883
96:4 216–17

96:4–6 415
96:5 429
96:6 . . . . 495, 1035
96:7. 417
96:7–10. 417
96:10. . 32, 372, 388, 395
96:13. . . . . . . 981, 1037
97 . . . . 432, 888
97:1 . . .32, 372, 395, 426,
426, 908, 1024
97:2. . . . . . 219, 428, 460
97:2–5. 431–2
97:3–4 634
97:5. 995
97:6. . . . . 429, 508
97:7. . . . . . . 433, 454–55
97:7–10. 429
97:8. 428
97:9. . . . . 216, 405
97:10. 430
97:11–12 430
97:17. 418
98:1. . . . . 883, 1037
98:1–3. 436
98:2. 437
98:3. . . . . 441, 460
98:4 454
98:4–6 437
98:6 . . . . 989, 1042
98:7–9. 440
98:9. . . . . 981, 1037
99 . . . . 432, 888
99:1. . 372, 395, 443, 995
99:1–3. 443
99:4 32
99:5 842
99:6 28
99:6–9 . . . . . . 445, 449
99:7. 446
99:8 446
100 1024
100:1. 454
100:1–3. 450
100:2 . . . . 451, 454
100:3 . . . . 176, 452
100:4–5 453
100:5 460
101 . . . . 455, 589
101:2–3. 460
101:3–8. . . . . . 461, 464
101:8. 465

102 . . . . . 455, 819, 949
102:1. 961
102:1–11 470
102:2. 822
102:6. 823
102:9. 472
102:12–22. 471–474
102:15. 905
102:19. 473
102:23. 979
102:23–27. 477
102:25. 497
102:26. 909
103 . . . . . 455, 537, 999
103:1. 481
103:1–2. 481
103:3–6 482
103:7. . . . . 28, 516
103:7–19. 484
103:8. . . . . 173, 659
103:9–10. 485
103:14–16. 486
103:15–17. 845
103:18. 603
103:19. 487
103:20. 150
103:20–22 . .488, 496, 763
104 1013
104:1. 601
104:1–4 494
104:3–4 497
104:5–9 1024
104:5–18. 497
104:6 261
104:7–9. 498
104:10–18. . . . . 501, 506
104:10–30 1024
104:13. 991
104:13–14. 1009
104:14–15. 483
104:19. 506
104:19–23. 499
104:24. . . . . . . 500, 991
104:25–26 501
104:27. 993
104:27–30. 502
104:29–30 919
104:31–35. 502
105 . . . . . . 28, 599, 629
105:1. 605
105:1–7. 513–14

105:5. .513, 554, 883, 991
105:8–15. 515–17
105:16–22. 517
105:23–28. 517
105:26. 28
105:38. 637
105:43–45 519
106 . . . . . . 28, 599, 637
106:1. 552
106:4–5 531
106:7. 554
106:9–11 535
106:13. 802
106:14. 546
106:16. 28
106:19–23. 536
106:22 . . . 883, 921, 991
106:24–27 537
106:28–33 538–39
106:34–39 . .539–40, 560
106:37. 546
106:40–46 541–42
106:44 954
106:48 . . . . 23, 324, 763
107 . . . . . . .28, 811, 1013
107–150 . . . . 23, 28
107:1. 552
107:1–3 551
107:2. 571
107:2–3. 28
107:3. 561
107:8. 605
107:15. 883
107:17–22 556
107:20. 556
107:22. 909
107:23–32. 557
107:25. 557
107:29. 557
107:33–41. 557
107:42–43. 559
108–110 21
108:1–4. 566
108:4. 670
108:5–6 568
108:7–9. 569
108:10–13. 570–72
108:13–14. 999
109 816
109:1–5. 579–80
109:6–7 580–81

109:8. 586
109:8–9 568
109:8–19. 581–82
109:20–25 882–83
109:26–29 583
109:30–35 583–84
109:31. 733
110 . . . 315, 382, 596–97
110:1–3. 591–93
110:3. 592
110:4–7. 593–94
110:5. 733
111–18 22
111 607
111:1–2 600–1
111:2 909
111:3 . . . . 601, 823
111:3–6. 601–2
111:4 . . . . 602, 659, 826
111:6 . . . . 602, 909
111:7–10 602–4
111:8 603
112 . . . . 616, 705
112:1 . . . . 610, 648, 802
112:2–5. 610–12
112:3. 611
112:4. . . . . 611, 659
112:6–9. 612–13
112:9. . . . . 107, 619
112:10 613–14
113 . . . . . . 755, 908, 977
113–18 . . . . . . .599, 620,
638, 669
113:1 862
113:1–3 620–21
113:2. 619
113:3 628
113:4–6. 621–22
113:5–6. . . 821, 887, 905
113:7. 758
113:7–9 622–23
114:1–2 630–31
114:3–4. 631–33
114:5–6. 633
114:7–8. 634
115 . . . . . . 755, 919, 977,
981, 115
115:1–3 643–46
115:2 . . . . 36, 652, 671–2
115:3 . . . . . 645, 712, 821,
870, 887

115:3–8. 867
115:4–6. 873
115:4–8. . . .646–48, 906
115:8 . . . . 31, 621
115:9–11 . . 648–49, 677,
731, 867, 873
115:12–13 648–49
115:14–15 649–50
115:15 . . . 732, 863, 1000
115:16 650
115:16–18 650–51
115:17 . . . . 306, 1018
115:22 975
115:28 494
116 708
116:1–2 657
116:3–6. 658
116:7–9. 660–61
116:8–9. 666
116:10–11 661
116:12–14 662–663
116:15–16 663–64
116:17–19 664
116:19 867
117:1 . . . . 481, 669
117:2 . . . . 670, 1000
118 766
118:1 . . . . . 531, 552, 868
118:1–4. 677
118:2–3. 481
118:4–5. 665
118:5. 722
118:5–14. 760
118:5–18 . . . . . .677, 682,
684, 689
118:7. 666
118:14 681
118:17 . . . . 909, 999
118:19–28 682–86
118:22–23. 688
119 . . . 34, 140, 599, 966
119:1–2. 902
119:1–8. 705–6
119:5–8. 1012
119:9. 1012
119:9–16. 706
119:13 659
119:14 . . . . 183, 611
119:17–24 708
119:23 707
119:25–32. 707

119:27 812
119:29. 945
119:32. 710
119:33–40. 708
119:41–48 708–9
119:52. 920
119:54 718
119:57–64. 710
119:73–74. 658
119:73–80. 710–11
119:75 440
119:81–88 711–12
119:84 323
119:89–96. 712
119:90. 823
119:97–104. 712
119:105–12 713
119:113–20 713
119:121–28 714
119:129–36 714–15
119:137–44 715
119:145–52 715
119:153–60 715–16
119:161–68 716
119:169–76 716–17
120–34 . . . . 22, 30, 720,
819, 846
120 . . . . . . 636, 850, 930
120:1. 721–2
120:1–7. 580
120:3–4 754
120:4. 794
120:5–7 724
120:7. 806
121 . . . . 755, 931
121:1 751
121:1–2 730–31
121:2 . . . . . 32, 722, 1000
121:3–4. 723–4
121:5–6. 733
121:7–8 . . . . . . 734, 810
121:8. 621
122 289
122:1–2 . . . 740, 795, 863
122:3–5. 741–3
122:6–9 . . .743–44, 806
123 944
123:1 . . 33, 712, 748, 821,
887, 1018
123:1–2. 750–2
123:2. . . . . 870, 933

123:3 769
123:3–4 . .735, 753–54, 757
123:4 811
124 . . . . 836, 978
124:1 563
124:1–2 . . . . . . 791, 810
124:1–5 760–63
124:2 494
124:4–5 735
124:6 863
124:6–7 763–64
124:8 . . . . .33, 494, 735,
        764, 1000
125 836
125:1–2 770–71
125:2 . . . . 621, 795
125:3 . . . . . 735, 771–73
125:4–5 773–74
125:5 . . . . 801, 806
126 . . . . 262, 836
126:1 795
126:1–3 . . . . 474, 780–83
126:2 810
126:4 735
126:4–6 783–85
126:6 814
127 . . . . 21, 801
127:1 . . . . 756, 810
127:1–2 791–93
127:3–5 793
128:1 806
128:1–4 801–4
128:5 . . . . 795, 863
128:5–6 804–6
129:8 863
129 . . . . 776, 836
129:1–5 . . . . 735, 810–13
129:3–4 756
129:5 795
129:5–8 813–15
130 472
130:1–2 821–22
130:3–4 822–24
130:5–6 824–25
130:7 846
131 750
131:1 831–2
131:2 832–33
131:3 846
131:8 621
132:1–5 839–41

132:3–4 810
132:5 . . . . 150, 1000
132:6–10 841–43
132:11–12 843–45
132:12 795
132:13 . . . . 795, 874
132:15 863
132:17 107
133 750
133:1 . . 852–53, 858, 867
133:2–3b 853–6
133:3 . . . .290, 856, 863,
        867, 874
134 . . . . . . 750, 975, 999
134:1 867
134:1–2 860–2
134:2 1040
134:3 . . . . . 494, 862–3,
        867, 874
135 . . . . . . 629, 637, 135
135:1 862
135:3 880
135:5–7 869–71
135:5–12 880
135:8–14 871–72
135:6 645
135:15–16 763
135:21 763
136 . . . . 637, 136
136:1 . . . . 531, 552, 868
136:1–3 882
136:4–9 882–83
136:10–15 884–85
136:16–22 885
136:23–25 886
136:26 . . . . . . 712, 1018
137 . . . . 59, 297, 137
137:1–4 893–5
137:5–6 896–97
137:7–9 897–900
137:9 . . . . 920, 943
138 726
138:1–3 906
138:4 979
138:4–6 . . . . 710, 907–8
138:7–8 909–10
139:1–6 916–18
139:7–12 919–20
139:8 908
139:13–18 920–23
139:18 1032

139:19–24 924
140 708
140:1–5 930–32
140:1–6 956
140:2–9 942
140:4 943
140:6–8 932
140:9–11 934–35
140:12–13 935
141:1 822
141:1–3 . . . . . . 937, 941
141:3 937
141:3–6 942–43
141:7–10 944
141:9–10 956
142 . . . . 25, 847
142:1–2 950–51
142:3 956
142:3–4 951–53
142:5 953
142:6–7 954
142:7 605
143 . . . . 472, 819
143:1–2 961
143:3–6 962–64
143:5 . . . . 909, 978
143:7–12 964–67
143:8 825
144 . . . . 503, 872
144:1 763
144:1–2 . . . . 32, 975–76
144:3–4 976–77
144:5–7 887
144:5–8 977–78
144:9 . . . 436, 1029, 1037
144:9–11 978–79
144:12–14 979–80
144:15 . . . . 802, 981
145 32
145:1 1003
145:1–2 989–990
145:3 1008
145:3–7 990–91
145:4 909
145:5 . . . . 601, 1022
145:5–6 832
145:8–9 . .659, 991, 1035
145:9 909
145:10 991
145:10–13 908
145:11–13 992

145:14–15 1003
145:14–16 . . . . 889, 1001
145:14–20 992–94
145:20 36
145:21 . . . . 955, 994
146 . . . . .21, 23, 211, 324
146:3–4 999
146:5 802
146:5–9 999–1000
146:6 1029
146:10 1002
147:1 867
147:1–6 1007
147:2–3 1001
147:8–9 . . . . 32, 998
147:12 998
147:15 569
147:18 569
148:1–6 1018
148:7–14 1019–23
148:89 32
149 201
149:1 . . . . 436, 1029
149:1–4 1029
149:2 998
149:4 1001
149:5–7 843
149:5–9 1032–35
149:7 568
150 . . . . 201, 1037
150:1–2 1040–41
150:2 1044
150:3–5 1041–43
150:4 202
150:6 1043

Proverbs

1:7 . . . . 266, 604
1:13 611
1:32 659
2:10 852
3:3 802
3:4 604
3:6 . . . . 774, 806
3:13 705
3:13–14 851
4:1–8 851
5:4 1036
6 614
6:6–8 796
6:6–11 793

6:9–11 . . . . 796, 797
6:16 63
8 501
8:20 219
8:32 802
9:10 604
10–22 789
10:3 1002
10:6 1002
10:4–5 793
10:12 261
10:13 943
10:27 806
10:30 . . . . 771, 1002
11:8 1002
11:18 1002
11:29 851
12:24 793
13:24 943
14:5 659
14:21 802
16:3 345
16:5 388
16:19 388
16:20 802
17:6 851
19:25 943
21:31 796
22:3 659
22:22–23 370
23:9 918
24:25 852
24:30–34 793
26:3 943
26:18–19 724
28:14 802
29:18 802
31:1 . . . .
682 . . . .
31:23 610

Ecclesiastes

1:2 . . . . 391, 976
2:17–26 500
6:12 852
7:20 937
7:25 145
8:3 645
9:7–8 . . . . 498, 854
10:17 . . . . . 610, 705, 802
11:19 969

Isaiah

1 211
1:17 390
2 474
2:3 897
2:7 646
2:8 415
2:11–12 388
3:17 898
5:1–7 . . . . 189, 194
5:5–6 195
5:7 185
5:29 920
6 . . . 225, 444, 447, 1018
6:1–8 908
6:3 503
6:5 166
7:18 680
8:7 377
9:4 . . . . 772, 812
11:1 845
11:10 672
12 422
12:1–6 911
12:4–5 414
13:11 237
14 593
14:5 772
14:7 954
14:12 593
14:13 103
14:31–32 291
19 422
19:21 943
20:5 813
21:13–17 725
24:4–13 438
24:8 438
24:21–22 1034
26:19 856
28:22 664
28:23 141
28:25 832
30:2–3 733
30:7 291
30:27 680
33:19 631
35:5 1001
35:7 638
36:13–20 644
37:26–27 814

37:27 813
38:7 85
38:18 1018
40–55 . . . .645, 652, 782,
      870, 905, 1031
40–66 . . . . . . 471, 1028
40:3 . . . . 561, 774
40:10 794
40:22 798
40:22–23 625
41 652
41:14 552
41:29 906
42:1 1031
42:5 883
42:7 . . . . 555, 1001
42:10 . . . . . . .436, 982,
      1029, 1037
42:13 670
42:18 580
43:8 1001
43:18–20 561
43:19 638
44:6 552
44:7 624
44:9–20 906
44:17 932
44:23 451
44:24 883
45:2 555
45:14 . . . . 625, 1034
45:18 625
46:1–7 906
46:10 645
47:4 552
48:17 552
49:7 782
49:8 1031
49:9 . . . . 555, 1001
49:12 552
49:19 762
49:23 782
49:26 840
51:1–2 538
51:3 786
51:4 219
51:5–7 1031
51:6 475
51:9 1020
51:10 821
51:11 782–83

51:17 104
52:7 806
52:12 831
54 1011
54:1 649
54:17 862
55 329
55:3 . . . . 974, 1031
55:3–5 843
55:11 556
56 648
56:3 978
56:6 978
57:15 1014
58 938
58:1 631
58:11–12 980
59:2 1033
59:9–10 219
60 495
60:9 1031
60:16 552
61:1 . . . . 414, 1001
61:1–4 1040
61:2 1008
63:2 964
63:19 952
66 754
66:18–24 116

Jeremiah
1:4 706
2 533
2:2 811
2:4–8 815
2:26 813
2:30 682
3:2 731
4:5 741
4:23–26 785
4:26 786
4:27 786
5:3 682
5:15 630
5:19 895
7:5–7 390
7:10 862
7:22 955
7:33 169
8:15 806
8:19 895

9:8 931
10:13 867
10:14 873
11:4 . . . . . 932, 955, 968
13 116
13:16 555
15:1 446
15:11 791
22:3 390
23:5 845
24:7 968
25:15 104
25:35 953
26:18 812
27:2 664
29:5 893
30–33 782
30:11 682
30:22 . . . . 932, 968
31:4 1030
31:8 682
31:15 123
31:20 835
31:31–33 827
31:32 157
31:34 452
32:7 921
32:18–19 173
32:27 1015
32:38 968
32:44 781
33:11 868
33:15 845
33:36 781
34:13 . . . . 907, 955
34:20–21 763
35:11 741
37:4 734
41:10 894
44:10 962
44:29 85
49:12 104
50:9 1029
50:33 1001
51:34 762

Lamentations
1:15 150
2:9 . . . . 85, 291
2:16 762
2:20 900

3:6 963
3:24. 953
3:31. 571
3:32. 173
3:34. 962
4 817
4:10. 900
4:21. 898
5:20–22 1031

Ezekiel
1:3. 706
1:5–28 443
1:7. 774
1:25. 1040
2:1–10. 815
4:3. 918
5:5. 746
8:1. 918
11:20. 968
13:9. 293
14:11 968
16 533
16:35–42 898
16:53. 781
17:1–10 189
18:6. . . . . 731, 751
20:6 955
20:9 . . . . 642, 967
20:23. 538
20:44 967
21:7. 613
22:25. 763
22:30. 537
23:24. 1029
23:32–34. 104
25:12–14. . . . . 571, 898
27:34. 821
34 . . . . 184, 1008
34:1–10. 131
34:11–16. 131
34:16. 1008
36:22 . . . . 643, 967
36:28. 932
38:12. 746
38:15. 553
39:2. 553
39:23. 103
44:7. 978
44:9 978
44:10–16. 873

47 805

Daniel
3:16–18. 357
7:13–14 196
9 819
9:9. 823
12:1. 923

Hosea
1 185
1–3 171
2:17. 811
2:25. 407
10 189
10:14. 146
11:3–4. 835
13:6. 831
13:8. 835
13:14. 666
14:1. 899
14:5. 856

Joel
2:2. 680
2:13. 279
2:16. 1029
2:17. 644
3:4–8 723

Amos
1:12. 899
2:14. 953
3:4. 192
5:1–17 . . . . 585, 815
5:15. 795
9 754

Obadiah
1–15 571
10–14 898
11 898

Jonah
1:7. 733
1:14. 645
2 821
2:2. 763
2:3. . . . . 557, 763
2:5. 557
3:10. 733

Micah
1:4. 613
3:12. 812
4:2. 897
5:2. 842
7:10. 644
7:11. 1012
7:18. 711

Nahum
1:3. 173
1:13. 664
3:10. 899

Habakkuk
1:5–11. 102
2:1–4. 101
2:15–16. 104
3 . . . . 573, 635, 636, 977
3:1–13. 102
3:6 981
3:13. 898

Zephaniah
1:16. 1043
2:2. 1012
3:5. 812
3:12. 680

Haggai
1:3–11. 784
1:6–11. 980
1:10. 856
2:20–23 590

Zechariah
1:12. 81
1:18. 766
1:21. 766
2:11. 766
2:15. 669
3:4. 823
3:8. 845
4:7. 684
7:8–10. 390
10:5. 813
10:6. 670
10:10. 649
11:17 415
12:3. 669
12:7. 1031

13:2. 231
14:16. 897

Malachi
1:2–5. . . . . 784, 924
2:11. 895
3:5. 390
3:10. 602
3:16. 923

Matthew
3:8. 439
4:1–11. 353
4:6 354
4:24. 733
5–7 999
5:3b. 617
5:6. 818
5:4–48 240
5:10b. 617
5:43–48 175
5:44 370
6:10. 465
6:19–34. 75
7:13–14. 947
7:13–27. 75
8:23–27 . . 133, 383, 506
8:26. 498
11:15 211
11:20–34. 108
11:25. 1012
13:9. 211
13:24–30, 36–50 75
13:43. 211
14:23–36. 133
17:15 733
18:1–4. 836
20:1–16. 196
21:5. 688
21:9. 688
21:33–41. 196
21:33–46. 688

Mark
1:2–3. 946
1:15. 995
3:31–25. 857
8:27. 849
9:5–6 166
9:33–34 849
10:17. 849
11:19 688
12:1–12. 196

14:36. 148
15:43. 76

Luke
1 889
1:37. . . . . 638, 1015
1:47–55 834
1:72–73. 525
3:31 329
3:38. 329
4:1–13. 353
4:9–12. 353
8:22–25 383
11:47–51 533
14:26. 924
19:38. 688
20:42–43 595
22:18–19 134
22:42. 108

John
1:3. 1014
1:5. . . . . 495, 920
1:14. . . . . 164, 341, 433
1:16. 77
2 . . . . 273, 858
2:19–22. 91
3:6–17 491
3:16. 560
4:9–10 560
6:31. 163
10 . . . . 226, 408
10:10. . . . . 77, 341
10:11 408
10:34–38 225
12:13 688
13:34–35. 525
14:6. 424
15 . . . . 196, 198
15:5. 345
15:16. 876
15:15 . . . . 345, 798
15:25. 76
17 857
17:12 736
17:21, 23 858
19:10–11 95

Acts
1–4 . . . . 296, 329
2:34. 596

2:42–47 525
7:10. 525
9:2. . . . . 256, 946
19:9. 256
19:18. 946
22 946
22:4. 946
23 . . . . 256, 946
24:14. 946

Romans
1:18. 273
1:18–20. 420
3 546
3:1–8. 937
3:5. 273
3:10–18 969
3:17. 937
3:22. 970
4:1–18. 757
5:8. 828
5:1–11 547
5:20–21 547
5:20–6:2. 269
6:11–14. 547
8:12–29. 757
8:19–22. 438
8:20–22 775
8:28. 383
8:28–31. 356
8:28–39 75
8:29. 384
8:30. 876
8:31. 766
8:31–33. 241
8:31–39. . . . . . . 99, 596
8:34. 596
8:35. 767
8:38–39 901
8:39. 737
11:33 133
12:1–2. 457
12:14–21 240
12:18–21 . . . . . 175, 370
14:10–11 440
15:12 673

1 Corinthians
1:18. 1013
1:18–31 266
1:26–28a. 1013

Scripture Index

1:27. 957
3:16–17. 92
3:20. 397
4:3–5 440
8 224
10 546
10:1–5. 525
10:6 546
10:19–20. 224
10:20. 546
12:11 345
15:55. 666

2 Corinthians
5:6–7 652

Galatians
2:16. 719
4:1. 756
4:1–7. 756
4:4 756
4:5–6 757
4:7. 757
5:1. 971
5:2–5 8
5:6. 9

Ephesians
1:3–14. 876
1:7–8. 490
1:20. 596
2:4–5 687
2:11–22. 257

Philippians
1:6. 250
2:5–11. 605
2:10. 628
4:10–19. 308

Colossians
1:15. 422
1:15–20. . . . . . 506, 605
2:13–15. 120
3:1. 596
3:6 273

1 Timothy
6:17. 506

2 Timothy
1:19 876
3:12–15. 775
3:14. 775
3:16. 586
4:1. 370

Hebrews
1:1–4. 506
1:3. 596
1:6. 433
1:10–12. 477
2:11 384
4:1–13. 408
4:11 408
4:14–16. . . . . . . 92, 448
7–10 255
7:23–28. 92
8:1. 596
9:23–28 255
9:26. 341
10:11–14 255
10:12. 596
10:14. 255
10:19–25. 78
10:24–24 400
10:25. 256
11 161
11:8–16 517
12:2. 596
12:2–3. 597
12:23–24. 397
12:28. 597

James
1:17. . . . . 77, 506
1:22. 615
2:26. 615
3:9. 861
3:17. 615
4:11–12. . . . . . . 397, 440
5:4. 585
5:5. 615
5:6. 585

1 Peter
1:15–16. 287
1:17. 287
1:17–19 343

2:9. 876
2:9–10. 638
3:22. 596
4 775
4:5–6 397
4:12. 775
4:19. 775

1 John
1:5. 495
1:14. 164
4:1–6 8
4:9–10 560
4:10. 560

Revelation
1:5. 329
2:7, 11, 17, 29 211
3:6, 13, 22. 211
4:8 475
5:5. 118
5:6. 118
5:9. . . . . 436, 982
5:9–10. 456
6 . . . . 119, 397
7:9–10. 456
11:17–18 448
12:15. 378
13:1. 378
14:6–13. 108
14:13. . . . . 436, 982
14:10. 108
15 456
15:3–4 . . . . 286, 368
15:4. 286
16 273
16:5–7 368
17:1, 15 378
19 902
19:11 422
19:11–21 902
19:14. 546
20 397
21:1. 383
21:24. 119
21–22 . . . . 119, 329, 506

Subject Index

Abraham, 91, 158, 231, 255, 256, 269, 327, 417, 422, 464, 515–18, 542, 665, 876

acrostic psalms, 19, 27, 29, 598, 600, 602, 604, 607–8, 610–11, 702–3, 713, 881, 986–88

anger, 82, 83, 95–96, 115, 149, 151–53, 156, 157–58, 171–72, 188, 262–63, 269–70, 272–73, 236–37, 471, 484–85, 487, 539, 613, 680, 905, 992

ark of the covenant, 146, 158–59, 316, 443–44

arrogance, 63, 68, 107, 237, 389, 389, 390–91, 463, 762, 766, 831, 835

Asaph/Asaphite, 21, 25, 57, 59, 60–61, 80, 98, 110, 121–22, 127, 140, 155, 167–68, 182–83, 199, 200, 214–15, 228–29, 244, 276, 289, 314, 866, 905, 950

Assyria/Assyrians, 112, 114–15, 119–20, 146, 185–86, 189, 197, 221, 233–34, 553, 644, 680, 772, 813–15, 1010

atheism, 64, 285–87

Babylon/Babylonians, 81–83, 85–86, 89, 95, 97–98, 102–2, 110–11, 113, 168–69, 172, 174, 177, 178, 186, 189, 221, 224, 233, 236, 260, 262, 291, 296, 377, 533, 552–53, 555, 560, 593, 624, 638, 653, 682, 733, 746, 772, 785–86, 891–92, 891–901, 955, 994, 1001, 1030, 1035

blessed (ʾashre), 24, 30, 32, 34, 106, 247–48, 254, 318–19, 392, 417, 461, 531, 533, 601, 609–11, 615, 617–18, 705, 794–95, 800–2, 852, 981

chaos (Chaoskampf), 32, 36, 87, 88–89, 93, 94, 219, 291, 317, 351, 352, 376, 377, 378, 384, 385, 497, 553, 557, 634, 920, 978, 1020, 1030

courts (of the temple), 245–46, 251, 295, 351, 418, 453, 455

Creator, 32, 33, 64, 68, 70–71, 73, 77, 86–89, 94, 334, 344, 372, 387, 402, 413, 416, 419, 494–504, 650, 735, 863, 882, 883, 915, 921, 998, 999, 1000, 1021, 1023–24, 1029–30

didactic poetry, 34, 141, 154, 375, 396, 512, 515, 520, 543, 559, 605, 629, 679, 945

Divine Assembly, 215–17, 219, 222–25, 316

doubt, 59–61, 65–68, 75, 84, 266

Edom, 178, 233–34, 566, 570–71, 897–98

enemy (enemies), 20, 26, 31, 35–36, 39–40, 83–86, 88–89, 108, 115–16, 120, 127, 151, 158, 188, 209, 217, 230, 231, 235–41, 245, 283, 290, 292, 297, 308, 323, 352, 363, 365, 449, 470–71, 553, 567, 570–71, 574, 578, 581–88, 590, 593, 595–96, 613, 637, 658, 670, 678, 680, 681, 704, 707–8, 710, 715–16, 719, 721, 723, 727, 761, 763, 765–66, 771, 810, 812–14, 816, 842, 886–87, 909, 912, 915, 923–24, 930, 934, 948–50, 952, 960, 962, 965

exodus, 82–83, 85–86, 128, 132, 147, 151, 175, 185–86, 189, 191, 202–6, 280, 340, 401, 484, 514, 518–20, 603, 606, 629, 631–32, 682–83, 686–87, 884, 1035–36

fear of the LORD, 141, 266, 282, 338, 486, 598–99, 604, 609–12, 613–14, 667, 800–2, 806, 808

Feast of Tabernacles, 201–4, 244

forgiveness, 91, 158–59, 173–74, 254–55, 260–64, 266–68, 271–72, 341–42, 409, 466, 480–82, 484, 486, 489, 820, 822–24, 826, 827–29

foundations of the earth, 160–61, 219, 475, 497

God of Jacob, 104, 202, 999–1000, 1003

hand
  right hand, 70, 86, 121, 126–27, 137, 158, 183, 192–93, 312–13, 317, 346, 435, 569, 574, 580, 584, 592–94, 681, 686, 733, 920, 952
  hand (of Yahweh), 79, 86, 87, 94–95, 101, 103–4, 108, 183, 189, 190, 193, 208, 213, 311, 317, 320, 361, 364, 393, 396, 437, 482, 502, 537, 573, 598, 603, 636, 681, 884, 909–10, 917, 926, 959, 977
  human hands, 57, 110, 113, 121, 123, 130, 224, 227, 297, 333, 340, 425, 527, 541, 641, 713, 714, 722, 751, 772–73, 794, 810–12, 814, 862, 931, 963, 978, 993
heavens, 32–33, 64, 71, 75, 100, 114, 118, 144, 149–150, 163, 191, 216–17, 222, 268, 306–7, 316–17, 375–77, 416, 419, 485–86, 494, 495–97, 504–5, 557, 565, 568–69, 570, 572–74, 620–24, 627, 636, 643, 645–46, 649–52, 712, 731, 742, 750, 752, 754, 756, 765–66, 776, 821, 846, 863, 870, 881, 883, 887, 901–3, 908, 919, 921, 973, 977, 979, 981, 1000, 1002, 1011, 1018–22, 1036–37, 1040
hesed ("steadfast love"), 29, 126, 263, 267, 315, 318, 454, 460, 483, 486–87, 531, 551–52, 554, 557, 559, 563, 565, 567, 572, 581–83, 646, 670–71, 673, 676, 686, 708–9, 711, 716, 825–27, 881–82, 888–89, 906, 910, 965, 967–68, 991, 1010
holy mountain, 35, 290, 447, 592, 682
honor, 177, 253, 281, 353, 364, 464, 487, 583, 592–4, 619–20, 643, 966, 976, 989, 1032, 1035
horn, 102, 104–7, 164, 201–3, 319, 331, 364, 497, 613, 746, 845, 1022

idols, 31, 156–57, 176, 222, 415–16, 420, 429, 454–55, 462, 644–49, 651–52, 866, 873, 877, 906, 1025
imprecation/imprecatory, 59, 104, 169, 175, 177–79, 242, 273, 577, 810,

813–14, 816–18, 893, 895, 896–97, 899–901, 915, 924, 935
inclusio, 532, 619, 658, 661, 676, 801, 802, 843, 851, 866, 893, 895, 915, 955, 986, 998, 1007, 1018, 1032, 1035
inheritance, 169, 176, 221–22, 389, 393, 532, 603, 756, 794, 871–72, 876, 886, 895

Jacob, 143, 149, 172, 202, 221, 260, 290, 514–17, 518, 630–31, 637, 840, 857, 868, 876
Jesus, 75–76, 91–92, 95, 108, 118, 120, 133–34, 163–64, 175, 196, 211, 225–26, 239–240, 254–55, 272–74, 296, 306, 329, 343, 353–54, 383, 397, 408, 422–23, 433, 440, 457, 465, 477, 506, 525, 560, 595–96, 605, 627, 687–88, 828, 857–59, 901, 946–47, 970, 983, 995, 1012
judge, 64, 74, 90, 98, 100, 102–3, 112–14, 116–18, 120, 140, 220, 362, 374, 387–88, 396–98, 417, 432, 434, 436, 438, 440

king(s)
  Divine King, 22, 28–29, 32–33, 36, 39–40, 130, 557, 558, 568, 573, 600–2, 604, 622–25, 627, 631–4, 637, 652, 750, 752, 766, 844–45, 847, 869, 871, 882–84, 886–89, 900, 902, 908–9, 911, 914, 935–36, 956–57, 977, 982, 984, 987, 988, 992, 993–94, 996, 998–99, 1001–4, 1009, 1011–12, 1018, 1022–23, 1029–30, 1034–37, 1041–44
  Israelite king(s), 31, 70, 80, 89, 105, 107–8, 131, 160–62, 184, 193, 195–96, 216, 220–21, 250–51, 295, 314–15, 318–22, 324–29, 376, 385, 427, 432, 449, 460, 462, 465, 544, 565, 590, 592, 594–95, 645, 658, 662, 679, 689. 742, 772, 785, 844–46, 848, 906, 979
  kings of nations, 33, 112, 117, 119, 329–30, 333–34, 336, 357, 364, 375, 378, 517, 589, 739, 872, 886, 900, 905, 907–8, 910–11, 914, 932, 980, 1003, 1021–22, 1028, 1033–36

Korah/Korahite, 21–22, 25, 243–44, 259–60, 276, 289, 299, 761, 905, 950

lament, 19, 20, 25, 26, 28–30, 37, 58–59, 66, 81, 84, 86–87, 89, 98, 113, 122–23, 125, 168, 170, 179, 195, 200, 210, 215, 250, 276, 304, 307–8, 313–18, 323, 330, 339, 389, 396, 468, 470–75, 481, 579, 583, 656, 664–65, 683, 704, 707, 712, 715–16, 720–21, 724, 752, 810, 819, 928–30, 935, 945, 948–50, 956, 970, 1045
lament, communal, 36, 80–1, 101, 105, 110–11, 212, 396, 582, 749, 753–54, 757, 780, 813, 894, 944
light (Yahweh as), 112–13, 219, 252–53, 334, 337, 391, 430, 495, 638, 825, 920

Marduk, 224, 377, 895, 990, 1041
Melchizedek, 255, 589, 593–596
Meribah, 206, 208, 405, 539
messiah/messianic, 92–95, 105, 164, 195–96, 273, 329, 341, 368, 397, 590, 595–96, 688
moon, 88, 96, 201–3, 329, 499, 501, 505, 733, 735, 883, 1019, 1024
Mount Zaphon, 103, 290, 553, 561, 844

name (divine), 36, 83, 86, 89–90, 98–100, 111, 117, 169, 174, 176–77, 192, 194, 237, 282, 286, 320, 339–40, 361, 412, 444, 453, 455, 473–74, 534, 582–83, 603, 620–21, 625–26, 643–44, 659, 664, 680, 685, 709, 742, 814, 820, 822–23, 838, 866–67, 872, 875, 882, 935, 955, 957, 989, 1022, 1024, 1040
nations, 29, 31–33, 85, 87, 116–17, 119, 168–72, 174–75, 177–78, 189–90, 218, 220–21, 225, 229–233, 238–39, 276, 280–81, 289, 291, 327, 412, 415, 417–18, 421–22, 429–30, 436–40, 443–444, 451–455, 514, 517, 522, 530, 538–39, 567–68, 590, 592–93, 595, 620, 622, 643–47, 651, 671–72, 679–80, 745–46, 810–11,

866–67, 871–72, 883 890–91, 905, 907–08, 1021–22, 1027–29, 1033–34, 1036

parallelism, 19, 63, 89, 100, 114, 116, 336, 376, 502, 553, 630, 722, 726, 730, 744, 820, 951
Passover, 134, 204, 374, 519, 536, 599, 620
penitential psalms, 472, 819
Persia/Persians, 234, 328, 590–91, 605, 612, 644, 649, 680, 744, 773, 807, 886–87, 901, 907, 990, 1010, 1041
pilgrimage, 33, 90–91, 201, 203, 244, 248–55, 351, 354, 737, 739–41, 744–45, 747, 838, 846, 853
poetry, 19, 107, 113, 427, 427, 473, 555, 591, 602, 702, 723, 881, 933, 983
poor, 80, 109, 115, 180, 218, 222, 225–27, 277–78, 285, 287, 370, 392, 395, 434, 457, 558–59, 565, 581–82, 584–85, 590, 612, 615–16, 618–20, 622–23, 626, 660, 717, 773, 845, 847, 891, 906, 908, 935, 942, 950, 956, 974, 989, 992–93, 998, 1001–4, 1006, 1009–10, 1012, 1031, 1037
praise, 19–20, 22, 27, 29, 40–41, 59, 66, 104, 115, 124–25, 128, 135, 180, 183–84, 201–202, 211–12, 256, 280, 305, 307–8, 315–16, 324, 330, 360–61, 405, 413–15, 419, 420, 424, 347–38, 441, 450–51, 453–55, 457–58, 474, 480–81, 488–89, 494, 500–2, 512–14, 530, 535, 542–43, 566, 568, 579, 583, 600, 610, 619–20, 623, 627, 629, 650, 669–70, 689, 763, 860–61, 866, 868, 873, 875, 978, 9896, 904, 906, 907, 915, 954–955, 973, 975, 978, 986, 989, 996–998, 1006–7, 1009–10, 1013, 1017–19, 1025–26, 1033, 1039, 1041

Rahab (chaos), 289, 291, 311, 1020
Red Sea, 127, 129–30, 132, 147, 148, 520, 530, 534, 536, 551, 631–32, 687, 884–85
refuge, 32–33, 73, 208. 284, 294, 333, 335, 348, 350, 368, 395, 678–79, 687, 720, 776, 944–46, 952–53, 975

righteous, 24, 34–35, 62, 73–75, 101,
104–5, 108, 116, 158, 273, 305, 321,
337–38, 360, 365–66, 370, 392–94,
396, 420, 430, 440, 464–65, 469,
519, 522, 572, 609, 613–17, 619,
659, 663, 683084, 714–16, 718,
761, 770–73, 776, 789, 806, 812,
815, 935, 940, 943–944, 955, 957,
961–62, 969, 1001–04
righteousness, 35, 105, 115, 173, 219,
266–69, 318, 326, 331, 363–64,
380, 420, 428, 430, 437, 439–40,
445, 473, 484, 487, 531–32, 547,
598, 601, 609, 616–17, 683, 775,
812, 818, 843, 902, 960, 966,
968–69, 993
rock (Yahweh as), 32, 72, 166, 321,
366, 368, 395, 402, 625, 943, 945,
975, 984

sacrifices, 77, 81, 91, 92, 118–19, 151,
163–65, 170, 246, 252, 255–57,
294, 328, 417, 446, 448, 538–39,
645, 657, 662, 664, 683, 870
sea, 87–88, 93, 103, 133, 291, 316–17,
373, 377–78, 403, 419, 498, 501,
552–53, 557, 561, 631, 633, 821,
870, 1000, 1023
Septuagint (LXX), 80, 150, 185, 195,
221, 249, 418, 433, 498, 554, 578,
646–47, 650, 656, 677, 681, 725,
726, 734, 736, 780, 781, 795,
811–16, 854, 861, 862, 899, 921,
931, 933, 942, 952, 965, 974, 975,
986, 1006, 1023
servant(s), 169–70, 174, 177, 265, 278,
284, 322–24, 460, 488, 519, 521,
523–24, 582, 663–64, 707–9, 711,
714, 719, 861–63, 868, 886, 906,
950, 960, 966, 968, 989
shalom, 36, 62, 187, 264–68, 531, 725,
742–44, 774, 806–7
shame, 161, 170, 237, 284, 323, 429,
582, 583, 594, 689, 706, 709, 719,
750, 753, 757, 813, 814, 847
Sheol, 283, 302, 304, 306–8, 504, 556,
659–63, 707, 762–63, 919, 936,
946, 962, 964, 1017
shepherd, 82, 105, 130–32, 154–55,
160, 183–84, 197, 408, 415, 455,
1007–8

sleep, 124, 158–59, 181, 732–33, 793,
796, 797, 923
Solomon, 26, 92, 160, 189, 244, 246,
251, 295–96, 326, 625–26, 742,
790, 843–44
Solomonic temple, 246, 385, 771
Shema, 142, 207, 282
sickness 384, 470, 556, 564
suffering, 36, 65, 68, 80, 83, 85, 97–98,
114, 123, 170, 186–88, 195, 205,
217–18, 278, 301–6, 470–72,
554–55, 560, 751, 815–16
sun, 88, 91, 112, 251–53, 499, 500–1,
505, 567, 621, 773–74, 793, 883,
1024

tabernacle, 146, 157–58, 293–94, 380,
418, 433, 442, 703, 854, 922
temple, 59, 67, 71, 80–1, 84, 90–92,
97–99, 112, 119, 160, 167–70,
201–2, 209, 244–48, 251, 257,
290, 293–94, 328–29, 365–66,
380, 443–44, 453, 651, 675,
682–83, 795, 840, 862, 1032,
1040, 1042
thanksgiving, 59, 99, 116, 368, 370,
453, 455, 551, 554, 656–58,
661–62, 664, 666–68, 675–76,
679, 682, 685, 689, 716, 720–21,
759, 763, 810, 904, 928, 939, 973
theophany, 69, 129, 236, 420, 422, 425,
427–28, 431–33, 496, 498, 503,
536, 632, 635, 884, 926, 977, 1042
torah, 59, 62, 67, 145, 149, 183, 282,
380, 392, 428, 446, 448, 465,
497, 521–22, 525, 599, 602–4,
606, 615, 702–19, 773, 806, 847,
857, 908, 945, 966, 1006, 1012,
1044–45

vengeance/revenge, 170, 177–78, 370,
387–88, 585, 810, 901–2, 924,
1028, 1033–34, 1036

warrior (divine), 112–13, 116–18, 129,
158–59, 188–90, 206, 209, 235,
237, 245, 247, 320, 375–76, 432,
436, 438, 565, 570, 573–74, 636,
794, 977, 981, 982–84, 1029, 1037
wicked, 24, 35–36, 61–69, 71, 72,
73–77, 103–5, 107–8, 217, 227,

236–37, 252, 283, 350, 360, 362–65, 368, 387, 389, 390–95, 410, 462, 464–65, 494, 580–81, 609, 613–14, 710, 713, 717, 719, 726–27, 752, 788, 771–77, 789, 806, 811–13, 816, 832, 846, 888, 910, 924, 929, 931, 933, 939–40, 942–48, 965, 987, 994, 1002, 1009

wickedness, 118, 153, 173, 339, 366, 388, 390, 395, 547, 558–59, 772, 796

wilderness, 28, 96, 140, 148–49, 151, 154, 164, 201, 520, 550, 553, 562, 634–35, 637–38, 714, 757, 811, 842, 880, 884–85

wisdom, 24, 29, 74, 80, 141–42, 300, 314, 338, 345, 354, 391, 486, 501,

522, 535, 551, 559, 604, 606, 608, 610–11, 614, 705, 712, 789–790, 800–2, 850, 852–53, 915–16, 949, 999, 1002

wrath, 115–16, 151, 171–72, 188, 262, 270, 272, 273, 303, 337–40, 388, 470, 594, 680, 1003

Zion, 33, 83, 84, 111–12, 116, 159–60, 162–63, 244, 248–50, 276, 289–93, 294–95, 382, 428, 430, 433, 443, 455, 470, 472, 476, 592, 728, 731, 738–39, 770–71, 780–81, 786, 804–5, 813, 838–39, 844, 846–47, 850–56, 860, 862–63, 891, 896, 998, 1000, 1026

Author Index

Adams, James Truslow, 797–98
Adams, Samuel L ., 807
Allen, Leslie C., 43, 45, 62, 66–68,
70–71, 82, 86, 104, 107, 123–24, 127,
129–30, 143, 152, 157, 159, 186–87,
193, 195, 203, 216, 231, 247, 261,
279, 281–82, 301, 305, 323, 348–49,
351, 356, 362, 388, 393, 417, 445,
451, 460, 476, 499, 512, 529, 530
Alter, Robert, 43, 278, 283–84, 290,
292, 312, 319–21, 322, 336, 338,
347–48, 388, 404, 413, 421, 427, 429,
445, 470–71, 484, 488–89, 497, 500,
514, 518, 531–32, 537, 833, 852, 1034
Anderson, A. A., 43, 62–63, 151, 314,
352, 375, 377–78, 390, 403, 449,
484, 537, 730, 779, 1027
Armitage, David, 544
Arnold, Bill, 316, 718, 954
Athanasius, 34
Attridge, Harold W., 44, 408, 433, 477
Augustine, 13, 653, 797
Avalos, Hector, 482–83
Bader, Christopher, 626–27
Ballhorn, Egbert, 44, 590, 862, 868, 992
Bar-Efrat, Shimon, 45, 893, 896–97
Barré, Michael, 656
Barth, Christoph, 45, 665, 1014
Barth, Karl, 1014
Bartholomew, Craig G., 48, 177, 345,
727–28
Barton, John, 35
Bass, Dorothy C., 748
Bauckham, Richard, 410, 912
Bautch, Richard J., 45, 819
Beale, Greg K., 93
Bechtel, Lyn M., 45, 757
Becking, Bob, 45, 894–95, 898
Bell, Rob, 410
Bellinger, Jr., William H., 22, 43, 45, 52,
604, 622, 657, 661, 679, 833, 850,
852, 899–900, 935, 966, 1022
Berquist, Jon L., 980
Beyerlin, Walter, 45, 555, 642, 780, 831
Birkeland, Harris, 45, 579, 765

Blenkinsopp, Joseph, 794
Blomberg, Craig, 6, 92
Bonar, Andrew A., 449
Bonhoeffer, Dietrich, 466–67, 858–59
Booij, Th., 45, 364, 589
Botha, Phil, 45, 54, 565, 567–68, 611,
751–52, 887
Braude, William G., 24
Briant, Pierre, 612, 1010
Briggs, Charles Augustus, 43, 246, 671
Briggs, E. G., 43, 246, 671
Brown, Michael L., 861
Brown, William P., 30–32, 34, 45, 72,
567, 592, 764, 797, 802, 831, 861,
920, 945, 946
Broyles, Craig C., 43, 45, 62, 66–68,
70–71, 82, 86, 104, 107, 123–24, 127,
129–30, 143, 152, 157, 159, 186–87,
193, 195, 203, 216, 231, 247, 261,
279, 281–82, 301, 305, 323, 348–49,
351, 356, 362, 388, 393, 417, 445,
451, 460, 476, 499, 512, 529, 530
Brueggemann, Walter, 43, 46, 58–59,
61, 413, 464, 540, 546–47, 604, 636,
657, 661, 679, 717, 726, 728, 821,
833, 874–75, 899–900, 935, 966,
1022, 1044–45
Buechner, Frederick, 777–778
Buggle, Franz, 902
Bullock, Hassell C., 46, 132, 307, 371
Burge, Gary M., 6, 53, 91, 738
Burns, Robert, 106
Buysch, Christoph, 904, 908, 940, 942,
950, 979
Calvin, John, 13, 30, 490, 586, 653–54
Carpenter, Eugene, 869
Casey, Edward S., 727–28
Ceresko, Anthony, 46, 1035–36
Cheung, Simon Chi-Chung, 46, 802
Childs, Brevard, 20–21, 25, 26 , 950
Clifford, Richard J., 43, 46, 89, 93, 523,
651, 929
Collins, Suzanne, 912
Cone, James, 467
Cook, Edward, 284

Cornelius, Izak, 46, 505, 794
Creach, Jerome F. D., 32–33, 46, 73, 334–35, 1003
Croft, Steven J. L., 46, 579
Crossan, John Dominic, 214, 219, 226
Crow, Loren D., 46, 739, 749, 761, 764, 781, 786, 801, 830, 832, 855
Crüsemann, Frank, 56, 702, 759–60
Currid, John D., 46, 520
Dahood, Mitchell, 43, 217, 553, 680–81, 753, 781, 830, 1027
Daly-Denton, Margaret, 46, 163
Davidson, Robert, 43, 561, 580, 593, 596, 640, 710–711, 717, 721, 801, 921, 924, 993
Davis, Ellen F., 46, 438–39
deClaissé-Walford, Nancy L., 14, 21, 24, 43, 45, 54, 611, 677, 765, 769, 782, 833, 835, 851, 893, 916, 973, 977, 1028
Dick, Michael, 54, 647
Dobbs-Allsopp, F. W., 46, 933
Dockery, David S., 1030
Donner, Herbert, 781, 872
Doyle, Brian, 47, 853
Duhm, Bernard, 701–702
Dussaud, René, 885
Dystra, Craig, 748
Eaton, John H., 43, 47, 62, 69–70, 82, 84, 100, 105, 107, 113, 116, 123, 125, 127, 141, 154–55, 160, 168–69, 195, 204–205, 216–18, 233, 245, 249, 251, 278, 285, 290, 291, 336–37, 339, 362, 364, 378, 445, 453, 476, 481, 483, 501, 502, 505, 517, 532, 534, 579
Ego, Beate, 47, 240, 536, 546, 553, 622, 662, 735, 812
Eidevall, Göran, 47, 722–23
Els, P. J., 657
Emerton, J. A., 47, 55, 126, 141
Feldmeier, Reinhard, 560, 828, 925
Firth, David, 21, 47, 56, 106, 178–179, 847
Fleming, Daniel, 47, 792
Fokkelman, J. P., 47, 867
Freedman, David N., 47–48, 432, 898, 1042
Fretheim, Terrence, 173, 247, 758, 961
Froese, Paul, 626–27
Füglister, Notker, 1034
Gane, Roy, 187

Garland, David, 857
Garland, Diana, 857
Gerstenberger, Erhard S., 43, 47, 352, 413, 551, 602, 629, 656, 684, 702, 725, 769–70, 772, 780, 784, 791, 810, 852–53, 882, 886, 916, 951, 960, 973, 982, 1029
Gillingham, Susan E., 43, 47, 132, 296, 884
Goheen, Michael W., 526
Goldingay, John, 43, 114, 117, 122, 124, 126, 130, 140, 142, 145, 150, 153, 155–56, 168, 171, 175, 18586, 191–92, 202, 204–206, 220, 234–35, 248–49, 260, 266, 279, 282, 285, 292, 304, 317, 321, 325, 348, 350, 362–64, 389, 402–403, 416–417, 420, 426, 444, 463, 483, 487, 498, 513–14, 531, 534–35, 539, 542, 550–51, 553, 556, 558–559, 583, 590, 592, 600, 612, 620, 626, 629, 644, 670, 676–79, 681, 704, 721, 723, 731, 739–40, 760, 771, 790, 792–93, 800, 804, 813, 832–34, 841, 847, 852, 855, 867–68, 870, 873, 882, 891–92, 894, 901, 904, 918, 924, 931, 934, 943–44, 950, 955, 966, 988, 995, 1001, 1007, 1012, 1033–34, 1043
Gosling, F. A., 46, 146
Goulder, Michael D., 47, 579, 679, 705, 725, 880, 892, 906, 960, 965, 1027
Grant, Jamie A., 47–48, 106, 177, 287, 296, 310, 324, 326, 378, 448, 471, 486, 495
Grant, Robert, 1004
Grisanti, Michael A., 753
Grogan, Geoffrey W., 44, 306, 323
Guillaume, Alfred, 894
Guldi, Jo, 544
Gunkel, Hermann, 13, 19, 20, 48, 667–669, 819, 915, 964, 1027
Harman, Allan H., 731
Hartley, John E., 924
Hauge, Martin R., 48, 936
Hays, Richard B., 968, 970
Heibert, Theodore, 48, 432
Heim, Knut M., 48, 325, 329
Hemming, Jo, 95
Hemming, Nigel, 95
Hess, Richard S., 48, 224–225
Holman, Jan, 48, 914

Holst, Søren, 48, 658, 678, 967
Hossfeld, Frank-Lothar, 24, 27, 44, 60,
  63–64, 67, 70–27, 82, 84–85, 89, 99,
  104, 113, 115–17, 123, 143, 153–54,
  157, 168, 175, 187, 194, 200, 204,
  218–19, 225, 230, 233–34, 245, 249,
  262, 283, 284–85, 293, 347, 349–50,
  352, 356, 360–61, 365–66, 368, 373,
  375, 394–95, 402, 404, 408, 416,
  419–420, 422, 426–428, 436, 444–
  446, 452, 455, 464, 474, 476, 481,
  498, 500, 505, 518, 520, 531–32, 535,
  538–39, 550–51, 553, 555, 557–59,
  565, 567–8, 570, 583, 585, 592, 594,
  596, 600, 604, 612, 614–15, 621,
  631–32, 634, 642, 644, 646, 648,
  650, 657, 662, 669, 670–72, 677,
  679, 681, 683–85, 702–704, 710–12,
  714, 720–25, 730–32, 740–41, 744,
  749–50, 752, 756, 761, 763, 772,
  776, 780–81, 783, 789, 792–93,
  801–804, 807, 811–812, 821, 823,
  826, 835, 855, 860, 866, 867, 869,
  871, 873, 880, 883–84, 892, 894–95,
  897, 910, 916–17, 919, 922–23, 930,
  932, 941, 950, 956, 960, 974, 976,
  978–79, 981, 987, 989, 992, 994, 997,
  999, 1001, 1006, 1109, 1017, 1020,
  1026–27, 1029–30, 1034–37, 1039,
  1041–42, 1044
Howard Jr., David M., 48, 396
Huff, Douglas, 466
Hughes, Dwei A., 48, 287, 486
Human, Dirk, 48–49, 89, 796, 879, 880
Hurvitz, Avi, 645
Inge, John, 727
Jacobsen, Thorkild, 377
Jacobson, Rolf A., 24, 43, 49, 52, 572,
  605–606, 765, 769, 782, 833, 835,
  851, 874, 893, 899, 916, 973, 977
Janowski, Bernd, 36, 49, 578, 657, 659,
  662–63, 678, 821, 920, 936, 938, 1024
Jensen, Joseph E., 49, 98, 105, 110
Jeremias, Jörg, 49, 51, 452, 551
Jones, Greg, 829
Jones, Ivor H., 1042–43
Kaminsky, Joel, 875–76
Kee, Min Suc, 49, 216
Keel, Othmar, 49, 553, 556, 592,
  648, 658, 762, 771, 821, 862, 885,
  931–32, 952, 963, 1000, 1010

Keesmaat, Sylvia C., 49, 330, 397, 440,
  545
Keet, Cuthbert C., 49, 721, 724, 790,
  833
Kelly, Douglas F., 181
Kimelman, Reuven, 49, 986, 988
Kirkpatrick, A. F., 44, 230, 336, 338, 377,
  447, 461, 470, 498, 503–504, 513
Kitz, Anne Marie, 49, 581
Kline, Meredith G., 50, 407
Klingbeil, Martin, 50, 981
Knierem, Rolf, 823
Knowles, Melody, 50, 745–46
Koch, Klaus, 27, 50, 827
Kohl, Margaret, 56, 848, 906
Körting, Corinna, 50, 739
Kramer, S. N., 990, 1041
Kraus, Hans-Joachim, 31, 36, 44,
  66, 68, 70, 123–24, 147, 156, 169,
  188–89, 191, 247, 252, 558, 565,
  601, 620, 637–38, 643, 647, 664,
  670, 672, 680, 682, 685, 688,
  720–21, 730, 733–34, 763, 765, 769,
  774, 779, 794, 801, 807, 824, 840,
  853, 885, 892, 898, 922, 935, 960,
  966, 1008, 1027, 1037
Krawelitzski, Judith, 50, 645, 870
Kselman, John S., 50, 99–100, 1002
Kuntz, J. Kenneth, 806
Labahn, Michael, 50–51, 355, 962, 981
Ladd, George E., 50, 423, 492, 507
Leuenberger, Martin, 50, 552, 590,
  863–64, 867
Levenson, Jon, 50, 438, 704–705
Lewis, C. S., 109, 151
Liess, Kathrin, 51, 953, 962–63
Limburg, James, 51, 734
Lindars, Barnabus, 992
Lo, Allison, 47, 310
Lohfink, Norbert, 51, 354, 1001–1002,
  1027
Longman, Tremper, 2, 6, 13, 44, 47, 51,
  66, 88, 105–106, 117, 331, 413, 438,
  573, 983
López, Félix García, 51, 354, 358
Luc, Alex, 823
Luther, Martin, 11, 13, 111, 731, 829
MacDonald, Nathan, 207, 223
MacIntyre, Alasdair, 607
Malchoz, Christian, 51, 880, 883
Martin-Achard, Robert, 672

Martin, Ralph P., 605
Mays, James L., 44, 51, 70–72, 87,
   89–90, 94, 102, 104, 114, 120,
   123–26, 171, 207, 212, 218, 248,
   253, 373, 376, 379, 385, 414,
   455–58, 471, 473, 478, 483, 488–49,
   504, 515–16, 533, 535, 560, 578,
   657, 664, 673, 688, 725, 731, 735,
   747, 752, 784, 801, 823, 836, 888,
   903, 911, 974, 1015, 1027, 1040
McCann, Jr., J. Clinton, 22, 24, 29,
   31, 44, 56, 58, 71, 131, 185, 187,
   191, 193, 201–202, 231, 236, 267,
   335, 387, 391, 557, 562, 566, 581,
   602–603, 670, 676, 679–680, 687,
   715, 719, 721, 743, 748, 749, 801,
   838, 841–842, 860, 906, 908, 940,
   957, 988, 995, 1002–1004, 1023,
   1027, 1031, 1040
McConville, J. Gordon, 47, 51, 310, 540
McKelvey, Michael G., 51, 367, 387,
   456–58, 460, 476, 485, 530
Mejía, Jorge, 51, 551
Menken, M. J. J., 44, 46, 49–50, 52, 55,
   163, 286, 330, 355, 397, 408, 506
Merton, Thomas, 36
Mettinger, Tryggve N. D., 31, 52, 620
Middleton, J. Richard, 52, 88
Milbank, John, 597
Miller, Patrick D., 46, 52, 58, 61, 108,
   115, 124, 227, 406–7, 494, 496–97,
   499, 501, 521, 573, 666–67, 705, 827
Mitchell, David C., 52, 204, 725, 731
Moberly, R. W. L., 770
Moltmann, Jürgen, 848
Mowinckel, Sigmund, 11, 19, 20, 52,
   373–374, 426, 579, 642, 679, 874,
   875
Moyise, Steve, 44, 46, 49–50, 52, 55,
   163, 286, 330, 355, 397, 408, 422,
   448, 456, 506, 546
Münnich, Maciej M., 990, 1041
Murphy, Roland E., 51–52, 58, 345, 741
Nasuti, Harry P., 52, 605, 622, 874
Nelson, Richard D., 52, 633–634
Niehaus, Jeffrey J., 52, 431–33, 646
Noll, Stephen F., 443
Northcott, Michael S., 419
Nouwen, Henri, 788
O'Connor, Michael, 55, 718, 943, 964
O'Dowd, Ryan, 53, 302

Oesterley, W. O. E., 44, 223, 330, 390
Ogden, Graham, 741
Ollenburger, Ben C., 53, 738
Ortberg, John, 737
Otto, Rudolf, 431–32, 830, 958
Peels, H. G. L., 53, 310
Perdue, Leo, 53, 614, 796
Peterson, Eugene, 745–46, 798, 849,
   947, 1014
Phillips, Elaine A., 53, 308–9, 575
Phillips, J. B., 575
Platt, David, 798
Poole, Charles E., 957
Prinsloo, Willem S., 1032
Prothero, Rowland E. , 58, 358
Rabe, Norbert, 898
Rasmussen, Michael, 280
Reid, Daniel G., 51, 117, 573
Richter, Sandra L., 53, 621
Riede, Peter, 53, 582, 680, 764
Roberts, J. J. M., 81, 85, 617–18, 978
Roberts, James A., 617–18
Röllig, Wolfgang, 781
Rooker, M. F., 53, 432
Rösel, Martin, 822
Ross, Allen P., 989
Scaioloa, Donatella, 53, 1001
Schaefer, Konrad, 44, 60–1, 63, 65–6,
   71, 85, 89–90, 113, 144, 147, 206,
   209, 230, 317, 337, 347, 351, 360,
   364–5, 394, 402, 419, 454, 471–2,
   481, 485–6, 502, 536, 542, 790
Schmid, Konrad, 53, 560, 568, 569,
   579, 624, 663, 754–55, 915, 1018
Schoville, Keith N., 1022
Scoralick, Ruth, 54, 603, 872, 885
Seybold, Klaus, 27, 44, 579, 645, 656,
   804, 880, 887, 892, 898, 915, 960
Shaeffer, Francis A., 53, 337, 525
Sheldrake, Philip, 727
Shoemaker, Stephen H., 832
Smick, Elmer B., 54, 223
Snyman, Fanie, 54, 671
Soll, William M., 54, 704
Spieckermann, Hermann, 560, 828
Starbuck, Scott A., 25
Stetzer, Ed, 689
Stokes, Ryan, 580
Stott, John R. W., 477–78
Swart, Ignatius, 659, 678
Talbert, Charles H., 617

Tate, Marvin E., 28, 44, 84–86, 98, 101, 104, 124, 131, 150, 157, 184, 189, 195, 200, 204, 206, 217, 221, 252, 569, 935

Taylor, William R., 937

Tennant, Timothy C., 358

Terrien, Samuel, 44, 88, 112, 151, 172, 192, 202, 220, 265, 335, 348, 375, 380, 395

Tickle, Phyllis, 716

Tournay, Raymond, 54, 568, 571, 1028, 1033

Tsevat, Matitiahu, 54, 221–222

Tucker, Jr., W. Dennis, 22, 45, 52, 54, 519, 559, 565, 572–73, 582, 584, 622, 660, 677, 712, 744, 753–54, 813, 847, 850, 867, 901, 906, 942, 974, 989, 1001, 1009

Turkle, Sherry, 562–63

Ursinus, Zacharias, 1025

van Dam, Cornelis, 710, 953

van der Meer, William, 54, 594

van der Merwe, Christo H. J., 54, 722, 751, 761, 791, 805, 869, 896, 934

Van Leeuwen, Raymond, 266, 486

van Rensburg, J. F. J., 54, 887

Volf, Miroslav, 902

von Nordheim, Miriam, 594

von Waldow, H. E., 54, 540

Wakely, Robin, 659, 678

Walker, Christopher, 54, 647

Wallace, Howard Neil, 55, 925–27

Walsh, J. P. M., 901

Walsh, Jerome T., 55, 544, 901

Waltke, Bruce K., 55, 718, 943, 964

Walton, John, 55, 216–217, 221, 231, 290, 305, 307, 317, 361, 378, 496, 505, 562, 1019

Warden, Duane, 1024

Watson, Wilfred G. E., 55, 854, 992

Weber, Beat, 55, 461

Weinfeld, Moshe, 407

Weippert, Helga, 803

Weippert, Manfred H. E., 55, 732, 803, 872

Weiser, Artur, 44, 252, 340, 403 426, 671–72, 702, 940, 1027

Wenham, Gordon J., 47, 94, 310

Wesselschmidt, Quentin F., 44, 663

Westbrook, Raymond, 55, 490

Westermann, Claus, 55, 763, 915, 956

Whitekettle, Richard, 55, 190

Whybray, Norman R., 55, 141

Willard, Dallas, 213, 1025, 1038

Williams III., H. H. Drake, 55, 397

Wilson, Gerald H., 14, 19, 20–28, 44, 45, 55, 59, 61, 76, 83, 99,105, 114, 122, 131, 168, 184, 247, 290, 300, 319, 324–326, 373–374, 380, 387, 451, 565, 595, 742

Wittman, Derek, 1027

Witvliet, John D., 1025

Wolff, Hans Walter, 56, 906, 922, 963, 1024

Wolterstorff, Nicholas, 937

Wright, Christopher J. H., 232, 327, 354–55, 414, 420, 422, 443, 462, 473, 507, 514, 522–23, 526, 587, 817–18

Wright, N. T., 56, 462, 507, 587, 817–18

Younger, K. Lawson, 6, 235

Zenger, Erich, 24, 27, 44, 48–49, 53, 56, 60, 63–4, 67, 70–2, 82, 84–5, 89, 99, 104, 113, 115–17, 123, 143, 153–54, 157, 168, 175, 179, 187, 194, 200, 204, 218–19, 225, 230, 233–34, 245, 249, 262, 273, 283, 284–85, 293, 347, 349–50, 352, 356, 360–61, 365–66, 368, 373, 375, 394–95, 402, 404, 408, 416, 419–420, 422, 426–428, 436, 444–446, 452, 455, 464, 474, 476, 481, 498, 500, 505, 518, 520, 531–32, 535, 538–39, 550–51, 553, 555, 557–59, 565, 567–8, 570, 583, 585, 592, 594, 596, 600, 604, 612, 614–15, 621, 631–32, 634, 642, 644, 646, 648, 650, 657, 662, 669, 670–72, 677, 679, 681, 683–85, 702–4, 710–12, 714, 720–25, 730–32, 740–41, 744, 749–50, 752, 756, 761, 763, 772, 776, 780–81, 783, 789, 792–93, 801–4, 807, 811–812, 821, 823, 826, 835, 855, 860, 866, 867, 869, 871, 873, 880, 883–84, 892, 894–95, 897, 910, 916–17, 919, 922–23, 930, 932, 941, 950, 956, 960, 974, 976, 978–79, 981, 987, 989, 992, 994, 997, 999, 1001, 1006, 1109, 1017, 1020, 1026–27, 1029–30, 1034–37, 1039, 1041–42, 1044

Zevit, Ziony, 56, 850

Zimmerli, Walther, 56, 530, 608